Lecture Notes in Computer Science 4331

Commenced Publication in 1973
Founding and Former Series Editors:
Gerhard Goos, Juris Hartmanis, and Jan van Leeuwen

Editorial Board

Geyong Min   Beniamino Di Martino
Laurence T. Yang   Minyi Guo
Gudula Ruenger (Eds.)

Frontiers of High Performance Computing and Networking – ISPA 2006 Workshops

ISPA 2006 International Workshops
FHPCN, XHPC, S-GRACE, GridGIS, HPC-GTP
PDCE, ParDMCom, WOMP, ISDF, and UPWN
Sorrento, Italy, December 4-7, 2006
Proceedings

Springer

Volume Editors

Geyong Min
University of Bradford, Bradford, UK
E-mail: g.min@brad.ac.uk

Beniamino Di Martino
Seconda Universita' di Napoli, Roma, Italy
E-mail: beniamino.dimartino@unina.it

Laurence T. Yang
St. Francis Xavier University, Antigonish, Canada
E-mail: lyang@stfx.ca

Minyi Guo
University of Aizu, Fukushima 965-8580, Japan
E-mail: minyi@u-aizu.ac.jp

Gudula Ruenger
Chemnitz University of Technology, Chemnitz, Germany
E-mail: ruenger@informatik.tu-chemnitz.de

Library of Congress Control Number: 2006937143

CR Subject Classification (1998): F.1, F.2, D.1, D.2, D.4, C.2, C.4, H.4, J.3

LNCS Sublibrary: SL 1 – Theoretical Computer Science and General Issues

ISSN   0302-9743
ISBN-10   3-540-49860-5 Springer Berlin Heidelberg New York
ISBN-13   978-3-540-49860-5 Springer Berlin Heidelberg New York

Springer is a part of Springer Science+Business Media

springer.com

© Springer-Verlag Berlin Heidelberg 2006
Printed in Germany

Typesetting: Camera-ready by author, data conversion by Scientific Publishing Services, Chennai, India
Printed on acid-free paper   SPIN: 11942634   06/3142   5 4 3 2 1 0

Preface

This proceedings volume contains the refereed and revised papers presented at the ten workshops held in conjunction with the 4th International Symposium on Parallel and Distributed Processing and Applications (ISPA 2006), in Sorrento, Italy, December 4-6, 2006. The objective of the workshops is to provide an outstanding international forum for academics, educators, engineering, and industrial professionals to contribute and to disseminate innovative and state-of-the-art research, to report, discuss and exchange experimental or theoretical results, experience, work-in-progress, and case studies on high-performance computing and networking. These workshops are:

- FHPCN 2006: Workshop on Frontiers of High-Performance Computing and Networking
- XHPC 2006: Workshop on XEN in HPC Cluster and Grid Computing Environments
- S-GRACE 2006: Workshop on Semantic Grid Applications in Computing and Engineering
- GridGIS 2006: Workshop on Fertilization of Grid Computing and Geographic Information Systems
- HPC-GTP 2006: Workshop on High-Performance Computing in Genomic Proteomics and Transcriptomics
- PDCE 2006: Workshop on Parallel and Distributed Computing in Engineering
- ParDMCom 2006: Workshop on Parallel and Distributed Multimedia Computing
- WOMP 2006: Workshop on Middleware Performance
- ISDF 2006: Workshop on Information Security and Digital Forensics
  UPWN 2006: Workshop on Ubiquitous Processing for Wireless Networks

The FHPCN 2006 workshop constituted 40 papers that were carefully selected from manuscripts submitted for potential publication at the conference. These papers are organized in four special tracks: System Architectures; Middleware and Cooperative Computing; Techniques, Algorithms and Applications; and Advanced Networking. Each of the additional nine workshops focused on a particular theme of high-performance computing and networking and complemented the spectrum of the main conference and FHPCN workshop.

We would like to thank the ISPA 2006 General Co-chairs, Beniamino Di Martino, Jack Dongarra, and Laurence T. Yang for their guidance and vision, and the Program Co-chairs, Minyi Guo and Hans Zima, for their support and encouragement. We deeply appreciate the tremendous efforts and contributions of the Chairs of individual workshops. Our thanks also go to all authors for their valuable contributions and to all Program Committee members and reviewers for providing timely and in-depth reviews. Last but not least, we deeply appreciate

Lan Wang, Shihang Yan, Xiaolong Jin, and Mimmo Di Sivo for their great help
and hard work with editing the proceedings.

Geyong Min
Gudula Rünger
ISPA 2006 Workshop Co-chairs
Beniamino Di Martino
Jack Dongarra
Laurence T. Yang
ISPA 2006 General Co-chairs
Minyi Guo
Hans Zima
ISPA 2006 Program Co-chairs

International Workshop on XEN in HPC Cluster and Grid Computing Environments

(XHPC 2006)

The XEN virtual machine monitor is reaching wide spread adoption in a variety of operating systems as well as scientific, educational and operational usage areas. With its low overhead, XEN allows for concurrently running large numbers of virtual machines, providing each with encapsulation, isolation and network-wide CPU migratability. XEN offers a network-wide abstraction layer of individual machine resources to OS environments, thereby opening options for new cluster- and grid high-performance computing (HPC) architectures and HPC services. With XEN finding applications in HPC environments, this workshop brought together researchers and practitioners active on XEN in high-performance cluster and grid computing environments.

XHPC 2006 also provided a forum for scientists, engineers, and researchers to discuss and exchange their new ideas, novel results, work in progress and experience on all aspects of virtualization in HPC environments. It covered a wide range of theoretical and applied topics in the area of virtualization including XEN in cluster environments, compute job entry and scheduling, MPI on virtual machines, system sizing, network architectures for XEN clusters, XEN on large SMP machines, performance measurements, management of XEN clusters, dynamic scheduling and load-leveling, and power management in HPC clusters.

We are very proud to have received many high-quality submissions. We conducted a rigorous peer review process for each submission, with the great support of all Program Committee members. Based on the reviews, we selected 11 papers to be included in this program. We congratulate the authors of accepted papers, and regret that many quality submissions could not be included due to the time and space limit.

Finally, we would like to take this opportunity to thank the authors of all the submissions for their contribution. We would also like to thank the Program Committee members for their efforts in reviewing the submissions. Finally, we would like to thank Gudula Rünger and Geyong Min for their guidance in the organization of this workshop.

Hope you all enjoy the workshop proceedings.

Michael Alexander
XHPC 2006 Workshop Organizers

Workshop Chair

Michael Alexander   WU Vienna, Austria

Program Committee

Franck Cappello	INRIA, France
Stephen Childs	Trinity College, Ireland
Claudia Eckert	Fraunhofer Institute, Germany
Bill Gardner	University of Guelph, Cananda
Rob Gardner	HP Labs, USA
Marcus Hardt	Forschungszentrum Karlsruhe, Germany
Klaus Ita	WU Vienna, Austria
Sverre Jarp	CERN, Switzerland
Thomas Lange	University of Cologne, Germany
Ronald Luijten	IBM Research Laboratory, Zurich, Switzerland
Franco Travostino	Nortel CTO Office, USA
Andreas Unterkircher	CERN, Switzerland

International Workshop on Semantic GRid Applications in Computing and Engineering

(S-GRACE 2006)

As an extension of current computing grids, a semantic grid is characterized as an open system in which information, computing resources and services are given well-defined meaning in standard ways. This approach helps bring resources virtually together and makes it easier for resources to be discovered and processed automatically. It also opens research opportunities for scientists and engineers. This workshop aims to provide a forum for researchers to discuss and share their findings and ideas in semantic grid applications in computing and engineering, and to envision the future work in this area. This year we are very proud to have received many high-quality submissions. We conducted a rigorous peer review process for each submission, with the great support of all Program Committee members. Based on the reviews, we selected nine papers to be included in the program. We congratulate the authors of accepted papers, and regret that many quality submissions could not be included due to the time and space limit. Taking this opportunity, we would like to thank all the authors for their contributions to the program. We would also like to thank the Program Committee members for their efforts in reviewing the submissions. In conclusion, we would like to thank the ISPA Workshop Chairs Geyong Min and Gudula Rünger for their excellent work in driving and supporting us in the various phases of workshop development.

Xubin (Ben) He
Wenbin Jiang
Beniamino Di Martino
Young-Sik Jeong
Laurence T. Yang
S-GRACE 2006 Workshop Organizers

Executive Committee

Steering Chair:	Laurence T. Yang, St. Francis Xavier University, Canada
General Co-chairs:	Beniamino Di Martino, Second University of Naples, Italy
	Xubin He, Tennessee Technological University, USA
Program Co-chairs:	Young-Sik Jeong, Wonkwang University, Korea
	Wenbin Jiang, Huazhong University of Science and Technology, China

Program Committee

Huajun Chen	Zhejiang University, China
Xiaowu Chen	Beihang University, China
Christian Engelmann	Oak Ridge National Laboratory, USA
Jizhong Han	Chinese Academy of Sciences, China
Sung-Kook Han	Wonkwang University, Korea
Youn-Hee Han	Korea University of Technology and Education, Korea
Dongwon Jeong	Kunsan National University, Korea
Rodrigo de Mello	University of São Paulo, Brazil
Li Ou	Tennessee Technological University, USA
Stephen Scott	Oak Ridge National Laboratory, USA
Ruppa K. Thulasiram	University of Manitoba, Canada
Juan Tourino	University of A Coruna, Spain
Guojun Wang	Central South University, China
Tao Xie	San Diego State University, USA
Naixue Xiong	JAIST, Japan
Zhiyong Xu	Suffolk University, USA
Pingpeng Yuan	Huazhong University of Science and Technology, China
Yifeng Zhu	University of Maine, USA
Hai Zhuge	Chinese Academy of Sciences, China

International Workshop on Fertilization of Grid Computing and Geographic Information Systems (GridGIS 2006)

The development of Geographic Information Systems (GIS) sciences and technologies motivates the concern of the next-generation GIS, including multi-resources distributed, high-performance computation and data transfer, and collaborative platform of virtual organization for multiple end users. Grid technology offers the prospect of enabling new types of applications and new ways of working in the area of GIS. Grid computing and geographic information system (GridGIS) is a science at the intersection of grid computing and GIS. It is characterized by modern grid computing technology, by information sharing between geographically distributed sites, and by real-time decisions.

This workshop aims to provide a forum for examining the state of the art of GridGIS. The main objectives are the definitions of theoretical and conceptual fundamentals of GridGIS, the description of applications and the related common fundamental problems as well as the determination of research directions to improve the understanding and applications of GridGIS. It also provides a venue for scientists to network with their peers working in similar fields.

It covers a wide range of theoretical and experimental topics in the area of GridGIS including:

- Definition and Architecture of GridGIS, including spatial information grid theory and technologies
- GridGIS middleware for security, error disposal, and the management of resources, tasks, users, login, messages, duplication, and logging
- Algorithms in GridGIS, including cooperative computing of spatial information, parallel, distributed, and intelligent data processing algorithms, etc.; Security of GridGIS
- Integration of remote sensing and global positioning systems (GPS) with GridGIS
- Data access service, metadata management and information service
- Applications of GridGIS, including online spatial decision support system, location-based service, telegeoprocessing, telemonitoring, Digital Earth, public emergency prevention and monitoring, etc.

We are pleased to have received a number of high-quality submissions. We conducted a rigorous peer-review process for each submission, with the support of all Program Committee members as well as a group of external reviewers. Based on the reviews, we selected five papers to be included in this program. We congratulate the authors of accepted papers, and regret that many excellent submissions could not be included due to the time and space limit.

Taking this opportunity, we would like to thank the authors of all the submissions for their contributions to the program. We would also like to thank the Program Committee members and external reviewers for their efforts in reviewing the papers.

Yong Xue
Chenghu Zhou
GridGIS 2006 Workshop Organizers

Workshop Co-chairs

Yong Xue	IRSA, Chinese Academy of Sciences, China
Chenghu Zhou	IGSNRR, Chinese Academy of Sciences, China

Program Committee

Ken Fisher	London Metropolitan University, UK
James King	London Metropolitan University, UK
Eunjoo Lee	London Metropolitan University, UK
Romas Mikusauskas	London Metropolitan University, UK
Peter Oriogun	London Metropolitan University, UK
Karim Ouazzane	London Metropolitan University, UK
Costas Varotsos	University of Athens, Greece
Yong Xue	IRSA, Chinese Academy of Sciences, China
Chenghu Zhou	IGSNRR, Chinese Academy of Sciences, China
Honglei Zhu	Clarke University, USA

International Workshop on High-Performance Computing in Genomic Proteomics and Transcriptomics

(HPC-GTP 2006)

Data mining and machine learning techniques have been widely applied in many practical problems. The ever-increasing growth of data arising in diverse areas has urged the development of high-performance methods, software and tools to extract useful information from data and to derive knowledge.

Genomics, proteomics and transcriptomics are among the most important areas where information obtained from very large datasets can assist medical researchers in understanding the structure and functions of the humane genome, discovering new personalized drugs, and diagnosing genetic diseases.

The problems arising in these areas have some unique characteristics. First, the quantity of data produced is going to exponentially increase in the next few years, leaving a stable gap of two orders of magnitude between known sequences and identified structures. Furthermore, the data are often updated, which, for example, poses problems to the training step of supervised learning techniques. Finally, the data have the unusual feature of comprising a very large number of variables. Indeed, publicly available datasets can contain data with tens of thousands of characteristics, which are updated regularly. This tendency is going to result in the need for algorithms that can handle such complexity in the next few years.

Due to the size and efficiency problems, it is likely that such very large databases will only be processed or mined using loosely connected supercomputers. Since standard data mining and machine learning algorithms do not achieve a good performance in the considered computational paradigm, special algorithms must be designed to exploit that strong computational infrastructure.

The HPC-GTP 2006 workshop, held in conjunction with The International Symposium on Parallel and Distributed Processing and Applications (ISPA 2006), aimed to bring together researchers who use high-performance computing to solve these computationally demanding problems in genomics, proteomics and transcriptomics. It represents a first attempt to collect the existing expertise in the field and engage researchers in this exciting and rapidly growing research area. Finally, special thanks to all authors for their contributions to the program. We would also like to thank the Program Committee members and external reviewers for their efforts in reviewing the submissions.

Mario R. Guarracino
Panos M. Pardalos
Laurence T. Yang
HPC-GTP 2006 Workshop Organizers

General Chairs

Mario R. Guarracino   National Research Council, Italy
Panos M. Pardalos   University of Florida, USA
Laurence T. Yang   St. Francis Xavier University, Canada

Program Committee

Mario Cannataro   University of Catanzaro, Italy
Vipin Chaudhary   Wayne State University, USA
Maria Luisa Chiusano   University of Naples "Federico II," Italy
Claudio Cifarelli   University of Rome "La Sapienza," Italy
Amitava Datta   University of Western Australia, Australia
Ivanoe De Falco   ICAR-CNR, Italy
Andrei Doncescu   LAAS-NCSR, France
Ryoko Hayashi   Kanazawa Institute of Technology, Japan
Chun-Hsi Huang   University of Connecticut, USA
Chokchai Leangsuksun   Louisiana Tech, USA
Tao Li   Int. University of Florida, USA
Wenjun Li   UT Southwestern Medical Center, USA
Yiming Li   National Chiao Tung University, Taiwan
Jun Ni   University of Iowa, USA
Clara Pizzuti   ICAR-CNR, Italy
Oleg Prokopyev   University of Florida, USA
Onur Seref   University of Florida, USA
El-Ghazali Talbi   LIFL, France
Domenico Talia   University of Calabria, Italy
Ernesto Tarantino   ICAR-CNR, Italy
Gerardo Toraldo   University of Naples "Federico II," Italy
Albert Zomaya   University of Sydney, Australia

International Workshop on Parallel and Distributed Computing in Engineering (PDCE 2006)

This workshop is an international forum for engineers, developers, and researchers to share experiences, discuss new ideas, and present results on all aspects of parallel and distributed computing applied to engineering. It covers contributions from academia and industry applied to all branches of engineering, such as aeronautical, agricultural, automotive, bioengineering, biological, biomedical, chemical, civil, computer, control, electrical, electronics, environmental, forest, industrial, manufacturing, materials, mechanical, mechatronic, metallurgical, naval, nuclear, optical, transportation, petroleum. Papers may describe new architectures, algorithms, methods, techniques, tools and software applications.

Topics of interest include, but are not limited to: methods for parallel and distributed applications development; parallel and distributed algorithms; parallel and distributed application software; parallel and distributed dedicated architectures; parallel and distributed numerical methods; parallel and distributed optimization methods; parallel and distributed reconfigurable computing; parallel and distributed simulations; performance analysis of parallel and distributed applications; real-time parallel and distributed computing; techniques for parallel and distributed applications development; and tools for parallel and distributed applications development.

This year we are very proud to have received 26 high-quality submissions. We conducted a rigorous peer-review process for each submission, with the great support of all Program Committee members as well as a group of external reviewers. Based on the reviews, we selected eight papers to be included in this program. We congratulate the authors of accepted papers, and regret that many quality submissions could not be included due to the time and space limit.

Taking this opportunity, we would like to thank the authors of all the submissions for their contributions to the program. We would also like to thank the Program Committee members and external reviewers for their efforts in reviewing the submissions. Finally, we would like to thank Geyong Min and Gudula Rünger, the ISPA 2006 Workshop Co-chairs, for the guidance in the organization of this workshop.

Alvaro L. G. A. Coutinho
Carlos Augusto P. S. Martins
Jairo Panetta
José Eduardo Moreira
José Nelson Amaral
Petr Ya. Ekel
Witold Pedrycz
PDCE 2006 Workshop Organizers

Executive Committee

General Co-chairs: Carlos Augusto P.S. Martins
                      Pontifical Catholic University of Minas Gerais, Brazil
                      Petr Ya. Ekel
                      Pontifical Catholic University of Minas Gerais, Brazil
Workshop Co-chairs: Alvaro L. G. A. Coutinho
                      Federal University of Rio de Janeiro, Brazil
                      Carlos Augusto P. S. Martins
                      Pontifical Catholic University of Minas Gerais, Brazil
                      Jairo Panetta
                      National Institute for Space Research, Brazil
                      José Eduardo Moreira
                      IBM Thomas J. Watson Research Center, USA
                      José Nelson Amaral
                      University of Alberta, Canada
                      Petr Ya. Ekel
                      Pontifical Catholic University of Minas Gerais, Brazil
                      Witold Pedrycz
                      University of Alberta, Canada

Program Committee

Eugênio Sper Almeida	National Institute for Space Research, Brazil
José Nelson Amaral	University of Alberta, Canada
Marcelo Cintra	University of Edinburgh, UK
Walfredo Cirne	Federal University of Campina Grande, Brazil
Alvaro L. G. A. Coutinho	Federal University of Rio de Janeiro, Brazil
Tiaraju Asmuz Divério	Federal University of Rio Grande do Sul, Brazil
Petr Ya. Ekel	Pontifical Catholic University of Minas Gerais, Brazil
Djalma Mosqueira Falcão	Federal University of Rio de Janeiro, Brazil
Sergio Takeo Kofuji	University of São Paulo, Brazil
Eugene Levner	Holon Academic Institute of Technology, Israel
Carlos Augusto P. S. Martins	Pontifical Catholic University of Minas Gerais, Brazil
Wagner Meira	Federal University of Minas Gerais, Brazil
Rodrigo Fernandes de Mello	University of São Paulo, Brazil
Alba Cristina M. A. de Melo	University of Brasilia, Brazil
José Eduardo Moreira	IBM Thomas J. Watson Research Center, USA
Philippe Olivier A. Navaux	Federal University of Rio Grande do Sul, Brazil
Jairo Panetta	National Institute for Space Research, Brazil
Witold Pedrycz	University of Alberta, Canada
Edison Zacarias da Silva	State University of Campinas, Brazil
Maria Helena Murta Vale	Federal University of Minas Gerais, Brazil

International Workshop on Parallel and Distributed Multimedia Computing

(ParDMCom 2006)

In recent decades, multimedia computing has emerged as an important technology to generate content based on images, video, audio, graphics, and text. Furthermore, the recent new development represented by high-definition(HD) and interactive television will generate important computing problems connected with the creation, processing, and management of multimedia content. Dealing with HD multimedia content (image, video and sound) will generate a huge volume of data to process, which can lead in a natural way to parallel and distributed computing. Moreover, the inherent data parallelism of multimedia content data makes this type of computing a natural application area for parallel and distributed processing.

This workshop aims to merge the recent research achievements in developing new theories, algorithms, architectures, systems and integrated multimedia platforms that exploit parallel and distributed computing. The papers included in this workshop reflect current trends in the parallel and distributed multimedia computing research areas with topics such as parallel and distributed algorithms for multimedia, parallel and distributed architectures for multimedia, and multimedia content creation, processing, and management using parallel and distributed architectures.

Many people contributed to the success of ParDMCom 2006. We wish to thank the Program Committee members and the external referees for their great work. We would also like to express our gratitude towards the ISPA 2006 organizers for their help in this whole process.

Agustinus Borgy Waluyo
Shu-Ching Chen
Hui Huang Hsu Ma Lin
Sabin Tabirca Laurence T. Yang
Jianhua Ma
ParDMCom 2006 Organizers

Executive Committee

Steering Co-chairs:	Laurence T. Yang, St. Francis Xavier University, Canada
	Jianhua Ma, Hosei University, Japan
General Co-chairs:	Shu-Ching Chen, Florida International University, USA
	Hui-Huang Hsu, Tamkang University, Taiwan

Program Co-chairs: Agustinus Borgy Waluyo, Monash University, Australia
Sabin Tabirca, National University of Ireland at Cork, Ireland
Man Lin, St. Francis Xavier University, Canada

Program Committee

Marios C. Angelides	Brunel University, UK
Bernady O. Apduhan	Kyushu Sangyo University, Japan
Dorin Bocu	Transiylvania University of Brasov, Romania
Hsuan T. Chang	National Yunlin University of Science and Technology, Taiwan
Lawrence Y. Deng	St. John's University, Taiwan
Michael Ditze	University of Paderborn, Germany
Xubin He	Tennessee Technological University, USA
Jason C. Hung	Northern Taiwan Institute of Science and Technology, Taiwan
Ismail Khalil Ibrahim	Johannes Kepler University Linz, Austria
Wenbin Jiang	Huazhong University of Science and Technology, China
Qun Jin	Waseda University, Japan
James Joshi	University of Pittsburgh, USA
Hong-va Leong	Hong Kong Polytechnic University, Hong Kong, China
Qing Li	City University of Hong Kong, Hong Kong, China
Alex Zhaoyu Liu	University of North Carolina at Charlotte, USA
Hongli Luo	Indiana University-Purdue University Fort Wayne, USA
Vishv Malhotra	University of Tasmania, Australia
Paul McKevitt	Ulster University, UK
John O'Mullane	National University of Ireland at Cork, Ireland
Mei-Ling Shyu	University of Miami, USA
Ling Tan	Monash University, Australia
Guojun Wang	Central South University, China
Zhiyong Xu	Suffolk University, USA
Xiaochuan Yi	AT&T, USA
Zhiwen Yu	Nagoya University, Japan
Chengcui Zhang	University of Alabama at Birmingham, USA
Chi Zhang	Florida International University, USA

International Workshop on Middleware Performance

(WOMP 2006)

Middleware technologies consist of various components that form the infrastructure or plumbing of distributed applications. Middleware performance plays a critical role in the end-to-end performance of distributed applications, which are characterized by a constant variation of location and intensity of users and/or their service. Middleware, based on existing and emerging technologies such as CORBA, .Net, EJB, Jini, Grid, Web Services, etc., should provide mechanisms to support applications to handle highly dynamic environments. This relies on awareness about the performance of middleware in order to assure certain degrees of service quality, such as response time or availability.

Ensuring adherence to performance requirements in middleware-based applications demands the characterization of metrics, measurement techniques, evaluation methods and benchmarks. The complexity of the design of such applications makes even more stringent the need for methodologies and tools that help the software designer in evaluating the impact of different alternatives in middleware on the application quality.

WOMP 2006 provided a forum for the growing community of scientists, researchers and software engineers interested in performance of middleware-based distributed applications, including essentially all kinds of measurement, analysis, prediction and testing, from requirements to software architecture, to design, to implementation. Performance analysis is intended in the very broad sense of analyzing nonfunctional quantitative aspects of such applications. This workshop focused on methods, measures, and tools for performance of distributed application developed from middleware. This includes middleware infrastructure, interaction paradigms, communication protocol, software architecture, middleware applications, other nonfunctional quality attributes, etc., and their relationship with performance.

This year we accepted papers that highlighted interesting research issues and provided insightful solutions. We were delighted to see contributions of accepted papers from three aspects. First, the performance evaluation and modeling issues are addressed in the context of emerging middleware domains including grid applications, Web services and context-aware mobile applications. Second, topics cover a wide spectrum including empirical evaluation and studies, analytical modeling, performance management tools and software architecture design. Third, papers address practical needs for methods, tools and models to be applicable to middleware systems.

All these contributions form a basis for inspiring and promoting fruitful discussions on the creation, use and refinement of methods, measures, and tools for performance of distributed applications developed from middleware. We thank our reviewers who made a considerable effort to review the papers.

We hope you find the workshop proceedings beneficial and enjoyable.

Carlos Juiz
Andrea D'Ambrogio
Yan Liu
WOMP 2006 Workshop Co-chairs

Workshop Co-chairs

Carlos Juiz	University of the Balearic Islands, Spain
Andrea D'Ambrogio	University of Rome "TorVergata," Italy
Yan Liu	NICTA, Australia

Program Committee

Mariacarla Calzarossa	University of Pavia, Italy
Shiping Chen	CSIRO, Australia
Lawrence Chung	University of Texas at Dallas, USA
Vittorio Cortellessa	University of L'Aquila, Italy
Mariela Curiel	University Simón Bolvar, Venezuela
Lorenzo Donatiello	University of Bologna, Italy
Ian Gorton	Pacific Northwest National Lab, USA
Gnter Haring	University of Vienna, Austria
Giuseppe Iazeolla	University of Rome "TorVergata," Italy
Yan Jin	Swinburne University of Technology, Australia
Helen Karatza	Aristotle University of Thessaloniki, Greece
Samuel Kounev	Cambridge University, UK
Ming Li	Deakin University, Australia
José Merseguer	University of Zaragoza, Spain
Dorina Petriu	Carleton University, Canada
Ramon Puigjaner	University of the Balearic Islands, Spain
Nary Subramanian	University of Texas at Tyler, USA
Antony Tang	Swinburne University, Australia
Cho-Li Wang	University of Hong Kong, Hong Kong

International Workshop on Information Security and Digital Forensics

(ISDF 2006)

During the last few years, the IT community has witnessed the rapid growth of the information security and digital forensics sector with the introduction of many new concepts and technologies. Such developments have been influenced by the growing popularity of the Internet as well as the availability of powerful computers and high-speed networks.

However, modern society is increasingly victimized by the exponential growth of criminal activities in cyberspace. Computers are misused for many illegal activities, such as e-mail espionage, credit card fraud, spam and software piracy, which result in invasion of privacy and disruption of daily lives. As a result, the necessity for prevention and prosecution of cyber-crime is also growing rapidly. This workshop is organized to bring together the international community of researchers and practitioners of information security and digital forensics in order to address this critical issue.

The objective of ISDF 2006 was to serve as a forum to present current and future work as well as to exchange research ideas in the field of information security and digital forensics. The workshop successfully attracted the participation of many researchers and practitioners, resulting in the submission of 45 papers. They were all thoroughly reviewed by the Program Committee members and external reviewers, and they selected 12 papers to be presented at the workshop.

We, the Co-chairs, extend our gratitude to the Program Committee members and external reviewers for their excellent work and their active participation in the creation of this technical program. We also thank all the authors for making this workshop possible. Finally, we extend special thanks to Yunseong Choi, who helped us organizing the workshop.

We hope you enjoy the workshop proceedings.

Kuinam J. Kim
Dong Chun Lee
Sung-Jae Yu
Sangho Lee
ISDF 2006 Workshop Organizers

Executive Committee

Steering Co-chairs: Kuinam J. Kim, Kyonggi University, Korea
Dong Chun Lee, Howon University, Korea
Sangho Lee, Kyonggi University, Korea
Program Chair: Jingyuan (Alex) Zhang, University of Alabama, USA

Program Committee

Junheun Jeung	Sunmoon University, Korea
Moung Ju Kim	Seoul Women's University, Korea
Sang Chun Kim	Kangwon University, Korea
Jae Choul Moon	STG Security, USA
Sangseo Park	The University of Melbourne, Australia
Sungjae Yu	Jungbu University, Korea

International Workshop on Ubiquitous Processing for Wireless Networks

(UPWN 2006)

Traditionally, wireless systems are considered for voice communication. However, wireless networks are becoming more popular for data processing. Since wireless communication guarantees freedom of movement, it can provide easier access from anywhere. Hence, wireless networks are a vital element for ubiquitous processing. Ubiquitous processing for wireless networks (UPWN) aims for seamless, secure, and intuitive access to the various ubiquitous computing networks for distributed processing. As the need for ubiquity grows, there has been great effort to support ubiquitous computing environments through distributed and parallel processing over networks. This conference provides an international forum for the presentation and showcasing of recent advances in various aspects of ubiquitous processing for wireless networks. It reflects the state of the art in computational methods, involving theory, algorithms, numerical simulation, error and uncertainty analysis and/or novel applications of new processing techniques in engineering, science, and other disciplines related to ubiquitous computing wireless networks. At the conference, discussions on specific themes of interest to the participants were included.

This workshop is a unique opportunity for developers, administrators, researchers, and service providers of ubiquitous computing to meet. It can provide an inside view of new paradigms in parallel and distributed processing for ubiquitous networking.

We are very proud to have received a large number of high-quality submissions. Based on the reviews, with the great support of all Program Committee members as well as a group of external reviewers, we selected 12 papers out of 38 submitted papers to be included in these proceedings. We regret that many quality submissions could not be included. Once again, we would like to thank all the authors of all the submissions for their contribution. We would also like to thank the Program Committee members and the external reviewers who did the peer review for the successful workshop. I owe special thanks to Geyong Min and Gudula Rünger, who served as ISPA 2006 Workshop Co-chairs and proceedings editors, for their guidance in organizing this workshop.

Keecheon Kim
UPWN 2006 Workshop Organizer

Executive Committee

General Chair: Keecheon Kim, Konkuk University, Korea
Program Co-chairs: Jongwon Choe, Sookmyung Women's University, Korea
                        Yan Ma, Beijing University of Post and Telecommunication, China
Steering Co-chairs: Michael Ha, Sprint Nextel Communications, USA
                        Sang Lee, Microsoft, USA
                        Oshiito Oyama, Tsukuba University, Japan

Program Committee

Jinsung Choi   LG Electronics, Korea
Hyunseung Choo   Sungkyunkwan University, Korea
Koji Okamura   Kyushu University, Japan
Vincent Tang   NUS, Singapore

Reviewers

Nael Abuhalaweh
Marcos D. de Assuncao
Rocco Aversa
Junguk Baek
Jacir L. Bordim
Anu Bourgeois
Patrick Bridges
Rajkummar Buyya
Wentong Cai
Valentina Casola
Liang Cheng
Eunjung Cho
Guojing Cong
Ewa Deelman
Frederic Desprez
Joerg Diederich
Falko Dressler
Iain Duff
Brett Estrade
Hafiz Farooq
Noria Foukia
Franco Frattolillo
Satoshi Fujita
Akihiro Fujiwara
Marc Garbey
Wolfgang Gentzsch
Jonathan Giddy
Luc Giraud
Minyi Guo
Suman Gupta
Lee Joon Heo
Annika Hinze
Adrinan Hong
Tsung-Chuan Huang
Nisar Hundewale
Shuichi Ichikawa
Yasushi Inoguchi
Chuzo Iwamoto
Fakhra Jabeen
Young-Sik Jeong
Xiaohong Jiang
Kazuki Joe
Hirotsugu Kakugawa
Daniel S. Katz
Andre Kerstens
Byungcheol Kim
Jik-Soo Kim
Kyong Kim
Hiroaki Kobayashi
Biplab Kumer
Dongeun Lee
Jaeil Lee
Hyukjoon Lee
Sunghung Lee
Jaehuann Leem
Kuan-Ching Li
Yiming Li
Maryline Markursius
Stefano Marrone
Susumu Matsumae
Hiroshi Matsuo
Antonino Mazzeo
Nicola Mazzocca
Lois Curfman McInnes
Rodrigo de Mello
Simon Miles
Reiko Miller
Eiji Miyano
Christine Morin
Syed Naqvi
Elth Ogston
Daniel Olmedilla
Hong Ong
Benno Overeinder
Marcin Paprzycki
Michael Philippsen
Massimiliano Rak
Ulrich Ruede
Shoichi Saito
Amal El F. Seghrouchni
Yongtae Shin
Wei Shyy
Roy Sterritt
Heinz Stockinger
Hussein Suleman
Alan Sussman
Hiroyuki Takizawa
Kiyofumi Tanaka
Feilong Tang
Michela Taufer
Tomoaki Tsumura
Laslo Varga
Yuri V. Vassilevski
Salvatore Venticinque
Cho-Li Wang
Dajin Wang
Guojun Wang
Joe Shang-Chieh Wu
Chao-Tung Yang
Ouklel Yang
Baoliu Ye
Jae Yong
Jaepil Yoo
Il-Chul Yoon
Liu Yun
Jose Alberto F. Zepeda
Jingyuan Zhang

Table of Contents

Track 2: Middleware and Cooperative Computing

Track 3: Techniques, Algorithms and Applications

Track 4: Advanced Networking

XHPC 2006 Workshop

S-GRACE 2006 Workshop

GridGIS 2006 Workshop

WOMP 2006 Workshop

ISDF 2006 Workshop

UPWN 2006 Workshop

DNA: Diameter NEMO Applications Based on Binding Update Integration

Youngjin Ahn[1], Tae-Jin Lee[1], Hyunseung Choo[1], and Sungchang Lee[2]

[1] School of Information and Communication Engineering
Sungkyunkwan University, 440-746, Suwon, Korea
{yjahn, tjlee, choo}@ece.skku.ac.kr
[2] Department of Telecommunications
Hankuk Aviation University, 200-1, Goyang, Korea
sclee@hau.ac.kr

Abstract. NEtwork MObility (NEMO) technology leads to manage not only host mobility but also the mobility of an entire network. For practical usage, mobile users should however be authenticated by their service provider when accessing foreign networks. AAA for NEMO (AFN) [8] provides a solution to perform the AAA mechanism, based on NEMO Basic Support (NBS). When we consider the AAA mechanism, the binding update procedure (BU) would also be performed when Mobile Router (MR) does frequent handoffs between Mobile Networks. These two procedures (Authentication and BU) result in additional overhead if they are performed separately. Therefore, both are considered for formulating an integration scheme. An efficient solution is proposed by integrating the binding update message into the Diameter protocol, in order to reduce traffic overhead and routing delay. The proposed scheme is analyzed in terms of measurement factors of transmission time and processing time. As a result, the proposed scheme outperforms AFN up to 8~35% in terms of routing delay.

1 Introduction

NEtwork MObility (NEMO) is technology that supports and manages group mobility. It ensures session continuity for all nodes in the Mobile Network, when the Mobile Router (MR) changes its point of attachment to the Internet. Whenever the Mobile Network moves to foreign networks, the MR dispenses with handoff overhead of each Mobile Network Node (MNN) inside the MR, which efficiently manages the network resources by making connections hierarchical. Hence, the IETF NEMO Working Group actively researches into the MR and Network Mobility.

In order to extend NEMO for practical use by Internet service providers, authentication, authorization, accounting (AAA) should be provided to support NEMO. In using the AAA mechanism, the structure is provided for authenticating a MR or MNN, and establishing Security Associations (SAs) between

G. Min et al. (Eds.): ISPA 2006 Ws, LNCS 4331, pp. 1–10, 2006.

entities. The representative protocols of AAA are RADIUS, TACACS+, and Diameter. Among these protocols, Diameter is the most suitable protocol for making NEMO secure with respect to roaming, scalability, and flexibility. Diameter adapts to various network environments. It also adapts NEMO for authenticating an MNN. A MR embracing an MNN should have the capability to use the Diameter protocol for the MNNs.

In the case of AAA application for Mobile IPv6 (MIPv6), some mechanisms are proposed to authenticate mobile devices for use on the Internet. The study for the Diameter MIPv6 application has begun with [5] and [10]. Even though both provide AAA using Diameter, [10] is more efficient than [5] because [10] enables the Diameter message to support embedded Binding Update. For NEMO, Kwon et al. proposed AAA for NEMO (AFN) [8], and provided the Diameter application protocol for adapting to the NEMO Basic Support protocol (NBS) [6]. This proposal allows an MR to authenticate MNNs behind the MR.

Although AFN provides a proper solution for AAA, it is also necessary to consider additional signaling overhead for handoff, when processing the BU message. Therefore, the new Diameter NEMO Application (DNA) scheme is proposed by integrating the BU message in the Diameter message, particularly when MNNs frequently move from one domain to another, and are based on NBS. The proposed DNA is analyzed and it is demonstrated that the proposed scheme is more efficient than AFN in terms of routing delay and network traffic overhead.

In this paper, related work on the study of AAA protocol with MIPv6 and NEMO is first introduced in Section 2. In Section 3, an integration scheme is proposed to minimize traffic overhead and delay. A model is derived to measure the delay of AFN and the proposed DNA in Section 4. Finally, Section 5 concludes this paper and discusses future work.

2   Related Works

The Diameter base protocol [2] can be extended to several applications such as NAS [3], MIPv4 [1], and MIPv6 [10] applications. The MIPv4/v6 applications that support a mobile node (MN) are authenticated and authorized, and SAs between entities are made by distributing the security keys when the MN is roaming foreign networks. The Diameter for MIP consists of three entities: home AAA server (AAAH), local AAA server (AAAL), and attendant. AAAH is located in the MN's home network. When an MN moves into a foreign network, AAAH authenticates the MN through the Diameter message exchanges. AAAL in the foreign network enables the MN to use of its network resource after the authentication procedure. The attendant is an entity providing a service interface between the MN and AAAL. It can be an access router (AR) in MIPv6 [7] and a foreign agent (FA) in MIPv4 [11]. Diameter defines a format in the form of Attribute Value Pairs (AVPs). Fundamental AVPs are provided in the base protocol [2], and additional AVPs for supporting MIP property are defined in MIP application documents. Diameter for MIPv4 has already been standardized while that for MIPv6 still remains open as an Internet draft, to make extension more certain. Furthermore, it is necessary to provide Diameter to NEMO applications for roaming in foreign networks.

Prior to NEMO consideration, MIPv6 applications for Diameter should be studied. Diameter MIPv6 applications are proposed by Dupont et al. [5] and Le et al. [10]. Both of the proposed applications define new AVPs for application to MIPv6 in Diameter packet format. The AVPs are located in the transport layer and Diameter entities use them to perform Diameter message exchanges. In these protocols, a node has a Network Access Identifier (NAI) to identify its unique device instead of its home address (HoA). Since AAAL receives a NAI included in a request message, it can route to its AAAH, authenticating the requester. Hence, the NAI is the essential parameter in the Diameter MIPv6 protocol. The MN itself does not support the Diameter protocol because it should be transparent to the AAA mechanism. It is assumed that the MN has long-term SA only with its AAAH. Both AAAH and AAAL share a secure channel.

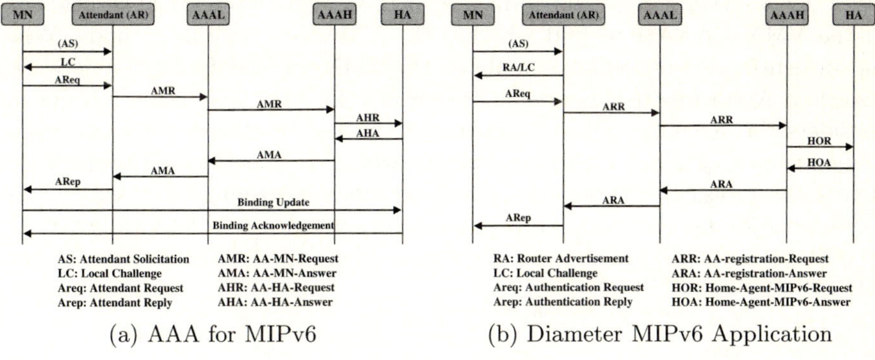

(a) AAA for MIPv6   (b) Diameter MIPv6 Application

Fig. 1. The solutions for adapting AAA to MIPv6

Fig. 1, (a) depicts message flows of AAA for MIPv6 proposed by Dupont et al. [5] and (b) describes those of Diameter MIPv6 application by Le et al. [10]. The attendant corresponds to the AR, and each domain has an AAA server, as AAAL and AAAH to be used by the Diameter protocol. The home agent (HA) is used for routing when the MN is located in the visited link. Fig. 1 (a) and (b) appears to be similar with regard to the message flow. When the MN moves to a new foreign domain and transmits an authentication request message to the attendant, it converts the message to the Diameter message, to check the permission. This message includes AAA parameters and key materials. However, Fig. 1(b) supports the binding update embedded in Diameter message exchange, while (a) does not support this update. (b) is efficient because of reducing additional overhead when the MN moves frequently and performs inter-domain handoff. In (b), AAAH can dynamically detect the HA's address through the Dynamic Home Agent Address Discovery (DHAAD) mechanism, using the Diameter AVP related to MIPv6, in the event that the MN does not know its HA address. Therefore, (b) makes better use of AVPs than (a), and can be remarkably flexible.

4   Y. Ahn et al.

AAA for NEMO (AFN) [8] is a Diameter application protocol for adapting
to NEMO. The architecture and message exchanges in this scheme are not quite
different to the Diameter MIPv6 application described above, but are in the
nested mobile network environment. This protocol is based on NEMO Basic
Support (NBS) [6] and supports Mobile Network session continuity. In the NBS
protocol, when the Top Level MR (TLMR) moves to another subnet, each MR
nested in TLMR makes a tunnel to forward packets to its HA. In the case of
the nested Mobile Network, tunnel processing is piled up to the nested level,
and packets from the visiting mobile node (VMN) should bypass each MR's HA
until arriving at a communicating correspondent node, called pinball routing.

Fig. 2 depicts the message flow to authenticate the VMN in a foreign network.
When a VMN comes to the MR's realm, the MR becomes the attendant and
the VMN requests the authentication message to the MR. The MR makes a
Diameter message to request VMN's authentication and then forwards this to
it's AAAH through the NBS tunnel. From the point of view of VMN's, the
MR's AAA server can be the VMN's AAAL, so that the message is forwarded
to the VMN's AAAH to find whether the VMN is a legitimate node. When
the authentication procedure completes, the VMN can use the foreign network's
resources. According to this scheme, it provides the AAA protocol to NEMO and
considers the AAA procedure in Diameter message exchange when requesting
authentication. Then, the Binding Update procedure is performed by the VMN.
Hence, the protocol induces extra overhead, due to exchanging messages twice
on registration for the usage of foreign network resources.

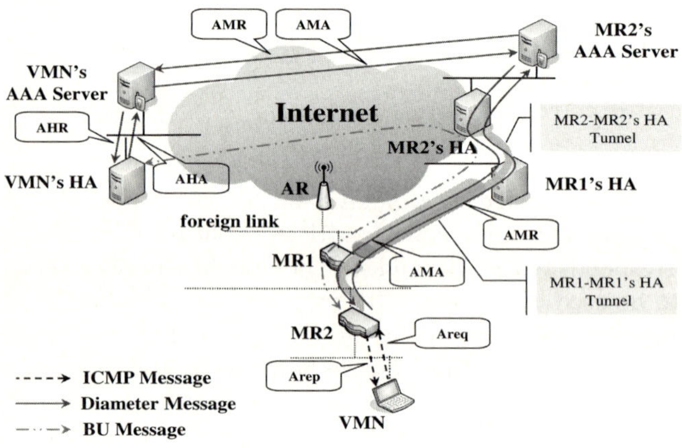

Fig. 2. The architecture of AFN

3   Proposed Diameter NEMO Application

3.1   Motivation

As discussed in Section 2, AFN based on the NBS protocol does not consider
handoff signaling overhead but considers authentication message exchange. If a

node frequently moves from one domain to another, it not only requests the AAA procedure to be authenticated by its AAAH, but it also requires a BU procedure in each handoff. These two procedures should occur successively, in common handoff situations, and result in overhead from double message exchange. To reduce this burden, a new scheme which integrates the BU message into the Diameter message is proposed, and the scheme is designated as Diameter NEMO Application (DNA).

The proposed DNA process may have several advantages in terms of efficiency. First, it lifts the burden when sending two different messages, *i.e.*, Diameter message and BU message. If a node has frequent mobility, it must send authentication requests and location registration messages. It can present serious overhead when initiating fast roaming. Secondly, it is possible to carry out additional work related to HA such as DHAAD. The DHAAD procedure is a merit of the MIPv6 protocol because it can allocate an MN's HA address to the MN when the MN does not have an HA address, or wants to change it's HA address. Finally, the proposed integrating procedure reduces traffic overhead causing by MN's sending BU message in the foreign network. With regard to scalability, it is important to note that the signaling storm may have occurred from the signaling traffic.

3.2 DNA Flow Messages and Header Format

New messages that the DNA exchanges are provided to support Diameter in integrating a VMN's location registration in the authentication procedure. Prior to introducing these messages, several parameters contained in the message

Table 1. DNA flow messages

Message Name	Description: *Parameters*	Type
Attendant Solicitation (AS)	Router solicitation including AAA security option	ICMP
Attendant Advertisement (AA)	Router advertisement including AAA security option	ICMP
Authentication Request (AReq)	Authentication request message including BU : $NAI, HoA, HAA, LC, HC, KM, BU$	ICMP
Authentication Reply (ARep)	Authentication reply message including BA : NAI, HoA, HAA, KM, BA	ICMP
Diameter-NEMO-Registration-Request (DRR)	Authentication request with diameter message : $NAI, HoA, HAA, HC, KM, BU$	Diameter
Diameter-NEMO-Registration-Answer (DRA)	Authentication answer with Diameter message : $NAI, HoA, HAA, HC, KM, BA$	Diameter
Home-Agent-Diameter-NEMO-Request (HDR)	Home agent request with Diameter message : HAA, BU, KM	Diameter
Home-Agent-Diameter-NEMO-Answer (HDA)	Home agent answer with Diameter message HAA, BA, KM	Diameter

exchanges, are provided. NAI is the Network Access Identifier for identifying where the MR or VMN originates, and provides the routing path, along which MR or VMN is authenticated. BU and BA are the Binding Update and Binding Acknowledgement messages, respectively. These messages are used in transparent routing, to maintain session continuity for the Internet service. The HoA (Home address) and HAA Home Agent Address are the required addresses for routing during MR or VMN handoff. LC is the local challenge with a random value, and should be generated by the attendant. HC is MR or VMN's host challenge and the value used to authenticate a MR or VMN by the AAAH. It is an encrypted value of LC for creating the session key between requester and AAAH. KM is the Keying Material used to establish a temporary security association (SA) between entities, such as VMN-HA and VMN-AAAL. Based on these message parameters, it is important that the foreign network validates visiting nodes and allocates resources to these nodes. According to the above parameters, new flow messages are created and sent to each entity. The new messages are described in Table 1.

To support binding update in the Diameter procedure, BA/BU AVPs are extended and the Diameter message header has an additional flag N. The N flag set informs AAA servers that the message comes from the Mobile Network. When the AAAL receives the Diameter message from a remote attendant (MR) in the foreign network, the IP address header of this message contains the source, destination, and home address option (HAO) address. Since the AAAL does not have the binding cache of the MR, it requests MR's binding information from its HA, using a signaling process, and refers to the HA for the validity of the addresses in the message header. Therefore, the attendant should set the N flag so it transmits the Diameter message to its AAA server.

3.3   DNA Description

In this section, the details for the proposed DNA are described. In Fig. 3, an example of DNA topology is provided. The VMN enters the nested Mobile Network, carrying out the authentication procedure with the binding update to use the resources of the foreign network. Although the original resource of the Internet is serviced by the AR's link, the VMN should to be authenticated to MR2's AAAL at the VMN's standpoint because it shares MR2's network resources. Each MR's link has a hierarchically different Mobile Network Prefix (MNP). The VMN optionally sends the AS (Authentication Solicitation) signal in order to attach to the MR2's link, and then it receives the AA (Authentication Advertisement) as a router advertisement message which includes LC. After the VMN makes its CoA from AA message, it sends AReq message to the attendant (MR2). The attendant constructs the DRR message from the VMN's request information and sends the message to its AAAL (MR2's AAA server) to authenticate the VMN. Since the MR2 is nested to MR1, the MR1 receiving the DRR message makes a tunnel between the MR1 and it's HA for mobility transparency. Since this procedure is based on the NBS protocol, the Diameter message exchanges are also performed by tunneling process. When AAAL receives the DRR, it relays the message to the AAAH (VMN's AAA server) to check the validity of the VMN. When the AAAH receives the DRR message, it authenticates the VMN and recognizes the BU AVP. The BU message including keying materials for when the Diameter message is delivered to the VMN's HA and the HA not only performs AAA processes, but also binding registration. The reverse route (HDA-DRA-ARep) includes the information of authentication and BA.

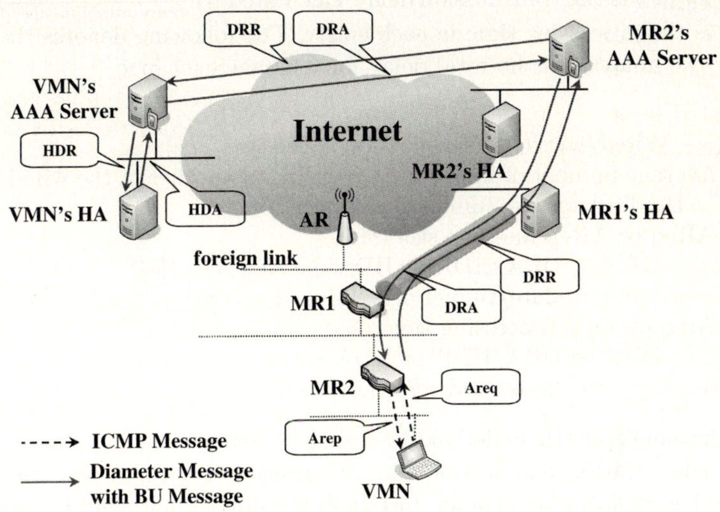

Fig. 3. The authentication procedure of DNA message

The dynamic Home Agent Address Discovery (DHAAD) function could be used to learn the address of HAs in the home network. The MR or MN may not know the HA's address at the home link. In the event that a VMN does not know it's HA's address, it sends and receives the DHAAD message. This message provides the HA's address on the home network. The BU message contains the DHAAD message in the HAO field in MIPv6. In the DNA scheme, this message can instead be embedded to in Diameter's AVP, and the MR/MN acquires its HA's address. Therefore, the DNA does not need to transmit the DHAAD message separately. The DHAAD AVP field could be encrypted by the Diameter protocol.

4   Performance Evaluation

4.1   Modeling

There are several assumptions to compare these schemes fairly. The delay is considered as performance measurement and the processing capacity of all nodes is identical. The transmission speed of wired routers is 10 times faster than that

of wireless routers. The propagation and queuing delay is not considered in the
evaluation because they are not seriously influential. Each domain is uniformly
distributed in the Internet and the distance between entities is simply one hop in
the same domain. The general processing delay of wired routers is not considered.

The delay factors are evaluated as a measurement. The end-to-end delay generally consists of transmission delay and processing delay. That is, $D_{TOT} =
H \cdot (D_{TRANS} + D_{PROC})$, where H is the number of hops. D_{TOT} means the total
delay. D_{TRANS} is the transmission delay, calculated by $\frac{packet\ size(bit)}{transmission\ speed(bit/sec)}$.
D_{PROC} is the processing time in each entity. The following denotes the param-
eters for the analysis of the total delay for massage exchange.

N – Nested level
B_{wd}/B_{wl} – Wired/wireless Transmission speed (bit/sec)
H_{avg} – Average number of hops from an entity to another in the wired network
S_{bu}/S_{tu} – Binding update/tunnel header size (bit)
S_{areq} – AReq or ARep message size (bit)
S_{drr}/S_{hdr} – DRR or DRA/HDR or HDA message size (bit)
T_{bu}/T_{tu} – Binding update/tunnel processing time (sec)
T_{areq} – Areq or Arep processing time (sec)
T_{drr}/T_{hdr} – DRR or DRA/HDR or HDA processing time (sec)
T_{ref} – Message verification and reference time (sec)

The performance metric is derived to compare each scheme in terms of authentication and location registration time. Examples of each scheme are show in
Fig. 4 and generalize the formula. In Fig. 4, the dotted line/solid line means the
wireless/wired link, respectively. The box indicates the domain boundary.

$$
\begin{aligned}
D_{TOT_{AFN}} = 2\Bigg[& \frac{1}{B_{wl}}\left\{ S_{areq} + S_{bu} + N \cdot (S_{drr} + S_{bu}) + 2\sum_{k=1}^{N} k \cdot S_{tu} \right\} \\
& + \frac{1}{B_{wd}}\left\{ \left((N+1)(S_{drr} + S_{bu}) + 2\sum_{k=1}^{N} k \cdot S_{tu}\right) \cdot H_{avg} + S_{drr} + S_{hdr} \right\} \\
& + T_{areq} + T_{drr} + 2T_{bu} + 4N \cdot T_{tu} + 3T_{ref} + 2T_{hdr} \Bigg]
\end{aligned}
$$

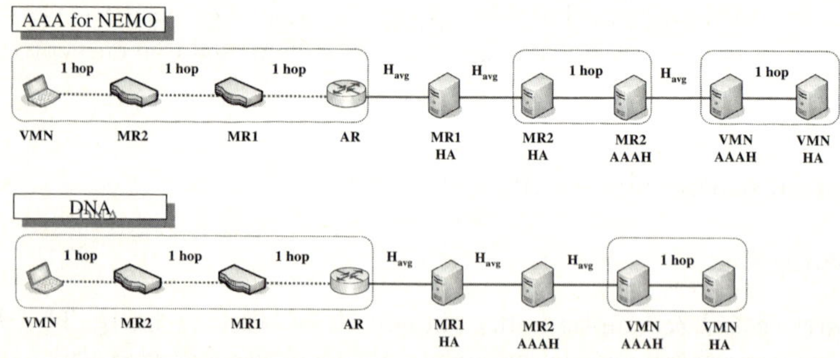

Fig. 4. Flow models of AFN and proposed DNA

$$D_{TOT_{DNA}} = 2\left[\frac{1}{B_{wl}}\left\{S_{areq} + S_{bu} + N \cdot S_{drr} + \sum_{k=1}^{N-1} k \cdot S_{tu}\right\}\right.$$

$$+ \frac{1}{B_{wd}}\left\{\left((N+1)S_{drr} + \sum_{k=1}^{N-1} k \cdot S_{tu}\right) \cdot H_{avg} + S_{hdr}\right\}$$

$$\left. + T_{areq} + T_{drr} + 2T_{bu} + 2(N-1)T_{tu} + 3T_{ref} + 2T_{hdr}\right]$$

4.2   Analytical Results

The total delay of AFN and DNA is evaluated. The following values are used
for evaluation of the described schemes, as presented in Table 2:

Table 2. Parameters for performance evaluation

S_{bu}	S_{tu}	S_{areq}	H_{avg}
40×8	20×8	256×8	10
S_{hdr}	S_{drr}	B_{wd}	B_{wl}
256×8	512×8	10^8	10^7

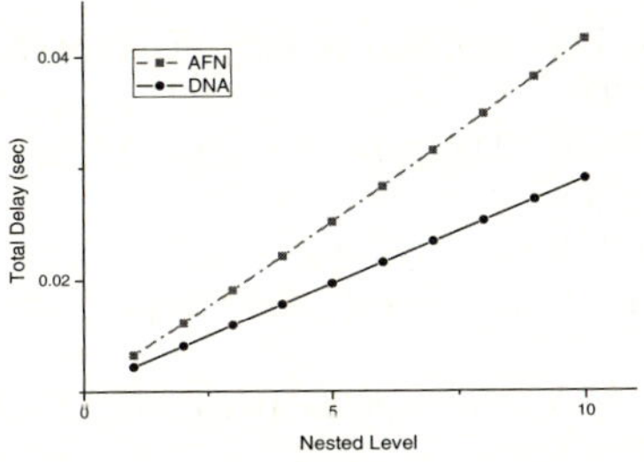

(a) Total delay vs. nested level

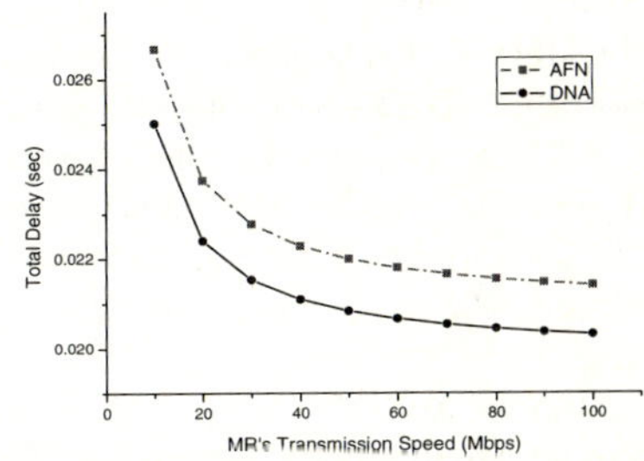

(b) Total delay vs. MR's transmission
speed in level 5

Fig. 5. Total delays for nested levels and MR's transmission speed

The analysis results are presented in Fig. 5. Fig. 5(a) presents the total delay
in terms of nested level in the Mobile Network, and Fig. 5(b) indicates the
total delay when the MR changes transmission speed. The degree at which the
changing transmission speed influences total delay is the goal of experiments,
since the wireless environment does not guarantee the MR's bandwidth. The
results from two plots demonstrate that the proposed DNA outperforms AFN in
terms of the total delay, *i.e.*, delays of Diameter message exchange and binding
update procedure. It is demonstrated that DNA is more efficient than AFN, up
to 8~35% along the variance of nested levels.

5   Conclusion

The more mobile devices emerge, the importance of NEMO technology increases. The research on Diameter NEMO Application is active as soon as the AFN protocol is introduced as an Internet draft. In this paper, a new combining scheme for AAA is proposed. In addition, a new analysis model is proposed to evaluate the total delay of message exchange. It is demonstrated that the proposed DNA approach is more efficient than AFN in terms of delay. As a future work, the route optimization scheme in Diameter NEMO application will be researched.

Acknowledgement

This research was supported by the Ministry of Information and Communication, Korea under the Information Technology Research Center support program supervised by the Institute of Information Technology Assessment, IITA-2005-(C1090-0501-0019). Corresponding author: H. Choo.

References

1. P. Calhoun, T. Johansson, C. Perkins, and T. Hiller, "Diameter Mobile IPv4 Application," IETF, RFC 4004, August 2005.
2. P. Calhoun, J.Loughney, E. Guttman, G. Zorn, and J. Arkko, "Diameter Base Protocol," IETF, RFC 3588, September 2003.
3. P. Calhoun, G. Zorn, D. Spence, and D. Mitton, "Diameter Network Access Server Application," IETF, RFC 4005, August 2005.
4. A. Conta and S. Deering, "Internet Control Message Protocol (ICMPv6) for the Internet Protocol Version 6 (IPv6) Specification," IETF, RFC 2463, December 1998.
5. F. Dupont and M. Laurent-Maknavicius, "AAA for mobile IPv6," IETF, draft-dupont-mipv6-aaa-01, November 2001.
6. V. Devarapalli, R. Wakikawa, A. Petrescu, and P. Thubert, "Network Mobility (NEMO) Basic Support Protocol," IETF, RFC 3963, January 2005.
7. D. Johnson, C. Perkins, and J. Arkko, "Mobility Support in IPv6," IETF, RFC 3775, June 2004.
8. T. Kwon, S. Baek, S. Pack, and Y. Choi, "AAA for NEMO," IETF, draft-kwon-aaa-nemo-00, July 2005.
9. C. de Laat, G. Gross, L. Gommans, J. Vollbrecht, and D. Spence, "Generic AAA Architecture," IETF, RFC 2903, August 2000.
10. F. Le and C. E. Perkins, "Diameter Mobile IPv6 Application," IETF, draft-le-aaa-diameter-mobileipv6-04, November 2004.
11. C. Perkins, "IP Mobility support for IPv4," IETF, RFC 3220, January 2002.
12. J. Vollbrecht, P. Calhoun, S. Farrell, L. Gommans, G. Gross, B. de Bruijn, C. de Laat, M. Holdrege, and D. Spence, "AAA Authorization Framework," IETF, RFC 2904, August 2000.

Towards Real-Time Processing of Monitoring Continuous k-Nearest Neighbor Queries[*]

HaRim Jung, Sang-Won Kang, MoonBae Song, SeokJin Im,
Jongwan Kim, and Chong-Sun Hwang

Department of Computer Science and Engineering
Korea University
1, 5-Ga, Anam-dong, Sungbuk-gu, Seoul, Korea
{harim, swkang, mbsong, seokjin, wany, hwang}@disys.korea.ac.kr

Abstract. This paper addresses the problem of monitoring continuous k-nearest neighbor (k-NN) queries. In order to support highly dynamic environments, where objects and/or queries are frequently moving, monitoring continuous k-NN require real-time updated results when objects and/or queries change their locations. Thus, it is important to minimize time delay for maintaining up to date the results. In this paper, we present the monitoring method to shorten time delay for updating continuous k-NN queries based on the notion of result region and the minimum bounding rectangle enclosing all objects inside each cell, referred to as $cMBR$, in the main-memory grid index structure. Simulations are conducted to show the efficiency of the proposed method.

1 Introduction

This paper addresses the problem of monitoring continuous k-nearest neighbor (k-NN) queries in a mobile computing environment. Given a set of moving (or static) objects and a set of moving (or static) query points, monitoring continuous k-NN query continually updates the closest k objects to each query point during the running time of each query. Because continuous queries have long running time, monitoring continuous queries focuses more on CPU-time efficient continuous maintenance of the results than initial result computation for each query. Thus, we are not concerned with initial k-NN evaluation and we assume that initial result of each query is available.

Since the large set of queries and objects update their location asynchronously, it is inefficient to update the index and re-evaluate each query results whenever any query and/or object moves [8]. Therfore, we periodically update the index and re-evaluate all query results affected by the motion of objects at fixed time interval Δt. Under the periodic update method, the query results easily deviate from the actual result due to the mobility of objects and/or queries.

[*] This work was supported by the Second Brain Korea 21 Project and the Korea Research Foundation Grant funded by the Korea Government(MOEHRD) (KRF-2005-041-D00665).

G. Min et al. (Eds.): ISPA 2006 Ws, LNCS 4331, pp. 11–20, 2006.

In order to provide real-time updated results for continuous k-NN query, it is critical to minimize Δt. In this paper, we utilize the notion of result region and minimum bounding rectangle enclosing all objects inside each cell, referred to as $cMBR$, in the main-memory grid index structure. The result region and $cMBR$ lead to save CPU-time for needless distance computation. Based on the notion of result region and $cMBR$, we present methods for index maintenance and query re-evaluation to shorten CPU-time for monitoring continuous k-NN queries.

The rest of this paper is organized as follows. Related work for monitoring continuous k-NN queries is discussed in Section 2. In Section 3, we present our technique covering index structure, incremental query re-evaluation algorithm, and optimizations. Section 4 presents the performance evaluation. Finally we conclude the paper in Section 5.

2   Related Work

Traditional algorithms for answering k-NN queries have been introduced by Roussopoulos et al. [2]. They assume a set of static objects indexed with R-tree-like structures [1] and present branch-and-bound R-tree traversal algorithm to avoid the examination of the entire index contents by utilizing two distance metrics, $MINDIST$ and $MINMAXDIST$. These two metrics provide a lower and an upper bound on the actual distance of object o from query point q respectively. In [4], the authors proposed modified branch-and-bound algorithm based solely on $MINDIST$ without reducing efficiency. In [5], the best-first search algorithm which achieves the optimal I/O performance has been proposed. It maintains a priority queue of the entries visited so far in ascending order by $MINDIST$.

Various techniques that consider answering k-NN queries under dynamic environments, where objects or queries are constantly moving have been proposed [6,7]. These techniques utilize spatial or temporal validity information for answering continuous k-NN queries. These techniques do not assume that queries run continually over the database and focus on efficient query evaluation for a single snapshot query.

Recently, motivated by LBSs, methods for monitoring continuous k-NN queries were proposed in [9,10]. These methods focus on maintaining query results for multiple long running queries in a CPU-time efficient way. They use a grid-like index structure for easy and fast maintenance.

Yu et al. [9] propose two main-memory indexing approaches with different scenarios for monitoring exact continuous k-NN queries over moving objects: object indexing and query indexing. With object indexing approach, overhaul query re-evaluation and incremental query re-evaluation, referred to as Yu-CNN, are suggested. Query indexing approach, which is suit for the case that the number of queries is very small, indexes query points instead of objects. Authors also introduce hierarchical extension of object indexing approach for improving performance when objects are not uniformly distributed.

Xiong et al. [10] propose SEA-CNN. SEA-CNN deals with incremental monitoring of continuous k-NN queries by considering only moving objects that may influence the query results. SEA-CNN assumes that objects are indexed with grid structure in secondary-memory and focuses on incrementally re-evaluating the query results without considering the evaluation of initial k-NN evaluation. SEA-CNN also considers the motion of queries.

Both Yu-CNN and SEA-CNN utilize previous k-NNs for re-evaluating query results. In particular, the search scope for the new query result is set to be the circular region centered at query point q with radius equal to the distance between q and the previous NN that is currently furthest as shown in Figure 1(a). However the search scope of both Yu-CNN and SEA-CNN is approximated with the collection of cells in the grid G. Every shaded cell c should be visited and the objects that fall in c should be considered, even if they do not constitute the actual result, in order to guarantee the correct result. Figure 1(b) illustrates the approximated search scope. Although all objects inside bold-lined cells do not constitute the actual NNs of q they must be examined.

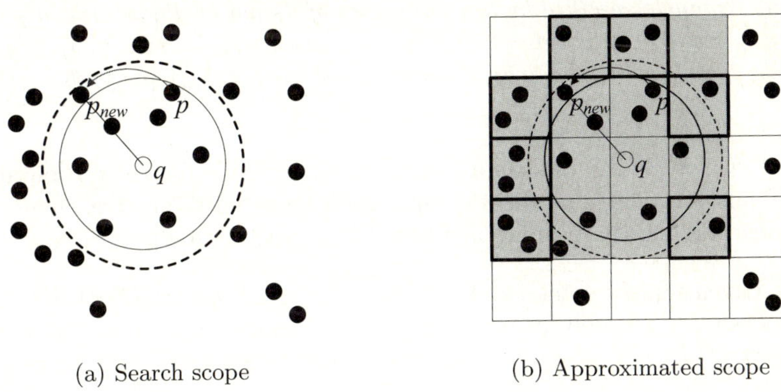

(a) Search scope   (b) Approximated scope

Fig. 1. Search scope and approximated search scope (k=7)

In order to avoid visiting needless cells, we propose continuous k-NN monitoring method based on the notion of result region and $cMBR$ in Section 3.

3 Monitoring of Continuous k-NN Queries

Like existing methods mentioned in Section 2 [9,10], we assume two-dimensional data space and given a set of query points in the data space, we periodically re-evaluate the k-Nearest Neighbors (k-NNs).

We focus on re-evaluating query answers in a CPU-time efficient way by reducing unnecessary computation for monitoring k-NN queries. In other words, we focus on reducing time interval between two consecutive re-evaluation periods. Since what is important in monitoring continuous k-NN queries is to continually maintain k-NNs over time and to minimize time delay Δt caused by re-evaluation, we do not deal with initial k-NN evaluation.

We use grid index for simple and fast maintenance under dynamic environment. The grid index G is two-dimensional array of cells generated by uniformly partitioning the data space with its size=$\delta \times \delta$. Each cell, denoted as $c_{i,j}$, at column i and row j (starting from low-left corner), contains every object with its coordinates (obj_x, obj_y), where $\lfloor x/\delta \rfloor = i$, $\lfloor y/\delta \rfloor = j$. Additional structure are also used for efficiency.

3.1 Preliminaries

In this section, we give definitions of $cMBR$ and pruning heuristic that are necessary for the description of our algorithm for monitoring continuous k-NN queries. Data structure for our method is also presented.

Definition 1. *Given a cell $c_{i,j}$ and objects $Obj = \{obj_i, 1 \leq i \leq n\} \in c_{i,j}$ with their coordinates (obj_x, obj_y), $cMBR_{i,j}$ is a two dimensional minimum bounding rectangle specified by two endpoints of its major diagonal $min\_point = (x_{min}, y_{min})$ and $max\_point = (x_{max}, y_{max})$, where $x_{min} = min(\forall obj_x)$, $y_{min} = min(\forall obj_y)$, $x_{max} = max(\forall obj_x)$ and $y_{max} = max(\forall obj_y)$ for $\forall (obj_x, obj_y)$ of $Obj \subset c_{i,j}$.*

With the use of $cMBR$, we can avoid visiting needless cells that do contain the result. Thus, we reduce needless computation for monitoring continuous k-NN queries by utilizing the pruning heuristic PH presented in [2].

- PH: Given a query point q and $cMBR_{i,j} \subset c_{i,j}$, if $MINDIST(cMBR_{i,j}, q) <$ kth_dist, $c_{i,j}$ is safely pruned because it cannot contain the object nearer than kth NN, where kth_dist is distance between kth NN and query q.

During the monitoring k-NN queries, we maintain main-memory based grid index structure and additional information.

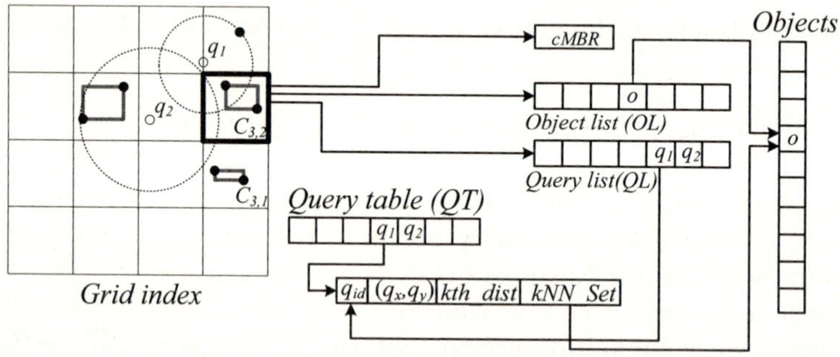

Fig. 2. Grid index structure and query table

Figure 2 illustrates the index structure. Each cell $c_{i,j}$ in the grid G maintains its $cMBR_{i,j}$ and OL, the list of objects within its extents. In addition, $c_{i,j}$ has the lists of queries whose result regions intersect with the $c_{i,j}$, referred to as query list QL.

Query table QT stores the queries that are currently running with their ids, coordinates, kth_dist, and current k-NNs. By using kth_dist, we determine the result region of each query q (i.e., the circular region centered at the query point q with radius equal to kth_dist).

3.2   Static Query Monitoring over Moving Objects

In this section, we present monitoring scheme for static k-NN queries. We assume that the initial result of each query q is available. By using the initial result of each q, we incrementally maintain the index and re-evaluate the result of q in every re-evaluation period if location updates of objects occur. In particular, for each cell $c_{i,j}$ in G, we takes the following steps:

1. Check if any of the inner objects moves out of $c_{i,j}$, denoted as obj_{out}. If so, obj_{out} is deleted from the object list of $c_{i,j}$. Each q in the query list of $c_{i,j}$ is checked whether q contains obj_{out} in its kNN_set. In case obj_{out} is in kNN_set of q and obj_{out} moves out from the result region of q, obj_{out} is deleted from kNN_set of q, kth_dist is set to $dist(q, obj_{out})$ and q is marked as affected.

2. Check if any of the inner objects moves within $c_{i,j}$, denoted as obj_{within}. If so, each q in the query list of $c_{i,j}$ also should be checked. In particular, for each q in the query list of $c_{i,j}$,
   - if q is marked as affected, q is ignored.
   - if obj_{within} is in kNN_set of q and obj_{within} moves out from the result region q, obj_{within} is deleted from kNN_set of q, kth_dist is set to $dist(q, obj_{within})$ and q is marked as affected.
   - if obj_{within} is not in kNN_set of q and obj_{within} moves into the result region of q, kth NN of q is deleted from kNN_set and obj_{within} is inserted into kNN_set. Then the order of kNN_set and the result region of q are updated.

3. Check if any of the outer objects moves into $c_{i,j}$, denoted as obj_{in}. If so, obj_{in} is inserted into the object list of $c_{i,j}$. Then, every q that is not marked as affected in the query list of $c_{i,j}$ is checked. If obj_{in} moves into the result region of q from step 2, the kth NN of q is deleted from kNN_set and obj_{in} is inserted into kNN_set. Then, the order of kNN_set and the result region of q are updated.

After above steps, we re-evaluate each affected query q_{aff}. We utilize priority queue and pruning heuristic PH for efficient query re-evaluation. Figure 3 illustrates the re-evaluation algorithm to retrieve the new kNN_set of q_{aff}. For each affected query q_{aff}, we first initialize the priority queue (line 1 in Figure 4) and enqueue all cell entries $\{c_{i,j}, MINDIST(cMBR_{i,j}, q)\}$ whose $MINDIST(cMBR_{i,j}, q)$ has less than $q_{aff}.kth\_dist$ (line 2-4 in Figure 3). Then,

16   H. Jung et al.

enqueued elements are visited. Finally, we update the new kNN_set and kth_dist (line 5-9 in Figure 3). After termination of the re-evaluation algorithm, the result region is updated.

As shown in Figure 4, when re-evaluate the affected queries, although the search scope of proposed method (cells inside the bold line in Figure 4(a)) is the same as that of Yu-CNN and SEA-CNN (cells inside the bold line in Figure 1(b)), we enqueue only shaded cells (in Figure 4(b)) into the priority queue. Thus, the number of distance computation for objects is reduced.

Algorithm 1

Input. G: grid index, q_{aff}: affected query

Procedure.

initialize the priority queue

for each cell $c_{i,j}$ that intersects with the result region of q_{aff} **do**

    if $MINDIST(cMBR_{i,j}, q) \leq q_{aff}.kth\_dist$ **then**

        enqueue every cell entry $\{c_{i,j}, MINDIST(cMBR_{i,j}, q)\}$

    end if

while entry has key $< q_{aff}.kth\_dist$ and priority queue is not empty **do**

        dequeue the next entry of the queue

    for each $obj \in c_{i,j}$ in the cell entry **do**

        if $dist(obj, q_{aff}) < q_{aff}.kth\_dist$ **then**

            update $q_{aff}.kNN\_set$ and $q_{aff}.kth\_dist$

        end if

    end for

end while

update the result region of q_{aff} in G

Fig. 3. Re-evaluation algorithm for static affected query

Although the query re-evaluation algorithm reduces the search scope of affected query q_{aff} and the number of visited cells, thus leads to shorten each re-evaluation time interval Δt due to reduction of the number of distance computation for objects, CPU-time for query re-evaluation is further reduced by using the notion of the result region.

Let Up_{obj} be the set of location updates of objects. Clearly, if the result region of q contains at least k objects after Up_{obj}, we can simply compute distance from the objects that fall in the result region to q. Then we form the new result of q without using re-evaluation algorithm. For this purpose, each q maintains additional counter, sorted list $q.in\_list$ for incoming objects and sorted list $q.out\_list$ for outgoing objects during the re-evaluation. Only if the number of outgoing objects Num_{out} is greater than the sum of the number of incoming objects Num_{in} and the number of remaining objects Num_{rem}, we mark q as affected and re-evaluate q by using Algorithm 1. However, in order to reduce the search scope, we set $q.kth\_dist$ to distance between the query point q and $\{Num_{out} - (Num_{in} + Num_{rem})\}th$ element of $q.out\_list$.

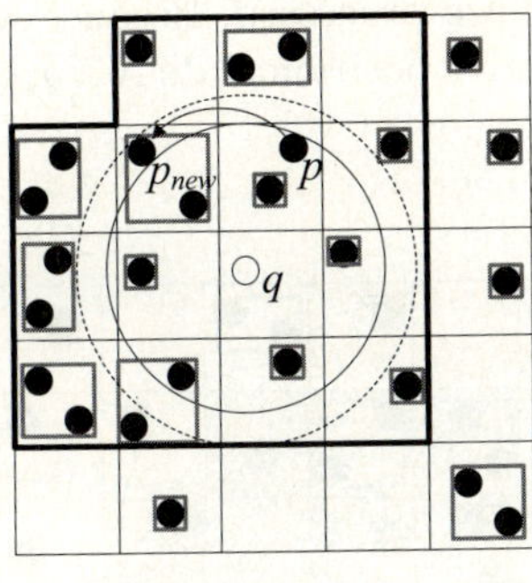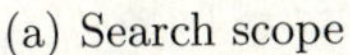

(a) Search scope

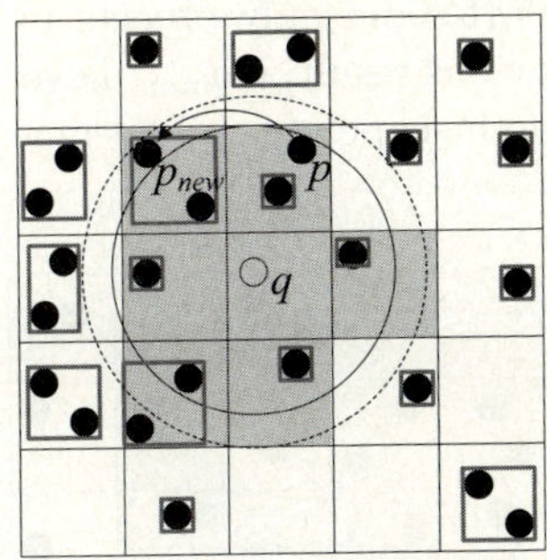

(b) Enqueued cells

Fig. 4. Search scope and enqueued cells of proposed method (k=7)

3.3   Moving Query Monitoring over Moving Objects

In this section, we consider query re-evaluation for moving query points over moving objects. In case a query q updates its location, we maintain query results incrementally based on the previous result, similar to SEA-CNN, and compare our proposed method with SEA-CNN because Yu-CNN does not consider the motion of queries.

When the moving query point q_{mov} changes its location q_{old} to a new location q_{new}, SEA-CNN sets the search scope of q_{mov} to the circular region centered at q_{new} with radius equal to $kth\_dist_{prev} + dist(q_{old}, q_{new})$, where kth_dist_{prev} is the previous kth_dist of q_{mov}. This guarantees that at least k objects are inside the search scope of q_{mov}. Although SEA-CNN incrementally re-evaluates the query result, it visits the cells more than necessary to answer the result due to the unnecessarily increased search scope.

To reduce the unnecessary increase of search scope when the queries move, we utilize the distances between queries and previous kNN_set. Specifically, when the moving query q_{mov} changes its location q_{old} to a new location q_{new} ,we mark the q_{mov} as affected irrelevant to whether it is affected by moving objects or not. In other words, it is unnecessary to check this query being affected by the motion of objects. Then, we set the search scope of moving query point q_{mov} to the circular region centered at q_{new} with radius equal to $max\{dist(q_{new}, NNq(k)_{prev})\}$, where $NNq(k)_{prev}$ is the previous kNN_set of q_{mov}. After update of the search scope of q_{mov}, we re-evaluate the new kNN_set of q_{mov} utilizing Algorithm 1 in Figure 3.

Figure 5 illustrates the search scope of SEA-CNN and the proposed method. As illustrated in Figure 5(a), SEA-CNN visits needless cells to guarantee the correctness of the result because it does not utilize $NNq(k)_{prev}$. Furthermore, when q_{mov} moves, the search scope of SEA-CNN is always larger than the previous result region irrelevant to the direction of the q_{mov} and all objects in the shaded cells must be processed. Compared to SEA-CNN, the search scope of the proposed method is much smaller than that of SEA-CNN as illustrated in

Figure 5(b) and only objects in bold-lined cells are processed. Because we use the previous result, if q_{mov} moves toward the relative position of its $NNq(k)_{prev}$, the search scope of q_{mov} becomes much smaller.

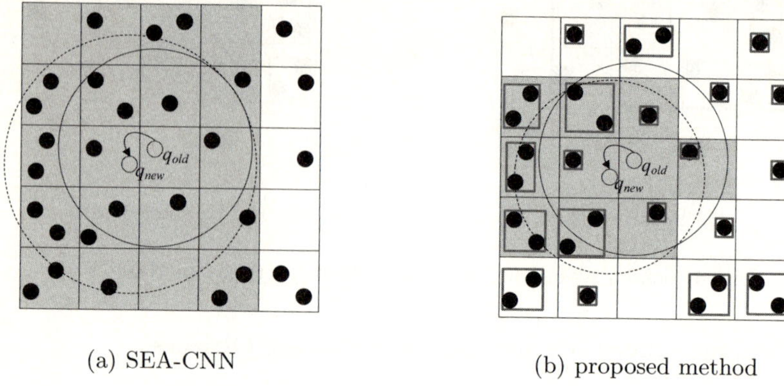

(a) SEA-CNN   (b) proposed method

Fig. 5. Search scope when q_{mov} moves($k{=}7$)

4   Performance Evaluation

In this section, we evaluate the performance of our proposed method. We compare our method with current methods for monitoring continuous k-NN queries (Yu-CNN and SEA-CNN).

All the experiments are performed on a Pentium M 1.2GHz machine with 1GB RAM. As the experimental data sets, we use object points and query points that are generated by pseudo-random number generator. We set k to 10. We first compare the performance of the proposed method with varying the number of objects and the number of queries for static queries with Yu-CNN and SEA-CNN. Then, we compare the performance of proposed method for moving queries with only SEA-CNN because Yu-CNN does not consider the motion of queries. The granularity of the grid index G is set to 64×64 because all methods (including our proposed method) show good performance in 64×64 grid index setting. The number of objects is varied from 10(K) to 100(K) and the number of queries is varied from 1(K) to 10(K) in the experiments.

Firstly, we compare CPU-time of proposed method for re-evaluating static queries with that of Yu-CNN and SEA-CNN. Figure 6 shows the effect of the number of objects and the number of queries. We set the number of queries to 1 (K) and measure the CPU-time with varying the number of objects, then set the number of objects to 10 (k) and measure the CPU-time with varying the number of queries. As illustrated in Figure 6(a), CPU-time of all the three methods is increasing as the number of objects rises. However, our proposed method outperforms Yu-CNN and SEA-CNN. CPU-time of all the three methods is also increased linearly to the number of queries similar to the effect of the number of objects as shown in Figure 6(b) and our proposed method shows the best

Table 1. Simulation parameters

Parameter	Setting
Number of objects	10, 20, 40, 60, 80, 100 (K)
Number of queries	1, 2, 4, 6, 8, 10

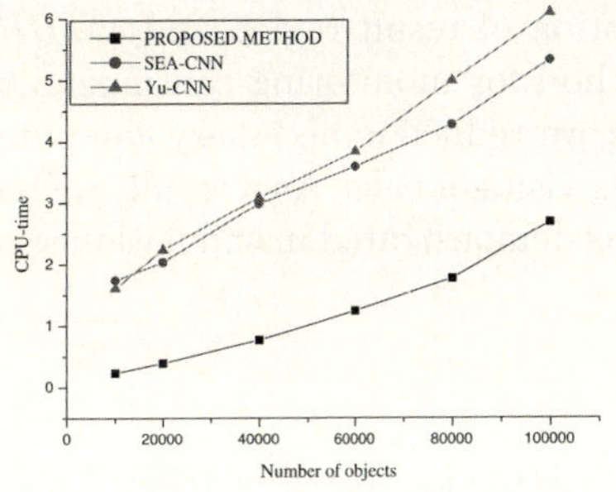

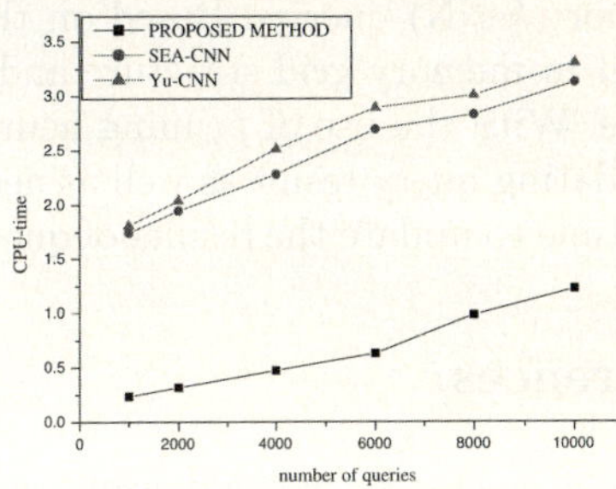

(a) Varying the number of objects   (b) Varying the number of queries

Fig. 6. Effect of the number of objects and queries

performance as the number of queries is increased. This is because proposed method utilizes the notion of $cMBR$ to reduce needless visits of cells and the result region.

Next, we compare the performance of proposed method with SEA-CNN, when both objects and queries are moving. We set the number of queries to 1 (K) and measure the CPU-time with respect to the number of objects. As illustrated in Figure 7, the performance of both proposed method and SEA-CNN degrades rapidly in comparison with the performance when queries are static, as the number of objects is increased. However, our proposed method shows better performance. This is due to the fact that proposed method utilizes previous k NN set in addition to the notion of $cMBR$ and the result region. Thus, our proposed

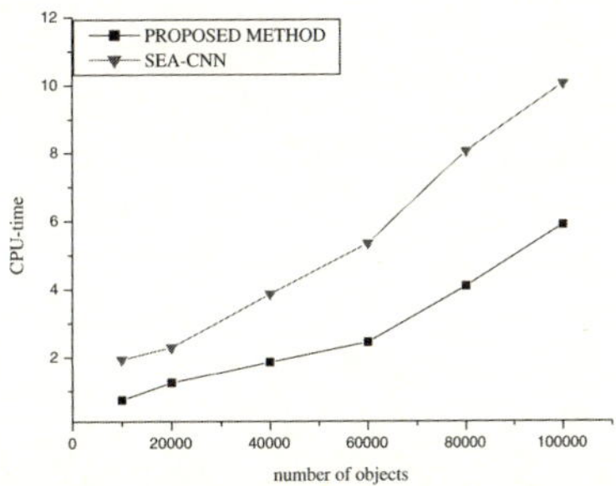

Fig. 7. Effect of the number of objects for moving queries

method reduces the search scope for re-evaluation compared with SEA-CNN which only uses previous radius of the result region.

5   Conclusion

In this paper, we investigate the problem of monitoring continuous k-nearest neighbor (k-NN) queries. Based on the notion of result region and $cMBR$, we present in-memory grid structure and method for monitoring continuous k-NN queries. With the use of pruning heuristic, we reduce unnecessary computation for updating query result as well as needless visits of cells. As a result, we reduce CPU-time to update the results of queries as demonstrated in simulation studies.

References

1. A.Guttman, "R-trees: a dynamic index structure for spatial searching," *In SIG-MOD*, 1984.
2. N.Roussopoulos, S.Kelley, and F. Vincent, "Nearest neighbor search," *In SIGMOD*, 1995.
3. Apostolos Papadopoulos and Yannis Manolopoulos, "Performance of Nearest Neighbor Queries in R-Trees," *In ICDT*, 1997.
4. K. L. Cheung and A. W. C. Fu, "Enhanced nearest neighbor search on the R-tree," *In SIGMOD*, 1998.
5. Gisli R. Hjaltason, Hanan Samet, "Browsing in Spatial Databases," *ACM Transactions on Database Systems*, 1999.
6. Y.Tao and D. Papadias, "Time-parameterized queries in spatio-temporal databases," *In SIGMOD*, 2002.
7. J.Zhang, M. Zhu, D. Papadias, Y. Tao, and D. Lee, "Location-based spatial queries," *In SIGMOD*, 2003.
8. Dmitri V. Kalashnikov, Sunil Prabhakar, Susanne E. Hambrusch, "Main Memory Evaluation of Monitoring Queries Over Moving Objects," *Distrib. Parallel Databases*, 15(2):117-135, 2004.
9. Yu, X., Pu, K., Koudas, N, "K-Nearest Neighbor Queries Over Moving Objects," *In ICDE*, 2005.
10. Xiong, X., Mokbel, M., Aref, W, "SEA-CNN: Scalable Processing of Continuous K-Nearest Neighbor Queries in Spatio-temporal Databases," *In ICDE*, 2005.

Comparison of SBA – Family Task Allocation Algorithms for Mesh Structured Networks

Leszek Koszalka, Michal Kubiak, and Iwona Pozniak-Koszalka

Chair of Systems and Computer Networks, Faculty of Electronics,
Wroclaw University of Technology, 50-370 Wroclaw, Poland
leszek.koszalka@pwr.wroc.pl

Abstract. In the last years, computer networks with mesh structure become a common computing platform. It is very important to find free resources for executing incoming jobs in a short time. The objective of the paper is a comparison between five task allocation algorithms. The evaluation of algorithms properties has been carried out with utilization of the designed and implemented experimentation system. The investigations have been concentrated on complexity as the introduced measure of efficiency. Moreover, a concept of an experimentation system allowing research for allocation in dynamic mode is presented.

1 Introduction

Nowadays, there is a constant need for higher and higher computing power as the software development advances and its basic requirements grow. Instead of using faster and faster processors we can combine several standard execution units and thus create a parallel system for which computing efficiency is far greater than the average of system components [9], [10]. A reasonable way is to design a structure of such a system in a shape of 2- or 3-dimensional mesh (Fig. 1 and Fig. 2).

The main reason is that mesh oriented systems have some very interesting properties like regularity, modularity and also scalability (e.g. [5], [6], [11]). That is why these systems are a very important issue for the implementation of any kind of parallel algorithms when using many execution units (EUs) simultaneously.

Obviously, if we desire to make a full use of the advantages that such a construction gives us, there has to be very efficient task disposition algorithm available. Effective task allocation algorithms are required when we are trying to reduce costs of the network and at the same time preserving the same high computing power. In the literature, many ideas of such algorithms for task allocation purposes have been proposed (e.g. [2], [3], [5], [6], [7], and [8]).

In this paper, we concentrate on the family of so-called stack–based algorithms (SBA) [6], in particular on algorithms proposed by the authors, including BFSBA, SSBA [3] and WSBA [1]. Evaluating properties of the algorithms has been done via simulation using the designed and implemented experimentation system. The main goal of the conducted experiments was inspection of efficiency of the five algorithms considered, including four algorithms from SBA-family.

G. Min et al. (Eds.): ISPA 2006 Ws, LNCS 4331, pp. 21 – 30, 2006.
© Springer-Verlag Berlin Heidelberg 2006

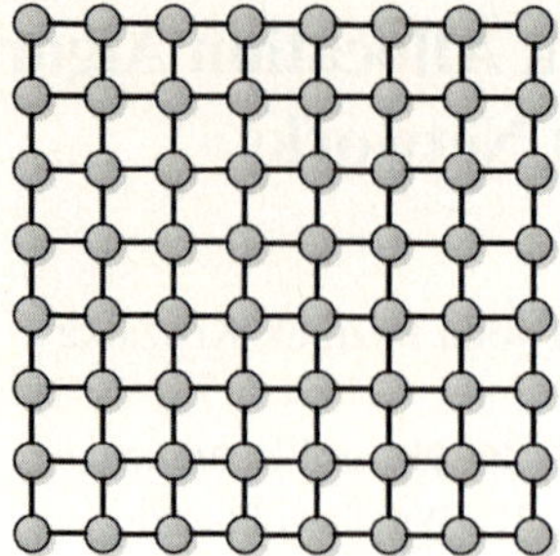

Fig. 1. 2D mesh with 64 EUs

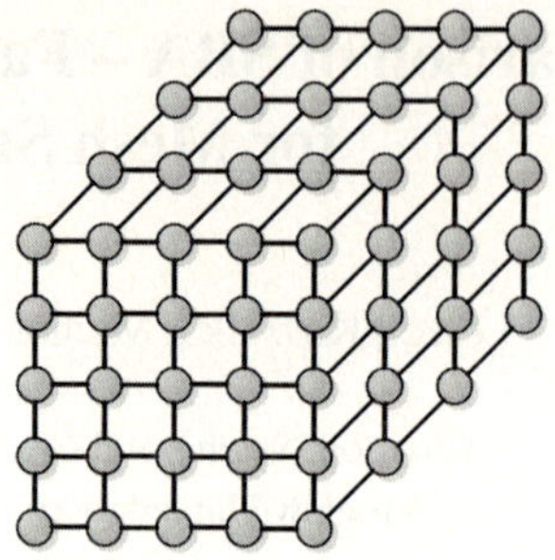

Fig. 2. 3D mesh with 100 EUs

The rest of the paper is organized as follows: Section 2 contains short description of task allocation problem and all algorithms considered. In Section 3 we present our experimentation system. In Section 4 some results of investigations are shown and discussed. In Section 5 new ideas of experimentation system for allocation in dynamic mode (allocation with reallocation) are shortly described. Section 6 contains final remarks.

2 Task Allocation Algorithms

In general, the goal of mesh algorithm in MPP (Massive Parallel Processing) [4] is to allocate a set of rectangular tasks onto the free submeshes of a rectangular processor mesh. When a given task is allocated it occupies a number of processing elements completely until it is finished.

Terms and Notions. Let us introduce some terms and definitions concerning mesh structured networks (without loss of generality with reference to 2D meshes).

A *mesh M(L, W)* is a rectangular structure (Fig. 1) composed of the number of $L \times W$ *nodes*, where L denotes length and W denotes the width of the mesh. This structure may be described as a matrix in which rows and columns are counted beginning with left-upper corner of the mesh. The *submesh S(l, w)* is a rectangular set of $(l \times w)$ nodes that pertain to the mesh $M(L, W)$. A given submesh is described by $\{<x_1,y_1>, <x_2,y_2>\}$, where $<x_1,y_1>$ and $<x_2,y_2>$ are the nodes located in its upper left corner and its lower right corner, respectively.

For algorithms description purposes the following notions are introduced: *Free submesh* or *Candidate Block* (*CB*) is a submesh in which every node is free i.e. it is not at the moment preoccupied with previously allocated tasks. *Busy submesh* (*BS*) is a submesh in which at least one node was already assigned to execute a task. *Total busy submesh* contains only busy nodes. *Coverage* (*C*) is a set of nodes such that using one of them as a *free node* makes a given task to be overlapped with *BS*. *Reject Area* (*RA*) contains nodes such that using any of them as *free node* makes a crossing of the boundary of the mesh by a given task [6].

Assumptions. The paper mainly concerns task allocation in static mode i.e. the following assumptions have been taken into consideration: (i) Any task that is waiting in a queue to be accomplished on the mesh $M(L,W)$ is rectangular. The ith task T_i, where $i=1,2,...,N$ requires a free submesh of known size i.e. $T_i=S(l_i, w_i)$ or $T_i=S(w_i, l_i)$. (ii) The total number of available nodes in the entire mesh is never smaller than the total number of nodes required by N tasks, (iii) Tasks execution times are longer than the predicted total time of their allocation - execution times may be considered as infinite.

Task Allocation Problem. The problem in the static case can be stated as follows:

- *given*: the 2D or 3D mesh, the set (queue) of N tasks with known sizes,
- *problem*: allocation of tasks within the mesh,
- *goal*: to ensure the possibly smallest complexity i.e. the shortest total
- allocation time T_N of N tasks.

Complexity is a value describing the time needed for carrying out all computations required by a given allocation algorithm. This term is regarded as the total number of elementary operations made during the whole allocation process.. This method of time measurement can be justified, because computations are conducted in a multitask computational environment. When we utilize operations by counting then we have opportunities for isolating the complexity of a specific thread – it is especially convenient and reasonable for the future research along with ideas described in Section 5.

Description of Algorithms. We focus on comparison between allocation algorithms such as *FS* (Full Search), which is a simple classic algorithm [1], and algorithms which belong to so-called SBA-family, including

- *SBA*   (Stack Based Algorithm)
- *SSBA*   (Sorted Stack Based Algorithm)
- *BFSBA*   (Best Fit Stack Based Algorithm)
- *WSBA*   (Window Stack Based Algorithm)

FS Algorithm. It begins searching a given mesh from the node $<0, 0>$ for every single task. Nodes are checked row by row until a free node is found. Next, it is checked, whether this free node may be regarded as the left-upper corner of a task being allocated i.e. a free submesh matching a given task may be formed. If this is the case, the task is allocated within this submesh and all nodes occupied by this task become a busy submesh. Then, the next task in a queue is allocated, and so on.

SBA Algorithm. In the beginning, for each task from a queue, the algorithm creates the coverage set C. Next, it creates an initial CB by subtracting the RA from the entire mesh. Then, it puts the initial CB together with the set C for the first task from the queue onto the stack. From now, the algorithm works in a loop. At first, it checks whether the stack is not empty. If it is true, the algorithm checks from the top of the stack whether the position of the set C is null. If it is not, *SBA* tests intersecting C and CB from the top of the stack, and (i) if they have at least one shared node then the top of the stack is popped up from the stack, C is spatially subtracted from CB, and the newly created CBs are pushed up onto the stack with C for the next task from the queue, (ii) if they have not got any shared node, *SBA* exchanges C with the next from the queue without any operation with the stack. When a CB with an empty C position appears on the top of the stack, the desired base block is obtained. Each node from this base block can be returned as the left-bottom node of a submesh in which a given task can be allocated. Finally, an incoming task is accommodated and a new item can be added to the set of busy submeshes.

SSBA Algorithm. The main idea of SSBA consists in reducing the number of tests for intersecting. It has been done by sorting the BS queue [9] through checking the coordinates of the recent CB and C, before doing a test for intersecting. Checking begins with comparing horizontal coordinates of CB and C. Next, if the horizontal coordinates are equal, the vertical coordinates are to be compared, etc. If C has greater coordinates than CB then the remainder of items in the queue has greater coordinates. Thus, at that point a free submesh has been found.

BFSBA Algorithm. The improvement consists in no-rotating when sizes of the considered task are all equal. Some modification called the Better Fit has been applied to SBA. The modified algorithm chooses CB with the minimal height and with the minimal horizontal position. This operation is not extra time-consuming because it can be done during standard run of the SBA scheme.

WSBA Algorithm. The basic idea of the algorithm consists of presenting knowledge of accessible allocation space (i.e. all free nodes available into mesh) in the form of the set of maximum submeshes (*maximum windows*) for any task being allocated.

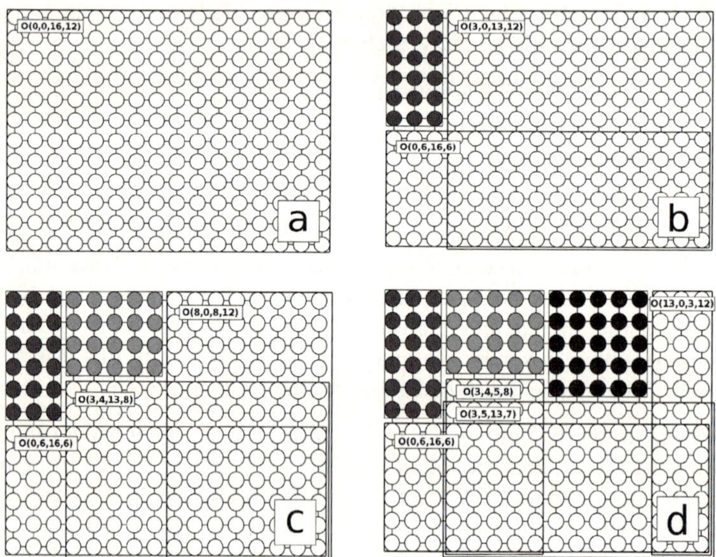

Fig. 3. An example of allocation using *WSBA* with the number of allocated tasks equal to: (a) zero, (b) one, (c) two, (d) three

Maximum windows should have the least as possible common nodes. These windows are placed on the inner stack of the algorithm (window stack) and they are sorted according to left-upper corner, at first along columns, next along rows. The incoming task is always located in the first window on the stack that is large enough to contain it. After successful allocation, the windows on the stack are updated following the rules: (i) none of windows would contain the nodes taken by that allocated task, (ii) a window which is contained in the other window has to be popped from the stack, (iii) windows are cut into maximum windows that do not contain the busy nodes. The algorithm operates in a loop. The idea of maximum windows is shown in Fig. 3 (e.g. O(3,0,13,12) means – left-upper corner as node <3,0> , width of 13 and length of 12).

3 Experimentation System

Following ideas presented in [3], the experimentation process concerning task allocation may be regarded as an input-output system (see Fig. 4).

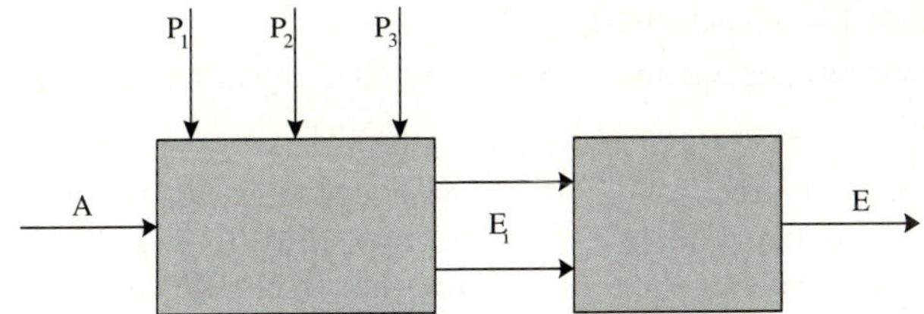

Fig. 4. Allocation process as an input-output system

The observable inputs are constituted by the parameters of the allocation process (symbolized by P$_i$ in the figure), the controllable input is the allocation algorithm (symbolized by A) chosen by the user. The output values can be indices of performance obtained from experiments (symbolized by E$_i$) and the introduced measure to the efficiency (denoted as E) of the series of experiments.

In order to carry out experiments a simulation environment was created in JAVA with application dedicated to work within multi-task environment (MS Windows, Java 1.4.1 SDK). It allows to visualize the state of the allocation process. The experimenter has opportunities to form a design of experiment by determining the inputs, including:

- W and L – parameters (P$_1$) concerning mesh size,
- N - the total number of tasks in a queue as the parameter (P$_2$),
- the parameters (P$_3$) of probability distribution of sizes of incoming jobs - available: (i) normal distribution with *mean* from 1 to 50 and *standard deviation* being less than the mean, (ii) uniform distribution within [1,50]; the random values of w and h are generated separately in both cases,
- the percentage of mesh utilization i.e. the ratio of the sum of products w_i and h_i for all N tasks and the area of the entire mesh given by product WxL,
- A - the allocation algorithm (available *FS*, *SBA*, *SSBA*, *BFSBA*, and *WSBA*).

4 Investigations

The main goal of the simulation experiments was to investigate (for different A) the relationship between complexity (measure of efficiency) and "deterministic" input parameters, including P_1 and P_2. The values of P_3 - probabilistic input were generated 100 times for the same deterministic inputs in order to make results (mean values of complexity) more accurate and thus more reliable. The percentage of mesh utilization was not greater than 75% during all experiments. In respect to the deterministic inputs three cases were considered.

- *Case #1*. Relationship between complexity and the total number of tasks for relatively small mesh ($W=L=30$).
- *Case #2*. Relationship between complexity and the mesh size (for $30<W<120$ and $30<L<120$).
- *Case #3*. Relationship between complexity and the total number of tasks for relatively large mesh ($W=L=130$).
- We concentrated on the proposed WSBA algorithm, trying to evaluate its properties.

Case #1. As it may be seen in Fig. 5 the *WSBA* algorithm appears to be less effective than the commercial algorithm (*SBA*) and their modifications (*SSBA* and *BFSBA*). By looking at the chart we can even guess that a major coefficient of its complexity is exponential. As expected, the algorithm which is based on full search (*FS*) was the worst one.

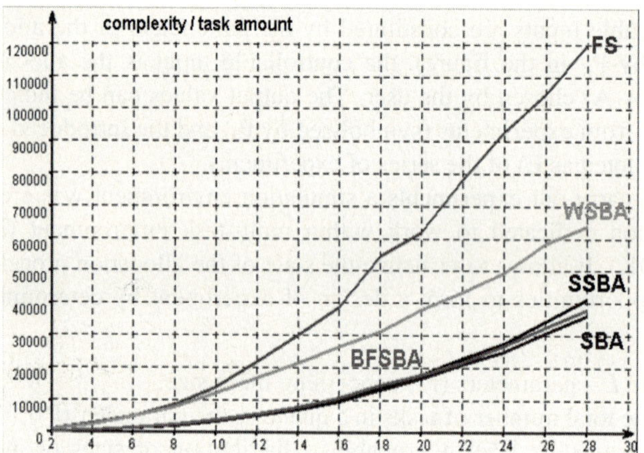

Fig. 5. Complexity vs. total number of tasks for relatively small mesh (30x30)

Case #2. We tested many times the WSBA algorithm trying to find the ranges of inputs at which this algorithm could be recommended. It has materialized in the situation when (i) mesh sizes were greater than 70, and (ii) generation of sizes of tasks ensures that 75% of the entire mesh would be covered by them, approximately. In Fig. 6, the advantage of *WSBA* over other members of *SBA*-family can be observed.

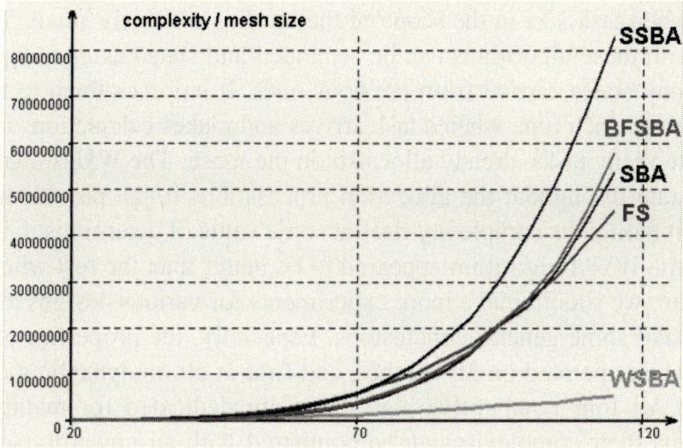

Fig. 6. Relationship between complexity and mesh size

Case #3. We anticipated that with a constantly growing amount of tasks and for rela-tively large mesh, the *WSBA* algorithm can supersede all of its competitors. It was confirmed by the obtained results (see Fig. 7).

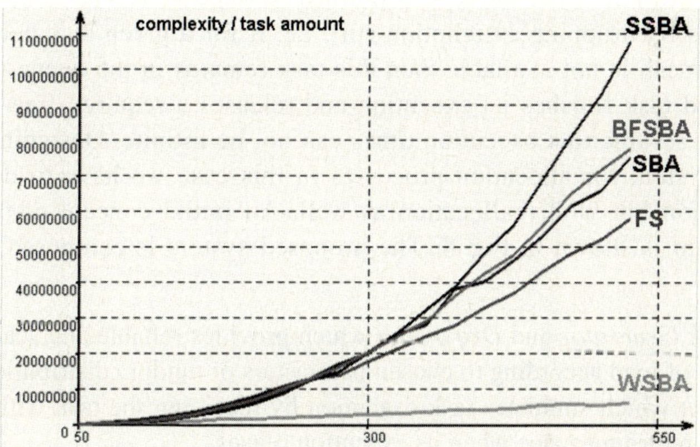

Fig. 7. Relationship between complexity and the total number of tasks for a relatively large mesh (130x130)

This phenomenon given by *WSBA* is directly related to the inner free submeshes available throughout the whole allocation process. Along with this algorithm a given task is allocated into the first free submesh that is capable of handling the task, thus placing the task into a mesh and then updating a stack are very fast activities.

Discussion. We have noted that the *WSBA* is more effective for larger meshes. The construction of *SBA, SSBA* and *BFSBA* algorithms makes their effectiveness vulnerable for the case when task size in the scope of the mesh is relatively small. The allocation of any task with these algorithms can be separated and stated as an independent problem without any states carried from previous ones. It enforces them to reinstate their inner assumptions each time when a task arrives and makes calculations more complex when there are many tasks already allocated on the mesh. The *WSBA* algorithm carries on its inner state throughout the allocation process thus it can provide almost instant task allocation though its complexity rises at some value of deterministic inputs.

Although the *WSBA* algorithm appeared to be better than the rest when operated in the static mode, we should make more experiments for various designs of experiments in order to make some general conclusions. Especially, the properties of *WSBA* need to be tested when operated on 3D meshes, and first of all, in dynamic mode of allocation process. All four competitive algorithms are dedicated for mainly single task allocation, thus their complexity can be compared with an upwardly set task queue. The *WSBA* algorithm keeps the mesh state within so it is expected to have a problem with task reallocation issue.

5 Development of Experimentation System

We may distinguish two modes of allocation process, the static mode and the dynamic mode. The static mode was defined in Section 2. The dynamic mode is characterized by dropping assumption (iii), i.e. if for a given task being allocated the free submesh is not available then this task remains in the queue until another just allocated task finishes its execution and releases a required free submesh. In this case we assume that execution times can not be infinite. Designing an experimentation system for allocation processes in this case we have to deal not only with allocation but with reallocation as well. An initial concept of the kernel of such a system is shown in Fig. 8. The proposed system is composed of modules, including

- *Task Generator* and *Dispatcher* which provides reliable and scalable generation of load according to chosen parameters of random distributions.
- *Mesh* which simulates task execution by receiving the task with coordinates and returning space when its execution ceases,
- *Algorithm* which is finding a free submesh for tasks received from *Task Dispatcher* taking into account recent information about freed submeshes.
- *Captain* which provides a way to conduct batch experiments and to navigate all the other modules.

To achieve most reliable processor time measurements, all modules should be implemented as a separate applications which communicate through *Server* module over the TCP/IP protocol (see solid lines in Fig. 8). Dotted lines are visualization of control routines within the system.

Such a distributed implementation within the Linux system is being tested, actually.

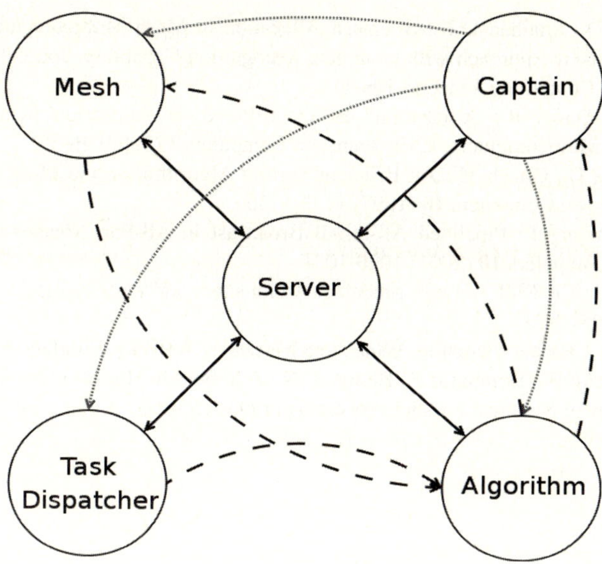

Fig. 8. Logical system architecture confronted with its physical dependencies

6 Final Remarks

The main conclusion resulting from the research is that in the static mode the *WSBA* is by far the best algorithm tested in the case when we need to allocate a huge amount of tasks but *SBA, BFSBA* and *SSBA* turn out to be useful when the total number of tasks in the queue is relatively smaller.

The further research will concentrate on evaluating task allocation algorithms properties in the dynamic mode with using the proposed experimentation system. Moreover, we are looking for efficient allocation algorithms based on dynamic programming approach,

References

1. Koszalka L., Kubiak M., Pozniak-Koszalka I.: Allocation Algorithm for Mesh-Structured Networks, Proc. of IARIA ICN'06 Conf., ICN5: Management, Mauritius, IEEE Computer Society Press (2006)
2. Chang C., Mohapatra P.: An Integrated Processor Management Scheme for Mesh-Connected Multicomputer System, Proc. of Int. Conf. on Parallel Processing, (1997)
3. Koszalka L., Lisowski D., Pozniak-Koszalka I.: Comparison of Allocation Algorithms for Mesh-Structured Networks with Using Multistage Experiment, LNCS 3984, Springer-Verlag (2006) 58-67
4. Batcher K.E.: Architecture of Massively Parallel Processor, Proc. of Intern. Conf. on Computer Architecture (1998) 174-179

5. Sharma D.D., Pradhan D.K.: Submesh Allocation in Mesh Multicomputers Using Busy List: A Best-Fit Approach with Complete Recognition Capability, Journal of Parallel and Distributed Computing **1** (1996) 106-118
6. Byung S., Das C.R.: A Fast and Efficient Processor Allocation Scheme for Mesh-Connected Multicomputers, IEEE Trans. on Computers **1** (2002) 46-59
7. De M., Das D., Ghosh M.: An Efficient Sorting Algorithm on the Multi-Mesh Network, IEEE Trans. on Computers **10** (1997) 1132-1136
8. Yang Y., Wang J.: Pipelined All-to-All Broadcast in All-Port Meshes and Tori, IEEE Trans. on Computers **10** (2001) 1020-1031
9. Agarwal A.: The MIT Alewife Machine: Architecture and Performance, Computer Architecture (1995) 2-13
10. Kasprzak A.: Packet Switching Wide Area Networks, WPWR, Wroclaw (1997) /in Polish/
11. Liu T., Huang W., Lombardi F., Bhutan L.N.: A Submesh Allocation for Mesh-Connected Multiprocessor Systems, Parallel Processing (1995) 159-163

Scalable Overlay Multicast Architecture[*]

Choonsung Rhee, Sunyoung Han[**], Byounguk Choi, and Jungwook Song

Dept. of Computer & Information Communication Engineering, Konkuk University
1 Hwayang, Gwangjin, Seoul 143-701, Korea
{csrhee, syhan, buchoi, swoogi}@cclab.konkuk.ac.kr

Abstract. We have introduced loosely-coupled TCP connection in order to support efficient and reliable overlay multicast. We have also defined new service type to the flow label of IPv6 header and proposed the architecture that offers differentiated service. In order to realize this proposal, we used separate buffer of a different kind in accordance with its service type. The architecture we propose supports subnet multicasting in a bid to prevent the degradation that has occurred due to the increased number of total users, and we have optionally adopted FEC (Forward Error Correction) so that the receiver can rectify the error. In order to verify the effect of the proposed solution, we simulated our experiment in an environment that is similar to the actual service environment.

1 Introduction

In order to efficiently utilize multimedia services, introducing multicast technology is a must. However, the current situation bears many issues when these technologies are to be adopted. Slow introduction of IP multicast led overlay multicast debut that processes multicast function in the upper layer of application level without changing the current network base [1,2,3]. This method not only resolves most of the issues raised in IP multicast, but also it eases the way multicast technology is added since it is easily applicable to the existing internet architecture. However, overlay multicast is less efficient than IP multicast.

We employed two different techniques in order to support efficient and reliable multicast [4,5,6]. The first one is the modified loosely-coupled TCP connection initially introduced by ROMA [6], and the other one is to provide differentiated service according to the packet type by defining the new service types to the flow label of IPv6 header.

---

[*] This research was supported by the MIC(Ministry of Information and Communication), Korea, under the ITRC(Information Technology Research Center) support program supervised by the IITA(Institute of Information Technology Assessment).

[**] Corresponding author.

G. Min et al. (Eds.): ISPA 2006 Ws, LNCS 4331, pp. 31–36, 2006.

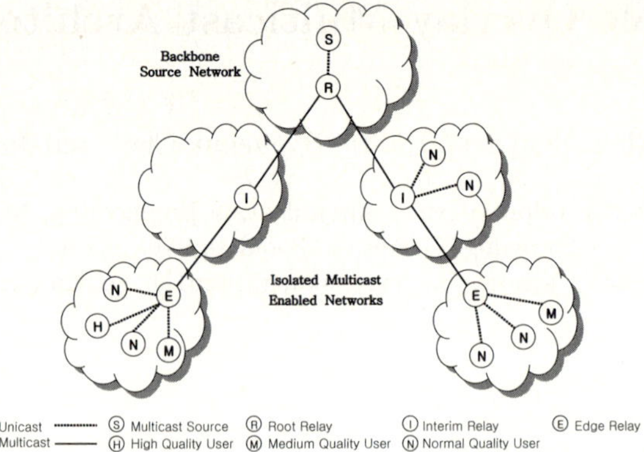

Fig. 1. The architectural model of the suggested overlay network

2   Architectural Model

2.1   Components

The basic environment we have in mind is a hybrid network where both multicast and non-multicast exist. We built overlay multicast network as it is shown in Fig. 1 when the whole configuration of IP multicast network is not fully completed.

Relay: Relay plays a role as both a multicast data deliverer and a constituent in building multicast tree. Our proposed structure is separated into three categories as below.

- **Root Relay:** Root Relay which is a root of multicast tree belongs to the backbone source network along with media service that is a multicast source.
- **Interim Relay:** Interim Relay lies in the middle of multicast tree, and it is separated into two types. In the first type of relay, no user is interested in receiving multicast service to the subnet, and it simply functions as a multicast data deliverer to the other relay. Differentiated transport can be done according to the designated value of flow label. In the other type of relay, users who receive multicast service to the subnet exist, and it performs additional functions other than the basic transports. It creates data including FEC according to the designated value in the flow label as well as delivers multicast data to the subnet multicast subscribers[7].
- **Edge Relay:** Edge relay, located on the edge of multicast tree, delivers multicast data to the end-users in the subnet. It optionally creates FEC according to the designated value in the flow label.

End-User: End-user as a terminal receiving multicast data, de-encapsulates overlay multicast header in the received multicast data. Moreover, it rectifies the error itself in case the error occurs according to whether it includes FEC or not. The proposed architecture separates end-user into three types as below.

- **High Quality User:** High Quality User receives faster data transport service than the general data, and it also guarantees reliable data transmission.
- **Medium Quality User:** Medium Quality User receives a bit faster data transport service than the ordinary users, and it also guarantees reliable data transmission.
- **Normal Quality User:** Normal Quality User receives normal-speed data transport service, and it does not guarantee reliable data transmission.

2.2   Features

Our new model has the following features.

- **Reliability:** Reliable transmission that IP multicast does not provide is distributed via overlay multicast network. For a reliable transmission, we used loosely-coupled TCP connection and unicast tunneling between each relays. We also employed optional FEC algorithm for subnet multicast areas.
- **QoS:** In order to support QoS, we defined a new type in the flow label of IPv6 header. According to this newly defined type, we differentiated data transmission speed by using different buffers.
- **Low Latency:** We minimized end-to-end delay of multicast data that requires fast speed by using buffers with different transmission speed. By using FEC, we reduced delays from re-transmitting the lost data.

2.3   QoS and Reliable Transmission

Flow Label Field as a newly added field in IPv6, eases real-time traffic control or packet that requires the same processing. We defined a new type in the flow label in order to send differentiated multicast packet as well as reliable data. The types for differentiated transmission are mutually exclusive. The newly defined type in low 8-bit of flow label is as follows.

- 10000000
  It is used for differentiated transmission. This data that demands best quality services provide faster transport service than other packets.
- 11000000
  It is used for differentiated transmission. This data that demands intermediate standard services provide a bit faster transport service than other ordinary packets.
- 11100000
  It is used for reliable transmission. It enables the receiver to rectify the error itself by creating FEC in case of subnet transmission.

Fig. 2 depicts the architecture for reliable and differentiated data transmission. The architecture we propose is a modified version of loosely-coupled TCP connection that was initially introduced by ROMA. Transmission between relays uses reliable TCP while transmission between relays and end-users in the subnet uses UDP. The left side of Fig. 2 is the incoming data while the right

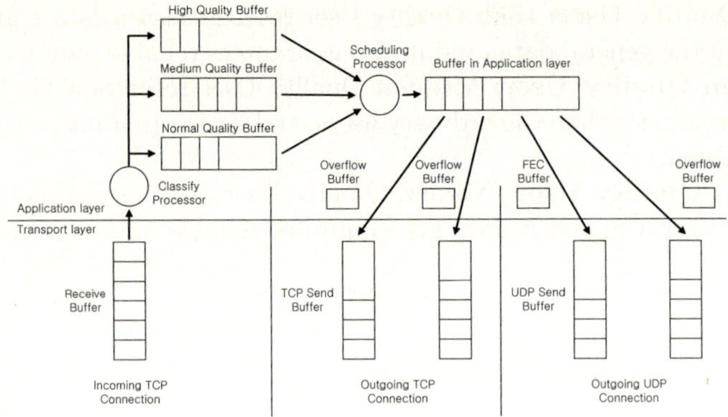

Fig. 2. The Architecture for reliable data transmission and QoS

side shows the movements of outgoing data. Relays that received data via reliable TCP connections use three buff-ers for the data processing. Relays separate multicast packet into three categories and store in high/medium/normal quality buffer according to the type defined in the flow label. Data transport method in relays is classified into two types. The first method is TCP transmission that is meant to send multicast data to other relays, and the other one is multicast transmission for end-users in the subnet. In TCP transmission for other relays, transport and overflow buffer exist per each corresponding relays. In multicast transmission for subnets, FEC buffer exists for reliability and overflow buffer for the transmission itself. Relays determine whether it should create FEC according to the designated type in the flow label before delivering multicast data to end-users in the subnet.

We adopted a way of using TCP between relays, and optionally creating FEC and sending it to multicast according to the designated value of flow label in the subnet. This method enhances the performance of real-time streaming service in overlay multicast through combined use of TCP, UDP and FEC.

3   Performance Evaluation

In fact, not only we constructed a small network in order to evaluate the performance of our proposed architecture, but also we implemented a simulation using one of the network simulators called OMNeT++ to evaluate the performance in a broader range [8]. For overlay multicast service, we configured a network with 3 different sources and 14 relays. Fig. 3 illustrates a testbed environment built by using OMNeT++.

In order to measure delays in the simulation, we adopted delays between each relays differently from 5 ms to 20 ms considering special features of the network. Multicast packet is able to move to other networks only via relay that works as a multicast router, and 3 sources are connected to relay3, relay6 and relay7 respectively. Test environment embraces 3 multicast groups, and each

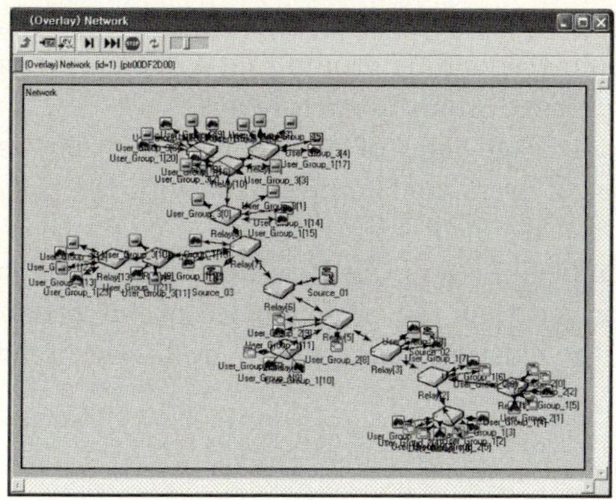

Fig. 3. The overlay multicast network to be simulated

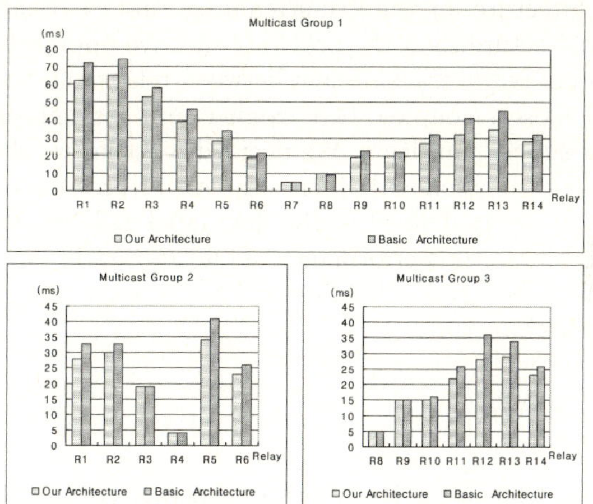

Fig. 4. Simulation results 1

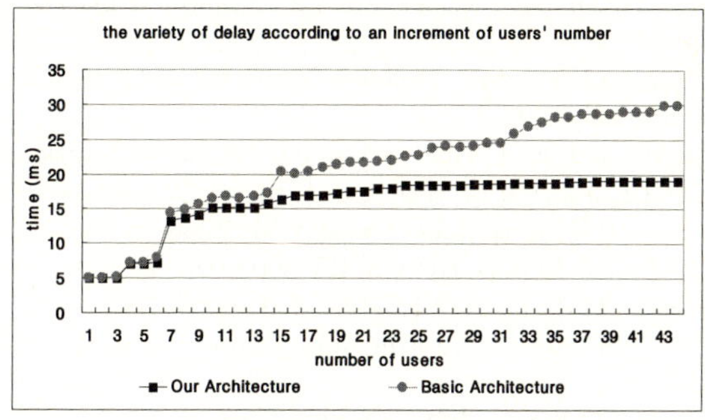

Fig. 5. Simulation results 2

user receiving services is connected to interim and edge relay that constructs multicast tree of the corresponding group. Fig. 4 depicts a result of delays shown from sources per multicast group to each relays.

We also measured average delay of the whole relays that was generated due to the increased number of users, and compared it with the basic overlay multicast architecture. Fig. 5 is a result of average delay of relays that was generated due to the increased number of users. As it is depicted in the simulation result of Fig. 4 and 5, we verified that the performance of our proposed architecture is more superior than the existing basic overlay multicast architecture.

4 Conclusion

In this paper, we introduced a novel overlay multicast architecture suitable for distributing stream. We examined and analyzed the problems arose from overlay multicast architecture for the live streaming, and eventually came up with more efficient architecture than the previous one. We approached the transport issue in two different ways; transmission between relays and transmission in the subnet. We used loosely coupled TCP connections for unicast-tunneling, and optional FEC for subnet multicast. We decided whether we should use FEC in subnet multicast transmission and differentiated transmission between relays according to the type newly defined in the flow label of IPv6. We also simulated some models to evaluate the performance of our approach. We verified that this architecture guarantees higher reliability and lower delay than the existing basic overlay multicast architecture.

References

1. P. Francis, Yoid: "Extending the Multicast Internet Architecture", 1999, White paper
2. J. Byers, J. Considine, M. Mitzenmacher, S. Rost: "Informed Content Delivery Across Adaptive Overlay Networks", ACM SIGCOMM, Aug 2002
3. Y. Chu, S. G. Rao, H. Zhang: "A Case For End System Multicast", ACM SIGMETRICS, 2000
4. R. Buskens, M. Siddiqui, S. Paul: "Reliable Multicast of Conrinuous Data Streams", Bell Labs Tech, Journal, 1997
5. S. Paul, K. Sabnani, J. Lin, S. Bhattacharrya: "Reliable Multicast Transport Protocol(RMTP)", IEEE Journal on Selected Areas in Communications, Apr 1997
6. G. Kwon, J. Byers: "ROMA: Reliable Overlay Multicast with Loosely Coupled TCP Connections", Technical Report BU-CS-TR-2003-015, Boston University, 2003
7. L. Rizzo, L. Vicisan:"RMDP: an FEC-based Reliable Multicast protocol for wireless environments", Mobile Computing and Communications Review, Volumn 2, Number 2, 1998
8. OMNeT++ version 3.2, http://www.omnetpp.org

On the Design of a Dual-Execution Modes Processor: Architecture and Preliminary Evaluation

Md. Musfiquzzaman Akanda, Ben A. Abderazek, and Masahiro Sowa

National University of Electro-Communications
Graduate School of Information Systems
1-5-1 Chofugaoka, Chofu-shi, 182-8585 Tokyo, Japan
`akanda@sowa.is.uec.ac.jp`

Abstract. In this work, we propose a novel dual-execution modes processor, named *Functional Assignment Register Machine* (FaRM), which supports both Queue and Stack execution models in a single and simple processor core.

The hardware elements, instruction formats and the major hardware components of the processor are presented in sufficient detail. We also give a preliminary evaluation result of the designed processor. From our preliminary evaluation results, we found that FaRM processor achieves about 65MHz speed and can execute both Queue and Stack execution models correctly. We also found that the novel architecture is implemented without considerable additional hardware when compared with conventional architectures with similar hardware configurations.

Indexwords: Dual-execution modes, Design, Queue, Dynamic Switching Mechanism, Parallel.

1   Introduction

Nowadays, as we enter into an era of constant demand for faster and compatible processors as well as different internet and network appliances using different processor architectures, it becomes extremely complicated and costly to develop a separate processor for every execution model that satisfies this demand. Internet applications, which are generally *stack − based*, need high execution speed or high performance as defined by the literature. However, recently the term "high performance" is questioned again by many processor designers and computer users. Some consider that high performance means high execution speed or low execution time of some given applications. Others define "high performance" differently. They consider that processors which support several execution models are the favourite candidates for high performance "award", since switching from processor to processor lead to difficulty and waste of time. This is true especially when users have different applications written for different execution models (i.e., Stack and RISC model). In this case, users are forced to run these two applications separately on different machines. In conventional machines, this problem

G. Min et al. (Eds.): ISPA 2006 Ws, LNCS 4331, pp. 37–46, 2006.
© Springer-Verlag Berlin Heidelberg 2006

was somehow solved using direct software translation techniques. However, these techniques still suffer from slow translation speed. Sun Microsystems proposed another alternative and designed its Stack-based Java processor, so that Java code can execute directly [2,6,7]. According to its designers, the JavaChip-I, for example, is a highly efficient Java execution unit design. It delivers up to 20 times the Java performance for x86 and other general-purpose processor architectures and up to five times the performance obtained by just-in-time (JIT) compiler. It is evident that in term of reduced execution time, the solution is better than translation (indirect) or JIT schemes, but in term of compatibility, the processor still suffers from not being able to execute other codes. Supporting another execution model will eventually lead to more complex hardware.

We realized that supporting different instruction sets could yield superior operational attributes to those architectures that support a single instruction set. Our objectives are clear; first, we knew that to reduce die size and improve performance, dual execution mechanism should be implemented in the FaRM pipeline as a finite state machine rather than a traditional microcoded engine. Second, the solution would have to dynamically calculate Queue and Stack locations to architectural registers called Shared Storage Unit (SSU). Thus avoiding the need for a translation stage. Finally, the resulting architecture would have to perform 16-bit fetches in order to fetch up to four instructions at once.

To this end, we propose in this work a dual-execution modes processor architecture named FaRM processor. It addresses the above problems as a pure-play architectural paradigm and integrates Stack and Queue execution models right into a single core. This is achieved dynamically with a $mode-switching$ scheme and a $sources-results$ locations computing unit [1].

The rest of this paper is organized as follows: in section 2, we present a detailed description of the proposed processor architecture. Section 3 gives the design result and analysis. The last section gives our conclusion.

2 System Architecture Description

The FaRM architecture is a 32-bit processor, which supports a subset of the Queue instruction set (QEM) and Stack instruction set (SEM)[1]. The QEM mode uses a first-in-first-out Queue data structure as the underlying control mechanism for the manipulation of operands and results. In addition, the QEM is analogous to the stack execution model (SEM) in that it has operations in its instructions set which implicitly reference an operand queue just as a stack machine has operations that implicitly references an operand stack. Each instruction removes the required number of operands from the front of the operand queue, performs some computations, and stores the result of computation into the operand queue at the specified offsets from the head of the Queue. The operand Queue occupies continuous storage locations. A special register called Queue Head (QH) contains the address of the first operand in the operand Queue. Operands are retrieved from the front of the Queue by reading the location indicated by the QH pointer. Immediately after retrieving an operand, the QH is incremented so that it points to the next operand in the Queue. Results are returned to the rear of the operand Queue indicated by the Queue Tail (QT). When switched for Stack-based mode, the switching circuitry and the FaRM Computing Unit (FCU) perform the job of executions mode switching. The FCU calculates the sources and destination for corresponding instructions.

In SEM execution mode, operands (implicitly referenced) are retrieved from the Top of the operand stack and results are returned back into the Top of the operand stack. For example, consider a *sub* instruction. In SEM mode, the *sub* instruction pops two operands from the top of the operand stack (SP), computes the difference and pushes the results back into the top of the stack. In QEM mode, the *sub* instruction removes two operands from the front of the operand Queue, computes their difference, and puts the results at the rear of the operand Queue indicated by the QT pointer. In the former case, the result of the operation is available at the SP. In the later case, the result is behind any other operand in the Queue. This will have an enormous impact to effectively exploit pipelined ALU where normal SEM obviously cannot guarantee. The details explanation of the novel queue computing model is given in [1,3,5].

2.1   Instruction Set Architecture

The dual-execution modes processor architecture uses a single shared instruction set for both Queue (FQM) and Stack (FSM) execution models. In FQM, the architecture supports a subset of a produced order parallel Queue processor instructions set [3]. FaRM's instruction set features are: (1) shared instruction set, (2) simple and has relatively small number of instructions and (3) fixed length instructions. All instructions are 16-bits wide and allowing simple instruction fetch, decode stages and facilitate pipelining of the processor where the upper part specifies the type of instruction (opcode), and says how to interpret the value (operand) stored in the lower part. In the current version of our implementation, we target our processor for small applications where our concerns focus on the ability to execute FaRM codes on a processor core with small die size and acceptable power consumption characteristics.

2.2   Pipeline Structure

FaRM processor is a pipelined architecture. It has six pipeline stages and is based on a 16-bit instruction set architecture. The basic block diagram of the architecture is given in Fig. 1. The processor consists of the following units: (1) Instruction Fetch Unit (FU), (2) Decode Unit (DU), (3) FaRM Computation Unit (FCU), (4) Issue Unit (IU), (5) Execution Unit (EXE), and (6) Shared Storage Unit (SSU).

Instructions fetch: The fetch unit fetches 4*16-bits instructions/cycle from the program memory and inserts them into the fetch buffer.

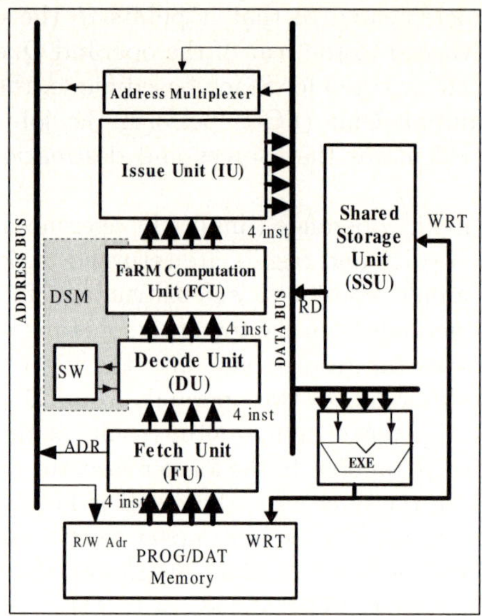

Fig. 1. Hybrid FaRM system architecture

Instructions decode: Decodes the instructions opcodes and operands. The decode unit (DU) has 4 decode circuits (DC) and 1 Mode Selector Register (MS). The later, is set to "0" or "1" according the the type of execution modes.

Address Computing: The processor's computation unit reads information from the decode unit and uses them to compute the instruction sources and destination locations for booth Queue and Stack execution models.

Instructions issue: The issue stage issues ready instructions to the execution unit. Memory and registers dependency are checked in this unit/stage. This unit also checks the sources availability.

Execution: The execution unit (EXE) executes issued instructions and sends the results to the Shared Storage Unit (SSU) or the data memory. The EXE consists of: 4 Arithmetic logical units (ALU), 2 Shift units, 4 Set register units, 4 Load/Store units, 4 Move unit, 1 Compare unit and 1 Branch unit.

Write Back Unit: The write back unit writes the result back to the PROG/DATA memory or SSU. The SSU is a 32*16 registers. The dual-execution mechanism (DSM) consists of a switching circuitry (SW) and a dynamic computation unit (FCU). The FCU unit calculates the sources and destinations for instructions in both FQM and FSM modes. A block diagram of the DSM mechanism is illustrated in Fig. 2. The DSM detects the instruction mode by decoding the operand of the *switch* instruction. After it detects the mode, it inserts a *mode − bit* for all instructions between the current and the next *switch* instruction.

The dynamic address computation mechanism has two mapping algorithms: (1) FaRM Queue Computing (FQMAP) and (2) FaRM Stack Computing (FSMAP).

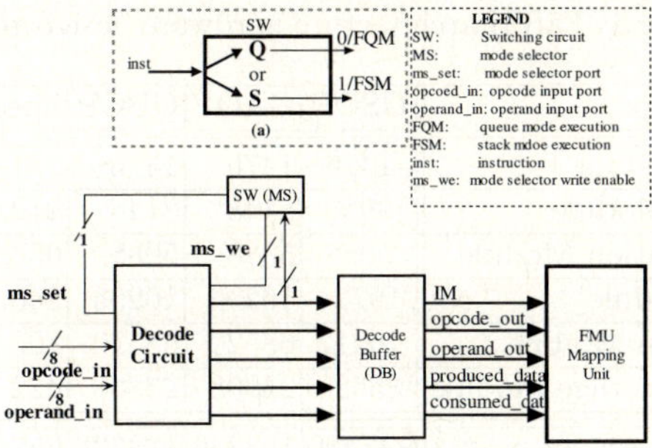

Fig. 2. DSM basic block diagram

In FQM, each instruction needs to know its QH and QT values. The above values are easy to know in serial Queue execution model, since the QH is always used to fetch instruction from the operand queue and the QT is always used to store the result of the computation into the tail of the operand Queue. However, in the parallel execution scheme the above values are not explicitly determined. This is due to the fact that previous instructions are simultaneously executed and may not be completed in order. The mechanism for calculating the *source*1 address for the queue computation is given in Fig. 3(a). The computing unit keeps the current value of the QH and QT pointers. Four instructions arrive to this unit each cycle. For the first instruction the number of consumed data (CN) (8-bit field) is added to the current QH value (QH0) to find the first operand and the number of produced data (PN) (8-bit field) is added to the current QT value (QT0) to find the result address (QT1) of the first instruction. The other three instruction's

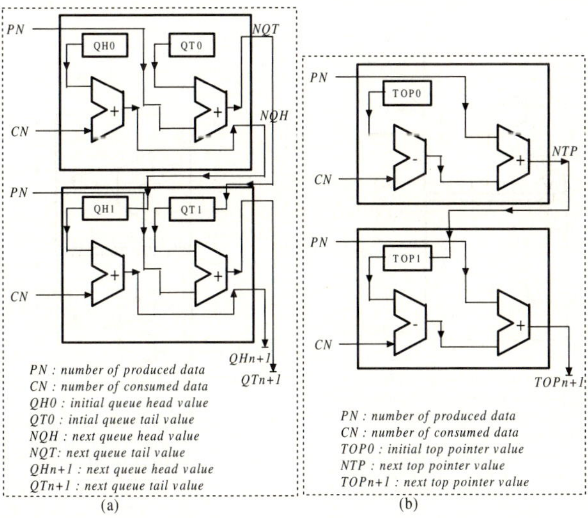

Fig. 3. Address calculation mechanism for source1 and destination: (a) FQM computing circuit; (b) FSM computing circuit

Table 1. FaRM architecture hardware design results

Description	GSOP	GAOP	GBOP	Speed(MHz)
Fetch Module	1476	1476	1476	231.80
Decode Module	9960	8148	8148	212.54
Computation Module	5088	5088	5088	65.27
Issue Module	19224	16296	16296	240.85
Execution Module	76212	68520	68520	108.39
Shared Storage Module	35520	23808	23808	422.12
FaRM processor	147480	123336	123336	65.27

first operand and result addresses are calculated similarly. The second operand (*source2*) of a given instruction is the first calculated by adding the address *source1* to the displacement (OFFSET) that comes with the instruction. Fig. 4(a) shows the hardware mechanism used for calculating the second operand.

In FSM, the execution is based on pure stack model. The mechanism for calculating the *source1* and *destination* address in this mode is shown in Fig. 3(b). The computing unit keeps the current value of the TOP pointer. Four instructions arrive to the FCU unit each cycle. For the first instruction the *source1* address is taken from the current top pointer value (TOPn-1). The number of consumed data (CN) (8-bit field) is subtracted from the current TOP value (TOPn-1) and then the number of produce data (PN) is added to find the result address (DESTn-1) of the first instruction. The other three instruction's first operand and result addresses are calculated similarly as indicated in Fig. 4(b). The second operand (*source2*) is calculated by subtracting from current top pointer value (TOPn-1) one. Fig. 4(b) shows the hardware mechanism used for calculating the second operand.

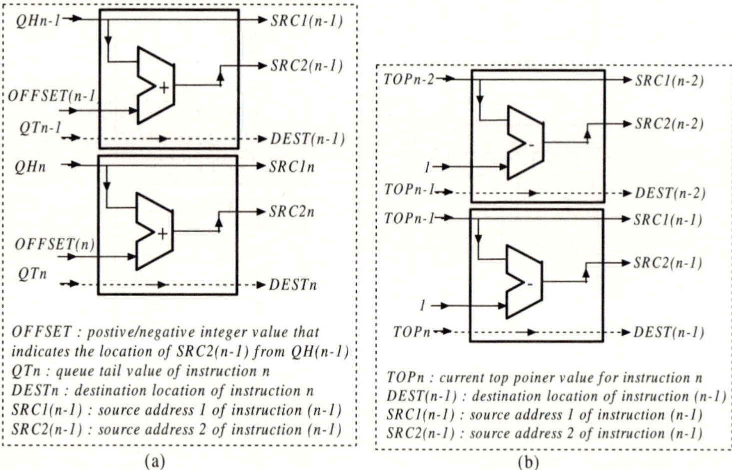

Fig. 4. Source2 calculation mechanism (a) FQM computing circuit; (b) FSM computing circuit

3   Results and Analysis

We have developed the FaRM processor architecture in verilog HDL. After synthesizing the HDL code, the designed processor gives us the ability to investigate the actual hardware performance and functional correctness. It also gives us the possibility to study the effect of coding style and instruction set architecture over various optimizations. For the processor to be useful for these purposes we identified the following requirements (1) High-level description: the format of the FaRM design description should be easy to understand and modify; (2) Modular: to add or remove new instructions, only the relevant parts should have to modify. A monolithic design would make experiments difficult; and (3) the processor description should be synthesizable to derive actual implementation.

To simplify the functional verification we have developed a front-end tool, which displays the internal state of the processor. The states displayed include: the state of each pipeline stage, SSU contents and data memory contents. We can easily extend the front-end tool to display several other states at each pipeline stage. For visibility, we only show the state of the SSU and the data memory - the two states are enough for checking the correctness of a simulated benchmark program. This approach allows monitoring the program execution as each instruction passes through the pipeline and identifies functional problems by tracing processor state change. We captured the input and output signals changes for several cases.

High-level verification is mainly used to verify functional correctness. Low-level problems such as timing violation cannot be verified directly with high-level verification tools. To ensure correctness of low-level implementation details, interfaces and timing, we use gate-level simulation for ensuring compliance with design specifications. We specified timing and other constraints using a unified user constraints file with the core modules. We used Altera Quartus II tools and Stratix FPGA EPS1 target device.

3.1   Complexity and Speed Comparison Results

As we earlier mentioned, the proposed architecture was designed in hardware with Verilog HDL and synthesised with Altera Quartus II synthesizable tools. Several test benches were used to verify the correctness of the architecture for both Stack and Queue execution models.

Table 1 shows the design results of the FaRM system architecture when synthesised for Stratix FPGA device over speed, area and combined optimisations. The complexity of the processor is given in terms of gates for each module and the whole processor core. The synthesize result gives the number of Logic Elements (according to[9] a gate is equivalent to 12 logic elements (LE)). In average, the processor achieves about 65 MHz speed for Stratix FPGA device.

We also compared the proposed FaRM system performance in terms of (1) execution capability, (2) complexity and (3) speed, to three synthesizable processors (JOP, S-JOP and PQP processors). The JOP processor is a Java Optimised architecture based on stack execution model with its own instruction set, called microcode [4]. Java byte codes are translated into microcode instructions or sequences

Table 2. Hardware Parameters used during synthesis stage for various processor architectures. S-JOP is a simplified (without bytecode support) JOP architecture.

Description	FaRM	PQP	JOP	S-JOP
Instruction Width (IW)	16-bits	16-bits	8-bits	8-bits
Fetch Width (FW)	8 bytes	8 bytes	1 byte	1 byte
Decode Width (DW)	8 bytes	8 bytes	1 byte	1 byte
Storage Register	16 (Shared)	16	16	16
Arithmetic Logic	1	1	1	1
Load/Store	1	1	1	1
Branch	1	1	1	1
Set Register	1	1	0	0
Execution mode	Dual	Single	Single	Single
Application program type	Queue, Stack	Queue	Bytecode, Stack	Stack
Supporting instructions	55	54	43	43

Table 3. Speed and complexity comparison

Achitecure	GSOP (Gates)	GAOP (Gates)	GBOP (Gates)	SSOP (MHz)	SAOP (MHz)	SBOP (MHz)
FaRM	147480	123336	123336	65.27	65.20	65.20
JOP	36048	35472	35472	80	80	80
PQP	144012	120852	120852	108.39	108.39	108.39
S-JOP	31212	28944	28944	80	80	80

of microcode. The S-JOP processor is a simplified version of JOP architectures and supports only stack native instruction set. For fair comparison, we removed the bytecode decoding circuitry part form the base JOP processor since our core's instruction set do not support them yet. Finally, the PQP processor is a produced order parallel queue architecture developed at Sowa Laboratory [3,5,8]. It supports a subset of the produced order queue instruction set architecture [3]. All instructions are 16-bit wide.Table 2 shows the design parameter of various processor architectures (FaRM, PQP, JOP and S-JOP).

Table 3 shows the complexity (in terms of gates number) and the speed for each processor over various optimisations: (a) GSOP- gates count for speed optimisations, (b) GAOP gates count for area optimisation, (c) GBOP gates count for balanced optimisation, (d) SSOP- speed for speed optimisations, (e) SAOP- speed for area optimisation, and (f) SBOP- speed for balanced optimisations. In average, the additional hardware needed by our dual-execution core is acceptable (Figure 5). Consequently, we found that FaRM, PQP, JOP, and S-JOP cores achieve about 65MHz, 80MHz, 108MHz, and 80MHz respectively. These results show that FaRM core is a little slower (about 18.5 %) than the other architectures. This comes for the execution mode switching mechanism delays, which needs additional hardware. For overall performance, we conclude that the complexity and the achieved speed

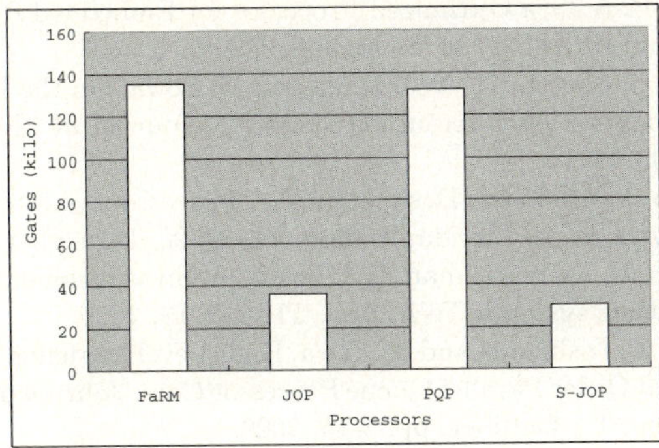

Fig. 5. Hardware complexity comparison

of our dual-execution modes core are acceptable. Complexity can be reduced more if aggressive optimisations techniques are adopted.

4   Conclusion

In this paper, we proposed a dual-execution modes processor and we presented its evaluation results. The architecture shares a single instruction set and supports both Queue and Stack execution modes in a single and simple processor core. This is achieved dynamically with an Execution-Mode-Switching (ESM) and Sources-Results-Computing mechanisms.

We presented the novel aspects of the dual-execution mechanism and a detailed description of the FaRM architecture. From our preliminary evaluation results, we found that FaRM processor achieves about 65MHz speed and can execute both Queue and Stack execution models correctly. It is implemented without considerable additional hardware when compared with conventional architectures with similar hardware configurations. For example, when compared with PQP core, only about 2.19% more gates are required.

Finally, we conclude that, although the proposed architecture is still in its preliminary design phase, it is expected that the system will have a bright future especially for applications requiring small memory footprint and tight resources.

References

1. M. M. Akanda , B. A. Abderazek and M. Sowa, An Efficient Dynamic Switching Mechanism (DSM) for Hybrid Processor Architecture, EUC 2005, LNCS Vol. 3824, pages77-86, December, 2005.
2. R. Radhakrishnan, D. Talla, and L. K. John, Allowing for ILP in an embedded Java processor, Proceedings of the 27th International Symposium on Computer Architecture, pages 294-305, June 2000.
3. M. Sowa,B. A. Abderazek, and T. Yoshinaga, FARM Processor, Parallel Queue Processor Architecture Based on Produced order computation model, Int. Journal of Supercomputing, HPC, Vol.32, No.3, June 2005, pp.217-229.

4. M. Schoeberl, JOP: A Java Optimized Processor for Embedded Real-Time Systems, PhD thesis, Vienna University of Technology, 2005.
5. B. A. Abderazek, S. Shigeta, T. Yoshinaga and M. Sowa, On the Design of Register-Queue Based Processor Architecture (FARM-rq), Journal of LNCS Vol. 2745, pp. 248-262, July 2003.
6. N. VijayKrishnan, Issues in the Design of JAVA Processor Architecture, PhD dissertation, University of South Florida, Tampa, FL-33620. December 1998.
7. R. Radhakrishnan, N. Vijaykrishnan, L. John and A. Sivasubramanium, Architectural issues in java runtime systems, Tech. Rep. TR-990719, 1999.
8. B. A. Abderazek, T. Yoshinaga and M. Sowa, High-Level Modeling and FPGA Prototyping of Produced Order Parallel Queue Processor Core, Journal of supercomputing, Volume 38, Number 1 / October, pp. 3-15, 2006.
9. STRATIX devices: www.altera.com/products/devices/stratix/

Pseudo Share Data Cache in Multiprocessor: PSDMP*

Pengyong Ma, Xiao Hu, Shuming Chen, and Yang Guo

School of Computer Science and Technology,
National University of Defense Technology, Changsha. 410073 China
pyma@nudt.edu.cn,
mapy@sohu.com

Abstract. With the development of semiconductor technology, multicore is integrated on one chip [1]. In CMP, more than one core accessing the shared data will cause memory access conflict and the problem of cache coherence. Cache coherence is a precondition for the system to function correctly. So it is a key problem in CMP. In this paper, we propose a new pseudo sharing level one data cache in a chip multiprocessor architecture (PSDMP). In PSDMP, the request of memory access will be propagated on a ring chain. This method can reduce both the complexity of the design and the load of L2 cache. Simulation results show that performance of PSDMP improves about 30% averagely than another CMP which uses MESI protocol, especially the best is about 100% for the parallel applications which has many inter-processor communications for modifying shared data. In one word, PSDMP is promising processor architecture.

1 Introduction

As the feature size of the integrated circuit manufacturing process continues to shrink, more and more transistors can be integrated on a single chip. It is predicted that there will be several billion transistors on a chip by the year 2010. So a single chip can integrate more complex functions, even multiple processor cores. CMP (Chip Multi-Processor) has been widely used in high performance processors. It will be a technology trend for future processors.

Multiple processor cores in CMP communicate by the shared cache. Every processor core has its own internal cache. There maybe several copies in multiple caches for one memory block. It will cause the problem of data coherence. To provide an efficient programming model and ensure the correctness of program execution, the designer must guarantee the cache coherence.

Generally, there are two main methods to resolve the cache coherence [2]: software-based method and hardware-based method [3] [4] [5] [6]. Software depends on programmers and the compilers. Programmer must know the trace of the program run and the architecture of the chip. It is very rigorous for most programmers and it will result in fewer people taking full advantage of the multi-core processor. On the other hand, compiler must distinguish the uncacheable data. During program execution the cacheable data enters the low levels cache and the uncacheable data remains in the

---

* This work is supported by National Natural Science Foundation of China(60473079).

share memory. It is quite restrictive by compiler. Moreover, lots of data can't be buffered in the lower levels cache and that will reduce the chip's performance.

On snoopy multiprocessor machines, every private cache maintains the coherence protocol. Generally, every cache controller changes the data's state depending on bus requests and the data previous state. Snoopy protocol's drawback is its scalable limitation. Directory protocol can solve this limitation; but it needs large memory to store the directories. Otherwise, to achieve high performance, the protocol always divides one transaction into multi-phases, which supports several requests simultaneously. It is difficult to maintain many temporary states [5].

In CMP, several threads run simultaneously, the memory access delay is large and the data bandwidth is the system's bottleneck. How to design a simple and high performance coherence protocol is a challenge.

In this paper, we propose a new architecture: PSDMP. Every core can access other L1Ds through a ring. Data request and response are accomplished on the ring. One data block has several copies in L1Ds. The copies are distinguished between master and slave depending on Master bits. After several benchmarks were run, we find that this architecture can reduce the memory load of L2 and enhance the chip's performance.

2 Model Proposed

In our CMP model, the core is "YHFT"-DSP. "YHFT"-DSP is two clusters and VLIW architecture. It can issue 8 instructions which include two memory instructions at most in one clk cycle [7] [8]. The chip has two-level cache; L1D is a 4K-bytes, two-way set associative cache with 4 single port memory blocks in one way. It can support two memory accesses in a cycle. Figure 1 is the L1D architecture [9] [10].

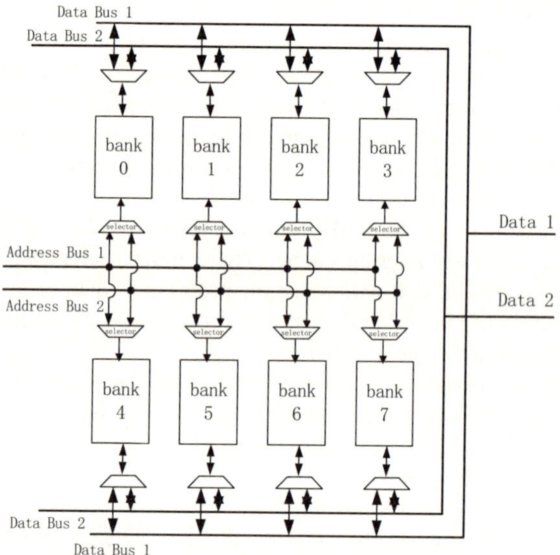

Fig. 1. It is the first level Cache architecture of "YHFT"-DSP, L1D has 8 *banks*; both instructions access every *bank* through the crossbar [9] [10]

On the assumption that there are 4 cores in one chip, if we adopt SMPDCA(shared multi-ported data Cache architecture)[11]; It will need a crossbar between 32 memory banks and 8 memory accesses. The access delay will spend several cycles and the hardware will increase rapidly. To solve this problem, we propose PSDMP. The core's L1Ds are linked by a ring. Every L1D cache is independent, but one core can access other L1Ds by the ring. When a load/store instruction arrives, if it hits its L1D only, the operation is same as in single core chip. If it hits other L1Ds, the core will issue request word on the ring. When other cores receive a request, they will insert a stall cycle or wait their L1Ds idle to return data or write the data to memory.

The request word will propagate as far as possible on the ring. For example, if there is only one request word on the ring, it will reach the destination in current cycle, otherwise it will be buffed in chain buffer as far as possible. Figure 2 is the frame of PSDMP with 4 cores.

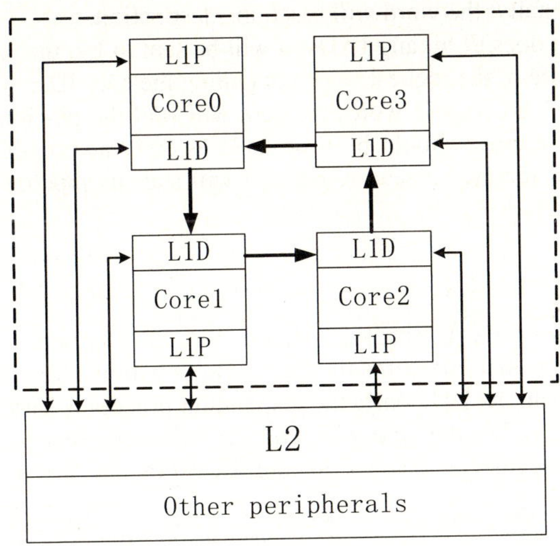

Fig. 2. There are 4 "YHFT"-DSP cores in the broken line rectangle with *L2* and *the other peripherals* outside. Four *L1Ds* are linked by the ring. Every core can access other *L1Ds* through the ring.

3   Design and Implementation

3.1   Read Access

After a load instruction issued, the address will be calculated out. Cache controller compares the address with the data in Tags, if it hit its L1D, the succeed steps are same as in single core chip; if the access doesn't hit itself L1D but other core's, the core will send request to the near core which include the data. The request word has three segments: Source core ID, Dst core ID, and the data address.

Source core ID	Dst Core ID	Address

Source core ID is the core's ID which contain the requested data. It has 2 bits to distinguish one from four cores. Dst core ID is the core's ID which sends the request word.

The read request propagates on the ring, when it arrives at a core, the core compares the Source core ID with it's, if equal, it will hold the request and stall its pipeline one cycle to fetch the data from its L1D, then it sends the data with the destination core ID on the ring. If not equal, it will transfer the request word to the next core by the ring. The request will reach the destination finally and disappear on the ring.

The read response word has three parts: Dst core ID, Ready and the data.

Dst core ID	Ready	data

The core which sends the request word will wait for data all along. When the response word arrives, it compares the Dst core ID with it's, if equal, it accepts the data and holds the response word; otherwise, it hands the response word to the next core by the ring. Finally, the word will reach the destination.

If a read request doesn't hit any L1Ds, it will be sent to L2, the response is same as in single core despite of the request word containing the core ID.

After sending a read request word, the core will stall the pipeline until the request data return, so the request should be responded as early as possible. When the core containing the data receives a read request, it will stall its pipeline to fetch the data immediately.

3.2 Write Access

The write access is similar as reading. After a store instruction issued in the execute stage, the cache controller compares the high address with the Tag data to judge hit or miss. If the access hits its L1D only, the responding process is same as in single core chip; if it hits other L1Ds, the core will send the write request word on the ring. The word contains four segments: destination core ID, width, data and address.

Dst core ID	Width	Data	Address

Because a write access maybe hits other three L1Ds, destination core ID contains three 2-bits ID to indicate that which L1Ds will update the data.

When a core receives a write request word, it compares the Dst core ID with itself. If three Dst core IDs equal it's, the request will be buffered in the write buffer and the core will hold the request word. If one or two Dst core IDs equal their ID, the core will buffer the request word and modify the corresponding Dst core ID to the remains and then transfer the request word to the next core. The core updates a byte, half word or a word depending on Width segment.

Figure 3 shows the process how a write request word propagates on the ring. From up to down it illustrates the steps of that how the request word passes the cores.

Write request word propagates as same as read request word on the ring. The difference between them is that once a core sends write request word on the ring; it considers that the write access is finished. So when the core receives a write request word, the request is not responded until that L1D is idle or the write buffer is full. On the contrary, once accepting a read request, the core will respond it immediately. If a write request doesn't hit any core, it will be sent to L2.

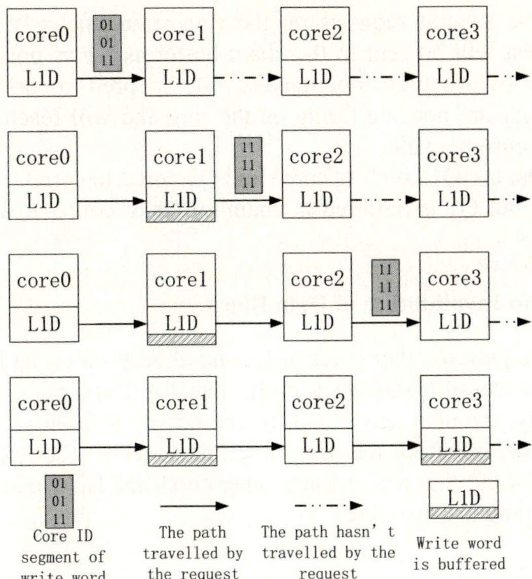

Fig. 3. *Core0* sends the write request and it propagates on the ring. The *Dst core ID* is *"01, 01, 11"*. This means that this write access hits *core1* and *core3*'s *L1D*s. When the request reaches *core1*, according to *Dst core ID*, *core1* finds that it should update its *L1D*; then it buffers the request. But *"11"* doesn't equal its ID, *core1* modifies the *Dst core ID* from *"01, 01, 11"* to *"11, 11, 11"* and transfers the request word to *core2* on the ring. *Core2* finds that three *Dst core IDs* are not equal to its ID, so it transfers the request word to *core3*. *Core3* finds that three *Dst core IDs* equal its ID, so it buffers the request word and eliminates it form the ring.

3.3   Conflict Handling

There are four cores sending request on the ring, it will bring conflict. How to solve this problem? If each of these requests is buffered in every core and transmitted in the next cycle, it will lessen the efficiency. For example, when core0 sends request to core3, the request will not arrive at core2 until 3 cycles later even though the ring is idle. One other method is to build a 4*4 crossbar connecting every core, but it needs lots of hardware. PSDMP needs only a ring chain and a chain buffer in every core.

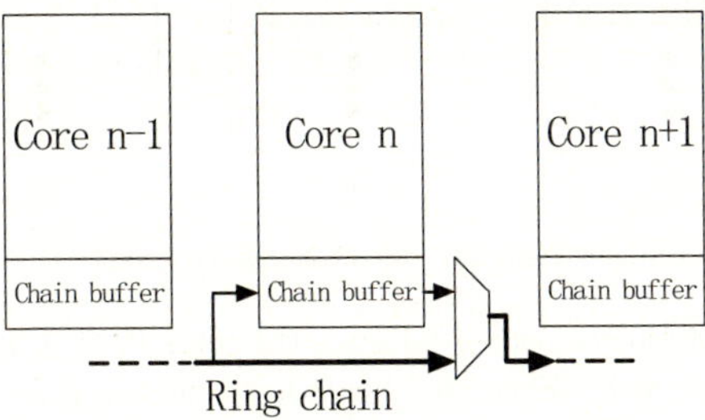

Fig. 4. When *core n-1* sends request to *core n+1*, if core n sends or transmits other request at the same time, the request of *core n-1* will be buffered in the *chain buffer* of *core n* and be sent to *core n+1* in the next cycle

So there may be several requests on the ring simultaneously. When a conflict happens, the request will be sent to the chain buffer as far as possible. As Figure 2 shows, if there are two requests simultaneity, one is core0 to core1 and the other is core2 to core3. They are not interfering on the ring and will reach their destinations respectively at the current cycle.

If the two request are Q1:core0 to core3 and Q2:core2 to core0. At current cycle T, Q2 reaches core0; but Q1 is buffered in chain buffer of core2, it will reach core3 in time T+1.

3.4   Allocation and Invalidation of Data Block

Every core sends request to other cores or L2 and allocates a cache line for read miss. On the contrary, it doesn't allocate a cache line for write miss. According to the principle of locality, the next access will be the nearby data very possibly. So if not allocate a cache line and fetch this miss line, the sequent read accesses will access other core's L1Ds or L2, this will enhance other cores and L2's load, especially it will break program running in other cores.

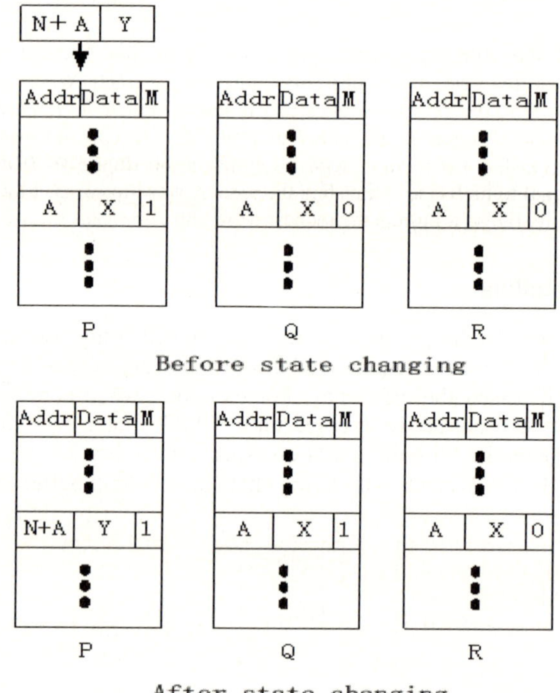

Fig. 5. It is the process of *Master symbol* shifting. The cores *P, Q, R* have the copies of data *X*. The line's *Master bit* is 1 in *P*. When data line whose address is *N+A* (N is multiple of the memory's size) enters *P*'s cache, it has to sacrifice the data *X*. *P* doesn't need to write back the data *X*, it only needs *Q* to set the corresponding *Master* bit. This process reduces the data exchanging between L2 and L1Ds, lightens the load of L2 in CMP, lessens the stall cycles of program and enhances the chip's performance.

The core doesn't allocate a cache line for miss write, because once the write request is sent on the ring, the core considers that this operation is complete and runs the program continually. Otherwise, it has to stall the program to wait the data back.

In PSDMP, one data block may have several copies in L1Ds; the difference with other coherence protocols is that the copies are same. So when the cores receive a flush or a snooping request, it needs only one core to return the dirty data, others just clear their valid bits. Master bit is used to distinguish the master and slave data line. Every cache line has a Mater bit; all Master bits are reset to 0 at the beginning. Once a core has a read miss and gets the data from L2, the corresponding Master bit will be set to 1. It means this core has the dominion of this cache line. When L2 invalidates this line, the L1D with Master bit being 1 check whether it needs to write back this line. L2 only waits for the master line's ACK signal.

When a read request misses in it's L1D but hits more than one L1Ds of other cores, the core only sends request to the nearly core without considering Master bit because these copies are same. This method will balance the load; otherwise the Master line will work hard.

The Master symbol maybe transferred when a core sacrifice a Master cache line. If other cores have the data's copies, they don't write back the dirty data to L2. The only work is to transfer the Master symbol.

4   Simulation Results and Analysis

In our simulation environment, the CMP cores are "YHFT"-DSP 700, the simulator is VCS and programs run in SUN Co. blade 2000. To evaluate the benefit of PSDMP, the evaluation is performed using a cycle-accurate.

Programs are compiled in "YHFT" IDE (integrated design environment) at first, then export the binary codes and run them in "YHFT"-DSP 700. Then each program is divided into 4 tasks and compiled. Finally these tasks run in 4 cores PSDMP and 4 cores chip with MESI protocol. During compiling, the optimize level is the same. L2 is set as RAM in chip, data and programs are loaded in RAM during simulation.

Because the core is "YHFT"-DSP, the programs are typical benchmarks in digital signal processing. It includes minerror, bitrev, dotp_sqr, fir, matrix, FFT.

Minerror performs a dot product on 256 pairs of 9 element vectors and searches for the pair of vectors which produces the maximum dot product result. It is used in the VSELP vocoder codebook search.

Bitrev performs the address bit-reversal of the input array.

Dotp_sqr performs two array's dot product and stores it in R. It also squares each element of input and accumulates it in G. The size of each array is 1024.

Fir assumes the number of filter coefficient is a multiple of 4 and the number of output samples is a multiple of 2. It operates on 16-bit data with a 32-bit accumulate. The size of coefficient array is 8; the size of input array is 1032 and 1024 of output.

Matrix performs two matrixes multiply. In this program, the sizes of two matrixes are both 32*32.

FFT calculates a 128 dot FFT with radix 2.

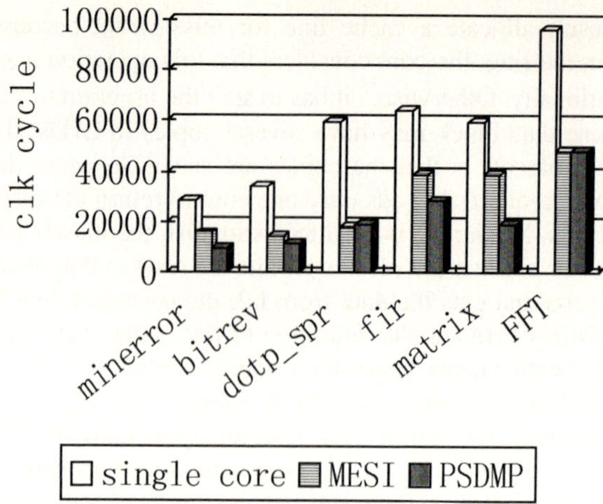

Fig. 6. It shows six programs running time in the *single core*, 4 cores with *MESI* protocol and 4 cores of *PSDMP* respectively. The *y-axis* shows the running time of the programs and the numbers came from detailed simulation. The times of MESI and PSDMP are the longest in 4 tasks.

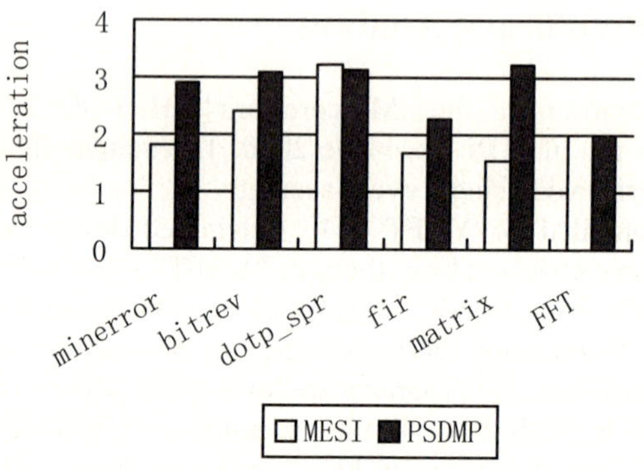

Fig. 7. It shows the *acceleration* of 4cores with *MESI* protocol and *PSDMP* relative to single core chip. On average *PSDMP* produces good acceleration (2.9, 3.1, 3.1, 3.5, 3.2 and 2.0). Whereas 4 cores with *MESI* protocol produces poor acceleration (1.8, 2.4, 3.2, 1.8, 1.5 and 2.0). *PSDMP* improves performances exceed 30%. It is clear that *PSDMP* is the better architecture.

As Fig. 6 and Fig. 7 showing, PSDMP improves performances exceed 30% comparing with MESI protocol. There are several main causes of it.

Firstly, pseudo sharing L1Ds improves the hit rate. The pseudo hit delay is shorter than the delay of waiting for the data from L2. When an access misses in its own cache but hits on other L1Ds, it can get the data in the next cycle if the ring is idle. The delay is 2.9 cycles on average by simulation. On the contrary, it is at least 7 cycles from L2.

Secondly, PSDMP reduces the conflicts of access L2. The bandwidth of shared L2 is always the bottleneck of system. The chip needs lots of data especially in DSP. During simulation, we find that in the chip with two cores the conflicting rate of access L2 is 30%; it will exceed 70% in 4 cores chip. In PSDMP, it doesn't need to access L2 if the miss data has been loaded in other L1Ds. It needs to do nothing but one L1D returning this data line. Once it sacrifice a Master cache line and allocate this line for the new data and if the sacrificial line's copies are loaded in other L1Ds too, it doesn't need write back the dirty date, the only work is to set other core' Master bit. Compared with MESI protocol, it doesn't exchange data with L2.

Finally, PSDMP doesn't maintain the complex coherence protocol. A write operation will update all copies by the ring, so all copies are same.

PSDMP is very fit with computing much data. It is especially suitable to the program which imports lots of data and modifies them, such as Fir and Matrix in Figure 7. Because in PSDMP, it needn't to invalidate other copies while it modifies the date.

Of course, PSDMP has its drawbacks. One core needs to stall its pipeline a cycle to fetch data for other core while accepting a read request. The write requests needn't to stall pipeline, but it needs write buffers to store them. Furthermore, the core's Tag must have multi ports. Through these ports, other cores access the Tag to determine whether the access hits this L1D.

5   Conclusions

Today, more processors are integrated in a chip; it causes the problem of cache coherence. No matter MSI, MESI or Dragon, it is complex to maintain the coherence. Moreover, if messages exchange between programs too frequently, it will lead to cache thrashing. In addition, multicore access L2 frequently, the bandwidth of L2 will limit the chip's performance seriously. Therefore, on the base of the detailed analysis of these factors, this paper proposes a new architecture of CMP: pseudo sharing the level one cache and then makes a detailed simulation.

Compared with the CMP using MESI protocol, PSDMP architecture has four strong points as follows: the higher rate of data hit; the lesser data access of L2; the shorter delay time of data sacrifice and the lower hardware spending to maintain coherence. Through simulation, it indicates that at average the performance of PSDMP improves about 30% than the CMP with MESI protocol.

Its drawback is that the Tags must be a multi-port memory.

References

1. Tang Zhimin: Prospect of tera-scale microprocessors. Imformation Technology Letters, No.8, 2004
2. FENG Li, Chen Ji-lu, Zhao Zhen-bo: Establishment of LC memory model and Cache consistency protocol. Journal of North China Electric Power University, Oct, 2002
3. Vinod Viswanath: Multi-log Processor Towards Scalable Event Driven Multiprocessors. DSD'04

4. Taeweon Suh: Supporting Cache Coherence in Heterogeneous Multiprocessor Systems. DATE'04
5. Daniel J.Sorin: Specifying and Verifying a Broadcast and a Multicast Snooping Cache Coherence Protocol. IEEE Transactions on Parallel and Distributed Systems, Vol.13, NO.6, June 2002
6. Guang R.Gao and Vivek Sarkar: Location Consistency-A New Memory Model and Cache Consistency Protocol. IEEE Transactions on Computers, Vol.49, NO.8, August 2000
7. WAN Jiang-Hua, CHEN Shu-Ming: MOSI: a SMT Microarchitecture Based On VLIW Processors. Chinese Journal of Computer, Vol.39, 2006
8. Chen Shuming, Li Zhentao: Research and Development of High Performance YHFT Digital Signal Processor. Journal of Computer Research and Development, Vol.43, 2006
9. Ma Pengyong, Chen Shuming, Li Guokuan: The Design of Cache Controller Supporting Two Parallel Cache Accesses. High Technology Letters, 2002
10. ZHANG Dan-Yu, MA Peng-Yong, CHEN Shu-Ming: The Mechanism of Miss Pipeline Cache Controller based on Two Class VLIW Architecture. Journal of Computer Research and Development, 2005
11. HUANG Guang-Qi, LI Zi-Mu, ZHOU Xing-Ming, DOU Yong: Shared Multi Ported Data Cache Architecture: SMPDCA. Chinese Journal of Computer, Dec, 2001

Further Improvement of Manik et al.'s Remote User Authentication Scheme Using Smart Cards

Jai-Boo Oh, Jun-Cheol Jeon, and Kee-Young Yoo[*]

Department of Computer Engineering, Kyungpook National University,
Daegu 702-701, South Korea
jboh0515@hotmail.com, jcjeon33@infosec.knu.ac.kr, yook@knu.ac.kr

Abstract. In 2006, Manik et al. proposed a novel remote user authentication scheme using bilinear pairings. Chou et al. identified a weakness in this scheme and made improvements. In addition, Thulasi et al. noted that both Manik et al.'s and Chou et al.'s schemes are vulnerable to forgery and replay attacks. In this paper, we analyze the previous schemes based on a timestamp and provide further comments together with an improved scheme using a nonce.

Keywords: Authentication, Bilinear Pairing, Forgery Attack, Replay Attack, Off-line guessing Attack.

1 Introduction

With the rapid growth of computer networks and the use of the Internet, the security of various types of data transmissions using public networks, such as electronic commerce, business transaction and government services has, become more and more important. Remote user-authentication schemes have become one of the most important research topics.

In 1981, Lamport [1] proposed a famous hash-based password authentication scheme. The scheme required the remote server system to maintain a password table to verify user legitimacy. In maintaining a verification table, that is a risk of password disclosure and issues in managing costs. To avoid these problems, several authentication schemes have been proposed [2, 3, 4, 5]. Hwang and Li [4] proposed a new authentication scheme using smart cards, which didn't require a password table. Recently, Manik et al. [6] proposed a remote user authentication scheme using bilinear pairings. Chou et al. [7], however, identified that this scheme had some flaws which could lead to a replay attack. They suggested a modified scheme to prevent such an attack. Thulasi et al. [8] pointed out that Chou et al.'s modified scheme is still susceptible from replay attacks. They identified that Manik et al.'s scheme has other weaknesses.

In this paper, we analyze the problems of the above schemes and propose an efficient protocol to avoid such attacks. The rest of this paper is organized as follows: Section 2 defines notations used in this paper. Section 3 briefly reviews previous schemes and provides comments regarding Manik et al.'s scheme. Section 4 offers further comments, as well as our improved scheme and a security and performance analysis. Concluding remarks are presented in Section 5.

---

[*] Corresponding author.

G. Min et al. (Eds.): ISPA 2006 Ws, LNCS 4331, pp. 57–64, 2006.

2 Preliminary

In this section, we refer to the basic definition of the bilinear map, the Bilinear Diffie-Hellman Generator, and related computational problems which are used throughout this paper. Most of the results in this section come from [9, 10].

Bilinear Map: Let G1 be an additive group of a large prime q and let P be a generator of G1. Let G2 be a multiplicative group with the same order q. A pairing is a map ê: G1 × G1 → G2 which has the following properties:

(1)   The map $\hat{e}$ is bilinearity: Given $P, Q, R \in G_1$, we have
$$\hat{e}(P, Q + R) = \hat{e}(P, Q)\,\hat{e}(P, R) \text{ and } \hat{e}(P + Q, R) = \hat{e}(P, R)\,\hat{e}(Q, R) .$$
Consequently, for any $a, b \in Z_q$:
$$\hat{e}(a{\cdot}P, b{\cdot}Q) = \hat{e}(P, Q)^{ab} = \hat{e}(a{\cdot}b{\cdot}P, Q)$$
$$= \hat{e}(P, a{\cdot}b{\cdot}Q) = \hat{e}(b{\cdot}P, Q)^{a} = \hat{e}(b{\cdot}P, a{\cdot}Q) .$$
(2)   The map $\hat{e}$ is non-degenerate: If P is a generator of G_1, then $\hat{e}(P, P)$ is a generator of G_2. In other words, $\hat{e}(P, P) \neq 1$.
(3)   The map $\hat{e}$ is efficiently computable.

Bilinear Diffie-Hellman Generator: Boneh et al. first formally set up the bilinear Diffie-Helman definitions and defined some assumptions and complex problems in [11].

Randomized algorithm: If the following conditions are satisfied, we say that a randomized algorithm $\mathcal{G}$ is a bilinear Diffie-Hellman (BDH) parameter generator.

(1) Takes a security parameter k for integer ≥ 1.
(2) $\mathcal{G}$ runs in polynomial time in k.
(3) $\mathcal{G}$ outputs a prime q, the description of groups G_1, G_2 of the prime order q and bilinear map $\hat{e}$: $G_1 \times G_1 \rightarrow G_2$.

Bilinear Diffie-Hellman problem: Let $< G_1, G_2, \hat{e} >$ be the output of $\mathcal{G}$ (k) and let P be a generator of G_1. The bilinear Diffie-Hellman (BDHP) in $< G_1, G_2, \hat{e} >$ is as follows: Given $< P, a{\cdot}P, b{\cdot}P, c{\cdot}P >$ with uniformly random choices of $a, b, c, \in Z_q^{*}$, compute $\hat{e}(P, P)^{abc}$.

BDH assumption: The BDH assumption states that no probabilistic polynomial time algorithm has a non-negligible advantage in solving the BDHP for $<G_1, G_2, \hat{e}>$ generated by $\mathcal{G}$ on input k.

Related Hard Problems: Many pairing-based cryptographic protocols are based on the hardness of BDHP for their security. Other computational problems related to pairing-based protocols are as follows:

(1) **Discrete Logarithm Problem** (DLP): Given two elements $P, Q \in G_1$, find an integer $a \in Z_q^{*}$, such that $Q = a{\cdot}P$ whenever such an integer exists.
(2) **Computational Diffie-Hellman Problem** (CDHP): Given $(P, a{\cdot}P, b{\cdot}P)$ for any $a, b \in Z_q^{*}$, compute $a{\cdot}b{\cdot}P$.

(3) **Decisional Diffie-Hellman Problem** (DDHP): Given $(P, a \cdot P, b \cdot P, c \cdot P)$ for any $a, b, c \in_R Z_q^*$, decide whether $c = a \cdot b \bmod q$.

Cryptographic Hash Function:

(1) $H_1 : \{0, 1\}^* \rightarrow G_1$, is a public one-way hash function that maps a message of arbitrary length into a non-zero point of G_1, as described in [12].
(2) $H_2 : \{0, 1\}^* \rightarrow Z_q$, is a key derivation function, typically a secure hash function.

3 A Review of Previous Schemes

In this section, we briefly review the previous schemes and cryptanalysis of Manik et al., Chou et al., and Thulasi et al..

3.1 Manik et al.'s Scheme

Setup phase: The remote server (RS) selects a secret key s and computes the server's public key, $Pub_{RS} = s \cdot P$. Then, the RS publishes the system parameter $< G_1, G_2, \hat{e}, q, P, Pub_{RS}, H_1>$.

Registration phase: This phase is invoked whenever U_i initially registered or re-registered to the RS.

(1) U_i submits his/her identity, ID_i and password PW_i to the RS.
(2) On receiving the registration request, the RS computes $Reg_{IDi} = s \cdot H_1(ID_i) + H_1(PW_i)$.
(3) The RS personalizes a smart card with ID_i, Reg_{IDi}, H_1 and this is sent to U_i over a secure channel.

Authentication phase: This phase is invoked whenever U_i wants to login to the RS. This phase is further divided into login and verification phase.

Login Phase: U_i inserts a smart card into a terminal and keys the ID_i and PW_i. If the ID_i is identical to the one that is stored in the smart card, the smart card performs as follows:

(1) Computes $DID_i = T \cdot Reg_{IDi}$, $V_i = T \cdot H_1(PW_i)$, where T is the user system's time-stamp.
(2) The login request $< ID_i, DID_i, V_i, T >$ is sent to the RS over a public channel.

Verification phase: This phase is invoked whenever the RS receives U_i's login request.

(1) The expected valid time interval $\Delta T \geq (T^* - T)$ is verified.
(2) Checks whether $\hat{e}(DID_i - V_i, P) = \hat{e}(H_1(ID_i), Pub_{RS})^T$. If it holds, the RS accepts the login request; otherwise, it is rejected.

Password change phase: This phase is invoked whenever U_i wants to change its password.

(1) U_i inserts the smart card to a terminal and keys ID_i and PW_i. If ID_i is identical to the stored key in the smart card, proceeds to the step (2); otherwise, terminates the operation.
(2) U_i submits a new password PW_i^*.
(3) The smart card computes a new
$$Reg_{IDi}^* = Reg_{IDi} - H_1(PW_i) + H_1(PW_i^*) = s \cdot H_1(ID_i) + H_1(PW_i^*) \,.$$
(4) The password has been replaced by the new password PW_i^* and the smart card has replaced the previously stored Reg_{IDi} value by Reg_{IDi}^* value.

3.2 Chou et al.'s Improvement of Manik et al.'s Scheme

Chou et al. [6] noted that the verification in [5], $\hat{e}(DID_i - V_i, P) = \hat{e}(H_1(ID_i), Pub_{RS})$ holds valid even when $DID_i' = DID_i + a$ and $V_i' = V_i + a$ where $a \in G_1$, as shown below.

$$\begin{aligned}
\hat{e}(DID_i' - V_i', P) &= \hat{e}(DID_i + a - V_i - a, P) \\
&= \hat{e}(DID_i - V_i, P) \\
&= \hat{e}(H_1(ID_i), Pub_{RS}) \,.
\end{aligned}$$

Chou et al. proposed a different verification technique as $\hat{e}(DID_i, P) = \hat{e}(T \cdot s \cdot H_1(ID_i) + V_i, P)$ to avoid the subtraction effect of [5].

3.3 Thulasi et al.'s Cryptanalysis

Chou et al. modified Manik et al.'s verification as $\hat{e}(DID_i, P) = \hat{e}(T \cdot s \cdot H_1(ID_i) + V_i, P)$. Thulasi et al., however, pointed out that this verification also is valid for $DID_i' = DID_i + a'$ and $V_i' = V_i + a'$ where $a' \in G_1$, as shown below.

$$\begin{aligned}
\hat{e}(DID_i', P) &= \hat{e}(DID_i + a', P) \\
&= \hat{e}(DID_i, P)\hat{e}(a', P) \\
&= \hat{e}(T \cdot s \cdot H_1(ID_i) + V_i, P) \, \hat{e}(a', P) \\
&= \hat{e}(T \cdot s \cdot H_1(ID_i) + V_i + a', P) \\
&= \hat{e}(T \cdot s \cdot H_1(ID_i) + V_i', P) \,.
\end{aligned}$$

Forgery attack: The tuple $<ID_i, DID_i, V_i, T>$ is sent to the RS over a public channel. Any adversary who tapped these can compute T^{-1}. An adversary can compute Reg_{IDi}, and $H_1(PW_i)$, as below.

$$\begin{aligned}
Reg_{IDi} &= T^{-1} \cdot DID_i = T^{-1} \cdot T \cdot Reg_{IDi} \,. \\
H_1(PW_i) &= T^{-1} \cdot V = T^{-1} \cdot T \cdot H_1(PW_i) \,.
\end{aligned}$$

An attacker, who knows Reg_{IDi} and $H_1(PW_i)$, can form the valid tuple $< ID_i, DID_i', V_i', T'>$ for the time stamp T^* by computing, $DID_i' = T' \cdot Reg_{IDi}$, $V_i' = T' \cdot H_1(PW_i)$. The scheme is vulnerable against replay and forgery attacks. Anyone can forge the login request, so it is also possible for an insider to lead an inside attack.

Weakness in the password change phase: In the password change phase, a user submits the ID_i, old password PW_i, and new password PW_i^*. The verifing equation is $Reg_{IDi}^* = Reg_{IDi} - H_1(PW_i) + H_1(PW_i^*)$, but they didn't verify the validity of the old password. Therefore, anyone who knows the ID_i and has a smart card can change the secret value Reg_{IDi} in the smart card.

4   Further Comments and the Improved Scheme

In this section, we illustrate further flaws on Manik et al.'s scheme and provide an improved one. Also we provide a security analysis.

4.1   Further Weaknesses of Manik et al.'s Scheme

Besides the replay and forgery attacks on Manik et al,'s scheme, it is still insecure against a guessing attack. As Thulasi et al. has identified, an adversary can compute Reg_{IDi} and $H_1(PW_i)$ by multiplying T^1 to the right side of the equation $DID_i = T \cdot Reg_{IDi}$, $V_i = T \cdot H_1(PW_i)$. Then, the secret value is only one parameter, such as Reg_{IDi} or $H_1(PW_i)$. An adversary can easily identify values which are kept in a smart card, and the following off-line guessing attack is possible:

Off-line guessing attack: As an active adversary knows the value of Reg_{IDi} and $H_1(PW_i)$, he/she can guess the password through the repetition of guessing and verification.

A comment on the password change phase: Thulasi et al. showed that there is no verification regarding the validity of the old password, however if the password change phase is operated after checking the validity of the inputted password, the phase does not have any problems.

4.2   Our Improved Scheme

The previous scheme is vulnerable against forgery, replay, and guessing attacks. One of the key reason for those weaknesses is that Reg_{IDi} and $H_1(PW_i)$ can be revealed based on the computation of the inverse of T. The following procedure illustrates our improved scheme.

Setup phase: The remote server (RS) selects a secret key $s \in Z_q^*$. Then, RS publishes the system parameter $< G_1, G_2, \hat{e}, q, P, H_1, H_2 >$.

Registration phase:
R1   User U_i submits his identity, ID_i and password PW_i to the RS.
R2   On receiving the registration request, the RS computes $Reg_{IDi} = s \cdot H_1(ID_i) + H_1(PW_i)$.
R3   The RS personalizes a smart card with the ID_i, Reg_{IDi}, H_1, H_2 parameters. They sent to U_i over a secure manner, such as face-to-face.

Authentication phase: The authentication phase is divided into login and verification phases.

Login Phase: The user U_i inserts a smart card into a terminal and keys the ID_i and PW_i. The smart card performs the following operations:

L1   Checks to see whether the ID_i is identical to the one that is stored in the smart card.
L2   Generates a nonce $n_i \in Z_q^*$.
L3   Computes $V_i = n_i \cdot P$.

L4   Computes $W_i = H_2(ID_i \| V_i \| T)$ where T is the user system's time stamp.
L5   Computes $X_i = Reg_{IDi} - H_1(PW_i) = s \cdot H_1(ID_i)$.
L6   Computes $DID_i = n_i \cdot W_i \cdot X_i$.
L7   Computes $C_i = DID_i \oplus X_i$.
L8   Sends the login request $< ID_i, V_i, C_i, T >$ to the RS over a public channel.

Verification phase:
V1   Verifies the expected valid time interval $\Delta T \geq T^* - T$.
V2   Extracts $DID_i = C_i \oplus s \cdot H_1(ID_i)$.
V3   Computes $W_i = H_2(ID_i \| V_i \| T)$.
V4   Checks whether $\hat{e}(DID_i, P) = \hat{e}(s \cdot H_1(ID_i), V_i)^{W_i}$. If it holds, the RS accepts the login request; otherwise, it is rejected.

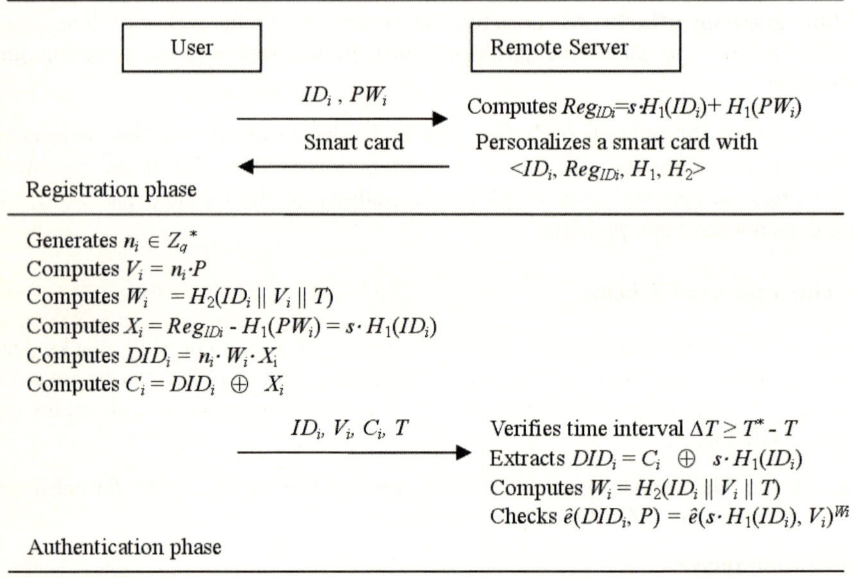

Fig. 1. Proposed remote authentication scheme using bilinear pairings

4.3   Validation and Security analysis

In this Section, we analyze the security of our proposed scheme.

Correctness: The validity in V4 of the verification phase is examined in the following.

$$\hat{e}(DID_i, P) = \hat{e}(n_i \cdot W_i \cdot X_i, P)$$
$$= \hat{e}(n_i \cdot W_i \cdot s \cdot H_1(ID_i), P)$$
$$= \hat{e}(W_i \cdot s \cdot H_1(ID_i), n_i \cdot P)$$
$$= \hat{e}(s \cdot H_1(ID_i), V_i)^{W_i}.$$

Replay attack: If an adversary replays an intercepted valid login request and the RS receives the request at time T'_r, the delay time is $\Delta T \leq T' - T$. Then, the replay attack does not work because the time interval exceeds the admissible delay time ΔT. Only a valid time stamp can be passed through the verification phase.

Forgery attack: In the login phase, an adversary can get the tuple $<ID_i, V_i, C_i, T>$, however, he cannot extract Reg_{IDi} or $H_1(PW_i)$ from the equation, $V_i = n_i \cdot P$ and $C_i = DID_i \oplus X_i$, since an adversary cannot find the nonce n_i or the server secret s. Thus, the correct DID_i or W_i cannot be computed, nor can an adversary pass V4 in the verification phase. The login request will fail.

Insider attack: In our scheme, we assume that remote server is protected through access control. Then, RS secret s is protected from an adversary. If the user login request is password-based and the RS maintains a password or verifier table for login request verification, this attack can be achieved by an insider of RS. In our scheme, however, the user login request is based on the user's password, as well as RS's secret and a nonce which is not maintained in the verifier table. Thus, our scheme can withstand this attack.

Moreover, our scheme can simply prevent the scenario of many logged-in users with the same login-ID, functioning/operating at the same time, as the other person cannot login to the RS without the smart card. In our scheme, the RS does not posses any password or verifier table for user verification, so our scheme can also withstand a stolen verifier attack.

5   Conclusion

Several researchers have indicated that Manik et al.'s scheme has security flaws, but it is difficult to improve their scheme in a given environment because of their fundamental problems. Thus, we have demonstrated that Manik et al.'s scheme has fundamental flaws in the construction of parameters and has been designed an efficient scheme based on employing a nonce and two kinds of hash operations. Moreover we have shown that our verification provides validity and security satisfaction. Our scheme has only one path that needs to be authenticated by the RS and minimal computational costs so that it can be efficiently used for remote user authentication.

Acknowledgement

This work was supported by grant No. R01-2006-000-10614-0 from the Basic Research Program of the Korea Science & Engineering Foundation.

References

1. L. Lamport: Password authentication with insecure communication. Communication of ACM 24 (1981) 770-772
2. E. J. Yoon, and K. Y. Yoo: More Efficient and Secure Remote User Authentication Scheme using smart cards. IEEE CS ICPADS (2005) 73-77
3. H. M. Sun and L. H. Li: An efficient remote user authentication scheme using smart cards. IEEE Transactions on Consumer Electronics 46 (2000) 958-961

4. M. Hwang and L. Li: A new remote user authentication scheme using smart cards. IEEE Trans Consumer Electronics 46 (2000) 28-30
5. W. Yang and S. Shieh: Password authentication schemes with smart cards. Computers and Security 18 (1999) 727-733
6. Manik. L. Das, Ashutosh Saxena, V. P. Gulati, D. B. Phatak: A novel remote user authentication scheme using bilinear pairings. Computers & Security 25 (2006) 184-189
7. J. S. Chou, Y. Chen, J. Y. Lin: Improvement of Manik et al.'s remote user authentication scheme. http://eprint.iacr.org/2005/450.pdf
8. Thulasi Goriparthi, Manik. L. Das, Atul Negi and Ashutosh Saxena: Cryptanalysis of recently proposed Remote User Authentication Schemes. http://eprint.iacr.org/2006/28.pdf
9. I. Blake, G. Seroussi, and N. Smart: Elliptic curve in cryptography. Cambridge University press (1999)
10. S. S. Al-Riyami: Cryptographic Schemes based on Elliptic Curve Pairings. Ph.D Thesis, University of London (2004)
11. D. Boneh and M. Franklin: Identity-based encryption from the Weil pairing, Advances in Cryptology (Crypto'2001), Lecture Notes in Computer Science, Springer-Verlag, Berlin Heidelberg New York 2139 (2001) 213-229
12. N.P. Smart: An identity based authenticated key agreement protocol based on the Weil pairing, Electronics Letters 38 (2002) 630-632

Dynamic Load Balancing on Non-homogeneous Clusters

Marcelo R. Naiouf[1], Laura C. De Giusti[2], Franco Chichizola[3],
and Armando E. De Giusti[4]

Instituto de Investigación en Informática LIDI (III-LIDI)[5]
Facultad de Informática – Universidad Nacional de La Plata
La Plata - Buenos Aires - Argentina
{mnaiouf, ldgiusti, francoch, degiusti}@lidi.info.unlp.edu.ar

Abstract. This paper discusses the dynamic and static balancing of non-homogenous cluster architectures, simultaneously analyzing the theoretical parallel speedup as well as the speedup experimentally   obtained.

A classical application (Parallel N-Queens) with a parallel solution algorithm, where processing predominates upon communication, has been chosen so as to go deep in the load balancing aspects (dynamic or static) without distortion of results caused by communication overhead.

Four interconnected clusters have been used in which the machines within each cluster have homogeneous processors although different among clusters. Thus, the set can be seen as a N-processor heterogeneous cluster or as a multi-cluster scheme with 4 subsets of homogeneous processors.

At the same time, three forms of load distribution in the processors (Direct Static, Predictive Static and Dynamic by Demand) have been studied, analyzing in each case parallel speedup and load unbalancing regarding problem size and the processors used.

Keywords: Parallel Processing, Load Distribution, Static and Dynamic Load Balancing.

1 Introduction

1.1 Cluster and Multi-cluster Architectures

A cluster is a type of parallel/distributed processing architecture consisting of a set of interconnected computers that can work as a single machine. The machines that make up a cluster can be homogeneous or heterogeneous, this being an important factor for the analysis of performance that can be obtained from a cluster as a parallel machine [1][2][3].

---

[1] Full-time Professor, School of Computer Sciences. UNLP.
[2] PhD student. UNLP Scholarship. Assistant Profesor, School of Computer Sciences. UNLP.
[3] PhD student. CONICET. Assistant Profesor, School of Computer Sciences. UNLP.
[4] CONICET Main Researcher. Full-time Professor, School of Computer Sciences. UNLP.
[5] This project is financially supported by the CIC and the YPF Foundation.

G. Min et al. (Eds.): ISPA 2006 Ws, LNCS 4331, pp. 65 – 73, 2006.

A multi-cluster architecture consists in interconnecting two or more clusters to configure a new parallel machine. The characterization of global performance parameters of a multi-cluster is complex owing to the number of intervening clusters, the degree of heterogeneity of processors and the inter-cluster communication system. On occasions, a combination of interconnected homogeneous clusters, configuring a heterogeneous multi-cluster is used.

1.2   Load Balancing in Heterogeneous Architectures

For the type of known work problems (e.g. matrix multiplication) a "predictive" static load balancing considering the calculation power of the multi-cluster processors can be obtained; however, many real problems have a variable or dynamic workload depending on the data [4][5][6][7]. In these cases, it is necessary to adjust data or processes allocation dynamically while the application is being executed.

Besides, in a multi-cluster scheme in which applications are resolved with the Master-Slave paradigm, any dynamic balancing solution used, implies a communication overhead that will be affected by the complexity of the communication scheme among the nodes of the different clusters.

1.3   Types of Problems with Variable Workload

There are certain types of data parallelism problems for which it is possible to perform a static balancing allocation of the total workload. In these cases, provided there is a heterogeneous architecture, it will be possible to define a predictive $F(P_i, Wt)$ function where P_i is the calculation power of processor i and Wt the total work This function allows to distribute data "a priori" among processors [8].

If there is a variable workload due to the data particular characteristics (e.g. data arrangement, identification of image patterns), it is not possible to have a predictive function that assures load balancing among processors. Thus, it will be necessary to have a dynamic allocation policy that can be combined with a predictive initial distribution of a percentage of the total data [5][9].

Any dynamic allocation policy used implies some overhead degree of communication, which will be more complex to model and predict in a heterogeneous multi-cluster architecture.

2   Characterization of Type of Application of Interest

As analyzed in the introduction, there are different research axes on dynamic load balancing problems in multi-cluster architectures.

An architecture model in which heterogeneity appears only in machines with different clusters and can be compared to a calculation power function of the machines of each cluster has been determined.

Finally, the focus of this experimental work has been put on one type of the problems in which communication time among Tc processes is not significant, considering Tp ($Tp \gg Tc$) local processing time.

This restriction allows to identify the differences among the static and dynamic load balancing schemes more clearly without overlapping an important communication overhead not relate to the distribution.

3   Load Distribution Models to be Studied and Theoretical Speedup to Be Achieved

Three ways of data parallelism implementation will be used:

- *Direct Static Distribution (DSD)* where the total workload *Wt* will be allocated to the architecture *B* processor in a homogeneous manner, so that each processor will have *Wt/B*, regardless the $F(P_i, Wt)$ function. This distribution is used as a lower bound reference.
- *Predictive Static Distribution (PSD)* where the total workload *Wt* will be allocated to the architecture *B* processor at the moment of starting the application, according to the prediction $F(P_i, Wt)$ function.
- *Dynamic Distribution upon Demand (DDD)* where a *Li* percentage of the total *Wt* workload will be allocated to the architecture *B* processor at the moment of starting the application, according to the prediction $F(P_i, W_i)$ function and then, each processor will demand more work on the part of the Master, as its task is being completed.

The *Li* value and the amount of additional work to be allocated to each processor on demand are experimental research parameters that depend on the application and the relation between *Tp* and *Tc*.

The theoretical speedup to be achieved by multi-cluster architecture will be a $G(P_i)$ function. The experimental measuring of the real speedup should directly correlate with the degree of balancing achieved with the total *Wt* work allocation during the execution of the application.

4   Contribution of This Work

- An expression for heterogeneous cluster calculation power is presented, considering individual processor power and heterogeneity. Also theoretical analysis of unbalance and maximum speedup attainable is presented.
- A Master-Slave model with 4 heterogeneous clusters among them operating as a (*B*=42) multi-cluster with an additional processor as Master has been studied, checking the theoretical analysis on processors heterogeneity and maximum speedup attainable.
- One problem case was studied, which responded to the hypothesis *Tp* >> *Tc*, with the three load distributions proposed (DSD, PSD, DDD) to carry out the data parallelism, specially comparing with the theoretical parallel speedup. This speedup was achieved in view of the calculation power of the processors, and the load unbalancing taking into account the parameters *B*, *Wt*, P_i y *Li* mentioned before.

5   Application to Parallel Solution on a Heterogeneous Multi-cluster of the N-Queens Problem

The N-queens problem consists in placing N queens on an NxN board in such a way that they do not attacks one another [10][11][12]. A queen attacks another one if they are in the same diagonal, row or column .

5.1   Sequential Solution

An initial solution to the N-queens problem, using an sequential algorithm, consists in trying all possible location combinations of the queens on the board, keeping those that are valid and disrupting the search whenever this is not achieved. Considering that a valid combination can generate up to 8 different solutions, which are rotations of the same combination, the number of distributions to be evaluated can be reduced. The best sequential algorithm found for this problem is based on this fact [13][14][15].

5.2   Parallel Solution Proposed Based on the Function of the Load Distribution Models

For the parallel solution of this problem, the queen is placed on one or more rows, and all the solutions for that initial arrangement are obtained. Each processor is in charge of solving the problem for a subset of said solutions, in this way, the whole system works with all the possible combinations of those rows.

When working with a heterogeneous architecture, the amount of work (combinations) that each processor must solve vary according to the existing relation regarding calculation power. To be able to distribute the work in a balanced way, it is convenient to use "fine grain", that is, many combinations of little work each, so as to level up the work done by each machine, and resolve several of them. To this aim, the first four rows are used to form each of the combinations to resolve [16].

In this way, different N^4 combinations are obtained to be distributed among all the heterogeneous processors, N being the board size. This distribution is carried out by using those motherhoods mentioned in III.

6   Experimental Results Obtained

In this section, the tests carried out are presented together with the results obtained, regarding the speedup metrics and the unbalancing described below.

6.1   Metrics Used

To measure the load unbalancing among the processors that intervene in a parallel application, the relative work difference obtained is calculated with formula (1), where $Work_i = machine\ time_i$ [2].

$$Unbalance = \frac{\max_{i=1..B}(Work_i) - \min_{i=1..B}(Work_i)}{average_{i=1..B}(Work_i)}. \tag{1}$$

The speedup metrics is used to analyze the algorithm performance in the parallel architecture as indicated by formula (2).

$$Speedup \;=\; \frac{SequentialTime}{ParallelTime}. \tag{2}$$

In the case of a heterogeneous architecture, the "Sequential Time" is given by the time of the best sequential algorithm executed in the machine with the greatest calculation power [1][17][18].

To evaluate how good the speedup obtained is, it is compared with the theoretical speedup of the architecture upon which work is being carried out. The speedup considers the relative calculation power of each machine with respect to the power of the most powerful machine [19]. The theoretical speedup is calculated with formula (3), where B is the number of machines of the architecture used, y P_i is the relative calculation power of the *machine i* regarding the best machine power. This relation is expressed in the formula (4).

$$TheoreticalSpeedup \;=\; \sum_{i=1}^{B} P_i . \tag{3}$$

$$P_i = \frac{sequentialTime\,(powerfulMachine)}{sequentialTime\,(m_i)}. \tag{4}$$

6.2 Experiments

The experiments were done on a multi-cluster architecture consisting of four clusters: an 16 Pentium IV 2.4 Ghz homogeneous cluster of 1 Gb memory.

- an 10 Celeron 2 Ghz homogeneous cluster of 128 Mb memory.
- an 8 Duron 800Mhz homogeneous cluster of 256 Mb memory.
- an 8 Pentium III 700 Mhz cluster homogeneous cluster of 256 Mb memory.

Communication within each cluster is done via an Ethernet web, using a switch for communication among clusters.

The language used for the implementations is C together with the MPI library to handle communications among processors.[20]

Tests were carried out using 42 machines, adding one for the dynamic distribution, acting as master, and with different board sizes. (N = 17, 18, 19, 20, 21).

In the case of dynamic distribution, it was experimented with different percentages of initial distribution. (Li = 0, 5, 10, 15, 20, 25, 50).

6.3 Results

The data of Table 1 shows the percentage of load unbalancing produced by the algorithm for the Direct Static, Predictive Static and Dynamic upon Demand distributions with different Li values. Some of these results can be seen in figure 1.

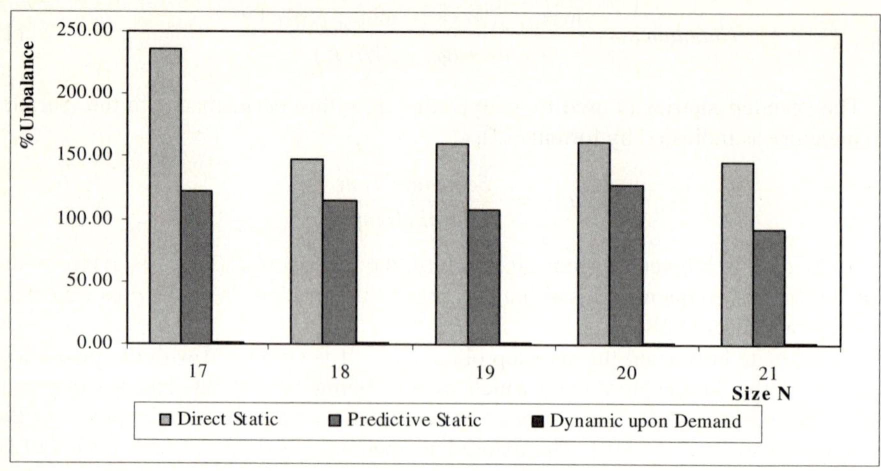

Fig. 1. Graph of Percentage of Load Unbalancing of Direct Static, Predictive Static and Dynamic upon Demand Distributions (*Li*=15). *N*=17,18,19,20,21

Table 1. Percentage of Unbalancing for each test

Size	Direct Static	Predictive Static	Dynamic upon Demand						
			0%	5%	10%	15%	20%	25%	50%
17	236.09	122.37	2.81	1.65	0.13	0.14	0.12	0.12	106.09
18	148.30	115.20	20.93	12.10	0.04	0.04	1.63	27.29	150.29
19	160.66	107.62	152.91	92.72	0.04	0.05	3.91	9.92	131.61
20	162.02	128.21	0.03	0.03	0.03	0.03	0.03	24.09	131.19
21	145.60	92.91	0.03	0.03	0.03	0.03	0.03	16.48	117.34

Table 2 presents the speedup obtained for each test mentioned before together with the optimal speedup (or theoretical) calculated for this machine combination. Table 3 shows the total time for each test.

Table 2. Speedup

Size	Optimum	Direct Static	Predictive Static	Dynamic upon Demand						
				0%	5%	10%	15%	20%	25%	50%
17	31	10.62	17.75	24.13	24.72	24.96	25.14	25.38	23.30	13.49
18	31	12.99	17.31	30.07	30.15	30.20	30.25	29.78	24.00	12.00
19	31	12.21	18.22	30.79	30.59	30.76	30.90	30.12	28.63	13.28
20	31	12.46	15.99	30.85	30.89	30.91	30.95	30.99	24.90	13.21
21	31	13.52	19.76	30.98	30.98	30.99	31.00	30.99	27.10	14.30

Figure 2 shows the speedup obtained with each of the distribution algorithms for some of the tests in Table 2, together with the optimal speedup of this architecture.

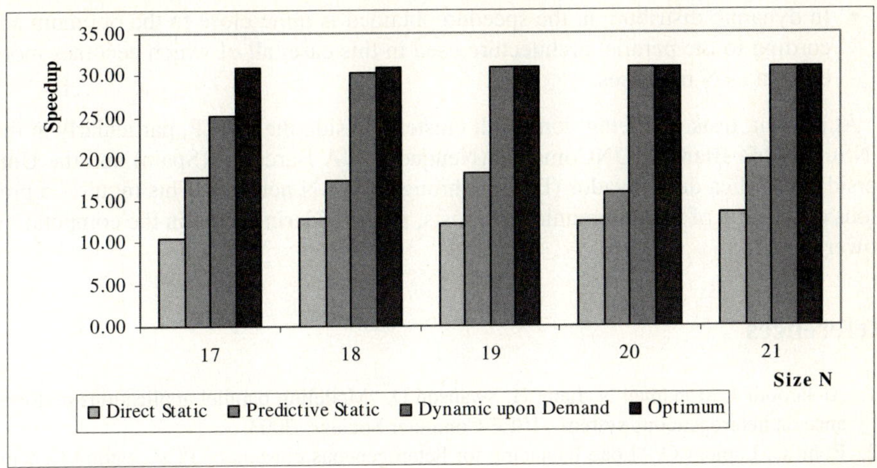

Fig. 2. Speedup of the Direct Static, Predictive Static and Dynamic upon Demand Distributions (Li=15) and Optimum. N=17, 18, 19, 20, 21.

Table 3. Algorithm Total Time

Size	Direct Static	Predictive Static	Dynamic upon Demand						
			0%	5%	10%	15%	20%	25%	50%
17	4.70	2.81	2.07	2.02	2.00	1.99	1.97	2.14	3.70
18	27.91	20.94	12.06	12.02	12.00	11.98	12.17	15.10	30.19
19	228.16	152.95	90.50	91.09	90.57	90.18	92.51	97.33	209.76
20	1795.20	1399.46	725.15	724.19	723.68	722.92	721.90	898.45	1693.51
21	13957.76	9554.65	6094.24	6094.46	6090.92	6090.52	6090.63	6966.64	13205.15

7 Conclusions and Work Guidelines

Analyzing the results obtained from the experimental work, we can come to the following conclusions:

- Experimental results are coherent with theoretical analysis of unbalance and maximum speedup attainable.
- For the type of problems where Tp>>Tc (as the N-Queens problem that requires a minimal communication among machines), if the work is data-dependent it's essential the choice of data distribution among clusters, to achieve an almost optimal speedup.
- Naturally, algorithms that take into account the calculation power of each machine for work distribution have a better behavior than Direct Static distribution. This improvement is clearly expressed in the load balancing and the speedup.
- Among the algorithm that take into account the calculation power, it can be seen that the algorithms that distribute dynamically can assign work in a more balancing way among the machines (as seen in Graph 1), without much affecting the final time of execution (as shown by the speedup en Graph 2 and the data of Table 3).

- In dynamic distribution, the speedup obtained is quite close to the optimum according to the parallel architecture used in this case, all of which becomes more evident as N increases.

At present, tests are being done with clusters outside the UNLP, particularly at the UNSur (Bahía Blanca), UNComahue (Neuquen), UA Barcelona(Spain) and the Universidad Católica del Salvador (Brasil), through a WAN network. This requires a previous evaluation of the communication costs, for considering them in the computation power model.

References

1. Al-Jaroodi J, Mohamed N, Jiang H, Swanson D. "Modeling parallel applications performance on heterogeneous system". IEEE Computer Society, 2003.
2. Bohn C, Lamont G. "Load balancing for heterogeneous clusters of PCs". Future Generation Computer Systems, Elsevier Science B.V., Vol 18, 2002, pp 389-400.
3. Leopold C. "Parallel and distributed computing. A survey of models, paradigms, and approaches". Wiley Series on Parallel and Distributed Computing. Albert Zomaya Series Editor, 2001.
4. Baiardi F, Chiti S, Mori P, Ricci L. "Integrating load balancing and locality in the parallelization of irregular problems". Future Generation Computer Systems, Elsevier Science B.V., Vol 17, 2001, pp 969-975.
5. Naiouf M. "Procesamiento paralelo. Balance dinámico de carga en algoritmos de sorting". Tesis doctoral. Universidad Nacional de La Plata, 2004.
6. Watts J, Taylor S. "A practical approach to dynamic load balancing". IEEE Transactions on Parallel and Distributed Systems, 9(3), March 1998, pp. 235-248.
7. Dongarra J, Foster I, Fox G, Gropp W, Kennedy K, Torczon L, White A. "The Sourcebook of Parallel Computing". Morgan Kauffman Publishers. Elsevier Science, 2003.
8. Ross K, Yao D. "Optimal load balancing and scheduling in a distributed computer system". Journal of Association for Computing Machinery, 38 (3): 676-690.1991.
9. Hui C, Chanson S. "Improve strategies for dynamic load balancing". IEEE Concurrency, pages 58-67. 1999.
10. Dongarra J, Foster I, Fox G, Gropp W, Kennedy K, Torczon L, White A. "The Sourcebook of Parallel Computing". Morgan Kauffman Publishers. Elsevier Science, 2003.
11. Bruen A, Dixon R. "Then n-queens problem. Discrete mathematics". 12:393-395, 1997.
12. De Giusti L, Novarini P, Naiouf M, De Giusti A. "Parallelization of the N-queens problem. Load unbalance analysis". Workshop de Procesamiento Paralelo y Distribuido (WPPD), Congreso Argentino de Ciencias de la Computación (CACIC'03), 2003.
13. Hedetniemi S, Hedetniemi T, Reynolds R. "Combinatorial problems on chessboards: II". Chapter 6 in domination in graphs: advanced topic, pag 133-162, 1998.
14. Bernhardsson B. "Explicit solution to the n-queens problems for all n". ACM SIGART Bulletin,2:7,1991.
15. Somers J. "The N-queens problem a study in optimization". www.jsomers.com/nqueen_demo /nqueens.html.
16. Takaken, "N-queens problem (number of solutions)". http://www.ic-net.or.jp/home/takaken/e/queen/.
17. De Giusti L., Chichizola F. "Optimización de N-queens Paralelo". Technical report III-LIDI. 2006.

18. Grama A, Gupta A, Karypis G, Kumar V. "Introduction to parallel computing". Second Edition. Pearson Addison Wesley, 2003.
19. Jordan H, Alaghband G. "Fundamentals of parallel computing". Prentice Hall, 2002.
20. Tinetti F. "Cómputo paralelo en redes locales de computadoras". Tesis Doctoral. Universidad Autónoma de Barcelona, 2004.
21. Snir M., Otto S., Huss-Lederman S., Walker D., Dongarra J., "MPI: The Complete Reference", The MIT Press, Cambridge, Massachusetts ,1996.

L2-Cache Hierarchical Organizations for Multi-core Architectures

Mario Donato Marino

Computing Engineering Department- Polytechnic School - University of Sao Paulo
mario@regulus.pcs.usp.br

Abstract. Nowadays the market is moving to have multiple cores on the same chip (Chip Multiprocessors - CMP) with a multi-sliced L2 which is shared by 2 cores. CMPs with 8 cores can already be found, and future CMPs will have more than 8 cores. Typical implementations of CMPs share the L2 cache among the processors and have 2 cores sharing the same L2. We are interested in investigating the behavior of the pair: L2 sharing x L2 cache size. So, we construct models of two different organizations of CMPs: (i) tiles, with L1 and L2 private, interconnected through a router; (ii) tiles with L1 private and L2 shared among processors. The (ii) organization is evaluated with different numbers (2, 4) of cores sharing the same L2 slice and also, the L2 shared slice size is changed (1 MB, 2MB and 4 MB). With a total number of 32 cores, the proposed configurations of (ii) organization are evaluated with a full-system simulation under SPLASH-2 benchmarks. By applying both techniques, results show that the execution time is improved of about 18.9% for Ocean, 88.8% for Raytrace,and 31.8% for Volrend.

1   Introduction

The adoption of chip multiprocessors, CMP [19,20] or multi-core architectures, is spreading all over the markets: commercial, industrial, domestic and gaming [12]. Several 2-core [9,10,11] solutions are already available for commercial, domestic and gaming purposes. An 8-core [17] solution is available for the web-server market. A 9-core [12] solution will soon be released for video game applications. Next-year road maps promises machines with 4 and also 16 [21] or more cores. Better dissipation, scalability, performance [13] and less energy [3,18] consumption, when compared to a wider processor, are the central reasons for adopting the CMPs.

Many cores inside the chip cause higher latencies due to wire delays [2,3,19,24] when compared to a wider core. The other consequence of having many cores is the need of more data to run several tasks in parallel. Present solutions concentrate [9,10,11] on increasing the bandwidth and/or on sharing some parts of their caches and maintaining others private. In this paper we are investigating the latter way.

The main feature of the solutions which focus on sharing are the data reusing. Data reusing is obtained by sharing a slice of L2, thinking on a multi-banked or

G. Min et al. (Eds.): ISPA 2006 Ws, LNCS 4331, pp. 74–83, 2006.

multi-sliced solution for L2. Designs and implementations of L2 through multi-sliced banks have been preferred [1,2,3,6,7,13,25] due to their low latency and better hit rate.

Hierarchical cache hierarchies with multi-sliced banks are built with replications of a tile. Each tile contains a processor, L1 cache and L2 cache. It's possible to use a set of processors with the L1 next level pointing to the same L2, which is denominated L2 shared cache cluster or L2 shared slice. Differently from the previous studies[1,2,3,21], which have investigated particular solutions, the main contribution of this paper is to evaluate the behavior of the hierarchical caches with these features investigating the pair: L2 size x number of processors sharing the L2, changing both parameters and how they are related. Following this idea, we constructed different hierarchical organizations of multi-sliced L2 caches and evaluated them with different numbers of shared clusters (different numbers of processors sharing the same cluster) and different L2 cache sizes, through a full-system simulation and running SPLASH-2 [15] benchmarks. In order to implement those evaluations, we consider a cluster as a set of cores; this paper compares 3 different organizations with (i) 32 L2 cache clusters of 1 core, (ii) 16 L2 cache clusters of 2 cores and (iii) 8 L2 cache clusters of 4 cores. These 3 configurations were also evaluated with 3 different L2 cache sizes. Other contribution of this article is to investigate CMPs with 32 cores which have more than 2x or 4x number of cores which previous papers [1,2,3,21] have investigated.

The rest of the paper is organized as follows. Section 2 describes possible multi-core organizations. Section 3 discusses the methodology and Section 4 presents results. Section 5 concludes our work.

2   CMP: Internal Organization

In this section we describe some configurations considered for tiled CMPs. They are based on a tile replicated in a 2-D mesh configuration, where each tile contains: (i) its processor, with a L1 instruction and L1 data caches; (ii) one L2 cache; (iii) a connection to the network. Figures 1a and b illustrate that.

Thinking of L2, its possible to have L2 private or shared. In order to be accessible by several processors, it's possible to implement L2 shared via multi-port or multi-slices. As we have said before, multi-slicing implementations[1,2,3,6,7,13,25] have been preferred because of their best performance. Based on the way the caches are connected in a hierarchical implementation, we propose a nomenclature for them: (i) private L1 data cache and private L2: *L1pL2p* configuration is illustrated in figure 1a; (ii) private L1 data cache and *i* processors sharing one L2 slice: *L1pL2si;* for example, L1pL2s2 if we have 2 processors sharing L2; L1pL2s2 configuration is illustrated in figure 1b and better described in the next item.

Figure 1a illustrates L1pL2p , which is the most simple one: a replication of a traditional tile, i.e., each tile has one CPU (processor or core), and each processor has its private L1 data cache and L1 instruction cache. Both L1 data and instruction caches are connected to a private L2. Each L2 is connected to

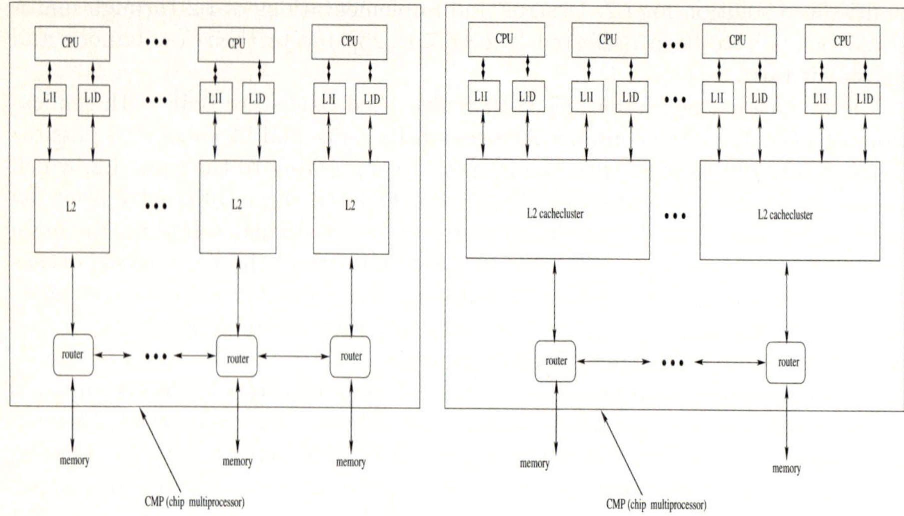

Fig. 1. a: L1pL2p; b: L1pL2s

another L2 and to the memory, through a router. Except for the memory, the sets of tiles (core + L1 + L2 + internal buses + router) are inside the chip. When a cache line is required by one processor, on a L1 miss, before going to the memory, the line is searched from another L2 cache, through the network, avoiding off chip accesses, that maximizes locality inside the chip. The number of hops needed to find the data on the remote L2 caches and the coherence messages may cause a congestion in this bus[21].

Figure 1b ilustrates L1pL2s configuration, which is similar to the ones proposed by Barroso[13] and Zhang[1]. Each tile has one CPU with its private L1 data and L1 instruction caches, which are connected to a shared cluster L2 (multi-sliced L2): each cluster of L2 is shared among 2, 4 or more processors, i.e., a set of processors sharing L2, as viewed at figure 1b. The sets of tiles (CPU + L1 + L2 + internal buses) are inside the chip. Previous papers [1,9,13] have shown the superiority of the scheme L1pL2s over the L1pL2p. The superiority of L1pL2s over L1pL2p is responsible for the industry migration from configuration L1pL2p to L1pL2s. The recent processors dual-core IBM Power5[10] and Intel Core 2 [11], the next AMD K8[9], and also the 8-core Niagara[17] are examples of sharing a L2 slice with 2 processors. Figure 1b illustrates a CMP with some shared clusters L2, each of these shared by 2 CPUs.

L1pL2s cache clusters communicate with the others by the network, via router, with the distributed directory held as a replicated set of L2 tags. Each CPU has its private L1 data and L1 instruction caches, which are connected to a shared cluster L2: each cluster of L2 may be shared among 2, 4 or more processors, i.e., a set of processors sharing the same L2 cache cluster. The main advantage of having a set of processors sharing the same L2 is that one of them can reuse a line brought by the other processor firstly originated from memory. So, if there is a miss in L1, the line is searched in a L2 cache cluster through the network, which is a way to move lines from remote L2s. If the line is found in the L2 cache cluster, network is avoided (congestion).

Table 1. Summary of L1pL2si simulation parameters

parameter	considered values
Processor	UltraSparc III, in order, IPC=1
# of processors	32 processors
i processors sharing L2	2 and 4
L1 cache line size	64 B
L1 cache associativity	4-way
L1 dcache size	32 kB, 64 kB, 128 kB and 256 kB
L1 icache size	32 kB
L1 latency	3 cycles
L1 replacement policy	LRU
L2 cache line size	128 B
L2 cache associativity	4-way
L2 latency	6 cycles
L2 replacement policy	LRU
MESI transaction	7 cycles - L2
1-hop latency	4 cycles - L2
# of processors sharing L2	1, 2 and 4
cluster of shared L2	32, 16 and 8
cache size:L2 cache cluster	1 MB/cluster, 2 MB/cluster
memory latency	200 cycles

3   Methodology

Since the main goal of the paper is to evaluate the impact of having more processors sharing the same L2 slice, we have changed the number of processors in the configurations L1pL2si [2 and 4 processors] and evaluate its impact on the execution time, hit rate and memory breakdown. We have considered, for each i (number of processors sharing the same L2 = 2 and 4) a different L2 cache cluster size: 1 MB, 2 MB and 4 MB. For the results section, for example, the L1pL2s4.2MB configuration means 4 processors sharing the L2 slice and having L2 cache size equals to 2 MB. Different models based on these configurations were constructed and be evaluated. The methodology used here is the same as the used in similar studies[1,13,2,21].

Different configurations of the models developed were run on Simics 2.0.16 [14] in order to perform a full system simulation. In these configurations, dedicated models of the L1, L2, the network and the memory were considered. These models consider contention and bandwidth.

For this paper, a technology of 70 nm and 24 FO4 processor clock cycle are assumed. Each CPU is an UltraSparc III, in-order issue, with an ideal pipelining and IPC = 1. Considering L1, we assume dcaches of 32 kB, 64 kB, 128 kB and 256 kB, 64B-line write-back, 4-way associative. By running Cacti[29] we obtain 1 to 2 cycles for the access memory times, which added to a conservative wire delay assumption results on a 3-cycle access time. When it comes to each slice of L2, we assume 1 MB, 2 MB and 4 MB as the cache size for each cache cluster, 128B-line write-back, 4-way associative. The number of processors sharing L2 varies from 1 (L1pL2p) to 2 (L1pL2s2) and 4 (L1pL2s4). When it comes to memory, we assume infinite memory with a 200-cycle latency.

We have chosen all the applications from SPLASH-2 [15] benchmarks, as they have been used for years by the research community to evaluate shared memory architectures, so we consider them as a representative benchmark. All SPLASH-2 benchmarks were compiled with gcc 4.0.0 and run for class-A input sizes. The time is measured in number of cycles.

4   Simulation Results

We evaluate the results of the simulations considering the following parameters: execution time (speedup), number of coherency messages and memory events (memory breakdown accesses).

Figures 2 and 3a show the execution time obtained from our experiments. We have chosen the basis version with L1 and L2 of 1MB both privates, i.e., L1pL2p.1MB the one which will be compared against the best ones in terms of execution times: (i) Barnes and Volrend: the configuration L1pL2s2.4MB has the lowest execution time; when compared to L1pL2p.1MB, L1pL2s2.4MB is 7.6% faster for Barnes and 31.8% for Volrend; (ii) FMM: the configuration L1pL2s2.2MB has the lowest execution time; when compared to L1pL2p.1MB, L1pL2s2.2MB is 0.6% faster; as a general behavior we can say that, as it's showed in the figure 2, all configurations produce about the same execution time; (iii) Ocean, Radiosity and Raytrace: the configuration L1pL2s4.4MB has the lowest execution time; when compared to L1pL2p.1MB, L1pL2s4.4MB is 18.9% faster for Ocean, 4.9% for Radiosity and 88.8% for Raytrace; (iv) Water: L1pL2s4.2MB has the lowest execution time; L1pL2s4.2MB is 29.3% faster, when compared to L1pL2p.1MB.

Figure 3b shows the behavior of the coherence traffic inside the chip. Considering the same L2 sizes, by confronting L1pL2p with L1pL2si (i is the # of processors sharing the same L2 cache) , the number of invalidate messages does not increase at the same proportion as i multiplied by the number of invalidates of L1pL2p. This can be justified by the fact that the sharing among the processors saves a lot of invalidations, contributing to the reduction of their number; as a consequence, the speedups are improved.

Considering Barnes, L1pL2p.1MB has a high L1 hit rate of about 95.7%, i.e., most data fit in L1. Fixing i, i.e., the number of processors which shares the L2 cache, and considering different L2 slice sizes, comparing L1pL2p with L1pL2si, we've noticed that the L1 hit rate: (i) decreases from 95.7% to 86.3% L1pL2p (L2 private); (ii) it increases from 84.3% to 89.2% (1MB to 2 MB); (iii)

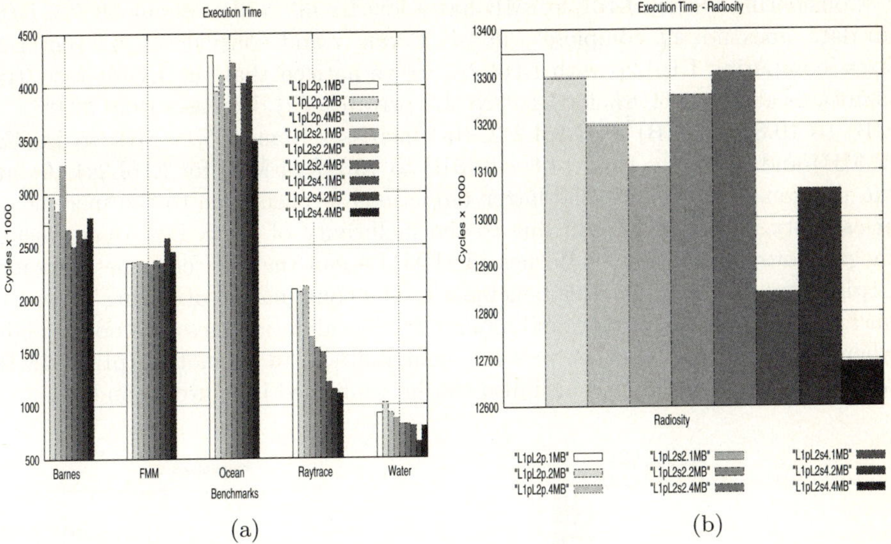

Fig. 2. a, b: Execution time - SPLASH2 benchmarks

it decreases from 89.2 % to 84.5% (2MB to 4MB) for L1pL2s2 (two processors sharing one L2 slice); (iv) it increases from 75.22% to 78.6% (1 MB to 2 MB); (v) and decreases from 78.6% to 70.1% (2MB to 1 MB) for L1pL2s4 (four processors sharing one L2 slice). When it comes to the coherency messages (figure 3b), (I) fixing i and increasing L2 slice size increases the number of coherency messages maintains about the same. (II) Fixing L2 slice size and changing i from 2 to 4: (1) it increases of up to 80% for 1 MB when compared to L1pL2p; (2) increases of up to 50% for 2MB and 4 MB when comparing to L1pL2p. Concluding, L1sL2s2.4MB has the best speedups (execution times) as seen in figure 2. This can be justified because L1sL2s2.4MB has the best combination of L1 high hit rate / L2 hit rate /low number of L2 invalidates.

About FMM, L1pL2p.1MB has a good L1 hit rate of about 87.2%. Fixing i, i.e., the number of processors which shares the L2 cache and considering different L2 slice sizes, comparing L1pL2p with L1pL2si, we've noticed that the L1 hit rate (i) decreases from 87.2% to 60.8% L1pL2p (L2 private); (ii) L1 hit rate maintains in about 63.5% changing from 1MB to 2 MB; (iii) decreases from 63.5% to 44.7% (2MB to 4MB) for L1pL2s2 (two processors sharing one L2); (iv) L1 hit rate increases from 75.22% to 78.6% (1 MB to 2 MB); (v) decreases from 36.09% to 29.9% when changing from 1MB to 4 MB for L1pL2s4. Concerning about coherency messages, figure 3b shows that if L2 slice size is increased (maintaining i) or if i is increased (maintaining L2 slice size), the number of invalidation messages increases but not in the same proportion as i or the cache size, which means that by sharing or by increasing L2 slice sizes minimizes the emission of this kind of traffic. The best combination of L1 hit / L2 hit / L2 miss rates/ coherency messages imply that L1pL2s2.2MB has the best speedup as noticed in figure 2a.

Considering Ocean, L1pL2p.1MB has a low L1 hit rate of about 59.7%, i.e., its data does not fit completely in L1. Fixing i and considering different L2 sizes, comparing L1pL2p with L1pL2si, we've noticed that the L1 hit rate: (i) maintains at about 60.8% for L1pL2p (L2 private); (ii) decreases from 32.0% (1 MB) to 19.8% (4 MB) for L1pL2s2; (iii) increases from 9.9%(1 MB) to 14.6% (2 MB) and decreases from 14.6% (2MB) to 13.2% (4 MB) for L1pL2s4. As in the previous benchmarks, the latter reductions in occur due to the increment of capacity misses in L1 and due to the inclusivity of L1 in L2. Analogously, the previous observation for Barnes and FMM about the coherency messages for L1pL2si are also valid for this benchmark. The combination of having a low L1 hit rate and high L2 hit rate, and a number of invalidation messages not so high when compared to the other versions, contribute to to promote L1pL2s4.4MB to have the best speedup, which also can be confirmed in figure 2a and 3b.

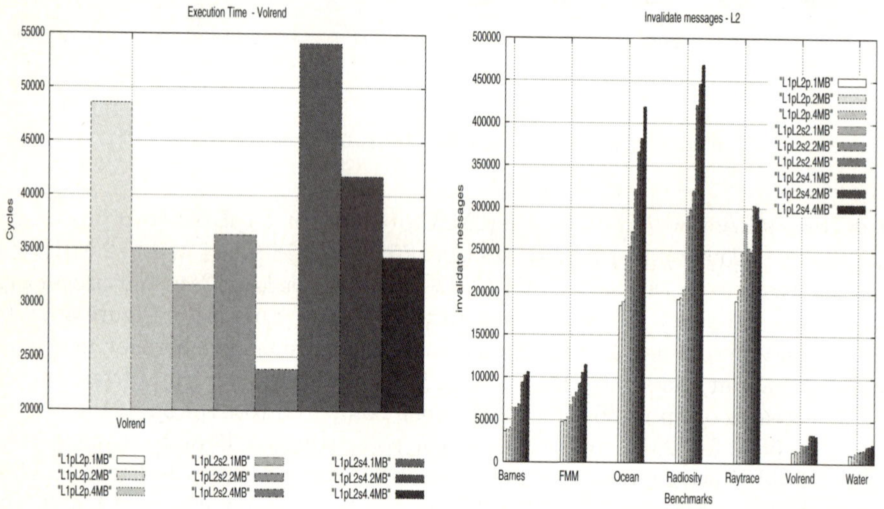

Fig. 3. a: Execution time - Volrend; b: Total number of invalidates of L2

Confronting all benchmarks, Radiosity is the one which has the highest L1 hit rate (about 99.3%) for L1pL2p.1MB, which means that most data completely fit on L1. Fixing i and considering different L2 sizes, comparing L1pL2p with L1pL2si, we've noticed that the L1 hit rate: (i) maintains at about 98.0% for L1pL2p (L2 private); (ii) it decreases from 98.6% (1 MB) to 97.1% (4 MB) for L1pL2s2; (iii) it maintains at 97.2% from 1 MB to 2 MB and decreases from 97.2% (2MB) to 96.22% (4 MB) for L1pL2s4. The effect of sharing L2 among several processors didn't affect Radiosity because of its high L1 hit rate, i.e., because the core of the benchmark fits inside L1. When it comes to the L2 miss rates, fixing i and changing the L2 slice size or fixing the L2 cache slice size and varying, both assumptions produce L2 miss rates close to 0.0%, which was previewed when we commented about its high L1 hit rates. The combination of having a high L1 hit rate and the highest L2 hit rate with an adequate number of invalidate messages((figure 3b)), contribute to to promote L1pL2s4.4MB to have the best speedup, which also can be confirmed in figure 2b.

In Raytrace, L1pL2p.1MB has a good L1 hit rate of about 85.2%, which means that most data completely fit on L1. Fixing i and considering different L2 sizes, comparing L1pL2p with L1pL2si, we've noticed that the L1 hit rate decreases from: (i) 85.2% to 68.6% for L1pL2p (L2 private); (ii) from 77.6% (1 MB) to 60.4% (4 MB) for L1pL2s2; (iii) from 69.0% (1MB) to 53.4% (4 MB) for L1pL2s4. As in the previous benchmarks, the latter reductions occur due to the increment of capacity misses on L1 and due to the inclusivity of L1 in L2. When it comes to the coherency messages (figure 3b), (i) fixing i and increasing L2 slice size cause the increment of the number of them by 50% when L2 size is changed from 1 MB to 2 MB and 10% from 2 MB to 4 MB. (ii) Fixing L2 slice size and changing i from 2 to 4: it increases of up to 20% (L1pL2s4) for 1 MB when compared to L1pL2p; decreases of 10% (L1pL2s4) for 2MB when comparing to L1pL2p; for 4 MB decreases of 3.5% when comparing to L1pL2p. The combination of having a high L1 hit rate and the highest L2 hit rate with number of invalidation messages not so high when compared to the other versions, contribute to to promote L1pL2s4.4MB to have the best speedup, which also can be confirmed in figure 2a.

In Volrend, L1pL2p.1MB has a high L1 hit rate of about 90.6%, which means that most data completely fit on L1. Fixing i and considering different L2 sizes, comparing L1pL2p with L1pL2si, we've noticed that the L1 hit rate: (a) decreases from 90.6% (1 MB) to 65.0% (4 MB) for L1pL2p (L2 private); (b) decreases from about 69.0% (1 MB and 2 MB) to 48.0% (4 MB) for L1pL2s2; (c) increases from 51.4% (1MB) to 54.0% (2 MB), but decreases from 54.0% (2 MB) to 45.0% (4 MB) for L1pL2s4. As in the previous benchmarks, the latter reductions occur due to the increment of capacity misses on L1 and due to the inclusivity of L1 in L2. As a conclusion, both sharing L2 among processors and increasing L2 slice sizes have benefited the speedups of Volrend. When it comes to the coherency messages (figure 3b), fixing i and increasing L2 slice size increases the number of coherency messages maintains about the same. Also, by fixing L2 slice size and changing i from 2 to 4: (i) it increases of up to 80% for 1 MB when compared to L1pL2p; (ii) increases of up to 50% for 2MB and 4 MB when comparing to L1pL2p. The combination of having a high L1 hit rate and the highest L2 hit rate with number of invalidation messages not so high when compared to the other versions, contribute to to promote L1pL2s2.4MB to have the best speedup, which also can be confirmed in figure 3a.

For Water, L1pL2p.1MB has a high L1 hit rate of about 93.1%, which means that most data completely fit on L1. Fixing i and considering different L2 sizes, comparing L1pL2p with L1pL2si, we've noticed that the L1 hit rate: (a) decreases from 93.1% (1 MB) to 76.7% (4 MB) for L1pL2p; (b) decreases from about 82.0% (1 MB and 2 MB) to 70.3% (4 MB) for L1pL2s2; (c) increases from 65.7% (1MB) to 7.6% (2 MB), but decreases from 77.6% (2 MB) to 60.1% (4 MB) for L1pL2s4. The same justification adopted in previous benchmarks is valid for Water: the latter reductions in occur due to the increment of capacity misses on L1 and due to the inclusivity of L1 in L2. When it comes to the number of coherency messages (figure 3b), fixing L2 slice size and changing i from 2 to 4: (i) for 1 MB and 2 MB L2 cache slice sizes, the number of coherency messages increases of up to 100% when L1pL2s4 is compared to L1pL2p, and 90% when L1pL2ps4 is compared to L1pL2p, for 4 MB L2 cache slices; fixing i and increasing L2 slice size increases the number of coherency messages maintains about the same. The combination of having a high L1 hit rate and the highest L2 hit rate with number of invalidation messages not so high when compared to the other versions, contribute to to promote L1pL2s4.2MB to have the best speedup, which also can be confirmed in figure 2a.

5   Conclusions

The goal of this study is to evaluate how pair size versus number of processors sharing L2 affects the performance of the parallel applications of SPLASH-2, considering the most adopted implementation of L2 (multi-sliced). As a general guide conclusion, for 4 of 7 benchmarks evaluated, this study extends previous works verifying the possibility of sharing L2 among 4 processors can even improve the speedups, comparing to traditional implementations with just 2 cores per L2. Very promising results were obtained: about 18.9% for Ocean, 88.8% for Raytrace, and 31.8% for Volrend. So, the combination of L2 sharing and increment of L2 slice size can be perfectly applied, providing good speedups, respectively due to the the reduction of conflict and capacity misses. We intend to make other tests also with other scientific benchmarks[22], such as SPEC, and other commercial benchmarks.

References

1. Zhang M., Asanovic K., Victim Replication: *Maximizing Capacity while Hiding Wire Delay in Tiled Chip Multiprocessors*, ISCA 2005, USA.
2. Chisti Z., Powell M.D., and Vijaykumar T.N., *Optimizing Replication, Communication, and Capacity Allocation in CMPs*, ISCA 2005, USA.
3. Kumar R., Zyuban V., Tullsen D.M., *Interconnections in Multi-core Architectures: Understanding Mechanisms, Overheads and Scaling*, ISCA 2005, USA.
4. Waingold E. et al, *Baring it all to Software: Raw Machines*, Computer 1997.
5. Evaluation of the Raw Microprocessor: An Exposed-Wire-Delay Architecture for ILP and Streams, Taylor M.B et all, Proceedings of ISCA 2004.
6. Nagarajan R.N., Sankaralingam K., Burger D., Leckler S.W., *A Design Space Evaluation of Grid Processor Architectures*, ISCA 2001.
7. Sankaralingam K., Nagarajan R.N., *Liu H., Kim C., Exploiting ILP, TLP, and DLP with the Polymorphous TRIPS Architecture*, IEEE, 2003.
8. Cascaval C. et al, *Evaluation of a Multithreaded Architecture for Cellular Computing,*, 2002.
9. http://www.amd.com
10. http://www.ibm.com

11. http://www.intel.com

12. http://www.research.scea.com/research/html/CellGDC05/index.html

13. Barroso L et al., *Piranha: a scalable architecture based on single-chip multiprocessing*, ISCA, 2002.

14. http://www.simics.net

15. Woo S. Ohara M., Torrie E., Singh J.P., Gupta A.; The SPLASH-2 programs: Characterization and Methodological Considerations. In Proceedings of the 22nd. Annual Symposium on Computer Architecture, p. 24-36, 1995.

16. Rakesh Kumar, Dean M. Tullsen, Norman P. Jouppi, Parthasarathy Ranganathan. *Heterogeneous Chip Multiprocessors*, Computer, vol. 38, no. 11, pp. 32-38, November, 2005.

17. http://www.sun.com

18. Chun Liu, Anand Sivasubramaniam, Mahmut Kandemir. *Optimizing Bus Energy Consumption of On-Chip Multiprocessors Using Frequent Values*, pdp, p. 340, 12th Euromicro Conference on Parallel, Distributed and Network-Based Processing (PDP'04), 2004.

19. K. Olukotun et al., *The Case for a Single-Chip Multiprocessor*, Proceedings of the Seventh International Symposium on Architectural Support for Parallel Languages and Operating Systems, October, 1996.

20. Huh J. Burger D., *Kecler S. Exploring the design space of future CMPs*, PACT, 1997.

21. Villa F., Acacio M., Garcia J., *Memory Subsystem Characterization in a 16-Core Snoop-Based Chip-Multiprocessor Architecture*, L.T. Yang et al. (Eds.): HPCC 2005, LNCS 3726, pp. 223232, 2005. c Springer-Verlag Berlin Heidelberg, 2005.

22. Curstis-Maury et all, An Evaluation of OpenMP on Current and Emerging Multi-threaded/Multicore Processors, IWOMP, Eugene, Oregon, USA, June 1-4, 2005.

23. Kumar R., Tullsen D.M., *Heterogeneous Chip Multiprocessors*, Computer, 2005.

24. Chisti Z., Powell M.D., and Vijaykumar T.N., *Distance Associativity for High-Performance Energy-Efficient Non-Uniform Cache Architectures*, In Proceedings of the 36th Annual International Symposium on Microarchitecture (MICRO), pages 55-66, December, 2003.

25. Kumar R., Jouppi N. P., Tullsen D.M., *Conjoined-core Chip Multiprocessing*, In 37th International Symposium on Microarchitecture, December, 2004.

26. Kumar R., Zyuban V., Tullsen D.M.; Interconnections in Multi-core Architectures: Understanding Mechanisms, Overheads and Scaling, ISCA, Wisconsin-Madison, USA, 2005.

27. Nayfeh B.A., Hammond L., Olukotun K., Evaluation of Design Alternatives for a Multiprocessor Microprocessor, ISCA, May, 1996.

28. Marino M.D., Preliminary evaluation of interconnection latency on a CMP with multisliced-L2, XXI South Symposium on Microeletronics, Porto Alegre, Brasil, May, 2006.

29. Shivakumar P., Jouppi N.P., *Cacti 3.0: An integrated cache timing, power and area model*. Technical report, Compaq Computer Corporation, Aug 2001.

Automatic Guidance of a Tractor Using Distributed Applications

Jaime Gómez[1], Antonio Carlón[1], José Fernando Díez[1], Mario Martínez[1],
Daniel Boto[1], and Luis Manuel Navas[2]

[1] Departamento de Teoría de la Señal, Comunicaciones e Ingeniería Telemática,
Universidad de Valladolid, Valladolid, Spain
`{jgomez, acarlon, josdie, mmarzar, dboto}@tel.uva.es`
[2] Departamento de Ingeniería Agrícola y Forestal. Universidad de Valladolid, Spain
`lmnavas@iaf.uva.es`

Abstract. In this paper it is presented a platform to be used in an agricultural scenario. This platform has been built using distributed applications developed by interconnected modules. The modules are communicated by sockets on TCP/IP. The architecture allows the programmer to develop a high number of interconnected applications with a high level of flexibility. Different modules will be used depending on the application. One of the developed applications is the autonomous guidance of a tractor using GPS and electronic compass. This and other applications have been tested with success in a real world environment.

1 Introduction

Distributed applications are the solution to our problems when we are developing a complex system that could be hard to debug. When many people join to build a common project, the discussions about what programming language must be used appear early. By using distributed applications, we can program each application in a different language and then, join them in a common project so that the applications fulfil the objectives when they are joined.

Also, when we need different applications to run faster, it is easy to install them in different computers and join them to get a more powerful result. Distributed applications can also be installed in different locations. In our case, the *Route Guidance Application* will run in a portable computer onboard and the *Monitorization Application* could run in the user's home.

Besides, security is another goal that we can get by using distributed applications.

2 Objectives

The main goal for this project is to get a distributed system that must be capable of automatically guiding a tractor through an agricultural plot using a GPS and an electronic compass.

The system must also be scalable so that other tasks could be accomplished. The developed modules have to be as simple as possible, easy to use for the final user

G. Min et al. (Eds.): ISPA 2006 Ws, LNCS 4331, pp. 84–93, 2006.

(usually without technical knowledge) and the platform must allow the modules to be programmed in different languages. On the other hand, the final system has to be so flexible that one module could be modified without affecting the rest of them.

3 Development

First, we are going to describe the hardware used in this project.

The tractor must have a GPS receiver mounted to know in each moment the position of the vehicle, an electronic compass to allow the system to correct errors in direction, and a number of video cameras to be used by the *Module of Artificial Vision*. The tractor must also have a portable computer onboard to make the necessary calculations for the guidance.

The tractor also has an *Electronic Module* capable of controlling the steering, the accelerator and the work tools.

The whole system includes a base station that consists in a portable computer near the plot. The onboard equipment and the base station are communicated at data link level by means of wireless 802.11.

The scheme of the devices can be seen in Fig. 1.

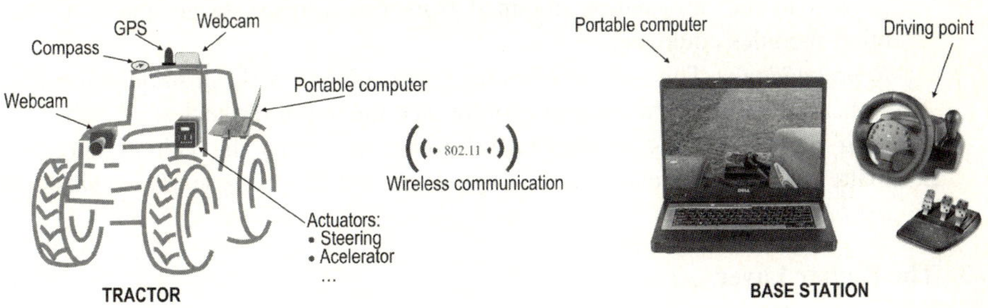

Fig. 1. The hardware scheme

The software developed for this project includes applications in order to:

- Help the driver in the manual guidance of the vehicle.
- Make a distance guidance of the tractor. The tractor can be driven from the base station. The video captured from the cameras onboard will be presented on the monitor of the base station.
- Guide automatically the tractor using *artificial vision*. In this case, the driver will guide the tractor in the heads of the route, and the system will take control in the rest of the plot.
- Guide automatically the tractor using *GPS* and electronic compass. First of all, the application will make the route based on a bunch of parameters. Then, the system will automatically guide the vehicle through this path.

The software has been developed based on a three layer protocol. The scheme of the model can be seen in Fig. 2. As we can see, the lower the layer, the more specific the application is.

3.1 The Lower Layer

The lower layer of the system includes the input/output modules and communicates the hardware platform with the medium layer.

In this layer we have two main types of modules:

- *Input modules.* These modules take data from the hardware devices and transform it into a language that could be read by the rest of the system. In this type, we can include the GPS, the compass and the video cameras.
- *Output modules.* These modules convert the data from the system into commands that could be read by the actuators. These actuators can, for instance, spin the wheel or press the accelerator.

3.2 The Medium Layer

The medium layer takes the information from the lower layer and makes the necessary calculations to accomplish a task. Then, it generates a bunch of commands to be sent to the lower layer, and information to be sent to the higher layer.

The following modules are included in this layer:

- *Positioning.* This module takes the information from the GPS receiver and joins it to the information obtained from the compass to get the data that other modules could use.
- *Route guidance.* This module takes the information from the *positioning module* and calculates the correct position of the steering to follow the desired path.
- *Split detection.* This module takes information from the video camera to make the necessary calculations to guide the vehicle using *guidance based in artificial vision*.

3.3 The Higher Layer

This layer takes the information from the other layers and presents it to the user, either in the onboard computer or in the base station. The user can interact with the applications of this layer to make the system work properly.

The modules included in this layer are:

- *Guidance assistance.* This module helps the driver presenting him a light bar that informs of the worked zones.
- *Tele-guidance.* This module allows the user to guide the vehicle using a steering wheel installed on the base station. The tractor will follow the commands of the driver.
- *Autonomous guidance based in artificial vision.* This module takes information from the split detection module and moves the steering using border detection.
- *Combination of tele-guidance and autonomous guidance.* This module allows the driver to guide the vehicle using tele-guidance but it also allows the system to guide automatically the tractor in certain moments.
- *Monitorization.* This module allows the user the guidance from the base station and informs him of the zones which have been worked. It also allows the driver to stop the tractor at any moment.

3.4 Communication Between Layers

The three layer based system provides the system with a high level of flexibility. The division of the different tasks in modules allows the developer to add new modules at any time without changing the whole system.

The communications between layers is made following the scheme of Fig. 2. It shows the modules used in each application. For example, the *route server module* communicates with the *GPS module* and the *route-guidance module*, and the *route-guidance module* takes data from the *positioning module* that uses the *GPS, compass and movement modules*.

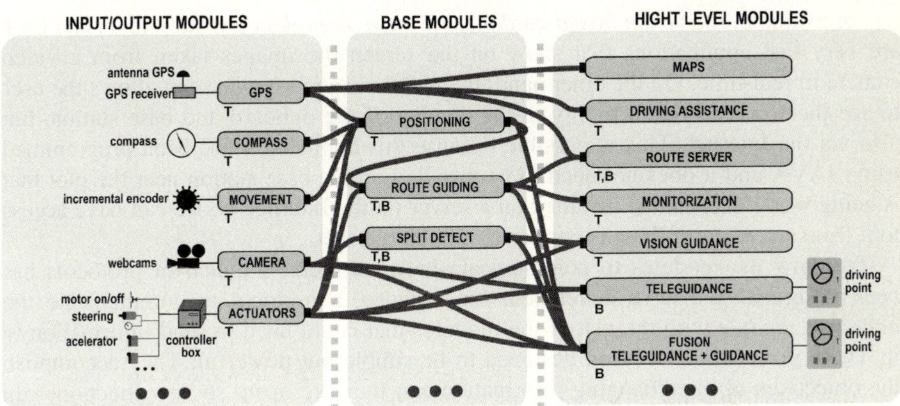

Fig. 2. Communication between layers

The main advantage of the development of the system using a model based in distributed applications is that the different modules can be written in different program languages.

The communication between the onboard equipment and the base station is made via wireless 802.11, and the communication between the layers inside of the system is made using sockets.

The advantage of the sockets is that we can find them in most of the programming languages, and they use the standard TCP/IP to make the communications, so the development of any application based on this standard will be fast, easy and powerful. We can see the communications scheme in Fig. 3.

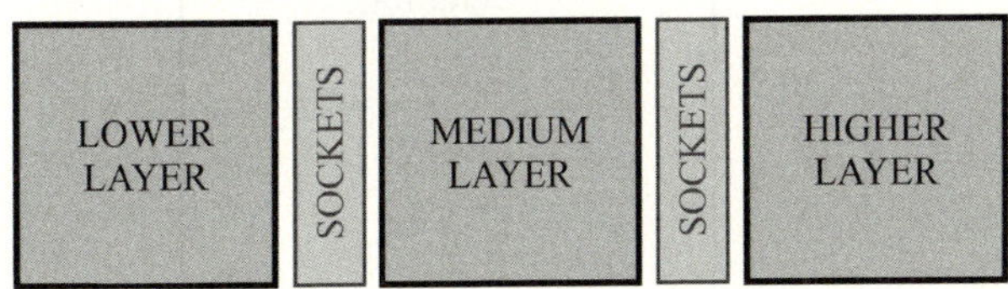

Fig. 3. Using sockets

The development of the lower layer modules has been made using LabView in combination with C and Matlab. The combination of these three platforms allows the lower layer to be easy to change in the development phase and powerful and fast in the final application.

The medium layer has been built using LabView and C, and the higher layer has been developed using a lot of programming languages. For example, the *vision based guidance* has been built using Visual C++, and the *monitorization system* has been developed using JAVA.

This work style can appear to be chaotic, but it allows the developer to have a high level of independence from other developers and allows the final user to have a more flexible application.

For example, the *vision based guidance* or the *tele-guidance* written in Visual C++ are very fast applications that show on the screen the images taken from a video camera in real-time. On the other hand, the *monitorization application* allows the user to see the worked zone not only in the display of the onboard and base station, but also via the Internet. This is possible because this application has been programmed using JAVA and it does not need to be installed on the base station near the plot that is being worked. It can be installed on a server on the Internet, so we can have access to it from anywhere if there is connection to the Internet.

To allow the modules to communicate between them, a bunch of protocols has been designed. We have developed, for instance, a protocol to communicate the *actuators module* with the rest of the modules that could need to send information to it. These protocols have been designed to be simple but powerful. They accomplish the objectives of interchanging information and they are open, so new functions can be easily added to accomplish new tasks.

To illustrate how the protocols work, let us explain a couple of them.

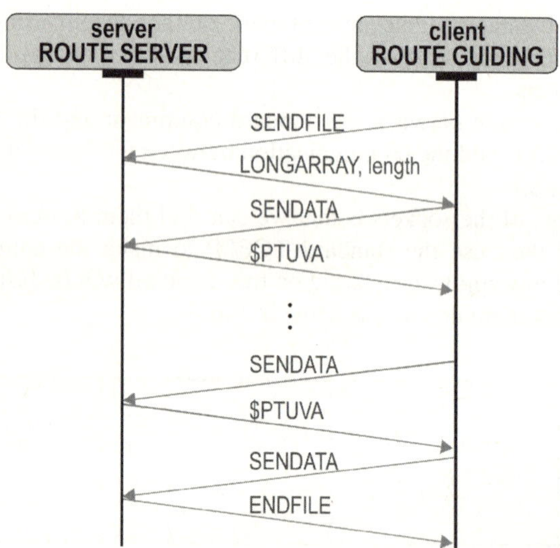

Fig. 4. Sentences interchanged by the server of files

The *server of files protocol* works over TCP/IP as we have seen before. To ask the server for a file, the client will send a message to the server. This message is called SENDFILE. Then, the server will answer with a message that will include the length of the file. Then, the client will ask for each line and the server will send them. When the server reaches the end of the file, it answers with an ENDFILE message. The interchange of information can be observed in Fig. 4.

Some modules only send information periodically. This is the case of the *GPS module* which sends messages every 200 ms. Fig. 5 shows the sent messages, and table 1 shows the information contained in these messages.

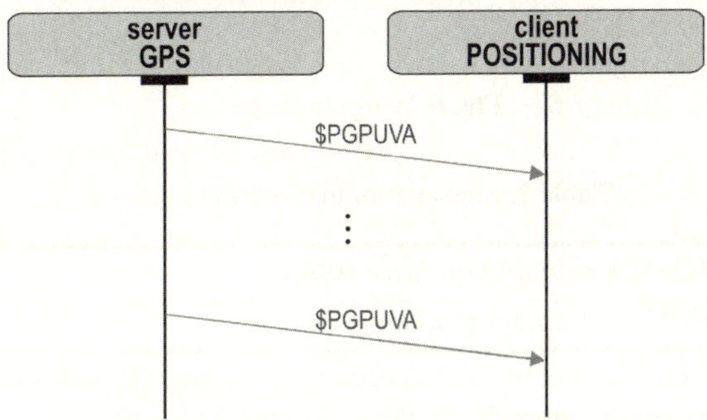

Fig. 5. Sentences sent by the *GPS module*

Table 1. Contents of the sentence PGUVA sent by the *GPS module*

PGPUVA *Navigation Sentence*
$PGPUVA, hhmmss.ss, a, pppppp.pppppp,qqqqqq.qqqqqq, nnnnnnn.nn, eeeee.ee, vv.vv, dd.dd, xx.xx, aa.aa, *hh
1) hhmmss.ss: UTC Time
2) a: *Navigation Receiver Warning*
3)pppppp.pppppp: *Latitude*
4)qqqqqq.qqqqqq: *Longitude*
5) nnnnnnn.nn: UTM Northing
6) eeeee.ee: UTM Easting
7) vv.vv: Speed (m/s)
8) dd.dd: Heading *GPS* (radians)
9) hh: *Checksum*
$PGPUVA,104032.25,A,4140.1375,00442.2053,4716696.00,473063.94,09.02, 01.20,01.32,02.27,*hh

The messages sent between applications are the centre of the developed protocols. Each communication has very well-defined messages to interchange information. The webcam protocol is shown in Fig. 6.

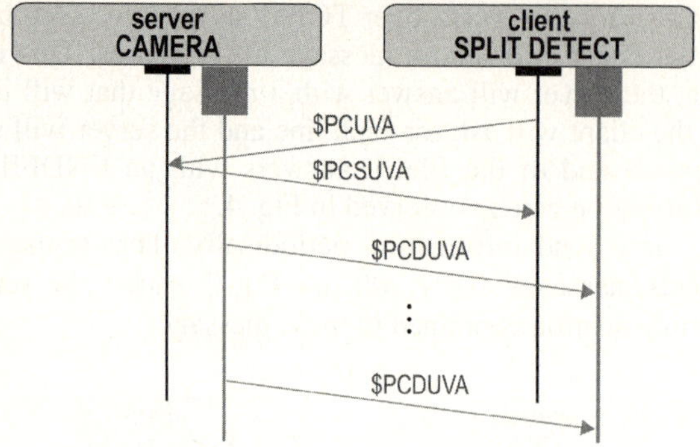

Fig. 6. Webcam protocol

Table 2. Messages of the *webcam protocol*

PCUVA *camera module input*
$PCUVA,for,cam,pto,*hh
1) for: Format of the required video image (RGB/COM) 2) cam: Number of the desired camera (1 .. N) 3) pto: Listen port (client) 4) hh: *Checksum*
$PCUVA,RGB,1,11300,*CHECKSUM

Camera module input

PCSUVA *Camera module ouput*
$PCSUVA,an,al,for,cam,pto,*hh
1) an: Image width (pixels) 2) al: Image height (píxels) 3) for: Format of the video image (RGB/COM) 4) cam: Number of the desired camera (1 .. N) 5) pto: listen port (client) 6) hh: *Checksum*
$PCSUVA,320,240,RGB,1,11300,*CHECKSUM

Camera module output

PCDUVA *Video information*
$PCDUVA,lon,inf,*hh
1) lon: Data size 2) inf: Video information to be sent 3) hh: *Checksum*
$PCDUVA,230400,inf,*CHECKSUM

Video information sent by the *camera module*

The messages defined for the *webcam protocol* are shown in Table 2.

The three layer based system and the communication protocols specifically developed for the system based on the TCP/IP standard allow the whole system to be more flexible, more scalable, easy to develop and easy to use.

4 Results

We have tested the whole system on an agricultural plot in Aguilar de Bureba, Burgos (Spain).

The main test consists in the guidance of a tractor in a plot. First of all, we walked around the plot carrying a PDA with a GPS receiver to get the coordinates for the border of the desired work zone.

Then, we determined the parameters that we were going to use, such as the width of the farm implement, the type of path (interlaced or non-interlaced), and other parameters. Then, we obtained the path which was going to be followed by the tractor from the border of the plot [1] [2] [3] [4] [5].

This path is loaded in the main application (the *Route Guiding module*), to guide the tractor through the path. In Fig. 7 we can see the graphic block diagram for the *actuator module*.

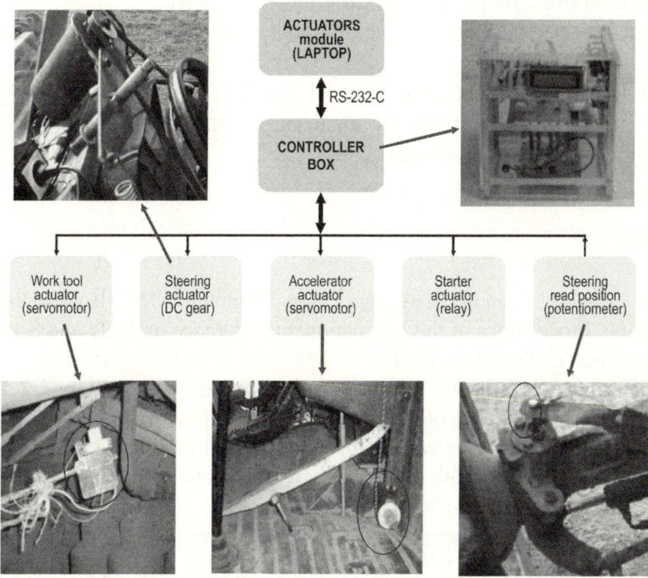

Fig. 7. Connection to *Actuator Module*

To improve the accuracy in the positioning, due to economical GPSs receivers are used, the *positioning module* mixes data from GPS receiver and from electronic compass [8][9][10].

The *monitorization application* runs in the base station and is communicated with the onboard computer. It receives the followed route and displays it on the screen.

We made several tests and they were successful. One result is shown in Fig. 8.

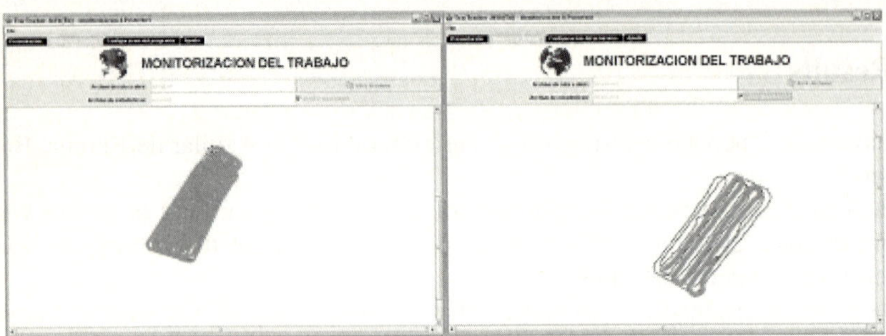

Fig. 8. The path which must be followed (in red) and the worked zone (in green)

5   Conclusions

We have obtained a distributed system which guides a tractor without the intervention of any human operator except in the beginning of the work.

The system has been created to be scalable, easy to use and to debug, and the modules are built separately.

The modules have been programmed in different programming languages according to fulfil the objectives of each of them, so that each module can be modified without affecting the others.

References

1. H. Choset and P. Pignon. Coverage Path Planning: The Boustrophedon cellular decomposition. Proceedings of the International Conference on Field and Service Robotics, Canberra, Australia, December, 1997
2. T. Arai, D. Kurabayashi, J. Ota and E. Yoshida. Cooperative sweeping by mobile robots. IEEE International Conference on Robotics and Automotion, pages 1744-1749, 1996
3. Yi Guo and Zhihua Qu, "Coverage control for a mobile robot patrolling a dynamic and uncertain environment," the 5th World Congress on Intelligent Control and Automation, Hangzhou, China, pages.4899-4903, 2004
4. B. Thuilot L. Cordesses, P.Martinet and M. Berducat. Gps based control of a land vehicle. Proceedigs of the 16th IAARC/IFAC/IEEE International Symposium on Automation and Robotics in Construction. ISARC'99, Madrid, Spain, pages 41-46, 1999
5. E. Nebot, S. Sukkarieh, H. Durrant-Whyte. "Inertial navigation aided with GPS information". Proceedings of Fourth Annual Conference on Mechatronics and Machine Vision in Practice. Toowomba, Australia. 1997
6. O. Connor, T. Bell, G. Elkaim. "Automatic steering of farm vehicles using GPS". Proceeding of the 3rd International Conference on Precision Agriculture. Minneapolis. 1996

7. O'Connor, M.L., Elkaim, G.H., and Parkinson, B. W. Kinematic GPS for Closed-Loop Contro of Farm and Construction Vehicles, Proceedings of ION GPS-95, Palm Springs, CA, Sept. 1995, pp 1261-1268
8. Farrell J.A., Givargis T.D., Bart J.M. "Real-time differential carrier phase GPS-ided INS". IEEE Transactions on Control Systems Technology. 2000(8) pages 709-721
9. T. Aono, Y. Matsuda, T. Kamiya. "Position estimation using GPS and dead reckoning". Proceedings of th 1996 IEEE/SICE/RSJ International Conference on Multisensor Fusion and Integration for Intelligent Systems. Washington D. C. 1996

RCMP: A Reconfigurable Chip-Multiprocessor Architecture

Raphael Fonte Boa, Dulcinéia Oliveira da Penha, Alexandre Marques Amaral,
Márcio Oliveira Soares de Souza, Carlos Augusto P. da Silva Martins,
and Petr Yakovlevitch Ekel

Pontifical Catholic University of Minas Gerais (Brazil)
`rfonteboa@ieee.org, dulcineia.penha@ieee.org,`
`alexmarques@ieee.org, marcioss@yahoo.com.br, capsm@pucminas.br,`
`ekel@pucminas.br`

Abstract. Current parallel architectures are not optimized to all different kinds of applications since they can vary in requirements and resource needs. An ideal system to attend different applications should be able to fit their different characteristics and resource needs and to improve application performance. Our objective is to design and to develop a system architecture that can be reconfigured to fulfill many kinds of the application requirements and run with a reduced communication overhead. Our main goal is a new Reconfigurable Chip-MultiProcessor architecture that improves adaptability to have better performance, regardless of the application requirements. Our results and its analysis show that our architecture provides greater flexibility and scalability and still obtains performance gain over one multiprocessor architecture. Our main contribution is a Reconfigurable Chip-Multiprocessor architecture, composed of reconfigurable processing, storage and interconnection elements.

1 Introduction

Current superscalar microprocessors are very used around the world. These architectures support multi-issue instruction parallelism with branch-prediction and instruction reordering capabilities. In addition, as the issue-windows increase, the issue queues are quadratic increased. This implies in complexity increasing and performance loss [1]. One alternative to run applications with better performances is to use parallel architectures. These architectures target performance gains over sequential ones, dividing applications in independent parts.

Traditional parallel machines can reduce the response time of some applications, depending on their data processing independency. However, multiprocessors usually have fixed and static architectures. Therefore, they may not be adequate to all kinds of applications, since these applications can vary in storage, processing and response time needs. For instance, if an application starts requiring more performance, and the multiprocessor is not able to achieve this requirement, it will not allow any adaptation. Moreover, multicomputers have a significant overhead due to communications among their processing elements (PE). For instance, if an application has a fine-grained workload, it will require too much communication. Therefore its performance will be limited by the network latency and bandwidth.

G. Min et al. (Eds.): ISPA 2006 Ws, LNCS 4331, pp. 94 – 103, 2006.

Hence, two problems were considered in this paper. First problem is the low optimization of the most common parallel machine architectures (multiprocessors and multicomputers) to suit different kinds of application requirements. The other is the great communication overhead presented in multicomputer and multichip multiprocessor machines.

The objective of this work is to design and to develop a system architecture that can be reconfigured to fit different application requirements and run with a reduced communication overhead. This overhead can be reduced with a single-chip parallel system [2]. The fitness for application requirements can be solved with a reconfigurable architecture [3]. Therefore, we propose a Reconfigurable Chip-Multiprocessor (RCMP) architecture, which have a flexible and parallel architecture integrated in a single-chip. Our main goal is an RCMP architecture that improves flexibility and scalability to achieve better performances, regardless of the application requirements.

2 Related Works

The most important advantage of CMPs (Chip Multiprocessors) is to explore the thread level parallelism that many applications present. Among papers presenting CMPs and its advantages over traditional processor solutions, we highlight the most relevant in the context of our research.

In Barroso et. al. [4], a chip multiprocessor research prototype is presented. Besides the Alpha processor cores, it has a two level cache hierarchy and additional circuit to provide some scalability. Piranha achieves performance gains by combining several simple processor cores, instead of trying to outperform with some complex cores. The results show that although a Piranha's single core has worse performance than the evaluated processors, the whole system has a performance gain of up to 2.9 times over those processors. Although Piranha does improves performance making use of a CMP architecture and address the scalable characteristic by providing a manner to add up new chips to the system, it does not provide flexibility and scalability within the chip, as presented by our architecture. Scaling a Piranha system is done through increasing the number of nodes, as in a multicomputer system.

Lee et. al. [5] presents a multiprocessor microarchitecture, called RAPTOR. It integrates four RISC (Reduced Instruction Set Computer) processors, using the SPARC version 9 instruction set architecture. It also integrates a graphics co-processor and an external cache controller. A great amount of simulations were performed to verify the described model and no performance evaluation was done. In the same way Piranha presents a few issues, the architecture provides no flexibility within the chip, and unlike Piranha, it provides no easy way to scale RAPTOR based systems, as our architecture does.

Nikitovic et. al. [6] presents an adaptive CMP that allows dynamically disabling some processing cores targeting energy savings. This is done without performance loss, according to the workload needs. This system was designed focusing mobile terminals. The performance and energy savings were evaluated using high level simulation models. The results showed that, high energy savings without performance loss can be achieved by disabling cores, not considering others techniques, such as frequency and voltage scaling. This approach brings versatility and ways of saving energy, one of the most important trends these days. In our architecture, this can be done by turning off the power supply of unused chip areas or chip elements not only processors but I/O devices, memories and others.

3   Reconfigurable Chip-Multiprocessor Architecture

We propose a reconfigurable chip multiprocessor architecture (RCMP), as shown in Figure 1. Our architecture makes use of reconfiguration concepts [3] to suit different workloads features and different resource requirements. In order to fulfill a wide variety of requirements and resource needs, our architecture presents the ability to reconfigure all its architectural elements, processing elements (PE), storage elements (SE) and interconnection elements (IE) as shown in Figure 1. Our architecture reconfiguration is not constrained to a specific reconfigurable block as other architectures are [7] [8].

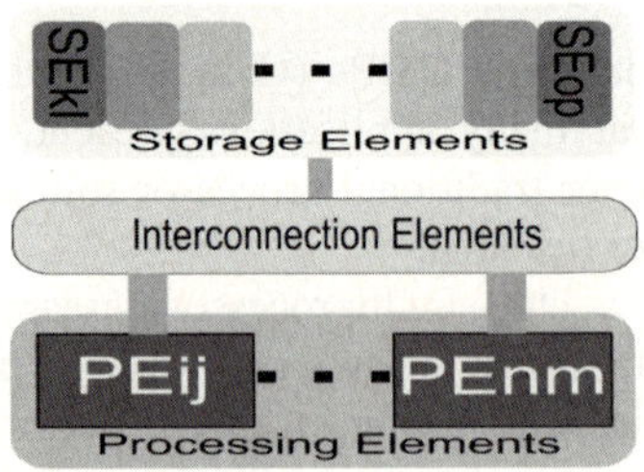

Fig. 1. RCMP (Reconfigurable Chip-Multiprocessor)

The number of architectural elements may vary in quantity, configuration and type. To suit different processing needs, the PEs can have several configurations and the number of PEs can be altered, while SEs can be reduced or increased to fit the application memory requirements. The topology is defined by how the IEs interconnect the PEs and SEs and it can change. Therefore the communication among these elements can happen through many ways. Our architecture can be homogeneous or heterogeneous, that is, different elements can compose the architecture. One example would be a superscalar and a RISC processor, configured and working together. The memory architecture used by the two processors could be different. This configuration makes the architecture heterogeneous. The element types and configurations may be different and groups of elements, although being of same types, do not have to be equally configured or to implement the same logic.

The PEs can be either general-purpose processors, specific-purpose processors or even dedicated hardware. Depending on the workload characteristics, different type of processing elements can be arranged and configured. Heterogeneous setups can merge PEs with different architectures, different word width, different clock rates and different purposes. The fact of being able to have different clock rates in each PE makes the architecture flexible to workloads that cannot be divided equally among multiple processors. To achieve a better timing while executing a workload, PEs can be configured with a job assigned based clock frequencies.

The SEs are also reconfigurable and can have their configuration changed at any time. SEs may be shared or non-shared register files, private or shared primary memories, caches or buffers. The SE word size can vary depending on the PEs architectures and to which PE or IE the memory connects to. SEs bottleneck problems can be overcome by configuring the SEs to support different number of simultaneous access, different clock rates and different policies. The SEs can be used to improve interprocessor communication on fine-grained workloads, when configured as shared register-files. This suits our architecture to workloads designed to execute in multiprocessors. On the other hand, memory policies based on the NORMA (No Remote Memory Access) model can be configured to suit multicomputer workloads. The SEs can have different access policies such as CREW (Concurrent Read, Exclusive Write), cache policies can also be different among the several on-chip SEs.

To interconnect the homogeneous and/or heterogeneous PEs and SEs, distinct IE configurations can be used. The IEs can interconnect elements with different word width, different throughput speed and different access policies. The interconnection architecture can be a BUS communication topology, crossbar interconnections or direct simplex communication links. An IE that connects two PEs having different word-widths, can implement a conversion scheme that buffers the remainder parts of one of the PEs data and deliver them to the second PE as several smaller data fragments.

This paper only presents the RCMP architecture, highlighting its internal elements and the ability to reconfigure the architecture internally. Although, the RCMP can be seen as a constructive block of a more complex architecture, composed of several RCMPs organized in a variety of configurations. Since the RCMP architecture is flexible and scalable, when used as constructive blocks by another architecture, in a higher abstraction level, the resulting architecture will also be flexible and scalable. For instance, the RCMPs can be configured in a pipeline fashion to explore time and space parallelism together. This can result in greater performance gains, since pipeline techniques are well known solutions to achieve performance improvements.

4 Implementation Results

We chose digital image processing (DIP) area to verify the proposed architecture since its operations are widely used in many applications e.g. games, digital T.V., digital videos, and so on. Besides, DIP operations demand high computational resources since they have considerable amounts of composed data (matrices). Beyond the operation algorithm complexity, DIP requires an inherited matrix manipulation algorithmic complexity, which is $O(n^2)$ where n is the matrix dimension.

Among DIP operations, convolution is one of the most used one since it is applied on several image filters. Because of that fact, we choose convolution operation as our case study. Also, this operation can be parallelized since there is no data dependency, because a convolution operation is composed of a filter kernel that is moved along an image modifying its pixels. The kernel center pixel new value is the mean of the multiplication of image area where the kernel stands and the correspondent filter kernel values. Equation 1 formally describes the convolution operation.

$$P[x][y] = \sum_{u=u-\frac{k}{2}}^{\frac{k}{2}} \sum_{v=v-\frac{k}{2}}^{\frac{k}{2}} I[x+u][y+v] \times M[u][v] \qquad (1)$$

The convolution operation can be used in both static (images or photographs) and dynamic (videos) image applications. The existent fixed and static parallel architectures cannot suit different image applications since they can vary in storage, processing and response time needs. Our architecture can be used in both types of image applications because it can be reconfigured to fit their different characteristics and resource needs and to improve application performance.

4.1 Convolution Implementation

We implemented a program that performs convolution operations on 512x512, 1024x1024 and 2048x2048 images, and executes over our proposed architecture. The application is a convolution filter executed on an image.

To execute the image-processing application, we implemented three instances of our CMP architecture with one, two and four Processing Elements (PEs). Depending on the CMP configuration, the execution is sequential or parallel. In the case of parallel configurations, with more than one PE, the convolution operation is parallelized and the image is divided into n parts, where n is the number of PEs. Each part is assigned to a specific PE, responsible for computing the convolution on the image segment.

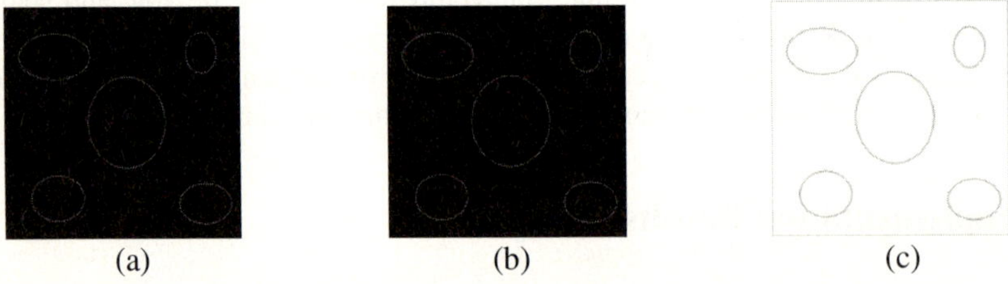

(a)   (b)   (c)

Fig. 2. (a) Input Image. (b) Filtered image. (c) Negative-image of filtered image.

The architecture presents an important feature, its ability to be reconfigured to suit different workload resource needs. We used this feature to divide the image to be processed into different number of blocks depending on the RCMP configuration. This flexibility on the number of PEs available for usage is a source for achieving performance improvements. In order to verify our convolution implementation we executed a high-pass filter in a 512x512 image, showed in Figure 2.a. Figure 2.b shows the results of the filtering operation. The Figure 2.c shows the negative image of the filtered one. We used the negative image to verify our implementation. The edges of the negative image are not part of it, we included edges in order to show the real negative image dimensions.

4.2 Reconfigurable Chip-Multiprocessor Architecture Implementation

Our architecture neither specifies the implementation platform nor the solution used to implement the architectural elements. To implement our architecture's prototypes, we used FPGA technology, and the chosen reconfigurable device was the Xilinx XC2V1500. We used softcores to implement the architectural elements, which are supplied by Xilinx together with Embedded Development Kit (EDK).

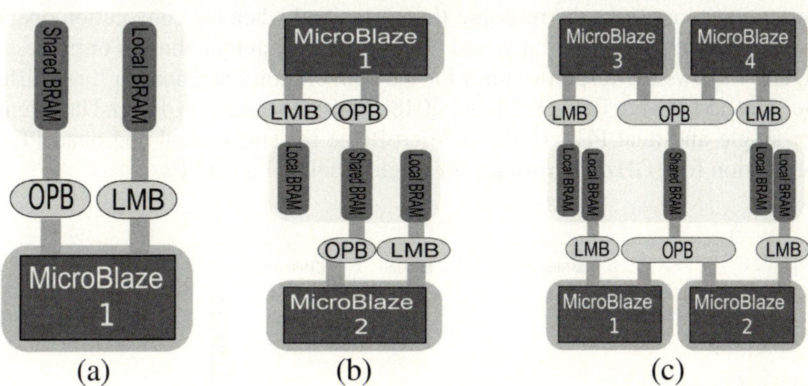

Fig. 3. Implemented instances of RCMP proposed architecture: (a) Single-Processor, (b) Dual-Processor, (c) Quad-Processor

The MicroBlaze softprocessor was used as the PE, which is a 32-bit RISC machine with a three stage in-order single issue pipeline. This processor was configured to run at the highest frequency available with the chosen implementation device, 100 MHz. All of our instances had each processor connected to a private local SE, which stored the convolution program. This SE was connected to the processor through the LMB (Local Memory Bus), a high-speed simplex connection to the processor to local memory.

The data to be processed was stored in a data buffer shared among the processors. This SE was connected to an OPB (On-Chip Peripheral Bus) that stands for general-purpose interconnection. All the processors in a configuration have access to the shared memory (data buffer). Each processor had a 16 KB local memory storing program data and code, and in all configurations the shared memory was 32 KB.

We implemented three configurations of our proposed architecture, a single processor (Fig. 3.a), a dual processor (Fig 3.b) and a quad processor (Fig 3.c) instance. Configurations with an odd number of PEs were not implemented due to the workload partitioning characteristics. Although not limited by the proposed architecture, our prototypes only present static reconfiguration, and no kind of dynamic reconfiguration was implemented.

5 Experimental Results

To compare our architecture with commercial ones, we implemented the convolution operation using multi-thread in C programming language. We executed the in a Dual convolution Pentium III, running at 1GHz , with a 10-stage pipeline, 32 KB L1-cache (instruction+data), a 256 KB L2-cache and 640 MB main-memory. The operating system is Linux-based with an SMP kernel. During the tests only kernel processes were running. This was done to achieve the minimum process concurrency rates possible while measuring program response times.

The Dual-Pentium has the limitation of having only two PE. As this number is fixed, we executed two versions of the convolution program: sequential and parallel (with two threads). In our tests we used an equal number of threads and PEs since our intention was to measure the response times obtained when the convolution operation is executed using parallelism only, and not concurrency among threads or process.

Figure 4 shows the response times for the convolution operation for three different image sizes (512x512, 1024x1024 and 2048x2048), executed on 1GHz-Dual Pentium III for single and dual PEs, 100MHz-MicroBlaze for single, dual and quad PEs and the projection for 1GHz-MicroBlaze for single, dual and quad PEs.

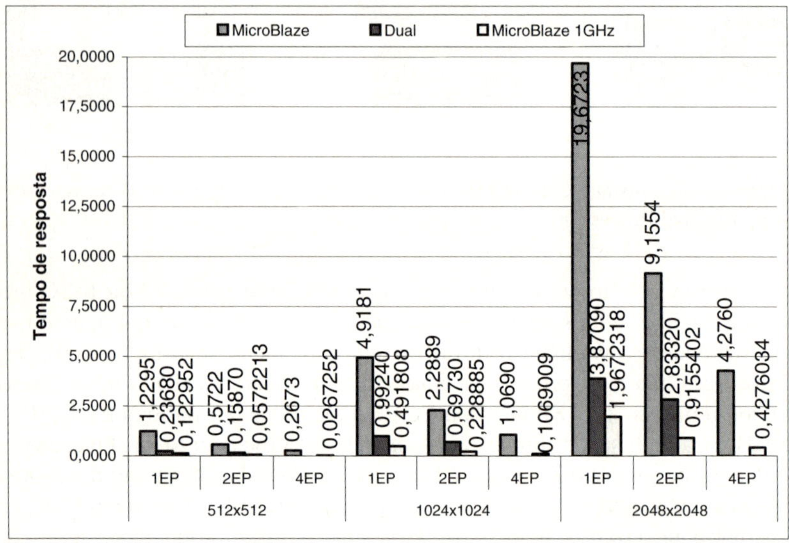

Fig. 4. 100MHz-MicroBlaze, 1GHz-Dual Pentium and 1GHz-MicroBlaze response times for different image-sizes and different number of PEs

The values for quad-PEs could not be measured on the Dual Pentium since it has a limited non-scalable and non-flexible architecture. As shown in Figure 4, the worst case of 100MHz-MicroBlaze response times is only five times greater than the 1GHz-Dual Pentium III. This result fulfills our expectations since the MicroBlaze have a frequency ten times smaller than the Dual Pentium, and none of the architectural improvements that the later has, such as ten-stage pipeline, cache memories and other superscalar improvements.

Although the 100MHz-MicroBlaze presents worst results than 1GHz-Dual Pentium, when we scaled the MicroBlaze frequency to 1GHz, we obtained response times better than the Dual Pentium ones, as we can observe in Figure 4. The scaled MicroBlaze best case response time was 3.9 times smaller than Pentium. Therefore we can observe that the 100 MHz prototypes had a performance worse than Pentium due to the frequency difference between both.

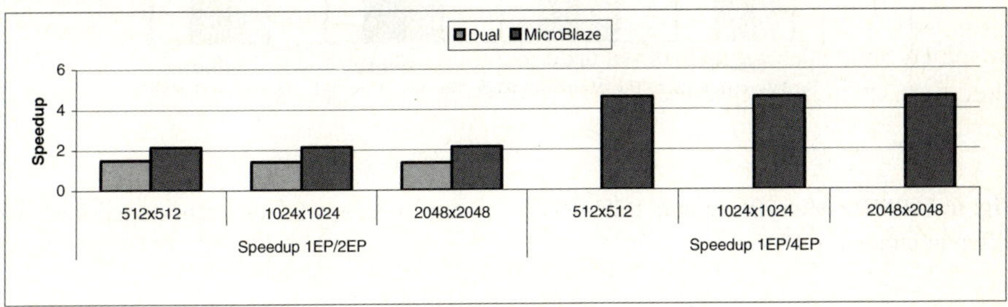

Fig. 5. 100MHz-MicroBlaze and 1GHz-Dual Pentium speedups for different image-sizes and different number of PEs

The Figure 5 presents the dual-PEs over the single-PE speedups of our 100MHz implementations and Pentium tests. Besides that, it presents the speedup of our implemented prototypes, quad-PE over single-PE.

As analyzed before, the MicroBlaze performed five times worse than Pentium. This is due to the implementation device frequency limitation and Pentium architectural improvements. Although, when increasing the number of PEs, the MicroBlaze achieved a speedup greater than two, while Pentium had its values below 1.5. The MicroBlaze speedups greater than two, can be explained by the fact that the convolution application, executed in configurations with multiple PEs, requires less cycles to complete. This behavior is under investigation by the researchers.

The quad-PE speedup values were greater than four, and they can be explained by the same reasons of the dual-PEs behavior. The quad-PEs results also show how the flexibility of our architecture and its FPGA implementation can be used to improve application performance, and how a fixed architecture such as Pentium III cannot provide different resource configurations to different applications.

Figure 6 presents the speedups of the Dual-Pentium over our 1GHz-MicroBlaze projection and our 100MHz-MicroBlaze over Dual-Pentium for different image sizes convolved using single and dual-PE configurations. Considering the MicroBlaze 1GHz projection, we can observe in Figure 6 that if the implementation device 100MHz frequency limitation is overcome our architecture can achieve a significant speedup when compared to Dual-Pentium III. These results can be seen in the first group of columns in Figure 6 and can be explained by the fact that we have improved the MicroBlaze frequency by ten and its response times were about five times greater than Dual-Pentium as shown in the second (right to left) column groups in Figure 6.

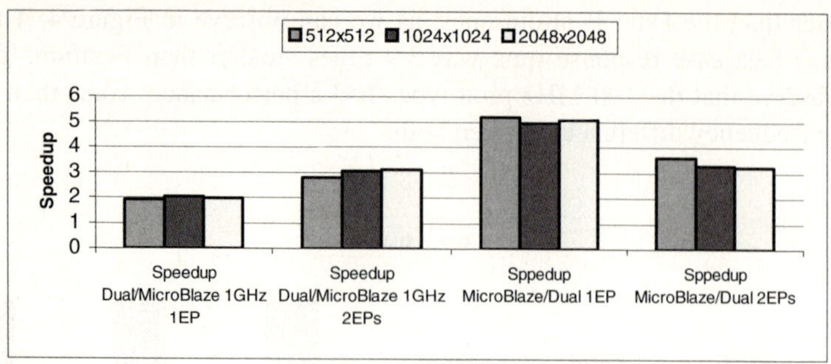

Fig. 6. 100MHz-MicroBlaze and 1GHz-Dual Pentium speedups for different image-sizes and different number of PEs

Our prototypes overcame Pentium times even though they have a simpler architecture with no cache memory and no superscalar improvements. This happens because we do not use any operating system (OS) thus having no overhead on sharing memory or assigning programs to specific processors. Besides, our architecture is highly flexible and, as shown in our implementation and results, the gains obtained are due to the ability to reconfigure the architecture to better suit different applications needs. Our architecture, just like Pentium, is a general purpose architecture, although we used no OS in our tests. The Pentium and other existent architecture, lacks scalability and flexibility. This can be seen in Figures 4, 5 and 6 where the values for quad-PE configurations could not be measured for Pentium, since it has only two processors and this number is fixed.

The results presented and analyzed in this section, highlights the advantages brought by a reconfigurable architecture. Our architecture can improve performance better than a fixed architecture such as Dual Pentium-III SMP Machine. Due to the use of reconfiguration techniques, we can configure our architecture to better suit different applications, and different resource requirements. This makes our architecture capable of addressing a wide variety of applications, and classes of applications such as coarse-grained or fine-grained workloads. As shown in the results, if the MicroBlaze frequency could be increased, the response time results could be even better than the currently obtained ones.

6 Conclusions and Future Works

In this paper we presented the RCMP architecture. This architecture is proposed to provide scalability and flexibility to a variety of workloads and still be able to execute them with high performance. Three prototypes of our architecture were implemented, featuring single, dual and quad PEs, thus we were able to measure the response times of the convolution program, running in all three instances. These values were used as a comparison base to verify our architecture gains and performance improvements.

We reached our objectives and the implemented prototypes confirm that the architecture can improve application performance and be reconfigured to better suit different application resource needs and requirements. Targeting achieving better performances, our architecture can be implemented with some dedicated circuits (ASICs) without any architectural change. The obtained results showed that the proposed architecture performance gain over a Dual Pentium-III is a matter of clock frequency. By scaling the architecture prototype clock frequency, our architecture would outperform the Dual Pentium III.

Our main contribution is the proposal and verification of a novel CMP architecture targeting reconfiguration to address different application workloads. Although we could only run our prototypes at 100 MHz, through the projection, we were able to observe that if implemented with ASIC technology or in a device without the 100 MHz frequency limitation, such as Xilinx Virtex 5 (500 MHz), we can outperform a market headed general purpose architecture such as Pentium III, and provide flexibility and scalability along with performance gains.

Some further works are: the implementation of the architecture with dedicated processing elements targeting a specific application; prototyping in higher speed devices, with higher clock frequencies; and architectural improvements, such as cache memories and autonomous job scheduling. We also intend to implement dynamic reconfiguration to verify which gains can be obtained with an adaptive CMP architecture; heterogeneous setups where different processors address different workloads requirements and resource needs and we intend to use some kind of OS.

References

1. D. Burger; et al. Scaling to the End of Silicon with EDGE Architectures Computer, IEEE Computer Society, Vol. 37, No. 7, pp 44-55, July 2004.
2. L. Hammond, A. N. Basem, K. Olukotun. "A Single-Chip Multiprocessor". In Computer Magazine, IEEE Computer Society, vol.30, no.9, pp. 79-85, Sept., 1997.
3. K. Compton, S. Hauck. "Reconfigurable Computing: A Survey of Systems and Software". ACM Computing Survey, Vol. 34, No. 2, pp. 171-210, 2002.
4. L. A. Barroso, K. Gharachorloo, R. McNamara, A. Nowatzyk, S. Qadeer, B. Sano, S. Smith, R. Stets, and B. Verghese. "Piranha: a scalable architecture based on sigle-chip multiprocessing". In Proceedings of the 27st Annual International Symposium on Computer Architecture, pages 282--293. IEEE Computer Society Press, 2000.
5. L. Sang-Won, S. Yun-Seob, K. Soo-Won, O. Hyeong-Cheol, and H. Woo-Jang. "Raptor: A single chip multiprocessor". In The First IEEE Asia Pacific Conference on ASICs, pages 217--220, 1999.
6. M. Nikitovic and M. Brorsson. "An adaptive chip-multiprocessor architecture for future mobile terminals". In Proceedings of International Conference on Compilers, Architecture, and Synthesis for Embedded Systems (CASES'02), pp. 43-49, Oct 2003.
7. Ye, Z. A., Moshovos, A., Hauck, S., and Banerjee, P., "CHIMAERA: A High-Performance Architecture With a Tightly-Coupled Reconfigurable Functional Unit," In Proceedings of the 27th International Symposium on Computer Architecture, pp. 225-235, 2000.
8. D. B. Gottlieb, J. J. Cook, J. D. Walstrom, S. Ferrera, C.-W. Wang, and N. P. Carter, "Clustered programmable-reconfigurable processors", in Proceedings of the IEEE International Conference on Field Programmable Technology, December 2002, pp. 134-141.

Virtual Link: An Enabler of Enterprise Utility Computing

Krishna Kant

Intel Corporation
`krishna.kant@intel.com`

Abstract. Dynamically provisioned virtual clusters provide a means of consolidating servers in a data center and for supporting utility computing. Data centers typically sport a large number of (layer 2) switches and very few routers, yet, the existing layer-2 QoS are not well developed. This paper proposes the notion of *virtual link* as an interconnection abstraction to provide granular QoS. The paper also presents an experimental study comparing virtual link based congestion control against other alternatives for emerging 10 Gb/sec Ethernet links. It is shown that virtual links can provide desired capabilities with a small perturbation to existing standards and can work well in mixed legacy environments.

1   Introduction

Utility computing refers to the notion of treating the entire data center as a pool of resources (computes, storage, special functions, etc.) which can be assigned dynamically to various applications as needed. Utility computing almost demands cluster capable applications and is greatly helped by a single unified fabric over which resources of various sorts can be accessed efficiently. We shall call the set of nodes allocated to a given application as a "virtual cluster". The obvious advantage of the consolidation is the increase in server utilization, which is often found to be in 5-10% range in current data centers. The ability to grow or shrink individual virtual clusters can be used to adapt physical resources to dynamically changing application needs and to minimize power consumption.

A unique feature of commercial data centers is that *most of the interconnect devices in a data center are (layer 2) switches, rather than (layer 3) routers.* In fact, smaller networks may not even have any routers except at the edges. The main reasons for this are low cost, lower latency, and almost zero configuration effort, for switches. Given such an environment, *layer3 QoS features (e.g., diffserv, intserv, etc.) are inadequate within a data center.* Furthermore, a blind implementation of these features at layer 2 is undesirable as it would take away the advantages of switches over routers. For example, setting up DSCP parameters is known to be very tricky [6] and requires detailed knowledge of the flows. Instead, our goal here is to define simpler mechanisms that can be largely automated.

A *virtual cluster* can be thought of as the realization of a clustered application and includes the *virtual nodes* (VN's) on which the application runs, and the

G. Min et al. (Eds.): ISPA 2006 Ws, LNCS 4331, pp. 104–114, 2006.

virtual paths (VP's) over which these VN's communicate. We call the node as virtual since it could well be implemented via a virtual machine running on a physical node. A virtual path between VN's can be further viewed as a sequence of one or more *virtual links* (VL), where a VL is defined to span only a *layer 2 domain*. [An L2 domain is the set of layer 2 devices (switches) delimited by layer 3/4 devices (routers & servers)]. Thus, a VP results by stitching together VL's at the intervening routers, if any. Note that the communication between VN's that belong to the same physical node may use some efficient local mechanism and is not addressed here.

The outline of the paper is as follows. Section 2 discusses related work in the field. Section 3 discusses the support required for establishing, tearing down and using virtual links. Section 4 discusses the QoS, congestion control and reconfiguration issues related to virtual link. Finally, section 5 compares virtual link based congestion control against endpoint control.

2   Related Work

Virtual LAN (VLAN) is a standardized mechanism (802.1q/p) for segmenting an Ethernet network into "islands" such that traffic from of VLAN is not accessible to another VLAN. The flows in each VLAN can be differentiated based on the 3-bit CoS (*class of service*) field in the extended Ethernet header. VLANs are inadequate for providing virtual cluster abstraction since they are intended to be static and do not provide any congestion control mechanisms.

The IEEE task force on Ethernet congestion management, known as 802.1ar, is currently examining ways of improving congestion notification and management [4]. The main objectives of this effort are to enable switches to mark packets and allow endpoint layer-2 to do 802.1x type link flow control at the level of individual "virtual pipes" or CoS classes. Adding an ECN like feature [7] at layer2 that TCP can exploit has also been considered here. These capabilities are certainly helpful in supporting the virtual link concept addressed in this paper.

The label switched paths (LSPs) defined for the well known MPLS (multi-protocol label switching) scheme provide virtual communication channels that can pack a high degree of sophistication in terms of traffic engineering [1]. For example, an extension of RSVP, called RSVP-TE, can be used for reserving resources on LSPs (RFC3209). This helps to automate the setup. However, a direct implementation of these layer-3 features would make the switches too complex and expensive, and is not desirable.

The extension of Ethernet to metro distances needs to deal with several issues including inadequacy of 4096 VLANs, scalability of broadcast procedures, and, QoS and congestion control [2]. One method to provide QoS over MAN areas is to make use traffic engineered MPLS paths and then run Ethernet protocol on top of this. An alternative approach is to extend Ethernet frame format slightly via *VLAN stacking*, also known as *Q-in-Q* mechanism. The former scheme is unsuitable for data centers; the latter scheme can be used, but will require some further extensions as discussed in section 3.1.

3   Supporting Virtual Links

Supporting virtual links requires some additional features which are listed below and discussed in subsequent subsections.

1. A pair of send & receive queues to which one or more virtual links can be mapped. We call these as *virtual queue pairs* (VQP) or simply VQ's.
2. Every packet needs to carry additional information to use the appropriate queues.
3. A signaling mechanism to setup, teardown and update virtual links.
4. A mechanism to convey switch congestion to the L2 boundary and local propagation and handling at higher (i.e., L3 or L4) level.

3.1   Virtual Link Queues

Virtual link queues are necessary to provide isolation between VL's and to control scheduling policies. Currently, the only queuing differentiation available in the Ethernet is via the IEEE 802.1p/q standard, which adds a 4-byte TCI (tag control info) field to Ethernet frames. Fig.1(a) shows the Ethernet-II frame format and Fig.1(b) shows the details of TCI field. As stated earlier, the CoS bits are intended for traffic prioritization and are similar to IP layer ToS (type of service) bits. CoS bits provide for only 8 queues, which is inadequate in the VL context. Also, the purpose of CoS bits is prioritization (e.g., giving control messages – such as the signaling messages that we will introduce – higher priority over others), and not really appropriate for VL application.

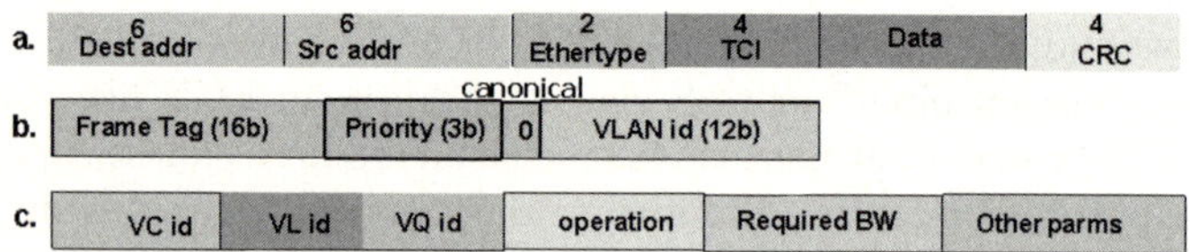

Fig. 1. a) Ethernet-II frame format, b) 802.1 header, c) Signaling msg format

The L2 Ethernet frames associated with IP and other higher layer protocols should be able to convey the queue id to the switches on the path. This can be done either by carrying the VQ id directly (say, 4-5 bits) or by carrying both VL and VC id's which can be mapped to VQ id's locally at each switch. Although the latter scheme is lot more flexible, it requires many more bits in the Ethernet frame. Finding extra bits in Ethernet frames is quite challenging w/o perturbing the standards substantially; therefore, we henceforth assume that VQ id's are carried directly.

Several approaches are possible to convey VQ id in Ethernet frames, but all of them have some impact on standards. One simple idea is to designate, say, 64 high end VLAN bit patterns (out of a total of 4096) for 32 VQ id's leaving 1 bit worth of information for congestion indication use. This along with canonical bit (unused currently) can satisfy congestion indication requirements. Within a data center, the number of VLANs is generally quite limited and thus the reduction in the number of possible VLANs is not an issue. The more serious issue is the potential use of high end VLAN bit patterns in real data centers. A somewhat different idea is to exploit the Q-in-Q type of encoding used in metro Ethernet, which basically adds additional Ethertype and TCI fields in the frame [2] (See Fig 1(a)). As stated earlier, these fields are used for transportation of frames between LAN segments. This encoding does require minor firmware updates to the switches. However, if we want to use the outer TCI bits for VQ-id and congestion indication, we will have to create yet another outer Ethertype so that the scheme does not conflict with metro Ethernet usage. The main advantage of doing so is that we now gain 4 bytes in each frame, which can be used to carry VL or VC ids, if we so desire. The down side is higher processing overhead and reduction of maximum data length by another 6 bytes.

The VQ id can be used by switches to implement a variety of scheduling mechanisms, including weighted round robin (WRR) for dividing available BW between competing flows. This is straightforward and not discussed any further.

3.2   Signaling Support for VL's

The signaling protocol is needed to provision VC's automatically since a manual provisioning is a recipe for non-use. The signaling requires a new Ethernet frame type similar to the one in Fig.1(a) but with a different Ethertype value.

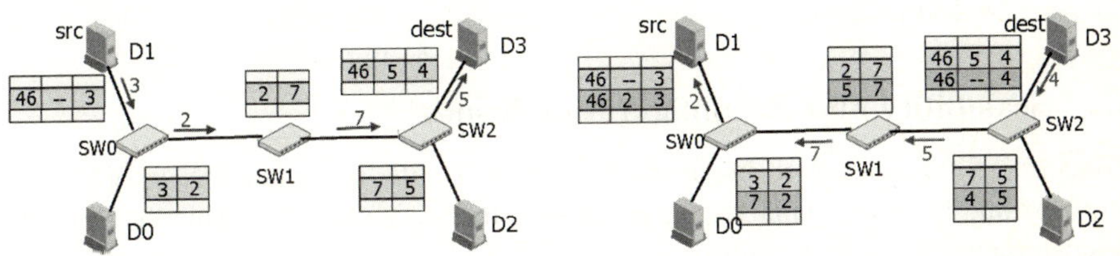

Fig. 2. Illustration of VL setup in a L2 domain: a) Forward, b) Backward

Fig 1(c) shows the generic format for signaling messages using this new ethertype. Here, the operation field indicates VL operations, including VL_initf, VL_initb and VL_ack for VL setup and a few others for VL teardown and parameter update. The field "other parms" include additional information that may be necessary for setting up queue thresholds.

Virtual links can now be setup by sending a special message, say *VL_initf*. This message starts with the local VQ's number and wiggles its way through the switches on the path to the L2 end. At each switch, it sets up the queue translation table (QTT). Fig. 2(a) illustrates this process for setup of a VL (with id 46) from server D1 to D3 via switches 0-2. To start with, layer 2 of D1 creates the table entry (46, −, 3) indicating that VQ 3 is used for VL 46 at this node. It then sends a VL_initf message to SW0. SW0 locally allocates a VQ id (say, 2) and creates a table entry (3,2) indicating that what comes with VQ 3 must go into VQ 2. The table will also store the VC id, requested BW, and other QoS parameters (if any), but these are not shown for simplicity. SW0 then changes the VQ id in the VL_initf message to 2 and forwards it to SW1. This process continues until the message reaches D3, which too sets up its table entry. This table entry (46, 5, 4) says that a packet for VL 46 coming with VQ id 5, will be placed in VQ 4. Note that *the dynamic allocation of VQ ids makes it easy to allocate only as many queues as are really required.*

The operations in Fig. 2(a) only take care of forward VL setup. When D3 receives this message, it needs to echo a *VL_initb* message towards D1, which effectively does the same thing in the other direction. Fig. 2(b) shows the tables at the end of complete setup. For simplicity, we have numbered send & receive VQ's identically, but this is not essential. Since messages can be lost, we also need some handshake mechanism (e.g., like the one in TCP or SCTP) to recover. The details of this are straightforward and will be omitted. Finally, we also need signaling messages to tear down virtual links and to adjust their parameters.

The above setup procedures are not claimed to be unique – ATM, Frame Relay, and most significantly MPLS LDP all use a similar scheme (with minor variations of the theme). In fact, it is possible to do VL setup by extending MPLS LDP protocol so that the switches examine the LDP messages [1]. We do not follow this approach to avoid the need for MPLS capabilities.

The setup scheme can be extended to establish virtual paths, by successively establishing virtual links across routers. The main difficulty here is the need to reestablish VL's as the routing table entries change. For lack of space we do not discuss the details here.

3.3   Scalability and Reconfiguration Issues

Conceptually, it is nice to use a distinct virtual path for every VN to VN communication; however, this can quickly become unscalable. In this section, we discuss issues related to limited usage of VL's.

To start with, we note that the main motivation for VL's is to isolate flows corresponding to *different* virtual clusters. Thus, if two or more VL's of a given VC happen to pass through a switch, they should all use the same virtual queue at this switch. Although this can be enforced easily in the VL setup procedure given in the last section, it is possible to simplify things even further. Note that the end result of setting up all VL's of a VC is to reserve a queue at each switch port encompassed by this VC. This can be done trivially by reaching all VN's of the VC from any given node.

The establishment of virtual paths across routers could get rather complex and may impact layer3. Fortunately, if the application is configured properly, the inter-router traffic should be smaller and less latency sensitive than the traffic within L2 domains. In this case, we can forego keeping any VL distinctions for paths that cross router boundaries. Or, such paths can be aggregated into a small set of "pipes" that exploit diff-serv and other IP level QoS features. For example, all IPC traffic may go through one pipe, all storage through another, etc. The main attraction of this approach is that it limits the scope of VL's and thus enhances scalability w/o and substantial performance implications.

The idea of aggregating multiple VL's into a smaller number of "pipes" or classes can be taken further to enhance scalability. In particular, the queue pairs are established based on the characteristics of applications running in the VC's; and thus the number of simultaneous queues is limited by the number of such characteristics identified.

Let us now briefly address the issue of dynamic reconfiguration of virtual clusters. We assume that any traffic flow that doesn't use VL concept is routed via VQ 0. The addition of a node to a VC is straightforward and will allocate new queues only at new switches/routers that are used by this VC. However, deletion of nodes from a VC must ensure that VQ's are not deleted until they become completely unused. This can be addressed easily via a reference count type of scheme.

4   Layer 2 Congestion Control

Any discussion of QoS is incomplete w/o examining congestion control issues since, for the most part, QoS is relevant only during congestion scenarios. The Ethernet standard only provides the 802.1x (so called Xon/Xoff) flow control. Unfortunately, this scheme applies to the entire link and does not provide flow control at the level of individual flows. Thus, packets may be dropped for individual flows. A reliable transport protocol such as TCP or SCTP will react to packet drops and reduce flows; however, *dropping packets in a data center environment is highly undesirable* because of high data rates, bursty traffic, and long latencies suffered by retransmitted packets. It follows that we need some mechanism in switches to explicitly convey congestion situation to the endpoints.

A workable layer 2 congestion control scheme in switches must support two basic functions: (a) Congestion detection and feedback to layer 2 edge, and (b) Congestion control at or above layer2 edge. In the following, we discuss these aspects briefly and then show that the congestion control can be simplified by using virtual links.

Congestion detection is best done via queue thresholds which need to be set judiciously. The VL signaling mechanism can be used for setting the thresholds. The threshold crossing at a switch can be carried to the L2 edge in many ways, as discussed in [4]. The basic schemes include implicit feedback (i.e., forward or backward packet marking), explicit feedback (sending feedback packets from endpoints), or mixed. Implicit schemes are generally preferred since they do not increase traffic during congestion; however, they require additional bits in the packets.

The congestion feedback mechanism discussed above brings the feedback only to the L2 edge. How this feedback is used depends on various congestion control options as illustrated in Fig. 3. In particular, bringing the feedback from a router to the endpoint may either be via ECN (as a result of backpressure on the router),

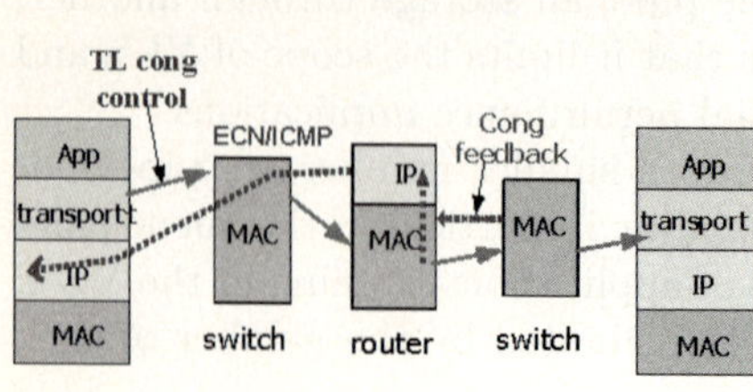

Fig. 3. Congestion Feedback and control

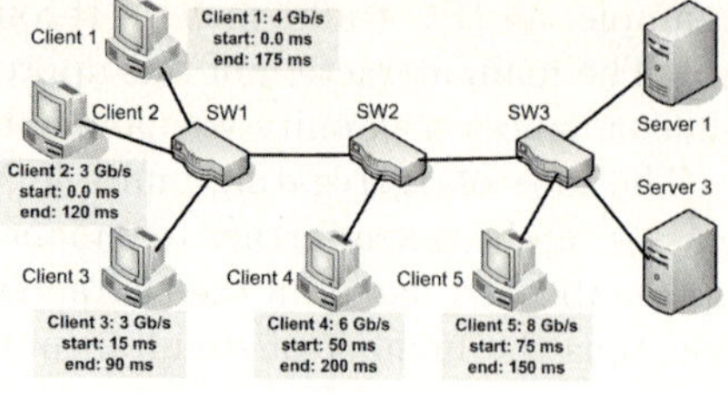

Fig. 4. Full Test Network

or explicitly via ICMP message. The consequences of latter mechanism are not considered here due to lack of space.

5   Experimental Study of L2 Congestion Control

In this section, we compare virtual link based congestion control against other alternatives in order to exhibit the pros and cons of virtual link based congestion QoS and congestion management.

5.1   Congestion Control Mechanisms

For simplicity, let's limit discussion to applications that use primarily a reliable connection oriented communication mechanism (e.g., TCP or SCTP). Now, if no VL support is available, the congestion will eventually manifest itself as packet loss followed by the transport reaction to it. (We used TCP-Reno in these experiments.) This is the baseline scenario studied here and is designated as L4-loss.

A slightly enhanced scheme is to enable the switches to report congestion via the ECN mechanism, except that it is implemented at layer 2. We further assume that TCP will examine these layer-2 ECN bits as well and take the same action as with layer-3 ECN bits. We call this the L4-ECN method.

Climbing up the feature ladder, we assume switches can mark packets for congestion but don't do any traffic differentiation. We still assume an appropriate signaling procedure to set congestion thresholds at switches. The idea now is to do an intelligent flow control at the endpoint NIC and thereby enforce proper BW allocation to various flows. We call this scheme as L2-FC. A concrete example of such and scheme is explored in [3,5].

Here we describe the scheme in [5] only briefly. Initially, each L2 endpoint sends out probes (or special signaling messages) to discover paths to all other endpoints of this L2 domain. All these paths are then constantly monitored for congestion at the endpoint. The feedback scheme is the *mixed feedback* discussed earlier. In particular, a switch on the path updates the congestion indicator if its current congestion level is higher than the one in the probe. Via this mechanism, each L2 endpoint is able to maintain the maximum congestion level along each path. This congestion level along with the desired weight (or relative BW) for various flows is used to do a bang-bang control for forcing the congestion along the path down to a predefined nominal value.

The final scheme studied is the VL based congestion control, which we call L4-VL. Although this scheme requires features (a)-(f), the congestion control is still at the endpoint TCP level (hence the name L4-VL). This scheme requires very little support from the endpoint NIC and does not require a sophisticated congestion control to be built into the NIC. On the other hand, the scheme provides no support for throttling UDP flows.

5.2 Congestion Control Performance

In this section we provide a detailed experimental comparison of the congestion performance the schemes L4-Loss, L4-ECN, L2-FC and L4-VL. For the comparisons, we used the OPNET simulation package which provides comprehensive implementations of all relevant networking layers (MAC, IP, TCP, ...) and pre-built models of many commercial switches and routers. It also provides a few application layers (e.g., database, FTP, VOIP, etc.). Yet substantial development work was required in order to implement the following features: a) switch level traffic differentiation, b) Endpoint layer 2 flow control, and c) Application level flow control. The simulated network is shown in Fig. 4. It is important to note here that the "clients" in Fig. 4 are not really the end-clients (usually outside the Enterprise), but rather other servers (e.g., mid-tier servers making DB requests) residing within the Enterprise.

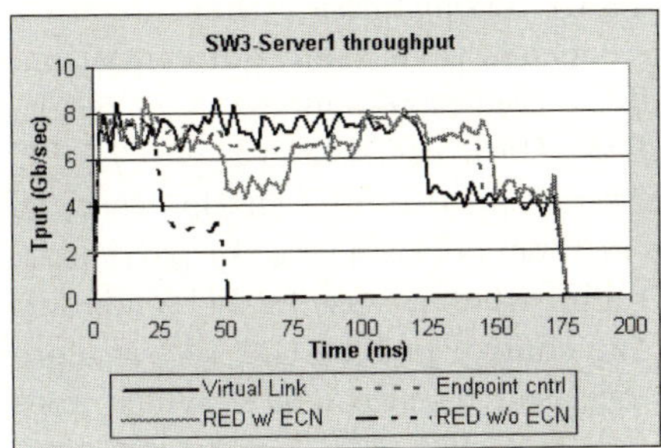

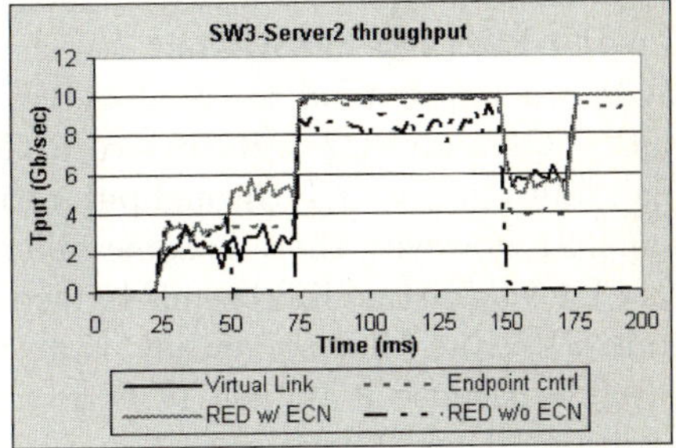

Fig. 5. Throughput of VC1 client 1   **Fig. 6.** Throughput of VC1 client 2

All links in Fig. 4 follow the IEEE 10 Gb/s standard. This is done to emphasize the emerging high speed data center environment. The physical cluster here is divided up into 2 virtual clusters:

VC1: This includes clients 1 & 2 and server1. Here both clients 1 and 2 generate database traffic over TCP.

VC2: This includes clients 3, 4 & 5 and server2. Each of these clients also generates database traffic over TCP.

In both cases, the traffic is 100% database updates which means that the congested flow direction is from client to server. (This scenario was chosen for simplicity; the mechanisms do work well irrespective of the direction of congestion.) The update sizes are assumed to be exponentially distributed with a mean of 8KB. The interarrival times of clients are uniformly distributed with maximum value twice that of the minimum value. The mean traffic driven by each client plus the start and stop times of each client are shown in Fig. 4. The start and stop times are staggered so that we can have a number of overload scenarios.

Figs 5 and 6 show, respectively, the achieved throughput for VC1 and VC2 respectively. Here the intent is to give 2/3rd of the BW to VC1 and 1/3rd to VC2. In other words, we expect VC1 to receive 6.67 Gb/s throughput under stress conditions.

We start with the traffic evolution for VC1 by referring to Fig 5. For the first 15 ms, only clients 1&2 are on, and together drive 7 Gb/s. Not surprisingly, this traffic is carried properly in all cases. At 15 ms, client 3 comes on and the total traffic driven over SW1-SW2 link is 10 Gb/s. Without the ECN (case L4-Loss) the highest traffic source (Client 1) experiences heavier losses than others and effectively shuts down. As a result, the VC1 throughput drops down to 3 Gb/s (Client 2 rate) for this case. This type of "shut-down" scenario was observed consistently in many situations and points to the inadequacy of depending on just the packet losses. In contrast, ECN is still capable of controlling the backlog effectively (case L4-ECN), though not quite as well as cases L4-VL & L2-FC.

At time 50ms, client 4 comes on. The total BW driven through SW2-SW3 link is now 16 Gb/s and we are under severe congestion. Case L4-Loss now experiences a connection reset due to too many retransmission timer expiries. Case L4-ECN still survives but now shows its deficiency – w/o any differentiation, TCP will simply tend to equalize BW of all the congested sources. As a result, both VC1 and VC2 will achieve 5 Gb/s BW. Both cases L4-VL and L2-FC maintain close to 2:1 throughput ratio between the two VCs in this case, as required, however, there is some difference in their performance. In particular, case L4-VL (virtual link) tends to favor VC1 a bit whereas case L2-FC (endpoint control) favors VC2 somewhat. Note that the control in case (L4-VL) is more variable because it is just TCP driven as opposed to case L2-FC which does additional layer 2 flow-control.

At time 75ms, client 5 also comes on. Since this simply adds to the existing overload, no change is expected. Surprisingly, however, case L4-ECN shows an increase in VC1 throughput! To understand this, notice that until time 75ms, the link from SW3 to Server2 was not saturated, but now it does get overloaded. Consequently, TCP connections at clients 3-5 all back off hard (more so at client 3) and this allows for higher VC1 throughput.

At time 90 ms, client 3 goes off. This has no impact on case L4-VL but both cases L2-FC and L4-ECN have a throughput increase because of less VC2 traffic. In fact, almost the entire VC1 traffic is able to get through in all three cases primarily because Client 4 continues to remain mostly shutout due to congestion on SW3-Server2 link. At time 120 ms, Client 2 also goes off, thereby reducing VC1 rate down to 4 Gb/s. Client 5 then goes off at time 150 ms, but it does not affect VC1 traffic (because client 5 traffic has little interference with it). Finally, at time 175 ms, VC1 traffic turns off completely.

Let us now briefly examine VC2 throughput in Fig 6. The behavior here is in some ways complementary to that in Fig 5, since a favoring of VC1 implies a disfavoring of VC2 and vice versa. The only point worth noting is that at time 175 ms, when VC1 traffic turns off completely, VC2 traffic actually surges to fill the link because of the earlier backlog.

6   Conclusions

The main conclusion from the above and several other studies is that switch level congestion detection and marking are essential for an acceptable performance. A TCP level congestion control driven by this marking (L4-ECN) can control the congestion but is unable to provide the desired QoS. Finally, both L2-FC and L4-VL schemes can provide decent congestion control and QoS. However, the two have somewhat different characteristics. The L4-VL scheme requires more perturbation to the switch infrastructure, but does require embedding sophisticated flow control in the NICs. The L2-FC scheme can also suffer from scalability issues in large L2 networks.

A crucial consideration in proposing new features for existing networks is compatibility with legacy implementations. With the L2-FC scheme, a legacy NIC will (a) ignore any congestion feedback and (b) will not even participate in the probing done by the newer NICs. The consequence of (a) is eventual TCP-level action based on packet losses. The consequence of (b) is imprecise accounting of paths and path flow control at the newer NICs and hence inaccurate control. In the L4-VL scheme, a non-VL capable switch will not understand signaling messages and would simply pass them on along the path. The normal packets also will not get any differentiation at these switches but will be silently forwarded along. Thus, if the legacy switches are not the sources of severe congestion, the whole system will continue to perform well. If the legacy switches do experience congestion, the flows through them will be governed by the default TCP behavior (i.e., TCP's tendency to equalize flows).

Acknowledgements. The author would like to thank Gary Mcalpine for assistance in detailed implementation and experimentation. Thanks are also due to Raj Ramanujan for discussions relating to some of the ideas in the paper.

References

1. "QoS Support in MPLS networks", MPLS/Frame Relay alliance whitepaper, May 2003.
2. G. Chiruvolu, An Ge, et. al., "Issues and approaches on extending Ethernet beyond LANs", IEEE Computer, March 2004, pp 79-86.
3. G. Mcalpine, M. Wadekar, et. Al., "An architecture for congestion management in Ethernet clusters", IEEE IPDPS Workshop 9, April 2005, Denver, CO.

4. H. Barraas, M. Wadekar, et. al., "Problem Space for Ethernet Congestion Management", IEEE 802.1ar Congestion Management Group Presentation, sept 2004.
5. G. Mcalpine, "Congestion Management for Switched Ethernet", Proc. of high perf. interconnects for distributed computing, July 2005.
6. S.H. Low, F. Paganini, et. al., "Linear stability of TCP/RED and a scalable control", Computer Networks, vol 43, no 5, pp633-647, 2003.
7. http://www.icir.org/floyd/ecn.html (collection of annotated references on ECN).

Pervasive Open Spaces: A Transparent and Scalable Dome-Based Pervasive Resource Allocation System

Amgad Madkour[1,*] and Sherif G. Aly[2]

The American University In Cairo, Egypt
[1]amadkour@eg.ibm.com
http://amgadmadkour.pioneersawg.com
[2]sgamal@aucegypt.edu

Abstract. Scalability imposes itself as a great setback for pervasive computing research. This paper presents a novel approach for scalable resource allocation which harnesses the power of scalable systems by creating what we call an open space. The fundamental concept behind open spaces lies in utilizing resources beyond user's current location within a pervasive computing environment, while accommodating user mobility patterns. We discuss the idea of domes that form an open space environment. We also discuss how resources are allocated and migrated through domes. We present a schema of how resources can be dynamically allocated and shared between users within the environment in a transparent and efficient manner. We also discuss how we accommodate user mobility to eventually achieve an open space structure.

1 Introduction

Pervasive computing defines a vision of bringing computers closer to people[1,2]. The main idea is to have machines adapting to human environments rather than forcing humans to undergo such adaptation. Pervasive computing enlightens this vision by providing ubiquitous services to users on an anytime, anywhere basis. This paper addresses a number of resource-related pervasive computing challenges mainly as it deals with localized scalability and uneven conditioning [3].

The dilemma of localized scalability exists when the interactions between users and their environments grow in sophistication as the devices in the computing environment itself also grow in sophistication.Uneven conditioning on the other hand exists when resource-hungry users need more resources than what is currently available to them. One solution for such problem was proposed by Project Aura [5]. The solution informs users of a better spot to obtain a service, as well as the resources necessary for the required task. However, such approach requires knowledge of the exact task at hand, along with intelligence about the distribution of resources.

---

* To whome correspondance should be addressed, Amgad Madkour is currently a Research Engineer in IBM Egypt Research and Development Group.

G. Min et al. (Eds.): ISPA 2006 Ws, LNCS 4331, pp. 115–124, 2006.

In this work, we also take scalability into consideration. Scalability should be recognized as a primary factor that influences the architecture and implementations of pervasive systems, similar to what has been done in distributed systems [9].

The paper is organized as follows: In section 2 we describe the related work. In sections 3 and 4 we define what Open Spaces are, and describe the basic components that form them. In sections 5, 6 , 7 and 8 we discuss resource allocation, mobility and limitations issue, and explain how resources are managed and released from our domes respectively. In section 9 and 10 we present the implementation and experimentation of the system.

2   Related Work

One of the main challenges is to define categories to tackle the issue of scalability. Buckholz and Popien in [8] divided the scalability issue into a number of dimensions: First, a numerical dimension that deals with the number of users in an environment, and second, a geographic dimension that deals with the distance between nodes in the environment that provides services. A third dimension, namely administrative, deals with execution control over the system.

Many survey papers state different paradigms of how both context aware services and users interact in accordance with their environment. Some scenarios assume that both the user and context services are located beside each other. Other scenarios assume that users are distant from context services, while still obtaining services by other means [8]. One such example is the conference assistant system that does not face scalability problems because of the assumption that its environment is small enough to handle the requests it receives from room visitors, and hence, scalability does not constitute a major issue [7]. The aim is to realize a more global approach to solving pervasive computing requirements where environments do not pose a limitation [8].

In this work, we also find great intimacy between work done in distributed file systems and the proposed idea of Open Space in pervasive systems. Scale-related aspects in distributed file systems were tackled by the Andrew and Coda distributed file system [9]. Location transparency was one of the main requirements which enabled the system to have users unaware of where files are allocated and stored.Some researchers consider pervasive computing to be a form of grid computing since both of them utilizes the idea of using free or unused resources [10,11,12].

3   Open Spaces

Open spaces is a pervasive environment that harnesses the power of scalable systems in terms of available resources. Open spaces uses hybrid concepts from distributed file systems, and grid computing and clusters to use any available resources of the system. Clusters help in defining a region of inter-related resources. We refer to cluster-like regions in our work as domes, which are explained later.

We use concepts of grid computing in extending our view of the system, where we exploit available resources in a certain region.

We created a paradigm that allows a pervasive environment to have an extendable and expandable grid capable of foreseeing beyond its current location. Users requesting resources in the Open Space will neither be bound by their current location, nor their current cluster (dome). The Open Space structure handles user requests on a more global scale in an invisible and transparent manner. It uses inter-dome communication to satisfy user requirements instead of the user searching for required resources.

Open Spaces is a two-part system that depends on both the infrastructure of the dome, as well as sharable user devices. As a pervasive environment, the system defines a protocol of communication between the dome and user devices so that the dome would be able to use shared resources of devices. This requires a layer to be present on user devices that will control its shared resources in the Open Space environment. Such layer is responsible for keeping the dome up to date about the resources status available at each device.

The types of resources that we deal with can vary from memory, processing or storage resources. Resource discovery is done when any user enters the Open Space environment and such user devices broadcast their current resources. Once the user device sends information to its relevant dome about the current status of its resources, and the amount that it will share, the dome keeps track of the device movement in the whole environment and acquires resources when it needs them.

We defined a resource allocation mechanism that maximizes the chances of a user performing resource consuming tasks, even if the user is using a device with limited resources. The choice of which dome to acquire resources from is based on the allocation mechanism that we have defined as explained in later sections.

We developed an application to perform complete simulation of our system in order to observe various interactions between the entities. We simulated user devices with a predefined sharable amount of resources and showed when and how the device communicated with the dome in order to synchronize its available resources. We also implemented inter-dome and intra-dome communications to show how resource acquisition is performed. We also simulated user movement in the Open space environment and showed how the environment handles user mobility within the domes.

4   The Open Space Structure

Open Space consists of a number of overlapping and enclosing domes that communicate with each other forming an Open Space pervasive environment. Figure 1 shows how we can have two overlapping domes aiding each other to provide resource allocation services for their users.

4.1   The Dome

A dome is a physically defined space that contains a number of wireless access points. Such access points are used to reply on user resource requests within the

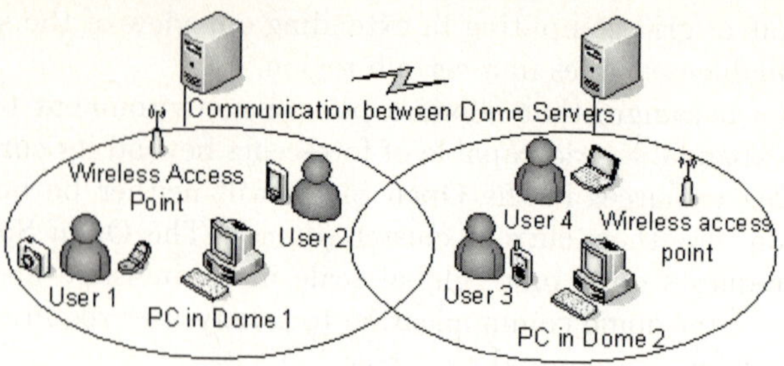

Fig. 1. Two domes populated with users. Each dome is equipped with usable resources that can be shared within the environment and managed by dome servers.

perimeter of the dome. The dome itself may have a collection of other micro domes within it. The main motivation is that each dome will enclose a number of local resources and mobile users in a specified region. It will also be the single point of contact for users that wish to request resources.

The structure of the domes themselves can either be static, or may change dynamically. However, within this work, we consider for the time being dome structures that are static. In other words, each dome can represent a building or a campus, or a subset of a campus. Each dome can have resources such as computing devices similar to the ones mentioned in Figure 1. Such computing devices are local to that specific dome.

We define wireless services that cover the perimeter of the dome. Therefore, if a user is outside the range of any dome, the user will obviously not be able to receive the domes services. Each statically defined dome is equipped with a dedicated machine. We will refer to the machine as server which is a normal computing device with reasonable processing and storage power. In our simulation of the system, we defined the server to be equipped with a middleware called the iKernel. The iKernel is responsible for the managing requests and allocation of resources to and from users. We discuss iKernel in details in later sections.

4.2   The Dome Architecture

We have two architectures that will aid us in the development of domes: The first architecture may have macro domes that enclose micro domes. This allows us to have a wireless cluster of domes that intercommunicate together to allocate resources for their users. This cluster maintains user location and resources when roaming between enclosed domes. The intercommunication frees the user to commute from one dome to another without worrying about losing resources, thus removing the burden of location constraints, as with the case of hand-over in cellular phones. The cluster mechanism will only operate if the whole cluster of micro domes is inside a macro dome, which in turn is responsible for managing the mobility of the user. This guarantees quality of service to the user as the transition from one micro dome to another is still tracked by the macro dome itself, which in turn holds the entire micro domes cluster.

The second architecture deals with a broader integration of domes. With such architecture, we have two domes that have no macro domes. For those domes to communicate they have to overlap in order to share resources between each other efficiently. In the first architecture, we depended on the existence of a macro dome that would facilitate and maintain communication between the micro domes.

5   Resource Allocation and Limitations

We introduce how resource allocation is performed when a user needs more resources than what his current device offers. After the user enters a dome, his resources will be reported to the dome according to a specific policy that is defined by the iKernel, as well as the middleware residing on the user device. When the user allocates any resource on his device, the current amount will also be reported to the dome. A policy governs the amount of resources that the user shares within the dome. The amount can either be predefined or the user could choose to allow sharing of his resources when the device is in idle state. These policies aim to govern the misuse or unfairness of resource sharing inside the dome. In this paper we assume that the resources will be allocated from idle state devices.

5.1   Resource Allocation Mechanism

In case the dome cannot allocate enough resources for the current user, the dome will proceed with the following procedures:

The dome's iKernel will query its overlapping domes about their resources and try to allocate the required amount of resources for the user. The minimum logical amount of overlapping domes should be two domes. The user device middleware sends a message to the dome that passes the request to its iKernel. The iKernel searches the resources that have been reported and attempts to determine the most appropriate resources to satisfy the user request. The iKernel then sends a message to the device informing it of the coordinates of were to acquire the resources needed. When the user device receives the request, it starts to perform its task on peer to peer basis with the device that shared this resource.

In case the first procedure fails to acquire the resources, the domes iKernel sends a message to the macro dome and tries to request information about resources. Each dome can have only one macro dome which encloses it. The macro dome replies with a message to the requesting dome informing it of the availability of the requested resources. If the macro dome fails, it recursively tries to search for resources on its overlapping domes then its macro dome and so forth. When resources are found, the message is sent recursively back to the initiating dome which in turn passes a message to the user informing him of the resources coordinates. Each dome follows the same procedure explained before to allocate the resources for the user.

In case both these procedures fail, the user will be in pending state inside the dome, until the required resources can be allocated.

6   Releasing Resources

Resources are released by the user when the user completely exits the dome. The resources are returned back to the allocating dome, to be eventually reallocated to users who may have a pending request. Any remaining resources are allocated to any new user entering the dome. In case the user leaves a dome with some of his resources still allocated, the dome actually tries to compensate for the resources it will loose due to the departure of the user and tries to reallocate them from its own resources. It will follow the same sequence we mentioned before in case that it couldnt allocate enough resources.

7   Resource Mobility

We have two mobility scenarios in our dome environment. The first is Intra-mobility in which the user may move from the macro dome into a micro dome. The resources allocated from the macro dome will remain until the micro dome that the user enters inside confirms that it has the necessary resources for the user. The second scenario is Inter-mobility in which the user may move from one macro dome to another macro dome. The main difference between the scenario we have mentioned and the current one is that we want to connect larger regions or domes together, where each region has its own pervasive environment.

8   Resource Management

The resources types shared among domes may include processing, memory, or storage. Each dome is equipped with what is called a shared resources pool. This pool includes all resources that are present at a certain point in time in the dome, and the dome uses that pool to allocate resources for users requesting them. Resources are not restricted to those local to the dome, but also include ones that are associated with the user.

In case the policy of the user allows sharing of his own resources, then when the user enters a dome, the resources that he has shared are placed inside the pool. This scenario would be very effective if the user has idle resources which another user maybe in dire need of to satisfy required resources.

Considering that we are in a pervasive environment, conventional operating systems will not be of much help. We need a special layer to manage the devices, as well as their resources (hardware or software). Such layer must have an efficient management and allocation system. We have included in our simulation what we mentioned before as a compact iKernel. The iKernel monitors all users entering the dome, which in turn allocates and reallocates resources to them accordingly. The iKernel has a defined mechanism to obtain resources as fast as possible using the shortest path that is available to it. Our current schema assumes access to overlapping domes, then access to macro domes. We believe that this schema yields best results due to distance issues.

The iKernel will determine the closest and most appropriate dome to start allocating resources from according to the mentioned schema. Another responsibility of the iKernel is keeping track of any new domes that may be created. This is done by a central server which keeps the iKernels of domes updated with the environment. Such policy ensures that the creation of a new dome is monitored by the central server whose only task is to keep track of created and removed domes.

9   Open Space Implementation

9.1   iKernel

The iKernel is the core of the Open Space architecture were it is responsible for management and allocation of requests from and to the user. The iKernel, which maintains a basic queue data structure to keep track of requests and resources that are currently available on a first come first serve manner also checks the shortest path between the requesting device and the nearest available resource by sorting a copy of system resources every time it receives a request to guarantee that the user receives resources from the nearest neighbor on a first come first serve queue. In our application, we created domes and their iKernel's each on a separate thread to fully simulate real deployment simulation.

The iKernel performs a number of major operations including checking for resources, processing resource removal and allocating/reallocating resources.

9.2   Device Middleware

The second component is the middleware that resides on the user device. This layer is the interface between the device resources and the iKernel in order for the device to use shared resources from the dome. Such layer broadcasts its resources upon entry by sending a report after each operation is done on the device. The middleware is also responsible for establishing a peer to peer connection with the device that contains the resources that the user or the system requires. After the device finishes the task the middleware sends a message to the dome to return the resources.

9.3   Dome Manager Server

The third and final component is the dome manager server which includes a layer that keeps information about current domes in an environment, and synchronizes with the rest of the domes on its list. As such, domes would be aware of candidate domes to acquire resources from. The update about newly available domes to the rest is done when a dome is added to the list of the dome manager server.

10   Experiment

We conducted three experiments using our simulator to demonstrate the behavior of our system as relates to the delay incurred upon allocating various resources. The three experiments were conducted to demonstrate such resource allocation delay behavior in three scenarios, namely in the presence of overlapping,macro and without the presence of domes.The ultimate objective of the experiments is to prove that the utilization of dome-based structures can decrease the overall delay resulting from the search and allocation of resources.

10.1   Experimental Setup

For our experiments, we identify the presence of domes in our simulator using 2-D planar coordinates. Each dome has an X and Y coordinates, as well as a radius. We also assumed that resource allocation delay is proportional to the proximity of the resources physical presence from the requesting device.Two types of delays exist, namely REQD, and COMD. The former specifies the time taken to locate and allocate a resource, and the latter specified communication delay to utilize the required resource. The total delay TOTAL is the summation of REQD and COMD.In the simulation, we fixed the location of the first user (DEV1) at X and Y coordinates (100,100). We then relocated the second user (DEV2) to two new locations. Both users are in different domes. DEV1 will attempt to acquire 256 MB of memory, however, it only owns half this amount, namely 128 MB of memory. We then measure the delay in terms of allocation and utilization for the three previously mentioned scenarios.

10.2   Experimental Results

The experiments show the effect of different scenarios mentioned earlier on the overall delay that is incurred. We assume that for each scenario, one user is fixed and the other user moves in three different locations. We show the overall delay that is incurred in each location.In the graph illustrated in Figure 2, we show the resulting delays between two devices without the intervention of domes. This is the conventional scenario that devices go through in order to search for resources. The device first attempts to contact the nearest device to establish a connection. After that the second device then replies with the availability of its resources and its approval of the first device process. This delay is even a best case scenario, where the device successfully found the resources it requires from the first trial. From our experiment we showed that we incurred a major delay overhead simply to find the appropriate resource to use.

In our dome based system, the dome is delegated to search for the appropriate resources necessary to satisfy the user device, which in turn decreases the delay because the device communicates with the dome to obtain information about where to acquire the resources from, instead of searching for the resource by itself. Furthermore, the dome does not have to search for available devices upon receiving a resource request, but rather, since resources are already registered by devices upon entry into the dome, the resource search time is significantly decreased.

In the graph illustrated in Figure 3, the time delay in both the overlapping and macro dome scenario is very close since the delays are primarily influenced by the

A Case for Non-blocking Collective Operations

Torsten Hoefler[1,3], Jeffrey M. Squyres[2], Wolfgang Rehm[3],
and Andrew Lumsdaine[1]

[1] Indiana University, Open Systems Lab, Bloomington IN 47405, USA
{htor, lums}@cs.indiana.edu
[2] Cisco Systems, San Jose, CA 95134 USA
jsquyres@cisco.com
[3] Technical University of Chemnitz, 09107 Chemnitz, Germany
{htor, rehm}@cs.tu-chemnitz.de

Abstract. Non-blocking collective operations for MPI have been in discussion for a long time. We want to contribute to this discussion and to give a rationale for the usage these operations and assess their possible benefits. A LogGP model for the CPU overhead of collective algorithms and a benchmark to measures it are provided and show a large potential to overlap communication and computation. We show that non-blocking collective operations can provide at least the same benefits as non-blocking point to point operations already do. Our claim is that actual CPU overhead for non-blocking collective operations depends on the message size and the communicator size and benefits especially highly scalable applications with huge communicators. We prove that the share of the overhead of the overall communication time of current blocking collective operations gets smaller with bigger communicators and larger messages. We show that the user level CPU overhead is less than 10% for MPICH2 and LAM/MPI using TCP/IP communication, which leads us to the conclusion that, by using non-blocking collective communication, ideally 90% idle CPU time can be freed for the application.

Keywords: Collective communication, Overlap, Non-blocking communication, Message passing (MPI).

1 Introduction

Non-blocking collective operations and their possible benefits have already been discussed at meetings of the MPI standardization committee. The final decision to not include them into the MPI-2 standard fell at March 6, 1997[1]. However, the fact that the decision was extremely marginal (11 yes / 12 no / 2 abstain) suggests that the role of non-blocking collective operations is still debatable. Our contention is that non-blocking collective operations are a natural extension to the MPI-2 standard. We show that non-blocking collective operations can be beneficial for a class of applications to utilize the available CPU time more efficiently and decrease the time to solution of these applications significantly.

---

[1] See: http://www.mpi-forum.org/archives/votes/mpi2.html

G. Min et al. (Eds.): ISPA 2006 Ws, LNCS 4331, pp. 155–164, 2006.

Further, we discuss two main problems of blocking collective communication which limit the scalability of applications.

First, blocking collective operations have a more or less synchronizing effect on applications which leads to unnecessary wait time. Even thought the MPI standard does not define other blocking collective operations than MPI_BARRIER to be strictly synchronizing, most used algorithms force many processes to wait for other processes due to data dependencies. In this way, synchronization with a single process is enforced for some operations (e.g., a MPI_BCAST can not be finished until the root process called it) and the synchronizing behavior of other operations highly depends on the implemented collective algorithm. In either case, pseudo-synchronizing behavior often leads to many lost CPU cycles, a high sensitivity to process skew (e.g., due to daemon processes which "steal" the CPU occasionally and introduce a pseudo-random skew between processes [1,2]), and a high sensitivity to imbalanced programming (e.g., some processes do slightly more computation than others each round).

Second, most blocking collective operations can not take much advantage of modern interconnects which enable communication offload to support efficient overlapping of communication and computation. Abstractly seen, each supercomputer or cluster consists of two entities, the CPU which processes data streams and the network which transports data streams. In many networks, both entities can act mostly independently of each other, but the programmer has no chance to use this parallelism efficiently if blocking communication (point-to-point or collective) is used.

Another rationale to offer non-blocking semantics for collective communication is an analogy between many modern operating systems and the MPI standard. Most modern operating systems offer possibilities to overlap computation on the host CPU with actions of other entities (for example harddisks or the network). Asynchronous I/O and non-blocking TCP/IP sockets are today's standard features to communicate. The MPI standard offers non-blocking point-to-point communication which can be used to overlap communication and computation. It would be a natural extension to offer also a non-blocking interface to the collective operations.

The next section describes related work in the field of overlap of computation and communication and the avoidance of synchronization. Section 2 gives some information about possible benefits of non-blocking collective communication. Section 3 presents benchmark results for a selected set of operations followed by a conclusion of this work.

1.1 Related Work

The obvious benefits of overlapping communication with computation and leveraging the hardware parallelism efficiently with the usage of non-blocking communication is well documented. Analyses [3,4,5] try to give an assessment of the capabilities of MPI implementations to perform overlapping for point-to-point communications. Many groups analyze the possible performance benefits for real applications. Liu et al. [6] showed possible speedups up to 1.9 for several parallel programs. Brightwell et al. [7] classifies the source of performance advantage for overlap and Dimitrov [8] uses overlapping as fundamental approach to optimize parallel applications for cluster systems. Other studies, as [9,10,11,12] apply several transformations to parallel codes to enable overlapping. However, little research has been done in the field of non-blocking collectives. Studies like [13,14] mention that non-blocking collective operations would be beneficial but do not provide a measure for it. Kale et al. [15] analyzed the applicability of a non-blocking personalized exchange to a small set of applications in practice. However, many studies show that non-blocking communication and non-blocking collectives *may* be beneficial. Our work contributes to the field because we actually assess the potential performance benefits of a non-blocking collective implementation.

2   Possible Performance Benefits

The most obvious benefits of non-blocking collective operations are the avoidance of explicit pseudo synchronization and the ability to leverage the hardware parallelism stated in Section 1. The pseudo-synchronizing behavior of most algorithms cannot be avoided, but non-blocking collective operations process the operation in the background, which enables the user to ignore most synchronization effects. Common sources for de-synchronization, process skew and load imbalance are not easily measurable. However, results can increase the application running time dramatically, as shown in [16]. Theoretical [17] and practical analyses [18,16] show that operating system noise and resulting process skew is definitively influencing the performance of parallel applications using blocking collective operations. Non-blocking collective operations avoid explicit synchronization unless it is necessary (if the programmer wants to wait for the operation to finish). This enables the programmer to develop applications which are more tolerant of process skew and load imbalance.

Another benefit is to use the parallelism of the network and computation layers. Non-blocking communication (point-to-point and collective) allows the user to issue a communication request to the hardware, perform some useful computation, and ask later if it has been completed. Modern interconnect networks can perform the message transfer mostly independently of the user process. The resulting effect is that, for several algorithms/applications, the user can overlap the communication latency with useful computation and ignore the communication latency up to a certain extent (or totally). This has been well analyzed for point-to-point communication (see Section 1.1). Non-blocking collective operations allow the programmer to combine the benefits of collective communication [19] with all benefits of non-blocking communication. The following subsections analyze the communication behavior of current blocking collective algorithms and implementations and show that only a fraction of the CPU time is involved into communication related computation. In relation to previous studies we show, theoretically and practically, that a similar percentage, in many cases even more, idle CPU time as with non-blocking point-to-point communication can be gained. We assume that the biggest share of the remaining (idle) CPU time can be leveraged by the user if overlap of communication and computation together with non-blocking collective communication can be applied.

2.1   Modelling CPU and Network Activity

This subsection gives an estimation of the theoretical CPU idle time during a collective operation. The CPU idle time during the communication will be modelled and benchmarked. Precise models for collective operations are presented in [20] and for barrier synchronization in [21]. Both studies show that the LogP [22] or LogGP [23] model is able to predict the communication time sufficiently accurately if the processes enter the collective operation simultaneously.

We analyze the three collective operations MPI_BARRIER, MPI_ALLREDUCE, and MPI_BCAST without loss of generality, in detail. As shown in [24,25,26], these three operations are frequently used in real applications. However, the results can also be applied to all other collective operations.

We assume the usual LogP/LogGP communication parameters (**L**atency, **o**verhead, **g**ap, **G**ap ber byte and **P**rocessors) and γ to assess computation:

We derive simplified LogGP models for networks adhering the properties defined in Section 2.2 in [21] (full bisectional bandwidth; full duplex; unlimited forwarding rate; L, o are constant; $o > L > g$). We model point-to-point message based implementations with logarithmic running time ($O(log_2 P)$) of all three operations. We assume the dissemination principle to perform MPI_BARRIER (1), analyzed in [21]. Our model for MPI_ALLREDUCE (2) assumes a simple binomial tree reduce implementation followed by MPI_BCAST and our MPI_BCAST (3) model assumes a binomial tree implementation (compare proposed models in [20]).

$$t_{barr} = (2o + L) \cdot \lceil log_2 P \rceil \tag{1}$$

$$t_{allred} = 2 \cdot (2o + L + m \cdot G) \cdot \lceil log_2 P \rceil + m \cdot \gamma \cdot \lceil log_2 P \rceil \tag{2}$$

$$t_{bcast} = (2o + L + m \cdot G) \cdot \lceil log_2 P \rceil \tag{3}$$

If we come back to the two entities, which are the network and the processor, mentioned in Section 1, we realize that each parameter is "accounted" at a specific entity. The processor is only used by o and γ while the network is used to perform the message transmission (L,g,G). Using this information, we can divide the equations presented above up into processing and network parts:

$$t_{barr}^{CPU} = 2o \cdot \lceil log_2 P \rceil \quad t_{barr}^{NET} = L \cdot \lceil log_2 P \rceil \tag{4}$$

$$t_{allred}^{CPU} = (4o + m \cdot \gamma) \cdot \lceil log_2 P \rceil \quad t_{allred}^{NET} = 2 \cdot (L + m \cdot G) \cdot \lceil log_2 P \rceil \tag{5}$$

$$t_{bcast}^{CPU} = 2o \cdot \lceil log_2 P \rceil \quad t_{bcast}^{NET} = (L + m \cdot G) \cdot \lceil log_2 P \rceil \tag{6}$$

We see that both, t^{CPU} and t^{NET} scale logarithmically with P. However, on modern interconnects the parameters can differ significantly. The following section provides an analysis of these parameters for modern interconect networks.

2.2   Fitting the Model to Modern Architectures

Modern interconnect architectures, like InfiniBand^{TM}, Quadrics^{TM}, or Myrinet^{TM}, which are used for HPC systems, try to offload a huge share of the communication into the network interface card. Traditional networks, like Ethernet (without offloading), still use the CPU extensively to process network protocols like TCP/IP. However, also Ethernet has been optimized for lower host overhead with simplified protocols [27] as well as direct user level access and protocol offloading [28]. All these new networks and approaches aim to reduce the overhead of the main CPU involved in communication (o parameter). The L parameter is usually greater than the o in modern networks, and the gap between t^{CPU} and t^{NET} grows with the message size as $G \cdot m$ is added. This enables efficient overlapping of computation and communication for point-to-point communication which has been described in the related work section. However, this idea can also be applied to collective communication. As one can see in equations (4),(5),(6), the gap between Network and CPU occupancy also grows with the number of involved processors P. This leads us to the prediction that especially blocking collectives which communicate large data chunks with many processors should be mostly utilizing the network (with an idle CPU). The only exception could be reduction operations, like MPI_ALLREDUCE, because they include processing (reduction) of values on the host CPU. However, in most cases, the bandwidth of the CPU should be much higher than the network bandwidth. In the following section, we evaluate these theoretical expectations with a custom benchmark set which measures the CPU usage during blocking collective operations.

3   Benchmark Results

We implemented a benchmark which measures the CPU utilization for different MPI collective operations. The benchmark uses the standard `gettimeofday()` and `getrusage()` functionality of modern operating systems to measure the idle time. It issues collective calls with different message sizes and communicator sizes. The benchmark methodology is described as pseudocode in Listing 1.1. The `getrusage()` call returns system time and user time used by the running process separately. We chose a high number of iterations (10000) in the inner loop (`max_iters`, Line 5) to be able to neglect the overhead and relative impreciseness of the system functions. We conducted the benchmark for different MPI implementations shown in Table 1.

Many MPI libraries are implemented in a non-blocking manner which means that the CPU overhead is, due to polling, 100% regardless of other factors. Only LAM/MPI with TCP/IP and MPICH2 with TCP/IP used blocking communication to perform the collective operations. However, it is totally correct to use polling to perform blocking MPI collective operations because, at least for single threaded MPI applications, the CPU is unusable anyways and polling has usually slightly lower overhead than interrupt based (blocking) methods.

```
for( proc=1; proc<nproc; proc=proc*2) {
  create_communicator(nproc, comm);
  for( size=1; size<maxsize; proc=proc*2) {
4   gettimeofday(t1); getrusage(r1);
    for( i=0; i<max_iters; i++)
      MPI_Coll(comm, size, MPI_BYTE, ...)
    getrusage(r2); gettimeofday(t2);
8 }}
```

Listing 1.1. Benchmark Methodology (pseudocode)

Table 1. Tested MPI Implementations

Implementation	Networks
LAM/MPI 7.1.2	InfiniBand, TCP/IP
MPICH2 1.0.3	TCP/IP
Open MPI 1.1a3	InfiniBand and TCP/IP
OSU MVAPICH 0.9.4.	InfiniBand

We investigated all collective operations for LAM/MPI and MPICH2 and want to discuss the frequently used MPI_ALLREDUCE (cf. [26]) in detail. Both MPI_ALLREDUCE implementations exhibit a similar behavior and use only a fraction of the available CPU power for communicators with more than 8 nodes. MPICH2 causes in the average of all measurement points less than 30% CPU load while LAM/MPI consumes less then 10%. We see also that the data size plays an important role because there may be switching points in the collective implementation where the collective algorithms or underlying point-to-point operations are changed (e.g., 128kb for MPICH2). However, this overhead includes the TCP/IP packet processing time spent in the kernel to transmit the messages which is measured with the `getrusage()` function as system time. User level, kernel-bypass, and offloading communication hardware like InfiniBand, Quadrics or Myrinet does not use the host CPU to process packets and does not enter the kernel during message transmission. Figure 1 shows the user level CPU usage (without TCP/IP processing) for both examples from above. It shows that the CPU overhead for MPI_ALLREDUCE, which implies a user level reduction operation in our case, is below 10% in the average for MPICH2 and below 3% for LAM/MPI. These figures show also that the share of CPU idle time grows with communicator and data size. Other collective operations which are not shown here due to space restrictions exhibit a similar behavior.

However, generally speaking, the time to perform a collective operation grows also with communicator and data size. This means that the overall (multiplicative) CPU waste is even higher. Figure 2 shows the absolute CPU idle time of both implementations, several collective operations, and a fixed communicated data size with varying communicator sizes. The effect of growing CPU waste during blocking collectives is clearly visible. Especially the MPI_ALLTOALL

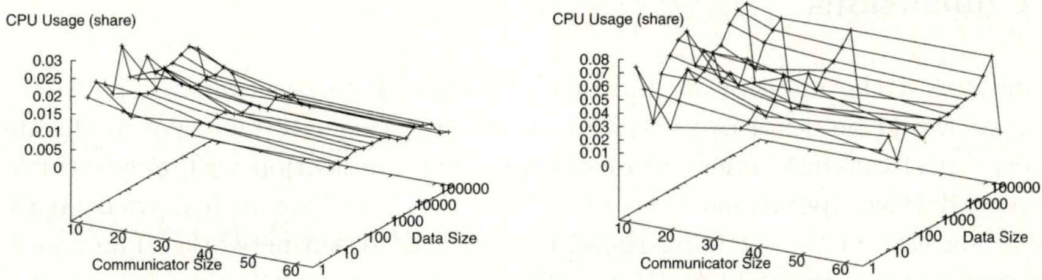

Fig. 1. MPI_ALLREDUCE (user time) overheads for LAM/MPI (left) and MPICH2 (right)

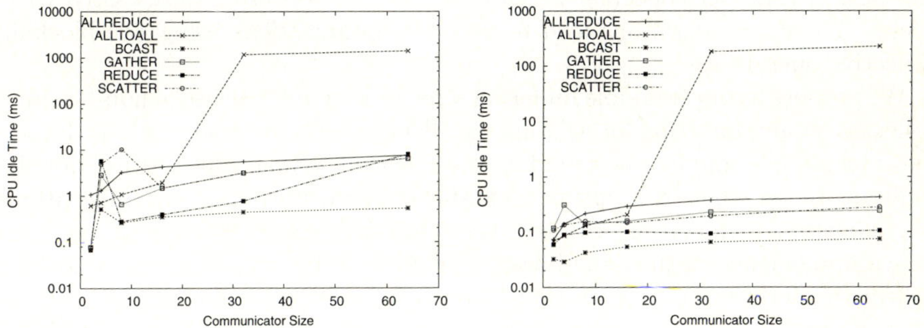

Fig. 2. CPU idle time for some collective functions with varying communicator sizes for a constant data size of 1kB (left: LAM/MPI, right: MPICH2)

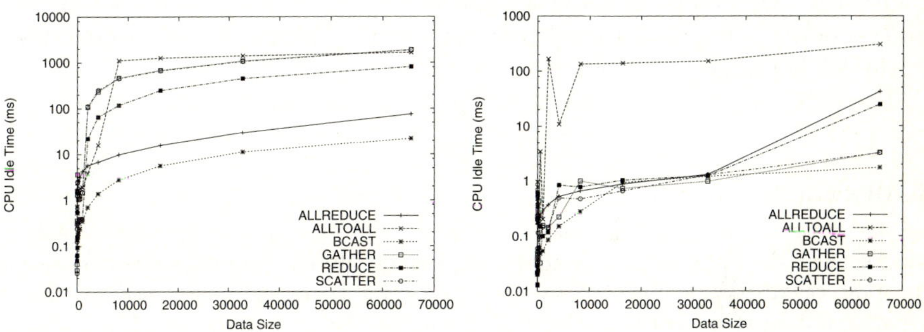

Fig. 3. CPU idle time for some collective functions with varying data size for a constant communicator size of 16 processes (left: LAM/MPI, right: MPICH2)

operation, which usually scales worst, shows high CPU idle times with a growing number of participating processes.

Figure 3 shows that absolute CPU idle time of both implementations, for a fixed communicator size, and varying data sizes. The CPU waste is even higher and scales worse than for the varying communicator size, nearly linearly with the data size (the figures are plotted with a logarithmic scale).

4 Conclusions

We show that the addition of non-blocking collective operations to the MPI-2 standard would be a natural extension to the existing interface. We model the potential performance benefit of overlapping communication with computation during collective operations. The model is proven and quantified with an extensive analysis of the CPU overhead for TCP/IP based networks. The results show clearly that, using TCP/IP, more than 70% of the CPU time is wasted in average during blocking collective operations. We assume that the gap is more than 90% for offloading based networks such as InfiniBand, Quadrics or Myrinet which do not process messages on the host CPU. Absolute measurements show the wasted time per collective which can easily be converted into wasted CPU cycles. These considerations lead to possible optimizations using non-blocking collective operations.

We propose a simple double buffering scheme to enable the use of non-blocking collective communication for existing parallel applications or algorithms. Examples include [29] and can be found at the LibNBC webpage [30]. Other double-buffering based schemes to optimize parallel implementations of more algorithms (e.g. Gaussian elemination) can be easily derived.

We implemented a portable library (LibNBC, [31]) supporting non-blocking collective operations on top of MPI-1 and port scientific applications to use the new semantics. However, implementing collective semantics on top of MPI-1 cannot easily take advantage of special hardware features to support collective communication (e.g., a hardware barrier [32]). We are planning to move the non-blocking collective implementation into the extensible Open MPI collective framework [33] to enable hardware optimized non-blocking collectives. We do also propose a MPI-2 extension [34] to support non-blocking collective operations in the MPI standard.

The NBC library is available at: `http://www.unixer.de/NBC/`.

References

1. Wagner, A., Buntinas, D., Panda, D.K., Brightwell, R.: Application-bypass reduction for large-scale clusters. In: 2003 IEEE International Conference on Cluster Computing (CLUSTER 2003), IEEE Computer Society (2003) 404–411
2. Terry, P., Shan, A., Huttunen, P.: Improving application performance on hpc systems with process synchronization. Linux J. **2004**(127) (2004) 3
3. Iancu, C., Husbands, P., Hargrove, P.: Hunting the overlap. In: PACT '05: Proceedings of the 14th International Conference on Parallel Architectures and Compilation Techniques (PACT'05), Washington, DC, USA, IEEE Computer Society (2005) 279–290
4. III, J.W., Bova, S.: Where's the Overlap? - An Analysis of Popular MPI Implementations (1999)
5. Lawry, W., Wilson, C., Maccabe, A.B., Brightwell, R.: Comb: A portable benchmark suite for assessing mpi overlap. In: CLUSTER, IEEE Computer Society (2002) 472–475

6. Liu, G., Abdelrahman, T.: Computation-communication overlap on network-of-workstation multiprocessors. In: Proc. of the Int'l Conference on Parallel and Distributed Processing Techniques and Applications. (1998) 1635–1642

7. Brightwell, R., Underwood, K.D.: An analysis of the impact of mpi overlap and independent progress. In: ICS '04: Proceedings of the 18th annual international conference on Supercomputing, New York, NY, USA, ACM Press (2004) 298–305

8. Dimitrov, R.: Overlapping of Communication and Computation and Early Binding: Fundamental Mechanisms for Improving Parallel Performance on Clusters of Workstations. PhD thesis, Mississippi State University (2001)

9. Calland, P.Y., Dongarra, J., Robert, Y.: Tiling on systems with communication/-computation overlap. Concurrency - Practice and Experience **11**(3) (1999) 139–153

10. Baude, F., Caromel, D., Furmento, N., Sagnol, D.: Optimizing metacomputing with communication-computation overlap. In: PaCT '01: Proceedings of the 6th International Conference on Parallel Computing Technologies, London, UK, Springer-Verlag (2001) 190–204

11. Danalis, A., Kim, K.Y., Pollock, L., Swany, M.: Transformations to parallel codes for communication-computation overlap. In: SC '05: Proceedings of the 2005 ACM/IEEE conference on Supercomputing, Washington, DC, USA, IEEE Computer Society (2005) 58

12. Abdelrahman, T.S., Liu, G.: Overlap of computation and communication on shared-memory networks-of-workstations. (2001) 35–45

13. Dubey, A., Tessera, D.: Redistribution strategies for portable parallel FFT: a case study. Concurrency and Computation: Practice and Experience **13**(3) (2001) 209–220

14. Brightwell, R., Riesen, R., Underwood, K.D.: Analyzing the impact of overlap, offload, and independent progress for message passing interface applications. Int. J. High Perform. Comput. Appl. **19**(2) (2005) 103–117

15. Kale, L.V., Kumar, S., Vardarajan, K.: A Framework for Collective Personalized Communication. In: Proceedings of IPDPS'03, Nice, France (2003)

16. Petrini, F., Kerbyson, D.J., Pakin, S.: The case of the missing supercomputer performance: Achieving optimal performance on the 8, 192 processors of asci q. In: Proceedings of the ACM/IEEE SC2003 Conference on High Performance Networking and Computing, 15-21 November 2003, Phoenix, AZ, USA, CD-Rom, ACM (2003) 55

17. Agarwal, S., Garg, R., Vishnoi, N.: The impact of noise on the scaling of collectives: A theoretical approach. In: 12th Annual IEEE International Conference on High Performance Computing, Goa, India (2005)

18. Jones, T., Dawson, S., Neely, R., Jr., W.G.T., Brenner, L., Fier, J., Blackmore, R., Caffrey, P., Maskell, B., Tomlinson, P., Roberts, M.: Improving the scalability of parallel jobs by adding parallel awareness to the operating system. In: Proceedings of the ACM/IEEE SC2003 Conference on High Performance Networking and Computing. (2003) 10

19. Gorlatch, S.: Send-receive considered harmful: Myths and realities of message passing. ACM Trans. Program. Lang. Syst. **26**(1) (2004) 47–56

20. Pjesivac-Grbovic, J., Angskun, T., Bosilca, G., Fagg, G.E., Gabriel, E., Dongarra, J.J.: Performance Analysis of MPI Collective Operations. In: Proceedings of the 19th International Parallel and Distributed Processing Symposium, 4th International Workshop on Performance Modeling, Evaluation, and Optimization of Parallel and Distributed Systems (PMEO-PDS 05), Denver, CO (2005)

21. Hoefler, T., Cerquetti, L., Mehlan, T., Mietke, F., Rehm, W.: A practical Approach to the Rating of Barrier Algorithms using the LogP Model and Open MPI. In: Proceedings of the 2005 International Conference on Parallel Processing Workshops (ICPP'05). (2005) 562–569
22. Culler, D., Karp, R., Patterson, D., Sahay, A., Schauser, K.E., Santos, E., Subramonian, R., von Eicken, T.: LogP: towards a realistic model of parallel computation. In: Principles Practice of Parallel Programming. (1993) 1–12
23. Alexandrov, A., Ionescu, M.F., Schauser, K.E., Scheiman, C.: LogGP: Incorporating Long Messages into the LogP Model. Journal of Parallel and Distributed Computing **44**(1) (1995) 71–79
24. Vetter, J.S., Mueller, F.: Communication characteristics of large-scale scientific applications for contemporary cluster architectures. In: IPDPS '02: Proceedings of the 16th International Parallel and Distributed Processing Symposium, Washington, DC, USA, IEEE Computer Society (2002) 96
25. Brightwell, R., Goudy, S., Rodrigues, A., Underwood, K.: Implications of application usage characteristics for collective communication offload. Internation Journal of High-Performance Computing and Networking **4**(2) (2006)
26. Rabenseifner, R.: Automatic mpi counter profiling. In: 42nd CUG Conference, CUG Summit 2000. (2000)
27. Hoefler, T., Reinhardt, M., Mehlan, T., Mietke, F., Rehm, W.: Low overhead ethernet communication for open mpi on linux clusters. In: Submitted to EuroPVM'06. (2006)
28. Shivam, P., Wyckoff, P., Panda, D.: Emp: zero-copy os-bypass nic-driven gigabit ethernet message passing. In: Supercomputing '01: Proceedings of the 2001 ACM/IEEE conference on Supercomputing (CDROM), New York, NY, USA, ACM Press (2001) 57–57
29. Hoefler, T., Gottschling, P., Rehm, W., Lumsdaine, A.: Optimizing a Conjugate Gradient Solver with Non-Blocking Collective Operations. (2006) Accepted for publication at the ParSim 2006 Workshop.
30. LibNBC: http://www.unixer.de/NBC (2006)
31. Hoefler, T., Lumsdaine, A.: Design, Implementation, and Usage of LibNBC. Technical report, Open Systems Lab, Indiana University (2006)
32. Hoefler, T., Mehlan, T., Mietke, F., Rehm, W.: Adding Low-Cost Hardware Barrier Support to Small Commodity Clusters. In: 19th International Conference on Architecture and Computing Systems - ARCS'06. (2006) 343–350
33. Squyres, J.M., Lumsdaine, A.: The Component Architecture of Open MPI: Enabling Third-Party Collective Algorithms. In: Proceedings, 18th ACM International Conference on Supercomputing, Workshop on Component Models and Systems for Grid Applications, St. Malo, France (2004)
34. Hoefler, T., Squyres, J., Bosilca, G., Fagg, G., Lumsdaine, A., Rehm, W.: Non-Blocking Collective Operations for MPI-2. (2006)

Using Agreement Services in Grid Computing[*]

Michel Hurfin[1], Jean-Pierre Le Narzul[2],
Julien Pley[1], and Philippe Raïpin Parvédy[1]

[1] INRIA Rennes / IRISA, campus de Beaulieu, 35042 Rennes cedex, France
{hurfin, jpley, praipinp}@irisa.fr
[2] GET ENST Bretagne / IRISA, campus de Rennes, 35512 Cesson-Svign, France
jlenarzu@irisa.fr

Abstract. The major purpose of a Grid is to federate multiple powerful resources into a single virtual entity which can be accessed transparently and efficiently by external users. As a Grid is usually an unreliable system involving heterogeneous resources located in different geographical domains, distributed and fault-tolerant resource allocation services have to be provided. In particular when a crash occurs tasks have to be re-allocated quickly and automatically, in a completely transparent way from the users' point of view. This paper presents PARADIS, an adaptive middleware based on a set of basic agreement services that has been integrated within an experimental Grid dedicated to genomic applications.

Keywords: Grid computing, dependability, agreement, task allocation.

1 Introduction

The major purpose of a Grid is to federate powerful distributed resources (computers, clusters, storage facilities, ...) within a single virtual entity which can be accessed transparently and efficiently by external users. In our study, we consider a Grid composed of heterogeneous resources provided by various institutions. These potential contributors correspond to well-established institutions that agree to share their resources and to trust each other. An example of such a grid has been designed in the context of a project founded by the French Ministry of Research called "ACI GénoGRID". This experimental Grid is dedicated to genomic applications and relies on the software presented in this paper. Its interest is twofolds. First, it federates resources belonging to genomic/bioinformatics centers dispatched in the western part of France and thus provides to each biologist a potentially higher computing power. Second, as this Grid is dedicated to a well-identified community of users who share mutual interests and agree on some data workflows, the amount of common information accessed and maintained through the Grid (programs, files and databases) is huge.

We consider that a Grid is a federation of domains controlled by independent and autonomous institutions. In each domain, an administrator is in charge of managing the level of participation of its own institution in terms of computing

* This work is supported by the cooperation project CAPES/COFECUB 497/05.

G. Min et al. (Eds.): ISPA 2006 Ws, LNCS 4331, pp. 165–174, 2006.
© Springer-Verlag Berlin Heidelberg 2006

power. The decision to include or to exclude some (or even all) local resources from the Grid can be taken at any time by the local administrator without any coordination with the others. A domain delimits a sub-part of the whole system in which synchrony assumptions are guaranted. Indeed, resources within a domain are connected through local area networks. Bounds on the transmission delay exist and are known. For security purpose, interactions between domains can be limited to a group of machine, one per domain that is responsible to interact with the other domains. In a large scale Grid, the only reasonable assumption is to consider that this set of proxies (belonging to different domains) corresponds to an asynchronous distributed system. Such a system is characterized by the lack of a global synchronized clock, and puts no bound on the transmission delay of messages.

In this general context, we address two major issues that both require a continuous adaptation to the changing computing environment: *resource allocation* and *dependability*. We aim at developing services that allow a Grid user to continuously take full advantage of the computing power offered by the Grid. Whatever the circumstances, a complete transparency and a quick response time are expected by the customers. To achieve this goal, all the dynamic changes of the computing capacity of the Grid have to be observed and appropriate adaptations must be performed. Most of the variations are due to an evolution of the set of resources (failure, decision of the administrator, ...). In that case, each time a resource disappears or appears, the tasks queuing for execution have to be distributed among the remaining resources in an efficient way. But even when the set of resources is stable, the proposed mechanisms have also to cope with unreliable estimation of the workload of each resource. First, for some particular applications, the duration of a task cannot be estimated precisely. This may create a difference between the estimated workload used by the task allocation mechanism and the real workload. Second, the administrator of a domain may refuse that his resources are exclusively devoted to the Grid. Some local applications can be launched concurrently by members of the institution without using the Grid mechanisms. In that case the workloads of the used resources increase without any control. In the above cases, adaptive mechanisms are necessary to adjust the task allocation with regards to these unforecast workload changes.

We propose to address both issues (resource allocation and dependability) in an homogeneous way using a slightly modified group concept. More precisely, all interactions between domains corresponding to distinct organizations are managed by a small group of registered processors (exactly one per domain). Each member of this group acts as a *master* for its own domain and interacts with the other members of the group to build consistent observations (1) of current workloads in each domain and (2) of the current composition of the group. In that sense, we argue that, in a distributed system prone to failures, an agreement service is a key concept to transform several local views into a single global one without opting for a centralized control approach and thus without having a single point of failure. An agreement service allows all the domains to acquire the same set of accurate data describing the current state of the Grid. Based on this unanimous observation, each domain can locally enact the right adaptation to react to the observed changes.

The overall paper is organized as follows. Section 2 outlines the relationships with some related works. Section 3 focuses on the interactions between a user and the Grid. Section 4 presents the multi-levels structure of the Grid that is a key characteristic of our approach. Section 5 discusses the use of agreement services to address the resource allocation issue and the dependability issue. Section 6 presents some algorithms and the architecture of the PARADIS middleware .

2   Related Work

Grid computing projects [4,1] and public-resource computing projects [3] are related to our work. Both share the objective of federating multiple computing resources for use by cpu-intensive applications. Although it should be easier to address the dependability issue in Grid computing platforms (i.e. institutional projects) than in public-resource platforms, we observe that very few projects has included sophisticated mechanisms for tolerating and masking failures.

In some systems [9,10,7], resources are managed by a controller in charge of dispatching the tasks within the grid. This controller is also in charge of detecting the failures of the resources and of reallocating the tasks. Of course, the controller may also crash and thus particular mechanisms have to be provided to mask the failure of a controller. In [7], a failed controller can be recovered by restarting it on another machine. Data that is necessary to initialize the state of a new controller is kept in a file (or a database) and is updated periodically by the single active controller. Primary back-up mechanisms have been proposed in [10] to implement a centralized and reliable control service. As pointed in [9], implementing such a mechanism in an asynchronous system is far from being trivial. Thus, the authors suggest to use an active replication mechanism to add fault-tolerant properties to the controller. An atomic broadcast service is used to ensure that all the replicas observe the same sequence of requests.

In all these works, the control is done by a set of replicas that have to observe the state of the whole grid. In this paper, we investigate a new approach in which the control is not centralized in a particular domain. Any institution that provide some resources also provide at least one controller. Thus, the control is equally shared across all the participants and no organization plays a central role. For political reasons, this strategy is more appropriate. Additionally, the controller attached to a particular domain is the only one that may observe the state of the resources within its domain. As it only provides a partial information to the other controllers, no controller has a view of the whole grid. For security and confidentiality reasons, this stategy is also more appropriate.

3   Interactions Between a User and the Grid

In our approach, the preliminary registration of any application that will be executed in the Grid is mandatory and has to be done once. In every domain, a copy of the application code and copies of the accessed data banks are created. Then, a biologist can launch one of his favorite applications from anywhere through one of the identified web portals. Once the submission is done, the Grid user has no more to interact with the Grid to ensure the completion of his application. When his execution terminates the user is informed by an email.

To benefit from the fact that many genomic applications can easily be split into several independent elementary tasks, we impose some simple programming rules. The main constraint is related to the high-level structure of the code corresponding to the application. This code has to be divided into two different parts: (1) an unique main task and (2) one or several elementary tasks. The functional activities that have to be performed are described within the elementary tasks. On the contrary the role of the main task consists mainly in initiating and coordinating the activations of these elementary tasks. This control activity is done using a set of three additional primitives called SUBMIT, WAIT and KILL. Once the input data needed to execute an elementary task is available (extracted either from the inputs provided to the global application by the user or from the result returned by a elementary task previously executed), the execution of the elementary task is submitted by the main task using the non-blocking primitive SUBMIT. The WAIT primitive allows to block the progress of the main task till all the mentioned elementary tasks have been completed. The WAIT primitive is necessary to create a synchronization point when two sets of elementary tasks have to be executed in sequence. The last primitive allows to stop the execution of the specified elementary tasks. The role of supervision played by the main task also includes the gathering of results returned by the elementary tasks and the final generation of a unique result file accessible from the Web portals. In our approach both elementary tasks and main tasks are taken into account by the load balancing mechanism.

4   A Two-Level Organization

The Domain Level: A domain is a set of heterogeneous nodes which communicate in a synchronous way. A node can be either a resource of the Grid or a machine devoted to control activities. The management of the domain is organized according to the master-slave model: in each domain, a single node named the *master* is selected to manage all the other nodes (named the *slaves*). In particular, the master has to schedule all the tasks carried out in its domain. At any time, the master can check the loads of its slaves. This information is used to compute an appropriate local scheduling of tasks. The composition of the domain is dynamic and consequently the computing capacity of the domain can increase or decrease. We assume that resources always join or leave the domain by requesting to the master. Nodes fail only by crashing. A faulty node behaves according to its specification until it stops prematurely and definitively its computation. As a domain is synchronous, all the crashes can be detected in a reliable way. When the crash of a resource is detected by the master, the master distributes again the tasks (previously allocated to the faulty node) among the remaining resources. The crash of the master has also to be tolerated. Some nodes (the *heirs*) are preselected to replace the master when it disappears. Thanks to a leader election protocol, a single heir is allowed to replace the previous master. If no node can replace the master, all the domain becomes unavailable. Of course, during the computation, the heirs have to keep track of the whole knowledge of their master. As the role of these backups is just to ensure that there is not a single point of failure per domain, we will no more discuss about them.

The Grid Level: The Grid is an asynchronous network connecting different domains. To avoid a flood of the Grid, only one node per domain is allowed to communicate with the other domains, this node is called the *proxy*. All the proxies of the Grid constitute a group. In practice, a single node per domain acts both as the proxy and the master. Like the composition of a domain, the composition of the network of domains is also dynamic. Through invocations of the *join* and *leave* operations, the local administrator of a domain can decide (independently from the other administrators) to add or remove his own domain from the Grid whenever he wants (maintenance and repair, alternating periods of private and public use of the local resources, ...). A domain is unavailable if no node of this domain can act as a proxy/master (occurrence of crash failures) or if the domain has been disconnected from the Grid (occurrence of communication failures, temporary partitions). On one hand, join and leave operations are intentional and broadcast to all the members. On the other hand, evolutions caused by occurrences of failure are unpredictable and are not necessarily observed by all the members of the group. The lack of bounds on communication delays makes impossible to distinguish a slow proxy from a failed proxy. In the proposed solution, each proxy is coupled with a failure detector module which maintains a list of domains that it currently suspects to be unavailable. These failures detectors are said "unreliable" because, the detection of a failed proxy by other proxies may be delayed or an available proxy can be mistaken for a faulty one by some proxy [2]. We assume that the failure detector belongs to the class of failure detectors denoted $\Diamond \mathcal{S}$: this class has been proved to be the weakest one enabling to solve a problem, called the Consensus problem, that is very close to the agreement problems we have to solve.

5   Agreement Problems

To address the resource allocation issue and the dependability issue, we propose a solution based on the use of agreement services by the set of proxies. All the required services are provided by the Eden framework and developed on top of a consensus service. In the consensus problem, each process proposes an initial value and then executes a consensus algorithm until one of the proposed values is decided. Eden makes use of the unreliable failure detector concept to provide Paradis with a reliable group communication service. Eden is based on a Generic Agreement Framework, called GAF, described in [6]. In GAF, different instantiations of the GAF parameters lead to generate different algorithms that solve efficiently several agreement problems. An instantiation is given by a concrete agreement component that implements the interface of a particular agreement service.

We identify three concrete agreement components which are: (1) Atomic Broadcast; It ensures that messages sent to the group of proxies are delivered in the same order to all the members. (2) Weak Interactive Consistency; It ensures that all the members that propose a value decide a same vector of values. The difference with a classical consensus is that the decided value should not be one of the proposed values but a vector of the proposed values. (3) Group Membership; It is in charge of managing the computation and installation of new views whenever it is necessary. One important property of this service states that all members of the group should reach consensus about the current membership (who is in the group and who is not). They share a consistent knowledge of the past history of the group, namely, the *join* and *leave* operations already executed and the failures suspected to have occurred.

Eden publishes a unified interface to the concrete agreement components needed by Paradis. This unified interface exports three operations: BROAD-CAST, PROPOSE and RECEIVE. The BROADCAST operation is used by a proxy to disseminate messages to the other proxies. It relies upon the service of the Atomic Broadcast component to ensure that every proxy will receive messages in the same order. The PROPOSE operation allows a proxy to propose a score for a given task. The Weak Interactive Consistency component used to implement it ensures that every proxy will decide the same vector of scores. Finally, the RECEIVE method is the counterpart of the BROADCAST and PROPOSE operations; it ensures that every proxy will receive decisions on the vector and messages in the same order. The Group Membership component is used to provide a proxy with information about suspected remote proxies. A proxy gets this information through the RECEIVE operation of the Eden interface.

6   Architecture of Paradis

At every domain, the master/proxy has to manage the domain itself and the coordination with the other masters/proxies. These two distinct roles are played by two modules: **Domain Manager** and **Grid Manager**. The two modules and the Web portal communicate via the exchange of notification events.

6.1   The Domain Manager

The execution of a main task or the execution of a set of elementary tasks is asked through the generation of a request. This request is broadcast to all the Domain Managers (DMs) using an atomic broadcast service. All the tasks mentioned in the request will be executed within a single domain but perhaps by different resources of this domain. As the resources are different and have perhaps different workloads, the time required to execute a task may vary from one machine to another. In Paradis, a bid mechanism is used to find, at a given time, the best domain and the best distribution of the requests on the resources.

First let us assume that a request R_i is composed of a single task. When a DM receives R_i from the GM, it determines which resource of its domain is the most appropriate to execute the task by computing, for every resource Res_j, a bid $bid_{i,j}$ (also called a score) representing the capability of Res_j to treat R_i as quickly as possible. Actually, this bid corresponds to the estimation of the time needed to complete R_i (waiting time before execution included). Thus it takes into account the current workload of a resource and the estimated execution time defined when the application has been registered. If R_i cannot be executed on Res_j for incompatibility reasons, then $bid_{i,j} = \infty$. Once the DM has computed the bids for all its resources, it will select the one Res_{win} with the lowest bid. If this bid is over a dynamic threshold (whose initial value is defined for each type of task and increases after each new computation of the bid of the task), the bid is also set to ∞. When the request does not contain a single task to execute, but a bag of tasks, there are many ways to calculate the bids, depending on the strategy you want to implement. You may want to get the first result as soon as possible, or you may prefer to get the whole bunch of results as soon as possible.

Once a bid has been computed, it is transmitted by the DM to the GM. At the grid level, the bids are used to make auctions between the different domains. Thanks to agreement protocols, all the GM agree on a single vector of bids (one per domain of the Grid). The auction is won by the domain that has proposed the lowest bid (different from ∞). The use of a dynamic threshold allows to postpone the decision when the resources are already too busy.

When a DM (which has proposed the lowest bid) receives some request R_i to treat from the Grid Manager (GM), it determines again which resource Res is the most appropriate to execute it. If Res is not available at this moment, then it adds the request to a list $Wait\_Req$ of requests to execute. Once Res is available, the DM executes the task T_i contained in R_i. Then it removes R_i from $Wait\_Req$ and add it to the list Exe_Req of the requests that are being executed. Once T_i is completed and has returned the result $result_i$, Res sends a message $\langle END, R_i, result_i \rangle$ to the DM. The DM removes then the request from Exe_Req and notifies the GM that R_i is completed and has returned the result $result_i$ thanks to the notification $\langle END, R_i, result_i \rangle$.

The task T_i contained in R_i may correspond to a main task. In this case, the execution of T_i generates some new requests R_{new} each time the SUBMIT function is called. In that case, the DM notifies the GM that there is a new request R_{new} to send on the grid thanks to the notification $\langle REQUEST, R_i \rangle$.

In case there is no available resource to execute the task T_i contained in R_i (it is the case if the resource that was supposed to execute it has left the domain), the DM has to notify the GM that it cannot treat R_i. This corresponds to the notification $\langle GIVEUP, R_i \rangle$.

6.2   The Grid Manager

The role of a Grid Manager (GM) is to manage the distribution of the tasks over the grid. It connects its own domain, represented by the Domain Manager (DM), with the other domains. It communicates with the other GMs via Eden and with its coupled DM through notification events. It manages two lists of tasks: a list of requests to allocate (called "Buffer") and a list of requests that are already allocated but not terminated (called "Allocations") .

Figure 1 presents the protocol executed by the GM. It consists of two parts: Actions in Part 1 are in response to messages received from the other GM through Eden; Actions in Part 2 follow notification events coming from the coupled DM or the portal.

Part 2 presents the 4 kinds of notification events a GM can receive from its local DM or from the local portal. When a request is submitted to the grid by a portal or by a DM, the GM is notified of this submission and broadcasts the request to all the GM through the BROADCAST function of EDEN. A notification of the end of the treatment of a request, of the kill of a request, or of the giving up of a request[1] received from the local DM is broadcast likewise.

Any message broadcast by a GM is received by every GM (sender included) via the Receive_Message() function of EDEN. This function returns the four types of messages broadcast by GMs (REQUEST, END, KILL, GIVEUP) in Part 1 and two additional messages types: DECIDE and REMOVE. Part 1 concerns the reactions to these messages.

- $\langle$REQUEST, $R\rangle$ informs the GM that there is a new request R to treat. It adds R to *Buffer*, a FIFO that contains all the requests that are not allocated yet (5).

- $\langle$DECIDE, $[bid_1, bid_2, ..., bid_n]\rangle$ returns the bids of all the domains for request $Req_{current}$ (6). The deterministic function Allocate() determines which domain D_{win} has proposed the best bid (7). The GM stores the information that $Req_{current}$ will be executed on D_{win} in the list Allocations (8). If D_{win} corresponds to the domain of the GM, then the latest forwards $Req_{current}$ to its DM thanks to the function Execute() (10). Now that there is no current auction, a new one can be started, the GM is ready to bid (9).

- $\langle$END, $Req, result\rangle$ informs the GM that the request Req has been treated and returned the result *result*. Then, the GM removes Req from the list Allocations (12) and call the function Store_Result(Req, *result*) (13). This function will not "automatically" store the results: it will store it only if the request had been submitted to the grid by the local DM or the local portal.

- $\langle$KILL, $Req\rangle$ informs the GM that the request Req has to be killed (recall that the code of the main task includes three primitives SUBMIT, WAIT and KILL). The execution of the task is stopped (15) and the request if removed from the list Allocations (16).

- $\langle$GIVEUP, $Req\rangle$ informs the GM that the domain in charge of Req has not been able to treat it. The GM removes Req from Allocations and adds it again to Buffer (19).

- $\langle$REMOVE, $D_k\rangle$ informs the GM that the domain D_k just left the grid (Either after having called the Leave() function of EDEN or having left without a warning. In this case, the leave of D_k have been detected by the Failure Detection

---

[1] This may happen if the domain does not have any resource to treat the request any more.

Grid Manager GM_x
Part 1
(1)   State $\leftarrow$ Join(D_x); Allocations $\leftarrow$ Init_Allocations(State);
(2)   Buffer $\leftarrow$ Init_Buffer(State); ready_to_bid $\leftarrow$ True;
(3)   While (True) do
(4)   switch $msg \leftarrow$ Receive_Message() :
(5)   case $\langle$REQUEST, $Req\rangle$: Buffer $\leftarrow$ Buffer $\cup\{Req\}$;
(6)   case $\langle$DECIDE, $[bid_1, ..., bid_n]\rangle$:
(7) $D_{win} \leftarrow$ Allocate ($[bid_1, ..., bid_n]$);
(8)   Allocations $\leftarrow$ Allocations $\cup\{(Req_{current}, D_{win})\}$;
(9)   ready_to_bid $\leftarrow$ True;
(10)   If $D_{win} = D_x$ then Execute($Req_{current}$); endif;
(11)   case $\langle$END, $Req, result\rangle$:
(12)   Allocations $\leftarrow$ Allocations $\setminus\{(Req, \_)\}$;
(13)   Store_Result ($Req, result$);
(14)   case $\langle$KILL, $Req\rangle$:
(15)   If $\{(Req, D_x)\} \in Allocations$ then Kill(Req); endif;
(16)   Allocations $\leftarrow$ Allocations $\setminus\{(Req, \_)\}$;
(17)   case $\langle$GIVEUP, $Req\rangle$:
(18)   Allocations $\leftarrow$ Allocations $\setminus\{(Req, \_)\}$;
(19)   Buffer $\leftarrow$ Buffer $\cup\{Req\}$;
(20)   case $\langle$REMOVE, $D_k\rangle$:
(21)   If $D_k = D_x$ then exit(); endif;
(22)   Foreach (Req_l, D_k) in Allocations do
(23)   Allocations $\leftarrow$ Allocations $\setminus\{(Req_l, D_k)\}$;
(24)   Buffer $\leftarrow$ Buffer $\cup\{Req_l\}$;
(25)   done;
(26)   endswitch;
(27)   If ready_to_bid then
(28)   If ($Req_{current} \leftarrow$ Extract_Buffer()) not NULL then
(29) $local\_bid \leftarrow$ compute_bid(D_x, $Req_{current}$);
(30)   PROPOSE ($local\_bid$);
(31)   ready_to_bid $\leftarrow$ False;
(32)   endif;
(33)   endif;
(34) done;
Part 2
(35) While (True) do
(36)   Upon reception of notification (from portal or D_x), notification $\in$
(37) $\{\langle$REQUEST, $Req\rangle, \langle$END, $Req, result\rangle,$
(38) $\langle$GIVEUP, $Req\rangle, \langle$KILL, $Req\rangle\}$
(39)   Broadcast (notification);
(40) done;

Fig. 1. Grid Manager's protocol

module of Eden.). The GM removes from the list *Allocations* all the requests
that had been allocated to D_k (23-24) and add them to the list *Buffer*.

When there is no current auction being processed, a new one can start if there is some request to allocate in the buffer (27-28). The execution of Extract_Buffer leads to remove the first request from the list Buffer and to store it in $Req_{current}$. Then, the GM calls the function compute_bid(D_x, $Req_{current}$) (29). This call makes the local DM compute the bid for the execution of $Req_{current}$ on the resources of the domain. The GM sends then this bid to Eden (30) and puts a lock on ready_to_bid to avoid concurrent bids (31).

7   Conclusion

This paper presents PARADIS, an adaptive system based on a Consensus building block that has been designed and implemented in a Grid dedicated to genomic applications. Resource allocation and dependability are issues that require a continuous adaptation to the changing computing environment. An agreement service is used by all the domains to acquire the same set of accurate data describing the current state of the Grid. Based on this unanimous observation, each domain can enact the right adaptation to react to the discovery of changes.

References

1. J. Almond and M. Romberg, The Unicore project: Uniform access to supercomputing over the web. *Proc. of the 40th Cray User Group Meeting*, 1998.
2. T. Chandra and S. Toueg, Unreliable Failure Detectors for Reliable Distributed Systems. *JACM*, 43(2):225-267, 1996.
3. W. Cirne, F. Brasileiro, N. Andrade, L. Costa, A. Andrade, R. Novaes, and M. Mowbray, Labs of the World, Unite!!! *J. of Grid Computing*, 4(3): 225-246. 2006.
4. I. Foster and C. Kesselman, "The Globus Project": A Status Report. *Proc. of the 7th IEEE Heterogeneous Computing Workshop*, pp. 4–19, 1998.
5. M. Hurfin, J.-P. Le Narzul, J. Pley, and P. Rapin Parvdy, A Fault-Tolerant Protocol for Resource Allocation in a Grid dedicated to Genomic Applications *Proc. of the 5th Int. Conference on Parallel Processing and Applied Mathematics, (PPAM 2003)*.
6. M. Hurfin, R. Macdo, M. Raynal, and F. Tronel, A General Framework to Solve Agreement Problems. *Proc. of the 18th IEEE Int. Symposium on Reliable Distributed Systems (SRDS'99)*, pages 56-65, 1999.
7. J. In, P. Avery, R. Cavanaugh, L. Chitnis, M. Kulkarni and S. Ranka, SPHINX: A Fault-Tolerant System for Scheduling in Dynamic Grid Environments. 19th International Parallel and Distributed Processing Symposium (IPDPS 2005).
8. Mobach, D.G.A. Overeinder, B.J. Brazier, F.M.T., A WS-Agreement Based Resource Negotiation Framework for Mobile Agents , In: *Scalable Computing 2006: Practice and Experience*, Vol. 7, No 1, pp. 23-36.
9. X. Zhang, F. Junqueira, M. Hiltunen, K. Marzullo, and R.D. Schlichting, Replicating Nondeterministic Services on Grid Environments. *Proc. of the 15th International Symposium on High Performance Distributed Computing (HPDC-15)*, June 2006.
10. X. Zhang, D. Zagorodnov, M. Hiltunen, K. Marzullo and R.D. Schlichting, Fault-tolerant Grid Services Using Primary-Backup: Feasibility and Performance. *Proc. of the IEEE International Conference on Cluster Computing*, pages 105–114,2004.

An Open Environment for Compositional Software Development

Ewa Ochmańska

Warsaw University of Technology, Faculty of Transport
00-662 Warsaw, Poland
`och@it.pw.edu.pl`

Abstract. The paper describes a concept of an open cooperative web platform for developing, designing and executing "compositional" applications, here interpreted as instances dynamically composed of three kinds of semantically interrelated resources. The resources include interoperable components, textual schemas describing their functionality and structuring rules as well as textual definitions of application structure and content. The described open software environment is built on top of emerging XML based standards and technologies of web and grid services. Its functionality comprises managing application resources and transforming them into contextual GUI which supports activities of developing, composing and executing applications. Users and developers contribute to evolutional growth of application resources by creating new definitions, specifying new schemas and implementing components. Semantic Web concepts with RDF/RDF Schema language are applied to organize resource pools accessible in the environment framework.

1 Introduction

The imposing progress of software technologies supporting web based distributed computing, certainly due to the open collaborative practices applied for developing related standards and tools, has led to important solutions for sharing, combining and reusing information, strongly based on the XML technology. The vision of Semantic Web, as a pool of web information resources integrated by machines into a global database, inspired tools describing data semantics like RDF and OWL.

The efforts concerned in sharing, combining and reusing application software to process this information have resulted in service-oriented approach, presently dominating but still less mature. The above mentioned collaborative practices did not prove equally helpful for the needs of application software development. In spite (and in some extent as a result) of the constantly growing use of Internet information resources and web based applications, there is still deficiency of effective principles for producing software and productive re-using of existing software on the web application level. In recent years many activities have been concentrated on searching and elaborating of methods for reusing ready-made pieces of software – leading to component based solutions, and of procedures and tools for cooperative software development [1, 2].

Increasing demand for sharing information and application resources across the web resulted in the emerging technology of web services. Service-oriented concepts

G. Min et al. (Eds.): ISPA 2006 Ws, LNCS 4331, pp. 175–184, 2006.

are currently perceived as most promising solution for Internet based heterogeneous distributed applications. Web services supplemented by state awareness have been also adopted in the context of grid infrastructures, providing middleware platform for transparent controlled use of computing resources by means of cooperative web based technologies [3].

The paper attempts to propose a particular light-weight approach to implement ideas of collaborative and component oriented software engineering in a loosely coupled frame of open distributed environment, in an infrastructure of web and grid services. The idea of the environment openness implies rather "open software resources" for virtual communities of users and developers than the classical meaning of "open source software". The approach focuses on creating methodology for sharing and evolving software resources in the way similar to that in which currently data and knowledge resources are being shared and evolved in the web. Functionality for using and developing component-oriented software for various application domains is built on top of above mentioned XML based web technologies. Presented solutions are founded on a methodology for defining, creating and executing application instances, which has been developed and previously applied for PDES simulation models [4]. Here the method is generalized to cope with different categories of "compositional" applications and with other functional areas of the proposed environment. Such an environment will support virtual communities of users and developers, involved in developing, composing and exploiting various categories of software applications, for which certain common characteristics can be defined on the category-specific level.

On general, method-specific level – developing, composing and dynamic creating of application instances is category independent, however relying on descriptions of their structure and content according to specifications of their semantic categories, being processed and transformed as corresponding XML based descriptive resources, organized by means of RDF statements. XML Schema is used for defining general language and its category-specific dialects to describe compositional applications. Using XML/XML Schema for description and validation is complemented with a somewhat novel concept of inverse transformation of resulting schemas to support user oriented functionality of the environment by a context-dependent GUI.

Model-driven in principle, the presented light-weight approach builds on popular XML related web standards. Nevertheless, it can be utilized as a supporting level also for heavier, strictly defined solutions. Dependencies between application content description and implementation of components may be established basing on any of presently available methods for component based software modeling and automatic code generation, which tend to XML. This is the case e.g. for OMG solutions related to MDA with UML/XML and UML/RDF transformation [5].

The second section explains ideas of applying web technologies in the framework of three-dimensional XML based processing of application resources in the proposed software environment. Its interrelated functional areas: • composing and executing applications; • supporting user/developer in exploiting and creating application resources; • providing and managing distributed pools of resources for virtual communities of users/developers are discussed in the successive sections. Concluding remarks point new semantic web technologies as a horizon for further research.

2   Web Technologies Used in the Environment

The concept of compositional application bases on the observation that particular categories of component-based applications can be built of similar types of similarly structured components. An instance of such application can be dynamically composed of semantically interrelated descriptive and programmatic resources: textual schema describing components and their possible composition for a semantic category of applications; textual definition describing contents and structure of an application; programmatic implementation of interoperable components.

Assuming that the above mentioned textual descriptive resources are formulated using XML notations, we enter the broad area of existing and dynamically emerging XML related web standards and technologies, providing us with wide possibilities to organize a user- and developer-oriented distributed environment for compositional applications:

- Firstly, XML based definition of an application structure and content can be validated against an appropriate schema describing semantics of the corresponding application category, and the application instance can be composed by a standard implementation of an XML parser, the same for any application of a given category and basically common for any category of applications designed in the frame of the presented methodology.

- Secondly, XML-based schemas and definitions describing application semantics can be treated by the rich arsenal of XML transformation tools in order to generate sophisticated interface for user/developers, guiding them though activities related with executing applications, defining them in accordance with proper semantic rules, specifying and implementing new categories of applications.

- Thirdly, the whole world of XML-based technologies for distributed web and grid architectures is available to organize schemas, defini-tions and components into virtual pools of distributed resources for compositional applications, accessible through communities of users and developers in an open software environment.

The functional areas corresponding to the above mentioned concepts are organized in three overlapping circles on Fig1., thus depicting their mutual correlations. The centre of the figure, where all the circles are intersecting, represents resources for compositional applications, as the basis for each sub-area of the environment functionality.

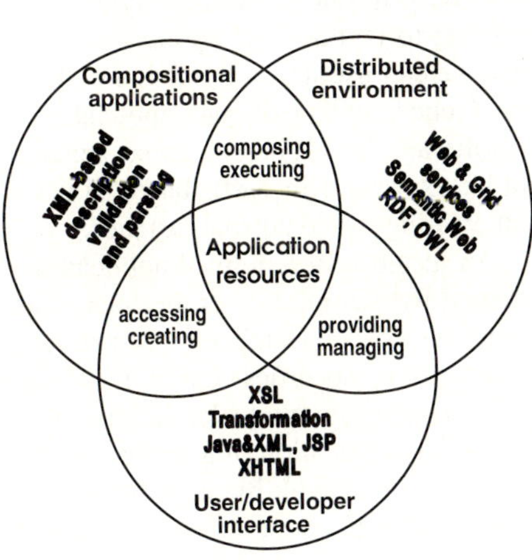

Fig. 1. XML-related standards and technologies supporting the open software environment

The functions of composing and executing applications, using XML-based standards and tools of the left upper circle of the figure to validate resources and to process them into executable instances of applications, are self-contained and independent of underlying system. A compositional application can be automatically executed after instantiating a proper structure of components by parsing its definition validated against corresponding schema, without any intervention of a user, on a single machine as well as in a configuration distributed across the web.

The second functional area concerns accessing application resources in order to use them as well as creating new resources by defining applications, specifying semantic categories and creating corresponding components. All these functions are placed in the sub-area marked by the lower circle on Fig. 1, representing intelligent contextual GUI driven by XSL Transformations completed by other standards and tools to bi-directionally transform information between a virtual pool of application resources and a user. The second circle augments the system configuration by the presence of users, whose actual access to the environment is governed by the third functional area.

As a matter of fact the user-oriented functionality, to support exploiting and evolving application resources, is designed for virtual communities of users collaborating in the distributed environment rather then for a single user. The right upper circle on the figure introduces the functions and means to embed the environment in the web – again making use of XML-based nature of resources for compositional applications. Those functions, focused on providing and managing application resources, will be supported by tools of Semantic Web on top of the web and grid services architecture.

3 Instantiating an Application

Compositional application semantics comprises description of possible types of its components and rules for their possible structuring to compose an application. After specifying a schema describing such semantics, we can use it as a guideline to define applications conforming to the specification. Hence, compositional application is understood as a piece of component-based software belonging to some semantic category, for which rules of composition can be expressed in XML based notation. Interconnected elements of Fig. 2 participate in creating its executable instance.

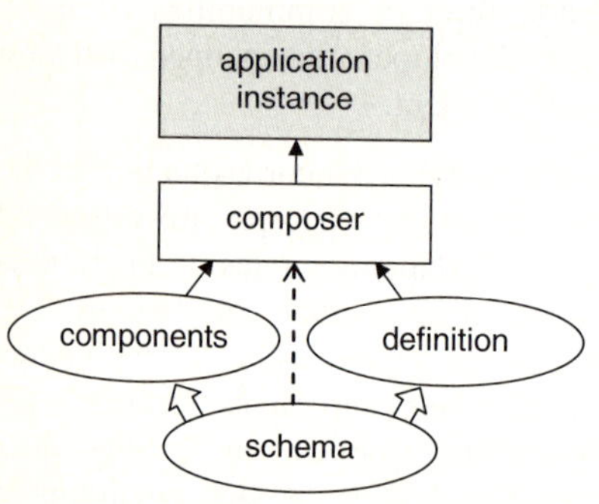

Fig. 2. Composing an application instance

An instance of a defined application is created by a composer as the interrelated structure of instantiated components. A definition specifies components and their structuring (mutual relations) for a particular application of a given semantic category described by a corresponding schema. A schema describes components' semantics, their interfaces and composing rules for a specific application category.

The thin black arrows on the figure mark input and output of executable program used for composing application:

its input comprises a definition of an application and a set of components, its output embodies an executable instance of application. The dashed arrow represents validating role of a schema for the application composer. The thick white arrows mark two semantic dependencies, crucial for the consistency of application resources:

- A textual definition of application has to be derived from a proper textual schema.
- Application components have to be implemented in accordance with their textual description enclosed in a proper textual schema.

Expressing semantic rules for compositional applications in XML-based languages, the basic approach consists in applying XML format to define an application and XML Schema to specify its semantic category. The composer program instantiates an application during standard process of parsing an XML document, validated against a proper schema. Such approach has been proved useful in the case of DES applications [4]. (An example, outlining an XSD schema for an application category from this domain, is shown in Section 6.) However, relatively new standards for describing data semantic concepts in the frame of web resources, can offer stronger means to express semantics of compositional applications, as we suggest in conclusions.

The issues of dependencies between textual description of component semantics and their implementation have to be considered, taking into account the state-of-the-art methods for software resources description and automated generation, in particular implementing components as Java classes in Java & XML development frame.

Both dependencies marked by thick white arrows on the figures are to be forced by the regime of data-driven GUI to the software environment, with functionality derived from the context of descriptive resources for particular application categories, described in the following section.

4   Contextual User Interface to the Application Resources

The pool of resources for compositional applications will be used and evolved by participants of virtual communities, acting in the distributed web based software environment with functional structure shown on Fig. 3. Depending on the users' scope of interest, aims and competences, they can play following different roles listed below in order of increasing expertise:

- user, just executing some defined earlier application, providing proper input data and consuming results
- advanced user, defining application of some selected category, according to his or her particular needs
- developer/programmer introducing a new category of applications to a pool of resources, accessible by his or her virtual community, by specifying schema and providing (implementing and/or referring) proper components.

All the above mentioned activities of users can be performed in the frame of a sophisticated contextual GUI, derived from application descriptive resources by means of XML transformations. As it is shown on Fig. 3, transforming application resources to that "intelligent" GUI lies in the central point of the environment functional structure and supports all its basic functions.

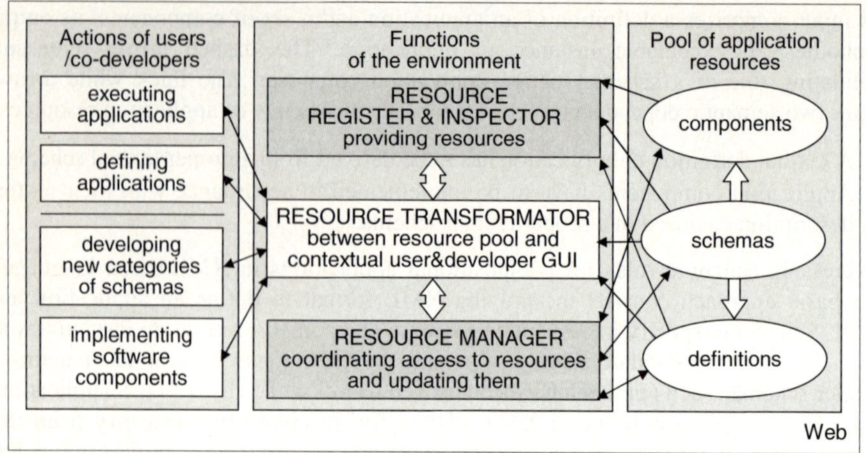

Fig. 3. Functional structure of the open software environment

Textual interface to the environment requires some "acting regulations" for particular roles of users and developers, to formally design corresponding GUI functionalities as well as mechanisms for proper transformation of application resources. Using existing XSL standards for XML transformation, completed with Java APIs for XML and JSP, the functions of GUI (hosted by a web browser or another client agent) can be automatically generated from semantic descriptions contained in XML definitions and schemas. E.g. a schema can be transformed into a contextual creator guiding users through successive steps of defining applications belonging to a particular semantic category, but tailored to their needs.

Furthermore, depending on the roles played by users, their GUI-based actions produce "feedback" information completing and augmenting accessible application resources. Definitions, schemas and components – produced by them inside their contextual GUI – have to be transformed into proper formats before adding to the resource pool. Software engine performing those bi-directional transformations co-operates with other basic parts of the system. Two of them are also shown on the figure. Register/ inspector and manager participate in accessing resources as well as in organizing and managing them. Both those parts represent another functional area of the presented environment, which is discussed in the next section.

The issues of instantiating and executing compositional applications seem to be omitted on the figure. Note however, that the instantiation procedure described in the previous section can also be viewed as an act of transforming application resources, performed in the background of user-oriented interface. Controlling distributed execution of application components, which should also be considered in the frame of the presented approach, has to be placed in its third functional area, as related to the distributed net configuration of the software environment.

5 Underlying Distributed System Architecture

Attempting to implement the open cooperative environment on the web platform, we organize pools of resources for compositional applications, to be accessible for virtual communities of their users and developers, in a loosely coupled distributed system architecture following current services-oriented trends, as outlined on Fig. 4.

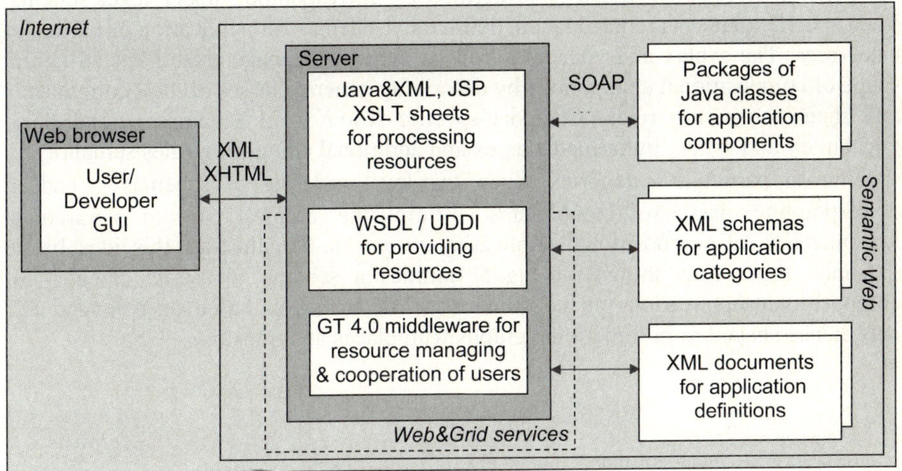

Fig. 4. An architectural outline of the environment

The following aspects of the above outline are to be noticed.

- Middleware layer of open source Globus 4.0 Toolkit [6] is responsible for managing application resources and organizing virtual communities of their users and developers. Management concerns consistency of application resources, access rights to resource pools, security, quality of execution etc.
- Providing access to automatically updated and selected resources distributed in the web demands an effective way to register and find them, which is offered by platform-independent mechanisms for accessing and discovering, proper to web and grid services with WSDL/UDDI standards and their extensions.
- Grid services also bring in additional feature of state-consciousness useful for the more advanced mode of composing and executing application as a set of distributed concurrent components.
- Communicating with resources in distributed web based environment – as well those in textual XML format as programmatic ones – is organized with use of SOAP communication protocol.
- Assuming users/developers communication with the environment via web browser, the formats resulting of transforming application resources to GUI content, discussed in the previous section, follow XML/XHTML standards.
- As we may have to do with advanced semantics to describe certain categories of application resources, and their general compositional rules as well – solutions based on Semantic Web concepts come to play.

6 Organizing Resources for Compositional Applications

The resources for compositional applications can be organized hierarchically. After deciding a background structure for compositional applications of a certain domain, the general description language is defined by corresponding upper level schema. Then specific dialects are introduced, defined by schemas for application of particular categories. The syntax and vocabulary of the general language establishes structural shape of compositional applications by describing general classes of their components and their composing rules. Category-specific lower level schemas extend basic vocabulary and syntax by refined classes and additional composing rules semantically specific to particular categories. Such two-level ordering of schemas – and of corresponding classes of components – forms the simplest case of hierarchical systemization of compositional application resources. To illustrate this idea by an example, the listing shown on Fig. 5 outlines a schema for some category of compositional applications in the domain of PDES models based on extended P/T nets, hence shaped as bi-directional graphs with places and transitions.

```xml
<?xml version="1.0"?>
<xsd:schema  xmlns:xsd="http://www.w3.org/2001/XMLSchema"
             xmlns="http://model.resources.edu">
    <!--semantic clases of places-->
    <xsd:include schemaLocation="http://model.resources.edu/xsd/places.xsd"/>
    <!--semantic clases of transitions-->
    <xsd:include schemaLocation="http://model.resources.edu/xsd/transitions.xsd"/>
    <!--general classes of place, transition and process,
        lists of general places and transitions, basic rules for bi-graph composition-->
    <xsd:redefine schemaLocation="http://model.resources.edu/xsd/ptnet.xsd"/>
        <xsd:complexType name="ListOfPlaces">
            <xsd:complexContent>
                <xsd:restriction base="ListOfPlaces">
                    <!--redefined list with category-specific semantic classes of places-->
                    ...
                </xsd:restriction>
            </xsd:complexContent>
        </xsd:complexType>
        <xsd:complexType name="ListOfTransitions">
            <xsd:complexContent>
                <xsd:restriction base="ListOfTransitions">
                    <!--redefined list with category-specific semantic classes of transitions-->
                    ...
                </xsd:restriction>
            </xsd:complexContent>
        </xsd:complexType>
    </xsd:redefine>
    <xsd:complexType name="ThisCategory">
        <xsd:complexContent>
            <xsd:extension base="Proces"/>
            <!--category-specific composition rules for semantic components-->
            ...
        </xsd:complexContent>
    </xsd:complexType>
</xsd:schema>
```

Fig. 5. An outline of a schema for a category of compositional applications

In general, resources can be organized in more levels of hierarchy – by introducing other domains, sub-domains or sub-categories. Moreover, the resulting trees are not necessarily disjoint; they may have common nodes, for it is possible (and desirable) that some components, along with their descriptive and programmatic resources, are used (re-used) by several categories. Note that the described hierarchical dependence concerns application schemas – derived by redefining (extending, restricting) of higher-level elements, as well as components – implemented by diversifying and specializing higher-level classes. The third kind of resources, application definitions are created at the semantic category level; however a horizontal dependence may be taken into account when merging definitions (possibly of different semantic categories) into a new definition of more composite application.

All application resources reside in the web and of course they are identified by their URIs. XML-based descriptive kinds of resources are organized by target namespaces of schemas for application categories according to their origins, levels of semantic classifications etc. The resulting ways of identification are used in mutual references between particular resources: Schemas for application categories refer to their semantic fragments and higher-level ancestors. Schemas of semantic components refer to their implementations. Definitions refer to their parts (member definitions) and to proper schemas. All above mentioned references are integrating resources needed to compose an application instance.

In spite of those built-in references in the form defined by XML/XML Schema specifications, we need an independent description of mutual dependencies between various resources accessible in virtual pools of the presented software environment. The following table illustrates the principle of describing compositional application resources by RDF statements. The rows contain exemplary RDF graphs for two types of references between resources of the category of applications outlined on Fig. 5.

Table 1. RDF graphs of references between application resources

Type of references	RDF graph
From schema for application category to its ancestor and to schemas for semantic components	http://model.resources.edu/xsd/thisCategory.xsd *http://resources.edu/references/base* http://model.resources.edu/xsd/ptnet.xsd *http://model.resources.edu/semantic/places* http://model.resources.edu/xsd/places.xsd *http://model.resources.edu/semantic/transitions* http://model.resources.edu/xsd/transitions.xsd
From schema for semantic places to implemented semantic place components	http://model.resources.edu/xsd/places.xsd *http://resources.edu/references/component* http://model.resources.educlasses/p1.class ... *http://resources.edu/references/component* http://model.resources.educlasses/pN.class

7 Conclusions

The approach presented in the paper has been applied in the modelling & simulation area, using XML data description meta-language in conjunction with XML Schema. Aiming for generalization of this idea to encompass a variety of semantic application categories in different domains, stronger semantic means should be introduced, as extensions to emerging XML-based standards of Semantic Web. General semantic rules for compositional approach as well as category-specific rules for particular semantic categories of applications can be described by languages for data and knowledge semantics like OWL, possibly extended by "annotations" to these standards specific for compositional approach.

Semantic XML-based concepts, widely used to organize (structure, describe, find) data and services, should be extended for organizing (structuring, describing, finding, composing and developing) compositional applications. Transforming pure semantic (textual) information about application categories and particular applications into dynamic, context dependent GUI will support process of using and augmenting software resources by virtual communities of software users and developers.

An important feature of the proposed distributed software environment is its implicit self-evolving. The described methodology and architectural frame can stimulate constant spontaneous but controlled growth of compositional software resources.

The approach is service-oriented, basing on the widespread technologies of web services and on their grid-oriented functionalities. Except for "compositionality", it poses in fact no limits for application specifics. Any new semantic category can be introduced by means of textual XML-based description in correspondence with proper software components.

It should be stressed that the proposed approach does not restrict compositional applications to service-oriented frame. Current standards of web and grid services are just exploited in order to provide the functionality of the environment. Nature of application components can be strongly diversified among various application categories, going outside and over classical definition of component, and in particular representing web services.

References

1. Zhou J., Stålhane.T.: A Component-based Reference Model for Web-based Systems, Proc. the 8th IASTED International Conference on Software Engineering and Applications, November 9-11, 2004, MIT Cambridge, MA, USA
2. Goguen J., Kai Lin. Web-based Support for Cooperative Software Engineering. Annals of Software Engineering, Vol.12, No.1, 2001
3. Open Grid Services Infrastructure (OGSI). http://www.ggf.org/ogsi-wg
4. Ochmańska E.: An Approach to Web-oriented Discrete Event Simulation Modeling. Proceedings of the ICCS, Kraków 2004. LNCS 3036, Springer-Verlag 2004
5. MDA Specifications: The Architecture of Choice for a Changing World. www.omg.org/mda/specs.htm
6. Globus Toolkit 4.0 Release Manuals. http://www.globus.org/toolkit/docs/4.0/

A Survivable Distributed Sensor Networks Through Stochastic Models

Dong Seong Kim and Jong Sou Park

Network Security Lab., Hankuk Aviation University, Seoul, Korea
{dongseong, jspark1}@gmail.com

Abstract. The previous security architectures and mechanisms for distributed sensor networks only focus on confidentiality, integrity and authentication. The distributed sensor networks should have the ability to provide essential services in the presence of attacks and failures, and recover full services in a timely manner. In this paper, we present stochastic models for survivable distributed sensor networks. We define states of cluster based sensor networks and analyze the distributed sensor networks using stochastic models in mathematical manner. The evaluation results with the proof of concept scenario show our approach has a feasibility to design survivable distributed sensor networks.

1 Introduction

The security for distributed sensor networks is one of the challenging issues. Recently, a lot of studies have proposed survey on security [6, 9, 18, 21] and security architecture [1, 8, 11, 16, 17, 23] and security mechanisms [2, 7, 12, 15] for distributed sensor networks. They mostly focus on security in terms of confidentiality, integrity and authentication. The distributed sensor networks should provide their essential function in the presence of failures, intrusions. This property can be considered as survivability of distributed sensor networks. Over the past few decades, a considerable number of studies have been made on survivability for conventional networks [3, 4, 8, 10]. But previous studies on survivability for conventional networks are infeasible since they haven't considered the resource constraints on sensor nodes in distributed sensor networks. Also, several studies [13, 14, 19] have been conducted on survivability for sensor networks. However, they use 'survivability of sensor networks' in term of link connectivity and stability between sensor nodes. The connectivity and stability issues are also important to survivability of sensor networks but they are lack of consideration of security. We view our approach as an initial contribution towards designing a survivable distributed sensor networks. In order to provide survivability of distributed sensor network, in this paper, we propose stochastic models for survivable distributed sensor networks. We simplify cluster based distributed sensor networks as stochastic models and evaluate the models through numerical model analysis with proof-of-concept scenarios.

G. Min et al. (Eds.): ISPA 2006 Ws, LNCS 4331, pp. 185 – 194, 2006.

2 Related Works

There are a lot of surveys on security for distributed sensor networks survey. In this paper, we introduce some relevant survey papers here. For securing a wireless sensor network, Law and Havinga [9] summarized how to secure a wireless sensor network using host and network-based defense guidelines. Shaikh *et al.*[18] proposed hypothetical security framework for the distributed wireless sensor networks in order to achieve highest level security and overall energy efficiency. The paper only addresses requirements for securing distributed sensor networks in viewpoint of key management, routing protocol, intrusion detection system, and trust management. F. Hu *et al.* [6] analyzed security challenges in wireless sensor networks and summarized key issues and current solutions. There are several works in the area of security architecture for distributed sensor networks. Walters *et al.* [21] surveyed the major topics in wireless sensor network security, and presented the obstacles and the requirements in the sensor networks security. Undercoffer *et al.* [1] proposed security protocol for sensor networks. Zia *et al.* [23] proposed a security framework for wireless sensor networks. Schmidt *et al.* [17] proposed a security architecture for mobile ad hoc network. The proposed design and prototype implementation results of pairwise key management and cipher for a cluster based sensor networks. Savola *et al.* [16] proposed an architecture for security management in self organizing mobile to estimate security level of ad hoc network nodes. This architecture is very similar to that of distributed intrusion detection system in mobile ad hoc network. Liu *et al.* [11] presented a design of a generic software architecture based on tiny active agents for sensor networks and identify the key research issues for optimizing the architecture for the constrained environment in sensor networks. As the subcomponents of security architecture, A. Perrig *et al.* [15] proposed SPINS which has two secure building blocks; SNEP provides data confidentiality, two party data authentication, and data freshness and microTESLA provides authenticated broadcast. K. Jones *et al.* [7] proposed a new frequency hopping strategy. Park *et al.* [12] proposed a lightweight security protocol particularly, rekeying mechanism. Karlof *et al.* [2] propose a link layer security architecture named TinySec. However, most of previous literature only concerns data confidentially, integrity, authentication, and other cryptographic countermeasure. In typical application scenarios, sensor nodes are spread randomly over the terrain under scrutiny and collect sensor data. Sensor network has to fulfill its mission, in a timely manner, in the face of intrusions, attacks, accident and failures in hostile environment. This is connected to survivability. R. Ellison *et al.* [4] proposed how to design survivable network system with a case study. But this is only for general network system design not for resource constrained distributed sensor networks. Liu *et al.* [10] proposed a general framework for network survivability. This paper showed how to derive survivability measures based on different definitions. Knight *et al.* [8] surveyed and summarized the concept of survivability. In this paper, we follow the definition of survivability introduced by Ellison *et al.* [3]; survivability is the ability of a network computing system to provide essential services in the presence of attacks and failures, and recover full services in a timely manner. Although K. Paul *et al.* [14] proposed survivable ad hoc networks; they only considered survivability in terms of link stability and path stability in mathematical form. Paul *et al.* [13] also addressed survivability of ad hoc network in terms of routing and transmission algorithm. Snow [19] also addressed the reliability and survivability of wireless and mobile networks. But they didn't pay attention to survivability with respect to security concepts. S. Zhu *et al.* [22] proposed LEAP (Localized Encryption and Authentication Protocol) and a key management protocol for sensor networks. They analyzed LEAP and survivability only in viewpoint of key management such individual key, group key cluster key and pairwise shared key. We propose a survivable distributed sensor network model which focuses on survivability related to security point of view. Our proposed model and its description will be presented in next section.

3   A Survivable Distributed Sensor Networks Model

The realistic implementation and test for distributed sensor networks is not easy. The stochastic model is easier to design and simulate distributed sensor networks. In order to reflect realistic sensor network model to our stochastic model, we use a cluster based model for distributed sensor networks due to its advantages in terms of cost and energy [5]. The conceptual example of cluster based model is depicted in Figure 1. The sensor nodes are deployed in some applications fields. The sensor nodes select a cluster head nodes and build several clusters. The sensor nodes exchange necessary keys to utilize security mechanisms applied in distributed sensor networks [7, 11, 15, 22]. Each sensor node send collected data to its cluster head node, and cluster head node send the collected data to base station. A base station is connected with the access point to the legacy network such as Internet or satellite communication. We assume that base stations are secure against any type of attacks. Sensor network can be compromised by adversary. According to state of each sensor node in a cluster, the state of cluster also can be expressed. We model the life time of each cluster consisting of sensor nodes as a finite set of states. The transition of a state can be influenced by many parameters (the parameters reflect state of sensor networks will be mentioned in section 4) and it exhibits random behavior. This randomness can be modeled by some well known stochastic models such as Poisons process, Markov Chain, semi-Markov process and so on [20]. The stochastic models are managed by base stations or higher level by user. Our model utilizes software rejuvenation method to provide survivability of distributed sensor networks. The more detailed stochastic model is presented in section 3. Our model monitors the state of each cluster and counteract with respect to the state of cluster based on stochastic model. If a sensor node in a cluster is compromised (e.g. cluster 1 in Figure 1), the stochastic model changes its state according to the stochastic model. The software rejuvenation method kills the malicious nodes and isolates the node out of a single sensor cluster. But if total number of compromised sensor nodes is larger than some predefined threshold value (see cluster 2, in Figure 2), the cluster will not be operated any more. Then, the overall sensor networks also exclude the cluster. If head node gets compromised (Cluster 4 in Figure 1), it's a very critical case, the sensor node with the transmission range of the head node have to immigrate to other cluster. Global intrusion detection systems in sensor networks should monitor and detect malicious node and report them to another sensor cluster head and add them to their new cluster members. The proposed stochastic models are presented in next subsection.

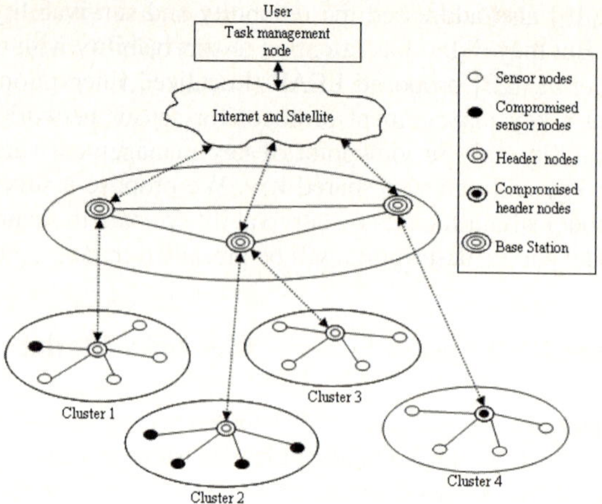

Fig. 1. A Cluster based Model for Distributed Sensor Networks

3.1 Semi-markov Process for a Cluster Based Sensor Network Model

As the behaviors of attacks, system responses to the attacks, intrusion detection, and repairing mechanism cause sojourn time of some states to be non-exponential. Simple Markov chain cannot represent this system and we build a cluster based model as semi-Markov Process (SMP). SMP model for cluster based sensor network for distributed sensor networks is depicted in Figure 2. In this paper, our model consisted of 7 states; healthy state H, suspicious state S, compromised state C. The cluster starts with *healthy state H*, *adaptation state A*, *rejuvenation state R*, *graceful degradation state GD*, and *failed state F*. In order to build survivable distributed sensor network, the model have to keep the cluster in healthy state as long as possible. If any kind of intrusions into the resistance mechanisms is occurred using known or unknown vulnerabilities, the cluster transits its state to *susceptible state S*. This state is a critical one because adversary wants to exploit the vulnerabilities and try to make sensor nodes compromised. If the intrusion detection systems for distributed sensor networks can successfully detect the state, it takes necessary actions and the cluster returns back to the *healthy state*. A successful exploitation by the adversary causes the system to transit its state to *compromised state C*, and then unwanted damage follows. Consequently, the model can be represented by the states {H, S, C}. For the simplicity of the model, we assume time and effort by adversary equivalently and use interchangeably. Traditional security mechanism has little countermeasure to take actions after attacks. If intrusion detection system can identify the compromised state of a cluster of sensor networks, it triggers the transition from *compromised state C* to *adaptation state A*. This is a decision making state and the actions of survivability commence from here. It assesses the impact of damages occurred and determines the appropriate strategies for recovery of sensor networks. The actions to be taken depend on the requirements of the survivability and types of attack detected. If the critical requirements of the system are integrity and confidentiality, then system is switched to *rejuvenation state R*. We adopt software rejuvenation to counteract the adversary's actions by killing or resetting the malicious node(s) and/or compromised node(s) online and brought the cluster to *healthy state H*. It is noted that only compromised nodes are killed or reset. And if it is sensed that the rejuvenation would not be successful, it will entered to *failed state F*. On the other hand, if the requirement is availability of the system, then adaptation mechanism triggers the system to enter *graceful degradation state GD* where it provides minimum and essential services. Accordingly, we can formulate our model responses during and after attack by the states {*A, R, GD, F*}. Unlike the traditional security systems which have deterministic responses, this response model exhibits randomness in determining the appropriate strategies for recovery, discovering attacks and the assessment of damages. Therefore, the stochastic model can be represented as {X (t): t ≥ 0} and state space X_s = {*H, S, C, A, GD, R, F*}. In next sub section, we analyze the SMP model using embedded Discrete Time Markov Chain (DTMC).

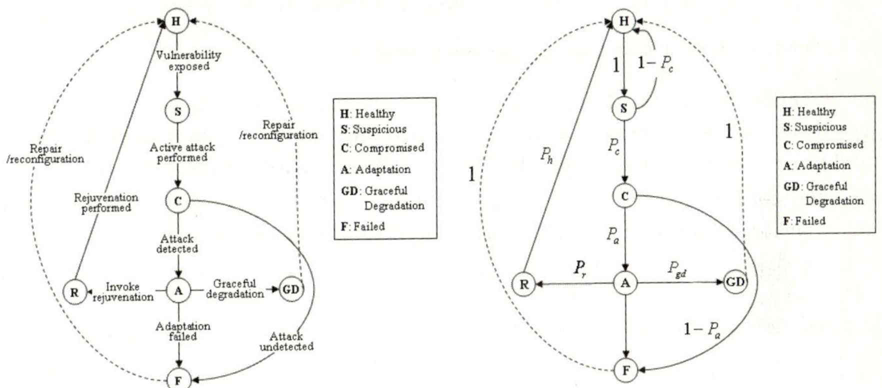

Fig. 2. Semi Markov Process model for a cluster based sensor networks

Fig. 3. State Transition Diagram of Embedded DTMC of SMP model

3.2 Discrete Time Markov Chain of SMP

The transition from one state to another in an SMP can be thought as two steps transitions logically. In the first stage, the process remains in state *i* for an amount of time given by h_i (t), where h_i (t) is the sojourn time distribution of state *i*. In the next stage, the process changes its state from *i* to *j* with the transition probability P_{ij} [16]. Therefore, SMP is a combination of transition probability matrix **P** and a vector of sojourn time distribution h_i (t). As a result, the SMP shows the behavior of a Markov Chain at the time of state transition. Figure 3 depicts the embedded Discrete Time Markov Chain (DTMC) of the SMP model. According to the state transition diagram of Figure 3, the steady state probabilities and other parameters of model are denoted as;

P_c = Probability that makes successful attack when the system is in suspicious state

P_a = Probability that successful attack is detected by intrusion detection system

P_r = Probability that software rejuvenation is triggered by adaptation mechanisms

P_h = Probability that software rejuvenation turns the system to healthy state

P_{gd} = Probability that system goes to graceful degradation state

h_H = Mean sojourn time the system remains in healthy state

h_S = Mean sojourn time the adversary to exploit vulnerabilities until attack is successful

h_C = Mean sojourn time the intrusion detection system to detect the attack and trigger the adaptation state

h_A = Mean sojourn time to apply the appropriate strategy for recovery

h_R = Mean sojourn time to apply rejuvenation

h_{GD} = Mean sojourn time the system is in graceful degradation state under attacks

h_F = Mean sojourn time the system is in failure state

Our intention is only to describe and analyze the steady state model. The transient analysis of the model requires actual probability distribution of the parameters which is out of the scope of this paper. The state probability vectors of the embedded DTMC and SMP are $v[v_H, v_S, v_C, v_A, v_R, v_{GD}, v_F]$ and $\pi[\pi_H, \pi_S, \pi_C, \pi_A, \pi_R, \pi_{GD}, \pi_F]$, respectively. To obtain the steady state probabilities, we need to solve the equation

$$v = vP \tag{1}$$

P is the transient matrix of DTMC, we compute the steady state probabilities of $\{\pi_i,\ i \in X_s\}$ of the SMP by using equation,

$$\pi_i = \frac{v_i . h_i}{\sum_j v_j . h_j} \tag{2}$$

Where h_i is the mean sojourn time of state i. Moreover for steady sate case, we also have,

$$\sum_i v_i = 1,\ i \in X_s \tag{3}$$

Rewriting equation (1) in the its elemental form we have,

$$v_H = v_S(1 - p_c) + v_{GD} + v_R p_h + v_F ,$$
$$v_S = v_H, v_C = v_S p_c , v_A = v_C p_a , v_{GD} = v_A p_g , v_R = v_A p_r , \tag{4}$$
$$v_F = v_C(1 - p_c) + v_A(1 - p_g - p_r) + v_R(1 - p_h)$$

Now, by solving the above equations using equation (3) we have,

$$v_H = \frac{1}{(2 + 2p_c + p_c p_a + p_c p_a p_r - p_c p_a p_r p_h)} \tag{5}$$

Rest of the values can be found in similar way. Lets assume the sojourn time of states be $h\{h_H, h_S, h_C, h_A, h_R, h_{GD}, h_F\}$. Therefore, steady state probability of healthy state H is given by,

$$\pi_H = \frac{v_H.h_H}{v_H.h_H + v_S h_S + v_C h_C + v_A h_A + v_{GD} h_{GD} + v_R h_R + v_F h_F} \tag{6}$$

$$\text{where,} \quad v_H = \frac{1}{2 + 2p_c + p_c p_a + p_c p_a p_r - p_c p_a p_r p_h}$$

Rest of the values can be calculated in similar way. If we assume the sojourn time distribution of State H and State S have uniform distributions—U(0, T_H) and U(0, T_S), then equation (6) can be rewritten as,

$$\pi_H = \frac{v_H.\dfrac{T_H}{2}}{v_H.\dfrac{T_H}{2} + v_S T_S / 2 + v_C h_C + v_A h_A + v_{GD} h_{GD} + v_R h_R + v_F h_F} \tag{7}$$

$$\text{where,} \quad v_H = \frac{1}{2 + 2p_c + p_c p_a + p_c p_a p_r - p_c p_a p_r p_h}$$

In next section, we evaluate our model using proof of concept example.

4   Evaluation and Analysis

In this section, we evaluate our model suing proof of concept scenario examples. In this paper, we focus on analyzing our model in terms of status of nodes' state. A survivable sensor networks should be in compromised state as short as possible and in healthy state as long as possible. So suppose that the mean time of compromised state C is less than that of both states H and S. On the other hand, rejuvenation must be faster than any other activities to avoid denial of service attack. Accordingly, suppose that the mean time of being in state R is shorter that that of F and GD. Under these constraints, the followings the values are randomly chosen for our evaluation in time unit.

$$h_H = 0.6, \ h_S = 0.35, \ h_C = 0.2, \ h_{GD} = 0.5, \ h_A = 0.4, h_R = 0.3, \ h_F = 0.4 \tag{8}$$

For the case of DTMC, the steady state probabilities or the proportions of time each state spends are,

$$v_H = 0.3337, \ v_S = 0.3337, \ v_C = 0.1168, \ v_A = 0.0934,$$
$$v_R = 0.0280, \ v_{GD} = 0.0561, \ v_F = 0.0383 \tag{9}$$

For the case of SMP the steady state probabilities are,

$$\pi_H = 0.4621, \ \pi_S = 0.2696, \ \pi_C = 0.0539, \ \pi_A = 0.1078,$$
$$\pi_{GD} = 0.0194, \ \pi_R = 0.0518, \ \pi_F = 0.0354 \tag{10}$$

Suppose that the number of sensor nodes are deployed in a cluster is 100 out of multiple clusters of sensor nodes. From equation (10), we can conclude by above observation that about 46 nodes are in healthy state while the number of nodes being stayed in compromise, rejuvenation and failure state are 5, 5 and 4, respectively. This statistics reveals the long term conditions of the distributed sensor nodes in a cluster.

Furthermore, we can determine the effect of rejuvenation and adaptation upon the two extremity of the sensor networks; healthy and failure state. Figure 4 reveals that rejuvenation can preclude the system to enter failure state. As the transition probability of successful rejuvenation P_h decreases, the steady state probability of the system being stayed in failure state (v_F for DTMC and π_F for SMP) increases.

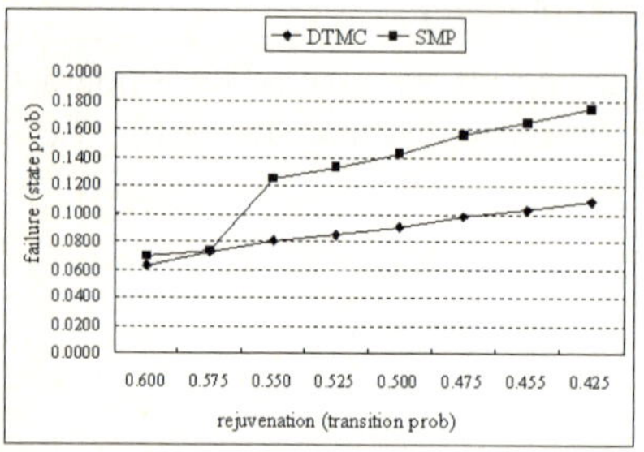

Fig. 4. Failure State Prob. vs. transition prob. of rejuvenation

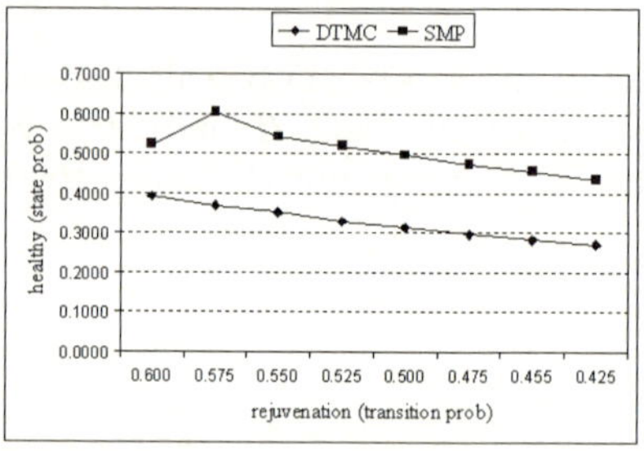

Fig. 5. Healthy state prob. vs. transition prob. of rejuvenation

Figure 5 also shows that the probability of system being stayed in healthy state decreases with probability of successful rejuvenation P_h. Figure 6 represents that the steady state probability of being stayed in failure state (v_F for DTMC and π_F for SMP) decreases as probability of triggering adaptation mechanism p_a increases.

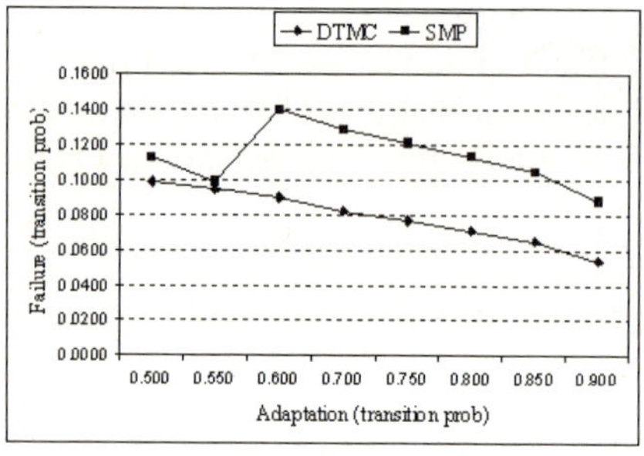

Fig. 6. Failure state prob. vs. transition prob. of adaptation

In this paper, we have only concentrated on building a framework of survivability model for DSN. We have described and analyzed the steady state model of our framework. SMP model can be scaled or modified if we add some more criterions.

The stochastic model only concerns, up to now, number of compromised nodes in a single cluster, and if we sum up all clusters into one, this model has scalability to support large number of sensor cluster with large number of sensor nodes. In addition to security related parameters such as compromised nodes, energy consumption in routing and data dissemination is also important issues in distributed sensor networks. And more detailed policy for rejuvenation as well as reconfiguration will be studied.

5 Conclusions

In this paper, we have proposed a model of survivable distributed sensor networks. Our approach adopts software rejuvenation to rejuvenate the sensor nodes under attack or and compromised in a single cluster of sensor networks. We analyzed our model in mathematical manner and showed that software rejuvenation and adaptation mechanisms based on SMP and DTMC can extenuate the failure probability while increases the probability of the sensor networks being stayed in healthy state.

In future works, we will extend the proposed model to cover the large number of sensor networks and consider other parameters such as energy consumption and data dissemination and so on.

Acknowledgement

This research was supported by the MIC (Ministry of Information and Communication), Korea, under the ITRC (Information Technology Research Center) support program supervised by the IITA (Institute of Information Technology Advancement) (IITA-2006-C1090-0603-0027).

References

1. Avancha, S., Undercoffer, J. L., Joshi, A., Pinkston, J.: Security for Sensor Networks. Wireless Sensor Networks, Kluwer Academic (2004) 253–275
2. Karlof, C., Sastry, N., Wagner, D.: TinySec: A Link Layer Security Architecture for Wireless Sensor Networks, In. Int. Conf. on Embedded Networked Sensor System, ACM Press (2004) 162–175
3. Ellison, B., Fisher, D., Linger, R., Lipson, H., Longstaff, T., Mead, N.: Survivable Networks Systems: An Emergin Discipline. Technical Report, CMU/SEI-97-TR-013, Software Engineering Institute, Carnegie Mellon University (1997)
4. Ellison, R. J., Linger, R. C., Longstaff, T., Mead, N. R.: Survivable Network System Analysis: A Case Study, IEEE software, IEEE Computer Society, Vol. 16, No. 4 (1999) 70–77
5. Heinzelman, W. R., Chandrakasan, A., Balakrishnan, H.:Energy-Efficient Communication Protocol for Wireless Microsensor Networks. In. Proc. of the 33rd Annual Hawaii Int. Conf. on System Sciences, IEEE Computer Society (2000) 3005–3014
6. Hu, F., Tillet, J., Ziobro, J., Sharma N.: Secure Wireless Sensor Networks: Problems and Solutions. J. on Systemics, Cybernetics and Informatics, Vol.1, No.9 (2004)
7. Jones, K., Wadaa, A., Olariu, S., Wilson, L.: Towards a New Paradigm for Securing Wireless Sensor Networks. New Security Paradigms Workshop, ACM Press (2003) 115–121

8. Knight, J.C., Strunk, E.A., Sullivan, K.J.: Towards a Rigorous Definition of Information Security Survivability, In. Proc. of the DARPA Information Survivability Conf. and Exposition, IEEE Computer society (2003) 78–89

9. Law, Y. W., Havinga, P. J. M.: How to Secure a Wireless Sensor Network. In. Proc. of Int. Conf. on Intelligent Sensors, Sensor Networks and Information Processing, IEEE Computer society (2005) 89–95

10. Liu, Y., Trivedi, K. S.: A General Framework for Network Survivability Quantification. In. Proc. of the 12th 12th GI/ITG Conf. on Measuring, Modelling and Evaluation of Computer and Communication Systems (2004) 369–378

11. Liu, Z., Wang, Y.: A Secure Agent Architecture for Sensor Networks. In. Int. Conf. on Artificial Intelligence (2003)

12. Park, T and Shin, K.: LiSP: A Lightweight Security Protocol for Wireless Sensor Networks, ACM trans. on Embedded Computing Systems, Vol. 3, No. 3. (2004) 634–660

13. Paul, K., Choudhuri, R. R., Bandyopadhyay, S.: Survivability Analysis of Ad Hoc Wireless Network Architecture. Mobile and Wireless Communication Networks, Lecture Note in Computer Science Vol. 1818, Springer Verlag (2000) 31–46

14. Paul, K., Choudhuri, R. R., Bandyopadhyay, S.: Survivable Ad Hoc Wireless Networks: Some Design Specifications. In. Int. Conf. on Multiaccess, Mobility And Teletraffic for Wireless Communications, Kluwer Academic Publishers (2000) 147–158

15. Perrig, A., Szewczyk, R., Wen, V., Culler, D.E., Tygar, J.D.:SPINS: security protocols for sensor netowrks. In. Proc. of Int. Conf. on Mobile Computing and Networking. ACM Press (2001) 189–199

16. Savola, R.: Architecture for Self-Estimation of Security Level in Ad Hoc Network Nodes. In. Proc. of the 3rd Australian Information Security Management Conf. (2005) 88–94

17. Schmidt, S., Krahn, H., Fischer, S., Watjen, D.: A Security Architecture for Mobile Wireless Sensor Networks, Security in Ad-hoc and Sensor Networks, Lecture Notes in Computer Science, Vol. 3313. Springer-Verlag, Berlin Heidelberg New York (2005) 166–177

18. Shaikh, R. A., Lee, S., Song, Y., Zhung Y.:Securing Distributed Wireless Sensor Networks: Issues and Guidelines. In. Proc. of Int. Conf. on Sensor Networks, Ubiquitous, and Trustworthy Computing, IEEE computer society (2006) 226–231

19. Snow, A.P., Varshney, U., Malloy, A.D.: Reliability and Survivability of Mobile and Wireless Networks. IEEE Computer, IEEE Computer Society, Vol. 33, No. 7 (2000) 49–55

20. Trivedi, K.S.: Probability and Statistics with Reliability, Queuing, and Computer Science Applications. 2nd edn. John Wiley & Sons (2001)

21. Walters, J. P., Liang, Z., Shi, W., Chaudhary, V.: Wireless Sensor Network Security: A Survey. In: Xiao, Y. (eds) : Security in Distributed, Grid, and Pervasive Computing, Auerbach Publica-tions, CRC Press. (2006)

22. Zhu, S., Setia, S., Jajodia, S.: LEAP: Efficient security mechanisms for large-scale distributed sensor networks. In. Proc. of the 10th ACM Conf. on Computer and Comm. Security, ACM Press (2003) 62–72.

23. Zia, T., Zomaya, A.: A Security Framework for Wireless Sensor Networks. In. Sym. Sensor Applications, IEEE Computer Society (2006) 49–53

Design and Analysis of the M2LL Policy Distributed Algorithm for Load Balancing in Dynamic Networks

Jacques M. Bahi[1], Raphaël Couturier[1], and Abderrahmane Sider[2],[*]

[1] Laboratoire d'Informatique de l'Université de Franche-Comté (LIFC). IUT de Belfort-Montbéliard, BP 527, 90016 Belfort Cedex, France
{jacques.bahi, raphael.couturier}@iut-bm.univ-fcomte.fr
[2] Département d'Informatique, Université Abderrahmane Mira de Béjaïa, Route de Targa Ouzemmour Béjaïa 06000, Algérie
abd_sider@yahoo.fr

Abstract. Load balancing a distributed/parallel system consists in allocating work (load) to its processors so that they all have to process approximately the same amount of work or amounts in relation with their computation power. In this paper, we present a new distributed algorithm that implements the M2LL policy (*Most to Least Loaded*). M2LL aims to indicate pairs of processors, that will exchange load, taking into account actually broken edges as well as the current load distribution in the system. The M2LL policy fixes the pairs of neighboring processors by selecting with priority the most loaded and the least loaded of each neighborhood. Our main result is that the M2LL distributed implementation terminates after at most $(n/2).d_t$ iterations where n and d_t are respectively the number of nodes and the degree of the system at time t.

Keywords: load balancing, dynamic networks, M2LL policy, distributed algorithms.

1 Introduction

Solving of large-size problems and speeding up the execution for small instances are the main purposes of parallel algorithms and architectures. Nowadays, the need for parallelism is becoming critical in many fields of science ranging from simulating fluid molecular dynamics and particle mechanics [7] to solving of large optimization and scientific problems [6]. The data-parallel model for parallelization is based on splitting the data that has to be processed over several processing units. The amount of data that is allocated to processors has to be controlled because of two main reasons: the data associated with each processor may increase or decrease depending on the computation being carried out and the processors may have heterogeneous speeds. That is what makes load balancing

---

[*] Third author wishes to acknowledge gratefully the help of first authors and of Pr. M. Kerkar from the Departement of Physics of the University of Bejaia, Algeria.

G. Min et al. (Eds.): ISPA 2006 Ws, LNCS 4331, pp. 195–204, 2006.

a fundamental problem that have to be addressed in the development of parallel/distributed software. It consists in allocating, according to a load balancing algorithm, the load to processors in relation to their computing powers. Load balancing algorithms are usually characterized as static/dynamic, global/local, sender/receiver initiated and/or synchronous/asynchronous [16,14,17,8].

Local load balancing algorithms are very attractive, because with this scheme, processors know and use only direct neighboring load and load is exchanged only with direct neighbors. These algorithms are iterative by nature, since they tend to balance the load *globally* (in the system) by successively balancing the load *locally* (in each neighborhood). The most popular local iterative algorithms are those named FOS (*First Order Scheme*) [9,7,19,10,11,15] and their derived form called DE (*Dimension Exchange*) [9,13,18]. The difference between diffusion and dimension exchange resides in their ability to communicate with different nodes. If a node can perform simultaneous communications with its neighbors then diffusion is used to exchange load information in parallel with all of them (in a single step of the algorithm). If not, then dimension exchange may be used and in this case, a node exchanges load information, cyclically, with each of its neighbors (only one per iteration). These algorithms were designed in a context of spreading usage of computing clusters formed by connecting machines by a rapid Ethernet-like network. But the recent evolution of network architectures toward the use of the Internet gives rise to a new execution environment for distributed computing. It is well known that the Internet is subject to contention and temporary link failures and processors may crash and recover. In this work, we deal with this concern supposing that the number of processors does not change and that a processor knows its living links and to what other processors it can send/receive messages. A link is alive if it can transmit a message in each direction [1]. Diffusion on dynamic networks has been investigated in [5,12,4]. Dimension Exchange on hypercube architectures with broken edges has been studied in [3]. In this paper, we focus on adapting the most efficient DE-type algorithm named GDE (*Generalized Dimension Exchange*) [18] so that it takes into account broken edges. This enhanced version of GDE, called GAE (*Generalized Adaptative Exchange*), can be conducted according to several policies [2]. We present a local, distributed and synchronous algorithm to implement the M2LL (*Most to Least Loaded*) policy. M2LL is used by the GAE algorithm for load balancing and aims at determining, for each iteration of GAE, all the pairs of nodes that will have to exchange work. This process has to ensure that the determined pairs are those that minimize the local unbalance of each neighborhood. Fixed pairs are different from an iteration to another depending on load differences between nodes and available live links. In order to take into account broken edges at a given moment, we suggest the following solution: broken links are simply not considered for finding a pair, moreover, nodes only deal with their neighbors that have not chosen their pair yet.

In section 2, we first present an analysis of the problem. As we will see later, a processor may face many problems, so we introduce messages that must be exchanged to resolve them coordinately. Section 3 gradually presents how processors resolve these problems with the concepts of the "interest" for load balancing and that of the "preference". In the last section, we detail the GAE algorithm with the M2LL policy and we conclude with future work.

2   Problem Analysis

A distributed-memory parallel system of n processors connected with an interconnection network is modelled by a graph $G = (V, E)$ where vertexes V and edges of E respectively represent the processors and links between them. Let E_B^t be the set of broken edges in the graph G at time (iteration) t, $N_i^t = \{j \in V : (i, j) \in E \wedge (i, j) \notin E_B^t\}$ the set of neighbor nodes of processor i at time t and let $|N_i^t| = b$. The aim of M2LL is to find for each processor i, a neighbor node $j \in N_i^t$ called its pair and noted $pair_i^t$. If i is the most loaded of $N_i^t \bigcup \{i\}$, then the processor j has to be the least loaded in N_i^t and vice versa. The load of a processor is a non-negative integer or real value noted w_i^t.

2.1   The Point of View of a Processor

A processor starts by exchanging its load level with each of its neighbors. This is achieved through a message having the form $\{id, iteration, load\}$ where id is an identifier of the sending node and *iteration*, the current iteration of the GAE algorithm. Thus, each processor knows the load of each of its neighbors and can order them by increasing load: $w_{j_0}^t \leq w_{j_1}^t \leq \ldots \ldots \leq w_{j_{b-2}}^t \leq w_{j_{b-1}}^t$. From the point of view of processor i which made it, this order implies that:

1. If $w_i^t \geq w_{j_{b-1}}^t$ then i is the "most loaded" of its neighborhood (if the inequality is strict) or, in the general case, belongs to the set of the "most loaded" nodes.
2. If $w_i^t \leq w_{j_0}^t$ then i is the "least loaded" of its neighborhood (if the inequality is strict) or, more generally, belongs to the set of the "least loaded" nodes.
3. If $w_{j_0}^t < w_i^t < w_{j_{b-1}}^t$ then i is neither the "most loaded" nor the "least loaded" of its neighborhood.

In the last case, processor i cannot choose directly with which of its neighbors it will balance its load. The idea that will allow it to choose a pair is to progressively remove j_0 and/or j_{b-1} by letting these nodes find firstly compared to node i, with whose of their respective neighbors they will exchange load. Whenever a processor neighbor of i takes its decision, it is removed from the list of possible pairs of node i. The removing is performed after receiving a "decision message" of the form $\{id, iteration, subiteration, decision\}$ sent by the processor id to all of its neighbors. *Subiteration* is associated with the current iteration of the M2LL algorithm which is executed many times by a processor until it takes a decision which in turn is transmitted in the boolean value *decision* and simply means whether the processor id is to be removed or not. Processor i has to send such a message after every M2LL sub-iteration to its neighbors which are not decided yet so that they can update load orders of their respective neighborhoods. For the time being, we will confine to case 1 and 2, since a processor in situation 3 will finish, after some M2LL sub-iterations (see 3.4) to be in either of them.

2.2   A Problem of Choice

In case 1, processor i belongs to the set of the "most loaded" nodes of its neighborhood. From its point of view, node j_0 is the "least loaded" in this neighborhood. If another processor in $j_1, j_2, \ldots$ has the same load as j_0, it should also be considered. In case 2, the situation of processor i is inverted relatively to case 1. Indeed, i belongs now to the set of the "least loaded" of its neighborhood and consequently, it should take as pair the node j_{b-1} or nodes $j_{b-2}, \ldots$ if they have the same load as j_{b-1}. So, we can see that whenever some processors have the same (maximum or minimum) load and they belong to a common neighborhood, then it will be necessary to "choose" one of them by some means to be defined. Solving of this issue, referred to as the "problem of choice", is given in section 3.3.

2.3   A Problem of Different Points of View

Until now, we investigated the situation of the neighborhood of processor i from the point of view of i. However, since M2LL is distributed, every processor has its own point of view of the load order that prevails in its neighborhood. For example, let's suppose that node i sees (views) it is in case 1. The question is how do processors $j_0, j_1 \ldots$ (that are the least loaded from the point of view of node i), see things in their respective neighborhoods. It is possible that they see processors i and $j_{b-1}, j_{b-2} \ldots$ as the "most loaded". In this situation, nodes $j_0, j_1 \ldots$ should choose a processor among i and $j_{b-1}, j_{b-2} \ldots$ according to the devised solution for the "problem of choice". But it may be also that one or each of them sees another processor, say h, more loaded than node i is. In this latter case, M2LL specifies that processor j_0 and/or j_1 chooses the "most loaded" to them (node h) and not choose i or one among $j_{b-1}, j_{b-2} \ldots$. Moreover, if processors i and $j_{b-1}, j_{b-2} \ldots$ know that one or several processors among $j_0, j_1 \ldots$ consider another node more loaded than they are, then they can remove it (or them) from the list of the "least loaded" nodes of their respective load orders. This will somewhat simplify the resolution of the "problem of choice" since the set of equally loaded processors is reduced.

Case 2 shows two analog problems. Indeed, processor j_{b-1} may see a node h less loaded than i and $j_0, j_1 \ldots$. Again M2LL states that it should choose h and, if i and $j_0, j_1 \ldots$ know this information, they can remove j_{b-1}.

2.4   A Problem of Centered Load

In the previous section, for case 1, we pointed out that j_{b-1} may see a processor h less loaded than j_0. It is clear too, that h may be more loaded than j_{b-1}. We can see now, that node j_{b-1} must be provided with some means to measure the "distance" that separate it from processors h and j_0. This measure should apply for h whatever its load is in comparison with the load of node j_{b-1}. Suppose that these distances are respectively $distance_{j_{b-1}}(h)$ and $distance_{j_{b-1}}(j_0)$. If $distance_{j_{b-1}}(h) > distance_{j_{b-1}}(j_0)$ then processor j_{b-1} should choose h. If

$distance_{j_{b-1}}(h) < distance_{j_{b-1}}(j_0)$ then the processor j_{b-1} should choose node j_0. A particular case arises when $distance_{j_{b-1}}(h) = distance_{j_{b-1}}(j_0)$ and $w_{j_0} < w_{j_{b-1}} < w_h$. We say that processor j_{b-1} has a "centered load" between j_0 and h. Notice that, this problematic situation is visible only to processor j_{b-1}. We have to pay attention to this problem because it can cause a real deadlock for the algorithm if it happens for all processors and no global knowledge about it is permitted. Symmetrically, processor j_0 also may experience a "centered load" between a processor h from its own neighborhood and node j_{b-1}. In the next section, we will define the distance used by M2LL and show how it enables the distributed solution of different points of view. Then we will look more closely to the problem of choice taking into account the particular case of centered loads.

3   A Graduate Presentation of Our Solution

Definition 1 (Interest of a Processor for Load Balancing). *The interest of a processor j for load balancing from the point of view of a neighbor i, at time t, is the quantity*

$$interest_i^t(j) = \left| w_j^t - w_i^t \right| \geq 0. \tag{1}$$

In other words, it is the absolute value of the difference of their loads. It makes it possible for processor i to measure its unbalance with its neighbor j. Notice that the interest is symmetric for both nodes on a given non broken edge. If processors and links are either of heterogenous computation powers or bandwidths then the interest of processor j for load balancing should be weighed by the (i, j) link bandwidth f_{ij} and by the powers s_i et s_j. Consequently, the interest for load balancing can be expressed by: $interest_i^t(j) = \frac{1}{f_{ij}} \left| \frac{w_j^t}{s_j} - \frac{w_i^t}{s_i} \right|$.

Definition 2 (The Best Interest). *The best interest of processor i, noted $BestInterest_i^t$, is the highest interest (unbalance) in the neighborhood N_i^t.*

$$BestInterest_i^t = \max_{k \in N_i^t} \left(interest_i^t(k) \right) \tag{2}$$

If, as we mentioned it before, any other processor h is less loaded than node j_0, then considering node j_{b-1}, we obtain $interest_{j_{b-1}}^t(h) > interest_{j_{b-1}}^t(j_0)$ which implies $BestInterest_{j_{b-1}}^t > BestInterest_{j_0}^t$. The best interest represents a measure of a processor's point of view and is the maximum unbalance it sees in its neighborhood. If it communicates it to its neighbors then they can assess whether it can be a partner in the process of looking for a pair. This is performed by letting every processor send a message which has the form $\{id, iteration, subiteration, Interested_{id}^t, BestInterest_{id}^t\}$. The meaning of the $Interested$ boolean component is postponed to end of section 3.1. This message type will be exchanged locally during a stage that we call interest exchange phase. Based on collected information after this exchange, processor j_{b-1} selects among nodes $j_0, j_1 \ldots$, those that still consider it as the most loaded. For example, if node j_0 sends an interest message containing $BestInterest_{j_0}^t$

such that $BestInterest^t_{j_0} = BestInterest^t_{j_{b-1}}$ then node j_{b-1} can end up to a sure knowledge it is more loaded than processor j_0. But if $BestInterest^t_{j_0} > BestInterest^t_{j_{b-1}}$ then node j_{b-1} now knows with certainty that processor j_0 has in view some other processors h more loaded than j_{b-1} and can then proceed to remove j_0 from its list of processors having minimal load. Thus, in addition to enabling processors to solve the different points of view problem, the measure of the best interest offers to both nodes j_{b-1} and j_0, the possibility to limit their set of processors that present a problem of choice.

Definition 3 (The Set of Interesting Processors). *The set of interesting processors for node i is defined by:*

$$B^t_i = \left\{ j \in N^t_i : BestInterest^t_j = BestInterest^t_i \right\} \tag{3}$$

B^t_i is the set of processors that have the same maximal unbalance as i, they may be more or less loaded than i and its elements are the only processors that will likely form a pair with i.

3.1   The Most Interesting Processor and the Pair Processor

Let $B^t_i = \{b_0, b_1, b_2 \ldots \ldots\} \subseteq N^t_i$ be the set of interesting processors for node i after the last interest exchange phase in a M2LL sub-iteration at GAE iteration t. The solving of the problem of choice by a processor i lets it deterministically find its most interesting processor, noted $MostInteresting^t_i$, for the current M2LL sub-iteration. $MostInteresting^t_i$ necessarily belongs to B^t_i.

It is easy to see that if a processor computes B^t_i then $B^t_i \neq \emptyset$ and at minimum, the cardinality of B^t_i is equal to 1. In this case, this unique processor is the most interesting processor. Whenever the cardinality of B^t_i is greater than 1, processor i has to solve its problem of choice (see details in **3.3**). Figure 1 shows two of three possible cases in a set B^t_i. In the first one (case (a)), processor 2 has a centered load between two or several processors. We can see that processor 2 has a centered load problem to solve. In order to detect it, it is sufficient to processor 2 to verify whether two or more interesting processors have different loads. Cases (b) shows another situation where processor 2 is the least loaded against the entirety of the B^t_2 set. In the third case (not depicted for space reasons), node 2 is the most loaded.

Case with a Centered Load Problem. In figure Fig.1(a), we let processor 2 choose one node among the least loaded ones, i.e. among 0 and 1. This implies that it is the most loaded in the pair being formed. Thus, this scheme makes it possible to ensure load sharing by favoring load migration from over-loaded to under-loaded regions. And finally, the problem of choice for processor 2 is between $\{0, 1\}$ and not $\{3, 4\}$. Let $L^t_i = \{b_j \in B^t_i : w^t_{b_j} < w^t_i\}$ be the set of interesting processors that have smaller load than that of i and let $Pref(.)$ be a given solution for the problem of choice. The most interesting processor for a node facing a problem of a centered load is defined according to formula 4.

$$MostInteresting^t_i = Pref(L^t_i) \ \ if \ \ (|B^t_i| > 1) \wedge \neg(|L^t_i| = |B^t_i| \vee |L^t_i| = 0) \tag{4}$$

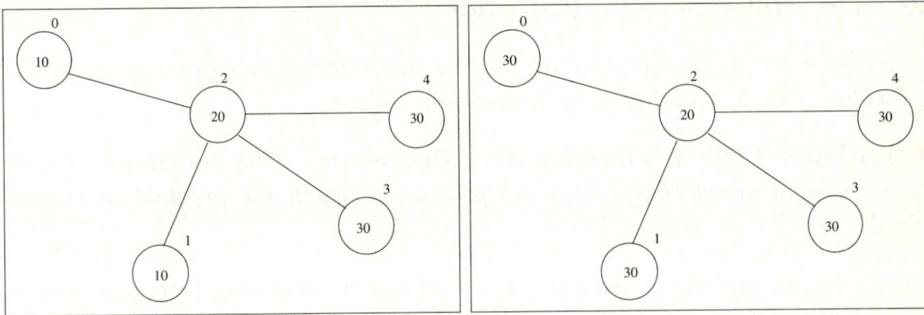

(a) Load of processor 2 is centered between that of nodes $0, 1$ and $3, 4$

(b) Processor 2 is the least loaded in relation with all its interesting processors

Fig. 1. The Set of Interesting Processors and the Problem of Choice

Case Without a Problem of Centered Load. If a processor does not face a problem of centered load then it is necessarily in a second case: its load is minimum (cf. processor 2 in Fig.1(b)) or maximum (not depicted) against two or more neighbors. In this case, the choice of the most interesting processor is equivalent to solving the problem of choice. For example, processor 2 will have to choose from $\{0, 1, 3, 4\}$. More generally, the most interesting processor is obtained by formula 5.

$$MostInteresting_i^t = Pref(B_i^t) \ if \ (|B_i^t| > 1) \wedge (|L_i^t| = |B_i^t| \vee |L_i^t| = 0) \quad (5)$$

Now it is time to explain the content of the $Interested_i^t$ component of interest exchange messages. A processor i sends a message containing $false$ to all nodes in B_i^t except its most interesting processor for which it will be $true$.

The Pair Processor. A processor i that found node j as its most interesting processor can conclude that $pair_i^t = j$ iif $MostInteresting_i^t = j$ and $MostInteresting_j^t = i$. Whenever the node i finds its pair j, a simple comparison of their load will make it clear which is the most loaded and which is the least loaded and consequently, the direction of the load migration.

3.2   The Decision of a Processor

A processor j is declared to have taken its decision by a processor i and noted $decided_i(j) = true$ iff: i) $interest_i(j) \leq 1$ or ii) $(i, j) \in E_B^t$ i.e. the (i, j) link is broken at time t or iii) $pair_j^t$ exists according to 3.1. Moreover, a processor considers that it has taken its own decision and is noted $decided_i(i) = true$ iff: i) $\forall j \in N_i : decided_i(j) = true$ or ii) $pair_i^t$ exists according to 3.1. After one M2LL sub-iteration, each processor sends to all its neighbors a decision message that contains its current state $decided_i(i)$ in the decision component. Based on this information, neighbors that have not taken their own decision yet can eliminate it from their respective load orders.

3.3   The Preference of a Processor

A processor i that considers node j as its most interesting processor according to formula 4 or 5 is said to have a preference for j.

Definition 4 (The Preference of a Processor). *The preference of a processor, simply noted $Pref(.)$, is the process by which the problem of choice is solved.*

A very simple preference consists in: i) arbitrarily choosing (the first, the last or the node with lower identity) or ii) randomly choosing one of the conflicting elements. In the following paragraph, we offer a solution that allows to maximize the number of formed pairs. Besides, we address the problem of centered load, when it spans the network and can lead to repetitive non-coinciding choices.

A Choice Based on the Degree of Freedom. The freedom degree of an interesting processor is defined by the number of nodes that presents the best interest for it; that is $|L_i^t|$ or $|B_i^t|$. The preference based on this number consists in favoring neighbour nodes that have a low degree of freedom when looking for the most interesting processor. The problem amounts then to choose one node from L_i^t or B_i^t that has the minimum freedom degree. Moreover, in order to avoid the repetition of non-coinciding choices during two or more sub-iterations, we associate a memory with least loaded nodes to store the freedom degree of their more loaded neighbors. By iterating between nodes with stable freedom degrees, least loaded processors are ensured to get coinciding choices after some finite sub-iterations number.

3.4   M2LL Termination

Proposition 1. *If the network topology (broken edges) does not change during its execution then M2LL terminates after a maximum of $(n/2)d_{max}^t$ sub-iterations. Besides, the safety of M2LL is ensured by means of the decision concept and the choice based on the preference ensures its correctness.*

Proof. Let d_{max}^t be the degree of the graph $G = (V, E, E_B^t)$ at iteration t of GAE and suppose it does not vary before $t+1$. If in the worst case non-coinciding choices arise in the network, our solution ensures that a pair of processors would take their own decision after a maximum of d_{max}^t sub-iterations. The number of possible pairs being at worst $(n/2)$, it follows that $(n/2)d_{max}^t$ M2LL sub-iterations will be necessary if they should all be formed.

4   The GAE Algorithm with the M2LL Policy

Algorithm 1 shows the GAE load balancing algorithm with the M2LL policy.

In stage 2, each processor exchanges load information *locally* on living links then keeps iterating (lines 5-12) within M2LL until it finds a pair or that knows

---

Algorithm 1. Generalized Adaptive Exchange (GAE) with the M2LL policy

1. $decided_i^t(i) = false; Pair_i^t = UNKNOWN;$ // GAE starts here
2.   Exchange load information with neighbors;
3.   bool $localBalance_i^t = \forall j \in N_i^t : |w_j^t - w_i^t| \leq 1;$
4.   **if** $(localBalance_i^t = false)$ **then** {
5.   **while** $(\neg decided_i^t(i))$ **do** { // M2LL sub-iterations begin here
6.   Find the processor $MostInteresting_i^t;$
7. $\forall j \in N_i^t :$ **If** $\neg decided_i^t(j)$ **then** exchange $MostInteresting_i^t$ with j ;
8.   Find $pair_i^t;$
        $Pair_i^t = j \Leftrightarrow \exists j \in N_i^t : \neg decided_i^t(j) \wedge MostInteresting_i^t = j \wedge MostInteresting_j^t = i$
9.   **if** $(Pair_i^t \neq UNKNOWN)$ **then** $decided_i^t(i) = true;$
10. $\forall j \in N_i^t :$ **If** $(\neg decided_i^t(j))$ **then** exchange $decided_i^t(i)$ with j ;
11.   **if** $(Pair_i^t = UNKNOWN)$ **then** $decided_i^t(i) = \exists j \in N_i^t : \neg decided_i^t(j);$
12.   } **end while** // M2LL sub-iterations end here
13.   **if** $(decided_i^t(i) = true)$ **then** {
14.   **if** $(Pair_i^t = j \neq UNKNOWN)$ **then** $w_i^{t+1} = w_i^t + \lambda(w_j^t - w_i^t);$
15.   **else** $w_i^{t+1} = w_i^t;$
16.   Apply load migration;
17.   } // GAE ends here
18.   }

---

all its neighbors took their decision. During one M2LL sub-iteration, a processor exchanges two kinds of messages: interest exchange and decision messages. At step 7, the outcome of formula 4 or 5 is sent to adjacent nodes that are "not decided yet". The finding of the most interesting processor allows each node to eventually find a pair. The necessary condition is stated in step 8. In the last stage (line 10), each processor indicates to its neighbors participating in the actual M2LL sub-iteration whether it has found a pair by a decision message. If so, its neighbors that have not succeeded to take their decision after the actual sub-iteration, remove it from their respective load orders.

5   Conclusion

In this paper we present a distributed algorithm for implementing the M2LL policy. M2LL takes into account broken edges and may be used on either static or dynamic topologies. The detailed analysis of load situations that can arise in a given neighborhood, has made it possible to state the different problems a processor may be faced when choosing its pair. Then, we detail our solution based on the key notions of the "interest" of a processor for load balancing and that of the "preference" of a processor whenever many of its neighbors present the "best interest". Finally, we investigate M2LL termination and describe how it is used by the GAE load balancing algorithm. In perspective, we plan to experimentally compare the behavior of the GAE M2LL algorithm against the RFOS diffusion-type algorithm [4] on dynamic networks.

References

1. W. Aiello, B. Awerbuch, B. Zkfaggs, S.Rao, "Approximate load balancing on dynamic and asynchronous networks", *Proc. of the 25th annual ACM symposium on Theory of computing*, pages: 632–641, 1993.
2. J.M. Bahi, R. Couturier, and F. Vernier, "Load Balancing on Dynamic Network", *Technical Report RR-2002-1, LIFC, Université de Franche-Comté*, September 2002.
3. J.M. Bahi, R. Couturier, F. Vernier, "Broken Edges and Dimension Exchange Algorithm on Hypercube Topology", *Proc. of the 11th Euromicro Conference on Parallel, Distributed and Network-Based Processing (Euro-PDP'03)*, 2003.
4. J.M. Bahi, R. Couturier and F. Vernier, "Accelerated diffusion algorithms on general dynamic networks", *Proc. of 5th Int. Conference, PPAM Czestochowa, Poland*, LNCS Vol. 3019 : 77–82. PPAM, Springer-Verlag Heidelberg, 2003.
5. J.M. Bahi and J. Gaber, "Load Balancing on Networks with Dynamically Changing Topology", *Europar Conference, Lecture Notes on Computer Science* : 175–182, 2001.
6. J.M. Bahi, R. Couturier, P. Vuillemin ,"Solving nonlinear wave equations in the grid computing environment: an experimental study", in JCA (Journal of Computational Acoustics), 14(1), June 2006.
7. J. Boillat, "Load balancing and poisson equation in a graph", *Concurrency: Practice and Experience*, 2(4):289-313, 1990.
8. A. Cortes, A. Ripoll, M.A. Senar and E. Luque, "Performance Comparison of Dynamic Load-balancing Strategies for Distributed Systems", *IEEE Proc. of the 32th Hawai Int. Conference on System Sciences*, Vol.8 : 8041–8051, 1999.
9. G. Cybenko. "Dynamic load balancing for distributed memory multiprocessors", *Journal of Parallel and Distributed Computing*, Vol. 7 :279-301, 1989.
10. R. Diekmann, A. Frommer, and B. Monien, "Efficient schemes for nearest neighbor load balancing" *Parallel Computing*, Vol. 25 (7) : 789-812, 1999.
11. R. Elsasser, B. Monien, and R. Preis, "Diffusion Schemes for Load Balancing on Heterogeneous Networks", *Theory of Computing Systems*, vol. 35, pp. 305–320, 2002.
12. R. Elsasser, B. Monien,S. Schamberger, "Load Balancing in Dynamic Networks", I-SPAN, 2004.
13. S. H. Hosseini, B. Litow, M. Malkawi, J. McPherson, and K. Vairavan, "Analysis of a graph coloring based distributed load balancing algorithm", *Journal of Parallel and Distributed Computing*, 10(2):160–166, Oct. 1990.
14. V. Kumar, G.Y. Ananth, V.N. Rao, "Scalable load balancing techniques for parallel computers", *Technical Report 91-55, Dept. of Computer Science, University of Minnesota*, 1991.
15. T. Rotaru and H.H. Nageli, "Dynamic load balancing by diffusion in heterogeneous systems", *Journal of Parallel and Distributed Computing*, 64 :481–497, 2004.
16. M. H. Willebeek-LeMair, A. p. Reeves, "Local vs. Global Strategies for Dynamic Load Balancing", *Proc. of the Int. Conference on Parallel Processing*, Vol. 1 : 569–570, 1990.
17. M. H. Willebeek-LeMair, A. p. Reeves, "Strategies for Dynamic Load Balancing on Highly Parallel Computers", *IEEE Trans. on Parallel and Distributed Systems*, Vol. 4 N° 9 : 979-993, Septembre 1993.
18. C.Z. Xu and F.C.M. Lau, "Analysis of the Generalized Dimension Exchange Method for Dynamic Load Balancing", *Journal of Parallel and Distributed Computing*, 16:385–393, 1992.
19. C.-Z. Xu and F.C.M. Lau," Optimal parameters for load balancing with the diffusion method in mesh networks", *Parallel Processing Letters*, 4(2) :139–147, 1994.

An Artificial Fish Swarm Algorithm Based and ABC Supported QoS Unicast Routing Scheme in NGI[*]

Xingwei Wang, Nan Gao, Shuxiang Cai, and Min Huang

College of Information Science and Engineering, Northeastern University, Shenyang, 110004, P.R. China
`wangxw@mail.neu.edu.cn`

Abstract. In this paper, by introducing knowledge of fuzzy mathematics, probability theory and gaming theory, a QoS unicast routing scheme with ABC supported is proposed based on artificial fish-swarm algorithm. Simulation results have shown that it is both feasible and effective with better performance.

1   Introductions

NGI (Next Generation Internet) is becoming an integrated network [1-4] converged seamlessly by heterogeneous multi-segment multi-provider sub-networks, such as terrestrial-based, space-based, fixed and mobile sub-networks, etc. Its backbone and access links become diversified. Several kinds of links may coexist on each hop for the user to choose along the end-to-end path. It is possible for the user to be ABC (Always Best Connected) [3-4] to NGI, the user can connect with NGI anytime, anywhere in the currently best way and can switch to the better way adaptively and transparently whenever it comes forth, and thus the so-called global QoS (Quality of Service) roaming should be supported seamlessly [5]. QoS routing is essential and ABC should be supported [4]. However, some characteristics of NGI, such as its heterogeneity and dynamics, influence of terminal and even network mobility, unavoidable message transfer delay and its uncertainty, etc., make it hard to describe the network status used when routing in NGI exactly and completely. On the other hand, the user QoS requirements are affected largely by a lot of subjective factors and often can not be expressed accurately, therefore the flexible QoS description should be provided. ABC means a user can get the best available connection anytime, anywhere, however, 'best' itself is a fuzzy concept, depending on many factors, such as user QoS requirement, cost a user willing to pay, user preference, terminal ability and access network availability, etc. In addition, with the gradual commercialization of network operation, ABC is not a user's own wishful thinking and thus need to consider both the network provider profit and the user profit with both-win supported [6].

---

[*] This work is supported by the National Natural Science Foundation of China under Grant No. 60673159; Program for New Century Excellent Talents in University; Specialized Research Fund for the Doctoral Program of Higher Education; the Natural Science Foundation of Liaoning Province under Grant No. 20062022.

G. Min et al. (Eds.): ISPA 2006 Ws, LNCS 4331, pp. 205–214, 2006.

In this paper, by introducing knowledge of fuzzy mathematics, probability theory and gaming theory, a QoS unicast routing scheme with ABC supported is proposed. In order to deal with imprecise network status information and flexible user QoS requirement, it uses range to describe the user QoS requirement and the edge parameter and introduces the user satisfaction degree function, the edge evaluation function and the path evaluation function. Based on artificial fish-swarm algorithm, it tries to find a QoS unicast path with Pareto optimum under Nash equilibrium on both the network provider utility and the user utility achieved or approached. Simulation results have shown that the proposed scheme is both feasible and effective with better performance.

2   Problem Description

2.1   Network Model and Routing Request

A network can be modeled as a graph $G(V, E)$, V is node set and E is edge set. $\forall v_i, v_j \in V(i, j = 1, 2, ..., |V|)$, there maybe exist several edges (representing different kinds of links) between them. Just for simplicity, the node parameters are merged into the edge ones in this paper. Therefore, $\forall e_l \in E$, consider the following parameters: available bandwidth $[Bw_{l_L}, Bw_{l_H}]$, delay $[Dl_{l_L}, Dl_{l_H}]$ and error rate $[Ls_{l_L}, Ls_{l_H}]$. A QoS unicast routing request is described as follows: $< [bw\_rq_L, bw\_rq_H], [dl\_rq_L, dl\_rq_H], [ls\_rq_L, ls\_rq_H], C_u >$, and its elements represent the user bandwidth, delay, error rate requirement and the upper limit of the cost the user will to afford respectively.

2.2   Edge Parameter Probability Model and User Satisfaction Degree Function

The probability $Ge_B(bw_l)$ of e_l guaranteeing to provide a user bandwidth bw_l and the satisfaction degree $Se_B(bw_l)$ for the user to get bandwidth bw_l on e_l actually are defined as follows:

$$Ge_B(bw_l) = \begin{cases} 1 & bw_l \leq Bw_{l_L} \\ (\frac{Bw_{l_H} - bw_l}{Bw_{l_H} - Bw_{l_L}})^k + \delta_B & Bw_{l_L} < bw_l \leq Bw_{l_H} \\ 0 & bw_l > Bw_{l_H} \end{cases} \tag{1}$$

$$Se_B(bw_l) = \begin{cases} 1 & bw_l \geq bw\_rq_H \\ e^{-(\frac{bw\_rq_H - bw_l}{bw_l - bw\_rq_L})^2} + S_1 & bw\_rq_L \leq bw_l < bw\_rq_H \\ 0 & bw_l < bw\_rq_L \end{cases} \tag{2}$$

$$\delta_B = \begin{cases} \varepsilon & bw_l = Bw_{l_H} \\ 0 & \text{otherwise} \end{cases} \tag{3}$$

$$S_1 = \begin{cases} 1 & bw_l = bw\_rq_L \\ 0 & \text{otherwise} \end{cases} \tag{4}$$

If the available bandwidth on P is bw_P, the satisfaction degree $SP_B(bw_P)$ for the user to get bw_P on P actually can be computed using formula (2), i.e. $SP_B(bw_P) = Se_B(bw_l)$.

Assume that the delay value is evenly distributed in $[Dl_{l_L}, Dl_{l_H}][7]$, the probability $Ge_D(dl_l)$ of the delay on e_l equaling to dl_l and the user satisfaction degree $Se_D(dl_l)$ to the delay traversing through e_l being dl_l actually are defined as follows:

$$Ge_D(dl_l) = \begin{cases} \frac{1}{Dl_{l_H} - Dl_{l_L}} & Dl_{l_L} \leq dl_l \leq Dl_{l_H} \\ 0 & \text{otherwise} \end{cases} \tag{5}$$

$$Se_D(dl_l) = \begin{cases} 1 - e^{-(\frac{dl\_rq_H - dl_l}{dl_l \cdot \sigma_1})^2} & dl_l \leq dl\_rq_H \\ 0 & \text{otherwise} \end{cases} \tag{6}$$

If the delay on P is dl_P, the user satisfaction degree $SP_D(dl_P)$ to the delay experienced by the user actually on P being dl_P can be defined as follows:

$$SP_D(dl_P) = \begin{cases} 1 & dl_P \leq dl\_rq_L \\ 1 - e^{-(\frac{dl\_rq_H - dl_P}{dl_P - dl\_rq_L})^2} + S_2 & dl\_rq_L < dl_P \leq dl\_rq_H \\ 0 & dl_P > dl\_rq_H \end{cases} \tag{7}$$

$$S_2 = \begin{cases} \varepsilon & Jp = 1 \wedge dl_P = dl\_rq_H \\ 0 & \text{otherwise} \end{cases} \tag{8}$$

Assume that the error rate value is evenly distributed in $[Ls_{l_L}, Ls_{l_H}]$, the probability $Ge_L(ls_l)$ of the error rate on e_l equaling to ls_l and the user satisfaction degree $Se_L(ls_l)$ to the error rate on e_l being ls_l actually are defined as follows:

$$Ge_L(ls_l) = \begin{cases} \frac{1}{Ls_{l_H} - Ls_{l_L}} & Ls_{l_L} \leq ls_l \leq Ls_{l_H} \\ 0 & \text{otherwise} \end{cases} \tag{9}$$

$$Se_L(ls_l) = \begin{cases} 1 - e^{-(\frac{ls\_rq_H - ls_l}{ls_l \cdot \sigma_2})^2} & ls_l \leq ls\_rq_H \\ 0 & \text{otherwise} \end{cases} \tag{10}$$

If the error rate is ls_P on P, the user satisfaction degree $SP_L(ls_P)$ to the error rate on P being ls_P can be defined as follows:

$$SP_L(ls_P) = \begin{cases} 1 & ls_P \leq ls\_rq_L \\ 1 - e^{-(\frac{ls\_rq_H - ls_P}{ls_P - ls\_rq_L})^2} + S_3 & ls\_rq_L < ls_P \leq ls\_rq_H \\ 0 & ls_P > ls\_rq_H \end{cases} \tag{11}$$

$$S_3 = \begin{cases} \varepsilon & Jp = 1 \wedge ls_P = ls\_rq_H \\ 0 & \text{otherwise} \end{cases} \tag{12}$$

Among them, $k > 0$; S_i is a modification function ($i = 1, 2, 3$); Jp is the hop number of the end-to-end path; ε is a positive decimal fraction much smaller than 1; σ_1 and σ_2 are regulation factors for adjusting magnitudes of the corresponding satisfaction degree values.

2.3   Edge and Path Evaluation Function

The edge and path evaluation functions represent their adaptability membership degrees to the user QoS requirements respectively.

Assume that the bandwidth occupied actually by the user on e_l and on P are Bw_{l_o} and Bw_{P_o} respectively, $Bw_{l_o} \leq Bw_{l_H}$, $Bw_{P_o} = Min_{e_l \in P}\{Bw_{l_o}\}$. Often Bw_{l_o} and Bw_{P_o} are equal. The adaptability membership degree function of Bw_{l_o} and Bw_{P_o} to the user bandwidth requirement, that is, the edge and path bandwidth evaluation function $EB_e(Bw_{l_o})$ and $EB_P(Bw_{P_o})$ are defined respectively as follows:

$$EB_e(Bw_{l_o}) = Se_B(Bw_{l_o}) \cdot Ge_B(Bw_{l_o}) \tag{13}$$

$$EB_P(Bw_{P_o}) = SP_B(Bw_{P_o}) \cdot \prod_{e_l \in P} Ge_B(Bw_{P_o}) \tag{14}$$

Assume that the delay experienced by the user on e_l and P actually are Dl_{l_t} and Dl_{P_t} respectively, $Dl_{P_L} = \sum_{e_l \in P} Dl_{l_L}$, $Dl_{P_H} = \sum_{e_l \in P} Dl_{l_H}$, $Dl_{l_t} \leq Dl_{l_H}$, the adaptability membership degree function of Dl_{l_t} and Dl_{P_t} to the user delay requirement, that is, the edge and path delay evaluation function $ED_e(Dl_{l_t})$ and $ED_P(Dl_{P_t})$ are defined respectively as follows:

$$ED_e(Dl_{l_t}) = \frac{\int_{Dl_{l_L}}^{Dl_{l_H}} Se_D(Dl_{l_t}) \cdot Ge_D(Dl_{l_t})d(Dl_{l_t})}{\int_{Dl_{l_L}}^{Dl_{l_H}} Ge_D(Dl_{l_t})d(Dl_{l_t})} \tag{15}$$

$$ED_P(Dl_{P_t}) = \frac{\int_{Dl_{P_L}}^{Dl_{P_H}} SP_D(Dl_{P_t})d(Dl_{P_t})}{\int_{Dl_{P_L}}^{Dl_{P_H}} d(Dl_{P_t})} \tag{16}$$

Assume that the error rate experienced by the user on e_l and P actually are Ls_{l_a} and Ls_{P_a} respectively, $Ls_{P_L} = 1 - \prod_{e_l \in P}(1 - Ls_{l_L})$, $Ls_{P_H} = 1 - \prod_{e_l \in P}(1 - Ls_{l_H})$, $Ls_{l_a} \leq Ls_{l_H}$, the adaptability membership degree function of Ls_{l_a} and Ls_{P_a} to the user delay requirement, that is, the edge and path delay evaluation function $EL_e(Ls_{l_a})$ and $EL_P(Ls_{P_a})$ are defined respectively as follows:

$$EL_e(Ls_{l_a}) = \frac{\int_{Ls_{l_L}}^{Ls_{l_H}} Se_L(Ls_{l_a}) \cdot Ge_L(Ls_{l_a})d(Ls_{l_a})}{\int_{Ls_{l_L}}^{Ls_{l_H}} Ge_L(Ls_{l_a})d(Ls_{l_a})} \tag{17}$$

$$EL_P(Ls_{P_a}) = \frac{\int_{Ls_{P_L}}^{Ls_{P_H}} SP_L(Ls_{P_a})d(Ls_{P_a})}{\int_{Ls_{P_L}}^{Ls_{P_H}} d(Ls_{P_a})} \tag{18}$$

Thus, the comprehensive quality evaluation function of the edge and the path $EC_e(e_l)$ and $EC_P(P)$ are defined respectively as follows:

$$EC_e(e_l) = \alpha_B \cdot EB_e(Bw_{l_o}) + \alpha_D \cdot ED_e(Dl_{l_t}) + \alpha_L \cdot EL_e(Ls_{l_a}) \tag{19}$$

$$EC_P(P) = \alpha_B \cdot EB_P(Bw_{P_o}) + \alpha_D \cdot ED_P(Dl_{P_t}) + \alpha_L \cdot EL_P(Ls_{P_a}) \tag{20}$$

Among them,α_B, α_D and α_L represent the relative importance of the bandwidth, delay and error rate to the user QoS requirement respectively,$0 \leq \alpha_B, \alpha_D$, $\alpha_L \leq 1$, $\alpha_B + \alpha_D + \alpha_L = 1$. $EC_e(e_l)$ and $EC_P(P)$ are used to reflect the user's satisfaction degree to e_l and P.

2.4   Gaming Analysis

There are two players in the game, that is, the network provider and the user. The user has n gaming strategies corresponding to n bandwidth allocation levels, denoted as$< Bw_{o_1}, Bw_{o_2}, ..., Bw_{o_n} >$. Bw_{o_x} indicates the bandwidth occupied actually by the user on the edge under his xth strategy. The network provider has m strategies corresponding to m bandwidth prices, denoted as $< pc_1, pc_2, ..., pc_m >$, and reflecting different relationship between supply and demand and different edge quality. Each strategy is composed of bandwidth base price and floating price; base price is determined by the network provider according to the edge type and does not take part in gaming; floating price is determined by gaming between the network provider and the user according to the delay and error rate of the edge. Under the strategy pair$< Bw_{o_x}, PB_y + PF_y^{zw} >$, the cost CT_{xy}^l paid by the user for using bandwidth Bw_{o_x} of e_l is as follows:

$$CT_{xy}^l = PB_y \cdot Bw_{o_x} + PF_y^{zw} \tag{21}$$

Accordingly, the cost CT_P paid by the user for using P is as follows:

$$CT_P = \sum_{e_l \in P} CT_{xy}^l \tag{22}$$

Define the network provider and user utility matrix on e_l is $[< uu_{xy}^l, nu_{xy}^l >]_{n \times m}$. where n rows and m columns are corresponding to the user's n gaming strategies and the network provider's m gaming strategies respectively. $< uu_{xy}^l, nu_{xy}^l >$ denotes the user's utility uu_{xy}^l and the network provider's utility nu_{xy}^l on e_l under the strategy pair $< Bw_{o_x}, PB_y + PF_y^{zw} >$. uu_{xy}^l and nu_{xy}^l are computed respectively as follows:

$$uu_{xy}^l = \frac{C_l(Bw_{o_x}) \cdot EC_e(e_l)}{CT_{xy}^l} \cdot \Lambda \tag{23}$$

$$\Lambda = \begin{cases} e^{-\rho \frac{(Bw_{o_x} - bw\_rq_H)}{bw\_rq_H}} & Bw_{o_x} \geq bw\_rq_H \\ 1 & Bw_{o_x} < bw\_rq_H \end{cases} \tag{24}$$

$$nu_{xy}^l = \frac{CT_{xy}^l - C_l(Bw_{o_x})}{C_l(Bw_{o_x})} \cdot \Omega \tag{25}$$

$$SD = \frac{Bw_{o_x}}{Bw_{l_H}} \tag{26}$$

$$\Omega = \begin{cases} e^{-\frac{\lambda_1}{Bw_{o_x}} \cdot (k_1 \cdot PB_y + k_2 \cdot PF_y)} & SD < \delta \\ 1 - e^{-\lambda_2 \cdot Bw_{o_x} \cdot (k_1 \cdot PB_y + k_2 \cdot PF_y)} & SD \geq \delta \end{cases} \tag{27}$$

Among them, $C_l(Bw_{o_x})$ is the cost of using Bw_{o_x} on e_l; Λ and Ω are regulation factor of the user utility and the network provider utility respectively; SD is a indicator of bandwidth supply and demand relationship; δ is a preset threshold; k_1, k_2, λ_1, λ_2 and ρ are regulation coefficients; $\lambda_1, \lambda_2, \rho > 0$, $0 \leq \delta, k_1, k_2 \leq 1$, $k_1+k_2 = 1$. When the bandwidth Bw_{o_x} actually got by a user exceeds bw_rq_H, the exceeded amount of bandwidth is useless for meeting with the user bandwidth requirement, however it has influence on meeting with the other users' bandwidth requirement. Therefore, the more the excess is, the more severely the user utility should be punished, which can prevent a user from attempting to occupy more bandwidth greedily even if it has got enough bandwidth. SD reflects bandwidth supply and demand relationship on an edge. The larger the value of SD is, the more demanding the bandwidth is on the edge. When the value of SD is greater than δ, the demand for bandwidth exceeds its supply on an edge; at this time, Ω is an increasing function of price, that is, the network provider utility increases with price, and the more demanding the bandwidth is, the faster the utility increases. When the value of SD is less than δ, the supply of bandwidth exceeds its demand on an edge; at this time, Ω is a decreasing function of price, that is, the network provider utility increases when the price decreases, and the more sufficient the bandwidth is, the faster the utility increases. k_1 and k_2 reflect the relative influence of the basic price and the floating price of the bandwidth on the network provider utility.

Assume that the edges in the graph corresponding to the links in the network are provided by Q network providers, the user utility and the hth network provider utility on P are defined respectively as follows:

$$TU_P = \frac{\sum_{e_l \in P} uu^l_{xy}}{Jp} \tag{28}$$

$$TW^h_P = \frac{\sum_{e_{l_h} \in P} nu^{l_h}_{xy}}{Jp_h} \tag{29}$$

In formula (29), e_{l_h} denotes the edges provided by the hth network provider on P, $nu^{l_h}_{xy}$ denotes the hth network provider utility on e_{l_h}, and Jp_h denotes the number of the edges provided by the hth network provider on P. Obviously, $\sum_h Jp_h = Jp$.

The goal of gaming on an edge is to determine an optimal strategy pair under which the network provider utility and the user utility achieve or approach Pareto optimum under Nash equilibrium. $< uu^l_{x^*y^*}, nu^l_{x^*y^*} >$ with Nash equilibrium achieved in $[< uu^l_{xy}, nu^l_{xy} >]_{n \times m}$ should meet with:

$$\begin{cases} uu^l_{x^*y^*} \geq uu^l_{xy^*} \quad x = 1, 2, ..., n \\ nu^l_{x^*y^*} \geq uu^l_{x^*y} \quad y = 1, 2, ..., m \end{cases} \tag{30}$$

Pareto superiority of $< uu^l_{xy}, nu^l_{xy} >$ on e_l is defined as follows:

$$PA^l_{xy} = \frac{1}{\alpha \cdot \frac{1}{uu^l_{xy}} + \beta \cdot \frac{1}{nu^l_{xy}}} \tag{31}$$

In formula (31), α and β are the preference weight to the network provider and to the user respectively, $0 \leq \alpha, \beta \leq 1$, $\alpha + \beta = 1$. Obviously, the larger the value of PA^l_{xy} is, the stronger the Pareto superiority of the network provider utility and the user utility is under the corresponding strategy pair.

In $[< uu^l_{xy}, nu^l_{xy} >]_{n \times m}$, if there exists only one $< uu^l_{x^*y^*}, nu^l_{x^*y^*} >$, it is the optimal network provider and user strategy pair; if there exist more than one or no $< uu^l_{x^*y^*}, nu^l_{x^*y^*} >$, compare their Pareto superiority and select the strategy pair with the largest value of PA^l_{xy} as the optimal network provider and user strategy pair (if there exist more than one such strategy pairs, select one randomly).

2.5   Mathematical Model

It is described as follows:

$$Maximize\{EC_P(P)\} \tag{32}$$

$$Maximize\{TU_P\} \tag{33}$$

$$Maximize\{TW^h_P\} \tag{34}$$

$$Maximize\{TU_P + \sum_h TW^h_P\} \tag{35}$$

s.t.

$$Bw_{P_o} \geq bw\_rq_L \tag{36}$$

$$Dl_{P_L} \leq dl\_rq_H \tag{37}$$

$$Ls_{P_L} \leq ls\_rq_H \tag{38}$$

$$CT_P \leq C_u \tag{39}$$

3   Algorithm Design

Artificial fish-swarm algorithm [8] is an artificial life computing method by simulating fish swarm behavior, trying to make the global optimum emerge out of fish swarm by seeking the local optimum of individual fish.

3.1   Solution Expression and Generation

An artificial fish is corresponding to a problem solution, i.e. a QoS unicast path. A solution is denoted as a vector and the edges of the path from source to destination constitute the vector's elements. The number of vector dimensions is the solution length and its maximum is regarded as standard length. If a solution does not reach the standard length, use the last edge of the path to extend and make the vector reach the standard length. The initial solution is generated by the random path algorithm [9].

3.2   Fitness Function and Distance

The fitness function of the solution corresponding to the artificial fish fs_k is defined as follows:

$$FT(fs_k) = \cfrac{1}{\cfrac{1}{EC_P(fs_k)} \cdot \sum_{e_l \in P} \cfrac{NE_l}{PA_{xy}^l}} \tag{40}$$

$$NE_l = \begin{cases} 1 & \text{Nash equilibrium} \\ > 1 & \text{Non-Nash equilibrium} \end{cases} \tag{41}$$

The distance between two artificial fishes is defined as follows:

$$d(k, v) = \| fs_k - fs_v \| \tag{42}$$

$d(k, v)$ is the number of different elements between fs_k and fs_v, and use $D_k(k, v)$ to denote the set of these different elements in fs_k.

3.3   Artificial Fish Behavior and Its Selection

Use VD_k to denote the perceptive distance of fs_k and all fs_v which meet with the condition $d(k, v) < VD_k$ form the neighborhood of fs_k. Let Sp be the artificial fish movement step and θ be congestion degree factor. The prey behavior is as follows:

Step1: Set the maximum non-movement times CN; set the counter of non-movement times $Cn = 0$.

Step2: For fs_k, select a fs_v from its neighborhood randomly.

Step3: If $FT(fs_v) > FT(fs_k)$, fs_k moves forward one step to fs_v, $s = Random(Sp)$, $Cn = 0$; if $s > d(k, v)$, $s = d(k, v)$; select s edges from $D_k(k, v)$ randomly to do transformation and make them the same as the corresponding edges of fs_v, $d(k, v) = d(k, v) - s$.

Step4: $Cn = Cn + 1$. If $Cn \leq CN$, go to Step2; otherwise, fs_k move one step randomly, $s = Random(Sp)$, and select s edges from fs_k randomly to do transformation.

The swarm behavior is as follows:

Step1: Determine the neighborhood of fs_k and its corresponding artificial fish set R_k, $nf = |R_k|$.

Step2: Determine the central position $fs_c = (e_1^c, e_2^c, ..., e_{len}^c)$ of all artificial fishes in R_k, where e_x^c is the most frequently used edge by artificial fishes in R_k on the xth vector element (if there are several such edges, select one from them randomly).

Step3: If $\frac{FT(fs_c)}{nf} > FT(fs_k) \cdot \theta$, fs_k executes Step3 in the prey behavior and move forward one step to fs_c; otherwise, execute the prey behavior.

The follow behavior is as follows:

Step1: For fs_k, select an fs_v from R_k with the largest $FT(fs_v)$ (if there are several such artificial fishes, select one from them randomly), $fs_{max} = fs_v$, $FT_{max} = FT(fs_v)$.

Step2: Determine the number nf of artificial fishes in the neighborhood of fs_{max}. If $\frac{FT_{max}}{nf} > FT(fs_k)\cdot\theta$, fs_k executes Step3 in the prey behavior and move forward one step to fs_{max}; otherwise, execute the prey behavior in section 3.3.

For behavior selection, fs_k execute prey, swarm and follow behavior by simulation and get fs_{k_p}, fs_{k_s} and fs_{k_f} respectively, then select the corresponding behavior with the largest value among $FT_p(fs_k)$, $FT_s(fs_k)$ and $FT_f(fs_k)$ to do.

3.4   Algorithm Procedure

The procedure of the proposed QoS unicast routing algorithm is described as follows:

Step1: Initialization. Set artificial fish-swarm scale to be N; starting from v_s, generate N artificial fishes according to section 3.1.

Step2: Check whether each fs_k meets with formula (36)-(39) or not: if so, go to Step3; otherwise, regenerate an artificial fish to substitute fs_k according to section 3.1, go to Step2.

Step3: For each fs_k, compute the user utility and the network provider utility on each edge according to formula (23) and (25), play game according to section 2.4(3), compute $FT(fs_k)$ according to formula (40), and denote fs_k with the current largest fitness value as fs_{k^*}.

Step4: Set the values of VD_k, Sp and θ; initialize the call-board and record the current fs_{k^*} on it; set the iterative times to be I and $j = 1$.

Step5: Each fs_k select one behavior to do according to section 3.3.

Step6: For each fs_k, check whether it meets with formula (35)-(38) or not: if so, go to Step7; otherwise, regenerate an artificial fish to substitute fs_k according to section 3.1, go to Step5.

Step7: For each fs_k, compute $FT(fs_k)$ according to formula (40); if $FT(fs_k) > FT(fs_{k^*})$, update the call-board and $k^* = k$.

Step8: If $j = I$, output fs_{k^*} as the problem solution, the end; otherwise, $j = j + 1$, go to Step5.

4   Conclusion

Simulations of the proposed QoS unicast routing scheme have been done on NS2 (Network Simulator 2)[10]. Assume that there are three network providers providing satellite, cellular and fixed links respectively, that is, there are three kinds of links for a user to choose on each hop along the path. The proposed scheme, the proposed microeconomics based fuzzy unicast QoS routing scheme in [11], and the unicast routing scheme based on Dijkstra algorithm [12] have been simulated on some physical and virtual network topologies. Simulation results have shown that the proposed scheme is both feasible and effective with better performance. In future, our study will focus on improving its practicality, developing its prototype system and extend it to multicast scenario.

References

1. Fawzi, D., Seshadri, M.: Challenges of Personal Environments Mobility in Heterogeneous Networks. Mobile Networks and Applications,Vol.8, No.1. (1982) 7–9
2. Willie, W.: Open Wireless Architecture and Enhanced Performance. IEEE Communications Magazine, Vol.41, No.6. (2003) 106–107
3. Gustafsson, E., Jonsson, A.: Always Best Connected. IEEE Wireless Communications, Vol.10, No.1. (2003) 49–55
4. Gabor, F., Eriksson, A.: Aimo Tuoriniemi: Providing Quality of Service in Always Best Connected Networks. IEEE Communications Magazine, Vol. 41, No. 7. (2003) 154–163
5. Theodore, B. Z., Konstantinos, G. V., Christos, P., et al: Global Roaming in Next-Generation Networks. IEEE Communications Magazine, Vol.40, No.2. (2002) 145–151
6. Quan, X. T., Zhang, J.: Theory of Economics Game. Beijing: China Machine Press, (2003)
7. Lorenz, H., Ariel, O.: QoS Routing in Networks with Uncertain Parameters. IEEE/ACM Transactions on Networking, Vol.6, No.6. (1998) 768–778
8. Li, X. L., S, Z. J., Q, J. X.: An Optimizing Method Based on Autonomous Animals: Fish-swarm Algorithm. Systems Engineering-Theory & Practice, Vol.22, No.11. (2002) 32–38
9. West, D.B: Introduction to Graph Theory. Beijing: China Machine Press. (2004) 136–142
10. Xu, L. M., Pang, B., Zhao, R.: NS and Network Simulation. Beijing: Posts & Telecom Press. (2003) 1–9
11. Wang, X. W., Hou, M. J., Wang, J. W., et al.: A Microeconomics-based Fuzzy QoS Unicast Routing Scheme in NGI. Springer LNCS 3824, (2005) 1055–1064
12. Wang, Z., Crowcroft, J.: QoS Routing for Supporting Resource Reservation. IEEE Journal on Selected Areas in Communications, Vol.14, No.7. (1996) 1228-1234

An Efficient Parallel Algorithm for Ultrametric Tree Construction Based on 3PR*

Kun-Ming Yu[1], Jiayi Zhou[2,**], Chun-Yuan Lin[3], and Chuan Yi Tang[4]

[1] Department of of Computer Science and Information Engineering, Chung Hua University
[2] Institute of Engineering Science, Chung Hua University
[3] Institute of Molecular and Cellular Biology, National Tsing Hua University
[4] Department of Computer Science, National Tsing Hua University
300, Hsinchu, Taiwan, R.O.C
[1] yu@chu.edu.tw, [2] jyzhou@pdlab.csie.chu.edu.tw,
[3] cyulin@mx.nthu.edu.tw, [4] cytang@cs.nthu.edu.tw

Abstract. In the computational biology and taxonomy, to construct phylogenetic tree is an important problem. A phylogenetic tree can represent the relationship and histories for a set of species and helpful for biologists to observe existent species. One of popular model is ultrametric tree, and it assumed the evolution rate is constant. UPGMA is one of well-known ultrametric tree algorithm. However, UPGMA is a heuristic algorithm, and it can not guarantee the constructed tree is minimum size. To construct minimum ultrametric tree (MUT) has been shown to be an NP-hard problem. In this paper, we propose an efficient parallel branch-and-bound algorithm with 3-Point Relationship (3PR) to reduce the construction time dramatically. 3PR is a relationship between a distance matrix and the constructed phylogenetic tree. The main concept is for any two species closed to each other in a distance matrix should be also closed to each other in the constructed phylogenetic tree. We use this property to mark the branching path with lower priority or higher, then we move the lower ranked branching path to delay bound pool instead of remove it to ensure the optimal solution can be found. The experimental results show that our parallel algorithm can save the computing time and it also shows that parallel algorithm with 3PR can save about 25% of computing time in average.

Keywords: phylogenetic tree, minimum ultrametric tree, parallel branch-and-bound algorithm, 3-point relationship, 4-point relationship.

1 Introduction

To construct phylogenetic trees is an important problem in the computational biology and in taxonomy, the phylogenetic tree can represent the histories for a set of species and helpful for biologists to observe existent species or evaluate the relationship of them. However, the real evolutionary histories are unknown in practice. Therefore, many methods had been proposed and tried to construct a meaningful phylogenetic tree, which is closing to the real one.

---

* The work is partially supported by National Science Council. (NSC 94-2213-E-216 -028).
** The corresponding author.

G. Min et al. (Eds.): ISPA 2006 Ws, LNCS 4331, pp. 215–220, 2006.

In the input of distance matrix, a phylogenetic tree is constructed according to the distance matrix [10,11]. In general, these values are edit distances between two sequences of any two species. There are many different models and motivated algorithmic problems were proposed [1,9]. However, most of optimization problems for phylogenetic tree construction have been show to be NP-hard [2-4,6,7]. An important and commonly used model is assumed that the rate of evolution is constant. Based on this assumption, the phylogenetic tree will be an ultrametric tree (*UT*), which is rooted, leaf labeled, and edge weighted binary tree. Because many of these problems are intractable and NP-hard, biologists usually construct the trees by using heuristic algorithm. The Unweighted Pair Group Method with Arithmetic mean (*UPGMA*, [1]) is one of the popular heuristic algorithms to construct *UTs*.

Although construct *MUTs* is an NP-hard problem, it is still worthy to construct for middle-size of species. Thus, it seems possible to find an optimal tree using exhaustive search. Nevertheless, for n species, the number of rooted and leaf label tree is, it grows very rapidly. For example, $A(10) > 10^7$, $A(20) > 10^{21}$, $A(30) > 10^{37}$. Hence, it is impossible to exhaustively search for all possible trees even n are middle-size. Wu *et al.* [13] proposed a branch-and-bound algorithm for constructing *MUTs* to avoid exhaustive search. The branch-and-bound strategy is a general technique to solve combinatorial search problems.

In this paper, 3-Point Relationship (3PR) is used to construct *MUTs* more efficiently. 3PR is the relationship between a distance matrix and the constructed phylogenetic tree. The concept is that in triplet of species (a, b, c), any of two species which is closed to each other in the distance matrix should aslo be closed to each other in the constructed phylogenetic tree in a distance matrix. The experimental results show that *PBBU* with 3PR can reduce about 25% computation time both in sequential and parallel algorithms.

The paper is organized as follows. In section 2, some preliminaries for sequential branch-and-bound algorithm and 3PR are given. Parallel algorithm is described in section 3. Section 4 shows our experimental results, and final section is our conclusions.

2 Preliminaries

In this paper, we present *PBBU* with 3PR for construct minimum ultrametric tree. In the following, we denote an unweighted graph G=(V,E,w) with a vertex set V, an edge set E, and an edge weight function w. Some definitions are given as follows:

Definition 1: A distance matrix of n species is a symmetric $n \times n$ matrix M such that $M[i, j] \geq 0$ for all $M[i,i]=0$, and for all $0 \leq i, j \leq n$.

Definition 2: Let $T = (V, E, w)$ be an edge weighted tree and $u, v \in V$. The path length from u to v is denoted by $d_T(u,v)$. The weight of T is defined by $w(T) = \sum_{e \in E} w(e)$.

Definition 3: For any M (not necessarily a metric), *MUT* for M is T with minimum $w(T)$ such that $L(T) = \{1,...,n\}$ and $d_T(i, j) \geq M[i, j]$ for all $1 \leq i, j \leq n$. The problem of finding *MUT* for M is called *MUT* problem.

***Definition* 4:** Let P be a topology, and $a,b \in L(P)$. $LCA(a,b)$ denotes the lowest common ancestor of a and b. If x and y are two nodes of P, we write $x \rightarrow y$ if and only if x is an ancestor of y.

***Definition* 5:** The distance between distance matrix and rooted topology of phylogenetic trees is consistent if $M[i,j] < \min(M[i,k], M[j,k])$ if and only if $LCA(i,j) < LCA(i,k) = LCA(j,k)$ for any $1 \le i,j,k \le n$. Otherwise is contradictory.

2.1   Sequential Branch-and-Bound Algorithm for MUTs

In the *MUT* construction problem, the branch-and-bound is a tree search algorithm and repeatedly searches the branch-and-bound tree (*BBT*) [8,14] to find a better solution until optimal one is found. The *BBT* is a tree which can represent a topology of *UTs*. Assume that the root of *BBT* has depth 0, hence each node with depth i in BBT represents a topology with a leaf set $\{1,...,i+2\}$.

2.2   3-Point Relationship (3PR)

3PR is a logical method to check the *LCA* relation for any triplet of species (a, b, c) in a distance matrix, which is preserved or not in the constructed phylogenetic trees. For any two species (a, b), $LCA(a, b)$ denotes the least common ancestor of (a, b). If (x, y) are two nodes in a phylogenetic tree, $x \rightarrow y$ is written if x is an ancestor of y. For a triplet of species (a, b, c) in the distance matrix M, if the distance $M[a, b]$ of species a and b is less than $M[a, c]$ and $M[b, c]$, $LCA(a, c) = LCA(b, c) \rightarrow LCA(a, b)$ (as $((a, b), c)$; in Newick tree format). For a triplet of species (a, b, c), it is contradictive if the least common ancestor relation in a distance matrix is not preserved in the constructed phylogenetic tree. *3PR* can be used to evaluate the qualities of constructed phylogenetic trees. A phylogenetic tree is considered unreliable if the number of contradictive triplets is large. The evaluated result may be useful for biologists to choose a feasible phylogenetic tree construction tool.

3   Parallel Branch-and-Bound Algorithm with 3PR

Parallel Branch-and-Bound Algorithm with *3PR* (*PBBU* with *3PR*) is designed on distributed memory multiprocessors and the master-slave architecture. The *PBBU* uses a branch-and-bound technique to avoid exhaustive search of possible trees. For load-balance purpose, the master processor (*MP*) contains a *Global Pool* and each slave processor (SP) has Local Pool, moreover we use new data structure instead of the link list to store *BBT*.

In [5], *3PR* is applied as a tree evaluation method. We use this property to put lower rank branching path to Delay Bound Pool (*DBP*) when selecting branch path in the branch-and-bound algorithm. For example, Table 1 is the distance matrix and Figure 1 shows two candidates when inserting the third species c. In *PBBU* without *3PR*, both (a) and (b) candidates need to be added to the pool when branching. However, topology of (b) is closing to distance matrix, it obtained higher rank, and (a) has lower rank. In *PBBU* with *3PR*, only (b) (with higher rank) candidate will be selected due to the distance of a and c is greater than the distance of b and c. This result is based on the conception that in a triplet of species (a, b, c), any of two species which is closed to each other in the distance matrix should also be closed to each other in the corresponding phylogenetic tree in a distance matrix. However, it cannot be directly used to bound another branching path, and *PBBU* with *3PR* put others candidates to the *DBP* to ensure the optimal solution can be found.

Table 1. Distance matrix

	a	b	c
a	0	25	20
b	25	0	15
c	20	15	0

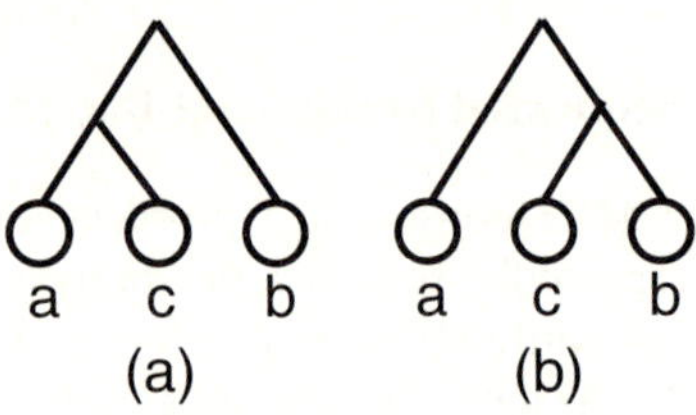

Fig. 1. Candidate *BBT*

4   Experimental Results

In the experimental results, we implement *PBBU* and *PBBU* with *3PR* on a Linux based PC cluster. Each computing node is an AMD Athlon PC with a clock rate of 2.0 GHz and 1GB memory. Each node is connected with each other by 100Mbps network. There are two data sets used to test our algorithms. One is a random data set, which is generated randomly. The distance matrix in the random data set is metric and the range of distances is between 1 and 100. Another is a data set composed of 136 Human Mitochondrial DNAs (*HMDNA*), which is obtained from [12]. Its distance matrix is metric and the range of distances is between 1 and 200. In order to eliminate the problems of data dependence, for each testing data, we run 10 instances. Then we compare the average, median, and worst cases.

Figure 2 and 3 show that *PBBU* with *3PR* and delay bound technique can find the optimal solution and save about 25% of computation time than *PBBU* without *3PR*. Because *3PR* technique move lower ranking candidates which disaccording to *3PR* to delay bound pool, after that, the better bounding value can be found early. Afterward it can bound more candidates to decreasing computation time.

Figure 4 is the speed-up ratio of *HMDNA* data set. We observed that the speed-up ratio of *3PR* is better than it without *3PR*. Furthermore, the difference between *3PR* and without *3PR* is larger when the number of processors increasing. Because of the tighter bounding value can be found quickly with more processors. It also shows that our algorithm is scalable in large number of computing resources. Figure 5 shows the computation time of 16 processors of *PBBU* with *3PR* for different number of species. We can observe that the computation time grow rapidly when the number of species increasing. Moreover, the reduced proportion between *PBBU* and *PBBU* with *3PR* is increasing with larger number of species. We consider that large number of species contains more candidates that a tighter bounding value which can be obtained from *3PR* technique can also bound grater number of candidates; it can decreasing the computation time.

Without 3PR vs. With 3PR (HMDNA)

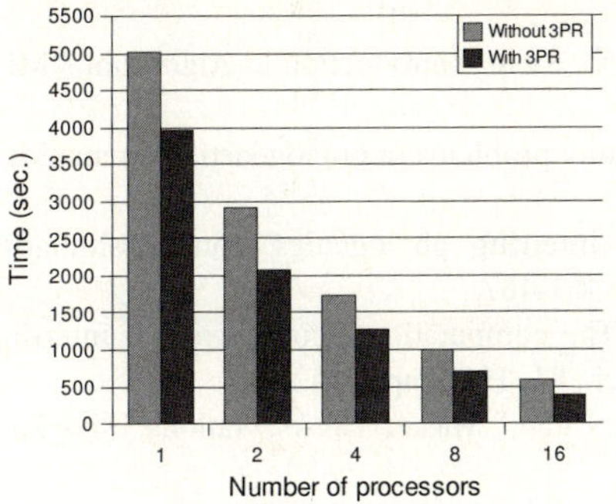

Fig. 2. 3PR vs. Without 3PR (HMDNA)

Without 3PR vs. With 3PR (Random)

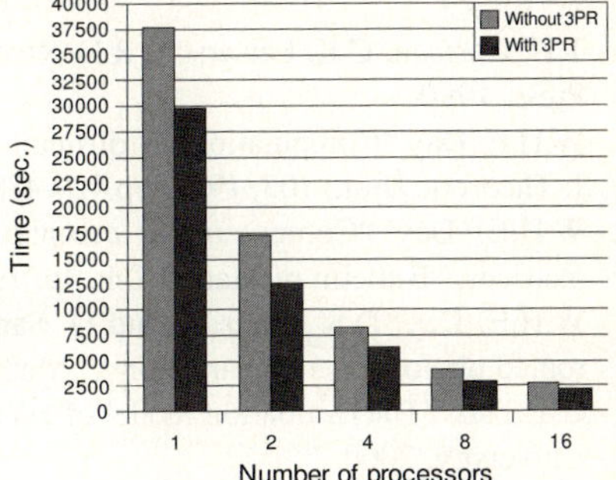

Fig. 3. 3PR vs. Without 3PR (Random)

Speed-up (HMDNA)

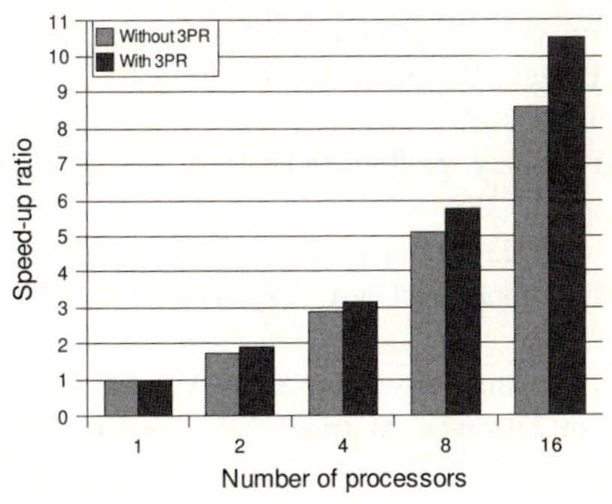

Fig. 4. Speed-up ratio (HMDNA)

Computing time (16 processors)

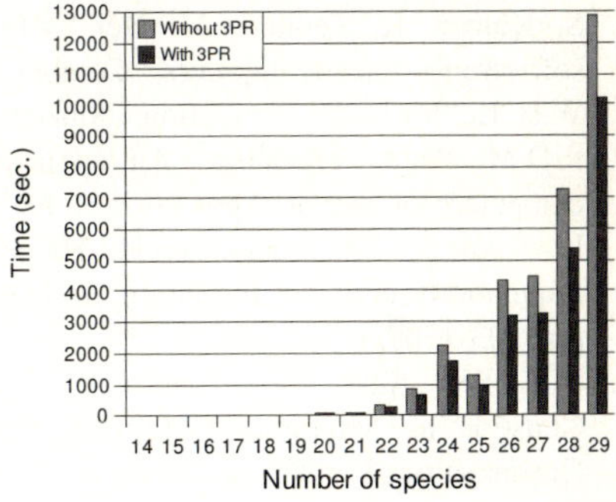

Fig. 5. Computing time (16 processors)

5   Conclusions

In this paper, we have designed *PBBU* with *3PR* for constructing *MUTs* problem. The *3PR* is the relationship between distance matrix and constructed evolutionary tree. It moves candidates which do not fit *3PR* to delay bound pool in branch-and-bound algorithm. After that, we can obtain the tighter bounding value quickly and uses it to bound more candidates. In order to evaluate the performance of our proposed algorithm, a random data set and a practical data set of *HMDNA* are used. The experimental results show that *PBBU* with *3PR* can find optimal solution for 36 species within a reasonable time on 16 PCs. Furthermore, the speed-up ratio shows the performance of our algorithm is good in our PC cluster environment. Moreover, the results also show that *PBBU* with *3PR* can save about 25% in average of computing time than *PBBU* without *3PR*, and it assured the results are optimal with the delay bound technique.

References

1. T.H. Cormen, C.E. Leiserson, R.L. Rivest and C. Stein "Introduction to Algorithm," MIT Press, 1990.
2. W.H.E. Day "Computationally difficult parsimony problems in phylogenetic systematics," J. Theoretic Biol., 103, 1983, pp.429-438.
3. W.H.E. Day "Computational complexity of inferring phylogenies from dissimilarity matrices," Bulletin of Math. Biol., 49, 1987, pp.461-467.
4. W.H.E. Day, D.S. Johnson, and D. Sankoff "The computational complexity of inferring rooted phylogenies by parsimony," Math. Biosci., 81, 1986, pp.33-42.
5. C.T. Fan, "The evaluation model of evolutionary tree," Master Thesis, Nationa Tsing Hua University, 2000.
6. L.R. Foulds "Maximum savings in the Steiner problemin phylogeny," J. Theoretic Biol., 107, 1984, pp.471-474.
7. D. Gusfield "Algorithms on Strings, Trees, and Sequences, computer science and computational biology," Cambridge University Press, 1997.
8. M.D. Hendy and D. Penny "Branch and bound algorithms to determine minimal evolutionary trees," Math. Biol., 59, 1982, pp.277-290.
9. S. Kumer, K. Tamura, M. Nei "MEGA: Molecular Evolutionary Genetics Analysis software for miceocomputers," Comput. Appl. Biosci., 10, 1994, pp.189-191.
10. W.H. Li "Molecular Evolution," Sinauer Associates, 1997.
11. R.D.M. Page "TreeView: An application to display phylogenetic trees on personal computers," Comput. Appl. Biosci., 12, 1996, pp.357-358.
12. L. Vigilant, M. Stoneking, H. Harpending, K. Hawkes and A.C. Wilson "African Populations and the Evolution of Human Mitochondrial DNA," Science, 253, 1991, pp.1503-1507.
13. B.Y. Wu, K.M. Chao, and C.Y. Tang "Approximation and Exact Algorithms for Constructing Minimum Ultrametric Trees from Distance Matrices," J. Combinatorial Optimization, 3, 1999, pp.199-211.
14. C.F. Yu and B.W Wah "Efficient Branch-and-Bound Algorithms on a Two-Level Memory System," IEEE Trans. Parallel and Distributed Systems, 14, 1988, pp.1342-1356.

Exploring Financial Applications on Many-Core-on-a-Chip Architecture: A First Experiment

Weirong Zhu[1], Parimala Thulasiraman[2,*],
Ruppa K. Thulasiram[2], and Guang R. Gao[1]

[1] Department of Electrical and Computer Engineering, University of Delaware,
Newark, DE, USA
[2] Department of Computer Science, University of Manitoba Winnipeg,
MB, Canada
{thulasir, tulsi}@cs.umanitoba.ca,
{weirong, ggao}@weirong@capsl.udel.edu

Abstract. Computational requirements for solving models of financial derivatives, for example, the option pricing problems, are huge and demand efficient algorithms and high performance computing capabilities. This demand has been rekindled by the recent developments in the mobile technology making wireless trading a possibility. In this paper, we focus on the development of a Monte-Carlo algorithm on a modern multi-core chip architecture, Cyclops-64 (C64) under development at IBM as the experimental platform for our study in pricing options. The timing results on C64 show that various sets of simulations could be done in a real-time fashion while yielding high performance/price improvement over traditional microprocessors for finance applications.

1   Introduction

Research in financial derivatives is one of the important areas of computational finance. Finance models used for evaluation and forecasting purposes to help the investor with the selection process typically lead to large dynamic, nonlinear problems that have to be solved in a short time span to beat the competitors in the market place. The computational requirements for solving such financial models are huge and demand efficient algorithms and high performance computing capabilities [1].

In our study, we focus on development of a Monte-Carlo algorithm with historic volatility and GARCH (Generalized Auto Regression Conditional Heteroskedasticity) fitted volatility to price options accurately on Cyclops 64 (C64), a modern many-core-on-a-chip architecture. The purpose is to facilitate pricing of options in a real time fashion. Moreover, our earlier studies using Monte-Carlo technique for the option pricing problem on distributed architectures yielded results [2,3] that are not amenable for real-time implementation, an important requirement for current day trading scenario.

---

* Corresponding author.

G. Min et al. (Eds.): ISPA 2006 Ws, LNCS 4331, pp. 221–230, 2006.
© Springer-Verlag Berlin Heidelberg 2006

This is a first and preliminary study in option pricing on a many-core-on-a-chip architecture. This study opens up many more studies and has many implications: (i) this could be a fore-runner for futuristic embedded architectures such as mobile devices where the current chip technology could be replaced by a CMP (Chip Multi Processor); (ii) wireless trading is becoming a reality in the recent past [4,5,6] and the current work could become a fore-runner for real-time wireless trading; (iii) experience from the current study encourages us to look into other computing techniques popularly used in finance, for example, binomial lattice and finite-differencing technique for implementation on many-core-on-a-chip architecture to enable real time trading.

1.1   Background and Related Work in Option Pricing

A *Call Option* [7] is a contract that gives the right to its holder (i.e. buyer) without creating an obligation, to *buy* a pre-specified underlying asset at a pre-determined price (*strike price*). Usually this right is created for a specific time period (*maturity date*), e.g. six months. A *Put Option* gives to its holder the right to *sell*. If the option can be exercised only at its expiration/maturity date (i.e. the underlying asset can be sold only at the end of the life of the option), the option is referred to as an European style Call/Put Option (or *European Call/Put*). If it can be exercised on any date before its maturity, then the option is referred to as an American style Call/Put Option (or *American Call/Put*).

Black and Scholes [8] proposed a model to price option, which has become a classical and celebrated model for pricing options. This model is basically a stochastic partial differential equation with option price as the unknown and underlying asset price and the time being dependent variables together with various parameters such as volatility of the asset price, expiration date, strike price and interest rate. In the current study future asset prices are generated with random number generated in the Monte-Carlo (MC) simulation and volatility is generated by two methods: historic volatility (based on the past changes in the asset price) and GARCH fitted volatility. Clark [9] and Thulasiram et al. [10] developed parallel algorithm for the binomial lattice approach [11] to price options. Use of fast Fourier transform (FFT) technique for option pricing was introduced by Carr and Madan [12]. Extending this model, Barua et al. [13] have developed an efficient parallel algorithm to enable quicker and accurate pricing of options by introducing data swapping technique in FFT. Mayo [14] evaluated American options using the implicit finite-difference method giving a fourth order accuracy in the log of the asset price and second order accuracy in time. Thulasiram et al. [15] designed a second order L_0 stable algorithm for the pricing problem which achieves the same error bound as that of the traditional Crank-Nicholson scheme, while at the same time assures that the error will not propagate. Srinivasan [16] used the quasi MC simulation technique for option pricing while Rahmail et al. [2] used the traditional MC simulation to study the effect of incorrect volatility for underlying assets on option pricing errors.

MC simulation is a forward-based procedure. Option pricing via MC can be divided into three basic steps: (1) simulate the stochastic process underlying

stock returns, where each realization is a sample path; (2) evaluate the value of
the option in a backward manner in order to find the early exercise point and
obtain a sample point estimate; and, (3) average over multiple sample estimates
to form an interval estimate that includes some measure of precision (e.g., standard error). Obviously, the existence of the precision measure is an advantage of
MC over other numerical methods.

In this study, we explore the possibility of expediting the MC simulation using
a many-core-on-a-chip architecture in the hope that future hand-held devices will
be embedded with CMP architectures and hence achieving parallelism on such
devices.

2   Cyclops-64 Architecture

The Cyclops64 (C64), based on a cellular architecture, is a Many Core System
on Chip (SoC) petaflops supercomputer (see Figure 1) project under development at IBM T.J. Watson Laboratory. C64 system consists of 13,824 C64 chip,
connected by a 3D mesh network. The C64 chip architecture (Figure 2) consists
of 160 hardware thread units, half as many floating point units, same amount
embedded SRAM memory banks, an interface to off-chip DDR SDRAM memory,
and bidirectional inter-chip connection ports on a single silicon chip. Each of the
80 processors have two thread units, a floating point unit, and two SRAM memory banks of approximately 32KB each. Five processors share a 32KB instruction
cache. Instead of data cache, a portion of each thread unit's corresponding on-
chip SRAM bank is configured as the scratchpad memory (SP). Therefore, a
thread unit can achieve fast access to its own SP, i.e., one cycle for a store,
and two cycles for a load. The remaining sections of all on-chip SRAM banks
together form the global memory that is uniformly addressable from all thread
units. The C64 also employs the Network-on-Chip (NoC) concept, all on-chip

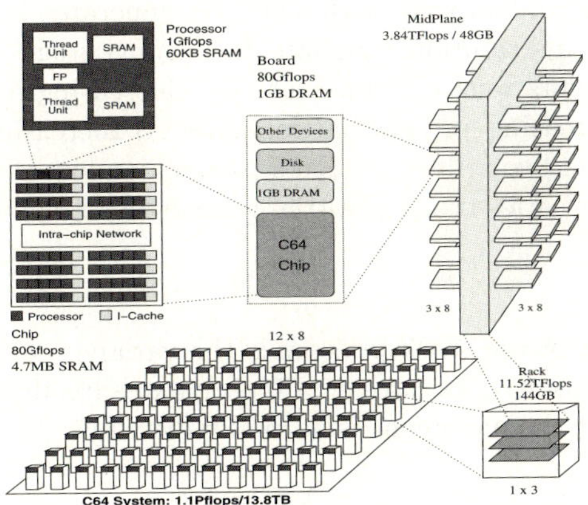

Fig. 1. Cyclops 64 Supercomputer

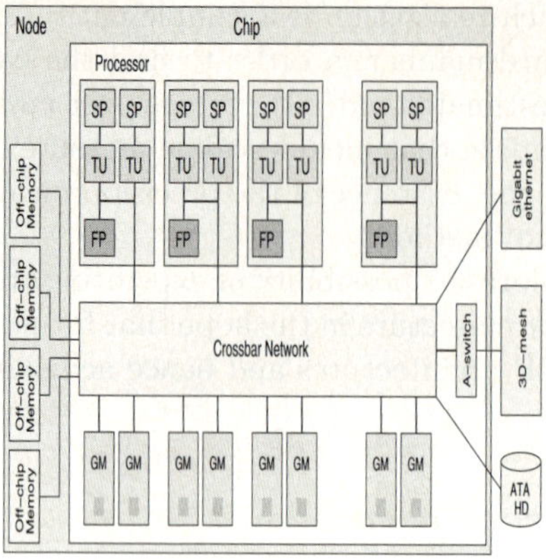

Fig. 2. Cyclops 64 Node

resources are connected to a 96 ports on-chip crossbar network, which provides a 4GB/s bandwidth per port per direction, 384 GB/s per direction in total. This huge bandwidth sustains all the intra-chip traffic communication.

3 Experimental Results

3.1 Monte Carlo Experiment Design

In the Black-Scholes option pricing model volatility is not observable. In the experiments we consider the following: (a) use of historical volatility of continuously compounded stock returns; (b) use of GARCH-fitted volatility of continuously compounded returns.

During the experiments we generated stock price series under the assumption that prices follow a random walk with drift. We generated increments using the normal probability distribution function. In various stages of the experiment volatility of increments was: (i) Constant; (ii) Decreasing; (iii) Increasing; (iv) Stochastic; (v) Decreasing and stochastic; and, (vi) Increasing and stochastic.

Using the generated volatilities σ_t and a pseudo-random number generator, we generate stock price series that follow the geometric Brownian motion process:

$$lnS_t = \gamma + \delta lnS_{t-1} + \nu_t \qquad (1)$$

where γ is the drift in the stock price, σ is the variance rate (volatility) of the stock price, In equation 1 we have $\gamma > 0$ to make sure that prices do not fall below zero and that the increment is normally distributed:

$$\nu_t \approx N(0, \sigma_t^2) \qquad (2)$$

We assumed the continuously compounded interest rate of 5% and the flat and deterministic yield curve, as it is assumed in the Black-Scholes model. Expiration date was set at 3 months from the starting point (time t), and strike price was varyied from 5 to 105 with the step size of 20. The starting prices P_0 in all cases were \$5.00. Using these parameters, we calculated call prices for the non-dividend paying stocks for each point in time t using all inputs as known. The formula used in calculations is the classical option pricing formula (see [7]). Next, we calculated option prices with all the same inputs but measured volatility.

In the first run of the experiment we estimated conditional volatilities and used them in the option pricing formula. In the second run of the experiment we estimated historical and GARCH-fitted volatilities of continuously compounded stock returns [17]. After calculating option prices (C^{TRUE}) using known data and option prices using observable and measured data ($C^{MEASURED}$), we calculated the option pricing error E in the following way:

$$E = C^{MEASURED} - C^{TRUE} \tag{3}$$

This would give us a dollar estimate of the error in case of using an improper measure of volatility in the Black-Scholes option pricing formula.

The experimental results on C64 have both the pricing and performance results. We describe our experimental design for the current study to compute the option values under two volatility criteria and the errors resulting from their use for computing the option values. On a AMD-K7-II processor, with 6 possible exercise prices, 6 patterns of volatility, and 1000 data points, one run of the experiment using the E-Views statistical package for only 20 iterations took 4 hours and 45 minutes.

Figure 3 depicts one of the many sets of pricing errors that results from the experimental study. This graph shows, which of the data generating processes creates larger errors when we use GARCH-fitted volatility of continuously compounded returns. The x-axis in all these figures corresponds to the strike prices ranging from \$5 -\$105 and the y-axis corresponds to the option pricing errors: -0.004 to 0.003 in fig 3 (a); -0.05 to 0.03 in fig 3 (b); -0.06 to 0.01 in fig 3 (c); -0.04 to 0.04 in fig 3 (d); -20.0 to 140.0 in fig 3 (e); -0.20 to 0.06 in fig 3 (f).

Figure 3 (a) corresponds to constant volatility, Figure 3 (b) corresponds to decreasing volatility, Figure 3 (c) corresponds to increasing volatility, Figure 3 (d) corresponds to stochastic volatility, Figure 3 (e) corresponds to decreasing and stochastic volatility, Figure 3 (f) corresponds to increasing and stochastic volatility. The six legends below each of these figures identify the prices starting from \$5 to \$105 in steps of \$20 for respective figures.

During the experiments the drift component of the stock price is \$0.006t, where t stands for the number of days. Therefore, we are able to plot call pricing error against various exercise prices and unconditional expectations of stock prices ($E[S_t] = 0.006 * t$). In this part of the experiment, $GARCH$ model is estimated for the sample size k with the mean equation that regresses continuously compounded returns on a constant. We generate fitted volatility and record the last value h_k. This is our input into the Black-Scholes formula for calculating the measured call price, $C_k^{MEASURED}$. Next, we add one more data point to the stock price series, estimate the GARCH model for the sample of

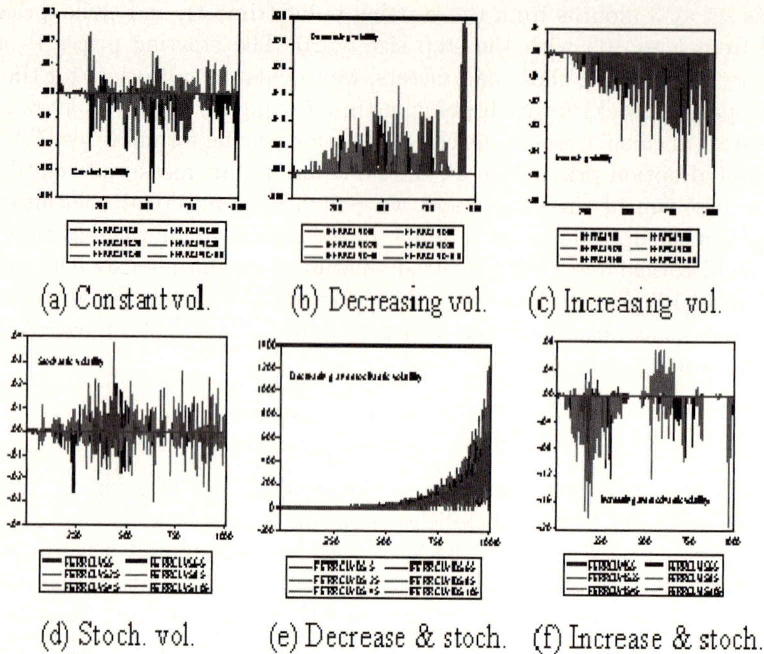

(a) Constant vol.   (b) Decreasing vol.   (c) Increasing vol.

(d) Stoch. vol.   (e) Decrease & stoch.   (f) Increase & stoch.

Fig. 3. Option pricing errors for stock prices generated using various patterns of volatility, average across series. GARCH-fitted volatility estimates based on continuously compounded returns are used to generate option prices.

$k + 1$ observations, and use h_{k+1} to calculate $C_{k+1}^{MEASURED}$. Using this process, we generate the time series of measured call prices $C_t^{MEASURED}$.

As we can infer from Figure 3, in some cases (for example, cases b and e) option pricing errors grow with higher sample size. This can be attributed to the non-stationarity of option prices: as sample size increases, sample volatility of data approaches infinity. Therefore, we get upward-biased estimates for the volatility of stock prices. The comparative statistics of Black-Scholes model show that call price increases when stock price volatility increases. Therefore, upward-biased estimates of stock prices result in upward-biased estimates of option prices. This situation could result in a false belief that there exists a Put-Call-Parity arbitrage strategy based on erroneously calculated call prices. In case of constant and stochastic volatility of prices (Fig. 3 (a and d)) the situation is not as clear. Option pricing errors seem to be fluctuating around zero on the average.

In the following subsection, we demonstrate the performance results of running the simulation on the C64 architecture.

3.2   Monte Carlo Simulation on C64

The performance of the Monte Carlo algorithm on C64 is compared to different representative off-the-shelf processors: AMD Opteron 250, Intel Centrino, and Intel Pentium 4. The basic configurations of those processors are shown in Table 1. The computation conducted on C64 is simulated with the FAST simulator [18], which is a functionally accurate simulation tool set for the C64 cellular architecture. The parameter setting for 4 different simulations is shown in Table 2.

Table 1. Processor Configurations

Processor	Clock Rate	Cache	off-chip Memory	Compiler
Cyclops-64 Thread Unit	500MHz	No data cache 5MB on-chip SRAM memory	1GB DRAM	gcc-3.2.3 for C64
AMD Opteron	2.4GHz	1MB L2 cache	3GB	gcc-3.2.3 for x86_64
Intel Centrino	1.86GHz	2MB L2 cache	512MB	gcc-3.3.6
Intel Pentium4	3.2GHz	512KB L2 cache	1GB	gcc-3.4.3

Table 2. Parameters for Monte Carlo Simulation

Parameter	begprice	step	variety	ARSIZE
sim-1	5	20	6	1000
sim-2	5	40	8	1000
sim-3	5	40	8	2000
sim-4	5	100	10	5000

For C64, a portion of each SRAM bank can be configured as the scratchpad memory (16KB, in this case), which guarantees fast and predictable access latency for the corresponding owner thread unit. For the Monte Carlo simulation, we carefully design the code, such that the intermediate results of the computation can completely fit into a thread unit's scratchpad memory. Only the latest i^{th} simulation results were stored on-chip for the next $(i+1)^{th}$ simulation. The previous 1, ... , $i-1$ results were stored off-chip.

We performed on average ten runs on each of the machine and obtained the execution times as shown in Figure 4 for the simulation parameters chosen in Table 2, where *begprice* is the beginning price of the simulation, *step* is the step size on price, *variety* is the number of volatility patterns, and *ARSIZE* is the number of data points in each simulation.

In the Monte Carlo simulation all the thread units can work independently during the simulation. Since all the intermediate data needed for a thread unit's computation can fit into its own scratchpad memory, there is no runtime competition and conflict for shared resources, such as global on-chip memory. Through calculations for all four groups of simulations, for the Monte Carlo option pricing simulation, we can conclude that 1 C64 node delivers the performance equivalent to 18 Opteron 250 CPU, 32 Intel Centrino CPU, and 28 Intel P4 3.2GHz CPU. The approximate price for a C64 node would be quite similar to machines built with those CPUs compared. The speedup of the parallel version can increase linearly with the number of threads used (this is also demonstrated with

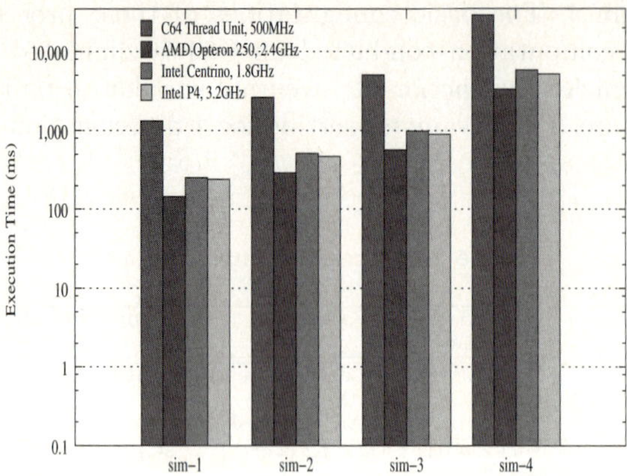

Fig. 4. Execution Time of Monte Carlo Simulation

the simulation). Therefore, the C64 delivers huge *performance/price* improvement over traditional microprocessors for computational finance applications. Moreover, for the Monte Carlo simulation, since all data fits into the scratchpad memory, all the computation is performed locally for each thread units and the power on the very long wires going to and from the crossbar is saved. In such a situation, the power consumption of a C64 node is lower than or close to machine built with conventional microprocessor. Given a C64 node delivers tens of times performance, the C64's *performance/power consumption* ratio is much higher compared to other microprocessors. Unlike a traditional microprocessor, which dies if any parts on the chip is broken, the C64 chip can still be in working condition, even if one or more thread units/memory banks fail.

4   Conclusions

The current work is a first attempt to study (option pricing using Monte-Carlo simulation). We showed that the use of incorrect volatility of the asset prices in the Black-Scholes model would result in moderate to large errors in option prices. We conclude that 1 C64 node delivers the performance equivalent to 18 Opteron 250 CPU, 32 Intel Centrino CPU, and 28 Intel P4 3.2GHz CPU. This translates to high *performance/price* and *performance/power consumption* improvement over traditional microprocessors for computational finance applications.

Acknowledgement

Part of this work was conducted while the second and third authors were visiting University of Delaware in Summer 2005. These authors acknowledge the financial support from Natural Sciences and Engineering Research Council of Canada and the University Research Grant Program of the University of Manitoba. The first and last authors would like to acknowledge the support from

IBM, in particular, Monty Denneau, who is the architect of IBM Cyclops-64 architecture, ETI, the Department of Defense, the Department of Energy (DE-FC02-01ER25503), the National Science Foundation (CNS-0509332), and other government sponsors. We would also like to acknowledge other members of the CAPSL group at University of Delaware, who provide a stimulus environment for scientific discussions and collaborations, in particular Juan del Cuvillo, and Ziang Hu.

References

1. E. J. Kontoghiorghes, A. Nagurnec, and Berc Rustem. Parallel Computing in Economics, Finance and Decision-making. *Parallel Computing*, 26:207–509, 2000.
2. Sergiy Rahmayil, Ilona Shiller, and Ruppa K. Thulasiram. Different Estimators of the Underlying Asset's Volatility and Option Pricing Errors: Parallel Monte Carlo Simulation. In *Proc. Intl. Conf. on Computational Finance and its Applications*, pages 121–131, Bologna, Italy, April 2004.
3. Gong Chen, Ruppa K. Thulasiram, and Parimala Thulasiraman. Distributed Adaptive Quasi-Monte Carlo Algorithm for Option Pricing on HNOWs Using mpC. In *Proc. 9th Annual Simulation Sympoisum*, pages 90–97, Huntsville, AL, April 2006.
4. Kiran Kola. WAMAN:Web-mining-Assisted Mobile-computing-enAbled on-line optioN pricing- a software architecture towards autonomic computing. Master's thesis, Department of Computer Science, The University of Manitoba, Winnipeg, MB, Canada, May 2006.
5. H. Kargupta, B. Park, S. Pittie, L. Liu, D. Kushraj, and K. Sarkar. Mobimine: Monitoring the stock market from a pda. *SIGKDD EXplorer*, 3:37–46, 2002.
6. U. Varshney and R.J. Vetter. Mobile commerce:framework, applications and networking support. *MONET*, 7:3–4, 2002.
7. John C. Hull. *Options, Futures and Other Derivatives*. Prentice Hall, Upper Saddle River, NJ, 5 edition, 2002.
8. F. Black and M. Scholes. The pricing of options and corporate liabilities. *J.Political Economy*, 81:637–654, January 1973.
9. Iain J. Clark. Option Pricing Algorithms for the Cray T3D Supercomputer. *Proceedings of the first National Conference on Computational and Quantitative Finance*, September 1998.
10. R. K. Thulasiram, L. Litov, H. Nojumi, C. T. Downing, and G. R. Gao. Multi-threaded Algorithms for Pricing a Class of Complex Options. In *Proc. Intl. Parallel and Distributed Processing Symp. (IPDPS01)*, San Francisco, CA, April 2001.
11. J.C. Cox, S.A. Ross, and M. Rubinstein. Option pricing: A simplified approach. *J. Financial Economics*, 7:229–263, 1979.
12. Peter Carr and Dilip B. Madan. Option Valuation using the Fast Fourier Transform. *The Journal of Computational Finance*, 2(4):61–73, 1999.
13. Sajib Barua, Ruppa K. Thulasiram, and Parimala Thulasiraman. High Performance Computing for a Financial Application using Fast Fourier Transform. In *LNCS Vol. 3648, Proc. European Parallel Computing Conference (EuroPar05)*, pages 1246–1253, Lisbon, Portugal, aug-sep 2005.
14. A. Mayo. Fourth Order Accurate Implicit Finite Difference Method for Evaluating American Options. In *Proc. Intl. Conf. on Computational Finance 2000*, London, England, June 2000.

15. Ruppa K. Thulasiram, Chen Zhen, Amit Chhabra, Parimala Thulasiraman, and Abba Gumel. A second order l_0 stable algorithm for evaluating european options. *Intl. Journal of High Performance Computing and Networking (in press)*, 2006.
16. Ashok Srinivasan. Parallel an Distributed Computing Issues in Pricing Financial Derivatives through Quasi Monte Carlo. In *Proc. Intl. Parallel and Distributed Processing Symp. (IPDPS02)*, Fort Lauderdale, FL, April 2002.
17. M. Chesney and L. Scott. Pricing European Currency Options: A Comparision of the Modified Black-Scholes and a Random Variance Model. *Journal of Financial and Quantitative Analysis*, 24:267–284, 1989.
18. Juan del Cuvillo, Weirong Zhu, Ziang Hu, and Guang R. Gao. FAST: A functionally accurate simulation toolset for the Cyclops64 cellular architecture. In *Workshop on Modeling, Benchmarking, and Simulation (MoBS2005)*, Madison, WI, June 2005.

A Distributed Simulation-Based Computational Intelligence Algorithm for Nanoscale Semiconductor Device Inverse Problem

Yiming Li and Cheng-Kai Chen

Department of Communication Engineering, National Chiao Tung University,
1001 Ta-Hsueh Road, Hsinchu 300, Taiwan
ymli@faculty.nctu.edu.tw

Abstract. In this paper, a distributed simulation-based computational intelligence algorithm for inverse problem of nanoscale semiconductor device is presented. This approach features a simulation-based optimization strategy, and mainly integrates the semiconductor process simulation, semiconductor device simulation, evolutionary strategy, and empirical knowledge on a distributed computing environment. For a set of given target current-voltage (I-V) curves of metal-oxide-semiconductor field effect transistors (MOSFETs) devices, the developed prototype executes evolutionary tasks to solve an inverse doping profile problem, and therefore optimize fabrication recipes. In the evolutionary loop, the established management server allocates the jobs of process simulation and device simulation on a PC-based Linux cluster with message passing interface (MPI) libraries. Good benchmark results including the speed-up, the load balancing, and the parallel efficiency are presented. Computed results, compared with the realistic measured data of 65 nm n-type MOSFET, show the accuracy and robustness of the method.

1 Introduction

Technology computer-aided design (TCAD) in semiconductor industry nowadays is continuously playing a central role in metal-oxide-semiconductor field effect transistors (MOSFETs) device fabrication [1-6]. For a set of given current-voltage (I-V) curves of MOSFETs, inversely searching out an optimal fabrication configuration forms an engineering's inverse problem [7-9]. Conventional try-and-error procedure has been used to seeking acceptable fabrication recipe. Unfortunately, such work has significantly encountered serious challenges, and simultaneously complicates the development of next generation technology due to evident variations of electrical characteristics in modern 65 nm MOSFETs [10-12], for example. Any computationally efficient approach is therefore required and also benefits sub-65 nm MOSFET's era. A simulation-based evolutionary TCAD methodology provides an alternative to new technology development. It is known that time cost of computation of the process simulation and device simulation dominates the efficiency of the simulation-based computational intelligence method. This approach may work in real world applications once distributed computing techniques [13-22] could be properly incorporated.

In this work, a distributed implementation of the simulation-based computational intelligence technique [8] is presented for solving the semiconductor inverse problem on a

PC-base Linux cluster. This approach successfully integrates a two-dimensional (2D) process simulation, device simulation, computational intelligence algorithm [13, 23-24], and empirical knowledge on our own cluster with message passing interface (MPI) libraries. According to achieved and accumulated experience from semiconductor foundry, different empirical knowledge is implemented in the developed prototype. It plays a good starting point in the loop of evolutionary processes. Fabrication steps are analyzed in the stage of semiconductor process simulation. To simulate the device characteristics of 65 nm MOSFETs and beyond, quantum mechanical effects are taken into consideration to accurately describe device's transport phenomenon. A set of 2D density-gradient-drift-diffusion equations [1-2] is numerically solved with an adaptive computing technique [1-6]. A hybrid genetic algorithm, combining genetic algorithm with numerical optimization method [23-24], is advanced in the simulation-based computational intelligence approach. The prototype of the simulation-based computational intelligence algorithm is implemented in our PC-based Linux cluster, which is functioned with 16 CPUs. Based upon a management server of the distributed system, all jobs of the process and device simulations are gathered in a queue. The server is then dynamically allocated the jobs to each CPU of the cluster. For a set of specified target of I-V curves as well as electrical characteristics, the prototype will perform process and device simulations and search out several suitable process recipes, such as doping profiles. The stopping criterion is subject to a given error tolerance between the simulation and the specification of designed target.

Compared with realistic experimental data and process recipe, the achieved results confirm the capability of the implemented prototype for a 65 nm n-type MOSFET (N-MOSFET) on the PC-based cluster. The accuracy and computational performance in terms of difference benchmarks are obtained. Distributed realization of the simulation-based computational intelligence algorithm not only is of great worth in advanced TCAD development but also provides a novel way to diagnosis of device characteristics in sub-65 nm MOSFETs era. This paper is organized as follows. In Sec. 2, we state the methodology. In Sec. 3, results and discussion are presented. Finally, we draw conclusions.

2   The Evolutionary Technique and Distributed Implementation

The developed distributed simulation-based computational intelligence algorithm includes 2D simulations of process and device, computational intelligence algorithm, and empirical knowledge of fabrication technology. Architecture of the proposed system is shown in Fig. 1. We utilize the distributed computation technique on the hybrid evolutionary system and external simulators. The distributed system management bridges the PC clusters and the simulation-based evolutionary system together. It allocates the computing resources while the evolutionary system perform optimization task. The simulation of process and device, shown in Algorithm 1, performs simulation of several important fabrication processes to obtain the device geometry of MOSFET and the corresponding doping profile. The output of the process simulation is then used in the device simulation to examine device characteristics. Both the target and simulated I-V curves are the input of the optimization kernel. After evolutionary process, a set of newest updated parameters is proposed and suggested for the next simulation of process and device. This work features the computational intelligence approach in the inverse problem of the doping profile. The developed evolutionary prototype, shown in Algorithm 1, is mainly relying on a hybrid genetic algorithm.

This evolutionary technique works together with several practically empirical rules that are necessary for pre-process of optimization, and significantly play good initial-starting (and re-starting) points for all evolutionary steps. In this investigation, only the hybrid genetic algorithm among evolutionary algorithms is enabled due to a moderate number (about 30 parameters) of parameters to be optimized.

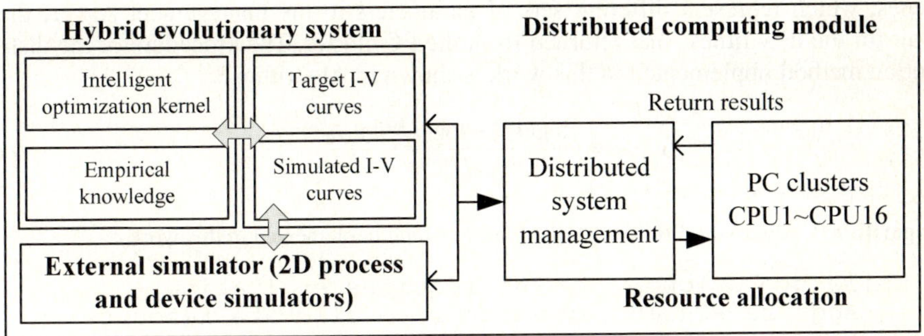

Fig. 1. A system diagram for the proposed system

Algorithm 1. A procedure of the proposed optimization system to solve the semiconductor device inverse problem

```
While optimal recipe is not found
    Use current recipe to simulate I-V curves:
        Perform process simulation
        Obtain doping profile
        Perform device simulation
        Obtain simulated I-V curves
    Evaluate error (target and simulated I-V curves)
    Generate new recipe with empirical knowledge
```

Algorithm 2. A procedure of the inverse modeling problem

```
Initialize GA environment
Generate initial process recipes
While device electrical characteristic is not converged
    Invoke process simulator to obtain doping profile
    While I-V curves are not converged
        Invoke device simulator
        Retrieve I-V characteristic from device simulator
        Evaluate result (I-V curves and device electrical
characteristics)
    End while
End while
```

As shown in Algorithm 2, with a set of selected process recipes and device model parameters, the external numerical programs are called to perform simulations of process and device to retrieve the newest I-V curves and device characteristics. Together with the specified target of I-V curves, the results are used in the calculation of the newest fitness score, and then the newest parameters are suggested for next simulation and optimization. The fitness score is used to evaluate how well the solution being tested that fits the desired outcome. Given by Eq. (1), the drain current (I_D) means the simulated data and the I_D^{target} is the specified target to be achieved. We distributed the external simulation programs, which are the dominant parts of the CPU time. In the procedure of the hybrid genetic algorithm, we only need to pass the genes, which represent different sets of parameters to the management server, then wait for the new fitness that returned from the PC cluster. The procedure of the distribution method implemented in this work is shown in Algorithm 3.

$$\text{fitness} \equiv (\frac{\log(I_D) - \log(I_D^{\text{target}})}{\log(I_D^{\text{target}})})^2 \qquad (1)$$

Algorithm 3. A working flow of the distribution which implemented in this work

```
While evolutionary system requires evaluation
    Acquire PC-Cluster manager to allocate resource
    For each assigned PC-Cluster's CPU
        Calls external simulator for simulation
        Return results to PC-Cluster manager
    End for
    PC-Cluster manager returns results to evolutionary
system
End while
```

The physical-based empirical knowledge directly indicates the relationship of the parameters and the tendency of device characteristics. During optimization processes, once a larger error occurring in certain region of the I-V curves is observed, empirical rules will be employed to destroy the evolution, which may result in different mutation and is useful in the iteration loop of simulation and optimization. We adopt the relationship of the target of the I-V curves to be optimized and several most concerned physical quantities. For different regions of the I-V curves, we can firstly tune the corresponding process or device parameters by following the empirically built-in rules in our evolutionary prototype. The corresponding pseudo code of several considered empirical knowledge of fabrication technology is shown in Algorithm 4.

Algorithm 4. A procedure of the considered experimental engineering knowledge

```
Empirical Knowledge for MOSFET IV-Optimization
    For each I-V point PT in I-V curves
    {
        If( PT.voltage < 0.0 )
          PT in Band-to-band tunneling model region
        Else if( PT.voltage >= 0.0 && PT.voltage < 0.6)
          PT in VT.Implementation region
        Else if( PT.voltage >= 0.6 && PT.voltage < 0.8)
          PT in Saturation region
        Else
          PT in Mobility model region
    }
```

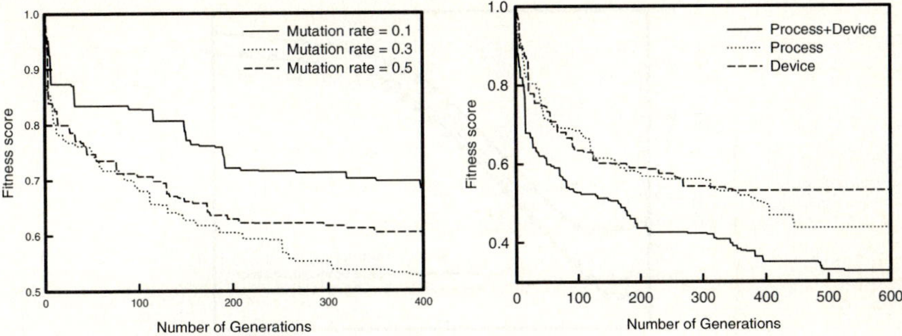

Fig. 2. (a) Performance comparisons among three different mutation rates, and (b) the performance comparisons among three different evolutionary strategies. There are totally 31 process and device's parameters to be optimized in the case of process and device simulations.

3   Results and Discussion

To inversely extract the doping profile of the designed 65 nm MOSFET for the given target of the I-V data, the implemented evolutionary prototype is running on our PC-based Linux cluster system with 16 CPUs. Figure 2a shows the comparison of the three distinct GA configurations with different mutation rates for only device parameters optimization. It is shown that the mutation rate = 0.3 has the best convergence behavior. Under the same setting, the fitness score versus the number of evolutionary generations is shown in Fig. 2b. It depicts the performance of the evolutionary technique with three different calibration strategies. If we partially optimize the process parameters or the device parameters, the accuracy of extraction is limited. Results suggest that it is necessary to extract process and device parameters simultaneously. For the given target, if the inverse extraction considers only the parameters of device modeling in the 2D device simulation, the fitness suggests that the proposed optimization methodology seems to be invalid even for a long time evolution process. For the simulation-based evolutionary technique with only the process-related parameters (i.e., only the parameters of the doping profile), a better fitness score is expected. However, the methodology with simultaneously considering the parameters of the process and device physics impressively confirms its computational efficiency.

The extracted I-V curves for the explored 65 nm MOSFET are shown in Fig. 3. The symbols are the desired target to be optimized, the solid lines are the final achieved result, and the dashed lines are the original I-V characteristics corresponding to the initial setting on the process and device simulations. We note that the target can ideally be regarded as the realistic silicon data after fabrication and measurement. For the 65 nm MOSFET, the optimized doping profiles are shown in Fig. 4. The derivation of the ratio of the on- and off-state currents consists of several mechanisms, such as the level of the off-state current significantly affected by the implantations of the threshold voltage, the lightly doped drain (LDD), and source/drain. The on-state current is directly proportional to the adjustment of device's mobility model, and the implantations of the threshold voltage and LDD. Table 1 shows the partial list of process parameters to be extracted with their numeric ranges for the explored 65nm N-MOSFETs and the extracted results.

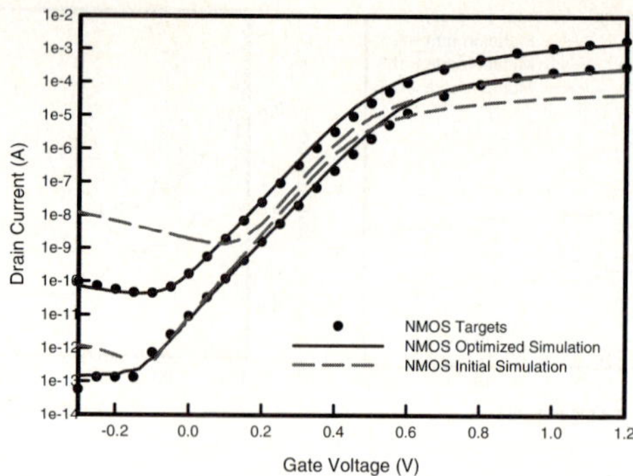

Fig. 3. The achieved accuracy of the extracted I-V curves for the 65 nm N-type MOSFET. The device is with the gate length L = 65 nm and device width W = 1 μm. Results are simultaneously obtained with considering device and process configurations. Symbols are measured data and lines are eventually optimized result.

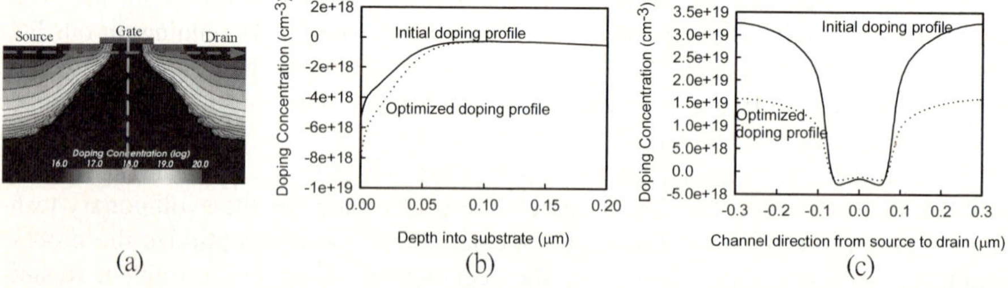

(a)   (b)   (c)

Fig. 4. (a) A plot of the extracted doping profile of the 65 nm N-MOSFET. The result is corresponding to the finally optimized I-V curves shown in Fig. 4. (b) Orange cutting-line (horizontal direction) plots for the corresponding doping profiles from surface into substrate which locates at the center of the device channel. (c) Pink cutting-line (perpendicular direction) plots for the corresponding doping profiles from the source side to the drain side below the device surface 50 nm.

Difference of the doping profile between the initial setting and final optimized results is shown in Fig. 4b. For the corresponding doping profiles, perpendicularly cutting-line plots from surface into substrate which locates at the center of the device channel are shown in Fig. 4b. A 30% difference is observed on the surface (i.e., the position at 0 μm). The plot along the channel from the source side to the drain side below the device surface 50 nm is shown in Fig. 4c. The difference is more than 50% shown in the both sides of the device channel (i.e., near the source and drain sides, respectively). Figure 5 is the achieved speed-up and efficiency for three different optimization configurations, where the speed-up is the ratio of the execution time of the simulation codes on a single processor to that on multiple processors. The efficiency of the distributed system is defined as the speed-up divided by the number of CPUs. It is found that the speed-up is about 13 for the simulation running on a

Table 1. A partial list of process parameters to be extracted with their numeric ranges for the explored 65nm N-MOSFETs

Process parameters	Numeric range	The calibrated results for 65nm N-MOSFET
Well Imp. Energy	200 ~ 500 KeV	462
Well Imp. Dose	5e+12 ~ 5e+13 cm^{-2}	2.6e+13
Well Imp. Tilt	0 ~ 45 (degree)	5
LDD Imp. Energy	10 ~ 50 KeV	30
LDD Imp. Dose	5e+12 ~ 5e+13 cm^{-2}	3.7e+13
LDD Imp. Tilt	0 ~ 45 (degree)	30
LDD Imp. Rotation	0 ~ 360 (degree)	43
S/D Imp. Energy	10 ~ 80 KeV	17
S/D Imp. Dose	1e+13 ~ 1e+14 cm^{-2}	2.1e+13
S/D Imp. Tilt	0 ~ 45 (degree)	2

Table 2. The achieved load balancing of the prototype running on the cluster with 16 CPUs with respect to three different population (Pop) sizes

CPU \ Pop size	Time (min) 8	16	32
#1	250	492	1042
#2	259	501	1023
#3	234	511	982
#4	231	530	987
#5	229	481	1002
#6	245	521	1034
#7	225	481	1021
#8	254	485	1012
#9	--	512	990
#10	--	532	1015
#11	--	498	986
#12	--	492	989
#13	--	487	996
#14	--	490	1031
#15	--	482	1027
#16	--	521	981
$\frac{Max - Min}{Max} \times 100\%$	13.12%	9.2%	5.8%

16-CPUs PC-based cluster system, and the efficiency is maintained at about 80%. Due to properties of distributed genetic algorithm without data exchanging, the presented work achieved to high performance. Preliminary results, shown in Table 2, are the achieved load balancing of the established system. The distributed management server properly maintains the load of each CPU in the cluster. For three different population sizes, the maximum difference of the calculation time ranges from 5.8% to 13.2% where the optimization configuration is extracting process and device parameters simultaneously. Small population size troubles the distribution in the evolutionary process and results in poor load balancing among CPUs. Increase of population sizes improves the load balancing among CPUs.

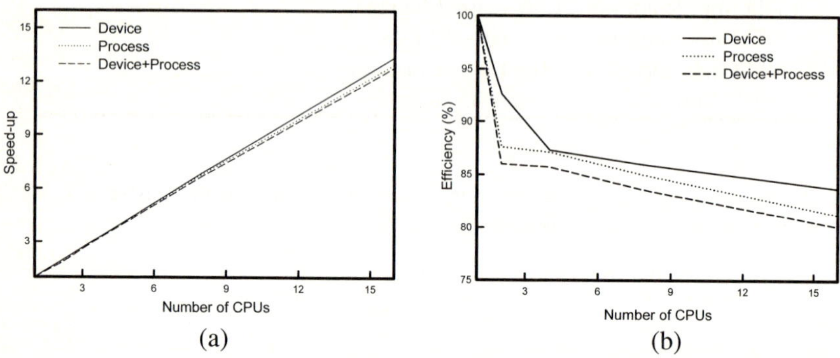

Fig. 5. The achieved performance versus the number of CPUs for three different optimization configurations, where (a) is the speed-up and (b) is the achieved efficiency

4 Conclusions

We have presented a distributed realization of the simulation-based computational intelligence algorithm for semiconductor device inverse doping profile problem. The prototype has successfully implemented on our PC-based cluster and tested on the 65 nm MOSFET devices. In the evolutionary processes, various process and device parameters have simultaneously been considered, and therefore the doping profiles of the 65 nm MOSFETs were successfully extracted according to the desired target which reflects realistic measured silicon data well. Performed on the PC-based Linux cluster with MPI libraries, preliminary performance of the distribution with dynamic job allocating has been achieved in terms of the speed-up and the efficiency. We are currently extending this approach to explore the inverse doping profile problem with minimization of the characteristic fluctuation for sub-65 nm MOSFET devices.

Acknowledgments

This work was supported in part by Taiwan National Science Council (NSC) under Contract NSC-94-2215-E-009-084, Contract NSC-95-2221-E-009-336, and Contract NSC-95-2752-E-009-003-PAE, by the MoE ATU Program, Taiwan, under a 2006 grant, and by the Taiwan Semiconductor Manufacturing Company under a 2005-2007 grant.

References

1. Li, Y., Chou, H.-M., Lee, J.-W.: Investigation of Electrical Characteristics on   Surrounding-Gate and Omega-Shaped-Gate Nanowire FinFETs. IEEE Trans. Nanotech. 4 (2005) 510-516
2. Li, Y., Chou, H.-M.: A Comparative Study of Electrical Characteristic on Sub-10 nm Double Gate MOSFETs. IEEE Trans. Nanotech. 4 (2005) 645-647
3. Li, Y. Yu, S.-M.: A Two-Dimensional Quantum Transport Simulation of Nanoscale Double-Gate MOSFETs using Parallel Adaptive Technique. IEICE Trans. Inf. Syst. E87-D (2004) 1751-1758
4. Li, Y.: A Parallel Monotone Iterative Method for the Numerical Solution of Multidimensional Semiconductor Poisson Equation. Comput. Phys. Commun. 153 (2003) 359-372
5. Li, Y., Sze, S. M., Chao, T.-S.: A Practical Implementation of Parallel Dynamic Load Balancing for Adaptive Computing in VLSI Device Simulation. Eng. Comput. 18 (2002) 124-137
6. Li, Y., Liu, J.-L., Chao, T.-S., Sze, S. M.: A new parallel adaptive finite volume method for the numerical simulation of semiconductor devices. Comput. Phys. Commun. 142 (2001) 285-289
7. Binder, T., Heitzinger, C., Selberherr, S.: A Study on Global and Local Optimization Techniques for TCAD Analysis Tasks. IEEE Trans. CAD. 23 (2004) 814-822
8. Li, Y., Yu, S.-M., Chen, C.-K.: A Simulation-Based Evolutionary Technique for Inverse Problems of Sub-65nm CMOS Devices. In: Kosina, H., Selberherr, S. (eds.): Book of Abstracts of the 11th International Workshop on Computational Electronics. Technische Universit¨at Wien (TU Wien), Institute for Microelectronics, Vienna, Austria (2006) 69-70
9. Dupre, L., Slodicka, M.: Inverse problem for magnetic sensors based on a Preisach formalism. IEEE Trans. Mag. 40 (2004) 1120-1123
10. Li, Y., Yu, S.-M.: Comparison of Random Dopant-Induced Threshold Voltage Fluctuations in Nanoscale Single-, Double-, and Surrounding-Gate Field Effect Transistors. Jpn. J. Appl. Phys. 45 (2006) 6860-6865
11. Li, Y., Yu, S.-M.: Study of Threshold Voltage Fluctuations of Nanoscale Double Gate Metal-Oxide-Semiconductor Field Effect Transistors Using Quantum Correction Simulation. J. Comput. Elec. 5 (2006) 125-129
12. Li, Y., Chou, Y.-S.: A Novel Statistical Methodology for Sub-100 nm MOSFET Fabrication Optimization and Sensitivity Analysis. In Extended Abstract of the 2005 Int. Conf. Solid State Devices and Materials (2005) 622-623
13. Cantú-Paz, E.: Efficient and Accurate Parallel Genetic Algorithms. Kluwer Academic Publishers, Boston (2000)
14. Goldberg, D. E.: Genetic Algorithms in Search, Optimization and Machine Learning. New York: Addison-Wesley (1989)
15. Thierauf, G., Cai, J.: Parallel evolution strategy for solving structural optimization. Eng. Struct. 19 (1997) 318-324
16. Schoneveld, A., de Ronde, J. F., Sloot, P. M. A.: Task Allocation by Parallel Evolutionary Computing. J. Paral. Distribu. Comput. 47 (1997) 91-97
17. Migdalas, A., Toraldo, G., Kumar, V.: Nonlinear optimization and parallel computing. Paral. Comput. 29 (2003) 375-391
18. Van Veldhuizen, D. A., Zydallis, J. B., Lamont, G. B.: Evolutionary computing and optimization: Issues in parallelizing multiobjective evolutionary algorithms for real world applications. In: *Proc. ACM Symp. Appl. Computing* (2002) 595-602

19. Nanda, P. K. Ghose, B., Swain, T. N.: Parallel genetic algorithm based unsupervised scheme for extraction of power frequency signals in the steel industry. IEE Proc.: Vision, Image and Signal Processing. 149 (2002) 204-210
20. Lee, C.-H., Parl, K.-H., Kim, J.-H.: Hybrid parallel, evolutionary algorithms for constrained optimization utilizing PC clustering. In: Proc. Congress on Evolutionary Computation. 2 (2001) 1436-1441
21. Cantú-Paz, E., Goldberg, D. E.: Efficient parallel genetic algorithms: theory and practice, Comput. Meth. Appl. Mech. Eng. 186 (2000) 221-238
22. High, K.A., LaRoche, R. D.: Parallel nonlinear optimization techniques for chemical process design problems. Comput. Chemical Eng. 19 (1995) 807-825
23. Li, Y., Cho, Y.-Y.: Intelligent BSIM4 Model Parameter Extraction for Sub-100 nm MOSFET Era. Jpn. J. Appl. Phys. 43 (2004) 1717-1722
24. Li, Y.: A Hybrid Intelligent Computational Methodology for Semiconductor Device Equivalent Circuit Model Parameter Extraction. In: Anile, A.M.; Alì, G.; Mascali, G. (eds.): Scientific Computing in Electrical Engineering. Springer-Verlag, Berlin Heidelberg New York (2006) 345-350

Monitoring Distributed Systems for Safety Critical Software: A Goal-Driven Approach and Prototype-Tool

Guido Pennella[1], Christian Di Biagio[1], Alessandro Colicchia, Gianfranco Pesce[2], and Giovanni Cantone[3]

[1] MBDA-Italy SpA, Via Tiburtina, Roma, Italy
`{guido.pennella, christian.di-biagio}@mbda.it`
[2] Centro di Calcolo e Documentazione, Università degli Studi di Roma "Tor Vergata",
Via O. Raimondo, Roma, Italy
`gpesce@ccd.uniroma2.it`
[3] Dip. di Informatica, Sistemi e Produzione, Università degli Studi di Roma "Tor Vergata",
Via O. Raimondo, Roma, Italy
`cantone@uniroma2.it`

Abstract. The reference company for this paper – a multination organization, Italian branch, which works in the domain of safety-critical systems - evaluated the major tools that the market provides for testing safety-critical software, as not sufficiently featured for her quality improvement goals. Once that we had transformed those goals in detailed technical requirements, and evaluated that it was possible to realize them conveniently in a tool, we passed to analyze, construct, and eventually utilize in field the prototype "Software Test Framework". This tool allows non-intrusive parallel measurements on different hard-soft targets of a distributed system running under one or more Unix standard OS. This paper reports on the characteristics of Software Test Framework, its architecture, and results from a case study. Based on comparison of results with previous tools, we can say that Software Test Framework is leading to a new concept of tool for the domain of safety critical software.

Keywords: Software engineering, Distributed and parallel systems, Hard Real-time Systems, Performance-measurement Tools.

1 Introduction

The development of safety critical software in industrial settings is usually influenced by user non-functional requirements that concern the load (e.g. the usage of the CPU and Memory in a period) of any computing node in a certain scenario, which is specified not exceed a fixed level.

Before designing safety-critical or mission-critical real-time systems, a specification of the required behaviour of the system should be produced and reviewed by domain experts. As the implementation advances, eventually it completes, the system is thoroughly tested to be confident that it behaves correctly. In fact, recently, the concept of software verification and validation has been extended up to include quality assurance for new digitalized safety-critical systems (EPRI, 1994). The test of the system's temporal behaviours seems best done when using a monitor, i.e. a system

G. Min et al. (Eds.): ISPA 2006 Ws, LNCS 4331, pp. 241–250, 2006.

able to observe and analyze behaviours shown by another remote system (a.k.a.: the "target"). Several authors (e.g. (Tsai, 1995) suggest that it is useful and practical using monitors to analyze the behaviour of a real-time system. Such a monitor could be used either as an "oracle" (Weyuker, 1982) – or reporting on system failures – as detected by the same monitor performing in the role of supervisor (Simser, 1996) – respectively. In safety-critical applications, the system should be monitored by another safety system to ensure continued correct behavior. To achieve these goals, observed behaviors must be quickly accepted or rejected; this task is quite difficult to enact when complex real-time systems are involved, and the requested response time is not the range of human capabilities. Additionally, software practitioners cannot diagnose, troubleshoot, and resolve every component affecting a critical software performance by using just manual methods.

The goals (Basili, 1994) of the present paper are concerned with: (i) Expressing the reference company need of testing safety-critical software in terms of conveniently feasible features and capabilities for the purpose measuring system test performances, by focusing on measurement of CPU and memory loads, performance monitoring of distributed heterogeneous processes and their threads, intrusiveness, and other key attributes, from the point of view of the reference organization practitioners, in the context of critical software development; (ii) Developing a new software tool that meet those needs. (ii) Characterizing that tool, comparing it with other testing tools, accepting it by a case study, and eventually accrediting the tool in field.

In the remaining of the present paper, Section 2 analyze lacks of ready-to-use software available to market. Section 3 transforms the reference organization's needs and goals in required testing features. Section 4 presents the philosophy, architecture, and functionalities of Software Test Framework (STFW), a new prototype tool, which is based on those features. Section 5 shows results from a case study, which involved the se of STFW. Section 6 briefly compares STFW with major professional tools that the market provides. Section 7 presents some conclusions and points to future research.

2 Monitoring Tools: Off the Shelf Software Analysis

All the major tools for monitoring hard real-time software seems to present substantial limits with respect to the ideal technology of our reference company.

Overall, all those tools shows a main limit: no one of them provides a module built right for acquiring and sending-out data. Of course, they carry out those activities, but in different, often broad, ways. Let T1, T2, and T3 denote three tools analyzed (it is not our role to advertise or counter-advertise tools; so we do not mention tool's names) as, in our best knowledge, the most known system-load monitoring tools.

In particular T1 is not so much intrusive, and sensitive data are continually refreshed. However, they reside on the target, which is expected to be not in charge of providing utility functions. T2 accesses the target system through TCP/IP, where no sensor is installed: because of the consequent usage of system calls, the tool is strongly intrusive. T3 is non-intrusive, but the set of data it is able to acquire is very limited.

As a conclusive remark, the real trouble with traded tools seems to be that they assume the point of view of the "System Administrator", so answering questions like: "What is the behaviour of my system". Vice versa, as already mentioned, what our reference company needs is a "Software Engineer" view, so answering questions like: "What is the problem", "Where is the problem", "How system's machines interact during a problem" "Who generated the problem".

3   Testing Features

Based on the expected use cases and the resulting requirements, a list of testing features (F) follow, which characterize a software test framework and is able to satisfy the needs that our reference organization expressed. Each of the shown features is augmented with the F's: (i) function or capability, (ii) measurement model applied (in round brackets), (iii) relative importance or weight, as expressed by the involved stakeholders [in square brackets] (not yet valorized).

- Heterogeneous targets monitoring (N|(Y, # heterogeneous target types) [w1].
- Average CPU percentage used during data acquisition on a target system. CPU and memory (see F3) occupancies are calculated under their maximum load, i.e. when all possible data are required for acquisition, and the acquisition interval is the one suggested by the tool producer, respectively (%) [w2].
- Memory occupancy on a target system (%) [w3].
- Persistent data repository and management (N|Y) [w4].
- Tailor the test system to suit special user needs or purposes (N|Y) [w5].
- Un-intrusiveness (Intrusiveness:: time for data acquisition in seconds) [w6].
- Distributed targets monitoring. TCP/IP over Ethernet (N|Y) [w7].
- Plug-in architecture (N|Y) [w8].
- System CPU (idle and used) percentage measurement (N|(Y,%)) [w9].
- System memory load (free and occupied) measurement (N|(Y, MB)) [w10].
- Process CPU (idle and used) percentage measurement (N|(Y, %)) [w11].
- Process memory load (free and occupied) measurement (N|(Y, MB)) [w12].
- Thread CPU (idle and used) percentage measurement (N|(Y, %)) [w13].
- Thread memory load (free and occupied) measurement (N|(Y, MB) [w14].
- Support multi platform for all the major operative systems (N | (Y, Checkbox for Lynux, Solaris, AIX, Linx, POSIX etc., respectively)) [w15].
- Allow regression testing (N|Y) [w147]
- Utilize software sensors (N|Y) [w17].
- Cost ($) [w18].

Let us note that features above are intentionally not concerned with software fault tolerance (Randell, 1975), which we decided not to taken in consideration in this first iteration of our work.

4   Software Test Framework

Software Test Framework is a complex analysis tool that deals with capturing resource occupation data of all target machines composing the distributed system.

In order to introduce minimal perturbation in the target system, STFW is developed for performing flexible non-intrusive as-accurate-as-possible measurements. These results can be achieved by employing a distributed architecture, which works on different computers in such way that only the measurements operations are performed on the target system, leaving the most complex elaborations and activities, such as the graphical plot, to other computers.

4.1   Architecture

STFW is build-up by three macro-units:

1. **Target:** it resides on each target machine and is responsible of the execution of the measurements and the optimization of the sensor. It is build-up by two sub-units:
    a.   **Test Manager** (TM): its task is to opportunely tailor the Sensor
    b.   **Sensor:** its task is to acquire information.
2. **Analysis System:** it does not reside on a target computer but on a different machine; it is responsible of the analysis, interpretation and visualization of data sent by Sensor, both in real and in deferred time. It is build-up by three sub-units:
    a.   **Data Manager:** it is responsible for the interpretation of information sent by Sensor, and forward the Data Plotter
    b.   **Data Plotter:** is able to graphically plot data that Data manager sends
    c.   **GUI** (Graphical User Interface): sends Test Manager the information to acquire, as specified by the user
3. **Repository:** it historicizes test related data; it does not reside on a target computer but on a different machine.

The most interesting features and capabilities of STFW are:

- STFW supports regression test
- STFW supports data repository
- STFW supports threads monitoring
- Sensor is a tailor-made software
- Sensor is not intrusive
- Sensor supports process multiple instances
- Acquisitions form different targets are synchronous in the same conversation.

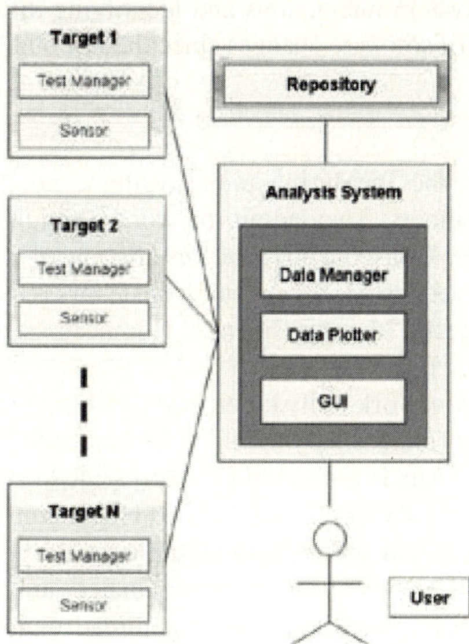

Fig. 1. ST-FW Architecture

4.2 Usage

STFW is very easy to use. In the first step, the user sets the IP addresses of the Target and Repository sub-system, respectively. Now, the user is allowed to start the test. After a small time (1 − 20 sec), in which the Test Manager (TM) recompiles Sensor to acquire only the specified information (Sensor loads only the needed modules), data plotting is started on the user screen and, in parallel, the repository is populated.

The user, during the first step, can load and lunch a historicized test: as result, the user is allowed to compare two different test in the same plot, the one historicized, and the other one in running. Moreover, once a test is finished, the user can choose graphical or numerical presentation of results; plots are presented for each acquisition time.

4.3 Regression Test

STFW provides EXnee, which is an integrated and enhanced version of Xnee. This is a free software tool, which is able to record and playback all events used by the X Server. So, each time a user moves the mouse or digits a button on the keyboard, Xnee records these events and is then able to reproduce all those actions. In this way, Xnee is able to replicate all the activity performed by the user in the same temporal sequence.

After a session of events is recorded, an STFW user can reproduce that session every time that s/he wants. For instance, let a user start the execution of, and then interact with, a (critical) software application. Of course, if the user makes decision to change that software, Xnee allows that user (and all the authorized colleagues) to start replication of all those interactions. Once that such a replication has been started, Xnee is able to proceed autonomously (the physical presence of user is no more requested) by replicating the user-system interactions and identifying differences in behaviors, if any, due to the injection of software changes since the last build (regression test).

4.4 Tailoring

In our best knowledge, the measuring tools available are "heavy" both for data-producers and data-consumers. They admit the worst configuration only, so that they acquire all possible data. Consequently, the installation of all their data-acquisition modules is permanently requested. As a result, consumers receive data that they never requested. As a further result, the intrusiveness is unnecessary high; in fact, it is proportional to the amount of data acquired.

Instead, STFW is a framework, fully tailor-made: tailoring introduces improvements both on the producer side (unnecessary modules are not loaded), and the consumer side (only explicitly requested data is processed and represented to the consumer).

In particular, concerning the consumer side, STFW is configurable to the different operational environments.   In order to allow the (static) specialization of STFW to the particular operational environment, some parameters are specified for the framework (i.e. operating system, process monitoring, thread monitoring etc.); parameters are easily handled, due the STFW modular structure.

With respect to other monitoring technology, two turning point makes STFW a new concept tool:

Concerning the target machine, STFW reduces the occupancy of the system resources in term of memory and CPU percentage occupied, because only user-required data is acquired (no overload of the system resources), and memory allocation is minimal (only the requested modules are loaded, which correspond to the requested data).

Concerning the consumer side, this is allowed to choose a-priori the data to acquire, so not having to discriminate a-posteriori among all the received information for the interesting data.

4.5 Intrusiveness

Intrusiveness represents the OS load for a software application. It is complementary to, and can be quantified in terms of, CPU percentage and amount of memory used by the application software itself in situation of maximum performance.

STFW is able to guaranty CPU occupancy under 1%, while acquire data with a minimal interval of 1 second. Measures can be even more accurate specifying the only processes or threads to be monitored in order to introduce the lighter computation possible. Let us note that major tools suggest acquiring data on the target system with sampling period not less than 3 or 10 seconds, respectively. Such a STFW advantage derives from its tailoring features (see Section 3.4) and the system architecture of the Target module.

In distributed systems also network as to be considered as a limited resource. STFW communication protocol between sensor and GUI is implemented in order to transmit the only information required choosing a flexible and dynamic payload format. This means that even if a target's specific information is required in the configuration phase(i.e a particular process name), only available data will be transmitted.

4.6 Parallelism, Synchronization, and Heterogeneity

Based on the architecture of our tool (see above), STFW supports data acquisition in parallel from different – in case, heterogeneous - targets.

This leads STFW to be the eligible tool to analyze machines in distributed computation scenarios even when heterogeneous SO are present. On a target machine, a test is build-up by a configuration phase.

and a subsequent conversation phase for data acquisition. When all the Sensors have been configured, they synchronize on the reception of a start message. Following the reception of this message, all Sensors start to acquire their data and finally sending those data to the consumer.

Let us note that, in order to compare consistent data, starting and completing synchronously acquisitions from different targets is an essential requirement. Because the end of a communication time-window is in the control of the consumer, it is enough to start (multi-point to point) communications at the "same" time, as STFW actually does (notice that latencies - as introduced both by the TCP/IP over Ethernet, and the OS scheduler – are negligible in common test environments, compared to sampling interval).

4.7 Data Repository

The whole information, as each Sensor acquires, is stored in a relational data base (DB). In order to keep intrusiveness in control, the DB is installed on the computer that hosts the Analysis System, or any other machine but different from the ones where Sensors are installed.

Storing data in a repository is useful because it allows reusing previous test cases, analyzing previous results, and comparing such previous results with those generated by running test cases.

4.8 Process and Thread Monitoring

STFW is able to acquire information about processes and threads, as in the followings:

- PID: Process Identifier
- TID: Thread Identifier
- PPID: Parent PID
- S: Status; can be Ready, Running or Waiting
- MO: Memory occupancy; is the sum of the amount of memory allocated for the stack, the executable file, and data.
- CPUO: CPU occupancy; is the percentage of CPU used.

TID does not apply to processes. In case of threads, MO evaluates the stack size (a thread shares text and data with its parent process).

5 Case Study

Let us present results from a case study, where we compared in real-time the behaviors of two applications running on two Single Board Computer (SBC). Monitored attributes were the system's target CPU occupancy, and the full information associated to the execution of two processes, Ubench 2.0 and Sensor, respectively. The Ubench's job consists in computing senseless mathematical operations for 3 minutes, and then, in the successive 3 minutes, performing senseless memory allocation and disallocations (Ubench, 2006). The job of Sensor consists in auto-monitoring activities.

We conducted the case study in an industrial environment, built-up by three calculus nodes, as in the followings: (1) Thales – Vmpc6a Single Board Computer (SBC) with Lynx OS, (2) Concurrent - Intel SBC with Linux Red Hat Enterprise, and (3) x86 PC with Windows XP. Those nodes are one to each other connected through an Ethernet LAN.

Each SBC was arranged to performed in the role of target system, and had its own Test Manager and Sensor installed. The Windows PC was arranged to perform in the role of consumer, and hosted the graphical console. Following the start of the GUI, we passed to configure the targets by entering "CPU", "Ubench" and "Sensor" and then pressing the OK button. When the Sensors were compiled, installed and ready to send data, we pressed the START button and then two plotting windows appeared on the PC screen, which showed the required information only. Figure 2 shows an instance of process-monitoring windows in STFW.

6 Comparative Analysis

Table 1 shows the limits of commercial measuring tool above mentioned with respect to STFW. Anyway, the reader should notice that STFW is just a prototype (but in its second internal release).

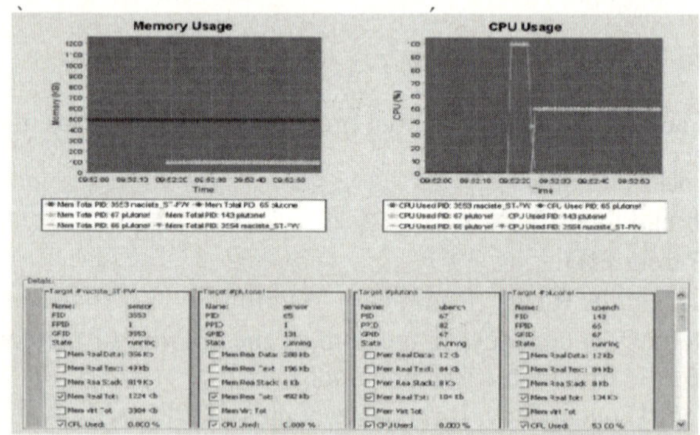

Fig. 2. Process-monitoring windows in STFW

Table 1. Characterization of T1, T2 and T3 monitoring tools (N≡0|Y≡1; Li ≡ Linux 2.6; Ly ≡ LynxOS; S ≡ Solaris)

F	m	T1	T2	T3	STFW
F1	0..1	0	0	0	1
F2	%	3	60	3	1
F3	MB	1	0	0,5	<2
F4	0..1	0	0	0	1
F5	0..1	0	0	0	1
F6	(sec.)	3	10	1	1
F7	0..1	0	1	0	1
F8	0..1	0	0	0	1
F9	0..1	1	1	1	1
F10	0..1	1	1	1	1
F11	0..1	1	0	0	1
F12	0..1	1	0	0	1
F13	0..1	0	0	0	1
F14	0..1	0	0	0	1
F15	SO list	Li, Ly, S, AIX	Li	S	Li, Ly, S, AIX
F16	0..1	0	0	0	1
F17	0..1	0	0	0	1
Cost	0..1Y	0	$$$	0	0

7   Conclusion and Future Work

We have presented the philosophy, architecture and features of a new tool, STFW, for testing time-behavior of safety-critical systems, and briefly compared that tool with major system performance measurement tools, as available from the market, in our best knowledge. STFW resulted to be much more supportive than other tools for our reference professional engineers. The most important features, which make STFW really a competitive tool, are: (i) Tailor-made non-intrusive data sensing; (ii) Synchronous conversations for acquiring state information from distributed targets; (iii) Repository of test cases for reuse, and their results for comparative analysis; (iv) Thread monitoring, (v) Ability to perform regression test.

Thanks to STFW, each product can be validate and verified in real-time by monitoring and comparing results from different tests, and reproducing complete scenarios build-up by different machines. Next step will be to extend STFW to VxWorks^{TM} (VxWorks, 2006), the world wide known SO for real-time system, and the most utilized for the control of automata.

References

1. Basili, V. R., Caldiera, G., and Rombach, H. D., *The Goal Question Metric Approach*, Encyclopedia of Software Engineering, Wiley&Sons Inc., 1994.
2. EPRI, Handbook for verification and validation of digital systems, Vol.1: Summary, EPRI TR103291, Vol.1, 1994.

3. IEEE, IEEE/EIA 12207.0-1996 Industry Implementation of International Standard ISO/IEC 12207: 1995 (ISO/IEC 12207) Standard for Information Technology Software Life Cycle Processes, in *IEEE/EIA* 12207.0-1996, 1998, pp. i-75.
4. Leveson. N. G., Software safety: Why, what, and how. *Computing Surveys*,18(2):125-163, June 1986.
5. Isaksen U., Bowen J. P., and Nissanke N., *System and Software Safety in Critical Systems*, December 1996.
6. Lilja D. J., *Measuring Computer Performance*, Ed. Cambridge University Press, 2000.
7. Randell B., System Structure for Software Fault Tolerance, *IEEE Trans. on Software Engineering*, vol. SE-1, no. 2, pp.220-232, 1975.
8. Simser D. and R.E. Seviora, Supervision of Real-Time Systems Using Optimistic Path Prediction and Rollbacks, *Procs. Int'l Symp. Software Reliability Eng.* (ISSRE), pp. 340–349, Oct. 1996.
9. Tsai J.J., Yang S.J., Monitoring and Debugging of Distributed Real-Time Systems, *J.J. Tsai and S.J. Yang, eds.*, IEEE CS Press, 1995.
10. Ubench 2.0™ , http://www.phystec.com/download/ubench.html (last access, March 2006).
11. Weyuker E.J., On Testing Non-Testable Programs, *The Computer J.*, vol. 25, no. 4, pp. 465–470, 1982.
12. VxWorks http://www.windriver.com (last access, April 2006).

A Profiling Approach for the Management of Writing in Irregular Applications

M.B. Ibáñez, F. García, and J. Carretero

Universidad Carlos III de Madrid,
Departamento de Informática, Av. Universidad 30,
28911 Leganés (Madrid), Spain

Abstract. Parallel file systems often work guided by APIs which provide hints to access storage in a coordinated manner. Nevertheless, the current APIs do not offer the expressiveness necessary to specify I/O operations conveniently in irregular applications. We characterize the state of irregular applications that precedes the performance degradation of the parallel file system and we propose a schedule based on profile information.

1   Introduction

Large-scale applications that manipulate huge datasets obtain poor I/O performance on modern parallel machines. Although there are parallel computers with theoretical peak performance greater that 1 Tflops/sec, real applications running on high-performance computers achieve I/O bandwidths of at most a few hundred MB/sec [9].

Parallel file systems such as PVFS [1], GPFS [4] provide a high-performance I/O infrastructure to handle large I/O requests but they perform poorly when deal with numerous small requests. Parallel file systems often work guided by APIs such as MPI-IO [5] which provide hints to access storage in a coordinated manner [10], [7], [3]. The hints are proved to be useful when there is some regularity on the data access pattern. Nevertheless, there is an important class of parallel scientific applications that perform accesses to data through one or more levels of indirections and change their data access patterns during execution. For these irregular applications, the current APIs do not offer the expressiveness necessary to specify I/O operations conveniently. Thus it is necessary to determine the conditions under which current APIs are helpful, when to change the optimization strategy to a new one able to coordinate I/O accesses more efficiently.

This paper deals with periodical checkpointing I/O of irregular and dynamic applications. It focus on characterization of irregular data access patterns that provokes unexpected behavior from GPFS. Finally, the paper shows the benefits of rescheduling writings based on profile information.

The rest of the paper is organized as follows. In Section 2, we describe the data consistency technique used by GPFS. Section 3 presents the relevant characteristics of our benchmark. In Section 4 we present a characterization of data patterns that degrades performance of parallel file systems, and we also show how to predict an imminent performance degradation for write access times by identifying unsafe variations in the time that tasks spend writing data. In Section 5

G. Min et al. (Eds.): ISPA 2006 Ws, LNCS 4331, pp. 251–259, 2006.

we present a user-programming solution based on independent and contiguous requests using MPI-IO. Finally, Section 6 concludes the paper.

2   Synchronizing Parallel Data Accesses in GPFS

The IBM General Parallel File System (GPFS) is a scalable, high performance file system, available on the RS/6000 SP parallel supercomputing and on Linux clusters [4],[8]. The system is a client/server architecture. It consists of compute nodes (I/O clients) that have equal access to a set of shared disks through a switching fabric. The GPFS disk drives are attached only to the I/O servers.

GPFS provides coherent caching at the client, optimized prefetching techniques, and guarantees recoverability from any single point of failure. GPFS uses data-shipping to guarantee user data consistency in applications that do not require POSIX semantics, a technique that is partitioned and centralized. Data-shipping binds each GPFS file block to a unique I/O node which is responsible for all the accesses to this block. The blocks are distributed to the I/O nodes in round-robin manner. GPFS forwards I/O operations to the node responsible for a particular data block rather than migrate access permission to the node trying to write the data.

3   Molecular Dynamics Benchmark

Our benchmark is based on a N-body problem known as molecular dynamics (MD). MD simulations consider the interaction of particles within a defined volume. Each particle interacts with the others within a specified cutoff radius. At each time step, it is necessary to compute forces and update positions and velocities of all particles. In the integration of the motion equations, the bodies can move independently, leaving one area of the space and entering to another one. In order to adapt to these changes, the application recalculate periodically which particles can interact with which. Because of the dynamic nature of the problem, the access pattern used to compute forces, temperature, energy and pressure of the system in MD application is irregular (see Figure 1). The indirectly referenced loop bounds of the inner j loop vary across iterations of the outer i loop.

The irregularity of the access pattern makes difficult and expensive to optimimize parallel accesses to the file, the optimizations must be repeated when the distribution of the molecules changes. Therefore, this kind of applications represent a challenge to parallel file systems.

4   Experimental Results

Our experimental platform is a Linux cluster [2], installed at *Universidad Politécnica de Madrid*'s CeSViMa center. The cluster consists of 180 nodes, -168 compute nodes and 12 I/O nodes- interconnected through Myrinet and GigaEthernet. Each node is a dual processor Power970 at 2.2 GHz, 4GB of RAM, and runs

```
DO i = 1, nlocal
    DO j = nnlist(i), nnlist(i + 1) − 1
        G = G + function(x(nlist(j)))
    END DO
END DO
```

Fig. 1. Irregular pattern of MD program

Linux with 2.6.5 kernel. We use MPI as communication library (MPICH-1.2.6-1 implementation) and the IBM GPFS file system to store the files. Our tests run on one processor per compute node and use the Gigabit Ethernet network.

4.1   Reference Patterns

Our profiling approach is based on a set of measures taken over a system where the tasks have similar amount of data distributed uniformly through the file, and the tasks perform fine-grain writings.

The first experiment is aimed at evaluating the write performance of GPFS for discontiguous access patterns. We collect time information varying the number of tasks from 1 to 8 and the size of the file from 1 to 8 blocks (in our system, 1 block has 512KB). Each task writes an equal number of bytes scattered randomly across the entire file. The tasks write the entire file without holes or overlap. The test does not use MPI_Datatypes to create a mapped view of the file, instead each task calculates the offset at which to access the file.

The measurements shown in Figure 2 demonstrate how I/O time decreases when the number of tasks is increased and the benefit of working with small files and a great number of processors. Figure 3 shows the average difference between the time spent by the tasks in each execution. From this figure we conclude that the standard deviation of time values is smaller for larger data files. We observed a range of values for files of 4MB from 0.0360 secs to 0.0381 secs, that is a difference of only 5.5% between the faster task and the slower one.

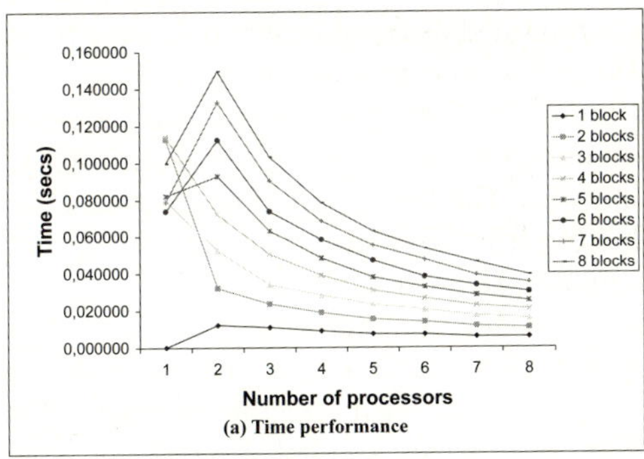

Fig. 2. Write performance of GPFS for discontiguous access patterns on a balanced system

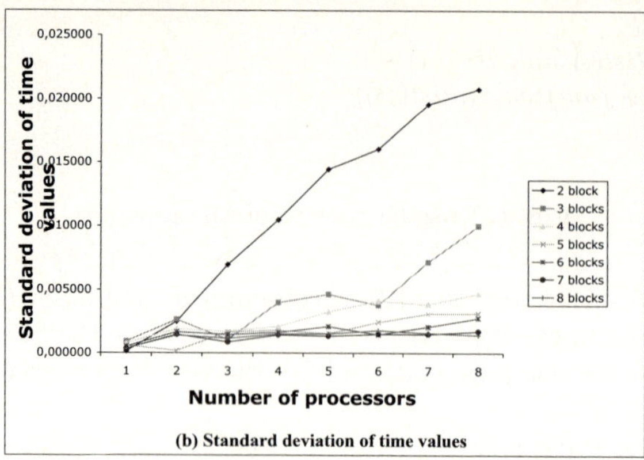

Fig. 3. Standard deviation of time values of GPFS for discontiguous access patterns on a balanced system

4.2   Test on Highly Unbalanced Systems

The next set of experiments represents steps of a MD-simulation which starts with a balanced substance and evolves towards highly unbalanced distribution of its molecules. When the substance is highly unbalanced, it has discontiguous access patterns. These kind of patterns provoke execution failures during checkpointing. We start by presenting experiments with three processors writing different amount of data in a file. Each processor uses fine-grain data accesses through the entire file.

Every experiment S is characterized by a *distribution matrix* which columns are labeled by the blocks of a file and the rows by the processors of the experiment, an element $S_{i,j}$ represents the percentage of data that the processor P_i writes in the block B_j.

In order to identify the balanced degree of a substance S, we define its *distance* d with regard to the balanced substance S_0 as the value obtained of the addition of the values of the matrix $|S - S_0|$. High distance values indicate substances more unbalanced. S is renamed as S_d in order to emphasize its balanced degree.

Figure 4 shows the evolution of a substance which starts with a uniform distribution of data among its three processors (S_0), continues with an increase in the amount of data handled by process P_1 (S_{265} and S_{279}), until a step where process P_1 writes almost all the file (S_{359}). The execution of experiments S_{265}, S_{279} and S_{359} fails due to GPFS difficulty to handle fine-grain data accesses with a data distribution among processors very unbalanced.

The previous failed behavior was reproduced in 17 of 37 experiments showed at Figure 5. We repeated each experiment 5 times and we observed that all the failures occur while GPFS deals with substances within the distance interval $[265, 359]$. We call this interval the *critical interval* and the substances in the interval *critical substances*. Thus, a way to prevent GPFS failures is to avoid the execution of critical substances using the distance metric.

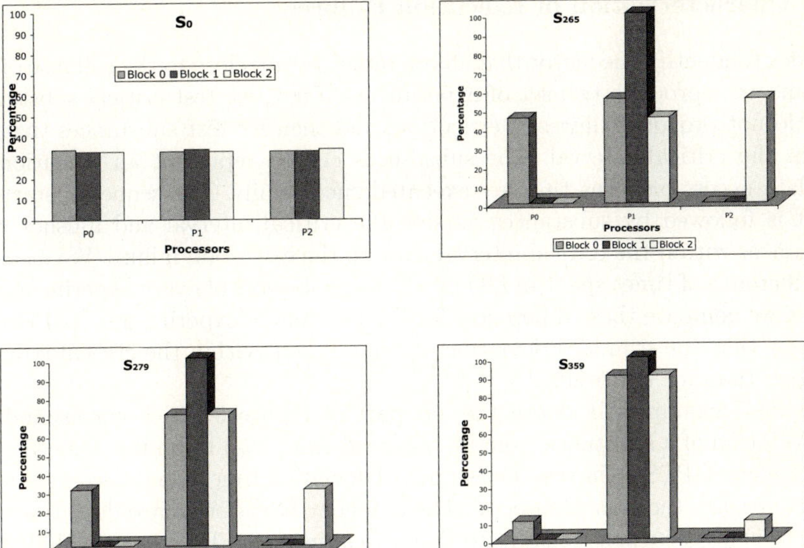

Fig. 4. Evolution of data distribution among processors in a N-body simulation

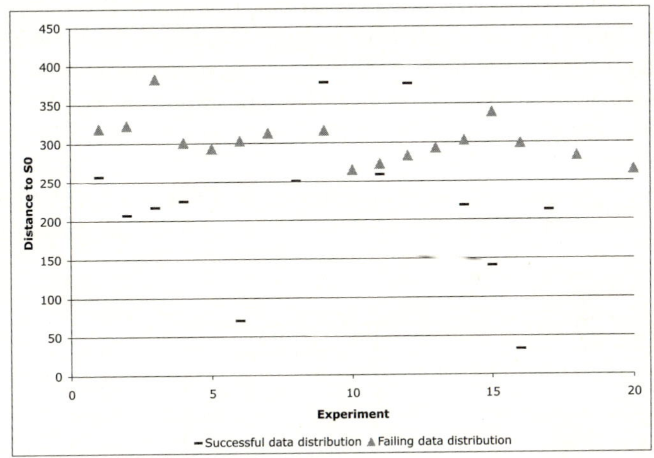

Fig. 5. Effect of data distribution on GPFS execution

Nevertheless, the distance metric is an inaccurate indicator of upcoming GPFS failures. At Figure 5 we also find critical substances that are handled correctly by GPFS. In order to characterize a state close to the collapse of the system, our next step is to analyze the behavior of critical substances that execute correctly.

4.3   Characterization of Execution Failures

In order to identify the factor that characterize a state close to the collapse of the system, we reproduce two set of experiments. First, we test critical substances that do not provoke failures of execution, and then we test substances that are not in the critical interval. The substances chosen represent an evolution on the data access patterns that are executed successfully. The sequence starts at S_0, it is followed by substances outside the critical interval and finishes with substances within the critical interval close to the execution failure. We measure the difference of times spent in I/O by all the processors of every experiment and finally, we compare these differences for the two sets of experiments. At Figure 6 we show that the standard deviation of experiments within the critical interval, is bigger than for the others.

Figure 7 examines in detail the left part of Figure 6 which corresponds to the evolution of a substance from its balanced state (S_0) to an unbalanced state (S_{283}) where GPFS collapses. The standard deviation time values becomes higher as we approach the critical interval. The tendency to the standard deviation time increase is bigger when we enter to the critical interval. Thus, we conclude that for standard deviation of time greater than 0.08 GPFS may collapse.

5   Proposed Approach

To solve the problem there are two alternatives, to hint GPFS to disable normal data shipping locking used by MPI-IO library or to schedule the writings to the file in a different way. The former alternative is not feasible due to the MPI implementation we use. We propose a schedule based on profile information gathered in the successive steps of a MD-simulation. The schedule is described by the algorithm at Figure 8.

The strategy presented follows two main steps. First, each iteration of the algorithm finds the task with time value more distant from the mean of $\mathcal{T}$ values,

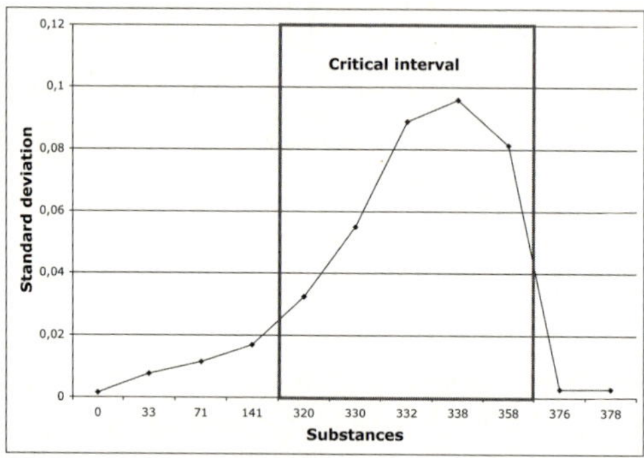

Fig. 6. Standard Deviation on times of execution of a set of benchmarks not failing in execution

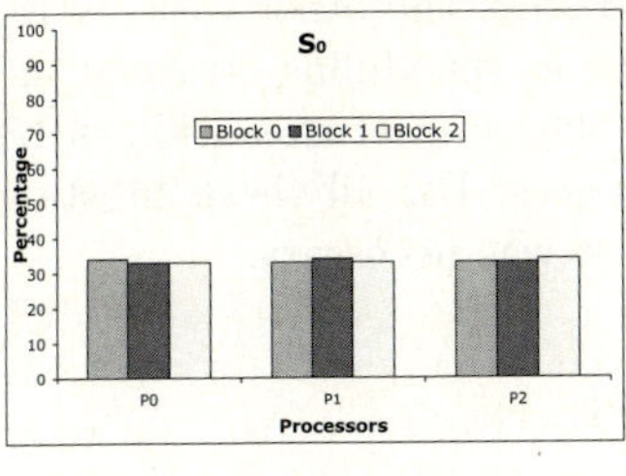

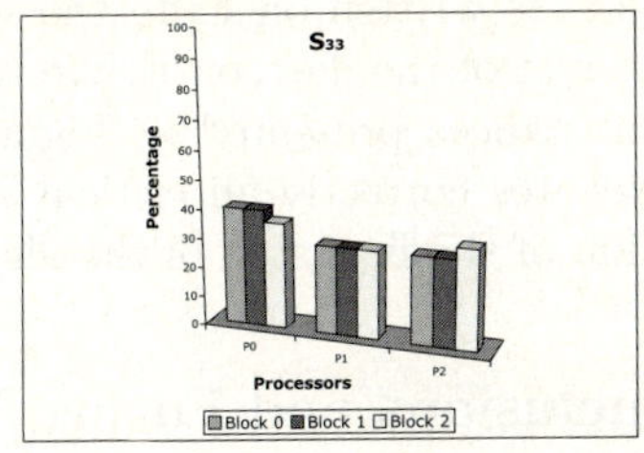

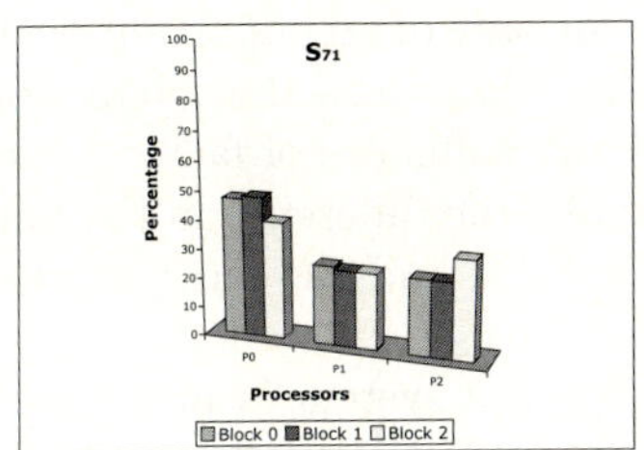

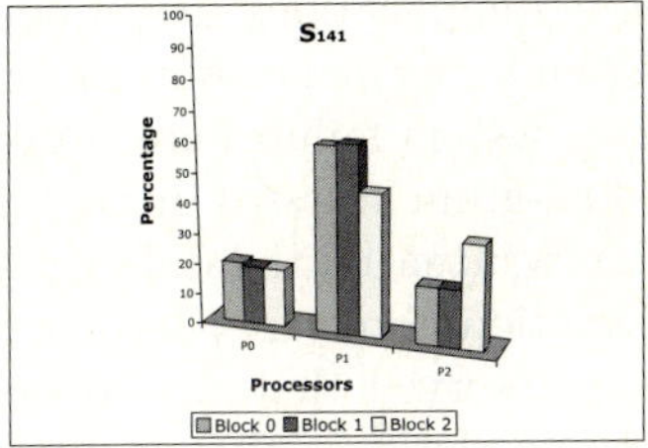

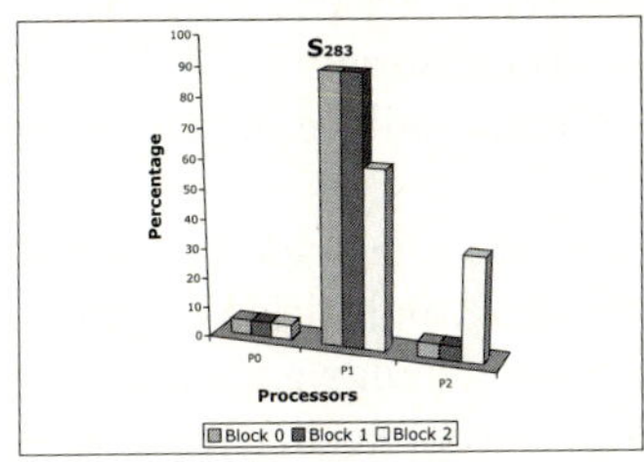

Fig. 7. Evolution of a substance from balance to highly unbalanced state

In what follows we use the following terminology.

$\mathcal{P} = \{P_0, P_1, ..., P_{n-1}\}$ are the set of processes that write on file F.

$\mathcal{T} = \{t_i | \ i \ \epsilon \ [0, ..., n-1], t_i \ is \ the \ time \ P_i \ spends \ writing \ on \ F\}$.

$\sigma_{\mathcal{T}}$ denotes the standard deviation of $\mathcal{T}$.

σ_{ideal} denotes the standard deviation of time values in the balanced substance.

1. while $(\sigma_{\mathcal{T}} + 0.08 \ > \ \sigma_{ideal})$
   $t_{max} = max \ \{t \ | \ t \ \epsilon \ \mathcal{T}\}$
   $P_{max} = P_i \ \epsilon \ \mathcal{P} \ \wedge \ t_i = t_{max}$
   to write P_{max}'s data on F using independent and contiguous requests
   $\mathcal{T} = \mathcal{T} - \{t_{max}\}$
   $\mathcal{P} = \mathcal{P} - \{P_{max}\}$
2. $\forall \ P_i \ \epsilon \ \mathcal{P}$: to write P_i's data on F using independent and contiguous requests

Fig. 8. Schedule based on profile information

and its data is written on F. In the second step, the other tasks write concurrently the rest of the data on F. We tested this scheduling strategy successfully on the substances presented at Figure 5, the time of execution is bigger but GPFS executes correctly all critical substances. For all these substances, only an iteration of the first step of the algorithm was necessary.

6   Conclusions and Future Work

In this paper we have shown that periodical checkpoint write operations of large-scale irregular applications, are responsible not only of an important degradation on file system performance but, in some cases, it provokes the collapse of the file system. File system failures are triggered by a confluence of factors, namely the tasks use fine-grain accesses through all the file, the difference in the quantity of information written by the different tasks is high, and the file system does not have information about user-level access patterns.

We have observed that the collapse of the file system is preceded by wide fluctuations in the time that highly unbalanced tasks spend writing data. Experimentally we have determined that a time fluctuation becomes critical when the standard deviation measured is greater of 0.08.

We have presented a user-programming solution based on independent and contiguous requests that avoid the failure of the file system once that a critical fluctuation is detected.

Although the solution presented depends on profile information gathered at runtime, it is useful on irregular applications such as N-body simulations because their data pattern accesses change gradually through the time. For other irregular applications, it is necessary to find measures based on distribution of data among tasks able to predict the imminent collapse of the system.

Acknowledgments

This work has been supported by the Spanish Ministry of Science under the TIN2004-02156 contract. The *Universidad Politécnica de Madrid*'s CeSViMa center supported the infrastructure used in this work.

References

1. Carns, P.H., Ligon III, W.B., Ross, R.B., Thakur, R. PVFS: A Parallel File System for Linux Clusters. 4th Annual Linux Showcase and Conference. (2000) pp. 317-327
2. Centro de Supercomputación y Visualización de Madrid (CeSViMa).: http://www.cesvima.upm.es
3. Ching, A., Choudgary, A., Liao, W.: Noncontiguous I/O through PVFS. Proceedings of the IEEE International Conference on Cluster Computing.(2002) pp. 405-414.
4. IBM.: IBM General Parallel File System High Performance Cluster File System. http://www-03.ibm.com/servers/eserver/clusters/software/gpfs.html

5. The MPI Forum: MPI-2: Extensions to the Message-Passing Interface (1997).
6. Prost, J.-P., Treumann, R., Blackmore, R., Hartman, C., Hedges, R., Jia, B., Koniges, A., White, A.: Towards a High-Performance and Robust Implementation of MPI-IO on top of GPFS. Euro-Par 2000, LNCS 1900, pp. 1253-1262.
7. Purakayastha, A., Ellis, C.S., Kotz, D.: ENWRICH: A Compute-Processor Write Caching Scheme for Parallel File Systems. The Fourth Workshop on Input/Output in Parallel and Distributed Systems (IOPADS). (1996). pp. 55-68.
8. Schmuck, F., Haskin, R.: GPFS: A Shared-Disk File System for Large Computing Clusters. FAST 2002 Conference on File and Storage Technologies. (2002) pp. 231–244
9. Thakur, R., Lusk, E., Gropp, W.: I/O in Parallel Applications: The Weakest Link. The International Journal of High Performance Computing Applications. Vol. 12, N. 4.(1998) pp. 389-395.
10. Thakur, R., Gropp, W., Lusk, E.: Data Sieving and Collective I/O in ROMIO. Proc. of the 7th Symposium on the Frontiers of Massively Parallel Computation. (1999) pp. 182-189

Parallel Thermo-Mechanical Modelling for Nuclear Waste Deposition

Jiří Starý, Ondřej Jakl, and Roman Kohut

Institute of Geonics, Academy of Sciences of the Czech Republic
stary@ugn.cas.cz, jakl@ugn.cas.cz, kohut@ugn.cas.cz

Abstract. The context of the paper is finite element solution of transient thermo-elasticity problems, motivated by the global need to simulate the operation of nuclear waste repositories. In this context, the paper deals with large-scale parallel processing of nonstationary heat equations, when the linear systems arising in each time step are solved by the overlapping domain decomposition method. The numerical experiments are performed on a large thermo-elasticity model simulating the behaviour of spent nuclear fuel stored using the Swedish KBS-3 method. The developed parallel codes are based on the OpenMP and MPI standards and their performance is investigated.

Keywords: Thermo-elasticity, finite element solver, parallelization, nuclear waste repository.

1   Introduction

One of the most urgent problems of the nuclear power industry is the management of radioactive waste. Nuclear fuel discharged from reactors continues to be radioactive for thousands of years and must somehow be disposed. In many countries they try to find a solution in constructing special repositories in rock formations hundreds of meters below the earth's surface. So far, the projects have not gone beyond experimental facilities. One of the most recognized methods of this type is the Swedish KBS-3 [5] and its prototype underground nuclear waste repository located at Äspö. Its relevance for us is emphasized by the fact that a similar conception of storage of the spent nuclear fuel is anticipated in the Czech Republic, too.

The topic of our current work is mathematical modelling and computer simulation of the complex phenomena related to the operation of the nuclear waste repositories such as that one at Äspö. In general, this topic involves demanding multiscale and multiphysics simulations of various coupled processes such as heat transfer, mechanical behaviour, water and gas flow and chemical interactions in a long-term period.

In this paper, we assume some simplification of the problem outlined above. Namely, we restrict ourselves to the modelling of thermo-mechanical processes which are not fully coupled. Nevertheless, the numerical solution of the thermal and mechanical parts leads to the repeated processing of large linear systems.

G. Min et al. (Eds.): ISPA 2006 Ws, LNCS 4331, pp. 260–268, 2006.

The principal task of ours is to find efficient and parallelizable iterative solution methods. For this purpose, we make use of the iterative solvers based on the conjugate gradient method with Schwarz-type preconditioners, advantageous from the parallelization point of view.

2 On Thermo-elasticity

We consider the finite element solution of thermo-elastic models with one-directional coupling through thermal expansion term in the constitutive relations. We suppose deformations to be very slow and not to influence temperature fields. Thus, we can split the problem into two parts. First, we determine the temperature distribution by the solution of the nonstationary heat equation. Second, we solve the linear elasticity problem at given time levels.

The thermo-elasticity problem is mathematically formulated as follows: Find the temperature $\tau = \tau(x, t)$ and the displacement $u = u(x, t)$,

$$\tau: \ \Omega \times (0, T) \to R, \qquad u: \ \Omega \times (0, T) \to R^3,$$

that fulfill the equations

$$\kappa \rho \frac{\partial \tau}{\partial t} = k \sum_i \frac{\partial^2 \tau}{\partial x_i^2} + Q(t) \qquad \text{in} \quad \Omega \times (0, T),$$

$$-\sum_j \frac{\partial \sigma_{ij}}{\partial x_j} = f_i \quad (i = 1, \ldots, 3) \qquad \text{in} \quad \Omega \times (0, T),$$

$$\sigma_{ij} = \sum_{kl} c_{ijkl} \left[\varepsilon_{kl}(u) - \alpha_{kl}(\tau - \tau_0) \right] \qquad \text{in} \quad \Omega \times (0, T),$$

$$\varepsilon_{kl}(u) = \frac{1}{2} \left(\frac{\partial u_k}{\partial x_l} + \frac{\partial u_l}{\partial x_k} \right) \qquad \text{in} \quad \Omega \times (0, T)$$

together with the corresponding boundary and initial conditions specified below.

The four expressions represent the heat conduction equation, equations of equilibrium, Hook's law and tensor of small deformations, respectively, with symbols having the following meaning: κ is the specific heat, ρ is the density of material, k are the coefficients of the heat conductivity, Q is the density of the heat source, σ_{ij} is the Cauchy stress tensor, ε_{kl} is the tensor of small deformations, f is the density of the volume (gravitational) forces, c_{ijkl} are the elastic moduli, α_{kl} are the coefficients of the heat expansion and τ_0 is the reference (initial) temperature.

For the heat conduction, we use the boundary conditions

$$\tau(x, t) = \hat{\tau}(x, t) \qquad \text{on} \quad \Gamma_0 \times (0, T),$$

$$-k \sum_i \frac{\partial \tau}{\partial x_i} n_i = q \qquad \text{on} \quad \Gamma_1 \times (0, T),$$

$$-k \sum_i \frac{\partial \tau}{\partial x_i} n_i = H(\tau - \hat{\tau}_{out}) \qquad \text{on} \quad \Gamma_2 \times (0, T),$$

simulation in the area of complex multiphysics modelling related with nuclear waste depositions.

Acknowledgement. This work is supported by the contract No. 105/04/P036 of the Grant Agency of the Czech Republic and by the grant No. 1ET400300415 of the Academy of Sciences of the Czech Republic.

References

1. R. Blaheta, P. Byczanski, R. Kohut, A. Kolcun, R. Šňupárek: *Large-Scale Modelling of T-M Phenomena from Underground Reposition of the Spent Nuclear Fuel.* In: P. Konečný et al (eds.): EUROCK 2005, Impact of Human Activity on Geological Environment. A.A.Balkema, Leiden, 2005, pp. 49–55.
2. X.-C. Cai: *Multiplicative Schwarz methods for parabolic problems.* SIAM Journal on Scientific Computing 15, 1994, pp. 587–603.
3. R. Kohut, J. Starý, R. Blaheta, K. Krečmer: *Parallel Computing of Thermoelasticity Problems.* In: I. Lirkov, S. Margenov, J. Wasniewski (eds.): Proceedings of the Fifth International Conference on Large-Scale Scientific Computing LSSC'05 held in Sozopol, Springer Verlag, Berlin, 2006, pp. 671–678.
4. B. Smith, P. Bjørstad, W. Gropp: *Domain decomposition. Parallel multilevel methods for Elliptic Partial Differential Equations.* Cambridge University Press, New York, 1996.
5. C. Svemar, R. Pusch: *Prototype Repository - Project description.* IPR-00-30, SKB, Stockholm, 2000.
6. *UPPMAX home page,* `http://www.uppmax.uu.se` (December 15, 2005).

A Markovian Sensibility Analysis for Parallel Processing Scheduling on GNU/Linux

Regiane Y. Kawasaki[1], Luiz Affonso Guedes[2], Diego L. Cardoso[1],
Carlos R.L. Francês[1], Glaucio H.S. Carvalho[1], Solon V. Carvalho[3],
João C.W.A. Costa[1], and Marcelino S. Silva[1]

[1] Department of Electrical and Computing Engineering, Federal University of Pará
(UFPA), 66.075-900,
Belém, PA, Brazil
{kawasaki, diego, rfrances, ghsc, marcelino}@ufpa.br
[2] Department of Computing Engineering and Automation, Federal University of Rio
Grande do Norte (UFRN), 59072-970,
Natal, RN, Brazil
affonso@dca.ufrn.br
[3] National Institute for Space Research (INPE), Computing and Applied
Mathematics Laboratory (LAC), P.O. Box 515, 12245-970,
São José dos Campos, SP, Brazil
solon@lac.inpe.br

Abstract. Parallel Computing has become a powerful tool to overcome certain types of computational problems in many areas such as engineering, especially due to the increasing diversity of platforms for execution of this type of application. The use of parallel computing over LANs and WANs is an alternative in the universe of dedicated environments (parallel machines and clusters), but, in some cases, it needs to imply QoS (Quality of Service) parameters, so it can execute efficiently. In this scenario, the deployment of resource allocation scheme plays an important role in order to satisfy the QoS requirements for parallel applications. In this paper we propose and present Markovian models for resource allocation (CPU allocation) schemes in a GPOS (General Purpose Operating Systems), aiming at offering an optimization method which makes the efficient performance of parallel and interactive applications feasible.

1 Introduction

In the last years, the set of platforms for the performance of parallel applications has become diversified. In the beginning, these environments were limited to some processor units linked by internal bus. However, today, typical platforms are great sets of computers linked by many different networks [1]. The points which caused that approach change were [2]: (a) the high cost for achievement and maintenance; (b) the use of highly specific purpose, which usually generates a high degree of idleness, characteristics which limited the achievement of parallel machines.

An alternative to this problem is to consider a differentiated treatment for the parallel processes, whenever demanded, by means of QoS approach [3]. However,

G. Min et al. (Eds.): ISPA 2006 Ws, LNCS 4331, pp. 269–278, 2006.

provision of QoS guarantees in GPOS or in other similar systems (like wireless and cellular mobile networks) is a complex issue due to problems such as those related to how to design the system behavior which needs process scheduling and admission control. It becomes even more challenging when in a system a specific process or groups of processes need a minimum of resource assurance. To do so, Call Admission Control (CAC) must act together with the process scheduler, so that, when the system detects that a determined application needs a resource assurance, it may adjust the system to provide it [4].

When it is needed to conjecture about the system performance, usually a model s constructed, which obtains its essential information. From this point, a performance analysis is carried out in order to explore and identify the system's behavior, bottleneck, bounds, etc [5]. Due to the necessity of investigating the feasibility of providing QoS to guarantee a minimum of resources to processes that need a differentiated treatment in a general purpose operating system, in case GNU/Linux, a performance model has been developed for the traditional GNU/Linux scheduler. Besides the traditional GNU/Linux model, a different model that reserves a percentage of the processor time for providing attention to parallel tasks has also been developed. By solving these models, their performance evaluation was compared to identify the changes in the system behavior due to reserving the resource.

This paper is organized as follows. In Section 2 it describes the analytical model of Linux scheduler architecture and a new scheduler model with resource allocation. The sensibility analysis is based on a detailed mathematical model followed by numerical results that are presented in Section 3, admitted with or without resource reservation models. Finally, in Section 4 it shows the final remarks of this work.

2   Linux Scheduler Analytical Model

The basic structure of the Linux scheduler is the process queue (*struct runqueue*). This *struct* is defined inside the archive *kernel/sched.c*. The current $O(1)$ scheduler keeps a *runqueue* per processor, which is responsible for containing all the executable processes of a given processor. Thus, if a process is inserted in a *runqueue* of a specific processor, it will only run on that processor [6]. Each *runqueue* contains two priority arrays [7]: active and expired. Priority arrays are data structures composed of a priority bitmap and an array that contains one process queue for each priority.

Linux scheduler and admission control is depicted in Fig.1. Higher (parallel jobs with QoS, kernel process) and lower priority jobs (compilers, browsers, parallel - without QoS jobs, and others) arrive at the system according to two mutually independent Poisson processes with parameters λ_1 and λ_2, respectively. For the sake of simplicity, it is assumed that both services require a negative exponential service time with rate μ. A job is removed from the active array if: (a) its processing is finished, with rate $qs_1\mu$ (for high priority jobs) and $qs_2\mu$ (for the other processes); or (b) it needs to be rescheduled to the high priority queue or low priority queue in the expired array, with rates $pr_1\mu$ or $pr_3\mu$, respectively. The scheduling of a job in the low priority queue in the active array is tied to the occupancy of the high priority queue in the active array in the sense that it will only be scheduled if the high priority queue in the active array is empty. When the processing queues are empty in an active array and there is a job to be processed in the expired array, these arrays are switched. This switching (via pointer) has an associated time of the $10^{-6}s$ [7].

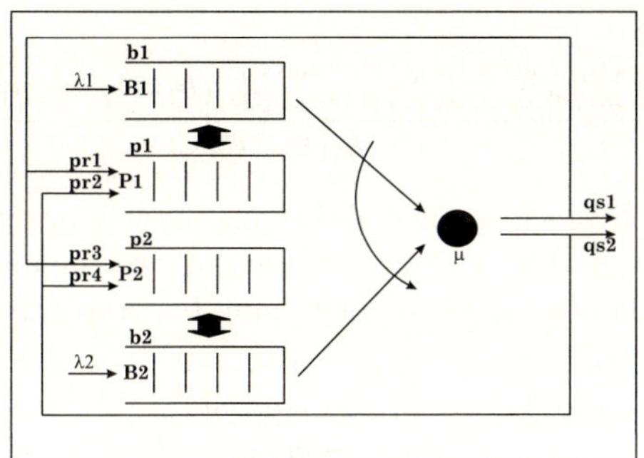

Fig. 1. System model

Given the assumptions presented above, it a Continuous-Time Markov Chain (CTMC) [8] model of the system, whose state is defined as:

$$s = (b_1, b_2, p_1, p_2, ac | 0 \le b_1 \le B_1; 0 \le b_2 \le B_2; 0 \le p_1 \le P_1; 0 \le p_2 \le P_2; ac = 0 \ \ or \ \ 1)$$

Where b_1 and p_1 are the number of processes in the high priority queues; and b_2 and p_2 are the number of processes in the low priority queues; and B_i is the buffer size of the queue i. At time, there is only one high priority queue in the active array and only one low priority queue in the active array, and the remainders are on the expired array. In order to indicate which queues are in these arrays it is used the variable ac, in such a way that if $ac = 0$, then the queues b_1 and b_2 will be in the active array and p_1 and p_2 in the expired array, and when $ac = 1$, vice-versa.

Using standard techniques for the solution of Markov chains, the steady-state probabilities of the CTMC are computed. Again because of the symmetry of the system only the performance measurements associated with the condition $ac = 0$ will be described, i.e., when b_1 and b_2 are in the active array, and p_1 and p_2 are in the expired array. Thus, let $p(b_1, b_2, p_1, p_2, ac)$ be the steady state probability of that Markov model, then the job blocking probability (Pb_i) of a job in the queue i, it is given by the probability of its priority queue is full. Eq. (1) shows, for instance, that probability for the high priority queue in the active array. The job blocking probability for other arrays may be computed at the same way.

$$Pb_1 = \sum_{b2=0}^{B_2} \sum_{p1=0}^{P_1} \sum_{p2=0}^{P_2} \pi(B_1, b_2, p_1, p_2, 0) \tag{1}$$

The mean delay of the high priority queue and the low priority queue in the active array may be computed as

$$Wb_1 = \frac{\sum_{b1=1}^{B_1} \sum_{b2=0}^{B_2} \sum_{p1=0}^{P_1} \sum_{p2=0}^{P_2} b_1 \pi(b_1, b_2, p_1, p_2, 0)}{\lambda_1 (1 - Pb_1)} \tag{2}$$

$$Wb_2 = \frac{\sum_{b1=0}^{B_1} \sum_{b2=1}^{B_2} \sum_{p1=0}^{P_1} \sum_{p2=0}^{P_2} b_2 \pi(b_1, b_2, p_1, p_2, 0)}{\lambda_2 (1 - Pb_2)} \tag{3}$$

Where, Pb_2 is the job blocking probability on the low priority queue. Likewise, since, at time, only p_1 and p_2 are in the expired array, the mean delay of the high priority queue and the low priority queue may be, respectively, computed as

$$Wp_1 = \frac{\sum_{b1=0}^{B_1} \sum_{b2=0}^{B_2} \sum_{p1=1}^{P_1} \sum_{p2=0}^{P_2} p_1 \pi(b_1, b_2, p_1, p_2, 0)}{\mu(pr_1 + pr_2)(1 - Pp_1)} \tag{4}$$

$$Wp_2 = \frac{\sum_{b1=0}^{B_1} \sum_{b2=0}^{B_2} \sum_{p1=0}^{P_1} \sum_{p2=1}^{P_2} p_2 \pi(b_1, b_2, p_1, p_2, 0)}{\mu(pr_3 + pr_4)(1 - Pp_2)} \tag{5}$$

Where, Pp_1 and Pp_2 are the job blocking probability on the high and the low priority queue in the expired array. The throughput of the jobs of the high priority queue and the low priority queue in the active array are, respectively, given by:

$$X_1 = qs_1\mu \sum_{b1>0}^{B_1} \sum_{b2=0}^{B_2} \sum_{p1=0}^{P_1} \sum_{p2=0}^{P_2} \pi(b_1, b_2, p_1, p_2, 0) \tag{6}$$

$$X_2 = qs_2\mu \sum_{b2>0}^{B_2} \sum_{p1=0}^{P_1} \sum_{p2=0}^{P_2} \pi(0, b_2, p_1, p_2, 0) \tag{7}$$

2.1   Reservation Model

In this section, an extended model is proposed in order to describe a static reservation allocation policy, where a percentage of the processor capacity (R) is allocated to process one class of applications (Fig. 2). Using this policy, we can divide the capacity of the processor in two variables, R (percentage reserved) used for applications with high priority and $(1 - R)$ for the other applications in the system.

The state of the CTMC of that system is defined as: $s = (b_1, b_2, p_1, p_2, bp, ac | 0 \le b_1 \le B_1; 0 \le b_2 \le B_2; 0 \le p_1 \le P_1; 0 \le p_2 \le P_2; 0 \le b_p \le B_p; ac = 0\,or\,1)$.

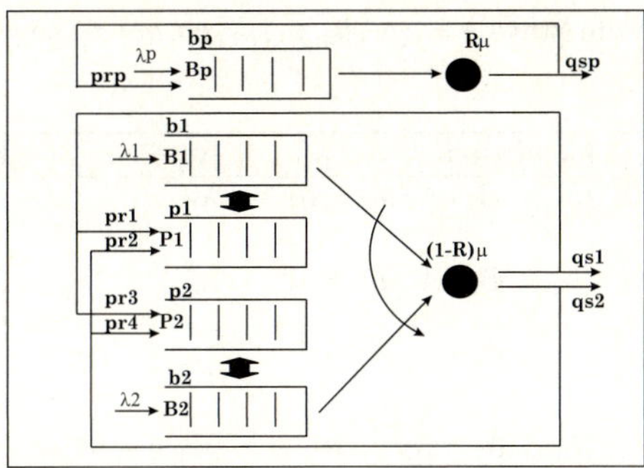

Fig. 2. Resource allocation

Transitions from state s to all possible successor states are reported in Table 1 along with their rates and conditions under which the transitions exist; the last column indicates the type of event to which a transition refers. When $ac = 0$, if a job is generated in the high priority queue in the active array, the occupancy of that queue, b_1, will increase by one unit. A rescheduled job from that queue will go to the high priority queue in the expired array with rate $pr_1(1 - R)$ or to the low priority queue in the expired array with rate $pr_3(1 - R)$. In the first case the job keeps the same priority and, in the latter, the priority is decreased. A job can leave the high priority queue in the active array, after finishing its processing with rate $qs_1(1 - R)$. An arrival in the low priority queue in the active array takes place with rate and increases b_2 by one unit.

Since the system under analysis is finite, when a buffer (active or expired arrays) is full an incoming or rescheduled job is blocked. After switching, the queues that were in the expired array (p_1 and p_2) become active and vice-versa. The variable bp represents parallel jobs. We assumed that $mtv = 10^{-6}$. The system is symmetric, which makes quite natural the match of the other transitions of the model.

The variable bp represents parallel jobs. We assume that $mtv = 10^{-6}$. The system is symmetric, which makes quite natural the understanding of the Table 1.

Due to the lack of space and for simplicity only the performance measurements of the high priority jobs (parallel) that demand QoS guarantees are presented. Assuming that $ac = 0$, the mean delay perceived by that processes are computed as

$$W_{pb} = \frac{\sum_{b_1=0}^{B_1} \sum_{b_2=0}^{B_2} \sum_{p_1=0}^{P_1} \sum_{p_2=0}^{P_2} \sum_{b_p=1}^{B_P} b_p \pi(b_1, b_2, p_1, p_2, b_p, 0)}{(\lambda_p + prpR\mu)(1 - Pb_p)} \tag{8}$$

Where Pb_p is blocking probability of high priority jobs that demand QoS guarantees derived as Eq.(1). The throughput is given by:

$$X_{pb} = qspR\mu \sum_{b_1=0}^{B_1} \sum_{b_2=0}^{B_2} \sum_{p_1=0}^{P_1} \sum_{p_2=0}^{P_2} \sum_{b_p>0}^{B_P} \pi(b_1, b_2, p_1, p_2, b_p, 0) \tag{9}$$

Table 1. Transitions from state $s = (b_1, b_2, p_1, p_2, bp, ac)$ to successor state t for jobs in priority policy

Successor State	Condition	Rate	Event
$(b_1 + 1, b_2, p_1, p_2, bp, ac)$	$(b_1 < B_1) \wedge (ac = 0)$	λ_1	A job arrives in high priority class
$(b_1, b_2 + 1, p_1, p_2, bp, ac)$	$(b_2 < B_2) \wedge (ac = 0)$	λ_2	A job arrives in low priority class
$(b_1 - 1, b_2, p_1, p_2, bp, ac)$	$(b_1 > 0) \wedge (ac = 0)$	$qs_1(1 - R)\mu$	A job from high class terminates
$(b_1 - 1, b_2, \theta, p_2, bp, ac)$	$(b_1 > 0) \wedge (ac = 0)$ $\begin{cases} \theta = p_1 + 1, \text{ if } p_1 < P_1 \\ \theta = P_1, \quad \text{ if } p_1 = P_1 \end{cases}$	$pr_1(1 - R)\mu$	A job is rescheduled to high priority class
$(b_1 - 1, b_2, p_1, \theta, bp, ac)$	$(b_1 > 0) \wedge (ac = 0)$ $\begin{cases} \theta = p_2 + 1, \text{ if } p_2 < P_2 \\ \theta = P_2, \quad \text{ if } p_2 = P_2 \end{cases}$	$pr_3(1 - R)\mu$	A job is rescheduled to low priority class
$(b_1, b_2 - 1, p_1, p_2, bp, ac)$	$(b_1 = 0) \wedge (b_2 > 0) \wedge (ac = 0)$	$qs_2(1 - R)\mu$	A job from low class terminates
$(b_1, b_2 - 1, \theta, p_2, bp, ac)$	$(b_1 = 0) \wedge (b_2 > 0) \wedge (ac = 0)$ $\begin{cases} \theta = p_1 + 1, \text{ if } p_1 < P_1 \\ \theta = P_1, \quad \text{ if } p_1 = P_1 \end{cases}$	$pr_2(1 - R)\mu$	A job is rescheduled to high priority class
$(b_1, b_2 - 1, p_1, \theta, bp, ac)$	$(b_1 = 0) \wedge (b_2 > 0) \wedge (ac = 0)$ $\begin{cases} \theta = p_2 + 1, \text{ if } p_2 < P_2 \\ \theta = P_2, \quad \text{ if } p_2 = P_2 \end{cases}$	$pr_4(1 - R)\mu$	A job is rescheduled to low priority class
$(b_1, b_2, p_1, p_2, bp + 1, ac)$	$b_p < B_p$	λ_p	A job arrives in QoS priority class
$(b_1, b_2, p_1, p_2, bp - 1, ac)$	$b_p > 0$	$qspR\mu$	A job from QoS class terminates
$(b_1, b_2, p_1, p_2, bp - 1, ac)$	$b_p > 0$	$prpR\mu$	A job is rescheduled, but before it is decremented
$(b_1, b_2, p_1, p_2, bp + 1, ac)$	$b_p < B_p$	$prpR\mu$	A job is rescheduled, but after it is incremented
$(b_1, b_2, p_1, p_2, bp, ac + 1)$	$(ac = 0) \wedge ((b_1 = 0) \wedge (b_2 = 0)) \wedge ((p_1 > 0) \vee (p_2 > 0))$	mtv	Change of arrays, b_1 and b_2 become expired
$(b_1, b_2, p_1, p_2, bp, ac - 1)$	$(ac = 1) \wedge ((p_1 = 0) \wedge (p_2 = 0)) \wedge ((b_1 > 0) \vee (b_2 > 0))$	mtv	Change of arrays, b_1 and b_2 become active

3   Performance Study

In this section some numerical results are presented to evaluate how adequate is the Markov model to scheduling GNU/Linux with and without resource allocation policy. First, we present the performance of the Linux Markovian model. For validation purpose, Linux scheduler was simulated by using an academic version of a powerful tool named ARENA©[9]. Some measures were obtained through system calls which collect data for later analysis, minimizing the overhead in kernel (this can be obtained in www.lprad.ufpa.br/parqos). Table 2 summarizes the parameters used.

Table 2. Input data

High Priority	Measures	Low Priority:	Measures
λ_1	7	λ_2	7,3
pr_1	0,1	pr_2	0
pr_3	0,09	pr_4	0,67
Avarage Buffer	5	Avarage Buffer	5

To validate the probability distributions adopted, models use input data obtained from the real system. In these data, Kolmogorov-Smirinov (K-S) goodness of fit tests were applied, using the trial version of BestFit©tool [10].

These data were used as parameters of probability distributions in question (Poisson for inter-arrivals times). The simulation results were collated with the performance measures obtained from the real system. As the numerical results of that comparison match (very similar), the values may be considered validated for the analytical model.

To implement CPU allocation policy it is important to study the CPU behavior. Assuming the table above, it represents a situation where scheduler is very busy and the inputs are Poisson traffic. A new application is added in λ_1, simulating a situation of great workload. Table 3 ilustrates the Markovian model output. As expected, higher the traffic load, bigger the throughput and, for that reason, longer the mean waiting time, longer is the blocking probability. In the table, 0% represents the system behavior performance with just λ_1 and λ_2. λ_p is derived from λ_1(5%, 10%, 20%, 30%, 40%) and represents the impact of adding an application to the system.

The investigation of the impact on increasing CPU allocation (sensibility analysis) is interesting because it shows the system behavior that determines at which extent the CPU is efficiently and fairly used by all processes. The data in which this analysis was conducted is described in Table 2, adding a load of 50% to λ_1 (originated by the parallel application).

The Fig. 3.a shows the processes active high priority (parallel processes), active low priority and expired low priority remain with values Queuing Waiting Time almost constant with respect to several CPU allocation (from 0 to 50%). This implies that the impact on the waiting time is low, for the processes high priority, active low priority and expired low priority, with respect to the increase

Table 3. Performance measurements

	0%	5%	10%	20%	30%	40%
Queue Waiting Time						
Active High Priority	0,21246	0,21491	0,21687	0,21943	0,22037	0,21995
Active Low Priority	0,59056	0,60058	0,60970	0,62533	0,63785	0,64774
Expired High Priority	6,05108	6,28370	6,48294	6,79442	7,01313	7,16437
Expired Low Priority	0,85739	0,87383	0,88871	0,91386	0,93334	0,94802
Blocking Probability						
Active High Priority	0,09701	0,10763	0,11827	0,13925	0,15940	0,17838
Active Low Priority	0,44159	0,44832	0,45431	0,46434	0,47214	0,47817
Expired High Priority	0,43127	0,44343	0,45346	0,46847	0,47854	0,48530
Expired Low Priority	0,45635	0,46216	0,46734	0,47591	0,48241	0,48723

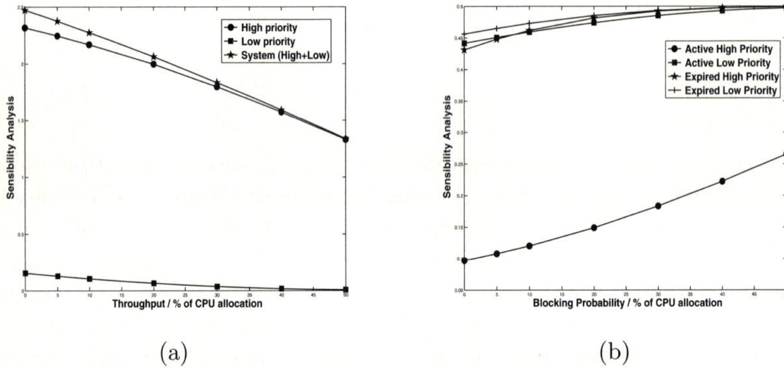

(a)   (b)

Fig. 3. (a) Queuing Waiting Time / % of CPU Allocation (b)Blocking Probability / % of CPU Allocation

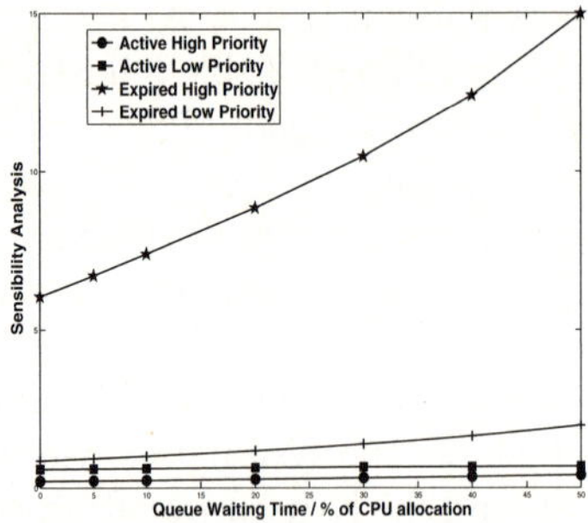

Fig. 4. Throughput / % of CPU Allocation

in the CPU allocation. On the other hand, the expired high priority processes have their time substantially increased when the CPU allocation gets larger. (for instance, 6 seconds of waiting to 0% of CPU allocation and 15 seconds to 50% of CPU allocation).

The blocking probability presents their worst values for active low priority, expired high priority and expired low priority (around 0.5 for 50% of CPU allocation) (Fig. 3.b). The smallest blocking probability is related to the active high priority processes.

Throughput is reduced approximately by 50% for both high priority and low priority processes (considering 0 to 50% of CPU allocation) (Fig. 4).

4 Final Remarks

In this paper, a Markovian Linux scheduler model has been presented and proposed for performance study and, in addition, an extended model, which uses static resource allocation policy. Through the sensibility analysis, it has been concluded that the performance of the parallel applications with QoS are greatly improved in its throughput. However, others applications have suffered some limitations. The contributions of this paper are: (1) Proposal of performance models for GPOS scheduler; (2) Proposal of a resource (CPU) allocation scheme in a parallel computing environment as well as showing through numerical results, obtained from its Markovian model, improvement of performance of parallel applications when compared to other applications.

Currently, we are implementing another extended model which uses dynamic CPU allocation policy. As future work, we are performing experiments with Markov decision process to find optimal admission control and scheduling strategies aiming at improving the resource (CPU and memory) allocation for parallel applications.

This work is supported by CNPq and CAPES.

References

1. Zhang, Y., Sivasubramaniam, A., Moreira, J., Franke, H.: Impact of Workload and System Parameters on Next Generation Cluster Scheduling Mechanisms. IEEE Transactions on Parallel and Distributed Systems, Vol. **12** (2001) 967-985.
2. Hwang, K., Xu, Z.: Scalable Parallel Computing - Technology, Architecture and Programming, WCB/ McGraw-Hill, (1998).
3. Niyato, D., Hossain, E.: Analysis of Fair Scheduler and Connection Admission Control in Differentiated Services Wireless Networks. IEEE International Conference on Communications, Vol. **5** (2005) 3137 - 3141.
4. Carvalho, G., Rodrigues, R., Francs, C., Costa, J., Carvalho, S.: Modelling and Performance Evaluation of Wireless Networks. Lecture Notes in Computer Science, Vol. **3124**. Heidelberg Germany (2004) 595-600.
5. Manolache, S., Eles, P., Peng, Z.: Schedulability Analysis of applications with Stochastic Task Execution Times. ACM Transactions on Embedded Computing Systems, Vol. **3**. November (2004) 706-735.
6. Chanin, R., Corrêa, M., Fernandes, P., Sales, A., Scheer, R., Zorzo, A.F.: Analytical Modeling for Operating System Schedulers on NUMA Systems, in Proc. of the 2nd International Workshop on Practical Applications of Stochastic Modelling, PASM05, University of Newcastle upon Tyne, UK, July (2005).

7. Love, R.: Linux Kernel Development, SAMS, 1st edn., (2003).
8. Wei, W., Wang, B., Towsley, D.: Continuous-Time Hidden Markov Models for Network Performance Evaluation, Performance Evaluation, Vol.**49**, (2002), pp. 129-146.
9. Rockwell Automatation - www.arenasimulation.com, accessed in 02/15/2006.
10. Palisade - www.palisade.com/bestfit, accessed in 02/18/2006.

Multiple Tasks Allocation in Arbitrarily Connected Distributed Computing Systems Using A* Algorithm and Genetic Algorithm*

Biplab Kumer Sarker[1], Anil Kumar Tripathi[2],
Deo Prakash Vidyarthi[3], Laurence Tianruo Yang[4], and Kuniaki Uehara[5]

[1] Faculty of Computer Science, University of New Brunswick, Fredericton, Canada
[2] Institute of Technology, Banaras Hindu University, Varanasi, India
[3] Jawaharal Nehru University, New Delhi, India
[4] Department of Computer Science, St. Francis Xavier University, Canada
[5] Graduate School of Science and Technology, Kobe University, Japan

Abstract. A number of algorithms is proposed for allocation of tasks in a DCS. Most of them did not consider allocation of various unrelated tasks partitioned into modules by taking into account the architectural capability of the processing nodes and the connectivity among them. This work considers allocation of disjoint multiple tasks with corresponding modules wherein multiple disjoint tasks with their modules compete for execution on an arbitrarily networked DCS. Two algorithms have been presented based on well-known A* algorithm and Genetic Algorithm techniques. The proposed algorithms consider a load balanced allocation for the purpose. The paper justifies the effectiveness of the proposed algorithms using several case studies.

1 Introduction

Task allocation problem is considered as a NP-Hard problem in the literatures [2]-[6], [8]-[11], [14], [9], even when processor capacities are not considered and thus many heuristic solutions are possible for this problem. Most of the algorithms for Task Allocation (TA) problem proposed by the scientists and researchers [2]-[6] so far, do make one or more assumptions. These consider a single task partitioned into corresponding modules for the execution and the repercussion of a single task allocation on a DCS. These also consider a few [5] or a large number of communicating tasks coming onto the DCS for processing [14]. Moreover, these works did not consider the connectivity of processing nodes, whereas in reality, a DCS receives a number of tasks from time to time for the execution. Factually, a DCS facilitates concurrent execution of modules belonging to various unrelated tasks [7], [12], [13]. The modules of any particular task, having IMC (InterModule Communication), do cooperatively execute and do not depend on the modules of the other tasks. This leads to the situation wherein, a processing node may be assigned modules belonging to different tasks. It is

---

* The corresponding author's email is sarker@unb.ca.

to mention that the real issue of task allocation must not ignore the possibility of multiple modules assignment of various tasks to the processing nodes in a dynamic fashion [7]. Task allocation algorithms also suffer from the number of constraints that are imposed by the task and the system as well [7].

Considering these views and furthermore taking into account the architectural capability of the processing nodes and the optimality of the solution guaranteed by A* based TA [2], in this paper we present two parallel algorithms for load balanced allocation in a DCS based on A* algorithm [18] and GA-the genetic behavior of the natural evolution. The paper is organized as follows. The next section discusses the load parameter for multiple tasks which is used in our case as a cost function to minimize turnaround time. This is the basis of effectiveness of the allocation. In section 3, the A* algorithm for task allocation is proposed. The next section discusses the proposed algorithm based on GA. Three case studies are exemplified using two algorithms in section 5. Section 6 compares the results of the proposed algorithms and discusses the effectiveness and scalability of the algorithms.

1.1   Assumptions

As the task allocation problem remains to be NP-hard, various heuristic solutions are proposed with one or more assumptions [2][18]. This work also makes certain assumptions that are as follows.

1. The processing nodes in the DCS are heterogeneous. The tasks are disjoint and have no inter-task communication. Only the modules within a task have interdependencies and communication requirements.

2. Execution and communication matrices for the task graphs are assumed to be given. These matrices are different for every task and calculated in units of time. While partitioning the task into modules, we assume that the memory requirements of the modules are also calculated.

3. The assumption of the availability of interconnection graph accommodates irregular type of interconnection networks.

Here, in this paper, the word 'processor' and 'processing node', 'assignment' and 'allocation' have been used to refer the same.

2   Load

The tasks submitted into a DCS are partitioned into suitable modules and then these modules are to be allocated to the processing nodes. Each task can be represented by a Task Graph $(TG) = (V_t, E_t)$, where (1) V_t is a set of vertices, each of which represents a module of the task $m_1, m_2, ..., m_n$ and (2) $E_t \subseteq V_t \times V_t$ is a set of edges each of which represents the Inter Module Communication (IMC) between the two modules at the end of the edge. We can also represent the network of processors $p_1, p_2, ..., p_n$ in a DCS as a Processor Graph $PG = (V_p, E_p)$; where vertices represent the processors and the edges represent the communication links between processors (see Fig.1). The goal of TA is to allocate the Task Graphs (TG) to a network of processors in a DCS (i.e. to PG) to achieve the minimum turn-around time of tasks [2].

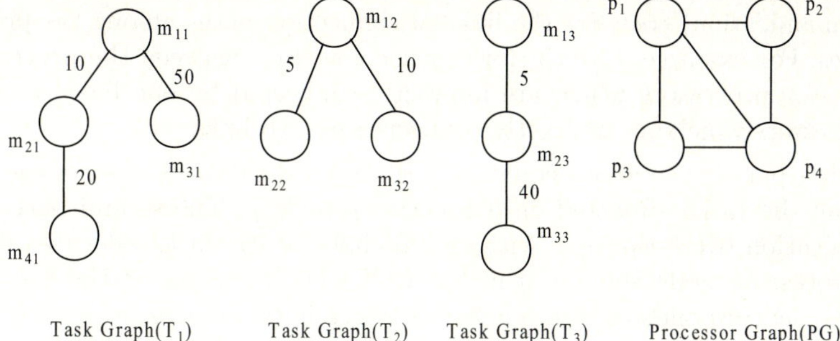

Fig. 1. Example of task graphs T_1, T_2 and T_3 with their modules and a DCS as processor graph

A processor's load comprises of all the execution and communication costs associated with its assigned modules of the task [6]. The time required by the heaviest-loaded processor will determine the entire tasks' completion time. So, the TA problem must find a mapping of the set of m modules of l tasks to n processors so as to minimize tasks completion time. Our goal is to allocate the modules in such a way that does not cause any processing node to be overloaded because an overloaded node may affect adversely in the turn around time of the tasks in a heterogeneous DCS.

The load in a processing node p is calculated as follows [18].

$$\sum_{l=1}^{k}\sum_{i=1}^{mi} X_{ilp}.M_{ilp} + \sum_{\substack{q=1\\q\neq p}}^{n}\sum_{l=1}^{k}\sum_{i=1}^{mi}\sum_{\substack{j=1\\j\neq i}}^{m}(C_{ijl} + CC_{pq}).M_{ilp}.M_{jlq} \qquad (1)$$

where $CC_{pq} = C_{fi}.L^i_{pq}$

X_{ilp} = execution cost of ith module of lth task on processing node p

C_{ijl} = Inter-Module Communication(IMC)Cost between i^{th} and j^{th} module of task l

M_{ilp} = assignment matrix of ith module of lth task on processing node p

$$M_{ilp} = \begin{cases} 1 & \text{if module } m_i \text{ of task } l \text{ is assigned to processor } p \\ 0 & \text{otherwise} \end{cases}$$

M_{jlq} = assignment matrix of jth module of lth task on any other processing node q

$$M_{jlq} = \begin{cases} 1 & \text{if module } m_j \text{ of task } l \text{ is assigned to processor } q \\ 0 & \text{otherwise} \end{cases}$$

L^i_{pq}= connection matrix of two processors p and q, describing the links (direct/ single indirect/ double indirect etc.) of connection paths among the processing nodes in Processor Graph (PG).

C_{fi}= coefficient matrix which has n entries describing the IPC (Inter Processor Communication) costs for the links of connection paths among the processing nodes. For example, C_{f1}=5 (for direct connection between the processors), C_{f2}=10 (for processors which are indirectly connected by one link), C_{f3}= 20 (for processors which are indirectly connected by two links) etc.

The first part of the above equation 1 is the total execution cost of the modules of all the tasks allocated on a processing node p. The second part is the communication overhead on p with the modules of the tasks allocated on the other processing node such as q in the DCS. The ith entry of the coefficient matrix C_{fi} corresponds to communication between two processors via i links. If processors p and q are not directly connected, we find L^2, multiply it by C_{f2}, (2nd field of C_f), and check whether this comes out to be non-zero; if it does, we replace L^1 in calculation with L^2; if not, we find out L^3 and multiply it with C_{f3} and check whether the product comes out to be non-zero. We continue like this until we find a non-zero value and then replace L^i in calculation with this (it is to be mentioned that we shall find a non-zero value within n multiplications, where n is the no. of processing nodes).

2.1   Global Table(GT)

To allocate the modules optimally so that no processor becomes overloaded, the load on each of the n processing nodes needs to be computed. By finding the processing node with heaviest load, the optimal assignment out of all possible assignments will allot the minimum load to the heaviest loaded processor. Thus it is necessary to consider realistic view that only a finite number of modules can be allocated to a processor depending on the architectural capability of the processing nodes in a DCS. Consequently, earlier algorithms [2], [5], [6] have continued to assume that all the modules will be eventually allocated no matter how large the memory requirements are, and/or how many modules a processor can accommodate and what is the current status of the system due to the existing allocation. These algorithms do not consider the requirement of allocation of modules of multiple tasks. In the proposed algorithms, we have shed off these unrealistic assumptions and make use of a data structure STATUS associated with every processor, which has two fields showing: the maximum number of modules that can be allocated to the processor and the memory capacity of the processor.

Whenever a module is chosen for allocation onto a processing node, the STATUS is checked and it is ascertained whether the processor can accommodate the module at hand. If not, another processor is chosen if available. The consequence might be that a certain module is not allocated at all. This data structure is implemented by constructing a Global table (GT) to maintain the track of maximum number of modules that can be allocated to a processing node depending upon its memory capacity. This is a dynamic table, which keeps the information of the remaining memory of nodes and the number of modules can be allocated on the nodes. Whenever a new task arrives, this GT is to be consulted and to be modified.

3   Algorithm for TA Using A*

In the A* algorithm [1], [2], for a tree search, it starts from the root, usually is called the start node (usually a null solution of the problem). Intermediate tree nodes represent the partial solutions, and leaf nodes represent the complete solution or goal. A cost function f computes each node's associated cost. The value of f for a node n, which is the estimated cost of the cheapest solution through n, is computed as

$$f(n) = g(n) + h(n) \tag{2}$$

where, $g(n)$ is the search-path cost from the start node to the current node and $h(n)$ is a lower-bound estimate of the path cost from current node to the goal node (solution), using any heuristic information available. To expand a node means to generate all of its successors or children and to compute the f value for each of them. The nodes are ordered for search according to the cost; that is, the algorithm first selects the node with the minimum expansion cost. The algorithm maintains a sorted list, called OPEN, of nodes (according to their f values) and always selects a node with the best expansion cost. Because the algorithm always selects the best-cost node, it guarantees an optimal solution [2].

To compute the cost function, $g(n)$ is the cost of a partial assignment at node n which is the load on the heaviest loaded processing node (p_i); this is done using the equation 1. For the computation of $h(n)$, two sets A_p (the set of modules that are already assigned to the heaviest loaded p) and U (the set of modules that are unassigned at this stage of the search and have one or more communication links with any module in set A_p), are defined. Each module m_i in U will be assigned either to p or any other processor q that has a direct or indirect communication link with p. So, two kinds of costs with each m_i's assignment can be associated: either X_{ilp} (the execution cost of m_i of task l on p) or the sum of communication costs of all the modules in set A_p that has a link with m_i. This implies that to consider m_i's assignment, it is to be decided whether m_i should go to p or not (by taking the minimum of these two cases' cost).

To support the run-time allocation of tasks to processors, we construct a manager-worker style parallel algorithm whose pseudo-code is given in sec. 3.1 and 4.2. One processor called the manager is responsible for keeping track of the assigned and unassigned tasks using a Global Table (GT) which is consulted and updated during every allocation. It always consists of the information about the total memory of the processing nodes and the remaining memory after assignment, no. of assigned modules and the remaining no. of modules can be assigned.

3.1   The Algorithm

1. *As a 'Manager' node, processor P_0 maintains the status of the Global Table (GT) for each processing node$(P_1, P_2, ..., P_n)$ termed as 'worker' in terms of available memory (M) and the modules that are already assigned to it.*
2. *'Manager' node maintains a list S of unallocated tasks with all modules (all tasks are in S at the beginning) and a list OPEN, empty at the beginning. Another list V is maintained by taking one Task ta from S and put it in another list V and reset OPEN.*
3. *The 'workers' checks possible allocation of modules in V using the $A*(2)$ algorithm and verifying STATUS of them by P_0; then allocate them; if not possible, deallocate the partially allocated modules of the task and move onto the next task, modifying the STATUS in between and update the Global Table (GT)by the Manager.*
4. *If S is not empty yet, go to step 2.*
5. *Stop (end of allocation).*

4   Algorithm for TA Using GA

A genetic algorithm emulates biological evolutionary theories to solve optimization problems [15]. The chromosomes in a GA population typically take the form of bit strings. But the chromosomes can take some other forms of string as well, such as letters, digits and integers [16]. The GA, most often requires a fitness function that assigns a score (fitness) to each chromosome in the current population. The fitness of a chromosome depends on how well that chromosome solves the problem at hand.

The fitness function in a genetic algorithm is the objective function that is to be optimized. It is used to evaluate the search nodes, thus it controls the GA [17]. As the GA is based on the notion of the survival of the fittest, the better the fitness value, the greater is the chance to survive.

Thus, the simplest form of GA involves three types of operators: selection, crossover, and mutation [16]. For the TA problem with multiple tasks allocation, we make the following assumptions:

1) The proposed algorithm makes use of a data structure for "chromosome" to describe allocations. It is an array of positive integers showing the index of the processing node to which a particular module is assigned. It has as many elements as the total number of modules of all tasks.

2) Initially all the elements are zero indicating that none of the modules are allocated to any of the processing node.

3) A data structure STATUS is associated with every processing node as described in Sec. 2.

4.1   The Fitness Function

The fitness function, in our problem, is the inverse of the load (the sum of loads on all the processors corresponding to a chromosome) described in the equation 1 of section 2.

4.2   The Algorithm

1. *"Manager" node randomly generate five chromosomes, verify STATUS and take one chromosome with maximum fitness value. Distribute the copy of chromosome to the "worker" nodes./* This fitness value is our threshold limit. Any chromosome below the threshold will be rejected and not included in the population. Each worker is considered as a processing node*/*

2. *Each worker nodes generate an initial population of 50 chromosomes above the threshold limit with that chromosome randomly.*

3. *SELECT: probability of selection of parents is linearly dependent on the fitness value. /* i.e. ax+b, where x is the fitness value, a and b are arbitrary values.*/*

4. *Perform crossover with probability P_c at a randomly chosen point.*

5. *If*
   Total no. of Chromosome(generated) < 100
   goto SELECT

6. *Pick up ten chromosomes randomly, using the probability of selection as in SELECT. Take out the one (chromosome) with maximum fitness.*

7. *Each "worker" sends its one (chromosome) with maximum fitness to the "Manager".*

8. *"Manager" receives chromosomes from the "workers" and take out the one (chromosome) with maximum fitness. This represents the allocation.*

4.3   Description of SELECT

To effectuate the probability of selection, we would produce several copies of the same chromosome. The idea is to take out chromosomes with their best fitness values randomly from all the chromosomes (included copies). Let there be P_a copies of chromosome a, where $a = 1 \ldots n$ and P_b copies of chromosome b, where, $b = 1 \ldots m$.

Then we would generate a random number (chromosome) r and find out, to which chromosome (a or b) this chromosome belongs. This can be done by the following expression i.e.

$$if \qquad \sum_{a=1}^{n} P_a \; < \; \sum_{b=1}^{m} P_b \tag{3}$$

then r belongs to chromosome b i.e. chromosome r is a copy of chromosome b.

However, this method would require memory for each copy of every chromosome. To save memory we could instead attach a field with each new chromosome generated. In this field we store an 'integer' number directly proportional to the fitness value of chromosome. Thus the chromosome represents 'X_i' copies of the chromosome, where 'X_i' is the number in its field and $i=1,2,\ldots n$.

When a chromosome is to be randomly selected, we generate a random number in the range from 1 to $\sum(X_1 + X_2 + \ldots + X_n)$, where X_i is the number in the field associated with the ith chromosome. Let us say, the number generated is Y and $X_1 + X_2 + \ldots + X_k < Y < X_1 + X_2 + \ldots + X_{k+1}$. Thus, the chromosome selected is X_{k+1}^{th} chromosome.

5 Implementation Results

In this section, we present three small examples with various number of TGs and PGs to justify the proposed algorithm with respect to allocation and status of the global table.

Case 1: We have considered a set of three tasks shown as TGs partitioned with their corresponding modules $T_1(m_{11}, m_{21}, m_{31}, m_{41})$, $T_2(m_{12}, m_{22}, m_{32})$, $T_3(m_{13}, m_{23}, m_{33})$ and a DCS as PG, consists of four processors (p_1, p_2, p_3, p_4) interconnected as shown in Fig. 2. Here, the IMC costs shown as in the figure 1 represent the communication costs between the modules of the tasks in time unit. For example, the communication cost between m_{11} (the first module of task T_1) with m_{21} (the second module of task T_1) is 10 unit. The adjacency matrix L^i_{pq} of processing nodes are assumed to be given which represents how the processing nodes are connected among each other. For example, the processing nodes p_2 and p_3 are not directly connected, so $L^1_{p2p3} = 0$. But they are connected with at least one indirect link (through p_1 or p_4). So, $L^2_{p2p3} = 1$.

The results for case 1: Total cost (communication and execution) using A* at all the processing nodes is 500 units. Total cost using GA at all the processing nodes is 120 units.

Case 2: The algorithm is implemented with other two cases. In case 2, a DCS consists of five tasks partitioned with their corresponding modules $T_1(m_{11}, m_{21}, m_{31}, m_{41}, m_{51})$, $T_2(m_{12}, m_{22}, m_{32}, m_{42})$, $T_3(m_{13}, m_{23}, m_{33}, m_{43})$, $T_4(m_{14}, m_{24}, m_{34}, m_{44}, m_{54}, m_{64}, m_{74})$, $T_5(m_{15}, m_{25}, m_{35}, m_{45}, m_{55}, m_{65}, m_{75}, m_{85})$ and a set of five processing nodes $(p_1, p_2, p_3, p_4, p_5)$ interconnected in some fashion.

The results for case 2: Total cost using A* at all the processing nodes is 1585 units. Total cost using GA at all the processing nodes is 213 units.

Case 3: A set of 8(eight) tasks with their corresponding modules $T_1(m_{11}, m_{21}, m_{31}, m_{41})$, $T_2(m_{12}, m_{22}, m_{32}, m_{42}, m_{52})$, $T_3(m_{13}, m_{23}, m_{33}, m_{43}, m_{53}, m_{63})$, $T_4(m_{14}, m_{24}, m_{34}, m_{44})$, $T_5(m_{15}, m_{25}, m_{35}, m_{45}, m_{55})$, $T_6(m_{16}, m_{26}, m_{36}, m_{46}, m_{56}, m_{66})$, $T_7(m_{17}, m_{27}, m_{37}, m_{47})$, $T_8(m_{18}, m_{28}, m_{38}, m_{48}, m_{58})$ and a set of 6(six) processors $(p_1, p_2, p_3, p_4, p_5, p_6)$ have been considered.

The results for case 3: Total cost using A* at all the processing nodes is 1380 units. Total cost using GA at all the processing nodes is 213 units.

6 Comparative Observations

From the results and the tables 1-6, it is observed that

a) The total cost (communication and execution) of the allocation for tasks using GA technique is much less than the cost of allocation using A* technique.

b) The tables show the status of allocation of every module of each task of the DCS. By comparing the Tables 2 and 3, it is observed that according to the Vth column (R_{mod}), the results using GA (Table 2) shows better allocation than the results using A*(Table 1). The results using GA achieves a good balanced load allocation than the results using A* considering the existing architectural

Table 1. The final status of the GT using A* for case 1

P_{node}	M_{mod}	M_{cap}	Mod_{assign}	R_{mod}	R_{mem}
p_1	4	10	$m_{21}m_{41}m_{22}$	1	1
p_2	3	8	$m_{12}m_{32}m_{23}$	0	2
p_3	4	9	$m_{13}m_{33}$	2	2
p_4	5	12	$m_{11}m_{31}$	3	5

Table 2. The final status of the GT using GA for case 1

P_{node}	M_{mod}	M_{cap}	Mod_{assign}	R_{mod}	R_{mem}
p_1	4	10	$m_{32}m_{13}$	2	5
p_2	3	8	$m_{21}m_{12}$	1	2
p_3	4	9	$m_{11}m_{31}m_{23}$	1	0
p_4	5	12	$m_{41}m_{22}m_{33}$	2	3

Table 3. The final status of the GT using A* for case 2

P_{node}	M_{mod}	M_{cap}	Mod_{assign}	R_{mod}	R_{mem}
p_1	10	50	$m_{21}m_{51}m_{12}m_{42}$ $m_{33}m_{43}m_{14}m_{34}$ $m_{64}m_{74}$	0	19
p_2	9	40	$m_{41}m_{22}m_{13}m_{24}$ $m_{25}m_{85}$	3	21
p_3	7	35	$m_{32}m_{23}m_{44}$ $m_{45}m_{65}$	2	21
p_4	6	30	$m_{11}m_{31}m_{54}m_{15}$	2	14
p_5	4	10	$m_{35}m_{55}m_{75}$	1	2

Table 4. The final status of the GT using GA for case 2

P_{node}	M_{mod}	M_{cap}	Mod_{assign}	R_{mod}	R_{mem}
p_1	10	50	$m_{11}m_{13}m_{14}$ $m_{44}m_{54}m_{74}$ $m_{35}m_{65}$	2	24
p_2	9	40	$m_{21}m_{51}m_{12}$ $m_{32}m_{33}m_{25}$ m_{75}	2	23
p_3	7	35	$m_{22}m_{42}m_{43}$ $m_{64}m_{24}m_{45}$	1	11
p_4	6	30	$m_{31}m_{41}m_{34}$ $m_{15}m_{55}$	1	14
p_5	4	10	$m_{23}m_{85}$	2	5

Table 5. The final status of the GT using A* for case 3

P_{node}	M_{mod}	M_{cap}	Mod_{assign}	R_{mod}	R_{mem}
p_1	10	50	$m_{21}m_{51}m_{12}m_{42}$ $m_{33}m_{43}m_{14}m_{34}$ $m_{64}m_{74}$	0	19
p_2	9	40	$m_{41}m_{22}m_{13}m_{24}$ $m_{25}m_{85}$	3	21
p_3	7	35	$m_{32}m_{23}m_{44}m_{45}$ m_{65}	2	21
p_4	6	30	$m_{11}m_{31}m_{54}m_{15}$	2	14
p_5	4	10	$m_{35}m_{55}m_{75}$	1	2

Table 6. The final status of the GT using GA for case 3

P_{node}	M_{mod}	M_{cap}	Mod_{assign}	R_{mod}	R_{mem}
p_1	10	70	$m_{21}m_{53}m_{15}m_{26}$ $m_{66}m_{17}m_{37}$ $m_{28}m_{48}$	1	28
p_2	8	50	$m_{31}m_{41}m_{14}m_{24}$ $m_{35}m_{36}m_{18}$	1	23
p_3	6	40	$m_{11}m_{25}m_{45}m_{55}$ m_{46}	1	26
p_4	7	35	$m_{42}m_{423}m_{33}m_{44}$ $m_{56}m_{27}m_{58}$	0	6
p_5	6	40	$m_{32}m_{13}m_{63}m_{16}$ m_{38}	1	22
p_6	6	33	$m_{12}m_{22}m_{52}m_{43}$ $m_{34}m_{47}$	0	9

capability of the DCS for case 1. Regarding case 2 and 3, comparing the results of the Tables 3-4 and 5-6, it is also noticed that the results using GA show a good balanced allocation based on the Vth column for each processing node than A*.

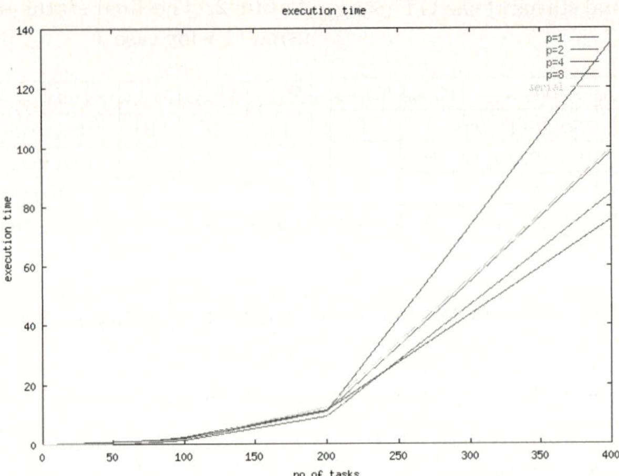

Fig. 2. Execution time using number of tasks = 400

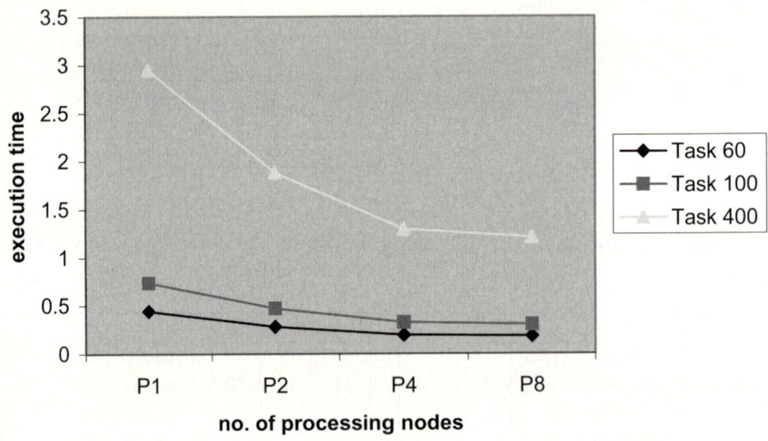

Fig. 3. Execution time using GA based algorithm for number of tasks = 60, 100 and 400, respectively

6.1   Experimental Results

To investigate the effectiveness and the scalability of our proposed algorithms we further experimented with large number of task graphs with corresponding modules. For simulation purpose, we used Sun Fire 12K, 8 processors based distributed multiprocessor systems and Message Passing Interface (MPI) as programming environment with 60, 100 and 400 tasks with the corresponding modules. It is to mention that the tasks graphs and the corresponding modules are generated randomly. It is found that for an amount of large number of tasks (400 tasks), our A* based parallel algorithm performed better (Fig. 2) than the results using 60 and 100 tasks [18], respectively . Thus, we concluded that for a large number of tasks our algorithm performed well and it is scalable with the large number of increasing tasks. However, GA based algorithm performed better for all the cases than A* based algorithm in terms of load balanced allocation and running time (see Fig. 3).

7 Conclusion and Future Work

We have considered the problem of allocation for multiple disjoint tasks partitioned into their corresponding modules and proposed two parallel algorithms for this purpose. We have taken into account the dynamic situation of arrival of tasks in arbitrarily networked DCSs and thus introduced a global table to handle this situation. Our algorithms have been implemented with several case studies. It has been shown that the algorithms are efficient in terms of good load balanced allocations among the processing nodes in DCSs. We found that the algorithm based on GA performs better. Furthermore, we have conducted experiments for a large number of tasks with the corresponding modules. Comparing the results obtained using our algorithms, it is evident that GA based algorithm can provide effective solution in terms of scalability and running time for the TA problem for a large number of tasks coming onto a DCS.

References

1. N.J. Nilson, *Problem Solving Methods in Artificial Intelligence*. McGraw Hill International Edition, 1971.
2. C.C. Shen and W.H. Tsai, "A Graph Matching Approach to Optimal Task Assignment in Distributed Computing System Using A Minimax Criterion", *IEEE Transactions on Computers*, vol. C-34, no. 1, pp. 197-203, 1985.
3. A.K. Tripathi, D.P. Vidyarthi and A.N.Mantri, "A Genetic Task Allocation Algorithm for Distributed Computing System Incorporating Problem Specific Knowledge", *International Journal of High Speed Computing*, vol. 8, no. 4, pp. 363-370, 1996.
4. A.K. Tripathi, B.K. Sarker, N. Kumar and D.P. Vidyarthi, "A GA Based Multiple Task Allocation Considering Load", *International Journal of High Speed Computing*, vol. 11, no. 4, pp. 203-214, 2000.
5. M. Kafil and I. Ahmed , "Optimal Task Assignment in Heterogeneous Distributed Computing System", *IEEE Concurrency*, vol. 6, no. 3, pp. 42-51, 1998.
6. Ramakrishnan, H.Chao, and L.A.Dunning, "A Close Look at Task Assignment in Distributed Systems", *Proceedings of IEEE Infocom-91*, pp. 806-812, 1991.
7. D.P.Vidyarthi, A.K.Tripathi and B.K.Sarker, "Allocation Aspects in Distributed Computing System", *IETE Technical Review*, vol. 18, no. 6, pp. 279-285, 2001.
8. P.Y.R.Richard Ma, E.Y.S.Lee and J. Tsuchiya, "A Task Allocation Model for Distributed Computing Systems", *IEEE Transactions on Computers*, vol. C-31, no. 1, pp. 41-47, 1982.
9. S.H.Bokhari, "On the Mapping Problem", *IEEE Transactions on Computers*, vol. C-30, pp. 207-214, March, 1981.

10. Pradeep K. Sinha, Distributed Operating System, IEEE Press, Prentice Hall of India Ltd., 1998.
11. A.S.Tanenbaum, Distributed Operating Systems, Prentice-Hall, Englewood Cliffs, 1995.
12. A.K.Tripathi, B.K.Sarker, N.Kumar and D.P.Vidyarthi, "Multiple Task Allocation with Load Considerations", *International Journal of Information and Computing Science (IJICS)*, vol.3, no.1, pp. 36-44, 2000.
13. D.P.Vidyarthi, A.K.Tripathi and B.K.Sarker, "Multiple Task Management in Distributed Computing System", *Journal of the CSI*, vol. 31, no. 1, pp. 19-25, 2001.
14. S. Menon, "Effective Reformulations for Task Allocation in Distributed Systems with a Large Number of Communicating Tasks", *IEEE Transactions on Knowledge and Data Engineering*, vol. 16, no.12, pp.1497-1508, 2004.
15. M. Sriniwas and L.M. Patnaik, "Genetic Algorithms: A survey", *IEEE Computer*, June, pp.44-52, 1994.
16. M. Mitchell, *An Introduction to Genetic Algorithm*, Prentice Hall of India. 1998.
17. A.K. Tripathi, D.P. Vidyarthi and A.N.Mantri, "A Genetic Task Allocation Algorithm for Distributed Computing System Incorporating Problem Specific Knowledge", *Int. Journal of High Speed Computing*, vol. 8, no. 4, pp. 363-370, 1996.
18. B.K.Sarker, A.K. Tripathi, D.P. Vidyarthi, K. Uehara and L.T.Yang, "Load Balanced Allocation of multiple Tasks in A Distributed Computing Systems", *Proceedings of EUC-2005*, L.T.Yang et al. (eds), LNCS-3824, pp. 584-596, 2005.

Panconnectivity and Pancyclicity of Hypercube-Like Interconnection Networks with Faulty Elements*

Jung-Heum Park[1], Hyeong-Seok Lim[2], and Hee-Chul Kim[3]

[1] School of Computer Science and Information Engineering,
The Catholic University of Korea, Korea
j.h.park@catholic.ac.kr
[2] School of Electronics and Computer Engineering,
Chonnam National University, Korea
hslim@chonnam.ac.kr
[3] Computer Science and Information Communications Engineering Division,
Hankuk University of Foreign Studies, Korea
hckim@hufs.ac.kr

Abstract. In this paper, we deal with the graph $G_0 \oplus G_1$ obtained from merging two graphs G_0 and G_1 with n vertices each by n pairwise non-adjacent edges joining vertices in G_0 and vertices in G_1. The main problems studied are how fault-panconnectivity and fault-pancyclicity of G_0 and G_1 are translated into fault-panconnectivity and fault-pancyclicity of $G_0 \oplus G_1$, respectively. Applying our results to a subclass of hypercube-like interconnection networks called *restricted HL-graphs*, we show that in a restricted HL-graph G of degree $m(\geq 3)$, each pair of vertices are joined by a path in $G \backslash F$ of every length from $2m - 3$ to $|V(G \backslash F)| - 1$ for any set F of faulty elements (vertices and/or edges) with $|F| \leq m - 3$, and there exists a cycle of every length from 4 to $|V(G \backslash F)|$ for any fault set F with $|F| \leq m - 2$.

1 Introduction

Linear arrays and rings are two of the most important computational structures in interconnection networks. So, embedding of linear arrays and rings into a faulty interconnection network is one of the important issues in parallel processing[9,13,15]. An interconnection network is often modeled as a graph, in which vertices and edges correspond to nodes and communication links, respectively. Thus, the embedding problem can be modeled as finding fault-free paths and cycles in the graph with some faulty vertices and/or edges. In the embedding problem, if the longest path or cycle is required the problem is closely related to well-known hamiltonian problems in graph theory. In the rest of this paper, we will use standard terminology in graphs (see ref. [3]).

* This work was supported by the Korea Research Foundation Grant funded by the Korean Government(MOEHRD) (KRF-2005-041-D00645), and also supported by the department specialization Fund, 2006 of The Catholic University of Korea.

G. Min et al. (Eds.): ISPA 2006 Ws, LNCS 4331, pp. 291–300, 2006.
© Springer-Verlag Berlin Heidelberg 2006

Definition 1. *A graph G is called f-fault hamiltonian (resp. f-fault hamiltonian-connected) if there exists a hamiltonian cycle (resp. if each pair of vertices are joined by a hamiltonian path) in $G\backslash F$ for any set F of faulty elements with $|F| \leq f$.*

On the other hand, if the paths joining each pair of vertices of every length shorter than or equal to a hamiltonian path are required the problem is concerned with panconnectivity of the graph. If the cycles of arbitrary size (up to a hamiltonian cycle) are required the problem is concerned with pancyclicity of the graph.

Definition 2. *A graph G is called f-fault q-panconnected if each pair of fault-free vertices are joined by a path in $G\backslash F$ of every length from q to $|V(G\backslash F)| - 1$ inclusive for any set F of faulty elements with $|F| \leq f$.*

Definition 3. *A graph G is called f-fault pancyclic (resp. f-fault almost pancyclic) if $G\backslash F$ contains a cycle of every length from 3 to $|V(G\backslash F)|$ (resp. 4 to $|V(G\backslash F)|$) inclusive for any set F of faulty elements with $|F| \leq f$.*

Pancyclicity of various interconnection networks was investigated in the literature. Recursive circulant $G(2^m, 4)$ of degree m was shown to be 0-fault almost pancyclic in [2] and then $m-2$-fault almost pancyclic in [12]. Möbius cube of degree m is 0-fault almost pancyclic[5] and $m-2$-fault almost pancyclic[8]. Crossed cube and twisted cube of degree m were also shown to be $m-2$-fault almost pancyclic in [17] and in [18]. Edge-pancyclicity of some fault-free interconnection networks such as recursive circulants, crossed cubes, twisted cubes was studied in [1], [7], and [6]. The work on panconnectivity of interconnection networks has a relative paucity and some results can be found in [4,10]. As the authors know, no results on fault-panconnectivity were reported in the literature.

Many interconnection networks can be expanded into higher dimensional networks by connecting two lower dimensional networks. As a graph modeling of the expansion, we consider the graph obtained by connecting two graphs G_0 and G_1 with n vertices. We denote by V_i and E_i the vertex set and edge set of G_i, $i = 0, 1$, respectively. We let $V_0 = \{v_1, v_2, \ldots, v_n\}$ and $V_1 = \{w_1, w_2, \ldots, w_n\}$. With respect to a permutation $M = (i_1, i_2, \ldots, i_n)$ of $\{1, 2, \ldots, n\}$, we can "merge" the two graphs into a graph $G_0 \oplus_M G_1$ with $2n$ vertices in such a way that the vertex set $V = V_0 \cup V_1$ and the edge set $E = E_0 \cup E_1 \cup E_2$, where $E_2 = \{(v_j, w_{i_j}) | 1 \leq j \leq n\}$. We denote by $G_0 \oplus G_1$ a graph obtained by merging G_0 and G_1 w.r.t. an arbitrary permutation M. Here, G_0 and G_1 are called *components* of $G_0 \oplus G_1$.

Vaidya *et al.*[16] introduced a class of hypercube-like interconnection networks, called *HL-graphs*, which can be defined by applying the $\oplus$ operation repeatedly as follows: $HL_0 = \{K_1\}$; for $m \geq 1$, $HL_m = \{G_0 \oplus G_1 | G_0, G_1 \in HL_{m-1}\}$. Then, $HL_1 = \{K_2\}$; $HL_2 = \{C_4\}$; $HL_3 = \{Q_3, G(8, 4)\}$. Here, C_4 is a cycle graph with 4 vertices, Q_3 is a 3-dimensional hypercube, and $G(8, 4)$ is a recursive circulant which is isomorphic to twisted cube TQ_3 and Möbius ladder with 4 spokes as shown in Figure 1. It was shown by Park and Chwa in [11] that every nonbipartite HL-graph is hamiltonian-connected.

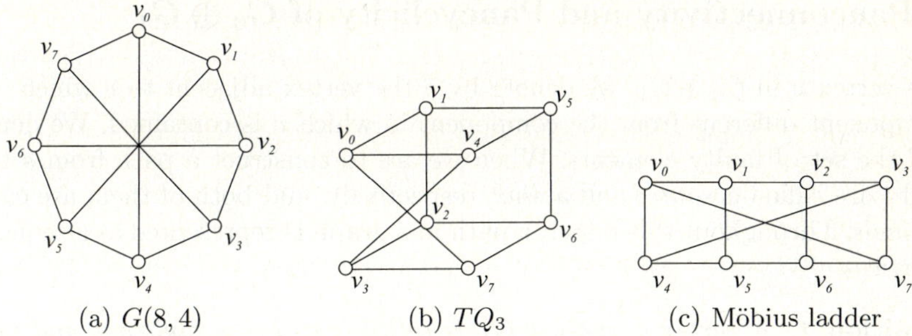

Fig. 1. Isomorphic graphs

In [13], a subclass of nonbipartite HL-graphs, called *restricted HL-graphs* was introduced which is defined recursively as follows: $RHL_m = HL_m$ for $0 \leq m \leq 2$; $RHL_3 = HL_3 \backslash Q_3 = \{G(8,4)\}$; $RHL_m = \{G_0 \oplus G_1 | G_0, G_1 \in RHL_{m-1}\}$ for $m \geq 4$. A graph which belongs to RHL_m is called an m-*dimensional restricted HL-graph*. Many of the nonbipartite hypercube-like interconnection networks such as crossed cube, Möbius cube, twisted cube, multiply twisted cube, Mcube, generalized twisted cube, locally twisted cube, etc. proposed in the literature are restricted HL-graphs. It was shown in [13] that every m-dimensional restricted HL-graph, $m \geq 3$, is $m - 3$-fault hamiltonian-connected and $m - 2$-fault hamiltonian. The result was utilized in [14] to find disjoint paths which cover all the vertices between source-sink pairs in restricted HL-graphs.

We first investigate panconnectivity and pancyclicity of $G_0 \oplus G_1$ with faulty elements. It will be shown that if each G_i is f-fault q-panconnected and $f + 1$-fault hamiltonian (with additional conditions $n \geq f+2q+1$ and $q \geq 2f+3$), then $G_0 \oplus G_1$ is $f + 1$-fault $q + 2$-panconnected for any $f \geq 2$. To study pancyclicity of $G_0 \oplus G_1$, the notion of *hypohamiltonian-connectivity* is introduced. A graph G is called f-*fault hypohamiltonian-connected* if each pair of vertices can be joined by a path of length $|V(G\backslash F)| - 2$, that is one less than the longest possible length, in $G\backslash F$ for any fault set F with $|F| \leq f$. We will show that if each G_i is f-fault hamiltonian-connected, f-fault hypohamiltonian-connected, and $f + 1$-fault almost pancyclic, then $G_0 \oplus G_1$ is $f + 2$-fault almost pancyclic for any $f \geq 1$.

Our main results are applied to restricted HL-graphs. We will show that every m-dimensional restricted HL-graph with $m \geq 3$ is $m - 3$-fault $2m - 3$-panconnected and $m - 2$-fault almost pancyclic. Both bounds $m - 3$ and $m - 2$ on the number of acceptable faulty elements are the maximum possible. Notice that f-fault q-panconnected graph is f-fault hamiltonian-connected, and that f-fault almost pancyclic graph is f-fault hamiltonian. Our results are not only the extension of some works of [8,17,18] on fault-pancyclicity of restricted HL-graphs, but also a new investigation on fault-panconnectivity of restricted HL-graphs.

2   Panconnectivity and Pancyclicity of $G_0 \oplus G_1$

For a vertex v in $G_0 \oplus G_1$, we denote by $\bar{v}$ the vertex adjacent to v which is in a component different from the component in which v is contained. We denote by F the set of faulty elements. When we are to construct a path from s to t, s and t are called a *source* and a *sink*, respectively, and both of them are called *terminals*. Throughout this paper, a path in a graph is represented as a sequence of vertices.

Definition 4. *A vertex v in $G_0 \oplus G_1$ is called* free *if v is fault-free and not a terminal, that is, $v \notin F$ and v is neither a source nor a sink. An edge (v, w) is called* free *if v and w are free and $(v, w) \notin F$.*

We denote by V_i and E_i the sets of vertices and edges in G_i, $i = 0, 1$, and by E_2 the set of edges joining vertices in G_0 and vertices in G_1. We let $n = |V_0| = |V_1|$. F_0 and F_1 denote the sets of faulty elements in G_0 and G_1, respectively, and F_2 denotes the set of faulty edges in E_2, so that $F = F_0 \cup F_1 \cup F_2$. Let $f_0 = |F_0|$, $f_1 = |F_1|$, and $f_2 = |F_2|$.

When we find a path/cycle, sometimes we regard some fault-free vertices and/or edges as faulty elements. They are called *virtual* faults. If G_i is f-fault hamiltonian-connected and $f + 1$-fault hamiltonian, $i = 0, 1$, then

$$f \le \delta(G_i) - 3, \text{ and thus } f + 4 \le n,$$

where $\delta(G_i)$ is the minimum degree of G_i.

2.1   Panconnectivity of $G_0 \oplus G_1$

Hamiltonian-connectivity of $G_0 \oplus G_1$ with faulty elements was considered in [13]. In this subsection, we study panconnectivity of $G_0 \oplus G_1$ in the presence of faulty elements. We denote by f_v^0 and f_v^1 the numbers of faulty vertices in G_0 and G_1, respectively, and by f_v the number of faulty vertices in $G_0 \oplus G_1$, so that $f_v = f_v^0 + f_v^1$. Note that the length of a hamiltonian path in $G_0 \oplus G_1 \setminus F$ is $2n - f_v - 1$.

Theorem 1. *Let G_0 and G_1 be graphs with n vertices each. Let f and q be nonnegative integers satisfying $n \ge f + 2q + 1$ and $q \ge 2f + 3$. If each G_i is f-fault q-panconnected and $f + 1$-fault hamiltonian, then*
(a) for any $f \ge 2$, $G_0 \oplus G_1$ is $f + 1$-fault $q + 2$-panconnected,
(b) for $f = 1$, $G_0 \oplus G_1$ with $2(= f + 1)$ faulty elements has a path of every length $q + 2$ or more joining s and t unless s and t are contained in the same component and $\bar{s}$ and $\bar{t}$ are the faulty elements(vertices), and
(c) for $f = 0$, $G_0 \oplus G_1$ with $1(= f + 1)$ faulty element has a path of every length $q + 2$ or more joining s and t unless s and t are contained in the same component and the faulty element is contained in the other component.

Proof. To prove (a), assuming the number of faulty elements $|F| \leq f + 1$, we will construct a path of every length l, $q + 2 \leq l \leq 2n - f_v - 1$, in $G_0 \oplus G_1 \backslash F$ joining any pair of vertices s and t.

Case 1: $f_0, f_1 \leq f$.

When both s and t are contained in G_0, there exists a path P_0 of length l_0 in G_0 joining s and t for every $q \leq l_0 \leq n - f_v^0 - 1$. We are to construct a longer path P_1 that passes through vertices in G_1 as well as vertices in G_0. We first claim that there exists an edge (x, y) on P_0 such that all of $\bar{x}$, $(x, \bar{x})$, $\bar{y}$, and $(y, \bar{y})$ are fault-free. There are l_0 candidate edges on P_0 and at most $f + 1$ faulty elements can "block" the candidates, at most two candidates per one faulty element. By assumption $l_0 \geq q \geq 2f + 3$, and the claim is proved. The path P_1 can be obtained by merging P_0 and a path P' in G_1 between $\bar{x}$ and $\bar{y}$ with the edges $(x, \bar{x})$ and $(y, \bar{y})$. Here, of course the edge (x, y) is discarded. Letting l' be the length of P', the length l_1 of P_1 can be anything in the range $2q + 1 \leq l_1 = l_0 + l' + 1 \leq 2n - f_v - 1$. Since $n \geq f + 2q + 1$, we have $2q + 1 \leq n - f_v^0$ and we are done.

When s is in G_0 and t is in G_1, we first find a free edge $(x, \bar{x})$ in E_2 such that $(\bar{x}, t)$ is an edge and fault-free. The existence of such a free edge $(x, \bar{x})$ is due to the fact that there are $\delta(G_1)$ candidates and that at most $f + 1$ faulty elements and the source s can block the candidates. Remember $f \leq \delta(G_1) - 3$. Assuming $x \in V_0$, a path joining s and x in G_0 and an edge $(\bar{x}, t)$ are merged with $(x, \bar{x})$ into a path P_0. The length l_0 of P_0 is any integer in the range $q + 2 \leq l_0 \leq n - f_v^0 + 1$. A longer path P_1 is obtained by replacing the edge $(\bar{x}, t)$ with a path in G_1 between $\bar{x}$ and t of length l'', $q \leq l'' \leq n - f_v^1 - 1$. The length l_1 of P_1 is in the range $2q + 1 \leq l_1 \leq 2n - f_v - 1$. We are done since $2q + 1 \leq n - f_v^0$ as shown in the previous subcase.

Case 2: $f_0 = f + 1$ (or symmetrically, $f_1 = f + 1$).

We have $f_1 = f_2 = 0$. First, we consider the subcase $s, t \in V_0$. Letting P' be a path in G_1 joining $\bar{s}$ and $\bar{t}$, we have a path $P_0 = (s, P', t)$ between s and t. The length l_0 of P_0 is any integer in the range $q + 2 \leq l_0 \leq n + 1$. To construct a longer path P_1, we select an arbitrary faulty element α in G_0. Regarding α as a *virtual fault-free element*, find a path P'' in G_0 between s and t. If α is a faulty vertex on P'', let x and y be the two vertices on P'' next to α; else if P'' passes through the faulty edge α, let x and y be the endvertices of α; else let (x, y) be an arbitrary edge on P''. The path P_1 is obtained by merging $P'' \backslash \alpha$ and a path in G_1 joining $\bar{x}$ and $\bar{y}$ with edges $(x, \bar{x})$ and $(y, \bar{y})$. If α is faulty vertex on P'', the length l_1 of P_1 is in the range $2q \leq l_1 \leq 2n - f_v - 1$; otherwise, we have $2q + 1 \leq l_1 \leq 2n - f_v - 1$. In any cases, we are done since $2q + 1 \leq n + 2$.

Secondly, we consider the subcase $s \in V_0$ and $t \in V_1$. We first find a hamiltonian cycle C in $G_0 \backslash F_0$ and let $C = (s = z_0, z_1, z_2, ..., z_k)$, where $k = n - f_v^0 - 1$. Assuming $\bar{z}_l \neq t$ without loss of generality, we can construct a path P_0 by merging $(z_0, z_1, ..., z_l)$ and a path in G_1 between $\bar{z}_l$ and t with the edge $(z_l, \bar{z}_l)$. The length l_0 of P_0 is any integer in the range $q + l + 1 \leq l_0 \leq n - f_v^1 + l$. Since l itself is any integer in the range $1 \leq l \leq n - f_v^0 - 1$, we have $q + 2 \leq l_0 \leq 2n - f_v - 1$.

Finally, we consider the subcase $s, t \in V_1$. We have a path P_0 in G_1 joining s and t, and the length l_0 of P_0 is in the range $q \leq l_0 \leq n - 1$. To construct a longer path P_1, we let $C = (z_0, z_1, z_2, ..., z_k)$ be a hamiltonian cycle in $G_0 \backslash F_0$, where $k = n - f_v^0 - 1$. If $\bar{s} \notin F$, we assume w.l.o.g. $\bar{s} = z_0$. Then, letting w.l.o.g. $\bar{z}_l \neq t$, P_1 is a concatenation of $(s, z_0, z_1, \ldots, z_l)$ and a path in $G_1 \backslash s$ between $\bar{z}_l$ and t. The length l_1 of P_1 is in the range $q + 3 \leq l_1 \leq 2n - f_v - 1$. If $\bar{s} \in F$, we let $(x, \bar{x})$ be a free edge such that $\bar{x}$ is adjacent to s. Then, letting w.l.o.g. $x = z_0$ and $\bar{z}_l \neq t$, P_1 is a concatenation of $(s, \bar{x}, z_0, z_1, \ldots, z_l)$ and a path in $G_1 \backslash \{s, \bar{x}\}$ between $\bar{z}_l$ and t. Here, the length l_1 of P_1 is in the range $q + 4 \leq l_1 \leq 2n - f_v - 1$. By the condition of $n \geq f + 2q + 1$ and $q \geq 2f + 3$, we can observe $q + 4 \leq n$. Therefore, we are done. This completes the proof of (a).

It immediately follows from Case 1 and the first and second subcases of Case 2, where the assumption $f \geq 2$ is never used, that for $f = 0, 1$, $G_0 \oplus G_1$ with $f + 1$ faulty elements has a path of every length $q + 2$ or more joining s and t unless s and t are contained in the same component and all the faulty elements are contained in the other component. Thus, the proof of (c) is done. To prove (b), assuming w.l.o.g. $\bar{s} \notin F$, it suffices to employ the construction of the last subcase of Case 2. Note that in the construction, G_1 is 1-fault q-panconnected. This completes the proof. $\square$

Corollary 1. *Let G_0 and G_1 be graphs with n vertices each. Let f and q be nonnegative integers satisfying $n \geq f + 2q + 1$ and $q \geq 2f + 3$. If each G_i is f-fault q-panconnected and $f + 1$-fault hamiltonian, then $G_0 \oplus G_1$ is f-fault $q + 2$-panconnected.*

2.2   Pancyclicity of $G_0 \oplus G_1$

In the presence of faulty elements, the existence of hamiltonian cycle in $G_0 \oplus G_1$ was considered in [13] as in Theorem 2. In this subsection, we investigate almost pancyclicity of $G_0 \oplus G_1$ with faulty elements. We denote by $H[v, w | G, F]$ a hamiltonian path in $G \backslash F$ joining a pair of fault-free vertices v and w in a graph G with a set F of faulty elements. $HH[v, w | G, F]$ is a hypohamiltonian path in $G \backslash F$ between v and w.

Theorem 2. *[13] Let a graph G_i be f-fault hamiltonian-connected and $f + 1$-fault hamiltonian, $i = 0, 1$. Then,*
(a) for any $f \geq 1$, $G_0 \oplus G_1$ is $f + 2$-fault hamiltonian, and
(b) for $f = 0$, $G_0 \oplus G_1$ with $2(= f + 2)$ faulty elements has a hamiltonian cycle unless one faulty element is contained in G_0 and the other faulty element is contained in G_1.

Before presenting our theorem on pancyclicity, we will give two lemmas. The proofs are omitted. They imply that to show an f-fault hamiltonian graph is f-fault almost pancyclic, it is sufficient to consider only vertex faults and further the maximum number of vertex faults. We call a graph G to be f-*vertex-fault almost pancyclic*, if $G \backslash F_v$ contains a cycle of every length from 4 to $|V(G \backslash F_v)|$ for any set of faulty vertices F_v with $|F_v| \leq f$.

Lemma 1. *Let a graph G be f-fault hamiltonian and f-vertex-fault almost pancyclic. Then, G is f-fault almost pancyclic.*

Lemma 2. *Let a graph G be f-fault hamiltonian and almost pancyclic when the number of faulty vertices $f_v = f$. Then, G is f-vertex-fault almost pancyclic.*

Theorem 3. *Let G_i be f-fault hamiltonian-connected, f-fault hypohamiltonian-connected, and $f + 1$-fault almost pancyclic, $i = 0, 1$. Then,*
(a) for any $f \geq 1$, $G_0 \oplus G_1$ is $f + 2$-fault almost pancyclic, and
(b) for $f = 0$, $G_0 \oplus G_1$ with $2(= f + 2)$ faulty elements is almost pancyclic unless one faulty element is contained in G_0 and the other faulty element is contained in G_1.

Proof. To prove (a), we let $|F| = f + 2$, and assume F has only vertex faults by virtue of the above two lemmas. Note that, by Theorem 2(a), $G_0 \oplus G_1$ is $f + 2$-fault hamiltonian. Assuming $f_0 \geq f_1$ without loss of generality, we will construct cycles in $G_0 \oplus G_1 \backslash F$. By the condition in the theorem, there exist cycles of length from 4 to $n - f_1$ in $G_1 \backslash F_1$. Also, the cycle of length $2n - f_0 - f_1$ exists. So, the construction of remaining cycles of length from $n - f_1 + 1$ to $2n - f_0 - f_1 - 1$ will be given.

 Case 1: $f_0 \leq f$.

 Subcase 1.1: $n > f_0 + 2f_1$.

There exists a hamiltonian cycle C_0 of length $n - f_0$ in $G_0 \backslash F_0$. On C_0, we have $n - f_0$ different paths P_k's of length k for every $1 \leq k \leq n - f_0 - 1$. Among them, there exists a P_k joining x_k and y_k such that both $\bar{x}_k$ and $\bar{y}_k$ are fault-free, since we have $n - f_0$ candidates and each of f_1 faulty vertices in G_1 can block at most two candidates. Then, $C = (P_k, HH[\bar{y}_k, \bar{x}_k | G_1, F_1])$ is a cycle of length $n - f_1 + k$, $1 \leq k \leq n - f_0 - 1$.

 Subcase 1.2: $n \leq f_0 + 2f_1$.

We find two free edges $(x, \bar{x})$ and $(y, \bar{y})$ in E_2. Such free edges exist since there are $n(\geq f + 4)$ candidates and $f + 2$ blocking elements. Note that there are no terminals. We will construct a cycle by merging $H[x, y | G_0, F']$ or $HH[x, y | G_0, F']$ with $H[\bar{x}, \bar{y} | G_1, F'']$ or $HH[\bar{x}, \bar{y} | G_1, F'']$. Here, F' (resp. F'') is a set of faulty elements in G_0 (resp. G_1) regarding some fault-free vertices as virtual faults. By taking account of $f - f_0$ vertices in $G_0 \backslash F_0$ excluding $\{x, y\}$ as virtual faults one by one, we can construct paths of length from $n - f - 2$ to $n - f_0 - 1$ between x and y. Also, by taking account of $f - f_1$ vertices in $G_1 \backslash F_1$ excluding $\{\bar{x}, \bar{y}\}$ as virtual faults one by one, we can construct paths of length from $n - f - 2$ to $n - f_1 - 1$ between $\bar{x}$ and $\bar{y}$. By merging two paths in G_0 and G_1, we can obtain cycles of length from $2n - 2f - 2$ to $2n - f_0 - f_1$. If $2n - 2f - 2 \leq n - f_1 + 1$, we will have all cycles of desired lengths. First, we have $2n - 2f - 2 \leq n - f_1 + 2$ since $(2n - 2f - 2) - (n - f_1 + 2) = n - 2f + f_1 - 4 \leq (f_0 + 2f_1) - 2f + f_1 - 4 = f_0 + 3f_1 - 2f - 4 = 2f_1 - f - 2 \leq 0$. Furthermore, careful observation on the above equation leads to $2n - 2f - 2 \leq n - f_1 + 1$ unless $n = f_0 + 2f_1$ and $f_0 = f_1$.

 For the remaining case that $n = f_0 + 2f_1$ and $f_0 = f_1$, it is sufficient to construct a cycle of length $n - f_1 + 1$. To do this, we claim that there exists an edge (x, y) in G_0 such that both $\bar{x}$ and $\bar{y}$ are fault-free. Let $W = \{w | w \in V_0 \backslash F_0,$

$\bar{w} \notin F\}$, and let $B = V_0 \setminus (F_0 \cup W)$. It holds true that $|W| \geq |B|$ since $|W| \geq n - f_0 - f_1 = f_1$ and $|B| \leq f_1$. Let C_0 be a hamiltonian cycle in $G_0 \setminus F_0$. If there is an edge (a, b) on C_0 such that $a, b \in W$, we are done. Suppose otherwise, we have $|W| = |B|$ and the vertices on C_0 should alternate in W and B. Since $G_0 \setminus F_0$ is hamiltonian-connected, we always have such an edge (x, y) joining vertices in W. Note that $|W|, |B| \geq 2$, and that if there are no edges between vertices in W, there can not exist a hamiltonian path joining vertices in B. Then, we have a desired cycle $(x, y, HH[\bar{y}, \bar{x}|G_1, F_1])$ of length $n - f_1 + 1$.

   Case 2: $f_0 = f + 1$.

We find a hamiltonian cycle C_0 in $G_0 \setminus F_0$, and let x_k and y_k be two vertices in C_0 such that both $\bar{x}_k$ and $\bar{y}_k$ are fault-free and there is a path of length k between x_k and y_k on C_0, $1 \leq k \leq n - f_0 - 1$. The existence of such x_k and y_k is due to the fact that the length of C_0 is at least three and $f_1 = 1$. Let P_k be the path of length k on C_0 whose endvertices are x_k and y_k. We construct cycles $(P_k, HH[\bar{y}_k, \bar{x}_k|G_1, F_1])$, $1 \leq k \leq n - f_0 - 1$, of length from $n - f_1 + 1$ to $2n - f_0 - f_1 - 1$. The hypohamiltonian path in G_1 between $\bar{y}_k$ and $\bar{x}_k$ exists since $f_1 = 1 \leq f$.

   Case 3: $f_0 = f + 2$.

We select an arbitrary faulty vertex v_f in G_0, regarding it as *a virtual fault-free vertex*, find a hamiltonian cycle C_0 in $G_0 \setminus F'$, where $F' = F_0 \setminus v_f$. The existence of C_0 is due to $|F'| = f + 1$. Let P_k be an arbitrary path of length k on $C_0 \setminus v_f$ whose endvertices are x_k and y_k, $1 \leq k \leq n - f_0 - 1$. Then, we have a cycle $(P_k, HH[\bar{y}_k, \bar{x}_k|G_1, \emptyset])$ of length $n - f_1 + k$ for every $1 \leq k \leq n - f_0 - 1$.

   The proof of (b) follows immediately from the proof of (a), where the assumption $f \geq 1$ is used only when $f_1 = 1$ in Case 2. $\square$

3   Restricted HL-Graphs

In this section, we will show that every m-dimensional restricted HL-graph is $m - 3$-fault $2m - 3$-panconnected and $m - 2$-fault almost pancyclic. Fault-hamiltonicity of restricted HL-graphs was studied in [13] as follows.

Theorem 4. *[13] Every m-dimensional restricted HL-graph, $m \geq 3$, is $m - 3$-fault hamiltonian-connected and $m - 2$-fault hamiltonian.*

3.1   Panconnectivity of Restricted HL-Graphs

By induction on m, we will prove that every m-dimensional restricted HL-graph, $m \geq 3$, is $m - 3$-fault $2m - 3$-panconnected. The proofs of lemmas are omitted.

Lemma 3. *The 3-dimensional restricted HL-graph is 0-fault 3-panconnected.*

To prove Lemmas 5 and 6, we employ a property on disjoint paths in $G(8, 4) \oplus G(8, 4)$ shown in Lemma 4. Two paths joining $\{s_1, s_2\}$ and $\{t_1, t_2\}$ such that $\{s_1, s_2\} \cap \{t_1, t_2\} = \emptyset$ are defined to be either s_1-t_1 and s_2-t_2 paths or s_1-t_2 and s_2-t_1 paths. Two paths P_1 and P_2 in a graph G are called *disjoint covering paths* if $V(P_1) \cap V(P_2) = \emptyset$ and $V(P_1) \cup V(P_2) = V(G)$, where $V(P_i)$ is the set of vertices in P_i.

Lemma 4. *For any four distinct vertices s_1, s_2, t_1, and t_2 in $G(8,4) \oplus G(8,4)$, there exists a vertex $z \notin \{s_1, s_2, t_1, t_2\}$ such that $G(8,4) \oplus G(8,4) \backslash z$ has two disjoint covering paths joining $\{s_1, s_2\}$ and $\{t_1, t_2\}$.*

Similar to Lemma 4, we can show that $G(8,4) \oplus G(8,4)$ has two disjoint covering paths joining every $\{s_1, s_2\}$ and $\{t_1, t_2\}$ with $\{s_1, s_2\} \cap \{t_1, t_2\} = \emptyset$.

Lemma 5. *Every 4-dimensional restricted HL-graph is 1-fault 5-panconnected.*

Lemma 6. *Every 5-dimensional restricted HL-graph is 2-fault 7-panconnected.*

By an inductive argument utilizing Theorem 1(a) and Lemmas 3, 5, and 6, we have Theorem 5.

Theorem 5. *Every m-dimensional restricted HL-graph, $m \geq 3$, is $m - 3$-fault $2m - 3$-panconnected.*

Corollary 2. *Every m-dimensional restricted HL-graph, $m \geq 3$, is $m - 3$-fault hypohamiltonian-connected.*

A graph G is called f-fault q-edge-pancyclic if for any faulty set F with $|F| \leq f$, there exists a cycle of every length from q to $|V(G \backslash F)|$ that passes through an arbitrary fault-free edge. Of course, an f-fault q-panconnected graph is always f-fault $q + 1$-edge-pancyclic. From Theorem 5, we have the following.

Theorem 6. *Every m-dimensional restricted HL-graph, $m \geq 3$, is $m - 3$-fault $2m - 2$-edge-pancyclic.*

3.2   Pancyclicity of Restricted HL-Graphs

To show that every m-dimensional restricted HL-graph is $m - 2$-fault almost pancyclic, due to Lemmas 1 and 2, we assume that the faulty set F contains $m - 2$ faulty vertices. The proofs of lemmas are omitted.

Lemma 7. *The 3-dimensional restricted HL-graph is 1-fault almost pancyclic.*

Lemma 8. *Every 4-dimensional restricted HL-graph is 2-fault almost pancyclic.*

From Theorem 3(a) and Lemmas 7 and 8, we have Theorem 7.

Theorem 7. *Every m-dimensional restricted HL-graph, $m \geq 3$, is $m - 2$-fault almost pancyclic.*

Corollary 3. *(a) Twisted cube TQ_m, $m \geq 3$, is $m - 2$-fault almost pancyclic[18].*
(b) Crossed cube CQ_m, $m \geq 3$, is $m - 2$-fault almost pancyclic[17].
(c) Multiply twisted cube MQ_m, $m \geq 3$, is $m - 2$-fault almost pancyclic.
(d) Both 0-Möbius cube and 1-Möbius cube of dimension m, $m \geq 3$, are $m - 2$-fault almost pancyclic[8].
(e) The m-Mcube, $m \geq 3$, is $m - 2$-fault almost pancyclic.
(f) Generalized twisted cube GQ_m, $m \geq 3$, is $m - 2$-fault almost pancyclic.
(g) Locally twisted cube LTQ_m, $m \geq 3$, is $m - 2$-fault almost pancyclic.
(h) $G(2^m, 4)$, m odd and $m \geq 3$, is $m - 2$-fault almost pancyclic[12].

References

1. T. Araki, "Edge-pancyclicity of recursive circulants," *Inform. Proc. Lett.* **88**, pp. 287-292, 2003.
2. T. Araki and Y. Shibata, "Pancyclicity of recursive circulant graphs," *Inform. Proc. Lett.* **81**, pp. 187-190, 2002.
3. J.A. Bondy and U.S.R. Murty, *Graph Theory with Applications*, 5th printing, American Elsevier Publishing Co., Inc., 1976.
4. J.-M. Chang, J.-S. Yang, Y.-L. Wang, and Y. Cheng, "Panconnectivity, fault-tolerant hamiltonicity and hamiltonian-connectivity in alternating group graphs," *Networks* **44**, pp. 302-310, 2004.
5. J. Fan, "Hamilton-connectivity and cycle-embedding of the Möbius cubes," *Inform. Proc. Lett.* **82**, pp. 113-117, 2002.
6. J. Fan, X. Lin, X. Jia, R.W.H. Lau, "Edge-pancyclicity of twisted cubes," in *Proc. of International Symposium on Algorithms and Computation ISAAC 2005*, pp. 1090-1099, Dec. 2005.
7. J. Fan, X. Lin, X. Jia, "Node-pancyclicity and edge-pancyclicity of crossed cubes," *Inform. Proc. Lett.* **93**, pp. 133-138, 2005.
8. S.-Y. Hsieh and N.-W. Chang, "Cycle embedding on the Möbius cube with both faulty nodes and faulty edges," in *Proc. of 11th International Conference on Parallel and Distributed Systems ICPADS 2005*, 2005.
9. S. Latifi, N. Bagherzadeh, and R.R. Gajjala, "Fault-tolerant embedding of linear arrays and rings in the star graph," *Computers Elect. Engng.* **23(2)**, pp. 95-107, 1997.
10. M. Ma and J.-M. Xu, "Panconnectivity of locally twisted cubes," *Applied Mathematics Letters* **19**, pp. 673-677, 2006.
11. C.-D. Park and K.Y. Chwa, "Hamiltonian properties on the class of hypercube-like networks," *Inform. Proc. Lett.* **91**, pp. 11-17, 2004.
12. J.-H. Park, "Cycle embedding of faulty recursive circulants," *Journal of KISS* **31(2)**, pp. 86-94, 2004 (in Korean).
13. J.-H. Park, H.-C. Kim, and H.-S. Lim, "Fault-hamiltonicity of hypercube-like interconnection networks," in *Proc. of IEEE International Parallel and Distributed Processing Symposium IPDPS 2005*, Denver, Apr. 2005.
14. J.-H. Park, H.-C. Kim, and H.-S. Lim, "Many-to-many disjoint path covers in hypercube-like interconnection networks with faulty elements," *IEEE Trans. on Parallel and Distributed Systems* **17(3)**, pp. 227-240, Mar. 2006.
15. A. Sengupta, "On ring embedding in hypercubes with faulty nodes and links", *Inform. Proc. Lett.* **68**, pp. 207-214, 1998.
16. A.S. Vaidya, P.S.N. Rao, S.R. Shankar, "A class of hypercube-like networks," in *Proc. of the 5th IEEE Symposium on Parallel and Distributed Processing SPDP 1993*, pp. 800-803, Dec. 1993.
17. M.-C. Yang, T.-K. Li, J.J.M. Tan, and L.-H. Hsu, "Fault-tolerant cycle-embedding of crossed cubes," *Inform. Proc. Lett.* **88**, pp. 149-154, 2003.
18. M.-C. Yang, T.-K. Li, J.J.M. Tan, and L.-H. Hsu, "On embedding cycles into faulty twisted cubes," *Information Sciences* **176**, pp. 676-690, 2006.

Embedding Starlike Trees into Hypercube-Like Interconnection Networks*

Jung-Heum Park[1], Hyeong-Seok Lim[2], and Hee-Chul Kim[3]

[1] School of Computer Science and Information Engineering,
The Catholic University of Korea, Korea
j.h.park@catholic.ac.kr
[2] School of Electronics and Computer Engineering,
Chonnam National University, Korea
hslim@chonnam.ac.kr
[3] Computer Science and Information Communications Engineering Division,
Hankuk University of Foreign Studies, Korea
hckim@hufs.ac.kr

Abstract. A *starlike tree* (or a *quasistar*) is a subdivision of a star tree. A family of hypercube-like interconnection networks called *restricted HL-graphs* includes many interconnection networks proposed in the literature such as twisted cubes, crossed cubes, multiply twisted cubes, Möbius cubes, Mcubes, and generalized twisted cubes. We show in this paper that every starlike tree of degree at most m with 2^m vertices is a spanning tree of m-dimensional restricted HL-graphs.

Keywords: Spanning trees, restricted HL-graphs, path partition, interconnection networks.

1   Introduction

Much research has been done to investigate whether an interconnection network contains a certain class of trees as spanning subgraphs. For spanning trees of hypercubes, one of well-known interconnection networks, various trees were investigated such as binomial trees, caterpillars[1], double-rooted complete binary trees[3], starlike and double starlike trees[2]. Other containment results can be found in [3]. This paper deals with starlike trees for spanning trees of a family of interconnection networks called restricted HL-graphs proposed in [6].

A *d-star* is a tree of degree d isomorphic to a complete bipartite graph $K_{1,d}$. A *d-starlike tree* (or a *d-quasistar*) is a tree formed from a d-star by the insertion of vertices of degree two into the edges. A *d-double starlike tree* is a tree obtained by connecting via an edge the roots of a d-starlike tree and a d'-starlike tree with $d' \leq d$. Examples of a d-star, a d-starlike tree, and a d-double starlike tree are shown in Figure 1. For two graphs G and H, G *spans* H if there is a one-to-one mapping ϕ of $V(G)$ into $V(H)$ such that if $(u, v) \in E(G)$ then

* This work was supported by grant No. R05-2003-000-11506-0 from the Basic Research Program of the Korea Science & Engineering Foundation.

G. Min et al. (Eds.): ISPA 2006 Ws, LNCS 4331, pp. 301–310, 2006.
© Springer-Verlag Berlin Heidelberg 2006

$(\phi(u), \phi(v)) \in E(H)$. A bipartite graph G is called *equitable* if G has a proper bicoloring such that both color sets have the same cardinality. Nebeský[4] showed that every equitable d-starlike tree with 2^m vertices, $d \leq m$, spans m-dimensional hypercube Q_m. No non-equitable d-starlike tree with 2^m vertices spans Q_m since Q_m itself is equitable. Kobeissi and Mollard[2] showed that every equitable d-double starlike tree with 2^m vertices, $d \leq 5$ and $d + 1 \leq m$, spans Q_m.

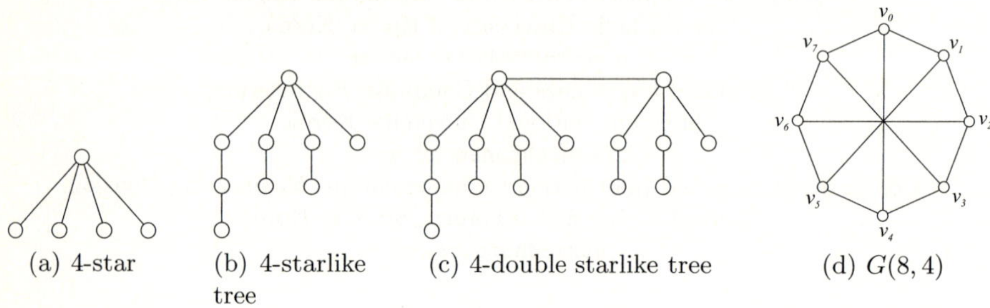

    (a) 4-star   (b) 4-starlike tree   (c) 4-double starlike tree   (d) $G(8,4)$

Fig. 1.

Many interconnection networks can be expanded into higher dimensional networks by connecting two lower dimensional networks. As a graph modeling of the expansion, we consider the graph obtained by connecting two graphs G_0 and G_1 with n vertices. We denote by V_i and E_i the vertex set and edge set of G_i, $i = 0, 1$, respectively. We let $V_0 = \{v_1, v_2, \ldots, v_n\}$ and $V_1 = \{w_1, w_2, \ldots, w_n\}$. With respect to a permutation $M = (i_1, i_2, \ldots, i_n)$ of $\{1, 2, \ldots, n\}$, we can "merge" the two graphs into a graph $G_0 \oplus_M G_1$ with $2n$ vertices in such a way that the vertex set $V = V_0 \cup V_1$ and the edge set $E = E_0 \cup E_1 \cup E_2$, where $E_2 = \{(v_j, w_{i_j}) | 1 \leq j \leq n\}$. We denote by $G_0 \oplus G_1$ a graph obtained by merging G_0 and G_1 w.r.t. an arbitrary permutation M. Here, G_0 and G_1 are called *components* of $G_0 \oplus G_1$.

Vaidya *et al.*[7] introduced a class of hypercube-like interconnection networks, called *HL-graphs*, which can be defined by applying the $\oplus$ operation repeatedly as follows: $HL_0 = \{K_1\}$; for $m \geq 1$, $HL_m = \{G_0 \oplus G_1 | G_0, G_1 \in HL_{m-1}\}$. Then, $HL_1 = \{K_2\}$; $HL_2 = \{C_4\}$; $HL_3 = \{Q_3, G(8,4)\}$. Here, C_4 is a cycle graph with 4 vertices, Q_3 is a 3-dimensional hypercube, and $G(8,4)$ is a recursive circulant which is isomorphic to twisted cube TQ_3 and Möbius ladder with four spokes (see Figure 1(d)). In [6], a subclass of nonbipartite HL-graphs, called *restricted HL-graphs* was introduced by the authors which is defined recursively as follows: $RHL_m = HL_m$ for $0 \leq m \leq 2$; $RHL_3 = HL_3 \backslash Q_3 = \{G(8,4)\}$; $RHL_m = \{G_0 \oplus G_1 | G_0, G_1 \in RHL_{m-1}\}$ for $m \geq 4$. A graph which belongs to RHL_m is called an *m-dimensional restricted HL-graph*. Many of the nonbipartite hypercube-like interconnection networks such as crossed cube, Möbius cube, twisted cube, multiply twisted cube, Mcube, generalized twisted cube, etc. proposed in the literature are restricted HL-graphs. Some works on HL-graphs and restricted HL-graphs were appeared in the literature; for example, hamiltonicity of HL-graphs[5], fault-hamiltonicity of restricted HL-graphs[6].

Concerning starlike trees as spanning trees of restricted HL-graphs, this paper shows two main theorems in the following.

Theorem 1. *Every d-starlike tree with 2^m vertices is a spanning tree of m-dimensional restricted HL-graphs for any $1 \leq d \leq m$. Furthermore, an arbitrary vertex of the restricted HL-graph plays a role of the root of the starlike tree.*

To prove Theorem 1, we rely on path partitionability of restricted HL-graphs. The path partition problem with which we are concerned in this paper is defined as follows. Given k distinct sources $s_1, s_2, \ldots, s_k$ in a graph G and k positive integers $l_1, l_2, \ldots, l_k$ with $\sum_{1 \leq i \leq k} l_i = |V(G)|$, a k-path partition is a set of k vertex-disjoint paths $\{P_1, P_2, \ldots, P_k\}$ such that each P_i is an s_i-path (that is, s_i is an endvertex of P_i) with l_i vertices and $\bigcup_{1 \leq i \leq k} V(P_i) = V(G)$. A graph G is called to be k-path partitionable if for any k distinct sources associated with positive integers l_i's with $\sum_{1 \leq i \leq k} l_i = |V(G)|$, G has a k-path partition.

Theorem 2. *Every m-dimensional restricted HL-graph is k-path partitionable for any $1 \leq k \leq m - 1, m \geq 2$.*

The two main theorems utilize fault-hamiltonicity of restricted HL-graphs. A graph G is called f-*fault hamiltonian* (resp. f-*fault hamiltonian-connected*) if there exists a hamiltonian cycle (resp. if each pair of vertices are joined by a hamiltonian path) in $G \backslash F$ for any set F of faulty vertices and/or edges with $|F| \leq f$. It was shown in [6] that every m-dimensional restricted HL-graph, $m \geq 3$, is $m - 3$-fault hamiltonian-connected and $m - 2$-fault hamiltonian.

Throughout this paper, a path in a graph is represented as a sequence of vertices. We denote by $H[v, w|G, F]$ a hamiltonian path in $G \backslash F$ joining a pair of fault-free vertices v and w in a graph G with a set F of faulty elements. G^m denotes an arbitrary m-dimensional restricted HL-graph. By definition, G^m is isomorphic to $G_0 \oplus G_1$ for some $m - 1$-dimensional restricted HL-graphs G_0 and G_1. For a vertex v in $G_0 \oplus G_1$, we denote by $\bar{v}$ the vertex adjacent to v which is in a component different from the component in which v is contained.

2   Proof of Theorem 1

Each subtree of a starlike tree forms a path. We denote by $T(a_1, a_2, \ldots, a_d)$ a d-starlike tree with root r and r-paths of length a_i, $1 \leq i \leq d$. The starlike tree has $\sum_{1 \leq i \leq d} a_i + 1$ vertices. We assume without loss of generality that $a_1 \geq a_2 \geq \cdots \geq a_d$.

Lemma 1. *For $d = 1, 2$, every d-starlike tree with 2^m vertices is a spanning tree of G^m, $m \geq 2$.*

Proof. Let $C = (x_0, x_1, \ldots, x_{2^m - 1})$ be a hamiltonian cycle in G^m. The d-starlike trees rooted at x_0 can be constructed by removing an appropriate edge from C. Precisely speaking, $C \backslash (x_0, x_{2^m - 1})$ and $C \backslash (x_{a_1}, x_{a_1 + 1})$ are the desired trees for $d = 1$ and $d = 2$, respectively. $\qquad\square$

Lemma 2. *Every 3-starlike tree with 2^m vertices is a spanning tree of G^m, $m \geq 3$.*

Proof. For $m \geq 4$, we first find $T(b, a_3)$ rooted at an arbitrary vertex in G_0 (or symmetrically in G_1), where $b = 2^{m-1} - a_3 - 1$. We have $b \geq 1$ since $a_3 + 1 \leq (2^m - 1)/3 + 1 < 2^{m-1}$ for any $m \geq 4$. Let the r-path of length b be r-z path, that is, z is an endvertex of the path. And then, we find a hamiltonian path $P = H[\bar{z}, \bar{r}|G_1, \emptyset]$ in G_1 between $\bar{z}$ and $\bar{r}$. We merge the r-z path and P with two edges $(z, \bar{z})$ and $(\bar{r}, r)$ into a cycle C of length $a_1 + a_2 + 1$. The tree can be obtained by removing an appropriate edge from C. Now, let $m = 3$. G^m is isomorphic to $G(8, 4)$. We construct a starlike tree rooted at v_0. When $a_3 = 1$, letting x be any vertex in $G(8, 4)$ adjacent to v_0, (v_0, x) is a path of length a_3 and the other two paths are obtained by removing an appropriate edge in a hamiltonian cycle in $G(8, 4)\backslash x$. When $a_3 \geq 2$ (by assumption, $a_1 = 3$ and $a_2, a_3 = 2$), we explicitly construct three paths (v_0, v_7, v_6, v_5), (v_0, v_4, v_3), and (v_0, v_1, v_2). This completes the proof. $\qquad\square$

Lemma 3. *Every 4-starlike tree with 2^m vertices is a spanning tree of G^m, $m \geq 4$.*

Proof. Let us consider the case of $a_3 + a_4 \leq 2^{m-1} - 2$ first. Let $T(b, a_3, a_4)$ be a starlike tree rooted at any vertex r in G_0, where $b = 2^{m-1} - a_3 - a_4 - 1$, and the r-path of length b be r-z path. The r-z path and $H[\bar{z}, \bar{r}|G_1, \emptyset]$ are merged with $(z, \bar{z})$ and $(\bar{r}, r)$ into a cycle of length $a_1 + a_2 + 1$. Removing an appropriate edge from the cycle results in a desired tree. Now, we assume that $a_3 + a_4 \geq 2^{m-1} - 1$, that is, $a_1 = a_2 = a_3 = 2^{m-2}$ and $a_4 = 2^{m-2} - 1$. When $m \geq 5$, similar to the previous case, the tree can be constructed by using $T(b, a_3 - 1, a_4)$ and $H[\bar{z}, \bar{r}|G_1, \{\bar{x}\}]$, where $b = 1$ and x is the endvertex of r-path of length $a_3 - 1$, $x \neq r$. The hamiltonian path exists since G_1 is 1-fault hamiltonian-connected. When $m = 4$, we find $T(3, 2, 2)$ in G_0. Let r-paths of length 2 be r-x path and r-y path, respectively. And then, we find a 3-path partition for $\bar{r}$, $\bar{x}$, and $\bar{y}$ with associated weights 4, 2, 2, respectively. The tree in G_0 and the 3-path partition in G_1 are merged into the desired tree. The existence of path partition is due to Lemma 5 in Section 3. $\qquad\square$

Lemma 4. *For $d \geq 5$, every d-starlike tree with 2^m vertices is a spanning tree of G^m, $m \geq d$.*

Proof. For the case of $a_1 > 2^{m-1}$, similar to the proof of Lemma 3, we find $T(b, a_3, a_4, \ldots, a_d)$ in G_0 with $b = 2^{m-1} - \sum_{3 \leq i \leq d} a_i - 1$. The r-z path, the r-path of length b is merged with $H[\bar{z}, \bar{r}|G_1, \emptyset]$ into a cycle of length $a_1 + a_2 + 1$. It suffices to remove an appropriate edge from the cycle. Now, we assume $a_1 \leq 2^{m-1}$. We let $a_2', a_3', \ldots, a_d'$ be positive integers satisfying (i) $1 + \sum_{2 \leq i \leq d} a_i' = 2^{m-1}$, (ii) $a_i' = a_i$ for $i = d - 1, d$, and (iii) $a_i' \leq a_i$ for every $2 \leq i \leq d - 2$. To show such a_i''s exist, we claim that $a_{d-1} + a_d + (d - 2) \leq 2^{m-1}$ for any $5 \leq d \leq m$. The proof of the claim is by a simple calculation using $a_{d-1} + a_d \leq 2(2^m - 1)/d$, and omitted here. Moreover, we can see that there exist a_i''s such that for some

p, $2 \leq p \leq d - 1$, $a_i' < a_i$ for all $2 \leq i < p$ and $a_i' = a_i$ for all $p \leq i \leq d$.
Then, we find $T(a_2', a_3', \ldots, a_d')$ in G_0. Let the r-path of length a_i' be r-z_i path
for each $2 \leq i < p$. To obtain a desired tree, it suffices to construct a $p - 1$-path
partition for $\bar{r}$ and $\bar{z}_i$ for all $2 \leq i < p$ with associated weights a_1 and $a_i - a_i'$'s,
respectively. We have $p - 1 \leq d - 2 \leq m - 2$. The existence of path partition is
due to Theorem 2. $\qquad \square$

3   Path Partitions

Given k distinct sources $s_1, s_2, \ldots, s_k$ in a graph G associated with k positive
integers $l_1, l_2, \ldots, l_k$, respectively, satisfying $\sum_{1 \leq i \leq k} l_i = |V(G)|$, a k-path par-
tition consists of k disjoint paths P_i with l_i vertices, $1 \leq i \leq k$, where each P_i
is an s_i-path. The *sink* of P_i is the endvertex of P_i different from s_i if $l_i \geq 2$;
if $l_i = 1$, s_i is the sink as well as the source of P_i. For $m = 2, 3$, Theorem 2
holds true since the path partitions are constructed straightforwardly from the
hamiltonian cycles/paths. For some l_i's, the 3-dimensional restricted HL-graph
$G(8, 4)$ has a 3-path partition for any 3 sources as follows.

Lemma 5. *$G(8, 4)$ has a 3-path partition for any three sources if $(l_1, l_2, l_3) =$
$(3, 3, 2)$, $(4, 2, 2)$, or $(5, 2, 1)$.*

Proof. The proof is by an immediate inspection and omitted here. $\qquad \square$

For $m \geq 4$, we will prove a stronger result than Theorem 2 claims. We are to
pose an additional constraint on the k-path partition that for any vertex subsets
W_i with $|W_i| \leq m - k$, $1 \leq i \leq k$, the sink of each s_i-path should never be
contained in W_i. Here, we assume $s_i \notin W_i$ whenever $l_i = 1$. Otherwise, no graph
has such a k-path partition. Moreover, we assume without loss of generality that
no sources are contained in W_i for all i. A graph G is called *strongly k-path
partitionable* if G has a k-path partition satisfying the additional constraint for
any s_i, l_i, and W_i, $1 \leq i \leq k$. Hereafter in this section, we will prove Theorem 3
by an induction on m.

Theorem 3. *Every m-dimensional restricted HL-graph G^m is strongly k-path
partitionable for any $1 \leq k \leq m - 1$, $m \geq 4$.*

Obviously, the theorem holds true for $k = 1$. From now on, we assume $k \geq 2$.

Lemma 6. *Every 4-dimensional restricted HL-graph $G(8, 4) \oplus G(8, 4)$ is strongly
k-path partitionable for any $2 \leq k \leq 3$.*

Proof. The proof is omitted due to space limit. $\qquad \square$

Let $m \geq 5$. We denote by k_0 and k_1 the numbers of sources in G_0 and G_1,
respectively. Of course, $k_0 + k_1 = k$. Let $I_0 = \{1, 2, \ldots, k_0\}$ and $I_1 = \{k_0 +
1, k_0 + 2, \ldots, k_0 + k_1\}$. We assume that $S_0 = \{s_i | i \in I_0\}$ and $S_1 = \{s_j | j \in I_1\}$ are
sets of sources contained in G_0 and G_1, respectively, and that $l_1 \geq l_2 \geq \cdots \geq l_{k_0}$

and $l_{k_0+1} \geq \cdots \geq l_{k_0+k_1}$. Let $W_i^0 = W_i \cap V(G_0)$ and $W_i^1 = W_i \cap V(G_1)$ for each $i \in I_0 \cup I_1$. We denote by $k\text{-PP}[\{(s_1, l_1, W_1), \ldots, (s_k, l_k, W_k)\}|G]$ a k-path partition in a graph G for s_i, l_i, and W_i, $1 \leq i \leq k$, if any. Let P_i be the s_i-path in the path partition, and let $t(P_i)$ be the sink of P_i. We let $L_0 = \sum_{i \in I_0} l_i$ and $L_1 = \sum_{j \in I_1} l_j$. If $L_0 = L_1$, we are done since the union of k_0-path partition in G_0 and k_1-path partition in G_1 results in a k-path partition in G^m. We assume without loss of generality $L_0 > L_1$.

3.1 $k = 2$

When $l_2 = 1$, we have $P_2 = (s_2)$ and $P_1 = H[s_1, x|G^m, \{s_2\}]$ for some vertex $x \notin W_1 \cup \{s_1, s_2\}$. When $l_2 = 2$, for some vertex y adjacent to s_2 with $y \notin W_2 \cup \{s_1\}$, we have $P_2 = (s_2, y)$ and $P_1 = H[s_1, x|G^m, \{s_2, y\}]$ for some vertex $x \notin W_1 \cup \{s_1, s_2, y\}$. Note that G^m is 2-fault hamiltonian-connected. Let $l_2 \geq 3$. We have two cases.

Case 1. $s_1, s_2 \in V(G_0)$.
When $|W_2^0| \leq m - 3$ and $l_2 < 2^{m-1}$, we find $2\text{-PP}[\{(s_1, l_1', \emptyset), (s_2, l_2, W_2^0)\}|G_0]$, where $l_1' = 2^{m-1} - l_2$. Let P_i' be the s_i-path in the 2-PP. Then, $P_2 = P_2'$ and $P_1 = (P_1', H[\bar{x}, y|G_1, \emptyset])$, where $x = t(P_1')$ and y is a vertex in G_1 with $y \notin W_1 \cup \{\bar{x}\}$. When $|W_2^0| \leq m - 3$ and $l_2 = 2^{m-1}$ $(l_1 = 2^{m-1})$, we let $P_2 = (H[s_2, \bar{x}|G_0, \{s_1\}], x)$ for some vertex x in G_1 with $x \notin W_2$ and $\bar{x} \neq s_1, s_2$, and let $P_1 = (s_1, H[\bar{s}_1, y|G_1, \{x\}])$ for some vertex y in G_1 with $y \notin W_1 \cup \{x, \bar{s}_1\}$. Finally when $|W_2^0| = m - 2$, we find $2\text{-PP}[\{(s_1, l_1', \emptyset), (s_2, l_2', \emptyset)\}|G_0]$, where $l_2' = l_2 - 1$ and $l_1' = 2^{m-1} - l_2'$. Let P_i' be the s_i-path in the 2-PP. Then, $P_2 = (P_2', \bar{x})$, where $x = t(P_2')$, and $P_1 = (P_1', H[\bar{y}, z|G_1, \{\bar{x}\}])$, where $y = t(P_1')$ and z is a vertex in G_1 with $z \notin W_1 \cup \{\bar{x}, \bar{y}\}$.

Case 2. $s_1 \in V(G_0)$ and $s_2 \in V(G_1)$.
When $|W_2^1| \leq m - 3$ and $l_1 \geq 2^{m-1} + 2$, we let x be a vertex in G_1 with $x \notin \{s_2, \bar{s}_1\}$ and assume $x \in W_1^1$ if $|W_1^1| = m - 2$. Find $2\text{-PP}[\{(x, l_1', W_1'), (s_2, l_2, W_2^1)\}|G_1]$, where $l_1' = 2^{m-1} - l_2$ and $W_1' = W_1^1 \backslash x$. Let P_1' and P_2' be the x-path and s_2-path in the partition, respectively. Then, $P_1 = (H[s_1, \bar{x}|G_0, \emptyset], P_1')$ and $P_2 = P_2'$. When $|W_2^1| \leq m - 3$ and $l_1 = 2^{m-1} + 1$, letting x be a vertex in G_1 with $x \notin W_1 \cup \{s_2, \bar{s}_1\}$, we have $P_1 = (H[s_1, \bar{x}|G_0, \emptyset], x)$ and $P_2 = H[s_2, y|G_1, \{x\}]$ for some vertex y in G_1 with $y \notin W_2 \cup \{x, s_2\}$. When $|W_2^1| = m - 2$ and $\bar{s}_2 \neq s_1$, let $(x_1, x_2, \ldots, x_{2^m-1})$ be an $\bar{s}_2$-s_1 hamiltonian path in G_0. Then $P_2 = (s_2, x_1, x_2, \ldots, x_{l_2-1})$ and $P_1 = (x_{2^m-1}, x_{2^m-1-1}, \ldots, x_{l_2}, H[\bar{x}_{l_2}, y|G_1, \{s_2\}])$ for some vertex y in G_1 with $y \notin W_1 \cup \{s_2, \bar{x}_{l_2}\}$. When $|W_2^1| = m - 2$ and $\bar{s}_2 = s_1$, for a vertex y in G_1 with $y \notin W_1 \cup \{s_2\}$, let $(x_1, x_2, \ldots, x_{2^m-1})$ be an s_2-y hamiltonian path in G_1. Then, $P_2 = (x_1, x_2, \ldots, x_{l_2-1}, \bar{x}_{l_2-1})$ and $P_1 = (H[s_1, \bar{x}_{l_2}|G_0, \{\bar{x}_{l_2-1}\}], x_{l_2}, \ldots, x_{2^m-1})$.

3.2 $1 \leq k_1 \leq k - 2$ $(k_0 \geq 2)$

First, we will develop a basic procedure PP-A for constructing a k-path partition. The procedure is applicable to the most of the subcases. Let $\bar{X} = \{\bar{x} | x \in X\}$ for a vertex subset X of $G_0 \oplus G_1$.

Procedure PP-A $(\{(s_1, l_1, W_1), \ldots, (s_k, l_k, W_k)\},\ G_0 \oplus G_1)$ ________________

1. Find l'_i and l''_i, $i \in I_0$, satisfying (A1) $l'_i + l''_i = l_i$, $1 \le l'_i \le l_i$, (A2) $\sum_{i \in I_0} l'_i = 2^{m-1}$, and (A3) $l'_i = l_i$ for some $i \in I_0$. Let $I'_0 = \{i \in I_0 | l''_i \ge 1\}$ and $k'_0 = |I'_0|$.
2. Find k_0-PP$[\{(s_1, l'_1, W'_1), \ldots, (s_{k_0}, l'_{k_0}, W'_{k_0})\}|G_0]$, where $W'_i = W_i^0$ if $l''_i = 0$; $W'_i = (\bar{W}_i^1 \cup \bar{S}_1) \backslash S_0$ if $l''_i = 1$; $W'_i = \bar{S}_1$ if $l''_i \ge 2$. Let x_i be the sink of s_i-path in the k_0-PP.
3. Find $k'_0 + k_1$-PP$[\{(\bar{x}_i, l''_i, W_i^1)|i \in I'_0\} \cup \{(s_j, l_j, W_j^1)|j \in I_1\}|G_1]$.
4. The two path partitions are merged with edges $(x_i, \bar{x}_i)$ for $i \in I'_0$.

Lemma 7. *When $L_0 \ge 2^{m-1} + 2$, Procedure PP-A constructs a k-PP unless (a) $k_0 = 2$, $k_1 = 1$, $l_1 = 2^{m-1}$, $l_2 = 2^{m-1} - 1$, $l_3 = 1$, and $\bar{s}_1 = s_3$, or (b) $k_0 = k_1 = 2$, $l_1 = l_2 = 2^{m-1} - 1$, $l_3 = l_4 = 1$, and $\{\bar{s}_1, \bar{s}_2\} = \{s_3, s_4\}$. There also exist k-PP's for the two exceptional cases.*

Proof. Unless $k_0 = 2$ and $l_2 = 2^{m-1} - 1$, we claim that there exist l'_i and l''_i, $i \in I_0$, satisfying additional two conditions (A4) $l'_i = l_i$ if $l_i \le 3$ and (A5) if $l_i \ge 4$, either $l'_i = l_i$ or $l_i = l'_i + l''_i$ with $l'_i, l''_i \ge 2$, as well as A1, A2, and A3. The proof of the claim is omitted. The k_0-PP exists in G_0 since $|W'_i| \le (m-1) - k_0$ for every i. Note that $k_1 = k - k_0 \le (m-1) - k_0$. The existence of $k'_0 + k_1$-PP in G_1 is straightforward.

For the case of $k_0 = 2$ and $l_2 = 2^{m-1} - 1$, in a very similar way, we will construct a k-PP excluding the two exceptional cases. The k-PP's for the exceptional cases will be obtained by using fault-hamiltonicity of G_0 and G_1. When $k_1 = 1$ and $l_1 = 2^{m-1} - 1$ ($l_3 = 2$), assuming w.l.o.g. $\bar{s}_1 \ne s_3$, we let $l'_1 = 1$ and $l'_2 = l_2$, and apply Procedure PP-A. Then, we obtain a desired k-PP. Let $k_1 = 1$ and $l_1 = 2^{m-1}$ ($l_3 = 1$). Unless $\bar{s}_1 = s_3$, letting $l'_1 = 1$ and $l'_2 = l_2$, Procedure PP-A is applied. For the exceptional case of (a), we first find 2-PP$[\{(s_1, l'_1, W'_1), (s_2, l'_2, W'_2)\}|G_0]$, where $l'_1 = 2$ and $l'_2 = l_2 - 1$. Let P'_i be the s_i-path in the 2-PP of G_0 and let $x_i = t(P'_i)$. Then, we have $P_2 = (P'_2, \bar{x}_2)$. To construct P_1, we show that there exists a vertex $y \notin W_1^1 \cup \{s_3, \bar{x}_2\}$ in G_1 such that $\bar{x}_1$ and y are joined by a hamiltonian path in $G_1 \backslash \{s_3, \bar{x}_2\}$. If $m \ge 6$, the existence of y is obvious since G_1 is 2-fault hamiltonian-connected. If $m = 5$, remembering $|W_1^1| \le 2$, the existence can be verified. Now, we have $P_1 = (P'_1, H[\bar{x}_1, y|G_1, \{s_3, \bar{x}_2\}])$.

When $k_1 = 2$, we have $l_1 = l_2 = 2^{m-1} - 1$ and $l_3 = l_4 = 1$. Unless $\{\bar{s}_1, \bar{s}_2\} \ne \{s_3, s_4\}$, assuming $\bar{s}_1 \ne s_3, s_4$, Procedure PP-A with $l'_1 = 1$ and $l'_2 = l_2$ produces a desired 2-PP. Now, we consider the case of $\{\bar{s}_1, \bar{s}_2\} = \{s_3, s_4\}$ and assume w.l.o.g. $\bar{s}_1 = s_3$ and $\bar{s}_2 = s_4$. When $m \ge 6$, we first choose a vertex y in G_1 with $y \notin W_2^1 \cup \{s_3, s_4\}$. Let $C_1 = (w_0, w_1, \ldots, w_{2^{m-1}-4})$ be a hamiltonian cycle in $G_1 \backslash \{s_3, s_4, y\}$. For each vertex v in G_0 adjacent to s_1 such that $v \ne s_2, \bar{y}$, we can construct a path P_v of length $2^{m-1} - 1$ in such a way that $P_v = (s_1, v, w_i, w_{(i+1) \bmod 2^{m-1}}, \ldots, w_{(i-1) \bmod 2^{m-1}})$, where $w_i = \bar{v}$. There are at least $m - 3$ such paths P_v. Among them, at least one path have the endvertex $w_{(i-1) \bmod 2^{m-1}} \notin W_1^1$. Note that $|W_1^1| \le |W_1| \le m - k = m - 4$. Let P_v be

308   J.-H. Park, H.-S. Lim, and H.-C. Kim

such a path. Then, we have $P_1 = P_v$ and $P_2 = (H[s_2, \bar{y}|G_0, \{s_1, v\}], y)$. When $m = 5$, there exists y in G_1 such that $y \notin W_2^1 \cup \{s_3, s_4\}$ and $G_1 \backslash \{s_3, s_4, y\}$ has a hamiltonian cycle. Let $C_1 = (w_0, w_1, \ldots, w_{12})$ be a hamiltonian cycle in $G_1 \backslash \{s_3, s_4, y\}$. There exist a vertex v in G_0 adjacent to s_1 such that s_2 and $\bar{y}$ are joined by a hamiltonian path in $G_0 \backslash \{s_1, v\}$. Then, we have $P_2 = (H[s_2, \bar{y}|G_0, \{s_1, v\}], y)$. Let $\bar{v} = w_i$. Assuming w.l.o.g. $w_{(i-1) \bmod 16} \notin W_1^1$, we have $P_1 = (s_1, v, w_i, w_{(i+1) \bmod 16}, \ldots, w_{(i-1) \bmod 16})$. Note that $|W_1|, |W_2| \le 1$. Therefore, we have the lemma. $\qquad \square$

Lemma 8. *When $L_0 = 2^{m-1} + 1$, Procedure PP-A constructs a k-PP (a) if for some $j \in I_1$, $\bar{s}_j \in S_0$, or (b) if for some $i \in I_0$, either $l_i \ge 3$ and $|W_i^1| < m - k$ or $l_i = 2$ and $\bar{s}_i \notin S_1 \cup W_i^1$. For the remaining cases, there also exist k-PP's.*

Proof. The proof is omitted due to space limit. $\qquad \square$

3.3 $k_1 = k - 1$ $(k_0 = 1)$

Let $\Delta = l_1 - 2^{m-1}$. Then, $L_0 - \Delta = L_1 + \Delta = 2^{m-1}$. We denote by P^R the reverse of a path P, that is, $P^R = (v_l, v_{l-1}, \ldots, v_1)$ for $P = (v_1, v_2, \ldots, v_l)$. A *concatenation* of two paths $(x_1, \ldots, x_p)$ and $(y_1, \ldots, y_q)$ is the path $(x_1, \ldots, x_p, y_1, \ldots, y_q)$.

Case 1.   for all $j \in I_1$, $l_j = 1$ or $l_j \ge 2$ and $|W_j^1| < m - k$.
When $k < m - 1$, we let α be a vertex in G_1 with $\bar{\alpha} \ne s_1$ and $\alpha \notin S_1 \cup W_1^1$ if $|W_1^1| < m - k$ or $\Delta = 1$; if $|W_1^1| = m - k$ and $\Delta \ge 2$, let α be a vertex in W_1^1 with $\bar{\alpha} \ne s_1$ and $\alpha \notin S_1$. We find $k\text{-PP}[\{(\alpha, \Delta, W_1')\} \cup \{(s_j, l_j, W_j^1)|j \in I_1\}|G_1]$, where $W_1' = W_1^1 \backslash \alpha$. And then, the k-PP in G_1 and $H[s_1, \bar{\alpha}|G_0, \emptyset]$ are merged with $(\bar{\alpha}, \alpha)$. Now, let $k = m - 1$. Notice that for all $j \in I_1$, $l_j = 1$ or $l_j \ge 2$ and $W_j^1 = \emptyset$. Letting $l_2' = l_2 + \Delta$, we find $k_1\text{-PP}[\{(s_2, l_2', W_1^1)\} \cup \{(s_j, l_j, W_j^1)|j \in I_1 \backslash 2\}|G_1]$. Let the s_2-path in the k_1-PP be $(v_1, v_2, \ldots, v_{l_2'})$ with $v_1 = s_2$, and let $x = v_{l_2+1}$ and $y = v_{l_2'}$. To obtain a k-PP, it suffices to construct P_1 and P_2. Let $P_2 = (v_1, \ldots, v_{l_2})$. If $\bar{x} \ne s_1$, we have $P_1 = (H[s_1, \bar{x}|G_0, \emptyset], v_{l_2+1}, \ldots, v_{l_2'})$. Assume $\bar{x} = s_1$. If $\Delta \ge 2$, we have $P_1 = (s_1, v_{l_2+1}, \ldots, v_{l_2'}, H[\bar{y}, z|G_0, \{s_1\}])$ for some vertex z in G_0 with $z \notin \{s_1, \bar{y}\} \cup W_1^0$. If $\Delta = 1$, we observe $l_2 \ge 5$. Letting $u = v_{l_2-2}$ and $v = v_{l_2-1}$, we find $3\text{-PP}[\{(\bar{u}, 2, W_2^0), (\bar{v}, 2^{m-1} - 3, W_1^0), (s_1, 1, \emptyset)\}|G_0]$. Then, P_2 is a concatenation of $(v_1, \ldots, v_{l_2-2})$ and the $\bar{u}$-path, and P_1 is a concatenation of $(s_1, v_{l_2'}, \ldots, v_{l_2}, v_{l_2-1})$ and the $\bar{v}$-path.

Case 2.   for some $j \in I_1$, $l_j \ge 2$ and $|W_j^1| = m - k$.
Let $a \in I_1$ be an index such that $l_a \ge 2$, $|W_a^1| = m - k$ $(|W_a^0| = 0)$, and $l_a \ge l_j$ for any $j \in I_1$ with $l_j \ge 2$ and $|W_j^1| = m - k$. Furthermore, we assume $\bar{s}_a \ne s_1$ if $l_a = 2$ and for some $j \in I_1$ with $j \ne a$, $l_j \ge 2$ and $|W_j^1| = m - k$. We first find $k_1\text{-PP}[\{(s_a, l_a', W_1^1)\} \cup \{(s_j, l_j, W_j^1)|j \in I_1 \backslash a\}|G_1]$, where $l_a' = l_a + \Delta$. Let the s_a-path in the k_1-PP be $(v_1, v_2, \ldots, v_{l_a'})$. Let $z = v_{l_a}$, $x = v_{l_a+1}$, $y = v_{l_a'}$, and $v = v_{l_a-1}$. And let $u = v_{l_a-2}$ if $l_a \ge 3$. We denote by Q_z the s_a-z subpath $(v_1, \ldots, v_{l_a})$ of the s_a-path. Let $R_z = (v_{l_a+1}, \ldots, v_{l_a'})$ so that the s_a-path is a concatenation (Q_z, R_z) of Q_z and R_z. Similarly, let $Q_v = (v_1, \ldots, v_{l_a-1})$ and $R_v = (v_{l_a}, \ldots, v_{l_a'})$, etc. To obtain a k-PP, it remains to construct P_a and P_1.

When $z \notin W_a^1$, we have $P_a = Q_z$ and $P_1 = (H[s_1, \bar{x}|G_0, \emptyset], R_z)$ if $\bar{x} \neq s_1$; if $\bar{x} = s_1$, $P_a = (Q_v, \bar{v})$ and $P_1 = (H[s_1, \bar{z}|G_0, \{\bar{v}\}], R_v)$.

Let $z \in W_a^1$. When $\bar{v} \neq s_1$, let $P_a = (Q_v, \bar{v})$. If $\bar{z} \neq s_1$, $P_1 = (H[s_1, \bar{z}|G_0, \{\bar{v}\}], R_v)$; otherwise, $P_1 = (s_1, R_v, H[\bar{y}, w|G_0, \{s_1, \bar{v}\}])$ for some w in G_0 with $w \notin \{s_1, \bar{v}, \bar{y}\} \cup W_1^0$. When $\bar{v} = s_1$ and $l_a \geq 3$, we have two constructions. If $k \geq 4$ or $k = 3$ and $|W_1^0| < m-k$, we find 3-PP$[\{(\bar{u}, 2, \emptyset), (s_1, 1, \emptyset), (\bar{y}, 2^{m-1}-3, W_1^0)\}|G_0]$. Then, P_a is a concatenation of Q_u and the $\bar{u}$-path, and P_1 is a concatenation of (s_1, R_u) and the $\bar{y}$-path. If $k = 3$ and $|W_1^0| = m-k$, letting $w \notin \{s_1, \bar{y}\}$ be a vertex in G_0 adjacent to $\bar{u}$, we have $P_a = (Q_u, \bar{u}, w)$ and $P_1 = (H[s_1, \bar{y}|G_0, \{\bar{u}, w\}], R_u^R)$.

When $\bar{v} = s_1$ and $l_a = 2$ $(s_a = v, \bar{s}_a = s_1)$, by the choice of s_a, for every $j \in I_1 \backslash a$, $l_j = 1$ or $l_j \geq 2$ and $|W_j^1| < m-k$. Let $k < m-1$ first. If $W_a^1 \backslash W_1^1 \neq \emptyset$, let t_1 be a vertex in $W_a^1 \backslash W_1^1$ and let $W_a' = W_a^1 \backslash t_1$ and $W_1' = \emptyset$; otherwise $(W_a^1 = W_1^1)$, let t_1 be a vertex in W_a^1 and let $W_a' = W_a^1 \backslash t_1$ and $W_1' = W_1^1 \backslash t_1$. Find k_1+1-PP$[\{(t_1, \Delta, W_1'), (s_a, l_a, W_a')\} \cup \{(s_j, l_j, W_j^1)|j \in I_1 \backslash a\}|G_1]$. If $W_a^1 \backslash W_1^1 \neq \emptyset$, P_1 is obtained by concatenating $H[s_1, \bar{w}|G_0, \emptyset]$ and the reverse of t_1-path in $k_1 + 1$-PP, where w is the sink of t_1-path. If $W_a^1 = W_1^1$ and $\Delta \geq 2$, P_1 is a concatenation of $H[s_1, \bar{t}_1|G_0, \emptyset]$ and the t_1-path in the $k_1 + 1$-PP.

If $W_a^1 = W_1^1$ and $\Delta = 1$, we have two constructions. For $m \geq 6$, we let b be an index in I_1 such that $l_b \geq l_j$ for any $j \in I_1 \backslash a$. Obviously, $l_b \geq 5$. Letting $l_b' = l_b + 1$, we find k_1-PP$[\{(s_b, l_b', W_1^1)\} \cup \{(s_j, l_j, W_j^1)|j \in I_1 \backslash b\}|G_1]$. Let the s_b-path in the k_1-PP be $(w_1, \ldots, w_{l_b}, w_{l_b+1})$, and let $p = w_{l_b-2}$ and $q = w_{l_b-1}$. There exists a vertex w in G_0 adjacent to $\bar{p}$ with $w \notin \{s_1, \bar{q}\} \cup W_b^0$. Then, we have $P_b = (w_1, \ldots, w_{l_b-2}, \bar{p}, w)$ and $P_1 = (H[s_1, \bar{q}|G_0, \{\bar{p}, w\}], w_{l_b-1}, w_{l_b}, w_{l_b+1})$. For $m = 5$ $(k = 3)$, let t_a be a vertex in G_1 adjacent to s_a with $t_a \notin \{s_b\} \cup W_a^1$. Let $P_a = (s_a, t_a)$. There exists a vertex w in G_1 with $w \notin \{s_a, t_a, s_b\} \cup W_1^1$ such that $G_1 \backslash \{s_a, t_a, w\}$ has a hamiltonian cycle C. Then, $P_1 = (H[s_1, \bar{w}|G_0, \emptyset], w)$. P_b is obtained by removing one of the two edges on C incident to s_b since $|W_b^1| < m - k = 1$. Finally, let $k = m - 1$. Note that $W_j^1 = \emptyset$ for any $j \in I_1 \backslash a$. Letting $l_b' = l_b + \Delta$, we find k_1-PP$[\{(s_b, l_b', W_1^1)\} \cup \{(s_j, l_j, W_j^1)|j \subset I_1 \backslash b\}|G_1]$. Let the s_b-path in the k_1-PP be $(w_1, \ldots, w_{l_b'})$ and let $x = w_{l_b+1}$. Then, we have $P_b = (w_1, \ldots, w_{l_b})$ and $P_1 = (H[s_1, \bar{x}|G_0, \emptyset], w_{l_b+1}, \ldots, w_{l_b'})$.

3.4 $k_1 = 0$ $(k_0 = k)$

Case 1. $k \leq m - 2$.

Let us first consider the case that there exists $i \in I_0$ such that $l_i = 1$ or $l_i \geq 2$ and $|W_i^0| < m - k$. We are to define l_i' and l_i'', $i \in I_0$, satisfying (i) $l_i' + l_i'' = l_i$, $1 \leq l_i' \leq l_i$, (ii) $\sum_{i \in I_0} l_i' = 2^{m-1}$, (iii) $l_i' = l_i$ for some $i \in I_0$ such that $l_i = 1$ or $l_i \geq 2$ and $|W_i^0| < m - k$, (iv) $l_i' < l_i$ for all i with $l_i \geq 2$ and $|W_i^0| = m - k$, and (v) $l_i' = l_i$ for all i with $l_i = 2$ and $|W_i^0| < m - k$, and either $l_i' = l_i$ or $l_i' \leq l_i - 2$ for all i with $l_i \geq 3$ and $|W_i^0| < m - k$. It is not difficult to see that there exist l_i''s and l_i'''s satisfying all the above five conditions unless (a) $k = 3$, $l_1 = l_2 = 2^{m-1} - 1$, $l_3 = 2$, $|W_1^0|, |W_2^0| < m - k$, and $|W_3^0| = m - k$, or (b) for some $p \in I_0$, $l_p \geq 2^{m-1} - (k-2)$, $|W_p^0| < m - k$, $l_i \geq 2$ and $|W_i^0| = m - k$ for any $i \in I_0 \backslash p$.

We let $W_i' = \emptyset$ if $l_i' = 1$; $W_i' = W_i^0$ if $2 \le l_i' = l_i$; $W_i' = \emptyset$ if $2 \le l_i' < l_i$. Then, $|W_i'| < m - k$ for every i. There exists a k_0-PP$[\{(s_i, l_i', W_i')|i \in I_0\}|G_0]$. Letting $I_0' = \{i \in I_0|l_i' < l_i\}$ and $k_0' = |I_0'|$, we find k_0'-PP$[\{(\bar{x}_j, l_j'', W_j^1)|j \in I_0'\}|G_1]$, where x_j is the sink of s_j-path in the k_0-PP. Merging the two PP's results in a desired k-PP. We omit the constructions of k-PP's using fault-hamiltonicity of G_0 and G_1 for the two exceptional cases (a) and (b) due to space limit. Now, we assume that for all $i \in I_0$, $l_i \ge 2$ and $|W_i^0| = m - k$ ($|W_i^1| = 0$). There exist l_i''s and l_i'''s satisfying (i) $l_i' + l_i'' = l_i$, $1 \le l_i' < l_i$ and (ii) $\sum_{i \in I_0} l_i' = 2^{m-1}$. We find a k_0-PP$[\{(s_i, l_i', \emptyset)|i \in I_0\}|G_0]$. And then, letting x_i be the sink of s_i-path in the k_0-PP in G_0, we find k_0-PP$[\{(\bar{x}_i, l_i'', \emptyset)|i \in I_0\}|G_1]$ and merge the two PP's.

Case 2. $k = m - 1$.

Recall the assumption $l_1 \ge l_2 \ge \cdots \ge l_k$. We first consider the case that $(k - 3) + l_{k-1} + l_k \le 2^{m-1}$ and $l_1 \le 2^{m-1}$. There are l_i' and l_i'', $i \in I_0 \backslash 1$, satisfying (i) $l_i' + l_i'' = l_i$, $1 \le l_i' \le l_i$, (ii) $\sum_{i \in I_0 \backslash 1} l_i' = 2^{m-1}$, and (iii) $l_{k-1}' = l_{k-1}$ and $l_k' = l_k$. We let $W_i' = W_i^0 \cup \{s_1\}$ if $l_i' = l_i$ and $|W_i^0| < m - k$; $W_i' = \bar{W}_i^1$ if $l_i' = l_i - 1$; $W_i' = W_i^0$, otherwise. Regarding s_1 as a non-source vertex virtually, we find $k_0 - 1$-PP$[\{(s_i, l_i', W_i')|i \in I_0 \backslash 1\}|G_0]$. Let the s_a-path in the $k_0 - 1$-PP passes through s_1, that is, the s_a-path be $(v_1, \ldots, v_{l_j'})$ with $v_{i+1} = s_1$ for some i. Let $I_0' = \{i \in I_0|l_i' < l_i\} \cup \{1, a\}$ and $k_0' = |I_0'|$. Clearly, $k_0' < k_0$. Letting x_i be the sink of s_i-path in the $k_0 - 1$-PP, we find k_0'-PP$[\{(\bar{x}_a, l_1 - l_j' + i, W_1^1), (\bar{v}_i, l_a - i, W_a^1)\} \cup \{(\bar{x}_i, l_i'', W_i^1)|i \in I_0' \backslash \{1, a\}\}|G_0]$. To obtain a k-PP, the two PP's are merged. For the case that $(k - 3) + l_{k-1} + l_k \le 2^{m-1}$ and $l_1 > 2^{m-1}$, regarding s_2 as a virtual non-source vertex, we can construct a k-PP in a similar to the previous case. For any $k = m - 1 \ge 4$, it holds true that $(k-3) + l_{k-1} + l_k \le 2^{m-1}$ unless $k = 4$ and $l_1 = l_2 = l_3 = l_4 = 2^{m-2}$. For the last subcase, a k-PP can be obtained using fault-hamiltonicity of G_0 and G_1. The construction is also omitted here.

References

1. T. Dvořák, I. Havel, J.-M. Laborde, and M. Mollard, "Spanning caterpillars of a hypercube," *J. Graph Theory* **24(1)**, pp. 9-19, 1997.
2. M. Kobeissi and M. Mollard, "Spanning graphs of hypercubes: starlike and double starlike trees," *Discrete Mathematics* **244**, pp. 231-239, 2002.
3. F.T. Leighton, *Introduction to parallel algorithms and architectures: arrays, trees, hypercubes*, Morgan Kaufmann Publishers, 1992.
4. L. Nebeský, "Embedding m-quasistars into n-cubes," *Czechoslovak Mathematical Journal* **38(113)**, pp. 705-712, 1988.
5. C.-D. Park and K.Y. Chwa, "Hamiltonian properties on the class of hypercube-like networks," *Inform. Proc. Lett.* **91**, pp. 11-17, 2004.
6. J.-H. Park, H.-C. Kim, and H.-S. Lim, "Fault-hamiltonicity of hypercube-like interconnection networks," in *Proc. of the IEEE International Parallel and Distributed Processing Symposium IPDPS 2005*, Denver, Apr. 2005.
7. A.S. Vaidya, P.S.N. Rao, S.R. Shankar, "A class of hypercube-like networks," in *Proc. of the 5th IEEE Symposium on Parallel and Distributed Processing SPDP 1993*, pp. 800-803, Dec. 1993.

Reconfigurable Interconnects in DSM Systems: A Focus on Context Switch Behavior

I. Artundo[1], D. Manjarres[1], W. Heirman[2], C. Debaes[1], J. Dambre[2],
J. Van Campenhout[2], and H. Thienpont[1]

[1] Department of Applied Physics and Photonics (TONA),
Vrije Universiteit. Pleinlaan 2, 1050 Brussel, Belgium
{iartundo, dmanjarres, christof.debaes, hthienpo}@tona.vub.ac.be
[2] Electronics and Information Systems Department (ELIS),
Universiteit Gent, Sint-Pietersnieuwstraat 41, 9000 Gent, Belgium
{wim.heirman, joni.dambre, jan.vancampenhout}@elis.ugent.be

Abstract. Recent advances in the development of reconfigurable optical interconnect technologies allow for the fabrication of low cost and run-time adaptable interconnects in large distributed shared-memory (DSM) multiprocessor machines. This can allow the use of adaptable interconnection networks that alleviate the huge bottleneck present due to the gap between the processing speed and the memory access time over the network. In this paper we have studied the scheduling of tasks by the kernel of the operating system (OS) and its influence on communication between the processing nodes of the system, focusing on the traffic generated just after a context switch. We aim to use these results as a basis to propose a potential reconfiguration of the network that could provide a significant speedup.

Keywords: Reconfiguration, interconnection network, distributed shared memory, multiprocessors, context switch.

1 Introduction

In DSM multiprocessor machines all the memory of the system is physically distributed among its nodes, and they can access data located in the memory of other nodes in a software transparent way. The interconnection network is thus part of the memory hierarchy and therefore high network latencies cause a significant performance bottleneck in program execution [1]. This situation will become worse in the future, as a result of increasing hardware performance, the rapid growth in instruction level parallelism and the use of multiple process contexts [2]. Reconfigurability in this aspect will allow the system to rearrange the interprocessor communications network to form topologies that are best suited for the particular computing task at hand, allowing for a network topology that closely matches the traffic patterns exhibited by the current application [3].

Optics is a great candidate to introduce fast interconnection networks in the architecture of multiprocessor systems [4]. By using optical interconnects at the scale of the link lengths found in multiprocessor machines, an increase in connectivity and higher communication bandwidths can be achieved, as well as the elimination of

G. Min et al. (Eds.): ISPA 2006 Ws, LNCS 4331, pp. 311–321, 2006.

frequency dependent cross-talk with galvanic isolation. One important aspect that has not been yet exploited so far is their inherent ability to switch the light paths easily in a data transparent way, paving the way towards adaptable network topologies.

It is necessary to determine the architectural for such networks and to propose an efficient way to reconfigure. For the leading low-cost solutions, a designer must overcome the fact that switching speed and connectivity do not come for granted, so it is necessary to find communication and reconfiguration schemes that not only overpass these limitations but try to use them at their advantage. Communication patterns lasting long enough compared to optical switching times must be found so that we can allow for a slow reconfiguration rate of the links in the topology. The frequent context switches that happen in modern operating systems are the perfect event to be used as a trigger, to establish a regular and profitable reconfiguration on the interprocessor communication network. The peak bandwidth and congestion expected in those intervals will be the key element in this study.

It is the goal of this work to investigate the communication patterns found on a DSM interprocessor network related to the task scheduling. We will first give an introduction to reconfigurability in interconnection networks. Later on, we will enter in detail on the context switch behavior of the operating system and the mechanisms to use it as a trigger for adapting the network to certain communication patterns. Finally, we will present the results obtained by running full system simulations of real parallel benchmarks and we will discuss them proposing a possible optical implementation of the system.

2   Reconfiguration in Interprocessor Networks

Through reconfiguration the system can adapt the interconnection network to better fit the real-time communication needs, which depend upon the application that is running in the machine. This will alleviate the large bottleneck affecting the current communication networks and moreover can serve as a backup network in case there is a failure in any of the components of the system.

The proposed interconnection network architecture for the DSM system consists of a fixed base network connecting all the nodes (processors and local memories), arranged in a torus topology. In addition, a certain number of freely reconfigurable point-to-point links will be provided (see Fig. 1) between nodes that are expected to have a large communication load. These new links can be used as direct shortcut connections to route the traffic between processor node pairs on the network. Afterwards, the extra links will be reassigned according to the new congestion measurements.

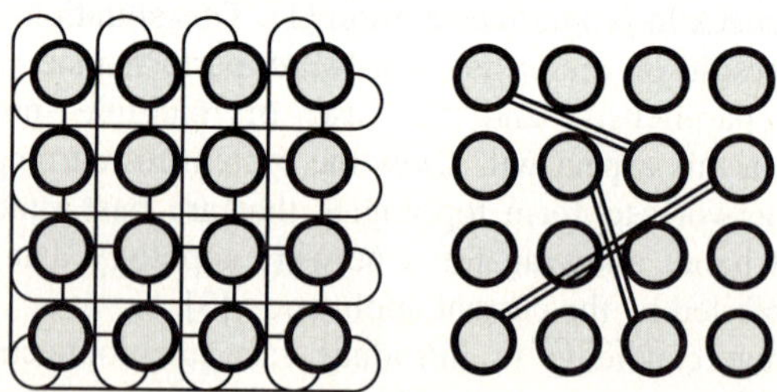

Fig. 1. Torus topology of the 16-node base interconnection network and reconfigurable optical layer with some assigned extra links

This setup, compared to the case where all links in the network are available to be used for the topology reconfiguration, has a number of advantages because the base network will always be available. It is therefore impossible to disconnect parts of the network, greatly reducing the complexity in the reconfiguration algorithms. However, this reconfigurability can offer advantages to a system considering some requirements are met beforehand.

In this study, we focus our architectural study primarily on the occurrence of events to act as trigger conditions that can lead to a reconfiguration. These events will be the context switches happening on the OS, expected to impose higher demands on the interconnection network during short intervals of time. The right placement of the extra links in the topology and the implementation of such a network are questions already treated in our previous works [5][6].

3   Context Switching in the Operating System

During normal execution, only one process per processor can be executed. After a certain time interval, this processor can switch to another process; this procedure is known as *context switch*. [7]. The OS used in this work, Solaris 9, has a good support for multiprocessor systems and it is based on a process-thread model where processes are divided in threads in order to be managed by the scheduler [8].

3.1   Scheduling of Processes and Threads, and Temporal Patterns

The OS uses several structures to define each process and thread, like indexed tables or arrays, describing every aspect involved in the process. After a processor has finished its allocated time-slot, a scheduler interrupts its execution, write all relevant processor state information to the memory space pointed by a context register and will pass execution to a next process.

The execution of different tasks is controlled by the scheduler, enabling processes and threads to work on one system by switching constantly between them on a short time interval. Previous works [9] have demonstrated the relationship between task scheduling and the end-point or network contention in dynamical interconnections, proposing new scheduling models that could be used to be aware of the communication layer state.

The process scheduler of Solaris is developed in a multilayer process-thread model. Solaris sets fixed time-slices that range between 20 ms and 200 ms for the lowest priorities in the system, which are the threads belonging to user processes. This means that it can be expected that the interprocessor network will be under heavy load with communication peaks at predetermined intervals of time, in correspondence with the tines when the context switches occur.. Overall, these intervals are in no way regular along time, because the execution is always being interrupted and continued. However, intervals in the order of tens or even hundreds of milliseconds will be long enough to be profitable for reconfiguration, even for slow switching technologies that can prepare and adapt the network to the expected burst of incoming traffic due to these process/context switches.

3.2 Reconfiguration Through the Context Switches

By a context switch, the kernel saves the state of the current running process or thread and then loads the state of the next one to be executed. Just after the context switch, the processor will work with a completely different set of code and data, therefore the data in the cache will be invalidated and a communication peak to this processor will occur to fill the caches. All these operations will generate a sudden burst of traffic on the network as these structures are moved from caches and memories. After an initial peak relativily high traffic can continue to the same destinations.

An OS that can make use of a reconfigurable interconnection network will need to track every context switch and keep record of the traffic patterns it generates. It will be able then to inform the interconnection hardware when and how a reconfiguration can take place. As there is no practical way to predict in advance the occupancy of the network due to the new traffic and its destination, the system will determine to which node most of the traffic was flowing last time the same context was run, and prepare the network in consequence for this expected increase of load. The reconfiguration would then be triggered always by a context switch. The performance gain obtained will be optimum in case the network reconfiguration fits the expected traffic to a certain destination after a context switch.

4 Simulation Environment

For studying all the aspects involved in these contexts switches and build a coherent reconfiguration architecture, we have established a full-system simulation environment based on the commercially available Simics simulator [10]. A more detailed description of our environment can be found in [11].

The interconnection network is a custom extension to Simics, where we modeled a 4x4 torus network with contention and cut-through routing. In our simulations, only two multithreaded benchmark applications were strictly run at the same time as the main load, so we can suppose with a high level of certainty that on a context switch we will switch between the benchmarking applications and no other default Solaris 9 daemons exist on the machine. We focus our results on two types of loads: in one case we have loaded the machines with two simultaneous runs of multitreading applications from the SPLASH-2 scientific benchmark [12]. In this case the Barnes algorithm is concurrently run with FFT, Radiosity, etc. Secondly, the Apache web server v.1.3 concurrently run with the SURGE request generator [13]. Each of the above user process will start 16 threads, so that at all time as much as 32 threads will be competing to be run on the 16 processors of the machine. Since in the proposed reconfiguration scheme, performance scales with the number of threads and processing nodes, our simulation results would benefit from higher processor counts. There was a certain level of noise (2-5%) on application runtimes, stemming from the initial state of the cache memories as well as other scheduled internal tasks of the OS at the beginning of the simulations.

Interrupts and system calls are managed by the OS in the machine, and in most cases do not require a whole process switch, so the context switches produced by them tend to be short and with low communication rates. We will not take them into account since their characteristics (in length and bandwidth consumption) did not offer a proper base to be used by a possible reconfiguration trigger. When filtering these short interrupts and system calls, we have only used execution intervals on every node lasting at least 10 ms.

5   Evaluating Communication and Reconfiguration

In this section we present a study of the dynamics of the context switches happening on the system, and show how they can be used as a reconfiguration trigger. To show a preliminary effect of such reconfiguration, we will use this data to run the simulations again, this time enhanced by the extra links placed between several pairs of nodes that are expected to have a high communication load due to a context switch.

5.1   Context Switch Communication Patterns

Within Simics, we have developed a module that monitors the occurrence of context switches in the simulated machine. From the possible events that can produce a context switch, we are mainly interested in process switches because they involve more data interchanged due to cache invalidation. In Table 1, values related to the average and maximum lengths of the contexts, as well as the number of switches, are presented during a 1400 ms SPLASH-2 and Apache benchmark execution.

Table 1. Time elapsed between several context switches

Application	Length (ms) Mean	Max	# Switches
SPLASH-2: FFT	9.94	12.96	303
SPLASH-2: Cholesky	7.89	13.35	3402
SPLASH-2: Ocean	10.35	14.10	3637
SPLASH-2: Radiosity	10.48	14.28	133
SPLASH-2: Barnes	14.42	224.236	111
Apache Web server	86.58	1119.081	115

The different behavior for every application and their interaction with the OS can be clearly seen here in the number of context switches occurred during simulation. Cholesky and Ocean were the more parallel multithreaded applications, resulting in much more switches on the system than the other ones. A large variation in the lengths can be observed for Barnes since mean and maximum values are highly separated. We have plotted in Fig. 2 histograms of the context durations for the execution of the Barnes algorithm and the Apache web server.

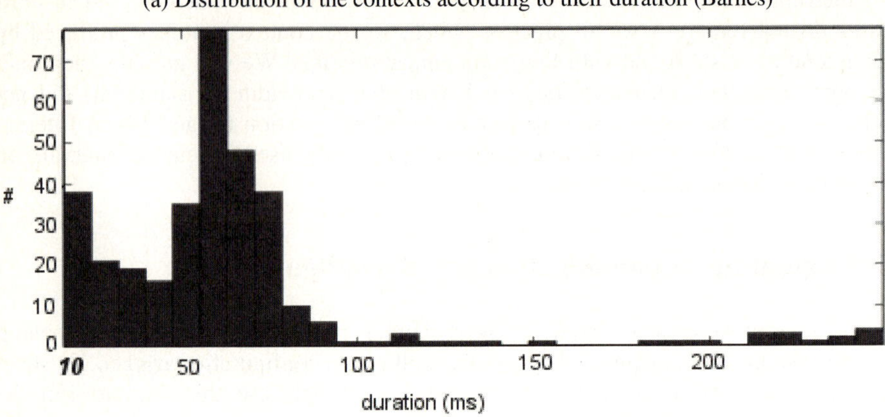

(a) Distribution of the contexts according to their duration (Barnes)

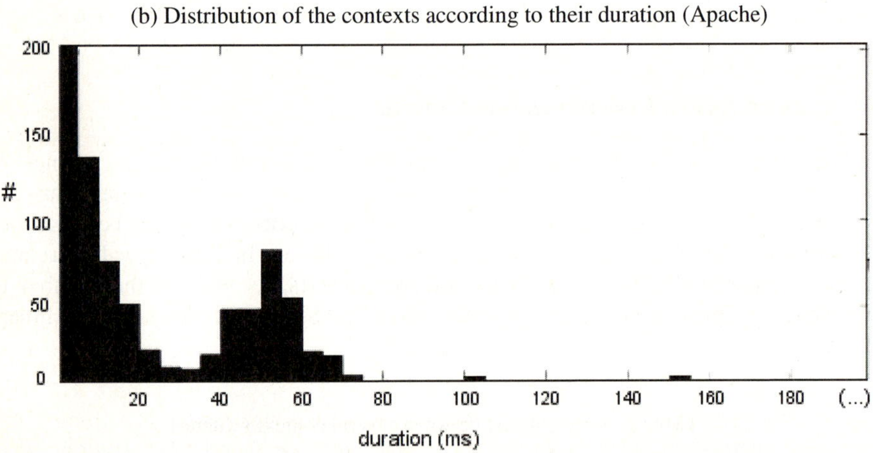

(b) Distribution of the contexts according to their duration (Apache)

Fig. 2. Histogram distribution of the length of the contexts for Barnes and Apache. More than 1300 contexts last for less than 10 ms, and we can clearly observe a second peak of contexts around 50 ms.

Despite the fact that we have already filtered the context switches per node with lengths not enough to be considered profitable to trigger a reconfiguration (< 1 ms), the majority of them have a short duration. It is remarkable that the number of longer contexts is still significant, taking into account that the simulation time was less than 1.5 seconds.

With Apache, the context lengths are considerably longer, with some contexts lasting for even more than one second. While in the Barnes simulations every node was sharing data and a lot of interaction occurred, in Apache the different concurrent processes are more independent and run during longer time intervals. The process that contains the Apache's kernel will receive the largest lump of traffic, resulting in a large amount of interprocessor communication on this node.

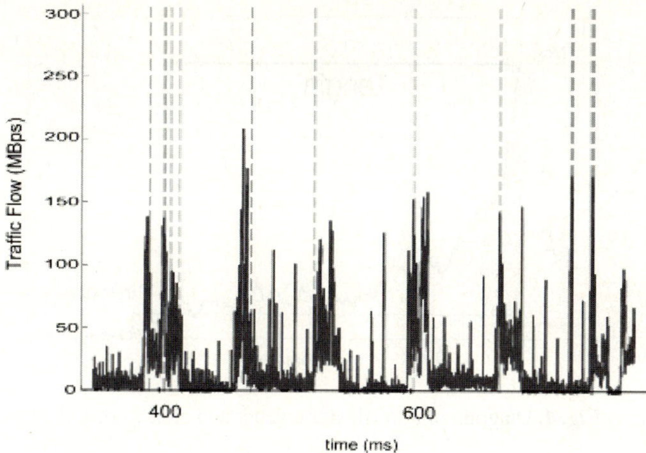

Fig. 3. Detail of outgoing traffic observed in a single node of the system during simulated time. Dashed lines are shown when a context switch occurs.

We show how the generated traffic is correlated with the context switches. In Fig. 3 the traffic flow of one single node is presented while context switches are indicated by vertical lines. At first glance, we can see how just after every context switch the bandwidth consumed on the network increases due to load/store operations from memories. This sudden rise, compared to the mean bandwidth consumed during the rest of the execution, is what we will consider a traffic burst. In some cases, we can even observe a peak of bandwidth consumption just before a context switch is happening, or even when no context switches are happening at all. This means that also other bursts of traffic are generated by the running application.

Next we focus on the time length of these bursts. Hereto, we first define exactly how the length of the burst is measured, i.e. the burst duration is the time difference between the moment of maximum bandwidth of the burst and the moment when traffic drops to 10% of that maximum (see Fig. 4). If we define $T_{k,l}(t)$ as the instant traffic flowing from node k to node l at time t, and τ^i_k the time where context switch i is happening at node k, we have that the bursts of traffic happening just after a context switch will be represented by:

$$B^i_{k,l}(t - \tau^i_k) = \Sigma\, T_{k,l}(t) \quad . \quad \tau^i_k \leq t < \tau^{i+1}_k \tag{1}$$

We can furthermore define $B^i_{k,l}$ as the average context switch traffic between nodes k and l, and B as the average traffic after a burst. The amount of traffic moved by a burst is therefore directly related to the burst length. However, this traffic measured on one node can go to or arrive from different destinations. The proposed reconfiguration scheme would only add one extra link to a pair of nodes and hence it is needed to predict which node pair is going to show the highest traffic for a next context switch.

After a context switch there was always one destination that was getting the majority of generated traffic, usually with a bandwidth that was 3-4 times higher than averaged traffic to other destinations. It will be critical to accurately know the final

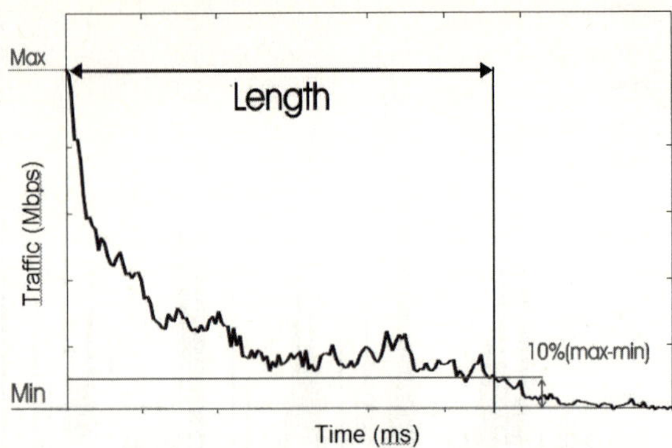

Fig. 4. Diagram of a traffic burst generated after a context switch

destination of this majority of this data communication in order to rearrange the topology and set the new extra link to the proper end node.

5.2 Context-Switch Triggered Reconfiguration

Once the behavior of the communication system was monitored and measured, we have a base to establish the reconfiguration scheme that is triggered by the context switches. Reassigning dynamically the extra links to different node pairs with the higher instant load is expected to result in a speedup of the application running on the system. No limits are imposed on which 16 node pairs are connected at each time (the results of adding more realistic constraints can be found in in [5][6]). Therefore, the 16 busiest node pairs in every reconfiguration interval can be directly connected by extra links according to measurements done on the previous reconfiguration interval.

This way, for the last part of this study we implemented a basic reconfiguration scheme. For this preliminary study on the effects of reconfiguration we had no insight on the scheduler of the Solaris OS, and therefore could not use any information on the prediction for when and to which process a processor will switch. To get however some insight into the excepted performance speed-up, we partitioned the simulated time in discrete reconfiguration intervals such that the topology changes take place at certain moments (see Fig. 7). These intervals should be long enough to amortize on the temporal cost of reconfiguration, during which the extra links are being repositioned and are unusable. The trigger event for a new reconfiguration would be a context switch happening on the system, and the length would be that of the new context. Of course, a prediction model is needed to adapt the network for the upcoming switch, as it is unknown *a priori* when a switch will happen.

As a basic prediction model, previously described in [14], we have divided the simulation time in reconfiguration intervals t_{reconf}. For now, we have not considered any down-time (due to extra link selection and optical switching, $t_{se}+t_{sw}$ as shown in Fig. 5) that occurs during network readjustments to keep the performance study independent of the chosen switching technology. As long as the reconfiguration interval is chosen to be significantly longer than both, this is a good approximation.

We have furthermore assumed equal characteristics for the extra links and the base network links, yielding the same average per-hop packet latency for both types of links. The destination node of the extra link will be that measured to have the largest bandwidth consumption on previous reconfiguration intervals.

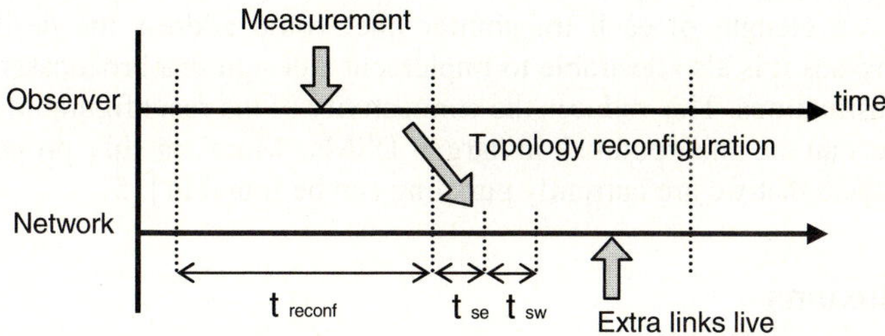

Fig. 5. In every reconfiguration interval, the system is monitoring the traffic flow, such that it can adjust the topology to accommodate the expected communication needs after a context switch

These connections are established just before a relevant context switch is expected. Of course, this will always be restricted to the prediction model used for determining the occurrence of a switch to a certain context and the destination of most of the traffic generated for that event. As computer communication is basically unpredictable, it is necessary to constantly monitor the communication flow on the network and extract valuable information on the detected traffic patterns, incorporating it into a prediction model that will do the reconfiguration job.

We proceeded with an implementation based on the accesses to the context register for determining the switches from the OS. In a real life case, we will not have perfect prediction of the context switches, and there will be a slight time shift between prediction and actual occurrence.

After adding the extra links on reconfiguration intervals triggered by context switches of no less than 100 μs, latency was greatly reduced for a large percentage of the traffic, and the base network was relieved so that less congestion occurred. We found speed-ups in the overall execution time between 8-11% for most of the SPLASH-2 applications. This can be translated into a larger improvement in communication latency that better reflects the performance gain directly obtained by the reconfiguration. Further work is still undergoing to more accurately implement the reconfiguration and obtain a better performance. A more pronounced gain is expected with a more precise prediction of the moment the context switches are happening and with a better determination of the most active communication partner after the context switch. Simulating also larger networks will lead to higher savings in hop distances between nodes and hence better performance improvements. Future work will include expanding the prediction model to more accurately follow the congestion on the network caused by different factors, and not only limited to context switches.

6 Reconfigurable Optical Network Implementation

Our proposal to build the reconfiguration layer of the interconnection network would consist of a wavelength tunable optical transmitter per processor node, broadcasting data on one of a fixed number of source wavelengths. Each processor node would also incorporate an optical receiver which is sensitive to one wavelength only. Hence, by tuning the wavelength of each transmitter one would address the destination. For scalability issues it is also desirable to implement a design that broadcasts to only to a subset of destinations. This reduces the connectivity of the reconfigurable network but the scheme can be incorporated in larger DSMs. More on this proposed optical implementation that we are currently pursuing can be found in [15].

7 Conclusions

The context switch offers a recurrent event that can be used as a base to predict high periods of heavy load in the internal communication of the machine. We can conclude that there are indeed clear intervals corresponding to switches with correlated bursts of high communication. Moreover, in many cases, the presence of these bursts is overlapped with peaks of traffic coming from the normal execution process and a reconfiguration which takes place on this moment can take profit for the whole context traffic.

However the observed variability of the context switch durations in this study requires more attention in distinguishing and predicting context switches by the operating system. We briefly showed the possibility of using these traffic bursts by a reconfigurable network that is able to modify its topology over the time, obtaining a first significant speed up around 9-11% in the overall execution time. This interconnect would be possible to implement by current slow, low-cost optical switching technologies.

References

1. Dai, D., Panda, D.K.: How Much Does Network Contention Affect Distributed Shared Memory Performance?, Proc. of the Int. Conf. on Parallel Processing, (1997) 454-461
2. Krewell, K.: Best servers of 2004: where multicore is the norm, Microprocessor report, January (2005)
3. Krishnamurthy, P.: "Reconfigurability of the interconnect architecture for chip multiprocessors", Proc. of the 4th International Symposium on Information and Communication Technologies, (2005) 136–141
4. Mohammed, E. et al.: "Optical interconnect system integration for ultra-short-reach application," Intel Technology Journal, Vol. 8, Num. 2, (2004)
5. Heirman, W., Artundo, I., Desmet, L., Dambre, J., Debaes, C., Thienpont, H., Van Campenhout, J.: "Speeding up multiprocessor machines with reconfigurable optical interconnects", Proc. of SPIE, Optoelectronic Integrated Circuits VIII, Vol. 6124 (2006) 156-167
6. Artundo, I., Desmet, L., Heirman, W., Debaes, C., Dambre, J., Van Campenhout, J., Thienpont, H.: Selective optical broadcasting in reconfigurable multiprocessor interconnects, Proc. of SPIE Photonics Europe, Vol. 6185, (2006)

7. Tanenbaum, A.S.: Modern Operating Systems 2nd ed., ISBN 0130313580, Prentice Hall, (2001)
8. Multithreading in the Solaris Operating System, Sun Microsystems technical whitepaper, (2002)
9. Sinnen, O., Sousa, L.A.: Communication contention in task scheduling, IEEE Transactions on Parallel and Distributed Systems, Vol. 16, (2005) 503-515
10. Magnusson, P.S., Christensson, M., Eskilson, J., Forsgren, D., Hållberg, G., Högberg, J., Larsson, F., Moestedt, A., Werner, B.: Simics: A Full System Simulation Platform, IEEE Computer, (2002) 50-58
11. Heirman, W., Dambre, J., Artundo, I., Debaes, C., Thienpont, H., Stroobandt, D., Van Campenhout, J.: Predicting Reconfigurable Interconnect Performance in Distributed Shared-Memory Systems. Integration, the VLSI Journal: Special Issue on System Level Interconnect Prediction (to appear), (2007)
12. Woo, S., Ohara, M., Torrie, E., Singh, J., Gupta, A.: The SPLASH-2 programs: characterization and methodological considerations, Proc. of the 22nd Annual International Symposium on Computer Architecture, (1995) 24-36
13. Barford, P., Crovella, M.: Generating representative web workloads for network and server peformance evaluation, Proc. ACM SIGMETRICS, (1998) 151-160
14. Heirman, W., Dambre, J., Van Campenhout, J.: Congestion Modeling for Reconfigurable Inter-Processor Networks, Proc. of the International Workshop on System Level Interconnect Prediction, (2006) 59-66
15. Artundo, I., Desmet, L., Heirman, W., Debaes, C., Dambre, J., Van Campenhout, J., Thienpont, H.: Selective Optical Broadcast Component for Reconfigurable Multiprocessor Interconnects, Journal on Selected Topics in Quantum Electronics: Special Issue on Optical Communications, Vol. 12 (2006) 828-837

Cross-Layer Scheduling Algorithm for WLAN Throughput Improvement

Sung Won Kim

School of Electrical Engineering and Computer Science, Yeungnam University,
Gyeongsangbuk-do, 712-749, Korea
`ksw@ieee.org`

Abstract. Throughput improvement is critical in wireless communication networks, since the wireless channel is often shared by a number of nodes in the same neighborhood. With cross-layer design, bandwidth can be shared more efficiently by competing flows in proportion to their channel conditions. In this paper, we propose a cross-layer design for throughput improvement in IEEE 802.11 wireless local area networks (WLANs). Our protocol is derived from the Distributed Coordination Function (DCF) in the IEEE medium access control (MAC) protocol. Simulation results show that the proposed method achieves the improved throughput compared with IEEE 802.11. An important feature of the proposed method is its backward compatibility, which allows the proposed method can work with legacy IEEE 802.11 nodes.

1 Introduction

IEEE 802.11 wireless local area networks (WLANs) [1] have become increasingly prevalent in recent years. In IEEE 802.11 WLANs, a channel is shared by all nodes in the neighborhood of an access point (AP). Dividing the limited channel bandwidth efficiently among nodes is an important and challenging problem.

Currently, there has been a shift in the design of recent generation wireless networks to support the multimedia services [2]–[4], so-called cross-layer design. To improve the system throughput by using the cross-layer design, bandwidth should be shared by all competing nodes proportional to a channel condition of each link. Links that have a better channel condition must be assigned higher priority, so that they can obtain higher bandwidth. The key challenge in WLAN is that there is no centralized scheduling server, as in the case of a router output port in a wireline environment. Instead, the scheduling operation is distributed among wireless nodes with packets to transmit.

An opportunistic scheduling algorithm that exploits the inherent multi-user diversity has been implemented as the standard algorithm in the third-generation cellular system IS-856 [5] (also known as high data rate, HDR). To enable the opportunistic multi-user communications, timely channel information of each link is required for an effective scheduling. Just as all the previous schemes have assumed, the exploitation of timely channel information is possible in cellular networks where the base station acts as a central controller and control channels are available for channel state feedback.

G. Min et al. (Eds.): ISPA 2006 Ws, LNCS 4331, pp. 322–331, 2006.

When it comes down to WLANs, it is difficult to utilize the multi-user diversity. The AP cannot track the channel fluctuations of each link because of the single shared medium and the distributed Carrier Sense Multiple Access with Collision Avoidance (CSMA/CA) Medium Access Control (MAC) protocol. Wang *et al.* [6] presented the opportunistic packet scheduling method for WLANs. The key mechanisms of the method are the use of multicast RTS (Request-To-Send) and priority-based CTS (Clear-To-Send) to probe the channel status information. Since their method requires the modification of RTS and CTS in the standard, the scheme cannot be directly applied into widely deployed IEEE 802.11 typed WLANs.

On the other hand, this form of the multi-user wireless system produces asymmetric traffic loads where most of the traffic loads converge into APs. For example, Internet access or mobile computing uses transmission control protocol (TCP) or user datagram protocol (UDP) in which the offered traffic load is strongly biased toward the downlink (from AP to nodes) against the uplink (from nodes to AP) or the direct link (from nodes to nodes). Thus, these traffic flows for the downlink are completely blocked due to the CSMA/CA MAC protocol in distributed environments.

To alleviate the bottleneck problem in the downlink and exploit the multi-user diversity in WLANs, we propose a cross-layer design combining the opportunistic downlink packet scheduling and MAC protocol. The remainder of this paper is organized as follows. The next section presents related works. Section 3 describes the proposed method. In Section 4, we investigate the enhancement of the proposed method with some numerical results. Finally, the paper is concluded in Section 5.

2   Related Work

2.1   IEEE 802.11 DCF

MAC protocol in the IEEE 802.11 standard consists of two coordination functions: mandatory Distributed Coordination Function (DCF) and optional Point Coordination Function (PCF). In the DCF, a set of wireless nodes communicates with each other using a contention-based channel access method, CSMA/CA. CSMA/CA is known for its inherent fairness between nodes and robustness. It is quite effective in supporting symmetric traffic loads in ad hoc networks where the traffic loads between nodes are similar.

The DCF achieves automatic medium sharing between compatible nodes through the use of CSMA/CA. Before initiating a transmission, a node senses the channel to determine whether or not another node is transmitting. If the medium is sensed idle for a specified time interval, called the distributed inter-frame space (DIFS), the node is allowed to transmit. If the medium is sensed busy, the transmission is deferred until the ongoing transmission terminates.

If two or more nodes find that the channel is idle at the same time, a collision occurs. In order to reduce the probability of such collisions, a node has to perform a backoff procedure before starting a transmission. The duration of this backoff is determined by the Contention Window (CW) size which is initially set to CW_{min}. The CW value is used to randomly choose the number of slot times in the range of $[0, CW - 1]$, which is used for backoff duration. In case of an unsuccessful transmission, the CW value is updated to $CW \times 2$ while it does not exceed CW_{max}. This will guarantee that in case of a collision, the probability of another collision at the time of next transmission attempt is further decreased.

A transmitter and receiver pair exchanges short RTS and CTS control packets prior to the actual data transmission to avoid the collision of data packets. An acknowledgement (ACK) packet will be sent by the receiver upon successful reception of a data packet. It is only after receiving an ACK packet correctly that the transmitter assumes successful delivery of the corresponding data packet. Short InterFrame Space (SIFS), which is smaller than DIFS, is a time interval between RTS, CTS, data packet, and ACK packet. Using this small gap between transmissions within the packet exchange sequence prevents other nodes from attempting to use the medium. As a consequence, it gives priority to completion of the ongoing packet exchange sequence.

2.2   Rate Adaptation

In [11], the auto-rate fallback (ARF) protocol for IEEE 802.11 has been presented. If the ACKs for two consecutive data packets are not received by the sender, the sender reduces the transmission rate to the next lower data rate and starts a timer. When, the timer expires or ten consecutive ACKs are received, the transmission rate is raised to the next higher data rate and the timer is canceled. However, if an ACK is not received for the immediately next data packet, the rate is lowered again and the timer is restarted. The ARF protocol is simple and easy to incorporate into the IEEE 802.11. However, as pointed out in [12], it is purely heuristic and cannot react quickly when the wireless channel conditions (e.g. signal to noise ratio, SNR) fluctuate.

In the above algorithms, the rate adaptation is performed at the sender. However, it is the receiver that can perceive the channel quality, and thus determine the transmission rate more precisely. Observing this, the authors in [13] have presented a receiver-based auto-rate (RBAR) protocol assuming that the RTS/CTS mechanism is there. The basic idea of RBAR is as follows. First, the receiver estimates the wireless channel quality using a sample of the SNR of the received RTS, then selects an appropriate transmission rate for the data packet, and piggybacks the chosen rate in the responding CTS packet. Then, the sender transmits the data packet at the rate advertised by the CTS. The simulation results in [13] show that the RBAR protocol can adapt to the channel conditions more quickly and in a more precise manner than does the ARF protocol, and thus it improves the performance greatly. Heusse *et al.* [14] have observed that in multi-rate WLANs, when certain mobile nodes use a lower bit rate than others, the performance of all nodes is considerably degraded. Specifically, the throughput of a high-bit nodes is down-equalized to that of the lowest bit-rate peer.

2.3   Throughput Fairness

Recently, throughput unfairness between the uplink and the downlink in IEEE 802.11 WLANs has received attention. In [7], the authors observe a significant unfairness between the uplink and the downlink flows when the DCF is employed in a WLAN. The TCP fairness issues between the uplink and the downlink in WLANs has been studied in [8]. Uplink flows receive significantly higher throughput than downlink flows. They find that the buffer size at the AP plays a key role in the observed unfairness, and propose a solution based on TCP receiver window manipulation. The fairness problem between uplink and downlink traffic flows in IEEE 802.11 DCF is also identified in [9]. Since in DCF, the AP and the nodes have equal access to the channel, when the downlink has a higher traffic load than the uplink, the downlink becomes a bottleneck. To solve this problem, the paper proposed a controllable resource allocation scheme between uplink and downlink flows, which adapts the parameters according to the dynamic traffic load. The scheme also improves the system utilization by reducing the collision probability. Wu and Fahmy [10] proposed a bandwidth sharing algorithm to achieve long-term throughput fairness in IEEE 802.11 WLANs. The algorithm does not require any change of the MAC frame format, which allows legacy IEEE 802.11 nodes to seamlessly coexit with the proposed method.

3   Cross-Layer Scheduling Algorithm

3.1   System Model

Each node can directly communicate only with the AP (uplink or downlink), since we focus on AP-coordinated wireless network. We propose that the AP determines the downlink channel access method according to the operation mode, DCF and ACF (AP Coordination Function). In DCF, the AP accesses the downlink channel by using the CSMA/CA. Nodes and AP use the DCF mechanism with RTS/CTS handshaking, where the next channel access should wait for DIFS and backoff window time after previous ACK packet. A two-way handshaking technique without RTS/CTS handshaking called basic access mechanism is not considered in this paper although our proposed method can be easily extended to the basic access mechanism. In ACF, the AP waits only for SIFS period instead of DIFS and backoff period. By shorting the interval period, the AP can access the channel without collision because all other nodes should wait at least DIFS period which is longer than SIFS period.

3.2   Multi-user Diversity

To switch between the two channel access methods, we propose that the AP has counters for the uplink and the downlink, denoted by $U(n)$ and $D(n)$, respectively. The counter values increase whenever there is a successful packet transmission in the uplink or the downlink. For example, when a packet is transmitted through the uplink at time n, the counter values are updated as

$$U(n) = U(n-1) + 1, \tag{1}$$

$$D(n) = D(n-1). \tag{2}$$

When $D(n) \geq U(n)$, which means the accumulated number of the downlink successful packet transmission is larger than that of the uplink, the operation mode of the AP is set to the DCF. On the contrary, when $D(n) < U(n)$, the operation mode of the AP is changed to the ACF. The two counters, $U(n)$ and $D(n)$, also update the values in the ACF and the operation mode will be changed to the DCF as soon as $D(n) \geq U(n)$. By using these two operation modes, more throughput is allocated to the downlink.

In DCF, the packet scheduling algorithm adopts the first-in first-out (FIFO) algorithm. In ACF, the AP schedules the packet based on the channel quality. Thus, the AP has to track the channel information. In order to track the latest channel quality, it is necessary to send the control packet to the node. However, this method will increase the overhead and need the modification of the IEEE 802.11 standard. Our design goal is that the proposed method can be implemented without the modification of the nodes already deployed in the system. Thus, we propose that the AP updates the channel quality of each link after every successful packet transmissions. The channel quality is reported from the physical layer by measuring the SNR of the CTS and ACK control packets. This estimation of the channel quality may not be the timely information. However, the estimation error is in the acceptable range as will be shown in the next section. Moreover, the proposed method can be implemented without the modification of the deployed nodes.

The AP lists all the communication links according to the channel quality. When the AP is in the ACF, the link that recorded the best channel quality in the previous successful transmission is given the first chance to transmit the packet in the queue. When there is no packet in the queue for that link, the next best channel quality link is given the second chance.

4   Performance Analysis

4.1   IEEE 802.11 DCF

Let N be the number of active nodes except AP. Then the probability that the successful packet transmission is performed by node n is given as

$$P_n = \frac{1}{N+1}, \quad \text{for } n = 1, 2, ..N. \tag{3}$$

The same probability applies to the AP. Let Γ be the maximum available system throughput. Then, the system throughput allocated to the downlink, Γ_d, and the uplink, Γ_u, are given as

$$\Gamma_d = \Gamma \times P_n = \Gamma \frac{1}{N+1}, \tag{4}$$

$$\Gamma_u = \Gamma \times (1 - P_n) = \Gamma \frac{N}{N+1}, \quad \text{for } n = 1, 2, ..N, \tag{5}$$

where the packet size is assumed to be the same for all the transmission. When the packet sizes for the uplink, S_u, and for the downlink, S_d, are different, (4) and (5) are changed to

$$\Gamma_d = \Gamma \, \frac{S_d}{S_u N + S_d}, \tag{6}$$

$$\Gamma_u = \Gamma \frac{S_u N}{S_u N + S_d}. \tag{7}$$

In this case, the ratio between the uplink throughput Γ_u and the downlink throughput Γ_u is given as

$$\frac{\Gamma_d}{\Gamma_u} = \left(\Gamma \, \frac{S_d}{S_u N + S_d} \right) \Big/ \left(\Gamma \frac{S_u N}{S_u N + S_d} \right) = \frac{S_d}{S_u} \times \frac{1}{N}. \tag{8}$$

Thus, in DCF, the allocated downlink throughput decreases as the number of nodes increases because the system throughput is shared equally between nodes.

This method is not efficient when the traffic load is asymmetric between the uplink and the downlink such as TCP and UDP. Even in the case of symmetric traffic load, the downlink traffic in DCF gets less throughput than that of the uplink and this causes the increased delay of the downlink traffic.

4.2   Simulation Parameters

We evaluate the performance of the proposed method by computer simulations. The IEEE 802.11 DCF is compared with the proposed method, named CROSS. The parameter values used to obtain numerical results for the simulation runs are based on the IEEE 802.11b direct sequence spread spectrum (DSSS) standard [1].

To reflect the fact that the surrounding environmental clutter may be significantly different for each pair of communication nodes with the same distance separation, we use the log-normal shadowing channel model [15]. The path loss PL in dB at distance d is given as

$$PL(d) = PL(d_0) + 10n \log(d/d_0) + X_\sigma, \tag{9}$$

where d_0 is the close-in reference distance, n is the path loss exponent, and X_σ is a zero-mean Gaussian distributed random variable with standard deviation σ. We set n to 3.25 and σ to 5.2 according to the result of measurements for an office building model [15]. To estimate $PL(d_0)$, we use the Friis free space equation

$$P_r(d_0) = \frac{P_t G_t G_r \lambda^2}{(4\pi)^2 d_0^2 L}, \tag{10}$$

where P_t and P_r are the transmit and receive power, G_t and G_r are the antenna gains of the transmitter and receiver, λ is the carrier wavelength, and L is the system loss factor which is set to 1 in our simulation. Most of the simulation parameters are drawn from the data sheet of Cisco 350 client adapter. The received power is

$$P_r(d) = P_t - PL(d). \tag{11}$$

The minimum received power level for the carrier sensing is set to -95 dBm, which is the noise power level. The long-term signal-to-noise ratio (SNR) is

$$SNR_L = P_t - PL(d) - \eta + PG, \tag{12}$$

where η is the noise power set to -95 dBm and PG is the spread spectrum processing gain given by

$$PG = 10 \log_{10} \frac{C}{S}, \tag{13}$$

where C is the chip rate and S is the symbol rate. Since each symbol is chipped with an 11-chip pseudonoise code sequence in the IEEE 802.11 standard, PG is 10.4 dB. The received SNR is varied by the Ricean fading gain δ. Under this model, the SNR of the received signal is

$$SNR = 20 \log_{10} \delta + SNR_L. \tag{14}$$

For the data rate in the physical layer for each communication link, we assume that the system adapts the data rate by properly choosing one from a set of modulation scheme according to the channel condition. The set of modulation schemes used in our simulation studies are BPSK, QPSK, 16QAM, 64QAM, and 256QAM. For simplicity, we ignore other common physical layer components such as error correction coding. With 1 MHz symbol rate and the above modulation schemes, the achieved data rates are 1, 2, 4, 6, and 8 Mbps, respectively.

We assume that all nodes except the AP are randomly distributed in the circle area with diameter 150 meters and move randomly at speed 0.1m/sec. The AP is located at the center of the area. To evaluate the maximum performance, traffic load is saturated in each nodes and the destination addresses of the packets are the AP. In the AP, there are N connections, each for one node, and packets are generated for each connections with the same pattern as those in each nodes. To make an asymmetric traffic load condition between uplink and downlink, the size of the downlink and uplink packets are 1024 and 64 bytes, respectively. The number of node N is set to 25. The effects of the uplink packet size and the number of nodes on the performance are also evaluated by the simulation.

4.3   Numerical Results

The effect of the uplink packet size on the downlink and uplink throughtput is shown in Fig. 1. The uplink packet size in the figure is normalized to 64 bytes. As explained in (7), the uplink throughput of DCF increases as the uplink packet size increases. This trend also applies to CROSS because the relative overhead size such as RTS, CTS, ACK, backoff, and collision period is reduced as the uplink packet size increases. DCF provides larger uplink throughput because it gives the same channel access chance to all the active nodes. Note that the most of the system throughput of DCF is allocated to the uplink which leads to the downlink bottle neck problems in asymmetric traffic load conditions. As explained in (8),

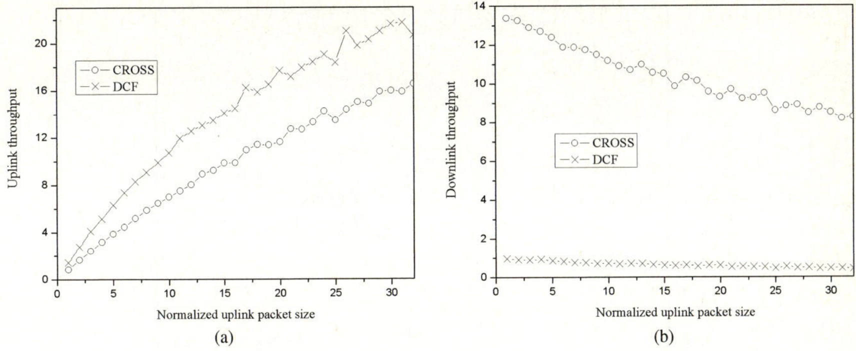

Fig. 1. Downlink and uplink throughput versus normalized uplink packet size

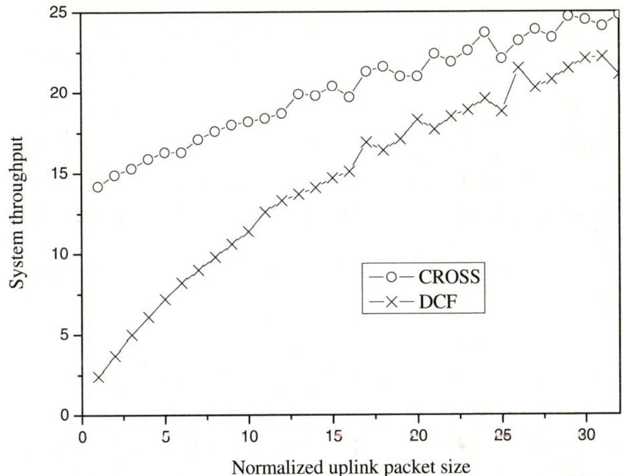

Fig. 2. The effect of the uplink packet size on the system throughput

the downlink throughput of DCF decreases as the uplink packet size increases. This trend also applies to CROSS. Compared with DCF, the proposed method provides larger throughput to the downlink and can mitigate the bottleneck problem of asymmetric traffic load condition.

The effect of the uplink packet size on the system throughput is shown in Fig. 2. As the uplink packet size increases, the system throughput increases. This is because the throughput increase of the uplink is more than that of the downlink. It is also shown that the proposed method outperforms than DCF.

The system throughput of the proposed method is compared with DCF in Fig. 3 by changing the number of nodes. In DCF, the system throughput decreases as the number of nodes increases. This decrease of the system throughput mainly comes from the increased collision between the packet transmissions. The probability of the packet collision increases as the number of nodes increases. On the contrary, the proposed method maintains a constant system throughput

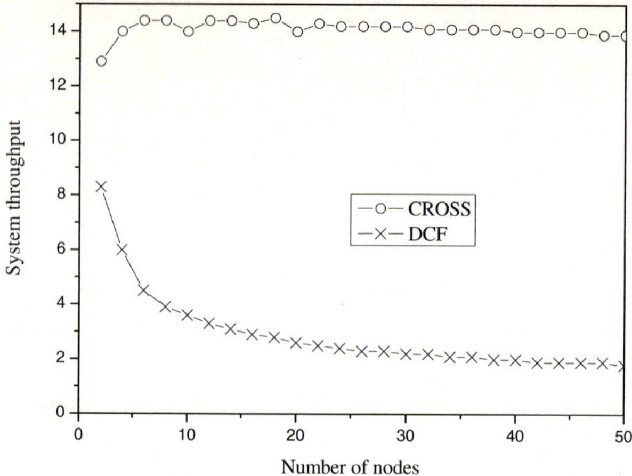

Fig. 3. The effect of the number of nodes on the system throughput

because it provides contention-free access method for the AP. Also note that the proposed method provides more system throughput than DCF because faster data rate is provided for the packet transmission during the ACF.

5   Conclusion

In order to increase the system throughput of WLAN, efficient cross-layer methods are actively worked. In this paper, we proposed the cross-layer method that combines the scheduling method, MAC layer protocol, and physical layer information. Depending on the channel conditions, channel access method and the scheduling method are dynamically changed. In the performance analysis and the simulation results, we showed that IEEE 802.11 DCF has the problem of throughput unfairness between the uplink and the downlink. It is also shown that the proposed method provides more system throughput than IEEE 802.11 DCF and alleviates the problem of throughput unfairness.

References

1. IEEE Std 802.11b-1999: Wireless LAN Medium Access Control (MAC) and Physical Layer (PHY) Specifications: Higher-Speed Physical Layer Extension in the 2.4 GHz Band. (1999)
2. Zhang, Y.J., Letaief, K.B.: Adaptive resource allocation and scheduling for multi-user packet-based OFDM networks. In: Proc. IEEE ICC 2004. Volume 5., Paris, France (2004) 2949–2953
3. Johnsson, K.B., Cox, D.C.: An adaptive cross-layer scheduler for improved QoS support of multiclass data services on wireless systems. IEEE J. Select. Areas Commun. **23** (2005) 334–343

4. Shakkottai, S., Rappaport, T.S., Karlsson, P.C.: Cross-layer design for wireless networks. IEEE Commun. Mag. (2003) 74–80

5. IS-856: CDMA 2000 standard: High rate packet data air interface specification. (2000)

6. Wang, J., Zhai, H., Fang, Y.: Opportunistic packet scheduling and media access control for wireless LANs and multi-hop ad hoc networks. In: Proc. IEEE WCNC 2004, Atlanta, Georgia (2004) 1234–1239

7. Grilo, A., Nunes, M.: Performance evaluation of IEEE 802.11e. In: Proc. IEEE PIMRC 2002, Lisboa, Portugal (2002)

8. Pilosof, S., Ramjee, R., Raz, D., Shavitt, Y., Sinha, P.: Understanding TCP fairness over wireless LAN. In: Proc. IEEE Infocom 2003, San Francisco, CA, USA (2003)

9. Kim, S.W., Kim, B., Fang, Y.: Downlink and uplink resource allocation in IEEE 802.11 wireless LANs. IEEE Trans. Veh. Technol. **54** (2005) 320–327

10. Wu, Y., Fahmy, S.: A credit-based distributed protocol for long-term fairness in IEEE 802.11 single-hop networks. In: Proc. IEEE WiMob 2005. (2005) 98–105

11. Kamerman, A., Monteban, L.: WaveLAN-II: A high-performance wireless LAN for the unlicensed band. Bell Labs Tech. J. **2** (1997) 118–133

12. Qiao, D., Choi, S., Shin, K.G.: Goodput analysis and link adaptation for IEEE 802.11a wireless LANs. IEEE Trans. Mob. Comput. **1** (2002) 278–292

13. Holland, G., Vaidya, N., Bahl, P.: A rate-adaptive MAC protocol for multi-hop wireless networks. In: Proc. IEEE/ACM MOBICOM 2001, Boston, MA, USA (2001) 236–251

14. Heusse, M., Rousseau, F., Berger-Sabbatel, G., Duda, A.: Performance anomaly of 802.11b. In: Proc. IEEE Infocom 2003, San Francisco, CA, USA (2003)

15. T. S. Rappaport: Wireless communications: principles and practices, 2nd Ed. Prentice Hall (2002)

Power Saving Mechanisms of IEEE 802.16e: Sleep Mode vs. Idle Mode*

Beomjoon Kim[1,**], Jaesung Park[2], and Yong-Hoon Choi[3]

[1] Department of Electronic Engineering, Keimyung University, Daegu, 704-701, Korea
bkim@kmu.ac.kr
[2] Department of Internet Information Engineering, The University of Suwon,
Gyeonggi-do, 445-743, Korea
jaesungpark@suwon.ac.kr
[3] Department of Information and Control Engineering, Kwangwoon University,
Seoul, 139-050, Korea
yhchoi@kw.ac.kr

Abstract. IEEE 802.16e standard specifies two mechanisms, sleep mode and idle mode, for the power-efficient operation of a mobile station (MS). Despite the common purpose, these two mechanisms are different in terms of MS's handover and wakening-up process. Recently, each of them is selected as a required feature in the system profile developed by WiMAX forum, which means that they should be implemented in a single MS for the certification. Therefore, the MS supporting the two mechanisms at the same time will require a method to make a better choice considering the situation that it is placed. As the first step toward designing the method, this paper focuses on evaluating the performance of sleep and idle mode in terms of terminal mobility. Analytic results verified by simulations show that idle mode performs better than sleep mode in supporting mobility.

1 Introduction

In IEEE 802.16 Working Group (WG), Task Group (TG) e has recently completed a project to specify a mobile broadband wireless access (BWA) system based on the baseline standard [1] that mainly concerns fixed terminals. The official standard of IEEE 802.16e-2005 [2] has been published in Feb. 2006.

In the mobile systems based on [2] such as Mobile WiMAX [3] and WiBro (Wireless Broadband) of South Korea, a mobile station (MS) will be powered by battery. Therefore, the power-efficient operation of a MS is one of the important factors that will affect the wide deployment of the Mobile WiMAX and WiBro systems. Reflecting the importance, the standard specifies two mechanisms, sleep

* The present research has been conducted by the Bisa Research Grant of Keimyung University in 2006 and the Research Grant of Kwangwoon University in 2006.
** Correspondence to: Beomjoon Kim, Dept. Electronic Engineering, Keimyung University, 1000 Sindang-Dong, Dalseo-Gu, Daegu, 704-701, Korea. Email: bkim@kmu.ac.kr

G. Min et al. (Eds.): ISPA 2006 Ws, LNCS 4331, pp. 332–340, 2006.

mode and idle mode, in order to achieve the low power consumption in a MS. These two modes lead a MS to very similar operation in that the MS is allowed to power down physical operations related to communicating with a base station (BS) and guaranteed delivery of downlink traffic by periodic messaging. However, they have a few substantial differences in MS's performing handover or returning to awake mode for normal operation.

Sleep mode is available only for the current serving BS, which means that if a MS in sleep mode moves away from the current BS's coverage and decides to perform handover, it has to quit sleep mode without any active connection. In fact, it is highly probable for the MS to request another sleep mode initiation after the handover because whether or not there is traffic to or from the MS has nothing to do with the handover. As a consequence, the handover process performed without regard to the existence of active connections may degrade the power saving efficiency of sleep mode due to uplink transmissions and downlink receptions during the handover process.

On the other hand, idle mode is originally designed to provide a seamless operation under the concept of 'paging group.' A paging group is comprised of a number of BSs, and each BS in the paging group may be regarded as identical by a MS in idle mode. It means that a MS can maintain idle mode as long as it stays within the paging group. Even in the case that the MS moves outside the paging group, rather a simple process may cover the change in its location, if secure location update [2] is available.

Despite the unnecessary handover process, sleep mode has an advantage of quick returning to awake mode for normal operation, i.e. without any additional procedures. It is because the MS in sleep mode maintains registered state with its current serving BS so that all the information and parameters needed for resuming communication are still valid. However, idle mode compromises the prompt transition to awake mode because de-registration from the network is forced at the initiation of idle mode. Every time a MS terminates idle mode, therefore, the process called 'network re-entry' should be performed before communicating with the BS where the MS is now attached. During the network re-entry, the MS has to obtain, negotiate, adjust, and update a set of parameters related to physical transmission, capability, and security.

As briefly discussed so far, sleep mode and idle mode have their own merit and demerit; sleep mode is more appropriate for the services that require a quick response like push-to-talk while idle mode is more appropriate for MSs moving fast. Accordingly, the WiMAX Forum has decided to include both sleep and idle mode as required features in the system profile for certification; it means that these two modes will be implemented in a single MS. In such a case, the MS will require a method to determine which mode is better to choose considering the requirements for applications running on it, its mobility, and etc. In order to design the method, the performance of sleep mode and idle mode need to be evaluated and compared in all aspects.

It is very recent that the official IEEE 802.16e standard has been published, so that there are only few works dealing with this issue. Although the work in [4] proposed a good model for evaluating the performance of sleep mode, it targets only sleep mode and based on the old version of the draft of the standard. Besides, MS's mobility is not considered at all. For more generalization, this paper evaluates the performance of idle mode as well as sleep mode, and investigates the affect of the MS's mobility on the performances of sleep mode and idle mode.

2 Description of Sleep Mode and Idle Mode

In this section, we provide a brief description of sleep and idle mode operations. For more details, readers are recommended to refer to the standard [2].

2.1 Sleep Mode

Basic Operation. Sleep mode may have three types of power saving classes that are differentiated by the traffic type of the associated service and corresponding sleep window management policy. In this subsection, we describe the basic operation of power saving class of type 1 that is designed for best effort services.

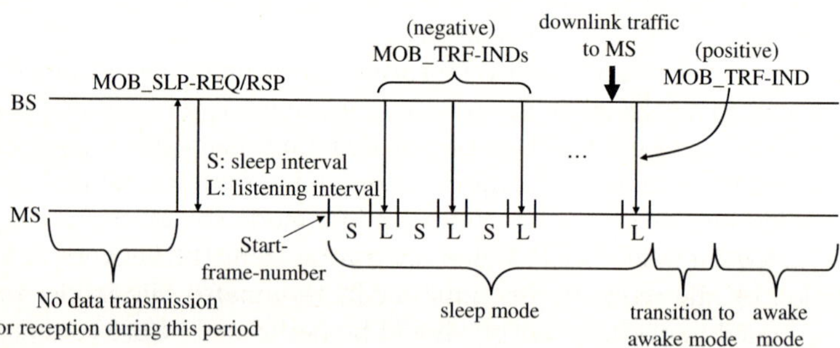

Fig. 1. Basic operation of power saving class of type 1 of sleep mode

Fig. 1 shows the basic operation of power saving class of type 1. If there has been no data transmission or reception for a time period, a MS may decide to enter sleep mode. In order to initiate sleep mode, the MS transmits a sleep request message (MOB_SLP-REQ) to the current serving BS. In response to the request message, the BS transmits a response message (MOB_SLP-RSP) which may approve the request. During this negotiation, several parameters related to the sleep mode operation are determined such as start-frame-number, initial-sleep window, listening window, final-sleep window base, final-sleep exponent, and so on.

After receiving the response message, the MS begins the sleep mode operation at the start-frame-number indicated by the response message. The sleep mode operation is interleaved with listening intervals, and a traffic indication message (MOB_TRF-IND) is received in every listening interval. The length of each listening interval is determined by the listening window. Between two listening intervals, sleep interval appears in which the MS may 'sleep.' The length of the sleep interval is determined by the sleep window.

Every time a MS receives a traffic indication message saying that there is no traffic to receive (a negative indication), the sleep window is increased by two until it reaches a maximum value. The maximum value of the sleep window is determined by

$$\textit{final-sleep window base} * 2^{\textit{final-sleep window exponent}}. \tag{1}$$

If there is downlink traffic addressed to the MS in sleep mode, it is notified by a positive indication at the very next listening interval. By receiving the positive indication, the MS terminates sleep mode and makes a transition to awake mode for normal operation.

Power Saving Class of Type 2 and 3. Unlike power saving class of type 1, the sleep window for power saving class of type 2, once defined, keeps the same value because it targets services with a constant transmission rate such as voice over IP (VoIP). The sleep window for power saving class of type 3 may also vary and is determined each time a sleep interval begins. This type of power saving class may be associate with the delivery of periodic control and management messages to the MS in sleep mode.

The power saving class of type 2 and 3 are somewhat different from type 1 because they are designed to transmit data for active services or periodic control and management messages; they do not require the function of traffic indication. Therefore, only power saving class of type 1 is considered in the rest of this paper.

Sleep Mode and Handover. Simply, sleep mode does not support inter-BS continuity. There may be a few reasons for this interruption, but the main reason is that the MS in sleep mode is regarded as still active but just conservative in its battery consumption. It means that the MS maintains a registered state with the current serving BS while in sleep mode. This concept facilitates the quick transition to awake mode because the serving BS keeps almost all the information about the MS.

For handover, however, the MS has to perform the same procedures as other MSs that operate in awake mode with active connections. Note that any uplink transmission to perform handover terminates sleep mode. Therefore, the sleep mode operation should be interrupted by handover, and the MS may initiate another sleep mode at the new serving BS after the handover, if necessary.

2.2 Idle Mode

Basic Operation. The idle mode operation is quite similar to sleep mode in that a MS repeats power-down and power-up till it exits idle mode by an indication of downlink traffic. The main difference is that idle mode adopts the concept of paging group in order to guarantee MS's seamless idle operation within a paging group. Fig. 2-(a) shows a paging group that is comprised of a number of BSs.[1] Every member BS of a paging group is set to have the same configuration related to the idle mode operation, and shares the list of idle MSs in the paging group so that idle MSs need not care about their location within the paging group.

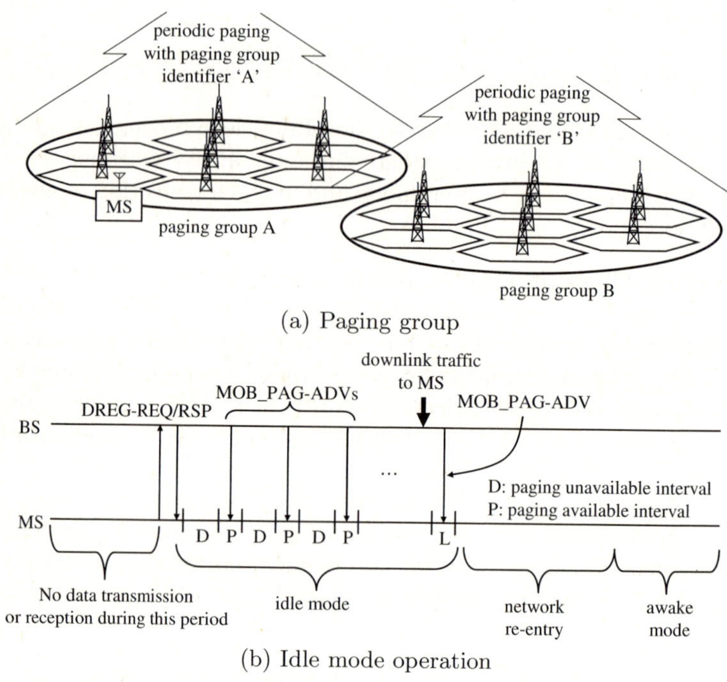

(a) Paging group

(b) Idle mode operation

Fig. 2. Idle mode operation with paging group

There are three main parameters: paging group identifier, paging cycle, and paging offset. They are determined at the initiation by exchanging the messages (DREG_REQ/RSP) as shown in Fig. 2-(b). Paging group identifier is shared by every member BS and included in every paging message (MOB_PAG-ADV) to inform the idle MSs of the paging group that they are located. Two remaining parameters, paging cycle and paging offset, are used for determining the starting point of each paging interval. They are also shared by every member BS so that MSs are able to receive the paging messages from any BS in the paging group. If the current frame number N_f meets the following condition

$$N_f \text{ modulo paging cycle } == \text{ paging offset}, \tag{2}$$

paging interval starts and continues for coming N frames. Note that the length of the paging interval N is already determined as a system parameter.

---

[1] How many BSs may be comprised in a paging group is up to the system design and service provider's requirement.

Paging and Network Re-entry. If there comes downlink traffic addressed to a MS in idle mode, every member BS in the paging group pages the MS at the very next paging interval. Unlike sleep mode, a MS cannot be registered to any BS. Therefore, a few BS-specific parameters used before entering idle mode will not be valid any more if the MS's current attachment BS has been changed. Therefore, when a MS terminates idle mode, it has to always perform the process called network re-entry to obtain, negotiate, adjust, and update the BS-specific parameters. The detailed procedures of the network re-entry process is up to its implementation; the standard [2] specifies an optimization to expedite the network re-entry process as an option.

Location Update. A MS in idle mode may travel outside the current paging group. It is known to MS by either missing the paging message at the expected paging interval due to the changed paging cycle and offset or the paging group identifier in the paging message if it happens to receive the paging message.

In such a case, the MS is needed to update the values of paging group identifier, paging cycle, and paging offset, which is referred to as location update (LU) process. After the location update process, idle mode continues. There are two kinds of location updates: secure and unsecure location updates. The secure location update process may be simpler than the network re-entry process while the unsecure location update requires the same procedures as the network re-entry process.

LU may be triggered by a timer. Even if there is no change in paging group, an idle MS has to perform LU before the timer is expired.

3 Evaluation Methodology

3.1 Cost Equations

The power consumed during sleep and idle mode is categorized according to the cost for:

- message transactions for handover, LU, or network re-entry
- decoding downlink frames in listening or paging interval.

Then, the cost equations of sleep mode (C_s) and idle mode (C_i) are expressed as the combination of the costs as follows:

$$C_s = C_l + C_h$$
$$C_i = C_p + C_u + C_e. \tag{3}$$

Here, C_l and C_p denote the costs for decoding the frames in listening interval and paging interval, and C_h, C_u, and C_e denote the costs for handover, LU, and network re-entry process. Each term of the cost equations is derived in a numerical way referring to [4], but the derivations are not included in detail in this paper due to page limit.

3.2   System Parameters

The value of parameters needed for calculating the cost equations are determined in consideration of ongoing discussions in WiMAX Mobile Task Group (MTG) [3], and they are summarized in Table 1. Concerning a parameter, the unit of frames may be converted to the unit of time under the assumption that the length of a frame is 5 msec [3], and vice versa.

Table 1. System Parameters for Sleep Mode and Idle Mode

parameter	definition	value
S_{min}	minimum sleep window	2 frames
S_{max}	maximum sleep window	1024 frames
L	listening window	2 frames
U	paging available interval	2 frames
V	paging unavailable interval	1024 frames
y	maximum distance of a cell from the center cell in a paging group	3
T_l	timer for location update	4096 seconds
R	cell radius	1 km

3.3   Approximation of Power Consumption

In order to calculate the cost equations derived in Section 3, a unit value of cost is assigned to α_l and α_p assuming that α_l is equal to α_p. Since no information is available yet about the actual power consumption of a network interface card implemented based on [2], the ratio between the power consumed by uplink transmission and downlink decoding is assumed to be 1, referring to [7] which discusses on the power consumption of a real network interface card for IEEE 802.11 Wireless LAN. Considering the usual four message transactions for ranging, capability negotiation, privacy key exchange, and registration, a single handover or network re-entry process is assumed to require the cost which is eight times higher than the unit cost. Also, only unsecure LU is considered so that location update requires the same cost as handover or network re-entry. Finally, we have

$$\beta_h = \beta_u = \gamma_e = 8\alpha_l = 8\alpha_p. \tag{4}$$

For simplicity, the unit cost is set to 1 in the calculation of each cost equation.

3.4   Simulation

For the purpose of verification, simulations are conducted with the parameters in Table 1. The detailed operations of sleep mode and idle mode are implemented through C programming. A simulation runs for inter-traffic arrival time that follows the exponential distribution. During the simulations, the number of the listening intervals, paging intervals, handovers, and location updates are captured and used for calculating the cost equations.

4   Result and Discussion

In Fig. 3, the total power cost are compared between sleep mode and idle mode in terms of MS's average cell-residence time in unit of minutes. Note that λ is converted to the number of traffic arrivals per day and set to 48 for this result.

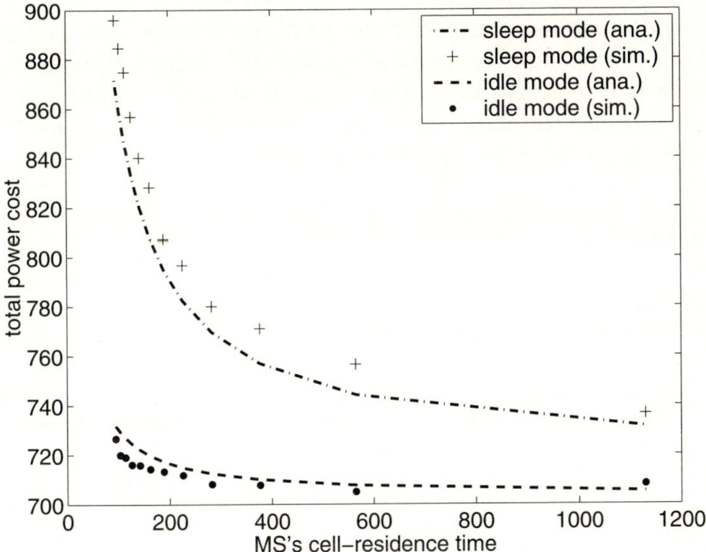

Fig. 3. Total cost of sleep mode and idle mode per MS's cell-residence time ($\lambda = 48$, R=1 km)

Overall power cost of sleep mode is much higher than idle mode. Especially, for a small value of the cell-residence time that corresponds to MS's high mobility, much more power is consumed in sleep mode than in idle mode, and the difference between the two decreases gradually as the cell-residence time increases. It is because the main factor that makes the difference is C_h that is applicable only to sleep mode. Note that the effect C_e is very marginal in this result because network re-entry is processed only once during idle-residence time.

Inversely, sleep mode may not be so bad for the MSs that are stationary or nomadic. For example, for a long cell-residence time, i.e. 1200 minutes or more, handover is not triggered so often that the power consumed by handover process may be regarded as trivial, if quick transition to awake mode precedes the power consumption. This issue is very interesting, although it is not managed in quantitative way at this moment. Another work is in progress for more understanding of this issue as our second step.

5   Conclusions

In this paper, we have analyzed the power saving efficiency of sleep mode and idle mode specified in IEEE 802.16e standard. As shown in the results, idle mode always performs better than sleep mode in supporting terminal mobility.

One thing we have to address here is that only one factor, mobility, has been considered to compare the performance of the two mechanisms. That is, the results do not capture the main advantage from sleep mode, quick transition to awake mode, because the performances of sleep mode and idle mode are evaluated only for a single session of sleep and idle mode operations. Currently, another work is in progress to evaluate sleep mode and idle mode in terms of latency in returning to awake mode with the detailed analysis of the power consumed during network re-entry from idle mode.

References

1. IEEE Std 802.16-2004: IEEE Standard for Local and Metropolitan Area Network - Part 16: Air Interface for Fixed Broadband Wireless Access Systems. (2004)
2. IEEE Std 802.16e-2005: Part 16: Air Interface for Fixed and Mobile Broadband Wireless Access Systems - Amendment 2: Physical and Medium Access Control Layers for Combined Fixed and Mobile Operation in Licensed Bands and Corrigendum 1. (2006)
3. The WiMAX Forum: available at http://www.wimaxforum.org/
4. Y. Xiao: Energy Saving Mechanism in the IEEE 802.16e Wireless MAN. IEEE Comm. Lett. **9** (7) (2005) 595-597
5. I. F. Alkyildiz and W. Wang: A Dynamic Location Management Scheme for Next-Generation Multitier PCS Systems. IEEE Trans. Wireless Comm. **1** (1) (2002) 178-189
6. K. L. Yeung and S. Nanda: Optimal Mobile-Determined Micro-Macro Cell Selection. In the proceeding of IEEE PIMRC'1995 (1995) 294-299
7. M. Stemm and R. Katz: Measuring and Reducing Energy Consumption of Network Interfaces in Hand-held Devices. IEICE Trans. Comm. **E80** (8) (1997) 1125-31

Routing Based on Ad Hoc Link Reliability

Kwonseung Shin[1], Min Young Chung[1], Jongho Won[2], and Hyunseung Choo[1],⋆

[1] School of Information and Communication Engineering
Sungkyunkwan University
440-746, Suwon, Korea +82-31-290-7145
{manics86, mychung, choo}@ece.skku.ac.kr
[2] Electronics and Telecommunications Research Institute
305-700, Daejeon, Korea +82-42-860-6632
jhwon@etri.re.kr

Abstract. An ad-hoc network is a group of mobile nodes acting as routers in infrastructureless networking situations. The ad-hoc node has a precondition of mobility, allowing path to be easily disconnected when transmitting data, thereby increasing network overhead. However, most ad-hoc routing protocols set up the path based only on the number of hops without considering other practical issues and factors. Here we consider a path with the least substantial number of transmissions (SNT) from source to destination based on reliabilities of links. This includes retransmissions due to unreliable links. In this paper, an efficient ad-hoc link reliability based routing (ALR) protocol suitable for mobile ad-hoc network in terms of SNT, is proposed. The network overhead and data transmission delay are reduced, by considering both ad-hoc link reliability and the number of hops. Our empirical performance evaluation comparing to AODV [1] shows that the enhancement is up to about 31% for SNT depending upon the mobility of nodes.

1   Introduction

An ad-hoc network [2] is a group of wireless mobile nodes, requiring no fixed network infrastructure such as base stations or access points. As a result of this advantage, ad-hoc networks can be used in military, emergency and relief scenarios. Nodes assist each other by conveying information, thereby creating virtual connections between each other. Routing protocols play an essential role in the creation and maintenance of these connections. Each node in the ad-hoc network acts as a router in a wired network. The mobility of these router-like nodes is a precondition of an ad-hoc network. Therefore, standard route protocols of wired networks cannot be directly applied. A considerable number of studies [1,3,4,5,6,7,8,9] have been conducted regarding the ad-hoc network.

As mentioned above, the ad-hoc network is a group of router-like nodes representing mobility. A path containing nodes that have high mobility is easily disconnected during data transmission, resulting in an increase in network overhead. Each node has varying ad-hoc link reliability which is a result of the

---

⋆ Corresponding author.

G. Min et al. (Eds.): ISPA 2006 Ws, LNCS 4331, pp. 341–350, 2006.

mobility characteristics. However, most ad-hoc routing protocols set up the path only using the number of hops, without considering the link reliability. Although link state routing algorithm [10] considering the delay and the reliability of link has proposed, it cannot be applied to the ad-hoc network containing the nodes which have high mobility.

In this paper, we propose an efficient ad-hoc routing protocol, considering a path with the substantial number of transmissions (SNT) from source to destination based on reliabilities of links. This reduces network overhead, and increases the efficiency of data transmission. The reliability of nodes can be computed by observing neighboring nodes. A detailed mechanism of computing the reliability from observed beacon messages, is currently being worked on. This paper focuses on the efficient routing protocol suitable for the dynamic ad-hoc network.

2   Related Work

The Ad-hoc On Demand Distance Vector (AODV) routing protocol [1] uses a reactive approach for finding routes. Thus, a route is established for transmitting data, only when it is required by the source node. When the source node desires initiating a path to the destination node, it broadcasts a Route Request (RREQ) message. Table 1 shows the fields of RREQ packet.

Table 1. RREQ packet

Field	Description
RREQ ID	A sequence number which identifies the particular RREQ when taken in conjunction with the originating node's IP address.
Hop Count	The number of hops from the Originator IP Address to intermediate nodes forwarding the RREQ.
Destination IP Address	The IP address of the destination for which a route is supplied.
Destination Sequence Number	The destination sequence number associated with the route. This represents the freshness of the route.
Originator IP Address	The IP address of the node originating the RREQ for which the route is supplied.

When an intermediate node receives a RREQ, it either forwards it on, or prepares a Route Reply(RREP) if it has a fresh route to the destination. The freshness of a route at the intermediate node is determined by comparing the destination sequence number in the RREQ. Intermediate nodes discard the duplicate copies when the RREQ has been received multiple times. The intermediate nodes set up a reverse path entry for the source node in its route table. In this way, the node knows where to forward a RREP to the source if a RREP is received later.

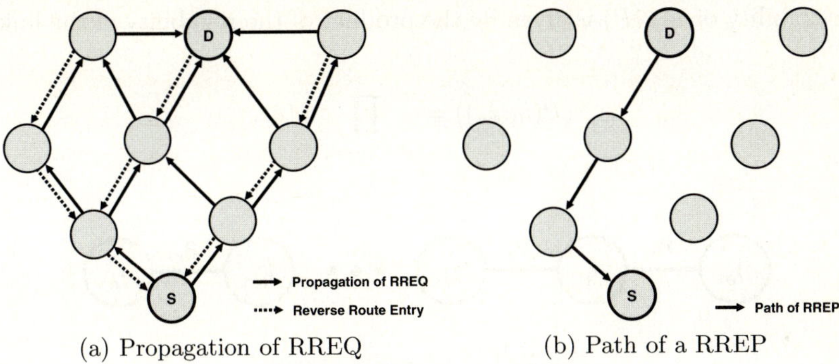

(a) Propagation of RREQ   (b) Path of a RREP

Fig. 1. Path discovery mechanism

When the destination node eventually receives the RREQ, it creates a RREP and unicasts it toward the source node. When an intermediate node receives the RREP, it sets up a forward path entry to the destination in its route table. In this way, the forward path from source to destination node is set up. Fig. 1 indicates the process of forwarding RREQ and RREP. Depending on only the number of hops, the AODV sets up the path. Therefore, when the node, which has high mobility, is in the path, the route is inefficient because it has a high probability of being disconnected.

3   The Proposed ALR Scheme

In this section, an efficient ad-hoc link reliability based routing (ALR) algorithm is proposed, considering both ad-hoc link reliability and the number of hops. The mobility of nodes in an ad-hoc network results in large variation of routing information. When many nodes exist in the network with high mobility, network overhead significantly increases. However, most ad hoc routing protocols set up the minimum hop path without considering the link reliability caused by the mobility of nodes. Hence, these protocols are inefficient in such dynamic environments. Therefore, a scheme which can represent both ad-hoc link reliability and the number of hops as a cost, is introduced. Then, an ad-hoc link reliability based routing protocol is proposed, by applying this scheme to the AODV.

3.1   Basic Mechanism

It can be considered that an ad-hoc network is represented by graph $G = (V, E)$ with n nodes and l links where V is a set of nodes and E is a set of links. Each link $e = (i, j) \in E$ is associated with ad-hoc link reliability $r(e)$. $(0 \leq r(e) \leq 1)$. The path is defined as a sequence of links, such that $(i_0, i_1) \rightarrow (i_2, i_3) \rightarrow \cdots \rightarrow (i_{n-1}, i_n)$, belongs to E. Let an ordering set $P(i_0, i_n) = \{(i_0, i_1), (i_1, i_2), \cdots, (i_{n-1}, i_n)\}$ denote the path from node i_0 to node i_n. The length of the path $P(i_0, i_n)$, denoted by $n(P(i_0, i_n))$, is defined as the number of links in $P(i_0, i_n)$.

The reliability of P $r(P)$ is given by the product of the reliability of the links in the P :

$$r(P(i_0, i_n)) = \prod_{e \in P(i_0, i_n)} r(e) \tag{1}$$

Fig. 2. The reliability of path

Fig. 2 represents a certain path $P(i_0, i_n)$ which its $n(P)$ is n and $r(P)$ is $\prod_{i=1}^{n} R_i$. R_k means the ad-hoc link reliability of link $(i_{k-1}, i_k) \in P(i_0, i_n)$. When a data packet is transmitted through a link, which has a reliability of R, the average number of transmissions is $\sum_{i=1}^{\infty} i(1 - R)^{i-1} R = \frac{1}{R}$. It is assumed that the i_0 transmits a data packet to the i_n through the path shown in Fig. 2. The i_0 has to transmit a data packet to i_1 an average of $\prod_{i=1}^{n} \frac{1}{R_i}$ times, because the $r(P(i_0, i_n))$ is $\prod_{i=1}^{n} R_i$. Similarly, because $r(P(i_1, i_n))$ is $\prod_{i=2}^{n} R_i$, the data packet has to be transmitted $\prod_{i=2}^{n} \frac{1}{R_i}$ times on average by i_2. The average number of transmission through the path $P(i_{n-1}, i_n)$ is $\frac{1}{R_n}$ using the same token. Therefore, when the source node is i_0 and destination node is i_n as presented in Fig. 2, the cost of path $c(P)$ can be represented as follows.

$$c(P) = \frac{1}{R_1 R_2 \cdots R_n} + \frac{1}{R_2 R_3 \cdots R_n} + \cdots + \frac{1}{R_n} = \sum_{i=1}^{n} \frac{1}{\prod_{j=i}^{n} R_j} \tag{2}$$

The value of $c(P)$ represents the substantial number of transmissions (SNT) when a data packet is forwarded. Hence, regarding the network overhead and delay, the path P with the minimum SNT, is the optimal path. In the subsequent section, AODV is improved, by applying the proposed basic mechanism.

3.2   Extended AODV

An additional field called SNT is employed. The value of $c(P)$ described in Section 3.1 is contained in the SNT field. In Fig. 2, it is assumed that the source node i_0 forwards RREQ to set up the path to i_n. In the RREQ, which is received by a certain intermediate node i_k, the cost of the path $P(i_0, i_{k-1})$ must have been recorded, because AODV uses a distributed routing algorithm. (2) can be rewritten as follows:

$$c(P) = (\cdots (((\frac{1}{R_1})\frac{1}{R_2} + \frac{1}{R_2})\frac{1}{R_3} + \frac{1}{R_3})\cdots)\frac{1}{R_n} + \frac{1}{R_n} \tag{3}$$

Therefore, the value of SNT_k which is recorded in the SNT field at i_k, is calculated as follows:

$$SNT_k = \frac{1}{R_k}(SNT_{k-1} + 1) \ , \ \text{where} \ SNT_0 = 0 \tag{4}$$

When the source node desires initiation of the path to the destination, it broadcasts a RREQ message with SNT written as 0. The intermediate node receiving the RREQ, forwards it with SNT computed by (4). Accordingly, the destination node is able to know the cost of each path.

Reverse Path Setup. In AODV, the intermediate nodes discard the duplicate RREQ. However, for proper operation of the proposed scheme, the RREQ received later which has a lower cost must also be forwarded. The number of hops and cost to the source node is maintained in each reverse path route entry. As multiple RREQs can be forwarded, there can be more than one reverse path. The number of hops in reverse path route entry is used to distinguish each path. This will be presented in the next section. The detailed process of forwarding the RREQ in the intermediate node is presented in Fig. 3.

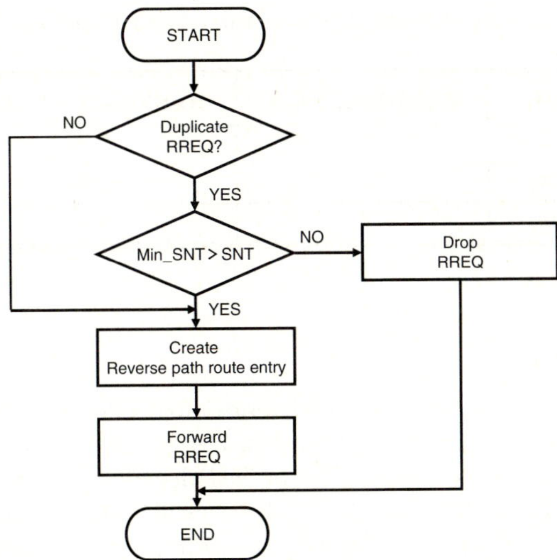

Fig. 3. The process of forwarding RREQ in the intermediate node

Forward Path Setup. The intermediate nodes receiving the RREP update in the route table. The cost to the destination node is maintained in each entry of the route table. In Fig. 2, the destination node i_n enters 0 in the SNT field and forwards the RREP. Then, a certain intermediate node i_k can obtain the cost to the destination node from following equation:

$$SNT_{k-1} = SNT_k + SNT_k \frac{1}{R_k} \ , \ \text{where } SNT_n = 0 \tag{5}$$

Another field, called *Path Length*, which represents the number of hops between source node and destination node, is employed. This field has a fixed value while the *Hop Count* is increased during the forwarding process. As described in previous section, several reverse path route entries may exist in some nodes. Intermediate nodes select the entry with the same *Hop Count* value as the subtracted *Hop Count* value from *Path Length* in the RREP.

Case Study. Fig. 4 is good illustrative example of the proposed mechanism. The ad hoc link reliability is marked at each edge. In the topology presented in Fig. 4, the path is set like solid arrows in Fig. 4(a) by AODV. The most reliable path is represented as solid arrows in Fig. 4(b). On the other hand, the proposed ALR scheme sets up the path as shown in Fig. 4(c), which is the least SNT path. The three kinds of paths are compared with regard to the number of hops, reliability, and SNT in Table 2. As mentioned in Section 3.1, the value of SNT means the substantial number of transmissions when a data packet is sent from source to destination. Therefore, the least SNT path is the most efficient path in the topology represented in Fig. 4.

Table 2. Comparison of three kinds of paths

Type of path	Length of path	Reliability of path	SNT
Minimum hop path	2	0.04	30
Most reliable path	5	0.656	6.476
Least SNT path	4	0.518	5.818

4   Performance Evaluation

Random graphs are the acknowledged model for different kinds of networks. There are many algorithms and programs, but the speed is usually the main goal, not the statistical properties. In the last decade the problem was worked by Waxman [11], Doar [12], Toh [13], Calvert et al. [14], and Kumar et al. [15]. They have developed fast algorithms to generate random graphs with different properties, similar to real communication networks. However, none of them have discussed the stochastic properties of generated random graphs. Rodionov and Choo [16] have formulated two major demands to the generators of random

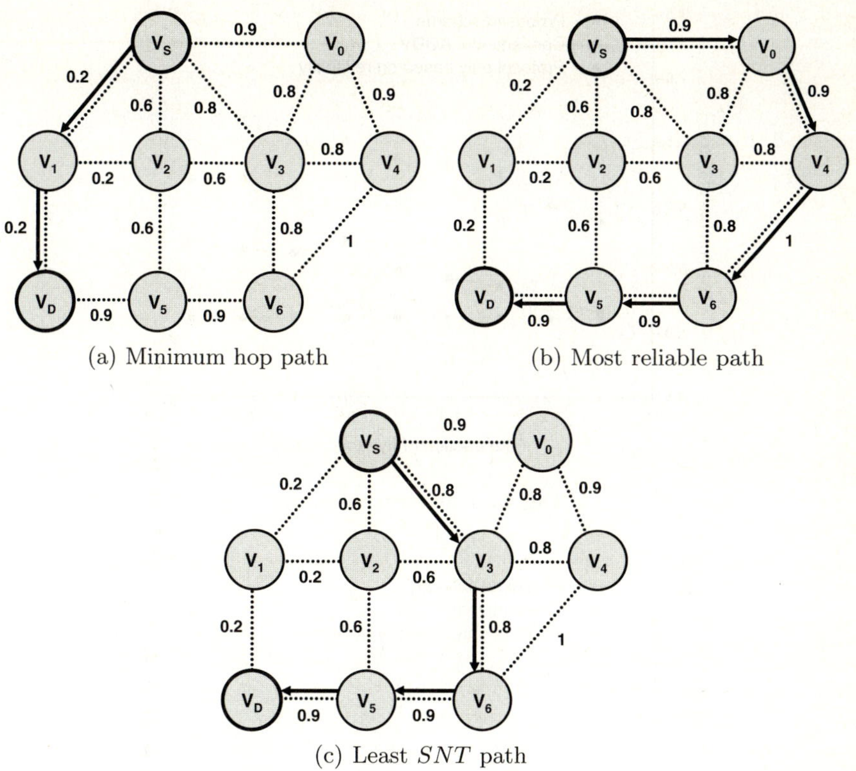

(a) Minimum hop path

(b) Most reliable path

(c) Least *SNT* path

Fig. 4. Three kinds of paths

graph: attainability of all graphs with required properties and the uniformity of their distribution. If the second demand is sometimes difficult to prove theoretically, it is possible to check the distribution statistically. The random graph is similar to real networks. The random networks used in this paper are generated by modifying Rodionov and Choo's mechanism to include properties of ad hoc netowrks. The proposed method of setting up the path is implemented in JAVA. The 10 different networks with 100 nodes are generated and locations of nodes are placed randomly with density of 0.003 $nodes/m^2$. The transmission radius of each node is set as $30m$. Nodes are divided into two types such as stable and dynamic nodes. The link reliability of each stable node is uniformly selected in $(0.9, 1)$ and that of each dynamic node in $(0.3, 0.9)$. In the first stage, the fraction of dynamic nodes is 0.1, and then the evaluation is performed, by incrementing the fraction of dynamic nodes by 0.1 until 0.9 for 10 different random ad-hoc networks.

The proposed ALR scheme is compared with conventional AODV with regard to the number of hops, ad-hoc link reliability, and the SNT. Fig. 5 presents the simulation results for the variation of the average number of hops. The *Protocol Only Based on Reliability* is the mechanism implemented to set up the most reliable path. Conventional AODV sets up the same path regardless of the

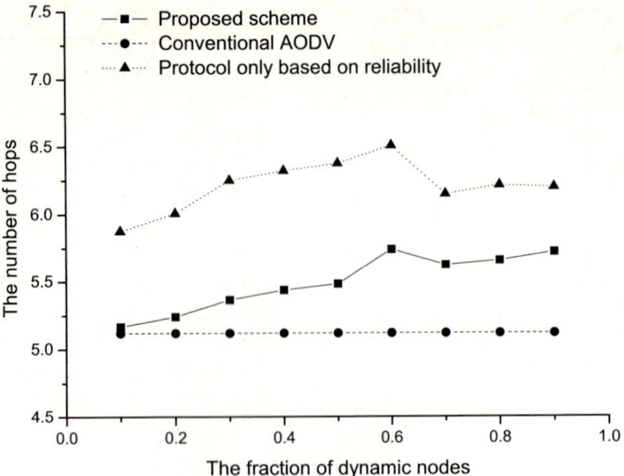

Fig. 5. The length of path

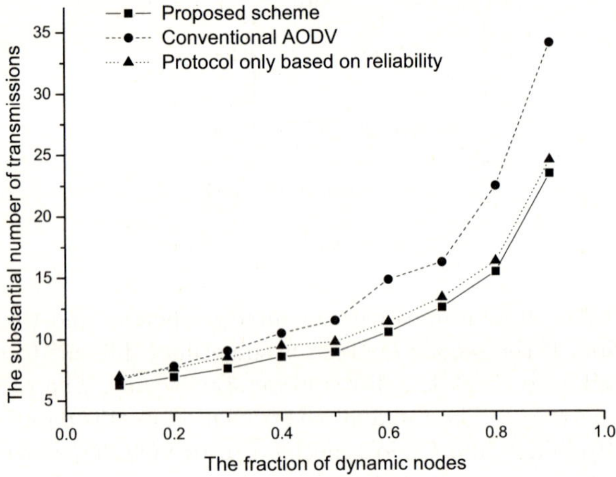

Fig. 6. The substantial number of transmissions

variation in path reliability. However, the proposed scheme sets up the different route to find more efficient path.

As described in Section 3.2, the value of SNT is the substantial number of transmissions when a data packet is transmitted from source to destination. Therefore, this value represents both network overhead and delay. Fig. 6 presents the variation of SNT according to incrementing the fraction of dynamic nodes. The proposed scheme sets up the least SNT path. Fig. 6 shows that the network overhead and data transmission delay are reduced up to 31.3% compared conventional AODV, when the fraction of dynamic nodes is 90%.

5   Conclusion and Future Work

In this paper, a scheme representing both ad-hoc link reliability and the number of hops as a cost, is introduced. Then, an ad-hoc link reliability based routing protocol is proposed, by applying this scheme to the AODV. It is demonstrated that this sets up the optimal path with regard to network overhead and data transmission delay in the ad-hoc network, with a precondition of mobility. Current work is focused on developing a detailed mechanism of computing the reliability from observed beacon messages.

Acknowledgments. This research was supported by Ministry of Information and Communication, Korea under ITRC IITA-2005-(C1090-0501-0019).

References

1. C. Perkins, E. Belding-Royer, and S. Das, "Ad hoc On-Demand Distance Vector (AODV) Routing," Network Working Group, Request for Comments: 3561. http://www.ietf.org/rfc/rfc3561.txt, 2003.
2. S. Corson and J. Macker, "Mobile Ad hoc Networking (MANET): Routing Protocol Performance Issues and Evaluation Considerations," Network Working Group, Request for Comments: 2501. http://www.ietf.org/rfc/rfc2501.txt, 1999.
3. R. Ogier, F. Templin, and M. Lewis, "Topology broadcast based on reverse-path forwarding routing protocol (TBRF)," Network Working Group, Request for Comments: 3684. http://www.ietf.org/rfc/rfc3684.txt, 2004.
4. C.-C. Chiang, "Routing in clustered multihop mobile wireless networks with fading channel," Proceedings of IEEE SICON, pp. 197-211, 1997.
5. E. T. Clausen and E. P. Jacquet. "Optimised Link State Routing Protocol (OLSR)," Network Working Group, Request for Comments: 3626. http://www.ietf.org/rfc/rfc3626.txt, 2003.
6. D. B. Johnson, David A. Maltz, and Yih-Chun Hu, "The Dynamic Source Routing Protocol for Mobile Ad Hoc Networks (DSR)," IETF MANET Working Group, INTERNET-DRAFT. http://www.ietf.org/internet-drafts/draft-ietf-manet-dsr-10.txt, 2004.
7. Y.-B. Ko, N.H. Vaidya, "Location-aided routing (LAR) in mobile ad hoc networks," Proceedings of the Fourth Annual ACM/IEEE International Conference on Mobile Computing and Networking (Mobicom'98), 1998.
8. S. Murthy J.J. Garcia-Luna-Aceves, "A routing protocol for packet radio networks," Proceedings of the First Annual ACM International Conference on Mobile Computing and Networking, Berkeley, CA, pp. 86-95, 1995.
9. L. Villasenor-Gonzalez, Y. Ge, and L. Lamont, "HOLSR: a hierarchical proactive routing mechanism for mobile ad hoc networks," IEEE Communications Magazine, vol. 43, no. 7, pp. 118-125, 2005.
10. G. Xue, "End-to-End Data Paths: Quickest or Most Reliable?," IEEE Communications Letters, vol. 2, no. 6, pp. 156-158, 1998.
11. B.M. Waxman, "Routing of Multipoint Connections," IEEE JSAC, vol. 9, pp. 1617-1622, 1993.
12. M. Doar, "A Better Mode for Generating Test Networks," IEEE Proc. GLOBECOM96, pp. 86-93, 1996.

13. C.-K. Toh, "Performance Evaluation of Crossover Switch Discovery Algorithms for Wireless ATM LANs," IEEE Proc. INFOCOM96, pp. 1380-1387, 1993
14. K.L. Calvert, M. Doar, and M. Doar, "Modelling Internet Topology," IEEE Communications Magazine, pp. 160-163, June 1997.
15. R. Kumar, P. Raghavan, S. Rajagopalan, D Sivakumar, A. Tomkins, and E Upfal, "Stochastic models for the Web graph," Proc. 41st
16. A.S. Rodionov and H. Choo, "On Generating Random Network Structures: Connected Graphs," Springer-Verlag Lecture Notes in Computer Science, vol. 3090, pp. 483-491, September 2004.

Tracking Anomalous Behaviors of Name Servers by Mining DNS Traffic

Yao Wang, Ming-zeng Hu, Bin Li, and Bo-ru Yan

Research Center of Computer Network and Information Security Technology,
Harbin Institute of Technology, Harbin 150001, Heilongjiang, China
{wangyao, mzh, libin, yanboru}@pact518.hit.edu.cn

Abstract. This paper seeks to quantitatively understand the nature of the current threat towards the common name servers. A new tracking technique based on statistical model is proposed to locate the anomalous name servers by analyzing the real-world DNS traffic. After summarizing the attacks towards DNS, the detection method based on associative feature analysis is presented. Experiments are conducted which highlighting both the payload anomaly and the data flow anomaly, and the experimental results reveal the efficiency of our method in detecting the anomalous behaviors of name servers.

1 Introduction

The Domain Name System (DNS) is a vital component of Internet infrastructure. As a hierarchical database distributed around the world, its primary function is to translate human-readable domain names to the corresponding IP addresses and providing the routing information of Email [1, 2]. As the most successful distributed system on the Internet, A great deal of daily network applications such as emails and web surfing all need DNS work properly. At the same time, many rising network applications ranging from load balance to service discovery also nearly depend on DNS. If an application fails to receive a reply for its DNS query, a denied service occurred; if a forged or malicious reply is received, a DNS hijacking happened. However, the key role of DNS is not seriously concerned about. Most regard the system as well behaved and quite reliable, yet there is surprisingly little data to support this claim. Actually, DNS has become prone to security intrusions and there are many configuration errors existed in the enormous global system [3], even in giant computer corporations such as Microsoft [4].The complexity of distributed system leaves DNS vulnerable to security threats, configuration errors, and system failures. Operators face the increasingly difficult task of finding and responding to unconscious failures and intended attacks.

In this paper, we proposed an associative feature analysis approach based on statistical models to track the anomalous behaviors of common name servers. In collaboration with a major commercial Internet Service Provider (ISP) in China, we captured and analyzed the real DNS traffic in the large-scale network environment.

The rest of the paper is organized as follows. After presenting the related work in Section 2, we give a brief overview of DNS attacks and the data set in Section 3. Subsequently, in Section 4, we describe the anomalous behavior detection methodology of name servers, and present the pragmatic analysis process of data set obtained

G. Min et al. (Eds.): ISPA 2006 Ws, LNCS 4331, pp. 351–357, 2006.

from the backbone with Section 5 detailing the results of this study. Finally, in Section 6, we conclude with a discussion of the results and implications for future work.

2   Related Work

Plenty of measures have been presented to study the performance and implementation errors of root servers. Danzig et al. performed an extensive study of the DNS traffic on the ISI (Information Sciences Institute) root server in 1992 [5]. They observed a variety of DNS implementation bugs such as recursion loops and poor failure detection algorithms. The finding is such errors incurred unnecessary wide-area DNS traffic by a factor of twenty. In 2001, Brownlee et al. [6] measured passively on the DNS traffic directed toward the F-root server and identified some queries repeated, to private address space or invalid top-level domains (TLDs), they also found some new errors such bogus *A* queries, source port zero and requests trying to update root servers. In a further work, Jung et al. [7] studied the prevalence of failures and errors interacting with root/gTLD servers. They observed that a significant fraction of lookups never receive an answer and furthermore, DNS server implementations continue to be overly persistent in the face of failures.

In spite of suffering from all kinds of attacks such as publicized DDoS attacks [8], the root servers themselves are well equipped and monitored closely to guard against these compromises, which make exploits towards the top-level servers arduous and cause adversary transfer their attentions to local name servers run by ISPs or large corporations. In contrast with root servers, local name servers are lack of enough ammunition to fight back intended attacks and unconscious failures. However, to the best of our knowledge, there are no efforts to detect the anomalous behaviors of common name servers systematically from the point of view of traffic analysis in a large-scale backbone environment. Furthermore, the unique characteristic of DNS data flow such as small in packet size and little in message amount make it more difficult to distinguish anomalous behaviors from normal ones.

3   Background

In this section, we analyze the real data of DNS traffic from a commercial ISP in China first and then summarizing the common characteristics of the prevalent DNS attacks.

3.1   Data Set

The network environment concerning in this study is backbone level. We captured two traces of DNS traffic as detailed in Table 1.

Table 1. Traces of DNS traffic gathered from backbone

Name	Size	Queries	Distinct queries
Trace 1	110.3M	216876	91648
Trace 2	289.6M	499505	200450

The percentage of each query type in the two traces is listed in Table 2. It shows that queries aiming at host address including both IPv4 and IPv6 contributed about half of the total number of queries. At the same time, *CNAME* lookups varied significantly from 17.17% in Trace 1 to 9.79% in Trace 2. Besides, there are still some malformed DNS queries with an illegal query ID such as "0" which often related with software bugs, misconfigurations and malicious attacks.

Table 2. Percentage of query types (%)

Query type	Ratio(Trace 1)	Ratio(Trace 2)
A	43.43	47.05
NS	0.17	0.22
CNAME	17.17	9.22
SOA	10.94	11.98
PTR	17.98	19.17
MX	2.26	2.57
TXT	0.15	0.21
AAAA	6.90	8.66
SRV	0.01	0.01
A6	0.80	0.67
ANY	0.16	0.20
Other	0.03	0.04

3.2 Taxonomy of DNS Attacks

The main kinds of DNS attacks are DNS Spoofing, Cache Poisoning, Denial of Service and Server Compromising respectively. We summarized their characteristics according to the attack attributes as showed in Table 3.

Table 3. Comparison of Attack methods of DNS

Attack type	Mode	Traffic	Target	Method	Difficulty
DNS Spoofing	P	small	C/S	spoofing	easier
Cache Poisoning	A	large	S	spoofing	easy
Denial of Service	A	huge	S	resource consumption	harder
Server Compromising	A	large	S	vulnerability intrusion	hardiest

Mode: P→passive   A→active   Target: C→client S→server

Table 3 shows that most attacks generated large traffic and targeted the name servers rather than clients. Therefore, by monitoring the query amount and the correlation between clients and servers, the anomalous behaviors of name servers can be detected.

4 Anomalous Behavior Detection Methodology for Name Servers

As mentioned, our study attempts to develop appropriate techniques that can effectively identify possible anomalous behaviors of name servers under the large scale network traffic. As we all know, the traffic-based method doesn't need to scan every bit of each packet, however, as an application level protocol, some payload of DNS packet such as odd value in query type is helpful in locating the range of anomalous behaviors. In fact, there are two kinds of anomalous behaviors, one is caused by intended attacks and another is caused by the vulnerabilities of name servers in software design, coding, or system configuration. The former can be detected by the traffic-based method, whereas the latter has to appeal to payload detection. So we present an associative detection method by mining not only attributes of traffic protocol but also specific payload of DNS packet. Of course, there is no "one size fits all" solution, but our approach can detect the anomalous behaviors of name servers more accurately and efficiently.

4.1 Statistical Models

By statistically analyzing traffic (either by sniffing or sampling packets), we were able to infer the overall anomalous behaviors of common name servers over time. Here we adopt the statistical models mentioned in [9] to identify the anomalous name servers.

Let x_1, x_2, ..., x_n be a random sample of size n from a p-dimensional normal distribution, the mean vector is given as formula (1):

$$\bar{x} = \frac{1}{n} \sum_{i=1}^{n} x_i \tag{1}$$

and the estimate of the covariance matrix is formulated as (2):

$$S = \frac{1}{n-1} \sum_{i=1}^{n} (x_i - \bar{x})(x_i - \bar{x})^T \tag{2}$$

For an assigned significance level α, if Δ_i is larger than Δ_*, then observation vector x_i is identified as an outlier. Here, each Δ_i is a function corresponding to the observation vector x_i, whereas the quantity Δ_* is the critical value to compare with Δ_i. The criterion for identifying the outliers is provided as (3):

$$\mathrm{Pr}\,obability[\Delta_i > \Delta_*] = \alpha \tag{3}$$

where Δ_i is given as formula (4):

$$\Delta_i = (x_i - \bar{x})^T S^{-1} (x_i - \bar{x}) \quad \text{for } i = 1, 2, ..., n \tag{4}$$

and Δ_* is given as formula (5):

$$\Delta_* = \frac{p(n-1)^2 F_{\alpha;p,n-p-1}}{n(n-p-1) + npF_{\alpha;p,n-p-1}} \tag{5}$$

4.2 Anomalous Behavior Detection Based on Associative Feature Analysis

We assign some features as the p-dimensional attribute to represent the DNS traffic. Basic features include source IP address, destination IP address, query type, action (query or response), and number of packets. Derived features include time-window based features which are constructed with similar characteristics during a given period time of T, since typically Denial of Service (DoS) and Cache Poisoning attacks involve hundreds of connections. The time-window based features here are listed as followed:

- CLT_QR: per client queries
- SRV_RS: per server responses
- CLT_QR_SRV: per client query the servers
- SRV_RS_CLT: per server response the clients

We separate the traffic according to action, the basic feature, which value 0 denoting query and value 1 denoting response respectively. At the same time, we divide the time-window based features into two groups: CLT_QR and CLT_QR_SRV designated to detect query frequency anomaly (QFA) and SRV_RS and SRV_RS_CLT designated to detect response frequency anomaly (RFA). Furthermore, payload anomaly (PLA) is detected according to formula (6):

$$P(t_i) = \begin{cases} 0, & t_i \in T_N \\ 1, & t_i \notin T_N \end{cases} \quad (\text{for } i = 1, 2, \ldots, n) \tag{6}$$

where $P(t_i)$ is the anomaly degree of each query type t_i and T_N is the set of normal query type defined in [2]. Then, the packets which $P(t_i)$ equals 1 will be picked out for further investigation.

5   Experimental Results

The results of PLA detection are demonstrated in Table 4(for Trace 1) and Table 5(for Trace 2) respectively. From the experimental results, we conclude that:

- The anomaly query type appeared most frequently in both the traces is Type 0, and this phenomena are explained by some offending ISPs as the result of global load balancing and geographic routing based on QoS algorithms. The packets appear to be harmless but very persistent. So the real cause needs further investigation.
- Some anomaly query types are launched by the same client such as Type 885 and 887 showed in Table 4. This suspicious client maybe a victim of software vulnerabilities, and it proved that our PLA detection is useful in DNS failure diagnosis.

Table 4. Anomaly Query Type(Trace 1)

Anomaly type	Number of IPs	Number of queries
0	4	36
39	1	1
375	1	13
885&887	1	20

Table 5. Anomaly Query Type(Trace 2)

Anomaly type	Number of IPs	Number of queries
0	9	175
39	3	3
301	1	1
349	1	4
611	1	7
887	1	16
1911	1	3

The results of the QFA detection of the trace data are presented in Fig.1.

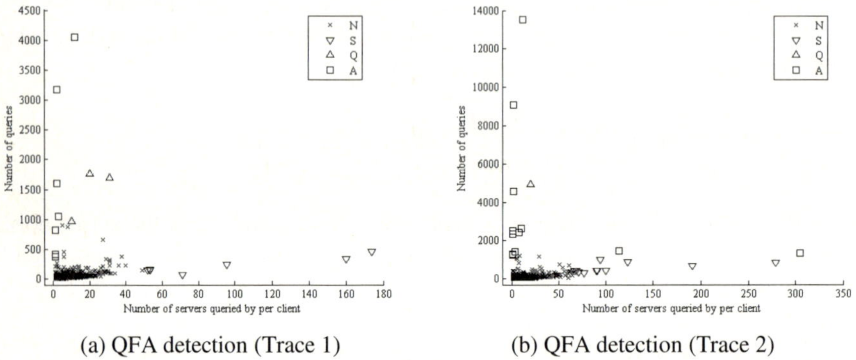

(a) QFA detection (Trace 1)   (b) QFA detection (Trace 2)

Fig. 1. QFA detection based on features of CLT_QR and CLT_QR_SRV

The points labeled N represent the normal query behaviors. The points labeled S are identified as an anomaly on the basis of CLT_QR_SRV alone; the points labeled Q are identified as an anomaly on the basis of CLT_QR alone; and points labeled A are identified as anomaly on the basis of associative feature analysis of the CLT_QR_SRV and CLT_QR at the significance level $\alpha = 0.001$. The anomalous queries launched by clients are detected more accurately in our QFA method than the isolated feature analysis. For example, as illustrated in Fig.1(b), if using only CLT_QR_SRV, the points which number of servers queried are 123,191 and 279 will be labeled as Anomaly because of their high values in CLT_QR_SRV, however, through our QFA detection, they are filtered accurately, and the point which queried 114 servers is labeled as anomaly.

Fig.2 demonstrates the results of RFA detection of the trace data based on SRV_RS_CLT and SRV_RS. The points labeled C are identified as an anomaly on the basis of SRV_RS_CLT alone; the points labeled SA are identified as a suspicious anomaly because some popular name servers usually served a great deal of clients and generated huge amount of responses, therefore, we will verify these points labeled SA combining with Large Scale Network Topology Measurement System in [10].

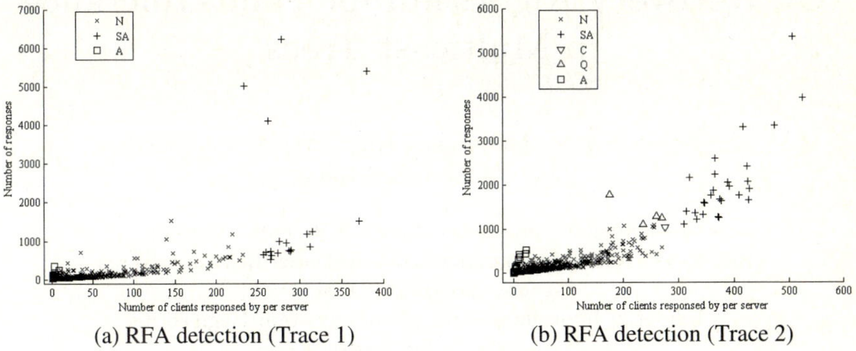

(a) RFA detection (Trace 1)   (b) RFA detection (Trace 2)

Fig. 2. RFA detection based on features of SRV_RS and SRV_RS_CLT

6   Conclusions and Future Work

In this paper, we outline an associative feature analysis approach based on statistical models to track the anomalous behaviors of common name servers. Through the detection of QFA, RFA and PLA, the anomalous behaviors of common name servers in the backbone are identified with an assigned significance level. The experimental results indicate the efficiency of our method in tracking the anomalous behaviors of name servers. To overcome the potential bias in the anomaly detection and to pinpoint the genuine causes of the anomalous behaviors, a further verification system is required to query the suspicious name servers in the future work.

References

1. Mockapetris, P.V.: Domain Names: Concepts and Facilities. RFC 1034, 1987
2. Mockapetris, P.V.: Domain Names: Implementation and Specification. RFC 1035, 1987
3. Pappas, V., Xu, Z.G., Lu, SW., Massey, D., Terzis, A., Zhang L.X.: Impact of Configuration Errors on DNS Robustness. In: SIGCOMM'04: Proceedings of the 2004 conference on Applications, technologies, architectures, and protocols for computer communications. ACM Press, New York (2004) 319–330
4. Thurrott, P.: Microsoft Suffers Another DoS Attack. http://www.winnetmag.com/ WindowsSecurity/Article/ArticleID/ 19770/WindowsSecurity 19770.html, 2001
5. Danzig, P.B., Obraczka, K., Kumar, A.: An Analysis of Wide-area Name Server Traffic: A Study of the Domain Name System. Proceeding of ACM SIGCOMM (1992) 281–292
6. Brownlee, N., Claffy, K., Nemeth, E.: DNS Measurements at a Root Server. IEEE Global Telecommunications Conference, San Antonio, TX (2001) 1672–1676
7. Jung, J., Sit, E., Balakrishnan, H., Morris, R.: DNS Performance and the Effectiveness of Caching. In: Proceedings of the First ACM SIGCOMM IMW, ACM Press (2001) 153–167
8. CAIDA. Nameserver DoS Attack October 2002. http://www.caida.org/projects/dns-analysis/, 2004
9. Ram, S., William, R.W.: A Statistical Technique for Computer Identification of Outliers in Multivariate Data. http://www.nasa.gov/centers/dryden/pdf/87795main_H-657.pdf
10. Zhang, H.L, Fang, B.X, Hu, M.Z.: A survey on Internet measurement and analysis. Journal of Software, (2003) 14(1):110–116

On Recovery Algorithm for Fault-Tolerance in Multicast Trees*

Seong-Soon Joo[1], Moonseong Kim[2], Yoo-Kyoung Lee[1],
and Young-Cheol Bang[3]

[1] Broadband Convergence Network Research Division
Electronics and Telecommunications Research Institute, Korea
`{ssjoo, leeyk}@etri.re.kr`
[2] School of Information and Communication Engineering
Sungkyunkwan University, Korea
`moonseong@ece.skku.ac.kr`
[3] Department of Computer Engineering
Korea Polytechnic University, Korea
`ybang@kpu.ac.kr`

Abstract. Since the multicast communication is the best technology to provide one to many communication, more and more service providers are using this technology to deliver the same service to multiple customers. These applications require seamless and real time services. With the deployment of the high-speed networks, real time services can be supported by reserving network resources in advance. In the case of seamless services, there should be no links or nodes failure in given networks. In real life networks, however, such failures are frequently happened more than we are expecting. In this paper, we propose a fault tolerant algorithm based on spanning trees that can be restorable using locally distributed mechanism in the case of multiple link-failures, if a tree existed. We also show that our algorithm can restore a multicast tree with constant recovery cost. We strongly believe our method can be generalized to apply to any type of tree-construction algorithm that requires the Quality of Service (QoS) in terms of reliability.

1   Introduction

Several protocols and algorithms have been developed and implemented for multicast communications. Algorithms for the tree construction in multicast protocols can be categorized as followings. Source-Based Algorithms (SBA) and Core-Based Algorithms (CBA) [1]. SBA constructs a tree rooted at source that originates and sends messages to each destination in the multicast group. SBA is currently used as the tree construction algorithm for Distance Vector Multicast Routing Protocol (DVMRP) [2], Protocol Independent Multicast Dense Mode (PIM-DM) [3], and Multicast Open Shortest Path First (MOSPF) [4]. On the other hand, CBA that is used for many-to-many multicasts selects a core node as

---

* Dr. Bang and Kim are the corresponding authors.

G. Min et al. (Eds.): ISPA 2006 Ws, LNCS 4331, pp. 358–367, 2006.

a root of the multicast tree. Then, a tree rooted at the core node is constructed to span all members in the multicast group. Thus, it is very important to select the best core node as much as possible. To send messages originated at source, messages are sent to the core and distributed to destinations along the path to the core node. Once messages are reached at the core node, messages are sent to remaining destinations. Multicast protocols that use CBA as a tree construction algorithm include Protocol Independent Multicast Sparse Mode (PIM-SM) [3] [5] and the Core-Based Tree (CBT) protocol [6] [7] [8] [9].

New communication services involving multicast communications and multimedia applications are becoming widespread. These applications require seamless and real time services within a certain delay bound. With the deployment of the high-speed networks and real time services can be supported by reserving network resources in advance. In the case of seamless services, there should be no links or nodes failure in given networks. In real life networks, however, such failures are frequently happened more than we are expecting. In the case that a node or link constituting a multicast tree fails, multicast members of subtree rooted at node that fails or has a failed outgoing link cannot receive message. This reason is that a multicast tree is disconnected. To support seamless and real-time services, hence, multicast routing should be reliable so that there must be a simple but very efficient mechanism that recovers from failures very fast.

In this paper, we introduce a very efficient algorithm for a spanning tree based multicast tree that can be restorable using locally distributed mechanism in the case of link-failure, if a tree exists. We also show that our algorithm can restore a multicast tree with constant recovery cost. We strongly believe our method can be generalized to apply to any type of tree-construction algorithm that requires the Quality of Service (QoS) in terms of reliability. The rest of the paper is organized as followings. In Section 2, we introduce motivation and preliminaries, and details of our algorithm is presented in Section 3. The performance evaluation is clearly analyzed in Section 4, and we conclude our paper in Section 5.

2   Preliminaries and Motivation

CBT forms a backbone within a connected group of nodes called cores. The backbone is formed by selecting one router, called the primary core, to serve as a connection point for the other cores, called secondary cores. Secondary cores remain disconnected from the primary core until they are required to join the multicast group. A router wishing to participate in the multicast communication sends a JOIN_REQUEST towards the nearest core. The message travels hop-by-hop on the shortest path to the core. When the message reaches a core or an on-tree node, a JOIN_ACK is sent back along the reverse path, forming a new branch from the tree to the requesting router. If the core that is reached is a secondary core and is off-tree, then it connects to a primary core using the same process.

In the event of a link failure, the child node that detects the failure follows a particular strategy in order to reconnect to the multicast tree. If that node's next hop to the nearest core is through one of its immediate children, it sends a message, called a FLUSH message, to its children. The FLUSH message travels down the tree, forwarded from parent to child, removing the connection between the parent and child. This message tears down the tree to the individual receivers, which then attempt to reconnect along their best path to a core. If the next hop to the core is not through a child, the detecting node attempts to reconnect itself by sending a REJOIN_REQUEST towards the nearest core and does not send the FLUSH message to its children. When the request reaches an on-tree node, that node returns a JOIN_ACK that rebuilds the branch down to the sending node. It also sends the REJOIN_REQUEST to its parent for forwarding to the primary core. The forwarding of the REJOIN_REQUEST back up the constructed tree is a mechanism used to detect loops that may have formed.

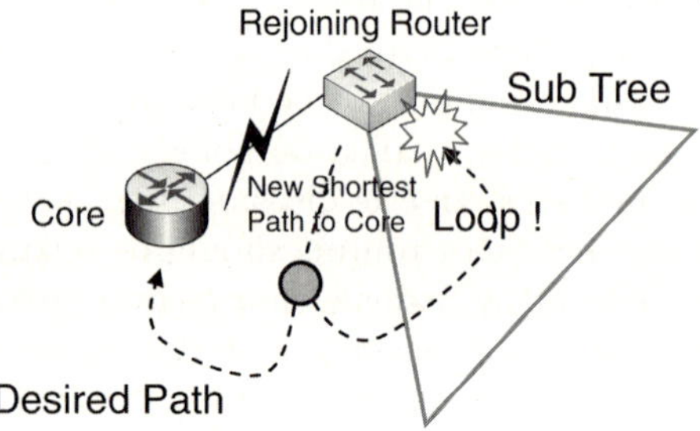

Fig. 1. Looping in a disconnected subtree

If a node receives a REJOIN_REQUEST that it originated, then a loop has formed, as shown in Fig. 1. The node detecting the loop removes the link to its parent by sending a message called a QUIT_REQUEST is received at the primary core, that core sends a unicast acknowledgment to the originator of the rejoin request to verify the absence of a loop. This unicast message is needed because if a loop had formed and the REJOIN_REQUEST was lost before it was returned to the originator, then the loop would not have been detected. However, if the originator never receives the acknowledgment, it can assume that a loop has formed, quit from its parent by sending a quit message, and attempt to rejoin again.

In order to resolve the problem of loops forming after link faults, the protocol specification of CBT [8] [9] was modified to eliminate the possibility of generating loops when faults are detected. Rather than trying to reconnect the subtree, the subtree is flushed and all group members in the subtree attempt to rejoin the tree individually (refer Fig. 4). This eliminates the problem of loop formation when rejoining the multicast tree. However, there are three drawbacks to this approach. A substantial delay in rebuilding the trees, a substantial increase in network traffic as the control messages, and overhead at the on-tree routers.

Schwiebert and Chintalapati have recently proposed a improved CBT for fault recovery [10], their algorithm hereafter referred to as ICBT. Although faults may seem to be uncommon events, the chance of faults is higher than one might expect. For example, it was recently observed that the Internet occasionally experiences periods of routing instability, also known as routing flaps, when the network can temporarily lose connectivity as floods of routing updates are processed [11]. This network instability could lead to timeouts that result in the flushing of subtrees due to these transient faults. Hence, authors modified the REJOIN_REQUEST in the original protocol. Instead of having the on-tree router sends the REJOIN_ACK, the REJOIN_ACK is sent by the core of the CBT (refer Fig. 5).

3   New Proposed Protocol Based on Spanning Trees

The REJOIN_REQUEST message generally was used to reconnect disconnected trees. But when the message routes through one of the descendants of the root of the disconnected subtree, a loop problem is formed (refer Fig. 1) and the tree is not reconnected. In the specification of CBT, the protocol eliminates the possibility of generating loop problem. Hence, the subtree is flushed and all multicast members in the subtree attempt to rejoin the tree individually (refer Fig. 4). But the method has lots of drawbacks, which are additional network traffic and extended reconnection time period. A recently proposed ICBT [10] rarely flushes the subtree (refer Fig. 5). It eliminates this overhead and delay in most cases. However, there exists the loop as ever. Though a descendant of the root of the disconnected subtree becomes the root of the disconnected subtree, ICBT cannot help avoiding the loop problem, repeatedly.

In order to reconnect with loop-free, we propose the new protocol based on Spanning Trees. For given a network, the core node firstly calculates the Spanning Tree and sends the Spanning Tree information to all nodes. Hence, each node of the network has the information which is neighbor nodes list in Spanning Tree. Also, the core node notifies that neighbor links are on-tree or off-tree. Initially, the set of on-tree links is current multicast tree as Fig. 2(a). The on-tree link is in multicast tree, otherwise it is off-tree in Spanning Tree. The multicast tree has to be composed of on-tree links. In the event, each node knows that its on-tree or off-tree links. This information is very important for quickly recovering. This example presents its using.

In the original specification of CBT, the root of the disconnected subtree would send a REJOIN_REQUEST toward the core using the appropriate unicast routing protocol. However, our proposed scheme needs not the appropriate unicast routing protocol, because all node has the neighbor node list information in Spanning Tree. Quite simply, the root of the disconnected subtree has to send a REJOIN_REQUEST toward neighbor nodes with not on-tree link, as shown in Fig. 2(b) and Fig. 3. As described in Fig. 2(c), if the neighbor node received the message is not on-tree router, then it forwards the message to neighbor node along the link in Spanning Tree, repeatedly. The subtree is, thus, reconnected as Fig. 2(d). Our proposed protocol has a constant recovery cost. It has been proved in next section.

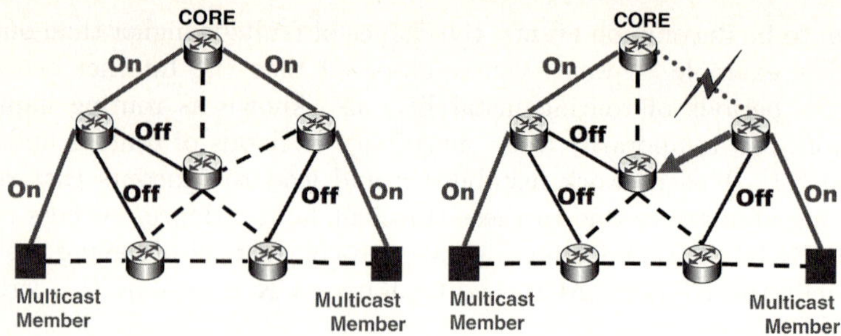

(a) Given network, Spanning Tree, (b) Link failure and recovery step 1 and initial multicast tree

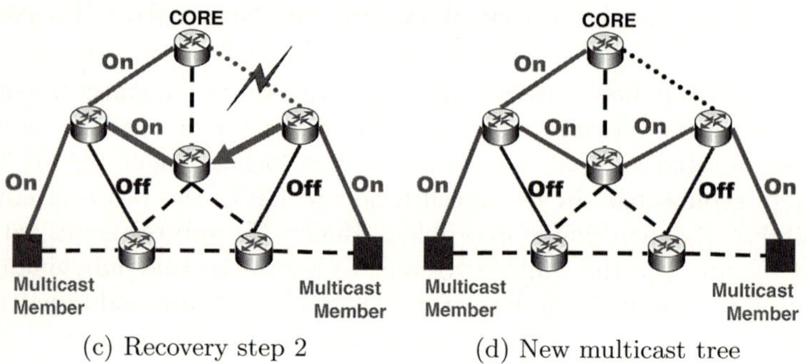

(c) Recovery step 2   (d) New multicast tree

Fig. 2. Scenario for proposed algorithm

4   Performance Analysis

Obviously, it is very difficult for us to make a precise performance comparison of all the schemes mentioned above in Section 2. So we just make simple scenario. We consider that a computer network is represented by a graph $G = (V, E)$ with $|V|$ nodes and $|E|$ links, where V is a set of nodes and E is a set of links, respectively. We assume that there exists a Spanning Tree, $\mathfrak{S}$, such that the tree degree is a constant, Deg, with tree height H. In other words, $|V| = \sum_{h=0}^{H} Deg^h$. Suppose there are $|M|$ nodes which are all members of multicast group M, and distribute uniformly in the $|V|$ nodes. We define the probability of multicast member existence is P_m. Hence, $|M|$ is $\sum_{h=0}^{H} \lfloor Deg^h \cdot P_m \rfloor$. And we obtain also the multicast tree $T(V_T, E_T) \subseteq \mathfrak{S}$, and then we can conjecture the range of $|E_T|$.

$$|M| - 1 \ \leq \ |E_T| \ \leq \ |V| - 1 \tag{1}$$

For the uniform random variable $|E_T|$, the expectation $E[\,|E_T|\,]$ is as follows:

$$|E_T|_{Avg} = E[\,|E_T|\,] \ = \ \left\lfloor \ \sum_{l=|M|-1}^{|V|-1} l \, / \Big(|V| - |M| + 1 \Big) \ \right\rfloor . \tag{2}$$

In order to resolve the problem of loops forming after link fault, the protocol specification of CBT [8][9] flushes the subtree and all group members in the subtree attempt to rejoin the tree individually. The average number of subtree's links is as follows:

$$|E_{subT}|_{Avg} = \left\lfloor \sum_{l=|M|-1}^{|E_T|_{Avg}} l \ / \Big(|E_T|_{Avg} - |M| + 2\Big) \right\rfloor . \tag{3}$$

And then the average number of group members in the subtree, $T_{subT}(V_{subT}, E_{subT})$ is $(|E_{subT}|_{Avg} + 1) \cdot P_m$. The probability such that a link (in $\Im$) is in on-tree is denoted P_{on} after flushing the subtree. Otherwise, $P_{off} = 1 - P_{on}$.

$$P_{on} = Prob\{ \ link \in T \setminus T_{subT} \ | \ ^\forall link \in \Im \ \} = \frac{|E_T|_{Avg} - |E_{subT}|_{Avg}}{|V| - 1} \tag{4}$$

For arbitrary node in the subtree, the average hop number of attempts for finding the on-tree node is as follows (See Fig. 3):

$$\sum_{i=1}^{C} i \cdot P_{off}^{i-1} \cdot P_{on} \tag{5}$$

where $C = |V| - (|E_T|_{Avg} - |E_{subT}|_{Avg} + 1)$.

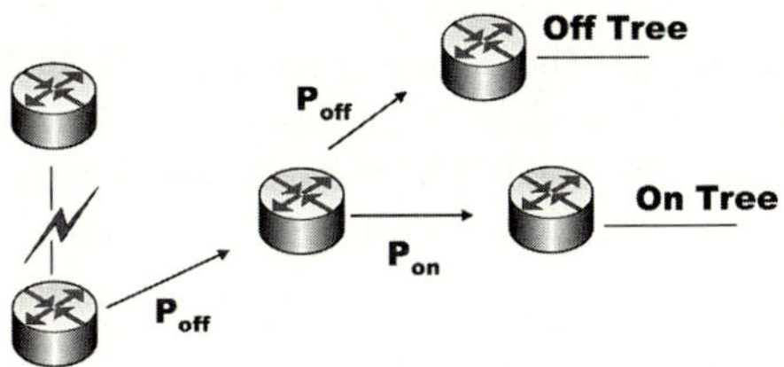

Fig. 3. Finding on-tree router

Since the on-tree router received REJOIN_REQUEST sends REJOIN_ACK, the recovery cost for CBT is as follows:

$$Cost_{CBT} = 2 \times \Big((|E_{subT}|_{Avg} + 1) \cdot P_m \Big) \times \sum_{i=1}^{C} i \cdot P_{off}^{i-1} \cdot P_{on} . \tag{6}$$

Let R_s be the root of the disconnected subtree and R_{on} be the first on-tree router received the REJOIN_REQUEST. After detecting link failure, R_s sends a LOOP_FORMED message to R_{on}. And then R_{on} becomes the root of the disconnected subtree. The average number of attempts for finding R_{on} (the Next Subtree Root 2, in Fig. 5) is as follows equation (8).

$$P_{onsub} = Prob\{ \ node \in V_{subT} \setminus \{R_s\} \ | \ ^\forall node \in V_T \setminus \{R_s\} \ \} = \frac{|E_{subT}|_{Avg}}{|E_T|_{Avg}} \tag{7}$$

$$\sum_{i=1}^{\infty} i \cdot P_{onsub}^{i-1} \cdot (1 - P_{onsub}) \tag{8}$$

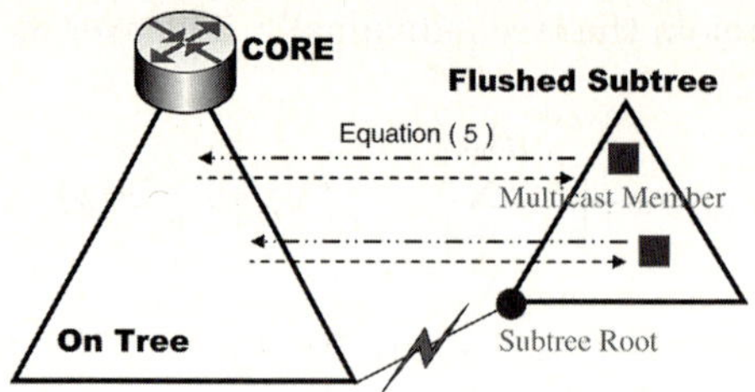

Fig. 4. CBT recovery mechanism

Also, each attempt's cost is as follows equation (10).

$$P_{on} \; = \; Prob\{ \; link \in T \setminus FL \; | \; {}^{\forall}link \in \mathfrak{F} \setminus FL \; \} \; = \; \frac{|E_T|_{Avg} - 1}{|V| - 2}, \tag{9}$$

where $FL = \{failure\ link\}$.

$$\sum_{i=1}^{|V|-1-|E_T|_{Avg}} i \cdot (1 - P_{on})^{i-1} \cdot P_{on} \tag{10}$$

When R_{on} receives the LOOP_FORMED message, it sends a REVERSE_EDGES message up the tree to R_s. R_s then sends a REVERSE_ACK toward R_{on}. A new REJOIN_REQUEST is initiated by R_{on}. Instead of having the on-tree router send the REJOIN_ACK, the REJOIN_ACK is sent by the core of the CBT in ICBT [10]. The average REJOIN_REQUEST and REJOIN_ACK cost are as follows equation (12).

$$\tilde{H} = \left\lfloor \log_{Deg} \left((|E_T|_{Avg} - |E_{subT}|_{Avg} - 1)(Deg - 1)/Deg + 1 \right) \right\rfloor \tag{11}$$

$$\sum_{h=0}^{\tilde{H}} h \cdot Deg^h / \left(|E_T|_{Avg} - |E_{subT}|_{Avg} - 1 \right) \tag{12}$$

Therefore, the average recovery cost for ICBT is as follows:

$$Cost_{ICBT} \; = \; 3 \times equation(10) \times equation(8) + 2 \times equation(12) . \tag{13}$$

However, our proposed protocol is assumed that one has the spanning tree $\mathfrak{F}$ information. So it has to easily find the on tree link node in $\mathfrak{F}$ with no loop. We calculate the average recovery cost is as follows equation (15).

$$P_{on} = Prob\{link \in Link \; | \; {}^{\forall}link \in LINK\} = \frac{|E_T|_{Avg} - |E_{subT}|_{Avg} - 1}{|V| - |E_{subT}|_{Avg} - 2}, \tag{14}$$

where $Link = T \setminus T_{subT} \setminus \{failure\ link\}$ and $LINK = \mathfrak{F} \setminus T_{subT} \setminus \{failure\ link\}$.

$$Cost_{Our} \; = \; 2 \times \sum_{i=1}^{|V|-1-|E_T|_{Avg}} i \cdot P_{off}^{i-1} \cdot P_{on}, \tag{15}$$

where $P_{off} = 1 - P_{on}$.

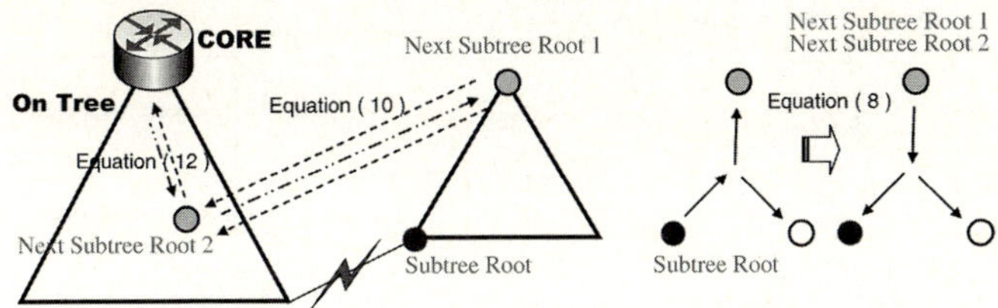

Fig. 5. ICBT recovery mechanism

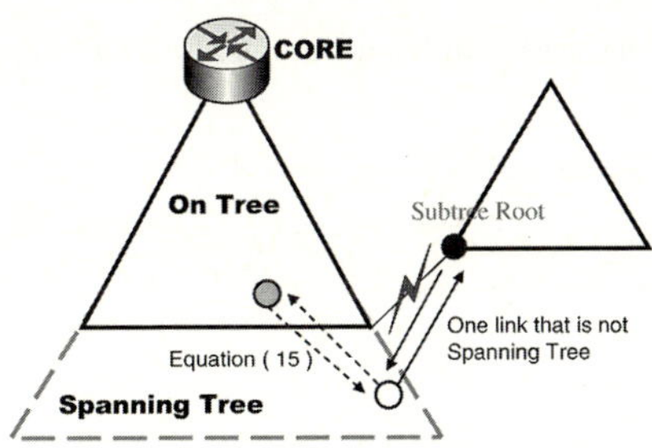

Fig. 6. Our recovery mechanism

We set several parameters to calculate the numerical result of each scheme. In Fig. 7, we take $Deg = 2$, $P_m = 0.2$, and $2 \leq H \leq 15$. In particular, $|V| = 65,535$ for $H = 15$. We can see that the performance of our proposed scheme is much better than those of the other two. Furthermore, $Cost_{Our}$ is an almost constant function.

Theorem 1. *Let Deg be a constant is great than 1. Then our recovery cost, $Cost_{Our}$, is always a constant when the height H is large.*

Proof. Since $Deg > 1$ and $|V| = \sum_{h=0}^{H} Deg^h$, $\lim_{H \to \infty} |V| = \infty$. Let P_m be a positive probability of multicast member existence. Then $0 < P_m \leq 1$. Since $|M| = |V| \cdot P_m$, $\lim_{H \to \infty} |M| = \infty$. Hence, because $|M| - 1 \leq |E_T|_{Avg} \leq |V| - 1$, $\lim_{H \to \infty} |E_T|_{Avg} = \infty$.

Since $|E_T|_{Avg} < |V|$, we take $|V| = k \cdot |E_T|_{Avg}$, $\forall k > 1$. $\lim_{H \to \infty} \left(|V| - 1 - |E_T|_{Avg} \right) = |E_T|_{Avg} \cdot \left(k - 1 \right) - 1 = \infty$. So, we obtain $2 \sum_{i=1}^{\infty} i \cdot P_{off}^{i-1} \cdot P_{on}$ as $Cost_{Our}$ when H is large.

$$2 \sum_{i=1}^{\infty} i \cdot P_{off}^{i-1} \cdot P_{on} = 2P_{on} \sum_{i=1}^{\infty} i \cdot P_{off}^{i-1} \approx 2P_{on} \sum_{i=1}^{\infty} \frac{d}{d\, P_{off}} P_{off}^i$$

$$\approx 2P_{on} \frac{d}{d\, P_{off}} \sum_{i=1}^{\infty} P_{off}^i = 2P_{on} \frac{d}{d\, P_{off}} \left(\frac{P_{off}}{1 - P_{off}} \right) = 2P_{on} \frac{1}{(1 - P_{off})^2}$$

$$= \frac{2}{P_{on}} .$$

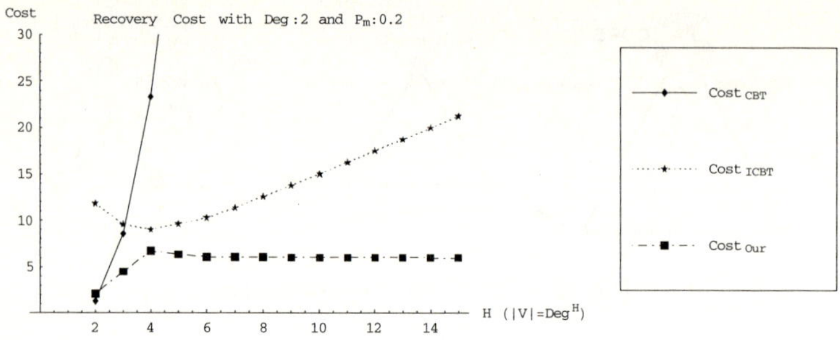

Fig. 7. Recovery costs under different H, $Deg = 2$, and $P_m = 0.2$

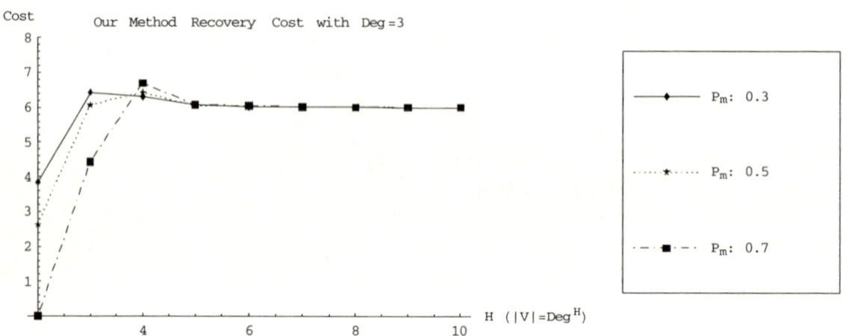

Fig. 8. Our protocol recovery cost under different H and $Deg = 3$

Since P_{on}, equation (14), is a constant, trivially, $Cost_{Our}$ is $\dfrac{2}{P_{on}} \in O(1)$. See Fig. 8. $\qquad\square$

5   Conclusion

With the proliferation of multimedia group applications, the construction of multicast trees satisfying the QoS requirements is becoming a problem of the prime importance. Furthermore, with the deployment of the high-speed networks, real time service can be supported by reserving network resources in advance. In the case of seamless services, there should be no links or nodes failure in given networks. However, such failures are frequently happened more than we are expecting in real life networks. In the case that a node or link constituting a multicast tree fails, multicast members of subtree rooted at node that fails or has a failed outgoing link cannot receive message. To support seamless and real-time service, multicast routing should be reliable so that there must be a simple but very efficient mechanism that recovers from failures very fast. In this paper, we propose a very efficient algorithm for a spanning tree based multicast tree that can be restorable using locally distributed mechanism in the case of multiple link-failures, if a tree exists. We also show that our algorithm can restore a multicast tree in constant recovery cost. We strongly believe our method can be generalized to apply to any type of tree-construction algorithm that requires the QoS in terms of reliability.

References

1. B. Wang and J. C. Hou, "Multicast Routing and its QoS Extension: Problems, Algorithms, and Protocols," IEEE Networks, January, 2000.
2. T. Pusateri, "Distance Vector Routing Protocol", draft-ietf-idmr-dvmrp-v3-07, 1998.
3. D. Estrin *et al.*, "Protocol Independent Multicast (PIM) Sparse Mode/Dense Mode," Internet draft, 1996.
4. J. Moy, "Multicast Extension to OSPF," Internet draft, 1998.
5. S. Deering *et al.*, "Protocol Independent Multicast-Sparse Mode (PIM-SM): Motivation and Architecture," Internet draft, 1998.
6. A. Ballardie, P. Francis, J. Crowcroft, "Core Based Trees (CBT)," ACM SIGCOMM, pp. 85-95, 1993.
7. A. Ballardie, "Core Based Trees (CBT) Multicast Routing Architecture," RFC 2201, Internet Engineering Task Force, September 1997.
8. A. Ballardie, "Core Based Trees (CBT version 2) Multicast Routing – Protocol Specification –," RFC 2189, Internet Engineering Task Force, September 1997.
9. A. Ballardie, B. Cain, and Z. Zhang, "Core Based Trees (CBT version 3) Multicast Routing – Protocol Specification –," Internet Draft, draft-ietf-idmr-cbt-spec-v3-01.txt, Internet Engineering Task Force, August 1998.
10. L. Schwiebert and R. Chintalapati, "Improved Fault Recovery for Core Based Trees," Computer Communications, vol. 23, pp. 816-824, 2000.
11. C. Labovitz, R. Malan, and F. Jahanian, "Internet Routing Instability," IEEE/ACM Transactions on Networking, vol. 6, pp. 515-528, 1998.

A Low Cost and Effective Link Protection Approach for Enhanced Survivability in Optical Transport Networks

Francesco Palmieri and Ugo Fiore

Federico II University, Centro Servizi Didattico Scientifico, Via Cinthia 45,
80126 Napoli, Italy
`{fpalmieri, ufiore}@unina.it`

Abstract. A well-recognized problem in high-speed all-optical networks is that fibres and switches frequently fail. When a network, designed in a non-robust way, encounters such kind of problem it can become highly vulnerable, i.e. experiencing large fractions of connections disruption. This makes resiliency a key issue in network design and thus efficient protection schemas are needed so that when a failure occurs, the involved traffic must be immediately rerouted over a predetermined backup path without affecting the user-perceivable service quality. In this paper we propose a new protection scheme, achieving robustness through a new low complexity link protection algorithm, which can be used to select end-to-end totally disjoint backup paths between each couple of nodes in a mesh network, providing restoration speeds comparable to ring restoration. Many research efforts in this area are targeted at optimization, with the objective of using as much capacity as possible while trying to guarantee adequate levels of protection. The design requirements for our scheme were instead simplicity and performance, aiming at providing a way of quickly computing backup paths for each link without taking resource optimization issues into consideration. We believe that the novel formulations and results of this paper, may be of interest for a network operator wishing to improve connections reliability, at a low implementation cost.

Keywords: Network resiliency, Link protection, Fast rerouting.

1   Introduction

Because of the convergence of voice, video, and broadband data services that has taken place in the last years, service providers' transport infrastructures now carry huge quantities of critical, delay and loss-sensitive traffic. In this environment backbone transport network robustness become a key element in network management and design and better than "best effort" protection against network failures will be one of the most important QoS parameters. Link and component faults in the network are, because of the statistical nature of these events, a serious issue that could impede achieving the reliable, timely delivery of data and the desired quality of service. In the past years backbone faults were only handled with redundancy and dynamic routing protocols that automatically updated, at the fault detection time, the network topology and computed new routes that avoid the failure, but in most cases the switchover time

G. Min et al. (Eds.): ISPA 2006 Ws, LNCS 4331, pp. 368–376, 2006.

due to the traditional routing protocol convergence was not fast enough to prevent real-time data and voice service disruptions. For example, in a modern all-optical wavelength switched network, allowing transmission speeds of up to 40 Gbps (OC-768), the failure of a network element (e.g., fiber link, cross-connect node, etc.) can cause the failure of hundreds of high speed optical channels, thereby leading to very large data loss [1], so fault processing and restoration times are required to be as short as possible (usually lasting less than 50ms) to avoid any user perceivable degradation. A straightforward solution for protecting mission-critical connections from a single link or node failure is to use a predetermined backup path, link or node-disjoint from the active one, from the same source (ingress) node to the same destination (egress) node. Such a failure-independent scheme can realize very fast restoration by eliminating route computation and ensures that no single failure can cause blocking on a network path. The problem of finding such pre-determined backup paths, operating as protection cycles around the failure is, therefore, strictly combinatorial on the network topology graph, without any relation to the probability of failures [2]. This technique has been originally introduced in SDH networks, typically based on a physical ring topology. On a network element failure in such a ring all traffic may be routed along the fault-free "curve" of the ring, given that enough capacity is available. Such a network element may be either a single fiber link or a node, hence these protection cycles provide protection against both link and node failures. Similarly, as carriers shift their attention from ring-based solutions to meshed networks, the same technique can be exploited to enable node as well as link protection in multi-homed meshes, by determining the better available path cycling around the failure. Resiliency (and hence robustness) in meshed networks can now be achieved by several mechanisms varying from path protection/restoration, through dedicated link protection, to shared path protection [3, 4, 5, 6, 7].

Our work focuses on the routing issue for protection switching. In particular, we study the probl em of finding for each link a totally disjoint near-optimal protection path in the network, so that a single link failure will not disrupt the network service that will be immediately restored along the pre-computed protection path. We are also implicitly concerned with finding for each link a set of backup path configurations that minimize the blocking probabilities. A connection over a link detecting a loss of signal may find itself blocked if no link or wavelength is available on the backup path, that is, any resource on its pre-determined backup path is being used at that moment by another connection (or failed on its own merit). However, the objectives of the different connections can be in conflict with each other and there may be many configurations in which reducing the blocking probability of one connection is only possible at the expense of increasing it for another. In this scenario, we propose a novel link protection mechanism that is characterized by a relatively good computational efficiency in determining near-optimal backup paths, and aiming to ensure through the above paths restoration speeds comparable to ring restoration. In fact these advantages made this type of link protection very suitable for MPLS-based networks [8] implementing fast restoration policies through pre-signaled backup paths. We considered a pure link protection mechanism, meaning that in case of link failure, the aggregated flow carried by the link is rerouted around the failed connection on the best available protection path, thus requiring an edge connectivity of at least 2 from the network, and that each link is assigned an available protection path. Our solution can cope with one failure at a time, and thus requires that all the previous failures (as well as repairs) have been taken care of and reported to the entity that computes the backup paths. This requires extensive signaling [7], and may be difficult and inefficient, especially if the rate of failures and repairs is high. The bandwidth on the protection paths can be reserved and therefore each link capacity can be divided into three categories: capacity allocated to primary connections, protection capacity reserved for restoration of connections affected by failures of other links, and unused capacity. Knowing the demands' volumes in advance, the network flows can be redistributed such that nearly 100% of connections affected by a link failure can be restored. Of course, this must be done at the cost of reducing the overall network utilization degree under normal conditions.

The outline of the rest of this paper is as follows. Section 2 presents some background material related to protection switching, to provide a better understanding of the context in which we propose our algorithm. The model, the basic ideas, and a detailed description of our algorithm are discussed in Section 3. Finally, Section 4 presents our conclusions and directions for future work.

2 Protection Switching Strategies and Choices

Protection switching is a mechanism conceived for providing reliable connection-oriented services resilient to network failures. With protection switching, a network provisions a protection (backup) path between the source and destination of each link or traffic engineered path when a connection request is initiated. The working and protection links and paths are routed in the network such that any network failure would affect at most one of them. In a normal situation, the source/destination pair of a connection communicate over the working link or primary path. However, when there is a network failure breaking the working path, the source and destination can immediately switch their communication channel to the protection path, so that transmission of data will not be disrupted by the network failure. From the perspective of the end users, the link failure is invisible to them as long as switching is fast enough. There are two prevailing schemes to guard against link failure in protection switching: path and link protection. Path protection reserves network resources for a preset protection path in addition to the primary path. Since it is impossible to foresee which link on the primary path will fail, the system allocates another path, which is completely link-disjoint from the primary path, that is, the primary path shares no common link with its associated protection path. When a link fails, the source and destination nodes of a call on the failed link are informed of the failure, and the communication is switched to the protection path that can be totally dedicated to the primary path, without any common resource with other backup paths or shared with other paths to improve network resource utilization.

On the other side, Link Protection reroutes all the connections on the failed link around it. When accepting a connection request, the link protection scheme will reserve the network resource for the associated protection path. Clearly, in link protection, the primary link and its backup path must be fiber-disjoint so that the network is survivable under single-fiber failures. Note that the protection path connects the two nodes adjacent to the failed link. When a link failure occurs, the node adjacent to and upstream of the failed link immediately redirects the traffic along the predetermined protection path to the node on the other end of the failed link to restore transmission. The backup path in link protection can be determined according to two different strategies, namely Dedicated and Shared link protection:

- In dedicated-link protection, at the time of connection setup, for each link of the primary path routing the connection, a backup path and wavelength are reserved around that link, and are dedicated to that connection.
- In shared-link protection, at the connection setup time, for each link of the primary path, a backup path and wavelength are reserved around that link. However, the backup wavelengths reserved on the links of the backup path may be shared with other backup paths. As a result, backup channels are multiplexed among different failure scenarios (which are not expected to occur simultaneously), and therefore shared link protection is more capacity efficient when compared with dedicated-link protection.

Both models have their pros and cons. When failure recovery must be instantaneous, it is adequate to use 1+1 protection, namely, transmit the same information on both the protection path and the primary path. Such a scheme, however, requires almost totally dedicated resources along each backup path and is normally useful only for the most critical traffic streams that are absolutely intolerant to recovery delay. Otherwise, if a small recovery delay is acceptable, the protection path need only be used as a backup after a failure on the primary path is detected. In that case, the backup path can be shared, fully or partially, among several links and connections. In general, however, it may not be possible to allocate a dedicated backup path on the same wavelength around each link of the primary connection path, thus dedicated link protection is very often totally unfeasible. Hence, we will not further consider dedicated-link protection.

In the context of this work we focus our attention on link protection since some advantages of link protection over path protection have certain direct implications in the area of network management and may be consequently of some interest for a network operator. The drawback with Path Protection is that information about a failure has to propagate back to the source nodes of all connections routed through the failed link. In some cases, the time taken for this propagation to the source may not be acceptable. Path protection only requires that the source and destination node be aware that a failure occurred somewhere along the primary path. Localization of the failure is not important, since protection takes place in the same way regardless of where the failure occurs. Thus, once the protection path has been set up, the network management does not need to have detailed knowledge of the nature of the failure to implement protection. Consequently, path protection can then be better handled by higher layer mechanisms. For link protection, local information is needed by the nodes adjacent to the failure, but there is no need to manage protection on a path-by-path basis. Very high speed protection arrangements, usually handled at the lower layer can therefore be better ensured by link protection. Typically the Network Management when handling protection requires a sufficiently detailed knowledge about the location of the failed link and of course about the available restoration paths. Thus, our choice is due to the fact that visibility by the network management system across layers may be useful for performing protection more efficiently. Link protection schemes usually allocate backup paths for each link separately for each path [9], [10], while aiming at optimizing resource usage. This has the advantage of providing easier service differentiation and better bandwidth utilization. However, all the computation required must be repeated at each connection request. This may not be efficient, if we recall that this kind of backup paths should be short-lived, and are deemed to be substituted by better-suited paths as soon as signaling provides them. In our model, paths are computed for each link, irrespective of usage. The drawback is that the entire link active capacity must be switched on the backup path, thus limiting the usable capacity of any link to half its residual capacity. However, this approach benefits of much faster backup path computation, that can be therefore performed more often, to accommodate for topology or traffic changes.

3 Our Link Protection Algorithm

We consider a circuit-switched all-optical network. There are n nodes and m links in the network and each link has a fixed number of wavelengths. In our resiliency model fixed alternate path rerouting is used to protect the traffic flowing on each link. This technique involves maintaining at least a pre-determined link disjoint route cycling around each link termination pair (v_i, v_j). The overall network is required to be totally resilient to any single link failure. The naïve algorithm for calculating all the protection cycles is based on temporarily removing one link at a time and solving the *Single Source Shortest Paths* (*SSSP*) problem for one of the terminations of the removed link. The whole protection framework can be modeled as below.

3.1 Problem Statement

Let $G=(V,E)$ be an undirected, unweighted graph. We let $|V|=n$ and $|E|=m$. The *distance* $\delta(v_i, v_j)$ from v_i to v_j in the graph is the smallest length of a path from v_i to v_j in the graph. We denote, for the generic link (v_i, v_j) the node v_i as the *start node* and v_j as the *end node*. The next hop $\pi(v_i, v_k)$ is the first node in the shortest path from v_i to v_k in the graph. If (v_i, v_j) is a link in the graph, and more than one equal-cost shortest path from v_i to v_k exists in the graph, we also denote by $\Pi(v_i, v_k)$ the set of next hops of the shortest paths from v_i to v_k. The algorithm computes the backup distances, i.e. the distances along the backup paths. For each edge (v_i, v_j) of the graph, the *backup distance* $\beta(v_i, v_j)$ is the minimum distance of vertex v_j from vertex v_i in $G\backslash(v, v_j)$. A *backup path* is one of the corresponding paths. We assume that G is bridge-connected. A *bridge* of a graph is a link whose removal disconnects the graph. The presence of bridges can be detected in linear time [11], so that a preprocessing phase can discover them and prevent further processing. Anyway, in line of principle, the occurrence of bridges should be avoided at network design time.

3.2 Outline of the Protection Path Selection Algorithm

The backup distance $\beta(v_i, v_j)$ is computed as follows: the alternate path from v_i to v_j, i.e. not comprising the edge (v_i, v_j) must touch an intermediate vertex v_k. The shortest backup path of (v_i, v_j) is then the composition of the shortest path from v_i to v_k, plus the shortest path from v_k to v_j, minimized over all the intermediate vertices. It should be noticed that the shortest path (in the initial graph) from v_i to v_k might include (v_i,v_j), and so that path would not provide a backup alternative in case of failure of (v_i,v_j). It is straightforward to verify if v_j belongs to the shortest path from the start v_i to an intermediate v_k. If it does, it must be the first hop, otherwise a shorter path could be obtained by short-cutting all the nodes traversed between v_i and v_j.

$$\pi(v_i,v_k) \neq v_j \ . \tag{1}$$

To check that the start node v_i does not belong to the shortest path from an intermediate v_k to the end node v_j, one should follow that path entirely, because by the same argument used above, if v_i belongs to such a shortest path, it can only be the next-to-last node (penultimate hop). But if the graph is undirected, the existence of a shortest path from v_k to v_j implies the existence of a shortest path from v_k to v_j, obtained by simply reversing the order in which nodes are traversed. Then, the same test as in (1) will suffice for determining the suitability of v_k as an intermediate node.

$$\pi(v_j,v_k) \neq v_i \ . \tag{2}$$

In cycles having an even number of vertices, it might also happen that, as in the leftmost graph in figure 1 below, the next hop of v_i going towards v_k is v_j, barring the use of v_k as a suitable intermediate node, and the next hop of v_j going towards v_l is v_i, barring the use of v_l as a suitable intermediate node.

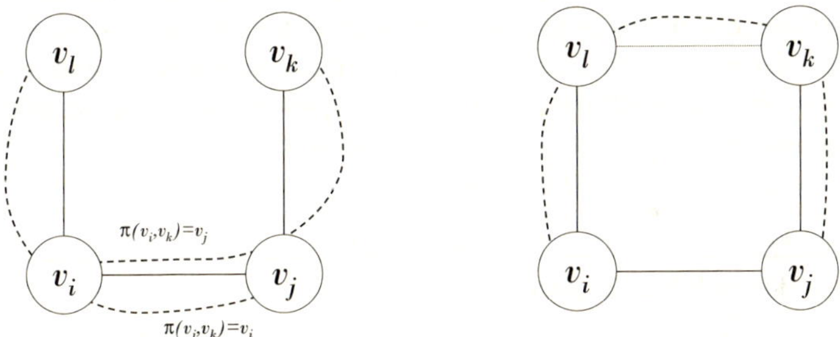

Fig. 1. Special case (left) and backup path for an even cycle (right)

When v_k is reachable from v_l, however, there exist other (equal-cost) paths from v_i to v_k and v_j to v_l, respectively using v_l and v_k as next hops, so that $|\Pi(v_i,v_k)| > 1$. Thus the alternate path to be used as backup path for the link (v_i,v_j) is given by the nodes in the cycle. A node v_k can't be used as a valid intermediate only when:

    a)   the shortest path from the end node to the intermediate v_k is unique, and
    b)   the start node is the next hop of that shortest path, that is, v_k is a valid intermediate node for the backup path of (v_i,v_j) iff

$$\left|\Pi(v_j,v_k)\right| > 1 \quad \vee \quad \pi(v_j,v_k) \neq v_i \ . \tag{3}$$

This condition is easy to check and doesn't increase the complexity of the inner loop.

can be arbitrarily chosen, the resulting sensor network tolerates sensors disconnections/connections due to failures of sensors. Next future works will concern other analysis and experiments and the introduction of path learning capability at nodes in order to achieve further performance improvements.

References

1. Li, X., Kim, Y., Govindan, R., Hong, W.: Multi-dimensional range queries in sensor networks. In: SenSys '03: Proceedings of the 1st international conference on Embedded networked sensor systems, New York, NY, USA, ACM Press (2003) 63–75
2. Moro, G., Monti, G.: W-Grid: a Cross-Layer Infrastructure for Multi-Dimensional Indexing, Querying and Routing in Ad-Hoc and Sensor Networks. In: P2P 2006: Sixth IEEE International Conference on Peer-To-Peer Computing, Cambridge, UK, IEEE Computer Society (2006) 210–220
3. Karp, B., Kung, H.: GPRS: greedy perimeter stateless routing for wireless networks. In: MobiCom '00: Proceedings of the 6th annual international conference on Mobile computing and networking, ACM Press (2000) 243–254
4. Intanagonwiwat, C., Govindan, R., Estrin, D., Heidemann, J., Silva, F.: Directed diffusion for wireless sensor networking. IEEE Trans.Netw. $11(1)$ (2003) 2–16
5. Ye, F., Luo, H., Cheng, J., Lu, S., Zhang, L.: A two-tier data dissemination model for large-scale wireless sensor networks. In: MobiCom '02: Proceedings of the 8th annual international conference on Mobile computing and networking, New York, NY, USA, ACM Press (2002) 148–159
6. Xiao, L., Ouksel, A.: Tolerance of localization imprecision in efficiently managing mobile sensor databases. In: MobiDE '05: Proceedings of the 4th ACM international workshop on Data engineering for wireless and mobile access, New York, NY, USA, ACM Press (2005) 25–32
7. Ratnasamy, S., Karp, B., Shenker, S., Estrin, D., Govindan, R., Yin, L., Yu, F.: Data-centric storage in sensornets with ght, a geographic hash table. Mob. Netw. Appl. $8(4)$ (2003) 427–442
8. Greenstein, B., Estrin, D., Govindan, R., Ratnasamy, S., Shenker, S.: Difs: A distributed index for features in sensor networks. In: Proceedings of first IEEE WSNA, IEEE Computer Society (2003) 163–173
9. Moro, G., Monti, G., Ouksel, A.: Routing and localization services in self-organizing wireless ad-hoc and sensor networks using virtual coordinates. In: ICPS'06: International Conference on Pervasive Services. IEEE Computer Society (2006) 243–246
10. Ouksel, A., Moro, G.: G-Grid: A class of scalable and self-organizing data structures for multi-dimensional querying and content routing in P2P networks. In: Agents and Peer-to-Peer Computing, Springer-Verlag (2004) 123–137

Making Wide-Area, Multi-site MPI Feasible Using Xen VM

Masaki Tatezono[1], Naoya Maruyama[1], and Satoshi Matsuoka[1,2]

[1] Tokyo Institute of Technology, 2-12-1 Ohokayama, Meguro, Tokyo, 152–8552 Japan
{masaki.tatezono, naoya.maruyama, matsu}@is.titech.ac.jp
[2] National Institute of Informatics, 2-2-1 Hitotsubashi, Chiyoda, Tokyo, 101–8430
Japan

Abstract. Although multi-site MPI execution has been criticized in the past as being "impractical" due to limitations in network latency and bandwidth, we believe many of the obstacles can be overcome by various means for wider classes of applications than previously believed. One such technique is transparent dynamic migration of MPI, coupled with aggressively performance-oriented overlay networks, assuming availability of gigabits of bandwidth on future WANs. The problem, of course, is to investigate the exact implications to application performances given the arsenal of such techniques, but such work has been quite sparse. Our current work involves using Xen as the underlying virtual machine layer to implement such migration, along with performance-optimizing migration strategies—this particular paper deals with performance evaluations of MPI on Xen VMs including what are the possible performance hindrances, implications of migrations, as well as the effect of variations in latencies and bandwidth parameters as realized by the overlay network using a software network emulator.

Keywords: MPI, cluster computing, grid computing, virtualization.

1 Introduction

Executing MPI on wide-area, multi-site clusters has been considered impractical. One of the reasons for this impracticality is heterogeneity of clusters. Using multiple clusters with different hardware and software is hard for typical applications users. Another reason is regarded as low performance of wide-area networks, imposing high communication overhead. Finally, the asymmetric networks caused by firewalls and NATs make multi-site MPI execution further difficult.

To achieve efficient multi-site MPI execution, we envision that the application user runs his programs on a *virtual cluster* that actually runs on multiple physical clusters connected with future high-speed wide-area networks. The virtual cluster hides heterogeneity of different system configuration using virtual machine monitors (VMMs) such as Xen [1]. It also hides the network asymmetry using overlay networks as a virtual network substrate. Moreover, it can exploit dynamic migration of VMs to use available resources more efficiently. For example, when a cluster of faster CPUs and larger memory becomes available for

G. Min et al. (Eds.): ISPA 2006 Ws, LNCS 4331, pp. 387–396, 2006.

use, an already-running virtual cluster can be migrated to the cluster for better performance.

There exists some past work that attempts to combine VMMs with overlay networks for multi-site MPI execution, such as Violin [2]. However, its evaluation of MPI performance has been done only with a single program, HPL, in a single site. Also, as far as we know, there is no performance evaluation on multi-site, wide area virtual clusters. Thus, the performance of more diverse set of applications, running on wide-area overlay networks, is still unknown and remains to be evaluated.

The primary purpose of this paper is a study of performance of MPI on a virtual cluster using Xen as a VMM and various overlay network configurations. First, we compare performance of NAS Parallel Benchmarks (NPB) on Xen-based virtual cluster with the native cluster with the same hardware configuration, consisting of up to 128 physical nodes. Next, we investigate the effect of overlay networks to application performance using different overlay network implementations.

These experimental studies show that the performance of Xen for MPI execution platform is comparable to native machines in terms of pure CPU performance. The average performance degradation of virtual clusters was less than 20%. We also show that doubling the number of nodes from 32 to 64 by adding another cluster cannot lead to speedups due to the bottleneck inter-cluster link. Based on these results, we discuss how to mitigate such network bottlenecks and the requirements to achieve high-performance MPI execution on virtual clusters.

2   Virtualization of Compute Hosts

We describe requirements on virtualization of compute hosts. First, the performance overhead should be minimal. Second, it must support light-weight dynamic VM migration. Third, it should not impose particular constraints to user-level programs; In other words, off-the-shelf MPI implementations and its applications should work with little adaptation.

With the recent advance in virtualization techniques, we see these requirements are achievable using available VMMs, such as Xen and VMWare ESX Server [3]. For example, Xen is reported to migrate a VM within 60ms on a LAN environment [4], with negligible CPU performance overhead [1]. Thus, we choose to use existing implementations of VMMs. We describe our current instance of this approach using Xen in Section 4.

3   Overlay Networks

We describe key requirements on underlying overlay networks where virtual compute hosts are hosted, and our approach to them.

3.1   Requirements

We require the following four criteria to be satisfied.

Providing Constant IP Addresses. To support migration of MPI processes, hosts' IP addresses need to be constant. The reason for this is that typical MPI implementations do not allow IP addresses to change at run time. We see this complexity should be handled by the overlay network layer, instead of the virtual cluster user.

Low Overhead. Since we intend virtual clusters as MPI execution platforms, the overhead needs to be kept minimal.

Security. To operate across WANs we need some level of security. At a minimum, we require overlay networks to have standard secure authentication mechanisms, such as SSL or SSH. Furthermore, since some user may require encryption of messages in communication links, it is preferable to be able to support message encryption.

Reachability of Compute Nodes. Typical MPI, such as MPICH [5], make a connection for each pair of participating processes, thus requiring that each process is able to connect to every other process. Although this requirement is not an issue on LAN clusters, such implementations cannot operate across firewalls and NATs. Even so-called "grid-enabled" MPI implementations, such as GridMPI [6] and MPICH-G2 [7], require each process to be globally accessible. Therefore, overlay networks have to provide reachability across firewalls and NATs even for compute nodes.

3.2   Approach

To achieve the requirements, we employ *site-to-site VPNs* as overlay networks. As depicted in Figure 1, in a site-to-site VPN, the physical gateway for each site establishes a secure connection to every other gateway. This achieves security by requiring authentication and possibly encryption of messages. By assuming the gateways are globally addressable with no firewalls, it provides reachability of compute nodes across firewalls and NATs.

The expected performance of this approach is superior to other alternatives, such as *client-to-server VPNs*, where each participating node connects to a single VPN server. Since packets traverse the additional layer only when crossing a site boundary, the expected performance overhead is less than that of the client-to-server VPN approach. A downside of this approach is that since it is the gateway of each LAN that makes a tunneling connection to every other gateway, it forces even underlying physical networks to join the virtual network, resulting in a significant change in the original network administration. We expect this is not necessarily a limiting barrier in HPC cluster environments.

4   Components of the Prototype Virtual Cluster

To evaluate the feasibility and performance of virtual clusters, we construct prototype virtual cluster environments using existing VMM and VPN implementations that satisfy our requirements.

As a VMM, we choose Xen for its performance and support of dynamic VM migration (a.k.a., live migration [4]). It optimizes virtualization performance by

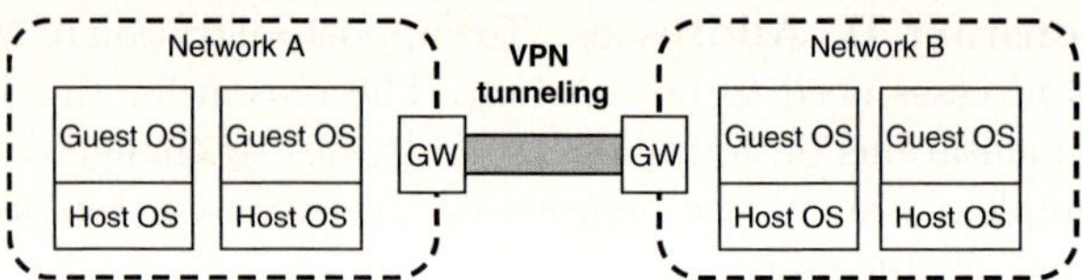

Fig. 1. Site-to-site VPN

para-virtualization, and is reported that the downtime during VM migration is as low as 60ms in a LAN environment [4].

Among existing implementations of overlay networks, we use OpenVPN, an open-source VPN implementation [8], and PacketiX, a commercial product by SoftEther Corporation [9], as sample implementations. Both implementations provide a software-emulated virtual Ethernet over the standard TCP/IP network. They support secure authentication and message encryption via SSL with X.509 certificates. Providing constant IP addresses is also doable by configuring a single-subnet site-to-site VPN. Although PacketiX employs performance optimization mechanisms, including parallel connections and automatic tuning of its number, its performance for HPC applications is still unknown.

5   Experimental Studies

To evaluate performance implication of virtual clusters, we conduct several experiments using our prototype virtual cluster. First, to examine the baseline performance of Xen-based virtual clusters , we compare performance of MPI applications on virtual compute nodes with native compute nodes. Note that to observe the overhead caused by host virtualization, we do not used VPNs for this experiment. Second, we evaluate the performance of virtual clusters on multi-site environments. In this study, we do not deploy the virtual clusters on real multi-site environments; rather we use software-emulated two-site clusters.

5.1   Experimental Setups

Our experimental platform consists of an x86 cluster, called PrestoIII cluster, a pair of VPN tunneling machines for each of OpenVPN and PacketiX, and a NIST Net network emulator.

PrestoIII: Base Evaluation Platform. PrestoIII cluster consists of 256 compute hosts of dual AMD Opteron 242 1.6GHz with 2GB of RAM, running Linux kernel v2.6.12.6. Each node has a gigabit Ethernet interface, connected to a 24-port gigabit switch of Dell PowerConnect 5224. As depicted in Figure 2, the entire cluster nodes are interconnected with twelve of the 24-port switches and an 8-port gigabit switch of 3Com SuperStack3 3848. Each of the Dell PowerConnect 5224 hosts 20 compute hosts, and is further connected to the 3Com switch with four 1Gbps uplinks.

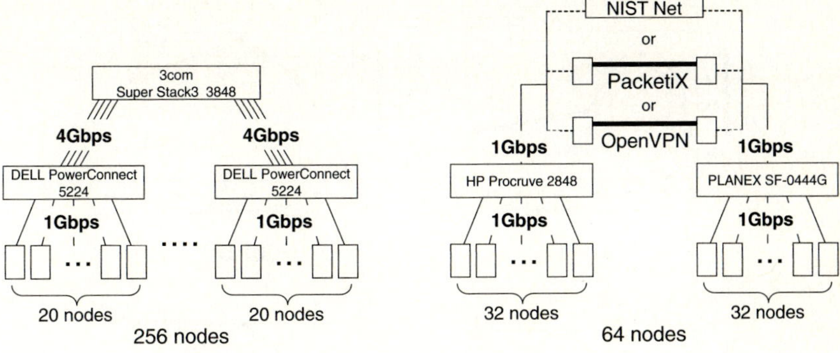

Fig. 2. PrestoIII Networking   **Fig. 3.** Overlay Network Testbeds

Virtual Machines. Each of the PrestoIII cluster nodes hosts a single VM (a.k.a., DomU), using Xen v3.0.2 on Linux kernel v2.6.16 with the Xen patch applied. Each VM and its host OS (a.k.a., Dom0) are assigned 512MB and 128MB of RAM, respectively.

Overlay Network Testbeds. Three kinds of overlay network testbeds are used: OpenVPN and PacketiX VPNs, and latency-inserted emulated two-site environments, as shown in Figure 3. To emulate a wide-area link, a software-implemented network emulator called NIST Net [10] is used. It allows to insert configurable amount of delay into a standard Linux packet router.

OpenVPN site-to-site VPN. Two 32-node clusters are created using PrestoIII compute nodes, each of which is interconnected with a 48-port gigabit switch. The switch is then connected to a VPN tunneling gateway implemented with OpenVPN v2.0.7. Its encryption and compression options are disabled. Each gateway runs on a node with the same configuration as the compute nodes of PrestoIII cluster, but with an additional gigabit NIC.

PacketiX site-to-site VPN. The PacketiX site-to-site VPN testbed is organized in the same way as the OpenVPN site-to-site testbed, except for the gateway machines. A pair of Windows XP machines with PacketiX v2.0 is used. They run on Intel Pentium4 662 3.6GHz with 1GB RAM, and two gigabit NICs. PacketiX's encryption and compression options are disabled.

Emulated Two-Site Clusters using NIST Net. This testbed differs from the other testbeds only on the inter-cluster link. The two clusters are interconnected by a linux router with NIST Net version 2.0.12b. It runs on AMD Athlon MP 2000+ 1.6GHz with 1GB of RAM, running Linux kernel v.2.4.31. It has two gigabit NICs, each of which is connected to one of the clusters via a gigabit switch.

Network and MPI Benchmark Programs. To evaluate latencies and bandwidths, NetPIPE v3.6.2 is used. For the studies of MPI performance, NPB v.3.1 with MPICH 1.2.7p1 is used.

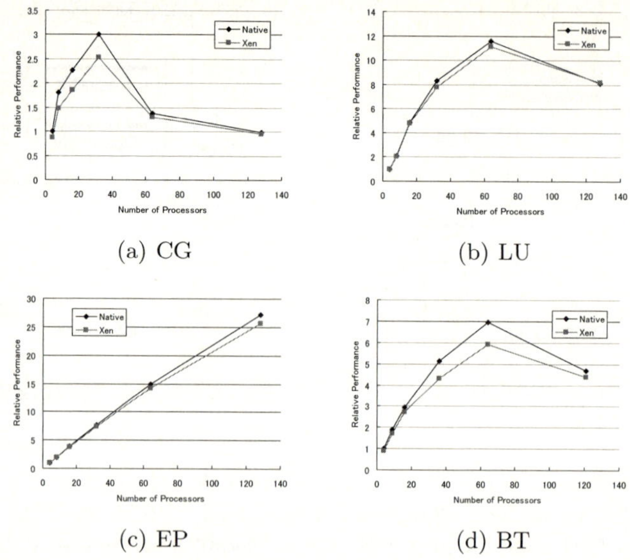

Fig. 4. The relative performance of NPB class B benchmarks

5.2   Network Benchmark Results on Xen VMs

To evaluate the performance of network I/O on Xen VMs, we compare the latency and bandwidth on Xen guest OSes with those on native and Xen host OSes. On two of the PrestoIII compute nodes, we used NetPIPE's ping-pong test, which bounces messages of increasing size between two processes.

The latencies on the Xen guest, Xen host, native OSes were 0.08ms, 0.05ms, and 0.04ms, respectively. The bandwidths on the Xen guest, Xen host, native OSes were 430Mbps, 883Mbps, and 896Mbps, respectively. Thus, the latency on the Xen guest OS was about twice as long as the native OS, while the bandwidth on the guest OS was about half of the native OS.

5.3   MPI Benchmark Results on Xen VMs

Figure 4 shows the performance of NPB CG, LU, EP, and BT class B on a cluster of Xen VMs and another cluster of native machines. The x-axes represent the number of processors used, while the y-axes the relative performance to the experiment using four processors. The performance metric is MOPS (i.e., mega operations per second).

Each graph in Figure 4 shows that the difference between the native and VMs is small: less than 20%, and nearly 0% in the case of EP and LU.

5.4   Network Benchmark Results on the Overlay Network Testbeds

Table 1 shows latencies and bandwidths of the site-to-site VPN and emulated two-site testbeds. We conducted the ping-pong tests over the OpenVPN and

Table 1. Latencies and bandwidth of the overlay networks

	Latency (ms)	Bandwidth (Mbps)
Native	0.04	896
OpenVPN	0.15	290
PacketiX	0.36	170
0ms	0.12	700
0.1ms	0.28	636
0.5ms	0.65	392

PacketiX gateway machines as well as the NIST Net router. The graph named "Native" in each figure shows the performance when no gateway or route is interposed between the two switches.

As shown in Table 1, the latency overhead by OpenVPN and PacketiX was 0.11ms and 0.32ms, respectively; The bandwidth of OpenVPN was decreased by a factor of three to five. To identify the reason of the low bandwidth, we measured the CPU usage of the OpenVPN gateway machines during the NetPIPE experiments. We see that on each gateway, the CPU usage was always close to 100%. We predict that the bandwidths of the VPN gateways are bound by CPU performance. Further analysis of the bottleneck remains to be conducted.

5.5 MPI Benchmark Results on the Overlay Network Testbeds

Figure 5 shows the results of four MPI benchmarks on the OpenVPN and PacketiX site-to-site VPN testbeds as well as emulated two-site testbeds. We configure the NIST Net emulator to impose delays of 0ms, 2.5ms, and 5.0ms. The 0ms-delay network gives the baseline performance using two clusters excluding the effect of VPN overhead. We also present the performance when 64 nodes in PrestoIII are used without the overlay networks to show the ideal performance of the 64-node cluster. The heights of the bars represent the relative performance of each configuration against the configuration using 32 native machines in a single cluster. The performance metric is MOPS. Note that the Y value greater than 1 means that its configuration achieves speedup by using 64 multi-site nodes against 32 nodes.

On these results, we point out three remarks. First, as expected, the performance of NPB EP is mostly irrelevant to underlying networks, and achieves a linear speedup using two 32-node clusters. Second, we see that the native machines and the Xen VMs exhibit almost the same performance patterns with respect to the variations in underlying networks. Third, the achieved speedups using two 32-node clusters are less than 1 for most cases except for EP, while those using a 64-node cluster are greater than 1.2 in both LU and BT. Thus, in these configurations, using two 32-node clusters does not make the performance better than a single 32-node cluster. On native machines, using OpenVPN degrades the performance of CG, LU, and BT, to 22%, 54%, and 28%, of the single 64-node cluster, respectively; the 0ms-delay network does to 31%, 79%, and 41%.

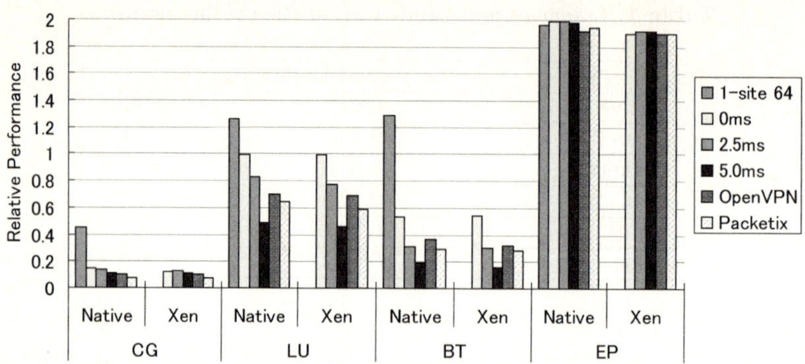

Fig. 5. Performance of the NPB benchmarks on the overlay networks

These results suggest that the most significant source of overhead of site-to-site VPNs comes from the inter-cluster link, not the VPN gateways.

6   Discussion and Future Directions

6.1   Performance Implications of Using VMs for MPI

The experimental results of MPI on Xen-based VMs using a physical single cluster shows that virtualization overhead ranges from 0% to 20% on 4–128-node clusters. Within four benchmarks, CG, which is the most communication intensive, exhibits the largest overhead. On the other hard, EP, which is mostly compute-intensive, achieves nearly the same performance as that on native machines. Therefore, we see that major source of overhead in MPI execution comes from its communication.

While some users would find 0–20% degradation unacceptable, we see that the advantage of VMs would outweigh for other users. One of such advantages is isolation of system environments. For example, virtual clusters allows the user to customize environments without modifying underlying resources. Such isolation is likely to be useful in resource-sharing environments such as computing centers.

6.2   Overlay Networks for MPI Execution

To improve the site-to-site VPN performance, we explore three directions. First, we will investigate optimization of collective operations. As discussed in Section 5.5, wide-area links are the most significant bottleneck in site-to-site VPNs. Thus, MPI performance could be improved by optimizing its collective operations for multi-site execution, as proposed by Kielmann et al. [11].

Second direction is to schedule wide-area communication based on load imbalance of parallel programs. Although load balancing is one of the research areas that have been received the most attention, the problem still exists in a wide variety of scientific programs. Our idea is to give a higher priority to the processes that are predicted to reach a barrier point later than the other processes. The VPN tunneling machine, in turn, could prioritize the messages to and from those higher-priority processes. We expect this priority-based scheduling to hide latencies of WANs to some extent.

Third, we will explore more advanced alternatives such as parallel implementations that use available multiple processors and nodes. Although the main bottleneck lies in wide-area links, we still expect there is a chance to improve the MPI performance by increasing the performance of VPN gateways.

7   Related Work

Virtual Workspace [12] deploys VMs by extending Workspace Service of Global Toolkit 4. Unlike our proposed virtual cluster vision, it does not do dynamic VM migration. Besides, in Virtual Workspace, no mechanism is provided for the reachability across NATs and firewalls. VioCluster [13] uses UML to virtualize compute nodes, and VIOLIN [2] as underlying overlay networks. With experimentation using HPL on a single-site VioCluster, they estimated the performance overhead of VioCluster is at most 15%. They have not evaluated performance of multi-site MPI executions.

There has been some work on MPI that extends the standard single-site MPI execution model to multi-site execution, such as MPICH-G2 [7], GridMPI [6], and MagPIe [11]. Although none of the past work can achieve the potential optimization through the VM migration, their optimized collective operations for wide-area links would be beneficial in our virtual cluster environments.

8   Conclusion

We have discussed the motivation and requirements of virtual clusters, and presented our current approach to them. It consists of Xen for virtualization of compute nodes, and site-to-site VPNs for overlay networks. The experimental studies suggest that, while the overhead caused by Xen VMs is relatively small, the underlying network can significantly degrade application performance. Finally, we discussed the possible strategies to mitigate the performance problem.

Our future work includes more elaborate performance studies as well as those discussed in Section 6. In addition, based on the detailed performance studies, we will explore the possibility of constructing performance models for MPI on virtual clusters. With the performance models, we plan to study global scheduling algorithms for virtual clusters on grids.

Acknowledgments

This work is supported in part by Japan Science and Technology Agency as a CREST research program entitled "Mega-Scale Computing Based on Low-Power Technology and Workload Modeling", and in part by the Ministry of Education,

Culture, Sports, Science, and Technology, Grant-in-Aid for Scientific Research on Priority Areas, 18049028, 2006.

References

1. Barham, P., Dragovic, B., Fraser, K., Hand, S., Harris, T., Ho, A., Neugebauery, R., Pratt, I., Warfield, A.: Xen and the art of virtualization. In: SOSP, Bolton Landing, New York (2003)
2. Jiang, X., Xu, D.: Violin: Virtual internetworking on overlay infrastructure. In: Department of Computer Sciences Technical Report CSD TR 03-027, Purdue University (2003)
3. VMWare: Esx server architecture and performance implications. White Paper (2005)
4. Clark, C., Fraser, K., Hand, S., Hanseny, J.G., July, E., Limpach, C., Pratt, I., Warfield, A.: Live migration of virtual machines. In: NSDI. (2005)
5. Gropp, W., Lusk, E., Doss, N., Skjellum, A.: A high-performance, portable implementation of the MPI message passing interface standard. Parallel Computing **22**(6) (1996) 789–828
6. GridMPI: Gridmpi project. `http://www.gridmpi.org/` (2006)
7. Karonis, N.T., Toonen, B., Foster, I.: MPICH-G2: A grid-enabled implementation of the message passing interface. Journal of Parallel and Distributed Computing (JPDC) **63**(5) (2003) 551–563
8. OpenVPN Solutions LLC: Openvpn. `http://openvpn.net/` (2006)
9. SoftEther Corp.: Packetix. `http://www.softether.comn/` (2006)
10. Carson, M., Santay, D.: NIST Net: A linux-based network emulation tool. SIGCOMM Comput. Commun. Rev. **33**(3) (2003) 111—126
11. Kielmann, T., Hofman, R.F.H., Bal, H.E., Plaat, A., Bhoedjang, R.A.F.: Magpie: Mpi's collective communication operations for clustered wide area systems. In: PPoPP, Atlanta, GA (1999) 131–140
12. Foster, I., Freeman, T., Keahey, K., Cheftner, D., Sotomayor, B., Zhang, X.: Virtual clusters for grid communities. In: CCGRID. (2006) 513–520
13. Ruth, P., McGachey, P., Xu, D.: Viocluster: Virtualization for dynamic computational domains. In: IEEE International Conference on Cluster Computing, Boston, MA (2005)

Virtualizing a Batch Queuing System at a University Grid Center

Volker Büge[1,2], Yves Kemp[1], Marcel Kunze[2], Oliver Oberst[1],
and Günter Quast[1]

[1] Institut für Experimentelle Kernphysik, Universität Karlsruhe (TH),
Postfach 6980, 76128 Karlsruhe, Germany
[2] Institut für Wissenschaftliches Rechnen, Forschungszentrum Karlsruhe,
Hermann-von-Helmholtz-Platz 1, 76344 Eggenstein-Leopoldshafen, Germany
`kemp@ekp.uni-karlsruhe.de`, `volker.buege@iwr.fzk.de`

Abstract. Computing clusters of High Energy Physics institutes at universities are often shared between different user groups, having their own requirements concerning the computing infrastructure. Those requirements can lead to incompatibilities between the needed operating systems, software packages, access policies or different grid middlewares. Some of the above incompatibilities can be solved by providing different portal machines for each group. Incompatibilities at the level of the shared worker nodes of the cluster are, however, difficult to overcome.

In this paper, an approach to overcome this incompatibility using the virtualization technique Xen is presented. Each physical worker node hosts different virtual machines, acting as virtual worker node for every group supported at the site. Ways to integrate this into an existing batch queue are shown.

The performance of different programs used in High Energy Physics on native and virtual machines are also presented.

Keywords: Xen, virtualization, batch queuing system, High Energy Physics.

1   Introduction

Computing clusters built at universities are often shared between several user groups. They can be member of the same institute working on different projects. Some clusters are also shared between groups from different institutes, or even departments of the same university. Often, the particular project software is complex and does not allow an easy recompilation on different platforms. Each project therefore has a preferred computing platform. The platforms are varying in terms of required hardware, installed operating system, and installed system software. Meeting the hardware requirements for all groups sharing a cluster can only be done during the planning phase of a cluster, and will potentially result in a compromise between different groups. Once the cluster is built, not much space is left for changes in the hardware requirements.

G. Min et al. (Eds.): ISPA 2006 Ws, LNCS 4331, pp. 397–406, 2006.

If groups agree on common hardware requirements, they had two choices for the operating system in the past: Either they install a common operating system on all worker nodes or they install subsets of the worker nodes with different operating systems in order to meet the specific needs of the different groups. Of course the ideal case is a common operating system. This ensures the most effective way of resource sharing, as every user can potentially access all nodes at all time. Only a common operating system on all nodes enables benefits from opportunistic use of the resources. There are, however, cases, where a common operating system for all computing nodes has disadvantages:

- The hardware has a mixed 32/64 bit architecture. In this case, the uniformity requirement forces the OS to be 32 bit, which does not make use of benefits of the 64 bit extensions. Some users could use these benefits for certain steps in their projects.
- The hardware consists of 64 bit processors. One group can only use a 32 bit operating system, whereas the other groups could bencfit from a 64 bit operating system.

In some cases, different groups cannot agree on one common operating system. Partitioning the cluster into different subsets of nodes is then the only feasible way of sharing at least some resources of the common infrastructure like storage, network or cooling. If the partitioning is static or varies only seldom, the opportunistic use of the computing resources is not possible. Dynamically changing the installed operating system to always map the needed computing resources to the installation is a difficult task, the switch from one operating system to another is rather time consuming.

Here virtualization comes into game: Using virtualization techniques it is easily possible to install and run different operating systems in virtual worker nodes on the same physical host at the same time. In contrast to the above "vertical partitioning" of the cluster, a "horizontal partitioning" using virtualization techniques is much more flexible, can integrate better into an existing cluster, and allows an optimal resource sharing of the computing resources. Figure 1 schematically shows the two different partitioning approaches.

Any partitioning of a cluster using virtualization techniques presents an additional layer of complexity to a cluster. In the following we will investigate

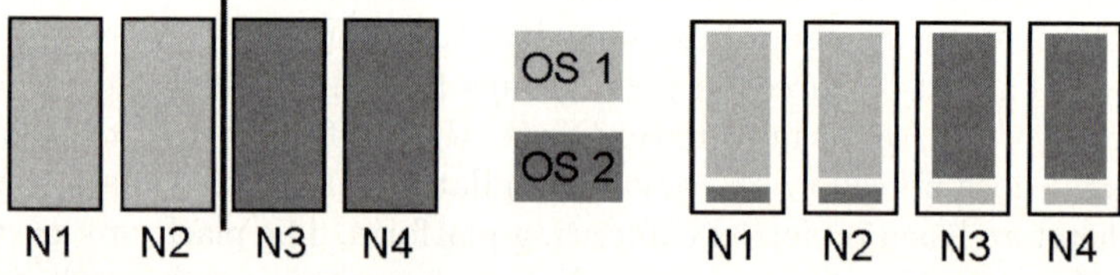

Fig. 1. A cluster of four physical hosts is partitioned vertically (left picture) and horizontally using virtualization techniques (right picture). In the horizontal partitioning scheme, all VMs are running at the same time, the resource allocation can be adjusted dynamically.

performance issues and present a proof-of-principle implementation of a horizontally partitioned cluster using virtualization techniques.

2   Computing Requirements of a Typical HEP Institute

Current and future data sources like the large HEP experiments at the Tevatron or the Large Hadron Collider (LHC) deal with large data production rates. Therefore the demand for computing power and mass storage has significantly increased over the past years.

For example the CMS detector [1] records the results of proton-proton collisions at a rate of 40 million per second. The average size of such a collision event is about 1.5 MB, which leads to a data rate of 60 TB per second. Online data reduction selects and records 150 events per second for further processing and reconstruction, leaving a data rate of $\approx$200 MB per second for storage [2]. In addition to the experiment data, events simulated with Monte Carlo techniques have to be generated and stored as well. This simulated data reflects our present knowledge or anticipations of the underlying laws of nature.

The CMS experiment alone will record up to 1.5 PB per year. Storage of similar size and significant computing time are required to provide the simulated data. The requirements of all four LHC experiments concerning computing power and storage space [2] in 2009 are:

- CPU: 200 Mega SpecInt2000
- disk space: 90 PB
- mass storage systems: 90 PB

In the case of the CMS collaboration more than 2000 physicists of 182 institutes of 38 nations need access to these computing and storage resources. Due to funding constraints and the requirement of redundant data storage it is not possible to build one large central computing facility which accepts the data and offers the needed computing resources to physicists. Instead, all four LHC and other HEP collaborations make use of grid technologies to interconnect distributed computing and storage. This approach offers the opportunity to integrate resources available at smaller sites into the grid. Many of the institutes in the collaboration already have clusters of different size. The main benefits of such an integration are:

- Minimization of idle times by allowing opportunistic use.
- Interception of peak loads.
- Shared deployment of common services.

As an example of such a typical institute cluster, the IEKP Linux cluster consists of 40 computing nodes (based on x86 or x86-64), 5 file servers with a total capacity of 20 TB and 6 portal machines for software development. The situation at the IEKP is typical also in another aspect: Its cluster serves three different groups which work on different large-scale international projects (CDF [3], CMS and AMS [4]), each having different software and different computing requirements. In terms of operating system these are:

- The CDF software is developed and tested with ScientificLinux Fermilab Edition version 3. ScientificLinux [5] is a Linux distribution mainly maintained by the Fermilab and CERN computing division and largely used in science. It is based on a recompiled RedHat Enterprise Server. The CDF software needs a 32 bit operating system.
- The CMS group favors the ScientificLinux CERN Edition version 3 at the moment. At the end of 2006, a transition is planned to ScientificLinux CERN Edition version 4.
- The AMS group does not have special operating system requirements. They would, however, benefit from a 64 bit operating system.

The IEKP cluster is not only serving local users from these three groups: The IEKP cluster is connected to the WorldWide LHC Computing Grid and the SAMGrid [6,7]. Users from all over the world can, provided they have the permissions, submit their jobs to the IEKP computing cluster. This is, however, only possible if the underlying operating system is standardized.

The operating system of the nodes is, by consensus, ScientificLinux CERN version 3. The schedules for a transition to a newer operating systems will vary among the different collaborations. Therefore, the cluster must either be partitioned vertically or horizontally.

Our implementation of the concept of horizontal partitioning using virtualization technologies is driven by the following demands:

- Enabling opportunistic use of computing resources.
- Providing both 32 bit and 64 bit operating systems.
- Local users and grid users run on different virtual worker nodes.
- Security and privacy improvements for all users provided by machine isolation.

Using virtualization techniques on the worker nodes and in the batch queuing system, clusters at universities shared among different user groups get the best possible performance out of their resources. The resources can even be shared across department boundaries and unused office computers can be integrated in a dynamic cluster during night time.

3   Virtualization of a Batch Queuing System

Users do not log in to the computing nodes, but they submit their jobs from a portal machine to a computing node via the batch queuing system. The prioritization of the jobs and users is done by a scheduler, which is either integrated into the batch queuing system, or a separate product interacting with the batch server. Maui/Torque [8,9] is an example of a frequently used batch system with a powerful scheduler also employed at the IEKP.

3.1   General Concepts of Batch System Virtualization

Three categories of batch queuing systems can be distinguished in terms of implementing a horizontal partitioning of a cluster:

- The batch queuing system provides control mechanisms for the virtual machines and can group different virtual machines to one physical host. In this case implementing a horizontal partitioned cluster means choosing the best fitting virtualization technique and providing the different operating systems.
- The batch queuing system does not provide native control mechanisms for the virtual machines. It has, however, the capability of grouping different virtual machines to one physical host. In addition to the choice of the virtualization technique and the preparation of the operating systems, one must implement the control mechanisms. Most batch queuing systems offer the possibility to run "prelude scripts". This feature can be used to adequately prepare the virtual machine before the execution of the job.
- The batch queuing system does not provide native control mechanisms for virtual machines. Grouping different virtual machines to one physical host is also not possible. In this case both features have to be implemented in around the batch queuing system.

The cluster virtualization we present in the following is based on the Maui/-Torque framework which falls into the third category. We therefore need a special program which we will present later in this paper. The general ideas of this approach can be adapted to other batch queuing systems. The concepts are also independent from the chosen virtualization product.

3.2   Choice of Virtualization Technique

Running one or several virtual machines on one physical host satisfies many different use cases: Various different virtualization techniques and virtualization products exist. A major application field for virtualization techniques is server consolidation. Another interesting use case is the horizontal partitioning of a cluster that will be discussed in this paper.

In order to benefit from the usage of virtualization techniques in a horizontally partitioned cluster, the following aspects have to be taken into account:

- Support of commodity operating systems like Linux or Windows.
- Acceptable overhead in performance.
- Easy installation and maintenance of virtual machines.
- Isolation of virtual machines from host system.
- Steering of virtual machines using scripts.
- Acceptable additional costs per existing physical host.

Several VMware [10] products, User Mode Linux (UML) [11] and Xen [12] have been investigated on with respect to the above requirements. The VMware player lacks the scripting abilities. The VMware ESX Server is a commercial product and might therefore not be affordable for smaller working groups. Benchmarks [13] show that Xen has a better performance than UML, making it the candidate of choice for such a partitioning. In order to measure the performance impact of Xen in a virtualized batch system, two additional benchmarks are conducted.

A first benchmark contains IO and CPU intensive standard applications of the CMS software framework like Monte Carlo simulations of particle collisions in High Energy Physics as well as simulations of the interaction of particles with matter. The execution of this benchmark on a native Dual Opteron system with 4 GB of memory and in a virtual machine, hosted on the same system shows a decrease of performance below 4%.

A second benchmark measures the execution time of an application based on the GalProp program [14] and used by the AMS group. This application can be compiled as a 32 bit and a 64 bit application. The benchmark was run on a Dual Opteron system with 2 GB of memory in a native 32 bit operating system. On an identical system a 64 bit version of the application was executed in a virtual machine. Both the VM and the host system are 64 bit systems. In this scenario the job execution takes 22% less CPU time than in the native 32 bit scenario.

The results of both benchmarks support the choice of Xen as virtualization technique for the following implementation of a horizontal partitioning of a cluster. The loss in performance is either minimal for native 32 bit applications. One can even see a gain in performance when using virtualization techniques to offer the user the optimal environment.

3.3   Preparation of the Worker Nodes

As we have seen in the previous section, we opt for the Xen virtualization technique, which we install on the physical node. The privileged domain, Dom0, only has the task to manage the virtual machines and eventually allow an ssh login from an administrator. User jobs running in the Dom0 would introduce a disparity between the Dom0 and the unprivileged domains, the DomUs. Instead, we use the benefits from the encapsulation in the virtual machines. This way, jobs running in a virtual machine cannot influence other virtual machines.

The operating system for the virtual machines is provided by the NFS server. It could also be installed locally into an image or a partition. As a first approach one would boot up the required operating system when a job needs to be computed in the virtual worker node. We do, however, not recommend this:

- Short jobs or interactive jobs should have a very short waiting time, ideally no waiting time at all if free resources are available. Booting up a DomU can take up to a couple of minutes, depending on the installation details and potential file system checks at boot time.
- The waiting time is even increased by another factor: The time the batch server needs to register the virtual worker node into its list of available resources.

We suggest another approach: Each virtual worker node which could potentially be required at some time is running all the time, but with a minimum of memory allocation. In our case, the virtual worker nodes are stable with only 32 MByte of dedicated RAM. Only the virtual worker nodes to which a job is submitted get a higher share of the total RAM. Using Xen, increasing the memory allocation for one DomU is almost instantaneous. Furthermore no time is lost for the registration of the virtual worker node with the batch server.

The CPU overhead of running several virtual worker nodes in parallel is minimal: Only the virtual worker node in which the user job is executed gets CPU time. All other virtual worker nodes do not have much CPU activity.

3.4   Integration into a Batch Queuing System

After having virtualized the computing nodes, one has to register the different nodes with the batch queuing system. As Maui/Torque cannot group virtual worker nodes to one physical host, this feature must be implemented around the batch queuing system in an external program.

The overall sketch of such a program is drawn in figure 2. The program is implemented as a daemon, which runs continuously. As a first step, the daemon must make sure that it has the full control over all nodes and all jobs. In the Maui/Torque wording, this is done by setting all nodes offline and all jobs to hold. At this moment no jobs can be submitted to any virtual worker node.

The daemon then queries the scheduler. A priority is assigned to each job waiting in the queue by the scheduler, according to fair share, expected running time, waiting time, and other criteria. The daemon sorts the jobs according to their priority. The priority assignment policy is not touched. This remains the task of the scheduler which is of utmost importance for shared computing centers with existing policies.

In a next step, the daemon determines the free resources by querying the batch queuing server. In this context, a free resource is a resource that can accept another job. Again, the daemon allows for implementing a site policy. One site could for example allow three jobs on one CPU, or one IO and one CPU intensive job per physical host. The daemon does not change this allocation policy. If there are free resources, the next jobs in the prioritized list are sent to the free resources.

Before sending a job to a virtual worker node, the physical host and the virtual worker node needs to be prepared. When the decision is made that a job should run on one virtual worker node, its memory allocation is set to the maximum possible. In addition, the state of the virtual worker node is set to "free", and the job is released. This way the daemon can control which job is submitted to which virtual worker node, ensuring that the job runs in the correct operating system, and that the physical host can offer resources to the virtual worker node.

After the job is submitted to the virtual worker node, the state of the node is set to "offline" again to make sure no other job can be submitted to this virtual worker node. After a short waiting period, the whole procedure is repeated again.

Such a daemon has been implemented in the Perl programming language. It has been interfaced to the Maui/Torque batch queuing system and is running on a test system at the IEKP.

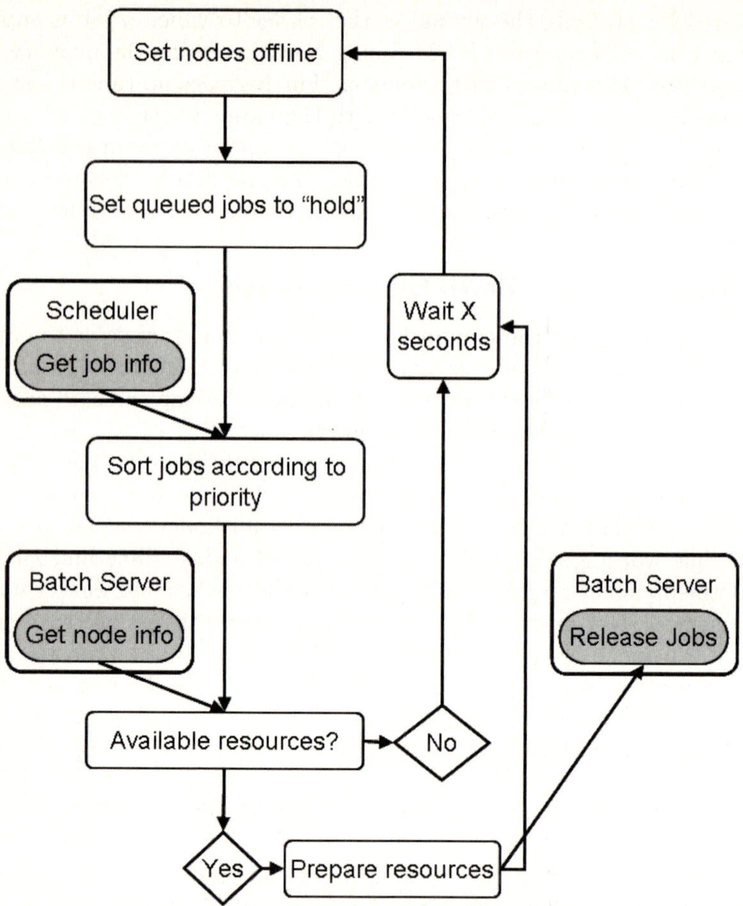

Fig. 2. General sketch of a daemon implementing the grouping of virtual machines to one physical host. The gray shaded areas represent standard interfaces to the external scheduler and batch system.

4   Conclusions and Outlook

When different groups with divergent operating system requirements want to concurrently share the same computing resources in a cluster, the cluster must be partitioned. A situation with many different groups is common at institutes of universities, one example being the cluster of the Institut für Experimentelle Kernphysik of the University of Karlsruhe.

When partitioning a cluster, one should chose a scheme with the following features:

– Flexibility in the response to changing occupancy patterns.
– Guarantee an optimal operating system for every job.

- Leave the choice of the base operating system to the system administrator.
- Only minimal changes to the base operating system and the batch queue.
- No change in existing prioritization policies.
- Good performance of the worker nodes.

The horizontal partitioning scheme presented in this paper matches all these requirements best.

The performance of the worker nodes is very good when using the virtualization technique Xen: A 32 bit HEP benchmark application does not show a noticeable drop in performance when run in a virtualized environment. Another benchmark application that can be recompiled as a 64 bit application fully benefits from virtual 64 bit worker nodes.

We present an implementation of a horizontally partitioned cluster using Xen on a test system at the IEKP. A program was written to group different virtual worker nodes to one physical host. This program interacts with the batch queuing system, but does not touch the prioritization policy or the resource allocation by the batch system. It would be preferable to have the node grouping feature already implemented in the batch system. This would increase the acceptance at computer centers as well as the overall stability and maintainability of a horizontally partitioned cluster.

The method of horizontal partitioning of a cluster using virtualization techniques is not restrained to existing clusters. Horizontal partitioning allows the formation of dynamic clusters in a decentral environment with computing resources from different administrative domains. As an example, office computers from different departments of a university or company can be combined to one cluster during night time and used by several groups, provided that they deploy virtual machines containing their operating system and their software. Even a mixed cluster of dedicated computing nodes and office computers can be imagined, providing a maximum of flexibility and hence the best possible utilization of computing resources.

Acknowledgments

We are grateful to Fred Stober, Iris Gebauer, Christophe Saout and the administration team of the IEKP. We wish to thank the Bundesministerium für Bildung und Forschung BMBF for financial support.

References

1. CMS Outreach, Compact Muon Solenoid Outreach Activities. `http://cmsinfo.cern.ch/`
2. LHC Computing Grid Technical Design Report. LCG-TDR-001, CERN-LHCC-2005-024, 20 June 2005.
3. CDF, Collider Detector at Fermilab. `http://www-cdf.fnal.gov/`
4. AMS, Alpha-Magnetic Spectrometer. `http://ams.cern.ch/AMS/ams_homepage.html`
5. ScientificLinux Homepage. `https://www.scientificlinux.org/`

6. Worldwide LHC Computing Grid Homepage. `http://lcg.web.cern.ch/LCG/`
7. CDF way to the Grid. S. Sarkar, I. Sfiligoi, 2005.
8. Maui Cluster Scheduler `http://www.clusterresources.com/pages/products/maui-cluster-scheduler.php`
9. Torque Resource Manager `http://www.clusterresources.com/pages/products/torque-resource-manager.php`
10. VMware Homepage. `http://www.vmware.com/`
11. User Mode Linux Homepage. `http://user-mode-linux.sourceforge.net/`
12. Xen Project Homepage. `http://www.cl.cam.ac.uk/Research/SRG/netos/xen/`
13. Xen: Scientific Use Cases and Performance Comparisons. M. Hardt, R. Berlich, 2005. Virtualization for Grid-Computing. M. Hardt, 2005.
14. GalProp Home page `http://www.mpe.mpg.de/~aws/propagate.html`

Power Management in Grid Computing with Xen

Fabien Hermenier, Nicolas Loriant, and Jean-Marc Menaud

OBASCO project
École des Mines de Nantes - INRIA, LINA
4, rue Alfred Kastler
44307 Nantes Cedex 3, France
{fabien.hermenier, nicolas.loriant, jean-marc.menaud}@emn.fr

Abstract. While chip vendors still stick to Moore's law, and the performance per dollar keeps going up, the performance per watt has been stagnant for last few years. Moreover energy prices continue to rise worldwide. This poses a major challenge to organisations running grids, indeed such architectures require large cooling systems. Indeed the one-year cost of a cooling system and of the power consumption may outfit the grid initial investment.

We observe, however, that a grid does not constantly run at peak performance. In this paper, we propose a workload concentration strategy to reduce grid power consumption. Using the Xen virtual machine migration technology, our power management policy can dispatch transparently and dynamically any applications of the grid. Our policy concentrates the workload to shutdown nodes that are unused with a negligible impact on performance. We show through evaluations that this policy decreases the overall power consumption of the grid significantly.

1 Introduction

The number of applications requiring gigantic storage and computational capabilities has increased the interest in grid computing in the last few years. At the same time, chip vendors have been producing more and more powerful CPUs at lower prices. Past work has mostly focused on designing efficient and scalable grids. Nevertheless, energy consumption has recently become a major concern for organisations running grids. Indeed, power consumption is an important portion of the total ownership cost, it determines the size of the cooling system and of the electrical backup power generators. The cost of a cooling system with the power consumption may sometimes exceed the grid initial investment. Moreover, intensive power consumption increases the chance of component failure. Thus, power consumption must be a key feature in grid design.

In the meantime and despite numerous users submitting jobs, a grid must rarely maintain peak performances constantly. For example, the average load of the grid of the École des Mines de Nantes subatomic research lab is about 70%. Moreover, many applications have specific needs *e.g.* middleware or operating system. For example, `Aliroot`(the application of the subatomic department of the École des Mines of Nantes), requires a specific middleware (Allien) and a

G. Min et al. (Eds.): ISPA 2006 Ws, LNCS 4331, pp. 407–416, 2006.

particular Linux distribution (Scientific Linux Cern). All those problems argues for a generic power management system adapted to grid.

In this paper, we present our prototype on power management for grid architectures. Our prototype is based on Xen virtual machine hypervisor so that our solution is transparent to user. Based on workload probes (CPU load, memory, NICs throughput *etc.*), the policy migrates virtual machines to concentrate the workload on fewer nodes of the grid, thus allowing unused nodes to be shut down. We present performance results over different application workloads and show the effectiveness of our algorithm.

The rest of the paper is organised as follows. Section 2 presents existing power management policies for cluster computing. Section 3 reviews the virtual machine technology and then Section 4 describes our implementation. Section 5 shows performance results and Section 6 concludes.

2   Energy Management

Most existing work on power management has focused on CPUs and laptops. Indeed, battery duration is a critical problem for users and CPU is by far the most power consuming component of a computer[1]. Today, most processors feature DVFS (Dynamic Voltage and Frequency Scaling) even server designed processor. A DVFS processor has a set of levels (voltage and frequency pairs). A default policy integrated in the BIOS can be overloaded by the operating system. OS and system select the level according to performance and temperature constraints.

The rest of this section describes IVS, CVS and VOVO, three power management policies for single system or clusters and the problem of computation migration in grid computing.

2.1   IVS – Independent Voltage Scaling

Independent Voltage Scaling is a node-local policy for power management. In this approach, every node must be a DVFS processor. Each node adjuts its processor voltage and frequency to the lowest possible value such that there is not much impact on performance. IVS is very simple and it does not require any specific environment or information about running applications. Elnozahy *et al.* [1] report power savings of up to 30% depending on applications. In order to minimize the impact on performance, Chen *et al.* [2] applied IVS only to nodes not in the critical path of running applications.

2.2   CVS – Coordinated Voltage Scaling

In contrast to IVS, Coordinated Voltage Scaling is a global policy. Each node periodically informs a monitor of its workload. The monitor evaluates the overall

---

[1] Although, network interfaces should not be neglected, especially in grids where low-latency NICs and Gigabit cards are common.

workload, estimates an average load and broadcasts it to every nodes. Then the nodes adapt their voltage and frequency to this average. This strategy tends to decrease the variance of the frequency distribution across the grid.

CVS is effective when the workload is uniformly distributed among nodes. Elnozahy *et al.* [1] evaluate the power savings of CVS to be about 25%. Nevertheless, the effectiveness of CVS is questionable when workload distribution is not uniform, indeed, nodes with an bigger workload are slowed down, thus decreasing the overall performance.

2.3 VOVO – Vary On, Vary Off

Pinheiro *et al.* [3] and Chase *et al.* [4] have proposed Vary On Vary Off, which dynamically adapts the number of nodes available according to the grid workload.

VOVO applies a workload concentration strategy. Similarly to CVS, a monitor estimates the overall workload, from which VOVO deduces the number of nodes required. When too many nodes are in use, jobs are migrated or balanced to concentrate the workload. Then unused nodes are simply shut down. The monitor may define a performance tolerance to possibly overload some nodes to further increase power savings.

VOVO has been found to give a power savings of 31% to 86% [1], indeed VOVO is fully effective when a large cluster is almost unused. However VOVO requires job migration technology, that can be implemented at several level. At the application level, users have to develop their own load balancer. While at the operating system level, a specific OS has to be installed on every machines and these must be identical. While this is rarely an issue in clusters, grids are more heterogeneous.

Designing the migration mechanism at the application[5], middleware, or operating system[6] levels is hardly feasible, as energy saving is an issue for organizations running grids, not for users developing applications. In our context, we suppose that grid are built by aggregations of primary cluster. Each cluster is managed by different organizations with their specific applications. Thus, various frameworks and middleware are used to develop grid applications. It is unfeasible to impose one of them on the entire grid as these are specific to the kind of applications developed (computationnal, data, services) [7].

3   Virtual Machines

The goal of a virtual Virtual machines is to provide each of multiple users with the illusion of having an entire computer (a virtual domain), all on a single physical computer (the host). This technology, also known as virtualization, differentiates from application virtual machines such as Sun Microsystem's Java Virtual Machine that isolates Java code from the underlying hardware and operating system thus releasing the developer with porting issues.

In a virtualized environment (see Figure 1), a piece of software called the hypervisor or the virtual machine monitor must enforce isolation between multiple virtual domains and must partition resources (CPUs, RAM, HDDs, NICs, *etc*) among them. The rest of this section describes virtualization and paravirtualization, the two major ways to implement an hypervisor.

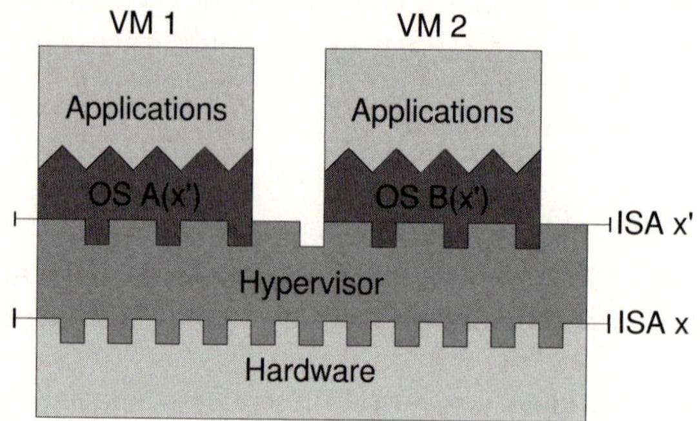

Fig. 1. Architecture of a Xen virtualised System

In contrast to emulation, virtualization reproduces the host architecture identically for the virtual machines. Hypervisors such as VMWare [8] run most instructions of the virtual domains directly on the host processor. The hypervisor must trap sensitive instructions that can not be executed safely such as TLB operations. While virtualization restricts the virtual architecture to the host one, it stills allows running unmodified OS images with much better performance than emulation.

Paravirtualization [9,10] has been introduced to overcomes the performance loses of virtualization due to sensitive operations. It explicitly requires porting the OS to a particular hypervisor. The architecture presented to the virtual machines slightly differs from the host architecture in order to eliminate "cooperatively" sensitive operations.

Virtualization thus makes it possible hosting a lot of virtual domains on the same machine without constraints. Each domain could use its own operating system, middleware or applications without risk of conflicts with others system. This advantages make that virtualization appreciable in grid computing: Cohabitation with the local organisation is safer and a migration mechanism of virtual domain makes deployment easier[11].

4   Our Solution

Our solution is a dynamic placement system for virtual domains on a grid virtualized with Xen (an hypervisor for each node). The placement algorithm aims to save energy by concentrating virtual domains on the smallest subset of nodes possible. Nodes not hosting virtual domains can be stopped, in order to reduce the overall power consumption. At present, the distribution criterion for virtual domains placement is based on CPU usage but could be extended to take other criteria into account, *e.g.*   network traffic or memory usage. Distribution of virtual domain is made with a minimal service interruption with xen migration mechanism[12]. The problem of data migration is solved by using a files server that exports operating systems and datas for each virtual domain.

Our solution is transparent for users of virtual domains and does not require any adaptations or specific operating system[2]. The architecture is based on a client/server model. A standard pre-made domain is running on each node. That domain, called Domain 0, runs a tool, the harvesting agent, that monitors CPU, memory and network. This supervisor monitors the resource usage of the node, and how this resources are divided among the node's virtual domains.

Each harvesting agent periodically sends a report to the decision agent which analyses them to get an overview of the grid and of its virtual domain resource usage. Then an algorithm determines actions to be taken by the various nodes (virtual domain migration, boot, shutdown).

4.1   Resource Collection

The harvesting agent uses functionalities offered by the `xenstat` library provides with Xen. This library allows the domain-0 to obtain statistics generated by the hypervisor, for each virtual domain, including information concerning allocated memory, bytes sent and/or received by the virtual network interface or the quantity of time used by the virtual CPU. By retrieving this information periodically, it is possible to know the percentage of CPU consumed by each virtual domains and, by summing them, the global CPU usage of the node (in this case, the result obtained does not consider the load of the hypervisor.) A report is made and sent to the decision agent. The harvesting agent is responsible for notifying the decision agent of changes in a node's state: When a node is stopped or ready to accept virtual domains, its harvesting agent send a departure or arrival notification, respectively. Thus, the decision agent knows the placement of virtual domains among the grid, and what nodes are available or offline.

4.2   The Decision Agent

This agent runs on its own machine. According to reports and notifications packets sent by nodes, the agent constructs two representations of the grid. A node based view gives information relative to the grid components: IP, MAC address, and state (online or offline) of each nodes. A virtual domain based view gives information about their location, their current resource consumption and the level of saturation of their host. The decision agent then uses this information to concentrate virtual domains in the smallest possible subset of nodes while avoiding saturation. The algorithm is based on two variables: a saturation and an underload threshold. Decisions are taken by comparing the current load of each node with its thresholds.

---

[2] Actually it requires to use a Xenified OS, but that limitation disappears with the help of hardware virtualization.

4. Chase, J.S., Anderson, D.C., Thakar, P.N., Vahdat, A.M., Doyle, R.P.: Managing energy and server resources in hosting centers. In: SOSP '01: Proceedings of the eighteenth ACM Symposium on Operating Systems Principles, Banff, Alberta, Canada, ACM Press (2001) 103–116

5. le Mouël, F., André, F., Segarra, M.T.: AeDEn : An adaptive framework for dynamic distribution over mobile environments. Annals of telecommunications **57** (2002) 1124–1148

6. Gallard, P., Morin, C.: Dynamic streams for efficient communications between migrating processes in a cluster. In: Euro-Par 2003: Parallel Processing. Volume 2790 of Lect. Notes in Comp. Science., Klagenfurt, Austria, Springer-Verlag (2003) 930–937

7. Krauter, K., Buyya, R., Maheswaran, M.: A taxonomy and survey of grid resource management systems for distributed computing. Software–Practice and Experience **32** (2002) 135–164

8. Berc, L., Wadia, N., Edelman, S.: VMWare ESX server 2: Performance and scalability evaluation. Technical report, IBM (2004)

9. Whitaker, A., Shaw, M., Gribble, S.D.: Scale and performance in the Denali isolation kernel. In: Proceedings of the 5th symposium on Operating systems design and implementation (OSDI), Boston, MA, USA (2002) 195–209

10. Barham, P., Dragovic, B., Fraser, K., Hand, S., Harris, T., Ho, A., Neugebauer, R., Pratt, I., Warfield, A.: Xen and the art of virtualization. In: Proceedings of the 19th ACM Symposium on Operating Systems Principles, Bolton Landing, NY, USA, ACM Press (2003) 164–177

11. Foster, I., Kesselman, C., Tuecke, S.: The anatomy of the grid: Enabling scalable virtual organizations. Lecture Notes in Computer Science **2150** (2001) 1–??

12. Clark, C., Fraser, K., Hand, S., Hansen, J.G., Jul, E., Limpach, C., Pratt, I., Warfield, A.: Live migration of virtual machines. In: Proceedings of the 2nd USENIX Symposium on Networked Systems Design and Implementation (NSDI '05), Boston, MA, USA (2005)

Dynamic Virtual Worker Nodes
in a Production Grid

Stephen Childs, Brian Coghlan, and Jason McCandless

Department of Computer Science, Trinity College Dublin
`childss@cs.tcd.ie`

Abstract. There is a growing body of opinion that virtual machines (VMs) provide a good environment for executing user jobs on Grid compute nodes. Sites which execute jobs in specially-created virtual machines can provide levels of isolation and customisation that are unobtainable when jobs run directly on the hardware. Various solutions have been proposed for initiating and controlling such dynamic virtual environments, but issues of integration with a production Grid middleware stack have not received much attention. In addition, solutions proposed to date often require significant user involvement in the process of locating and initiating VMs. We outline a scheme for transparently providing dynamically-instantiated VM-based worker nodes in the EGEE production grid. By extending server-side software, the use of virtual machines is made invisible to the user. Users simply specify the details of their required execution environment in the standard job description language. Resource brokers then locate sites that advertise support for that particular environment. Sites that support dynamic virtual worker nodes advertise support for the various environments that they know how to create; the site's compute element is responsible for instantiating a VM that conforms to the environment description requested and for executing the job in that VM's context. We also evaluate the VM management tools available to implement such a scheme and describe their possible integration with LCG and gLite middleware.

1 Introduction

The case for using VM-based worker nodes as the fundamental unit of execution in Grid computing has been well made by a number of researchers [1,2]. In brief, VMs provide enhanced security by isolating users from each other and from the real hardware, they allow comprehensive customisation (right down to the OS kernel level) of the environment in which users' jobs run and they make it easier to manage large systems by establishing a common hardware platform on which services are run.

There has been progress in defining processes for requesting, creating and controlling VMs in a Grid environment. The Globus Virtual Workspaces project has established generic abstractions, protocols and tools [3] that can be used with Dynamic Virtual Environments (DVEs) implemented in a variety of technologies. Their method is compatible with their web services-based Globus Toolkit

G. Min et al. (Eds.): ISPA 2006 Ws, LNCS 4331, pp. 417–426, 2006.

4 (GT4). An alternative system comes from researchers at the University of Florida: their In-Vigo project [4] also includes mechanisms for dynamic control of virtual machines.

Good work has been done on the lower levels of VM management in a Grid environment: languages and interfaces now exist for describing the desired properties of a VM and bindings are available to a variety of VMMs. However, work remains to be done to integrate such low-level mechanisms into existing Grid architectures. Until this is done, it will remain difficult to persuade users and site admins to use VMs as the primary execution environment, despite the benefits listed above. There are three main issues that need to be addressed to properly integrate dynamic worker nodes with a production Grid infrastructure.

1.1   Integration with Production Grids

The first issue is backward compatibility. Users want an execution environment configured according to their needs, with appropriate application software, compilers and libraries installed. They are not concerned with the implementation of this execution environment, as long as it is suitably configured. This implies that the details of VM configuration should be hidden from the user. Users employ their existing job description languages (e.g. Globus RSL [5], Condor ClassAds [6], EGEE JDL [7]) to describe their requirements, and the Grid middleware uses these requirements to locate (or initiate) an execution environment that conforms. These requirements will be used at various levels: a matchmaker (or resource broker) will use them to locate conforming sites, and the computing element (CE) at a particular site will use them as a recipe for creating new virtual WNs.

Another issue is security and accountability. As the Grid middleware is designed specifically to provide access to large numbers of resources within different administrative domains, it is vital to prevent the abuse of the technology to mount large-scale attacks. Virtual machines can potentially help in the task of securing the infrastructure. For example, they can be used to isolate a user's login session so that the effects of malicious activity are limited to a single virtual machine which can be easily suspended or shut down. The ability to suspend is likely to be a valuable diagnostic aid. It is important for the VM management to use the same security infrastructure as the other Grid services: in most production Grids today this implies compatibility with the Globus Security Infrastructure [8] (GSI) at least and preferably also support for role-based authorisation systems such as VOMS [9].

The third issue is that of complex inter-dependencies. Production grids are a complex ecosystem of interdependent software services. Careful thought needs to be given to the level in the Grid stack at which VM services should be implemented. There are many services whose interactions with the VM service need to be considered: matchmaking, information systems, job submission and file staging, local resource management systems (LRMS) and data management. For example, if worker nodes are to be created dynamically, the LRMS must be able to cope with the appearance and disappearance of nodes – the VM service will potentially need to communicate changes to the LRMS. At each level, the VM service will need to interact with other services to provide seamless integration that allows users to benefit from VM technology without having to drastically change their working practices. We will return to this topic in more detail in Section 2.

1.2   Target Grid Architecture

We now briefly describe features of the EGEE production grid that are relevant to this work; further details can be found in [10]. At each site there is one (or more) Computing Element (CE) which serves as an interface to the clusters at the site. In LCG, the CE runs a Globus 2.4 gatekeeper with jobmanagers that interface to various Local Resource Management Systems (LRMS); the LRMS has final reponsibility for scheduling the job on a worker node. Each site also hosts an information index (BDII) that aggregates information about resource capabilities at the site. Sites are then joined together to form a Grid via central BDIIs that aggregate the information from the various site BDIIs. Many central BDIIs are deployed, each of which effectively provides a custom view of the Grid. The other important central service is the Resource Broker (RB); again, there can be many of these deployed. RBs are responsible from matchmaking between users and sites: they search the resources advertised by sites and try to find the closest match to requirements specified by the user in his job description. Our goal is to provide backward compatibility from the user's point of view. This implies that modifications must be made by the resource provider at their site, rather than to the central services or the user's job submission code.

1.3   Guiding Principles

In order to implement a practical solution that is compatible with currently-deployed large-scale Grid infrastructure, we have adopted a number of guiding principles: the resource provider should manage the provision of virtual environments (so the use of VWNs should be transparent to the user); a single standard security scheme compatible with that deployed on the production Grid should be used; existing tools should be used as much as possible; details of VM management should be hidden from Grid users.

The aims of this paper are two-fold: firstly, to analyse the problem of integrating dynamic virtual worker nodes into a production Grid infrastructure, and secondly, to provide a preliminary sketch of how this might be implemented within the context of the EGEE grid.

2   Analysis of the Problem

We now break down the problem of integrating dynamic virtual worker nodes into its component parts.

2.1   Describing Execution Environments

A fundamental requirement is to provide users with a means of comprehensively describing the execution environment they need. This requirement already exists in the Grid world as users need to locate sites with worker nodes that have the software and OS required to run their job successfully. For example, the EGEE Job Description Language (based on Condor ClassAds) allows users to describe their job in terms of key-value pairs, using the GLUE Schema [11] to provide a standardised language for describing hardware and software capabilities. A system supporting dynamic virtual worker nodes requires that these descriptions can be used as input to a VM manager, enabling it to instantiate VMs with appropriate configurations. Therefore, there must be a scheme for translating user requirements into the specification language used by the VMM.

2.2   Transmitting User Requirements

It is not enough to decide on a common language for describing execution environment requirements: it must be possible to transmit these to all parties within the system who need them. Again, this requirement is not unique to the virtual worker node context — local batch systems also require as much information as possible on users' requirements in order to make good scheduling decisions. Unfortunately this is an area where the EGEE middleware is recognised to be weak: despite repeated requests from site admins and others, most of the information supplied by the user in their job description is discarded before submission to the site Computing Element. There is ongoing work to solve this problem in the gLite middleware [12].

2.3   Interaction with the Information System

The information providers at a site advertise the capabilities of that site's resources: installed versions of OS and middleware, CPU and memory capacity of compute nodes, VOs supported, number of CPUs available, etc. With dynamic virtual nodes, a site could advertise capabilities that are not actually online, but which can be quickly instantiated by creating VMs. For example, a site with system images for Fedora Core 4, Scientific Linux 3 and Debian could advertise support for all three OS even though only a subset of these might be running on worker nodes at a particular time.

The introduction of virtual worker nodes brings a new requirement for "truth in advertising". Sites currently advertise the number of CPUs available based on the capacities of the physical worker nodes. Information providers at a site with virtual VMs must be careful not to advertise resources that cannot be delivered. For example, it should only advertise as many free CPUs as it can create new VMs. We will return to this topic later on when outlining a sample implementation.

2.4   Efficient Initiation of VWNs

A number of techniques could be used here. Instantiated VMs should be left running after a job completes as long as there are free VM slots in the virtual cluster. This allows the CE to start incoming jobs that match that VM slot without VM startup overhead. In a multi-VM per node cluster, copy-on-write could be used to quickly start multiple VMs from a single image.

2.5   Multi-level Matchmaking

In existing Grids, matchmaking occurs at a relatively coarse grain: the RB selects a particular CE (representing one or more clusters) based on the requirements specified by the user. Dynamic worker nodes add at least two further locations where matchmaking is needed: firstly, the VM management service on the CE must decide on which VM host to initiate a new VM, and secondly the CE needs to be able to target a job to a particular virtual WN based on the requirements. The second requirement is not exclusive to dynamic virtual nodes, as it arises whenever clusters are significantly heterogeneous.

A CE/VManager could use an algorithm like this to select a destination WN: 1. A job arrives at the site from the resource broker; 2. The CE reads the requirements associated with the job and looks for a running and idle WN that meets those requirements; 3. If it finds a matching WN, it sends the job there; 4. If it doesn't find an active VM, it selects a suitable VM host and instantiates a new VM there conforming to the requirements. The process then resumes from step 2.

2.6   Compatibility with LRMS

The compute nodes at Grid sites are generally organised as homogeneous clusters managed using an LRMS such as Torque or LSF. The makeup of clusters normally changes quite rarely and so LRMSes do not always provide good support for dynamic reconfiguration. For example, in the popular Torque system, the list of nodes making up the cluster is defined in a configuration file that is only read at server startup. If worker nodes are to be created and destroyed dynamically, we need to define a good scheme for making the LRMS aware of the existence of nodes. This could be as simple as pre-configuring the LRMS with a large pool of compute nodes, providing slots which are then populated by individual VMs as they come up and down. Alternatively, a more sophisticated scheme could use the configuration API of an LRMS to directly inform it of changes in the state of the cluster due to VMs being created or destroyed.

The details of the interaction between the VM manager and any one LRMS will be dependent on the features supported by that LRMS; it may be necessary to define a generic control interface that is implemented by LRMS-specific plugins. What is important is that dynamic worker nodes can be integrated into an existing LRMS used by site admins to schedule access to their compute resources. If this process can be facilitated, it will make the use of VMs more attractive.

It should be noted that the constraints outlined above make Condor a particularly attractive candidate LRMS for virtual clusters: it natively supports matchmaking at a fine-grained level and is designed to cope with rapidly-changing pools of machines.

3   Evaluation of Potential Components

3.1   Specification and Requirements

One of the most important components of the system is a language for describing the capabilities of execution environments. Such a language is potentially used at multiple levels throughout the system: the user describes her desired execution environment at job submission time, a matchmaker searches the infromation system for matching resources, a virtual machine manager at a site potentially uses it to locate or create conforming VMs, and a VM image repository may use it to advertise the configurations available for use.

The GLUE schema is widely used on the Grid to describe the capabilities of sites. It is usually implemented using the Lightweight Directory Interchange Format (LDIF). The schema provides a detailed mapping for a wide range of resource properties including both hardware (CPU speed, memory size, etc.) and software (OS release, middleware version, VO-specific software tags, etc.).

The ClassAd format was developed within the Condor project and named by analogy to classified advertisements in newspapers that describe goods or services for sale. It is used by resources to advertise their capabilities and the kinds of jobs they are willing to accept, and by jobs to describe their characteristics and those they require from an executing site. A matchmaker performs a pair-wise comparison between job and resource ClassAds to work out where to execute a job. EGEE's JDL format is based on ClassAds and has a simple key-value structure.

The Globus Virtual Workspaces project includes a WSDL schema for describing virtual workspaces and their associated services. The attractions of this approach are compatibility with widely-deployed web services (include GT4). However, the current implementation seems to be quite limited compared to more mature techonologies.

3.2   VM Management

One of the most basic requirements is a control interface for creating, controlling and destroying VMs. The Grid middleware can either talk directly to the native control interface of a particular VMM or use a generic VM control interface which has plugins for specific VMMs. Whichever approach is taken, support for authentication and authorisation is essential.

The advantage of using native control interfaces is that all functionality of the VMM can be accessed directly. The main disadvantage is that new bindings have to be written for each VMM to be supported. Xen [13] exports an XML-RPC interface for managing VMs. This provides a standardised API that can be used from almost any language, either locally or remotely. However, the Xen system does not support GSI authentication. VMWare Server provides a scripting interface [14] that is accessible from COM or Perl; this would also need to be augmented with GSI security.

Alternatively, there are a number of generic APIs available for controlling dynamic virtual environments. Globus Virtual Workspaces [15] provides WSDL-based description of virtual environments and back-end plugins to implement them in various technologies including Xen virtual machines and Unix user accounts. This API is tightly integrated with GT4 and so natively supports Grid standards including GSI security and OGSA. The VMPlants system [16], implemented in Java, provides "VMShops" that are a front-end for requesting VMs, and "VMPlants" (installed on each physical resource) that support various VM

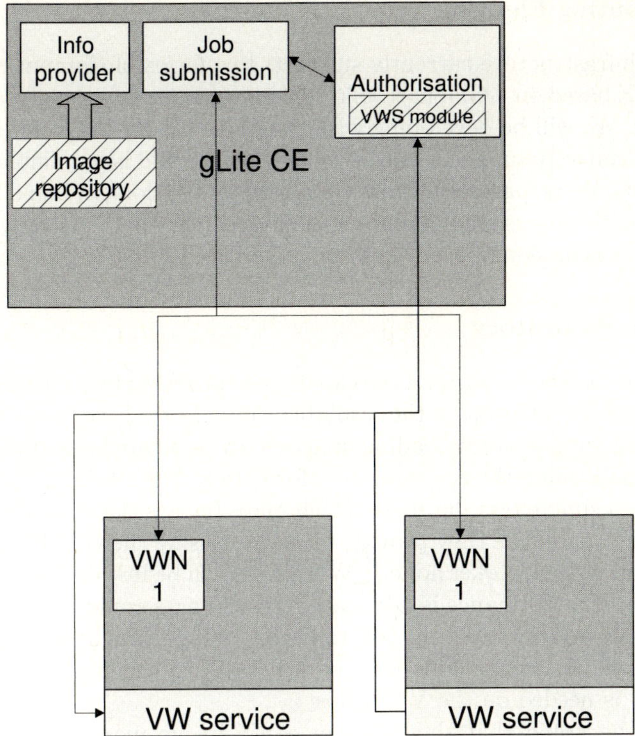

Fig. 1. Proposed architecture for integrating virtual WNs

implementations. It also provides a directed acyclic graph (DAG) notation for describing the configuration of VMs; this allows for good reuse of stored system images.

4   Proposed Architecture

4.1   VM Management

A virtual cluster manager (VCMan) runs on the CE at each site. VCMan interacts with the job submission service, the information provider, and with virtual machine creators (VW services) on each of the VM hosts in the cluster. Although VCMan is logically a single service, in practice it may be implemented as a set of plugins called by existing Grid services, rather than as a free-standing daemon.

All control interfaces should be secured using GSI authentication and accessed in the context of the user's proxy. If calls to VM services are made directly from the job submission control flow, this should happen automatically. We intend to install the Globus virtual workspace service on each VM host. We selected this technology because of its native support for GSI authentication and its interface to Xen.

4.2 Computing Element

The EGEE infrastructure currently supports two forms of Computing Element: the LCG2 CE based on a Globus Toolkit 2.4 gatekeeper, and the gLite CE, which uses Condor. We will be developing with the gLite CE for the following reasons: the gLite CE natively supports web services which should help in integration with Globus Virtual Workspaces; the gLite CE already uses Globus Virtual Workspaces code, albeit with a focus on dynamic account creation; work is already being done to improve transmission of user requirements to the gLite CE [12].

4.3 Image Repository

A system is needed for describing the capabilities provided by a particular file system image and for advertising the available capabilities. Eventually this process should provide support for uploading images with associated descriptions and automatically publishing the appropriate information. For our initial prototype we intend to use a simple text database which maps images (identified by filesystem paths) to the capabilities they provide (described using the GLUE schema).

For now, all virtual worker node (VWN) hosts will be installed with a standard set of images. If performance is adequate, these images could even be read from a mounted network file system. Alternatively, images might be automatically replicated to local storage (this may be necessary in any case if copy-on-write functionality is needed on the VWN host).

It should be noted that the problem of FS image management for virtual clusters is difficult to solve in general, and is an active area of research within the virtualisation community parallax:warfield:hotos:05. We hope that as this research progresses, standard solutions will become available that are suitable for use in a Grid context.

4.4 Information System

The CE publishes data that is a combination of static data set at configuration time and dynamic data retrieved by directly querying the state of the LRMS. For example, the operating system release is currently a static parameter, whereas the number of free CPUs is obtained from the LRMS. The information provider system supports a plugin architecture allowing new components to be written to populate a particular data set.

The first challenge is to advertise the capabilities of the site responsibly, representing the range of potential environments that can be created without presenting an misleading picture. For example, a site supporting VClusters does want to advertise the different flavours of OS it can support, but shouldn't present an excessive number of CPUs merely because it is able to create VWNs at will.

The GLUE schema allows for multiple clusters to be advertised by a site. This feature is already being used within EGEE to publish information that better reflects the structure of a heterogeneous site [17]. We will use this feature to publish multiple clusters for the different capabilities provided by VM images.

Memory sizes and CPU speeds are fixed for physical machines; for virtual machines, they depend on parameters set when the VM is created. To publish all possible combinations of software and hardware capabilities, an extremely large number of clusters would have to be configured. For the moment, we plan to publish one distinct cluster per OS as this is one of the most significant variables. The maximum memory published could be set either to the maximum available for VM creation, or to the maximum size of any one VM. Eventually the information published should be sourced dynamically from the capabilities described in the image repository. As a first step, we will statically configure a set of clusters corresponding to the installed VM images.

Figure 1 shows the various modules involved in our prototype: the hatched boxes represent new code. The virtual machines will be controlled via the authorisation control path, in the same way as account-based workspaces are currently created. The design is still at an early change and will almost certainly change as work progresses.

5   Conclusion

We have presented an analysis of the issues involved in integrating dynamic virtual WNs into a production Grid, with particular reference to the EGEE infrastructure. We envisage a backwards-compatible approach where resource providers modify their clusters and compute elements, but publish information in such a way that virtual environments are created straight from unmodified job submissions.

This paper is preliminary in nature and is intended to open up discussion on the functionality needed by VM management systems and Grid middleware if they are to be truly integrated. We hope to develop a working prototype in the near future, and to gain further insights through that development process.

References

1. Figueiredo, R.J., Dinda, P.A., Fortes, J.A.B.: A Case for Grid Computing on Virtual Machines. In: Proceedings of the International Conference on Distributed Computing Systems. (2003)
2. Keahey, K., Foster, I., Freeman, T., Zhang, X.: Virtual Workspaces: Achieving Quality of Service and Quality of Life in the Grid. Scientific Programming Journal (2006)
3. Keahey, K., Doering, K., , Foster, I.: From Sandbox to Playground: Dynamic Virtual Environments in the Grid. In: 5th International Workshop in Grid Computing (Grid 2004). (2004)
4. Adabala, S., Chadha, V., Chawla, P., Figueiredo, R., Fortes, J., Krsul, I., Matsunaga, A., Tsugawa, M., Zhang, J., Zhao, M., Zhu, L., Zhu, X.: From virtualized resources to virtual computing Grids: The In-VIGO system. Future Generation Computer Systems **21** (2005)
5. Globus: The Globus Resource Specification Language (RSL), specification 1.0. (`http://www-fp.globus.org/gram/rsl_spec1.html`)

6. Solomon, M.: The ClassAd language reference manual. `http://www.cs.wisc.edu/condor/classad/refman.pdf` (2004)

7. European Data Grid: The EDG job description language (JDL). (`http://server11.infn.it/workload-grid/docs/DataGrid-01-TEN-0142-0_2.pdf`)

8. Foster, I., Kesselman, C., Tsudik, G., Tuecke, S.: A security architecture for computational grids. In: Proc. 5th ACM Conference on Computer and Communications Security Conference. (1998) 83–92

9. Alfieri, R., Cecchini, R., Ciaschini, V., dell Agnello, L., Frohner, A., Gianoli, A., Lőrentey, K., Spataro, F.: VOMS, an authorization system for virtual organizations. In: 1st European Across Grids Conference, Santiago de Compostela, Springer-Verlag LNCS 2970 (2003) 33–40

10. Peris, A.D., Lorenzo, P.M., Donno, F., Sciaba, A., Campana, S., Santinelli, R.: LCG-2 user guide. LHC Computing Grid Manuals Series. `https://edms.cern.ch/file/454439/2/LCG-2-UserGuide.pdf` (2005)

11. Andreozzi, S., Burke, S., Field, L., Fisher, S., Konya, B., Mambelli, M., Schopf, J.M., Viljoen, M., Wilson, A.: GLUE schema specification version 1.2. `http://infnforge.cnaf.infn.it/glueinfomodel/index.php/Spec/V12` (2005)

12. Prelz, F.: Passing requirement information to the gLite CE via BLAHPD. In: HEPIX conference. (2006)

13. Barham, P., Dragovic, B., Fraser, K., Hand, S., Harris, T., Ho, A., Neugebauer, R., Pratt, I., Warfield, A.: Xen and the Art of Virtualization. In: Proceedings of the Nineteenth ACM Symposium on Operating Systems Principles, ACM (2003)

14. VMware: VMware scripting API user's manual. `http://www.vmware.com/pdf/Scripting_API_215.pdf` (2005)

15. Keahey, K., Foster, I., Freeman, T., Zhang, X., Galron, D.: Virtual Workspaces in the Grid. In: Proceedings of Europar 2005. (2005)

16. Krsul, I., Ganguly, A., Zhang, J., Fortes, J.A.B., Figueiredo, R.J.: VMPlants: Providing and Managing Virtual Machine Execution Environments for Grid Computing. In: Proceedings of the 2004 ACM/IEEE conference on Supercomputing. (2004)

17. Traylen, S.: How to publish different memory limits for different queues on the same ce. `http://goc.grid.sinica.edu.tw/gocwiki/How_to_publish_different_memory_limits_for_different_queues_on_the_same_CE` (2005)

Performance Models for Virtualized Applications[*]

Fabrício Benevenuto[1], César Fernandes[1], Matheus Santos[1], Virgílio Almeida[1],
Jussara Almeida[1], G.(John) Janakiraman[2], and José Renato Santos[2]

[1] Computer Science Department
Federal University of Minas Gerais - Brazil
{fabricio, cesar, mtcs, virgilio, jussara}@dcc.ufmg.br
[2] HP Labs
Palo Alto - USA
{john.janakiraman, joserenato.santos}@hp.com

Abstract. This paper develops a series of performance models for predicting performance of applications on virtualized systems. It introduces the main ideas of performance modeling and presents a complete case study of an application running on Linux that is migrated to a virtualized environment consisting of Linux and Xen. The paper describes the models, the process of obtaining measurements for the models and calculates performance metrics for the two environments. A validation of the results is also discussed in the paper.

1 Introduction

Virtualization can be understood as a technique to partition resources of a machine in multiple environments, creating a new level of indirection between physical resources and applications. Recently, virtualization technologies are experiencing a renewed interest as a way to improve system security, reliability, and availability, reduce costs, and provide flexibility. Particularly, such benefits are gaining popularity with Virtual Machines Monitors (VMM), providing software-based solutions for building shared hardware infrastructures.

Virtual machines provide a suitable environment to consolidate multiple services into few physical machines. Nevertheless, in order to migrate applications from physical machines to virtualized consolidated platforms, one needs to be able to estimate the performance these applications will achieve on the new environment. *Will migrated applications run with competitive performance as they run on their current environment? How many servers will be needed to create a virtual environment able to support the execution of the services provided, with acceptable performance? What is the best configuration of resources on the virtual environment for a certain application?* Therefore, there is a current need for new tools for predicting performance, providing information for resource allocation, and determining optimal system configuration. This work gives the first

---

[*] This work was developed in collaboration with HP Brazil P&D.

G. Min et al. (Eds.): ISPA 2006 Ws, LNCS 4331, pp. 427–439, 2006.

step in this direction. We propose simple queuing models for predicting the performance that applications, currently running on Linux system, will achieve if migrated to a Xen virtual system, with same hardware configuration. We further validate these models with experimental results.

The rest of the paper is organized as follows. The next Section presents related work. Section 3 discuss background on performance modeling. Section 4 reviews the main architectural aspects of Xen, describes the tools and the experimental environment used for the performance evaluation. Section 5 discuss experimental results, whereas Section 6 presents analytic equations for virtual systems and compares analytical and experimental results. Finally, Section 7 concludes the paper and presents directions for future works.

2   Related Work

Three popular virtual systems are VMware [11], Denali [12], and Xen [1]. VMware is responsible for several products using different virtualization strategies. Denali was projected to support a large number of VMs, where each VM is able to execute only one application. Unlike Denali, Xen was designed to support VMs able to execute an entire operating system and thus, more than one application. The focus of our model and analysis is the Xen VMM, which is briefly described in Section 4.1.

The first studies and applications of virtualization emerged in 1960, when virtualization was described as an evolution of the study of time sharing and multiprogramming [13]. One of the most popular virtual environments at that time was the IBM VM/370. Bard et. al proposed analytical models for VM/370 to estimate performance metrics such as CPU utilization, and developed a performance predictor tool for this environment [14].

More recently, queuing network models for performance prediction of virtual environments were proposed in [7,3]. However, the proposed models were not validated for any specific virtual architecture. In this work, we propose specific analytic models for the Xen architecture, validating these models with experimental results.

Recently, Cherkasova et al. [2] proposed a methodology to measure separately the CPU overhead on the IDD due to I/O operations of a guest VM. The idea is to count the cost and the number of page exchanges between a certain guest virtual machine and the IDD to estimate the amount of CPU usage of the IDD consumed in behalf of a certain virtual machine. Other studies also provided performance evaluation of applications running on Xen [8,4]. In common, all these efforts are based solely on experimental evaluation of Xen and its applications.

3   Performance Models

A *model* is a representation of a system. Performance models [7] are useful for predicting the values of performance measures of a system from a set of values of workload, operating system, and hardware parameters. Performance prediction is the process of estimating performance measures of a computer system for a given set of parameters. Typical performance measures include response time, throughput, resource utilization, and resource queue length. The input parameters to such a model fall into one of three categories: workload, basic software, and hardware parameters. The workload parameters describe the load imposed on the system of interest by the applications, i.e., the transactions submitted to it. The software parameters describe features of the basic software, such as the Xen virtual machine monitor overhead. Examples of such parameters are virtualization overhead, CPU dispatching priority, etc. Examples of hardware performance parameters include the components of the servers that supports a Xen system, such as processor speeds, disk latencies and transfer rates, and local area network speed. The output of a performance model is a set of performance measures, such as response times, throughput, and resource utilizations.

The emphasis of this paper is on how to build performance models for virtualized applications. We start out with simple models that provide bounds on some performance metrics. For example, one common question in the analysis of virtualized systems is "what is the maximum theoretical value of the arrival rate λ for a given virtualized system?" This question has an easy answer that depends solely on the service demands of all resources. Note that the service demand D_i, the utilization U_i, and the arrival rate λ are related by $\lambda = U_i/D_i$ for all resources i. Because the utilization of any resource cannot exceed 100%, we have that $\lambda \leq 1/D_i$ for all i's. The maximum value of λ is limited by the resource with the highest value of the service demand, called the bottleneck resource. Thus,

$$\lambda \leq \frac{1}{\max_{i=1}^{K} D_i} \tag{1}$$

In order to estimate more accurate performance metrics, models have to consider contention for resources and the queues that arise at each system resource—CPUs, disks, memory and communication devices. Queues also arise for software resources, such as threads, database locks, and protocol ports. The various queues that represent a virtualized system are interconnected, giving rise to a network of queues, called a queuing network (QN). A common question that could be answered by a queuing network model of a virtualized system is: "what will the average response time of application Y be when it is migrated from a pure Linux to a Linux/Xen environment that has the same system configuration?" To answer this question, we need models that present details of the system. The level of detail at which resources are depicted in a QN model of a virtualized system depends on the reasons to build the model and the availability of detailed information about the operation and availability of detailed parameters of specific resources. In other words, models depend on data collected by measurement tools in virtualized systems. The basic input parameters that we use in our performance models are service demands and arrival rates. Service demand is the sum of the service time at a resource (e.g. processor, disk, network) over all visits to that resource during the execution of a transaction or request. In a queuing network model, not all requests that flow through the resources of a system are similar in terms of the resources used and the time spent at each resource. Therefore, Workload may be broken down into several workload components, which are represented in a QN model by a *class* of requests. Different classes may have different service demand parameters and different workload intensity parameters. Classes of requests may be classified as *open* or *closed* depending on whether the number of requests in the QN is unbounded or fixed, respectively. Open classes allow requests to arrive, go through the various resources, and leave the system. In this paper we initially present a simple model that estimates bounds on the performance of a virtualized system and then we develop an open-class queuing network model that represents applications running on Linux and Xen.

4   Case Study

In order to demonstrate the causes of virtualization overhead on the Xen VMM, we provide a performance evaluation of three benchmarks running on Xen and Linux. Then, we use a simple case study of a Web server to validate the performance models. The goal is to predict the performance a Web server application, currently running on a non-virtual system, will achieve if migrated to a Xen virtual machine. Our research strategy consists of a performance study of a simple Web server which provides only static content. In addition to this case study, we presented some results to discuss which components of the Xen environment need to be considered in a model. Next, we briefly describe the Xen virtual machine monitor and Xen I/O model. Our discussion focuses on aspects which are more relevant for the performance evaluation presented. Then, we present the tools and the hardware platform used.

4.1   Xen Architecture

Xen is a free and open-source virtual machine monitor (VMM) which allows multiple (guest) operating system (OS) instances to run concurrently on a single physical machine. It uses paravirtualization, where the VMM exposes a virtual machine abstraction slightly different from the underlying hardware. The Xen system has multiple layers. The lowest and most privileged is called VMM. Each guest OS runs on a separate virtual machine called domain. The domains are scheduled by the VMM to make effective use of the available physical CPUs. Each application, running on a guest OS, accesses hardware devices via a special privileged virtual machine called *isolated driver domain (IDD)*, which owns specific hardware devices and run their I/O device drivers. All other domains (*guest domains* in Xen terminology) run a simple device driver which communicates with the driver domain to access the real hardware devices. Figure 1 provides an overview of Xen I/O model. The IDD can access directly the hardware devices it owns. However, a guest domain accesses the hardware devices indirectly through a virtual device connected to the IDD. The IDD maps through bridges or routing the physical interface to its virtual interface which communicates with the guest virtual interface. The guest domain exchanges requests and responses with the

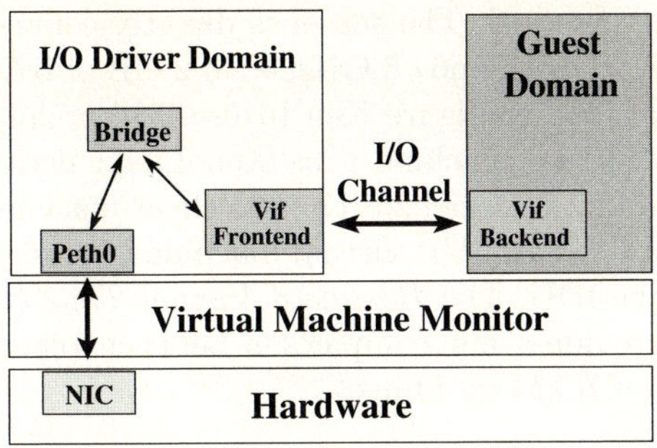

Fig. 1. Overview of Xen I/O model

IDD over an I/O channel. In order to avoid copying, references to page-sized buffers are transferred over the I/O channel instead of the actual I/O data.

4.2 Monitoring Framework

In order to develop performance models, we need to be able to measure the virtualized system. We developed an application called *Xencpu* to measure CPU busy time on Xen. This tool is based on the source code of *xm top* tool, provided with Xen, and was designed aiming at the automatic execution of our scripts. The CPU busy time on the Linux system is obtained based on information from */proc* directory. Disk busy time, on both Xen and Linux, was also obtained from the */proc* directory. Other parameters such as experiment duration and number of processed requests are obtained with scripts or from the benchmarks used.

4.3 Workload

The workload used is generated by the following benchmarks:

- **Web server:** we used httperf [9] as clients and Apache [10] version 2.0.55 as the Web server. The httperf is a tool which allows generating several HTTP workloads and measuring the performance of the Web server from the point of view of the clients. We run httperf on a client machine, sending requests with rate λ to the server, measuring throughput and server response time of the requests. The workload used is part of a set of workloads from SPECWeb99 [7] and it does not contain dynamic content.
- **Disk intensive application:** This benchmark consists of copying a 2 GB file from a directory to another, on the same partition. We use this benchmark to analyze the impact of disk activity on the virtual environment overhead.
- **CPU intensive application:** It consists on a kernel compilation, which evocates several functions, stressing system CPU.

4.4 Experimental Setup

For all experiments, we use a two 64-bit CPU 3.2 GHz Intel Xeon server, with 2 GB of RAM, one disk with 7200 RPM and 8 MB of cache, and two Broadcom

Realtek gigabit Ethernet card. The server is directly connected to a client machine, an one-CPU AMD Athlon64 3 GHz, with 2 GB of RAM, and two Realtek gigabit Ethernet card. We configure Xen to use i386 architecture. We use Xen version 3.0 and the virtual machine runs XenoLinux derived from Linux Debian Etch i386 distribution, kernel 2.6.12. The client machine also uses the same Linux distribution and kernel. The virtual machine is configured to use 512 MB of RAM as well as the IDD. The *Borrowed Virtual Time* (BVT) is used as the Xen scheduler. To provide a fair comparison between Linux and the Xen VM, we also use 512 MB of RAM on Linux.

5   Performance Evaluation

This Section presents an experimental performance study of applications running on the Xen VMM. Unlike previous work [2,8,4], the focus of our analysis is on collecting metrics to support the design and validation (next Section) of models for performance prediction. We configure the virtual environment with one IDD and one guest, each one using a different CPU. The Linux system uses two SMP CPUs. Each result is an average of 20 runs. With a confidence level of 90%, the results differ from the mean by 10% at maximum.

In order to demonstrate the causes of virtualization overhead on the Xen VMM, we compare the three benchmarks described in Section 4.3 running on Linux and Xen systems. Figure 2 shows a kiviat representation which compares CPU and disk utilization on Linux and Xen systems for the three benchmarks. In a kiviat graph each radial line, which starts on the central point 0, represents one metric with maximum value 1 [5]. We plot six metrics on this graph, namely, the CPU utilization on the two Linux CPUs, on the IDD and on the VM, and disk utilization on both systems. Each curve represents a benchmark. Observing the disk-bound benchmark curve, we see that disk utilization is 1 (i.e., 100%) for both systems, and the VM CPU utilization is slightly higher than the sum of the utilizations of the two CPUs on Linux. Note that there is a significant load on the IDD CPU, since it works as interface for the hardware to the VM. For the kernel compilation benchmark, the VM CPU utilization is 1, which is also the sum of the CPU utilizations of the two CPUs running Linux. Since this benchmark does not execute a representative number of I/O operations, the CPU utilization on the IDD is almost 0. Note that the disk activity is negligible for the Web server, but there is a considerable CPU processing on the IDD due to network I/O operations.

Based on these observations, we can conclude that the assignment of CPU resources to VMs and IDDs can affect critically system performance, since the IDD processing is significant for workloads which stress I/O operations. We discuss how to predict the performance of each of these components separately in the next Section. We focus the rest of our analysis on the Web server benchmark. Figure 2 shows that disk utilization is almost zero for this benchmark. Thus, we do not consider disk residence time in our experiments and models. Our Web server provides only static content and uses a hardware platform with two CPUs

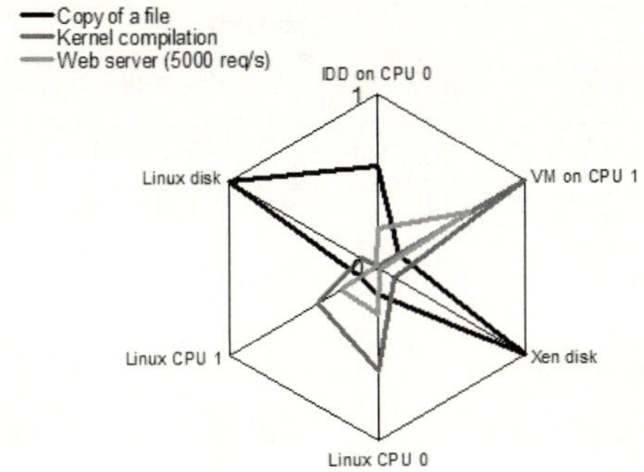

Fig. 2. Kiviat graph: comparison of CPU and disk utilization on Xen and Linux

and one disk. The two processors work in parallel on the Linux system. On the other hand, in a Xen environment the two CPUs are used to process each request. In the virtual environment, we assign one CPU for the IDD and one CPU for the guest VM. The requests are processed by the Web server running on the guest virtual machine. The VM is not able to access directly network and disk, and thus, it uses the IDD to access them. Figure 5 summarizes the experimental and analytical results. The analytical results will be explained on the next Section.

Figures 5(a) and 5(b) show the measured CPU utilization and demand as a function of request rate. Note that CPU utilization increases linearly with request rate for both IDD and VM. Moreover, the CPU utilization consumed by the IDD represents a significant overhead and must be considered by our models. As we will further discuss, the ratio between the CPU demands (and thus CPU utilizations) for the IDD and the VM is fairly constant over the range of request rates we experiment with. Figures 5(c) shows average response time as a function of request rate. As one might expect, average response time is significantly longer at the virtual environment for request rates greater than 7000 requests per second, when the server starts to become overloaded. Clearly, the VM is the bottleneck in the Xen system, and performance degrades significantly with $\lambda \geq 7800$ requests/sec. From this point on, the overloaded server experiences significant delays in accepting connections from the client, which causes httperf not to send requests on the ratio we desire, limiting our experiment to this ratio. The Xen virtual environment is able to provide the same throughput of the Linux system, at the cost of a higher CPU utilization.

6   Performance Models for Xen-Based Applications

This Section presents simple analytic models based on queueing network theory for applications running on the Xen virtual environment. Figures 3(a) and 3(b) present our model representations for the Linux system and the virtual environment using Xen VMM, respectively. These two systems are not equivalent, since in the Xen environment, the guest VM needs to use the IDD to access the hardware components. Note that Figure 3(b) represents the configuration of the XEN

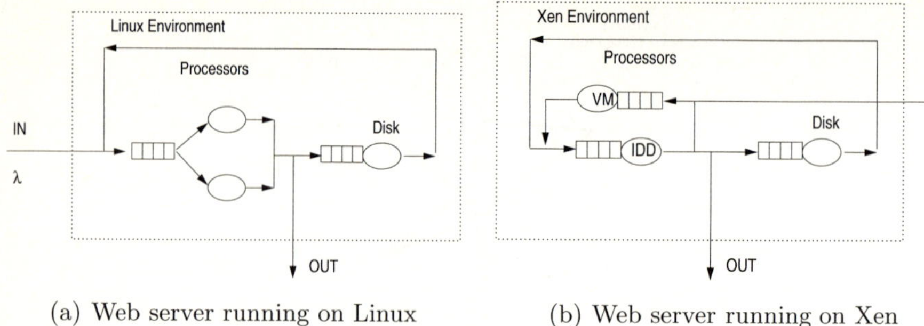

(a) Web server running on Linux   (b) Web server running on Xen

Fig. 3. Queue network model representation for Linux and Xen environments

system used in *our experiments*, with IDD and VM running on separate independent CPUs. Nevertheless, we note that alternative system configurations, where either IDD or VM receives only a fraction of a CPU, would lead to different model representations. In the rest of this Section, we discuss asymptotic bounds and average value equations for open class queuing network models, validating these bounds with the experimental results discussed in Section 5.

6.1   Asymptotic Bounds

Asymptotic bound analysis can be quite useful to determine the maximum load a system can support while still providing reasonable response times (i.e., before saturation). The maximum rate, λ_{max}, the system can support without saturation is given by equation 1. As discussed previously, the maximum request rate reached in our experiments is $\lambda = 7800$. Considering D_{CPU}^{VM} as the CPU demand for the VM, equation 1 yields a $\lambda_{max} \leq \frac{1}{D_{CPU}^{VM}} = \frac{1}{0.000127} = 7874$, which is very close to the measured value.

6.2   Queuing Network Model

This Section presents an analytical model for an application on the Xen VMM. The strategy for building the performance model is to define a *slowdown factor* [7,3] (i.e., S_v) of an application running on a virtual machine which is a function of the number of privileged instructions executed by the guest VM and of the number of instructions needed to emulate a privileged instruction. However, the fraction of privileged instructions executed by a VM and the average number of instructions required by the VMM to emulate a privileged instruction are not easy to be measured on a real system. We propose an equation to capture the overhead of virtualization of an application. The slowdown of a given application can be computed as the busy time of resource k on the virtual environment, B_k^{Virt}, divided by B_k the busy time of resource k to execute the same application on an equivalent non-virtual system.

$$S_v = \frac{B_k^{Virt}}{B_k} \tag{2}$$

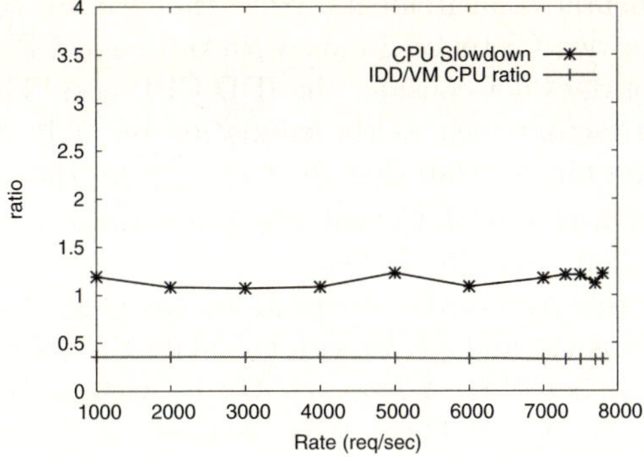

Fig. 4. Slowdown and $Cost_{VM_i}^{IDD}$ for the Web server benchmark

The slowdown can be interpreted as the overhead introduced by virtualization to execute a certain application. It means that applications running on virtual machines will see their CPU time increased S_v times. S_v will be used to calculate the input parameters (i.e., service demands) for the virtualized performance model. Queuing models will be used to predict the performance of applications migrating from non-virtual environments to virtualized environments.

As described in Section 4.1, the Xen architecture is divided in two different kinds of components: the IDD and the VMs. The Xen I/O model, also used by other virtual systems [12], use a page exchange mechanism between the IDD and the guest VM. In this context, the CPU time required by the IDD to process a package of 36 and 1448 bytes is the same if the number of page exchanges to deliver these packages are the same [2]. In order to compute the IDD CPU overhead (i.e., the CPU time demanded by the IDD) due to an application running on a guest VM we define $Cost_{VM_i}^{IDD}$ as:

$$Cost_{VM_i}^{IDD} = \frac{B_{CPU}^{IDD}}{B_{CPU}^{VM_i}} \tag{3}$$

where B_{CPU}^{IDD} is the portion of CPU time consumed on the IDD on behalf of the application running on the guest VM_i and $B_{CPU}^{VM_i}$ is the CPU time consumed by the guest VM_i. In [2], it is discussed how to isolate the CPU cost of the IDD of a certain VM, even when running multiple VMs simultaneously. Since the virtualization overhead is divided in these two kinds of components (IDD and VMs), we consider S_v as the overhead factor relative to the VM part of the virtualization slowdown. We estimate the IDD CPU utilization due to I/O operations of a certain VM, considering that $Cost_{VM_i}^{IDD}$ is constant relative to request rate, as supported by the experimental results shown in Figure 4.

Figure 4 displays the VM CPU slowdown and $Cost_{VM_i}^{IDD}$ as a function of λ. We compute S_v based on busy time measured on the VM and the sum of the busy time of the two CPUs on Linux. The slowdown obtained is around 1.2. For practical use, a table of slowdown factor per class of applications can be built from experimental measurements. Note that we are comparing the sum of busy time of the two CPUs on Linux with only one CPU on the VM, and the slowdown factor does not consider the IDD CPU cost. The slowdown factor stems from several factors such as the emulation of TCP checksum, which is done by hardware on Linux. Note that the $Cost_{VM_i}^{IDD}$ for the system under study is also constant and around 0.34. Considering this evidence, we assume $Cost_{VM_i}^{IDD}$ is also a constant in our analysis. In Section 7, we discuss how to generalize the model to represent this part of the overhead for any type of application.

Based on equations (2) and (3) we can calculate the service demand for the virtual environment. Let $VM_1, VM_2, ..., VM_n$ be virtual machines that share the same hardware platform. The service demand at resource k for the new environment, $D_k^{VM_i}$, is given by:

$$D_k^{VM_i} = D_k \frac{S_v}{P_{VM_i}} \tag{4}$$

where D_k stands for the demand of resource k for Linux running the same workload as VM_i, and P_{VM_i} is the speedup of the hardware of virtual machine VM_i compared to the non-virtualized hardware. Note that we do not use the same speedup for the IDD and VM, since these components can use different amounts of resources. For instance, we can configure a virtual environment assigning 1 CPU for the IDD and 3 CPUs for a certain VM. The utilization of resource k on VM_i can be obtained by the following equation:

$$U_k^{VM_i} = \lambda D_k^{VM_i} \tag{5}$$

The utilization can also be calculated based on the utilization measured on Linux, as we did for service demand. The $Cost_{VM_i}^{IDD}$ can be used to calculate the IDD demand for a certain class of applications as

$$D_{CPU}^{IDD} = D_{CPU}^{VM_i} \frac{Cost_{VM_i}^{IDD}}{P_{IDD}} \tag{6}$$

where P_{IDD} is the speedup of the IDD relative to a baseline Xen configuration. Note that the speedup of the IDD is not relative to the non-virtual system. We introduced P_{IDD} so that the model can predict resource allocation for the IDD.

Based on equations 4 and 5, the estimated residence time R_k at resource k for a open class system is given by:

$$R_k = \frac{D_k^{Virt}}{1 - U_k^{Virt}} \tag{7}$$

The response time, R^{Virt}, on the virtual system can be obtained as the sum of the residence time at all resources:

$$R^{Virt} = R_{CPU}^{VM} + R_{CPU}^{IDD} + R_{Disk} \tag{8}$$

Figure 5 represents, on the same graphs, both the experimental and the analytical results. We use the values of S_v and $Cost_{VM_i}^{IDD}$ presented on Figure 4

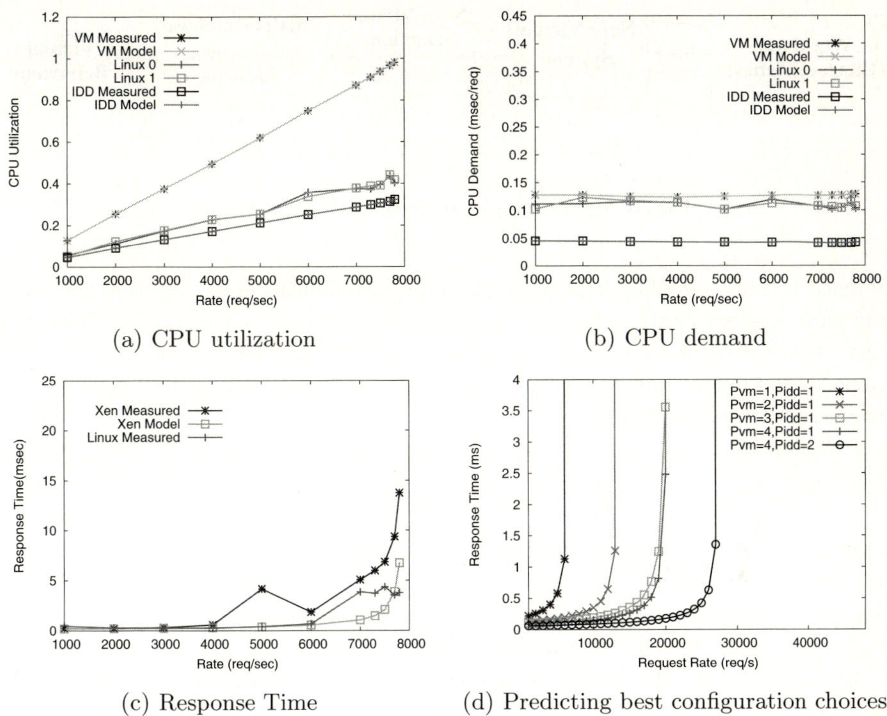

(a) CPU utilization

(b) CPU demand

(c) Response Time

(d) Predicting best configuration choices

Fig. 5. Analytical and experimental results for the Web server benchmark

as parameters for the models. Both, CPU demand and utilization models for Xen IDD and VM are exactly the same as the ones obtained with experimental measurements since the S_v and $Cost^{IDD}_{VM_i}$ factors were obtained with the same experiments. Figure 5(c) shows the calculated response time as a function of request ratio. When the request ratio is about to reach its upper bound, the response time start increasing quickly for both experimental and analytical results. The model response time is sub-estimating the measured response time, which was expected since there is a small network overhead and disk is not represented in the model. This result validates the proposed models and shows that they can be used to predict performance of an application running on a Xen VM.

In order to show another applicability of the models, consider a situation where one wants to know how powerful should be a hardware platform to support with quality of service high request ratios. Figure 5(d) exhibits the server response time as a function of the request rate for different speedups of the VM (P_{VM}), and different speedups of the IDD (P_{IDD}). We use the same slowdown factor and Linux demands of the experimental results for plotting the graph. As we increase the VM speedup the maximum request rate also increases. However, for $P_{VM} = 3$ and $P_{VM} = 4$ the maximal request rate is basically the same since the system bottleneck is the IDD. When the IDD speedup is increased, the maximum request rate is also increased. This example shows how models can

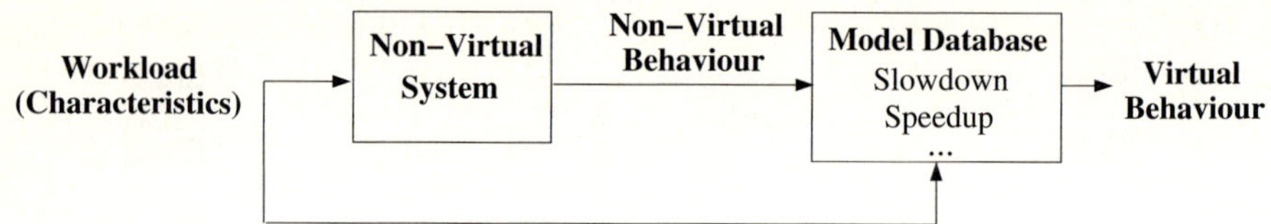

Fig. 6. Performance predictor tool architecture

be used to identify system bottleneck and consequently help to define the most adequate system configuration. Note that the virtual environment may need a high speedup compared to the non-virtual system to achieve the same performance. Increase in hardware cost may be counterbalanced by reduced costs in infrastructure management.

7   Conclusions and Future Work

This work proposes and validates simple analytic models to predict how applications will perform on Xen VMs, based on the performance of applications running on non-virtual environments. We envision two directions towards which our work can evolve. First, our assumption that $Cost_{VM_i}^{IDD}$ is constant, verified to be true for the web server benchmark in our experiments, may be relaxed. In other words, our models can be generalized to represent the overhead of the IDD performed on behalf of application programs as a special workload class in a multi-class queuing model [6]. In the case that $Cost_{VM_i}^{IDD}$ is not constant, the service demands of the special overhead class are load dependent. Second, we believe that our models can support the design of performance predictor tools as well as self-adaptive virtual systems. Figure 6 represents the design of a performance predictor tool where a database of benchmarks and their S_v (and other parameters) are used to predict the performance of applications. The main idea is to obtain metrics from the non-virtual environment and based on previously established information, such as slowdown, to estimate the performance of that application on the virtual environment. We plan to create such tool as a result of the consolidated models. Another interesting direction is to derive S_v experimentally, capturing metrics from the non-virtualized environment.

References

1. P. Barham, B. Dragovic, K. Fraser, S. Hand, T. Harris, A. Ho, R. Neugebauer, I. Pratt, and A. Warfield". Xen and the Art of Virtualization. In *Proc. of 19th ACM Symposium on Operating Systems Principles*, Oct 2003.
2. L. Cherkasova and R. Gardner". "measuring CPU overhead for I/O processing in the Xen virtual machine monitor". In *Proc. of USENIX Annual Technical Conference*, Apr 2005.
3. D. Menascé. Virtualization: Concepts, Applications, and Performance. In *Proc. of The Computer Measurement Group's 2005 International Conference*, Orlando, FL, USA, Dec 2005.

4. D. Gupta, R. Gardner, and L. Cherkasova". XenMon: QoS Monitoring and Performance Profiling Tool. Technical Report HPL-2005-187, HP Labs, Oct 2005.

5. R. Jain. *The Art of Computer Systems Performance Analysis: Techniques for Experimental Design, Measurement, Simulation, and Modeling.* John Wiley and Sons, INC, 1st edition, 1991.

6. D. Menasce, V. Almeida, and L. Dowdy. *Capacity Planning and Performance Modeling: From Mainframes to Client-Server Systems.* Prentice-Hall, Inc., Upper Saddle River, NJ, USA, 1994.

7. D. A. Menasce, L. W. Dowdy, and V. A. F. Almeida. *Performance by Design: Computer Capacity Planning By Example.* Prentice Hall PTR, Upper Saddle River, NJ, USA, 2004.

8. A. Menon, J. R. Santos, Y. Turner, G. Janakiraman, and W. Zwaenepoel". Diagnosing Performance Overheads in the Xen Virtual Machine Environment. In *Proc. of First ACM/USENIX Conference on Virtual Execution Environments (VEE'05)*, Chicago, IL, Jun 2005.

9. D. Mosberger and T. Jin". httperf: A Tool for Measuring Web Server Performance. In *Proc. of First Workshop on Internet Server Performance*, pages 59—67, Madison, WI, Jun 1998.

10. A. W. Site. http://httpd.apache.org.

11. VMWare Web Site. http://www.vmware.com.

12. A. Whitaker, M. Shaw, and S. Gribble". Scale and Performance in the Denali Isolation Kernel. In *Proc. of Operating Systems Design and Implementation (OSDI)*, Dec 2002.

13. Y. Bard. Performance Analysis of Virtual Memory Time-Sharing Systems. *Proc. of IBM Systems Journal*, 14(4):366–384, 1975.

14. Y. Bard. An analytic Model of the VM/370 System. *Proc. of IBM Journal of Research and Development*, 22(5):498–508, Set 1978.

Dynamic Virtual Clustering with Xen and Moab

Wesley Emeneker[1], Dave Jackson[2], Joshua Butikofer[2], and Dan Stanzione[1]

[1] Fulton High Performance Computing Institute
Arizona State University
[2] Cluster Resources
[1]{Wesley.Emeneker, dstanzi}@asu.edu,
[2]{jacksond, josh}@clusterresources.com

Abstract. As larger and larger commodity clusters for high performance computing proliferate at research institutions around the world, challenges in maintaining effective use of these systems also continue to increase. Among the many challenges are maintaining the appropriate software stack for a broad array of applications, and sharing workload across clusters. The Dynamic Virtual Clustering (DVC) system integrates the Xen virtual machine with the Moab scheduler to allow for creation of virtual clusters on a per-job basis. These virtual clusters can provide a unique software environment for a particular application, or can provide a consistent software environment across multiple heterogeneous clusters. In this paper, the overhead of Xen-based DVC vs. native cluster performance is examined for workloads consisting of both serial and MPI-based parallel jobs.

Keywords: Xen, HPC, Dynamic Virtual Cluster, Moab.

1 Introduction

With the proliferation of high performance compute clusters in research environments, the existence of several HPC clusters on a research campus is commonplace. Effectively leveraging the resources of multiple clusters in order to increase job throughput and decrease turnaround time is a difficult task. In many cases, it is relatively simple to physically interconnect the networks of multiple clusters on a limited geographic scale to form a campus area grid [2]. However, the simple existence of the network connections does not make it possible to share workloads between clusters. Among the many challenges, the software environments across clusters may be sufficiently different as to prevent portability of jobs, different filesystems may be available on different clusters, and resource management software must be aware of the various resources available.

The application of the Xen paravirtualization technology to cluster computing promises mitigation of the heterogeneous software environment problem by abstracting the software environment across clusters. This paper describes the design of a system integrating Xen, the Moab cluster scheduler, and the Torque resource manager which allows the automatic creation and destruction of "virtual clusters" within individual clusters or spanning multiple clusters. This system,

G. Min et al. (Eds.): ISPA 2006 Ws, LNCS 4331, pp. 440–451, 2006.

Dynamic Virtual Clustering (DVC), allows software environments customized to a particular group or job to be deployed on a per job basis as part of the normal operation of HPC clusters. The DVC system makes it practical to run jobs within a single cluster that requires a custom software environment, to run jobs intended for one cluster on a remote cluster transparently to the user, and even to run single jobs that span multiple clusters, all with no disruption to the "normal" cluster environment.

The rest of this paper looks at the possibilities of DVC and many of the issues encountered with dynamically creating and destroying clusters of virtual machines. Section 2 looks at work on using virtual machines in a distributed computing environments, and examines projects that may bring increased capability to cluster computing with Xen. After examining issues encountered when applying Xen to High Performance Computing (HPC), we propose a prototype DVC setup and parallel job preemption implementation in section 4. We also examine the initial implementation of DVC with the Moab cluster scheduler and characterize the overhead and performance of several workloads in section 6. In addition to the overhead and performance measurements, we show initial results for the preempt/restart plan presented in section 4. Finally, section 7 analyzes the results seen, and proposes improvements and features to be implemented before DVC can become a viable clustering setup.

2   Related Work

The merits of using Xen for High Performance Computing (HPC) have been examined in [5,1,8,14,10]. Several ideas for using virtual machines in a distributed fashion have been proposed and implemented [12], but very little application of Xen to HPC, especially in a campus area grid, has been done.

Many projects currently under development today are concerned with maximizing the performance and increasing the capability of virtual machines. Intel's Vanderpool and AMD's Pacifica CPU extensions[11,13] are examples of projects that aim to increase the capabilities of virtual machines.

The hardware virtualization support supplied by Intel and AMD allows multiple virtual machines to run on the same computer without requiring any modifications to the guest OS. While VMware has been doing this for many years, the loss of performance incurred by using VMware[5] makes it unsuitable for HPC clusters. The current Xen approach to virtualization requires the OS to be ported to the paravirtualized interface, which for some proprietary OSs may be impossible. By taking advantage of the Vanderpool and Pacifica technology, Xen will no longer require an OS to be ported in order to run it as a guest.

3   Dynamic Virtual Clustering

The goal of DVC is to allow any cluster job, whether serial or parallel, to run on any available cluster resource transparently. For multi-cluster use, DVC requires that the various clusters be connected in a campus area grid [2]. A campus

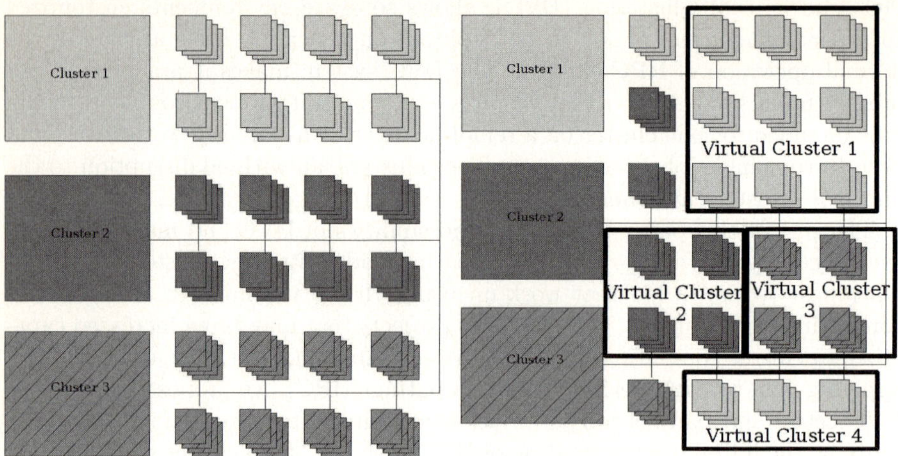

Fig. 1. A Campus Area Grid   **Fig. 2.** Virtual machines in a cluster environment

area grid requires that each cluster's internal network be connected so that all compute nodes across the grid are visible to one another, as depicted in figure 3. Once this connection is in place, DVC allows jobs to move between clusters, or even span them.

The three primary capabilities of DVC are:

1. The ability to run jobs within a cluster that would otherwise require modifications to the clusters software environment
2. The ability to run a job submitted to one cluster unmodified on a second cluster, even if the second cluster has a substantially different software stack.
3. The ability to transparently run a single job that spans multiple clusters, either to increase total throughput or to increase the maximum possible job size

In addition to these three additional capabilities, a properly constructed Xen-based DVC system has the ability to add transparent preemption/restart and migration to all jobs on the cluster.

Capability (1) above derives from the ability of a Xen VM to provide image customization. A Xen image can be created that has exactly the software stack required for a particular job, including the correct set of libraries, licenses, user accounts, etc. When a job requiring a particular image is to be run, the DVC system in conjunction with the resource management software:

1. Selects the correct Xen image for that job based on the queue to which the jobs was submitted or tags in the submission script
2. Stages this image to the nodes scheduled for the job
3. Boots the image on each node, supplying the appropriate network configuration information

4. Starts the appropriate resource management daemons within each VM in the virtual cluster, allowing jobs running inside the VMs to be monitored
5. Informs the resource management software of the existence of the new virtual nodes
6. Launches the job within the virtual nodes

When the job is completed, the DVC software must:

1. Detect the termination of the job
2. Shut down and remove all the VMs associated with the job
3. Inform the resource management software that the virtual nodes no longer exist

Once virtual clusters can be transparently created and destroyed in this manner, it is possible for jobs with widely varying software requirements to be run on a single cluster with substantially lower administration overhead than would otherwise be required. For example, jobs requiring different versions of MPI can be run each in their own virtual cluster without the need for scripts to change the default environment (e.g. changing a symbolic link to /usr/bin/mpirun), or without extensive use of environment variables.

The second capability of DVC stated above is the ability to load balance jobs between clusters.

If one cluster in the campus grid is heavily loaded, and other clusters are lightly loaded, DVC allows jobs to be forwarded (load balanced) to lightly loaded clusters. In this case, forwarding means jobs submitted to the heavily loaded cluster are executed on the lightly loaded cluster using the software image of the original cluster to which the job was submitted. The capacity of a cluster to run jobs is generally constrained by the number of processors in in the cluster. Using DVC to accomplish job migration has several advantages:

- Jobs do not need to be modified to account for differences between cluster software environments.
- Job capacity is increased by allowing multiple cluster's processors to be used.
- Increasing the job capacity decreases average job turnaround time.

For load balancing to occur, DVC follows the same procedures described above with the following addition.

1a. Find a cluster capable of running the job, and exchange job information

With this modification, job forwarding can be accomplished.

The third capability of DVC, cluster spanning, provides increased capability and increased capacity in a multi-cluster environment. Previous work[6,7] has demonstrated that spanning jobs across multiple clusters results in higher total throughput, even when limited bandwidth is available between clusters. Spanning jobs across clusters allows:

- Jobs too large for any single cluster to be run across multiple clusters. Given 2 32-node clusters, a single 64 node job could be spanned across them.

– When a job has insufficient resources on one cluster, the resources of multiple clusters can be combined to fulfill the job requirements. Given 2 32-node clusters each with 16 nodes free, a 32 node job can be spanned across the clusters to meet resource requirements.

Job spanning is more difficult for schedulers than capabilities 1 and 2. For spanning to occur, a scheduler must be able to determine which nodes are available for use, and be able to loan (give temporary control) them to the requesting scheduler. As with job migration, the following procedures must be changed:

1a. If no cluster can individually run the job, borrow nodes from one or more clusters
   (a) Notify the loaning scheduler to not schedule on borrowed nodes
   (b) Add borrowed nodes to local resource pool

Once the job is completed, additional steps must be taken to return the borrowed nodes to the originating cluster.

4. Remove borrowed nodes from resource pool
5. Notify loaning scheduler that borrowed nodes are available for scheduling

Although using VMs will degrade the performance of each individual host[5], the capabilities that VMs give may increase cluster utilization overall. Figure 3 shows several possibilities for cluster spanning and migration. In the drawing, each cluster has a different software image, but by using DVC we can use the required image on any cluster in the campus area grid.

While the possibilities of environment customization, job migration, and job spanning are enticing, there are many issues that must be dealt with before DVC can become useful.

4   Challenges in Dynamic Virtual Clustering

There are many potential benefits of using DVC in a multi-cluster environment. These include simplified cluster job spanning, easier administration, and better isolated and controlled cluster jobs. Despite these benefits, dynamically creating a cluster of virtual machines tailored to run a single job creates substantial overhead. Allocating and assigning resources, starting the tailored virtual machines, running the job, and finally destroying the virtual cluster are intimately involved with dynamically creating virtual clusters. Here we examine and propose solutions to the major issues of the initial implementation of Dynamic Virtual Clustering.

4.1   Design Decision 1: Assigning Network Addresses

Schedulers and resource managers must be aware of and know how to contact every node in the cluster, whether real or virtual. IPs and hostnames assigned to virtual machines must be capable of being looked up by the scheduler and resource manager. There are two main ways to assign IPs and hostnames to virtual machines and each method has its disadvantages.

Dynamic Assignment: DHCP is a common tool for assigning IP addresses in clusters. While this approach works well for real cluster nodes, for virtual nodes this technique presents difficulties. For virtual machines, the scheduler must be able to generate a list of unique MAC addresses that do not conflict with any node accessible in the network. The scheduler must be able to determine which MAC addresses are no longer in use, and be able to reassign and reuse them. However, most schedulers don't operate at the MAC address level, but rather at the IP or hostname level. Static assignment bypasses assigning MAC addresses and directly uses IPs and hostnames.

Static Assignment: With this approach to IP and hostname assignment, we require the environment to parse and use environment variables passed on the kernel command line. While each virtual machine will get a different IP and hostname, the variables passed to the kernel are incapable of changing for as long as the environment exists, therefore the assigned variables are "static". By using IPs and hostnames that are capable of forward and reverse DNS resolution, we can ensure that any virtual machine created will be able to be used by the controlling resource manager and scheduler.

This approach has distinct advantages over dynamic assignment. It is much simpler to define a set of names and IP addresses (instead of MACs) that can be looked up by the scheduler and resource manager and assigned to a VM. Additionally, by prepending a marker to the host's hostname, we have a simple way to both denote which machines are virtual.

Design Decision: Define a list of virtual machines hostnames and IPs in DNS or a host lookup file to ensure forward and reverse lookup capability. VM hostnames and IPs are assigned by prepending an arbitrary marker to the host's hostname (in this case, a "v_") to denote a virtual machine. The IPs are looked up by the scheduler and passed on the kernel command line when the VM is booted. In addition to this, the scheduler must also add the newly created host to the resource manager so that job can be scheduled on the VM.

4.2   Design Decision 2: Resource Management and Creation

In a virtual cluster the batch scheduler must be capable of controlling job execution and managing resources available to each virtual machine. Each node in a typical Torque cluster runs a "mom" that is capable of reporting job status and resource consumption to the scheduler as well as controlling job execution. Although virtual nodes are not as permanent as nodes in a real cluster, the scheduler must be able to control the execution of any job assigned to the virtual cluster. The temporary nature of virtual clusters implies that the Torque resource manager should not have a permanent list of all possible virtual nodes.

Design Decision: Each virtual node must have a "mom" reporting to a scheduler in order to be able to schedule jobs, monitor resource consumption, and control job execution on the virtual node. The batch scheduler must dynamically add or remove virtual nodes from the Torque resource manager upon creation or destruction of a virtual cluster.

4.3   Design Decision 3: Image Management

Managing VM images is a vital part of successfully deploying a Dynamic Virtual Cluster. Several steps must be taken to ensure that every node in the virtual cluster has the same and correct image.

Staging: Distributing VM images is a time consuming job. While it is possible to use a central NFS server as a repository for all images, each VM will generally require write access to the image. This requires either a separate image for each VM, or a Copy-On-Write image for each VM. The cost of either is substantial for a central repository.

The second approach to filesystem staging gives each host a copy of the filesystem to reside on a local disk. Any VM booted on a host can use the local image instead of a remote image, thereby removing one possible bottleneck. Even though this approach provides a few advantages over a central repository, the issue remains of using trusted images.

Trust: Trust is an important part of using VM images. In a homogeneous virtual cluster, each filesystem image must be identical to the base image that all VMs expect to use. By performing a hash of the local image, we can check (to a high degree of confidence) that a local image hash is identical to the precomputed remote image hash.

Removal: In the DVC setup proposed, each Xen VM is given a locally owned image that it can read and write. Because each VM is capable of modifying its local image, the possibility of image skew and image fill creeps in. Therefore, each image used by a VM is deleted after the VM is destroyed. The disadvantage to this approach is that an expensive copy operation must take place each time a VM is to run on the machine.

Design Decision: Each image is copied from a trusted location to a unique temporary location that only exists while the virtual machine exists.

4.4   Parallel Preemption and Restart

Checkpointing, preempting, and restarting parallel programs are notoriously hard problems. Although it is well understood how to checkpoint serial and parallel jobs at the application level [3,9], a synchronized save of distributed processes for a coherent distributed state is difficult. The Xen hypervisor is capable of saving the entire state (including the network state) of any guest domain running on a host. With the assumption that network communication between distributed processes uses a reliable protocol, we must save each environment in time to prevent any network timeouts from occurring, thus a coherent distributed state should exist.

Preempting and restarting distributed processes running inside Xen guest domains hinge on the synchronization of all saves. One method for preemption requires a script to open multiple ssh sessions simultaneously. Once each preemption requested guest is checked for existence, all requested guests are saved. A second method for preemption relies on the synchronized time of each host in the group of domains to checkpoint. While network time protocols cannot synchronize host clocks precisely, the clocks can be set to within a few milliseconds of each other. By relying on independent programs on each host that are set to save the state of a guest at a future time, we can reliably save the state of a set of distributed processes.

Design Decision: Use a script to open multiple ssh sessions in order to save multiple guest environments simultaneously.

5   Methodology

5.1   Initial Implementation

In order for DVC to become a transparent cluster service, the batch scheduler must be able to create VMs, run jobs inside them, and destroy them without user intervention. A basic DVC system has been implemented within the Moab cluster scheduler. This system has been used to test the overhead of VM creation, runtime, and clean up.

Moab: Moab is both a cluster scheduler and a policy engine. In addition to managing and running traditional cluster jobs, Moab is able to schedule in a grid environment where multiple clusters are presented as a pool of resources. Flexible policy settings within the Moab scheduler are able to ensure both fair use of resources and required levels of quality of service. These features, and the following specific capabilities, make Moab a good platform for implementing and deploying DVC:

- Borrowing nodes from other clusters running the Moab scheduler
- The ability to interface with multiple resource managers (TORQUE, LSF, SGE, bproc, etc.)
- Providing an interface allowing external scripts to give and receive data from Moab

As part of this project, in collaboration with Moab developers, several experimental capabilities have been added:

1. Detection of VM filesystem images available for virtualization on each physical node
2. Scheduler creation, destruction, and management of virtual nodes
3. Dynamic addition and removal of virtual nodes from resource manager
4. Job scheduling within virtual node clusters
5. Removal of VM host resources from scheduler

These capabilities, combined with the fact that TORQUE is a freely available, actively maintained, and widely used resource manager make the Moab/TORQUE combination a solid choice for deploying Dynamic Virtual Clustering.

Manual Virtualization: The first step towards creating a DVC system is to manually create virtual machines that the batch scheduler can identify and use for jobs. This step is accomplished in Moab with a set of plugin scripts that create virtual nodes and register them with the cluster for scheduling. With the VM creation scripts, Moab is able to construct a Xen domain configuration file on the fly with the necessary options (name, memory, fs image, etc.). In order to keep virtual machines on the same node separate, each virtual node has a unique directory containing the requisite filesystem images. With the virtual node setup and creation accomplished, it becomes possible to schedule on the new virtual node by registering the node with both the resource manager and scheduler.

Queue Virtualization: Building upon manual virtualization, queue virtualization is able to take any job submitted to a "virtualize" queue which will create the necessary virtual nodes, schedule the job on the recently created virtual cluster, and finally destroy the virtual cluster.

5.2   Experimental Setup

For this testing, two clusters were used- one 14 node cluster and one 12 node cluster. All nodes contained identical hardware.

- Host machine: CentOS 4.3, Xen Linux 2.6.16 domain-0
- Host specifications: Dual Xeon EM64T 3.6 Ghz processors, 8GB RAM, Gigabit Ethernet.
- Guest machine: CentOS 4.2, Xen Linux 2.6.16 domain-U, 1GB image size
- Resource Manager: Torque 2.1.0
- Batch Scheduler: Moab

All cluster nodes were connected with a single private Gigabit Ethernet switch.

6   Results

6.1   Test Plan

In this section, measurements are presented for the overhead associated with DVC. The types of overhead examined include the time required for the staging, configuration, booting, runtime and clean up of all VMs in a virtual cluster, as well as the amount of memory consumed.

The loss of CPU performance has been examined numerous times as seen in [1,10,14,4], and won't be shown here. For this set of measurements, VM disk usage was not a factor for 2 reasons:

1. All jobs used network mounted filesystems to read and write data. No user was allowed to write data to the VM disk.
2. The VM disk image is a constant size on the host hard disk.

The last major source of resource consumption is RAM. Consumed RAM is largely subject to the software environment of the virtual machine, but must be taken into account when dynamically creating virtual machines. The following sources of overhead in dynamic virtual clusters were measured.

- VC creation overhead: Filesystem staging, configuration creation, boot time
- Environment overhead: Memory

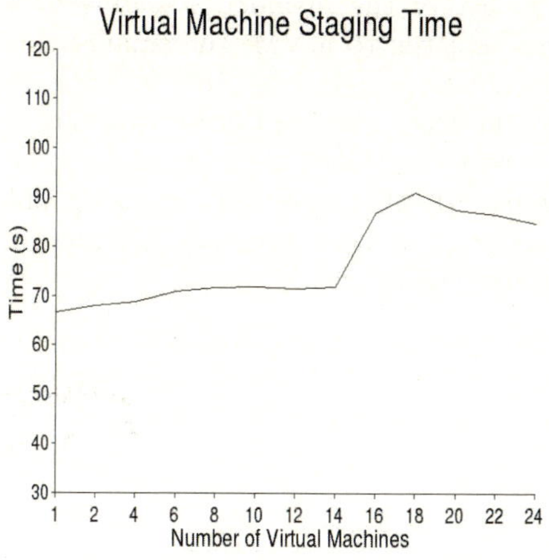

Fig. 3. VM Creation Overhead

Figure 3 shows virtual machine staging overhead. Each virtual cluster must be created on-the-fly, and it is desirable to do so in parallel in order to decrease wait time. However, there is significant overhead of 65-75 seconds involved in copying a 1GB image from a trusted location to 1-14 nodes. The jump in time from creating 14 VMs to creating 16 VMs occurs because 14 nodes is a self-contained cluster. Any more than 14 virtualized nodes requires nodes from the second cluster to be virtualized. After the jump in time from 14 to 16 virtual machines, the graph levels off to an average staging time of under 90 seconds when the second cluster is in use.

On top of this image overhead, VM boot time and extra resource consumption must be considered and are listed in table 1. The times presented in this table are the averaged results of 15 independent tests.

Table 1. Virtual machine overhead

Guest Startup	23 seconds
Guest Shutdown	11 seconds
Guest Destruction	< 1 second
RAM consumed by environment	50MB RAM

While the DVC scheme proposed in this paper does not require a guest to shutdown cleanly, the shutdown time is shown along with guest destruction time.

Combining each type of overhead, the average time-to-ready of each VM is approximately 2 minutes. While a 2 minute startup delay is acceptable for many cluster applications, for short running and development jobs the delay may take a large percentage of the total run-time.

6.2   Analysis

Each measured source of overhead decreases the capability of a virtual cluster; however, if the overhead is small, the advantages of using DVC can outweigh the overhead incurred by VM use.

- Creation: The time taken to stage and boot a virtual machine is the largest source of DVC at approximately 2 minutes. While this may seem significant, for a cluster job running more than 1 hour, a 3% increase in total run-time is incurred, a small difference compared to the normal run-time.
- Resource Consumption: Like creation time, RAM consumption by the VM environment subtracts only a small percentage from the available memory. Most new HPC nodes have at least 1GB of RAM per processor. Given that 50MB of memory is used by the VM, 5% of the memory available to a job would be wasted. As more memory is given to a VM, the smaller this percentage becomes.
- Destruction: VM destruction requires the least overhead of all those measured. However, improvements to DVC creation by allowing VM images to be reused instead of deleted can save staging costs at the price of increasing VM destruction time. With image reuse, we can cut DVC creation/destruction time from approximately 2 minutes to less than 1.

Given the overhead presented above and the loss of performance[5,1,4] incurred by VM use, the total loss of resources (CPU, RAM and time) is approximately 10%. While this percentage is non-trivial, the capabilities that DVC can give- job migration and cluster spanning- can allow us to increase the capability of multiple clusters.

6.3   Preempt and Restart

In order to verify the validity of the claim that parallel preemption and restart is possible with Xen, we attempted to preempt and restart the HPCC benchmark suite. Jobs using up to 8 nodes have been successfully preempted and restarted consistently. At the time of this writing, preempting and restarting larger jobs is not yet stable.

7   Conclusions and Future Work

Dynamic Virtual Clustering holds promise for multi-cluster environments. With the capabilities of customized software environments, job migration, and job spanning, we can more efficiently schedule clusters in order to increase throughput and decrease job turnaround time[7,6].

The use of virtual machine image customization makes it possible to customize cluster images and provide a homogeneous software environment on top of heterogeneous clusters. Forwarding jobs between clusters allows load-balancing of cluster jobs between heavily and lightly loaded clusters to increase job throughput and decrease turnaround time. Finally, DVC makes spanning jobs over multiple clusters possible to increase both the capability of a multi-cluster environment.

Future work includes modifying Xen to allow paused environments to be saved and restarted, modifying the Moab cluster scheduler to bring take into account resource consumption and image reuse, and deploying DVC in much larger clusters.

References

1. Paul Barham, Boris Dragovic, Keir Fraser, Steven Hand, Tim Harris, Alex Ho, Rolf Neugebauer, Ian Pratt, and Andrew Warfield. Xen and the art of virtualization. In *SOSP '03: Proceedings of the nineteenth ACM symposium on Operating systems principles*, pages 164–177, New York, NY, USA, 2003. ACM Press.

2. John Brooke, Martyn Foster, Stephen Pickles, Keith Taylor, and Terry Hewitt. Mini-Grids: Effective Test-Beds for GRID Application. In *Grid Computing - GRID 2000: First IEEE/ACM International Workshop*, page 158, 2000.

3. K. Mani Chandy and Leslie Lamport. Distributed snapshots: determining global states of distributed systems. *ACM Trans. Comput. Syst.*, 3(1):63–75, 1985.

4. B. Clark, T. Deshane, E. Dow, S Evanchik, M. Finlayson, J. Herne, and J.N. Matthews. Xen and the Art of Repeated Research. In Proceedings of the Usenix annual technical conference. July 2004.

5. Wesley Emeneker and Dan Stanzione. HPC Cluster Readiness of Xen and UML. In *In Proceeding of IEEE International Conference on Cluster Computing (Cluster 2006)* , 2006.

6. William Jones, Louis Pang, Dan Stanzione, and Walter Ligon. Bandwidth-aware Co-allocating Meta-schedulers for Mini-grid Architectures. *International Conference on Cluster Computing (Cluster 2004)*, 2004.

7. William Jones, Louis Pang, Dan Stanzione, and Walter III Ligon. Characterization of Bandwidth-aware Meta-schedulers for Co-allocating Jobs Across Multiple Clusters. *Journal of Supercomputing, Special Issue on the Evaluation of Grid and Cluster Computing*, 2005.

8. Nadir Kiyanclar, Gregory A. Koenig, and William Yurcik. Maestro-VC: A Paravirtualized Execution Environment for Secure On-Demand Cluster Computing. *ccgrid*, 2:28, 2006.

9. Friedemann Mattern. Efficient algorithms for distributed snapshots and global virtual time approximation. *Journal of Parallel and Distributed Computing*, 18(4), 1993.

10. Aravind Menon, Jose Renato Santos, Yoshio Turner, G. (John) Janakiraman, and Willy Zwaenepoel. Diagnosing performance overheads in the xen virtual machine environment. In *VEE '05: Proceedings of the 1st ACM/USENIX international conference on Virtual execution environments*, pages 13–23, New York, NY, USA, 2005. ACM Press.

11. Mendel Rosenblum and Tal Garfinkel. Virtual Machine Monitors: Current Technology and Future Trends. *Computer*, 38(5):39–47, 2005.

12. Nut Taesombut and Andrew A. Chien. Distributed Virtual Computers: Simplifying the Development of High Performance Grid Applications. 2004.

13. R. Uhlig, G. Neiger, D. Rodgers, A.L. Santoni, F.C.M. Martins, A.V. Anderson, S.M. Bennett, A. Kagi, F.H. Leung, and L. Smith. Intel Virtualization Technology. *Computer*, 38:48–56, May 2005.

14. X. Zhang and K Keahey. Evaluation of a Virtual Xen Cluster Using the Pallas MPI Benchmarks Suite, April 2005.

Performance Enhancement of SMP Clusters with Multiple Network Interfaces Using Virtualization

Peter Strazdins[1], Richard Alexander[2], and David Barr[2]

[1] Department of Computer Science, Australian National University
`Peter.Strazdins@cs.anu.edu.au`
[2] Alexander Technology, Canberra
`{richard, david}@alexandertechnology.com`
`http://www.alexandertechnology.com`

Abstract. Clusters of small-scale SMP/CMP nodes are becoming increasingly popular due to their cost-effectiveness. As these nodes are typically capable of supporting a number of network interfaces similar to the number of CPUs, the issue arises how to optimally configure the cluster for optimum communication performance. This paper evaluates a number of configurations on a 4-CPU Opteron cluster with multiple Gigabit Ethernet interfaces. Techniques include channel bonding and using independent communication pathways. With the latter, the use of virtualization via the Xen Virtual Machine Monitor offers the best potential to parallelize all stages of message transmission, for the case when multiple CPUs on a node are communicating simultaneously. Network-level microbenchmarks indicate the best performance is achieved with a configuration where guest virtual machines running on each CPU communicate directly with a dedicated interface, bypassing the virtual machine monitor. Channel bonding also proved to be more effective over multiple communication streams than over single.

1   Introduction

Cluster computers, assembled from COTS commodity-off-the-shelf compute nodes and communication networks, have proved a highly cost-effective solution to high performance computing demands, and have gained dominance in this market. COTS technology has provided high increases in computational speed for a given cost, but in terms of communication networks, the definition of COTS is not only less clear, but their performance increase has not matched that of the compute nodes. While (Gigabit) Ethernet continues to be the most widely used (and most strongly fits the COTS criterion) communication network, there are more specialized networks available, such as InfiniBand, Myrinet and Quadrics.

While low-end SMP nodes have long been seen as highly cost-effective in the cluster context [1,2,3], the recent advent of Chip Multiprocessing (CMP) promises an even higher price-performance advantage. CMP adds a new dimension to the question of the optimal number of CPUs for a cluster computer node. The key issue is that the communication and computational performance must be balanced for a cluster configuration to be cost-effective.

However, many of the COTS processor systems which may be selected for a cluster compute node come with motherboards supporting multiple I/O connections. Typically on these motherboards, the main system bus is connected to a number of PCI buses, each

G. Min et al. (Eds.): ISPA 2006 Ws, LNCS 4331, pp. 452–463, 2006.
© Springer-Verlag Berlin Heidelberg 2006

of which may have a number of slots where I/O devices can be connected. For example, the IWILL DK8-HTX motherboard for Opteron systems has AMD-8111 I/O Hub and AMD-8131 PCI-X Tunnel chips, between them having three PCI-X/PCI buses and 14 device slots, as well as two in-built Gigabit Ethernet controllers [4]. Since network interfaces are themselves I/O devices, this permits a considerable number of interfaces to be connected[1], which can potentially provide an aggregate communication bandwidth to match the nodes' aggregate compute performance for a moderate number of CPUs. As the network's cost (interface cards and switches) is typically a small fraction of an Ethernet-based cluster's overall cost [1], multiple network interfaces may prove to be similarly cost effective as multiple CPUs. This is particularly the case when the ports of the switch are under-utilized, in which case the extra cost is only in the cards, which for Gigabit Ethernet is typically under a few hundred dollars each.

In recent years, there has been a resurgence of interest in *virtual machines* (virtualized operating systems), largely due to the increased encapsulation that this offers, which in turn offers advantages in flexibility, security, performance isolation and migration [5,6]. There are various techniques which may accomplish this, but one offering both potentially high performance and high functionality is known as *para-virtualization*. Xen [5] is an x86-based virtual machine monitor for Linux which uses this technique. The para-virtualization approach of Xen offers an easy way of dedicating network interfaces to instances of virtual machines (which in turn may be running simultaneously on multiple CPUs).

This paper is concerned with an increasingly important issue in cluster design of how to determine the optimal number of CPUs and network interfaces per node, and of how to configure the interfaces. To this end, the paper evaluates various multiple network interface configurations on an SMP cluster with at least as many CPUs. In terms of configurations, we explore two broad possibilities for multiple CPU nodes: *channel bonding*, where all interfaces may be used to send parts of a message (individual packets, in the case of Ethernet [7]); and setting up independent network interfaces for a particular source (or destination) CPU. Our emphasis is on Gigabit Ethernet interfaces, due to their relatively low cost and wide deployment. A key issue in this context is the degree of parallelization possible over the stages of message transmission: the TCP/IP stack, the access of the network interfaces (either network interface cards (NICs) or chips), and the transmission across the communication channel. PCI bus configurations can also play an important role in this process. For independent network interface configurations, dedicating network interfaces to virtual machine instances offers the potential of parallelization over all stages of message transmission. Thus, this paper is will also explore the potential benefits, and overheads, of virtualization in these configurations.

This paper is organized as follows. Section 2 discusses related work, and defines the new contributions made in this paper. Background information on Xen and TCP/IP stack processing is given in Section 3. A variety of multiple network interface configurations that we will study is described in Section 4, with the experimental setup described in Section 5. Performance results are given in Section 6 and conclusions are given in Section 7.

---

[1] Although in practice, bus bandwidth limitations and the number of interrupt requests available would limit this number.

2   Related Work

There are a number of performance evaluations of cluster networks with SMP nodes in the literature (e.g. see [2,8] and the references within). These typically evaluate the effect of connecting cluster nodes with different networks (interface card and switch combinations), but use configurations with a single network interface for communication.

Gigabit Ethernet-based networks, due to their popularity, have also been evaluated. [7] examines the effects of channel bonding of a dual Xeon connected with dual Intel/Pro 1000 ports; it concluded that the channel bonding provided by the Linux kernel was mostly ineffective, and even degraded performance for medium-sized messages. However, it concluded that the related technique of *striping* the data at the socket level (which permits more independent TCP/IP stack processing for each interface) could almost double the bandwidth.

Network I/O performance has recently been recognized as an important issue for Xen [9]. Here, a multiple TCP stream configuration showed that the Xen 'driver domain' (see Section 3) achieved 69% and 100% of the native Linux's receive and send performance, respectively; whereas a normal (guest) VM under Xen achieved 33% and 20% respectively. Subsequent optimizations improved the driver domain's receive performance to 90%, and the VM's send performance to 90% [10]. The configuration used here is the most similar to ours so far, in that the experiment aggregated the performance of 4 server processes, each connected to an independent NIC (c.f. the `*.indep.4p` configurations of Section 4). However, the server was not an SMP, and the clients were on 4 separate machines; thus, their configurations emphasise the CPU overheads of Xen more than ours.

There has been recent interest in the use of virtualization for cluster computing. Key issues include reducing the performance (particularly for message passing) and management overheads, with preliminary solutions being proposed and evaluated [6]. The solution for reducing messaging passing overheads is called *virtual machine monitor bypass* (VMM-bypass), and is elaborated in [11]. This solution can be applied to networks with OS bypass capabilities (also known as *user-level communication*), in this case InfiniBand, which can similarly be used to bypass the virtual machine monitor. The results show that the performance of communication under bypass of the Xen monitor approaches that of the original InfiniBand driver. However, there is not a clear evaluation of how large the overheads were originally under Xen without bypass.

This paper's contributions are that it makes a comparison of various multiple network interface configurations for clusters with multiple CPU nodes. Techniques used include channel bonding and VMM-bypass; however the latter is used to set up independent communication channels, and is a more generic approach as it does not require OS bypass capabilities of the network. In the comparison of the multiple configurations, we also evaluate the overhead of Xen at the MPI level.

3   Background

This section gives background information which is relevant to the experiments on various the GigE network interface configurations described subsequently.

Various references [5,12,11] describe the approach of Xen to virtualization, which the reader is referred to. Xen requires one special guest VM, called *domain0*, to be present; this is used to manage a number of guest VMs. These guest VMs can communicate to each other using shared pages; communication to external VMs occurs through *a virtual interface*. Data is transferred via pseudo-device drivers to domain0; by default, only this domain has access the native device interfaces. Apart from the processing of interrupts, which are fielded first by the VMM, device access from domain0 proceeds very similarly as it would under the corresponding Linux kernel that XenoLinux is based on. For this reason, domain0 is also referred to as the 'driver domain' [10].

The Linux kernel 2.6 has sophisticated TCP/IP stack processing on multiple CPU systems. Due to its widespread importance, studies have recently emerged analysing the parallelization strategies used in Linux [13,14]. Two kinds of locks are required for TCP/IP stack processing: locks related to connection, and locks associated with particular sockets, with the latter typically requiring more frequent access.

Two broad parallelization strategies exist: *connection-parallel* and *message-parallel*, with the former being regarded as superior [13,14]. The message-parallel strategy parallelizes the processing (of different segments) of a single transmission; it can be employed when channel bonding is in use, but typically requires large message sizes to become effective. The connection-parallel strategy allows messages using different sockets to proceed in parallel; this eliminates contention on the per-socket locks [13], and thus explains why socket striping achieves better performance than channel bonding (as reported in [7]).

4   Multiple Network Interface Configurations

Figure 1 shows the configurations for nodes with 2 network interfaces (and 2 CPUs). The acronym NIC should be regarded here as denoting any kind of network interface, whether implemented on a card or on a chip (note also that some cards have dual interfaces). In each case, there are MPI process pairs 0 and 2, and 1 and 3; it can be assumed that communication only occurs between pairs. The diagram indicates communication paths between these processes, rather than physical connectivity. In fact, both connection paths (denoted Nic1 and Nic2) go through the same switch, and in all cases it is possible for any process to communicate with any other.

Configuration `driver.bond.2p` runs MPI processes on the driver domain (domain0), using channel bonding to combine the aggregate performance of the two connecting interfaces. Configuration `driver.indep.2p` is similar, except traffic between the pairs occurs independently on separate NICs; this is achieved by each node being given two IP addresses and binding each to two separate Ethernet interfaces (e.g. `eth1` and `eth2`). The `route add` command is used to route traffic to each of the IP addresses of the other node through one of these interfaces. MPI processes are then configured using a list of the four IP addresses. This ensures that different sockets are used for each stream, thus providing a simple way of ensuring that a connection-parallel strategy is employed.

Configuration `guest.bond.2p` requires two Xen guest domains (1 and 2) to be configured on each node, with the MPI processes being assigned to each of the four

VMs (with each assigned a different IP address). Communication occurs through domain0, which uses bonding of the two NICs. Configuration `guest-byp.indep.2p` is similar, except it uses VMM-bypass: i.e. the NICs are unbound from domain0 and each independently bound to one of VMs. As Xen binds a VM to a CPU (see Section 4.1), this results in processes and NICs being automatically bound to a specific CPU.

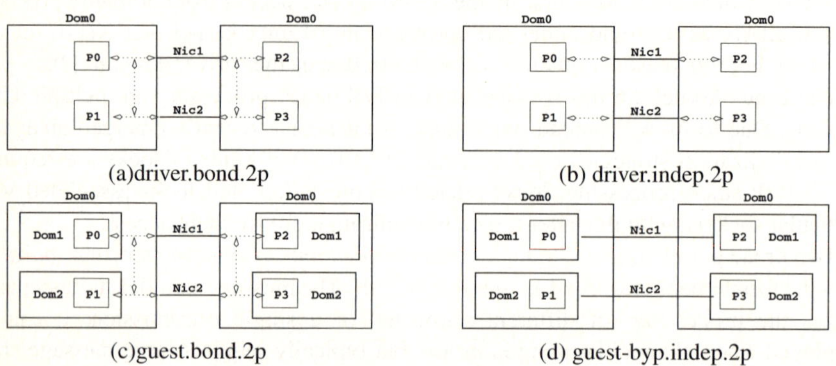

(a)driver.bond.2p

(b) driver.indep.2p

(c)guest.bond.2p

(d) guest-byp.indep.2p

Fig. 1. 2-way NIC configurations

For a baseline comparison, there are also 2 process (1 pair) versions of these configurations, denoted similarly but with the suffix '.1p'. There are similarly 4 pair versions of the above configurations, which use 4 NICs (and use 4 CPUs, with 4 IP addresses per node), denoted with the suffix '.4p'.

In terms of parallelization of the TCP(/IP) stack, the `guest-byp.indep.*` configurations offers fully independent processing for multiple network interfaces. The host-indep.* configurations offer socket-level parallelism, whereas the *.bond.* configurations offer connection-level parallelism.

The characteristics of intra-node communication are also of interest (this would correspond to a situation as on Figure 1, except P0 and P2 are on one node, and P1 and P3 are on the other). For the `driver.*` configurations, these will occur via a shared memory transport. For the `guest*.*` configurations, these occur via *virtual interfaces*, implemented in turn by *event channels*, which can exchange data by shared pages [11]. If this is the case, while there would be some overhead of invoking the Xen VMM (to service requests in the event channels), there need be little or no copying overhead for the data.

4.1   Modifying Xen for domain0 Bypass

Normally, guest domains under Xen perform I/O via a *virtual interface* to domain0; domain0 then accesses these hardware devices directly [12]. This is done by setting the `vif` variable in the guest domain's configuration file.

If this is omitted, no virtual interfaces are set up; however, an actual (PCI-connected) network interface can be set up to perform I/O instead [12]. This can be specified in the guest domain's configuration file by setting the `pci` variable to the desired bus

and slot number, e.g. to connect to the card on slot 4 of PCI bus 3, the setting is
`pci=['03,04,0']`.

The binding of a guest domain to a single CPU is similarly specified in its configuration file. It remains to ensure that before the guest domains are brought up, these slots are unbound from domain0, and, for maximum efficiency, the interrupt requests arising from that slot are directed to the same CPU. In Linux, this can be done by creating a file `/proc/irq/`i`/smp_affinity` which contains the CPU's number, where i in the interrupt request number of that slot.

Note that in this context, the VMs form the nodes of a (virtual) cluster which will be used to run parallel jobs and so must 'trust' each other; thus, there is less of a security issue here in bypassing Xen's driver domain.

5   Experimental Setup

We use a 2 node cluster for our experimentation. Each node consists of dual SMP dual-core 2.2 GHz AMD Opteron processors with a 2-way 64 KB level 1 data cache and an 8-way 512 unified L2 cache, and 4 GB of RAM. The nodes have an IWILL DK8-HTX_815 motherboard, with 800 MB/s HyperTransport links. The motherboard has in-built dual Intel 82541GI/PI GigE controllers. External NICs can be connected to two slots connected to the same 64-bit 33/66/100 MHz PCI-X bus, and to one slot connected to a third 32-bit 66 MHz PCI 2.2 bus. For external NICs with dual Ethernet ports, this permits up to 8 Gigabit Ethernet interfaces on this motherboard.

One of the in-built GigE chips is configured to Ethernet interfaces `eth1` (the other is needed by the driver domain as a control interface). A Pro/1000 MT NIC with an Intel 82541PI chip is configured to `eth4`. The nodes also have a Pro/1000 MT NIC (Intel 82546GB chips) with dual interfaces; these are configured to `eth2` and `eth3`. Inspection of the Linux device driver code indicates that the 82546 chip supports *segmentation bypass*, i.e. offload of some of the IP stack, but that there is no offload for the 82541 chip. Note that the same device driver is used for all interfaces. The `lspci` command indicates `eth1`, `eth2` and `eth3` are on PCI bus 3, which is running at 66 MHz in 32-bit mode (total bandwidth of 240 MB/s), and that `eth4` is on PCI bus 1, also running at 66 MHz in 32-bit mode.

The networks are configured with am Ethernet Message Transfer Unit of 4148 bytes - sufficient to hold a 4KB payload under TCP/IP. This value was found to be optimal under elementary network bandwidth tests.

The system software is based on the Linux Dapper Drake 6.0.6 distribution, with a XenoLimux 3.2.2 kernel. This is based on the Linux kernel 2.6.16 SMP, which both the driver and guest domains are based on. gcc 4.0.3 comes with this distribution. The channel bonding driver, when used, is that which comes with the Linux kernel.

5.1   Benchmark Programs

Our benchmark programs use the MPICH-2 MPI implementation under the MVAPICH-2 package from the Ohio State University [15]. MPI is configured to only use interfaces `eth1` to `eth4`.

To test raw communication performance, we use the latency and bandwidth (uni- and bi-directional) benchmarks program, also available under the MVAPICH-2 package [15,8]. The latency tests give the averaged timings for $r = 100$ ping-pong tests[2]. The uni-directional bandwidth test is for $g = 64$ one-way messages followed by an acknowledgement, repeated $r = 20$ times. The bi-directional bandwidth tests are similar, except each nodes posts g receives and then sends g messages. All tests have a warm-up period of $r/10$ un-timed messages (of the same length as those to be measured).

The latency test is useful as it represents the communication performance of where a node on the 'critical path' of a parallel computation is waiting on a message. The uni-directional bandwidth test is aimed to demonstrate the maximum one-way bandwidth performance. It models pipelined communication, such as is used in applications such as parallel Linpack. The bi-directional tests can show saturation effects (in the PCI bus and/or network interfaces); it also models important communication patterns such as all-to-all exchange.

The benchmarks use `MPI_Wtime()` to measure time, which in this case, is based on `gettimeofday()`. This should return the actual wall time irrespective of whether running on real or virtualized hosts.

These benchmarks normally run as 2 MPI processes. For our experiments, they were modified to run as pairs of MPI processes; in this case 1, 2, or 4 pairs being of interest. Also, calls to `sched_setaffinity()` were used to bind processes to the CPU corresponding to their process number. Timings for each pair are recorded. Our methodology involves performing 10 timings for each data point on an otherwise quiescent system; while the average is of most interest, variations may indicate 'stress' on the kernel and/or an asymmetry in the loads over each CPU from message processing.

5.2   System Integrity Issues

The use of 4 network interfaces in the 4 CPU nodes initially created problems. It caused communication-intensive applications to hang or crash. The problem was traced to the handling of interrupt requests, due to the limited number available on the DK8-HTX motherboard. Some local disk I/O interrupts, as they shared the same interrupt number as one of the network devices were lost.

The solution was to configure the operating system (domain0) to implement its filesystem on a network bootable RAM disk rather than the local disk.

This problem does however indicate a practical limitation to the number of network interfaces that can be used simultaneously on a given motherboard.

6   Results

In Section 6.1, we report the performance of the single pair configurations. Native Linux performance is also included and the bandwidths of the separate interfaces are also measured. From this, we can evaluate the overhead of Xen and gain a baseline to understand the performance of multiple interfaces, which is presented in Section 6.2.

---

[2] r is increased by a factor of 10 for small messages.

6.1 Baseline Performance

For single pair performance (interface `eth1`), the unidirectional bandwidth approaches 110 MB/s, close to the theoretical maximum of Gigabit Ethernet (125 MB/s), for all but the `guest.bond.1p` configuration. The bi-directional case is similar, except the bandwidth approaches 135 MB/s. In both cases, the `*.indep` configurations perform best, being virtually indistinguishable from each other. Similar to [7], channel bonding in the driver domain gives lower performance, especially in the 1KB – 256 KB region, but in the unidirectional case for messages over 1 MB it has slightly faster performance. The performance of the `guest.bond` configuration, which performs communication via Xen's virtual interfaces to domain0 (which in turn is configured to use channel bonding) approaches 50MB/s in both cases – much lower than the others; this trend we will see maintained. The bandwidth across `eth2` and `eth3` was about 15% faster in the bi-directional case, and `eth4` was slower with a maximum bandwidth of 90 MB/s.

For the latency tests, the results are similar to the unidirectional bandwidth case, with the bandwidth increasing sharply at 1 KB. However, `driver.bond` suffers a greater (30-50%) performance loss over the 32 – 256 KB range. Table 1 summarizes performance at the endpoints.

Table 1. Inter-node Latency Test Performance summary for 1-pair configurations

	`*.indep`	`driver.bond`	`guest.bond`
time at 1 B (μs)	87	91	106
B/W at 4 MB (MB/s)	107	105	51

The above experiments were also run under native Linux (based on the same kernel and distribution as for XenoLinux) with independent channels; we call this the `native.indep.1p` configuration. The results were identical to `driver.indep.1p`, except that the latency test yielded a marginally higher bandwidth of 109 MB/s (at 4 MB); this indicates the messaging performance under domain0 is essentially identical to native Linux.

Intra-node performance was measured similarly, by running the MPI processes on the same physical host; the results a summarized in Table 2. The `driver.*` configurations use a shared memory transport; the `guest*.*` configurations use virtual interfaces; by comparison with Table 1, this has a very similar bandwidth to that of inter-node communication. The uni- and bi-directional bandwidths for large messages were the same as for the latency tests.

Table 2. Intra-node latency test performance summary for 1-pair configurations

	`driver.*`	`guest*.*`
time at 1 B (μs)	18	530
B/W (MB/s) at 4 MB	30	50

6.2   Multiple Interface Performance

Figure 2 gives the bandwidths for 2 pair performance (using interfaces `eth1` and `eth4`). Figure 3 gives the performance for 4 pairs; configuration `guest.bond.4p` is omitted here, due to it being insufficiently stable to complete the tests.

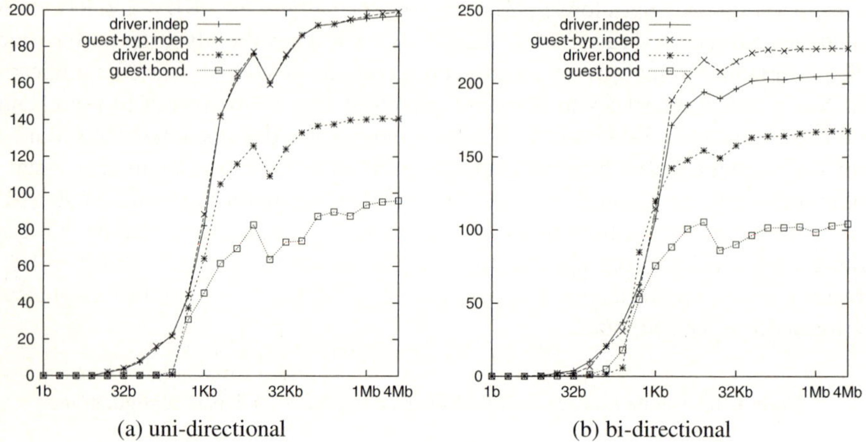

(a) uni-directional   (b) bi-directional

Fig. 2. Bandwidth (MB/s) versus message size for 2-pair configurations

For the latency tests (not graphed), the results are similar to the 1-pair tests, with again `driver.bond` suffering a 30-50% performance loss over the 32 – 256 KB range. Table 3 summarizes performance for large messages.

Table 3. Latency test bandwidth at 4 MB for 2- and 4-pair configurations

	driver.indep	guest-byp.indep	driver.bond	guest.bond
2-pairs	172	200	144	86
4-pairs	296	296	256	–

Overall, it can be seen that the `*.indep` configurations consistently give the best performance, with the `guest-byp.*` configuration performing the same on some tests, and ≈ 10% better on others. In the 4-pair case, it achieves 300 MB/s and 345 MB/s for uni- and bi-directional bandwidth, respectively. This is comparable with the maximum expected uni-directional bandwidth, which is 354 MB/s; this is the sum of the bandwidth on PCI bus 3 (264 MB/s) plus the bandwidth over `eth4` (90 MB/s – see Section 6.1).

Comparing the results in Section 6.1 and Figures 2–3, we see a clear (although sub-linear) increase in bandwidth as network interfaces (and communication streams) are added. In particular, `driver.bond` improves its performance as communication intensity increases, and also demonstrates benefit from multiple communication streams.

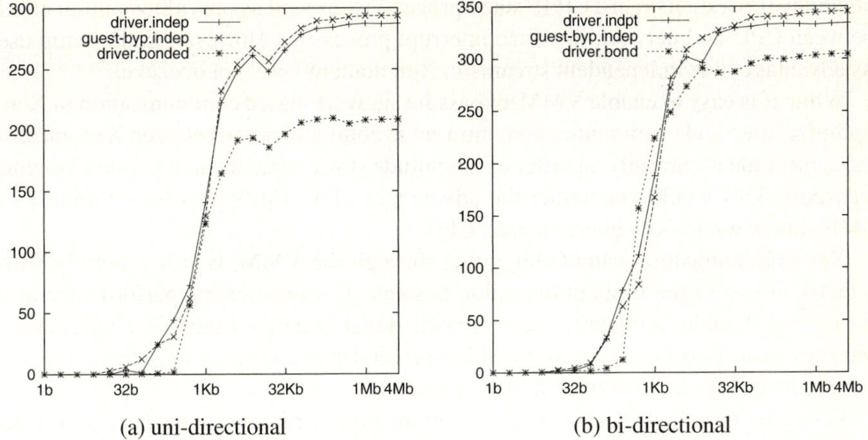

(a) uni-directional   (b) bi-directional

Fig. 3. Bandwidth (MB/s) versus message size for 4-pair configurations

However, from extrapolating the trends, it seems likely that there would be diminishing returns from adding more interfaces, at least on the motherboard used.

It should be noted that there was a significant variation in the measurements for the `driver.indep.4p` tests (the averaged results are over 10 measurements). The `driver.bond` configurations experienced some variations, but these were significantly reduced once CPU affinity was imposed. CPU affinity did not however seem to have a large impact on average performance. `guest-byp.indep` showed very small variability in all tests; it can be noted that affinity is enforced in the `guest*.*` configurations.

The `native.indep.2p` results were indistinguishable from that of the `driver.indep.2p`. However, the `native.indep.4p` results showed conflicting differences over `driver.native.4p`: the latency test showed a bandwidth of only 256 MB/s at 4MB, but the uni-directional bandwidth was much higher, peaking at 335 MB/s. Bi-directional bandwidth shows great variability in the 4–64 KB range, peaking at 382 MB/s at 8 KB, but decreased to 300 MB/s after 256 KB. In this situation, while communication performance is different in domain0 over native Linux, neither shows conclusively better performance overall.

7   Conclusions and Future Work

Our preliminary experiments on a 4 CPU Opteron-based Gigabit Ethernet clusters indicate that worthwhile improvements in communication bandwidth can be achieved by using multiple network interfaces. With one communication stream per process pair, configuring streams to run independently across separate interfaces generally yielded significantly better performance than did channel bonding. However, relatively better gains for channel bonding were observed as the number of streams and communication intensity increased. The best performance came from configurations using Xen virtualized hosts with VMM-bypass for network I/O. This is because it has the greatest potential of parallelism in TCP/IP stack processing, as well as providing natural affinity between CPU and network interface interrupt processing. However, in the setup used, its advantage over independent streams in Xen domain0 was not decisive.

While it is easy to enable VMM-bypass for network-based communication in Xen to optimize inter-node communication, intra-node communication between Xen guests on the same node is currently an order of magnitude slower than the native shared memory transport. This would counteract the advantages of VMM-bypass for configuring an SMP cluster with a Xen guest on each CPU.

Xen communication bandwidth, going through the VMM, is still generally within a factor of two of the best configuration possible. Communication performance of the Xen driver domain (domain0) closely matched that of native Linux for single network interfaces and 1-pair configurations, although for 4-pair configurations, there was some variability but no decisive overall difference.

Future work includes optimizing communication performance between Xen guests on the same node; this could be implemented as a shortcut to a shared-memory transport in the virtual interface implementation. Once this is done, application-level performance could be meaningfully evaluated over the configurations studied here. Other directions for future work include evaluating these effects on nodes of different motherboards; particularly interesting will be the 8 CPU case.

It is foreseeable that virtualization, with a combination of VMM-bypass and optimization, may actually offer performance advantages in SMP clusters. As well as permitting some advantages in average performance, configurations of one virtual machine per CPU show low variability in performance, due to the increased encapsulation afforded by para-virtualization.

Acknowledgements

The authors thank Alistair Rendell for helpful suggestions in the experimentation and the preparation of the manuscript. We also thank Tony Breeds for setting up the software distribution and some of the result-generating infrastructure used in this work, and thank Brendan Howe for technical support.

References

1. Aberdeen, D., Baxter, J., Edwards, R.: A 98c/MFLOP Ultra-Large Scale Neural Network Training on a PIII Cluster. In: Proceedings of Supercomputing 2000. (2000)
2. Capello, F., Richard, O., Etiemble, D.: Understanding performance of SMP clusters running MPI programs. Future Generation Computer Systems **17** (2001) 711–720
3. Pukayastha, A., Guiang, C.S., Schulz, K., Minyard, T., Milfeld, K., Barth, W., Hurley, P., Boisseau, J.R.: Performance Characteristics of Dual-processor HPC Cluster Nodes based on 64-bit Commodity Processors. In: Proceedings of the Linux Clusters Institute (LCI) International Conference: the HPC Revolution. (2004)
4. Advanced Microelectronic Devices: AMD Microprocessor Solutions. (http://www.amd.com/us-en/Processors)
5. Barham, P., Dragovic, B., Fraser, K., Harris, S.H.T., Ho, A., Neugebauer, R., Pratt, I., Warfield, A.: Xen and the Art of Virtualization. In: Proceedings of SOSP 03: the Nineteenth ACM Symposium on Operating Systems Principles, Ney York, ACM (2003) 164–177

6. Huang, W., Liu, J., Abali, B., Panda, D.: A Case fopr High Performance Computing with Virtual Machines. In: Proceedings of ICS06: International Conference of Supercomputing, Cairns (2006)
7. Turner, D., Oline, A., Chen, X., Benjegerdes, T.: Integrating New Capabilities into NetPIPE. In: 10th European PVM/MPI User's Group Meeting, Venice, Springer (2003) 37–44
8. Liu, J., Chandrasekaran, B., Wu, J., Jiang, W., Kini, S., Yu, W., Buntinas, D., Wyckoff, P., Panda, D.: Performance Comparison of MPI Implementations over Infiniband, Myrinet and Quadrics. In: Proceedings of the SuperComputing 2003 Conference, Phoenix (2003)
9. Menon, A., Jose Renato Santos, a.Y.T., Janakiraman, G., Zwaenepoel, W.: Diagnosing Performance Overheads in the Xen Virtual Machine Environment. In: First ACM/USENIX Conference on Virtual Execution Environments (VEE'05). (2005) 13–25
10. Menon, A., Cox, A.L., Zwaenepoel, W.: Optimizing Network Virtualization in Xen. In: Proceedings of the 2006 USENIX Annual Technical Conference, Boston (2006) 15–28
11. Liu, J., Huang, W., Abali, B., Panda, D.: High Performance VMM-Bypass I/O in Virtual Machines. In: Proceedings of the 2006 USENIX Annual Technical Conference, Boston (2006)
12. University of Cambridge Computing Laboratory: The Xen virtual machine monitor. (http://www.cl.cam.ac.uk/Research/SRG/netos/xen)
13. Willmann, P., Rixner, S., Cox, A.L.: An Evaluation of Network Stack Parallelization Strategies in Modern Operating Systems. Technical Report TR06-872, Rice University Computer Science (2006)
14. Bhattacharya, S.P., Apte, V.: A Measurement Study of the Linux TCP/IP Stack Performance and Scalability on SMP systems. In: Proceedings of the 1st International Conference on COMmunication Systems softWAre and middlewaRE (COMSWARE), New Delhi (2006)
15. Nowlabs, Ohio State University: MVAPICH2 Toolset. (http://nowlab.cse.ohio-state.edu/projects/mpi-iba/)

Architectural Characterization of VM Scaling on an SMP Machine

Padma Apparao, Ravi Iyer, and Don Newell

Systems Technology Lab
Intel Corporation
padmashree.k.apparao@intel.com

Abstract. The use of virtualization as a means to consolidate multiple applications on the same server platform continues to grow in the datacenter. However, the performance implications in a virtualized environment are not yet thoroughly understood for key commercial server workloads. In this paper, our goal is to provide architectural insights into the performance of server application scaling in a virtualization environment. We do so by studying the scaling behavior of a compute intensive application, namely SPECjbb2005 which is a commercial Java server benchmark. When comparing to native execution, the performance of a single virtual machine running SPECjbb2005 appears to be comparable. However, as the number of virtual machines is increased, the performance degradation was found to be significant. A detailed investigation into overheads of virtual machine scheduling and context switching overhead was conducted. Based on this investigation, we show how the number of instructions executed per operation, the cycles per instruction, and the cache misses and the TLB misses all are affected when scaling virtual machines. We also compare the performance of the simultaneously running virtual machines and discuss fairness and prioritization implications of scheduling decisions.

Keywords: virtualization, servers, performance, scalability, Xen, architectural characterization, Java.

1 Introduction

While virtualization [11]has been around for several decades, it has re-emerged in recent years as an effective means to consolidate multiple applications on to a single platform. Several companies are now providing hardware and software virtualization solutions [1,[6][7][13][21]as they see a growing rate of adoption. Applications with a varied set of requirements can share the same physical resources (cores, memory, I/O devices, etc) and provide benefits in terms of reduced total cost of ownership to the server administrator. Virtualization techniques are also used to provide benefits such as security, isolation, debugging, binary compatibility and performance monitoring. In this paper, our primary focus is on evaluating the performance characteristics of a commercial server application when running in a virtualized environment.

As virtualization-based usage models are adopted, researchers are now attempting to analyze the overheads involved [4][5]and look for solutions. However, there are only a

G. Min et al. (Eds.): ISPA 2006 Ws, LNCS 4331, pp. 464–473, 2006.

limited number of studies that focus on the architectural characteristics of virtual machine execution. In this paper, we study the performance and scalability of a compute-intensive commercial server workload (SPECjbb2005) running within virtual machines. Our measurement-based methodology employs an Intel Xeon platform with two cores running at 3.3 GHz frequency. We run our workloads on the Xen hypervisor and employ several performance tools (Oprofile/Xenoprofile [[2][20], top/xmtop and hardware performance counters) to extract overall system performance (CPU utilization, context switches, etc) and architectural behavior (instructions, cycles per instruction, cache misses, TLB misses, etc). For comparison, we also measure the performance of SPECjbb2005 in a native (non-virtualized) platform. We expect that the findings from out study will be useful to VMM architects and platform architects as it provides insight into performance bottlenecks.

The rest of the paper is organized as follows: In section 2, we provide background on the various virtualization techniques used commercially. We also discuss the typical overheads for virtualization. In Section 3, we describe the platform under test, the tools and methodology used for measurement and analysis. Section 4 presents the results and analysis of SPECjbb2005 wherein we present the raw performance of SPECjbb in native and virtualized environments. We look at the scaling of VMs and the how the virtualization overheads change with scaling. At the end of this section we present the scheduling effects and the effects on the virtualization overheads. Finally, we discuss a methodology for developing a performance model to project VM scaling. Section 7 summarizes this work and provides a direction for future work in this area.

2 Overview of Virtualization

The most recent virtualization solutions are either based on total virtualization or para-virtualization. In this virtualization models, multiple virtual machines are supported on top of the host machine running the same ISA. Earlier versions of virtualization provided support for unmodified guest operating systems (OS) to execute without any awareness of the underlying virtualization layer. This total virtualization [19] demands relatively complex implementation of hypervisor which depends on techniques like ring compression and binary patching to enable this environment. This complexity and performance overhead in the hypervisor can be reduced by making the host hardware and the guest operating system aware of virtualization. First is referred to as hardware assisted virtualization. Recently processor vendors like Intel and AMD are adding hardware support for virtualization [1,13] which reduces the burden on the hypervisor by providing the virtualization and isolation hooks in the processor hardware.

While hardware supported virtualization makes the hardware aware of virtualization, para-virtualization (Fig. 1) makes the guest OS aware of virtualization. This provides an environment where the guest operating system works in concert with the hypervisor to provide an efficient and simpler virtualization environment. Current developments in Xen/Linux and Microsoft Windows® virtualization solutions are moving in this direction. In this paper we focus on Xen, the popular open source para-virtualized virtual machine monitor (VMM) based on Linux.

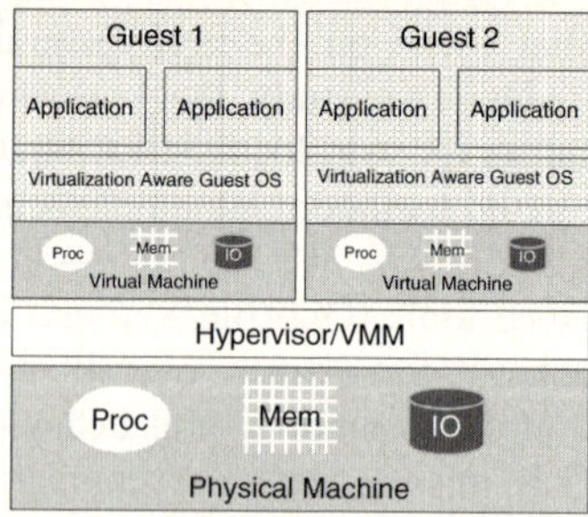

Fig. 1. Para-virtualization Architecture

2.2 Virtualization Overheads

The function of the hypervisor is to own and control physical resources of the host and expose virtual machines to guests running on it. The resources virtualized are processor, memory and IO. Depending on the mode of virtualization, the complexity and cost of virtualization varies. For example the cost of para-virtualization is much lower as compared to total virtualization. Overheads of virtualization are caused by the guest VM making access to platform resources such as processor, memory, and IO. All these result into a trap in the   include traps into the hypervisor (the VMM) which handles the VM access. Typical overheads are page faults, context switches and interrupts. The VMM intervenes to provide the necessary resources to the VM and this impacts the performance of the workload running in the guest VM. In this paper we quantify the overheads of running SPECjbb2005 in a VM and also show how these overheads change with scaling and the architectural effects of the overhead events.

3 Workloads and Methodology

In this section, we describe the workloads and evaluation methodology for characterizing virtualization performance. We chose SPECjbb2005 [24]as the compute intensive workload as it is well known server benchmark and does no I/O.

3.1 The SPECJBB2005 Benchmark

SPECjbb is a server-side benchmark for evaluating the performance of the servers running online transaction processing (OLTP) workloads. SPECjbb resembles TPC-C [25] but is implemented in Java and emulates a 3-tier system with emphasis on the middle tier. The benchmark is extremely sensitive to heap size and memory management; and is essentially compute and memory intensive as a result.

3.2 Platform Configuration

The system we have chosen for performing our performance work is an Intel Xeon system with two processors and 16GB memory. Each processor is an Intel Pentium 4 processor (with no hyperthreading) with three levels of cache (16KB L1, 1MB L2 and

8M L3). We use the Xen (xen-unstable version 3.0.2) with built in support for PAE (page address extensions for large memory sizes). When running natively we run single and 8 multiple instances of SPECjbb to study scaling. In case of virtualization, Xen could only support 16GB of memory and therefore we were able to run only 4 VMs with 3GB each.

3.3 Performance Profiling Tools

In native linux, one can use standard tools like sar, vmstat, iostat, top, etc., to look at performance data. However, under virtualization, to measure number of interrupts received by each guest VM, there is no easy way other than instrumenting the VMM. The unstable version of Xen we have used for our characterization work has Xenoprofile [2]a CPU performance profiling tool. The lack of java support in Oprofile (and Xenoprofile) forced us to use Xen enabled Emon for gathering performance counter information for SPECjbb. We could gather and calculate metrics like CPI, MPI, Pathlength, DTLB and ITLB page walks events with the tools mentioned above.

4 Performance of SPECjbb2005

In this section, we describe the raw performance of SPECjbb2005 when running natively and inside VMs. As the single VM performance was not very interesting due to only 2-3% degradation, we focused on VM scaling.

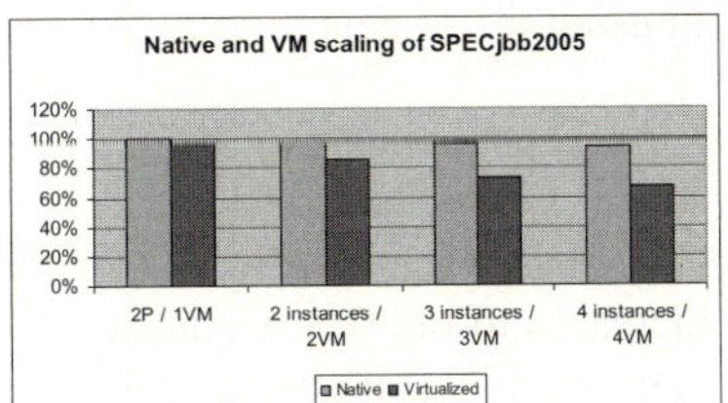

Fig. 2. SPECjbb2005 Performance Scaling

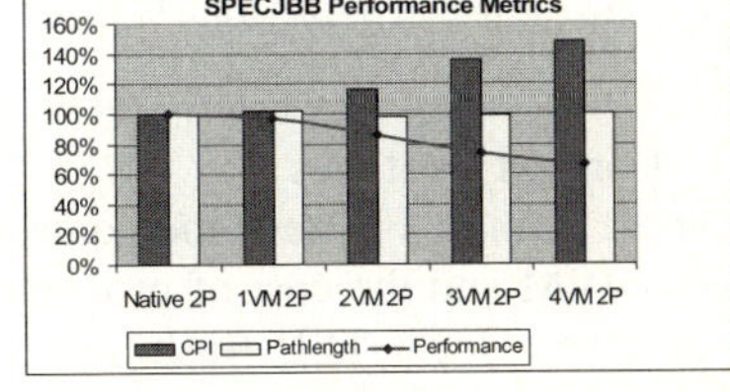

Fig. 3. Architectural Characteristics

4.1 VM Scaling Performance

Figure 2 shows the performance impact when running multiple instances of the benchmark natively and in multiple VMs each with 2 virtual cpus. All the performance data (y-axis) is normalized to single benchmark instance running natively. In each pair of bars, the first bar shows native performance and the second bar shows performance in virtualized case. The drop in performance is much higher in case of virtualization due to the higher overhead of context switches in a virtualized environment.

As seen in Figure 3 the pathlength (instructions per java operation) has remained constant across all the configurations while the CPI has increased by about 20% for each additional benchmark instance we created. Figure 4 shows MPI (misses per instruction) numbers for trace, L2 and L3 caches and TLBs as well as flush statistics for trace cache and TLBs. All the data is normalized to the single instance of the benchmark running natively. The increase in trace cache and ITLB flushes indicate increased context switch activity which affects performance. Figure 5 shows breakdown of CPI into various components. From this we can say that L2 and L3 MPI increase has contributed most to the CPI increase. This increase in MPI suggests that scheduling algorithms used by VMM may not be cache friendly.

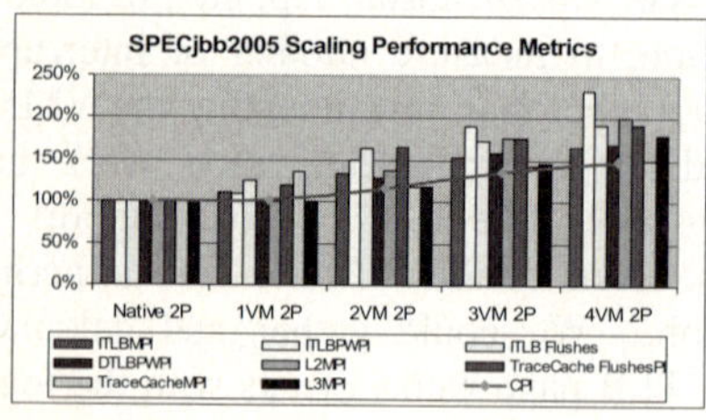

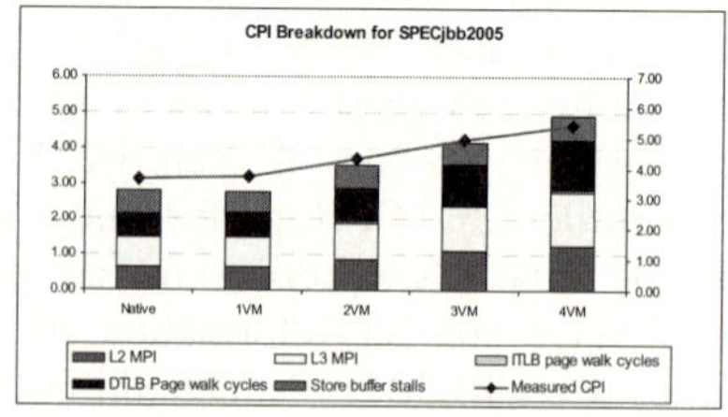

Fig. 4. Micro-Architectural Characteristics   **Fig. 5.** CPI Breakdown

4.2 Virtualization Overheads

The overheads of virtualization are due to context switches, interrupts and page faults, which are enhanced from native Linux performance due to the extra layer of VMM software. When running natively we saw every little overhead going from 1VM to 4VMs. We calculated the time spent in processing say a context switch, a local TLB flush, interrupt processing and page fault handling using instrumentation of the source code.

4.2.1 Context Switches

As can be seen in Figure 6 the context switches events/sec increase by 3000% from 1VM to 4VM and the cost of processing these increases to 600%. A context switch will involve a local TLB flush and may on a smp machine involve a global iTLB flush (flush of all TLBs). A secondary effect of a context switch is the pollution of the cache by the switched out process. So when the process is rescheduled again it has to load its cache again and hence experiences a number of L2 misses. In the case of our workload we have seen an increase of 2x in the L2 MPI which contributes significantly to the CPI. Similarly the instrumentation to count the number of local TLB flushes shows an increase by about 2x going from 1VM to 4VMs with the throughput per event going down by 3x. The iTLB flushes have a direct impact on the performance because when the iTLB is flushed on a context switch, when the process is brought back in it will experience a lot of iTLB misses for the next process which may results in a page walk. The data presented earlier in Figure 4 shows that the iTLB MPI increases by 1.5x, the L2 MPI increases by 2x and the iTLB page walk stall cycles also increase by 2x. All these contribute to the CPI for the workload as was shown earlier in Figure 5.

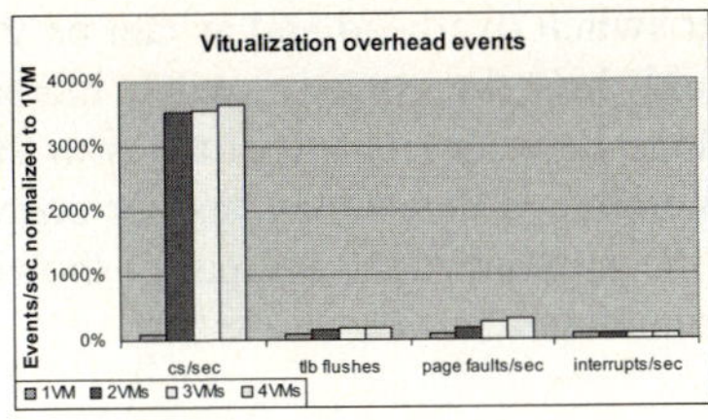

Fig. 6. Overhead events

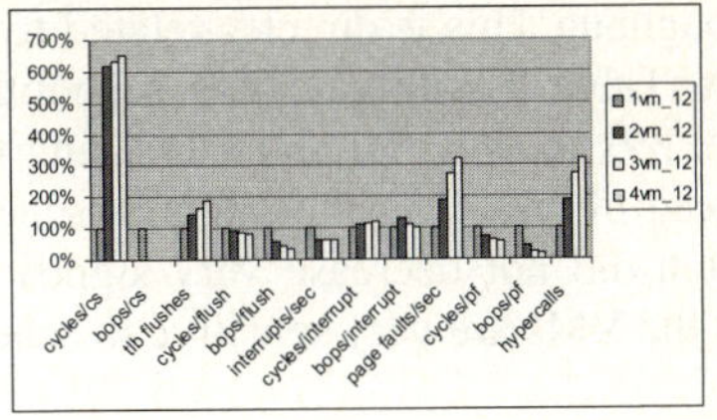

Fig. 7. Overheads events and their costs

5   VM Scheduling Policies

Since one of the interesting evolving usage models in enterprise computing is utility or pay-per-use computing models (like Azul [[6],[7]]), an interesting study was to find out how the different scheduling policies affect the performance of individual VMs and what impact this has on the virtualization overheads.

Table 1. Virtualization overheads with scheduling parameters

Scheduling parameters	Throughput	cs/sec	tlb flushes/sec	interrupts/sec	page faults/sec
default	100%	100%	100%	100%	100%
s21_21_21_37	129%	7%	113%	154%	105%
s20_20_20_40	140%	9%	114%	154%	99%
s19_19_19_43	132%	10%	91%	155%	101%

Table 1 shows the effect of the scheduling parameters on the virtualization overheads. We notice that as we change the scheduling overheads the context switch rate drops considerably. In the default case dom0 is given a time slice of 15ms out of every 20ms and even though dom0 (cpu0) is not running the benchmark, it will be scheduled and that actually impacts the performance. By lowering the time slice for dom0 to 5 ms and adjusting the parameters we were able to drop the context switch rate.

Table 2. Scheduling and its effects on Context Switches

	Throughput	cs/sec	cycles/cs	bops/cs
1vm_012	1.00	1.00	1.00	1.00
2vm_012	0.83	36.76	6.10	0.02
3vm_012	0.71	37.25	6.21	0.02
4vm_012	0.64	38.29	6.39	0.02
4VM (with selective scheduling)	0.89	3.47	5.70	0.26

Another interesting data point that we observed was with default scheduling the 4VMs could achieve only 64% of the 1VM throughput. However adjusting the scheduling parameters we could get the scaling to be much better (89%) of the 1VM throughput. This is directly related to the context switch overhead and as can be seen from Table 2 with selective scheduling we could drop the context switch increase from 39x to only 3x, and increasing the work done between context stitches to 26% instead of only 2% (with default scheduling). We noticed that the cycles per context switch did not decrease very significantly but the number itself decreases showing that the VMs are very sensitive to scheduling parameters.

6 Inferences on VM Modeling Approach

Our experiments have given us insight into the various overhead involved with virtualization and their costs and impacts on performance. With this, one can develop a model to project the performance of a large number of VMs. For example, we start with the known configuration and the performance in that configuration. We then look at all the events that add overhead, such as context switches, interrupts, page faults, and traps etc. We can compute the direct impact of these overheads by measuring the instructions executed for these overheads, the indirect impact of these overheads is the contribution to the CPI and Pathlength. As mentioned in earlier sections, the overhead events contribute to the CPI and their costs can be almost directly correlated to the CPI increase.

In order to estimate the pathlength behavior, we need to understand the additional system events (such as context switches and page faults) that occur due to virtualization. In order to estimate the CPI behavior, each of the architectural events (like L2 MPI and TLB Misses) needs to be modeled. In this section, we provide a summary of these two behaviors based on the individual components.

Table 3. Virtualization overheads

	Throughput	cs/bop	cycles/cs	flushes/bop	cycles/flush	interrutps/bop	cycles/interrupt	pf/bop	cycles/pf
1VM	15059	0.002951391	2097	0.001599	2645	0.003381	25074	0.230119	773
2VM	12517	0.309907326	7625	0.003099	2330	0.004063	26414	0.526396	560
3VM	10714	0.365448945	7779	0.004159	2202	0.004725	27108	0.895911	497
4VM	9600	0.419439583	8011	0.005278	2036	0.005253	28164	1.172152	455

As can be seen from Table 3 the context switches increases significantly from 1Vm to 2VMs and then starts to stabilize and thus can be treated almost as a constant in our model. The cycles/context switch increase slightly as we scale. We notice a similar kind of behavior with page faults and in order to understand page faults in greater depth for our model, we need to understand the instructions executed during a page fault and how it would impact the pathlength and performance. SPECjbb2005 being a compute intensive workload does not have many interrupts and the tlb flushes are also within noise. In summary the context switches is the key parameter that is changing as we scale the VMs.

If we fit the points to a curve, the equation turns out to be a linear one.

Equation: - y=0.0006x +0.0015

Such a characterization needs to be done for more cache sizes and configurations to capture the entire parameter space and the effects of scaling VMs.

Other parameters such as tlb misses, page walks, also can be characterized in a similar fashion. Once all of the parameters are well understood, the CPI can be estimated by using an equation similar to

System CPI = Core CPI + MPI*memory latency* Blocking factor + TLBmisses * page walk latency * blocking factor

The blocking factor is the fraction of time that the processor/core is stalled waiting for the resource unit and it is determined by experimental measurements and simulations various platform characteristics such as bus frequency, core frequency and core micro-architecture. The Core CPI is a function of architectural events that actually cause a slow down, such as an iTLB miss, a dTLB miss, a store buffer stall, a trace cache miss etc. Knowing the virtualization overheads and their costs, one can calculate their contribution to the CPI.

In this paper, we only presented some examples of architectural characterization. A more detailed investigation into this and the development of a full virtualization model is underway.

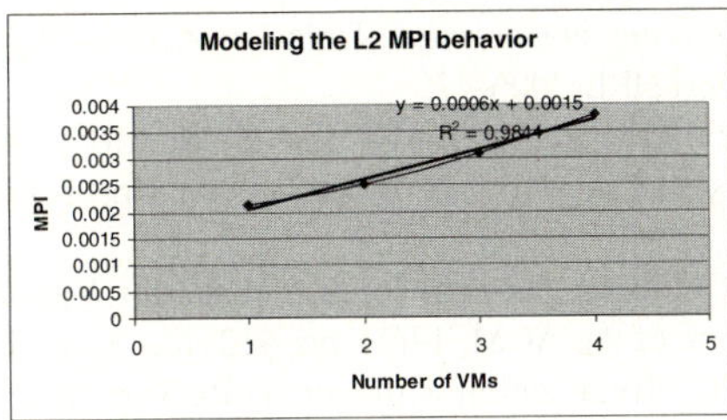

Fig. 8. Modeling of L2 MPI behavior

7   Summary and Future Work

In this paper we have presented our experiments with a compute intensive workload namely SPECjbb2005 to understand its behavior in a virtualized environment. Our experiments showed that the workload does not suffer from much performance degradation while running virtualized. A significant degradation of 36% was seen as we scale the VMs from 1 to 4. Of the various overheads in virtualization, this workload is purely affected by the context switches. We instrumented Xen code to count the number and the cost of context switches, the itlb flushes, page faults, and interrupts to account for the loss in performance. We have shown that the context switch overhead increases dramatically with only 4VMs. The indirect impact of these overheads is the change in the architectural metrics like CPI the major contribuor of which are L2 MPI and iTLB and dTLB MPI. We finally present an introduction to a model whereby one can project the scaling of a workload for a large number of VMs.

In this paper we have the overheads introduced due to virtualization but we have not been able to point this to the functionality in the VMM where these overheads are arising due to the lack of java profiling tools.in a virtualized environment. In our future work we want to experiment with more workloads that stress other virtualization techniques (e.g. network and disk I/O).

References

[1] Advanced Micro Devices. AMD64 Virtualization Codenamed "Pacifica" Technology, Secure Virtual Machine Architecture Reference Manual, May 2005.

[2] A. Menon, J. R. Santos:, http://xenoprof.sourceforge.net/xenoprof_2.0.txt (Accessed June 2006).

[3] A. Menon, A. Cox, W. Zwaenepoel, Optimizing Network Virtualization in Xen, 2006 USENIX Annual Technical Conference.

[4] A. Menon et al. Diagnosing Performance: Overheads in the Xen Virtual Machine Environment. In First ACM/USENIX Conference on Virtual Execution Environments (VEE'05), June 2005.

[5] A Singh. An Introduction to Virtualization. http://www.kernelthread.com/publications/virtualization (Accessed June 2006)

[6] Azul Virtual Machine Software, Azul Systems. http://www.azulsystems.com/products/cpools_avm.ht

[7] Azul Compute Pools, Azul Systems. http://www.azulsystems.com/products/cpools.html

[8]   B. Clark et al. Xen and the Art of Repeated Research. In proceedings of USENIX 2004 Annual Technical Conference, Boston, MA.

[9] D. Gupta et al. Enforcing Performance Isolation Across Virtual Machines in Xen.HP Labs, Technical Report HPL-2006-77.

[10] D. Reed, I. Pratt, P. Menage, S. Early, and N. Stratford. Xenoservers: Accountable Execution of Untrusted Programs. In Workshop on Hot Topics in Operating systems, 1999.

[11] G. J. Popek, R. P. Goldberg, "Formal Requirements for Virtualizable Third Generation Architectures," Comm. of the ACM, 17(7), pp. 412-421, July 1974.

[12]   H. K. F. Bjerke. HPC Virtualization with Xen on Itanium. MSc Thesis. July, 2005.

[13] Intel Virtualization Technology Specification for the IA-32 Intel Architecture, April 2005

[14] J.E. Smith, and R. Nair. Virtual Machines: versatile platforms for systems and processes. Morgan Kaufmann publishers. May 2005.

[15] J. F. Kloster, J. Kristensen and A. Mejlholm. Efficient Memory Sharing in the Xen Virtual Machine Monitor. Technical Report. Department of Computer Science, Aalborg University, Jan 2006.

[16] K. Duda and D. Cheriton, "Borrowed Virtual Time (BVT) Scheduling: Supporting Lantency-sensitive Threads in a GeneralPurpose Scheduler," in Proceedings of the Seventeenth ACM Symposium on Operating Systems Principles (SOSP'99), Kiawah Island Resort, SC, December 1999, pp. 261--276.

[17] K. Lawton: Bochs: http://en.wikipedia.org/wiki/Bochs (Accessed June 2006).

[18] L. Cherkasova and R. Gardner. Measuring CPU Overhead for I/O Processing in the Xen Virtual Machine Monitor. In Proceedings of the USENIX Annual Technical Conference, April 2005.

[19] M. Rosemblum and T. Garfinkel. Virtual Machine Monitors: Current Technology and Future trends. IEEE Computer, 38(5): 39-47, 2005.

[20] Oprofile. http://oprofile.sourceforge.net (Accessed June 2006).

[21] P Barham, B. Dragovic, K. Fraser, et al. "Xen and the Art of Virtualization." SOSP 2003.

[22] P. Barham et al. Xen and the Art of Virtualization. In proceedings of the ACM symposium on operating systems principles, Oct 2003.

[23] R. Sailer et al. Building a MAC-Based Security Architecture for the Xen Open-Source hypervisor. ACSAC 2005 -21st Annual Computer Security Applications Conference, ASCA, September 2005.

[24] SpecJbb2005 Java Server Benchmark. SPEC. http://www.spec.org/jbb2005/

[25] TPC-C Online Transaction Processing BenchmarkTPC. http://www.tpc.org/tpcc/default.asp

[26] SWsoft Virtuozzo, "Top Ten Considerations for Choosing a Server Virtualization Technology".

[27] SWsoft Virtuozzo "An Introduction to OS Server Virtualization and a New Approach to Server Consolidation."

Paravirtualization for HPC Systems*

Lamia Youseff[1], Rich Wolski[1], Brent Gorda[2], and Chandra Krintz[1]

[1] Department of Computer Science
University of California, Santa Barbara
[2] Lawrence Livermore National Lab (LLNL)

Abstract. In this work, we investigate the efficacy of using paravirtualizing software for performance-critical HPC kernels and applications. We present a comprehensive performance evaluation of Xen, a low-overhead, Linux-based, virtual machine monitor, for paravirtualization of HPC cluster systems at LLNL. We investigate subsystem and overall performance using a wide range of benchmarks and applications. We employ statistically sound methods to compare the performance of a paravirtualized kernel against three Linux operating systems: RedHat Enterprise 4 for build versions 2.6.9 and 2.6.12 and the LLNL CHAOS kernel. Our results indicate that Xen is very efficient and practical for HPC systems.

1   Introduction

Virtualization is a widely used technique in which a software layer multiplexes lower-level resources among higher-level software programs and systems. Examples of virtualization systems include a vast body of work in the area of operating systems [32, 31, 25, 30, 4, 16], high-level language virtual machines such as those for Java and .Net, and, more recently, virtual machine monitors (VMMs). VMMs virtualize entire software stacks including the operating system (OS) and application, via a software layer between the hardware and the OS of the machine. VMM systems enable application and full-system isolation (sand-boxing), OS-based migration, distributed load balancing, OS-level check-pointing and recovery, non-native (cross-system) application execution, and support for multiple or customized operating systems.

Virtualization historically has come at the cost of performance due to the additional level of indirection and software abstraction necessary to achieve system isolation. Recent advances in VMM technology however, address this issue with novel techniques that reduce this overhead. One such technique is paravirtualization [1] which is the process of strategically modifying a small segment of the interface that the VMM exports along with the OS that executes using it. Paravirtualization significantly simplifies the process of virtualization (at the cost of perfect hardware compatibility) by eliminating special hardware features and instructions in the OS that are difficult to virtualize efficiently. Paravirtualization systems thus, have the potential for improved scalability and performance over prior VMM implementations. A large number of popular VMMs employ paravirtualization in some form to reduce the overhead of virtualization including Denali [1], IBM rHype [41], Xen [28, 40, 11], and VMWare [20, 33, 38]. Moreover, hardware vendors now employ new ways of enabling efficient virtualization in

---

* This work is sponsored in part by LLNL and NSF (CNS-0546737 and ST-HEC-0444412).

G. Min et al. (Eds.): ISPA 2006 Ws, LNCS 4331, pp. 474–486, 2006.

the next-generation processors [37, 29] which have the potential to further improve the performance of VMM-based execution.

Despite the potential benefits, performance advances, and recent research indicating its potential [22, 44, 15, 19], virtualization is currently not used in high-performance computing (HPC) environments. One reason for this is the perception that the remaining overhead that VMMs introduce is unacceptable for performance-critical applications and systems. The goal of our work is to evaluate empirically and to quantify the degree to which this perception is true for Linux and Xen.

Xen is an open-source VMM for the Linux OS which reports low-overhead and efficient execution of Linux [40]. Linux, itself, is the current operating system of choice when building and deploying computational clusters composed of commodity components. In this work, we study the performance impact of Xen using current HPC commodity hardware at Lawrence Livermore National Laboratory (LLNL). Xen is an ideal candidate VMM for an HPC setting given its large-scale development efforts [28, 42] and its availability, performance-focus, and evolution for a wide range of platforms.

We objectively compare the performance of benchmarks and applications using a Xen-based Linux system against three Linux OS versions and configurations currently in use for HPC application execution at LLNL and other super-computing sites. The Linux versions include Red Hat Enterprise Linux 4 (RHEL4) for build versions 2.6.9 and 2.6.12 and the LLNL CHAOS kernel, a specialized version of RHEL4 version 2.6.9.

We collect performance data using micro- and macro-benchmarks from the HPC Challenge, LLNL ASCI Purple, and NAS parallel benchmark suites among others, as well as using a large-scale, HPC application for simulation of oceanographic and climatologic phenomena. Using micro-benchmarks, we evaluate machine memory and disk I/O performance while our experiments using the macro-benchmarks and HPC applications assess full system performance.

We find that Xen paravirtualization system, in general, does not introduce significant overhead over other OS configurations that we study – including one specialized for the HPC cluster we investigate. There is one case for which Xen overhead is significant: random disk I/O. Curiously, in a small number of other cases, Xen improves subsystem or full system performance over various other kernels due to its implementation for efficient interaction between the guest and host OS. Overall, we find that Xen does not impose an onerous performance penalty for a wide range of HPC program behaviors and applications. As a result we believe the flexibility and potential for enhanced security that Xen offers makes it useful in a commodity HPC context.

2 Background and Motivation

Our investigation into the performance implications of coupling modern virtualization technologies with high performance computing (HPC) systems stems from our goal to improve the flexibility of large-scale HPC clusters at Lawrence Livermore National Laboratory (LLNL). If virtualization does not impose a substantial performance degradation, we believe it will be useful in supporting important system-level functionalities such as automatic checkpoint/restart and load balancing.

For example, several researchers have explored OS and process migration, such as Internet Suspend/Resume [21] and μDenali [39]. Recent studies on OS image migration [17, 12] illustrate that migrating an entire OS instance with live interactive services is achievable with very little down time (e.g. 60ms) using a VMM. To be effective in a production HPC environment, however, the operating system and language systems must all be commonly available and standardized to ease the system administration burden. Thus it is the virtualization of Linux (the basis for a large proportion of cluster installations) that is of primary interest.

In addition, it is possible for one cluster to run different Linux images which aids software maintenance (by providing an upgrade path that does not require a single OS "upgrade" event) and allows both legacy codes and new functionality to co-exist. This is important for legacy codes that execute using a particular version of the OS and/or obsolete language-level libraries that depend on a specific OS kernel release level. VMMs also enable very fast OS installation (even more when coupled with effective checkpointing), and thus, their use can result significant reductions in system down time for reboot. Finally, VMMs offer the potential for facilitating the use of application-specific and customized operating systems [22, 44, 15, 19].

Though many of the benefits of virtualization are well known, the perceived cost of virtualization is not acceptable to the HPC community, where performance is critical. VMMs by design introduce an additional software layer, and thus an overhead, in order to facilitate virtualization. This overhead however, has been the focus of much optimization effort recently. In particular, extant, performance-aware, VMMs such as Xen [28], employ *paravirtualization* to reduce virtualization overhead. Paravirtualization is the process of simplifying the interface exported by the hardware in a way that eliminates hardware features that are difficult to virtualize. Examples of such features are *sensitive* instructions that perform differently depending on whether they are executed in user or kernel mode but that do not trap when executed in user mode; such instructions must be intercepted and interpreted by the virtualization layer, introducing significant overhead. There are a small number of these instructions that the OS uses that must be replaced to enable execution of the OS over the VMM. No application code must be changed to execute using a paravirtualizing system such as Xen. A more detailed overview of system-level virtual machines, sensitive instructions, and paravirtualization can be found in [34].

To investigate the performance implications of using paravirtualization for HPC systems, we have performed a rigorous empirical evaluation of HPC systems with and without virtualization using a wide range of HPC benchmarks, kernels, and applications, using LLNL HPC hardware. Moreover, we compare VMM-based execution with a number of non-VMM-based Linux systems, including CHAOS (a Linux distribution and kernel based on Red Hat Enterprise Release 4) that is currently employed by, and specialized for LLNL users and HPC clusters.

3   Methodology and Hardware Platform

Our experimental hardware platform consists of a four-node cluster of Intel Extended Memory 64 Technology (EM64T) machines. Each node consists of four Intel Xeon 3.40 GHz processors, each with a 16KB L1 data cache and a 1024KB L2 cache. Each node has 4GB of RAM and a 120 GB SCSI hard disk with DMA enabled. The nodes are interconnected with an Intel PRO/1000, 1Gigabit Ethernet network fabric using the ch_p4 interface with TCP/IP.

We perform our experiments by repeatedly executing the benchmarks and collecting the performance data. We perform 50 runs per benchmark code per kernel and compute the average across runs. We perform a *t-test* at the $\alpha \geq 0.95$ significance level to compare the means of two sets of experiments (e.g. those from two different kernels). The t-test tells us whether the difference between the observed means is statistically significant (see [23] and [8] for clear and readable treatments of the procedure we employ).

3.1   HPC Linux Operating System Comparison

We empirically compare four different HPC Linux operating systems. The first two are current releases of the RedHat Enterprise Linux 4 (RHEL4) system. We employ builds v2.6.9 and v2.6.12 and refer to them, respectively, as *RHEL2.6.9* and *RHEL2.6.12*.

We also evaluate the CHAOS kernel. CHAOS is the **C**lustered, **H**igh-**A**vailability, **O**perating **S**ystem [13, 10] from LLNL. CHAOS is a Linux distribution based on RHEL4 v2.6.9 that LLNL computer scientists have customized for the LLNL HPC cluster hardware and for the specific needs of current users. In addition, CHAOS extends the original distribution with new administrator tools, support for very large Linux clusters, and HPC application development. Examples of these extensions include utilities for cluster monitoring, system installation, power/console management, and parallel job launch, among others. We employ the latest release of CHAOS as of this writing which is v2.6.9-22; we refer to this system as CHAOS kernel in our results.

Our Xen-based Linux kernel (host OS) is RHEL4 v2.6.12 with a Xen 3.0.1 patch. Above Xen, the guest kernel is a paravirtualized Linux RHEL4 v2.6.12, which we configure with 4 virtual CPUs and 2GB of virtual memory. We refer to this overall configuration as *Xen* in our results. Xen v3 is not available for Linux v2.6.9, the latest version for which the CHAOS extensions are available. We thus, include both v2.6.9 and v2.6.12 (non-CHAOS and non-XEN) in our study to identify and isolate any performance differences between these versions.

Table 1. Benchmark Overview

	Benchmark Category	Code Name	What it measures
Micro	Memory	Stream	Mem read/write rate (MB/s)
Micro	Disk I/O	Bonnie	Seq & Rand disk I/O (MB/s)
Macro	Parallel Benchmarks	NAS Parallel Benchmark; class C *Multigrid (MG) in: 512^3* *LU Solver (LU) in: 162^3* *Integer Sort (IS) in: 2^{27}* *Embarrassingly parallel (EP) in: 2^{32}* *Conjugate gradient (CG) in: 150000*	Total time (s) and millions of operations per second (Mops)
App	Scientific Simulations	MIT GCM exp2	Total time (s)

3.2 Benchmarks

We overview the benchmarks that we use in this empirical investigation in Table 1. The benchmarks set consists of micro-benchmarks, macro-benchmarks, and real HPC applications. We employ the same benchmark binaries for all operating system configurations.

Our micro-benchmark set includes programs from the HPC Challenge [24] and LLNL ASCI Purple Benchmark suite [3]. The programs are specifically designed to evaluate distinct performance characteristics of machine subsystems. In this work, we focus on memory and disk I/O benchmarks since the other macro-benchmarks and codes we use for evaluation test other performance characteristics more directly.

We use the HPCC/LLNL ASCI Purple benchmark Stream [36] to evaluate memory access performance. Stream reports the sustainable memory bandwidth in MB/s for four different memory operations: Copy (read/write of a large array), and three operations (Scale, Sum, and Triad) that combine computation with memory access to measure the corresponding computational rate for simple vector operations.

For evaluation of disk performance, we employ Bonnie [9]. Bonnie is a disk stress-test that uses popular UNIX file system operations. Bonnie measures the system I/O throughput for six different patterns of reads, writes, and seeks. We employ three different file sizes: 100MB, 500MB and 1GB for our experiments to eliminate any cache impact on measured performance.

To evaluate the full system and computational performance, we employ several popular macro-benchmarks from the NAS Parallel benchmark suite [6, 5]. The former set is from the NASA Advanced Supercomputing (NAS) facility at the NASA Ames Research Center. The suite evaluates the efficiency of highly parallel HPC computing systems in handling critical operations that are part of simulation of the future space missions. The benchmarks mimic the computational, communication, and data movement characteristics of large-scale, computational fluid dynamics (CFD) applications.

We also include an HPC application in our study, the General Circulation Model (GCM) from the Massachusetts Institute of Technology (MIT). GCM is a popular numerical model used by application scientists to study oceanographic and climatologic phenomena. GCM simulates ocean and wind currents and their circulation in the earth's atmosphere thousands of years in advance. A widely used implementation of GCM is made available by MIT Climate Modeling Initiative (CMI) team [27]. Researchers commonly integrate this implementation into oceanographic simulations. The MIT CMI team supports a publicly available version [2, 26], which we employ and refer to in this paper as *MIT GCM*. The MIT GCM package has been carefully optimized by its developers to ensure low overhead and high resource utilization.

The package includes a number of inputs. We use the sequential version of `exp2` for this study. Exp2 simulates the planetary ocean circulation at a 4 degree resolution. The simulation uses twenty layers on the vertical grid, ranging in thickness between 50m at the surface to 815m at depth. We configure the experiment to simulate 1 year of ocean circulation at a one-second resolution.

4 Micro-benchmarks

In this section, we evaluate the impact of Xen on specific subsystems of our cluster system. We consider memory and disk I/O subsystems.

4.1   Memory Access Performance

Sustainable memory bandwidth is another important performance aspect for HPC systems, since long cache miss handling can hinder the computational power attainable by any machine. To study the impact of paravirtualization on sustainable memory bandwidth, we use Stream [36], which we configure with the default array size of 2 million elements.

Figure 1 shows the results. CHAOS attains the highest memory bandwidth for all stream operations. This is the result of CHAOS optimizations by LLNL computer scientists for memory-intensive workloads. Surprisingly, Xen attains consistently higher memory bandwidth by approximately 1-2% for every operation over RHEL2.6.12. The t-value for the difference ranges between 12-14, indicating that the differences between Xen and RHEL2.6.12 measurements is statistically significant.

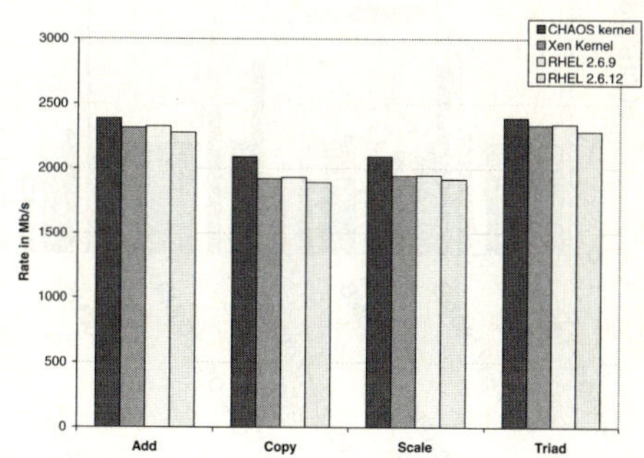

Fig. 1. Stream memory performance (Mb/s)

Since Xen uses asynchronous I/O rings for data transfers between the guest OS and the host OS, it is able to reorder requests and amortize each for better memory performance. The Xen I/O ring algorithm was wise enough to arrange the requests produces by domU on behalf of the stream code, and exploited their sequential nature to gain performance and memory bandwidth. On the other hand, these gains are less apparent between the Xen and RHEL2.6.9 configurations.

4.2   Disk I/O Performance

Disk performance of virtualized systems is also a concern for applications that perform significant disk I/O such as those for scientific database applications. To measure this performance, we use the Bonnie I/O benchmark. For the Xen kernel, we configure an LVM-backed virtual block device (VBD).

Bonnie reads and writes sequential character input and output in 1K blocks using the standard C library calls `putc()`, `getc()`, `read()`, and `write()`. For the Bonnie `rewrite` test, Bonnie reads, dirties, and writes back each block after performing an `lseek()`. The Bonnie random I/O test performs an `lseek()` to random locations in the file, then then `read()` to reads a block from that location. For these events, Bonnie rewrites 10% of the blocks.

Figure 2 shows the performance of Bonnie for the four kernels relative to the performance of CHAOS. The x-axis is the performance of the different disk I/O metrics, for different file sizes (y-axis). The first three bars in each group show the performance of the sequential output tests; the next two bars are for the sequential input test; the sixth bar is for the random test; and the last bar is total time.

Xen has a higher per-character output, per-block output, and rewrite rate for all file sizes relative to CHAOS. Xen performance is slower for sequential output rewrite for

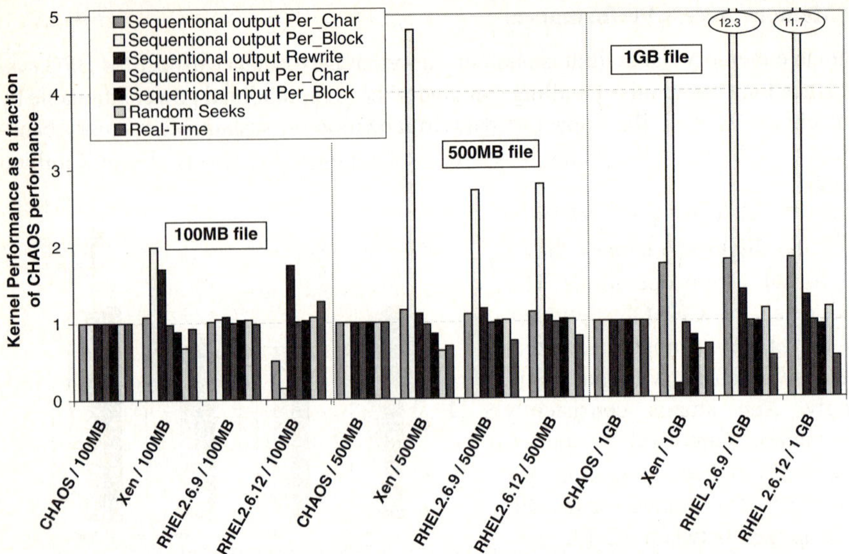

Fig. 2. Bonnie Disk I/O bandwidth rate and real-time relative to CHAOS performance

the 1GB file. CHAOS has not been optimized for disk I/O. The 1GB sequential output rewrite performance using Xen is the result of Xen's disk scheduling algorithm. As described previously, Xen used an I/O descriptor ring for each guest domain, to reduce the overhead of domain crossing upon each request. Each domain posts its request in the descriptor ring; the host OS consumes them as they are produced. This results in producer-consumer problem that the authors of Xen describe in [28]. The improvements from Xen I/O are the result of reordering of I/O requests by the host OS to enable highly efficient disk access. In the case of sequential output for 1GB files, the requests are very large in number and randomly generated across the file. This prevents Xen from making efficient use of the I/O rings and optimizing requests effectively. This effect is also apparent and significant in the results from the random seek tests. These results indicate that if random seeks to large files is a key operation in a particular HPC application, the Xen I/O implementation should be changed and specialized for this case. This scenario is fortunately not common in HPC applications.

The sequential character performance is not significantly different across kernels. However, for sequential input per block, Xen disk I/O speed lags behind the other three kernels by about 11-17%. This performance degradation is caused by Xen's implementation of I/O buffer rings. The default size of the buffer rings fail to optimize block input performance. However, tuning the I/O buffer rings in Xen Dom0 can improve on the performance for such workloads.

5   Macro-benchmarks

Paravirtualization offers many opportunities to HPC applications and software systems, e.g., full system customization, check-pointing and migration, etc. As such, it is

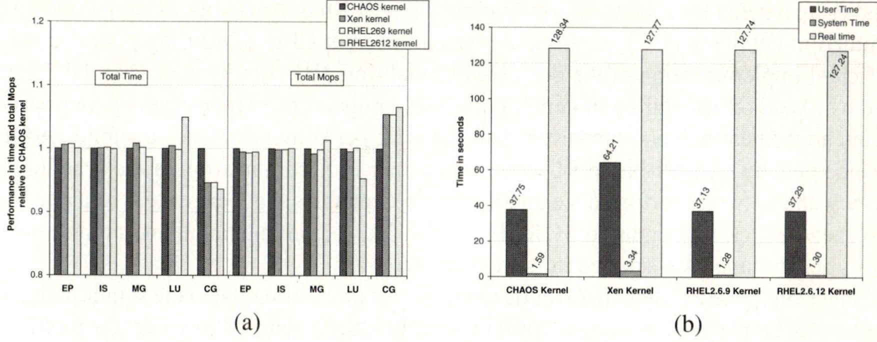

Fig. 3. Xen performance for NAS Benchmark and GCM Application. (a) shows the NAS Parallel Benchmark performance relative to CHAOS. The left half (first benchmark set) is for total time (lower is better); the right half is for Mops (higher is better). (b) is the MIT GCM performance in seconds (lower is better).

important to understand the performance implications that such systems impose for a wide range of programs and applications. We do so in this section for the popular NAS parallel benchmarks and the MIT GCM oceanographic and climatologic simulation system. This set of experiments shows the impact of using Xen for programs that exercise the complete machine (subsystems in an ensemble).

5.1   NAS Parallel Benchmarks (NPB)

For the first set of experiments we employ the NAS parallel benchmarks (NPB) as we describe in Section 3. The benchmarks mimic the computational, communicational and data movement characteristics of large scale computational fluid dynamics applications.

Figure 3 (a) shows the performance of the NPB codes(x-axis) for our different kernels relative to CHAOS (y-axis). *EP, IS* and *MG* are the Embarrassingly Parallel, Integer Sort, and Multi grid codes respectively, while *LU* is the Linear solver code and *CG* is the Conjugate gradient code. For all of the codes, we choose to run class C benchmark sizes to better asses the different performance implications of virtualization. We present two different metrics for each of the five benchmarks. The left five sets of bars reflect total execution time. The right five are for the total millions of operations per second (Mops) the benchmarks achieve.

All of the kernels perform similarly for EP, IS, and MG. The differences between the bars, though visually different in some cases, are not statistically significant when we compare them using the t-test with 95% confidence. This is interesting since the benchmarks are very different in terms of their behavior: EP performs distributed computation with little communication overhead, IS performs a significant amount of communication using collective operations, and MG employs a large number of blocking send operations. In all cases, paravirtualization imposes no statistically significant overhead.

LU decomposition shows a performance degradation of approximately 5% for RHEL2.6.12 for both total time and Mops. The reason for this is due to overhead this kernel places on computation. CHAOS optimizes this overhead away and RHEL2.6.9

makes up for this loss due to its low overhead on MPI-based network latency, which we studied in details in [43]. Xen implements a different CPU scheduling policy: a very efficient implementation of the borrowed virtual time (BVT) scheduler [14]. BVT and the overhead of scheduling in general positively impacts the Mflops rate of Xen-based sequential linear solvers. However, Xen network performance places a subtle performance penalty on MPI-based LU code performance. A combination of the scheduling policy and network performance enabled by Xen enables the Xen system to avoid the overhead which was endured by RHEL2.6.12. Xen's computational and communications performance was studied in more details in [43].

The *Conjugate Gradient* (CG) code computes an approximation to the smallest eigenvalue of a large sparse matrix. It combines unstructured matrix system vector multiplication with irregular MPI communications. CG executes slower using CHAOS than using the other kernels by about 5%. The statistical difference however was not significant, which may mean that the differences was introduced due to noise in the readings. We support this claim using the standard deviation of the 50 measurements that we collected using this kernel: This value is 31 for an average measurement of 607s, in terms of Mops this value is 12 for an average of 237s. In summary, Xen performs consistently comparable to CHAOS and the two RHEL kernels and delivers performance similar to that of natively executed parallel applications.

5.2   MIT GCM

To evaluate the use of virtualization for real HPC applications, we employ the MIT *General Circulation Model* (GCM) implementation. MIT GCM is a simulation model for oceanographic and climatologic phenomena. The execution of the MIT GCM using the `exp2` input, involves reading several input files at the beginning of the run for initialization, processing a computationally intensive simulation, check-pointing the processed data to files periodically, and outputting the final results to several other files. The total amount of data that is read and written by the system during each run is approximately 33MB. The individual writes are on the order of 200B per call to write() and the total size of each file is approximately 1MB.

We use the Linux time utility to measure the performance of MIT GCM which reports the time spent executing user code (User Time), the time spent executing system code (System Time), and the total time (Real Time). We present the results in Figure 3 (b). The y-axis is the time in seconds for the kernels shown on the x-axis.

From the experiments, we found Xen execution time of MIT GCM to be slightly faster than that for CHAOS. The difference however, is not statistically significant given a 95% confidence level. Similarly, the difference in performance between Xen and RHEL kernels is negligible.

Our experience with the system indicates that the difference between Xen and CHAOS is primarily due to the disk I/O activity. We also observe that Xen User Time and CPU usage is consistently and uniformly different from that of the other kernels. This is due to the way Xen computes user and system time in the Linux time utility in error. This is a Xen implementation bug that will be fixed in the next version of Xen.

These results are extremely promising, despite the time utility bug. They show that Xen achieves performance equal to that of the RHEL kernels and slightly better than that of CHAOS. In addition, our results from the prior section on disk I/O indicate that Xen is able to mask I/O overhead for common disk activities. Our results show, that Xen can satisfy the performance requirements of real HPC applications such as GCM. We plan to investigate how other applications behave over Xen as part of future work.

6   Related Research

The work related to that which we pursue in this paper, includes performance studies of virtualization-based systems. We investigate a wide range of metrics for HPC benchmarks, applications, and systems. We consider both subsystem performance for a number of important HPC components as well as full-system performance when using paravirtualizing systems for HPC cluster resources (IA64, SMP machines).

Other work investigates the performance of Xen and other similar technologies in a non-HPC setting [28, 11]. This research shows the efficacy and low overhead of paravirtualizing systems. The benchmarks that both papers employ are general-purpose operating systems benchmarks. The systems that the authors evaluate are IA32 and stand-alone machines with a single processor. Furthermore, those papers investigate the performance of the first release of Xen, which has changed significantly. We employ the latest version of Xen (v3.0.1) that includes a wide range of optimization and features not present in the earlier versions, as well as running on SMP machines.

Other work investigates the performance of Xen for clusters as part of an unpublished class project [18]. Researchers have also explored the impact of Xen on network communication [7, 35], the latter provides a minimal evaluation of Xen for an IA64 cluster. The authors of [35] investigate different network switch fabric on Linux clusters including Fast Ethernet, Gigabit Ethernet, and different Myrinet technologies. More recent studies evaluate other features of Xen such as the performance overhead of live migration of a guest OS [12]. They show that live migration can be done with no performance cost, and with down times as low as 60 mseconds. These systems do not rigorously investigate the performance overheads of doing so in an HPC setting.

7   Conclusions and Future Work

Paravirtualizing systems such as Xen, expose opportunities for improved maintenance and customization for HPC systems. In this paper, we evaluate the overhead of using Xen in an HPC environment. We compare three different Linux configurations against a Xen-based kernel. The three non-Xen kernels are those currently in use at LLNL for HPC clusters: RedHat Enterprise 4 (RHEL4) for build versions 2.6.9 and 2.6.12 and the LLNL CHAOS kernel, a specialized version of RHEL4 version 2.6.9. We perform experiments using micro- and macro-benchmarks from the HPC Challenge, LLNL ASCI Purple, and NAS parallel benchmark suites among others, as well as using a large-scale, HPC application for simulation of oceanographic and climatologic phenomena. As a result, we are able to rigorously evaluate the performance of Xen-based HPC systems relative to non-virtualized system for subsystems independently and in ensemble.

Our results indicate that, in general, the Xen paravirtualizing system poses no statistically significant overhead over other OS configurations currently in use at LLNL for HPC clusters – even one that is specialized for HPC clusters – in all but two instances. We find that this is the case for programs that exercise specific subsystems, a complete machine, or combined cluster resources. In the instances where a performance difference is measurable, we detail how Xen either introduces overhead or somewhat counter-intuitively produces superior performance over the other kernels.

As part of future work, we will empirically evaluate the Linux v2.6.12 CHAOS kernel as well as Infiniband network connectivity. In addition, we are currently investigating a number of research directions that make use of Xen-based HPC systems. In particular, we are investigating techniques for high-performance check-pointing and migration of full systems to facilitate load balancing, to isolate hardware error management, and to reduce down time for LLNL HPC clusters. We are also investigating techniques for automatic static and dynamic specialization of OS images in a way that is application-specific [22, 44].

References

[1] A. Whitaker and M. Shaw and S. Gribble. Scale and Performance in the Denali Isolation Kernel. In *Symposium on Operating Systems Design and Implementation (OSDI)*, 2002. "http://denali.cs.washington.edu/".

[2] A. Adcroft, J. Campin, P. Heimbach, C. Hill, and J. Marshall. *MIT-GCM User Manual*. Earth, Atmospheric and Planetary Sciences, Massachusetts Institute of Technology, 2002.

[3] LLNL ASC Purple Benchmark Suite. "http://www.llnl.gov/asci/purple/benchmarks/".

[4] J. D. Bagley, E. R. Floto, S. C. Hsieh, and V. Watson. Sharing data and services in a virtual machine system. In *SOSP '75: Proceedings of the fifth ACM symposium on Operating systems principles*, pages 82–88, New York, NY, USA, 1975. ACM Press.

[5] D. Bailey, T. Harris, W. Saphir, R. van der Wijngaart, A. Woo, and M. Yarrow. The nas parallel benchmarks 2.0. *The International Journal of Supercomputer Applications*, 1995.

[6] D. H. Bailey, E. Barszcz, J. T. Barton, D. S. Browning, R. L. Carter, D. Dagum, R. A. Fatoohi, P. O. Frederickson, T. A. Lasinski, R. S. Schreiber, H. D. Simon, V. Venkatakrishnan, and S. K. Weeratunga. The nas parallel benchmarks. *The International Journal of Supercomputer Applications*, 5(3):63–73, Fall 1991.

[7] H. Bjerke. HPC Virtualization with Xen on Itanium. Master's thesis, Norwegian University of Science and Technology (NTNU), July 2005.

[8] BMJ Publishing Group: Statistics at Square One: The t Tests, 2006. "http://bmj.bmjjournals.com/collections/statsbk/7.shtml".

[9] Bonnie Disk I/O Benchmark. "http://www.textuality.com/bonnie/".

[10] R. Braby, J. Garlick, and R. Goldstone. Achieving Order through CHAOS: the LLNL HPC Linux Cluster Experience, June 2003.

[11] B. Clark, T. Deshane, E. Dow, S. Evanchik, M. Finlayson, J. Herne, and J. N. Matthews. Xen and the art of repeated research. In *USENIX Annual Technical Conference, FREENIX Track*, pages 135–144, 2004.

[12] C. Clark, K. Fraser, S. Hand, J. G. Hansen, E. Jul, C. Limpach, I. Pratt, and A. Warfield. Live Migration of Virtual Machines. In *USENIX Symposium on Networked Systems Design and Implementation (NSDI '05)*, Boston, MA, USA, May 2005.

[13] Clustered High Availability Operating System (CHAOS) Overview. "http://www.llnl.gov/linux/chaos/".

[14] K. J. Duda and D. R. Cheriton. Borrowed-virtual-time (BVT) scheduling: supporting latency-sensitive threads in a general-purpose schedular. In *Symposium on Operating Systems Principles*, pages 261–276, 1999.

[15] Eric Van Hensbergen. The Effect of Virtualization on OS Interference. In *Workshop on Operating System Interference in High Performance Applications, held in cooperation with The Fourteenth International Conference on Parallel Architectures and Compilation Techniques: PACT05* , Septmber 2005. "http://research.ihost.com/osihpa/".

[16] S. W. Galley. PDP-10 virtual machines. In *Proceedings of the workshop on virtual computer systems*, pages 30–34, New York, NY, USA, 1973. ACM Press.

[17] J. Hansen and E. Jul". Self-migration of Operating Systems. In *ACM SIGOPS European Workshop (EW 2004)*, pages "126–130", "2004".

[18] H.Bjerke and R.Andresen. Virtualization in clusters, 2004. "http://haavard.dyndns.org/virtualization/clust_virt.pdf".

[19] E. V. Hensbergen. PROSE : Partitioned Reliable Operating System Environment. In *IBM Research Technical Report RC23694*, 2005.

[20] J. Sugerman and G. Venkitachalam and B. Lim. Virtualizing I/O devices on VMware workstations hosted virtual machine monitor. In *USENIX Annual Technical Conference*, 2001.

[21] M. Kozuch and M. Satyanarayanan. Internet suspend/resume. In *WMCSA '02: Proceedings of the Fourth IEEE Workshop on Mobile Computing Systems and Applications*, page 40, Washington, DC, USA, 2002. IEEE Computer Society.

[22] C. Krintz and R. Wolski. Using phase behavior in scientific application to guide linux operating system customization. In *Workshop on Next Generation Software at IEEE International Parallel and Distributed Processing Symposium (IPDPS)*, April 2005.

[23] R. J. Larsen and M. L. Marx. *An Introduction to Mathematical Statistics and Its Applications*. Prentice Hall, Third Edition, 2001.

[24] P. Luszczek, J. Dongarra, D. Koester, R. Rabenseifner, B. Lucas, J. Kepner, J. McCalpin, D. Bailey, and D. Takahashi. Introduction to the hpc challenge benchmark suite, March 2005. "http://icl.cs.utk.edu/projectsfiles/hpcc/pubs/hpcc-challenge-benchmark05.pdf".

[25] S. E. Madnick and J. J. Donovan. Application and analysis of the virtual machine approach to information system security and isolation. In *Proceedings of the workshop on virtual computer systems*, pages 210–224, New York, NY, USA, 1973. ACM Press.

[26] J. Marotzke and R. G. et al. Construction of the adjoint MIT ocean general circulation model and application to Atlantic heat transport sensitivity. *Journal of Geophysical Research*, 104(C12), 1999.

[27] MIT's Climate Modeling Initiative. "http://paoc.mit.edu/cmi/".

[28] P. Barham and B. Dragovic and K. Fraser and S. Hand and T. Harris and A. Ho and R. Neugebauer. Virtual machine monitors: Xen and the art of virtualization. In *Symposium on Operating System Principles*, 2003. "http://www.cl.cam.ac.uk/Research/SRG/netos/xen/".

[29] AMD Virtualization Codenamed "Pacifica" Technology, Secure Virtual Machine Architecture Reference Manual, May 2005.

[30] G. J. Popek and R. P. Goldberg. Formal requirements for virtualizable third generation architectures. *Commun. ACM*, 17(7):412–421, 1974.

[31] G. J. Popek and C. S. Kline. The PDP-11 virtual machine architecture: A case study. In *SOSP '75: Proceedings of the fifth ACM symposium on Operating systems principles*, pages 97–105, New York, NY, USA, 1975. ACM Press.

[32] R.A. Meyer and L.H. Seawright. A Virtual Machine Time Sharing System. In *IBM Systems Journal*, pages 199–218, 1970.

[33] M. Rosenblum and T. Garfinkel. Virtual machine monitors: Current technology and future trends. *Computer*, 38(5):39–47, 2005.

[34] J. E. Smith and R. Nair. *Virtual Machines: Versatile Platforms for Systems and Processes*. Morgan Kaufmann/Elsevier, 2005.

[35] P. J. Sokolowski and D. Grosu. Performance considerations for network switch fabrics on linux clusters. In *Proceedings of the 16th IASTED International Conference on Parallel and Distributed Computing and Systems*, November 2004.

[36] The memory stress benchmark codes: stream. `"http://www.llnl.gov/asci/purple/benchmarks/limited/memory/"`.

[37] Enhanced Virtualization on Intel Architecture-based Servers, March 2005.

[38] C. A. Waldspurger. Memory resource management in vmware esx server. *SIGOPS Oper. Syst. Rev.*, 36(SI):181–194, 2002.

[39] A. Whitaker, R. Cox, M. Shaw, and S. Gribble. Constructing services with interposable virtual hardware, 2004.

[40] Xen Virtual Machine Monitor Performance. `"http://www.cl.cam.ac.uk/Research/SRG/netos/xen/performance.html"`.

[41] J. Xenidis. rHype: IBM Research Hypervisor. In *IBM Research*, March 2005. "http://www.research.ibm.com/hypervisor/".

[42] XenSource. "http://www.xensource.com/".

[43] L. Youseff, R. Wolski, B. Gorda, and C. Krintz. Paravirtualization for HPC Systems. Technical Report Technical Report Numer 2006-10, Computer Science Department University of California, Santa Barbara, Aug. 2006.

[44] L. Youseff, R. Wolski, and C. Krintz. Linux kernel specialization for scientific application performance. Technical Report UCSB Technical Report 2005-29, Univ. of California, Santa Barbara, Nov 2005.

Xen-OSCAR for Cluster Virtualization

Geoffroy Vallée and Stephen L. Scott*

Oak Ridge National Laboratory, Oak Ridge, TN, USA
{valleegr, scottsl}@ornl.gov

Abstract. New virtualization solutions such as Xen allow users to execute hundreds of virtual machines on a single physical machine. The interest of these solutions have been proven for system isolation and security features, especially for Internet Service Providers (ISPs), as well as for high performance computing.

A natural question is to know if it is possible to use all these virtual machines at the same time, creating a virtual cluster. This might be an interesting solution for the development and the experimentation of cluster applications.

This document presents an extension of OSCAR for the deployment and the management of Xen virtual machines. We also analyze in this paper the interest of virtualization for the development, the testing and the experimentation of applications for clusters, in particular with the use of a fully virtualized cluster.

Keywords: para-virtualization, Xen, virtual cluster, OSCAR, system software management.

1 Introduction

Machine virtualization is an important topic today and seems to be a suitable solution for resource sharing providing to users a full virtual machine (VM) that can not corrupt the physical machine. The Xen Virtual Machine Monitor [4,13] provides such a secure and full-featured virtualization solution.

At the same time, Linux clusters are widely adopted as supercomputing infrastructure facilities. So a natural question is then to know if it is possible to use several virtual machines in order to create a "virtual cluster"; a virtual cluster being a cluster composed of both physical systems and virtual machines, just virtual machines (on a single or several physical machine), or a mix of physical and virtual machines. Previous studies have proven that the use of solution like Xen is suitable for high performance computing [8]. Of course, depending on the configuration of the virtual environment, a virtual cluster can not be as efficient as a real cluster because resources are shared by the VMs (concurrent access to physical resources). However virtual clusters may be interesting as development,

---

* ORNL's work was supported by the U.S. Department of Energy, under Contract DE-AC05-00OR22725.

G. Min et al. (Eds.): ISPA 2006 Ws, LNCS 4331, pp. 487–498, 2006.

testing and experimentation platform, even if today, no solution for system management of such environment is available, with a full set of features traditionally provided by system management software [7].

This paper presents an extension of OSCAR, system management tool for clusters, for the deployment and the management of Xen virtual machines. More precisely, this study of cluster virtualization using Xen aims to identify impact of such a solution for the development, testing and experimentation of cluster software. We look at virtualization as an "end-to-end" solution, from the deployment of the virtual cluster to the execution of parallel applications.

The remainder of this paper is organized as follows: Section 2 presents the terminology used in this document. Section 3 presentsXen-OSCAR , a tool for the deployement and management of a virtual cluster based on Xen VMs within a cluster. Section 4 concludes.

2   Terminology

The execution of a virtual machine (VM) implies that one or several virtual systems are running concurrently on top of the same hardware, each having its own view of available resources. The operating system (OS) of the VMs is called *guest OS*. VMs are running concurrently on top of the hardware. A *Hypervisor* manages this concurrent execution and does the mapping between the resource vision of the VMs and the real hardware. The Hypervisor is typically a small system running on side of the VMs therefore does not include drivers and specific mechanisms to access the physical hardware. Therefore, the Hypervisor is coupled to a traditional OS, called *host OS*.

Using virtual machines, it is possible to create a *virtual cluster*; cluster composed of virtual machines (it may also be composed of standard physical systems). If the cluster is only composed of virtual machines and on a single host OS, the cluster is called *fully virtualized cluster*.

3   Cluster Virtualization

The Hypervisor mechanism allows users to create multiple virtual machines on a single physical machine. These virtual machines can communicate together through the network: a virtual NIC is created by default on the host OS to communicate with the virtual machine; Xen also automatically creates a bridge on the host OS between all virtual NICs and the local system, allowing virtual machines to be on the same network as the host OS. Therefore, the use of virtual machines for the virtualization of compute nodes within a cluster is possible; using multiple virtual machines on multiple physical machines, or multiple virtual machines on a single physical machine, depending on the nature of the use (*e.g.* development or production).

Nevertheless, solutions like Xen were orginally intended for the virtualization of single machines and were not intended to provide a solution for virtual clustering. To have a complete solution for virtual clustering, several issues have to be addressed: (i) is it possible to use traditional solutions for system software management of clusters? (ii) is it possible to use traditional tools for the development and the profiling of applications? (iii) what is the virtualization impact on the execution of parallel applications traditionally executed on clusters?

Today, several tools (software suites) are available for the installation and management of clusters, like OSCAR [3,5] or Rocks [11,12]. The main goal of these projects is to ease the installation and the management of clusters by installing and managing the system, middleware, runtime and applications across the cluster.

These tools allow users to create and manage a Beowulf cluster without particular expertise in system and cluster management. For instance, OSCAR creates images on the head node and then deploys this image on all compute nodes.

Because of our famillarity with OSCAR, we are members of the core develoopement team, OSCAR has been selected as the clustering suite for this study. We also selected OSCAR because it allows users to define multiple images for compute nodes that may be based on different Linux distributions or providing a different software stack (*e.g.* MPI vs. PVM), enabling system customization (customization benefits are describe in Section 3.2).

3.1   OSCAR Overview

OSCAR allows one to install a cluster in 8 steps. During the first step, the user can choose software components (*e.g.* PVM , MPI) to be installed on the cluster. The second step configures these software components. The third step installs OSCAR packages [2] on the headnode, installing tools to create and deploy images for compute nodes. Software components on the headnode such as runtime and daemons are also installed on the headnode. The fourth step creates a image for compute nodes. The fifth step allows users to define the compute nodes, *i.e.*, the number of compute nodes and their IP addresses. The sixth step allows users to assign a MAC address to an IP address for each compute nodes. The DHCP server is also setup. Then compute nodes can be network booted. During the boot process, the compute nodes contact the headnode which assigns an IP address and then transfers the image. The seventh step configures the cluster (some software components need a specific action after the installation of the software itself, *i.e.* perform a post-installation action). Finally, the eighth step tests the cluster.

The creation and the deployment of images for the compute nodes is currently based on System Installation Suite (SIS) [15]. SIS is based on three components: (i) System Imager, (ii) System Installer and (iii) System Configurator. As described in the above OSCAR steps, first an image for compute nodes is created on the headnode (using System Imager) after which, it is possible to boot the compute nodes and to initiate the installation. Compute nodes are network booted. The headnode is contacted and based on the MAC address of the compute node, an IP address and an image are assigned. The image is transfered from the headnode to the compute node with the *rsync* command (via System Installer). When the image is copied on the compute node, System Configurator can perform any last updates on the system to finish the node configuration (*e.g.* setup the boot loader). It is then possible to reboot the compute node as the system has been installed.

OSCAR currently supports Red Hat Entreprise Linux, Fedora Core, Mandriva, Suse, and provides an experimental version for Debian. It also provides a large set of software components, for instance PVM, MPICH, LAM-MPI, OpenMPI, Ganglia, Torque, or SGE.

3.2 Xen-OSCAR: Tool for Cluster Virtualization

Xen-OSCAR is an extension of OSCAR allowing the use of Xen virtual machines on a single machine or on remote machines. For that, it is necessary to be able to deploy and manage host OS as well as the system of virtual machines.

Therefore Xen-OSCAR is composed of two components: (i) an OSCAR package for the creation of an image for the deployment of the host OS on remote machines, and (ii) a network abstraction layer that gives the illusion that virtual machines are standard physical computing resources (it is then possible to fully benefit from existing OSCAR features including mature project for system management).

Xen-OSCAR has been developed to allow users to setup a virtual Beowulf cluster which may be composed of a mix of physical machines and virtual machines, since a network abstraction (composed of the default bridging mechanisms provided by Xen and our network boot emulation) hides the virtual nature of Xen virtual machines without impling any restriction regarding standard machines (*i.e.* a system without any virtual machine).

Management of Host OS for Xen. The first challenge for the deployment of virtual machines within a distributed or a parallel environment is the deployment of the host OS. In the Xen case, the host OS has to be composed of a standard operating system plus the Xen kernel and Xen tools.

Therefore an OSCAR package for Xen has been created. This package, when selected for an OSCAR image, automatically installs and configures Xen into the image for compute nodes.

The standard OSCAR installation process may be then used to automatically deploy the host OS on remote machines. OSCAR also allows the user to specify the software stack that has to be installed on the host OS. For instance, since the host OS aims only at being the interface between the Hypervisor and virtual machines, clustering tools such as MPI may not be needed. Such software components can be easily removed from the image (OSCAR provides a simple interface for the selection of OSCAR packages, named *OSCAR Selector*). At the end OSCAR guarantees that no unecessary overhead will be created on the host OS by unecessary deamons or runtimes, allowing user to create a customized image for host OS. Another full-featured image for cluster computing will be created for VMs, as described in the following paragraph.

Management of Xen Virtual Machines. Once the host OS is deployed, it is then possible to deploy and create virtual machines. Comparing the installation of the Xen virtual machines and the real machines, major differences are the boot sequence and the file system used by the VMs.

For a physical machine, within a cluster, a device such as the disk or CDROM may boot compute nodes or a network boot mechanism such as PXE, allowing compute nodes to contact the head node to transfer the node image. With a virtual machine based on Xen, it is not possible to have a full boot sequence as network boot is not possible. An approach to address this issue is to simulate a boot sequence using a specialized virtual machine that acts like a bootable CDROM. This issue is detailed further in this section.

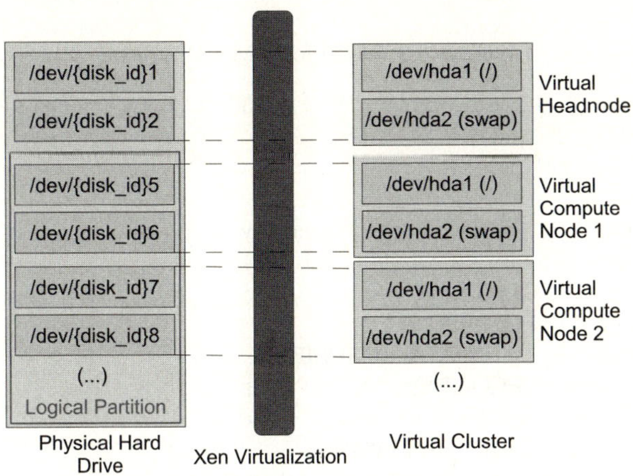

Fig. 1. Example of Mapping Between Physical Partitions and Partitions Used by Virtual Machines

For the "disk virtualization" the problem is different. Tools like OSCAR expect that a full hard drive is available for the system. This hard drive is first partitioned, formated, and then the system is installed. It is not possible to do that with a virtual machine because even if the virtual machine has the vision of a single hard drive (see Figure 1), partitions have to be described before the "boot" of the virtual machine. This issue is detailed further in this section.

To ease the use of virtual machines, a tool for virtual machine specification has been developed. This can be done through an XML file and allows the user to specify VM's characteristics via a simple high-level description. Listing 1.1 gives an example of such a configuration file for a virtual machine having 128 MB of memory, for which the system is installed on a 1000MB file (virtual block device), and having one virtual NIC, linked to the host OS (TUN/TAP) with the 00:01:02:03:04:05 MAC address. The XML DTD for such a profile is provided in Listing 1.2.

This configuration file is then analyzed for the creation of the Xen configuration file and for the initialization of the file system for the VM.

Listing 1.1. Example of VM Specification

```xml
<?xml version="1.0"?>
<profile>
        <name>VM1</name>
        <memory>128</memory>
        <image size="1000">/home/gvallee/temp/v2m/test_xen.img</image>
        <nic1>
                <type>TUN/TAP</type>
                <mac>00:01:02:03:04:05</mac>
        </nic1>
</profile>
```

Listing 1.2. DTD for VM's Profiles

```xml
<?xml version="1.0" encoding="ISO-8859-1"?>
<!--
DTD for V3M profiles.
-->
<!ELEMENT profile (name, type, memory?, image,
virtual_disks?, cdrom?, nic1?, nic2?) >
<!ELEMENT name (#PCDATA)>
<!ELEMENT image (#PCDATA)>
<!ATTLIST image size CDATA #IMPLIED>
<!ELEMENT memory (#PCDATA)>
<!ELEMENT virtual_disks (virtual_disk+)>
<!ELEMENT virtual_disk (#PCDATA)>
<!ATTLIST virtual_disk id CDATA #REQUIRED>
<!ELEMENT cdrom (#PCDATA)>
<!ELEMENT nic1 (type, mac)>
<!ELEMENT nic2 (type, mac)>
<!ELEMENT mac (#PCDATA)>
```

Virtual Network Boot. Because of the lack of a full boot sequence for Xen virtual machines, a *virtual network boot* is necessary for the installation of the VM's system via OSCAR. One approach is to use a Xen image to emulate a network boot. The goal of this image is: (i) to create a virtual compute node with a virtual hardware and (ii) to connect to the headnode to get configuration information, and (iii) initialize the virtual hardware and install the system. The protocol is based on protocol used by OSCAR to install real compute nodes (see Figure 2).

The Xen image for the emulation of a network boot is based on a minimal Linux distribution providing all the tools necessary for the installation of the compute node via OSCAR (such as DHCP, rsync, System Configurator) and a specific script to perform the node installation (based on SIS scripts). This script is automatically called after the boot on the VM, and automatically stops the VM when the system installation is done. Thus, for users, the installation process is completely transparent, the same as a standard OSCAR node installation. When the compute node is installed, Xen-OSCAR has changed the Xen configuration file for the VM in order to not emulate the network boot but to start the compute

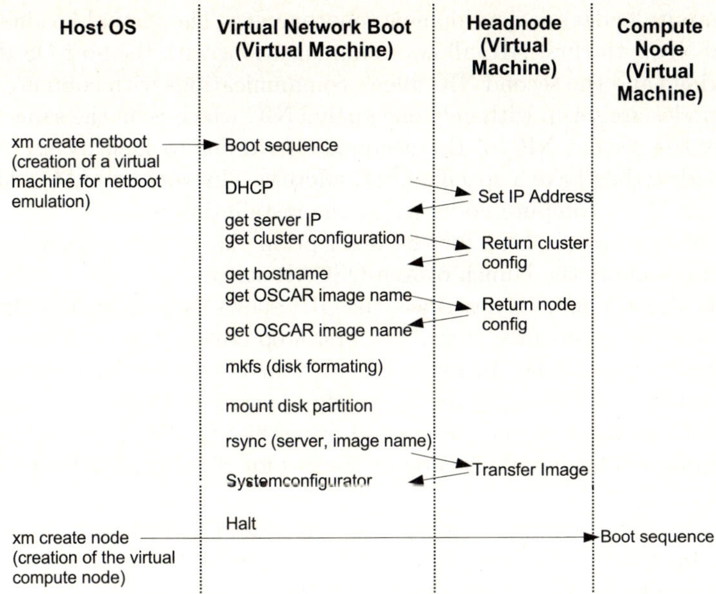

Fig. 2. Netboot Emulation for System Installation of Xen VMs Using OSCAR

node. User believes that it is the same VM as the one used during the installation process, the installation has been completely transparent to the user, thanks to our network abstraction for Xen VMs.

Disk Virtualization. In a physical cluster, quite frequently compute nodes have the same configuration; they use the same partitions to install the system and mount a network file system from the headnode. Since Xen allows the specification of the mapping between a disk partition or a file (used as virtual block device) and a virtual disk for a virtual machine, virtual compute nodes have the same disk configuration (in our case, we use the first partition of the first virtual IDE disk, for simplification purposes or files used as virtual block devices). This virtual partition is then mapped on a physical partition on the hard drive that is specific to a virtual machine (see Figure 1).

OSCAR partitions and formats the partitions of the disk of the compute nodes. It is not possible to do that with virtual compute nodes as partitions for the system have to be created and formated before to starting the VM and each of them have to be described in the Xen configuration file associated to the VM. Therefore, during the virtual network boot for the node installation, the hard drive does not have to be partitioned. Partitioning and formatting is automatically done before the initialization of OSCAR thanks to information users give through the VM configuration.

Fully Virtualized Cluster Case. To illustrate one possible use of Xen-OSCAR, we detail the use of a fully virtualized cluster (*i.e.*, a virtual headnode and virtual compute nodes) as development environment. The virtual headnode has two virtual NICs: the first NIC allows communications with the host OS through the Xen bridge and the second NIC allows communications with compute nodes. Compute nodes are setup with only one virtual NIC which is on the same virtual network as the second NIC of the headnode. In order to identify each of the compute nodes, they have a specific MAC address. This virtual MAC address is the identifier of the compute node during the installation process.

To use such a case, a GUI for the description the virtual cluster has been developed and allows the launch of Xen-OSCAR scripts.

Once the virtual cluster is described, the GUI allows users to initiate the setup of the virtual cluster in three steps. The first step creates the partitions on the physical disk for the virtual cluster and creates the file system for the headnode. In the second step, the image of the headnode is installed. During the third step, Xen-OSCAR automatically creates configuration files for Xen (for the headnode and the compute nodes) and also creates images for the virtual network boot of compute nodes.

Once the virtual hardware is setup and mapped on a physical partition, it is possible to boot the headnode.

Next section presents a study of such a fully virtualized cluster for development purpose.

3.3   Development of Applications Using a Virtual Cluster

To develop applications for clusters, developers need to have: (i) the appropriate environment (*i.e.* runtime and middleware such as MPI, PVM) and (ii) standard tools like debuggers and profilers.

Standard runtime and middleware for clustering are installed by OSCAR; a virtual cluster managed with such a tool may be used for the development of applications for clusters. However, developers have to remember that the execution on a virtual cluster is not comparable to the execution on a real cluster. For instance, processes of a parallel application may not be able to run at the same time because of concurrent access to the physical resources. Therefore, techniques like co-scheduling [6] cannot be applied on a virtual cluster and it may be difficult for the programmers to analyze the global execution behavior of the application using a virtual cluster.

Application debugging and profiling is much more difficult because these tools very often access low level information, executing protected processor instructions which are not virtualized by Xen. The kernel of the virtual machine is not running in the ring 0 of privileges and therefore the kernel (or kernel module or application) cannot execute low level protected instructions if they do not have a Hypervisor interface to do it. For instance, PAPI [1] or oprofile [10] cannot directly access some processor instructions (such as access to the *msr* register of x86 processors) and need to be ported to Xen. Oprofile has been ported to the Xen kernel (through a kernel patch) thanks to the Xenoprof [9] project.

3.4   Execution of Parallel Applications

Applications for clusters are mostly parallel applications like MPI applications. Therefore, it is critical to analyze the execution of such application using a virtual cluster. We do not try to analyze the efficiency of the execution as this is pointless since the use of a virtual cluster will not allow users to have performance comparable to a real cluster (because of the resource sharing). This analysis is aimed at determining if a virtual cluster may be used for experimentation, *i.e.* to analyze if the behavior of an application is representative and comparable to a real execution.

With a virtual cluster, virtual machines are scheduled on a single physical machine. Several studies on the execution of such an application on clusters has shown that to guarantee efficiency, communicating processes must run simultaneously in order to get the full benefit of parallelism [6]. Unfortunately, virtual machines cannot execute at the same time if the physical machine does not offer multiple processors, and even if the physical machine has multiple processors, there is no guarantee that virtual machines will be executed at the same time. Therefore, there is no guarantee that communicating processes can be executed in parallel and thus, they may be stopped everytime they want to communicate with another process on another virtual machine, decreasing the global performance of the application.

In this section, we study the impact of virtualization on the execution of MPI applications. We used a virtual cluster of 10 virtual machines, each virtual machine having 64MB of memory. The machine used is a Pentium 4, 1.7GHz with 1GBytes of memory and a 250GBytes EIDE hard drive. All experiments were made with Xen-2.0.6 which is based on the kernel-2.6.11.10. We used Xen-2.0.6 and we made evaluations with different Xen policies for the scheduling of virtual machines. Unfortunately it was not possible to boot the Xen kernel with the *Atropos* policy, the kernel froze during the boot sequence.

The benchmark used is Beff [14]. Beff calculates the effective bandwidth, *i.e.* the accumulated bandwidth of the communication network of parallel and/or distributed computing systems. Several message sizes, communication patterns and methods are used. The algorithm uses an average to take into account that short and long messages are transferred with different bandwidth values in real applications. We executed the benchmark with varying sizes of the MPI applications (from 2 processes up to 10 processes, with 1 process per compute node) and for each size we made 5 runs of the benchmark.

Figure 3 shows both the effective bandwith for different sized MPI applications (from 2 processes up to 10 processes with 1 process per compute node) and the bandwith for a ping pong communication between the two first MPI processes. The effective bandwith deceases according to the number of MPI processes. Moreover, the two scheduling policies offer the same kind of global performance. If the application is communication intensive, global performance is very poor and does not exceed 8 MB/second. Performances with the *Borrowed Virtual Time* policy is more constant: virtual machines with active processors have more time slices, therefore processes (and so virtual machines) blocked

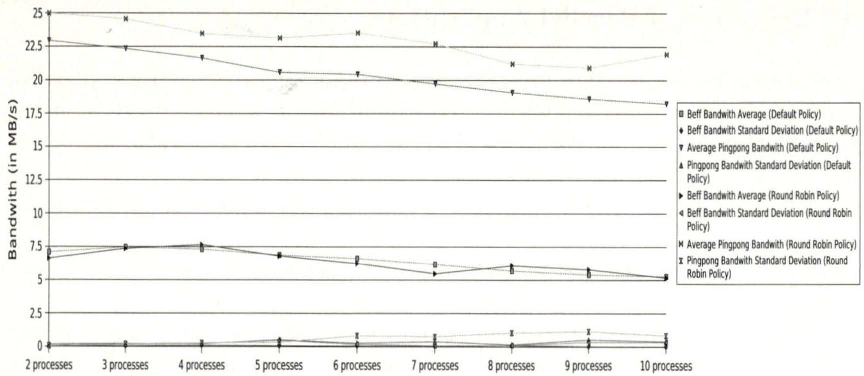

Fig. 3. Bandwith Performance (B*eff* Benchmark) for Both the Default and the Round Robin VM Scheduling Policy of Xen

because pending communications are penalized. On the other hand, with the round robin policy, all virtual machines have the same execution time and are scheduled periodically. Therefore, we can see that depending on the communication pattern of the application, global performance may vary. It is also interesting to note that even if the results may vary, the standard deviation is pretty good. Therefore results for a specific application can be considered as representative for execution on a virtual cluster.

The bandwith with the *Borrowed Virtual Time* policy decreases according to the number of MPI processes because the scheduling of the virtual machines is not lead by communications but only by computation. Therefore, there is no guarantee that the two virtual machines on which MPI ping pong processes are running are efficiently scheduled. In the other hand, the round robin policy guarantees that the two first MPI processes are scheduled one after the other (modulo allocation of time slices for other virtual machines) and therefore, performance does not decrease quickly as it does with the *Borrowed Virtual Time* policy. The standard deviation for the two scheduling policies is acceptable and results may considered as representative.

Figure 4 shows the latency for a ping pong communication between the two first MPI processes. The latency with the *Borrowed Virtual Time* policy increases according to the number of MPI processes. Communication is made through the memory of the physical machine and the scheduling of virtual machines being lead by the computing activity. Virtual machines that block often, *e.g.* blocking communications, are penalized. With the round robin policy, machines that block often because of I/O are not penalized as much. Moreover, results for the *Borrowed Virtual Time* policy do not have a good standard deviation, results are not constant and cannot be considered as representative. On the other hand, the standard deviation for the round-robin policy is good, results can be considered as correct. In conclusion, analyzing the MPI latency, the round robin policy is better than the *Borrowed Virtual Time* policy.

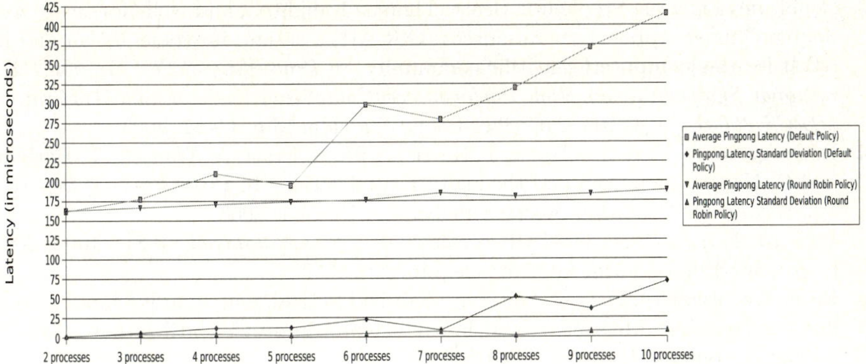

Fig. 4. Pingpong Latency (B*eff* Benchmark) with the Default VM Scheduling Policy of Xen

4   Conclusion

This paper presents a study of the use of virtual clusters based on Xen for the development of parallel applications and their experimentation. Our study shows that the use of a virtual cluster is not comparable to a physical cluster because: (i) the tools for cluster management, like OSCAR, have to be adapted in order to be used for the management of virtual clusters, (ii) development tools like profilers have to be ported on the Xen architecture, and (iii) the execution of parallel applications is deeply influenced by the scheduling policy of the VMs; the execution behavior may differ greatly between two experiments.

As part of the work to port existing cluster software to Xen, a set of tools, such as oprofile and OSCAR, have be adapted to Xen to ease the use of a virtual cluster. We also saw through the creation of Xen-OSCAR and the port of Papi that the modifications porting existing software to Xen is minimal. However, because all tools have not been ported to Xen, developers and users may not have their favorite environment for their virtual cluster.

Finally, hardware support for virtualization (the Intel VT technology and AMD Pacifia technology) is supported by the latest Xen release and should increase the interest in virtual clusters (no modifications should be needed for the execution of OSes, runtimes, middleware and applications). However, our experiments have shown that developers and users will still have to pay attention to the scheduling policy of the VMs.

References

1. S. Browne, J. Dongarra, N. Garner, G. Ho, and P. Mucci. A portable programming interface for performance evaluation on modern processors. In *The International Journal of High Performance Computing Applications*, volume 14, pages 189–204, 2000.
2. Core OSCAR Team. HOWTO: Create an OSCAR package, January 2004. http://oscar.openclustergroup.org/tiki-index.php.

3. Benoît des Ligneris, Stephen L. Scott, Thomas Naughton, and Neil Gorsuch. Open Source Cluster Application Resources (OSCAR) : design, implementation and interest for the [computer] scientific community. In *Proceeding of 17th Annual International Symposium on High Performance Computing Systems and Applications (HPCS 2003)*, pages 241–246, Sherbrooke, Canada, May 11-14, 2003.

4. B. Dragovic, K. Fraser, S. Hand, T. Harris, A. Ho, I. Pratt, A. Warfield, P. Barham, and R. Neugebauer. Xen and the art of virtualization. In *Proceedings of the ACM Symposium on Operating Systems Principles*, October 2003.

5. Richard Ferri. The OSCAR revolution. *Linux Journal*, (98), June 2002. http://www.linuxjournal.com/article.php?sid=5559.

6. Eitan Frachtenberg, Dror G. Feitelson, Fabrizio Petrini, and Juan Fernandez. Flexible coscheduling: Mitigating load imbalance and improving utilization of heterogeneous resources. In *ipdps*, April 2003.

7. Wei Huang, Jiuxing Liu, Bulent Abali, and Dhabaleswar K. Panda. A case for high performance computing with virtual machines. In *The 20th ACM International Conference on Supercomputing (ICS'06)*, June 2006.

8. Jiuxing Liu, Wei Huang, Bulent Abali, and Dhabaleswar K. Panda. High performance vmm-bypass i/o in virtual machines. In *USENIX Annual Technical Conference 2006*, June 2006.

9. Aravind Menon, Jose Renato Santos, Yoshio Turner, G. (John) Janakiraman, and Willy Zwaenepoel. Diagnosing Performance Overheads in the Xen Virtual Machine Environment. In *First ACM/USENIX Conference on Vitual Execution Environments (VEE'05)*, 2005.

10. Oprofile, 2003. http://oprofile.sourceforge.net.

11. Philip M. Papadopoulos, Mason J. Katz, and Greg Bruno. Npaci rocks: Tools and techniques for easily deploying manageable linux clusters. In *CLUSTER*, 2001.

12. Philip M. Papadopoulos, Mason J. Katz, and Greg Bruno. Npaci rocks: tools and techniques for easily deploying manageable linux clusters. *Concurrency and Computation: Practice and Experience*, 15(7-8):707–725, 2003.

13. Ian Pratt, Keir Fraser, Steven Hand, Christian Limpach, Andrew Warfield, Dan Magenheimer, Jun Nakajima, and Asit Mallick. Xen 3.0 and the art of virtualization. In *Proceedings of the Linux Symposium 2005*, volume 2, pages 65–78, Jul 2005.

14. Rolf Rabenseifner. Effective bandwidth (beff) benchmark. http://www.hlrs.de/mpi/b_eff/.

15. System installation suite. http://sisuite.org/.

Job Scheduling for
Loosely-Coupled Inhomogeneous Nodes
Using Data Envelopment Analysis

Michael Alexander

Wirtschaftsuniversität Wien
Department of Informations Systems,
Augasse 2-6, 1090 Vienna, Austria
malexand@wu-wien.ac.at

Abstract. Job Scheduling in high performance computing (HPC) clusters and
grids has traditionally been performed by job entry and management systems,
such as the Portable Batch System that place their emphasis on job management
and only to a lesser extent on job scheduling. In grid infrastructures and
emerging, virtual machine-based HPC environments, the previous assumption
on relative homogeneity of nodes does not hold any more. In contrast, loosely
coupled nodes in these settings are more heterogenous than ever. This places
new demands on job scheduling, where a large number of different nodes create
the problem of optimally laying out compute jobs across the network for
efficient resource allocation. The proposed approach presented utilizes non-
parametric Data Envelopment Analysis (DEA) to derive a workload-type
proximity factor for a given node type. An experimental factor determination is
performed using 5 physical and one virtual nodes.

Keywords: HPC, Job Scheduling, Xen, DEA, Data Envelopment Analysis.

1 Introduction

High performance computing (HPC) clusters and grids rely on batch job entry and job
scheduling systems [8] and [9] to manage compute jobs. In homogenous cluster
architectures, nodes are similar, so the emphasis is to level the load between them
through queues, priorities and job parameters. Yet in grid infrastructures, virtual
machine (VM) environments or heterogenous clusters, nodes may differ substantially
ranging from the class of machine to its individual population parameters such as
RAM etc. Hence, the run-time performance for a particular job type may not be a-
priori as universally understood as for homogenous clusters. Still, these distributed
compute networks tend to have their compute jobs allocated in similar mechanisms to
the orthodox homogeneous cluster case. This paper based on [1] and [2] presents a
novel approach to determine node affinity for a compute job by means of execution
efficiency measurement through non-parametric Data Envelopment Analysis (DEA).
It is shown, that the method can provide an efficiency affinity factor that could be
used to by schedulers to allocate compute jobs efficiently across the network.

G. Min et al. (Eds.): ISPA 2006 Ws, LNCS 4331, pp. 499–508, 2006.

2 Data Envelopment Analysis

Data Envelopment Analysis is a mathematical programming approach which allows for comparisons of decision making units (DMUs) with similar objectives.It uses the Linear Programming Method for numerical computation. DEA has first been described by Charnes et al. [6] with further refinements for optimal input-output targets by Thanassoulis and Dyson [13] and unit raking by Andersen and Petersen [4], amongst others.

DEA is a nonparametric efficiency analysis method, which uses an empirical production function describing the set of DMUs under consideration. Its main advantage to econometric and descriptive (such as ratio based and statistical) efficiency analysis is its ability to handle input and output vectors consisting of many elements which are common to complex systems. No assumptions on the form of the production function, common to parametric approaches, have to be made. Also, DEA is not susceptible to problems in parameter estimation, if e.g. input variables show conlinearity, or autocorrelation of an error term with the output variable is present. DEA determines the relative efficiency of units within the DMU set. Efficiency is determined as relative to a virtual (constructed) frontier curve, which describes the best possible achievable output for a given level of input. Statistical techniques, in turn, frequently measure the deviation from a medium reference curve. Furthermore, DEA allows for use of different units of input and output measure, such as time, cost, units of labor etc. A DMU is Pareto efficient, if no other DMU or combination of DMUs can improve one output, without lowering another output level or the increase of an input level.

The following diagram in [1] shows a simplified graphical representation of a DEA problem with two inputs x_1, x_2 and one output. The convex envelope is the efficiency frontier, spawning a hull over the feasible region.

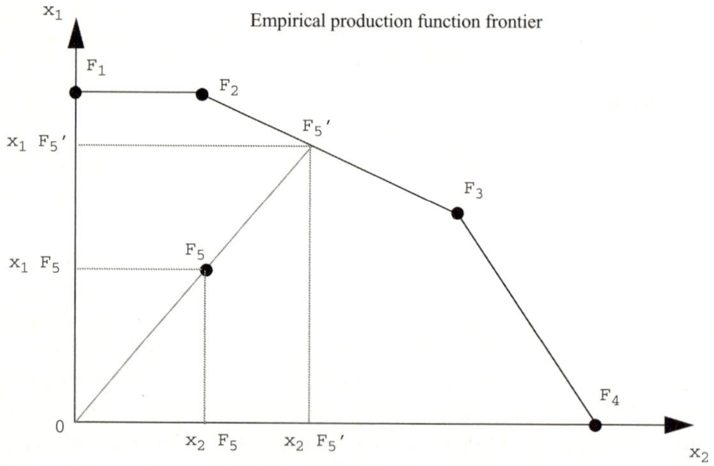

Fig. 1. DEA Efficiency Frontier Curve

x_1 and x_2 are two inputs, and $F_{1..5}$ denote the DMUs$_{1..5}$. F_{1-4} are all relatively efficient, being on the efficiency frontier. F5, in turn, is deemed inefficient. The graphical representation of the measure of X-inefficiency is given by the quotients of the rays:

$$\theta_{F5} = \frac{\overline{0F_5}}{\overline{0F_5'}} \tag{1}$$

The DMU's F_2 and F_3 are the peer units of F_5; their input times a scaling-down factor determined by linear programming produce the same output as F_5. Their unit weights, $l_{2,3}$ are described by the ray quotients $\overline{F_3F_5'}/\overline{F_3F_2}$ $\overline{F_2F_5'}/\overline{F_3F_2}$ respectively.

The principal idea, on which DEA is based, is to measure relative efficiency for a set of n DMUs not by using an average composite with fixed weights for inputs x_{ij}, but by allowing input weights to be variable for each x_{ij}. Hence, DMUs can be classified relatively efficient through strength in a particular factor. Generally, an $m+s$ dimensional supported hyperplane is formed. The generic equation for a hyperplane in R_{m+s} with the normal variables $\{m_{1..s}, u_{1..m}\}$ is:

$$\sum_{r=1}^{s} \mu_r y_r - \sum_{i=1}^{m} v_i x_i + w = 0 \tag{2}$$

with the conditions for fulfilling the "supported" criterion that a) all points having to be located on or below the envelope surface and b) at least one point has to be an element of the surface. The following figure is a graphical example representation of a VRS (variable returns to scale) surface.

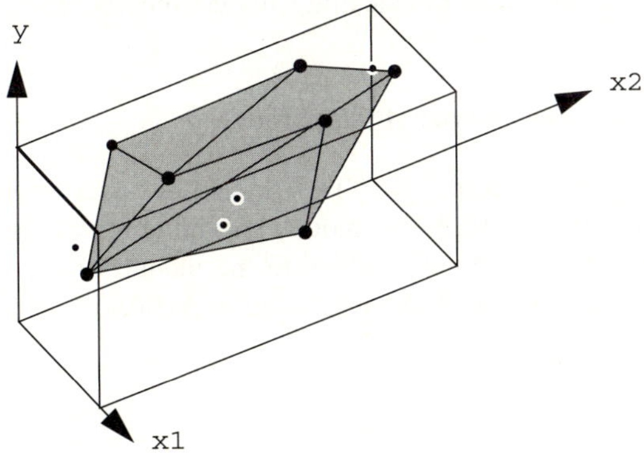

Fig. 2. VRS Surface Example (Source: Ali and Seiford [3], p. 122 - modified)

DEA, as introduced by Charnes et al. [6], is derived from the following mathematical programming problem, which maximizes the virtual (composite) output to input quotient. This is the output oriented form of the problem. Alternatively, an input oriented DEA problem minimizes the inputs, while holding the output level constant. Most DEA applications use the input oriented measure as the prime indicator, as does the following cluster node efficiency analysis.

$$\max h_0(u, v) = \frac{\sum_r u_r y_{r0}}{\sum_i v_i x_{i0}}$$

$$\text{s.t.} \quad \frac{\sum_r u_r y_{rj}}{\sum_i v_i x_{ij}} \leq 1 \quad \text{for } j = 0,\ldots,n \quad u_r, v_i \geq 0 \tag{3}$$

The nonlinear programming problem above is transformed into a linear programming (LP) for solving an LP problem for each DMU. Like other linear programming problems, DEA models can be formulated in one of two forms, which are reciprocal-dual against each other. Based on computational considerations for large problems, the form which has the lower number of constraints should be chosen. In DEA, the primal problem is also called multiplier problem, the dual problem is called an envelopment problem. Furthermore, DEA assumes that if DMU j is capable of producing a given input-output combination, another DMU can do the same. Restrictions here need modified DEA models by adding linear programming constraints.

The method carries disadvantages as well: the main one being, that in theory, in a system of m inputs and s outputs $m \times s$ efficient units are possible, supporting the hyperplane. Consequently, the strongest propositions DEA produces are those on inefficient units. Secondly, no statistical hypothesis testing methods are available. Thirdly, there are no provision for handling disturbance-random error, such as for measurement error.

2.1 Banker, Charnes and Cooper (BCC) Model

The Banker, Charnes and Cooper (BCC) [5] model is an extension of the original Charnes, Cooper and Rhodes (CCR) [6] model, providing for variable returns to scale. The following convexity constraint is added to the model for non-increasing returns as needed for compute nodes in which the addition of resources lead to a less proportional increase in output:

$$\sum_{j=1}^{n} \lambda_j \leq 1 \tag{4}$$

is added. The variable u_o denotes the corresponding returns to scale indicator in the primal. The BCC efficiency measure represents true technical efficiency, compared to the CCR model.

Primal BCC Problem

$$\max \sum_{r=1}^{s} \mu_r y_{r0} - u_0 \qquad\qquad (5)$$

$$\text{s.t.} \quad \sum_{i=1}^{m} \upsilon_i X_{i0} = 1$$

$$\sum_{r=1}^{s} \mu_r y_{rj} - \sum_{i=1}^{m} \upsilon_i x_{ij} - u_0 \leq 0 \qquad\qquad j = 1, ..., n$$

$$-\mu_r \leq -\varepsilon \qquad\qquad r = 1, ..., s$$

$$-\upsilon_i \leq -\varepsilon \qquad\qquad i = 1, ..., m$$

Dual BCC Problem

$$\min \theta_0 - \varepsilon \sum_{r=1}^{s} \bar{s}_r - \varepsilon \sum_{i=1}^{m} s_i \qquad\qquad (6)$$

$$\text{s.t.} \quad \sum_{j=1}^{n} y_{rj}\lambda_j - \bar{s}_r = y_{r0} \qquad\qquad r = 1, ..., s$$

$$\sum_{j=1}^{n} x_{ij}\lambda_j - \theta_0 x_{i0} + s_i = 0 \qquad\qquad i = 1, ..., m$$

$$\sum_{j=1}^{n} \lambda_j = 1$$

$$\lambda_j, \bar{s}_r, s_i \geq 0$$

The dual uses DMU weights and the slack variables.

2.2 Target Choice

Target choice models allow to determine input and output target levels which render relatively inefficient DMUs efficient. The determination of these optimal target levels is based on the projection of the inefficient DMUs towards the frontier.

Given that DEA does not distinguish between different regions under a frontier hyperplane, $q_j < 1$, $q_j < 1$ hence, the preferences for improvement are crucial. Fig. 3. shows three possible projections of F_3 on the efficiency frontier for an input minimization case. The most common approach is radial expansion, which is depicted by the ray $\overline{F_3 F_3'}$ going through (0,0). In the two input case shown, improvement priority can be on $X_{1,2}$ alternatively, shown by lines which lie

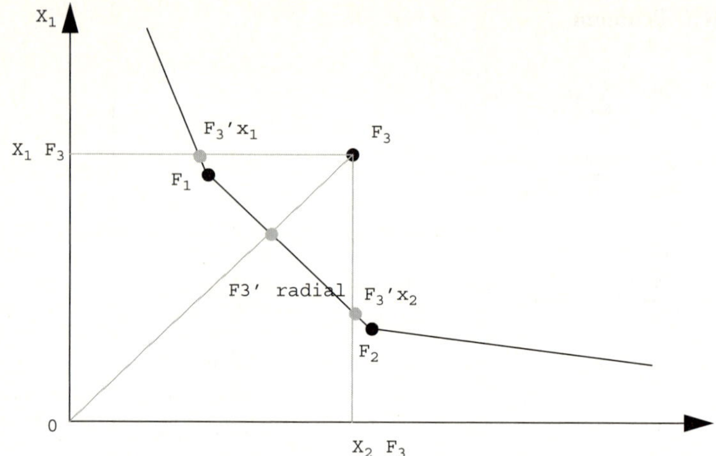

Fig. 3. Target Input Choice

orthogonally to the category axes. It is important to note that these extensions require separate minimization/maximization runs for each problem and can not be calculated from a CCR or BCC result, since changes in one input/output affect the whole input/output vector.

Thanassoulis and Dyson [13] have extended the CCR/BCC model for several preference cases. The study uses a radial type uniform input lowering strategy target choice strategy. Here, the solution presented is characterized by having a minimum in the sum of slacks weighted by the inverse average value on each input or output variable. Before, the radial efficiency is maximized. Alternatively, target choice could set a priority for each output variable expansion or input variable reduction, with an "infinite" size solution set. The model for target choice employed consecutively is based on Thanassoulis and Dyson's weights based general preference structure model.

$$\max \quad \sum_{r \in R_0} w_r^+ z_r - \sum_{i \in I_0} w_i^- p_i + \varepsilon \left(\sum_{i \in \bar{I}_0} d_i^- + \sum_{r \in \bar{R}_0} d_r^+ \right)$$

$$\text{s.t.} \quad z_r y_{rj_0} - \sum_{j=1}^{n} \beta_j y_{rj} = 0 \qquad r \in R_0$$

$$p_i x_{ij_0} - \sum_{j=1}^{n} \beta_j y_{rj} = 0 \qquad i \in I_0$$

$$\sum_{j=1}^{n} \beta_j x_{jr} - d_r^+ = y_{rj_0} \qquad r \in \bar{R}_0$$

$$\sum_{j=1}^{n} \beta_j x_{ij} + d_i^- = x_{ij_0} \qquad i \in \bar{I}_0$$

$$z_r \geq 1 \qquad \forall r \in R_0$$

$$p_i \leq 1 \qquad \forall r \in I_0$$

$$\beta_j \geq 0 \qquad \forall j$$

$$p_i, z_r \qquad \text{free} \, \forall i \in I_0 \quad \text{and} \, r \in R_0$$

$$d_i^-, d_r^+ \geq 0 \qquad \forall i \in \bar{I}_0 \qquad \text{and} \, r \in \bar{R}_0 \tag{7}$$

The model attaches the weights $w_r + w_i$-to the outputs/inputs which are modeled as factors z_r, p_i. The former represents the target output increase, the latter the input decrease. I, R are input-output index sets $I=\{1,...,i\}$ $R=\{1,...,s\}$. After specifying the relative priority of all i and s, the model gives the targets $(x_{ij0}", y_{rj0}")$.

3   Experimental Factor Determination

In the following experiment, five physical and one virtual node were used calculate the nodal type efficiency factor for a sparse matrix multiplication work-load using the JASPA benchmark tool [10]. The matrix A to generate computational load is a large dimension 90449 matrix with 2455670 non-zero elements [11] with the operation $\mathbf{B} = \mathbf{A} \times \mathbf{A}$. Table 1 lists the data for the respective nodes[1], whereby the input variable CPU denotes the central processing unit number of cores, cache, the total per CPU cache size in kB, RAM the random access memory per CPU, power the estimates power uage [7]

Table 1. Nodal Input Data

	CPU	Cache	RAM	Power	BogoMIPS	Cost	Matrix	IO
frankfurt	2	2048	2	250	5980.16	4500	6.026	62.3
boo	4	4096	2	300	5324	2200	5.477	90.9
clusterlogin	1	1024	1	200	5989.87	1100	6.102	62.5
pallando	8	1024	0.82	1200	1401	3000	10.816	47.0
xmbsp	2	1024	0.262	1200	1401	3000	10.811	11.5
athlon	1	256	0.5	180	2946.91	150	6.628	28.3

---

[1] The Nodenames:Type are {frankfurt:Dual Xeon Blade}, {boo:Dual Xeon 5160 MacPro), {clusterlogin:HP single P4}, {pallando:8-wayP3 SMP}, {xmbsp:Xen 2 VCPU VM as single VM on a phyiscal machine}, {athlon:Single Athlon). frankfurt ran Fedora Core 3 Linux, all other nodes Debian Sarge.

in watt under full load, BogoMIPS are Linux Kernel CPU delay loop measurement instructions per second per core, cost the estimates present market value of the node in Euro. The output variables here are the matrix multiplication total time in seconds and an IO value of reading 1GB sequentially from a raw disk device in seconds.

Table 2 and 3 give the efficiency factor results using a convex, non-increasing returns. input oriented BCC model with radial expansion and super-efficiency values for efficient nodes. The node *frankfurt* was found as the only one inefficient one which is consistent with a high DEA dimensionality of 14 (7 inputs and 2 outputs). The entries under the respective inputs and outputs are the weights resulting from the model run. The other nodes, using super-efficiency would still remain efficient with a maximum radial expansion of the inputs times the listed factor. Hence, the node found most efficient is *athlon* with the input:cost and the output:matrix supporting the hyperplane.

Table 2. Efficiency Factors (a)

Node	Efficiency Factor	CPU	Cache	RAM	Power	BogoMIPS	Cost
frankfurt	87.38%	0.00	0.00	0.00	0.00	0.00	0.00
boo	see[a]	0.01	0.00	0.00	0.00	0.00	0.00
clusterlogin	242.83%	0.82	0.00	0.00	0.00	0.00	0.00
pallando	see[a]	0.01	0.00	0.20	0.00	0.00	0.00
xmbsp	399.58%	0.50	0.00	0.00	0.00	0.00	0.00
athlon	874.67%	0.00	0.00	0.00	0.00	0.00	0.01

[a] Node remains efficient in the model on any increase in input reseources.

Table 3. Efficiency Factors (b)

	IO	Peers	Matrix
frankfurt	0.01	boo (0.23) clusterlogin (0.57) athlon (0.19)	0.06
boo	46.82	1	0.06
clusterlogin	0.05	1	0.53
pallando	90.25	0	56412.86
xmbsp	0.00	0	0.84
athlon	0.00	1	2.69

Table 4. Target Choice

Input, Output	Actual	Target	Improvement
Cost	4500	1191.22	-73.53
BogoMIPS	5980.16	5188.26	-13.24
Power	250	214.01	-14.39
RAM	2	1.14	-42.99
Cache	2048	1615.67	-21.11
CPU	2	1.74	-13.24
Disk IO	62.28	62.28	0
Matrix	6.03	6.06	0.55

Table 4 lists the resulting target choice values for the inefficient node *frankfurt*. In order to be efficient, the cost would have to be reduced to at least 1192.22 Euro, the BogoMIPs to 5188.24 and the power intake to at least 214.01 Watt etc., while the matrix multiplication output computation with the calculated input values is project to go up slightly to 6.06.

4   Conclusions and Future Work

This paper proposes the addition of a workload type-to node efficiency factor to HPC cluster and grid job scheduler algorithms. Using non-parametric Data Envelopment Analysis (DEA), pernode efficiency factors are derived from a select number of node specifica of differing data types and scales as inputs, that are mapped to reference nodal compute and IO workload performance figures. The method shows its utility in identifying the node a given sparse matrix multiplication and sequential disk IO workload would intuitively be most efficient to run on. High degree of heterogeneity in compute clusters and grids make an optimized workload to node allocation difficult to determine over all nodes. Hence, large cluster and grid networks of dissimilar virtual machines are believed to benefit from the proposed workload-to-nodal type efficiency measure based scheduling. Future work will include adding a parameterized Xen load-curve to the model in order to adapt the approach to a multiple virtual machine on a single physical node case.

References

[1] M. Alexander. Payment Systems Efficiency and Risk, Doctoral Thesis, University of Vienna, 1997.

[2] M. Alexander. Chapter Complex Decision Analysis using Non-Parametric Data Envelopment Analysis. In: *Qudrat-Ullah, H., Spector, M and Davidsen, P. Com-plex Decision Making: Theory and Practice.* Springer, 2006 (forthcoming).

[3] A. I. Ali and Lawrence M. Seiford. The mathematical programming approach to efficiency analysis. in: Fried, Harold O., C.A. Knox Lovell and Shelton S. Schmidt, ed. *The measurement of productive efficiency: techniques and applica-tions.* Oxford: Oxford University Press, 1993.

[4] P. Andersen, P. and N. C. Petersen. A procedure for ranking efficient units in data envelopment analysis. *Management Science* Vol 39 (October), 1993: 1261-1264.

[5] R.D Banker, A. Charnes and W. W. Cooper. Models for estimating technical and scale efficiencies in data envelopment analysis. *Management Science* 30, 1984: 1078-1092.

[6] A. Charnes, W. Cooper and E. Rhodes. Measuring the efficiency of decision making units. *European Journal of Operations Research* (2), 1978, pp. 429-444.

[7] F. Hermenier, N. Loriant and J.M. Hermenier. Power Management in Grid Computing with Xen. Workshop on XEN in HPC Cluster and Grid Computing Environments as part of ISPA'2006 (forthcoming).

[8] Cluster Resources. Moab Workload Manager.http://www.clusterresources.com

[9] Cluster Resources. TORQUE Resource Manager.http://www.clusterresources.com

[10] JASPA http://www.dl.ac.uk/TCSC/Staff/Hu_Y_F/SOFTWARE/JASPA/JASPA_1.0.tar.gz

[11] MatrixMarket. Matrix S3DKQ4M2. http://math.nist.gov/Matrix-Market

[12] Portable Batch System. http://www.openpbs.org

[13] E. Thanassoulis and R. Dyson. Estimating preferred target input-output levels using data envelopment analysis. *European Journal of Operations Research* (56), 1993: 80-97.

Semantic Description of Grid Based Learning Services

Gustavo Gutiérrez-Carreón, Thanasis Daradoumis, and Josep Jorba

Open University of Catalonia, Av. Tibidabo 39-43 - 08035 Barcelona, Spain
{ggutierrezc, adaradoumis, jjorbae}@uoc.edu

Abstract. Grid technology has emerged as a powerful tool to increase the capabilities of e-learning frameworks. Learning services are fundamental components representing functionalities that can be easily reused without knowing the details of how services have been implemented. On the one hand, a problem that still remains unsolved is how to use and integrate low-level learning services to compose more complex high-level services or tools that make sense to both tutors and learners. On the other hand, the approaches that are currently used to implement an e-learning framework developed with learning services based on the Grid are limited in semantic expressiveness for matching services and only support keyword based search. Due to the complexity of these two related problems, the paper focuses on the second one by proposing an initial model for Semantic Description of Grid based Learning Services based on OWL–S (Semantic Markup for Web Services) that facilitates learning service providers the description and categorization of atomic, simple or compose services and allow service requesters to specify their needs. This model aims at offering a mechanism for automatic Grid Learning Service discovery, invocation, composition and interoperation.

Keywords: Learning Grid, Learning Services, Semantic Web.

1 Introduction

Web services have fundamentally changed the way that e-learning frameworks were developed. IMS Global Learning Consortium[1] proposes an Abstract framework [1] representing a set of services used to construct an e-learning system in its broadest sense. One of the design principles for the abstract framework is the adoption of service abstraction to describe the appropriate e-Learning functionality (Figure 1).

Currently Globus Toolkit (GTS3) [2] is a set of a variety of tools that has been commonly used to implement Grid Services. In a Grid environment, service description is based on WSDL[3] and the fundamental message enveloping mechanism is SOAP[4]. WSDL provides a simple way for service providers to describe the basic format of requests to their systems regardless of the underlying protocol or encoding. Globus Metacomputing Directory Service (MDS) implements a standard Web Services interface to a variety of local monitoring tools and constitutes

---

[1] IMS develops and promotes the adoption of open technical specifications for interoperable learning technology.

G. Min et al. (Eds.): ISPA 2006 Ws, LNCS 4331, pp. 509–518, 2006.

the tool in GTS3 that is used to register Grid services while UDDI has been used in the web community for business service discovery. Both of them only support keyword based search and are limited in semantic description. Open Grid Service Architecture (OGSA) [5] identifies state modeling and management as a fundamental requirement for service-oriented architectures whereby the Web Services Resource Framework (WSRF [6]) defines conventional interfaces and behaviors for representing, abstracting, and manipulating the state in a Web services framework. The creation of a new grid service instance involves the creation of a new process in the hosting environment, which has the primary responsibility of ensuring that the services it supports adhere defined grid service semantics.

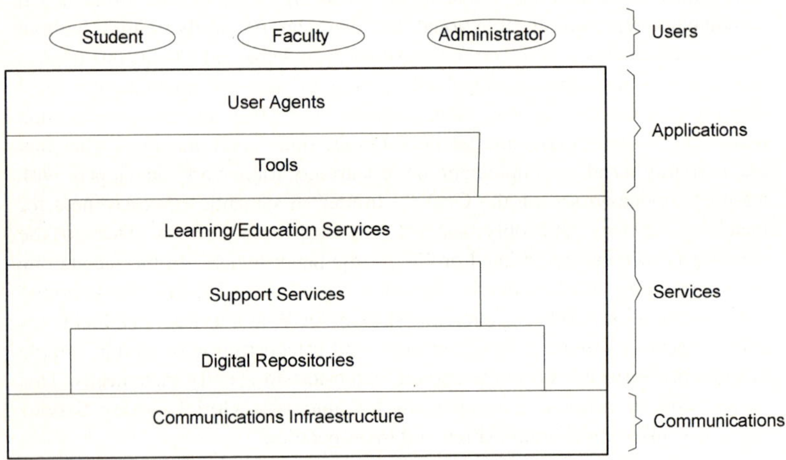

Fig. 1. A logical architecture for an eLearning system [1]

Powerful tools should be enabled by service descriptions across the Web service lifecycle. Semantic Markup for Web Services (OWL-S, formerly DAML-S)[7] is an ontology of services that makes these functionalities possible. These semantically rich descriptions enable automated machine reasoning over service and domain descriptions, thus supporting automation of service discovery, composition, and execution, and reducing manual configuration and programming efforts.

Learning objects become more and more available on the Web as well as services with well-defined machine interpretable interfaces. Automated composition of learning resources, exposed as web services, can then match a personalized learning need [8]. Semantic description offers a mechanism to generate annotation registries of a set of diverse learning resources over and above the course materials or learning objects in an e-learning framework. These annotations provide access to marked-up resources, which enables ontologically guided or semantic search. Semantic Learning Webs depend on four things: annotated educational resources, a means of reasoning about them, a means of retrieving the most suitable one, and a range of associated services [9].

The Semantic Grid merges the semantic web with grid computing and it emerges as an important alternative in e-learning systems in order to maintain dynamism in terms of resources, content and participants as well as to support effective E-learning strategies [10].

In this paper we propose a model for grid learning services semantic description based on OWL-S standard that can be used for both low-level learning services and more complex high-level ones. The rest of the paper is organized as follows: In section 2 we review some efforts for Grid based Learning Services semantic description and discovery. The proposed model is discussed in Section 3 whereby in Section 4 we apply the model in a Simple Sequencing Learning Service scenario supported by low-level services. Finally in Section 5, we present the conclusions and future work.

2   A Review of Grid Learning Services

Finding services with desired features becomes every time more challenging because the number of Web services is continually increasing. Current standards in Web Services and Grid communities (including UDDI and WSDL) do not directly support semantic description and discovery of services [11]. Semantic discovery is the process of discovering services capable of meaningful interactions, even though the languages or structures which they are described may be different [12].

2.1   Grid Learning Services Semantic Description

Some efforts in grid learning services semantic description are made in [13] with semantic search of Learning Services in a Grid Based Collaborative System. This work proposes a user-centric conception to model the abstractions that educators use to describe their learning activities. This method is based on a conceptual model of learning interaction that allows educators to search for services in an easy and suitable way without knowing about the functional specification of services and they only need information related to collaborative learning activities.

Another related work is OntoEdu [14] where ontologies are used to describe concepts of a networked education platform and their relations. In OntoEdu, the education ontology includes two big parts: an activity ontology (AO) and a material ontology (MO). The AO is implemented based on a service oriented approach with metadata descriptions using the OWL-S model. This project is oriented towards adaptability and automatic composition of the function user requested.

The SELF project [10] proposes an e-learning framework resulting from the integration of available technologies, specifically the semantic web, grid, collaborative and personalization tools, and knowledge management techniques. SELF provides intelligent search matching and inference support making use of semantic description tools. A main drawback of this project is that it makes use of technologies that are not specialized in learning systems.

Some initial efforts have been made in [8] who employed a semantic specification of learning objects (LOs) formatted in OWL-DL that can be used both to retrieve LOs from a repository satisfying a user request and to compose such discovered LOs in a courseware. The proposed approach also copes with non-exact solutions to the courseware composition.

2.2 Semantic Discovery and Grid Learning Services Matching

In general, a semantic discovery process relies on semantic annotations, containing high-level abstract descriptions of service requirements and behavior. Metadata is an essential element in semantic discovery with the capability to expand service descriptions with additional information. The achievement of dynamic composition and automation of services involves discovering new services at run time by software components without human interaction. SOAP provides description of message transport mechanisms and WSDL describe the interface used by each learning service. However, neither SOAP nor WSDL are of any help for the automatic location of learning services on the basis of their capabilities. Paolucci [11] comments that in order to enable automation of this process we need a meaningful description of the service and its parameters that can be processed automatically by tools and means to process the context of description by discovery engines.

In this sense, there are some works that aim to improve the semantic services capability of matching. On the one hand, in [12] Paolucci focuses primarily on comparing inputs and outputs of a service as semantic concepts represented in OWL to improve UDDI [15]. This work proposes a way of ranking semantic matching results. This ranking can be used in conjunction with other user-defined constraints to inform of an exact, or potentially useful web-service capability match. On the other hand, there are important lines of research that propose extensions to Web service description WSDL in two ways, annotated WSDL and WSDL-S files [16]. These approaches try to adhere to the current standards while trying to maximize semantic representations required for automation.

In sum, the works presented above try to provide a solution to the complex problem of grid learning services semantic description, but they are either limited in semantic expressiveness for matching services or they do not face at all the difficult task of using and integrating low-level learning services to compose more complex ones. Both these features could greatly enhance and facilitate the tutor's and learners' labor in a complex web-based learning scenario. For this reason, we present an initial effort towards developing a new model for grid-based learning services semantic description whose ultimate aim is to offer a mechanism for automatic Grid Learning Service discovery, invocation, composition and interoperation. This paper focuses on the first feature the details of which are described in the next section.

3   A Model for Semantic Description of Grid Based Learning Services

OWL-S is motivated by the need to provide three essential types of knowledge about a service [7] (Figure 2): the *Service Profile* describes what the service does by specifying the input and output types, preconditions and effects, the *Service Model* describes how the service works, the *Service Grounding* contains the details of how

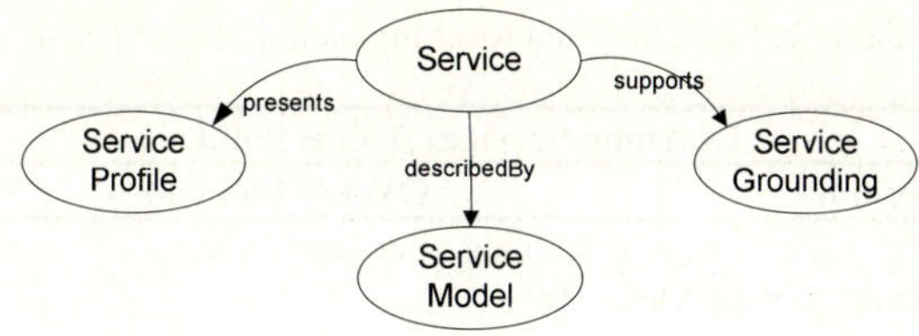

Fig. 2. The top level of the service ontology

an agent can access a service by specifying a communications protocol, parameters to be used in the protocol and the serialization techniques to be employed for the communication.

Our model proposes a mechanism using OWL-S to describe semantically a Grid Based Learning Service (GBLS). One the one hand, we identify the principle characteristics of a GBLS related to an e-learning environment and the activities that support it. On the other hand, we consider a Grid Based Learning Service (GBLS) as a granular functional component with some input information, a functional activity and some output information. In this sense we form two conceptual groups of properties to achieve a complete description of a GBLS: the Learning Services Identification (LSI) and the Learning Services Access Point (LSAP) (Figure 3).

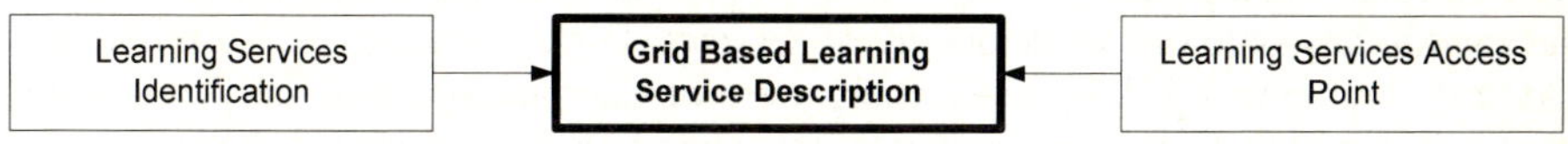

Fig. 3. Parts of the conceptual model for a GBLS semantic description

The LSI element constitutes a set of parameters used to define the principle characteristics of a GBLS. Table 1 describes it in more detail.

Table 1. LSI Elements

Learning Services Identification			
Element	**Description**	**OWL's Element**	**Parameter**
Name	The name of a service	Service Profile	ServiceName
Category	Depending on the e-learning framework, services providers could construct the domain of categories for each group of learning services	Service Profile	ServiceCategory
Description	General description of a service	Service Profile	textDescription

The LSAP element is characterized by the most important functional properties of a GBLS and is described in Table 2.

Table 2. Properties and resulting parameters of LSAP

Learning Services Access Point			
Element	**Description**	**OWL's Element**	**Parameter**
Activity	Activity in the e-learning framework supported by a service	Service Model	hasParameter
User	Defines the profile that makes use of a service (learner, teacher, another process, etc)	Service Model	hasParameter
Related Services	Specifies one or more services related to a service	Service Model	hasParticipant
Process	A service is described as a functional process	Service Model	Pocess
Errors	Specifies the errors resulting from the execution of a service	Service Model	hasParameter
Bindings	Definitions included in a WSDL description of a learning service	Service Grounding	WsdlAtomicProces sGrounding

On the one hand, the LSI contains basic information related to a learning service, allowing a user centric search. This model is generic enough to be implemented in any e-learning framework supported by GBLS and can be used for describing both low-level and composed services. In that sense, the domain of categories could be adapted to any ontology or taxonomy of services. For example, if we adopt the IMS Abstract Framework [1] Service's categories, we can obtain a taxonomy of learning tools supported by Common Services and they are in turn supported by Basic Services (Figure 4). On the other hand, LSAP allows the construction of an ontology domain for functional parameters related to the e-learning framework. This semantic description, in combination with the modifications suggested in [17], allows capability-based search as well as discovery of learning services based on the inputs and preconditions that need to be satisfied and on the outputs and effects that need to be produced. The *Bindings* element of LSAP is a parameter of WSDL describing the interface of each learning service. Both elements of the model are necessary to deal with the problem of using and integrating low-level services to compose more complex high-level services or tools. In particular, the LSAP describes grid-based learning services as processes, which allows one to specify whether a service is an atomic, simple o composite process as well as its relationship with the other services.

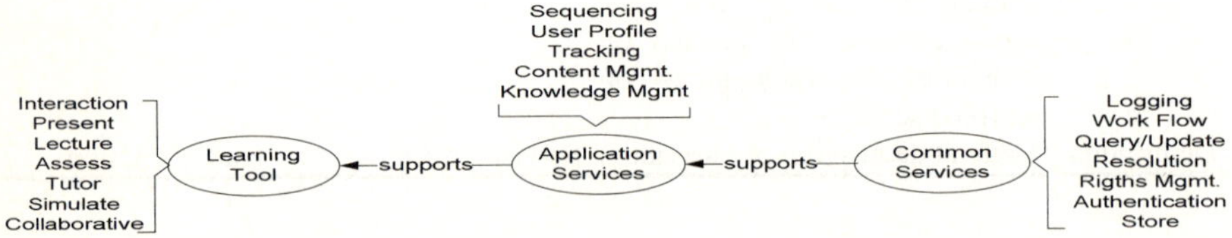

Fig. 4. Service Categories for the IMS Abstract Framework

4 An Example Scenario

At this stage of our research work, to implement and test our approach, we used a rather simple scenario which is based on a Simple Sequencing Services Tool formed by a collection of lower level services of the Carnegie Mellon Learning System Architecture Lab [18]. We point here that this tool has not been designed to be used in a Grid environment. However, we found that these services could be adapted to our definition and deployment and be used into a grid service environment since they are completely based on a web services specification. For this reason we decided to use this tool for the complete specification both of the Learning Service Identification and Access Point, which is required in our model representation. In this example, the Sequencing Control Service is supported by the set of low-level services shown in Figure 5.

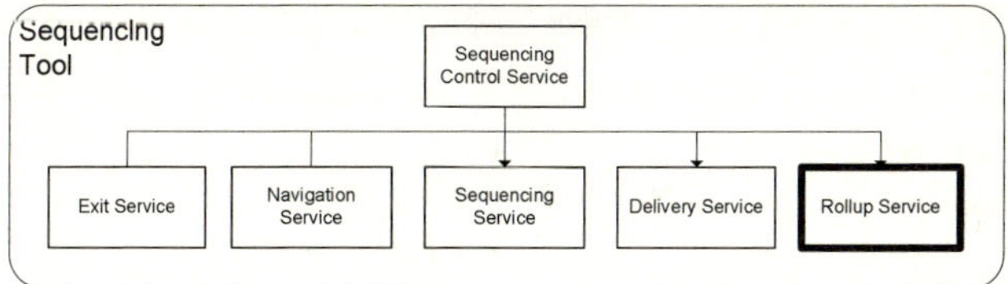

Fig. 5. A set of low-level services from the IMS Abstract Framework

For the sake of example, we are going to focus on the Rollup Services of the Sequencing Tool. This service description can be found in [18] and its properties are shown in Table 3. We used the OWL-S Editor tool [19] to implement our model's description. The graphical result of the model implementation is shown in Figure 6.

Table 3. Properties and resulting parameters of the model description that could be automatically linked using services semantic description

Property	Parameter Value
Name	Rollup Service
Category	Sequencing Control Services
Description	Perform the rollup process and update the tracking model for the learner
Activity	Activity tree
User	Learner
Errors	Data errors
	Processing Errors
Process	Overall Rollup Process
Bindings	WSDL file

In this Figure, we can observe that the relation of the services with each one of the parameters that define the model is represented by a link specifying each parameter in relation to the OWL-S model.

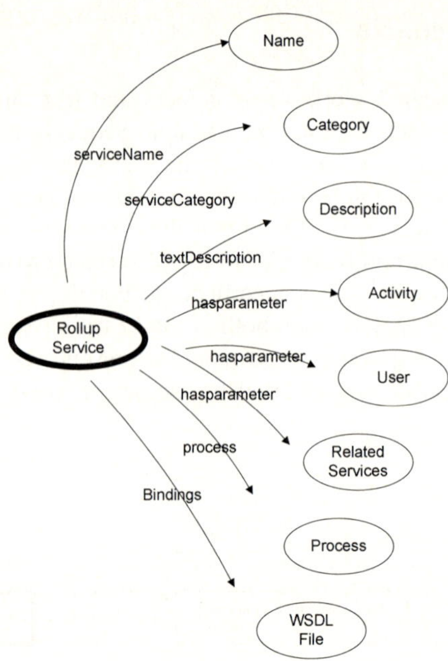

Fig. 6. The graphical result of the model implementation

An example of some request parameters and their OWL description in our model representation is shown below.

```
<process:Process rdf:ID="Process">
    <process:hasParameter>
      <process:Input rdf:ID="User">
         <rdfs:comment
rdf:datatype="http://www.w3.org/2001/XMLSchema#string">
              learner
         </rdfs:comment>
       <process:parameterType
rdf:datatype="http://www.w3.org/2001/XMLSchema#anyURI">
           http://www.w3.org/2001/XMLSchema#anySimpleType
       </process:parameterType>
      </process:Input>
    </process:hasParameter>
    <service:presents>
       <profile:Profile rdf:ID="Description">
        <profile:textDescription
rdf:datatype="http://www.w3.org/2001/XMLSchema#string">
Perform the rollup process and update the tracking Model for the learner
        </profile:textDescription>
         <profile:hasParameter rdf:resource="#learner"/>
         <service:presentedBy rdf:resource="#Rollup_Services"/>
         <profile:hasParameter rdf:resource="#end_activity"/>
         <profile:hasParameter rdf:resource="#root_activity"/>
         <profile:hasParameter rdf:resource="#activity_tree"/>
       </profile:Profile>
     </service:presents> ….
```

The model can be used in a similar way to develop the semantic description of the rest of the Rollup Service properties and resulting parameters.

The mechanism to process this OWL file, initially proposed in [18], throws a UDDI registry and is extended to send and receive semantic queries using a matchmaker. The OWL-S matching component in this architecture is tightly coupled with the UDDI registry.

5   Conclusions and Future Work

In this work we proposed a model for semantic description of Grid-based Learning Services (GBLS) to offer a new alternative for improving GBLS search and discovery. The model proposed is based on two principle characteristics of grid learning services: Service Identification and Services Access Point. Each one of these elements is related to some objects within an e-learning framework. We showed that, with the appropriate modifications of UDDI or a WSDL-S adaptation, this description can lead to an automatic discovery and invocation of GBLS. This model represents an alternative for semantic description of service properties, parameters and relationships, which facilitates services automatic discovery and invocation without human intervention while it provides sufficient information for human search. In the proposed model, GBLS are described as a process, which allows services to be invoked as an atomic, simple or composed process. The proposed model also supports a set of characteristics included in the grid learning service WSDL description. The current results of this work present a learning services conceptual description as well as an initial implementation and use of the model. On the one hand, future work aims at a full implementation and use of the model for searching, discovery and composition of GBLS in a real Learning Grid environment. On the other hand, we plan the construction of a complete conceptual model of interactions related to a learning collaborative scenario based on Grid.

References

1. IMS Global Learning Consortium, IMS Abstract Framework: White Paper, 2003
2. I. Foster. Globus Toolkit Version 4: Software for Service-Oriented Systems. IFIP International Conference on Network and Parallel Computing, Springer-Verlag LNCS 3779, pp 2-13, 2005.
3. E.Christensen, F.Curbera, GMeredith, and S.Weerawarana. Web Service Description Language (WSDL) 1.1 http://www.w3.org/TR/2001/NOTE-wsdl20010315, 2001
4. Martin Gudgin, Marc Hadley, Noah Mendelsohn, Jean-Jacques Moreau,Henrik Frystyk Nielsen, SOAP Version 1.2 Part 1: Messaging Framework, http://www.w3.org/TR/2003/REC-soap12-part1-20030624, 2003
5. Liang-Jie Zhang, Jen-Yao Chung, Qun Zhou, Developing Grid computing applications, 2002
6. I. Foster, K. Czajkowski, D. Ferguson, J. Frey, S. Graham, D. Snelling, S. Tuecke, Modeling and Managing State in Distributed Systems: The Role of OGSI and WSRF, Proceedings of the IEEE, 93(3), 2005.
7. Mike Dean, Guus Schreiber, Sean Bechhofer, Frank van Harmelen, James Hendler, Ian Horrocks, Deborah L. McGuinness, Peter F. Patel-Schneider, and Lynn Andrea Stein. OWL Web Ontology Language Reference, 2004.

8. Simona Colucci, Tommaso Di Noia, Eugenio Di Sciascio, Francesco M. Donin, Azzurra Ragone1, Semantic-Based Automated Composition of Distributed Learning Objects for Personalized E-Learning, 2004
9. Stutt and Enrico Motta , Semantic Webs for Learning: A Vision and Its Realization, Arthur, 2004
10. Zaheer Abbas, Muhammad Umer, Mohammed Odeh, Richard McClatchey, Arshad Ali, Farooq Ahmad, A Semantic Grid-based E-Learning Framework (SELF), NUST Institute of Information Technology, CCCS Research Centre, University of the West of England, 2005
11. Massimo Paolucci, Takahiro Kawamura, Rerry R. Payne, and Katia Sycara. Semantic matching of web services capabilities, 2002.
12. Massimo Paolucci, Takahiro Kawamura, Terry R. Payne, Katia Sycara, Importing the Semantic Web in UDDI, Robotics Institue, Carnegie-Mellon University, USA, 2002
13. Guillermo Vega-Gorgojo, Miguel L. Bote-Lorenzo, Eduardo Gómez-Sánchez, Yannis A. Dimitriadis, Juan I. Asensio-Pérez, Semantic Search of Learning Services in a Grid-Based Collaborative System, School of Telecommunications Engineering, University of Valladolid, 2003.
14. Cui Guangzuo, Chen Fei, Chen Hu, Li Shufang, OntoEdu: A Case Study of Ontology-based Education Grid System for E-Learning, Modern Education Technology Center at Peking University, 2004.
15. Luc Moreau, Simon Miles, Juri Papay, Keith Decker, Terry Payne, Publishing Semantic Descriptions of Services, University of Southampton, UK. 2005
16. Preeda Rajasekaran, John Miller, Kunal Verma, Amit Sheth, Enhancing Web Services Description and Discovery to Facilitate Composition, University of Georgia, Athens, 2004
17. Naveen Srinivasan, Massimo Paolucci. Katia Sycara, Semantic Web Service Discovery in the OWL-S IDE, 2006
18. Simple Sequencing Services, Carnegie Mellon Learning System Architecture Lab,2002
19. Daniel Elenius, Grit Denker, David Martin, Fred Gilham, John Khouri, Shahin Sadaati, and Rukman Senanayake, The OWL-S Editor – A Development Tool for Semantic Web Services, SRI International, Menlo Park, California, USA, 2004

A QoS Oriented Broker System for Autonomic Web Services Selection

Young-Jun Seo and Young-Jae Song

Dept. of Computer Engineering, Kyunghee University,
1, Sochen-dong, Gihung-gu, Yongin-si, Gyeonggi-do 446-701, Republic of Korea
`yjseo@khu.ac.kr`, `yjsong@khu.ac.kr`

Abstract. With the growing popularity of web services, web services standards enable the development of large-scale applications in open environments. In particular, they enable services to be dynamically bound. Unfortunately, current techniques fail to address the critical problem of selecting the right service instances. If one needs to be chosen among many similar web services, a service consumer needs quality information of web service in general. Therefore, a device that can share quality information among service consumers is needed in order to solve the problem of web service selection. This paper presents a design specification and service selection method of Agent-based QoS Broker(AQB) system on behalf of service consumers. An object-oriented approach has been used for system analysis by UML and it was possible to analyze static aspects and dynamic ones of the system. An agent selection rule has been used to select the part needed by an agent in the system. An interaction between agent's role and agent has been shown by diagram. An agent perform the function such as collection, feedback of QoS metrics value and service selection through broker.

1 Introduction

Recently, web service has come upon as an alternative in order to solve the problem of integrated technologies among enterprises. And web service integrate individual applications into low-cost and high-efficiency. According to IDC, the sales of web service related SW was expected 3 billion dollars in 2004 and this is only 1.6% of 188 billion dollars which is total amount of SW market that year. However, it is expected to be 11 billion dollars in 2008 by increasing 58% per year for 5 years[1].

But, there are some increasing problems to be solved as web service has become activating. The focusing element among these is the web service selection. The techniques(WSDL and UDDI) which are publishing and finding the present service depend on only static description of service interface and they have a disadvantage which is not able to describe runtime service selection based on nonfunctional attributes evaluation[2]. When it needs to choose one among the similar web services, service consumer generally needs quality information of web service. Therefore, a device that is able to share quality information among

G. Min et al. (Eds.): ISPA 2006 Ws, LNCS 4331, pp. 519–531, 2006.

service consumers is needed to solve the problem of web service selection. By using shared quality information, service consumers know quality reputation of required service. The purpose of QoS-oriented service selection is to select optimal web service for the current task and some particulars should be considered in the process as followed. There are more discussions on the using milestone of selection mechanism, the kind of information needed in the selection process, the achieving method of information, and the method of using information in the selection process.

This paper on behalf of service consumers defines the architecture of Agent-based QoS Broker(AQB) system which selects optimal web service autonomously and design specification. A theory of agent is accepted widely and suitable for related system developing in the circumstance of distributed and heterogeneous environment like web service[3]. So, in this paper I extracted agents by using agent selection rules and injected the roles into system design. Agent's roles could be divided into big three. First, it collects QoS metrics value while moving QoS brokers. Second, it selects the most appropriate service as comparing with measured QoS parameter. Third, it has to feed-back QoS metrics value of service which is selected by monitoring. QoS broker is a storage that shares QoS parameter of services as it collects and stores QoS metrics values and offers them to agents. Therefore, service consumer's application can choose an optimal web service that is suitable for quality preference and be possible to construct on run-time.

This paper is organized as followed. Section 2 introduces research trends of web service selection and a theoretical background of agent as related work. Section 3 describes problem domain of agent-based QoS broker system and design specification. Problem domain is described by system architecture and design specification does modeling by using UML. Section 4 describes the best web service selection method which find a service provider providing the optimum quality that the consumer needs in a position of service consumer. Comparative evaluation is done with established approaches through qualitative method in Section 5 and finally Section 6 describes conclusions and further research.

2   Related Work

This section explains research trends of web service selection and agent's characteristics.

2.1   Web Service Selection

The study of de Moor[4] proposed selection mechanism which web service selection is executed in the process of software development cycle. It does not depend on software developer to select service, but includes members of virtual community. Information can be achieved from community members while developing. However, it is not said clearly how to use information in the selection process.

In the research of Maximilien[5], the system is proposed that a proxy agent collects information for the service and interacts other proxy agents to maximize that information. Agents connect with service broker that is located between service consumers and providers. Service broker has not only rating of observed QoS, but also information for the service. Even though the method is not described in details, information is combined with historical usage and that information is used to select service.

Liu[6] suggested a dynamic selection mechanism that web service selection is executed based on QoS computation and policing on run-time. The system uses an extensible QoS computation model to select web service. Web service is so various that single static model cannot define all QoS parameter, on the other side domain-specific parameter for a service cannot apply to other services perfectly. Therefore, general quality criteria have been defined including execution price, execution duration, and reputation. Execution price is the cost that service requestor has to pay a service provider to use the service. Execution duration is the time that takes from the call service to getting back the result. Reputation is a parameter that can be described by user for the particular web service. These QoS parameters can be decided by getting information from service providers or execution monitoring from clients. In order to execute selection, central QoS registry of the system gets data collected from clients and store at a matrix of web service data. Each row of matrix presents web service and each column does QoS parameter. And it executes data computation like normalization. Clients are able to access registry and service will be provided based on preferred parameter by client.

Day[7] suggested a dynamic selection method based on QoS information. In that study, central forum system is used to state interaction between client and web services and it allows deducing an optimal service from a lot of potential services and selecting. While clients call a service, information for the call is marked up and central forum will be reported. Interaction describes QoS information from observing interaction attempt and system context information from the calling period. QoS information deals observed availability, reliability, and execution time of the service and system context information includes CPU, memory usage, and the numbers of bandwidth, running process. Clients deduce from these interactions to decide which service should provide good QoS. Clients can access various services information and deduce these data from rule-base expert system or naive Bayesian classifier. Expert system ranks each service based on observed values for the particular QoS parameter and user-defined weight. Classifier classifies service as one of the five categories, i.e. "excellent", "good", "adequate", "poor", and "terrible", based on observed QoS parameters.

3   Problem Domain and System Design

3.1   Problem Domain

Problem domain applied in this paragraph added QoS Broker and Agent Server to established web service architecture on the base of proposed architecture in

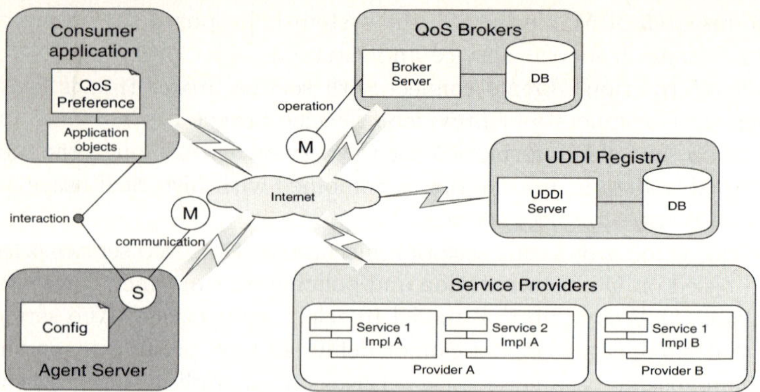

Fig. 1. System Architecture for Problem Domain

the study of Maximilien[2]. QoS Broker is used to share experience information of QoS among consumers. Agent Server generates an agent that helps selecting service with the optimal QoS. Agent is divided into mobile agent and static agent up to whether mobile is needed. Figure 1 shows whole structure of problem domain via system architecture. Here, agent with character of mobile was marked as M.

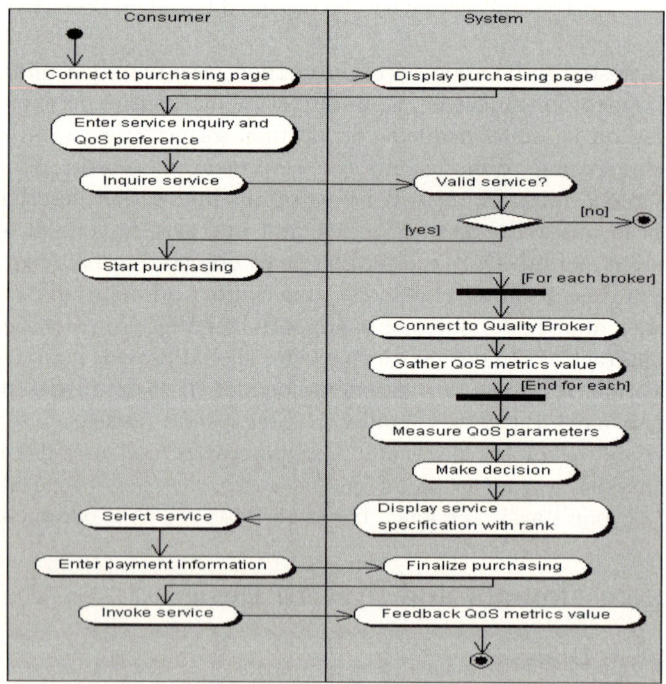

Fig. 2. Activity Diagram

3.2 Activity Diagram

Before discussing the functions provided by system, we need a business modeling process that can make us to grasp improved business. Therefore, Figure 2 describes specific business process by using activity diagram. To make sure of responsible domain, it employs swimlane. This swimlane does not connect to a class or an object. And swimlane except system can be an actor.

Step 1. Service consumer connects to purchasing page and inputs inquiry of service wanted and QoS preference.

Step 2. Before proceeding selection process, system decides if requested service is validity.

Step 3. If so, he/she starts purchasing and connects decentralized Quality Broker while moving agent. Agent collects QoS metrics value from each broker. This step continues until completing collecting from all brokers.

Step 4. QoS parameter is measured from QoS metrics values. For instance, in the case of availability parameter, it will be measured on the basis of the number of successful executions and total number of invocations.

Step 5. Agent of system selects the optimal service through Decision making procedure. In the Decision making procedure, QoS parameters are applied to decision making algorithm like PROMETHEE[8] and outranking relation of services are computed. According to this evaluation, the service of biggest value is the best choice.

Step 6. When service is to be chosen, payment information is inputted.

Step 7. Consumer invokes corresponded service with specification information, for example, WSDL, of selected service.

Step 8. After monitoring QoS metrics value while agent use service, it gives feedback to Quality Broker. Stored QoS metrics values will be used in the selection process of service hereafter.

3.3 Event Table

An event table can decompose complex system into manageable task units based on event. An event table includes rows and columns, representing events and their details respectively[9]. An event drives all system processing and happens specific time and place. Trigger is a data arrival or a point of time when system has to deal with. And source is an external agent or actor that supplies data to the system. A use case is an action that has to be operated by the system when an event happens. A response is an output produced by the system and a destination is an external agent or an actor what is received data from the system.

3.4 Use Case Diagram

Use case diagram is a graphic model which summarized functions that have to be supplied from new system and refers to event table in order to identify actor and use case. Actor will be identified by observing trigger and source column of

Table 1. System Event Table

Event	Trigger	Source	Use Case	Response	Destination
1. Consumer wants to check service validity	Service inquiry	Consumer	Check service validity	Service validity details	Consumer
2. Consumer places a purchasing	New purchasing	Consumer	Make a purchasing	Purchasing confirmation Transaction	Consumer Bank
3. Consumer changes or cancels purchasing	Purchasing change request	Consumer	Update purchasing	Change Confirmation Transaction	Consumer Bank
4. Consumer updates account information	Consumer account update notice	Consumer	Update consumer account	Change Confirmation	Consumer
5. Time to produce transaction summary reports	End of day		Produce transaction summary reports	Transaction summary reports	Consumer

event table and use table will be defined by observing use case column. If it is the case that one use case asks the service of another, the relationship <<include>> will be set up between two use cases. For example, "Make a purchasing" use case has to confirm validity of service first in Figure 3, there has been a relationship set up between "Check service validity" and <<include>>.

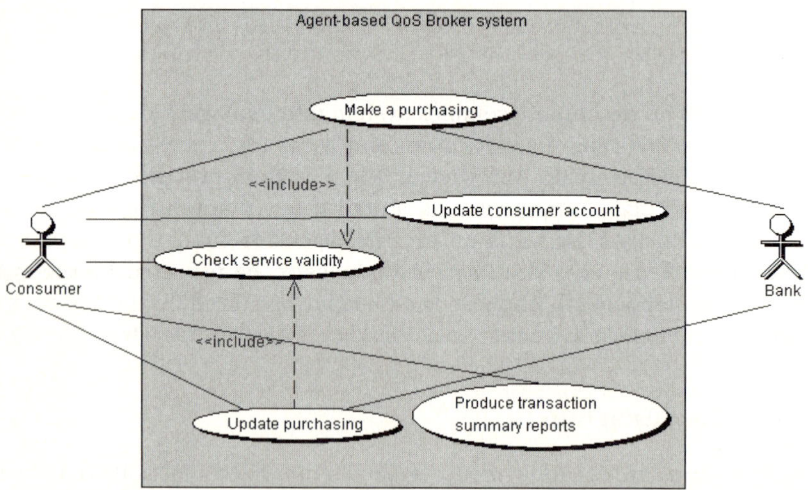

Fig. 3. Use Case Diagram

3.5   Class Diagram

Before describing class diagram, some class has to be chosen as an agent from classes. In this paper, I have classified agent into collaborative learning agent, interface agent, collaborative agent, and smart agent like Figure 4 with referring agent classification proposed by Nwana[10].

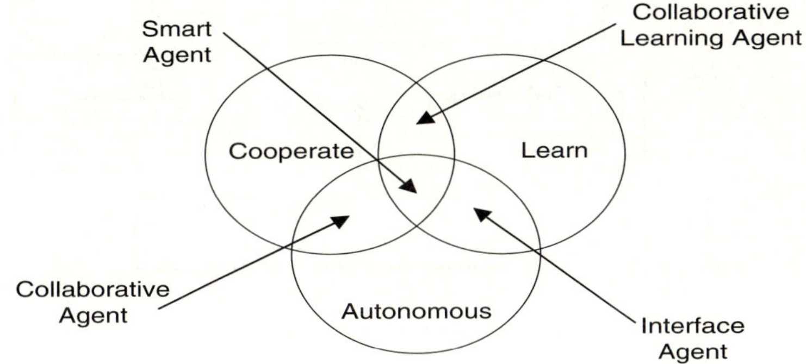

Fig. 4. A Part View of an Agent Typology[10]

However, not this classification is always clear and it is classified up to attribute emphasized especially. For instance, collaborative agent is rather emphasized agent to emphasize autonomous and cooperate attribute than learn attribute. Following Listing 1 is decision rule for three attributes to induce four types of agent[3].

1. Autonomous
   (a) Does it need internal knowledge?
   (b) Does it make decision by itself?
   (c) Can it be tolerant of unexpected or wrong inputs?
2. Learn
   (a) Is its knowledge updated continuously?
   (b) Does it interact with external entities?
3. Cooperate
   (a) Does it operate cooperatively?
   (b) Is it operated in multi-threaded style?

Listing 1. Agent Selection Rule[3]

Three agents have been chosen on the basis of design specification so far.

- Messenger Agent(Interface Agent - rule 1.a, 1.c, 2.b) : It roles a messenger between application of operates consumer and Decision Maker Agent. That is, if a consumer begins purchasing, it passes a corresponded request to Decision Maker Agent and shows the result to the consumer.

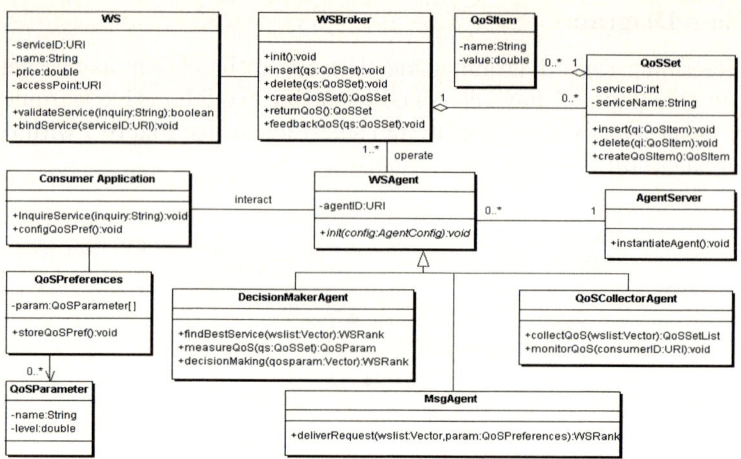

Fig. 5. Class Diagram

- QoS Collector Agent(Collaborative Agent - rule 1.a, 3.a, 3.b) : It operates a function that collects QoS metrics value of service while moving QoS brokers. It is very important for this agent to cooperate with other agents and it should be suitable for distributed environment. It also does feedback to Quality Broker after monitoring QoS metrics value while services are binding.
- Decision Maker Agent(Collaborative Agent - rule 1.a, 1.b, 3.a) : This is the main role and has an internal decision making algorithm. It deals ranking of services on the basis of QoS metrics value collected by QoS collector agent and decides the optimal service with the highest ranking.

Figure 5 is the class diagram including three selected agents.

3.6   Sequence Diagram

Sequence diagram shows the order of interaction among objects in the single use case. To identify all objects and actors on the scenario, it only uses object and act of each class diagram and use case diagram. Figure 6 is a sequence diagram in order to describe control flow of "Make a purchasing" use case. The next is an outlined explanation of Figure 6.

- Before purchasing service, to confirm whether service is valid.
- If valid, AgentServer sets up three agents for initialization.
- After QoSPreference of consumer application is delivered to MsgAgent, DecisionMakerAgent starts working for service selection.
- QoSCollectorAgent collects QoS metrics values from WSBrokers.
- Having collected, DecisionMakerAgent measures QoS parameter.
- Selection is done by delivering list of service with ranking information to consumer application and best service is binding.

- QoSCollectorAgent monitors QoS metrics value while binding and feedback to WSBroker.
- WSBroker inputs values from feedback related to QoSSet.

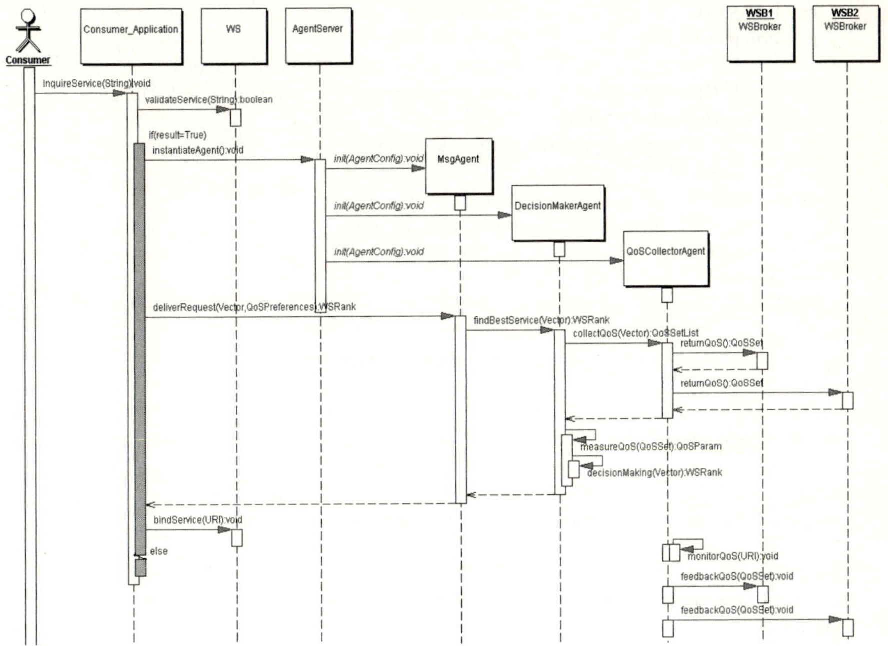

Fig. 6. Sequence Diagram

4   Service Selection Method

In order to select the best web service with result values calculated by 5 quality criteria, this paper adopted PROMETHEE approach among MCDM approaches and following three stages are necessary[8]. The algorithm can be summarized as follows:

At the first stage, weight, preference function and threshold by evaluation criteria were decided. In Min/Max, Max means an index which gives more positive influence to the relevant web service selection as the evaluation criteria value increases and Min means an opposite case. Weight is decided by experiences of the past and opinions of service consumers. Preference function is defined with 6 kinds and each function is selected by the type of criteria.

At the second stage, leaving flow, entering flow and net flow of the preference are calculated. First, the preference function value per quality criteria should be calculated and the preference function value $p_k(WSP_i, WSP_j)$ of the basis k means $p_k(f_k(WSP_i), f_k(WSP_j))$ which is the difference between WSP_i and WSP_j. The preference index $\Pi(WSP_i, WSP_j)$ is a measure for the intensity of

---

Algorithm 1. Pseudo Code of QoS Decision Making Algorithm

```
Define attributes of QoS criteria
Construct QoS Matrix
/* Compute preference function value between WS_i and WS_j */
While more QoS criteria Do
        For i=1 to N
                For j=1 to N
                        Compute difference evaluation value between WS_i and WS_j
                        If the more value increases, the more positive influence have then
                                If result > 0 then
                                        Compute preference function value
                                Endif
                        Else
                                        Set preference function value to zero
                                Endif
                        Endfor
                Endfor
Endwhile
/* Compute preference index value between WS_i and WS_j */
For i=1 to N
        For j=1 to N
                Compute weighted average of the preference function values between WS_i and WS_j
        Endfor
Endfor
/* Compute leaving, entering flow between WS_i and WS_j */
For i=1 to N
        For j=1 to N
                Compute average of the preference index values between WS_i and WS_j
        Endfor
Endfor
/* Compute net flow between WS_i and WS_j */
For i=1 to N
        Compute difference value between leaving flow and entering flow of WS_i
Endfor
Choose WS_i with maximum net flow value
```

---

the service consumer's preference for an alternative WSP_i in comparison with an alternative WSP_j for the simultaneous consideration of all quality criteria. It is basically a weighted average of the preference functions $p_k(WSP_i, WSP_j)$.

The outranking relation of alternatives is calculated by figuring out leaving flow(ϕ^+), entering flow(ϕ^-) and net flow(ϕ) like equation 1 with preference index $\Pi(WSP_i, WSPj)$.

$$\phi^+(WSP_i) = \frac{1}{N} \sum_{\substack{n=1 \\ n \neq i}}^{N} \Pi(WSP_i, WSP_n) \tag{1}$$

$$\phi^-(WSP_i) = \frac{1}{N} \sum_{\substack{n=1 \\ n \neq i}}^{N} \Pi(WSP_i, WSP_n)$$

$$\phi^{net}(WSP_i) = \phi^+(WSP_i) - \phi^-(WSP_i)$$

At the third stage, the outranking relation is evaluated. The higher the leaving flow and the lower the entering flow, the better the alternative. In case a complete pre-order is requested, PROMETHEE II yields the so-called net flows. As the net flow $\phi^{net}(WSP)$ of preference is higher, the relevant WSP means the more superior alternative.

5   Comparative Evaluation

Comparative evaluation between established approaches which are described earlier in related work and the approach proposed in this paper is the same as Table 2, each features are as followed[4,5,6,7].

Table 2. Comparative Evaluation of Web Service Selection Approaches

Approach / Features	de Moork[4]	Maximilien[5]	Liu[6]	Day[7]	AQB System
Employment time	Design-time	Run-time	Run-time	Run-time	Run-time
Kinds of Information	User, community requirements	Service locations, QoS ratings	QoS data	Client-specific data	QoS parameter
Methods of getting information	Involving users in development cycle	Proxy agents	Client feedback	Client feedback	Agents feedback
Methods of using information	No explicit method	No detail method	Normalization	Rule-base expert system, Naive Bayesian classifier	Multiple Criteria Decision Making

First, the employment time of selection mechanism. All comparable approaches apart from de Moor's approach selected web service dynamically on run-time. On the other hand, users and community members operated selection mechanism on design time by de Moor's approach.

Second, kinds of information needed in the selection process. Most researches except de Moor's approach used QoS data in the selection process. As a character of web service, at the time when consumer uses web service, quality is the main decision element to choose web service. So, approach presented in this paper has been only considered performance, safety, and cost related QoS parameter.

Third, methods of getting information. In Liu and Day's approach, client does feed-back QoS registry or forum system in direct. But, the approach proposed by with Maximilien use agent to feedback to broker.

Fourth, methods of using information in the selection process. There was no clear explanation how to use information in the process of selection in De Moor and Maximilien' approach. While Liu's approach operates the same computation such as normalization and Day' approach inducts through rule-base expert system or naive Bayesian classifier. Information was used for MCDM approach like PROMETHEE in the presented approach. When PROMETHEE compares with other approaches like MAUT and AHP, it has an advantage that even though comparative alternative has been added or deleted, it can overcome the problem that it has to operate pair-wise comparison again. Therefore, it is the appropriate approach[11] for the matter of web service selection that asks a lot of quality attributes which measured and evaluated at the same time.

6   Conclusion

This paper has presented the architecture of Agent-based QoS Broker system which agents on the basis of shared QoS through broker select service autonomously and the design specification. We used object-oriented approach by using UML for system analysis, and through this, we have been able to analyze static side and dynamic side of system. Agent selection rule has been used to select some part that agent needs from the system, and though diagram, interaction been shown among agent' role and agent. Agent operates QoS metrics value collection, service selection, feedback of QoS metrics value through broker. Especially, decision making result that happens from the procedure of agent' service selection supports consumer to bind the optimal service on run-time. In future work, we will expand our selection algorithm to take into account the trust relationship between brokers. Also, system architecture and design should be expanded in order to suit for service composition environment and there is a need to describe service selection algorithm inside.

References

1. Sandra Rogers, "Web Services Software 2004-2008 Forecast", IDC, Apr, (2004).
2. E. Michael Maximilien, Munindar P. Singh, "A Framework and Ontology for Dynamic Web Services Selection" IEEE Internet Computing, Vol. 8, No. 5, pp. 84-93, (2004).
3. Sooyong Park, Jintae Kim, Seungyun Lee, "Agent-Oriented Software Modeling with UML Approach", IEICE Transaction on Information and Systems, Vol.E83-D, No.8, Aug, (2000).
4. Aldo de Moor, Willem-Jan van den Heuvel, "Web service selection in virtual communities", In 37th Hawaii International Conference on System Sciences, Jan, (2004).
5. E. Michael Maximilien, Munindar P. Singh, "Agent-based architecture for autonomic web service selection", In Workshop on Web Services and Agent-based Engineering at Autonomous Agents and Multi-Agent Systems, (2003).

6. Yutu Liu, Anne Ngu, Liangzhao Zheng, "QoS computation and policing in dynamic web service selection (to appear)" In Proceedings of the WWW 2004, May, (2004).
7. Julian Day, Ralph Deters, "Selecting the best web service", In Proceedings of the IBM Centers for Advanced Study Conference (CASCON '04), pp.293-307, (2004).
8. Brans, J. and P. Vincke, "A Preference Ranking Organization method(The PROMETHEE Method for Multiple Criteria Decision-Making)", Management Science, Vol. 31, No. 6, (1985), 647-656
9. John W. Satzinger, Rober B. Jackson, Stephen D. Burd, "Systems Analysis and Design in a Changing World", Course Technology, (2002).
10. Nwana, H. S., "Software Agents: An Overview", Knowledge Engineering Review, Vol.11, No.3, pp.205-244, Oct, (1996).
11. K.H.Bennett, and others, "A Broker Architecture for Integrating Data Using a Web Services Environment", ICSOC, Vol.2910, pp.409-422, (2003).

XML Based Semantic Query Mechanism on Grid

Jinguang Gu[1,2] and Baowen Xu[2]

[1] College of Computer Science and Technology,
Wuhan University of Science and Technology, Wuhan 430081, China
[2] College of Computer Science and Engineering,
Southeast University, Nanjing 210096, China
{sam, bwxu}@seu.edu.cn

Abstract. Semantic heterogeneity and few compatible data sources are two problems in data grid service. This paper introduces a novel wrapper-mediator based semantic data grid service mechanism, it uses ontology based semantic information to wrap the heterogeneous data source, and employs mediator structure to supply accessing interface for the data sources. The extension of XML algebra with semantic query enhanced and semantic grid communication mechanism are also discussed to enable semantic querying on data gird environment.

1   Introduction

We witness a rapid increase in the number of web information sources that are available online. The World-Wide Web(WWW), in particular , is a popular medium for interacting with such sources[1]. How to integrate and query distributed and heterogeneity information, especially semi-structured and non-structured information is the problem we need to solve. Data grid technology is the standard means of realizing the needs. However, the studies in data grid technology still have the shortcomings as follows: 1)The flexibility of the grid technology is limited. Taking OGSA-DAI[2] for example, it only supports the limited related database and native XML database. However, most information on Internet comes from web-based semi-structured data environment, such as company web application and XML-based e-commerce platform; furthermore, OGSA-DAI does not have the effective mechanism for other data sources to be integrated into the grid environment. 2) The individual node in the grid environment may exist in varied semantic environment; different data resource is constructed in accordance with different semantic standard. The present data grid does not take into consideration the semantic heterogeneity among different nodes. Many projects are focusing these two topics about data grid, GridMiner[3] and OGSA-WEB[4] are two novel projects focusing on the first one, they use a OGSA-DAI compatible architecture to support semi-structure information sources on the internet; DartGrid II[5] and SemreX[6] are excellent projects focusing on the second topic.

This paper focusses on these two topics too. It employs a mediator-wrapper framework to support different information sources and enable semantic information operation on different grid nodes. And it uses XML query style language

G. Min et al. (Eds.): ISPA 2006 Ws, LNCS 4331, pp. 532–541, 2006.

to retrieve information from different grid nodes, because XML is rapidly becoming a language of choice to express, store and query information on the web, other kinds of web information such as HTML-based web information can be transferred to XML based information with annotation technologies. Users can query information with XML languages, XPath based languages such as XQuery, XUpdate are suitable for retrieving information in distributed integration systems. The remainder of this paper is structured as follows. Section 2 gives the general discussion about framework of the mediator-wrapper based semantic data grid (SDG for short), and proposes the knowledge fusion mechanism on the mediator node from the local wrapped grid nodes. Section 3 discusses the knowledge communication mechanism to support semantic querying and knowledge fusion. Section 4 discusses ontology enabled querying planning on XML based grid nodes, such as ontology enhanced XML query algebra and XML query planning algorithm. Section 5 summarizes the whole paper.

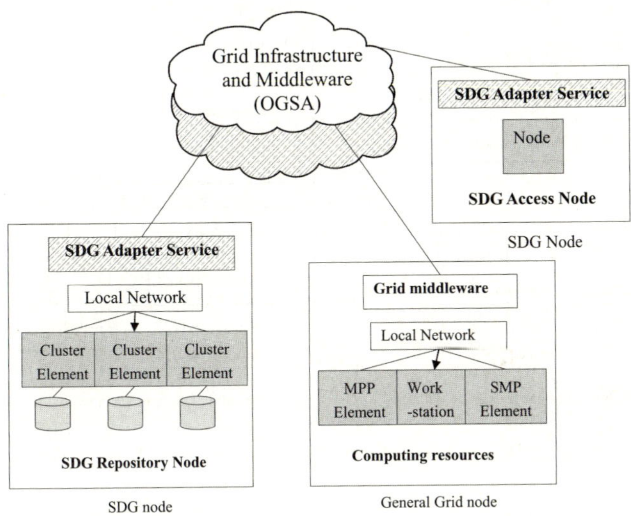

Fig. 1. General Architecture of Semantic Data Grid

2 Mediator-Wrapper Based Semantic Data Grid Service

Semantic Data Grid (SDG) must satisfy the following requirements:

- The architecture must be opening and compatible with existing standard such as the framework of OGSA[7] or WSRF[8] considering compatible with OGSA-DAI;
- It must provide flexible method for integrating various data sources including relational databases, Native XML databases, or Web based application systems;

– It must support the global semantics to the users who access semantic data grid.

The general architecture of semantic data grid can be illustrated in fig 1. It uses a semantic grid adapter service to support semantic operation on the gird. This paper employs a mediator-wrapper method to construct the adapter service, which can be expressed by figure 2(a). The function of the wrapper of local grid nodes is to describe its semantics and its mapping relationship with other nodes, the information source of these nodes include both free and commercial databases, flat files services, web services or web based applications, HTML files and XML files, and the semantic information of every local gird node is described with the language based on its ontology. The mediator node constructs the global semantics of the local nodes, the semantic communication mechanism between the mediator and wrapper nodes is discussed in the following section.

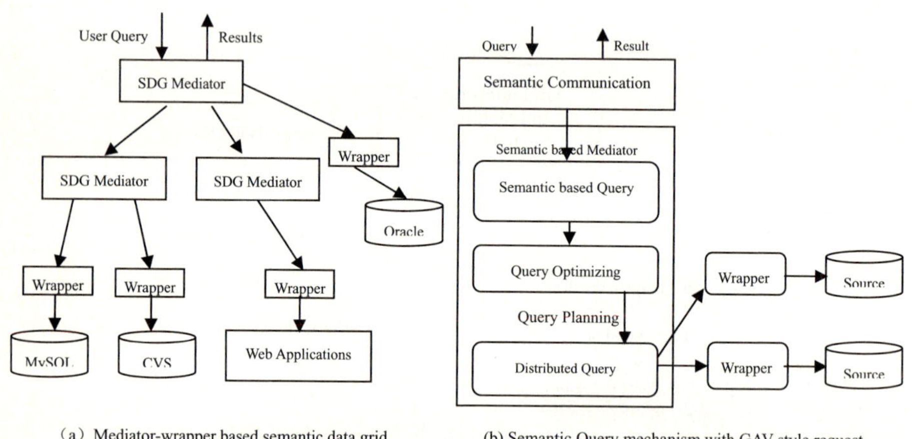

(a) Mediator-wrapper based semantic data grid   (b) Semantic Query mechanism with GAV style request

Fig. 2. Mediator-Wrapper based Semantic Data Grid

To support OGSA-DAI interface, this paper develops a Ontology to XML (OTX as short) algorithm to generate a virtual data source (VDS) of OGSA-DAI[9]. To illustrate the algorithm, we first define the ontology based knowledge on the mediators and wrappers.

Definition 1. *A knowledge schema is a structure* $KB := (C_{KB}, R_{KB}, I, \iota_C, \iota_R)$ *consisting of (1) two sets* C_{KB} *and* R_{KB}, *(2) a set* I *whose elements are called instance identifiers or instances, (3) a function* $\iota_C : C_{KB} \to \Re(I)$ *called concept instantiation, (4) a function* $\iota_R : R_{KB} \to \Re(I^+)$ *called relation instantiation.*

There are four basic relations: *part-of, kind-of, instance-of* and *attribute-of,* which denote respectively the relation between portion and whole, the relation of concept hierarchy, the relation between concept and instance, the relation of attributes. The OTX can be express in algorithm 1.

Algorithm 1. OTX

Input: $S = (C_S, R_S)$//parse ontology, acquire conceptual model
Output: XML Schema
1 **foreach** $c_i \in C_S$ **do**
2   **if** $kind\_of(c_i, c_x) \notin R_S$ **then**
3   output <complexType name=c_i+"Type"/ >
4   **else**
5   output <complexType name=c_i+"Type" base=c_x+"Type" derivedBy="extension">
6   **end**
7 **end**
8 **foreach** $CA_j \in CA(c_i)$ **do**
    // $CA(c_i) = \{CA_1, CA_2, \ldots, CA_p\}$ is the attribute of c_i, and $CA_i = (nCA_i, v_i)$
9   **if** $attibute\_of(c_y, c_i) \in R_S)$ **then**
10   output <element name="nCA_j" type=c_y+"Type"/>
11   **else**
12   output <element name="nCA_j" type="v_j"/>
13   **end**
14   output </complexType>
15 **end**
16 **foreach** $c_i \in C_S$ **do**
17   output <element name="c_i" type=c_i+"Type"/>;
18 **end**

---

3   Communication Mechanism with Semantic Grid

It is very important to develop a knowledge communication and coordinating mechanism to support the ontology fusion and semantic query on different data grid nodes. This paper employs a Knowledge Communication and Manipulation Language for Semantic Grid, or KCML for short to support this mechanism, which is an extension of the KGOL[10] language. One function of KCML is to coordinate with each grid node to build the mediator-wrapper architecture dynamically. The other function is to build global knowledge on the mediator and enable semantic query. The communication language is build on SOAP, following the expression of SOAP's class XML, supporting SOAP over HTTP, HTTPS or other rock-bottom communication protocol. The language could describe as:

$KCML ::= Ver|Operation|Sender|Receiver|Language|Content.$

The field *Ver* is for keeping Expanding, showing which version language was used. The new version language has compatibility downwards, supporting the old communication mechanism; *Operation* gives basic communication atom which will be described next; *Content* describes what is communicated; *Sender* defines sender's information, including user, address (such as IP ,e-mail,URL, port); *Receiver* defines receiver's information (usually, receiver should be Web Service or Grid Service), ,including type (HOST, Web Service or Semantic Web Service), address(such as IP address, e-mail, URL, port, if receiver is Web Service, also including service address), identifier; *language* defines which language is used this communication, including RDF/RDFs, DAML+OIL, OWL etc.

3.1   Basic Communication Atom

To simplify the content of this paper, we only discuss the atom of KCML language which support ontology fusion and semantic querying. The atom includes query operation, join operation and union operation etc. as following[11]:

- **Selection.** $\sigma_F(c) = \{x | x \in \iota_C(c) \wedge F(x) = true\}$ where F is composed of logic expression, supporting logic operation $\wedge, \vee, \neg, \forall, \exists, <, >, \leq, \geq, \neq, =$ and $\in$. c is concept element of knowledge instance;
- **Join.** $\bowtie (c_1, p, c_2) = \{x, y | x \in \iota_C(c_1) \wedge y \in \iota_C(c_2) \wedge p(x, y) = true\}$, where p is join condition, c_1 and c_2 is concept element;
- **Union.** $c_1 \cup c_2 = \{x | x \in \iota_C(c_1) \wedge x \in \iota_C(c_2)\}$, c_1 and c_2 is the same as above;
- **Minus.** $c_1 - c_2 = \{x | x \in \iota_C(c_1 \wedge \neg c_2)\}$, c_1 and c_2 is the same as above;
- **Projection.** $\pi_P(c) = \bigcup_{p_i \in P} \{y | \exists x, (x, y) \in \iota_R(p_i) \wedge x \in \iota_C(c)\}$, where c is concept element, P is a set of relationship and $P = \{p_1, p_2, \ldots, p_k\}$;

3.2   Semantic Fusion Atom

The mediator node constructs the global semantics of the local nodes based on ontology via ontology fusion mechanism[12] based on the ontology mapping patterns in gird environment, the patterns of ontology mapping can be categorized into four expressions: direct mapping, subsumption mapping, composition mapping and decomposition mapping[13], a mapping can be defined as:

Definition 2. *A **Ontology mapping** is a structure $\mathcal{M} = (\mathcal{S}, \mathcal{D}, \mathcal{R}, v)$, where $\mathcal{S}$ denotes the concepts of source ontology, $\mathcal{D}$ denotes the concepts of target ontology, $\mathcal{R}$ denotes the relation of the mapping and v denotes the confidence value of the mapping, $0 \leq v \leq 1$.*

A direct mapping relates ontology concepts in distributed environment directly, and the cardinality of direct mapping could be one-to-one. A **subsumption mapping** is a 6-tuple $\mathcal{S}_\mathcal{M} = (\mathcal{D}_m, \mathcal{R}_m, \mathcal{B}_m, \preceq_m, \mathcal{I}_m, v)$, where $\mathcal{D}_m$ is a direct mapping expression; $\mathcal{R}_m$ is the first target concept, which is the most specialized ontology concept. The mapping between the source ontology and $\mathcal{R}_m$ is denoted as **Root ontology concept mapping**; $\mathcal{B}_m$ is the last target concept, which is the most generalized ontology concept. The mapping between the source ontology and $\mathcal{B}_m$ is denoted as **Bottom ontology concept mapping**; $\preceq_m$ is inclusion relation between target ontology concepts; $\mathcal{I}_m$ is the inverse mapping. Subsumption mapping is used to denote concept inclusion relation especially in the multiple IS-A inclusion hierarchy. The **composition mapping** is a 4-tuple $\mathcal{C}_\mathcal{M} = (\mathcal{F}_m, \mathcal{A}_m, \mathcal{B}_m, v)$, where $\mathcal{F}_m$ is a direct mapping expression; $\mathcal{A}_m$ is chaining of role(s) between target ontology concepts; $\mathcal{B}_m$ is the last target symbol, which is the node of chaining target role(s), and composition mapping is used to map one concept to combined concepts. For example, the mapping *address=contact(country, state, city, street, postcode)* is a composition mapping, in which the concept *address* is mapped to combined concept *"contact, country, state, street, and postcode"* of local schema elements. The **decomposition mapping** is a 4-tuple $\mathcal{C_M} = (\mathcal{A}_m, \mathcal{B}_m, \mathcal{L}_m, v)$, where $\mathcal{A}_m$ is chaining of role(s) between source ontology concepts; $\mathcal{B}_m$ is the last target symbol, which is the node of chaining source role(s); $\mathcal{L}_m$ is a direct mapping expression. Decomposition mapping is used to map a combined concept to one local concept, and the example for the decomposition mapping is the reverse of the composition.

Algorithm 2. XPlan($\sigma(X, Y), FL$)

    Input: $\sigma(X, Y)$ is the query needed to be processed, FL is the fusion connection list.

    Output: P is the query planning sequence

1 $P \leftarrow \emptyset$, $S_q \leftarrow \emptyset$;

2 **foreach** $x \in X$ **do**

3   **switch** *Mappings of X node in fusion list FL* **do**

4   **case** *directfusion*

5           $P \leftarrow P + (\sigma(x, Y), \{\sigma(x, Y), \sigma(x_1 : S_1, Y), \sigma(x_2 : S_2, Y), \ldots, \sigma(x_n : S_n, Y)\}, \cup)$;

6   **case** *subsumption or composition*

7           $P \leftarrow P + (\sigma(x, Y), \{\sigma(x_1 : S_1, Y), \sigma(x_2 : S_2, Y), \ldots, \sigma(x_n : S_n, Y)\}, \cup)$;

8   **end**

9   **end**

10    $S_q \leftarrow S_q + \sigma(x_1 : S_1, Y) + \sigma(x_2 : S_2, Y) + \ldots + \sigma(x_n : S_n, Y)$;

11 **end**

12 **foreach** $\sigma(x, Y) \in S_q$ **do**

13   **foreach** $y \in Y$ **do**

14   **switch** *Mappings of Y concept in fusion list FL* **do**

15   **case** *directfunsion*

16           $P \leftarrow P + (\sigma(x, y), \{\sigma(x, y), \sigma(x : S_1, y_1), \sigma(x : S_2, y_2), \ldots, \sigma(x : S_n, y_n)\}, \cup)$;

17   **case** *subsumption*

18           $P \leftarrow P + (\sigma(x, y), \{\sigma(x : S_1, y_1), \sigma(x : S_2, y_2), \ldots, \sigma(x : S_n, y_n)\}, \cup)$;

19   **case** *decomposition*

20           $P \leftarrow P + (\sigma(x, y), \{\sigma(x : S_1, y_1 \wedge F), \sigma(x : S_2, y_2 \wedge F), \ldots, \sigma(x : S_n, y_n \wedge F)\}, \bowtie, F)$;

21   **end**

22   **end**

23 **end**

24 **end**

25 **return** P;

The KCML language must support the mapping patterns between different semantic nodes on gird, we use **Match** atom to support it, it can be defined as

$M(c, d, r) = \{(x, y) | x \in \iota_C(c) \wedge y \in \iota_C(d) \wedge (x, y) \in \iota_R(r)\}$, where c is different concept from d, r is relationship of mapping.

The knowledge stored at mediator can be described as the ontology fusion connections list, which can be described as definition 3. The corresponding fusion connection lists of the mapping patterns can be denote as $\mathcal{F}_{cd}$, $\mathcal{F}_{cs}$ and $\mathcal{F}_{cc}$ respectively.

Definition 3. *Fusion Connection is a structure* $\mathcal{F}_c(O_1 : C_1, O_2 : C_2, \ldots, O_n : C_n, \mathcal{M})$, *where* C_1 *denotes a concept or concept set of ontology* O_1, C_2 *denotes a concept or concept set of Ontology* O_2, $\mathcal{M}$ *denotes the mapping patterns between* C_1, C_2, $\ldots$ *and* C_n.

4   Semantic XML Query Rewriting and Planning

The semantic query in a mediator-based SDG can be express as figure 2(b). The user's request is rewritten and modified accordingly based on the global semantics, and is due processed optimally. Corresponding operation plan is made and passed by the wrapper to each data source node for operation. From above description, we know that this paper employs the GAV(Global as View) method to process the user's query[1]. The query can be described as an XML query with semantic enhanced, which can be described as an extension of XML algebra, and it will be discussed in the following subsection. Because common XML query languages such as XQuery and XUpdate can be transferred into XML query algebra, so the extension is manageable.

4.1   The Extension of XML Algebra with Semantic Query Enhanced

This paper extended XML algebra TAX[14] to enable semantic querying on mediated gird nodes, TAX uses *Pattern Tree* to describe query language and *Witness Tree* to describe the result instances which satisfy the Pattern Tree. The definition of pattern tree with ontology extension can be described as follows:

Definition 4. *An Ontology Enhanced Pattern Tree is a 2-tuple* $SPT := (T, F)$, *where* $T := (V, E)$ *is a tree with node identifier and edge identifier.* F *is a combination of prediction expressions.*

The prediction expression F supports the following **atomic condition** or **selection condition**[15]. Atomic condition have the form of X *op* Y, where:

- $op \in \{=, \neq, <, \leq, >, \geq, \sim,$ **instance of, isa, is_part_of, before, below, above**$\}$
- X and Y are conditional *terms*, which are attributes ,types,type values $v : \tau$ and $v \in dom(\tau)$, ontology concepts and so on;
- $\sim$ stands for the estimation of semantic similarity.

The selection condition is:

- Atom conditions are selection conditions;
- If c_1 and c_2 are selection conditions, then $c_1 \wedge c2$, $c_1 \vee c_2$ and $\neg c_1$ are both selection conditions;
- No others selection conditions forms.

4.2   XML Query Rewriting and Planning

The query planning is based on the semantic XML query rewriting technology. In order to simplify the discussion, this paper just pays attention to the query planning mechanism of the selection operation. Briefly, a selection operation can be expressed as $\sigma(X : S, Y)\ \{X \subseteq P_i \cup P_o, Y \subseteq PE\}$, where P_i is the input pattern tree, P_o is output pattern tree, PE is predication list, S denotes the site in which the query will be executed. We define two operators $\cup$ and $\bowtie$ to represent *Union* and *Join* operation separately, and define the operator $\Rightarrow$ to represent the query rewriting operation, and we use $\sigma(X : S_0, Y)$ or $\sigma(X, Y)$ to denote the user's query from the mediator site.

Firstly, we propose how to rewrite pattern tree (which is the X element of expression $\sigma(X, Y)$), there maybe several cases as follows:

1. X is one of the elements of input pattern tree or output pattern tree, and it is also a concept in the global ontology hierarchy. $X_i(1 \leq i \leq n)$ are the concepts for different local ontologies. X and X_i were combined into one concept in the integrated global ontology with strong direct mappings, which means that X and X_i can match each other, then we can rewrite X as $X \cup \bigcup_{1 \leq i \leq n} X_i$. The responding selection rewriting can be expressed as:

$$\sigma(X, Y) \Rightarrow \sigma(X, Y) \cup \sigma(X_1 : S_1, Y) \cup \sigma(X_2 : S_2, Y) \ldots \cup \sigma(X_n : S_n, Y) \quad (1)$$

2. The concept of X is generated by the subsumption mapping or composition mapping of $X_i(1 \leq i \leq n)$, then we can rewrite X as $\bigcup_{1 \leq i \leq n} X_i$. The responding selection rewriting can be expressed as:

$$\sigma(X, Y) \Rightarrow \sigma(X_1 : S_1, Y) \cup \sigma(X_2 : S_2, Y) \ldots \cup \sigma(X_n : S_n, Y) \quad (2)$$

And then, we propose how to rewrite the predication expressions (which is the Y element of the expression $\sigma(X, Y)$, there are also several cases, which can be described as follows:

1. If there are lots of concept $Y_i(1 \leq i \leq n)$ combined in the concept Y of global Ontology, we can rewrite Y as $Y \cup \bigcup_{1 \leq i \leq n} Y_i$. The corresponding selection rewriting can be described as:

$$\sigma(X, Y) \Rightarrow \sigma(X, Y) \cup \sigma(X : S_1, Y_1) \cup \sigma(X : S_2, Y_2) \ldots \cup \sigma(X : S_n, Y_n) \quad (3)$$

2. If the concept Y is generated by the subsumption mapping of $Y_i(1 \leq i \leq n)$, we can rewrite Y as $\bigcup_{1 \leq i \leq n} Y_i$. The corresponding selection rewriting can be described as:

$$\sigma(X, Y) \Rightarrow \sigma(X : S_1, Y_1) \cup \sigma(X : S_2, Y_2) \ldots \cup \sigma(X : S_n, Y_n) \quad (4)$$

3. If the concept Y is generated by the composition mapping of $Y_i (1 \leq i \leq n)$, suppose the composition condition is F, we can rewrite Y as $(Y_1 + Y_2 + \ldots Y_n) \cap F$. The corresponding selection rewriting can be described as:

$$\sigma(X, Y) \Rightarrow \sigma(X : S_1, Y_1 \wedge F) \bowtie \sigma(X : S_2, Y_2 \wedge F) \ldots \bowtie \sigma(X : S_n, Y_n \wedge F) \quad (5)$$

It is worth to point out that rewriting process may require a recursion in the transitivity property of semantic mapping. The query planning is a sequence, each node of the sequence can be denoted as $P_n = (Q_n, S_n, C_n, F_n)$, where Q_n is the query which is needed to rewrite, S_n is a set of sub query executed on different sites, C_n denotes the connection operator, in most time, it is $\cup$ or $\bowtie$ operator, F_n is the predication which denotes the connection conditions. P_n represents the query rewriting procedure of query Q_n. The query planning procedure of user's query $\sigma(X, Y)$ can be expressed in algorithm 2.

5 Discussion and Conclusion

Semantic data grid service mechanism we present in this paper wrapped various information source through ontology semantic, and used Mediator-Wrapper to support the heterogeneous data source, employed mediator structure to realize virtual data gird service which supports semi-structured information retrieving language. The extension of XML algebra with semantic query enhanced and semantic grid communication mechanism are also discussed to enable semantic accessing on data grid environment. However, query optimizing in distributed web sites and the capability of different nodes and network were not considered in the query planning mechanism discussed in this paper, future research will be focused on this topic.

Acknowledgment

This work was partially supported by a grant from the NSF (Natural Science Fundation) of China under grant number 60425206, and it was partially supported by a grant from NSF of Hubei Prov. of China under grant number 2005ABA235 and a grant from the NSF of Hubei Education Agency of China under grant number Z200511005.

References

1. Levy, A.Y., Rajaraman, A., Ordille, J.J.: Query heterogeneous information sources using source descriptions. In: Proceedings of the 22nd VLDB Conference, Mumbai, India, Morgan Kaufmann Publishers Inc (1996) 251–262
2. Antonioletti, M., Atkinson, M., Baxter, R., et al.: The design and implementation of Grid database services in OGSA-DAI. Concurrency and Computation: Practice and Experience **17** (2005) 357–376

3. Wöhrera, A., Brezanya, P., Tjoab, A.M.: Novel mediator architectures for Grid information systems. Future Generation Computer Systems **21** (2005) 107–114
4. Pahlevi, S.M., Kojima, I.: OGSA-WebDB: An OGSA-Based System for Bringing Web Databases into the Grid. In: Proceedings of International Conference on Information Technology: Coding and Computing (ITCC'04), IEEE Computer Society Press (2004) 105–110
5. Chen, H., Wu, Z., Mao, Y.: Q3: A Semantic Query Language for Dart Database Grid. In: Proceedings of the Third International Conference on Grid and Cooperative Computing (GCC 2004), Wuhan, China, LNCS 3251, Springer Verlag (2004) 372–380
6. Jin, H., Yu, Y.: SemreX: a Semantic Peer-to-Peer Scientific References Sharing System. In: Proceedings of the International Conference on Internet and Web Applications and Services (ICIW'06), IEEE Computer Society Press (2006)
7. Foster, I., Kesselman, C., Nick, J.M., Tuecke, S.: Grid Services for Distributed System Integration. IEEE Computer **35** (2002) 37–46
8. Czajkowski, K., Ferguson, D.F., Foster, I., et al.: The WS-Resource Framework. http://www.globus.org/wsrf/specs/ws-wsrf.pdf (2004)
9. Zhang, L., Gu, J.: Ontology based semantic mapping architecture. In: Proceedings of 2005 International Conference on Machine Learning and Cybernetics, Guang Zhou, China (2005) 2200–2205
10. Zhuge, H., Liu, J.: A Knowledge Grid Operation Language. ACM SIGPLAN Notices **38** (2003) 57–66
11. Sheng, Q.J., Shi, Z.Z.: A Knowledge-based Data Model and Query Algebra for the Next-Gereration Web. In: Proceedings of APWeb 2004, LNCS 3007 (2004) 489–499
12. Gu, J., Zhou, Y.: Ontology fusion with complex mapping patterns. In: Proceedings of 10th International Conference on Knowledge-Based, Intelligent Information and Engineering Systems, Bournemouth, United Kingdom, LNCS, Springer Verlag (2006) 738–745
13. KWON, J., JEONG, D., LEE, L.S., BAIK, D.K.: Intelligent semantic concept mapping for semantic query rewriting/optimization in ontology-based information integration system. International Journal of Software Engineering and Knowledge Engineering **14** (2004) 519–542
14. H.V.Jagadish, L.V.S.Lakshmanan, D.Srivastava, et al: TAX: A Tree Algebra for XML. Lecture Notes In Computer Science **2379** (2001) 149–164
15. Hung, E., Deng, Y., V.S.Subrahmanian: TOSS: An Extension of TAX with Ontologies and Simarity Queries. In G.Weikum, ed.: Proceedings of the 2004 ACM SIGMOD international conference on Management of data, Paris, France, ACM Press (2004) 719–730

A Novel Memory-Oriented OWL Storage System*

Dongwon Jeong[1], Myounghoi Choi[1], Yang-Seung Jeon[3], Youn-Hee Han[2],
Young-Sik Jeong[3], and Sung-Kook Han[3]

[1] Dept. of Informatics and Statistics, Kunsan National University,
Gunsan, Jeollabuk-do, 573-701, Korea
`{djeong, cmh775}@kunsan.ac.kr`
[2] School of Internet-Media, Korea University of Technology and Education,
Cheonan, Chungnam, 330-708, Korea
`yhhan@kut.ac.kr`
[3] Dept. of Computer Engineering, Wonkwang University,
Iksan, Jeollabuk-do, 570-749, Korea
`{globaljeon, ysjeong, skhan}@wku.ac.kr`

Abstract. A novel memory-oriented OWL storage system is proposed. Semantic Web is recognized as the next generation Web and OWL (Web Ontology Language) is one of the most important technologies to achieve the Semantic Web. Even though several memory-oriented storage systems have been proposed to manage and handle OWL documents, they still suffer from low performance. In this paper, we propose a new memory-based OWL storage system to resolve the problem. This paper describes the proposed storage model and shows the experiment and comparison result. The evaluation result shows our storage system provides higher performance than other systems. Therefore, it enables us to develop and provides high quality Semantic Web services.

1 Introduction

Semantic Web is recognized as a next framework for an advance of the current Web. To realize the Semantic Web, many technologies such as XML, RDF, RDF Schema, OIL, and DAML have been proposed [1, 2, 3, 4]. However, there still exit several issues such as no reasoning function and high implementation complexity due to various suggestions.

To resolve these issues, OWL (Web Ontology Language) has been developed as an international standard of W3C [5]. Recently, many Web pages have been building using OWL language to endow them with an intelligent function (Inference facility). We can verify the fact that one million or more Web pages have been built with OWL for about one year since OWL had been selected as the international standard. We believe that the OWL document will increase by geometric progression.

With this situation, one of the most crucial issues is how to efficiently store a very large OWL data into memory. There are two types of storages to load and manage OWL data. The first is memory-based (memory-oriented) storages that load OWL ontologies on memory, and the other is permanent storages that load OWL ontologies into such as relational databases or object-oriented databases [6, 7, 8, 9, 10, 11, 12, 13].

---

* This work was supported in part by MIC & IITA through IT Leading R&D Support Project.

G. Min et al. (Eds.): ISPA 2006 Ws, LNCS 4331, pp. 542–549, 2006.

The goal of this paper is to develop an enhanced memory-based storage model. In other words, it is on how to effectively load a very large OWL ontology on memory. To resolve this issue, several memory-based storage systems have been presented such as Sesame and OWLJessKB.

However, the previous systems have several issues to deal with very large OWL data sets (OWL ontologies). Most systems are based on the triple (3-tuple) model. Hence, it exponentially increases the structural complexity and requires high response time. Most of all, their memory-based loading time is time-consuming.

This paper proposes a novel memory-based loading system to efficiently load very large OWL data sets. Especially, this paper proposes a new memory-based storage model and shows the performance evaluation of the previous systems and our system, which is proposed in this paper.

The outline of this paper is as follows: Section 2 introduces the proposed storage model and Section 3 shows its implementation. Section 4 presents the evaluation methodology such as experiment data sets, system environment, and comparative item. Section 5 shows the evaluation result and Section 6 concludes this paper.

2   Framework of Storage System

This section describes the proposed memory-based storage model, i.e., in-memory-based loading system. In fact, storage systems could be classified into two types: Persistent storage system and memory-oriented storage system. We are studying on the relational database-based persistent storage system, but this paper just focus on the memory-oriented storage system.

2.1   Conceptual Storage Model

Fig. 1 illustrates the conceptual structure of the proposed storage model. In this figure, first, an OWL document is parsed to check its validation and extract a data set, which is suitable for the defined memory structure in the proposed system. In other words, the original OWL documents are translated to the memory storage structure model. Once the parsing operation is finished, the extracted data set is loaded on the memory. A user gives a query and the query processing agent obtains its result from the stored data set on memory. The query could be composed in SQL style or the others such as KIF, RQL, or SPARQL [15, 16, 17].

Currently, in our system, queries should be composed as SQL (SQL statement) and the query processing agent parse the queries and return the results to users. If it is in other languages, the agent translates it into a SQL statement. In addition, a module for reverse parsing might be added to show the query result as an OWL document.

2.2   Memory-Based Storage Model Definition

As shown in Fig. 1, the storage system input is a set of OWL ontologies and its result could be an OWL document or a value set. Operations for parsing and storing are required. The input ontologies are loaded on memory and stored into the defined memory storage structure. The proposed storage system also has operations to return query results to users. When they are sequentially denoted as I, OP, M, QP, and O, the proposed storage model is defined as Definition 1.

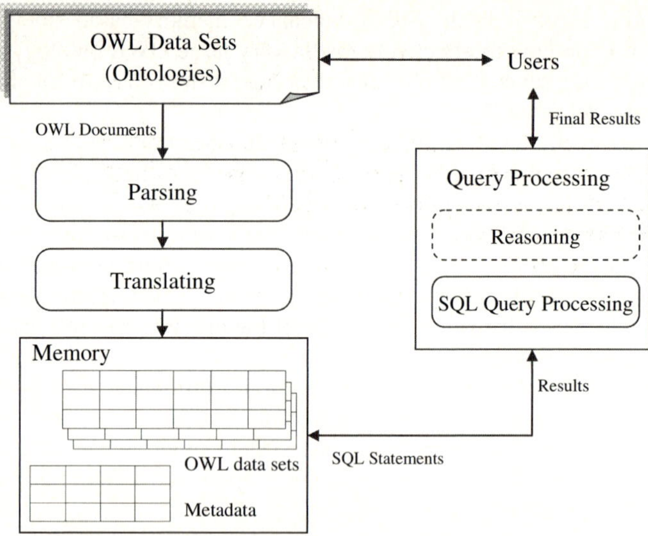

Fig. 1. Conceptual model of the proposed storage system

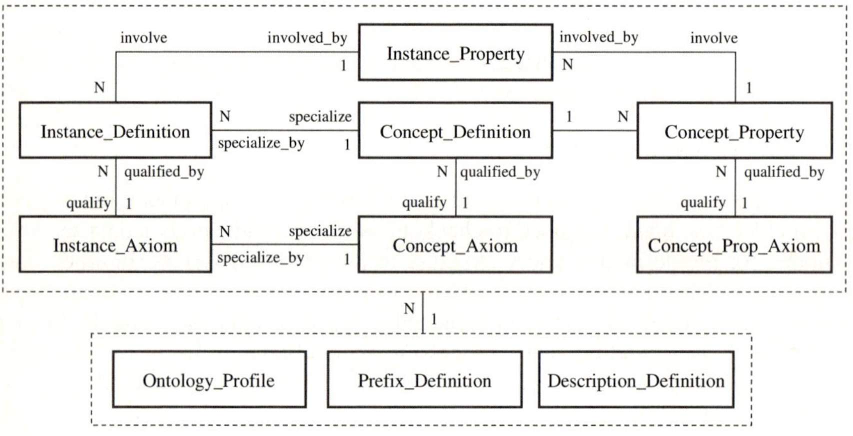

Fig. 2. Metamodel of the storage structure for loading and storing OWL data sets on memory

Definition 1. SM, denoting the proposed model, is defined as follows.

    SM = (I, OP, S, QP, O), where
        I: Original OWL documents (OWL data sets, OWL ontologies)
        OP: Operations for parsing and storing
        M: OWL data on memory
        QP: Operations for query processing including reasoning function
        O: Query results to be returned to users

Fig. 2 shows a metamodel of the defined storage structure (M in Definition 1) to store OWL data sets in memory. An OWL ontology basically consists of a triple (Subject, Predicate, Object). In this paper, both of Subject and Object are described as Concept or Instance. In the OWL specification, they are defined as Class and Individual. Ontology_Profile includes header information in OWL ontologies. Prefix_Definition respectively store full prefix names and an abbreviation of each full prefix.

3   Implementation

We implemented a prototype for the proposed storage model and Fig. 3 shows its snapshots. Fig. 3-(1) shows all of the parsing and translating results. The translation results are illustrated in Fig. 3-(2). Conversion accuracy of the implementation prototyping has been proved with several OWL ontologies. Especially, it satisfies the Web Ontology Language Test Cases by W3C.

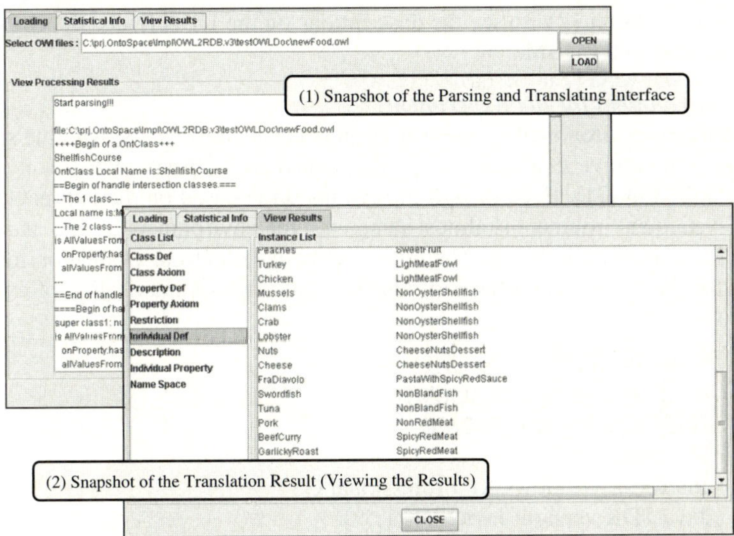

Fig. 3. Snapshot of the implementation

4   Evaluation Methodology

This section describes an evaluation methodology including the system environment, data sets for the experiment, and comparative items.

4.1   Target Systems and Experiment Environment

Target Systems
We already introduced the OWL storages in Section 1, but the target systems in this paper include Sesame and OWLJessKB. The others are not been considered because

they provide neither APIs for prototyping nor an exact storing model [20, 21]. Exactly, Sesame supports Sesame-DB and Sesame-Memory. Sesame-DB is a persistent storage system and Sesame-Memory is a memory-oriented storage system. This paper focuses on the evaluation of memory-based (memory-oriented) systems, thus Sesame-Memory is chosen as a target system.

Experiment Data Sets

We gathered several OWL ontologies, which are widely used to introduce to OWL or describe models and tools for OWL data management and used the sets to prove the translation precision of the proposed storage model. However, each ontology size is not acceptable for the performance evaluation. Therefore, we generated an OWL data set using a data generator (UBA), which has been developed by SWAT project team at Lehigh University [19]. The team proposed a permanent storage system and also presented the evaluation research results comparing it with several storage systems [20, 21]. We also generate the same data sets using the UBA. In other words, we created five OWL data sets: LUBM(1,0), LUBM(5,0), LUBM(10,0), LUBM(20,0), and LUBM(50,0). LUBM(N,S) denotes the dataset contains N universities using a seed value of S. Refer [21] to see the descriptions on the UBA (Univ-Bench Artificial Data Generator) and LUBM.

System Environment for the Experiment

Our experiment environment (System environment) is almost same with the setting in [21]. The comparative evaluation is accomplished by indirect comparison with the result described in [21]. Even though the evaluation is based on the indirect comparison, our system environment is almost same with the environment in [21] and most of all the CPU capability is lower. Therefore, we believe that our evaluation methodology provide the reliability of the experiment result. The summarization of evaluation is as follows:

- CPU: Pentium 4 (1.70 GHz)
- Memory size (RAM): 256MB
- Heap memory size: 512MB
- Hard dist size: 80GH
- Platform: Windows XP Professional OS
- Java SDK version: Java SDK 1.5.0
- DBMS: Oracle 10g

4.2 Comparative Item

The comparative item is the loading time. We repeated the experiment five times to obtain more precise evaluation results. As described, the data set includes five ontologies created with conditions LUBM(1,0), LUBM(1,0), LUBM(1,0), LUBM(1,0), LUBM(1,0), which contain OWL files for 1, 5, 10, 20, and 50 universities respectively. It means an ontology, created under a condition LUBM(1,0), consists of OWL files. Every university contains 15 or more departments. With these experiment sets, we estimate the loading time of each ontology (OWL file set). The loading time is the sum of parsing time and storing time the parsed data set to a database.

In this paper, we use the experiment result described in [21]. It means that the comparative evaluation is accomplished by indirect comparison. Even though the evaluation is based on the indirect comparison, our system environment is almost same with the environment in [21] and most of all CPU capability is lower. Therefore, we believe that our evaluation methodology provide the reliability of the experiment result.

5   Evaluation Results and Discussions

Table 1 shows the OWL data set loading time for all of the chosen target systems including the proposed system. Fig. 4 depicts how the loading time grows as the OWL set size increases. In Fig. 4, the dashed lines mean the systems cannot load corresponding data sets. First in case of OWLJessKB, it could not load the OWL data set generated with options from LUBM(5,0) to LUBM(50,0).

Table 1. Experimental evaluation result on loading time of the systems

	Data Set	The num. of Instances	Load Time(hh:mm:ss)
Sesame-Memory	LUBM (1, 0)	103,397	00:00:13
OWLJessKB			03:16:12
Proposed System			00:00:12
Sesame-Memory	LUBM (5, 0)	646,128	00:01:53
OWLJessKB			-
Proposed System			00:01:18
Sesame-Memory	LUBM (10, 0)	1,316,993	00:05:40
OWLJessKB			-
Proposed System			00:04:11

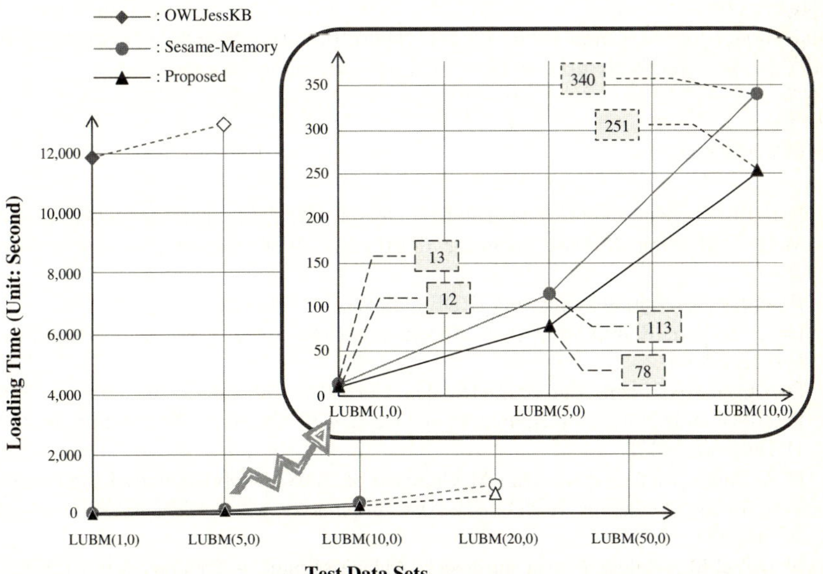

Fig. 4. Graphical description of the loading time experiment results

With LUBM(1,0) data set, OWLJessKB requires 12,000 seconds to load on memory. On the other hand, Sesame-Memory and our system take 13 seconds and 12 seconds respectively and our systems shows a little better loading performance. As for LUBM(5,0) and LUBM(10,0), both (Sesame-Memory:Our System) consume 113: 78 and 340:251 respectively. Both systems could not load data sets, LUBM(20,0) and LUBM(50,0). As a result, the proposed storage model is more efficient than the others.

6 Conclusion and Further Study

To realize the emerging Semantic Web, several technologies have been developing. Most of all, OWL is accepted as one of the most important and state-of-the-art technologies toward the ideal Semantic Web. There might be many issues and one of the most important issues is how to efficiently store a very large OWL data into memory, i.e., load and store into memory.

In this paper, a novel memory-based OWL storage model was proposed. With the simple introduction to the proposed storage model, the experiment result on the loading time has been described to show the predominance of our proposed storage model.

Further studies include additional and complementary experiments: (1) Query response time and (2) Query answer soundness (accuracy). This paper focused on the development of an efficient memory-oriented storage model. However, a new permanent storage model, which is better than existing models, should be developed for practical usability of OWL. Most of permanent models are based on the triple structure. However, almost all data are stored in relational database model. It means a relational model-based permanent storage model should be proposed to make reflect the current realistic situation. The proposed our storage model is designed using relational model concept not triple model. Therefore, we believe our memory-based model can be effectively used to develop a new persistent storage model.

References

1. François Yergeau, John Cowan, Tim Bray, Jean Paoli, C. M. Sperberg-McQueen, and Eve Maler, Extensible Markup Language (XML) 1.1, W3C Recommendation, 4 February 2004.
2. Resource Description Framework (RDF), http://www.w3.org/RDF/.
3. Dave Bechett, RDF/XML Syntax Specification (Revised), W3C Recommendation, 10 February 2004.
4. Dan Connolly, Frank van Harmelen, Ian Horrocks, Deborah L. McGuinness, Peter F. Patel-Schneider, and Lynn Andrea Stein, DAML+OIL Reference Description, W3C Note, 18 December 2001.
5. M.K. Smith, C. Welty, and D.L. McGuinness ed., OWL Web Ontology Language Guide, W3C Recommendation, 10 February 2004, http://www.w2.org/TR/2004/REC-owl-guide-20040210/.
6. Maria del Mar Roldan-Garcia and Jose F. Aldana-Montes, A Tool for Storing OWL Using Database Technology, November 2005.

7. Pan, Z. and heflin, J., DLDB: Extending Relational Databases to Support Semantic Web Queries, In Workshop on Practical and Scaleable Semantic Web Systems, The 2nd International Semantic Web Conference (ISWC2003), 2003.

8. Broekstra, J. and Kampman, A., Sesame: A Generic Architecture for Storing and Querying RDF and RDF Schema, The 1st International Semantic Web Conference (ISWC2002), 2002.

9. OWLJessKB: A Semantic Web Reasoning Tool, http://edge.cs.drexel.edu/assemblies/software/owljesskb/.

10. Grosof, B.N., Horrocks, I., Volz, R., and Decker, S., Description Logic Programms: Combining Logic Programms with Description Logic, In Proceedings of the 12th international World Wide Web Conference, 2003.

11. Horrocks, I., Li, L., Turi, D., Bechhofer, S., The Instance Store: Description Logic Reasoning with Large Numbers of Individuals, 2004.

12. SourceForge.net, Jena2 Database Interface - Database Layout, November 2004, http://jena.sourceforge.net/DB/layout.html.

13. Jena: A Semantic Web Framework for Java, http://jena.sourceforge.net/.

14. Jess: A Rule Engine for the Java Platform, http://herzberg.ca.sandia.gov/jess/.

15. Gensereth, M. and Fikes, R. Knowledge Interchange Format, Stanford Logic Report Logic, Stanford University, http://logic.stanford.edu/kif/kif.html.

16. G. Karvounarakis, A. Magkanaraki, S. Alexaki, V. Christophides, D. Plexousakis, M. Scholl, and K. Tolle, Querying the Semantic Web with RQL, Elsevier Science, Computer Networks and ISDN Systems Journal, Vol. 42, No. 5, pp. 617-640, August 2003.

17. Eric Prud'hommeaux and Andy Seaborne, SPARQL Query Language for RDF, W3C Candidate Recommendation, 6 April 2006.

18. Jeremy J. Carroll and Jos De Roo, OWL Web Ontology Language Test Cases, W3C Recommendation, 10 February 2004.

19. Yuanbo Guo, Data Generator(UBA): UBA1.7, http://swat.cse.lehigh.edu/projects/lubm/.

20. Yuanbo Guo, Zhengxiang Pan, and Jeff Heflin, An Evaluation of Knowledge Base Systems for Large OWL Datasets, Vol. LNCS 3298, 2004.

21. Yuanbo Guo, Zhengxiang Pan, and Jeff Heflin, LUBM: A Benchmark for OWL Knowledge Base Systems, Journal of Web Semantics, 2005.

An Ontology Matching Approach to Semantic Web Services Discovery

Beniamino Di Martino

Dipartimento di Ingegneria dell' Informazione
Facoltà di Studi Politici ed Alta Formazione Europea e Mediterranea "Jean Monnet"
Seconda Università di Napoli
beniamino.dimartino@unina.it

Abstract. In this paper we present an approach to semantic based Web Service discovery, and a prototypical tool, based on syntactic and structural schema matching, among an input ontology, describing a service request, and web services descriptions, at the "syntactic level" through WSDL, or at the semantic level, through service ontologies included in OWL-S, WSMO, SWSF and WSDL-S. The different input schema, WSDL descriptions, OWL ontologies, OWL-S, WSMO, SWSF and WSDL-S components, are represented in an uniform way by means of directed rooted graphs, where nodes represent schema elements, connected by directed links of different types, e.g. for containment and referential relationships. On this uniform internal representation a number of matching algorithms operate, including structural based algorithms (Children Matcher, Leaves Matcher, Graph and SubGraph Isomorphism) and syntactical ones (Edit Distance (Levenshtein Distance) and Synonym Matcher (through WordNet synonyms thesaurus).

1 Introduction

Semantic Web Services (SWS) enrich Web Services technology with formal, ontology based, description of services functionalities and capabilities at the semantic level, thus enabling semantic based discovery, composition, dynamic binding, orchestration. A number of frameworks and standards supporting such functionalities have been recently developed, including OWL-S [1] (previously DAML-S [2]), WSMO [3], SWSF [4] and WSDL-S [5] (previously METEOR-S [6]), mainly integrating Semantic Web languages RDF and OWL with Web services interface description languages (mainly WSDL [7]). Nevertheless such technologies are still immature and incomplete, and compete each other; in particular, they still do not provide viable and integrated solutions to the web Services discovery problem.

In this paper we present an approach to the semantic based Web Service discovery, and a prototypical tool, based on syntactic and structural schema matching, among an input ontology, describing a service request, and web services descriptions, at the "syntactic level" through WSDL, or at the semantic level, through service ontologies included in OWL-S, WSMO, SWSF and WSDL-S. Matching among OWL-S, WSMO, SWSF and WSDL-S descriptions is also provided, together with a functionality for "reverse" ontology syntesis, i.e. production of an OWL ontology from a WSDL description.

G. Min et al. (Eds.): ISPA 2006 Ws, LNCS 4331, pp. 550–558, 2006.

Our matching procedure takes as input two schemas and determines a mapping indicating which elements of the input schemas logically correspond to each other, together with a similarity measure indicating the plausibility of their equivalence. The different input schema, WSDL descriptions, OWL ontologies, OWL-S, WSMO, SWSF and WSDL-S components, are represented in an uniform way by means of directed rooted graphs, where nodes represent schema elements, connected by directed links of different types, e.g. for containment and referential relationships. On this uniform internal representation a number of matching algorithms operate, including structural based algorithms (Children Matcher [8], Leaves Matcher [8], Graph and SubGraph Isomorphism [9,10,11]) and syntactical ones (Edit Distance [12] (Levenshtein Distance) and Synonym Matcher (through WordNet [13] synonyms thesaurus).

The rest of the paper is structured as follows: Section 2 provides with a classification of ontology mapping approaches. Section 3 describes the procedure we have devised and the schema mapping algorithms we've implemented. Section 4 concludes the paper with description of future work.

2   Ontology Matching Approaches

Our approach to ontology and web services descriptions' comparison is based on schema matching models and techniques. In this section we briefly review the fundamental concepts on schema matching. See [19,20] for extensive review on generic schema matching, while [21,22] are more focused on ontology matching. A fundamental operation in the manipulation of ontologies is *match*, which takes two ontologies as input and produces a mapping between elements of the two ontologies that correspond semantically [19]. Match plays a central role in numerous applications, such as web-oriented data integration, electronic commerce, schema integration, schema evolution and migration, application evolution, data warehousing, database design, web site creation and management, and component-based development. A mapping is defined as a set of *mapping elements*, each of which indicates that certain elements of schema S1 are mapped to certain elements in S2. Furthermore, each mapping element can have a *mapping expression* which specifies how the S1 and S2 elements are related. The mapping expression may be directional, for example, a certain function from the S1 elements referenced by the mapping element to the S2 elements referenced by the mapping element, or it may be non-directional, that is, a relation between a combination of elements of S1 and S2. Currently, schema matching is typically performed manually, perhaps supported by a graphical user interface. Obviously, manually specifying schema matches is a tedious, time-consuming, error-prone, and therefore expensive process. Moreover, as systems become able to handle more complex databases and applications, their schemas become larger, further increasing the number of matches to be performed. The level of effort is at least linear in the number of matches to be performed, maybe worse than linear if one needs to evaluate each match in the context of other possible matches of the same elements. A faster and less labor-intensive integration approach is needed. This requires automated support for schema matching. To define the match operator, Match, we need to choose a representation for its input schemas and output mapping. In practice, a particular representation must be chosen, such as an entity-relationship (ER) model [23], object-oriented (OO) and database models [24,25], XML, or directed graphs. In each case, there is a natural correspondence between the building blocks of the representation and the notions of elements and structure: entities and relationships in ER models; objects and relationships in OO models; elements, subelements, and IDREFs in XML; and nodes and edges in graphs. Match is a binary operation that determine pairs of corresponding elements from their input operands. Match operates on metadata (schema elements) and an element in a match result can relate multiple elements from both inputs.

In the following we classify the major approaches to schema matching. An implementation of Match may use multiple match algorithms or *matchers*. This allows us to select the matchers depending on the application domain and schema types. Given that we want to use multiple matchers we distinguish two subproblems. First, there is the realization of individual matchers, each of which computes a mapping based on a single matching criterion. Second, there is the combination of individual matchers, either by using multiple matching criteria (e.g., name and type equality) within an integrated *hybrid matcher* or by combining multiple match results produced by different match algorithms within a *composite matcher*. For individual matchers, we consider the following largely-orthogonal classification criteria:

- *Instance vs schema:* matching approaches can consider instance data (i.e., data contents) or only schema-level information.
- *Element vs structure matching:* match can be performed for individual schema elements [26], such as attributes, or for combinations of elements, such as complex schema structures.
- *Language vs constraint:* a matcher can use a linguistic based approach (e.g., based on names and textual descriptions of schema elements) or a constraint-based approach (e.g., based on keys and relationships).
- *Matching cardinality:* the overall match result may relate one or more elements of one schema to one or more elements of the other, yielding four cases: 1:1, 1:n, n:1, n:m. In addition, each mapping element may interrelate one or more elements of the two schemas. Furthermore, there may be different match cardinalities at the instance level.
- *Auxiliary information:* most matchers rely not only on the input schemas S1 and S2 but also on auxiliary information, such as dictionaries, global schemas, previous matching decisions, and user input [27].

Many systems for schema matching have been developed, based on one or, more frequently, a combination of the methods described before. S-Match [28], Anchor-Prompt [29], COMA [8], Cupid [30]. QOM [31], are notable examples.

3 Semantic Web Service Discovery Based on Ontology Matching

The procedure we have devised, and the prototipe tool implemented, performs semantic discovery of Web services, based on structural and element level matching, among schema imported from OWL, WSDL, WSML and OWL-S web services descriptions. Such schema are represented by means of directed rooted graphs, where nodes represent schema elements, connected by directed links of different types, e.g. for containment and referential relationships. Our matching procedure takes as input two schemas and determines a mapping indicating which elements of the input schemas logically correspond to each other. The match result is a set of mapping elements specifying the matching schema elements together with a similarity value between 0 (strong dissimilarity) and 1 (strong similarity) indicating the plausibility of their correspondence.

Our matching procedure combines and integrates a number of matching algorithms, adopting two of the above described approaches:

- the structural approach, based on the application of the following algorithms: Children Matcher [8], Leaves Matcher [8], Graph and SubGraph Isomorphism [9,10,11].
- the linguistic or syntactic approach, based on application of: Edit Distance [12] (Levenshtein Distance) and Synonym Matcher (through WordNet [13] synonyms thesaurus).

In the following, we describe the chosen approaches, and corresponding matching components (matchers) we've implemented, in more detail.

Children Matcher: This structural matcher is used in combination with a linguistic-level matcher. It determines the similarity between two inner elements based on the combined similarity between their child elements, which in turn can be both inner and leaf elements. The similarity between the inner elements needs to be recursively computed from the similarity between their respective children. The similarity between the leaf elements is obtained from the linguistic-level matchers, e.g. Synonym Matcher or Edit Distance .

Leaves Matcher: This structural matcher is also used in combination with a linguistic-level matchers, e.g. Synonym Matcher or Edit Distance. In contrast to the Children strategy, this matcher only considers the leaf elements to estimate the similarity between two inner elements. This strategy aims at more stable similarity in cases of structural conflicts.

Graph and SubGraph Isomorphism Matcher: This structural matcher is based on the *VF algorithm* [3,4,5]. that is a deterministic matching method for verifying both isomorphism and graph-subgraph isomorphism. The algorithm has general validity, since no constraints are imposed on the topology of the graphs to be matched, and can exploit semantic information if available. We illustrate the VF algorithm in the following. Given two graphs $G_1 = (N_1, B_1)$ and $G_2 = (N_2, B_2)$, a mapping $M \subset N_1 \times N_2$ is said to be an isomorphism iff it is a bijective function that preservers the branch structure of the two graphs, that is, M maps each branch of G_1 onto a branch of G_2 and viceversa. M is said to be a graph-subgraph isomorphism iff M is an isomorphism between G_2 and a subgraph of G_1. We will assume that the graphs involved are *directed graphs*, i. e. a branch (i, j) is to be considered different from (j, i). The extension of the algorithm to undirected graphs is however trivial. The matching process can be suitably described by means of a State Space Representation (SSR). Each state s of the matching process can be associated to a partial mapping solution $M(s)$, which contains only a subset of the components of the mapping function M.

A partial mapping solution univocally identifies two subgraphs of G_1 and G_2, say $G_1(s)$ and $G_2(s)$, obtained by selecting from G_1 and G_2 only the nodes included in the components of $M(s)$, and the branches connecting them. In the following we will denote by $M_1(s)$ and $M_2(s)$ the projection of $M(s)$ onto N_1 and N_2 respectively, while the sets of the branches of $G_1(s)$ and $G_2(s)$ will be denoted by $B_1(s)$ and $B_2(s)$ respectively.

Edit Distance or Levenshtein Distance (LD): String similarity is computed from the number of edit operations (deletions, insertions, or substitutions) necessary to transform one string (s) to another one (t). The strings are first tokenized (i.e. converted to lower case and the punctuation is removed) and then stemmed using Porter Stemmer algorithm before applying the Edit Distance Algorithm. The result of this algorithm is then normalized to obtain a value between 0 and 1.

Synonym Matcher: this algorithm uses WordNet synonyms thesaurus to find synonyms, returning 1 if a synonym has found or 0 otherwise.

The above devised procedure defined has been implemented resulting in the prototype tool ***SchemaMatcher***. It performs syntactic and structural schema matching, among an input ontology, describing a service request, and web services descriptions, at the "syntactic level" through WSDL, or at the semantic level, through service ontologies included in OWL-S, WSMO, SWSF and WSDL-S. Matching among OWL-S, WSMO, SWSF and WSDL-S description is also provided, together with a functionality for "reverse" ontology syntesis, i.e. production of an OWL ontology from a WSDL description. It has been developed entirely in Java, by utilizing DOM parsers

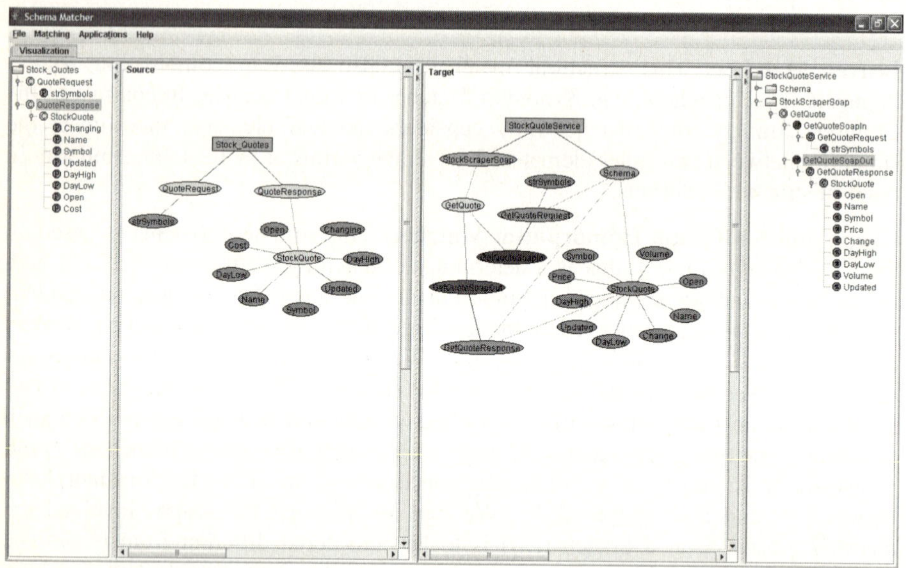

Fig. 1. *Schema* visualization, showing JTree and Graph representation of source and target schema

for XML and Java APIs for Wordnet synonyms thesaurus. The different input schema, WSDL descriptions, OWL ontologies, OWL-S, WSMO, SWSF and WSDL-S components, are represented in an uniform way by means of directed rooted graphs, where nodes represent schema elements, connected by directed links of different types, e.g. for containment and referential relationships. The set of structural and syntactic matchers described in the previous section operate on these uniform internal representations. These graphs are produced by different DOM (Document Object Model) parsers, which parse the different input schema and produce complete JTree structures (for for internal representation of all schema information and for graphical visualization), and the graph structures, representing only the information relevant for applying the matchers (schema elements and corresponding relations among them).

We present in the following the main working phases of *SchemaMatcher*.

First of all, the two schema to be matched, source and target, are loaded. It is possible to choose among OWL, WSDL, WSML and OWL-S descriptions; these can be loaded from local files, or remotely by providing their URI.

After the loading phase, DOM parsing is performed, and two graphs are produced and visualized together with their parsing trees, as illustrated in Figure 1.

It is possible to choose the application of a selection of the before described matching algorithms, (a syntactic similarity threshold for Edit Distance algorithm can also be selected), by means of the *pop-up window* illustrated in figure 2:

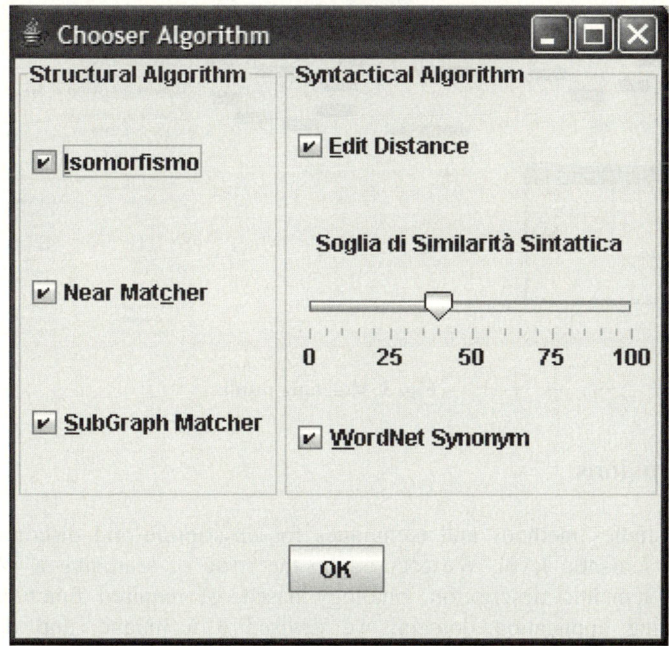

Fig. 2. Selection of matching algorithms

Once the matching algorithms' selection has been performed, the matching process starts; figure 3 depicts the results of the process. On the left panel, it is possible to browse the graphs in order to select mathing nodes and matching subgraphs. By double-clicking on a node of one of the two graphs, the corresponding node on the other graph is highlighted, and a joining line appears. If the selected node belongs to a structurally matching subgraph, the two matching subgraphs are highlighted as well. On the right panel the quantitative results of the matching process are displayed. In particular are reported: number of nodes of source and target scheme, number of matched nodes, and their percentages on total nodes, for syntactical and structural matching; for structural matching only: number of isomorph subgraphs, number of non-isomorph but similar subgraphs, with their relative distance measure (number of different nodes and archs). Finally, for each matching node are reported the results of syntactic matching, with e.g. Edit Distance measure or use of synonyms (1.0 value means that edit distance is 0, or they're synonyms).

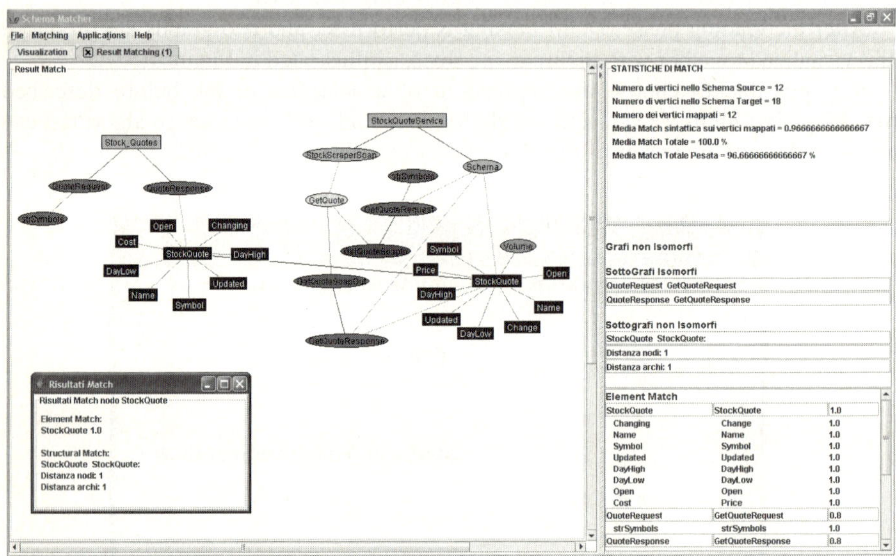

Fig. 3. Matching results

4   Conclusions

We have studies methods and techniques for description and discovery of Web Service at semantic level. We focused on the issue of searching a Web Service through a semantic description, ontology based, of required functionalities and corresponding application domain; we devised a technique, and developed a prototype, for uniform graph based representation of ontology and the different web service descriptions, and on integrated syntactic and structural matching of graph representations, including isomorphism properties.

Future work is oriented towards: - integrating NLP techniques for searching through UDDI natural language descriptions of web services, and mapping those with the query ontology; - automatic classification of web services, characterized by their WSDL descriptions, against a set of domain categories characterized by an ontology, by using matching techniques developed.

I'd like to acknowledge the implementing work done by my undergraduate students Angelo Martone and Carlo Baia.

References

[1] Martin et al., OWL-S 1.0 Release, http://www.daml.org/services/owl-s/1.0/owl-s.html

[2] Martin et al., DAML-S 0.9 Release, http://www.daml.org/services/daml-s/0.9

[3] Roman et al., *Web Service Modeling Ontology – Standard (WSMO – Standard)*, http://www.wsmo.org

[4] Steve Battle et al., Semantic *Web Services Framework (SWSF) Overview*, http://www.daml.org/services/swsf/1.0

[5] LSDIS and the University of Georgia, *Web Service Semantics - WSDL-S*, http://lsdis.cs.uga.edu/projects/meteor-s/wsdl-s

[6] LSDIS and the University of Georgia, *METEOR-S Semantic Web Services and processes*, http://lsdis.cs.uga.edu/projects/meteor-s

[7] R.Chinnici, M.Gudgin, J.Moreau, S.Weerawarana, *"Web Services Description Language (WSDL) Version 1,2"* - http://www.w3.org/TR/2002/WD-wsdl12-20020709

[8] H.H. Do, E. Rahm: COMA: System for Flexible Combination of Schema Matching Approach. VLDB 2002

[9] L.P. Cordella, P. Foggia, C. Sansone, M. Vento, Subgraph Transformations for the Inexact Matching of ARG, *Computing* suppl. 12, pp. 43-52, 1998.

[10] L.P. Cordella, P. Foggia, C. Sansone, M. Vento, Performance evaluation of the VF Graph Matching Algoritmh, Proc. of the 10th ICIAP, IEEE Computer Society Press, pp. 1172-1177, 1999.

[11] L.P. Cordella, P. Foggia, C. Sansone, M. Vento, Fast Graph Matching for Detecting CAD Image Components, Proc. of the 15th Int. Conf. on Pattern Recognition, IEEE Computer Society Press, vol. 2, pp. 1038-1041, 2000.

[12] Michael Gilleland, Merriam Park Software, *Levenshtein Distance Algorithm*, http://www.merriampark.com/ld.htm

[13] Princeton University, *"Wordnet a lexical database for the English language"* - http://wordnet.princeton.edu

[14] D.Booth, M.Champion, C.Ferris, F.McCabe, E.Newcomer, D.Orchard, *"Web Services Architecture"* - http://www.w3.org/TR/2003/WD-ws-arch-20030514

[15] N.Mitra, *"SOAP Version 1.2 Part 0:Primer"* - http://www.w3.org/TR/soap12-part0

[16] R.Chinnici, M.Gudgin, J.Moreau, S.Weerawarana, *"Web Services Description Language (WSDL) Version 1,2"* - http://www.w3.org/TR/2002/WD-wsdl12-20020709

[17] OASIS, *"About UDDI"* - http://www.uddi.org/about.html

[18] BPEL4WS Consortium. *Business Process Execution Language for Web Services.* http://www.ibm.com/developerworks/lib0rary/ws-bpel

[19] E. Rahm and P. Bernstein. A survey of approaches to automatic schema matching. *The International Journal on Very Large Data Bases (VLDB)*, (10(4)):334–350, 2001.

[20] P. Shvaiko and J. Euzenat. A survey of schema-based matching approaches. *Journal on Data Semantics (JoDS)*, IV, 2005.

[21] F. Giunchiglia, P.Shvaiko: Semantic matching. *The Knowledge Engineering Review Journal*, 18(3):265-280, 2003.

[22] Y. Kalfoglou and M. Schorlemmer. Ontology mapping: the state of the art. *The Knowledge Engineering Review Journal (KER)*, (18(1)):1–31, 2003.

[23] S. Bergamaschi, S. Castano, and M. Vincini. Semantic integration of semistructured and structured data sources. *SIGMOD Record*, (28(1)):54–59, 1999.

[24] V. Kashyap and A. Sheth. Semantic and schematic similarities between database objects: a context-based approach. *The International Journal on Very Large Data Bases (VLDB)*, 5(4):276–304, 1996.

[25] L. Palopoli., D. Sacca, D. Ursino. Semi-Automatic, Semantic Discovery of Properties from Database Schemas, Proc. IDEAS, 1998, 244-253

[26] F. Giunchiglia and M. Yatskevich. Element level semantic matching. In Proceedings of the Meaning Coordination and Negotiation workshop at the International Semantic Web Conference (ISWC), 2004.

[27] P. Bouquet, F. Giunchiglia, F. van Harmelen, L. Serafini, and H. Stuckenschmidt, Contextualizing ontologies. *Journal of Web Semantics*, (26):1–19, 2004.

[28] F. Giunchiglia, P. Shvaiko, and M. Yatskevich. S-Match: an algorithm and an implementation of semantic matching. In *Proceedings of the European Semantic Web Symposium (ESWS)*, pages 61–75, 2004.

[29] N. Noy and M. Musen. The PROMPT Suite: Interactive tools for ontology merging and mapping. *International Journal of Human-Computer Studies*, (59(6)):983–1024, 2003.

[30] J. Madhavan, P. Bernstein, and E. Rahm. Generic schema matching with Cupid. In *Proceedings of the Very Large Data Bases Conference (VLDB)*, pages 49–58, 2001.

[31] M. Ehrig and S. Staab. QOM: Quick ontology mapping. In *Proceedings of the International Semantic Web Conference (ISWC)*, pages 683–697, 2004.

[32] J. Euzenat and P.Valtchev. Similarity-based ontology alignment in OWL-lite. In *Proceedings of the European Conference on Artificial Intelligence (ECAI)*, pages 333–337, 2004.

Ontology-Based Composition of Web Services for Ubiquitous Computing*

Yang-Seung Jeon[1], Eun-Ha Song[1], Minyi Guo[2], Laurence T. Yang[3],
Young-Sik Jeong[1], Jin-Tak Choi[4], and Sung-Kook Han[1,**]

[1] Department of Computer Engineering, Wonkwang University,
344-2 Shinyong-Dong, Iksan, 570-749, Korea
`{globaljeon, ehsong, ysjeong, skhan}@wku.ac.kr`
[2] School of Computer Science and Engineering, Aizu University
Aizu-Wakamatsu, Fukushima-ken 965-8580 Japan
`minyi@u-aizu.ac.jp`
[3] Department of Computer Science, St. Francis Xavier University,
Antigonish, NS, B2G 2W5, Canada
`lyang@stfx.ca`
[4] Department of Computer Engineering, University of Incheon,
117 Dohwa-Dong, Nam-Gu, Inchon, Korea
`choi@incheon.ac.kr`

Abstract. Current Web service environment provide connection to individual services but is still deficient in semantic processing technology for the interoperability of Web services. The semantic processing of Web services is a key technology for the dynamic discovery and composition of Web services. Thus, the present study established Web service ontology to support ubiquitous environment and proposed a method of describing Web services in consideration of their functional and semantic aspects. In addition, it implemented a service interlocking and composition system by including a mediator function, which enables the composition of heterogeneous Web services, in the system.

1 Introduction

Current ubiquitous computing environments involve heterogeneous systems as well as various kinds of applications, protocols and formats[5] and, in order to integrate these components, we need standardized protocols and semantic description methods. Semantic description makes it possible to specify Web services using ontology technology and to deal with Web services semantically through knowledge processing rather than information processing. As the concept of the Web is growing broad, various types of new Web services are emerging, which have not been available in existing information infrastructure.

Today's standard Web service technologies [6,7,10] provide developers with connection to and use of individual services. However, they cannot interact with services and interpret them compositely, and cannot be used by ordinary people. That

---

* This paper was supported by Wonkwang University in 2006.
** Corresponding author.

G. Min et al. (Eds.): ISPA 2006 Ws, LNCS 4331, pp. 559–568, 2006.

is, the current Web service structure has the limitation that syntactic extension is possible but semantic components or semantic extension is almost impossible. To solve these problems, a number of technologies have been proposed including chorography and orchestration. Without semantic processing, however, Web services can hardly execute their functions properly. Thus, research on semantic Web service discovery and dynamic Web service composition is going on actively, and a solution is to ontology-based descriptions of Web Services. The present study proposes a method for describing Web services using ontologies, in order to support ubiquitous computing technology. Inside the system, D-Mediator (data mediator) and C-Mediator (control mediator) are used for the interoperation and composition of heterogeneous services.

This paper explains the Web service description methods of OWL-S, WSMO and WSBPEL[4,7,8], and describes the requirements and construction of ontology for Web Services. Lastly, we present a Web service composition system based on ontology for Web Services.

2   Background

This section introduces OWL-S, WSMO (Web Service Modeling Framework) and BPEL4WS (Business Process Execution Language for Web Services) [4,7,8], which are base technologies for Web service composition.

OWL-S is a representative semantic Web service language that extended DAML-S based on OWL[1]. By integrating OWL-based ontology technology with existing Web service description.

WSMO provides ontological specifications for the core elements of Semantic Web Services. In fact, Semantic Web Services aim at an integrated technology for the next generation of the Web by combining Semantic Web technologies and Web Services, thereby turning the Internet from a information repository for human consumption into a world-wide system for distributed web computing. Therefore, appropriate frameworks for Semantic Web Services need to integrate the basic Web design principles, those defined for the Semantic Web, as well as design principles for distributed, service-orientated computing of the Web.

BPEL4WS provides a language for specifying business processes and business interaction protocols. It can create a composite process by integrating different operations such as Web service call, data manipulation, error report, and process termination. Business processes are described in two ways – implementing executable business processes and describing non-executable abstract processes.

3   Ontology for Web Services

3.1   Requirements

WSDL (Web Service Description Language) [6], an existing Web service description language, describes only the functional information of services such as input parameters, output parameters, service providers and service locations, and has limitations in supporting the discovery, execution, composition and interoperation of

Web service. Because WSDL cannot describe semantic information of Web services, we need ontology-based Web service interface technology that can describe not only the syntax but also the semantics of services.

Here, services include not only the provision of static information through Web sites but also actions such as selling products and driving physical equipment. To utilize Web services, we need to describe services semantically so that software agents can interpret and process them autonomously.

3.2 Ontology Construction

Web services description ontology is established by extracting semantic information on the actions and objects of Web services opened and operated in Web service portal sites and UDDI Business Registry (UBR), which is run by IBM and Microsoft.

Fig. 1 is the relational of established Web service ontology. Web service ontology is composed of semantic descriptions of Web services such as actions and objects, which are domains to which actions are applied, functional descriptions of Web services such as the precondition on input parameters and the post-condition of output parameters, and other information required for describing Web services.

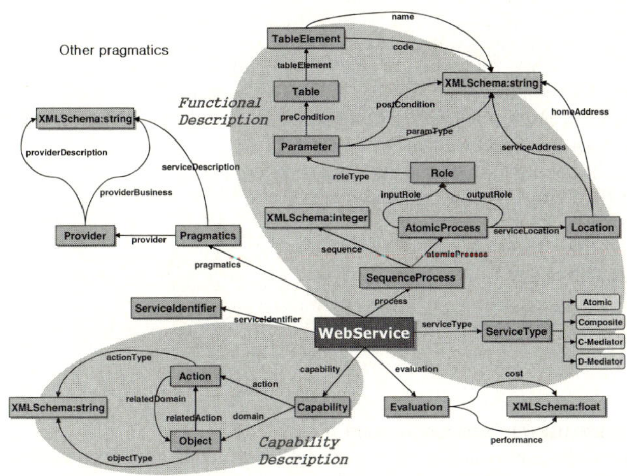

Fig. 1. Relational composition of Web services description ontology

As shown in Fig.1, if semantic annotation is provided for an email sending service using ontology, the action is 'send' and the object is 'email'. The functional description includes also information on the location of the email transmission service (location of WSDL), service provider and input/output parameters for the execution of the service. The modeled Web service description ontology is described using OWL, and ontology input is described using Protégé-2000.

In Fig. 1, rectangles are classes and arrows are properties. Extracted classes, properties and instances are entered as inputs. The instance of ServiceType class, which describes the type of service to be composed, should have Atomic, Composite,

C-Mediator or D-Mediator as its value. The Atomic type means that the service is not a composite but a single service, and the Composite type means a composite service created from the composition of services. In addition, C-Mediator and D-Mediator are service types used in matching parameters. C-Mediator is a service that extracts what it needs from service output parameters, and D-Mediator is a service that converts the type of the output parameter of a specific service to the type of the input parameter of a service to be matched.

4 Composition of Ontology-Based Web Services

4.1 Web Service Domain

Ontology-based semantic modeling means to define terms used in the concerned domain, establish relations among the terms, and implement the process. The process includes the classification of concepts, the establishment of the hierarchical relation of the classes, the definition of class properties, the diversities and constraints of the properties, and the creation of instances.

```
<?xml version="1.0"?>
<rdf:RDF xmlns="urn:sms.wonkwang.ac.kr/swpt#"
          xmlns:rdf="http://www.w3.org/1999/02/22-rdf-syntax-ns#"
          xmlns:rdfs="http://www.w3.org/2000/01/rdf-schema#"
       xmlns:owl="http://www.w3.org/2002/07/owl#"
       xml:base="urn: sms.wonkwang.ac.kr /swpt">
  <owl:Ontology rdf:about="urn: sms.wonkwang.ac.kr/c-onto"/>
  <owl:Class rdf:ID="CapAmazonMagazinSearch">
   <rdfs:subClassOf>
    <owl:Class rdf:ID="InsMagazine"/>
   </rdfs:subClassOf>
   <rdfs:subClassOf>
    <owl:Class rdf:ID="InsSearch"/>
   </rdfs:subClassOf>
</owl:Class>
… … …
<owl:ObjectProperty rdf:ID="serviceLocation">
  <rdfs:comment>Web service address with optional home address</rdfs:comment>
  <rdfs:domain rdf:resource="#AtomicProcess"/>
  <rdfs:range rdf:resource="#Location"/>
  <rdfs:type rdf:resource="urn://www.w3.org/2002/07/owl#UniqueProperty"/>
</owl:ObjectProperty>
```

Fig. 2. Web service described in ontology

Based on common words and shared understandings obtained from the process, we can achieve the consistency of communication in interoperation. Fig. 2 is a part of an OWL document describing Web service ontology input on Protégé-2000. The Web service ontology described in OWL enables semantic-based selection and composition of Web services, and information on input and output parameters; input and output conditions and service location is also extracted from the established ontology through the function description of Web services. Fig. 3 shows the screen of Web service ontology input on Protégé-2000.

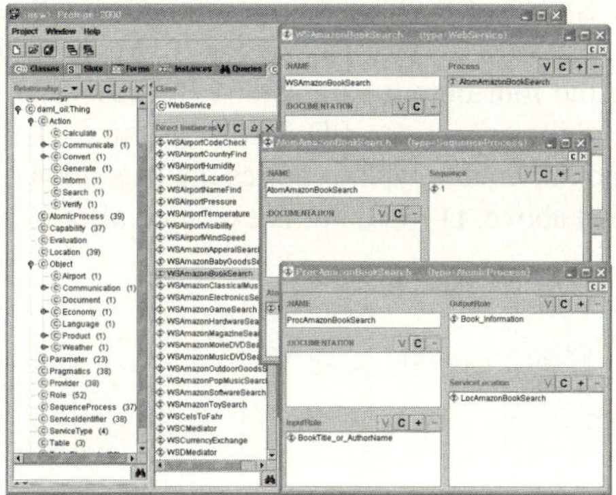

Fig. 3. Screen of Web service description ontology input

4.2   C-Mediator and D-Mediator for Composition

When two or more heterogeneous services are composed, two things should consider. One is the type collision in the matching of different data types. For example, type collision happens when a 'float' type output parameter of a service is matched with a 'string' type input parameter. The other thing to be considered is how to extract input parameters when a service has two or more output results. This problem does not need to be considered if all the results of the service match. However, if only some of returned output results match, a process to extract them is needed. This study implemented D-Mediator (Data-Mediator) for conversion between two different types to solve the type collision problem, and C-Mediator (Control-Mediator) for extracting necessary output parameters.

Fig. 4 (a) shows the mechanism of converting 'float' type output parameter S_1O_1 of service S_1 to 'double' type input parameter S_2I_1 of service S_2 through D-Mediator in matching parameters between two different services. For example, when composing exchange service S_2 that exchanges currencies by receiving the output parameters exchange rate (float type), exchange rate (double type) and exchange amount (double type) of service S_1 that calculates exchange rate between two currencies, type collision happens as in Fig. 4 (a). Here, the problem is solved as D-Mediator converts S_1O_1 (float type) of S_1 to S_2I_1 (double type) of S_2. Conversion from general string type (not numeric string type) to int or float type is not allowed, so is processed as an exception.

Fig. 4. (b) shows a mechanism of extracting only S_1O_1 and S_1O_4 out of output parameters S_1O_1, S_1O_2, S_1O_3 and S_1O_4 of service S_1 and matching them with input parameter S_2I_1 and S_2I_3 of service S_2. For example, when composing exchange service S_2 that exchanges currencies by receiving exchange rate (double type) and exchange amount (double type) and Amazon book search service S_1 that receives input parameters author name (string type) and book title (string type) and returns output parameters date of publishing (string type), publisher (string type) and price (float type). This process has not only type collision but also the parameter extraction problem. In this case, before the execution of D-Mediator, C-Mediator is executed first to extract parameters from the outputs of S_1 to be matched with the input parameters of S_2. In Fig. 4 (b), only S_1O_1 and S_1O_4 of Amazon book search service S_1 are matched with S_2I_1 and S_2I_3 of exchange service (S_2). Thus, C-Mediator is executed to extract S_1O_1 and S_1O_4 among the four output parameters. Because S_1O_1 and S_2I_3 are identical in type they do not need the execution of D-Mediator, but S_1O_4 (book price: float type) and S_2I_3 (exchange amount: double type) requires the execution of D-Mediator for their matching. As mentioned above, D-Mediator is executed after C-Mediator.

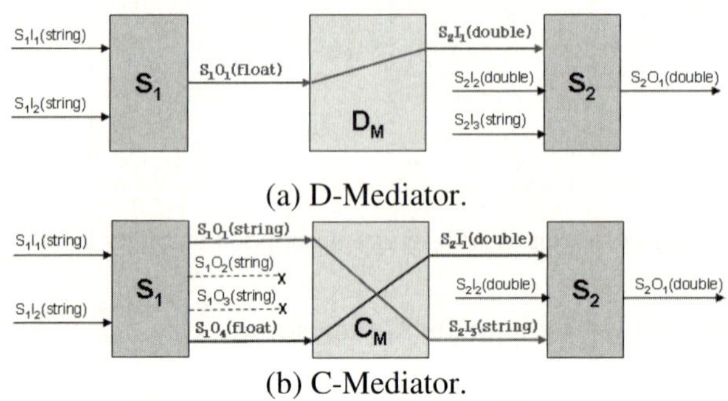

(a) D-Mediator.

(b) C-Mediator.

Fig. 4. Mediator for interoperability of Web services

D-Mediator and C-Mediator were implemented as Web services for consistency in composite service processing technology and easy reuse of composite services in the future. When D-Mediator and C-Mediator are described in Web service composition process, their values of property 'serviceType' are 'D-Mediator' and 'C-Mediator' respectively.

5 Implementation

5.1 Environment

The present system used Protégé 2000[13] as an ontology editor for our ontology, and OWL (Web Ontology Language) as a language for describing ontology. In addition, we used Jena 2.1 Ontology API[14] of HP Research Institute for parsing constructed ontology. The scope of ontology was defined to include Web service classification, Web service parameters information in WSDL and service management domain in UDDI.

Web services based on ontology allows for knowledge processing, service automatic discovery and composition, thus they can be applied to ubiquitous environment. In composition, the function of mediator was inserted, which provides interoperability between heterogeneous services. Communication between a service requester and the composition system was defined using SOAP[15]. In particular, SOAP message supports terminal equipment and communication.

5.2 System Architecture

Ontology-based Web service composition system is composed of three modules - Service Ontology, Service Composer, and System Manager.- and the architecture of the system is presented in Fig. 5.

Service Ontology provides semantic description for the data and the functionality of the Web services to be composed. The Repository supplies several types of meaningful information that Service Annotator needs in order to compose Web services in Service Composer.

The Service Composer is where Service Annotator performs actual service composition based on the provided service information of parameter, type and composition information etc. Service Composer is composed of Execution Controller that controls service execution, Data Manager that manages service parameters and converts the types of parameters between services to be composed, Composite Service Generator for composing actual services based on information on service execution in Execution Controller, and Parameter Match Maker that matches parameters between actual services based on the compatibility of the parameters of the services to be composed in Data Manager.

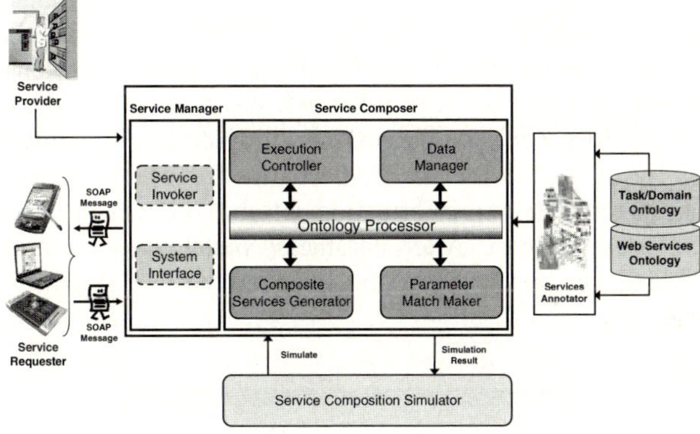

Fig. 5. Architecture of Web service composition system

In addition, there is Service Composition Simulator for efficient service composition before the composition of actual services if they can be composed.

System Manager executes actual services using service location information from Service Annotator and service match information in Service Composer. This is composed of Service Invoker to call services, and System Interface to pass service input parameters to the service to be called.

5.3 Example

Select a Web service to be composed. To add services to be composed, click the 'Continue' button. If all services to be composed have been selected, click the 'Composition' button to execute service composition of the selected services.

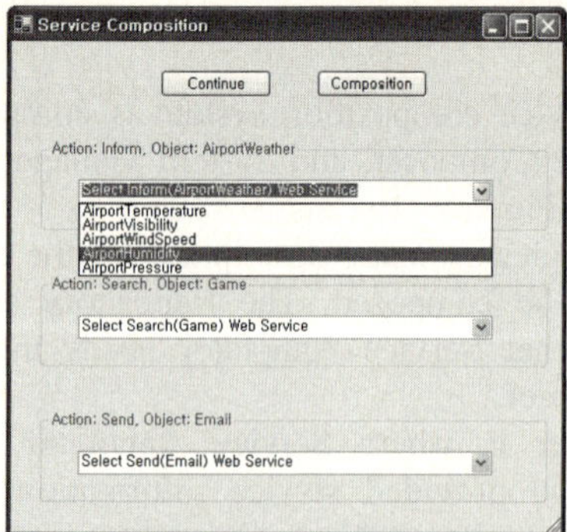

Fig. 6. Screen to select services to be composed

Fig. 6 shows an example that composes 'Inform' action and 'AirportWeather' object, 'Search' action and 'Game' object, and 'Send' action and 'Email' object. The combo box on the screen is a list of services extracted from Web service ontology.

Fig. 7 is a screen that matches the input and output parameters of AirportHumidity service that provides information on airport humidity, AmazonGameSearch service that finds game products in the Amazon site, and EmailSend service that send emails. Here, input parameter 'EmailBody' of EmailSend service is matched with output parameter 'Weather_Message' of AirportHumidity service. Then, the result of output parameter 'Weather_Message' of AirportHumidity service is automatically entered into the text box for the input of 'EmailBody' on the top of the service input window. Whether the parameter matching information set above is adequate can be tested by clicking the 'Simulate' button. After parameter matching is completed, click the 'Run' button to execute the Web service in a remote site provided by the actual service provider.

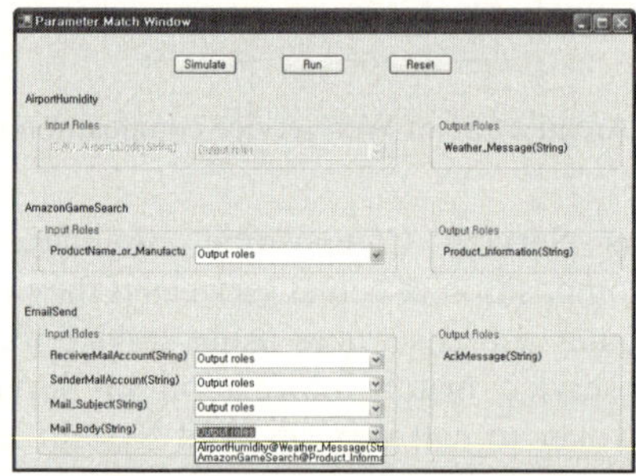

Fig. 7. Parameter matching screen

Fig. 8 shows the actual parameter inputting for executing Web services. If data are entered, the input data are transmitted in the form of SOAP message to the remote site where the service is located. The service host executes the requested service and

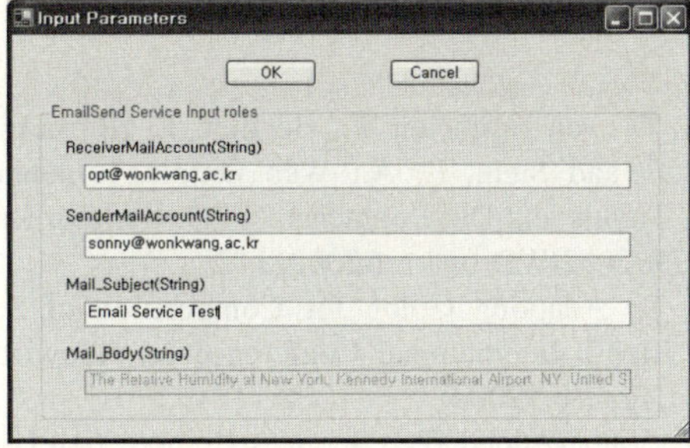

Fig. 8. Parameter input screen showing parameter matching information

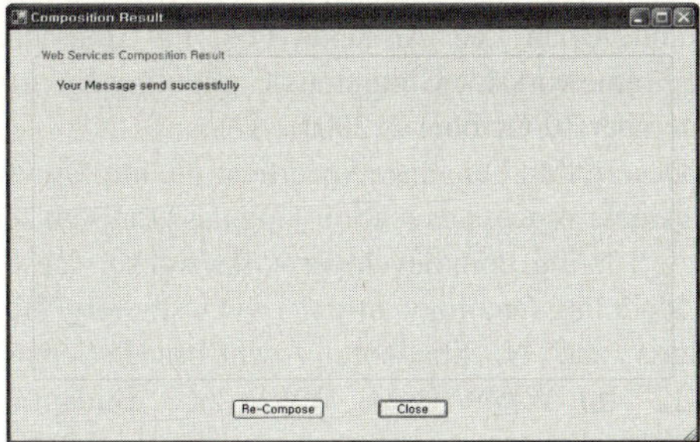

Fig. 9. Final results of service composition

returns the results to the client in the form of SOAP message. Fig. 9 is the final result from the execution of the service.

6   Conclusions

Current Web services provide developers with connection to and use of individual services, but interaction with the services and composite interpretation are impossible and ordinary people can hardly interpret and use the services. Web service description languages such as WSMF and BPEL4WS express the functional aspects of Web services, and OWL-S still has limitations in expressing the conceptual and semantic functions of Web services. Because these description methods cannot do Web service discovery and dynamic Web service composition, which are the most important semantics in Web services, they cannot attain the ultimate goals of semantic Web services. The present study proposed a new method of describing Web services by designing Web service ontology for the integrated expression of the functional and semantic aspects of Web services. In addition, by supporting semantic interoperability among Web services, ontology-based Web service composition serves the natural integration of heterogeneous applications inside and outside of a company as well as automatic system integration between business partners. Moreover, it facilitates automatic software integration and enables efficient interoperation among Web services.

References

1. Dean, M., Connolly, D., van Harmelen, F., Hendler, J., Horrocks, I., McGuinness, D.L., Patel-Schneider, P. F. and Stein, L. A.: Web Ontology Language (OWL) Reference Version 1.0. Recent Trends and Developments. W3C Working Draft 12 November 2002, http://www.w3.org/TR/2002/WD-owl-ref-20021112/
2. McIlraith, S., Son, T.: Adapting Golog for Composition of Semantic Web Services. Proceedings of the Eighth International Conference on Knowledge Representation and Reasoning, Toulouse, France, (2002)
3. Matskin, M., Rao, J.: Value-Added Web Services Composition Using Automatic Program Synthesis. Web Services, E-Business, and the Semantic Web, CAiSE 2002 International Workshop, WES 2002, Toronto, Canada, (2002)
4. W3C, OWL-S, http://www.w3.org/Submission/2004/SUBM-OWL-S-related-20041122/
5. Shankar R. Ponnekanti, Brian Lee, Armando Fox, Pat Hanrahan, and Terry Winograd ICrafter: "A Service Framework for Ubiquitous Computing Environments" Proceedings of Ubicomp 2001, September 30-October 2, 2001
6. W3C, Web Service Description Language Specification, http://www.w3.org/TR/wsdl
7. F. Curbera et al., Business process execution language for web services (BPEL4WS) 1.0, July 2002, http://www-106.ibm.com/developerworks/webservices/library/ws-bpel
8. W3C, Web Service Modeling Ontology, http://www.wsmo.org/TR/
9. N. Gibbins, S. Haris and N. Shadbolt. Agent-based Semantic Web Services. In Proceedings of the 12th Int. WWW Conf., WWW2003, Budapest, Hungary, 2003, ACM Press, 2003, pp. 710-717
10. L. Ardissono, A. Goy, and G. Petrone. Enabling conversations with web services. Proc. of the 2nd Int. Conf. on Autonomous Agents and Multiagent Systems, 2003, Melbourne, pp. 819-826
11. J. Rao, P. Kungas and M. Matskin. "Logic-based Web Service Composition: from Service Description to Process Model". Proc. of the IEEE Int. Conf. on Web Services, ICWS 2004, San Diego, California, USA, July 6-9, 2004, IEEE Computer Society Press
12. Tim Berners-Lee, James Hendler, Ora Lassila, "The Semantic Web", Scientific American, 2001.5
13. Standford Univ,. Protege, http://protege.stanford.edu/doc/users.html
14. HP Lab, Jena, http://jena.sourceforge.net/index.html
15. W3C, Simple Object Access Protocol, http://www.w3.org/TR/soap12-part0

Web Service Resource Framework Based Computing Service Framework for Computational Grid Applications

Eui Heo[1], Kyung-Lang Park[1], Oh-Young Kwon[2],
Oh-Kyung Kwon[3], and Shin-Dug Kim[1]

[1] Supercomputing Lab, Dept. of Computer Science, Yonsei University,
134 Shinchon-Dong, Seodaemun-ku, Seoul, 120-749, Korea
`{parousia, lanx, sdkim}@parallel.yonsei.ac.kr`
[2] Dept. of Computer Engineering, Korea University of Technology and Education,
P.O. BOX 55, Chonan, 330-600, Korea
`oykwon@kut.ac.kr`
[3] Korea Institute of Science and Technology Information,
P.O. BOX 122, Yusong, Daejeon, 305-806, Korea
`okkwon@kisti.re.kr`

Abstract. Grid and Web service technology can be used as a solution for the resource shortage problem. These two technologies are used to be applied to MPI (message passing interface) applications to design a framework to deploy MPI applications on OGSA (open Grid service architecture). In particular, we modeled MPI applications as WS-Resources. We call the WS-Resource "MPI resource" and it is composed of an MPI application and its associated dynamically created running environment. Thus, an MPI resource represents one MPI task. Through this model, MPI applications can be published to the world of the Grid. In addition, running environment is dynamically created from resources chosen among distributed idle resources on the Grid. Deployed MPI resources are utilized by other services. Especially in virtual organizations, MPI resources can have the roles responsible for computing task as computing resources for compute-intensive works and data resources for data-intensive works.

1 Introduction

Recently, Grid computing platforms are designed without any dependency to any specific middleware based on service-oriented architecture (SOA), which is evolved significantly. Thus, we can virtualize many types of resources widely and use those virtualized resources on the Grid. In addition, Grid comes to have the solid foundation from SOA standards [1].

On the other hand, MPI (massage passing interface) has been popular programming tool for high performance computing (HPC) users. Although MPI technology is old-fashioned, it is still useful for HPC users today. In particular, in accordance with the rapid performance improvement of CPU (central processing unit) and high-speed network, supercomputing technology utilizing distributed resources has been developed practically and MPI has been continually developed for this new computing

G. Min et al. (Eds.): ISPA 2006 Ws, LNCS 4331, pp. 569–578, 2006.

environment. Eventually, there have been many new trials to apply MPI technology to Grid environment for utilizing distributed and heterogeneous resources [2].

In service-oriented Grid environment, MPI tends to show new possibility. Many applications and computing resources can be provided by the Grid computing platform. In scientific area, high performance systems are required to analyze and process a large collection of data, perform complicated simulation, and verify many theories. In industrial area, high performance computing systems are required to design and simulate their products. In economic area, there are many needs of computing for analyzing hourly produced economic indicators.

In this situation, if MPI applications could be deployed on the Grid, many users can utilize many MPI applications running on the Grid platform, as a prominent source of computing and data system. Moreover, if MPI applications could be deployed on the Grid, and could be accessed publicly, it will accelerate collaboration of research in each discipline and cross-discipline by sharing produced data and information.

There are some approaches similar to ours. One research is focused on wrapping general legacy applications as services [3] [4]. They deployed applications, which are as workflow composed of legacy command line applications, as services. There is another research more similar to ours at the point of deploying especially MPI applications as services [5]. Our research is similar to those researches in the point of deploying applications on Grid service environment. However, we are interested in representing MPI applications as "resources" which come conceptually from WS-Resource of WSRF [6]. Representing MPI applications as not services but resources is beyond the difference of two words, service and resource. This transition will make the "MPI resources" more applicable to the diverse needs of users and applications on Grid.

We implemented a prototype of our work and got satisfactory results. It becomes possible to share MPI task using MPI resources. MPI resources allow sharing of computational tasks monitoring and those computational results. The overhead from the service structure was very small. The service proportion for MPI resource running time is 1~2% for about one minute time work. It becomes more less if the work time is longer. And the memory usage is very small. One MPI resource size is several kilobytes. Even though many MPI resources are created, the proportion of MPI resources becomes very slight.

In the rest sections, we first review more details of related works in section 2 and introduce the background of this paper, the concept of WSRF in section 3. Then we present our works about how MPI applications could be deployed and executed as WS-Resource, how MPI resources could be designed, and how the MPI resources could be utilized in VOs on OGSA as in section 4. In section 5, we evaluate our research. Finally, we discuss and conclude our research.

2   Related Work

There are various approaches to applying service concept to MPI applications. One interesting research is to implement MPI functions as services [7]. MPI processes running on different nodes exchange messages using the MPI function services. This approach is interesting, but not suitable for HPC that the performance is critical.

Because the messages frequently exchanged between processes are wrapped as SOAP messages and pass through the service container, so the overhead caused by service construct is very big and inevitable.

Another approach is exposing whole MPI application as a service, so underlying mechanism is abstracted [5]. This research focuses on "data-centric virtualization." Only input and output interfaces are exposed, and the data produced by MPI service can be utilized by other services. The form of data produced by legacy MPI applications is various, so routines using produced data must be implemented according to each circumstance. This approach is appropriate for MPI which is similar to our approach. In addition, we will state not only wrapping MPI applications as services but also running the application on the resources over Grid and MPI applications as resources on OGSA.

There are other methods wrapping applications as services, not limited to MPI applications [3] [4]. These approaches focus on deploying one legacy application or workflow composed of legacy applications as a service. MPI applications also can be deployed by those frameworks. However, in those frameworks the deployed applications are dependent on specific resources. Our framework is dedicated for computing functionality. In particular, we pay attention to the points of the Grid environment sharing idle resources and MPI application codes independent on machines. Therefore, we make MPI applications select resources from the distributed resources and run on those resources.

3   MPI Service Framework

In this section, we present a framework for the MPI WS-Resources, where MPI applications are considered as resources based on WSRF. For this, we first review shortly about WSRF and the concept of WS-Resource. Then we describe our framework.

3.1   WSRF, WS-Resource and MPI Resource

Grid uses SOA for its foundation, but it is insufficient for representing "stateful service" needed by OGSA. First, OGSI (open Grid service infrastructure) has been devised. However, OGSI has some conflicts with Web services. The alternative is WSRF [8], which is conformed to be applied to Web services. Moreover, it introduces new concept, WS-Resource. It is an advanced concept in virtualizing resources as services. Especially services and resources are strictly separated. WS-Resource can represent any entity. It can be either logical entities or physical resources. Finally, WS-Resource becomes the infrastructure of OGSA.

We get the concept of the "resource", the logical entity, from WS-Resource and we present MPI resource, the unit of one MPI task, which is composed of an MPI application and its dynamically created running environment. The MPI resource is the resource on OGSA, so it can be shared by virtual organizations (VOs). Especially MPI resources are the special resources responsible for performing computational tasks.

3.2 Overall Framework of MPI Service

Fig. 1 illustrates the overall MPI service framework. This framework is divided to three physical modules. The first one is the user Web interface accessing to MPI services. The second one is MPI service server providing computing services. The last one is computing resources required for performing the MPI applications.

MPI service server is composed of several components, i.e., application repository and Resource information service. Application repository contains descriptions about the MPI applications and parameter information required for running applications. Resource information service monitors the distributed resources in Grid, and keeps the information. These two components provide basic information for making MPI resources.

When user selects an application and submits parameters, the client program first queries MPI resource index to find already created resources, which have properties of the same application and parameters. If it exists, client program gets the endpoint reference (EPR). If it does not exist, client program requests MPI resource factory to make a new MPI resource.

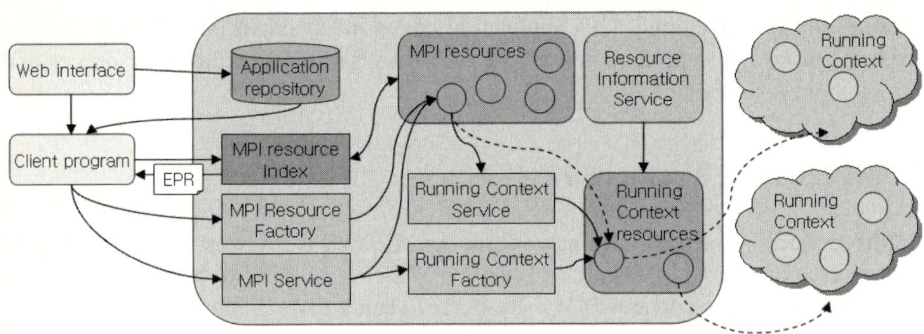

Fig. 1. MPI Service Framework

MPI service sets and gets the information of the MPI resource, performs operations of an MPI resource and monitors the MPI resource. When client requests an MPI service to run the application, the MPI service prepares the environment through running context factory. Running context factory dynamically creates a temporary running environment for MPI applications. It requests needed information to the resource information service and composes running environment. MPI resources have the EPR of a running context resource and can order running of an application on it.

The process is performed as follows. User accesses the client program through Web interface. User selects an MPI application registered in the application repository. User submits the parameters to the client through the Web interface. The client requests MPI resource index to query resources that have same application and parameters. If it is found, the EPR of the MPI resource is returned to the client program. If it is not found, client program requests making a new MPI resource to MPI resource factory. MPI resource factory requests necessary information to the application repository and makes a new MPI resource. Client program requests MPI service to use the MPI resource. MPI service requests running context resource factory to make a running context resource for the MPI resource. MPI service gets the EPR of the running context resource. The created running context resource generates the JSDL (Job Submission Description Language) based on the information of the application and the running environment. MPI resource orders the running context resource to submit the JSDL to the WS-GRAM at the front node of running environment. MPI resource gets the messages.

3.3 MPI Resource

When we try to design a framework of scientific applications on OGSA, we face several considerable points. Most scientific applications are performed in their own workflows. So we can consider wrapping the whole workflow as one service. In this case, application users can use the applications very simply and easily. But this design approach is restricted in some points. Resource utilization can be restricted and applications are performed on the restricted site. Therefore, we need to consider an approach separating computational task from the whole workflow for efficient resource utilization.

Another thing is to consider sharing MPI tasks on the Grid. We can consider sharing of MPI tasks and their results among the VOs. If several collaborating VOs are sharing some computational tasks from the beginning of running application, immediate data and information may be shared. These two points are mainly considered to design MPI resources.

MPI resources are created by the MPI resource factory and registered into MPI resource index. It is can be checked for reusing and sharing. Resource creation is occurred when the MPI resources required are not found in MPI resource index. When the MPI resource is not found, MPI factory creates a new MPI resource. MPI resource is initialized with the application information provided by application repository. When an MPI resource is requested to run, the MPI resource dynamically creates a running context resource, which provides running environment to MPI resources.

Application repository provides descriptions about MPI application when users contact the Web interface to select application list. In addition, it provides MPI resources with metadata that is necessary for running MPI resources such as required user parameters. When user wants to deploy his application as MPI resource, in advance, he must register his application to the application repository through Web interface by providing the information such as parameter number and description about the application, and upload his application code.

The properties of the MPI resources are described in WSDL as shown in Fig. 2. Especially element `Application` is defined as a complex type containing all information about the MPI applications. Application repository provides application description, parameter number, each parameter name, and file name.

MPI resource is almost a persistent resource. Created MPI resources reside in the service container until any destroy command is issued, and they can be reused and shared by other WS-Resources or services through MPI resource index. The size of MPI resource is very small. It is about several kilobytes. This is good in several points. The one is comparing parameters and the results from accumulated MPI resources. The second one is utilizing already produced data without any further

```
<xsd:element name="MPIResourceProperties">
<xsd:complexType>
  <xsd:sequence>
    <xsd:element ref="tns:ProcessNum" minOccurs="1" maxOccurs="1"/>
    <xsd:element ref="tns:FileLocation" minOccurs="1" maxOccurs="1"/>
    <xsd:element ref="tns:OutputMsg" minOccurs="1" maxOccurs="1"/>
    <xsd:element ref="tns:ErrorMsg" minOccurs="1" maxOccurs="1"/>
    <xsd:element ref="tns:Application" minOccurs="1" maxOccurs="1"/>
    <xsd:element ref="tns:ResourceList" minOccurs="1" maxOccurs="1"/>
    <xsd:element ref="tns:RunningContextEPR" minOccurs="1" maxOccurs="1"/>
  </xsd:sequence>
</xsd:complexType>
</xsd:element>
```

Fig. 2. MPI resource properties

execution. The last one is sharing computing works among VOs. When several VOs collaborate and especially share computational tasks, they can share MPI resources and results by sharing the EPR of those MPI resources.

3.4 Running Context Resource

Running context resource is to manage the environment dynamically created from the distributed resources on Grid. It is the result of our intention separating computational tasks from applications or workflows. MPI resources can utilize idle computing resources on Grid through the running context resources.

Resource information service monitors distributed computing resources and provides needed resource information for creating running context resources, such as OS, CPU, MPI library, compile command, run command, working directory, and WS-GRAM EPR. When the MPI service requests to create a running context resource, running context resource factory creates a new resource using the information from resource information service.

In particular, MPI resource can have running context composed of multiple distributed resources as shown in Fig. 3. The running context service queries resource information service to search a collection of resources that meet the conditions for

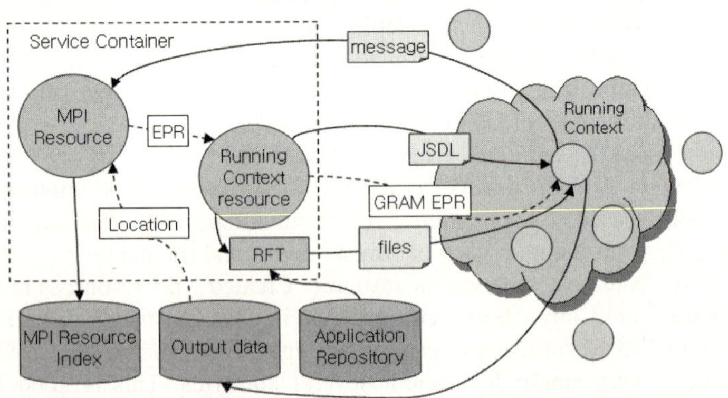

Fig. 3. MPI Resource and Running Context Resource

creating suitable running environment. For composing one running environment, resources must have same properties about CPU, OS, and MPI library because those properties directly influence compiling and file system. If resources are selected, the running context resource makes the resource list such as machinefile of MPICH-G2 or hostfile of Open MPI needed for running MPI application. Then it generates JSDL based on the information about the application to run, the parameters submitted, and the system information of the front node in the running context. In this way, the running preparation can be performed.

When an MPI resource orders its running context resource to run the application, then the running context resource submits JSDL to WS-GRAM of the front node. All the required files such as an MPI application and input files are staged-in through the file transfer service to working directory of the front node. WS-GRAM starts the application on the created running environment.

When application execution is finished, the MPI resource gets output messages, error messages and file location reference from WS-GRAM. Files produced by the application, are staged-out to the designated place described in MPI resource property. If this procedure is done, running context resource is destroyed automatically. The state of resources on Grid changes hourly, so the running context must be created dynamically and it can be destroyed when its execution is finished.

3.5 MPI Resource Index

MPI resource index service is the service for utilizing existing MPI resources. When a user wants to start an MPI resource, first, selects an application registered in the application repository, and then submits parameter values following the description of the application metadata. At this time, the client program requests MPI resource index service to find any running resources with the same application and submitted parameters. If matching MPI resources exist, it is not necessary to make a new MPI resource. The client program gets the EPR of the MPI resource and the user immediately can get the all information about the MPI resource running already without additional running time of the application.

3.6 The Roles of MPI Resources in VOs

We modeled the MPI resource as a special resource responsible for performing computing tasks on OGSA. The MPI resource can have two kinds of role in VOs. The one is as computing resource and another is as data resource.

Fig. 4 describes two scenarios between two VOs. MPI resources as computing resources are for compute-intensive works. Services linked with solid lines represent direct interaction. In this case, an MPI resource or an application service utilizes computing power of the linked MPI resource for its computing need. The data exchanging mechanism and the interfaces in this scenario must be designed tightly coupled. Because data exchange occurs directly between two entities. Therefore, this relationship is inflexible but efficient in compute-intensive and real time works. In Fig. 4, MPI resource 1 becomes a computing resource to an application service and MPI resource 2.

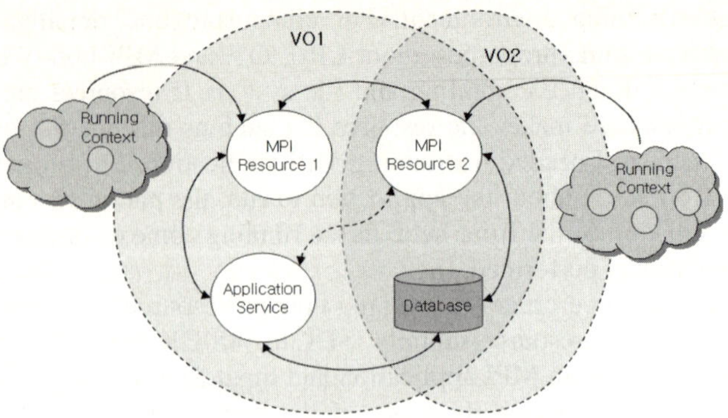

Fig. 4. MPI Resources in VOs

Another role is as a data resource. This is for data-intensive work. Massive data produced by MPI resources is staged out to the designated locations and MPI resources have the locations. Therefore, MPI resources can provide the access to the data indirectly. Indirect data provision is illustrated as dotted lines in Fig. 4. MPI resource 2 provides data to an application service. Actually, the data produced by MPI resource 2 is stored in the designated location and the application service gets the data from the location. This scenario can be implemented as the loosely coupled mechanism. The database can be designed to provide the same data to diverse services or resources by implementing various data providing interfaces.

Fig 4 also represents an MPI resource shared between two VOs. This is possible by simply sharing the EPR of the MPI resources. VO1 and VO2, both can monitor the MPI resource 2 and retrieve properties of MPI resource 2.

One important issue about MPI resources on OGSA is data flowing. There are several approaches. One is exchanging data in workflow through XML form and the other is through existing flat files. The former approach is good ultimately for SOA. Nevertheless, this approach is restricted in many cases as of now. First, all applications must be implemented as services or existing applications using flat files must be equipped by the data transforming service, which transforms XML data to flat files and flat files to XML data. In addition, if the data size is massive such as GBs or TBs, the transferring overhead caused by SOAP messages and service structure will be tremendous.

We choose the latter approach. At this present time, before the leap progress of SOA performance and network technology, we think the latter is more efficient approach. Therefore, we present data flow mechanism through providing reference to the data location. Yet we think exchanging data through XML form is possible and useful in limited cases such as the case that produced data is small enough to transfer as SOAP messages.

4   Evaluation

We implemented the MPI resource based on Globus Toolkit version 4 (GT4) Java WS Core. GT4 is installed in MPI service server and computing resources. MPI service server is chosen as a system with the CPU, AMD Athlon(tm) XP 2500+ and 512MB memory. And each computing resource has CPU, Pentium III 1.0 GHz and 1GB memory.

Following Table.1 and Fig. 5 depict the time consumption of an MPI resource by stages from creation to getting result messages. From this, we get the overhead caused by service structure. The ratio of service to total running time of an MPI resource is trivial level. The overhead caused by service structure is fixed, so, the total time and the ratio of service is in inverse proportion. This example is short-term job. Therefore, for the long-term job, the ratio will be much smaller.

Table 1. MPI resource running time by each stage and node number

Nodes	Creation	Preparation	Run	Get message	Service Ratio (%)
1	42	702	77308	54	1.02
2	48	685	45279	39	1.68
4	46	685	28567	38	2.62

Fig. 5 shows lazy initialization phenomenon [9]. The phenomenon occurs when clients or service containers are first started. It adds some more time when the service is first started, but the influence to whole is limited.

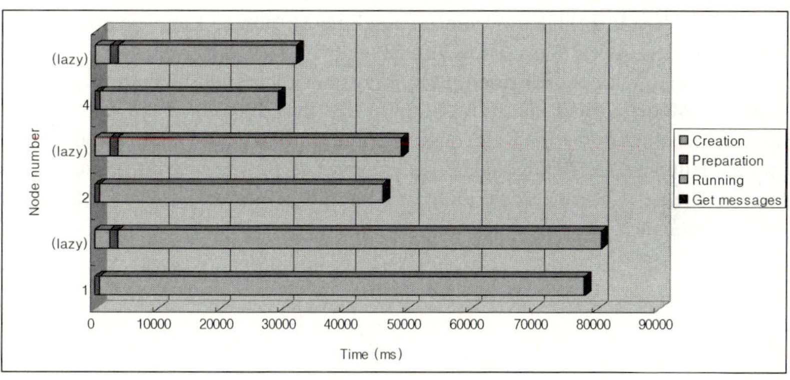

Fig. 5. MPI resource running time by each stage and node number

5   Conclusion

In this paper, we present a service framework of MPI applications for computational Grid. With this, we try to fulfill the diverse computing needs of application services on OGSA. Especially we model MPI resource on OGSA. MPI resource is modeled for being responsible for computational tasks. MPI resources can be members of VOs, and they become computing resources for compute-intensive application services and data resources for data-intensive services. Like the measured results above, the overhead caused by service structure is. The MPI resource may meet variety of computing needs to services on OGSA with trivial overhead.

References

1. I. Foster, C. Kesselman, J.M. Nick, S. Tuecke: Grid services for distributed system integration, IEEE Computer, Vol. 35-6, pp. 37-46 (2002)
2. Nicholas T. Karonis, Brian R. Toonen, Ian T. Foster: MPICH-G2: A Grid-enabled implementation of the Message Passing Interface. J. Parallel Distrib. Comput. 63(5): 551-563 (2003)
3. Dennis Gannon, Jay Alameda, Octav Chipara, Marcus Christie, Vinayak Dukle, Liang Fang, Matthew Farellee, Geoffrey Fox, Shawn Hampton, Gopi Kandaswamy, Deepti Kodeboyina, Charlie Moad, Marlon Pierce, Beth Plale, Albert Rossi, Yogesh Simmhan, Anuraag Sarangi, Aleksander Slominski, Satoshi Shirasauna, and Thomas Thomas: Building grid portal applications from a Web-service component architecture. Proceedings of the IEEE (Special issue on Grid Computing), 93(3):551-563, March (2005)
4. T. Delaitre, A.Goyeneche, P. Kacsuk, T.Kiss, G.Z. Terstyanszky, S.C. Winter: GEMLCA: Grid Execution Management for Legacy Code Architecture Design, Conf. Proc. of the 30 th EUROMICRO Conference. (2004)
5. E. Floros, Yannis Cotronis: Exposing MPI Applications as Grid Services. Euro-Par 2004: 436-443
6. Web Service Resource Framework (WSRF) TC, Web Services Resources specification 1.2, OASIS. (2005)
7. Diego Puppin, Nicola Tonellotto, Domenico Laforenza: How to Run Scientific Applications over Web Services. ICPP Workshops 2005: 29-33
8. Foster, I., Czajkowski, K., Ferguson, D.E., Frey, J., Graham, S., Maguire, T., Snelling, D., Tuecke, S.: Modeling and managing State in distributed systems: the role of OGSI and WSRF, Proceedings of the IEEE, Volume 93, Issue 3, March 2005 Page(s): 604 - 612
9. Taiani, F.; Hiltunen, M.; Schlichting, R.: The impact of Web service integration on grid performance, High Performance Distributed Computing, 2005. HPDC-14. Proceedings. 14th IEEE International Symposium on 24-27 July 2005 Page(s):14 - 23

Metropolitan-Scale Grid Environment: The Implementation and Applications of TIGER Grid*

Chao-Tung Yang[1,**], Tsu-Fen Han[1], Wen-Chung Shih[2], Wen-Chung Chiang[3], and Chih-Hung Chang[3]

[1] High-Performance Computing Laboratory
Department of Computer Science and Information Engineering
Tunghai University, Taichung 40704, Taiwan
ctyang@thu.edu.tw, g942814@thu.edu.tw
[2] Department of Computer and Information Science
National Chiao Tung University, Hsinchu 30010, Taiwan
gis90805@cis.nctu.edu.tw
[3] Department of Information Management
Hsiuping Institute of Technology, Dali, Taichung 412, Taiwan
wcchiang@mail.hit.edu.tw, chchang@mail.hit.edu.tw

Abstract. Internet computing and Grid technologies promise to change the way we tackle complex problems. Harnessing these new technologies effectively, it will transform scientific disciplines ranging from high-energy physics to life sciences. This paper describes a metropolitan-scale Grid computing platform named TIGER Project (standing for **T**aichung **I**ntegrating **G**rid **E**nvironment and **R**esource), which basically interconnects universities and high schools' Grid computing resources and sharing available resources among them, for investigations in system technologies and high performance applications. This novel project shows the viability of implementation of such project in a metropolitan city.

1 Introduction

Grid computing offers a model for solving massive computational problems using large numbers of computers arranged as clusters embedded in a distributed telecommunications infrastructure [1, 3, 4, 5, 7, 9]. Grid computing has the design goal of solving large problems for any single supercomputer, whilst retaining the flexibility to work on multiple smaller problems. Grid computing involves sharing heterogeneous resources (based on different platforms, hardware/software, computer architecture, computer languages), located in different places belonging to different administrative domains over a network using open standards [2, 8, 10, 12]. In short, it involves vitalizing computing resources. Numerous next generations, large scale advanced applications are being developed on innovative technology infrastructure. The development of new types of information technology infrastructure continues to

---

* This work is supported in part by National Science Council, Taiwan R.O.C., under grants no. NSC95-2213-E-029-004 and NSC95-2218-E-007-025.
** Corresponding author.

progress rapidly. It has been noted that one way to view the future is to visit an advanced technology research lab where innovative developers are creating powerful new architecture, protocols, and integrated systems. A number of these development efforts are directed at providing technology infrastructure with attributes that resemble common utility more than a specialized tool.

The basic idea of Grid computing is to create an infrastructure to harness the power of remote high-end computers, databases and other computing resources owned by various people across the globe through the Net. Grid computing involves connecting computers, processors and storage devices via a network in order to gain better overall performance by effectively utilizing unused resources. In the Grid computing world, people submit computing jobs to the grid and the grid system allots the required computing resources and processes the job. The development and deployment of computational Grids is focused on creating a more seamless and direct means of utilizing computationally based resources. The majority of Grid projects today are directed solving complex problems, which can are bandwidth, data, and compute cycle intensive, such as the types of problems encountered by large-scale e-Science.

This paper describes a metropolitan-scale Grid computing platform named TIGER Project (standing for **T**aichung **I**ntegrating **G**rid **E**nvironment and **R**esource) [3, 16], which basically interconnects universities and high schools' Grid computing resources and sharing available resources among them, for investigations in system technologies and high performance applications. This novel project shows the viability of implementation of such project in a metropolitan city. The successful implementation of the Grid computing infrastructure will certainly have far-reaching implications for the business, scientific and individual computing users. Different computational science research sectors, and for commerce, industrial and social service applications can benefit of such technology.

The remainder of this research paper is organized as follows. Section 2 introduces the implementation of TIGER, a metropolitan-scale Grid computing environment and description of each educational unit infrastructure. Later in section 3, we introduce ongoing research projects being investigated by our teams. Finally, in section 4, conclusions and future works are presented.

2   TIGER Grid Testbed

The TIGER Grid computing platform, which stands for Taichung Integrating Grid Environment and Resources, consists of three universities and two high schools, either public or private system, all located in Taichung City and County, Taiwan [3, 16]. The project of constructing such grid infrastructure was to increase each educational unit's computational power cluster resources and exchange

The educational unit's in Taichung, Taiwan participating at this project are Tunghai University (THU), Providence University (PU), HsiuPing Inst. of Tech (HIT), National Dali High School (DL) and at last, Li-Zen High School (LZ). They are interconnected among themselves by TANET (Taiwan Academic Network), of 1Gbps. The TIGER Grid platform was built of 32 computing nodes, 40 processors of different speed and total storage of more than 2TB in 2005. All these institutions are in Taiwan, and each is at least 10 Km from THU. Our all machines have Globus 4.0.1 or above installed. Figure 2 shows the status of various ports used for grid testbed in one monitor page. The detail hardware specification of each educational unit is listed in Table 1.

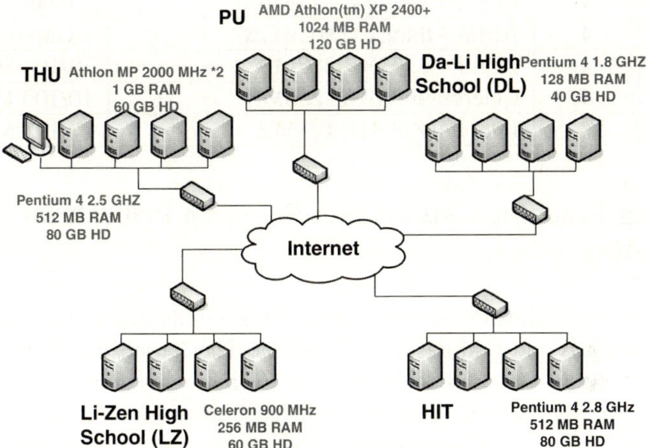

Fig. 1. TIGER Grid Platform

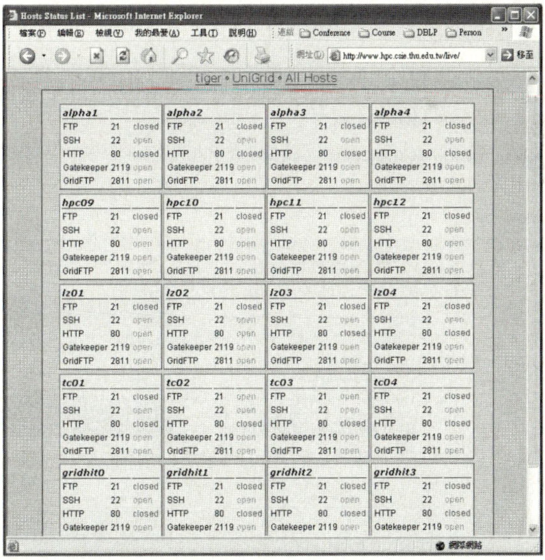

Fig. 2. The TIGER monitor page for status of various ports

Table 1. TIGER Grid participants and hardware specifications

Site	Nodes	CPU / Memory	Local Network
THU	4	Dual AMD MP 2000+, 1GB	10/100 Mbps
THU	4	Dual-Core Intel P4 2.8GHz, 512MB	1 Gbps
THU	4	Intel P4 2.8GHz, 512MB	1 Gbps
THU	4	Intel P4 3.0GHz, 512MB	1 Gbps
PU	4	AMD Athlon 2400+, 1GB	1 Gbps
HIT	4	Intel P4 2.8GHz, 512MB	10/100 Mbps
LZ	4	Celeron 900MHz, 256MB	10/100 Mbps
TC	4	Intel P4 1.8GHz, 128MB	10/100 Mbps

3   Ongoing Teaching Courses and Research Projects on Grid Computing

As we known, the Globus Project provides software tools that make it easier to build computational grids and grid-based applications. These tools are collectively called The Globus Toolkit (http://www.globus.org/). In our system, we adopted it as infrastructure for our BioGrid. The toolkit includes software for security, information infrastructure, resource management, data management, communication, fault detection, and portability. We use Globus toolkit 4.0.1 as middleware to construct a grid computing environment and conduct the experimentations for lecture used. Also, we used the monitoring system development by our laboratory to monitoring whole gird testbed. Figure 3 shows the snapshot of Ganglia tool on TIGER [3, 16].

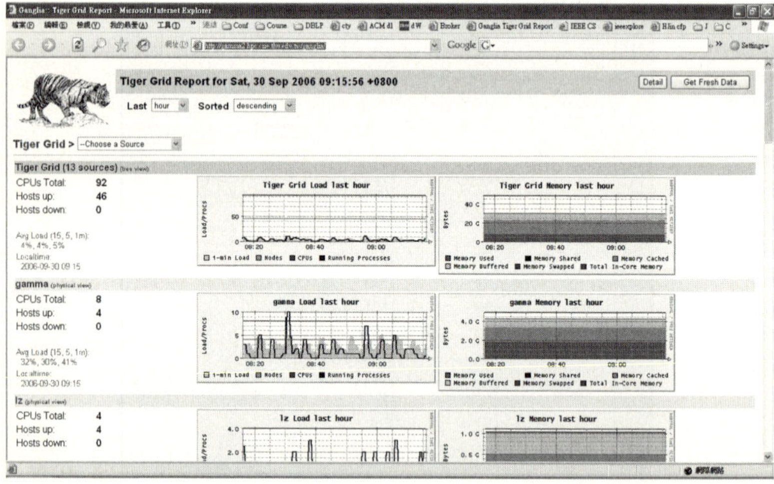

Fig. 3. The snapshot of grid testbed

3.1 Grid Resource Broker

As Grid Computing becomes a reality, there is a need to manage and monitor available resources world-wide, as well as a need to convey these resources to everyday users. This work describes a resource broker as shown in Figure 4 whose main function is to match available resources to user needs. The resource broker provides a uniform interface for accessing available and appropriate resources via user credentials [15, 16]. We also focus on providing approximate measurement models for network-related information using NWS for future scheduling and benchmarking.

We first propose a network measurement model for gathering network-related information (including bandwidth, latency, forecasting, error rates, etc.) without generating excessive system overhead. Second, we consider inaccuracies in real-world network values in generating an approximation values for future use. We constructed a grid platform using Globus Toolkit that integrates the resources of five schools in Taichung integrated grid environment resources (TIGER). The resource broker runs on top of TIGER. Therefore, it provides security and current information about available resources and serves as a link to the diverse systems available in the Grid.

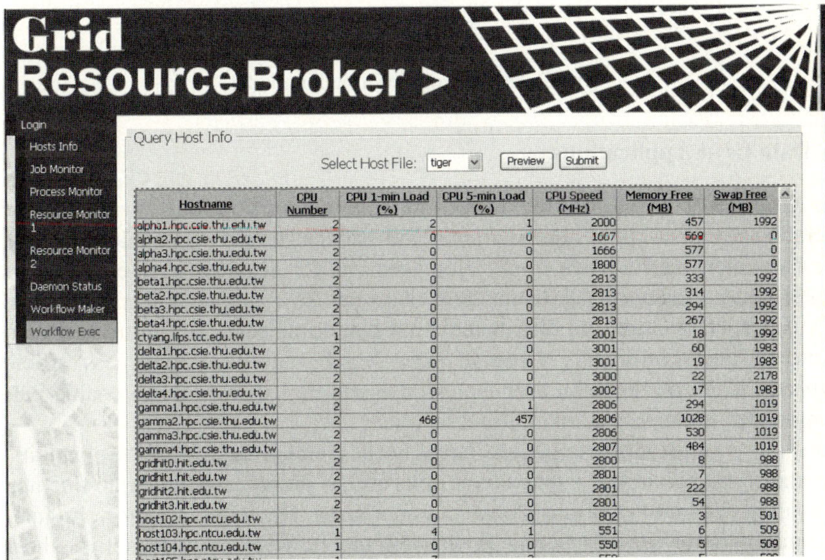

Hostname	CPU Number	CPU 1-min Load (%)	CPU 5-min Load (%)	CPU Speed (MHz)	Memory Free (MB)	Swap Free (MB)
alpha1.hpc.csie.thu.edu.tw	2	2	1	2000	457	1992
alpha2.hpc.csie.thu.edu.tw	2	0	0	1667	568	0
alpha3.hpc.csie.thu.edu.tw	2	0	0	1666	577	0
alpha4.hpc.csie.thu.edu.tw	2	0	0	1800	577	0
beta1.hpc.csie.thu.edu.tw	2	0	0	2813	333	1992
beta2.hpc.csie.thu.edu.tw	2	0	0	2813	314	1992
beta3.hpc.csie.thu.edu.tw	2	0	0	2813	294	1992
beta4.hpc.csie.thu.edu.tw	2	0	0	2813	267	1992
ctyang.lfps.tcc.edu.tw	1	0	0	2001	18	1992
delta1.hpc.csie.thu.edu.tw	2	0	0	3001	60	1983
delta2.hpc.csie.thu.edu.tw	2	0	0	3001	19	1983
delta3.hpc.csie.thu.edu.tw	2	0	0	3000	22	2178
delta4.hpc.csie.thu.edu.tw	2	0	0	3002	17	1983
gamma1.hpc.csie.thu.edu.tw	2	0	1	2806	294	1019
gamma2.hpc.csie.thu.edu.tw	2	468	457	2806	1028	1019
gamma3.hpc.csie.thu.edu.tw	2	0	0	2806	530	1019
gamma4.hpc.csie.thu.edu.tw	2	0	0	2807	484	1019
gridhit0.hit.edu.tw	2	0	0	2800	8	988
gridhit1.hit.edu.tw	2	0	0	2801	7	988
gridhit2.hit.edu.tw	2	0	0	2801	222	988
gridhit3.hit.edu.tw	2	0	0	2801	54	988
host102.hpc.ntcu.edu.tw	2	0	0	802	3	501
host103.hpc.ntcu.edu.tw	1	4	1	551	6	509
host104.hpc.ntcu.edu.tw	1	0	0	550	5	509

Fig. 4. The computational grid resource broker

3.2 Network Information Model

Network Weather Service (NWS) can measure point-to-point network bandwidth and latency that may be important for grid scheduling and load balancing [6]. NWS detects all network states during time periods selected by the user. Because this kind of site-to-site measurement results in $N(N\text{-}1)$ network measurement processes, the time complexity is $O(N^2)$. Our network model focuses on solving the problem of reducing this time complexity without losing too much precision.

In this work, we focus on providing approximate measurement models for network-related information as shown in Figure 5 by using NWS for future scheduling and benchmarking [17, 18]. We first propose a network measurement model for gathering network-related information including bandwidth, latency, forecasting, error rates, etc., without generating excessive system overhead. We then consider inaccuracies in real-world network values in generating approximation values for future use.

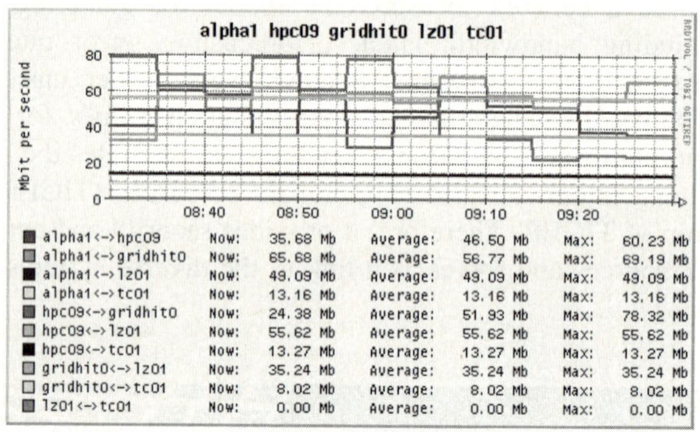

Fig. 5. The network information model

3.3 Data Grid Applications

Data Grids enable the sharing, selection, and connection of a wide variety of geographically distributed computational and storage resources for addressing large-scale data-intensive scientific application needs in, for instance, high-energy physics, bioinformatics, and virtual astrophysical observatories, among others. Data sets are replicated in Data Grids and distributed among multiple sites. Unfortunately, datasets of interest are significantly large in size, which may lead to access efficiency overheads. The co-allocation architecture was developed in order to enable parallel downloading of datasets from multiple servers.

Several co-allocation strategies have been coupled and used to exploit rate differences among various client-server links and to address dynamic rate fluctuations by dividing files into multiple blocks of equal sizes. However, a major obstacle, the idle time of faster servers having to wait for the slowest server to deliver the final block, makes it important to reduce differences in finishing time among replica servers. In this work, we propose a dynamic co-allocation scheme, namely Recursive-Adjustment Co-Allocation scheme, to improve the performance of data transfer in Data Grids. Our approach reduces the idle time spent waiting for the slowest server and decreases data transfer completion time [13, 19]. We also provide an effective scheme for reducing the cost of reassembling data blocks. Figure 6 shows the client tool for transferring files in parallel.

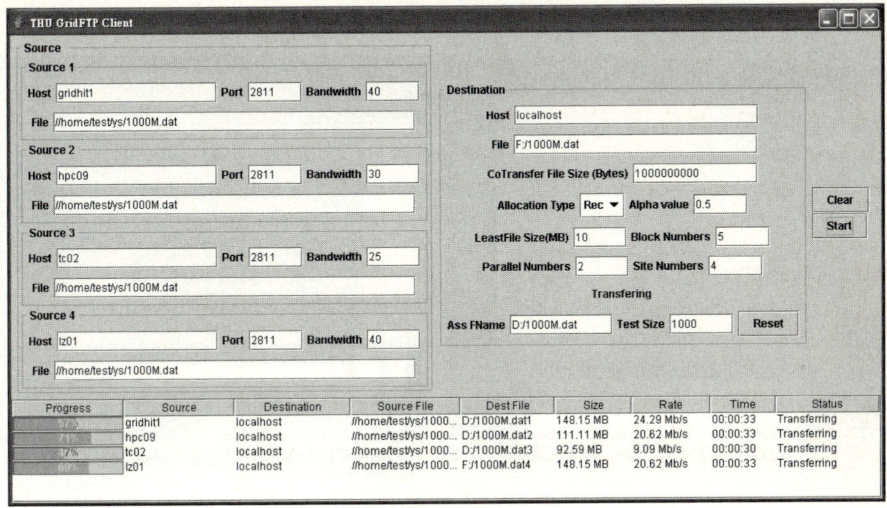

Fig. 6. The Gridftp client tool

3.4 Bioinformatics Grid Applications

Biology databases are diversified and massive; as a result, researchers must compare each sequence with a vast number of other sequences efficiently. A number of programs such as Blast, FASTA, ClustalW, etc., have been written to rapidly search a database for a query sequence. Comparison, whether of structural features or protein sequences, lies in the heart of bioinformatics. These activities require high-speed, high-performance computing power to search through and analyze huge amounts of data, and industrial-strength databases perform a wide range of data-intensive computing functions. The emergence of Grid computing and Cluster computing would meet these requirement. Biological data exists all over the world as various web services, which help biologists to search and extract useful information. The data formats produced from various biology tools are heterogeneous. It needs powerful tools to handle this issue. The process of information integration of heterogeneous biological data is complex and difficult.

This work also describes an approach to solve this problem by using XML technologies. We implement an experimental distributed computing application for bioinformatics [14]. Which consist of basic high-performance computing environment (Grid and PC Cluster system), multiple interface of user portal to provide a useful graphical interface as shown in Figure 7 for biologists who are not specialized in IT to be able to benefit directly from the usage of high-performance technology, and a translation tool for biology data to convert them into XML format.

3.5 Hybrid Parallel Loop Scheduling

For self-scheduling of parallel loops, we propose a general approach called HPLS (Hybrid Parallel Loop Scheduling) and conduct the experimental results on the TIGER. This approach utilizes performance functions to estimate the performance ratio of each

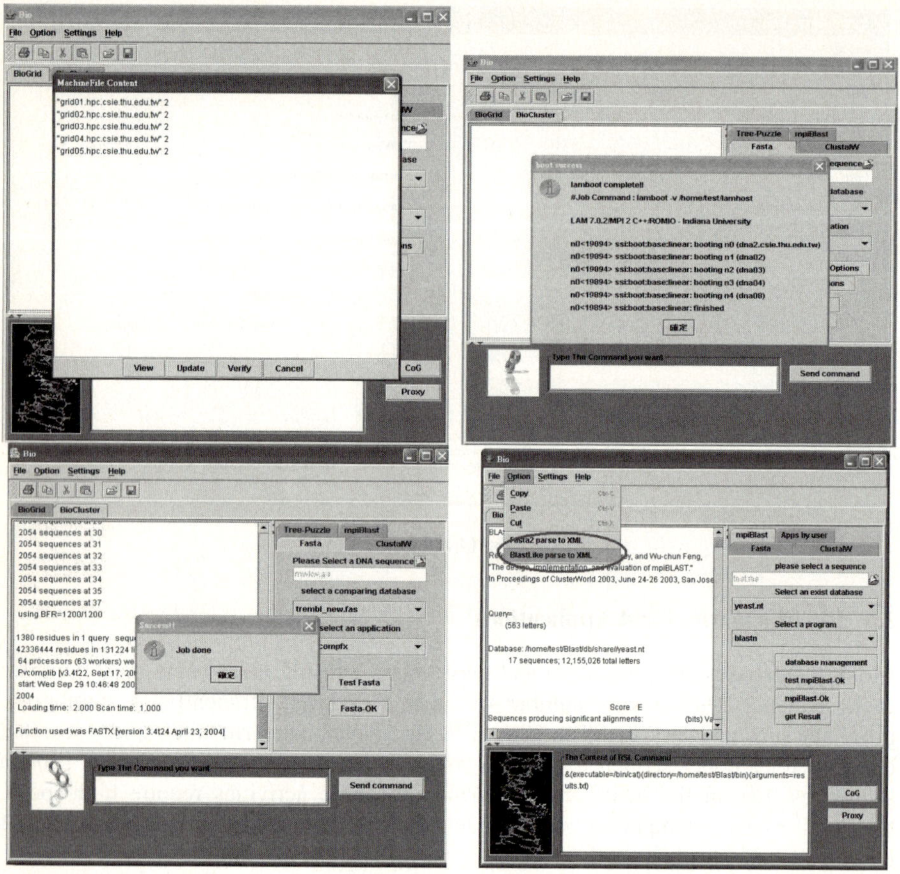

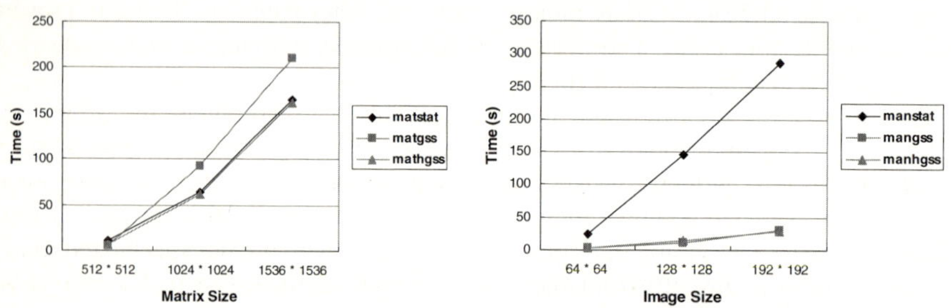

Fig. 7. The GUI of BioGrid for parallel bioinformtics

Fig. 8. Hybrid Parallel Loop Scheduling for Grids

node. To verify our approach, a testbed grid is built, and two types of application programs, matrix multiplication and Mandelbrot are implemented to be executed in this testbed. Empirical results in Figure 8 show that our approach can obtain performance improvement on previous schemes, for grid environments [11, 20, 21].

4 Conclusions

The rise of grid computing and its application discipline brings to computer science faculty members new opportunities and challenges, both in education and in research. In this paper, we described a metropolitan-scale Grid computing platform named TIGER Project (standing for **T**aichung **I**ntegrating **G**rid **E**nvironment and **R**esource), which basically interconnects universities and high schools' Grid computing resources and sharing available resources among them, for investigations in system technologies and high performance applications.. In addition, we also describe the on going related projects and previous results. With interdisciplinary collaboration and using this platform, researchers, faculties and students from computer science, chemistry, physics, biology and engineering programs can interact among themselves.

References

1. The Globus Project, http://www.globus.org/
2. MPICH-G2, http://www.hpclab.niu.edu/mpi/
3. TIGER Project, http://gamma2.hpc.csie.thu.edu.tw/ganglia/, 2006.
4. The Globus Alliance, http://www.globus.org/
5. The National Science Foundation Middleware Initiative, http://www.nsf-middleware.org/
6. Network Weather Service, http://nws.cs.ucsb.edu/
7. I. Foster et al., The Physiology of the Grid: An Open Grid Services Architecture for Distributed Systems Integration, available at http://www.globus.org/research/papers/ogsa.pdf
8. Ian Foster, Carl Kesselman, The Grid 2: Blueprint for a New Computing Infrastructure, Morgan Kaufmann Publishers Inc., San Francisco, CA, 2003.
9. William Gropp , Ewing Lusk , Anthony Skjellum, Using MPI (2nd ed.): portable parallel programming with the message-passing interface, MIT Press, Cambridge, MA, 1999.
10. H. Jordan, and G. Alaghband, Fundamentals of Parallel Processing; Prentice Hall, 2003.
11. Wen-Chung Shih, Chao-Tung Yang, and Shian-Shyong Tseng, "A Hybrid Parallel Loop Scheduling Scheme on Grid Environments," Grid and Cooperative Computing - GCC 2005: Fourth International Conference, Lecture Notes in Computer Science, vol. 3795, pp. 374-385, Springer-Verlag, November 2005.
12. B. Wilkinson and M. Allen, Parallel Programming: Techniques and Applications Using Networked Workstations and Parallel Computers, 2nd Edition; Prentice Hall, 2005.
13. Chao-Tung Yang, Chun-Hsiang Chen, Kuan-Ching Li, and Ching-Hsien Hsu, "Performance Analysis of Applying Replica Selection Technology for Data Grid Environments," PaCT 2005, Lecture Notes in Computer Science, vol. 3606, pp. 278-287, Springer-Verlag, September 2005.
14. Chao-Tung Yang, Yu-Lun Kuo, Kuan-Ching Li, and Jean-Luc Gaudiot, "On Design of Cluster and Grid Computing Environments for Bioinformatics Applications," Distributed Computing - IWDC 2004: 6th International Workshop, Lecture Notes in Computer Science, Springer-Verlag, Arunabha Sen, Nabanita Das, Sajal K. Das, et al. (Eds.), Kolkata, India, vol. 3326, pp. 82-87, Dec. 27-30, 2004.
15. Chao-Tung Yang, Chuan-Lin Lai, Po-Chi Shih, and Kuan-Ching Li, "A Resource Broker for Computing Nodes Selection in Grid Environments," Grid and Cooperative Computing - GCC 2004: Third International Conference, Lecture Notes in Computer Science, Springer-Verlag, Hai Jin, Yi Pan, Nong Xiao (Eds.), vol. 3251, pp. 931-934, Oct. 2004.

16. Chao-Tung Yang, Kuan-Ching Li, Wen-Chung Chiang, and Po-Chi Shih, "Design and Implementation of TIGER Grid: an Integrated Metropolitan-Scale Grid Environment," Proceedings of the 6th International Conference on Parallel and Distributed Computing, Applications and Technologies (PDCAT 2005), IEEE CS Press, December 5-8, 2005.
17. Chao-Tung Yang, Po-Chi Shih, Sung-Yi Chen, and Wen-Chung Shih "An Efficient Network Information Modeling using NWS for Grid Computing Environments," Grid and Cooperative Computing - GCC 2005: Fourth International Conference, Lecture Notes in Computer Science, vol. 3795, pp. 289-300, Springer-Verlag, November 2005.
18. Chao-Tung Yang, Po-Chi Shih, Cheng-Fang Lin, Ching-Hsien Hsu, and Kuan-Ching Li, "A Chronological History-Based Execution Time Estimation Model for Embarrassingly Parallel Applications on Grids," ISPA 2005, Lecture Notes in Computer Science, vol. 3758, pp. 425-430, Springer-Verlag, November 2005.
19. Chao-Tung Yang, I-Hsien Yang, Kuan-Ching Li, and Ching-Hsien Hsu "A Recursive-Adjustment Co-Allocation Scheme in Data Grid Environments," ICA3PP 2005 Algorithm and Architecture for Parallel Processing, Lecture Notes in Computer Science, vol. 3719, pp. 40-49, Springer-Verlag, October 2005.
20. Chao-Tung Yang, Wen-Chung Shih, and Shian-Shyong Tseng, "A Dynamic Partitioning Self-Scheduling Scheme for Parallel Loops on Heterogeneous Clusters," *International Conference on Computational Science - ICCS 2006, Lecture Notes in Computer Science*, vol. 3991, pp. 810-813, Springer, University of Reading, UK, May 28-31, 2006.
21. Wen-Chung Shih, Chao-Tung Yang, and Shian-Shyong Tseng, "A Performance-Based Approach to Dynamic Workload Distribution for Master-Slave Applications on Grid Environments," *Advances in Grid and Pervasive Computing - First International Conference, GPC 2006, Lecture Notes in Computer Science*, Editors: Yeh-Ching Chung, José E. Moreira, vol. 3947, pp. 73-82, Springer, Taichung, Taiwan, May 3-5, 2006.

A Plug-In Tool for Composing Web Services for Applications Development*

Olivia G. Fragoso D.[1], René Santaolaya S.[1], Mariana Guzmán R.[1,3],
Mario Guillén R.[1,2], and Manuel A. Valdés M.[3]

[1] Centro Nacional de Investigación y Desarrollo Tecnológico
Interior Internado Palmira s/n Col. Palmira,
Cuernavaca, Morelos, México CP62490
{ofragoso, rene, marianag}@cenidet.edu.mx
[2] Instituto de Investigaciones Eléctricas, IIE-GAR-26-3,
Reforma 113, Col. Palmira
Cuernavaca, Morelos, México CP62490
mguillén@iie.org.mx
[3] Universidad del Mar
Ciudad Universitaria s/n
Puerto Escondido, Oaxaca. CP 71980
valdes@zicatela.umar.mx

Abstract. Web services composition is currently the paradigm proposed to reduce the cost, time and effort in software development. At the same time, web services seem to fulfill reuse requirements that other technologies have not delivered yet. However, some software development tools do not completely satisfy the need for composing multiple web services. This paper describes tool to support in a semiautomatic way the composition of multiple web services, based on a composition process model. The tool can be used as a plug-in in some software development environments such as Eclipse. In addition, the generation of a template based on XML tags in a client application in order to facilitate the communication with the web services is also described.

1 Introduction

Applications development by composing web services is one of the current paradigms proposed to support organizations in reducing the cost, time and effort in the development of their applications. Web services are "software systems identified by a URL, whose public interfaces and bindings are defined and described using XML"[1]. When complex and large scale applications are developed, their execution logic involves the execution of more than one web service. Web services with different functionalities will have to interact among them in order to fulfill the requirements of the applications. This is known as web services composition [2].

Service composition can be realized for two reasons. One reason is the composition of web services that together execute a given functionality and return some data that a client application will use to continue with its execution. The other reason refers

---

* This work was partially funded by COSNET through the project 526.04-P.

G. Min et al. (Eds.): ISPA 2006 Ws, LNCS 4331, pp. 589–597, 2006.

to compose services into a higher-level service that encapsulates some logic of the client or the business; examples are the flight-hotel booking service [3] and the purchase-delivery service [4].

Some software development tools do not support the generation of stubs of multiple web services at a time. It does not help when software developers want to employ many web services in their applications since they have to select one web service at a time and generate its stub. This paper presents a plug-in tool to support in a semiautomatic way the composition of multiple web services based on a process model and the generation of a template in a client application in order to compose the web services. This tool facilitates the generation of the stubs of all selected web services. The plug-in tool can be used in JAVA based software development environments such as Eclipse. In addition, this plug-in tool allows the user to select all the web services necessary for the application and generates all the stubs at a time and stores them in only one file. None of the composition languages such as BPEL4WS, WSCI, XLANG, and WSFL were used in this work in order to enable the composition process, because the logic of applications depends totally on the designs that the developer must implement either writing it by hand, or generating the code directly from a design diagram using a code generator. Instead, tags similar to some constructs of the composition languages were defined for the automatic generation of a template in a client application, the messages involved in the composition and statements defining the sequence of execution.

Related work deals with problems at the integration level, such as in [6] where the author explains how to use the Microsoft SOAP toolkit to integrate web services with visual basic VB6 applications, and automatic or semi-automatic support for the composition and execution of web services using a process model [7], [2]. One commercial system is the BizTalk from Microsoft [8]. It models sequential, parallel and conditional structures of business processes that communicate web services. Triana [9] is a problem solving environment that uses a workflow diagram to specify the composition but its implementation was done using the WServe API. Other work refers to the definition of new languages to act as reference models to describe the logic of interactions among web services [10]. Some tools [11], [12] to compose web services for integrating information from different sources have been developed. A system for the generation of a high level web service that coordinates the interaction among component web services is described in [13]. Also, ontologies and semantic descriptors such as DAML-S are also being used to support the selection and composition of the web services [14], [15].

2   Motivation

The number of web services accessible to a software developer is growing very fast. It may seem an advantage for many developers. However, it also carries two huge problems. One of them is the selection of appropriate web services. The other problem refers to the composition of the selected web services when a set of them fulfills user requirements. Particularly, software developers expect that web services provide software reusability. Because of that, the tendency to employ more web services within their developments is going upwards at the same reason as new web services are being deployed. Moreover, some software development tools automatically support a limited composition of web services like the generation of the stub of one web service at a time, this is the problem dealt with in this paper.

3   Process Model for Composing Web Services for Applications

Figure 1 shows the process model for composing web services. The model consists mainly of 6 activities some of which are carried out by the developer and some are realized in an automatic way. Section 3 presents the interface of the plug-in tool and explains the activities of the process model as they are supported by the tool.

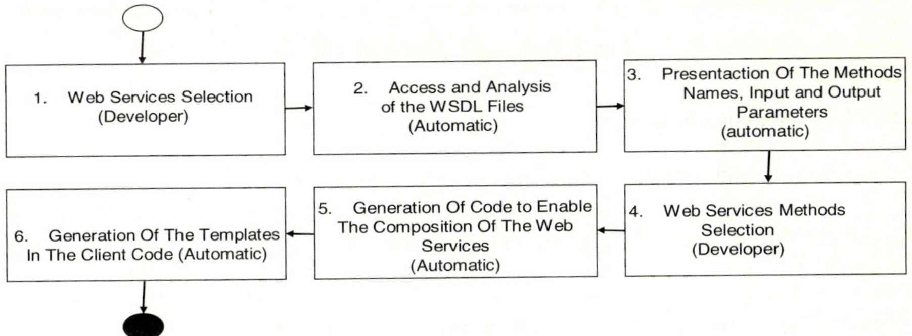

Fig. 1. Process model for composing multiple web services for applications

4   COMPOSITOR: A Plug-In Tool for the Composition of Multiple Web Services for an Application

Figure 2 shows a high level model of the tool named COMPOSITOR. In order to have COMPOSITOR working within the Eclipse environment, it must be plugged into the Workspace directory of Eclipse. Figure 2 shows two modules, *WSDL ANALYZER MODULE* and *COMPOSITION MODULE*. The WSDL (Web Service Definition Language) files are automatically analyzed to identify and to select the methods of the web services that an application will use. The *COMPOSITION* module generates the stubs to recognize the web services to be composed and also generates a template in a client application to send messages to the methods of the selected web services.

In figure 2, the user interface interacts with the module that performs the analysis of the WSDL files, since it is the developer who selects the web services to be composed. The composition module enables the use of the web services by generating the stubs to connect the application with the web services. The tool supports the process presented in figure 1 as described in the subsections below.

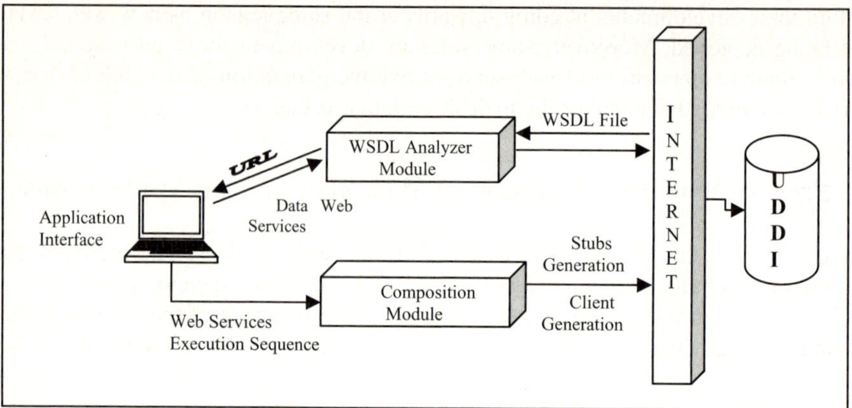

Fig. 2. Compositor High Level Model

4.1   Web Services Selection

Since the selection process is a problem itself, in this paper a selection approach is not dealt with. For the purpose of this work, the selection of the web services to be composed is done by hand directly by the developer of an application using a standard browser.

4.2   Access and Analysis of the WSDL files of the Web Services

The access to the WSDL files is done through the URL (Uniform Resource Locator) specified in the UDDI (Universal Description Discovery and Integration) directory. The analysis of the WSDL files of the web services selected is done with the purpose of obtaining information about the web services to be composed such as the methods names, and their input and output parameters that will be used by the application. This activity is supported by the API JDOM v2 [16].

4.3   Presentation of the Methods Names, Input and Output Parameters

The names of the methods and their parameters are presented in the upper white box of the interface shown in figure 3. The names *setMedidasAC(double in0), getAreaC() and inicializarAreaC()* are the names of the methods that correspond to one of the web services chosen for the composition.

4.4   Web Services Methods Selection

Once the information about a web service is presented to the developer in the upper white box in figure 3, he/she will select from the list the methods of the web services that will be executed and will return some data to the application being developed. The selected methods are shown in the white box placed in the middle of the interface also shown in figure 3.

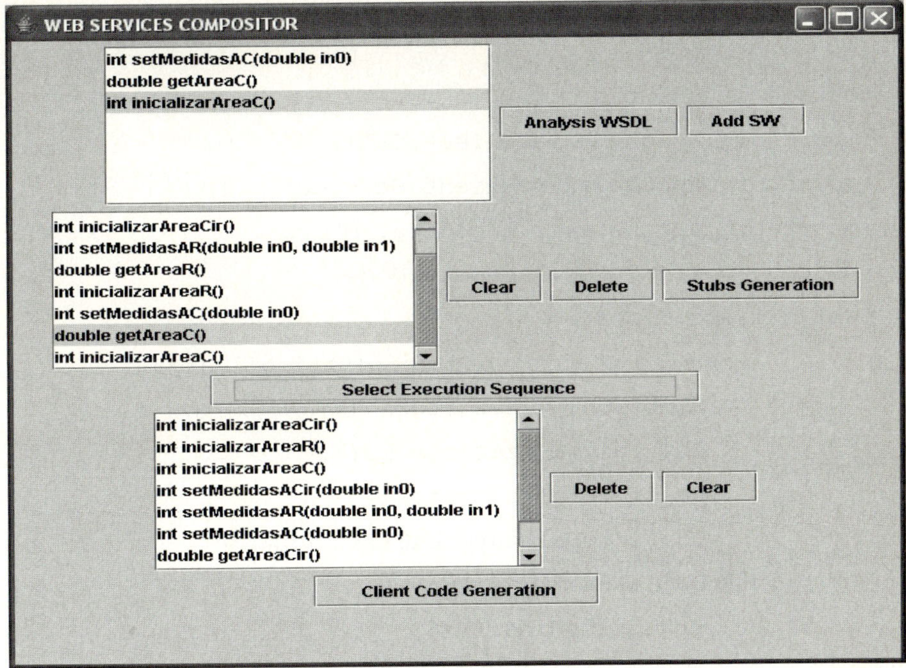

Fig. 3. COMPOSITOR user interface

4.5   Generation of the Code to Enable the Web Services Composition

Once the methods that will be used in the composition are selected, it is necessary to generate the stubs. Stubs will help the application to know about the web services to be composed. The stubs code is generated and stored by default in a file named *Stubs.java* and saved in the Workspace directory of the environment were the software developer is working.

4.6   Generation of the Template in the Client Code

After the stubs are generated, the developer must select the sequence of messages among the application and the web services by clicking on the method name shown in the white box placed in the middle of the interface in figure 3. The sequence is set as it appears in the lower white box of the interface shown in the same figure. In the example introduced in this paper, the first method to execute is *inicializarAreaCir()*, then *inicializarAreaR(), inicializarAreaC()* etc...

An output of this activity is a template that provides the developer with basic code instructions in JAVA language, which corresponds to the objects, messages and the sequence of execution of the web services selected by the developer. The template code is shown below beginning at the line *Obj.inicializarAreaCir();* where the user has to write the name the object that calls the *inicializarAreaCir()* method and to specify the parameters if they are required by the method signature. The same applies for all the lines where the name *Obj* appears.

Example of the template code in the client application generated automatically using the tags described in table 1.

```
package pruebaStub;

import org.apache.axis.client.Call;

import org.apache.axis.client.Service;

import org.apache.axis.encoding.XMLType;

import javax.xml.rpc.ParameterMode;

public class Cliente {
        public static void main(String[] args) {
          Stubs Obj = new Stubs ();
          Obj.inicializarAreaCir();
          Obj.inicializarAreaR();
          Obj.inicializarAreaC();
          Obj.setMedidasACir();
          Obj.setMedidasAR();
          Obj.setMedidasAC();
          Obj.getAreaCir();
          Obj.getAreaC();
          Obj.getAreaR();  }
```

The JAVA code shown above is generated based on tags similar to some constructs of the composition languages such as BPEL4WS, and XLANG. The tags are described in table 1. A slice of the XML file is shown below.

Code example of the XML file for supporting the generation of the template in the client application.

```
<?xml version="1.0" encoding="UTF-8" ?>

- <Composition>

- <Services>
        <Operation name="inicializarAreaCir" />
        <ParametroOut name="response" type="int" />
        <Service name="MyService" />
        <Port Location =
        "http://127.0.0.1:8080/axis/services/MyService
        " />

</Services>

- <Services>
```

```
            <Operation name="inicializarAreaR" />

            <ParametroOut name="response" type="double" />

            <Service name="Myservice2" />

            <Port Location=
            "http://127.0.0.1:8080/axis/services/MyService
            2" />

</Services>

</Composition>
```

Table 1. Tags defined to enable the generation of the template in the client application

TAG	Description
<Composition>	This is the root of the document
<Services>	This tag is contained within the root tag. Each instance of this tag contains the name of the service, a method name and its data
<Operation name>	This tag contains the name of the operation or method of the selected web service
<ParametrosIn name>	This tag describes the input parameters and their types, for the method to be invoked
<ParametroOut name>	This tag describes the output parameter and its type, of the method to be invoked
<Service name>	This tag describes the name of the web service where the method is contained
<Port Location>	This tag describes the URL address and the port of the web service to be composed

5 Tests

Initial functional tests on the plug-in tool were carried out, they showed that the tool performed as expected. It allowed to select several web services and to generate their stubs all of them at a time. Tests were performed for small applications and with small web services created specifically for the tests. However, it is necessary to scale up the tests to large real life applications in order to measure the benefits on saving software development time, reducing costs and effort. In addition, to evaluate if web services are the technology that enables large scale software reusability.

6 Conclusions

A plug-in tool like the one presented in this paper may help to overcome some deficiencies of widely used software development environments without having to restructure them. This tool has a very simple and small interface compared with the advantages it offers, because with a few steps the user habilitates the composition of several web services. In addition, all what the user needs to know about the web services is their URL addresses. The tests applied to the tool showed that it facilitated the work of the software developer, since it is very simple to install it in the Eclipse environment, the interface is small and a developer could have as many web services in his application as needed to comply with his requirements.

The composition process can also be used to generate new composite web services based on component web services. This can be done by encapsulating as a web service the template generated. Current research is also underway to determine the techniques that will yield the best results for the automatic selection of the web services to be composed either for integrating them into applications or for the generation of new composite web services. Work is also being done to model the logic of interactions among web services from a data flow model in order to support conditional and parallel structures, and to solve the adaptation of mismatches among the web services. In addition, the generation of client code in other languages such as C# is being taken into account.

A positive aspect of this work is that developers will not have to learn composition oriented languages. The tags defined in this work for the generation of the template in the client application are in XML format to facilitate its standardization. Future work will be carried out to substitute the XML tags with standard composition languages.

References

1. Dustdar, S., Schreiner, W.: A Survey on Web Services Composition. In: International Journal on Web and Grid Services. Vol.1, No 1. (2005). pp 1-30
2. Chandrasekaran, S., Miller, J.A., Silver, G.S., Arpinar B., Sheth A.P.: Composition, Performance Analysis and Simulation of Web Services. Masters Thesis, University of Georgia Athens. 2002
3. Pistore, M., Roberti, P., Traverso, P.: Process-Level Composition of Executable Web Services: "on-the-fly" versus once for all" Composition. In: Proceedings of the European Semantic Web Conference ESWC (2005), Heraklion, Grecia, 29 May – 1 June
4. Pistore, M., Barbon, F., Bertoli, P., Shaparau, D., Traverso, P.: Planning and Monitoring Web Service Composition. Workshop on Planning and Scheduling for Web and Grid Services,. ICAPS 04, (2004).Whistler, British Columbia, Canada, June 3-7
5. Wohed, P., van der Aalst, W.M.P., Dumas, M., ter Hofstede, A H.M.: Analysis of Web Services Composition Languages: The Case of BPEL4WS. Lecture Notes in Computer Science, Vol. 2813. Springer-Verlag, Berlin Heidelberg (2003) 200-215
6. Fomitchev, M. I. : Integrating XML web services with VB6 applications. Dr. Dobb´s Journal (2004), February
7. Traverso, P., Pistore, M.: Automated Composition of Semantic Web Services into Executable Processes, (2004) International Semantic Web Conference, ISWC
8. http://www.microsoft.com/latam/prensa/2002/feb/lan_vsnet.asp. 05/07/2004
9. Majithia, S., Shields, M., Taylor, I., Wang, I.: Triana: a Graphical Web Service Composition Toolkit. (2004) IEEE International Conference on Web Services, 514-521
10. Piccinelli G., Williams S.L.: Workflow: a Language for Composing Web Services. In: Proceedings of the 16th Euroean Conference on Object-Oriented Programming ECOOP. (2002). Malaga, Spain, Jun 11th

11. Ponnekanti, S. R., Fox, A.: SWORD A Developer Toolkit for Web Service Composition (2002) The Eleventh International World Wide Web Conference, Honolulu, Hi
12. Ko, I., Neches, R.: Composing Web Services for Large – Scale Tasks. In: IEEE Internet Computing. (2003) September-October, pp 52-59
13. Trianotti, M., Pistore, M., Calabrese, G., Zacco, G., Lucchese, G., Barbon, F., Bertoli, P. Traverso, P.: ASTRO: Supporting Composition and Execution of Web Services. (2005) Third International Conference on Service-Oriented Computing, Amsterdam, The Netherlands, 12-15 December
14. Narayanan, S., McIlraith, S. A.: Simulation, Verification and Automated Composition of Web Services. In: Proceedings of the 2nd WWW Conference. (2002). May
15. Wu, D., Parsia, B., Sirin, E., Hendler, J., Nau, D.: Automating DAML-S Web Services Composition Using SHOP2. Lecture Notes in Computer Science, Vol. 2870. Springer-Verlag, Berlin Heidelberg (2003) 195-210
16. www.jdom.org 20/10/2005.

Spatial Data Service Models in Grid Environment

Guoqing Li[1], Dingsheng Liu[1], Zhenchun Huang[2], Yi Zeng[1], and Yong Xue[3]

[1] China Remote Sensing Satellite Ground Station, CAS
`{gqli, dsliu, yzeng}@ne.rsgs.ac.cn`
[2] Department of computer science, Tsinghua University
`huangzc@tsinghua.edu.cn`
[3] Institute of Remote Sensing Applications, Chinese Academy of Sciences
`y.xue@londonmet.ac.uk`

Abstract. This paper presents the data service models in data grid and points out the well-known catalogue based grid data manage model CDM cannot satisfy the requirement of multi-resource grid data application. Combining with the need of spatial data application gird, this paper gives out another two models, broker-based model BDM and direct manage model DDM. Through experiments with these models, the detailed comparison among them is also been given here.

1 Introduction

Data operation is the basic grid kernel component not only in data grid but in computing grid, which includes replica, catalogue, query and discovery. The most important part of data operation is data manage model (DMM), which focuses on two facts, user-oriented data accessing mechanism and grid platform-oriented data providing mechanism. The research about DMM has been taken in almost all grid basic platform and many DMMs have been built to provide   important components. The Globus Toolkit contains a data management component that provides such services [1].

Storage resource broker system SRB, developed by SDSC, is the well used data grid middleware. SRB provides a uniform accessing interface for file system, archive system and database system, which hides the complex and specialty of storage system. It supports multi data resource management in WAN with operations of replica, accessing to replicated dataset, file collection and logical file invoking, and so on. Up to now, there are many application have used SRB as their basic grid data manage middleware.

Globus is designed firstly as a computing grid platform. With the developing of data grid application, new components about DMM has been added into Globus, which supports most data grid functions, such as fast transmission among grid nodes, data replica, finding of replicated dataset and metadata management. Globus is becoming the most important data grid platform, and some outstanding data grid middleware has been provided now, GRC, GridFtp and joint research on DATAGRID GDMP. Other research works have been taken by IBM, SUN, and LSF etc. OPeNDAP [2] also brings the professional data service middleware.

G. Min et al. (Eds.): ISPA 2006 Ws, LNCS 4331, pp. 598–602, 2006.

Spatial data is a special one comparing with other science data. Generally, spatial data includes all data relative to space address, and 80% information we have to deal with is spatial information [3]. The character of spatial data is not only the complex and different data structure, heterogeneous data organizing, massive storage, but also the various data service modes and application modes. So we can not use only one kind of uniform data model to describe so many kind of spatial data. The research on spatial grid DMM wants to explain the method how to deal with such complexity and massive data.

Special data types and different application models need special relative DMMs. The analysis of Globus and DATAGRID combined with our research on DMM in Spatial Information Grid (SIG) project, we provide three DMM models, data manage model based on catalogue (CDM), data manage model based on broker (BDM) and direct data manage model (DDM). Such models can be used in spatial data grid as well as other high complex data application grid.

2   Data Manage Model Based on Catalogue (CDM)

The typical CDM can be seen in Globus GRC and DATAGRID GDMP. As Figure 1 shown, in CDM model, grid provides centralized or distributed catalogue database and services. Catalogue service can work in two modes, activity query and passivity query, to update the data list synchronously. With activity query, catalogue queries every registered data services on schedule and recording the changing data information. In passivity query, data provider has to register new data and changed data on catalogue servers by itself. Catalogue

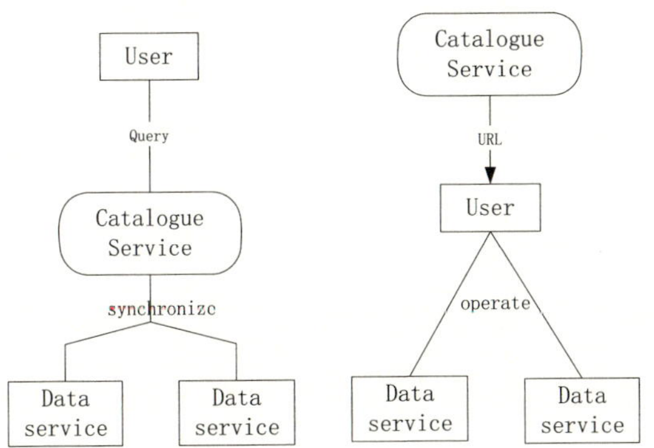

Fig. 1. CDM work mode

servers record the necessary parameters of such data list and build the uniform code GUID for these data. A data user firstly needs to send a query to catalogue service, and waiting for the feedback from catalogue service. The returned result is a resource URL, which can be organized in the uniform list format. User can select what he interested from the result list and invoke them in his following grid application. The following invoking need not the help of catalogue service, it can be finished with Peer to Peer protocols between data provider and data consumer.

User can get the query result very quickly with catalogue services in CDM, which is very similar the work mode of web page query mechanism, such as Google searcher. However, the problem encountered in CDM is creditability of result and the update cost of catalogue servers. Because the catalogue information of a large range query is always in very large size to be transferred and organized. The suitable algorithm should be developed to bring out high performance catalogue synchronization with multi data resources. Because catalogue updating always can not be finished in real time, the record storied in catalogue database can only show the status of data provider in the last catalogue update time.

There are three different times needed to be considered, data resource changing time, catalogue update time and user query time. If user query time is earlier then the catalogue update time and later then resource changing time, the query result will bring misunderstanding information. Creditability is coming from the difference of these operation times.

3   Data Manage Model Based on Broker (BDM)

It is the most important difference between BDM and CDM that BDM does not build upon catalogue service. There is a new service DMS (Data Manage Service or Data Mining Service) in instead of CDM, which is a broker service. BDM need not to maintain the catalogue database. There is no static global index database, as shown in Figure 2.

The key technology has to be built firstly in BDM is grid query data model (GQDM), which is a XML metadata architecture. GQDM selects the important components which are frequently appeared in user application and also have been defined and included in every main spatial metadata system. With such data description method,

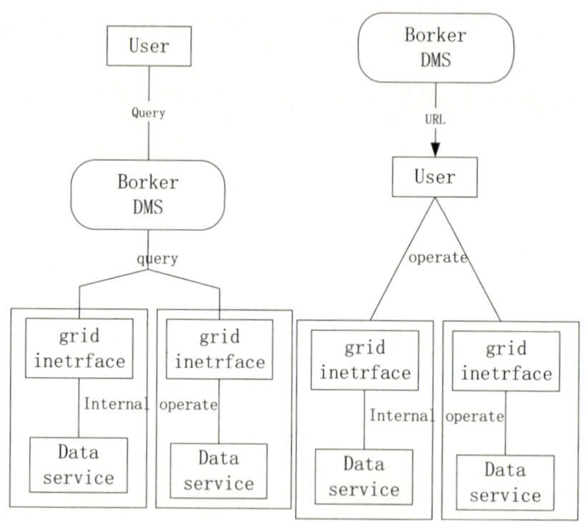

Fig. 2. BDM work mode

the grid data resource service interface, include file system and database system, will naturally contain the exchange interface between local metadata and GQDM grid metadata. As a result, a data provider needs not to synchronize the remote catalogue database with automatic or initiative method when he updates his data resource. When a gird user submit a query, DMS will accept his query and send a GQDM-based message to all data services which DMS can find from grid registration centre. The grid interface of data service will translate the GQDM-based message into local query parameters and start local query process. Reversely, the query result will be translated to be a GQDM-based message and send back to grid user or the portal directly.

For better performance, a cache service should be designed to save to the frequent accessed data invoking and data entities. In certain condition, we can storage the high probability data in cache service; user can operate data time after time. However, we have to consider the copyright conflict of cached data.

Apparently, the great problem of such broker-based DMM is the cost of each query, especially the time cost. Queries will cause direct operation to data service every time, so the time cost cannot be saved at all. In the other hand, such cost assures the reliability of query result. Short lift period is very important character of grid and grid service, which heavily affects the management of grid. Static offline index of metadata will cause misunderstanding of grid resource, for both service resource and data resource.

4   Directly Data Manage Model (DDM)

DDM is a simple data resource manage mode with only the grid basic registration and resource finding service, named RFS or RS. Generally, RS is designed to manage grid services. However, if the data complex is not very high and less massive, RS also can be used to register dataset, as shown in Figure 3. When user asks for data, the query message will be sent directly to RS. RS will check its database and return the result just like the service query.

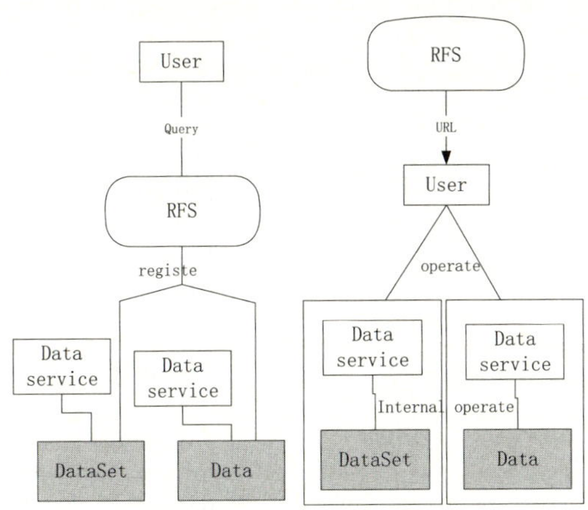

Fig. 3. DDM work mode

It is clear that DDM is belonging to another type of CDM. DDM also has a static database to storage the index data, and RS has to be act as such function to record and maintain such database. There is a remarkable dissymmetry that although user can search or register data independently, he has to know the exact interface of data service when he wants to use such data in grid application, however.

The best benefit of DDM is simple. User needs not waste time and money to build complex data service architecture and he can use the basic grid resource manage service directly, such as RS, which is provided by the common grid platform. Part of our research work on GIS has used DDM model, and many GIS vector area data is storied and serviced with DDM. Our registration service, RFS2.0 supports many levels registration and searching with P2P technology, such improvement overcomes the problem of query bottleneck. Some level RFS services have been defined as special data registration services.

5   Comparison and Analyses

Some experiments have been taken to monitor thus three models. Within the project of China Forestry Information Grid Testbed, a DDM data service has been used to manager the demo dataset, include vector data and grid image data. In the project of China Spatial Information Grid, we designed both CDM and BDM data developer at the same time. In this case, there are 11 grid datasets distributed around China. With bi-side authorization and special accepted service interface, CDM agent caches the metadata of 9 of 11 datasets in every certain time. While another BDM based portal is built to directly search all datasets which can be found from registration centre.

We compared these three server models in Table 1. Form table we can seen that these modes can be used in different grid with different scale and complex character. If to build a large scale grid, which needs strict data policy and cooperation mechanism, CDM is suitable, the query speed of which is very fast. If to build a small grid test bed or a scale limited grid with less data amount and without detail data description mode, DDM is good way, which is easy built and used. BDM is suitable for the middle scale and complex gird application, which is outstanding in its grid expansibility and veracity.

Table 1. Comparison of three DMM models

DMM type	CDM	BDM	DDM
Catalogue server	Need	Not need	Need
Query speed	Fast	Slowly	Fast
Reliability of query result	Low	High	Low
Update work of provider	Complex	Easy	Complex
Suitable grid scale	Large	Middle	Small
Invoking method	Direct	Direct	Additional information needed
Kernel components	Catalogue service	Broker service	Register service
Expansibility	General	High	Low
File type data resource query	Support	Support	Support
Database type data resource query	Not Support	Support	Not Support

Acknowledgement

The research works about this paper are supported by the Chinese key technology research projects 2003AA131050, 2002AA104110, in the key laboratory of China Remote Sensing Satellite Ground Station. Some experiments have been taken in China Spatial Information Grid and Chinese Forestry Information Grid.

References

[1] Bart Jacob, Grid computing: What are the key components?
[2] http://www.opendap.org/
[3] http://www-900.ibm.com/developerWorks/cn/grid/gr-overview/index_eng.shtml

Solving Spatio-temporal Non-stationarity in Raster Database with Fuzzy Logic

Rakefet Shafran-Natan and Tal Svoray

Dept. of Geography and Environmental Development, Ben-Gurion University of the Negev,
Beer-Sheva, 84105, Israel
{shafranr, tsvoray}@bgu.ac.il

Abstract. Vegetation dynamic in semi-arid regions is widely affected by climate and hydrological regimes. These regimes create a patchy landscape which, therefore, cannot be treated as stationary in space. Overall complexity significantly increases when the temporal component is added to the analysis. However, despite the complexity involved with variation in time, most of the temporal data storage in raster data-models is done using series of snapshot layers associated with a particular time event. The reason is mainly associated with resolution problems and limitations in controlling large databases with computer resources. Recently, the combination between spatial and temporal databases has become crucial in GIS modeling for solving spatial dynamic problems. We suggest hereby the use of fuzzy theory to apply stationary rules to non-stationary environment in raster database. The method is demonstrated as an analysis of vegetation dynamics in a semi arid environment. The results display the simplicity of the combination between spatially explicit rules and raster database which allow our method to analyze ongoing processes in cell ij at the same time resolution.

Keywords: fuzzy logic, raster, GIS, temporal, non-stationarity.

1 Introduction

Environmental researchers are facing the challenge of developing models for precise prediction of phenomena that change both in time and space [1]. The developments in remote sensing technology and in the accuracy of digital elevation models (DEM) open an opportunity to combine these data sources in raster geographic information systems (GIS) [2],[3]. Raster GIS are usually merged with time-area (TA) methods under the assumption of "stationarity" [1] to use high-resolution information for understanding the heterogeneity of the environment in multi-layer analysis [4]. Regression analysis is widely used in remote sensing and in raster GIS. Among regression methods, Ordinary Least Squared (OLS) is the most common for the establishment of spatial relationships between any two variables in the raster database. However, a relationship between two variables can differ significantly in space. Therefore, OLS may not always provide a reliable description of the relationships over different sites but rather some average impression over a region [4], [5]. Furthermore, the use of DEM for terrain analysis also assumes stationarity,

G. Min et al. (Eds.): ISPA 2006 Ws, LNCS 4331, pp. 603–609, 2006.

despite the high spatial variability of any given watershed [1]. The existence of sink and source zones may provide such a problem since topographic calculations of primary and secondary morphometric attributes assume a continuous flow along the slope (the contributing area) and from the slope to the channel (the sink). However, it is well known that in semi-arid regions, for example, the terrain is not continuous and therefore cannot be treated as stationary [6]. Statistical interpolation methods in many cases are used for predicting phenomena in space through a calculated surface including an isotropic spatial autocorrelation and stationary trend. These statistical assumptions do not hold for patchy, heterogeneous environments and the calculation methods are time consuming, need pre-processing of the date training and require a large number of calculation sets [7]. Semi-arid areas are characterized by large variability of environmental conditions in both space and time [8], [9]. Hydrology is the major determinant of vegetation dynamics which creates a patchy landscape [12]. Therefore, one can not assume spatial or temporal stationarity in this environment [1]. In addition, several shortages still occur in raster datasets concerning temporal analysis: 1) The layers are based on spatially static information which is attached to an attribute table and not updated during time. 2) Multiscale resolution can cause problems of data overlapping on a pixel basis. 3) Historical information is usually of low quality [10]. And 4) there are difficulties to control large raster databases with limited computer resources [11]. Here, we suggest a method for the representation of vegetation growth in patchy environments through process-based modeling which uses spatially and temporally explicit fuzzy modeling. The model is based on the synergy of three environmental sub–models with four climatic variables. The spatial cell resolution is 25x25m and the model is operated on a daily basis. The model simulates plant germination and production rate.

2 Methods

The use of spatio-temporal data has become crucial for analysis and development of dynamic models for better understanding cause and effect scenarios [20]. Fuzzy logic is a mathematical formulation that suggests solutions where there is lack of knowledge for absolute answers [13], or for spatial performance of areas with indeterminate borders [14]. The synergy between raster GIS, fuzzy formulation and expert knowledge allows to identify environmental features [15],[17],[14]. The GIS stores landscape complexity and fuzzy logic allows definition of rules in a detailed manner [16]. Therefore, the more the system is heterogeneous the advantage of the method is grown. Fuzzy formulation is usually composed of three primary elements: fuzzy sets, fuzzy membership functions and fuzzy logic joint membership functions [14]. Fuzzy set (A) could be defined as:

$$A \{x, (x)\} \ A = \mu \text{ for } x \in X \tag{1}$$

where x is the variable and $\mu_A(X)$ is the membership function of x in A [19]. The scientific literature provides numerous membership functions, including, for example, linear, trapezoidal, sigmoid and cosine [16]. The membership functions (MF's) define the degree of membership for each cell or attribute in the set (A) [14]. The membership value is subjective and should reflect the way by which the researcher grasps the phenomenon. The degree of membership is limited in the 0-1 range while 1 means complete membership. The set A was defined in our study as the set with optimal conditions for vegetation production. That is, the more rainfall amount increases the more water available to the plant and production is expected to be more intense. Therefore, the membership function we used in this case is linear positive:

$$x - \alpha / \beta - \alpha \tag{2}$$

X is the grid cell value or the record in the attribute cell (fuzzy set). Where, α is minimum value in the set, and β is the maximum [16]. To integrate the effect of all membership values (spatial and temporal), we used the joint membership function (JMF). There is several ways to perform a JMF and we have used the convex combination operation [14]. Eq 3 shows the operation where every MF for each fuzzy set A are the membership function $\mu(X1....Xn)$, and the weight (λ 1...7) [18].

$$JMF\left(X\right) = \lambda_1 \mu_{X1} + \lambda_2 \mu_{X2} + ... + \lambda_n \mu_{Xn} \tag{3}$$

The weights λ determine the extent by which each membership function contributes to the final set (daily germination or production prediction). Consequently, they represent a hierarchy of the variable's contributions to the JMF and, hence, each variable's value in the final predictive model [19].

In our model, the membership scores accumulate from the first rainfall event (day one). Germination conditions (JMFgermination) are calculated on a daily basis, until conditions for germination are fulfilled based on a threshold value that was set to 1. If a cell has germinated, it starts to accumulate daily conditions for productions (JMFproduction) until the end of the season. The model is written in AML and runs on ARCGIS 9.

3   Results and Discussion

This paper addresses the problem of modeling dynamic and non-stationry phenomena in raster GIS. Our method is based on fuzzy logic theory and it enables the generalization of intermediate layers in a temporal database. This approach can be easily generalized and applied to complex environments that take different stages of evolution [20]. The evolution, over time, in our case, occurs along the growing season where each cell accumulates the conditions for germination until they are satisfied. From this day, the cells, that have germinated, start to accumulate the daily conditions for production until the end of the season. Every cell on the grid germinates at different day according to available conditions (temperature) and resources (water). The germination phase begins from the second day after the first rainfall event (Julian day 295) and it ends after 12 days (Julian day 306 – fig. 1). Figure 1 clearly shows that every cell ends the germination phase in a different day and therefore, it also starts to accumulate daily condition for production in a different day (fig. 2).

The results in fig. 2 illustrate three different processes in the model on a specific Julian day (297). Each cell in the spatial location ij is the same cell for all three maps. Map 2.1 shows the germination date for each cell during four days (until day 297) and after the Meters first storm of the season (cells that did not germinate until that day

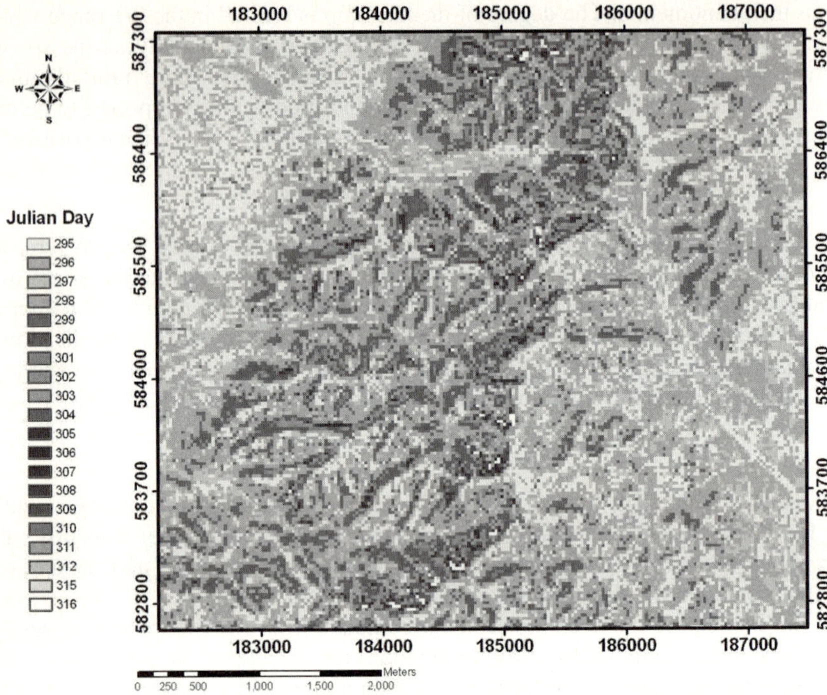

Fig. 1. The germination date in each cell on a Julian day (winter 1989-1990)

are assigned as zero). Map 2.2 presents a prediction for the production conditions on the Julian day 297. Cells that did not germinate until the Julian day 297 did not begin the production phase and assigned as zero. In map 2.3 the cells that did not germinate continue to accumulate environmental and temporal conditions until they will reach the threshold value that is satisfactory for germination. In map 2.3, areas with accumulated JMF production score below 1 did not germinate and cells with a score higher than 1 have germinated.

GWR calculates regression coefficient for every local point in space, based on a distance –weighted sub-sample of neighbors, on the basis that they may not remain fixed over space [21]. However, this modeling framework is highly computationally intensive and the weights must be re-calculated and the model re-run for each location. This method cannot calculate for large areas with large number of data points [4]. Our model enables to handle the spatio-temporal non-stationarity in raster environment, whereas every grid cell is assigned with a different membership score. The grid cell scores are not related to the other cells in the neighborhood and do not need large straining sets. In the model every cell is an independent entity which accumulates daily conditions although the same rules apply for the entire layer. As was shown previously, this method can inherent a stationary rules (MF's) to a peachy environment and analyze different ongoing processes in cell ij at the same time. Since all the variables get a membership value from zero to one, the outcome is a model that runs within a unified scale. We conclude that the spatial and temporal resolution of

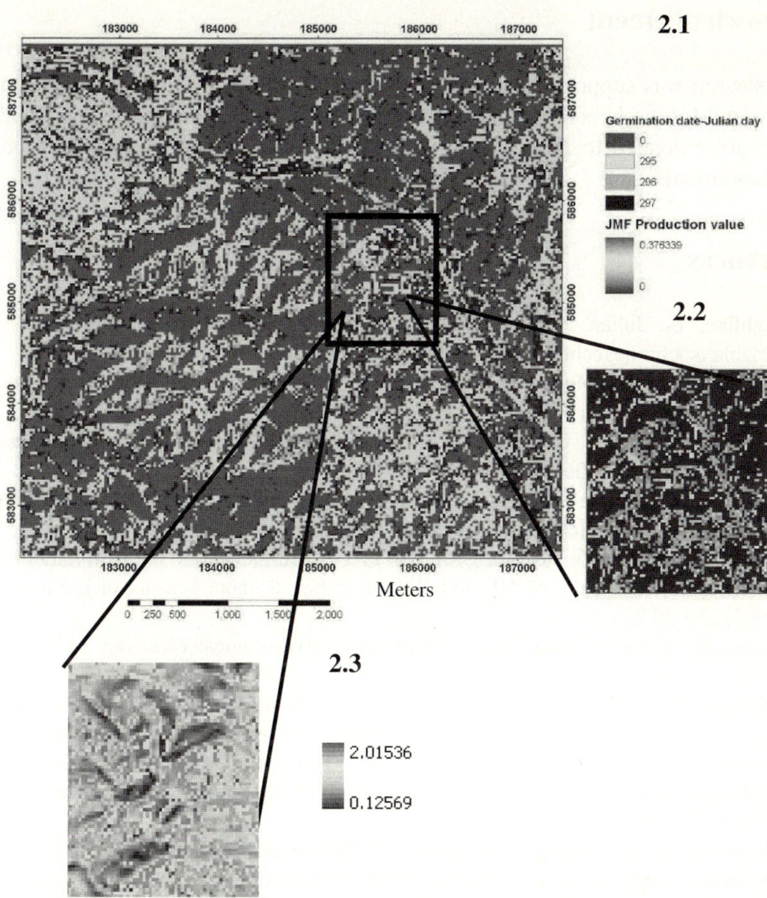

Fig. 2. The effect of germination date on production rate. 2.1: germination date in Julian days; 2.2: JMF production score; 2.3: JMF germination in accumulated values.

the prediction layer increases since fuzzy logic provides flexibility to the GIS database of spatio-temporal analysis. This flexibility is achieved by using the rules from expert knowledge to determine the membership function and the weight in the JMF function which contributes to the explanation of variation in the phenomenon.

4   Conclusions

We present here an approach to tackle non stationarity in raster GIS database in a heterogeneous environment. The results show that the model can describe non-stationary environment without the use of training sets or rigor statistical assumptions. The result characterizes in a rather realistic way spatio-temporally dynamic processes. The use of measured variables over large areas without difficulties and the simplicity of the techniques presented here can make the model suitable for wide raster applications.

Acknowledgement

This research was supported by THE ISRAEL SCIENCE FOUNDATION (grant No. 692/06) and by the Israeli Ministry of the Environment under contract no: 83217301. Thanks are extended to Amir Natan who read parts of the manuscript and provided useful comments.

References

1. Saghfian, B., Julien, P.Y., Rajaie, H.: Runoff hydrograph simulation based on time variable isochrone technique, Journal of Hydrology 261 (2002) 193-203.
2. McBratney, A.B., Mendonsa Santos, M.L., Minasny, B.: On digital soil mapping. Geoderma 117 (2003) 3-52.
3. Scull, P., Franklin, J., Chadwick, O.A., McArthur, D.: Predictive soil mapping: a review. Progress in Physical Geography 27 (2003) 171-197.
4. Osborne, P.E., Suarez-Seoane, S.: should data be partitioned spatially before building large scale distribution model? Ecological Modelling 157 (2002) 249-259.
5. Foody, G. M.: Geographical weighting as a further refinement to regression modeling: An example focused on the NDVI-rainfall relationship. Remote Sensing of Environment. 88 (2003) 283-293.
6. Beven, K., Freer, J.: A dynamic TOPMODEL. Hydrological Processes 15 (2001) 1993-2011.
7. Graniero, P.A., Robinson, V.B.: A Real–time Adaptive Sampling Method for Field Mapping in Patchy, Heterogeneous Environments. Transactions in GIS 7 (2003) 31-53.
8. Ludwig, J.A., Wilcox, B.P., Breshears, D.D., Tongway, D.J., Imeson, A.C.: Vegetation patchesand runoff-erosion as interacting ecohydrological processes in semiarid landscape. Ecology 86 (2005) 288-297.
9. Huenneke, L.F., Clason, D., Muldavin, E.: Spatial heterogeneity in Chihuahuan Desert vegetation: implication for sampling methods in semi-arid ecosystem. Journal of Arid Environments 47 (2001) 257-270.
10. Dragicevic, S., Marceau, J.D.: An application of fuzzy logic reasoning for GIS temporal modeling of dynamic processes. Fuzzy Set and Systems 113 (2000) 69-80.
11. Wu, H., Li, B., Stoker, R., Li, Y.: A semi-arid grazing ecosystem simulation model with probabilistic and fuzzy parameters. Ecological Modelling 90 (1996) 147-160.
12. Noy-Meir, I.: Desert Ecosystems: Environment and producers. Annual review Ecology and Systematics 4 (1973) 25-51.
13. Bojorquez-Tapia, L.A., Juarez, L., Cruz-Bello, G.: Integrating fuzzy logic, optimization, and GIS for ecology impact assessments. Environments Management 30 (2002) 418-433.
14. Burrough, P.A., MaCmillan, R.A., Van Deursen, W.: Fuzzy classification methods for determining land suitability from soil profile observation and topography. Journal of Soil Science 43 (1992) 193-210.
15. McBratney, A.B., Odeh, I.O.A.: Application of fuzzy set in soil science: fuzzy logic, fuzzy measurements and fuzzy decisions. Geoderma 77 (1997) 85-113.
16. Robinson, V.B.: A perspective on the fundamentals of fuzzy sets and their use in Geographic Information Systems. Transactions in GIS 7 (2003) 3-30.
17. Zhu, A.X., Hudson, B., Burt, J., Lubich, K., Simonson, D.: Soil mapping using GIS, expert knowledge, and Fuzzy logic. Soil Science Society America Journal 65 (2001) 1463-1472.

18. Baja, S., Chaphman, D.M., Dragovich, D.: A conceptual model for defining and assessing land management units using a fuzzy modeling approach in GIS environment. Environmental management 29 (2002) 647-661.
19. Svoray, T., Bar-Yamin, S., Henkin, Z., Gutman, M.: Assessment of herbaceous plant habitats in water-constrained environments: Predicting indirect effects with fuzzy logic. Ecological Modelling 180 (2004) 537-556.
20. Drgicevic, S. Maeceau, D.J., A fuzzy set approach for modeling time in GIS. International Journal of Information Science 14 (2000) 225-245.
21. Brunsdon, C., Fotheringham, S., Charlton, M.: Geographically weighted regression modeling spatial non-s.

Study on Grid-Based Special Remotely Sensed Data Processing Node in Grid GIS

Jianqin Wang[1], Yong Xue[2,3,*], Jianping Guo[2,4], Yincui Hu[2], Chaolin Wu[2], Lei Zheng[2,4], Ying Luo[2,4], Yi Xie[1], and YunLing Liu[1]

[1] College of Information and Electric Engineering, China Agricultural University, P.O. Box 142, Beijing, 10083, China
[2] State Key Laboratory of Remote Sensing Science, Jointly Sponsored by the Institute of Remote Sensing Applications of Chinese Academy of Sciences and Beijing Normal University, Institute of Remote Sensing Applications, Chinese Academy of Sciences, P.O. Box 9718, Beijing 100101, China
[3] Department of Computing, London Metropolitan University, 166-220 Holloway Road, London N7 8DB, UK
[4] Graduate School of the Chinese Academy of Sciences, Beijing, China
Tian1.wang@163.com, y.xue@londonmet.ac.uk

Abstract. Grid Geospatial Information Service (Grid GIS) system aims to study and develop grid-based uniform spatial information access and analysis system. Data resources of Grid GIS include not only original and traditional GIS data but remotely sensed data. Everyday, space missions involve the download, from space to ground, of huge amount of raw images that are stored in the ground stations geographically distributed. It is a practical pressing task to process these data resource in real time or almost real time and to effectively share spatial information among remote sensing community. Grid technology can provide access to a global distributed computing environment via authentication, authorization, negotiation and security tools. This paper discusses the key technologies of Grid-based special remotely sensed data processing node. First, the concept of Grid-based special remotely sensed data processing node is introduced. Following is the architecture and functions of this node. Based on this architecture, the tasks scheduling algorithm is presented. Finally we introduce the computing resource meta-module information registry and renewal mechanism of the Grid-based special remotely sensed data processing node for Grid GIS.

1 Introduction

Every day, dozens of satellites collect huge amount of images of the Earth, which are stored in ground stations geographically distributed. Remote Sensing data is characterized by largeness and instantaneousness. Naturally, it emerges three obvious problems for remote sensing community: (1) Remotely sensed data is very significant in some cases, such as fire and flood monitoring. So far real time processing in remote sensing confronts many difficulties in one single computer, or even impossibility.

---

* Corresponding author.

G. Min et al. (Eds.): ISPA 2006 Ws, LNCS 4331, pp. 610–617, 2006.

(2) Large amount of remotely sensed data processing module or algorithms, which are already exit, are the valuable resources in the Internet. They cannot be effectively used by the entire community but quietly stay in the disks of a few remote sensing specialists. Iterance of writing common remote sensing algorithms such as pre-processing algorithms "geometric correction" again and again will waste much time. (3) Large scale of remotely sensing sensed data geographically distributed need to be managed effectively.

Grid computing technology enables the virtualization of distributed computing and data resources such as processing, network bandwidth and storage capacity to create a single system image, granting users and applications seamless access to vast IT capabilities (http://cs.nju.edu.cn/people/yangxc/grid-computing.htm).

The Grid, itself, was born at a workshop at Argonne National Laboratory in September 1997, called "building a computational Grid", which was followed in 1998 by the publication of "The Grid: Blueprint for a New Computing Infrastructure" by Ian Foster of Argonne National Laboratory and Carl Kesselman of the University of Southern California (Foster and Kesselman 1998). "Grid" is used to refer to "a software system that provides uniform and location independent access to geographically and organizationally dispersed, heterogeneous resources that are persistent and supported" (Johnston et al. 2004). It has emerged as an important new field, distinguished from conventional distributed computing by its focus on large-scale resource sharing, innovative applications, and, in some cases, high-performance orientation (Foster et al. 2001). Foster et al. (2001) defined "Grid problem" as flexible, secure, coordinated resource sharing among dynamic collections of individuals, institutions, and resources –what they referred to as virtual organizations (VOs).

Today there are several Grid projects in remotely sensed information service. Aloisio *et al.* (2001) described how to provide comfortable, intuitive, yet powerful Web access to supercomputing. A Web-based, Grid-enabled application that processes, analyses, and delivers remote-sensing images provides an example of the technology at work. New image processing algorithms, which is distributed computing approach (Petrie *et al.* 2003), for remote sensed images are now being considered by Pacific Northwest National Laboratory. Aloisio *et al.* (2000) presented and discussed an architecture that allows transparent access to remote supercomputing facilities from a web gateway. The implementation exploits the Globus toolkit and provides users with fast, secure and reliable access to parallel applications. They showed the usefulness of their approach in the context of Digital Puglia, an active digital library of remote sensing digital data. Aloisio and Cafaro (2003) presented an overview of SARA/Digital Puglia (Synthetic Aperture Radar Atlas), a remote sensing environment that showed how Grid technologies and high performance computing can be efficiently used to build dynamic earth observation systems for the management of huge quantities of data coming from space missions and for their on-demand processing and delivering to final users. SARA/Digital Puglia is a Grid-enabled, high performance digital library of remote sensing images, developed in a joint research project with CACR/Caltech, ISI/USC and the Italian Space Agency. Grid-based Special Remotely Sensed Data Processing Node being built by Institute of Remote Sensing Applications, Chinese Academy of Science provides uniform super virtual computing power and share complex data processing module and algorithms in order to let users conveniently get all the remotely sensed information service as well as do shopping.

In this paper, we will discuss the key technologies of Grid-based special remotely sensed data processing node. First, the concept of Grid-based special remotely sensed data processing node is introduced. Following is the architecture and functions of this node. Based on this architecture, the tasks scheduling algorithm is presented. Finally we introduce the computing resource meta-data information registry and renewal mechanism of the Grid-based special remotely sensed data processing node for Spatial Information Grid (SIG).

2 Architecture of Grid-Based Special Remotely Sensed Data Processing Node

Remotely sensed data is one of the important spatial information resources. So, the study on spatial information Grid must involve the content of Grid-based remotely sensed data processing node.

2.1 Conception of Grid-Based Special Remotely Sensed Data Processing Node

The conception of Grid-based special remotely sensed data processing node has two meanings from different point of views.

- Physical perspective:
  From the perspective of Grid topological structure, Grid-based special remotely sensed data processing node is the physical resource entity that constitutes the spatial information Grid environment. The hardware includes PCs and/or high performance computers and the network infrastructure. The software is composed of software resources for remotely sensed data processing and middleware resources.
- Logical perspective:
  The logical meaning of the node is similar to VOs. It can help to search and process remotely sensed data across locations and organizations. The whole process of the node involves the management and sharing of virtual resources across different locations and heterogeneous environments. With integration of the above virtual resources, the node has the ability of remotely sensed data processing. And what's more, it can provide an integrated virtual resource for spatial information Grid.

2.2 Architecture of Grid-Based Special Remotely Sensed Data Processing Node

As one of the nodes of Spatial Information Grid (SIG), the Grid-based remotely sensed data processing node can not only manage all the resources and tasks of SIG, but also provide the computing resource for spatial information Grid. To accomplish above purposes, we present the architecture of the Grid-based special remotely sensed data processing node. Figure1 shows the architecture of the node.

There are computing resource, resource monitor, global scheduler, job queue database, remote sensing algorithms and models database, RFT server, meta-modules registering server and a serial of services in the architecture. The services include remote algorithm accepting service, resource monitoring service and so on. Meta-module service let users know about the knowledge of the remote sensing data processing algorithms of the node. More detail descriptions will be given in Section 4. In the Grid-based remotely sensed data processing node, RFT (Reliable File Transfer) service is responsible for the large amount of data transferring between the data server, node and users. The service can get data from remotely sensed data servers of spatial information Grid and provide the results for users. The node can provide processing algorithm resources. Also user can send their algorithms to the node to be executed when the algorithms provided by the node cannot accomplish user's purpose. Remote algorithm accepting service can help do this work. Resource monitoring service monitors all the computing resource of the node. The service collects status information of the computing resources and sends it to global task scheduler. The status information, which consists of the static and dynamic information, is useful for task scheduling. The global scheduler is responsible for manage all the tasks of the node. It is a vital component of the node. The tasks submitted to the node are immediately sent to job queue database. The tasks are recognized as records in database. When the task is finished, the record of the task will be deleted. There are two types of temporary files within the node, namely data temporary files and algorithm temporary files. The data received from data server of spatial information Grid is saved as data temporary files, which will be deleted after being processed. The codes accepted by remote algorithm accepting service is saved as temporary files, too. When users submit tasks, some other information, such as the estimated time and the path of data, are submitted at the same time. Tasks accepting service accepts the service request and the additional information. Figure 2 shows one example of tasks accepting service. The accepting service accepts the information and save it as the records of the tasks queue database.

3   Node Management and Tasks Scheduling

The resources of the node and submitted tasks should be managed well to maximize efficient of the node. Here we emphasize the tasks managing and scheduling.

The submitted tasks and additional information are accepted and saved in the tasks queue database by the tasks accepting service. There are two kinds of tables in the tasks queue database. The tasks are stored in the task description table and the additional information such as path of data is stored in the data description table. Each record in the data description table has a unique ID number, which is the same as the ID number of the corresponding tasks record in the task description table. The ID number is the primary key of the tables in the tasks queue database.

The task scheduler, which schedules the inner tasks of the node, accept the tasks, process the tasks, accept the data, send the results and manage the computing resource. Tasks scheduling is important for the node. The submitted tasks are stored in the tasks queue database. Then one of them will be picked out to execute based on some rules. The rules adopted by the node are described below. First the submitted tasks are grouped by the remote sensing algorithm, which it uses. One group is set up for one algorithm. Then we pick up one task of each group to be executed. For each group, all the priority ratio of tasks in the group will be calculated. Then the tasks with the minimal priority ratio will be picked out. All the selected tasks will be executed in order.

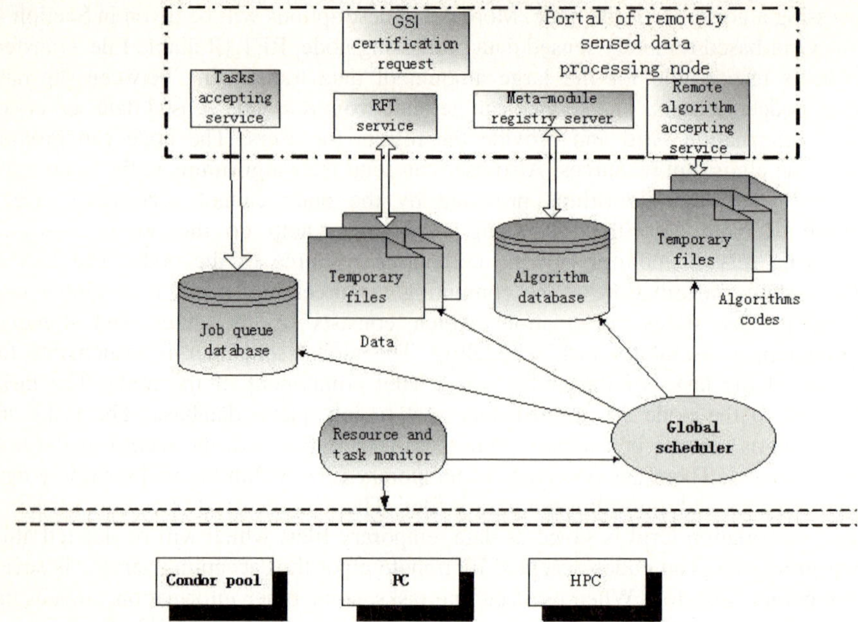

Fig. 1. Architecture of Grid-based Special Remotely Sensed Data Processing Node

4   Grid-Based Remote Sensing Meta-module Services

Grid technology is a very effective method for remotely sensed data processing service. Through it the existing remotely sensed data processing modules and algorithms resource can be shared seamlessly as a common service in Grid environment. It much more enhances the resource utility rate. In order to publish, describe, and manage Grid service data, the paper puts forward a Grid-based remotely sensed meta-module conception and corresponding structure. Combing the rule of this conception and OGSI technology, we define the Grid-based remotely sensed meta-module service data and Service Data Description language schema. Through remotely sensed Service Data Provider, the remote sensing service can be registered in the Registry Container of the special remotely sensed data processing Grid node. Users can also search and choose the proper services by demand line or Grid browser. After that, users can send a service request to Grid computing node according to the service data description.

4.1   Concept of Grid-Based Remote Sensing Meta-module

The Service Data Element (SDE) model provides standard mechanisms for querying, updating and adding and removing data associated with each Grid service instance.

```
                          Parameter
ReceivingService       Definition:
                          anyURL: InputDataPath;    float: Threshold value;

                          duration: Runtime;    String: ArithmeticName    ...
                       Handle
                       Definition:
                          ReceiveDataInfo(anyURL InputDataPath, String dataType, DataSize)
                              {   ...      }
                          ReceiveThreshold(float Threshold value)
                              {   ...     }

                          ReceiveRuntime(duration  Runtime)
                              {   ...     }

                          ReceiveModelDescription(String ArithmeticName)
                              {   ...     }

                          Other handle(otherparameterType otherparameter)
                            Local
                       Operation:

                          Oper1(Put the tasks into tasks queue database)
                          Oper2( Put the path of remotely sensed data into xml files )
                          Opern( Other operations )

                       } // ReceivingService
```

Fig. 2. Example of tasks accepting service

We defined the concept of Grid-based remote sensing meta-module as follows: *The metadata that describe serials of remotely sensed data processing modules and algorithms in order to publish and manage these resources in Grid environment.* The description of Grid-based remote sensing meta-module must include function representations of algorithms,p input and output descriptions, control parameter descriptions, etc. As Grid-based remote sensing meta-module, it must match these conditions:

- They must be described as the form of the Service Data Element (SDE) of Grid Service.
- Expression schema must match with the rule of the Grid Web Service Description Language (GWSDL)
- They can clearly describe the name, function, input and output parameter of the remotely sensed data processing module.
- The provided meta-module can be registered and updated in Grid environment.

Remotely Sensed meta-module SDD XML Schema is made up of six parts: domain name, version copyright, module information, module algorithm and running time, input information, output information.

4.2 Grid-Based Remotely Sensed Meta-module Service Registry

Combing Globus Open Grid Service Infrastructure (OGSI) rules and remotely sensed meta-module above, we provide the remotely sensed Grid service registry method.

Serials of remotely sensed data processing module service data, such as NDVI service, aerosol computing service, image classification service, etc., are registered in the registry container of the special remotely sensed data processing Grid node. For users, they can search the proper services from the service data through special portal made up of remote sensing service sets. There are two ways to find service through Grid service, one is based on demand line, and the other is Grid browser.

4.3   Grid-Based Remotely Sensed Meta-module Service Update

With the changes of remote sensing algorithms, the related meta-module information should be updated automatically. The registry container can accept the service update notifications and take actions including accepting the module update notification, deleting the old meta-module information and again registering of meta-module information.

The mechanism of update notification is push notification. Registry container subscribes to the notification of remote sensing meta-module update. If there is any information of module updating, the remote sensing SDE will send notification to the registry container.

Renewal information of meta-module will be registered at Registry Container in registry. Registry container can delete the old remotely sensed meta-module information and act as the observer.

Notification service instance of remotely sensed meta-module will be created by service factory. Registry container can get the notification information through describe service update information when the module renewing.

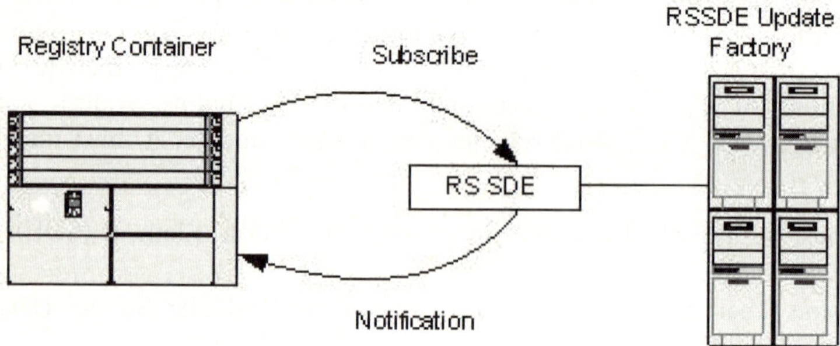

Fig. 3. Meta-module update based on Grid platform

5   Conclusions

Grid GIS is an infrastructure for spatial information collection and sharing by integrated management and processing in order to provide services as needed. SIG provides a basic technical architecture for integrated spatial data acquisition, data processing and applications as well as an intelligent spatial data processing platform and basic environment. Grid GIS aims to quickly process and analyse large amount of spatial data (from Terabyte to Petabyte) in near real time. Grid-based Special Remotely Sensed Data Processing Node is the important part of the Grid GIS. The node can provide RFT service, tasks accepting service, meta-module registry service and renewal service. Task schedule mechanism provides effective scheduler algorithm. Remotely sensed meta-module register by Service Data of OGSA and update by Notification mechanism.

Acknowledgement

This publication is an output from the research projects "Grid platform based aerosol fast monitoring modeling using MODIS data and middlewares development" (40471091) funded by National Natural Science Foundation of China (NSFC), China, "Dynamic Monitoring of Beijing Olympic Environment Using Remote Sensing" (2002BA904B07-2) and "863 Program - Remote Sensing Information Processing and Service Node" (2003AA11135110) funded by the MOST, China, "Digital Earth" (KZCX2-312) funded by Chinese Academy of Sciences, China, and "Research Fund for Talent Program" funded by China Agricultural University.

References

Aloisio, G., Cafaro, M., Kesselman, C., and Williams, R., 2001, Web access to supercomputing. Computing In Science & Engineering, Vol 3, Iss 6, pp 66-72.

Aloisio, G., Cafaro, M., Falabella, P., Kesselman, C., and Williams, R., 2000, Grid computing on the web using the globus toolkit. Lecture Notes In Computer Science, Vol 1823, pp 32-40.

Foster, I. and Kesselman, C. (eds.). The Grid: Blueprint for a New Computing Infrastructure. Morgan Kaufmann, 1999.

Foster, I. C. Kesselman, S. Tuecke The Anatomy of the Grid, Intl J. Supercomputer Applications, 2001.

Johnston, W. E., Gannon, D., Nitzbcrg, B., Tanner, L. A., Thigpen, B., and Woo, A., 2004, Computing and Data Grids for Science and Engineering, (URL: http://www.sc2000.org/techpapr/papers/pap.pap253.pdf).

Petrie, G. M., Dippold, C., Fann, G., Jones, D., Jurrus, E., Moon, B., and Perrine, K., 2003, Distributed Computing Approach for Remote Sensing Data. In Proceedings of the International Parallel and Distributed Processing Symposium (IPDPS 2003) held in Nice, France, on 22-26 April 2003, pp.

Xue Y., Wang. J, et al. Preliminary study of Grid computing for remotely sense information. International Journal of Remote Sensing, v 26, n 16, Aug 20, 2005, p 3613-3630.

Versioning and Consistency in Replica Systems

Hartmut Kaiser[1], Kathrin Kirsch[2], and Andre Merzky[3]

[1] Center for Computation & Technology, Louisiana State University
[2] Max Planck Institute for Psycholinguistics, Nijmegen
[3] Vrije Universiteit, Amsterdam

Abstract. Grid Replica systems are gaining foothold in real end user systems, and are used in an increasing number of large scale projects. As such, many of the properties of these systems are well understood.

This paper how to handle some minor shortcomings of todays data replica systems, in respect to consistency management, and to their ability to handle derived data sets. We think that both features will allow replica systems to gain wider acceptance in the GIS community.

1   Introduction

Distributed replica systems add real value to large data centric projects: an inspection of success stories like GriPhyN [1], LIGO [2,3] and the CERN Data Grid [4] show the central role replica systems play in their overall architecture. It is interesting that the number of *basic* concepts found in these replica system is small compared to the overall number of concepts provided by modern systems such as SRB [5,6]. Here, basic concepts are those provided by all replica systems and minimally *required* by all data management use cases [7,8].

- hierarchical logical name space with attributes (meta data)
- attribute access and manipulation
- data access and manipulation
- distributed architecture
- latency management
- back end system support

That list is, for example, completely implemented by the Globus Replica Location Service RLS [9,10], the CERN Replica Management System Reptor [11,12], the Storage Resource Broker SRB [5,6], and others. Successful deployment of these systems dominate todays landscape of data grids [1,2,3,4,13,14].

There exists, however, a set of use cases which, with the above set of properties, fail to be implementable, at least for large scale projects where scalability and maintainability are of increasing concern. We present 2 of these use cases in the next section, review the properties of existing replica systems in respect to these use cases in Sect. 3, and describe required additional properties in Sect. 4. We will propose a simple implementation on top of existing replica system in Sect. 5.

G. Min et al. (Eds.): ISPA 2006 Ws, LNCS 4331, pp. 618–627, 2006.

2   Discussion of Replica System Use Cases

2.1   Linguistic Scenario

The linguistic field of language acquisition is, although not commonly known, very data intensive and depends heavily on language corpora: for the linguistic analysis, human speech has to be recorded, transcribed and prepared as input for analysis tools. These steps are supported by Language Resource Archives (LRA), which also play a crucial role in development and testing of linguistic models, but also in language documentation and preservation [15,16].

The resource intensity of data collection and preparation, especially in longitudinal language acquisition studies, encourages *data sharing* in the linguistic community. This however results in branching of the original corpus and a redundancy of corpus work, as the technical infrastructure of existing LRA supports only one main version (usually the one of the corpus owner), in a specific format and layout (determined by the used LRA). The following use case (also shown in fig. 1) describes requirements for *data sharing* in a language acquisition scenario, but translates easily to other fields such as language documentation and preservation, which have similar needs for collaborative data management[1].

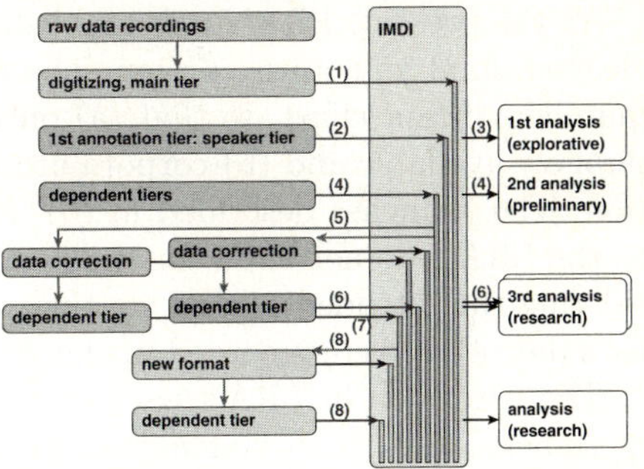

Fig. 1. The life cycle of linguistic data collection (simplified) can span years and is a large scale collaborative effort

(1) The recording of a longitudinal language corpus takes several months or years, depending on the design of the linguistic study. Video and audio tapes are digitized, in accordance with the format requirements of the used LRA, and form the first version of the main tier of the new corpus in that LRA.

(2) The first annotation, a transcription of the audio tier, is added, again conforming to the LRA standards.

(3) A first preliminary and exploratory data analysis is performed, allowing for planning of promising research topics, and motivating the addition of further, research-specific annotation tiers.

(4) New dependent tiers are added to the corpus (usually morpho-syntactic tiers), and allow a first detailed research analysis.

(5) Different research groups obtain limited access to the data. Data are not prepared for publication at this stage, so data sharing occurs in controlled conditions: read and write access control is required for all tiers.

---

[1] All steps described in this use case are very time intensive and expensive, as there are no automatic or semi-automatic ways to transcribe spoken child language.

(6) New tiers are added which allow for a final analysis of the data, in respect to the various research questions motivated by the preliminary analyzes in (3), (4) and (5). This causes a split of the corpus, as changes and additions on the main tier or on dependent tiers are caused by different research objectives.

(7) A public version of the corpus is prepared by several groups which obtained access in (5). That public version allows a variety of research groups to use the corpus and associated tiers for their work.

(8) Various tiers get subsequently added to the corpus by the public, and existing tiers continue to be changed by various groups, in various formats, increasing thereby the diversity, quality and usability of the published corpus.

At the present, LRA's only publish corpora as described in (7), as a single, cleaned, final and static version. The requirements vary with the LRA, but require significant effort, so that (a) only a small percentage of the data is made publicly available and (b) corpora are usually published years after their collection. The branches described in (5), (6) and (8) are not available for research as the LRA's do not allow for the coexistence of different corpus versions. Considering the intended corpus life time and usage (the linguistic community still uses data that were recorded in the 70s) this is an unfortunate situation.

The extension of LRA's with collaborative features will lower the entry requirements for smaller language collection projects, and would help to open their widely dispersed data collections to the community. It also would allow them to use the collaborative features of LRA's very early in the corpus lifetime.

2.2   Data Management in Geographic Information Systems

GIS draw their input data from a large variety of resources [17,18], which also implies a large variety of ownerships and copyrights [19]. Further, the transformation of these data, as required by any typical GIS system [20], imply the creation and maintenance of derived data sets, which, in our opinion, leads to similar collaborative requirements as the described linguistic use case.

The use case presented here is based on a scenario from the SCOOP hurricane forecasting project [21] (SCOOP: SURA Coastal Ocean Observing and Prediction). The Scoop-GIS has the goal to provide automated regular forecasts for gulf area hurricane tracks and storm surges. It models a data driven workflow using a central data archive as data repository for incoming, intermediate and resulting data sets. Although it is an realistic use case, it is not planned to implement it anytime soon: the SCOOP community is too small to be concerned about scalability. In particular, contrary to the scenario below SCOOP does not perform data replication and does not use collections.

(1) The National Hurricane Center in Miami, Florida (NHC), part of the National Oceanic and Atmospheric Administration (NOAA) provides the main input data for any hurricane forecast process. If a hurricane forms, the NHC provides track information for its 'center of pressure' in a 6 hour rhythm.

(2) NHC starts the execution of the workflow by placing the track data into the archive. That triggers the University of Florida (UF) which derives 4

additional tracks from the original NHC track by rotating that about ± 5 and ± 10 degree. The UF also calculates wind fields for all 5 tracks, and adds the wind fields to the archive. Meta data annotations are used to maintain dependency information between the various data sets.

(3) The placement of the wind fields triggers large simulation codes for various aspects of the cyclone system, for each wind field: Wave Watch 3 (WW3) simulations predict ocean wave amplitudes; ADvanced CIRCulation models (ADCIRC) predict storm surges in coastal regions, etc.

(4) The long running codes from (3) predict up to 72 hours of the cyclones development. Simulations snapshots are taken after 6 hours and are used as more realistic boundary conditions for the next run of the workflow. The simulation models hence need a couple of iterations to stabilize.

(5) Additional wind fields are sometimes provided by 3rd parties, e.g. by the Naval Research Laboratory of the US Navy (NRLMRY) or by the National Center for Environmental Prediction (NCEP). These wind fields start again predictive WW3 and ADCIRC simulations, but are, due to their singular inputs, not subject to the iterative boundary adjustment described in (4).

(6) The prediction outputs are stored in the data archive, and are used by SCOOP members and 3rd parties for automated or interactive visualizations, combining both static data sources (e.g. topological data), the original track data, and the predicted cyclone behavior over the next 72 hours.

(7) Both the 72 hour forecasts and the intermediate forecast results (such as the 6-hour snapshots) can be used to spawn off regional forecasts, leading to downscaled versions of step (3), (4) and (6).

2.3 Basic Operations in the Use Cases

The basic operations required in the presented GIS scenario are similar to those required by the linguistic scenario: derived data sets play a central role, and versioning, consistency, and access policies need to be addressed, by maintaining the scalability of the overall system.

Versioning and Consistency: A change to a data set creates a derived data set. Similar as in Concurrent Version Systems (as CVS or Subversion), such changes may get merged into the original data set, or create a *branch*, leaving the original data intact. Step (5) of the linguistic use case is a good example of that process. In the GIS scenario, the original hurricane track received by the NHC is used to create four derived tracks, which create new data sets (branches).

Ownership and Permissions: The owner of a data set decides who can read and/or write the data. If data are read-only, a private copy can still be created and changed. That process, however, must not pollute the original ownership and permissions. For example, the original hurricane track is owned by NHC. The UFL copies that track, and re-added four additional versions to the archive: these should have the same or less access permissions as the initial NHC track. In the linguistic use case, dependent tiers should share the same permissions as the tiers they depend upon, and should hence inherit these permissions.

3   Consistency and Scalability in Data Grids

The basic functionality of replica systems is simple: a replica catalog maintains a mapping between logical names (entities) and a set of distributed identical physical files (replicas). Often, entities are annotated with meta data.

In order to be scalable and performant in distributed environments, replica systems deploy a variety of latency hiding, data caching and other optimization techniques, which can make the implementation of a replica system non-trivial. The basic feature set described above is, however, easy to implement, and is representative for the majority of replica systems.

3.1   Consistency Considerations

The basic operations listed above have subtle implications for data consistency of replicas, but also for the consistency of the name space of the replica catalog. For example, as two remote users change two replicas of the same entry at the same time, the replicas will cease to be identical. Similarly, operations in the logical file hierarchy can result in inconsistencies.

The problem is somewhat simplified by the fact that name space and meta data are often held in a central (though often replicated) data bases [22]. Hence, consistency can be provided by insuring consistency of that data base, which is in itself a well understood and solved problem. Also, the replication of these data bases over a small and rather static set of services is well implementable [23,10].

Operations on the logical namespace are usually small and, in fact, often atomic. The same does not hold for operations on the replicas: the access patterns to the physical files are difficult to predict, and consist of potentially large numbers of small operations. The provision of consistency for the replicas therefore constitutes a significantly more difficult problem – see [22] for discussion.

3.2   Scalability Properties

Scalability issues of replica systems in respect to replica location management, selection, provisioning and transport are basically solved [10,9,12]. Data consistency, however, is expensive and impacts the scalability of these systems [22]. Todays grid replica system thus rarely provide consistency guarantees, and are often targeting on Write-Once-Read-Many use cases [10].

Scalability of ownership and permission enforcement are often provided by external systems, such as GAS [24] and GridShib [25]. These are known to scale well for large environments, allowing replica systems to profit from their scalability. It must be noted that the user level *management* of ownerships and permissions can be tedious. Domain specific interfaces are often required for that task [26]. We think that the scalability of ownership *management* breaks the shown use cases: the creation of derived data sets would require the intervention of the owner of the *original* data set, to approve or decline the derivations dependent on the data access policy intended for the *new* data set.

4 Data Versioning in Replica Systems

4.1 Consistency and Versioning

As discussed in the last section, consistency is usually considered to be a property of an instance of an entity which is under the management of the system: that entity is consistent if all its replicas are identical; it becomes inconsistent if one replica gets changed; and can become consistent again as these changes get propagated to all other replicas [22].

We want the reader to take the perspective of the end users: consistency then often means that any operation performed on any replica of an entry is reflected by any subsequent operation on any (same or other) replica of that entry.

For example, data written to a particular replica should be retrievable by a subsequent read operation on that entry. The entry would be inconsistent if that read operation would not return the new data, because it happened to get performed on a replica which is not yet in sync with the changed replica instance.

Now, from that perspective it would actually be simple to achieve consistency with the following scheme:

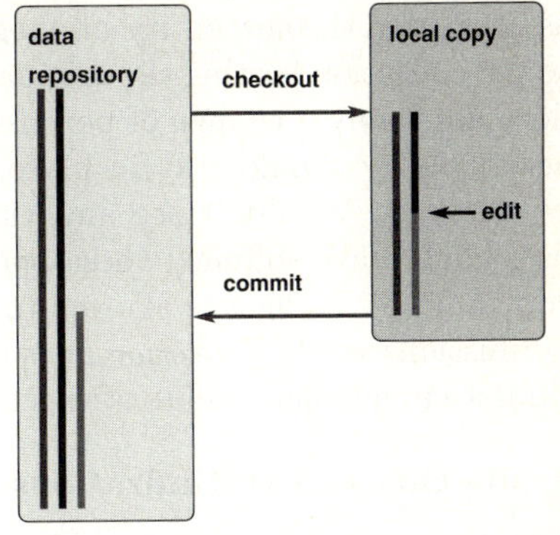

Fig. 2. Proposal: Changing a replicas results in a new version of its entity

1. A replica systems entry **A** is tagged to have an initial version id **A-1**, and has 2 replicas **A-1a** and **A-1b**.
2. A end user intends to perform a write operation on **A**. On `open()`, the replica system performs a `copy()` of any replica to **A-2a**, which is not yet published in the replica catalog. The user edits that replica.
3. On completion of the edit, the replica **A-2a** is published as *new entry*, which
   - is a new version of **A**, named **A-2**
   - has only one replica (that is **A-2a**)
4. **A-2** gets lazily replicated for availability etc., and slowly spreads in the system (**A-2b**).
5. Any subsequent read operation on **A** is automatically rerouted to the *newest* version **A-2**.

With the above schema, **A** never gets into an inconsistent state. The scheme does introduce, however, the possibility conflicts when multiple users edit **A** at the same time. We will discuss that point below, and propose a solution.

The schema involves only operations which are very well supported by todays replica systems, and are known to perform well, and to be scalable:

- replica selection based on meta data (version)
- replication (local copy, spreading of new entry)

- change meta data
- publish new entry

The reader might feel familiar with the described scheme – in fact it is the very scheme which is used by concurrent versions systems such subversion [27]: changes are performed on local copies of an entity, which is then synchronized with the central repository and with other, distributed copies. Changes *always* result in a completely new version of the entity – only performance optimizations lead to the more efficient exchange of differential updates.

The user causing the creation of a new version is the *owner* of that new version, as he created the new entity, and registered it to the system. For that, write access to the collection hosting the original entity is required. That change in ownership does not imply a change of permissions to other users – by default, the original access policy should stay in place. The new owner can however change access permissions. We don't see any violation of the security contract here, as the user could have softened these permissions by creating an unprotected private copy anyway, as he was allowed to create a copy in the first place. Further, the permissions for the *collection* does not change, so that the new access permissions cannot circumvent a more stringent access policy on that collection.

Trade-Offs and Optimizations

The approach to treat data edits implicitly as version bumps has two significant drawbacks. Firstly, the algorithm requires additional storage space as it increases the numbers of entities in the system on each edit, and all entity versions need to get replicated. Secondly, as mentioned above, it introduces conflicts when multiple users are editing replicas of the same entity.

It is tempting to shrug off the space trade-off as "insignificant in nowadays unlimited storage systems", but that would negate the communities these systems are targeting: large distributed VOs with extremely large data sets.

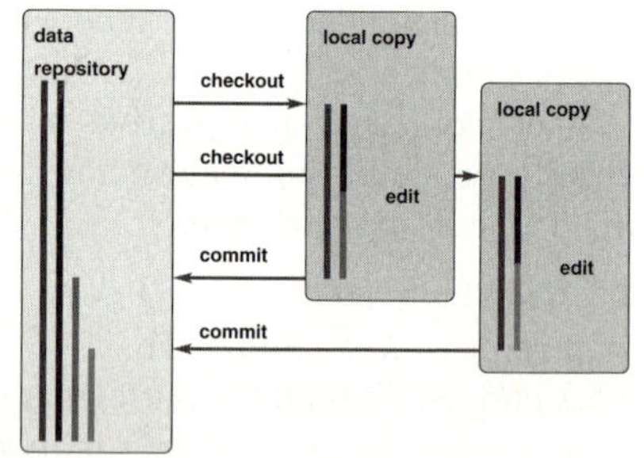

Fig. 3. Proposal: race conditions can effectively be avoided by modeling them as branching

We think, however, that (a) the algorithm as-is fits those use cases which have only a limited and comparably small number of write operations, and that (b) very simple space optimizations can be applied. Those space optimizations can, for example, weed out versions which are superseded by newer versions, have never been used, and are not explicitly tagged for keeping (e.g. for auditing).

Resolving Conflicts

Conflict could of course be resolved manually. That however seems impractical for large binary data we are considering here. The conflicts could also be resolved by treating all new replicas not only as new versions, but as *branches*.

In th linguistic use case, branching is effectively what happens in step (5): two groups change the content of a collection, incompatibly, at the same time: branching is the natural way to cope with such operations.

5   Implications for Data Grid Implementations

The previous sections motivated the introduction of two basic capabilities, versioning and branching, on top of conventional replica systems. Both operations can be build upon a very small set of basic operations:

- attach meta data to entities (version/branch information)
- update meta data consistently
- replica selection based on these meta data
- replication (local copies, spreading of new entries)
- publish new entries

As discussed in Sect. 3, these operations are all available in replica systems and perform and scale well. The most critical operation is the meta data update, as it requires consistency management for meta data – as discussed above, that is well understood and implemented in typical replica systems [10,12,22,23].

Further, the implementation of versioning and branching operations does not need to be atomic. The initial step is, in both cases, the creation of a replica which is not registered in the replica catalog – which is an supported operation. After changing that replica, it needs to be registered as new entry, i.e. with a new set of meta data – again a supported operation. The implementation of versioning and branching can hence, in our opinion, be implemented on top of existing and deployed replica systems, in user space (although an implementation as system extension would allow for more efficient space and availability optimization, as described earlier).

6   Conclusion

We propose to extend existing replica systems with scalability enhancing features: (a) automatic entity versioning on replica changes, and (b) automated branching on colliding replica changes. Combined with sticky permission and ownership policies of entity collections, this would allow for

- performant consistency on concurrent data changes
- scalable permission maintenance
- interactive collaborative usage of data
- community shared data maintenance

The only trade-off we are aware off is an increase in storage space, depending on the number of writes, which can be relieved by optimizing storage policies.

These features should allow to apply grid replica techniques to large scale GIS environments, and would allow the GIS community to benefit from the positive effects replica systems showed in other scientific and commercial environments.

We are aware that this paper is rather silent on the specific details of ownership and permission management, and their application to the described use cases. We felt that this topic was not adequately to be handled in the limited space available, and thus will present that in a future publication.

Acknowledgments

The presented ideas base on many discussions with colleagues at the Max-Planck-Institute for Psycholinguistics Nijmegen, Netherlands, at the Center for Computation and Technology at the Louisiana State University, USA, and in the Data Area of the Open Grid Forum [28].

References

1. Paul Avery and Ian Foster. The GriPhyN Project: Towards Petascale Virtual Data Grids. *The 2000 NSF Information and Technology Research Program*, 2000.
2. A. Abramovici, W.E. Althouse, R.W.P. Drever, Y. Gursel, S. Kawamura, F.J. Raab, D. Shoemaker, L. Sievers, R.E. Spero, and K.S. Thorne. LIGO-The Laser Interferometer Gravitational-Wave Observatory. *Science*, 256(5055):325–333, 1992.
3. E. Deelman, C. Kesselman, G. Mehta, L. Meshkat, L. Pearlman, K. Blackburn, P. Ehrens, A. Lazzarini, R. Williams, and S. Koranda. GriPhyN and LIGO, building a virtual data Grid for gravitational wave scientists. *High Performance Distributed Computing, 2002. HPDC-11 2002. Proceedings. 11th IEEE International Symposium on*, pages 225–234, 2002.
4. B. Segal, L. Robertson, F. Gagliardi, F. Carminati, and G. CERN. Grid computing: the European Data Grid Project. *Nuclear Science Symposium Conference Record, 2000 IEEE*, 1:2, 2000.
5. A. Rajasekar, M. Wan, R. Moore, W. Schroeder, G. Kremenek, A. Jagatheesan, C. Cowart, B. Zhu, S.Y. Chen, and R. Olschanowsky. Storage Resource Broker-Managing Distributed Data in a Grid. *Computer Society of India Journal, Special Issue on SAN*, 33(4):42–54, 2003.
6. C. Baru, R. Moore, A. Rajasekar, and M. Wan. The SDSC Storage Resource Broker. *Proceedings of the 1998 Conference of the Centre for Advanced Studies on Collaborative Research*, 1998.
7. Reagan Moore and Andre Merzky. Persistent Archive Concepts. Technical report, Global Grid Forum, December 2003. GFD.26.
8. Heinz Stockinger, Omer F. Rana, Reagan Moore, and Andre Merzky. Data Management for Grid Environments. *Lecture Notes in Computer Science*, 2110:151–160, 2001.
9. A.L. Chervenak, N. Palavalli, S. Bharathi, C. Kesselman, and R. Schwartzkopf. Performance and Scalability of a Replica Location Service. *High Performance Distributed Computing Conference (HPDC-13), Honolulu, HI, June*, 2004.
10. A. Chervenak, B. Schwartzkopf, H. Stockinger, B. Tierney, E. Deelman, I. Foster, W. Hoschek, A. Iamnitchi, C. Kesselman, and M. Ripeanu. Giggle: a Framework for Constructing Scalable Replica Location Services. *Proceedings of the 2002 ACM/IEEE conference on Supercomputing*, pages 1–17, 2002.
11. P. Kunszt, E. Laure, H. Stockinger, and K. Stockinger. Advanced Replica Management with Reptor. *5th International Conference on Parallel Processing and Applied Mathematics, Sept*, 2003.

12. L. Guy, P. Kunszt, E. Laure, H. Stockinger, and K. Stockinger. Replica Management in Data Grids. *Global Grid Forum*, 5, 2002.

13. C. Lagoze, W. Arms, S. Gan, D. Hillmann, C. Ingram, D. Krafft, R. Marisa, J. Phipps, J. Saylor, C. Terrizzi, et al. Core Services in the Architecture of the National Digital Library for Science Education (NSDL). *Arxiv preprint cs.DL/0201025*, 2002.

14. A. Solomonides, R. McClatchey, M. Odeh, M. Brady, M. Mulet-Parada, D. Schottlander, and S.R. Amendolia. MammoGrid and eDiamond: Grids Applications in Mammogram Analysis. *Proceedings of the IADIS Intl. Conference: e-Society*, pages 1032–1033, 2003.

15. Kathrin Kirsch. Working Cross-Platform: a case Study in Coding, Sharing and Analyzing Corpora. Presentation at the 27th annual meeting of the DGfS 2006 in Bielefeld: Workshop on Language Archives - Standards, Creation and Access (AG-6), February 2006.

16. D. Broeder, F. Offenga, D. Willems, and P. Wittenburg. The IMDI Metadata Set, Its Tools and Accessible Linguistic Databases. *Proceedings of the IRCS Workshop on Linguistic Databases, Philadelphia*, pages 11–13, 2001.

17. Z.R. Peng and M.H. Tsou. *Internet GIS: Distributed Geographic Information Services for the Internet and Wireless Networks*. Wiley, 2003.

18. Editor: George Percivall. OGC Reference Model (ORM). Technical report, Open Geospatial Consortium, September 2003.
`http://www.opengeospatial.org/specs/?page=orm`.

19. A. Matheus. Authorization for digital rights management in the geospatial domain. *Proceedings of the 5th ACM workshop on Digital rights management*, pages 55–64, 2005.

20. A. Vckovski and A.J. Vckowski. *Interoperable and Distributed Processing in Gis*. CRC Press, 1998.

21. Gabrielle Allen, Philip Bogden, Gerald Creager, Chirag Dekate, Carola Jesch, Hartmut Kaiser, Jon MacLaren, Will Perrie, Gregory Stone, and Xiongping Zhang. GIS and Integrated Coastal Ocean Forecasting. *Concurrency and Computation: Practice and Experience*, 00(2), 2006.

22. D. Dullmann, W. Hoschek, J. Jaen-Martinez, B. Segal, A. Samar, H. Stockinger, and K. Stockinger. Models for Replica Synchronisation and Consistency in a Data Grid. *10th IEEE Symposium on High Performance and Distributed Computing (HPDC-10)*, 2001.

23. T. Anderson, Y. Breitbart, H.F. Korth, and A. Wool. Replication, consistency, and practicality: are these mutually exclusive? *Proceedings of the 1998 ACM SIGMOD international conference on Management of data*, pages 484–495, 1998.

24. S. Cannon, S. Chan, D. Olson, C. Tull, V. Welch, and L. Pearlman. Using CAS to Manage Role-Based VO Sub-Groups. *Proceedings of Computing in High Energy Physics (CHEP'03)*, 2003.

25. T. Barton, J. Basney, T. Freeman, T. Scavo, F. Siebenlist, V. Welch, R. Ananthakrishnan, B. Baker, M. Goode, and K. Keahey. Identity Federation and Attribute-based Authorization through the Globus Toolkit, Shibboleth, GridShib, and MyProxy. *5th Annual PKI R&D Workshop, April*, 2006.

26. Open Grid Portals.
`http://www.opengridportals.org/space/Portlets/Security`.

27. B. Collins-Sussman, B.W. Fitzpatrick, and C.M. Pilato. *Version Control with Subversion*. O'Reilly, 2004.

28. Data Area of the Open Grid Forum (OGF).
`http://www.ggf.org/ggf_areas_data.htm`.

Design of GridGIS Architecture

Jianqin Wang[1], Yong Xue[2,4,*], Yuxin Jiang[1], Chenghu Zhou[3], Rongguo Chen[3],
Jianping Guo[2,5], Wei Wan[2,5], Lei Zheng[2,5], and Yi Xie[1]

[1] College of Information and Electrical Engineering, China Agricultural University,
P.O. Box 142, Beijing, 100083, China
[2] State Key Laboratory of Remote Sensing Science, Jointly Sponsored by the Institute of
Remote Sensing Applications of Chinese Academy of Sciences and Beijing Normal University,
Institute of Remote Sensing Applications, Chinese Academy of Sciences,
P.O. Box 9718, Beijing 100101, China
[3] Institute of Geographical Sciences and Natural Resources Research of Chinese Academy of
Sciences, Beijing 100101, China
[4] Department of Computing, London Metropolitan University, 166-220 Holloway Road,
London N7 8DB, UK
[5] Graduate School, Chinese Academy of Sciences, Beijing 100049, China
Tian1.wang@163.com, y.xue@londonmet.ac.uk

Abstract. Grid Geospatial Information Service (Grid GIS) system aims to study
and develop grid-based uniform spatial information access and analysis system.
Data resources of Grid GIS include not only original and traditional GIS data
but remotely sensed data. Analysis function is made up of not only single
spatial information access but complex and quick data processing. The Grid
GIS system can provide not only convenient and quick spatial information
access service but a second developing environment to satisfy all kinds of user
requirements. In this paper we mainly discuss Grid GIS system framework and
running-framework design. To clearly demonstration how to develop the Grid
GIS system, we describe service and interface criterion. Series of geospatial
information standards are also discussed to adapt system extend requirement.

1 Introduction

The term "the Grid" was coined in the mid 1990s to denote a proposed distributed
computing infrastructure for advanced science and engineering [1]. There are several
famous grid projects today. Access Grid (www.fp.mcs.anl.gov/fl/access grid) lunched
in 1999 and mainly focused on lecture and meetings-among scientists at facilities
around the world. European Data Grid sponsored by European Union, mainly in data
analysis in high-energy physics, environmental science and bioinformatics. Grid
Physics Network (GriDPhyN) [2] lunched in 2000 and sponsored by NSF mainly in
data analysis for four physics projects: two particle etectors at CERN's Large Hadron
Collider, the Laser Interferometer Gravitational Wave Observatory, and the Sloan
Digital Sky Survey. Information Power Grid [3] is the NASA's computational support
for aerospace development, planetary science and other NASA research. International
Virtual DataGrid Laboratory (iVDGL) sponsored by NSF and counterparts in Europe,

---

* Corresponding author.

G. Min et al. (Eds.): ISPA 2006 Ws, LNCS 4331, pp. 628–636, 2006.

Australia, and Japan in 2002. Network for Earthquake Engineering and Simulation labs (NEESgrid) (www.neesgrid.org) intended to integrate computing environment for 20 earthquake engineering labs. TeraGrid (www.teragrid.org) is the general-purpose infrastructure for U.S. science: will link four sites at 40 gigabits per second and compute at up to 13.6 teraflops. U.K. National Grid [5] sponsored by U.K Office of Science and Technology. Unicore (www.unicore.de) is a seamless interface to high-performance Education and Research computer centers at nine government, industry and academic labs.

EnvirGrid main goals are generalization of Earth Science application infrastructure to become GRID-aware, extend GRID access to European Environmental and Earth Science application to large science communities, to value adding and commercial communities, …, and demonstrate collaborative environment for Earth Science.

The application type of distributed geographical information system can be classified into seven types: original data downloading, static map displaying, metadata search, dynamic map browser, data pre-processor, GIS search and analysis based on Web, GIS software which can respond to net. The main aims of establishing distributed GIS are to provide distributed transaction processing, transparent operation between different system and data, also favorable interface and inter-operation, so, the geographical information can be shared furthest. Distributed geographical information system provides users with basic functions that include data operation, geographical measure and analysis, geographical decision-making support and so on.

"Grid" geographical information system [4] makes use of some geographical information servers with grid technology to construct the grid environment and implements grid scheduling, load-balance and quick geographical information service with the infrastructure provided by grid middleware.

2 Architecture Design

Providing users the framework which can marshal, share and co-process spatial information resource and GIS service distributed in different information center, we should work over software structure and running environment of distributed spatial data service system. Presently, many mature distributed inter-connection and processing technologies which have been applied into spatial information system to share the spatial information and service highly cost, be short of scalable and maintain difficultly that it can not meet the users' requirements. So, to solve the problems mentioned above, it is essential to research architecture of grid GIS software platform.

Because of the development situation of spatial information processing technology, the research of the architecture will focus on how to take advantage of grid technology and idea to organize and manage the existing spatial information resource effectively and on how to gather computing resource on the internet to quickly process spatial information. According to the analysis, a lot of the existing spatial information resource and high-performance computing resource distribute in wide area. So, the structure of the platform is important to implement spatial information sharing and co-processing. Fig.1 shows the architecture of grid GIS software platform.

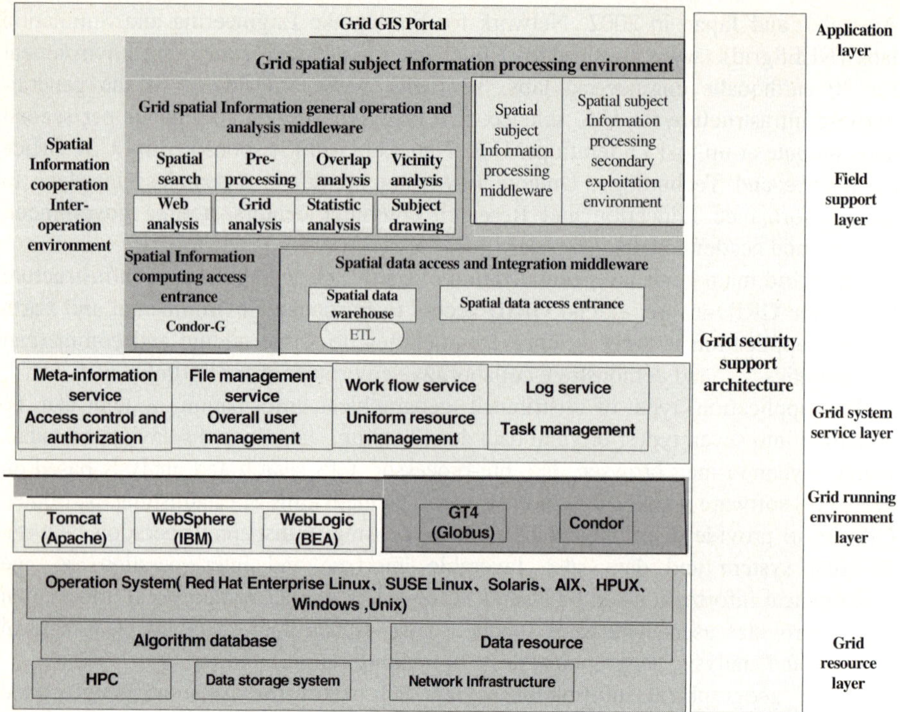

Fig. 1. Architecture of grid GIS software platform

(1) Grid resource layer

Grid GIS is a platform constructed on wide band infrastructure for spatial information processing and sharing, it involves the existing spatial data and data storage system and supports data online updating via spatial data collection equipment. It also supports general operation system, special operation system, embedded operation system. Computing resource includes existing computer clusters, distributed personal computers and homebred Shu Guang processor. Data resource includes all the spatial data which involves multi-scale basic geographical dataset, multi-origin remote sensor data, population distributing data, disease space distributing data, and agriculture space distributing data, mine energy space distributing data and so on. Some of them are structural or not. Data storage includes the existing heterogeneous and distributed database, also includes the new established information warehouse, all of which can be shared.

(2) Grid running environment layer

Grid running environment layer uses Vega GOS, GT4 (Globus toolkits 4) and Condor as rock-bottom running environment, of which Vega GOS and GT4 emphasize particularly on service developing, deployment and publication environment of information grid, and Condor would focus on computing environment of computing grid.

(3) Grid system service layer

Grid system service layer which locates on the top of grid running environment layer provides users with the basic grid system services of access control and authorization, overall user management, uniform resource management, task management, meta information service, file management service and so on.

(4) Field support layer

Field support layer consists of grid spatial data access and integration middleware which provides uniform spatial data access, grid spatial information general operation and analysis middleware and spatial subject information processing environment. Spatial subject information processing environment includes spatial subject information processing service and spatial subject information processing secondary exploitation environment which updates the software processing ability and advances its sharing degree to meet the different requirements and provide online developing environment. The spatial subject information processing software which gathers mass spatial data, information and computing nodes provides convenient spatial information processing service.

(5) Application layer

Application layer provides users grid GIS interface which includes embedded GIS, Web GIS (Web Geospatial Information Service), special GIS and desktop GIS.

3 Principle of System Deployment on Grid Computing Platform

GridGIS works under the grid architecture which isn't the same as traditional center control information system. This section provides an overview on the most common P2P topologies [5]. It discusses the general advantages and drawbacks that all P2P topologies have in common.

The A in Fig.2 denotes centralized topology which relies completely on a central server or on a set of well-known servers. There are several advantages when using a centralized topology. The structure is simple and management is easy. There are also drawbacks to it. The server overworks, and if the server fails to work, the nodes connected to it will become invalidate.

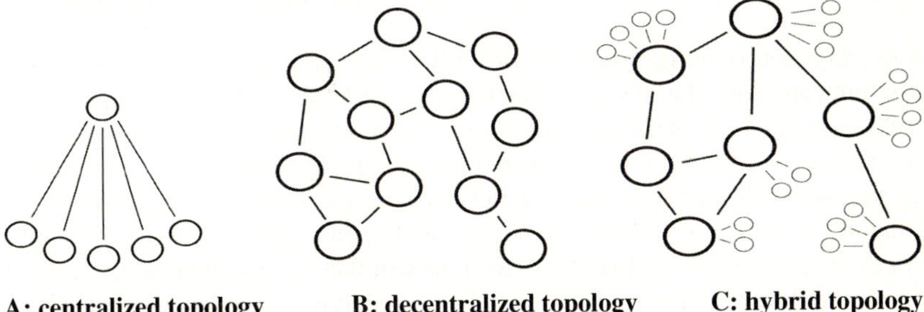

Fig. 2. Three main topologies

The B in Fig.2 denotes decentralized topology which does not depend on a central server.The advantages of it are reliable, easy to join and leave and have no single point of failure. Difficulty in management and low resource searching efficiency are considered as its drawbacks.

The C in Fig.2 denotes the Grid GIS hybrid topology which combines centralized topology with decentralized topology. It inherits some advantages from both topologies and better scalable than decentralized topology. In this paper, the hybrid topology is adopted. So, the structure of grid computing platform is described as follows:

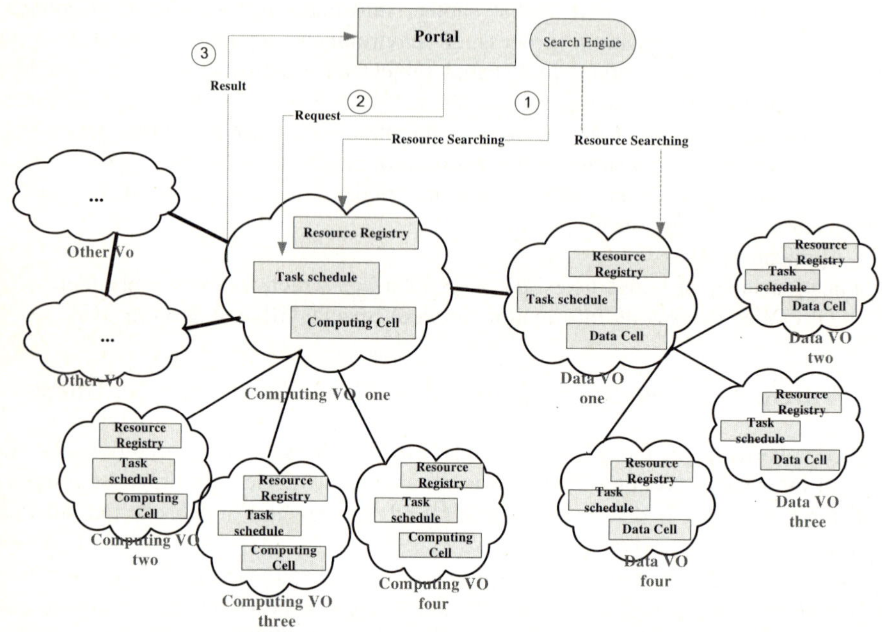

Fig. 3. Structure of Grid Computing Platform

4   Grid GIS System Management and Schedule Flow Design

Fig.4 displays the running-frame of grid GIS system. Portal gives the users interface to communicate with the system conveniently. Task scheduling management parses the tasks presented by users and hands out to corresponding nodes. Model algorithm library provides algorithm to advance processing efficiency. The whole resource search engine is to search resource which user needs from register center. The grid GIS mainly involves computing resource and data resource, user can apply for resources from the system after login. System searches for usable resources that have been registered to resource registry center after receiving the tasks presented by user, then parses the user's tasks. If the user applies for the data resources, system searches for specific resource through the resource registry center then return the data resources to user proxy. If the user applies for the computing resources, on the one hand, system must search for the data resources which computing nodes deal with, on the other hand, it should search for the usable computing nodes. Then the task

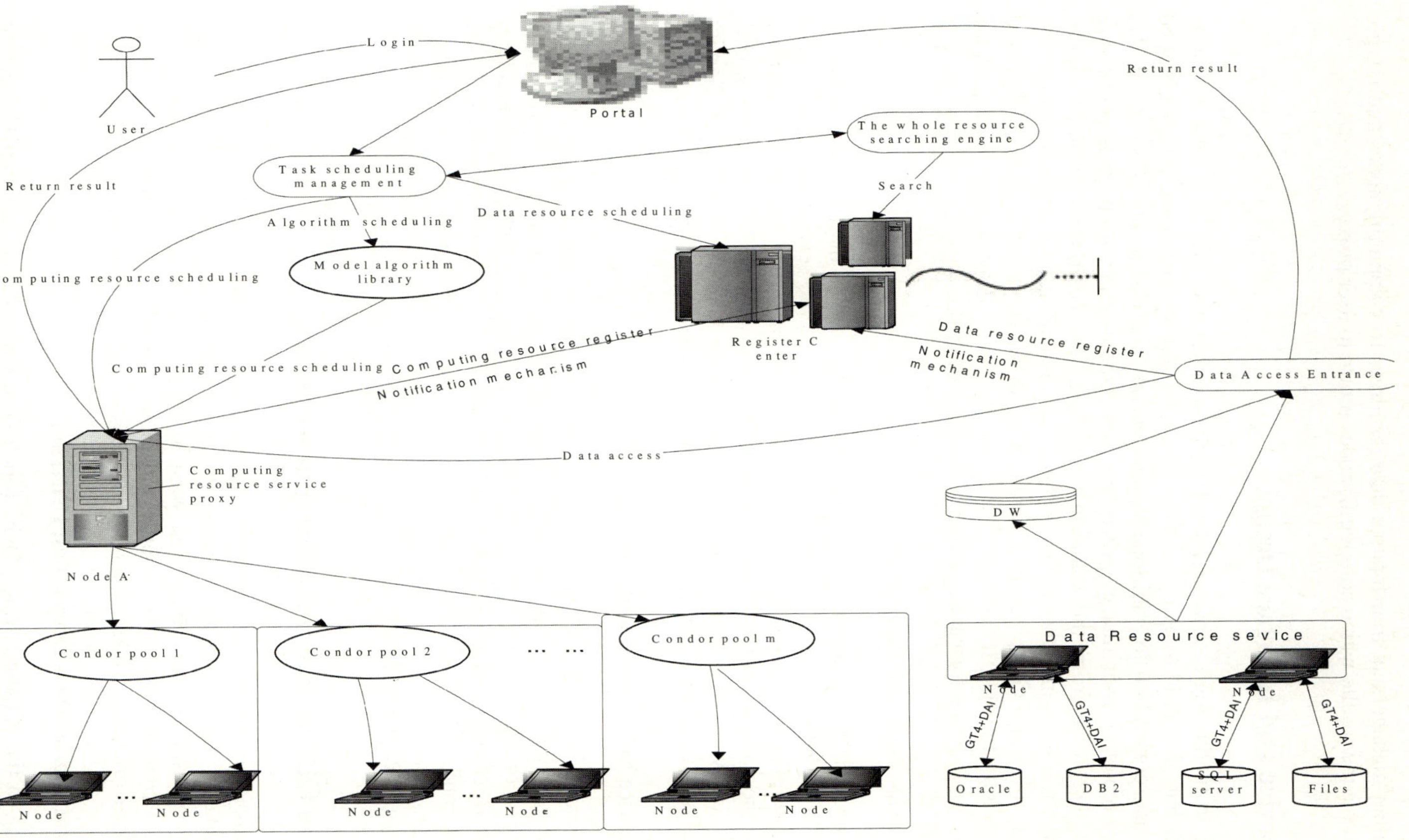

Fig. 4. Running-frame of grid GIS system

scheduling management transfers the data resources to computing nodes and merges and returns the results which computing nodes return to user proxy.

5 Service and Interface Design

Seeing from the logic structure, Grid GIS includes not only grid GIS operation system, but also field supporting layer. Seeing from the functions, besides unified access and connection to traditional heterogeneous and distributed GIS data, it also includes remote sensor images processing and remote information quick processing service. Different from the traditional software, the computing resource, model algorithm resource and other resources grid GIS involves can be shared. Seeing from the data which grid GIS processes, there are vector data and grid data. So, the system is so complicated that it must strictly define the grid GIS software development's interface and service format according to the view of grid.

5.1 Service Interface Description

The service interface definition in grid GIS service shows that what functions the service provides users with, other services which call the service have no need to know how to work the service but what functions it provides. The service interface goes by the name of PortType in Web Service. Based on the J2EE framework, Grid GIS service will adopt the format of Java class or GWSDL (Grid Web Service Description language) which adopts XML format to describe all the interfaces.

5.2 Service Deployment and Publication

All the interfaces in grid GIS system must be implemented with java program language. And the implemented interfaces must be published and deployed in term of grid syntax. The process of deployment is to take advantage of tool service which grid GIS tool layer provides to combine all the interfaces grid service needs and service codes, GWSDL document and Stub file together, then makes use of deployment descriptor to deploy. It tells the web server how to publish grid GIS service (the deployment descriptor exits in the format of WSDD (Web Service Deployment Descriptor).

6 Grid GIS System Standard and Criterion

The tremendous spatial data and information resources which Grid GIS involve are heterogeneous and distributed. It makes the sharing and access difficult. And also the computing resources are. So, if you want to manage the resources effectively and provide the users integrative spatial information access and processing service, studying an opening standard and criterion is absolutely necessarily.

6.1 Grid Spatial Data Description Criterion

Referring to the standard which OGC (open Grid Consortium) and FGDC (Federal Grid Data Consortium) established, we could work over metadata criterion which is fit for spatial data under Grid environment and establish the GGIS (Grid Geospatial Information Service) metadata standard.

6.2   Uniform Resource Description Criterion in Grid Environment

Grid GIS assembles and schedules the internet resources which include computing resource, data resource, model algorithm resource. Some of them are static resource, others are dynamic resource. So, to present the different resources with unified resource description, it is essential to establish corresponding resource description metadata criterion. it is convenient to dynamically and statically describe the different resources under Grid GIS environment with grid GIS resource description metadata criterion which is established Referring to the MDS grid resource description metadata and spatial information operation characteristic, the description is the basis of internet resources scheduling and tasks dispatching.

6.3   Spatial Information Process Inter-operation Language Criterion

Referring to the GML (Grid Markup Language) criterion to establish spatial information inter-operation criterion set which will be used in G-SML (Grid-Spatial-ML) cross-platform grid environment and will be compatible with all other spatial information processing operation descriptions, and also be fit for cross-platform operation.

6.4   Grid Spatial Data Access Interface Criterion

The data resource involved in grid GIS environment is stored in different places and the databases are heterogeneous. So it is essential to establish grid spatial data access interface criterion to access uniformly.

6.5   Grid GIS Middleware Criterion

Grid GIS is a platform which could dynamically extend spatial information sharing and quick processing and meet the different needs. The middlewares used in the supporting platform are dynamic, robust and extensible. Working over scientific grid GIS supporting middleware criterion has great meaning for platform dynamic, robust and extensible.

7   Conclusion

Grid Geospatial Information Service system aims to study and develop grid-based uniform spatial information access and analysis system. Grid computing technology can satisfy this system's complexity because of its characteristic. Grid GIS system is different from grid operation system. All kids of computing resource and data resource are managed and shared by Grid GIS system resource service proxy. Geographical distributed and heterogeneous Geospatial information data an be conveniently accessed by Globus Tookitsr4 and data access interface (DAI) [6]. Computing resource including high performance computer, workstation and personal computer are also be utilized by condor pool virtual organization to provide supercomputing power. Remotely sensed data can be processed in near real time by computing power in Grid

GIS system. In order to manage and schedule users requirements task schedule and manager is also needed. Task schedule and manager indexes information through index engine. Grid GIS system must follow the grid criterion and geospatial information standard to strength its extendedness characteristic. In this paper, we also describe the method of grid service interface and service deploy.

Acknowledgement

This publication is an output from the research projects "Aerosol fast monitoring modeling using MODIS data and middlewares development" (40471091) funded by NSFC, China, "Monitoring of Beijing Olympic Environment Using Remote Sensing" (2002BA904B07-2) and "Remote Sensing Information Processing and Service Node" funded by the MOST, China and "Research Fund for Talent Program" funded by China Agricultural University.

References

[1] Foster, I. and Kesselman, C. (eds.). The Grid: Blueprint for a New Computing Infrastructure. Morgan Kaufmann, 1999.

[2] Laura Gilbert, Jeff Tseng and Rhys Newman etc.Implications of virtualization on Grids for high energy physics applications .Journal of Parallel and Distributed Computing, Volume 66, Issue 7, July 2006, Pages 922-930 .

[3] Rudolf Eigenmann and Michael J. Voss .Towards a compilation paradigm for computational applications on the information power grid Mathematics and Computers in Simulation, Volume 54, Issues 4-5, 15 December 2000, Pages 307-320 .

[4] Zhanfeng Shen, Jiancheng Luo et al. Architecture design of grid GIS and its applications on image processing based on LAN Information Sciences 166 (2004) 1–17.

[5] D. Zeinalipour-Yazti, Vana Kalogeraki and Dimitrios Gunopulos. Exploiting locality for scalable information retrieval in peer-to-peer networks.Information Systems, Volume 30, Issue 4, June 2005, Pages 277-298

[6] M. Antonioletti, M. Atkinson, S. Laws, S. Malaika, N. Paton, D. Pearson, G. Riccardi, Web services data access and integration (WS-DAI), in: 13th Global Grid Forum, 2005.

Selection for Feature Gene Subset in Microarray Expression Profiles Based on a Hybrid Algorithm Using SVM and GA

Wei Xiong, Chen Zhang, Chunguang Zhou, and Yanchun Liang

College of Computer Science and Technology, Jilin University, Key Laboratory
of Symbol Computation and Knowledge Engineering of Ministry of Education,
Changchun 130012, China
ycliang@jlu.edu.cn

Abstract. It is an important subject to find feature genes from microarray expression profiles in the study of microarray technology. In this paper, a hybrid algorithm using SVM and GA is proposed. We first find a feature gene subset and filter most genes which are unrelated with diseases according to certain significant level, gene importance and classification efficiency by Least Square Support Vector Machine. Then we apply an improved genetic algorithm to carry out feature selection, in which the information entropy is used as a fitness function. At last, we apply the proposed feature selection algorithm to the two expression data sets of microarray, evaluate the feature gene subsets that are obtained in different conditions. Simulated results show that both good classification efficiency and the important genes which are related with diseases could be obtained by using the hybrid algorithm.

Keywords: feature selection, Support Vector Machine, genetic algorithm.

1 Introduction

The technology of microarray is a new technology with the development of life science and information technology. And the microarray is the most widely used technology in the fields of bioinformatics. The advent of microarray makes it possible to perform gene diagnosis and gene treatment.

Due to its low cost, high flux and high sensitivity, microarray is one of the important technologies for the study of functional genome, which is obviously better than the previous research model of single gene. But several challenging research tasks are largely overlooked because of the lack of an efficient analysis method.

Aiming at the above-mentioned problems, a feature selection method based on a SVM and GA hybrid algorithm is proposed to find a feature gene subset in this paper. At first, a feature gene subset is obtained and most genes which are unrelated with diseases according to certain significant level, gene importance and classification efficiency are filtered by Least Square Support Vector Machine. On the basis of it, we apply an improved genetic algorithm to carry out feature selection according to their contribution to classifying. In the proposed method, the crossover and mutation

G. Min et al. (Eds.): ISPA 2006 Ws, LNCS 4331, pp. 637–647, 2006.
© Springer-Verlag Berlin Heidelberg 2006

operators in the genetic algorithm are improved such that the feature gene number of the subset could be controlled during the process of genetic operation, and the information entropy is used as separate criterion, and then the selected feature subset is evaluated by Support Vector Machine and the method of leave-one-out. We apply the proposed feature selection algorithm to the two expression data sets of microarray, evaluate the feature gene subsets that are obtained in different conditions. Comparisons of the simulated experimental results using the hybrid algorithm with those using other algorithms show the effectiveness of the proposed algorithm.

2 Model and Steps of the Hybrid Algorithm

The process of obtaining feature gene subset is made up of five steps:

(1) Perform preprocessing for the data of microarray. Use the Standard Deviation to do the data filtering and choose the genes with higher Standard Deviation and arrange the genes in order.

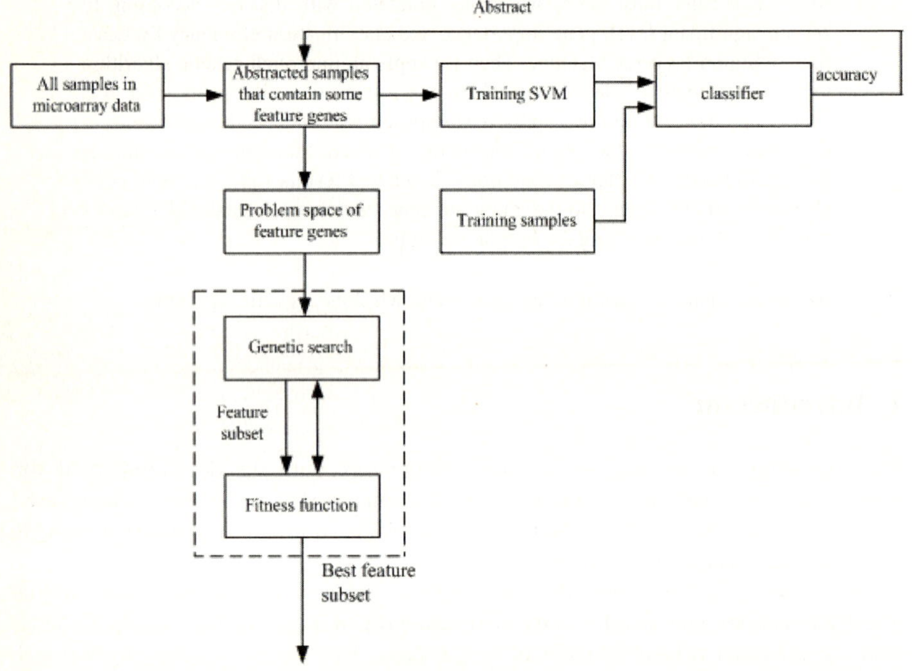

Fig. 1. Model of hybrid algorithm

(2) Use the Least Square Support Vector Machine (LSSVM) to construct a classifier. Firstly, select some samples to contain the training set and testing set, and then make selection to build up the certain quantity feature gene subset by the classified accuracy. This selecting and choosing process changes the gene number and compare the accuracy continuously.

(3) Compose the initial population with some individuals which have the feature genes selected by the LSSVM. And then make use of the improved genetic algorithm to perform genetic search. One individual is composed of some feature genes and a individual is a feature gene subset. Classify the initial training set with k-means clustering program, and then Classify the processed training set which has been taken part of genes that are not the feature genes out of the initial training set. The information entropy is used as the fitness function.

(4) Determine the individual whose fitness value is the largest one in the last generation. It is the best feature gene subset. The fitness value is the result computed by the information entropy.

(5) Evaluate the selected feature subset using SVM and the method of leave-one-out. Choose some of the samples to train and the others to test. Evaluate the result by the classified accuracy first and then observe the description and the function of the important feature gene selected. At last, compare the simulated experimental results using the hybrid algorithm with those using other algorithms, like Neural Network method.

The model of the feature gene subset selection is shown in Fig. 1.

3 Hybrid Algorithm of SVM and GA

3.1 Least Square Support Vector Machine

Support vector machine (SVM) was proposed by Vapnik and his research team based on statistical learning theory. The aim of SVM model is to construct the decision function takes the form [1, 2]:

$$f(x,w) = w^T \varphi(x) + b \tag{1}$$

where the nonlinear mapping $\varphi(\cdot)$ maps the input data into a higher dimensional feature space. In the LSSVM, the classification problem is formulated:

$$\min_{w,b,e} J(w,b,e) = \frac{1}{2} w^T w + \gamma \frac{1}{2} \sum_{k=1}^{N} e_k^2 \tag{2}$$

subject to the equality constraints

$$y_k [w^T \varphi(x_k) + b] = 1 - e_k, \quad k = 1,..., N \tag{3}$$

This corresponds to a form of ridge regression. The Lagrangian is given by

$$L(w,b,e;\alpha) = J(w,b,e) - \sum_{k=1}^{N} \alpha_k \{ y_k [w^T \varphi(x_k) + b] - 1 + e_k \} \tag{4}$$

with Lagrange multipliers α_k. The conditions for the optimality are

$$\frac{\partial L}{\partial W} = 0 \rightarrow w = \sum_{k=1}^{N} \alpha_k y_k \varphi(x_k)$$

$$\frac{\partial L}{\partial b} = 0 \rightarrow \sum_{k=1}^{N} \alpha_k y_k = 0$$

$$\frac{\partial L}{\partial e_k} = 0 \rightarrow \alpha_k = \gamma e_k, \quad k = 1,..., N$$

$$\frac{\partial L}{\partial \alpha_k} = 0 \rightarrow y_k[w^T \varphi(x_k) + b] - 1 + e_k = 0, \quad k = 1,..., N$$

$$(5)$$

for $k=1,...,N$. After elimination of e_k and ω, the solution is given by the following set of linear equations

$$\begin{bmatrix} 0 & -Y^T \\ Y & ZZ^T + \gamma^{-1}I \end{bmatrix} \begin{bmatrix} b \\ a \end{bmatrix} = \begin{bmatrix} 0 \\ \vec{1} \end{bmatrix} \qquad (6)$$

Where

$$Z = [\varphi(x_1)^T y_1,..., \varphi(x_N)^T y_N], \ y=[y_1,..., y_N], \vec{1}=[1,...,1], \alpha=[\alpha_1,...,\alpha_N]$$

and Mercer condition

$$\Omega_{kl} = y_k y_l \varphi(x_k)^T \varphi(x_l) = y_k y_l \psi(x_k, x_l) \qquad k,l = 1,..., N \qquad (7)$$

is applied. Hence, the classifier

$$f(x) = \text{sgn}(\sum_{k=1}^{N} \alpha_k^* y_k K(x \cdot x_k) + b^*) \qquad (8)$$

is found by solving the linear set of Equations (6)-(7) instead of quadratic programming. Different kernel functions construct different SVM model. In this paper, we use three kernel functions to construct three different SVM model, Linear function, Polynomial function and Rbf function.

3.2 Improved Genetic Algorithm

Compose the initial population with some individuals which only have the genes selected by the LSSVM. The genetic operation is performed on these individuals. The operators in the improved genetic algorithm are fitness proportional selection operator, the improved crossover operator, and the improved mutation operator. The fitness function is based on the information entropy.

(1) Selection operator
The selection operation is based on the fitness, in which the fitness proportional selection operator is used.
(2) Improved crossover operator
It is demanded that the number of feature genes must keep fixed during the process of the genetic operation, so an improved crossover operator is developed. In the

crossover operation, make sure that the 0 positions and the 1 positions in one individual that changed by crossover operator are in the same quantity. For either of two individuals, cross over several 0 positions in one individual and 1 positions in the other individual when the corresponding positions in the two individuals are not the same. For example, in Fig. 2:

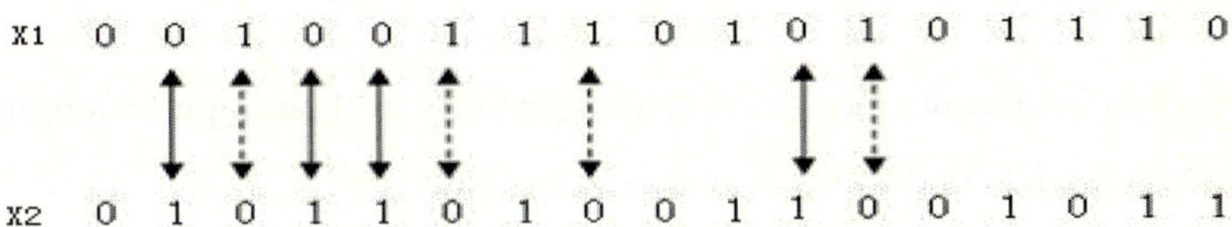

Fig. 2. The example of the improved crossover operator

(3) Improved mutation operator

For the same reason, an improved mutation operator is developed. When turning over a 1 position selected randomly in a individual, a 0 position is turned over.

(4) Fitness function

The construction of the fitness function is such an important part of genetic algorithm that it will affect the speed of convergence and the possibility of finding the best solution. In this paper, the fitness here corresponds to the separate criterion in feature extraction. The separate criterion based on the information entropy-gini impurity index is used in this paper [3].

Calculate the gini index of each category which is classified according to the current genetic individual. The fitness would be the reciprocal of the index sum. It can be written as:

$$f(G_i) = \frac{C}{\sum_{k=1}^{K} gini(\omega_k^i)} \tag{9}$$

Where C is an adjustment factor used to adjust the value of fitness, G_i represents the ith genetic individual after encoding, which is a feature gene subset. $\sum_{k=1}^{K} gini(\omega_k^i)$ is the sum of the index, in which:

$$gini(\omega_k^i) = \begin{cases} \dfrac{1}{2} H^2 \left[P(\omega_1 \mid \omega_k^i), P(\omega_2 \mid \omega_k^i),..., P(\omega_n \mid \omega_k^i) \right] & n_k^i \neq 0 \\ 1 & n_k^i = 0 \end{cases} \tag{10}$$

When n_k^i, the number of samples which belong to category k according to the individual G_i, equals to 0, the diversity of categories is supposed to be the maximum, with the value 1, otherwise, it equals to the gini index, in which :

$$H\left(P(\omega_1 \mid x), P(\omega_2 \mid x),..., P(\omega_n \mid x)\right) = -\sum_{i=1}^{n} P(\omega_i \mid x) \log P(\omega_i \mid x) \qquad (11)$$

square it under some condition, then we have

$$H^2\left(P(\omega_1 \mid x), P(\omega_2 \mid x),..., P(\omega_n \mid x)\right) = 2\left(1 - \sum_{i=1}^{n} P^2(\omega_i \mid x)\right) \qquad (12)$$

where $P(\omega_i \mid x)$ represents the conditional probability of the sample belonging to the category ω_i under the condition x, it must satisfy that:

$$\sum_{j=1}^{n} P(\omega_j \mid x) = 1 \qquad (13)$$

It represents the posterior probability that the samples which belong to the category k after reclassifying according to G_i belonged to the category j at the beginning. It satisfies apparently that:

$$\sum_{j=1}^{K} P(\omega_j \mid \omega_k^i) = 1 \qquad (14)$$

So the information entropy-gini impurity index can be suitable for evaluating the classified result of feature gene subset.

The program is terminated if the difference of the mean fitness values of two generations is smaller than a threshold value. Furthermore, a maximum number of generations is set to make sure the algorithm be terminated actually. Using the improved genetic algorithm we get the best feature gene subset.

4 Experiment

4.1 Data Acquisition and Preprocessing

Microarray data consists of p genes and n DNA samples. The data can be described using a $p \times n$ matrix $X = [x_{ij}]$ where x_{ij} represents the expression data of the ith gene g_i on the jth sample X_j. A vector can be used to represent a sample:

$$X_j = \{x_{1j}, x_{2j},..., x_{pj}\}$$

Suppose that there are p genes in the microarray. The length of genetic string would be p, and a p-featured se is denoted by a binary vector G:

$$G = \{g_1, g_2,..., g_p\}$$

Every position in the string represents whether the relative gene would be involved in the subset. For example, a five-featured set could be $G = \{g_1, g_2, g_3, g_4, g_5\}$, a string $\{1\ 1\ 0\ 1\ 0\}$ means that the subset is $G = \{g_1, g_2, g_4\}$.

Microarray expression profile has a lot of fuzzy data in it, which are no use for the classification. In order to obtain the right data for the next input used by SVM, microarray data need to be processed first. In the paper, a Standard Deviation process method is proposed to filter the expression data. The Standard Deviation is shown below:

$$S = \sqrt{\frac{1}{n}\left[(x_1 - \overline{x})^2 + (x_2 - \overline{x})^2 + ... + (x_n - \overline{x})^2\right]} \tag{15}$$

4.2 Results of Experiments and Analysis

In order to evaluate the proposed hybrid algorithm, we perform experiments on two data sets, which are published in website. One is Colon data set and another is leukemia data set.

(1) Colon data set
The colon set is from Affymetrix Company, which is an array with 62 tissue samples of 65000 oligonucleotide genes (40 tumors and 22 normal tissues). In the experiment, we use the data with 2000 human genes picked by Alon et al, the expression data come from the website [4]: http://microarray.princeton.edu/oncology/affydata/.

For obtaining the right data for the next input, the microarray data need to be preprocessed. The results are shown in Fig. 3:

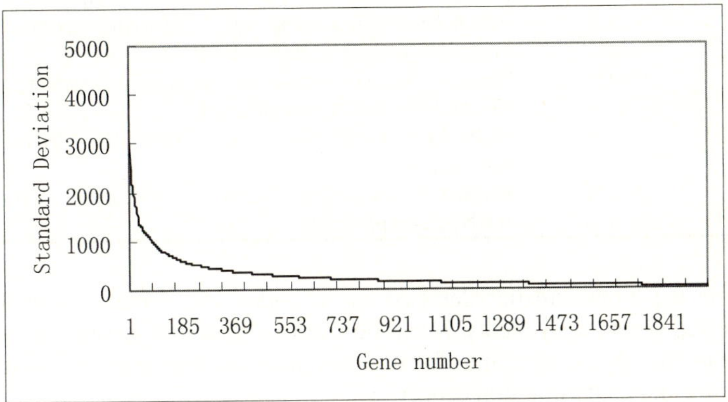

Fig. 3. Standard Deviation of 2000 genes in colon data set

Colon dataset contains two classes and it has 62 samples, among which 30 samples are for training and the remaining 32 samples are for testing. We use SVM with three kernel functions to evaluate the selected feature gene subset. The results are shown in Table 1.

The best result obtained using the hybrid algorithm is 20 genes. When the gene number is 20, the generation number is 800. The corresponding parameters in SVM need to be adjusted with gene subsets in different size. The result in this paper is also compared with the results obtained using other existing methods in references [5, 6]. The best accuracy obtained using a decision forest method combined with permutation method is 0.8767 when gene number is 39, and the best accuracy obtained using SVM method is 0.8390 when gene number is 20. The hybrid algorithm proposed with the best accuracy is 0.906 when the gene number is only 20.

Table 1. Evaluated results of subsets with different sizes

Gene Num	rbf	polynomial	linear
10	0.844	0.813	0.813
15	0.844	0.844	0.844
20	0.906	0.875	0.875
40	0.844	0.813	0.813
50	0.906	0.844	0.844

Because of the characteristics of gene selection, we not only need to get the good classification efficiency, but also obtain the important genes which are related with diseases. The results are shown in Table 2:

Table 2. Description of feature genes

Gene No.	Sequence	Gene description
U14973	Gene	Human ribosomal protein S29 mRNA, complete cds
T58861	3' UTR	60S RIBOSOMAL PROTEIN L30E (Kluyveromyces lactis)
Z22658	Gene	H.sapiens thrombin inhibitor mRNA
M26383	Gene	Human monocyte-derived neutrophil-activating protein (MONAP) mRNA, complete cds
T74896	3' UTR	SERUM AMYLOID A PROTEIN PRECURSOR (HUMAN)
R01221	3' UTR	Human transcription factor TFIIA small subunit p12 mRNA, complete cds

Search in the bioinformatics database in networks, and compare with the results obtained using other experiments, it can be confirmed that these selected genes play an important role as a central hub for the gene network that maps to the underlying pathological complexity of colon cancer [3].

(2) Leukemia data set

Leukemia data set is from Golub's paper, which is composed with 72 tissue samples of 7129 leukemia genes (25 Acute Myeloid leukemia (AML) and 47 Acute lymphoblastic leukemia (ALL)). In the experiment, we use the mcroarray expression data from the website [7]: http://www.broad.mit.edu/cancer.

In order to obtain the right data for the next input using SVM, the microarray data need to be processed first, then we can select some feature genes from all of the 7129 genes. The Standard Deviation results are shown in Fig. 4.

The data set has 72 samples, among which 38 samples are for training and the remaining 34 samples are for testing. We also use the SVM with three kernel functions to evaluate the selected feature gene subset. The results are shown in Table 3.

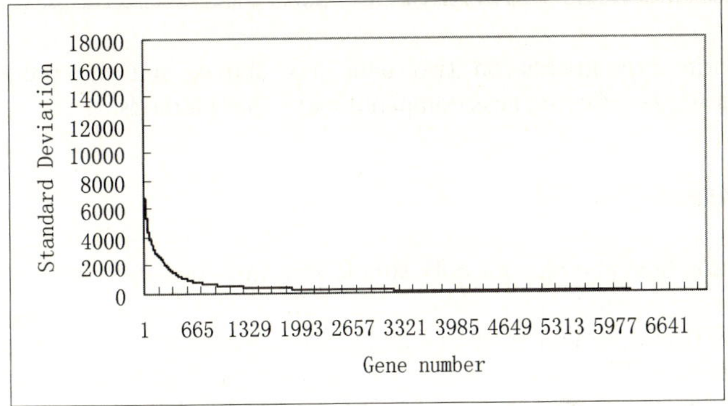

Fig. 4. Standard Deviation of 7129 genes in leukemia data set

Table 3. Evaluated results of subsets with different sizes

Gene num	rbf	polynomial	linear
10	0.941	0.941	0.941
15	0.971	0.971	0.971
20	0.971	0.941	0.941
40	0.971	0.971	0.971
50	0.971	0.971	0.971

The best result using the hybrid algorithm got is 15 genes. When the gene number is 15, the generation number is 1000, and the corresponding parameters in SVM need to be adjusted with gene subsets in different size.

The result in this paper is also compared with the results obtained using other methods in references [6-8]. The best accuracy obtained using a Neural Network method is 0.58, the best accuracy obtained using a SVM method is 0.971 when gene number is 20, and the best accuracy obtained by Golub et al is 0.853 when gene number is 50. In this paper, the proposed hybrid algorithm has the best accuracy of 0.971 when the gene number is only 15 compared with other methods.

Like the Colon dataset, we not only expect to get the good classification efficiency, but also obtain the important genes which are related with leukemia classification. The simulated experimental results are shown in Table 4.

Multiple lines of evidence from molecular biological studies imply that these genes are involved in leukemia development and progression, like M27891 [3]. Meanwhile, we also search in the bioinformatics database in networks, and compare the results with those obtained from other experiment, these feature genes concern the leukemia disease.

Table 4. Description of feature genes

Gene No.	Gene description
M27891	CST3 Cystatin C (amyloid angiopathy and cerebral hemorrhage)
L25931	LBR Lamin B receptor
M38690	CD9 CD9 antigen
X95735	Zyxin
M31667	CYTOCHROME P450 IA2

We perform experiments on two data sets above, and the proposed hybrid algorithm shows the effectiveness compared with other methods.

5   Conclusions

Support Vector Machine has not only simple structure, but also better performances, especially better generalization ability. Meanwhile, GA has advantages in implicit parallelism, global optimum searching and simple operability. So the proposed hybrid algorithm based on SVM and GA is equal to select the feature genes, and numerical results show that good effectiveness of the proposed hybrid algorithm is obtained.

It can be seen from the two experiment results that the classified accuracy of selected feature gene subset is high, and the genes play an important role in the disease. And we know co-expressed genes may work in the same biological process. So hunting the important feature gene has made it possible and generated enormous interests to systematically derive biological pathways and networks. It is a challenging and meaningful task to find feature gene and build gene networks.

Acknowledgments. The authors are grateful to the support of the National Natural Science Foundation of China (60433020), the science-technology development project of Jilin Province of China (20050705-2), the doctoral funds of the National Education Ministry of China (20030183060), and "985" project of Jilin University.

References

1. Suykens JAK and Vandewalle J. Least Squares Support Vector Machines Classifiers. Neural Processing Letters. 9 (1999) 293-300.
2. Jiang JQ, Wu CG, and Liang YC. Multi-Category Classification by Least Squares Support Vector Regression. Lecture Notes in Computer Science. 3496 (2005) 863-868.
3. Li X, Rao SQ, Wang YD, et al. Gene mining: a novel and powerful ensemble decision approach to hunting for disease genes using microarray expression profiling. Nucleic Acids Research. 9 (2004) 2685-2694.
4. Alon U, Barkai N, Notterman DA, Gish K, Ybarra S, Mack D, and Levine AJ. Broad Patterns of gene expression revealed by clustering analysis of tumor and normal colon tissues probed by oligonucleotide arrays. Proc. Natl. Acad. Sci. USA . 96 (1999) 6745-6750.
5. Lv SL, Wang QH, Li X, GU Z. Two feature gene recognition methods based on decision forest. China Journal of Bioinformatics. 3 (2004) 19-22.

6. Liu Q, Yang XT. Microarray Gene Expression Data Analysis Based on Support Vector Machine. Mini-Micro Systems. 3 (2005) 363-366.
7. Golub T R et al. Molecular Classification of Cancer: Class Discovery and Class Prediction by Gene Expression Monitoring .Science. 286 (1999) 531-537.
8. Toure A and Basu M. Application of neural network to gene expression data for cancer classification [C]. International Joint Conference on Neural Networks (IJCNN).1 (2001) 583-587.

Filtering Epitope Alignments to Improve Protein Surface Prediction

Brendan Mumey[1], Nathaniel Ohler[1], Thomas Angel[2], Algirdas Jesaitis[2], and Edward Dratz[3]

Department of [1] Computer Science, [2] Microbiology, [3] Biochemistry
Montana State University, Bozeman, MT, 59717, USA
mumey@cs.montana.edu

Abstract. In previous work, we developed a new algorithm to computationally predict the epitope, the antibody binding surface of a protein, based on aligning individual mimetic probe sequences derived from an experimental process called antibody imprinting for the protein of interest. A program called EPIMAP implements this algorithm and produces a list of the top-scoring alignment(s) of the probe to protein. Typically 50-100 probes sequences will be known experimentally and must be individually aligned using EPIMAP. The goal of the work reported in this paper is to select the most mutually compatible alignments (one for each probe used) in order to improve the accuracy of epitope prediction. We formalize this problem, show that it is NP-complete and describe an effective branch-and-bound search algorithm that works well in practice for inputs of interest. We show in our experimental results section that filtering alignments improves the accuracy the epitope prediction.

1 Introduction

Structural biology has contributed enormously to understanding of biological mechanisms. Examples abound, from the peptide alpha helix and the DNA structure to enzyme mechanisms, drug design and large macromolecular complexes, such as potassium channels or the ribosome. Whenever the structure of biological molecules has been determined the structures have almost invariably illuminated or even revolutionized the understanding of biological mechanisms. Proteins are the building blocks of biological structures; to understand their function we must learn their structure [2, 5]. A large fraction of protein structures of interest (50% or more) cannot be solved by the traditional approaches techniques such as X-ray crystallography and NMR. Recently, we developed a new algorithm to computationally predict the epitope, the antibody binding surface of a protein, based on aligning individual mimetic probe sequences derived from an experimental process called antibody imprinting for the protein of interest [1, 9]. Antibody imprinting requires antibodies against the target protein of interest, which are often available or can be made using a variety of standard methods [7]. Antibodies can either recognize continuous or discontinuous epitopes. Discontinuous epitopes provide the most useful structural information, because they can reveal distant segments of primary sequence that are

G. Min et al. (Eds.): ISPA 2006 Ws, LNCS 4331, pp. 648–657, 2006.

in close spatial proximity on the native, folded protein. Evidence to date indicates that most antibodies recognize discontinuous epitopes on protein surfaces [10]. The method works by screening the antibody for the target protein against a random peptide library. Such libraries consist of $\sim 10^{9\text{-}10}$ randomly generated short peptides sequences (usually 9-12 amino acid residues in length). Peptides that have a high affinity to the antibody are selected. We refer to these selected peptides as probe sequences. Typically 50-100 probes are found. Each probe mimics a portion of the surface of the epitope of the target protein. The computational problem addressed on our previous work was to align each probe individually to the target protein. These alignments are performed with a program called EPIMAP. For each probe, EPIMAP produces a set of the top-scoring alignments (these may include ties or the user may choose to generate suboptimal alignments). There are other computational methods to predict protein epitopes but all currently published methods make predictions based on the protein sequence alone and are limited to predicting linear epitopes (not discontinuous). See [11] and [3] for a survey of existing methods.

With the background above, the goal of the work presented here is to choose exactly one alignment for each probe so that the selected alignments are maximally mutually consistent. The advantage of this approach is that it can find the alignments that best fit together and filter out more spurious alignments that may have scored well due to chance. We refer to this as the *alignment selection problem* and formalize it below. As we show, solving this problem improves our ability to successfully predict protein epitopes.

We begin with some background on our existing epitope prediction software. EPIMAP takes as input a particular probe p and target t. It uses a branch-and-bound algorithm to determine the best alignment of p and t. Because inversions can occur in the alignment, finding the optimal alignment is itself a NP-complete problem. Alignments are scored with simple two part scoring scheme, $score(A) = S(A) - G(A)$, where $S(A)$ is the substitution score for A and $G(A)$ is the gap penalty cost for A. Substitution scores are found by looking up score in a substitution matrix M of each aligned pair of residues between p and t [4]. Gaps are scored using simple gap penalty function. This gap penalty function usually increases linearly until some maximum gap cost threshold is reached. Recently, we have also incorporated secondary-structure prediction into the gap cost function. If the target protein t is predicted to have secondary structure in a particular region (either alpha helices or beta sheets) then the gap cost function is modified slightly to account for the periodic nature of the 3d structure of the target residues in that region. When EPIMAP is run on a particular input p and t, there may be several top scoring alignments. Or, the user may choose to find a certain number of suboptimal solutions in addition to the overall top-scoring alignment(s). This paper considers the problem of selecting exactly one alignment for each probe in such a way that the resulting set of selected alignments is the most mutually compatible in the following sense: An individual alignment for a probe sequence may consist of several segments that have different orientations with respect to the primary sequence of the target. If alignments for different probes have overlapping segments on the target protein, then we score them based on whether the alignments agree on the alignment direction of the primary sequence. If a number of probes agree in the location and alignment direction of a region of the target protein, this is good evidence that that region is part of the true epitope.

<pre>
          98765   1234
          SRVKT   LLSK
          12345   9867
          VVTFF   WLKE
. . PGNLPNMLRDLRDAFSRVKTFFQMKDQLDNLLLKESLLEDFKGYLGCQALSEM . .
</pre>

Fig. 1. A sample overlapping alignment of two probes LLSKTKVRS and VVTFFEKLW against the target protein sequence. Note that both probes agree in the alignment directions of each segment (this can be seen by renumbering one of the probes in reverse order).

An important feature of the probes is that they are symmetric in the sense that if the order of the amino acids in a probe is reversed it will have the same affinity to the antibody. Thus we consider probes to have both a forward and backwards orientation, e.g. if the forwards orientation of a probe is LLSKTKVRS, then the backwards orientation of the same probe is SRVKTKSLL. As is shown above in Fig. 1, in typical probe-target alignments it is possible to have reversals of part of the probe in alignments. This most likely represents an internal 'twist' in the protein. This can happen when two discontinuous loops in the primary sequence of the protein pinch together to form the antibody epitope and one loop is twisted with respect to the other. Using both probe orientations, one can compare alignments with arbitrary directions while maintaining directional consistency within the individual alignments.

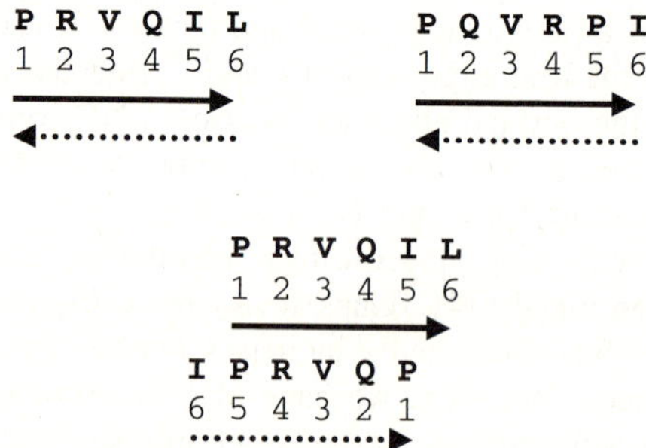

Fig. 2. The probe PRVQIL is aligned above another probe PQVRPI. Solid arrows indicate the forward orientation of a probe and dashed arrows represent the backward orientation. An oriented alignment of the two probes is shown. It should be noted that reverse oriented alignment would score as well.

A *match* is said to occur when alignments for two different probes have runs in the same direction (increasing or decreasing) at the same position on the target protein. If alignments for several probes align at the same position, some increasing and some decreasing, then the larger of the sum of increasing matches and the sum of decreasing matches is used. For instance, if five probes at position i are increasing, and three probes at position i are decreasing, then the score for position i is five. This lets us calculate a match score at each position in the target. The match scores are then summed over all of the target protein positions to give an *overall alignment compatibility score* for how well the selected set of alignments agree with one another. *The computational problem that we address is to select a single oriented alignment for each probe that maximizes the overall alignment compatibility score.* The selected alignments will be the most mutually consistent and in general will provide a more accurate prediction of the epitope of the protein of interest. In the next section we formalize the problem and describe a branch-and-bound algorithm to solve it. Following this, we show that formal problem is NP-complete (in fact, we can show that it does not admit a polynomial time approximation scheme unless P = NP). We then describe some initial experimental results and conclude with some ideas for future work.

2   Formalizing and Solving the Problem

To begin with, we formally define the alignment selection problem that takes as input a set of possible alignments as generated by the EPIMAP program and as output, selects a single alignment for each probe such that the selected alignments are optimally mutually compatible.

Alignment Selection Problem (ASEL).

Input: A set of probes $P=\{p_1,..,p_n\}$ and a set of possible alignments A_p for each probe p in P to specified target protein t. We assume A_p contains both the forwards and backwards representatives of each alignment.

Output: For each probe p, a single selected alignment s_p from A_p such that the overall alignment compatibility score of the selected alignments $\{s_p\}$ is maximized.

We use a branch-and-bound search strategy to solve ASEL in practice. The idea is to prune search branches that provably cannot contain the globally optimal solution. The central data structures used is a search tree T. Each internal node of T represents a partial solution where alignments for a subset of the probes have been selected. This is accomplished as follows: We view T as a rooted tree; the level of a node in T is simply the depth it is at from the root. Edges are considered to have the same depth as their originating parent node. We will use edges at level i to indicate which alignment is selected for probe i. So there will be $|A_i|$ edges leaving each node at level i. Thus leaf nodes (nodes at level $|P|$ in T) represent complete solutions where alignments have been selected for each probe in P.

To evaluate a search node in the tree, we simply compute the match score of each target position so far based on the partial selection of alignments. The search algorithm proceeds by expanding unexplored nodes in the tree until a leaf node is reached. When a leaf node is reached the overall alignment compatibility score of the solution represented by the leaf is computed and compared with the current best solution. If the new solution is better, then it is kept.

In order to improve the efficiency of the search, we employ a bounding technique to prune off internal nodes in the tree that cannot possibly lead to a solution that improves upon the current best. Let n be an internal node at level 1 in T. For any position i in the target, the best match score achievable by any leaf node that goes through n is bounded by n's current match score plus the number of unassigned probes that could be aligned to position i. By summing up the match score bounds, we can bound the total alignment compatibility score that is achievable by any leaf descendent of n. If this bound is less than score of the current best solution, then n (and its descendents) can be immediately pruned from T.

The order in which nodes are expanded in T is somewhat arbitrary. We have chosen to explore T in a round-robin fashion where each level is considered in turn and the best unexplored node at the current level is examined and its children are generated in T. This process continues until either the entire search tree is explored, and the provably best solution is found, or a pre-specified number of iterations is reached and search stops at that point and the current best solution is reported.

The worst-case complexity of this algorithm is $O(|A_1|\,|A_2| \ldots |A_n|\,|t|)$ as, in principal, every combination of ways to select an alignment for each probe must be considered. In practice, we are able to bound a significant fraction of this search space and determine the optimal solution. For larger inputs, we simply let the algorithm run a pre-set number of iterations and report the best solution found at that point. In the next section we prove that underlying problem is NP-complete.

Our current implementation of this algorithm is written in Java and is called EPIFILTER. The current version of the program is serial but we are investigating a parallel version in order speed up the computation. Searching the through the tree T can be fairly easily parallelized as each processor can search a different part of T independently, although there may be some load balancing issues. The only shared data required is the current best solution found.

3 Computational Complexity

In this section, we prove that the alignment selection problem is NP-complete using a reduction from the satisfiability problem 3SAT [6]. Briefly, this problem asks whether it is possible to find a truth assignment for a set of Boolean variables that will simultaneously satisfy (make true) every given clause. A clause is the logical OR of any three literals (a literal is either a variable or its negation).

Theorem 1. ASEL is NP-complete

Proof: Let I be a given instance of 3SAT. We will construct an instance I' of ASEL such that I is satisfiable if and only if I' has solution that achieves a specified alignment compatibility score. Let V be the set of variables used in I. For each variable, we will construct a new probe that has two possible alignments (forwards and backwards). The target positions of these alignments are determined by the clauses in I. For each literal that appears in clause, we add forward or backwards portions to the alignments for the corresponding variables as illustrated in Fig. 3.

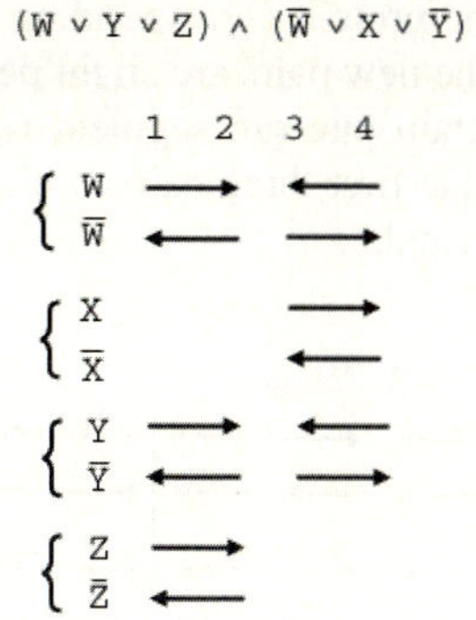

$$(W \vee Y \vee Z) \wedge (\overline{W} \vee X \vee \overline{Y})$$

Fig. 3. An example of a 3SAT instance being converted into an ASEL instance. Positions 1 and 2 represent the first clause, while 3 and 4 represent the second clause. Note the inverted variables have opposing directions to their counterparts. The brackets represent the alignment sets for each of the four probes.

We also include two additional special probes, each with only one alignment in the forward direction (right), spanning the full length of the protein. The purpose of this is to provide a forward direction bias to the optimal alignment selection. The forward direction will be interpreted as 'true' for the purposes of constructing a truth assignment of the variables later. Each clause has three literals so the match score for any target position depends on the directions of the selected alignments for three probes involved. For example, in Fig. 3, suppose that the alignments corresponding to W, X, $\overline{Y}$, and Z were chosen. Then positions 1 and 2 (corresponding to the clause ($W \vee Y \vee Z$)) would each have a match score of 4 (counting the two special probes not shown in the figure). Thus, the amount that each clause contributes to the total alignment score depends on the number of forward segments in the selected alignments of its associated variables.

# →	score
0	6
1	6
2	8
3	10

Fig. 4. This table summarizes the possible scores that a given clause can contribute to the overall alignment compatibility score. The amount depends on the number forward segments in the selected alignments for the probes corresponding to the clause's variables.

The goal of this construction is to be able to determine if all the clauses in I are satisfiable based on optimal alignment score of the ASEL instance being created. At this point, the satisfied and unsatisfied clauses are still indistinguishable. By definition, any given clause is satisfied if at least one of its literals is true. So, we produce a system of alterations to the ASEL instance such that satisfied clauses will produce a greater score than the unsatisfied clauses.

Each pair of positions on the protein corresponding to a single clause from I is replaced with nine new pairs. The new pairs are slight perturbations to the original pair. The first three pairs each contain one run segment reversed from the original. The second three pairs just repeat the first three pairs, while the last three pairs each contain two reversals from the original.

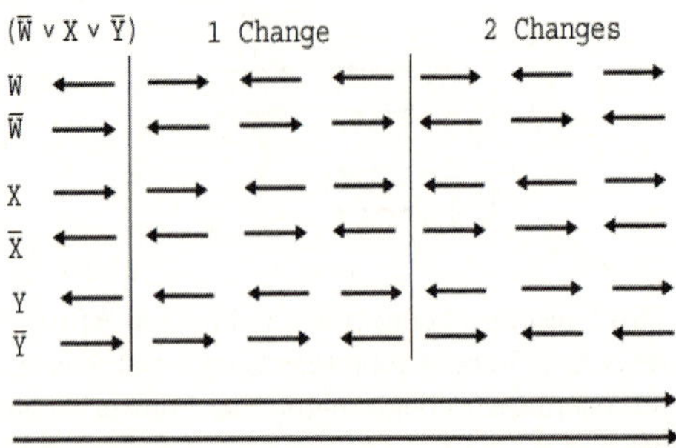

Fig. 5. The original alignment segments created by the clause, and the six new pairs created through alterations. (Nine new pairs are generated as the three pairs in the '1 Change' category are used twice.) The two full length arrows represent the two additional alignments mentioned above.

The resulting collection of pairs will score 60 for any unsatisfied clause and exactly 66 for any satisfied clause.

	$(\overline{W} \vee X \vee \overline{Y})$	1 Change			2 Changes			
	0	1	1	1	2	2	2	
#→	1	0	2	2	1	1	3	
	2	1	1	3	0	2	2	
	3	2	2	2	1	1	1	new scores
				*2				
scores		6	6	6	8	8	8	60
		6	8	8	6	6	10	66
		6	6	10	6	8	8	66
		8	8	8	6	6	6	66

Fig. 6. The top columns represent the possible new number of forward facing arrows given the number of changes to the original combination. The bottom columns represent their respective match scores. (Note the '1 Change' category is multiplied by two since each '1 Change' pair occurs twice.) The resulting final ASEL scores return 60 if the original clause was not satisfied and 66 otherwise.

These alignment sets constitute the ASEL instance I'. We claim that I is satisfiable if and only if there exists an alignment selection for I' with an overall alignment compatibility score of $66N$, where N is the number of clauses in I. This follows from the observation above that each clause contributes a score of 66 only if it is satisfied and 60 otherwise. This completes the reduction and the proof.

4   Experimental Results

To validate our EPIFILTER software, we selected a model system where the structure of the antibody epitope was previously known. We chose the interleukin protein IL10 and antibody 9D7. The primary amino acid sequence of recombinant human IL-10 is 160 amino acids long. The structure of the antibody-antigen complex of 9D7-IL10 was determined by x-ray crystallography [7] (PDB: 1lk3.pdb). From the x-ray crystal structure of the antibody (9D7) bound to its antigen (IL-10), the molecular contacts were determined using CPP4 [10]. The epitope for antibody 9D7 was then mapped employing the antibody imprinting method. Peptides that mimic the epitope on IL-10 that the antibody 9D7 binds to were selected from a random peptide phage display library. The amino acid sequences of the selected peptides (probes) were then aligned onto the primary sequence of the target IL-10 using EPIMAP. The 9D7 epitope on IL-10 is discontinuous; it is composed of two regions in the primary sequence that are close together in the folded protein but are not contiguous in the primary amino acid sequence of IL-10. Antibody 9D7 binds to two regions of IL10 composed of residues 71-83 and 125-137. The peptides that were selected by phage display primarily mapped to the 125-137 region of IL10. Amino acid residues from the 125-137 region on IL10 are bound most tightly by antibody 9D7 and probes selected mapped strongly to this region. By running EPIMAP, a set of potential alignments was found for each of 28 probe sequences; we chose to include the top three alignments for each probe, including ties. Due to ties, some probes had a many as 10 possible alignments. These alignments were then fed into the alignment selection program, EPIFILTER. As is shown in Fig. 7, EPIFILTER increases the predictability of the underlying epitope by increasing the alignment frequency in the true epitope region.

5   Conclusions

Antibody imprinting is a useful new way to derive structural information about proteins. The alignment selection problem improves upon our existing methods for epitope prediction based on antibody imprinting. Typically an individual probe may have several possible high-scoring alignments. By comparing these against the possible alignments of all the antibody-mimicking probes found, a consensus for what the true epitope is can be found. We have used a fairly simple model for scoring how compatible the selected alignments are, based on just counting up the number of alignments that agree in their orientation at each position in the target protein sequence. Other approaches such as considering the substitutability of the aligned probe sequences might lead to improved solutions but may add to additional computational expense. Another direction to explore is solving the alignment problem for all probes simultaneously. This would potentially greatly increase the size of the search space but could lead to better epitope predictions.

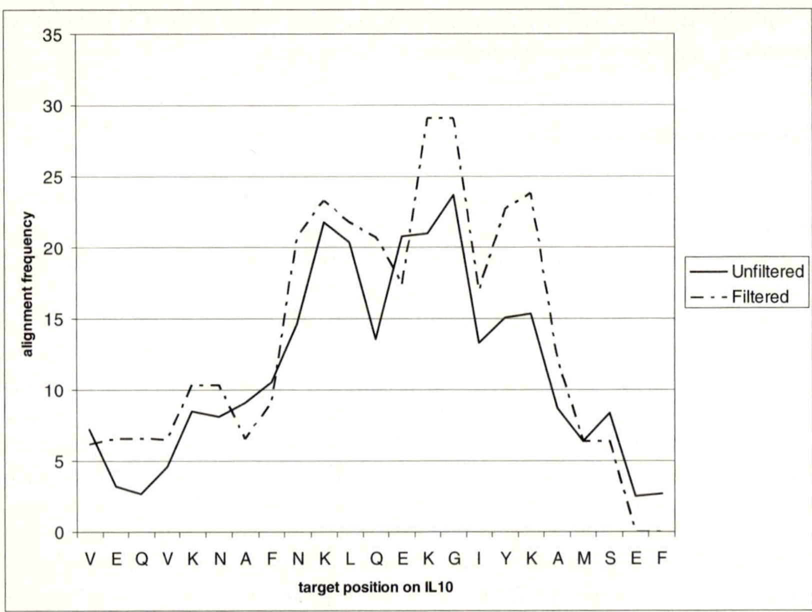

Fig. 7. Results for the protein IL10 to predict the epitope for the antibody 9D7. Residues KNAFNKLQEKGIY form the main portion of the actual epitope. Alignment frequency is the frequency that probes are aligned to particular partitions in the target (normalized if a probe has more than one alignment). The alignments selected by EPIFILTER strengthen and sharpen the prediction of the epitope. The position-dependent alignment frequencies of these selected alignments are given as the 'Filtered' line above. The alignment frequencies of the original alignment data set are shown as the 'Unfiltered' line.

References

1. Bailey, B., Mumey, B., Hargrave, P., Arendt, A., Ernst, O., Hofmann, K., Callis, P., Burritt, J., Jesaitis, A., Dratz, E.: Constraints on the Conformation of the Cytoplasmic Face of Dark-adapted and Light-excited Rhodopsin Inferred from Anti-rhodopsin Antibody Imprints. Protein Science, Vol. 12, No. 11. (2003)
2. Baker, D., Sali, A.: Protein structure prediction and structural genomics. Science 294(5540), (2001) 93–96
3. Blythe, M., Flower, D.: Benchmarking B Cell epitope prediction: Underperformance of existing methods. Protein Science, Vol. 14. (2005) 246-248
4. Bordo, D., Argos, P.: Suggestions for "safe" residue substitutions in site-directed mutagenesis. J. Mol. Biol., Vol. 217 (1991) 721–729
5. Branden, C., Tooze, C.: Introduction to Protein Structure, Garland Publishing, New York, NY. (1999)
6. Garey, M., Johnson, D.: Computers and Intractability: A Guide to the Theory of NP-Completeness, W.H. Freeman and Co. (1979)
7. Jesaitis, A., Gizachew, D., Dratz, E., Siemsen, D., Stone, K., Burritt, J.: Actin surface structure revealed by antibody imprints: Evaluation of phage-display analysis of anti-actin antibodies. Protein Science, Vol. 8 (1999) 760–770

8. Josephson, K., Jones, B., Walter, L., DiGiacomo, R., Indelicato, S., Walter, M.: Noncompetitive antibody neutralization of IL-10 revealed by protein engineering and x-ray crystallography. Structure, Vol. 10, No. 7 (2002) 981-987
9. Mumey, B., Bailey, B., Kirkpatrick, B., Jesaitis, A., Dratz, E.: Revealing Protein Structure: A new method for mapping discontinuous antibody epitopes to reveal structural features of proteins. J. of Computational Biology, Vol. 10 Issue 3-4 (2003) 555-567
10. Padlan, E.: X-ray crystallography of antibodies. Adv. Protein Chem., Vol. 49 (1996) 57–133
11. Roggen, E.: Recent Developments with B-Cell Epitope Identification for Predictive Studies, Journal of Immunotoxicology, Vol. 3, (2006) 1-13

A Grid Service Based on Suffix Trees for Pattern Extraction from Mass Spectrometry Proteomics Data

M. Cannataro and P. Veltri

University Magna Græcia of Catanzaro, Italy
`{cannataro, veltri}@unicz.it`

Abstract. The paper presents a Grid Service allowing to detect and extract the longest common sub-spectrum among a set of mass spectrometry spectra data. The system uses a novel pattern extraction algorithm named LCSS (Longest Common Spectra SubString) that adapts a very popular string matching technique based on Suffix Trees to spectra data. The basic LCSS algorithm made available as a Grid Service is used to implement a pattern extraction workflow on mass spectrometry dataset. First experimental results are presented.

Keywords: Pattern Extraction, Mass Spectrometry, Suffix Tree, Grid Services.

1   Introduction

Mass Spectrometry (MS) is a technique allowing to identify the masses of macromolecules in a compound. The mass spectrometer separates gas phase ions according to their m/z (mass to charge ratio) values [1]. The output of the spectrometer, said spectrum, is a (large) sequence of value pairs. Each pair contains a measured *intensity*, which depends on the quantity of the detected biomolecule, and a mass to charge ratio (m/z), which depends on the molecular mass of the detected biomolecule. Spectra are often analyzed through data mining techniques, such as classification (e.g. diseased vs healthy patients) or clustering (e.g. subclasses of samples corresponding to different types of the same disease). Since spectra may be affected by errors and noise, they are usually preprocessed before conducting any data mining or pattern extraction analysis.

Classifiers able to classify spectra in the proper classes usually make the classification with respect to few peaks (e.g. decision trees). A complementary approach could require that entire sub-spectrum are repeated among samples of the same class, thus it could be important to extract from a set of spectra some common pattern (i.e. a common sub-spectrum) that could be representative of a class. Pattern extraction is a technique widely used in bioinformatics and especially in protein sequence analysis. String-based pattern extraction works on strings representing protein sequences and a lot of algorithms have been developed for detecting and extracting common sub-strings or sub-sequences, such as those based on Suffix Trees [6]. The main reason to use string-based algorithms for extracting patterns from spectra is their high efficiency and their suitability to solve a lot of pattern extraction problems, such as exact string matching, common substring, common subsequence, longest common substring, longest common subsequence, repetitive structures in biological data, etc. [6].

G. Min et al. (Eds.): ISPA 2006 Ws, LNCS 4331, pp. 658–667, 2006.
© Springer-Verlag Berlin Heidelberg 2006

The paper describes a pattern extraction algorithm allowing to detect and extract the longest common sub-spectrum among a set of MALDI-TOF spectra [1]. The proposed algorithm, named LCSS (Longest Common Spectra SubString), adapts a very popular string matching technique, the Suffix Tree [6], to spectra data. A Grid Service implementation of the algorithm and a first performance evaluation is also presented.

The rest of the paper is organized as follows. Section 2 introduces MS data. Section 3 summarizes Suffix Trees. Section 4 presents the proposed pattern extraction algorithm, while Section 5 shows an application of the basic algorithm to extract common patterns from a multiple-spectra dataset. Section 6 discusses preliminary results, while Section 7 summarizes the paper and describes future work.

2   Mass Spectrometry Data

Mass Spectrometry (MS) is a technique allowing to identify the masses of macromolecules in a compound. The mass spectrometer separates gas phase ions according to their m/z (mass to charge ratio) values [1]. The sample can be inserted directly into the ionization source or can be separated into different components which enter the spectrometer sequentially. Common ionization techniques are Electrospray Ionization (ESI), Surface Enhanced Laser Desorption/Ionization (SELDI), and Matrix-Assisted Laser Desorption/Ionization (MALDI), coupled with different kind of mass analyzers such as Time Of Flight (TOF) or quadrupole ion traps. Mass Spectrometry output can be represented as a (large) sequence of value pairs (spectrum). Each pair contains a measured *intensity*, which depends on the quantity of the detected biomolecule, and a mass to charge ratio (m/z), which depends on the molecular mass of the detected biomolecule.

Mass spectrometry is emerging as an important tool for biomarker discovery. Body fluids as well as tissues can be routinely used to generate protein profiles, containing potential disease markers whether individual proteins or sets of interacting proteins. Data Mining is commonly used to discover biomarker patterns in spectra data [5], but a number of technical challenges need to be faced, among which is the extremely high-dimensionality of mass spectra. A typical mass spectrum has several thousands of attributes that exhibit a high degree of spatial redundancy. The exact number depends on the type of mass spectrometry instrument that is used, its resolution, and the mass range it covers.

Spectra preprocessing aims to correct intensity and m/z values in order to reduce noise, reduce the amount of data, and make spectra comparable [2]. *Binning* performs data dimensionality reduction by aggregating measured data into *bins*: a set of peaks from a spectrum is substituted with a unique peak $(I, m/z)$, whose intensity I is an aggregate function of the original intensities (e.g. their sum), and the mass m/z is usually chosen among the original mass values (e.g. the median value). *Peaks alignment* corrects errors on m/z measurements finding a common set of peak locations in a set of spectra, in such a way that all aligned spectra will have common m/z values for the same biological entities. Moreover, a small number of individuals are chosen to be included in clinical study, so pattern extraction has to deal with the problem of high dimensionality small sample size. Indeed, spectra can yet exhibit hundreds or thousands of peaks after preprocessing, thus string-based pattern extraction can complement data mining methods.

3 Suffix Trees

The main idea of the paper is to apply a string-based pattern matching algorithm, the Longest Common Substring algorithm based on Suffix Tree [6], to spectra data. Any string of length m can be represented by its m suffixes, and these suffixes can be stored in a data structure said Suffix Tree (ST). Given the string 'mississippi', 'miss' is a prefix, 'ippi' is a suffix, and 'issi' is a substring. Note that a substring is a prefix of a suffix.

If $T = t_1, t_2, ..., t_i, ..., t_m$ is a string, then $T_i = t_i, t_{i+1}, ..., t_m$, is the suffix of T that starts at position i. All suffixes of 'mississippi' are showed in Figure 1.

```
T1   = mississippi = T
T2   = ississippi
T3   = ssissippi
T4   = sissippi
T5   = issippi
T6   = ssippi
T7   = sippi
T8   = ippi
T9   = ppi
T10  = pi
T11  = i
T12  =                          (empty)
```

Fig. 1. All suffixes of 'mississippi'

Creating the ST requires time $O(m)$ and searching for a pattern P in it requires time $O(n)$, where n is the length of the pattern. An important aspect is the possibility to decouple the creation of the ST from the search of the pattern. These properties make the suffix tree an interesting data structure for implementing many string-based applications, e.g. multiple genome alignment in bioinformatics. The first linear-time suffix tree algorithm was developed by Weiner in 1973, after McCreight realized a more space efficient algorithm in 1976, and Ukkonen produced an "on-line" variant of it in 1995 [6]. The key to search fast in a suffix tree is that there is a path from the root for each suffix of the text. This means that at most n comparisons are needed to find a pattern of length n.

If the non-empty suffixes are sorted it is evident that some of them (may) share common prefixes. Two or more common prefixes share a common path from the root of the suffix tree. Now, a search of the (sub)string P must be a prefix of a suffix of T, if it occurs in T. The suffix tree for 'mississippi' is showed in Figure 2.

When there is more than one string to be searched a Generalized Suffix Tree (GST) can be created [6]. As the GST contains more than one string, each leaf node contains an identifier indicating the string associated with this suffix, and a second identifier indicating the position of the suffix. The Longest Common Substring (LCS) of two strings, T_1 and T_2, can be found by building a generalized suffix tree for T_1 and T_2: each node is marked to indicate if it represents a suffix of T_1 or T_2 or both. The deepest node marked for both T_1 and T_2 represents the longest common substring. Equivalently, one

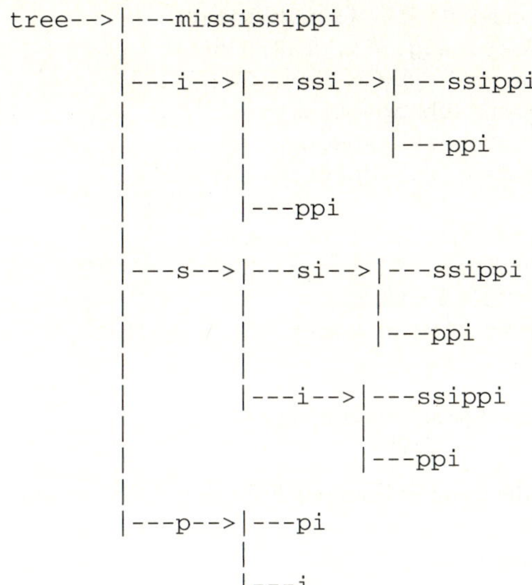

Fig. 2. The Suffix Tree for 'mississippi'

can build a (basic) suffix tree for the string $T_1\$T_2\#$, where '$\$$' is a special terminator for T_1 and '$\#$' is a special terminator for T_2. The longest common substring is indicated by the deepest fork node that has both '...$\$$...' and '...$\#$...'. Note that the 'longest common substring problem' is different from the 'longest common subsequence problem': an instance of a subsequence can have gaps where it appears in T_1 and in T_2, but an instance of a substring cannot have gaps. The algorithm for two strings can easily be extended to more strings.

4 The Longest Common Spectra Substring Algorithm

Since spectra data are couples of real numbers, $(intensity, m/z)$, a first problem is to transform spectra in strings so that suffix trees and generalized suffix trees can be computed. The simple approach proposed here is to sample intensity values mapping them onto discrete values each one corresponding to a letter of an alphabet. Let be A an alphabet of N symbols, and $maxIntensity$ and $minIntensity$ the maximum and minimum intensity values, the intensity domain can be partitioned into N quantization intervals $[minIntensity + (i * K), minIntensity + ((i+1) * K)]$, $i = 0, ..., N-1$, where $K = (maxIntensity - minIntensity)/N$ is the quantization level. Thus, a peak of intensity I it can be associated to the symbol A_j, if I belongs to the jth quantization interval. The proposed *Longest Common Spectra Substring* (LCSS) algorithm finds the longest common sub-spectrum in a set of mass spectra. Its pseudo-code is showed in Figure 3.

The current version of the algorithm compares two spectra S_1 and S_2. After the two spectra are converted into strings T_1 and T_2, the proposed algorithm builds the

```
LCSS(N: integer; S1, S2: spectrum; l, i, j: integer)
Input:  N; //size of the alphabet, e.g. 64, 128, 256
        S1, S2; //input spectra
Output: l; //length of the common sub-spectrum
        i, //position of the common sub-spectrum in S1
        j; //position of the common sub-spectrum in S2
{
T1 = spectrum2string(N,S1); //convert S1 intensities
T2 = spectrum2string(N,S2); //convert S2 intensities
GST = GenSuffixTree(T1, T2); //build the GST
LCS (l, i, j); //find the longest common substring in GST;
}
```

Fig. 3. The Longest Common Spectra Substring algorithm

Generalized Suffix Tree (GST) and then the Longest Common Substring (LCS) is computed by finding the deepest node marked for both T_1 and T_2. Since the algorithm provides the position of the LCS in T_1 and T_2, namely i and j, it is possible to extract the corresponding sub-spectrum from each spectrum S_1 and S_2 simply selecting the peaks (intensity, m/z) starting respectively at positions i and j. The two sub-spectrum can be compared to find how the quantization error impacts on the length of discovered sub-spectrum. Moreover, since the position of the sub-spectrum in both spectra deals with masses of molecules, the significance of the discovered common pattern can be evaluated with respect to the positions i and j. Very close positions mean that the common pattern refers to common masses, whereas very different positions may have few of significance.

5   Extracting Patterns from Mass Spectrometry Proteomics Data

To effectively compare spectra, they must be aligned, i.e. the same molecular component needs to have the same mass on each sample. Moreover, peaks intensities need to be normalized with respect to all dataset. Thus, before intensities can be quantified, spectra must be preprocessed. The work [2] surveys some recent spectra preprocessing algorithms including spectra normalization, binning, and alignment.

To compare multiple spectra the basic LCSS algorithm must be extended to face multiple strings. This can be obtained by building first the Generalized Suffix Tree of all the strings (or equivalently by building the basic Suffix Tree of the concatenation of all strings separated by proper delimiters), and by finding the Longest Common Substring that is computed by finding the deepest node marked for all the strings. The set of common sub-spectra found by the following procedure represents a common pattern in the dataset S that can be used as representative of spectra belonging to different classes, e.g. healthy and diseased patients.

The steps to extract the first longest common patterns from a spectra dataset $S = S_1, ..., S_N$ are the following:

1. Normalize spectra $S_1, ..., S_N$;
2. Reduce spectra dimension by applying a binning algorithm;

3. Align peaks;
4. Convert spectra $S_1, ..., S_N$ obtaining strings $T_1, ..., T_N$;
5. Set the Longest Common Spectra Substring as $LCSS = \emptyset$;
6. Extract $NextLCSS = [L, (start_1, end_1), ..., (start_N, end_N)]$ from $T_1, ..., T_N$;
   - L is the sub-spectrum length expressed as number of peaks,
   - $(start_1, end_1), ..., (start_N, end_N)$ are, respectively, the starting and ending positions of the common sub-spectrum in $S_1, ..., S_N$,
   - $minStart$ and $maxStart$ are the minimum and maximum starting positions of the common sub-spectrum in $S_1, ..., S_N$ (note that $minEnd = minStart + L$ and $maxEnd = maxStart + L$);
7. IF $NextLCSS = \emptyset$ THEN RETURN $LCSS$;
8. IF $(maxStart - minStart < shiftThreshold)$ AND $(L > lengthThreshold)$
   THEN $LCSS = LCSS \cup NextLCSS$
   ELSE discard $NextLCSS$;
   - $shiftThreshold$ and $lengthThreshold$ allow to reject a common sub-spectrum that presents a large shift inside spectra or that is very short;
9. Mark peaks belonging to the interval $[minStart, maxEnd]$ so that they are not considered in the search of the next sub-spectrum;
10. GOTO step 6.

The LCSS algorithm has been implemented as a service of MS-Analyzer [3], a software platform for the preprocessing, management and analysis of spectra data. It has been implemented and deployed on a Grid using the Globus middleware [4].

6   Performance Evaluation

A first performance evaluation considered the behavior of the core algorithm when finding the longest common sub-spectrum on a real spectra dataset. Notice that only the first common sub-spectrum is considered. In such study we measured, respectively, the LCSS execution time, the length and the positions of the discovered LCSS, and the difference (error) between the sub-spectrum evaluated on the first and the second input spectra, after recovering real intensity values. Such measurement were taken varying the quantization parameter N (i.e. the alphabet size).

The second study evaluated the performance of the LCSS Grid Service deployed on a small Grid composed by three computers. Execution times and spectra transfer times were measured considering one Grid Service invoked respectively, by 1, 3 and 6 clients installed on such a Grid.

6.1   The Proteomic Spectra Dataset

The input dataset is obtained by two set of experiments. In the first experiment, a biological human serum has been processed by a MALDI-TOF mass spectrometer obtaining the A_1 spectrum. Such processing has been repeated four times obtaining the spectra A_2, A_3, A_4, and A_5. Although they are replicas of the same sample, their values are not exact replicas of the A_1 values, due to noise and instrument perturbation. In the second experiment, the same serum of the first experiment has been mixed with two known proteins and, using the same approach, the spectrum B_1 and replicas B_2, B_3, B_4, and B_5, have been obtained. The adding of two proteins to the original serum produces some perturbation on the spectrum, yet maintaining some common sub-spectrum. Spectra A_1 and B_1 are showed in Figure 4, where the discovered LCSS is indicated by a circle. Each spectrum contains 34671 peaks and the masses range between 3999.749927 and 20000.324102 Dalton. In the same set of replicas, intensities for the same peaks can vary considerably, for instance the minimum and maximum intensities are respectively (3.63926, 5186.37) and (10.5301, 8024.88) for the spectra A_5 and A_2.

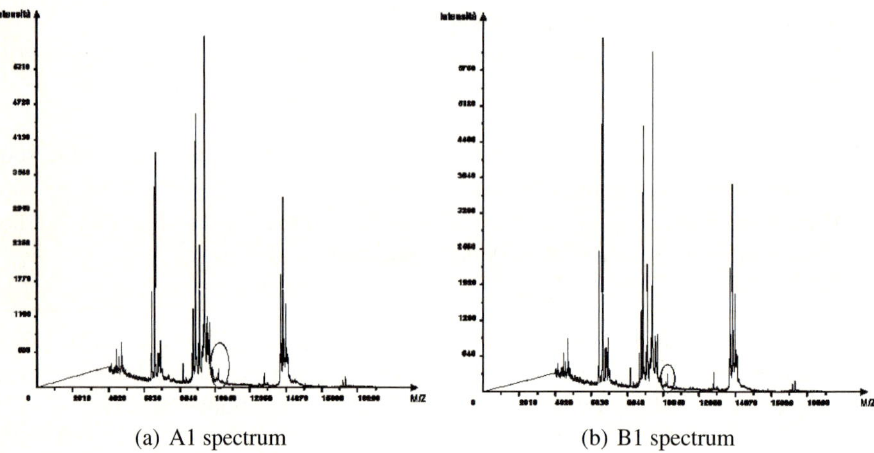

(a) A1 spectrum   (b) B1 spectrum

Fig. 4. Spectra A1 and B1 used in the experiments

6.2   Pattern Extraction Evaluation

Table 1 reports for the spectra A_1 and B_1, the LCSS length L, its initial position in A_1 and B_1, namely i and j, the shift $|i - j|$, and the 2-norm average relative error, when varying N. The *2-norm average relative* (2AR) error is defined as:

$$2AR = \sqrt{\frac{1}{L} \sum_{i=1,L} \left(\frac{|y_i - y_i'|}{y_i} \right)^2}$$

where $Y = [y_1, ..., y_L]$ and $Y' = [y_1', ..., y_L']$ are the intensity values of the common sub-spectrum starting, respectively, at position i and j on A_1 and B_1.

Similar results are obtained when searching the LCSS on the remaining spectra.

Figures 5(a) and 5(b) show, respectively, the LCSS excution time and the 2-norm average relative (2AR) error when varying N. Execution time decreases when the quantization level increases. In fact, for lower values of N the alphabet comprises a small set of characters so the strings obtained by the source spectra contain many similar characters. This increases the time requested to find the LCSS on the GST. Instead, an higher value of N, i.e. a richer alphabet, simplifies the search of the LCSS on the GST since there are less identical characters.

Table 1. Characteristics of LCSS varying N

N	L	i	j	$\|i-j\|$	2AR
64	4236	17992	17989	3	11.94096
96	1616	20060	19584	476	11.85594
128	495	22715	21936	779	11.423612
160	121	18762	18008	754	10.11193
192	30	20063	20060	3	0.11746

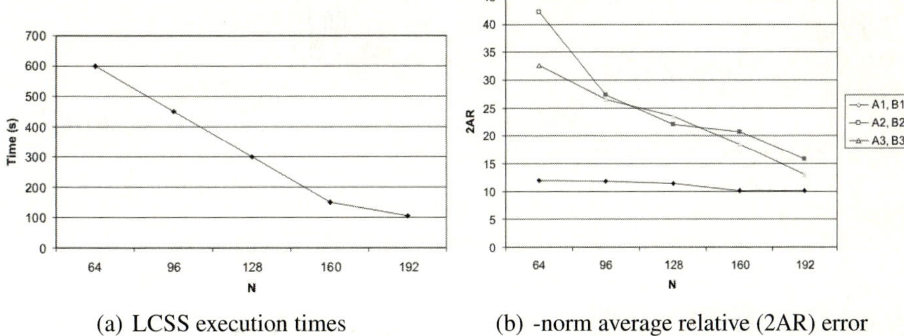

(a) LCSS execution times   (b) -norm average relative (2AR) error

Fig. 5. Performance of the LCSS Grid Service

On the other hand, a low N introduces great approximation and quantization error, so it happens that for low values of N the length of the LCSS increases (due to a worse quantization), the positions i and j of the sub-spectrum in the input spectra tend to be greatly unaligned and finally, the difference (error) between the sub-spectrum computed on the two spectra increases. On the contrary, large N increases precision (i.e. i and j alignment), reduces errors, but discover shorten sub-spectra.

Figure 6 shows the details of the LCSS discovered respectively in A_1 and B_1 for $N = 192$. It is possible to see a very high similarity between the sub-spectrum on each input spectra.

6.3   Grid Service Evaluation

The Grid Service implementing the LCSS algorithm receives a request containing the two input spectra from one or more clients, then finds and sends back the discovered LCSS (length and starting positions in input spectra). The client loads two spectra from the file system (e.g. A_1 and B_1), sends them to the Grid Service, and receives the discovered LCSS (see Figure 7). We conducted a set of experiments varying the number of clients that contemporarily send search requests to just one LCSS Grid Service. The number of clients C was respectively 1, 3, and 6.

Table 2 shows, respectively, the average times needed to send the spectra to the Grid Service (T_s), to execute the LCSS algorithm (T_e), to receive the results (i.e. length and position of the discovered LCSS) on the client (T_r), and the overall response time (T). It is possible to note that although the number of clients increases from 1 to 6, the overall response time per search increases only slightly: this is due to the parallel multi-threaded implementation of the LCSS Grid Service.

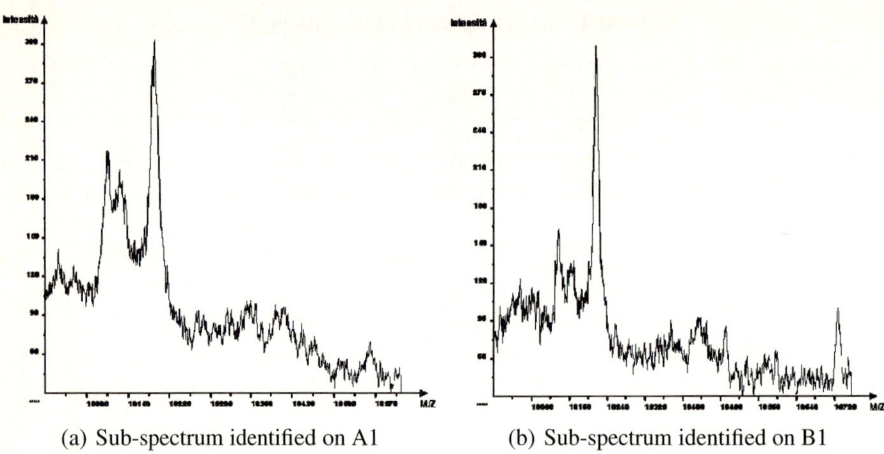

(a) Sub-spectrum identified on A1   (b) Sub-spectrum identified on B1

Fig. 6. Details of the identified sub-spectrum on A1 and B1

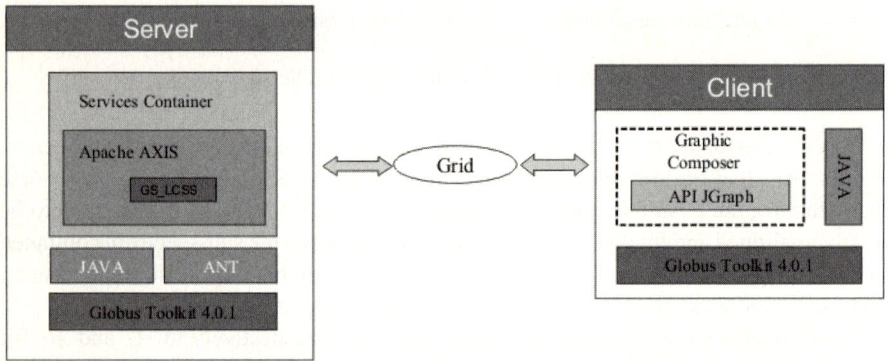

Fig. 7. LCSS Grid Service and Client

Table 2. Execution time for the LCSS Grid Service

C	Ts	Te	Tr	T
1	0.1405	588.745	0.0131	588.8975
3	0.1825	669.627	0.02295	669.837
6	0.2695	803.654	0.025	803.9485

7   Conclusions and Future Work

The paper presented a Grid Service for the detection and extraction of the longest common sub-spectrum among a set of spectra. The main contribution of the proposed system is the combination of a very popular string matching technique based on Suffix Trees with functions for the preprocessing and management of mass spectrometry data. The first performance results are encouraging so future work will regard the extension of the algorithm to face more than two spectra and to allow the contemporary detection of more sub-spectra. Since spectra data are huge, another research direction will regard the parallel implementation of the Grid Service, for instance executing the conversion of spectra to strings in parallel.

Acknowledgments

Authors are grateful to Walter Morelli and Umberto Mellace for their work on the implementation of the LCSS algorithm and Grid Service. A special thank to Marco Gaspari and Giovanni Cuda for providing the spectra dataset.

References

1. R. Aebersold and M. Mann. Mass spectrometry-based proteomics. *Nature*, 422:198–207, 13 March 2003.
2. M. Cannataro, P. Guzzi, T. Mazza, G. Tradigo, and P. Veltri. Preprocessing of mass spectrometry proteomics data on the grid. In IEEE Press, editor, *CBMS'05*, pages 549–554, 2005.
3. M. Cannataro, P. Guzzi, T. Mazza, G. Tradigo, and P. Veltri. Using ontologies for preprocessing and mining spectra data on the grid. *Future Generation Comp. Syst.*, 23(1):55–60, 2007.
4. Alliance Globus. The globus project. - http://www.globus.org/.
5. V. Gopalakrishnan, E. William, S. Ranganathan, R. Bowser, M. E. Cudkowic, M. Novelli, W. Lattazi, A. Gambotto, and B. W. Day. Proteomic data mining challenges in identification of disease-specific biomarkers from variable resolution mass spectra. In *Proceedings of SIAM Bioinformatics Workshop 2004*, pages 1–10, Lake Buena Vista, FL, April 2004.
6. Dan Gusfield. *Algorithms on Strings, Trees, and Sequences: Computer Science and Computational Biology*. Cambridge Univ Press, 1997.

Performance Evaluation of BLAST on SMP Machines

Hong-Soog Kim[1,2], Hae-Jin Kim[1], and Dong-Soo Han[1,*]

[1] School of Engineering,
Information and Communications University,
119 Munjiro, Yuseong-Gu, Daejeon 305-600, Korea
{kimkk, hjkim, dshan}@icu.ac.kr
[2] Electronics and Telecommunications Research Institute,
161 Gajeong-dong, Yusong-Gu, Daejeon 305-350, Korea
kimkk@etri.re.kr

Abstract. BLAST is a tool for finding biologically similar sequences to given query sequences in annotated sequence database. Since the number of sequences in the database increases at exponential rate, and the number of users drastically increases, the performance of BLAST is a primary concern to service sites like NCBI. NCBI developed a parallel BLAST for the speedup of BLAST using threads on SMP machines. But the speedup is still limited due to the architectural limitations of SMP machines. Distributed memory multiprocessor can be an alternative choice for cost-effective search in very large scale sequence data. However for an optimized configuration of Cluster systems and SMP machines, the performance study of BLAST on SMP machines is essential. In this paper, we analyze BLAST and BLAST algorithms to enhance the performance of BLAST on parallel machines and report the performance of BLAST on SMP machines. Some important runtime characteristics of BLAST are identified through the performance evaluation. According to our performance test, PC clusters or clusters of low-way SMP machines outperform high-way SMP machines in terms of cost-effectiveness. Besides, BLAST on Linux operating system shows better performance than BLAST on Solaris operating system in the same configurations.

1 Introduction

Many molecular biologists who are engaged in large scale genetic sequencing projects produce and announce ever-increasing amount of sequence data. As a consequence, GenBank, the primary repository for DAN sequence data, continues to grow at an exponential rate. It is known that GenBank contains roughly 15,849,921,438 nucleotides in 14,976,310 sequences as of 2001 [1]. Historically, GenBank has doubled its size in about 18 months, but that rate has accelerated to be doubled in every 15 months due to the enormous growth in data from expressed sequence tags (ESTs).

---

* Correspondence author.

G. Min et al. (Eds.): ISPA 2006 Ws, LNCS 4331, pp. 668–676, 2006.

Keeping pace with the ever increasing data is difficult task for biologists. The more sequence data biologists gather, the more useful sequence similarity algorithm is. But the more time it takes to search and compare sequences in the database. BLAST is one of the most popular sequence similarity algorithms in use today. Its running time is proportional to the size of the database and thus sequence similarity analysis using BLAST is becoming a bottleneck [2]. This indicates that huge sequence database can result in more serious problem. For example, if the size of database exceeds the size of physical memory of the system, BLAST program invoke frequent page faults while it scans the database.

Since the number of sequences in the database increases at exponential rate, and the number of users drastically increases, the performance of BLAST is a primary concern to service sites. Speedup of BLAST program can be achieved in three aspects: algorithmic enhancement, adoption of fast processor with more memory, and use of multi-processors.

Since its first release, BLAST has undergone various algorithmic enhancements in terms of speed and biological sensitivity. So, the current version of BLAST is approximately 10 times faster than the other conventional dynamic programming based similarity search algorithms. It is a heuristic algorithm that approximates the dynamic programming algorithm while its loss of sensitivity is negligible since it has rigid statistical background for determining the significance of search result. Therefore, algorithmic enhancement for speedup is out of our research scope.

In order to speedup BLAST, we can use faster processor. According to Moore's law, the processor speed doubles in roughly every 1.5 year. However, the size of sequence database doubles in every 1.3 year. Since the complexity of BLAST algorithm is proportional to the size of database and the database size increases faster than the processor speed, this approach cannot address such an inherent limitation.

Multiprocessor can give scalable speedup for existing application program if an appropriate parallelization technique is developed. Albeit the current version of BLAST is parallelized using thread facility to exploit symmetric multiprocessor (SMP) machine, it gives limited speedup on SMP system. Since the speedup of BLAST on SMP machine is not sufficiently scalable due to architectural limitations of SMP machine, we consider distributed-memory multiprocessor system like PC clusters or low cost SMP machines as an alternative multiprocessor type. However for the judicious decision on the combination of Cluster systems and SMP machines, the performance of BLAST on SMP machines must be analyzed in a comprehensive way.

In this paper, we analyze BLAST and BLAST algorithms to enhance the performance of BLAST on parallel machines and report the performance of BLAST on SMP machines. Some important run time characteristics of BLAST are identified through the performance evaluation. According to our performance test, PC clusters or clusters of low-way SMP machines outperformed high-way SMP machines in terms of cost-effectiveness. In the comparison of Linux and

Solaris operating systems, BLAST on Linux operating system showed better performance than BLAST on Solaris operating system.

Section 2 describes preliminary information on BLAST and Section 3 explains BLAST algorithm in detail. The BLAST performance results on SMP machines are in Section 4. We draw conclusion in Section 5.

2   BLAST Programs

BLAST (Basic Local Alignment Search Tool) [3,4,5] is one of the most widely used similarity search tools available to today's computational biologist. It rapidly identifies statistically significant matches between newly sequenced segments of genetic material or proteins and databases [1] of known nucleotide or amino acid sequences. Similarity search allows the scientist to make inferences about the structure and function of their discoveries or to screen new sequences for further investigation using more sensitive and computationally expensive methods. As the name implies, the search strategy is based on finding subsequences of query and subject sequences that have a large number of exact matches.

BLAST has undergone nearly continuous development since its initial release in 1990. A major effort has been expanded in the creation of multiple user interfaces, including a Web site that handles sequences submitted by members of the worldwide bioinformatics community for BLAST searches against the extensive set of databases maintained by National Center for Biotechnology Information (NCBI). The numerical methods implemented in BLAST software have also been refined and extended since 1990. Algorithmic development now proceeds at two sites: NCBI and Washington University. They distribute different versions of BLAST program suit (NCBI BLAST and WU-BLAST). Both sites have recently produced new versions of BLAST that are able to handle gaped alignments. This extension promises to continue important role of BLAST in genomic research for the time being. In this paper, we consider NCBI BLAST only and BLAST means NCBI BLAST here and after.

All versions of BLAST from version 1.4 on have provisions for running in parallel on (distributed) shared-memory multiprocessors. BLAST parallelization is quite straightforward. The work of comparing a particular query to all entries in a database falls naturally into subtasks consisting of assessment of a pair of a query sequence and a subject sequence. BLAST initializes respective subtasks of subject sequences that are processed by individual threads and then reassigns a subtask whenever each thread completes its workload. Hence the workload scheduling is dynamic.

---

[1] It should be clarify that term *database* refers simply to a usually large set of cataloged sequences. It does not imply any extra capabilities of fast access, data sharing, and so on, commonly found in standard database management systems. Therefore, *database* is merely a collection of sequences, although sequence information is copiously complemented with additional information such as the origin of the data, bibliographic references, sequence function (if known), and others.

Version 1.4 of BLAST uses a variety of vendor-specific constructs to implement parallelism. In the IRIX case, the parallel threads are created using *sprocs*. For the 2.0 version, NCBI has converted all Unix OS-based ports to the use of POSIX thread [6]. Regardless of the mechanism used to implement parallelism in BLAST, the use of multiprocessors is often quite effective in reducing the response time of BLAST run.

3   BLAST Algorithm

In this section, the overall structure of BLAST and detailed similarity assessment algorithm used in BLAST are explained. From the overall structure of BLAST programs, we identify the point where we can extend parallelized BLAST from SMP system to cluster system. From the detailed similarity assessment algorithm used in BLAST, we pinpoint the portion that is inevitably sequential and the portion that is potentially parallelizable in the algorithm.

3.1   Overall Structure of blastall Program

The *blastall*, the driver program for BLAST programs, behaves single interface permitting access to all five types of BLAST programs. It allows a user to specify a query sequence file and a database against which query sequences in the query sequence file is compared.

For the purpose of running the algorithm and computing overall statistics, *blastall* treats multiple databases as if they were aggregated into a single large virtual database that is mapped to the available virtual memory space on the machine performing the similarity search. Each query sequence in the query sequence file is searched against the entire subject sequences in the virtual database. Once the search is over similarity search is repeated for the next query sequence in the query sequence file. This is repeated until all the sequences in the file is processed. The computational cost of applying BLAST algorithm to a pair of sequences is proportional to the lengths of the sequences. However the rate of proportionality may vary for different databases and query sequences with respect to their contents. The pairwise comparison process has been made very efficiently through the use of a binary encoding of the sequences that substantially reduces memory requirements and an efficient implementation is made on finite automata. In order to extend the pairwise comparison to a complete search of one query sequence s against a number of databases $D_1, D_2, D_3, \ldots, D_n$, *blastall* uses an iteration as in Figure 1.

From parallel algorithmic paradigms' point of view, the NCBI-BLAST can be considered as phase parallel, process farm and work pool model [7]. The query sequences in a query file are iterated with synchronization. It corresponds to phase parallel (synchronous iteration paradigm). A master thread executes the essentially sequential part of the parallel program and creates a number of slave threads to execute parallel workload. It is corresponds to process farm (master-slave paradigm). A pool of work (subject sequences in sequence database) is

```
master thread
parse command line options and
set the query file, database files, BLAST program, etc.;
for each query sequence s in query file do {
  build neighborhood word list and its DFA for s;
  create or activate threads to run on different processors;
  synchronize the threads;
  initialize task into chunks of 500 subject sequences;
  while (chunk remained) do {
    allocate a chunk on demand to a thread;
  }
  join threads;
  sort hits in global hit list;
  and make data structure for alignments;
  report similarity search results for query sequence s
}

slave thread
request for next chunk of database sequences to master thread;
while (chunk allocated) do {
  for given query sequence s and each subject sequence
  in the subject sequences in the chunk do {
    search hits and extend hits;
    reap hit list by E_value;
    get lock for global hit list;
    merge thread local hit list into global hit list;
    release lock for global hit list;
  }
  request for next chunk of database sequences to master thread;
}
return ;
```

Fig. 1. Overview of blastall program

realized in a global data structure. Any free thread that fetches a piece of work (chunk) from the pool does similarity search and saves results into global search result. This corresponds to work pool model.

4   Performance Evaluation of BLAST on SMP Machines

In this section, we evaluate the performance of BLAST (especially for blastx) in order to inspect its behavior when the number of processes (threads) is increased with various size of query sequence.

4.1   Testing Environment

The hardware and software specification of the test platform, BLAST database, and query sequence are given in Table 1.

Table 1. Specification of SMP machine

Processors	8-way Intel Xeon Pentium III 700MHz with 1024KB L2 cache
Memory	2048 KB
O.S	Linux (kernel version 2.4.18) Sun Solaris 8
BLAST	Version 2.2.1 blastx
BLAST DB	nr (929,420 sequences; 291,584,220 total letters)
Query sequence	GI 20544475 Homo sapiens adenylate cyclase 2 (brain) (ADCY2) (total length: 6,551 letters)

In order to make variations on the length of query sequence, we generate query sequences of length from 100bp to 1200bp by truncating original sequence (GI: 20544475). In early state of testing, we experimented BLAST on Linux operating system. In that evaluation, we found that speedup stopped around four or five processors. In order to make sure whether this is the case for other operating systems, we conducted the same evaluation on Solaris 8 operating system.

4.2   Performance Evaluation Results

Figure 2 shows the execution time of *blastx* on an 8-way SMP machine with Linux operating system. The Y-axis specifies execution time in log-scale with base 2. For small size query sequences, the execution time reaches minimal at four or five processors while the execution time continuously decreases for longer query sequences. Figure 3 depicts the speedup in normal scale, which is calculated from Figure 2. From Figure 2, we can figure out the effective number of processors for a given query sequence size. From the experimental results, we can conclude that parallelized BLAST, which is distributed by NCBI, is more effective for longer query sequences. Because the experiment on Linux operating system showed that execution time for small size query sequences decreased only for certain number of

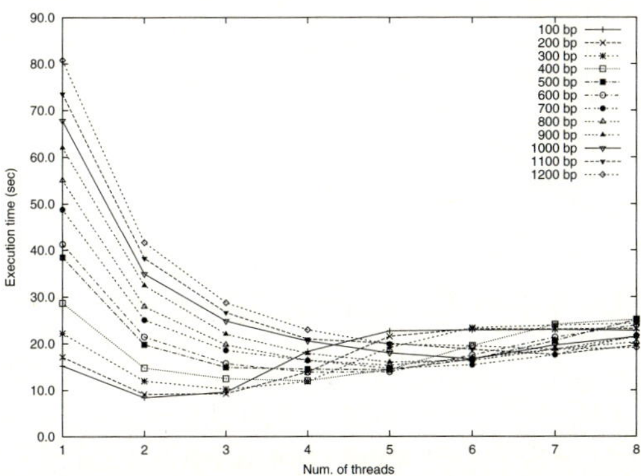

Fig. 2. Execution time on Linux operating system

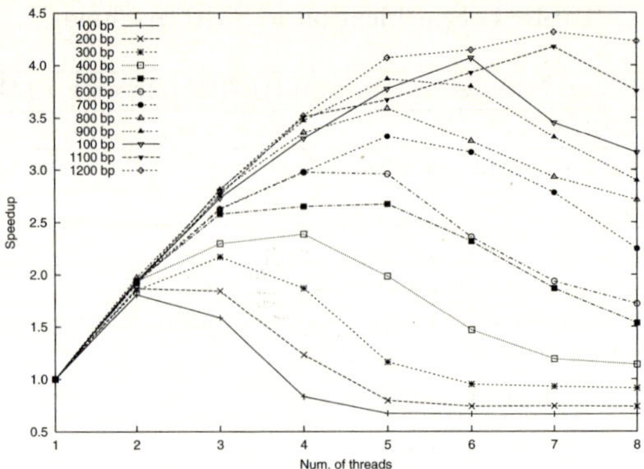

Fig. 3. Speedup on Linux operating system

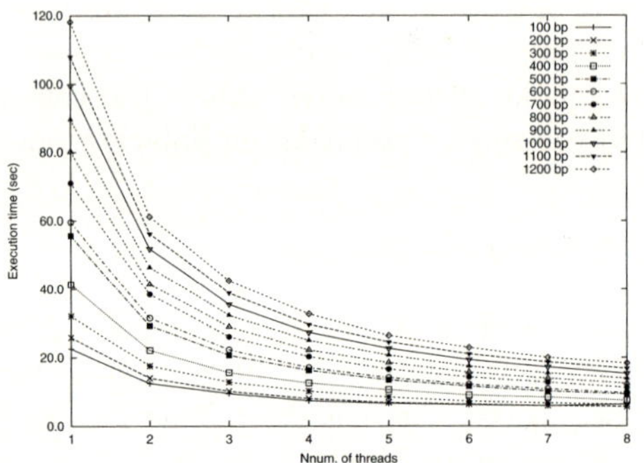

Fig. 4. Execution time on Solaris operating system

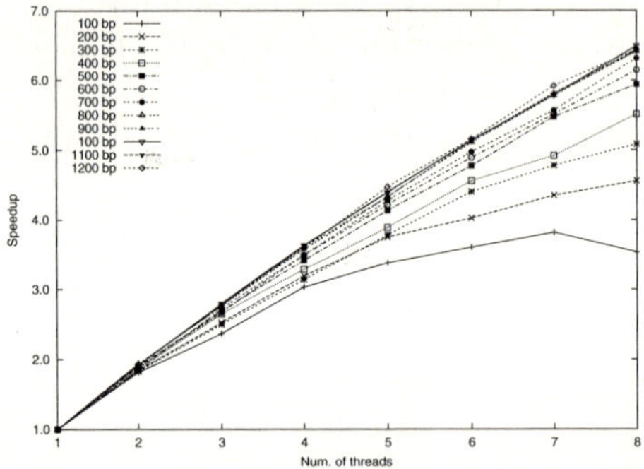

Fig. 5. Speedup on Solaris operating system

processors, we tested BLAST performance on different operating system, Solaris 8, which is known for its elaborate tuning for thread facility.

Figure 4 and Figure 5 shows the execution time (in log scale with base 2) and the speedup (in normal scale) on an 8-way SMP system with Solaris 8 operating

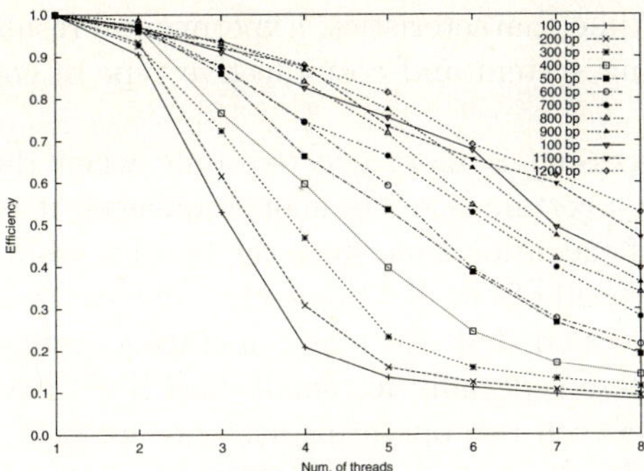

Fig. 6. Efficiency of Linux operating system

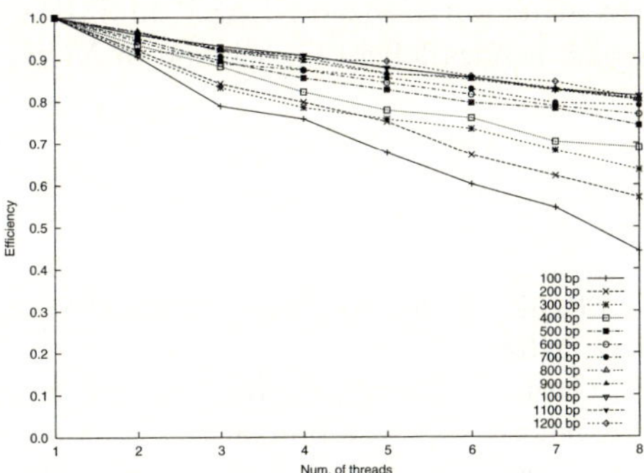

Fig. 7. Efficiency of Solaris operating system

system. Figure 6 and Figure 7 show the efficiencies of Linux and Solaris operating systems respectively. As depicted in the Figures, it is revealed that NCBI BLAST on Solaris operating system is more scalable as the number of processors increases in contrast to the experimental results on Linux operating system.

In most range of query sequence size and DOP (Degree of Parallelism), The performance of BLAST on Linux operating system outperforms the performance of BLAST on Solaris operating system. These results cannot be explained only by the thread facility of the given operating system because the two operating systems are different in many aspects such as file management, process management, memory management, etc. Since we aim to parallelize BLAST on cluster of PCs or small-sized SMPs eventually, the results give us a hint on the decision of operating systems for cluster systems.

5   Discussion and Conclusion

In this paper, the overall structure of BLAST algorithm, and the parallelizable portion and unparallelizable portion of BLAST algorithm are studied. For the preliminary experiment, we have evaluated BLAST on SMP machines and found some important run-time characteristics. Experimental results give us a hint on the choice of operating system and cost-effective type of computation node in cluster systems.

First, parallel processing is more effective only when the size of query sequence is longer than a certain size. For short sequences, it is worse to use more processors in terms of execution time since the benefits from parallel processing are less than the overhead of parallel processing. Second, in the same hardware configuration, it is revealed that the Linux operating system is superior to the Solaris operating system especially for small-sized SMP machines. The performance comparison between two operating systems indicates that the cluster of PCs or small-size SMPs (2-way or 4-way SMPs) is more cost-effective.

For the parallelization of BLAST on cluster systems, which has fundamentally different architecture from SMP machines, we need to develop upper level of parallelization on the existing parallelized BLAST on SMP system. In the future we are planning to devise a parallelization scheme of NCBI BLAST on cluster systems.

References

1. NCBI: Growth of GenBank. Technical report, National Center for Biotechnology Information (March 12, 2002)
2. Chi, E.H., Shoop, E., Carlis, J., Retzel, E., Ried, J.: Efficiency of shared-memory multiporceossors for a genetic sequence similiarity search algorithm. Technical report, Computer Science Dept., University of Minnesota (1997)
3. Altschul, S.F., Gish, W., Miller, W., Myers, E.W., Lipman, D.J.: Basic Local Alignment Search Tool. Journal of Molecular Biology **215** (1990) 403–410
4. Altschul, S., Gish, W.: Local alignment statistics. Methods in Enzymology **266** (1996) 460–480
5. Altschul, S., Madden, T., Schaffer, A., Zhang, J., Zhang, Z., Miller, W., Lipman, D.: Gapped BLAST and PSI–BLAST: A new generation of protein katabase search programs. Nucleic Acids Research **25** (1997) 3389–3402
6. Camp, N., Cofer, H., Gomperts, R.: High-Throughput BLAST. Technical report, Silicon Graphics, Inc. (1998)
7. Hwang, K., Xu, Z.: Chapter 12 Parallel Paradignms and Programming Model. In: Scalable Parallel Computing. McGraw-Hill Companies, Inc. (1998)

compPknots: A Framework for Parallel Prediction and Comparison of RNA Secondary Structures with Pseudoknots

Trilce Estrada, Abel Licon, and Michela Taufer

Computer Science Department, University of Texas At El Paso,
El Paso, TX 79968
{tpestrada, alicon2, mtaufer}@utep.edu

Abstract. Codes for RNA secondary structure prediction based on energy minimization are usually time and resource intensive. For this reason several codes have been simplified: in some cases they do not predict complex structures like pseudoknots, other times they predict structures with reduced lengths, or with simple pseudoknots. Each of these codes has its strengths and weaknesses. Providing scientists with tools that combine the strengths of the several codes is a worthwhile objective. To address this need, we present compPknots, a parallel framework that uses a combination of existing codes like Pknots-RE and Pknots-RG, to predict RNA secondary structures concurrently and automatically compare them with reference structures from databases or literature. In this paper compPknots is used to compare the predictions of 217 RNA structures from the PseudoBase database. Its parallel master-slave architecture provide scientists with higher prediction accuracies in shorter time.

1 Introduction

Nucleic Acid chains called RiboNucleic Acids (RNA) play critical roles in several processes in living organisms. In cellular protein synthesis, genetic information is expressed through RNA chains. In some viruses, RNA chains are carriers of genetic codes. RNA molecules are composed of 4 types of nucleotides or bases: adenine (A), cytosine (C), guanine (G) and uracil (U) that fold back on themselves thus pairing with each other. So for example C-G and A-U form stable *base pairs* with each other through the creation of hydrogen bonds between donor and acceptor sites on the bases. The *secondary structure* of an RNA molecule is the collection of base pairs. Since the experimental identification of RNA secondary structures is time demanding, in the past decades a significant effort has been made to build RNA structure predictions from sequence data using computational methods. A first approach consists of the computation of common foldings for a family of aligned, homologous RNAs. Usually, the alignment and secondary structure inference must be performed simultaneously, or at least iteratively and therefore methods that employ this approach for their predictions are not easy to automate and require significant human intervention. A second approach targets the structure prediction of single sequences based on the minimization of the free energy of a folding [1]. With the significantly increasing computing power, today's methods that employ this approach can be easily automated

G. Min et al. (Eds.): ISPA 2006 Ws, LNCS 4331, pp. 677–686, 2006.

and therefore are attractive methods to perform these predictions. Several motifs can be commonly found in RNA secondary structures: stem-loops (i.e., helix, hairpin loop, interior loop, buldge loop, multi loop) and pseudoknots.

Among the several motifs in an RNA molecule, the prediction of pseudoknots is particularly demanding in terms of data and computational power required for codes based on energy minimization methods. Therefore several codes that use the minimization of the RNA free energy of a folding often do not include pseudoknot predictions [2]. Because pseudoknots have been observed in several RNA molecules [3] omitting them from predictions can significantly affect the prediction accuracy. To reduce computation time and data storage, several codes that include pseudoknots have been implemented with significant simplifications: the Rivas and Eddy code (Pknots-RE) [4] can predict the secondary structure of very short RNA segments (of the order of hundreds of nucleotides) while RNA molecules are normally compounds of thousands of nucleotides; Reeder and Giegerich [5] have significantly reduced the complexity of the pseudoknots that their code, Pknots-RG, can predict. To solve the limitations of these codes on their own, a more effective approach would be to use the combination of both. Providing the user with a tool that combines the strengths of each of the single codes would be a worthwhile goal. Once predictions are performed, a comparison of the predicted secondary structures against experimentally observed structures is needed. The comparison of predicted RNA secondary structures is often performed manually using tools such as PseudoViewer [6]. This manual task is monotonous, highly sensitive to errors, and when the sequences are too long or too numerous, it is impossible for a human to do this in a feasible amount of time.

The above listed critical aspects point out the need for tools that (1) predict secondary structures of RNA segments, included pseudoknots, in parallel using combinations of energy based methods and (2) automatically compare the predictions against reference structures from databases or literature. We address this need in this paper by presenting a parallel framework, compPknots, for prediction and comparison of RNA secondary structures with pseudoknots. compPknots exploits the advantages of parallel computation using the MPI library MPICH to predict large numbers of RNA secondary structures using well-known RNA structure prediction codes such as Pknots-RE [4] and Pknots-RG [5] concurrently. Using compPknots, we evaluate the prediction accuracy of the single Pknots-RE and Pknots-RG predictions against their combined accuracy for a set of 217 RNA segments from the PseudoBase database [7]. Running the predictions in parallel on a Beowulf cluster using these two codes significantly reduced the execution time for the predictions of the 217 RNA segments.

The rest of the paper is organized as follows: In Section 2, we present an overview of the main biochemical concepts needed to understand this work and a short review of works in the field of RNA structure prediction. Section 3 describes the *compPknots* framework, its software components for parallel prediction and comparison of RNA secondary structures, and how to use it. Section 4 presents the evaluation of *compPknots* in terms of its prediction accuracy and performance. In Section 5 we conclude and present current work in progress.

2 Background and Related Work

A ribonucleic acid (RNA) is one of the two types of nucleic acids (Deoxyribonucleic acid DNA and Ribonucleic acid RNA) found in living organisms. An RNA molecule represents a long chain of monomers called nucleotides or bases. RNA contains four different nucleotides: adenine, guanine, cytosine, and uracil that are represented with the letters A, G, C, and U respectively. A sequence of these bases is strung together to form a long, single-stranded RNA molecule. The molecule, whose sequence may be up to thousands of bases long, tends to fold back on itself, mostly by pairing between complementary bases: C and G form a complementary base pair, and so do A and U. The *secondary structure* of an RNA molecule is the collection of base pairs that occur in its three dimensional structure. RNA secondary structures can be classified into two basic categories called *stem-loops* and *pseudoknots* (see Fig. 1). Both kinds of secondary structures on overlapping RNA viral genes have been implicated in important viral gene expression processes [8]. Pseudoknots have been also shown to be relevant in many RNA mediated processes. Examples are the self-splicing group I introns [9], ribosomal RNAs, or RNaseP. Recently, pseudoknots were located in prion proteins of humans, and confirmed for many other species [10].

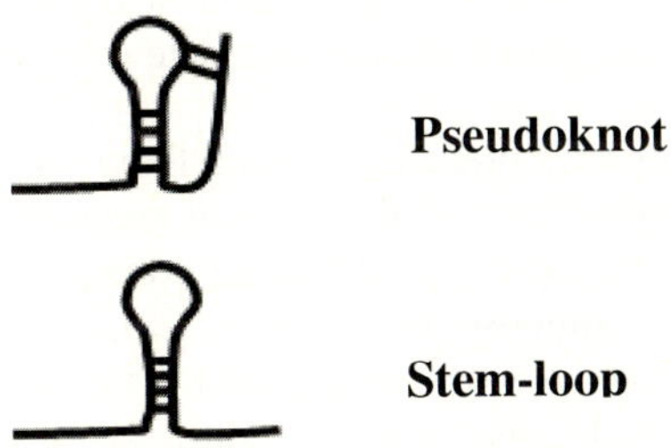

Fig. 1. Pseudoknot and stem-loop

With the current increased interest in the RNA functions, algorithmic support for analyzing structures that include pseudoknots is much in demand; determining such structures, including pseudoknots, has been shown to be an NP-hard problem. Only for more restricted classes of pseudoknots, polynomial algorithms have been implemented. Rivas and Eddy [4] developed a dynamic programming algorithm, Pkno ts-RE, for predicting optimal (minimum energy) RNA secondary structures, including pseudoknots. The algorithm has the worst case time and space complexities of $O(n^6)$ and $O(n^4)$ respectively. The implementation of the algorithm uses standard RNA folding thermodynamic parameters augmented by a few parameters describing the thermodynamic stability of pseudoknots and by coaxial stacking energies. Reeder and Giegerich [5] improved the complexity of the algorithm, reaching the $O(n^4)$ space and $O(n^2)$ time, by using the Minimal Free Energy (MFE) model. The runtime improvement, compared to Pknots-RE, results from an idea of canonization, while the space improvement results from disallowing chained pseudoknots. Uemura et al. [11] proposed an algorithm based on tree-adjoining grammar. The time complexities of their algorithm depends on the types of pseudoknots: it is $O(n^4)$ for simple pseudoknots and $O(n^5)$ or more for the other pseudoknots. Although the algorithm can always find optimal structures, tree-adjoining grammars are complicated and impractical for longer RNA sequences. Akutsu [12] analyzed Uemura's method and found that the tree-adjoining grammar was not crucial but the parsing procedure was. Since the parsing procedure is intrinsically a dynamic programming procedure, Akutsu re-formulated this method as a dynamic programming procedure without the tree-adjoining grammar. This method has not been implemented into a code yet.

compPknots aims to include a variety of codes to capture the strength of each single code. The current version of our framework presented in this paper includes Pknots-RE and Pknots-RG, but it can be easily extended to accommodate other existing codes for RNA predictions.

3 Components, Parallelization, and Usage of *compPknots*

compPknots is a framework that can integrate concurrent executions of existing codes for RNA secondary structure predictions such as Pknots-RE and Pknots-RG, with the capability of automatically measuring the level of prediction accuracy for these codes by using a comparison approach based on stacks. The framework is written in C and employs the MPICH library for concurrent predictions and comparisons. Its modular structure allows users to easily extend it to accommodate other codes and comparison techniques.

The current framework integrates predictions using Pknots-RE and Pknots-RG and their comparisons. For each input segment, the chain of nucleotides, or RNA segment, is read and its correctness is checked: this checking consists of verifying that only characters in the following list compose the chain: A, C, G, U, a, c g, and u. If comparisons are scheduled, the user provides *compPknots* with the file with the experimentally observed structures and *compPknots* schedules the corresponding comparisons. The observed secondary structures are traditionally represented in terms of strings of brackets, i.e., "(" and ")","[" and "]", "{" and "}", dots ".", and colons ":". Two paired nucleotides are represented with two closed brackets collocated in the string at the same position as the correspondent nucleotides in the input segment. A checking is required for the observed secondary structure to control whether it contains only characters in the following list: "[", "]", "{", "}", "(", ")", ".", and ":". Also predicted secondary structures are returned as a string of braces, parenthesis and dots. After checking the correctness of input segments and observed structures, *compPknots* can execute either Pknots-RE or Pknots-RG or both (default configuration). Finally, predicted secondary structures are compared with the observed structures provided in the input file and the statistics are then printed to the screen or stored to a file.

The comparison between a predicted structure and an observed structure is based on stacks: for the predicted structure and the observed structure the code allocates a pair of stacks for storing general stem-loops (predicted stem-loop stack and observed stem-loop stack) and a second pair for storing loops associated to pseudoknots (predicted pseudoknot stack and observed pseudoknot stack). Each pair of stacks is used twice for each assignment in case a pseudoknot is present. If a pseudoknot is not present, only the pair of stacks associated to the stem-loop is used. One bracket representing one of two paired nucleotides, e.g., "(" and ")" or "[" and "]", or one dot or colon, i.e., "." or ":", representing an unpaired nucleotide, is read at the time from both the predicted and observed structures. If an opening character appears, e.g., "(" or "[", its position in the RNA segment is stored in the corresponding stack based on the fact that the character is from the predicted or from the observed structure as well as on the fact that the code is going through a first set of parenthesis (a stem-loop) or is going through a second set without having completed a previous one (a pseudoknot). If the character is a closing one, e.g., ")" or "]", then the last element in the corresponding stack is removed. If a removal occurs at the same time from the predicted and observed stacks, the equivalent nucleotide positions are compared. If the positions are equal, the number of true predicted base pairs is incremented by one; otherwise the system increments the number of false predicted base pairs.

compPknots uses a master-slave paradigm to run predictions and comparisons, where the master is in charge of getting new jobs and dispatching them to available slaves. The master validates the correctness of RNA segments submitted for prediction as well as the correctness of observed RNA secondary structures before submitting them to the slaves. The master also receives the results of the predictions and comparisons and prints or stores them. Slaves are activated by the master that sends them the initialization parameters, e.g., what code to use for the prediction and whether to compare predictions with observed structures. Once the slave is active, it starts its prediction cycle in which it requests and gets new jobs. The cycle terminates if there is no job remaining. Fig. 2 shows the flow of tasks executed by the master and the slaves. The assignment of a single job at a time to the hosts helps prevent load imbalances: the length of jobs depends on the length of their RNA segment and whether the resources on the distributed system are dedicated or not.

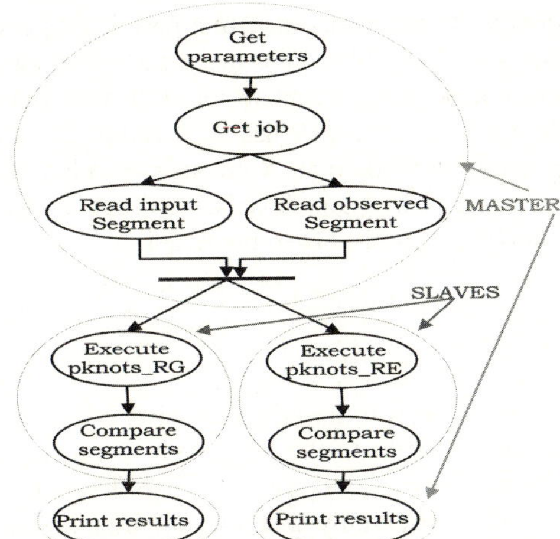

Fig. 2. Concurrent prediction and comparison in *compPknots*

compPknots is flexible in terms of capabilities that scientists can select for a given run. The user can, for example, choose whether to predict and compare a nucleotide segment provided to the code from the command line or several segments listed in a file, or whether to select just one of the RNA structure prediction codes and store the output to a file rather than printing it to the screen. A list of capabilities and possible input options are reported in [13]. For each RNA segment, the following metrics are returned to the scientist:

- Length of the RNA segment: Number of nucleotides or bases in the given segment.
- Total observed base pairs (*total pairs*): Number of base pairs in the observed secondary structure.
- Total predicted base pairs: Number of base pairs in the predicted secondary structure. This is the sum of true pairs and false pairs.
- True predicted base pairs (*true pairs*): Number of pairs predicted that are also in the observed secondary structure.
- False predicted base pairs (*false pairs*): Number of base pairs predicted that are not in the observed secondary structures. This is the sum of wrong predicted pairs and true pairs not detected.
- Sensitivity: Number of true pairs over the number of base pairs.

$$sensitivity = \frac{true\_pairs}{total\_pairs}$$

- Selectivity. Number of true pairs over the sum of true and false pairs.

$$selectivity = \frac{true\_pairs}{true\_pairs + false\_pairs}$$

- Total Energy: Energy of the RNA secondary structure.

The sensitivity and selectivity are two standard metrics that are used by scientists to quantify the accuracy of a prediction [14]. The sensitivity indicates whether the prediction has captured the secondary structure partially or completely. The selectivity indicates whether a prediction has introduced additional base pairs in the predicted secondary structure that are not present in the observed secondary structure. These metrics range from 0, i.e., the structure has been completed miss-predicted, to 1, i.e., in the case of a successful prediction. More in particular, if the sensitivity is 1, it means that all the observed base pairs have been correctly predicted. If the selectivity is 1, then no additional base pair has been predicted.

4   Evaluation

The evaluation of *compPknots* in this paper consists of two components: first of all, the framework is used to evaluate the effectiveness on the prediction accuracy of combining several prediction codes; then the performance analysis of predictions using each single code sequentially and the combination of both concurrently is evaluated.

For the *evaluation of the accuracy* of single codes, Pknots-RE and Pknots-RG, and their combination, we used 217 RNA segments and their experimentally observed secondary structures from the PsudoBase database choosing all the complete segments in this database, i.e., those segments that do not present nucleotides gaps in their brackets representation [7]. For the predictions with Pknots-RG, we scored the predicted structures exclusively on an energy base and we did not force pseudoknot identifications as possible in this code [5]. For the evaluation of the prediction accuracy of the single codes (considered separately), we considered 4 levels of sensitivity and selectivity, i.e., 0.0, $\lfloor 0.0 \rfloor - \lfloor 0.5 \rfloor$ in which the values 0.0 and 0.5 are not included in this range, $\lfloor 0.5 \rfloor - \lfloor 1.0 \rfloor$ in which the value 1.0 is not included in this range, and the last level being 1.0. We counted the number of predictions that fell into each level for the two metrics. Fig. 3 shows the number of predictions for the 4 levels for both Pknot-RE and Pknot-RG. As we can see in Fig. 3, sensitivity and selectivity in Pknots-RE and Pknots-RG have similar behaviors. With reference to the sensitivity, both codes have a significant number of structures that are completely miss-predicted i.e., the codes are not able to capture any base pairs. More in particular, for Pknots-RE, 6.4% of the predictions have no true pairs and 33.6% of the predictions capture all the true pairs. For Pknots-RG, 4.6% of the predictions are completely miss-predicted (which is less than for Pknots-RE) but fewer predictions capture all the true pairs (29.9% for Pknots-RG versus 33.6% for Pknots-RE). The remaining structures are partially predicted correctly, i.e., 59.9% for Pknots-RE and 65.4% for Pknots-RG. With reference to the selectivity, both the codes show the tendency to predict more base pairs than those observed experimentally: only for 29 RNA segments predicted by Pknots-RE (13.3% of the predicted secondary structures) the number of false pairs is zero. For RNA segments predicted by Pknots-RG only 34 predictions (15.6% of the predicted secondary structures) have no false pairs. In general with reference to the overall pool of RNA segments, we found that Pknots-RE has an average sensitivity of 73.3% and an average selectivity of 62.2% while Pknots-RG performs slightly better with an average sensitivity of 75.6% and an average selectivity of 64.7%.

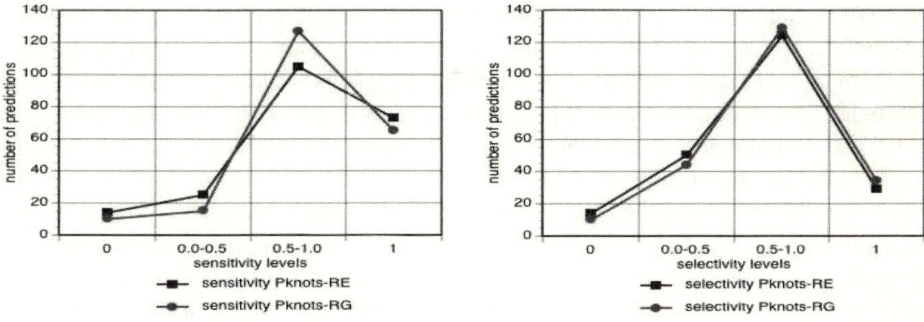

Fig. 3. Sensitivity and selectivity levels for 217 predicted RNA secondary structures using either Pknots-RE or Pknots-RG for predictions

If we consider the single predictions separately we can see that in several cases one of the two codes provides an accurate prediction while the other code performs poorly. An evaluation of the accuracy using a combination of both codes was performed using *compPknots* and the results are reported in [13]. In this comparison we combined different levels of sensitivity and selectivity of secondary structures predicted using the two codes, Pknots-RE and Pknots-RG concurrently. For each code we considered the follow levels: (1) both sensitivity and selectivity are zero, i.e.,

0{0}; (2) sensitivity and selectivity range within zero and one, i.e., 0.x{0.y}; (3) selectivity is one but selectivity is less than one because, despite the prediction capture all the true pairs, it also captures additional pairs that have not been observed experimentally (false pairs), i.e., 1{0.y}; and selectivity and sensitivity are both one, i.e., 1{1}. We observed that the cross prediction using both the codes increased the prediction accuracy significantly: we were able to predict correctly the complete secondary structure of 92 RNA segments for which the sensitivity was equal to one. This is equal to 42.3% of the pool of RNA segments considered. Also the selectivity was significantly improved: 22.2% of the secondary structures have both sensitivity and selectivity equal to one. The average sensitivity and selectivity were increased to 82.4% and 70.8% respectively proving how the combination of prediction codes can indeed increase the final accuracy for our 217 RNA segments.

Another important aspect of running the codes concurrently is the *execution time*. To address this issue, we ran the predictions using *compPknots* with each code as well as their combination on a Beowulf cluster at the University of Texas at El Paso. The cluster has a head node with 2 AMD Opteron processors, 4 GB memory, 3 TB of disk space (shared by all the nodes over NFS) and 64 compute nodes with 2 AMD Opteron processors, and 4 GB of memory each. Each prediction of the 217 RNA segments was repeated three times and the values reported are average times. The same set of 217 RNA segments were computed using *compPknots* with 1, 2, 4, 8, 16, and 32 processors. The segments have a length that ranges from 21 to 137 nucleotides or bases.

In our performance analysis, we observed that between the two codes, Pknots-RE is the most time and resource intensive. For Pknots-RE, the execution of the sequential prediction and comparison of the 217 RNA segments using one node of the cluster took an average of 1512 minutes, while the same execution using Pknots-RG took only 14.29 seconds. We also observed that the combined execution of the two codes was mainly dictated by two factors: the prediction using Pknots-RE and the execution times of the 10 longest RNA segments. In particular, the latter factor limited the scalability of *compPknots* with this set of RNA segments. Running *compPknots* with Pknots-RE and Pknots-RG with 2 processors took 837 minutes. This time went down to 475 and 260 minutes with 4 and 8 processors respectively. For 16 and more processors the time needed for this set of RNA segments did not scale any further as shown in Fig. 4.a. We measured the times for the prediction and comparison of the ten longest segments with length longer than 100 nucleotides, and compared these times with the total time to predict and compare all 207 remaining segments from our Pseudo-Base set. Fig. 4.b shows the times to run a Pknots-RE prediction in minutes (x-axis) for different RNA segments (y-axes, where the name of each segment is associated to its length -- number in parentheses). As we can see in the figure, the time for the prediction of segments such as BMV3, CCMV3, and CMV3, whose lengths are 137, 134, and 133 respectively, is comparable with the total time to execute the remaining 207 segments. This suggests that once we have more than 8 processors, those that receive the longest segments will determine the time of the whole simulation. In general, the scalability of *compPknots* executions depends on both the length and number of segments. Even a smart distribution of tasks across processors cannot solve load imbalances due to the executions of predictions in which a few segments dominate over the others because of their much larger length. These observations suggest two future improvement strategies for *compPknots*: the need for the parallelization of the

Pknots-RE code and the potential for *compPknots* to run effectively on clusters of heterogeneous nodes where longer segments are assigned to faster nodes and shorter segments are assigned to slower nodes.

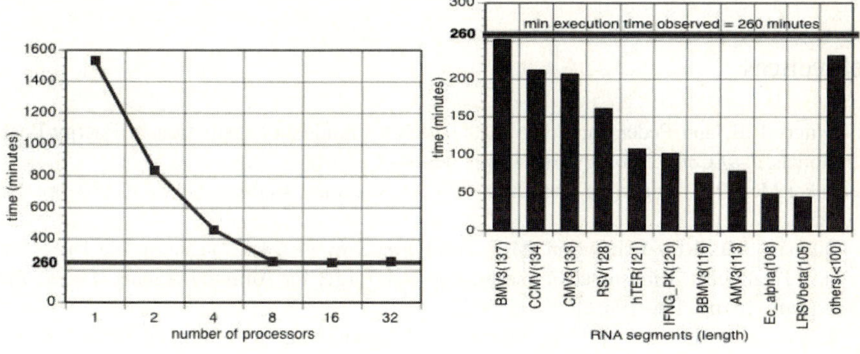

a. Execution time for 217 RNA segments   **b.** Segment execution time

Fig. 4. Performance analysis of *compPknots* for a set of 217 RNA segments

5   Conclusions and Future Work

In this paper we presented *compPknots*, a parallel software framework that given a set of RNA molecules, predicts their RNA secondary structures (including their pseudoknots) using a combination of existing prediction codes concurrently. It also allows users to automatically compare these predictions with reference structures from databases or literature, identifying the predictive accuracy of each RNA secondary structure. *compPknots* allowed us to run two codes concurrently for predictions, Pknots-RE and Pknots-RG, benefiting from the combined prediction capability of both. The combined execution of the codes allowed us to correctly capture a larger number of RNA secondary structures as oppose to using the single codes separately. The parallel framework based on a master-slave paradigm and implemented using MPICH allowed us to achieve results in a shorter amount of time. *compPknots* is a prototype that is part of a "smart" framework that automatically at run time selects RNA segments from large RNA molecule, predicts the secondary structures in parallel using a large variety of existing codes, and based on the comparisons of the collected results selects new RNA segments from the initial RNA chain to ultimately rebuild larger parts of this RNA molecule. We are currently extending *compPknots* to accommodate these features.

Acknowledgments

This material is based in part upon work supported by the Texas Advanced Research Program under Grant No. 003661-0008-2006. Financial support through the National Science Foundation (grant # EIA-0080940, "MII: Graduate Education for Minority

Students in Computer Science and Engineering: Extending the Pipeline" and grant # SCI-0506429, "DAPLDS - a Dynamically Adaptive Protein-Ligand Docking System based on multi-scale modeling") is acknowledged. We wish to thank Dr. Ming-Ying Leung, Prayook Tungjatooronrusamee, and Yash Dahl for their valuable advice during the implementation and testing of *compPknots*.

References

1. Lyngo, R.B. and Pedersen, C.N.S. (2000) RNA Pseudoknot Prediction in Energy-Based Models. *J. of Comp. Biology,* 7(3/4), pp. 409–427.
2. Zuker M. (1989) Computer Prediction of RNA Structure. *Methods Enzymol.* 180, pp. 262-288.
3. Dinman, J.D., Ruiz-Echevarria, M.J., and Peltz, S.W. (1998) Translating old Drugs into new Treatments: Ribosomal Frameshifting as a Target for Antiviral Agents. *Trends Biotechnol.,* 16, pp. 190–196.
4. Rivas, E. and Eddy, S. (1999) A Dynamic Programming Algorithm for RNA Structure Prediction including Pseudoknots. *Journal of Molecular Biology*, 285(5), pp. 2053-2068.
5. Reeder J. and Giegerich R. (2004) Design, implementation and evaluation of a practical pseudoknot folding algorithm based on thermodynamics. *BMC Bioinformatics*, 5(104).
6. Han, K. and Byun,Y. (2003) PseudoViewer2: Visualization of RNA Pseudoknots of any Type. *Nucleic Acids Res.,* 31, pp. 3432–3440.
7. Batenburg, F.H.D. van, Gultyaev, A.P., Pleij, C.W.A., Ng, J., and Oliehoek, J. (2000). Pseudobase: a Database with RNA Pseudoknots. *Nucl. Acids Res.,* 28(1).
8. L. Bidou, G. Stahl, B. Grima, H. Liu, M. Cassan, and J. Rousset: In Vivo HIV-I Frameshifting Efficiency is Directly Related to the Stability of the Stem-loop Stimulatory Signal. *RNA,* 3:1153-1158, 1997
9. Cech, T. (1988) Conserved Sequences and Structures of Group I Introns: Building an Active Site for RNA Catalysis a Review. *Gene*, 73, 259-271.
10. Barette, I., G. Poisson, P. Gendron, and F. Major (2001). Pseudoknots in prion protein mRNAs con_rmed by comparative sequence analysis and pattern searching. Nucleic Acids Research 29 (3), 753-758.
11. Uemura Y, Hasegawa A, Kobayashi S, and Yokomori (1995) Grammatically Modeling and Predicting RNA Secondary Structures. In *Proceedings of the Genome Informatics Workshop*, Universal Academy Press, Tokyo, pp. 67-76.
12. Akutsu, T. (2000) Dynamic Programming Algorithms for RNA Secondary Prediction with Pseudoknots, *Discrete Applied Mathematics,* 104, 45-62.
13. T. Estrada, A. Licon, and M. Taufer: CompPknots: a Framework for Parallel Prediction and Comparison of RNA Secondary Structures with Pseudoknots. *Technical Report UTEP-CS-06-42*, University of Texas, El Paso, September 2006.
14. Gardner P.P. and Giegerich R. (2004) A Comprehensive Comparison of Comparative RNA Structure Prediction Approaches. *BMC Bioinformatics*, 5(140).

On Integration of GUI and Portal of Cluster and Grid Computing Platforms for Parallel Bioinformatics*

Chao-Tung Yang[1,**], Tsu-Fen Han[1], Heng-Chuan Kan[2], and William C. Chu[3]

[1] High Performance Computing Laboratory
[1,3] Department of Computer Science and Information Engineering
Tunghai University, Taichung City 40704, Taiwan
ctyang@thu.edu.tw, g942814@thu.edu.tw, chu@csie.thu.edu.tw
[2] Biotechnology Group, Southern Business Unit
National Center for High-performance Computing
Hsinshi, Tainan County 74147, Taiwan
n00hck00@nchc.org.tw

Abstract. In this paper, we implement an experimental distributed computing application for parallel bioinformatics. The system consists of the basic cluster and grid computing environment and user portal to provide a useful graphical interface for biologists who are not specialized in Information Technology (IT) to be able to easily take advantages of using high-performance computing re-sources. Finally, we perform several experimentations to demonstrate that cluster and grid computing platform indeed reduces the execution time of the biology problem.

1 Introduction

Bioinformatics is the combination of biology and information technology. These include any computational tools and methods to manage, analyze and manipulate large sets of biology data. Thus, computing technologies are vital for bioinformatics applications. Biology problems often need to repeat the same task for millions of times such as searching sequence similarity over the existed databases or comparing a group of sequences to determine evolutionary relationship. In such cases, the high performance computers to process this information are indispensable. Biological information is stored on many different computers around the world. The easiest way to assess this information is to connect these computers together through the network. This approach requires high-performance computing infrastructures with access to huge databases of information.

Many advances in computing technology and computer science over the past 30 years have dramatically changed much of our society. The computing technologies today represent promising future possibilities. Currently, it is still very difficult for

---

* This work is supported in part by National Science Council, Taiwan R.O.C., under grants no. NSC95-2221-E-029-004 and NSC95-2218-E-007-025.
** Corresponding author.

G. Min et al. (Eds.): ISPA 2006 Ws, LNCS 4331, pp. 687–696, 2006.

researchers who are not specialized in IT to fully comprehend the power of the high-performance computing technologies. IT engineers are therefore playing an important role to improve the research environment. The mission imposed on us is to provide a user-friendly interface for scientists to benefit directly from using high-performance computing technologies. To face this problem, we develop three kinds of user interfaces. The user portal enables interactions between the application user and the application itself. It obtains parametric inputs for the problem and reports the results upon completion of the application's execution.

The rest of the paper is organized as follows. In section 2, a brief overview of Bioinformatics and the features of high-performance computing are described. In section 3, we report the implementation of our system. In section 4, we report the experimental results and performance comparisons. Finally, conclusions are given in section 5.

2 Background

2.1 Bioinformatics

Computer technology is used at nearly every stage of the drug development processes which compose of pre-clinical testing, research, and development. Bioinformatics allows researchers to analyze terabytes of data produced by the Human Genome Project [12]. It is the discipline of obtaining information about genomic or protein sequence data. This may involve searching sequence similarity of databases, comparing an unidentified sequence to the sequences in a database, or making predictions about the sequence based on current knowledge of similar sequences. Various databases of gene/protein sequence, gene expression, and related analysis tools all help scientists determine whether and how a particular molecule is directly involved in a disease process. That, in turn, aids in the discovery of new and better drug targets.

Sequence similarity search to a query can be found in a database by alignment algorithms and returning the highest scoring sequence. Examples of such software tools are the BLAST [18], FASTA [10], and Smith-Waterman algorithms [9]. BLAST and FASTA provide very fast searches within a sequence database.

Multiple alignments illustrate relationships between two or more sequences. When the sequences involved are diverse, the conserved residues are often key residues associated with maintenance of structural stability or biological function. Multiple alignments can reveal many clues about protein structure and function. The most commonly used software for multiple alignments is the ClustalW [5] package.

2.2 Cluster Computing

A Beowulf cluster [8] is a form of parallel computer, which is nothing more than a computer that uses more than one processor. There are many different kinds of parallel computer, distinguished by the kinds of processors they use and the way in which those processors exchange data. It takes advantage of two commodity components: fast CPUs designed primarily for the personal computer market and networks designed to connect personal computers together (in what is called a local area network or LAN). Beowulf clusters provide an effective and low-cost solution for delivering enormous computational powers to applications and are now used virtually everywhere. More specifically, a Beowulf cluster is a high-performance, high-throughput and high-availability computing platform [1].

To make use of multiple processes and executing each on a separate processor, we need to apply parallelism of computing algorithms. There are two common types of parallelism: MPI [14] and PVM [20]. PVM is a master-worker approach which is the simplest and easiest to implement. It relies on being able to break the computation into independent tasks. A master then coordinates the solution of these independent tasks by worker processes. MPI cannot (or cannot easily) be broken into independent tasks. In this kind of parallelism, the computation is broken down into communicating, inter-dependent tasks. Here we used LAM/MPI [15] for our cluster system and MPICH [16] for our Grid system.

2.3 Grid Computing

Grid computing [2][3] enables virtual organizations to share geographically distributed resources as they pursue common goals, assuming the absence of central location, central control, omniscience, and an existing trust relationship. In our system, we adopted a Grid middleware called Globus toolkit 4.0 [21] as the infrastructure for our BioGrid. The toolkit includes software for security, information infrastructure, resource management, data management, communication, fault detection, and portability. Java CoG [13] (Commodity Grid Kits) combines Java technology with Grid computing is used to develop advanced Grid services and accessibility to basic Globus resources. It allows for easier and faster application developments. It also encourages collaborative code reuses and avoids the duplicate efforts among problems involving environments, science portals, Grid middleware, and collaborative pilots.

3 Implementation

Our implementation can be divided into two parts: the basic high-performance computing environment and the user portals.

3.1 High-Performance Computing Environment

The high-performance computing environment comprises of the BioGrid [4][19] and BioCluster [6][7]systems. Both of them execute three bioinformatics software: mpiBLAST [17], FASTA and ClustalW. The hardware architecture is shown in Figure 1. In BioGrid portion, we construct a BioGrid testbed which includes four separated nodes. Each node is installed with Globus toolkit 3.0 for the Grid infrastructure, and MPICHG2 for message-passing.

The Redhat 9.0 Linux distribution is installed on each node. The idea of the Linux cluster is to maximize the performance-to-cost ratio of computing by using low-cost commodity components and free-source Linux and GNU software to assemble a parallel and distributed computing system. Software support includes the standard

Linux/GNU environment, compilers, debuggers, editors, and standard numerical libraries. Coordination and communication among the processing nodes are the key requirements of parallel-processing clusters. To accommodate this coordination, developers create software to carry out the coordination and hardware to send and receive the coordinating messages. Messaging architectures such as Message Passing Interface (MPI), and Parallel Virtual Machine (PVM), allow programmers to ensure that the controls and messages take place during the operation.

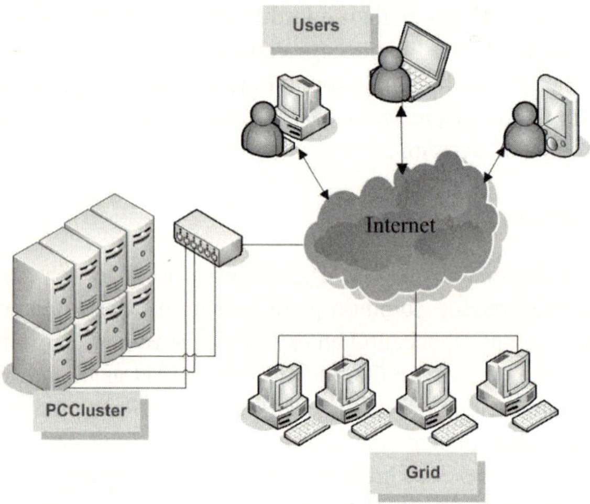

Fig. 1. The hardware architecture of our system

3.2 User Portal

The user portal enables interactions between the application user and the application itself. It obtains parametric inputs for the problem and reports the results upon completion of the execution. Our portal composes of three interfaces: Java-based Application, JSP web page and Pocket PC for easy control of the parallel bioinformatics software. Furthermore, we also develop various basic services for Grid and Cluster systems.

The Java-based application makes use of Java CoG kit to connect with the Grid system. There are some key characteristics of this application: (i) GridProxyInit, a JDialog to summit a pass phrase to Grid for extending expired date of certificate; (ii) GridConfigureDialog utilizes UITool of the CoG Kit for users to configure the number of process and host name of the Grid server; (iii) GridJob creates a GramJob instance which represents a simple gram job. It allows for submitting a job to a gatekeeper, canceling it, sending a signal command, registering and unregistering from callback; (iv) GetRSL provides a common interchange language to describe resources; (v) GlobusRun is a factory method for creating a previously exported credential.

The various components of the Globus Resource Management architecture manipulate RSL strings to perform their management functions in cooperation with other components in the system. For example, GetRSL combines the RSL string. JobMonitor uses two parameters, Gridjob and RSL to start up the GlobusRun and monitors the job process. Then, it submits jobs to the Grid server and receives the responses from the Grid server. GridFTP could upload DNA sequences to the Grid System. In addition to the functions that Java CoG kit provides, there are several APIs developed specifically for our system. For instance, ProxyDestroy destroys the CA Files to protect the Grid system. Note that the machine files can be configured from the application site for our system as shown in Figure 2.

For cluster, we also develop a series of capability. In server site, a program named CommandClient was written to receive the commands from the client. Users could configure the cluster system from the application site which includes information of how many CPUs being used, lam/mpi, PVM, lamhost file locations. And we can monitor the CPU and memory information to know which machines in our cluster system are alive. It also has the capability of lamboot and lamhalt from remote site as shown in Figure 3.

We implement GUI for Bioinformatics software applications on both of the Grid and Cluster systems. Only application service interface is visible, however, implementation details such as distributed processing and parallel processing are invisible from users.

The JSP web page utilizes a variety of advanced technologies such as JavaServer Pages, HTML, JavaScript, ActionScript (in Flash) and Tomcat. The portal composes of three parts: Machine Monitor, Bioinformatics software application and Job submission. Figure 5 demonstrates that the Machine Monitor (MM) can display critical information such as remote machine is still working or not and check if the Java CoG kit was installed on the machine. If the machine halts unexpected the Error Log delivers the details as seen in Figure 6.

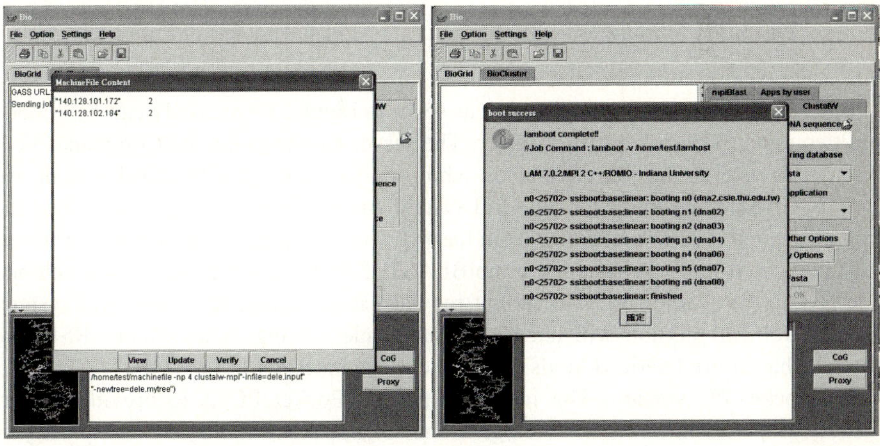

Fig. 2. Configure the machine file for Grid system

Fig. 3. The capability of lamboot and lamhalt from remote site

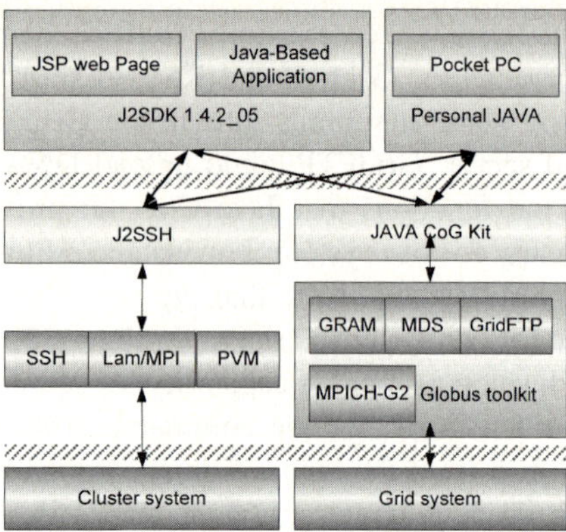

Fig. 4. The software architecture of our system

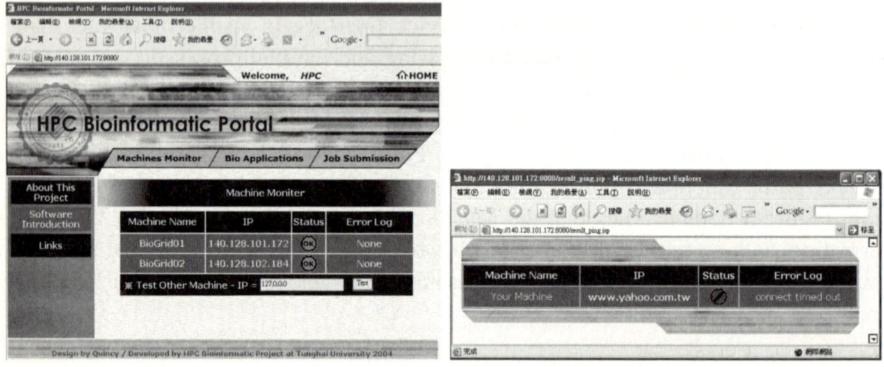

Fig. 5. The Machine Monitor   **Fig. 6.** Example of Error Log

Bioinformatics software application as seem in Figure 7 essentially can be divided into two parts: BioGrid and BioCluster. The server side exploits the CommandClient program to receive the job commands submitted to cluster. On the Grid system, we develop GridJob to submit jobs to Grid system and SimpleCreateProxy to extend the time of expired date of certificate from the JSP web. And the bioinformatics software tools integrated into our system are mpiBLAST, FASTA and ClustalW. Job submission (Figure 8) enables users to submit regular Linux command to our Grid system. Because Job Submission will not be operated unless using intact Globus RSL, the interface has offered various kinds of RSL hot keys for users.

For Pocket PC version, The main function of Pocket PC is to provide a user-friendly graphical interface for biologists and scientists to simplify the complexity of operating the bioinformatics software on the Grid and Cluster systems. Besides, it can configure the numbers of CPUs and IP addresses of the sever (Figure 9).

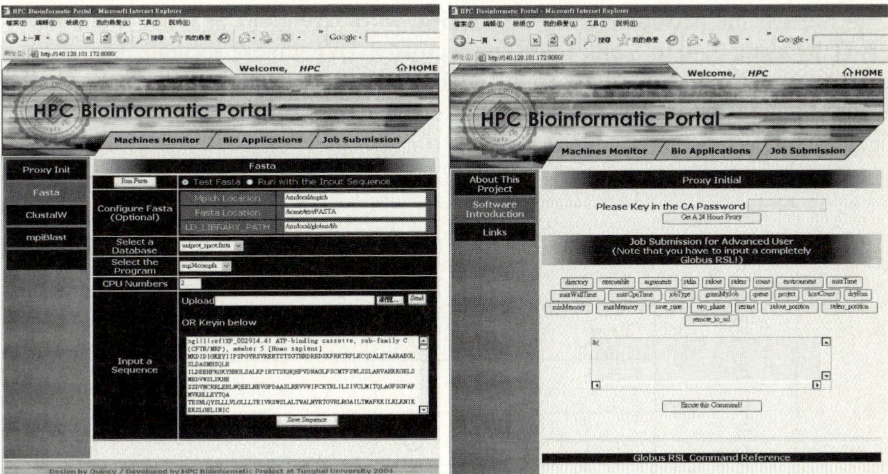

Fig. 7. The Bioinformatics software Application   **Fig. 8.** The Job Submission

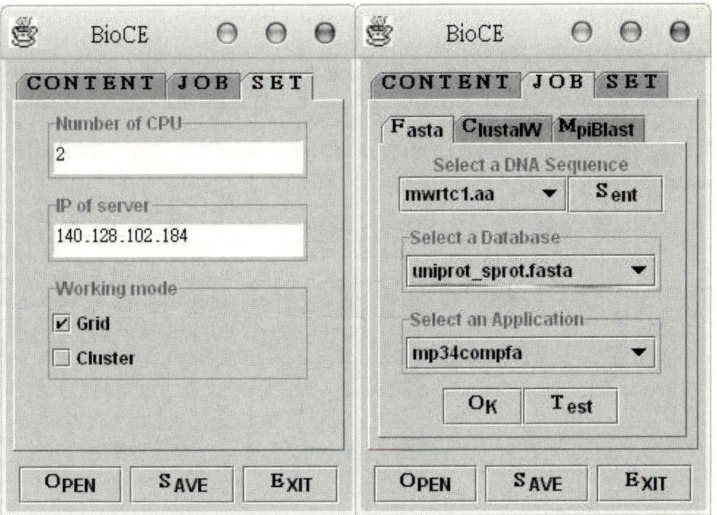

Fig. 9. System configuration and bioinformatics software application

4   Performance Evaluation

We conduct the experimentation on a 16-processor Linux PC cluster. Figure 10 shows experimental results of the parallel versions of all bioinformatics software. All parallel applications are executed by using from 2, 4, 8 to16 processors to compare the execution times. To obtain more accurate data, we execute five times per experiment and calculate the average time of execution. From the results, it is clearly found that the parallel system can reduce significant times from performing the sequence alignments.

We assess the performance of the BioGrid with executions of FASTA and mpiB-LAST by using 2, 4, to 8 processors, respectively. To get more accurate data, we also execute five times per experiment and calculate the average time of execution. Figure 11 demonstrates the performance comparisons of FASTA and mpiBLAST between our system and a generic Grid.

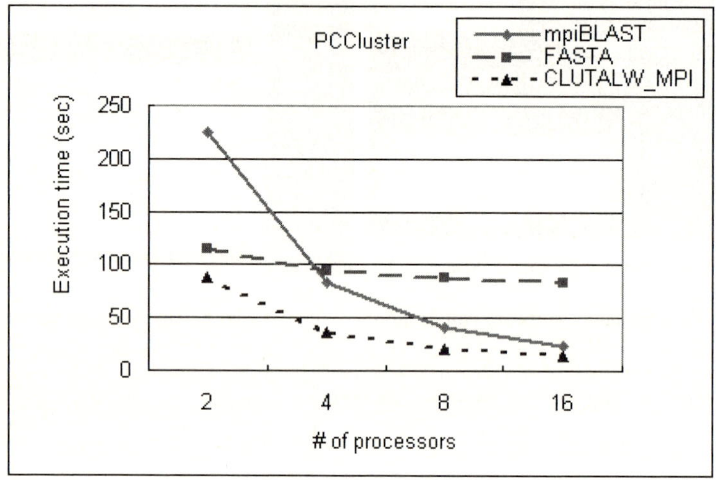

Fig. 10. The average execution times of all parallel versions of bioinformatics applications using processor numbers from 2 to 16

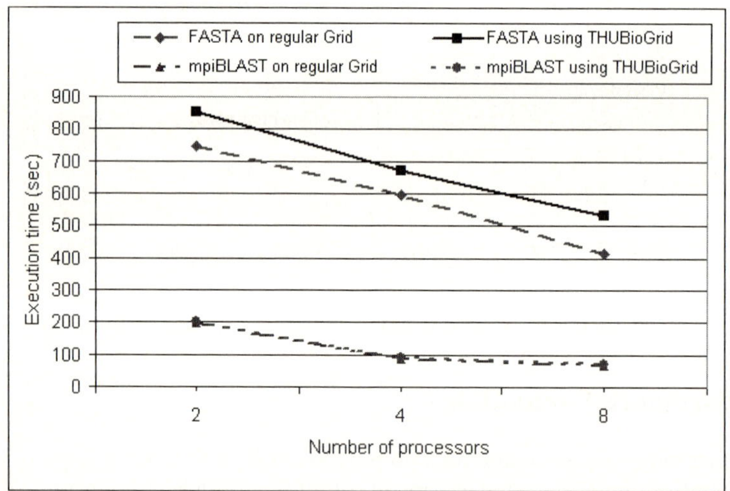

Fig. 11. The performance comparison of FASTA and mpiBLAST between the Application and regular Grid

5 Conclusions

In the paper, we have built the basic platform for high-performance computing environment using the Linux PC cluster and Grid. The experiment results illustrate that both environments save significant times in mapping and efficacy. It performs much better than regular computers. The user portals can help biologists and scientists to easily take control of the bioinformatics software as well as the Grid and Cluster systems. Multiple interfaces allow users to work with bioinformatics software from everywhere.

References

1. R. Buyya, High Performance Cluster Computing: System and Architectures, Vol. 1 and Vol. 2, Prentice Hall PTR, NJ, 1999.
2. Foster, C. K., eds., The Grid 2: Blueprint for a New Computing Infrastructure, Morgan Kaufmann, 2nd edition, 2004.
3. Foster, "The Grid: A New Infrastructure for 21st Century Science", Physics Today, Vol. 55, No. 2, 2002, pp. 42-47.
4. Michael Karo, Christopher Dwan, John Freeman, Jon Weissman, Miron Livny, Ernest Retzel, Applying Grid Technologies to Bioinformatics, Proceedings of HPDC-10'01, 2001, pp. 0441.
5. Kuo-Bin Li, "ClustalW-MPI: ClustalW Analysis Using Distributed and Parallel Computing," Bioinformatics, vol. 19, no. 12, pp. 1585-1586(2), 2003.
6. Trelles O., Andrade M.A., Valencia A., Zapata E.L., and Carazo J.M., Computational Space Reduction and Parallelization of a new Clustering Approach for Large Groups of Sequences, Bioinformatics, vol.14, no.5, 1998, pp.439-451.
7. Trelles O., "On the parallelization of bioinformatics applications," Briefings in Bioinformatics, May 2001, (vol.2) 2.
8. T. L. Sterling, J. Salmon, D. J. Backer, and D. F. Savarese, How to Build a Beowulf: A Guide to the Implementation and Application of PC Clusters, 2nd Printing, MIT Press, Cambridge, Massachusetts, USA, 1999.
9. Chao-Tung Yang, Yu-Lun Kuo, Kuan-Ching Li, and Jean-Luc Gaudiot, "On Design of Cluster and Grid Computing Environments for Bioinformatics Applications," Distributed Computing - IWDC 2004: 6th International Workshop, Lecture Notes in Computer Science, Springer-Verlag, Arunabha Sen, Nabanita Das, Sajal K. Das, et al. (Eds.), Kolkata, India, vol. 3326, pp. 82-87, Dec. 27-30, 2004.
10. Chao-Tung Yang, Po-Chi Shih, Sung-Yi Chen, and Wen-Chung Shih "An Efficient Network Information Modeling using NWS for Grid Computing Environments," Grid and Cooperative Computing - GCC 2005: Fourth International Conference, Lecture Notes in Computer Science, vol. 3795, pp. 289-300, Springer-Verlag, November 2005.
11. FASTA main page, ftp://ftp.virginia.edu/pub/fasta/
12. Human Genome Project, http://www.ornl.gov/sci/techresources/Human_Genome/home.shtml
13. Java Cog kit, http://www-unix.globus.org/cog/
14. MPI Forum main page, http://www.mpi-forum.org/
15. LAM-MPI (Message Passing Interface) main page, http://www.lam-mpi.org/

16. MPICH main page, http://www-unix.mcs.anl.gov/mpi/mpich/
17. mpiBLAST main page, http://mpiblast.lanl.gov/index.html
18. NCBI BLAST main page, http://www.ncbi.nlm.nih.gov/BLAST/
19. North Carolina Bioinformatics Grid (BioGrid) web site, http://www.ncbiogrid.org
20. PVM – Parallel Virtual Machine, http://www.epm.ornl.gov/pvm
21. The Globus Project, http://www.globus.org/

Combining Measures for Temporal and Spatial Locality

Jörg Dümmler[1], Thomas Rauber[2], and Gudula Rünger[1]

[1] Chemnitz University of Technology, Department of Computer Science, 09107
Chemnitz, Germany
{joerg.duemmler, ruenger}@cs.tu-chemnitz.de
[2] Bayreuth University, Angewandte Informatik II, 95440 Bayreuth, Germany
rauber@uni-bayreuth.de

Abstract. Numerical software for sequential or parallel machines with
memory hierarchies can benefit from locality optimizations which are
usually achieved by program restructuring or program transformations.
The choice of the program version that achieves the best performance is
usually complex as many dependencies have to be taken into account.
Thus program-based locality measures have been introduced to give programmers a guideline if a performance gain can be expected from a program restructuring. The novel contribution of this paper is the extension
of these locality measures to support spatial locality. These extended
measures are applied to two applications from scientific computing and
the obtained prediction is compared to benchmark results.

1 Introduction

Modern computer systems use a deep memory hierarchy including multiple levels of cache. Cache misses on these machines usually result in a waiting time of
multiple clock cycles and can slow down applications considerably. Hence, the
exploitation of the memory hierarchy provides the basis for an efficient execution
of a given application. The number of cache misses is influenced by hardware
specific parameters, e.g., the number of levels, the size and associativity of the
cache, and software dependent parameters like the locality of the memory accesses. A high temporal locality is reached, if accesses to the same memory
address lie closely together. An example is the repeated use of a scalar variable,
e.g., to control the iterations of a loop. A high spatial locality is achieved, if
accesses to neighboring memory locations lie closely together. An example is the
consecutive use of the elements of an array variable.

Extensive research has been made to find program transformations which
preserve the correctness of a program and increase the locality of the memory
accesses. Applications from scientific computing usually spend a large proportion
of the computing time in deeply nested loops. Therefore many transformations
to increase memory locality for loop nests have been proposed. Examples include
loop blocking or loop interchange, see [1] for a good overview. Deciding which
program version achieves the best performance is a complex task and depends
on the program code, the input data and on the target platform. In the general

G. Min et al. (Eds.): ISPA 2006 Ws, LNCS 4331, pp. 697–706, 2006.

case not all this information is available, e.g. when parts of the considered program are not available in advance. Examples are solvers for ordinary differential equations (ODEs) which are usually written as black-box code that can operate on arbitrary ODE systems described by a function f.

Program-based locality measures, which allow the comparison of memory locality of different program versions, have been introduced in [2]. These measures only rely on the program source and do not take hardware dependent properties into account. Hence, an exact prediction of the cache misses is not possible as a memory access can result in a cache miss on one platform and a cache hit on another platform with a bigger cache. Nevertheless, the program-based locality measures can be used in an optimizing compiler tool or by a programmer to make a platform independent decision which program version to use or which program tranformations to apply. It has been shown that these measures can successfully capture the effects of temporal locality. The contribution of this paper is the extension of these measures with support for spatial locality. We study the extended cost measures for matrix multiplication and show the importance of spatial locality. As a more complex example we examine three different versions of an iterated Runge-Kutta ODE solver.

The rest of the paper is structured as follows. Section 2 introduces the program-based locality measures and suggests an extension for the support of spatial locality. Benchmark results for different program versions of a matrix-matrix-multiplication and a comparison with the predictions by the locality measures is discussed in section 3. Section 4 discusses related work and Section 5 concludes the paper.

2   Locality Measures Supporting Spatial Locality

The starting point of this work are the program-based locality measures presented in [2] which try to capture the memory access locality of a scientific application in a single value. The resulting value only depends on the program version and the input data size but is independent from platform specific characteristics. These measures observe each storage location in isolation and are therefore not able to uncover changes in spatial locality which plays an important role as we will show in section 3. This section introduces an extended definition of these cost measures which combines the effects of temporal and spatial locality.

To capture the effects of changes in spatial locality, accesses to physically neighboring memory locations have to be considered. Since we only take the program text as an input, it is not always possible to tell which of the variables are physically neighboring. The placement of the statically declared variables is subject to the compiler, which usually allocates neighboring storage locations to variables that are declared in adjacent positions in the program source. But most memory accesses are usually made to dynamically allocated memory, whose physical location is determined by the underlying operating system and cannot be predicted from the program source. As a consequence, we only consider the spatial locality of memory accesses which are made to the same data structure.

The locality measure is defined as a function $\mu : P \times \mathbb{N} \to \mathbb{R}^+$ where P is a set of equivalent program versions, $n \in \mathbb{N}$ is the input data size, and $\mu(A, n)$ is the locality value for $A \in P$ and input data size n. Lower values of this measure correspond to a better memory access locality, e.g. if $\mu(A, n) < \mu(B, n)$ for program version A and B then A is expected to have a better locality behavior than B for input data size n.

Let V_s be the set of variables of a program version A, where all variables, scalar or array, are represented by a single element $v_s \in V_s$. The total number of accesses to a variable $v_s \in V_s$ is denoted as $l_{v_s} + 1 \in \mathbb{N}$. The finite sequence $T = t_1, t_2, \dots$ of consecutive natural numbers starting with $t_1 = 0$ represents the time indices of all memory accesses of a given program version. The *access sequence* of a given $v_s \in V_s$ is defined as the subsequence

$$n_0(v_s), n_1(v_s), \dots, n_{l_{v_s}}(v_s) \subset T$$

of the sequence T. Furthermore, for array variables it is important to know, which element was referenced by a memory access. This information is stored in the *offset sequence* of a variable $v_s \in V_s$ that is defined as the sequence

$$o_0(v_s), o_1(v_s), \dots, o_{l_{v_s}}(v_s) \quad \text{with } o_i(v_s) \in \mathbb{N}, \quad 0 \le i \le l_{v_s}.$$

For a scalar variable all elements of its offset sequence will be 0. We define the *spatial access distance* $d_{s_i}(v_s)$ of a variable $v_s \in V_s$ as

$$d_{s_i}(v_s) = \sqrt{(n_i(v_s) - n_{i-1}(v_s))^2 + (o_i(v_s) - o_{i-1}(v_s))^2}$$

with $1 < i \le l_{v_s}$. In case of an array variable, the *spatial access distance* between two consecutive accesses to this variable decreases, if either the temporal distance is reduced or if the offsets of the elements involved lie closer together, i.e. the spatial locality is increased.

Figure 1 (left) shows an example for the computation of the *access distances* as defined for the temporal locality measures. Each element of the array has its own *access sequence* and therefore spatial locality between neighboring elements cannot be detected. In constrast the *spatial access distances* as defined in this paper combine temporal and spatial information as shown in Figure 1 (right). There is only one *access sequence* and an additional offset sequence for the array X in the example. The euclidian distance between two consecutive memory accesses to an array is used to computate the *spatial access distances*.

Based on the *spatial access distances*, the *average spatial access distance* of a variable $v_s \in V_s$ is defined as

$$M_s(v_s) := \left(\sum_{i=1}^{l_{v_s}} d_{s_i}(v_s) \right) / l_{v_s}$$

Following the definition of the temporal locality measures in [2] we define the following new cost measures which combine temporal and spatial locality:

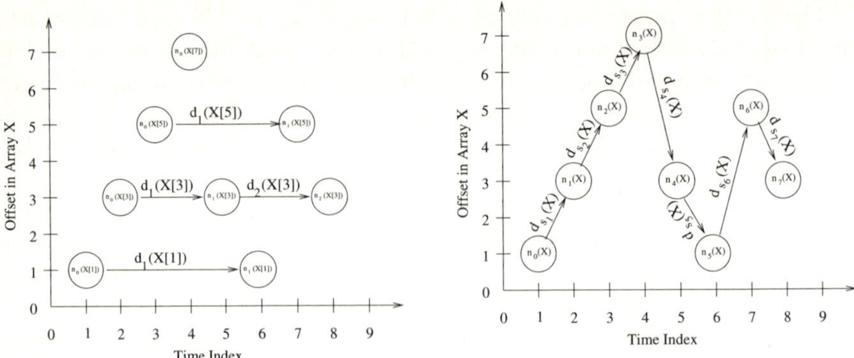

Fig. 1. Example for the calculation of the *access distances* $d_i(v)$ as defined in [2] (left) and $d_{s_i}(v)$ as defined in section 2 (right)

Arithmetic mean of access distances:
$$\mu_{s_{AM}}(A, n) := \left(\sum_{v_s \in V_s} M_s(v_s) \cdot l_{v_s}\right) / \sum_{v_s \in V_s} l_{v_s},$$
Arithmetic mean of average access distances:
$$\mu_{s_{AA}}(A, n) := \left(\sum_{v_s \in V_s} M_s(v_s)\right) / \#V_s,$$
Sum of access distances:
$$\mu_{s_{SA}}(A, n) := \sum_{v_s \in V_s} \left(\sum_{i=1}^{l_{v_s}} d_{s_i}(v_s)\right),$$
Square of quadratic mean of access distances:
$$\mu_{s_{SQ}}(A, n) := \sum_{v_s \in V_s} \left(\sum_{i=1}^{l_{v_s}} d_{s_i}(v_s)^2\right) / \sum_{v_s \in V_s} l_{v_s},$$
Logarithmic geometric mean of access distances:
$$\mu_{s_{LG}}(A, n) := \sum_{v_s \in V_s} \left(\sum_{i=1}^{l_{v_s}} \log_2 d_{s_i}(v_s)\right).$$

Note that these definitions of locality measures do not cover spatial locality that may be exploited between different variables. This is only a disadvantage if the application uses many small arrays and scalar variables. Applications from scientific computing often operate on large data structures that are addressed using only a few pointer variables. In this case, spatial locality between different variables only plays a negligible role. Moreover, from the programmer's point of view, the placement of variables to memory locations cannot be directly influenced, i.e., the spatial locality within a single data structure is usually the target for program modifications.

3   Benchmark Results

In this section, we present experimental results for different program versions and compare the resulting execution times to the predictions obtained by applying the locality measures. We use the multiplication of two square matrices as this is part of many applications from scientific computing and because the locality properties have been studied extensively. The program transformations used heavily rely on the exploitation of spatial locality. Therefore it is a good example to demonstrate the advantage of the extended measures. In the second example we study different program versions of an iterated RK solver for large ODE systems. These program versions use different computation schemes to calculate the argument vectors. The performance is influenced by temporal and spatial locality.

The program-based locality measures were calculated by utilizing a library in cooperation with a special simulation program. The simulation program mimics the memory access pattern of the target program version and calls special library function which accumulate all memory accesses and compute the cost measures. Memory accesses to index variables used for loop control were not considered, because, depending on the platform and the compiler, these variables are often stored in processor registers. In future versions a fully automated determination of the measures by a suitable compiler tool is planned.

The hardware characteristics of the platforms used for benchmark tests are summarized in Table 1.

Table 1. Platforms used for benchmark tests

Processor	Intel Xeon	Intel Itanium 2	Intel Pentium 3	Sun UltraSparc III
Clock Rate	2.0 GHz	900 MHz	650 MHz	750 MHz
L1 Cache	8K data + 12K micro-ops	16K data + 16K instr., 4-way	16K data + 16K instr., 4-way	64K data + 32K instr., 4-way
L2 Cache	512K, 8-way	256 KB, 8-way	256 KB, 8-way	8 MB, 2-way
L3 Cache	n/a	1.5 MB, 12-way	n/a	n/a

3.1 Multiplication of Two Square Matrices

As a first example we study different program versions for the multiplication of two matrices. Figure 2 (left) shows the pseudo code of a straight forward implementation. Through interchanging the loops in the second loop nest, six different program versions are derived, which are denoted as $mmm\_xyz()$, where x is the index variable of the outermost loop, y the index variable of the middle loop and z the index variable of the innermost loop.

Assuming a row-wise data layout for all matrices, program version $mmm\_ikj()$ offers the best locality properties[1]. This is due to a stride 1 data access to the matrices B and C in the innermost loop, which results in an optimal exploitation of spatial locality. The accesses to matrix A can benefit from temporal locality in the innermost loop and from spatial locality in the middle loop.

Loop blocking is another popular program transformation, which can increase temporal locality. In each of the six program versions one, two or all three loops

function *mmm_ijk()*:

```
for (i = 0; i < N; i++)
  for (j = 0; j < N; j++)
    C[i][j] = 0;
for (i = 0; i < N; i++)
  for (j = 0; j < N; j++)
    for (k = 0; k < N; k++)
      C[i][j] += A[i][k] * B[k][j];
```

function *mmm_ikj_3(bs)*:

```
for (i = 0; i < N; i++)
  for (j = 0; j < N; j++)
    C[i][j] = 0;
for (i = 0; i < N; i+=bs)
  for (k = 0; k < N; k+=bs)
    for (j = 0; j < N; j+=bs)
      for (ii = i; ii < min(i+bs, N); ii++)
        for (kk = k; kk < min(k+bs, N); kk++)
          for (jj = j; jj < min(j+bs, N); jj++)
            C[ii][jj] += A[ii][kk] * B[kk][jj];
```

Fig. 2. Pseudo code of a matrix-matrix-multiplication with loop ordering (i, j, k) (left) and with loop ordering (i, k, j) and loop blocking applied to all three loops (right)

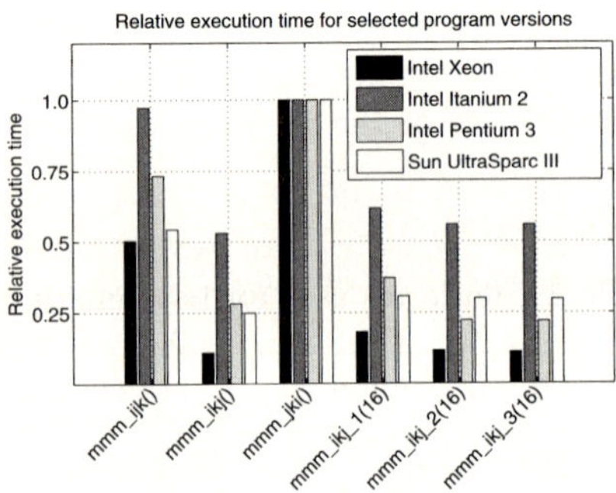

Fig. 3. Relative execution time of program versions of a matrix-matrix multiplication using 1024x1024 matrices on different platforms

can be blocked. This results in 18 additional program versions, which have the block size as a parameter. For simplicity we use the same block size for all loops. We denote these program versions as *mmm_xyz_n(bs)*, where x, y and z refer to the loop ordering, n gives the number of blocked loops and bs is the block size used. Figure 2 (right) gives the pseudo code of function *mmm_ikj_3(bs)*.

Figure 3 shows a selection of benchmark results scaled to a value of 1.0 for the slowest version, which was *mmm_jki()* in all cases. Considering the program versions without blocking, *mmm_ikj()* shows the best performance on all platforms. The speedup achieved depends on hardware characteristics, like the cache latency, and therefore differs from platform to platform. The block size leading to a minimum runtime is platform depend. We show a block size of 16, because it achieved competitive runtimes on all platforms.

Figure 4 shows on the left side the program-based locality measures for temporal locality as introduced in [2] and on the right side the extended cost measures introduced in this paper, both scaled to a maximum of 1. The temporal locality measures cannot predict the resulting runtime accurately, since temporal locality plays only a negligible role in the program tranformations. All spatial locality measures identify program version *mmm_jki()* as the one with the worst locality properties. The program versions with blocking and *mmm_ikj()* achieve the

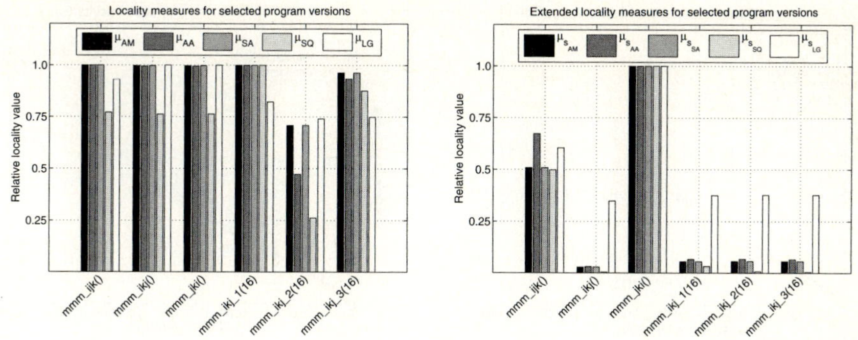

Fig. 4. Relative values of the temporal locality measures (left) and the spatial locality measures (right) for different program versions of a matrix-matrix multiplication

lowest spatial locality value and therefore are considered to have the best memory access locality. These results match with the runtime tests shown in Figure 3 and with the theoretical considerations in [1].

Altogether it can be stated, that the spatial locality measures are able to capture the locality properties of the different program versions of a matrix-matrix multiplication. These effects could not be uncovered using only the temporal locality measures.

3.2   Iterated Runge-Kutta Methods

As a more complex example from scientific computing we study the spatial locality measures with different program versions of solvers for initial value problems (IVPs) of ODEs. Large systems of ODEs arise, e.g. when discretizing time dependent partial differential equations (PDEs) in the spatial domain using the method of lines[3]. Iterated RK solvers are explicit methods which were derived from classical implicit methods. The advantage of the iterated RK methods is the data independence of the computation of the stage vectors admitting a parallel execution [4]. From the implicit system of equations it is possible to construct an explicit system by computing approximations $\mu_l^{(i)}$, $i = 1, \ldots, m$, for the stage vectors v_l, $l = 1, \ldots, s$, using a fixed point iteration starting with η_k and using a fixed number of steps m, which depends on the RK method.

The following computation scheme shows the core of an iterated RK solver, where h is the step size and a_{ij}, b_i and c_i are parameters of the underlying implicit RK method:

```
for (l = 1; l <= s; l++)
```
$$\mu_l^{(0)} = f(x_k, \ \eta_k);$$
```
for (i = 1; i <= m; i++)
    for (l = 1; l <= s; l++)
```
$$\mu_l^{(i)} = f(x_k + c_l h, \ \eta_k + h_k \textstyle\sum_{j=1}^{s} a_{lj}\mu_j^{(i-1)});$$
$$\eta_{k+1} = \eta_k + h_k \textstyle\sum_{j=1}^{s} b_i\mu_j^{(m)};$$

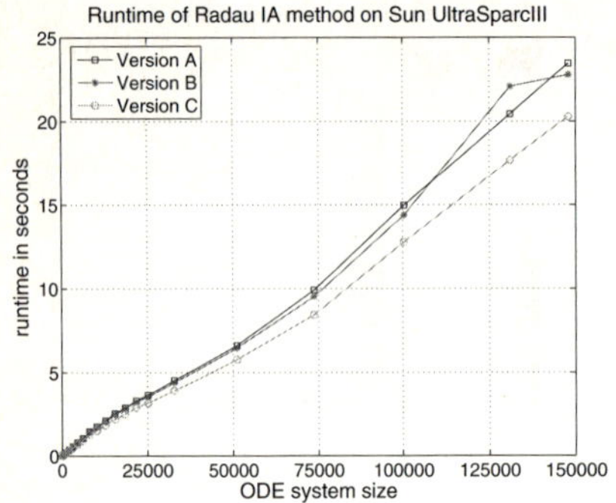
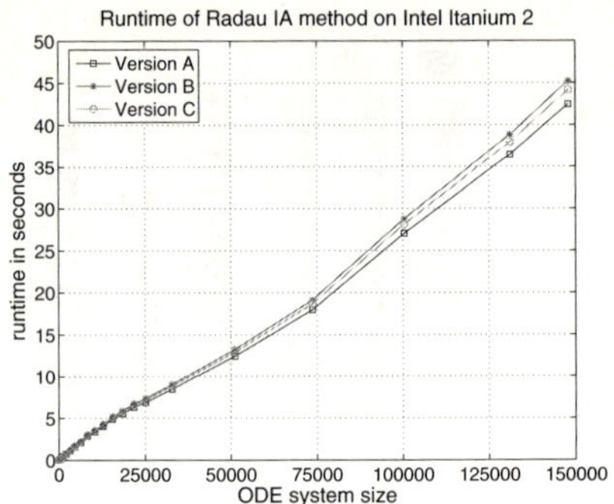

Fig. 5. Runtime in seconds of a Radau IA method applied to the Brusselator ODE on a Sun UltraSparc III (left) and on an Intel Itanium 2 (right)

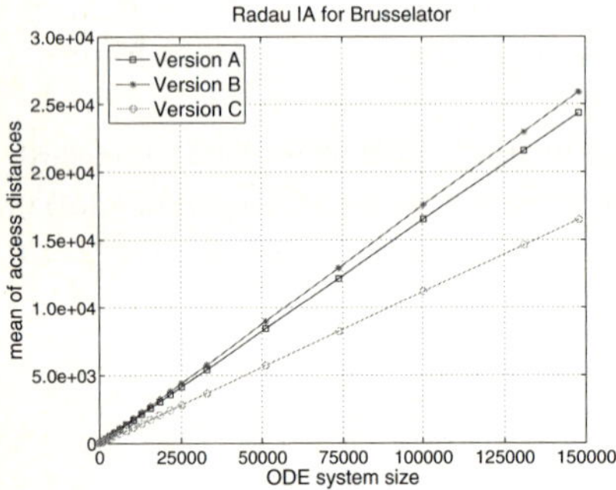
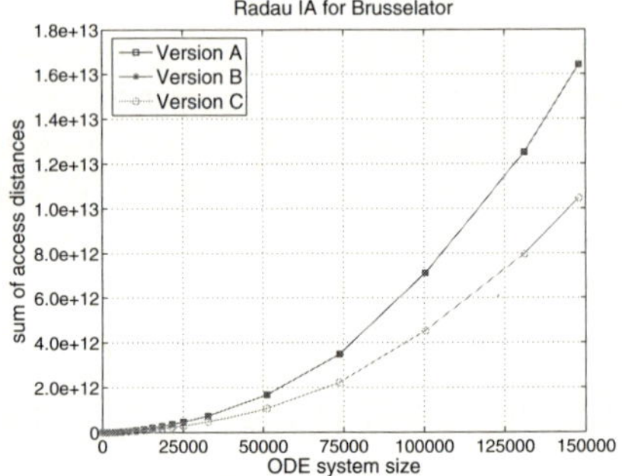

Fig. 6. Locality measures $\mu_{s_{AM}}$ (left) and $\mu_{s_{SA}}$ (right) for Radau IA applied to the Brusselator ODE

Version A: Program version A is a straightforward implementation of the computation scheme for iterated RK methods.

Version B: In this program version the computation of the argument vectors needed to calculate the approximation $\mu_l^{(j)}$ is modified. Separate argument vectors are introduced for each iteration, which results in a higher memory requirement and an additional multiplication per iteration. Some of the dependencies are resolved, so that further transformations are possible.

Version C: Through interchanging loops program version C is generated. Each computation is put in a separate loop nest, which results in an optimal exploitation of spatial locality. The computational and memory requirements are equal to those of version B.

To compare the performance of the three program versions we executed benchmark tests on different platforms. We use the Radau IA method [3] as basic RK method and solve the Brusselator equation [5] as example ODE system. The Brusselator equation is used to describe the reaction of two chemical substances with diffusion in the two dimensional space.

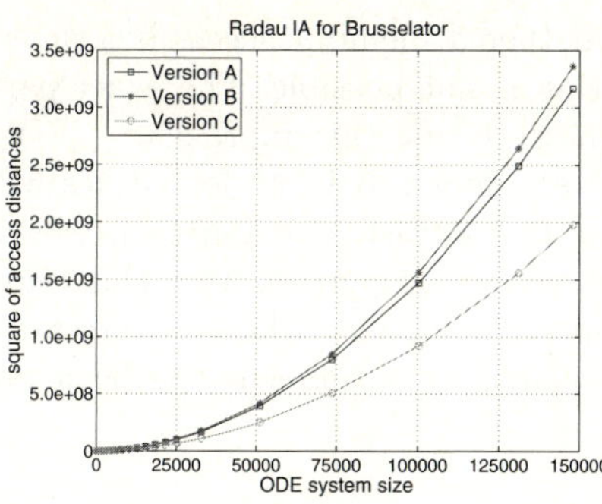
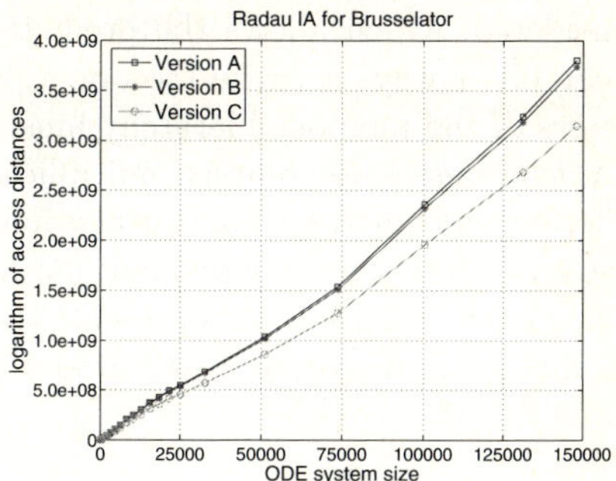

Fig. 7. Locality measures $\mu_{s_{SQ}}$ (left) and $\mu_{s_{LG}}$ (right) for Radau IA applied to the Brusselator ODE

Figure 5 shows the runtime for different system sizes on a Sun UltraSparc III processor and on an Intel Itanium 2 system. The performance of program versions **A** and **B** on the UltraSparc III platform are about equal, whereas program version **C** achieves an average speedup of 14%. On the Intel Itanium 2 the transformed program version **B** is 6% on the average slower compared to the original version **A**. The final program version **C** performs better than version **B** but cannot reach the performance of version **A**. This can be explained by the additional operations performed by versions **B** and **C** introduced by the transformation step.

Figure 6 (right) shows the spatial locality measure $\mu_{s_{SA}}$ for the program versions of an iterated RK solver. A similar result is obtained by applying measure $\mu_{s_{AA}}$. These two measures testify an about equal locality of memory accesses to program versions **A** and **B**. Program version **C** shows smaller locality values as expressed by the measures, i.e. is assumed to have a better memory access locality. The results obtained by cost measure $\mu_{s_{AM}}$ shown in Figure 6 (left) and by cost measure $\mu_{s_{SQ}}$ shown in Figure 7 (left) certify program version **B** a better memory access locality compared to version **A**. In contrast measure $\mu_{s_{LG}}$ presented in Figure 7 (right) yields a lower locality value and therefore a better memory access locality for program version **A**.

All spatial locality measures examined certify program version **C** the best memory access locality. The locality values of program versions **A** and **B** lie closely together for all measures. These result correspond with the measured runtimes on the Sun UltraSparc III processor very well. On the Intel Itanium 2 processor program version **A** achieves a smaller runtime. This program version requires fewer operations, which cannot be captured by the locality measures.

4   Related Work

An analytical examination of cache misses can be made by using cache miss equations, which can be used to calculate the position of cold misses and replacement misses in arrays. Direct mapped caches were analysed in [6] and the results generalized to associative caches in [7]. In [8] a worst case scenario is considered, which allows the prediction, whether a memory access is always a cache hit, always a cache miss or a prediction is not possible. The exact parameters of the memory hierarchy must be known to use this approach.

Cache misses for matrix-multiplication were analyzed in [9] for caches with different associativities and cache line sizes. In contrast, our approach tries to give an architecture independent measure of locality properties. An architecture-independent metric that represents the temporal behavior of data-movements of parallel programs in a distributed shared-memory environment has been presented in [10].

5   Conclusion and Future Research

In this paper we have introduced an extension to program-based locality measures which adds support for spatial locality. It has been shown that the spatial locality measures can be used to compare temporal and spatial locality properties of different program versions.

In future work we plan to add support for a fully automical determination of these measures. An extension of the cost measures to include the number of arithmetical operations is also possible. Another area of future research focuses on the extension of the cost measures for parallel programs.

References

1. Allen, R., Kennedy, K.: Optimizing Compilers for Modern Architectures. Academic Press, 522 B Street, Suite 1900, San Diego, CA 92101-4495, USA (2002)
2. Rauber, T., Rünger, G.: Program-based locality measures for scientific computing. International Journal of Foundations of Computer Science **15** (2004) 535–554
3. Hairer, E., Nørsett, S., Wanner, G.: Solving Ordinary Differential Equations. 2 edn. Volume 1. Springer (2002)
4. Rauber, T., Rünger, G.: Parallel Execution of Embedded and Iterated Runge-Kutta Methods. Concurrency - Practice and Experience **11** (1999) 367–385
5. Hairer, E., Wanner, G.: Solving Ordinary Differential Equations. 2 edn. Volume 2. Springer (2004)
6. Ghosh, S., Martonosi, M., Malik, S.: Cache miss equations: An analytical representation of cache misses. In: Int. Conf. on Supercomputing. (1997) 317–324
7. Ghosh, S., Martonosi, M., Malik, S.: Cache miss equations: a compiler framework for analyzing and tuning memory behavior. ACM Transactions on Programming Languages and Systems **21** (1999) 703–746
8. Ferdinand, C., Wilhelm, R.: Efficient and precise cache behavior prediction for real-time systems. Real-Time Syst. **17** (1999) 131–181
9. Lam, M., Rothberg, E., Wolf, M.: The cache performance and optimizations of blocked algorithms. In: Proc. of the 4th Int. Conf. on Architectural support for programming languages and operating systems, ACM Press (1991) 63–74
10. Rodriguez, B., Jordan, H., Alaghband, G.: A Metric for the Temporal Characterization of Parallel Programs. Journal of Parallel and Distributed Computing **46** (1997) 113–124

Parallel Processing Applied on the Electric Grounding Systems Design

Marco Aurélio S. Birchal[1], Maria Helena M. Vale[2], and Silvério Visacro[2]

[1] PUC Minas – Pontifícia Universidade Católica de Minas Gerais
GSDC – Computing and Digital Systems Group
Av. Dom José Gaspar, Belo Horizonte, 30535-910, Brazil
`birchal@pucminas.br`
`http://www.pucminas.br`
[2] UFMG – Universidade Federal de Minas Gerais, LRC – Lightning Research Center
Av. Antônio Carlos 6627, Belo Horizonte, 31270-910, Brazil
`{mhelena, visacro}@cpdee.ufmg.br`
`http://www.ufmg.br`

Abstract. Electrical engineering is a source of problems that can take advantage of the parallel processing on computing. It happens once the kind of numeric solution is often done by the evaluation of linear equations put in matrix style. Concrete encased grounding systems are a powerful answer to the grounding design problem. It uses the metal embedded in the concrete structure of the building as grounding electrodes. Nevertheless, the great demand of computer processing, necessary to calculate such a grounding system, makes it difficult to use sequential program implementation. This paper presents the basis of the engineering problem and a parallel tool, called PENCAPS, that implements the numeric solution developed to solve concrete encased electrode grounding systems.

1 Introduction

Grounding systems are a fundamental part of the electrical project of buildings. Most edifications are made with concrete foundations. The natural availability of the metal grid inside the concrete blocks turns it possible to use them as grounding electrodes. The electrode formed by the metal-concrete block junction is called concrete encased electrode [1]. Figure 1 shows this concept.

This kind of use has been made for many years with great effectiveness in lowering the total resistance of the grounding system. Nevertheless, the use of the concrete encased grounding has been done almost totally in an empirical way, lacking a mathematical formulation of its behavior.

The LRC (Lightning Research Center) Grounding Group, at UFMG – Federal University of Minas Gerais - studied the engineering problem as an application of the electromagnetic theory [2] and presented a mathematical model that can be solved by numeric method.

G. Min et al. (Eds.): ISPA 2006 Ws, LNCS 4331, pp. 707–716, 2006.

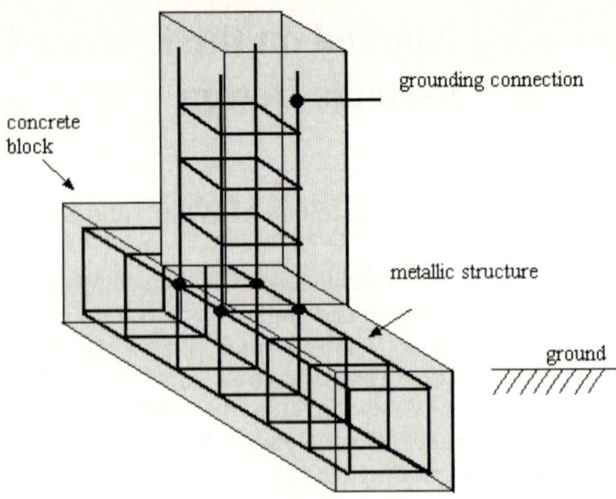

Fig. 1. A concrete encased electrode

A sequential program was developed [3], based on that model, proving the model to be effective. The program, however, couldn't handle realistic large size electrical systems, due to its processing limitations.

A new parallel application, called PENCAPS, was proposed and implemented to solve systems that demands great computational resources.

The rest of this paper treats the working model and details this application. Section 2 brings the mathematical numeric model that treats the concrete encased electrode problem. Section 3 discusses the design of concrete encased grounding systems. Section 4 shows the development of the application and details the parallel programming solution used on it. Section 5 shows a case study used to verify the application. Section 6 depicts and discusses the benchmark results and Section 7 shows the conclusions of the work.

2   Numeric Model

The solution of a grounding system consists on finding the total equivalent resistance of a given physical arrange of electrodes [4].

The numeric solution proposed by the authors involves the applying of the electromagnetic theory to find some relationships among the electrical variables involved in the problem.

The main differentiation of the solution proposed is to use the equivalence between the electrical current that passes through a surface section and its corresponding charge density. Figure 2 shows a concrete encased electrode and the fragmentation of its length in little surfaces. The faces of the concrete block also were divided into a mesh of surfaces.

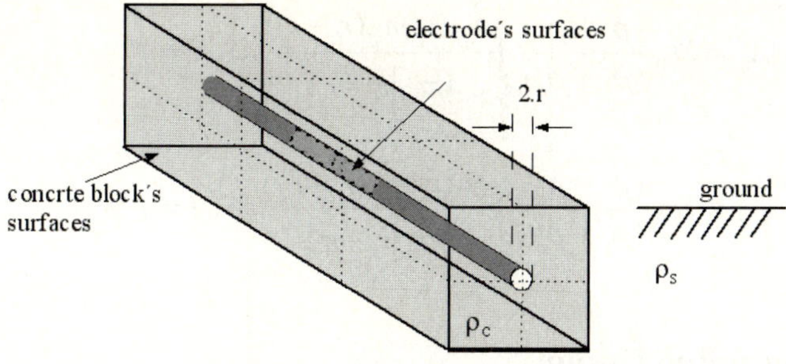

Fig. 2. Block and electrode surfaces

After applying boundary element method over each one of the surfaces of the electrode [5] and concrete block, one can write the relation given by Equation 1.

$$\eta_h(r) = \sum_{i=1}^{n} \eta_i N_i(r) \tag{1}$$

In this equation, $\eta_h(r)$ is the unknown value of the system and represents the set of charge densities of all the created surfaces. η_i is the charge contribution of each one of the surfaces over all others. N_i is a function that assumes zero or one, depending on specific conditions. Details of the proposed solution can be found in earlier works of the Group [2], [3], [5].

Equation 1 can be rewritten in the matrix form and, doing so, one can evaluate this by applying a linear equation system solver. Equation 2 shows this new representation form. In this equation, the values of the V_n vector represent the known electric potential for a given fault protection event.

The A_{ij} terms that form the main matrix are given by the equations 3 and 4, where ε_0 is the air permissivity, ρ_s and ρ_c are the resistivity of the soil and concrete, respectively; r_i and $r_i{}'$ are points over the surfaces.

The η_i vector has to be calculated.

$$\begin{bmatrix} V_1 \\ V_2 \\ \dots \\ V_n \\ 0 \\ 0 \\ \dots \\ 0 \end{bmatrix} = \begin{bmatrix} A_{11} & A_{12} & \dots & & \dots & A_{1n} \\ A_{21} & A_{22} & \dots & & \dots & A_{2n} \\ \dots & \dots & \dots & & & \dots \\ \hline & & & & & \\ & & & & & \dots \\ \dots & \dots & \dots & & & \dots \\ A_{n1} & A_{n2} & \dots & & \dots & (A_{nn}-1) \end{bmatrix} \cdot \begin{bmatrix} \eta_1 \\ \eta_2 \\ \\ \\ \dots \\ \\ \\ \eta_n \end{bmatrix} \tag{2}$$

The process of building matrix A is a time consuming one and can take advantage of the use of a parallel processing.

$$A_{ij} = 2\varepsilon_0 \frac{(\rho_s - \rho_c)}{(\rho_s + \rho_c)} \int_{S_j} \frac{N_j(r_j)n_i.(r_i - r_j)}{4\pi\varepsilon_o |r_i - r_j|^3} dS, \; i \neq j \qquad (3)$$

$$A_{ii} = 2\varepsilon_0 \frac{(\rho_s - \rho_c)}{(\rho_s + \rho_c)} \int_{S_i} \frac{N_i(r_i')n_i.(r_i - r_i')}{4\pi\varepsilon_o |r_i - r_i|^3} dS, \; i = j \qquad (4)$$

3 The Grounding Design

The design of a concrete encased grounding system comprises a set of tasks. Some of these steps are very time consuming and so, indicated to be parallelized.

Figure 3 shows the data flow of a grounding design and depicts which of those tasks can be done in parallel. The first step is the Geometry Construction, where the user specifies the geometry of the physical system and its electrical properties.

The second step is the automatic Mesh Generation. Here, the system collects the input data and builds a mesh of boundary elements.

The third and the most time consuming is the Matrix Generation, where the system builds the main matrix of the engineering problem to be solved. This is made by applying the electrical attributes on the previously generated mesh.

The forth step does the main calculation, where the problem is solved. It resolves the linear equation system formed by the main matrix and the electrical potential input vector. The last task is a post-processing one. It calculates the potential over given physical coordinate points, to plot the potential profile graphic.

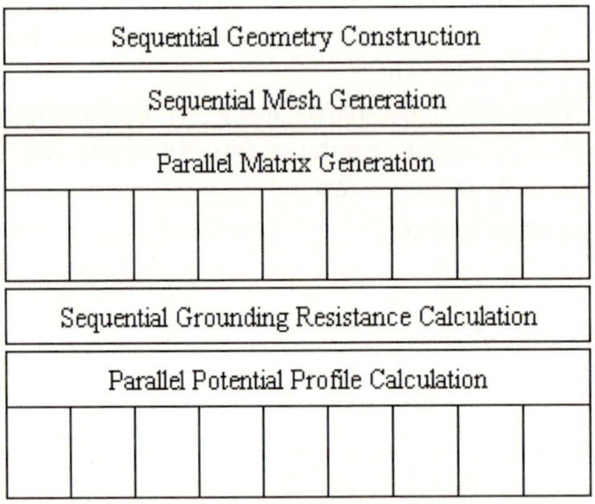

Fig. 3. Steps of a grounding design

4 The Parallel Program Application

The matrix A showed in the Equation 2 is a full matrix of large dimension, where each of its elements is an integral that can be double, in certain conditions. This leads the building of this matrix to be a great time consuming process that can forces one to decrease the complexity of the electrical system.

With the use of parallel processing on computing it is possible to increase the size of the electrical system to the limits of a real engineering problem and get it solved in a reasonable processing time.

The computational solution implemented in PENCAPS and showed in this work creates two different software tools, to handle with the design of a concrete encased electrode grounding system. Figure 4 shows the interactions between the tools – the front-end and the back-end – and the environment possibilities.

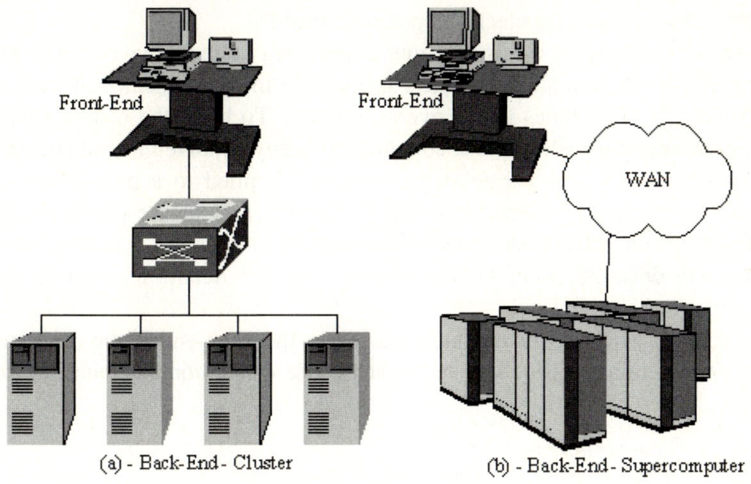

Fig. 4. The application architecture possibilities

4.1   The Front-End

The first tool is a sequential front-end application that helps the user to enter the engineering problem specifications, as the geometry details and electrical values to be applied to the physical elements. This tool does all the interactions between the design staff and the computer system, working as a user interface with graphics resources.

It also can plot the resulting electrical system geometry and the potential profile of a given fault. The sequential steps of the concrete encased grounding design are all done by the front-end. It manages the grounding project in a hierarchical way.

This can keep track on the relations among the different pieces of data that compounds the grounding project. The data are collected on input files and the results are calculated.

The front-end disposes the tasks that comprise the concrete encased grounding design in a tree, where all data can be reached. This kind of arrangement also brings a visual understanding of the entire process and the time sequence for the steps to be done.

4.2 The Back-End

The back-end is the parallel tool developed to achieve high performance where exists great processing demand.

It was written in C language with the MPI (Message Passing Interface) API [6]. This results in an application tool with good portability, making it suitable to run in many hardware platforms.

The parallel implementation. There are two distinct parallel functions implemented on the back-end. The first and main one is the building of the matrix A. The second is the parallel calculation of the electrical potential profile.

The matrix building is the more time consuming step of the concrete encased grounding design. A parallel procedure can increase the performance of such a task, what significantly contributes to the overall process. To build the matrix, one has to calculate each one of its cells, whose contents are heavy to solve integral equations.

This process has four separate steps, each one applied to a part of the matrix. These parts represent the interactions among the different nature physical elements (electrode-electrode interaction, electrode-concrete interaction, concrete-electrode interaction and concrete-concrete interaction). Figure 5 details the matrix building process.

The second parallel procedure implemented in the back-end is the calculation of the electrical potential profile. This is the last phase of the concrete encased grounding design.

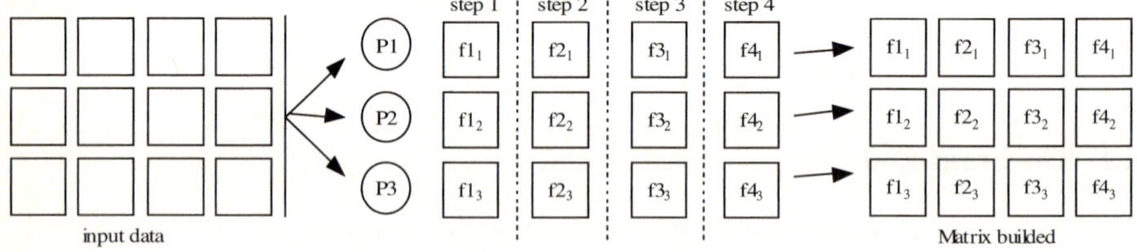

Fig. 5. The matrix building process

After obtaining the total equivalent grounding resistance, one can calculate the fault potential over the soil surrounding the grounding system.

This is very useful since, with the potential profile, one can evaluate the real risk conditions presented by the grounding system, in the presence of an electric fault.

The calculation process can become very time consuming, depending on the quantity of points to be evaluated. The more the points, the better the resolution of the resulting potential profile graphic.

The implemented parallel routine uses the master-slave model, where the master reads points and sends them to be calculated by the slaves. Figure 6 shows the scheme of this implementation.

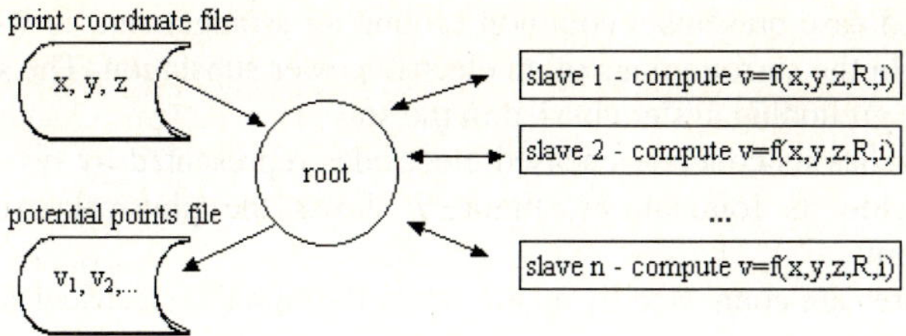

Fig. 6. Master-slave potential calculus

Complexity analysis. As discussed before, the main parallel routine is the matrix building one. It has four separate subroutines, each one dealing with a different kind of integral equation. The first equation has a loop of size n, where n is the number of line elements. This leads to an $O(n)$ complexity in this phase of the computation.

The second has an $O(n^2)$ complexity, due to an internal loop for solving a double integral equation.

The third subroutine solves an $O(m.n)$ equation, where m is the number of the four-sided polygons created by the mesh structure. The fourth, the heaviest subroutine, is $O(m^2)$.

In all cases, the problem is divided by p processors, leading the four subroutines complexity to $O(n/p)$, $O(n^2/p)$, $O(m.n/p)$ and $O(m^2/p)$, respectively.

The parallel implementation of the electric potential profile leads to an $O(n/(p-1))$ complexity, since the n points are distributed to p-1 slaves, once the master in this procedure doesn't process calculations but distributes the points to the slaves.

5   Case Study

The application was submitted to a case study [7], [8], in a way of collecting benchmark data and performance evaluation.

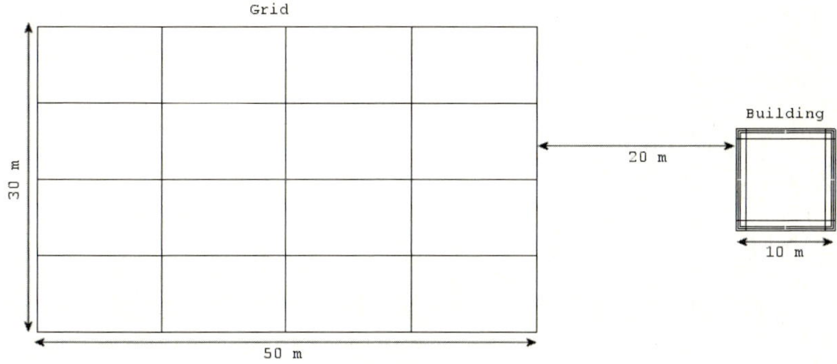

Fig. 7. Grounding structure of the case study

The proposed case presents a common grounding arrangement, in which an edification is found in the surroundings of an electric power substation. The substation has a grid electrode grounding system buried in the soil.

The building has its concrete encased electrodes represented by two encapsulated metal rings inside its foundations. Figure 7 shows the physical structure of the grounding system.

Both structures are connected by an air cable, through the electrical subdistribution transformer.

The calculated equivalent resistance of the proposed system was 27.1 Ω, considering 2500 Ω.m and 400 Ω.m the resistivities of the soil and of the concrete, respectively.

6 Results and Discussion

The case study was run over two different testbeds and the speedup [9] was calculated.

The first testbed is a distributed memory IBM RS/6000 SP supercomputer, with 42 120 Mhz risk processors. The second testbed is a cluster of 10 dual Pentium III 1 Ghz processors, with a gigabit Ethernet network. Both systems are located in the CENAPAD MG/CO (High Performance Processing National Center - Minas Gerais and Midwest Region) in Belo Horizonte, Brazil.

The same engineering problem was run over the two hardware platforms and the speedup was calculated as a function of the number of processors involved in the matrix building.

Figure 8 shows the execution time and the corresponding speedup, as a function of the number of processors used, when running over the IBM machine. As it shows, there is an initial dysfunction of the speedup when using less than 5 processors. However, for five processors or more, the speedup goes increasing as expected.

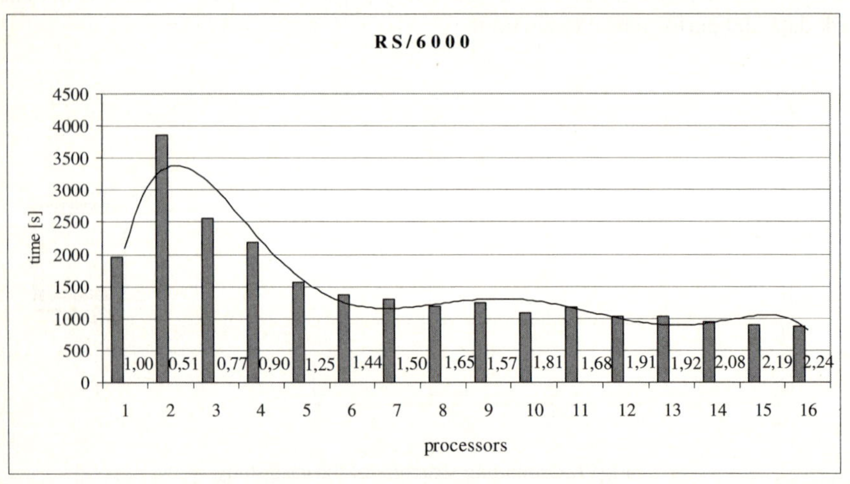

Fig. 8. Speedup over IBM RS/6000 SP

This initial behavior seems to happen as a result of the latency of the network, since the speedup increases when the set of values to be sent decrease once there are more processors running. One can also see that the increasing of processors for a number greater than 14, makes no great gains in speedup.

The second test, conducted over the cluster platform, had a much more predicted behavior, once the speedup responded as expected, in function of the number of processors being used. This is a more powerful platform, with quicker processors and network, as depicted by the Figure 9.

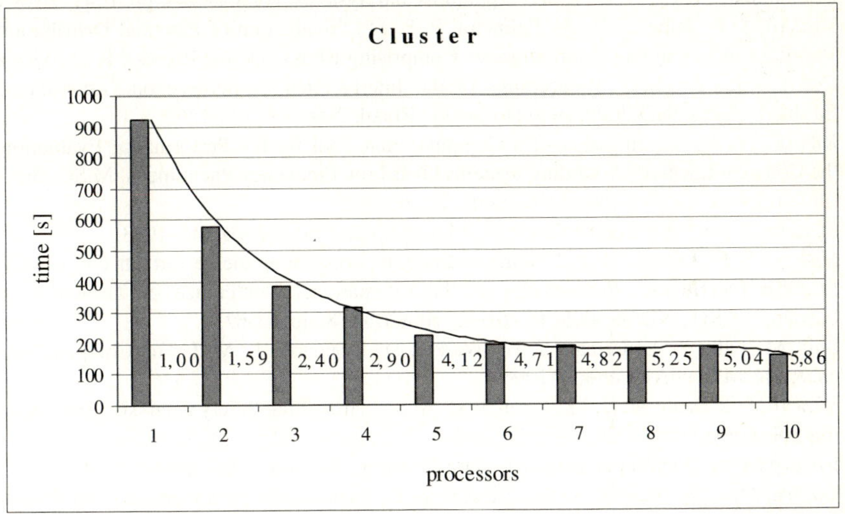

Fig. 9. Speedup over Pentium cluster

In this test, the speedup kept increasing as the number of processors grew. Nevertheless, the speedup stabilized after 8 processors, with not much gain in the speedup after this limit. In both cases, one can see that there was a considerable increase of performance, as the speedup got to 2.24 in the first case and to a much better 5.86 in second case.

7 Conclusion

Concrete encased electrode grounding systems are a complex kind of engineering problem that had been challenged designers on solving it. This work presented not only a numerical solution to accomplish this task but an efficient algorithm which implements that.

In a way of guaranteeing an efficient solution to the problem once it is a great computational resource consumer, the algorithm was implemented using parallel processing. The resulting computational application that was developed to perform such type of design proved to be a powerful tool that is able to efficiently solve large scale grounding problems. This valuable tool may help engineers on designing more reliable electrical protection systems. The case study presented in this work demonstrated the use of the software in a common situation that represents a typical engineering problem and the results obtained confirmed the worth of the application program.

References

1. Ufer, H. G., "Investigation and Testing of Footing-Type Grounding Electrodes for Electrical Installations", IEEE Trans. Power Apparatus and Systems, vol 83, 1964, pp. 1042–1048.
2. Visacro, S. F., Ribeiro, H. A., Palmeira, P. F. M., "Evaluation of Potential Distribution at Vicinities of Grounding Configurations Comprising Both Concrete Encased Electrodes and Conventional Meshes", Proceedings of the International Conference on Grounding and Earthing - GROUND´2000, Belo Horizonte, Brazil, 2000, pp. 123-126.
3. Ribeiro, H. A., Development of a Computational Tool for the Performance Evaluation of the Concrete Encased Grounding Systems Over Low Frequency Phenomena. M.SC Thesis – (in Portuguese), UFMG, Belo Horizonte, Brazil, 2000.
4. Visacro, S. F., Aterramentos Elétricos, Alphagraphics, Belo Horizonte, 1998.
5. Visacro, S. F., Ribeiro, H. A., "Some Evaluations Concerning the Performance of Concrete-Encased Electrodes", Proceedings of the International Conference on Grounding and Earthing - GROUND´98, Belo Horizonte, Brazil, 1998, pp. 63-67.
6. Snir, M., Otto, S., Lederman, S. H., Walker, D., Dongarra, J., MPI: The Complete Reference, The MIT Press, London, 1996.
7. Visacro, S. F., Vale M. H. M., Birchal, M. A. S., "Grounding Safety Analysis: Interconnecting Substation Grid to External Electrodes", Proceedings of the IX Symposium of Specialists in Electric Operational and Expansion Planning, Rio de Janeiro, Brazil, 2004.
8. Birchal, M. A. S., Vale M. H. M., Visacro, S. F., "Analysis of Risk Conditions on Interconnected Grounding Systems: Concrete Encased Electrodes and Grid", Proceedings of the International Conference on Grounding and Earthing – GROUND´2004, Belo Horizonte, Brazil, 2004, pp. 297-301.
9. Hennessy, J. L. D., Patterson, A., Computer Architecture a Quantitative Approach, 3rd ed. San Francisco: Morgan Kaufmann, 2002.

Implementing Overlapping Domain Decomposition Methods on a Virtual Parallel Machine

David Darjany[1,*], Burkhard Englert[2,**], and Eun Heui Kim[1,***]

[1] California State University Long Beach, Dept. of Mathematics and Statistics
Long Beach, CA 90840
`ddarjany@yahoo.com, ekim4@csulb.edu`
[2] California State University Long Beach, Dept. of Comp. Engr. & Comp. Science
Long Beach, CA 90840
`benglert@csulb.edu`

Abstract. To solve many partial differential equations of different types domain decomposition techniques were developed. Such algorithms are generally very well suited for implementation on a virtual parallel machine, simulated on a distributed system. While such algorithms are readily available and well established in the literature, authors do usually not concern themselves with questions of the practical implementability of their algorithms. In particular issues such as finding the optimal size of overlap in domain decompositions, finding the most effective number of subdomains or deciding whether to use exact or inexact subdomain solvers are beyond the scope of these results. In this paper we will address these questions. We first develop suitable domain decomposition algorithms for our virtual parallel machine. Through numerical experiments using our algorithms we then show that smaller linear systems work well even without any overlap while larger systems require that at least 10% of the subdomain size overlap to have convergency. The data also indicates that between 20% to 35% of the subdomain is the optimal overlap size. We next increase the number of subdomains and analyze its effect on the parallel solver. Our data shows that for a sufficiently large linear system computational speed of convergence improves significantly as the number of subdomains increases. We finally compare the effectiveness of exact and inexact domain solvers and show that the appropriate choice of the number of iterations in the worker algorithm, is much more efficient in the inexact solver than in the exact solver.

1   Introduction

Domain decomposition techniques have been developed in recent years for solving partial differential equations of various types including elliptic, parabolic and

---

* Research supported by the Dept. of Energy under grant DE-FG02-03ER25571.
** Research supported by the Dept. of Transportation under METRANS USC-111699.
*** Research supported by the Dept. of Energy under grant DE-FG02-03ER25571.

G. Min et al. (Eds.): ISPA 2006 Ws, LNCS 4331, pp. 717–727, 2006.

mixed type equations. In particular for elliptic problems, various domain decomposition algorithms are well developed, see for example the survey paper by Chan and Mathew [6] and the references therein for details. While these algorithms are readily available they are only little concerned with practical implementability on parallel clusters. In particular issues such as finding the optimal size of overlap in domain decompositions, finding the most effective number of subdomains or deciding whether to use exact or inexact subdomain solvers are not addressed in these papers. In this manuscript we will study these more practical aspects of these domain decomposition techniques. Evaluating the impact of the underlying hardware, however, is beyond the scope of this paper.

1.1   Domain Decomposition

In general, domain decomposition methods can be classified either as overlapping subdomain algorithms or nonoverlapping subdomain algorithms, based on a decomposition of the domain into a number of overlapping subregions or nonoverlapping subregions respectively. A comparison of some of the overlapping and nonoverlapping algorithms can be found in [4]. As it was discussed in [6] the overlapping method is generally easier to implement (the nonoverlapping method has so called interface problems) and it is easier to achieve an optimal convergence rate and often more robust. However extra work is needed in the overlapping regions. Furthermore, the overlapping method is not suitable for the discontinuous differential operator because of the discontinuities on the overlapped regions. The results in [2,5] show that the overlapping and nonoverlapping algorithms are basically related under a specific interface preconditioner.

In this manuscript we focus on the overlapping method and we briefly discuss the classical Schwarz alternating algorithms [4,6,7,8,9,10,13] based on overlapping subregions for a Poisson equation with a Dirichlet boundary condition:

$$\begin{cases} Lu \equiv -\Delta u = f(x,y), & \text{in } \Omega, \\ \quad u = g \quad \text{on } \partial\Omega. \end{cases} \tag{1}$$

It also works for a general elliptic equation with a Neumann or mixed boundary condition. For simplicity we consider Ω is covered by Ω_i, $i = 1,2$ where $\Omega_1 \cap \Omega_2 \neq \emptyset$. With an initial guess u^0, the Schwarz alternating algorithm constructs a sequence of iterations u^k, $k = 1, 2, ...$, where we first solve

$$\begin{cases} Lu_1^{k+1} = f \text{ in } \Omega_1 \\ u_1^{k+1} = u^k \mid_{\Gamma_1} \\ u_1^{k+1} = 0 \text{ on } \partial\Omega_1 \setminus \Gamma_1, \end{cases} \quad \text{and} \quad \begin{cases} Lu_2^{k+1} = f \text{ in } \Omega_2 \\ u_2^{k+1} = u_1^{k+1} \mid_{\Gamma_2} \\ u_2^{k+1} = 0 \text{ on } \partial\Omega_2 \setminus \Gamma_2, \end{cases}$$

where $\Gamma_1 = \partial\Omega_1 \cap \Omega$ and $\Gamma_2 = \partial\Omega_2 \cap \Omega$. Next u^{k+1} is then defined by

$$u^{k+1}(x,y) = \begin{cases} u_2^{k+1}(x,y) \text{ if } \quad (x,y) \in \Omega_2 \\ u_1^{k+1}(x,y) \text{ if } (x,y) \in \Omega \setminus \Omega_1. \end{cases}$$

Depending on the choices of Ω_i, $i = 1,2$, it can be shown that

$$\|u - u^k\| \leq \rho^k \|u - u^0\|, \quad \rho < 1.$$

The constant ρ can be close to one if the overlapping region is thin. See for example [11]. Depending on the number of subdomains and the geometry of the domain, there are so called "coloring methods" in implementing alternating methods, that is, to determine which subdomains get computed in what order, see [6] for details.

It is very well known that the Poisson equation arises in the study of stationary diffusions and waves, electric potential, steady fluid flow, Brownian motion and so on. We discretize the equation (1) by finite differences (it is also true for finite elements) to get a large sparse symmetric positive definite linear system:

$$Au = b. \tag{2}$$

There are many iterative methods to solve linear systems such as Jacobi, Gauss-Siedel, SOR and so on. In this manuscript we use the Gauss-Siedel iterative method since it is easy to implement and sufficiently efficient.

We note that for the Poisson equation (even for certain nonlinear equations), the domain can be scaled to be small. However since our goal is to implement and test the efficiency of these algorithms for large linear systems (2) when implemented over a distributed systems, we focus in this paper on solving (2) for a domain without any scaling.

1.2   Motivation

We now discuss some practical issues in implementing the overlapping subdomain method using our new algorithms. One of the issues is how to choose the size of the overlapping region, that is how to choose $\gamma = dist(\Gamma_1, \Gamma_2)/2 > 0$, where $dist$ is the standard Euclidean distance. Here for simplicity we assume that subdomains are evenly overlapped. It is pointed out in [3,6] that there are convergence theories which show that the bigger γ gets the fewer number of iterations is needed. However the convergence theories do not answer the question of how to choose γ appropriately in practice. The next practical issue is to choose an optimal number of subdomains. This issue is often governed by the geometry of the domain and naturally by the number of clusters available for parallel computing. Also, in the early stages of the iterations, to save computational cost, instead of finding exact solutions for subdomain problems, inexact subdomain solvers can be used. Inexact subdomain solvers can be formulated in two ways. One way is that when the differential operator has variable coefficients, the subdomain problems can be approximated by simpler forms, for example with constants (average valued) coefficients. The other way is that in solving the subdomain linear system of (2), it can be used by a few of Gauss-Seidel (or Jacobi, SOR, etc) iterations or replaced by some other inexact methods (ILU, ILUT). However in applications, it may result in the loss of convergence in the iterations.

In this manuscript, we focus on experiments of overlapping subdomain methods by varying the size of γ and by varying the number of subdomains. Furthermore we compare efficiencies of inexact subdomain solvers and exact solvers by varying the number of Gauss-Siedel iterations in subdomain solvers. We note that instead of using alternating methods (alternating subdomains), we run worker machines simultaneously. That is, with u^k, $k = 0, 1, ...$, in the domain $\Omega = \{0 < x < a, 0 < y < b\}$, the master machine sends each corresponding boundary data for each and every subdomains, worker machines then perform computations **simultaneously** and send the new data u^{k+1} back to the master machine. We repeat this until u^k converges. This simplifies the process of dividing the subdomains to alternate the computations, that is we do not need the so called coloring method to generate a sequential order of subdomains to work on them *one after the other*.

We discuss the algorithms in more detail in Section 2.

1.3   Our Contributions

Our contributions are based on our domain decomposition algorithms for a virtual parallel machine and are threefold:

- Using our algorithms we investigate what happens if we increase the size of the overlap relative to the size of the domain. We show that the results depend on the size of the linear system (the domain). Our data shows that smaller linear systems work well even without any overlapping while the larger systems require that at least 10% of the subdomain size overlaps to have convergency. The data indicates that between 20% to 35% of the subdomain is the optimal overlap size. We provide some numerical results in Section 3.
- We next increase the number of subdomains and analyze its effect on the parallel solver. Our data shows that for a *sufficiently* large linear system its computational speed improves significantly as the number of subdomains increases.
- We finally compare the effectiveness of exact and inexact domain solvers and show that the inexact solver with the appropriate choice of MS, the maximum number of iterations in the worker algorithm, is much more efficient than the exact solver. For a smaller linear system, a relatively small number of MS is sufficient to improve the efficiency, whereas for a larger system, a bigger number of MS is needed. Our data shows that as the size of the matrix increases about 250%×250%, the number MS must increase by about 1, 000 %.

2   Algorithms

In this section we describe the algorithms that we designed and used for the computations. Our virtual parallel machine is implemented over a distributed system. We designate one machine as *master* and the others as *workers*. We present the algorithm for Master machine in subsection 2.1 and for worker machines in subsection 2.2. Since implementations of virtual parallel machines are readily available over the internet, many users will not want to rewrite this code. Hence we also decided to perform our experiments using such available code packages. We implement *Lucio Andrades parmatlab v1.77 Beta - parallel computing toolbox* [1] for distributed computing on connected PCs.

This toolbox using matlab distributes processes to workers available over the intranet/internet. Each worker must be running a matlab daemon to be accessed.

The toolbox can operate in two possible modes: [MPMD mode] Multiple program-Multiple Data parallel model; the user has the control to send different matlab tasks to remote machines simultaneously and retrieve results later. [SPMD mode] Single program-Multiple Data parallel model; parallelization and management of remote workers is done automatically. Input data must be regularly ordered in matlab hyperblocks.

Our algorithm operates in MPMD mode.

Using this readily available toolbox has several advantages [1]: 1. No common file system is needed since all communications between tasks are through TCP/IP connections. 2. The parallel virtual machine does not need to know which workers are available, it'll will be listening until workers report ready. New workers can be added even after the process has been started. 3. Parallelization can be done over different dimensions (up to 5) at the same time and using contiguous, overlapping or constant hyper-blocks. Indexes can also vary for different input variables, the only restriction is that the total number of parallel elements should be the same. 4. The toolbox uses an improved version of the TCP/IP TOOLBOX 1.2.3 by Peter Rydesater [12]. In particular, serialization of data is achieved with a low-level MEX file, reducing the impact on computational efficiency. Serial data to Matlab variables is also done with a MEX file.

2.1   Master Algorithm

INPUT: size of main domain ($0 \leq x \leq a$, $0 \leq y \leq b$), number of sub-domains N, size of overlap (in # of mesh points), tolerance ϵ, maximum number of iterations for the master algorithm M, maximum number of iterations for the worker algorithm MS, function $f(x, y)$ (the nonhomogeneous term in the Poisson equation (1)), boundary function $g(x, y)$. In addition, exact solution for comparison purposes if known.

OUTPUT: the approximate solution to (1), total number of master iterations, execution time, error from exact solution (if supplied).

Or, message notifying that max number of iterations has been reached without convergence.

Step 1: Determine sizes of vectors based on domain definition (number of mesh points for interior domains, boundary domains and the full domain).

Step 2: Initialize g, w, the approximate boundary and function, respectively (we used an initialization function $w = 0$).

Step 3: Set up position vector, containing the bottom left corner of each domain (this is sent to the worker machine and then back so we know which domain we are receiving back).

Step 4: Initialize parallel session. Use *Lucio Andrades parmatlab v1.77 Beta - parallel computing toolbox* [1].

Step 5: WHILE (the counter $< M$) do Steps 6–9.

Step 6: Send each domain to a parallel worker machine. This is split up into 3 steps. First send the leftmost domain, then the middle domains, and lastly, the rightmost domain. The worker machines run a Poisson algorithm, which is described in Subsection 2.2.

Step 7: Receive each domain from parallel worker machines. They are received in random order, and reset to its proper location in the $w-$vector based on the returned start position of that particular domain.

Step 8: Check one column of a domain with its matching value from another domain. (What is checked is the left most domain of the overlap of each region).

If the difference between the two columns values is less than ϵ (we take $\epsilon = 10^{-2}$), for every overlap region, then mesh results together, using only one sub-domains data for each overlap. Graph the result.

Close the parallel session. STOP.

Step 9: Else, replace w by the newly computed solution, increment the counter and go to Step 6.

Step 10: Close the parallel session. STOP.

2.2   Worker Algorithm (Poisson Algorithm)

We implement the Gauss-Siedel iterative method and test for both an exact solver which is identical to the Gauss-Siedel iterations and an inexact solver which must execute the algorithm after MS, relative small, number of iterations even without convergence. In the algorithm there is no differences between the exact and the inexact solvers except the obvious one, MS for the exact is large and MS for inexact is small.

INPUT: the most current approximate solution of (1) $Wtemp$, the start position of where this data sits in the $x - y$ plane (lower left boundary) $startPos$, the nonhomogeneous function $f(x,y)$, the most current boundary data g corresponding to $Wtemp$, a vector holding (i) the mesh size $\Delta x = \Delta y$ (ii) number of y steps the data encompasses, (iii) number of x steps the data encompasses (iv) maximum number of iterations for the procedure to be performed, MS.

OUTPUT: the approximate solution W, $startPos$ which is the same as the input value, a Boolean result of whether or not the algorithm converged within the max number of iterations it was allowed to perform sol.

Step 1: Set up local variables from passed vectors

Step 2: Set up the vector b, the RHS of $Ax = b$, from the finite difference methods by using the boundary data g, the nonhomogeneous function f and $\Delta x = \Delta y$.

Step 3: WHILE ((I) the counter $< MS$ or (II) the error between the most recent and the previous approximation $> \epsilon$) do Gauss-Seidel iterations with the initial approximation $Wtemp$.

Step 4: Send the approximate solution W, $startPos$, sol to the master machine. STOP.

3   Numerical Experiments

For implementations, we use $f = 2\sin(\pi y/b) + (\pi/b)^2 x(a - x)\sin(\pi y/b)$ and $g = 0$ on the boundary so that the exact solution of the Possion equation (1) becomes $u_{exact} = x(a - x)\sin(\pi y/b)$ on $\Omega = \{0 < x < a, 0 < y < b\}$. We use PCs, Intel Pentium 4, 1.5 GHz, 256MB of RAM, 40GB hard drives. We are connecting PCs via a local area network. The operation system for PCs is Windows XP. The programming codes are written in Matlab version 6. In all of our experimentations, we use the mesh size $\Delta x = \Delta y = 10^{-1}$ and thus the tolerance $\epsilon = 10^{-2}$.

3.1   Varying Size of Overlap

By *subdomain size* we mean the following. For a given domain Ω we evenly subdivide Ω into N many nonoverlapping subdomains, say Ω_i', such that $\overline{\Omega} = \bigcup_{i=1}^{N} \overline{\Omega}_i'$ where $\overline{\Omega}$ means the closure of Ω. We let the size of Ω_i' be the *subdomain size*. We then extend Ω_i' to obtain an overlapping decomposition Ω_i of Ω for worker machines to perform computations.

CASE 1A: Domain $\Omega = \{0 < x < 3, 0 < y < 1\}$, number of subdomains is 3. Exact solver method is used for subdomain solvers. Subdomain size is 1.

In this case, we increase the size of the overlap from 0 to 0.5, that is the number of overlapping mesh points from 1 to 11. The number of iterations in the Master machine decreases as the size of overlap increases. However when the overlap size gets bigger than 0.2 (20%), the execution time jumps from $12.7s$ to $18.3s$. In fact this case shows that the fastest execution time is obtained when the size of the overlap is 0.2, which, however is very close to the case when the size of overlap is 0, and it gets slower beyond 0.3. We think that it is because beyond the overlap 0.3 the workers are solving unnecessarily large linear systems and thus it becomes inefficient. This suggests that the optimal size of the overlap is within 20% of the subdomain size.

Table 1. Case 1A

# of mesh points (Size of overlap)	# Iterations in Master	Execution Time in seconds	max $|u - u_{exact}|$
1(0)	6	12.8	6.256×10^{-3}
3(0.1)	5	13.8	1.332×10^{-3}
5(0.2)	4	12.7	1.512×10^{-3}
7(0.3)	4	18.3	1.656×10^{-3}
9(0.4)	3	19.1	1.636×10^{-3}
11(0.5)	3	19.0	1.668×10^{-3}

Table 2. Case 1B

# of mesh points (Size of overlap)	# Iterations in Master	Execution Time in seconds	max $|u - u_{exact}|$
1(0)	12	73.5	2.412×10^{-1}
5(0.2)	8	60.1	1.237×10^{-3}
9(0.4)	6	60.9	1.531×10^{-3}
11(0.5)	5	59.1	1.532×10^{-3}
13(0.6)	5	61.8	1.596×10^{-3}
15(0.7)	4	56.1	1.537×10^{-3}
17(0.8)	4	63.3	1.588×10^{-3}

CASE 1B: Domain $\Omega = \{0 < x < 6, 0 < y < 2\}$ and the number of subdomains are 3. Exact solver method is used for subdomain solvers. In this case the subdomain size is 4.

This case shows that for the overlap sizes which are bigger than 0.7 there is no improvement on both the number of iterations for the Master machine and the execution time. Only the first case does not converge and the fastest execution time is obtained when the overlap size is 0.7 which is 35% of the subdomain size.

3.2   Varying Number of Domains

CASE 2A: Domain $\Omega = \{0 < x < 6, 0 < y < 2\}$, and 15 mesh points overlaps. Exact Sub-domain Solver is used. Note that Ave. # of worker iterations means that average number of iterations in worker machines on the first (largest) master iteration.

Case 2A shows no improvement in the execution time as the number of subdomains increases. In fact the data shows that one subdomain, that is no distributed computing, is the fastest. This happens because the machines are spending most of their time to communicate with each other and thus we conclude that the size of the linear system (the domain) is not sufficiently large enough to see any improvement from distributing the algorithm.

Table 3. Case 2A

# of subdomains	# Iterations in Master	Execution Time in seconds	$\max |u - u_{exact}|$	Ave. # of worker iter's
1	1	43.9	1.618×10^{-3}	690
2	4	54.6	1.526×10^{-3}	598
3	4	55.9	1.537×10^{-3}	530
4	5	47.9	1.559×10^{-3}	484
5	5	46.7	1.487×10^{-3}	456

Table 4. Case 2B

# of subdomains	# Iterations in Master	Execution Time in seconds	$\max |u - u_{exact}|$	Total iterations
1	1	1572.2	1.397×10^{-3}	2758
2	11	1007.7	8.719×10^{-4}	5500
3	11	866.9	6.990×10^{-4}	8250
4	12	413.1	9.750×10^{-4}	12000
5	12	359.8	7.622×10^{-4}	15000

CASE 2B: Domain $\Omega = \{0 < x < 10, 0 < y < 4\}$ and 21 mesh points overlaps. Inexact Sub-domain Solver (250 iterations/worker machine) is used.

This case shows that the execution time decreases significantly as the number of sudomains (worker machines) increases. Unfortunately we only had 5 workers to test so we do not have any more data. It will be interesting to see how the execution time changes as the number of workers increases further.

3.3   Inexact vs. Exact Subdomain Solver

CASE 3A: Domain $\Omega = \{0 < x < 6, 0 < y < 2\}$ and 15 mesh points overlap. Number of Domains is 3.

Table 5. Case 3A: Inexact subdomain solver

MS: # of iter. in worker	# iter. in Master	Exec. Time in sec.s	$\max |u - u_{ex}|$	Total iter.s
3	64	66.3	2.695×10^{-1}	576
4	55	61.2	2.062×10^{-1}	660
5	48	53.6	1.717×10^{-1}	720
10	31	41.7	8.00×10^{-2}	930
15	24	42.3	4.11×10^{-2}	1080

In this case we obtained the results by varying the maximum numbers of iterations MS in the inexact solvers and the results of the exact solvers. The fastest execution time shown in the inexact subdomain solver is obtained when the maximum number of iterations in workers is set to $MS = 10$. So by comparing the execution time in the exact solver which is $52.4s$, we see that the inexact solver is faster when setting 10 as the number of iterations in workers.

Table 6. Case 3A: Exact subdomain solver

# of iter. in Master	# iter. in worker1	# iter. in w2	# iter. in w3	max $|u - u_{ex}|$
1	499	593	497	2.5425
2	441	484	428	1.975×10^{-1}
3	303	358	290	1.100×10^{-2}
4	195	200	183	1.540×10^{-2}
Totals:	1438	1635	1398	
Total iter.	4471			
Exec. time	$52.4s$			

Case 3B: Domain $\Omega = \{0 < x < 10, 0 < y < 4\}$ and 15 mesh points overlap. Four Domains. Without using the distributed algorithm, using 2552 iterations, we obtain an execution time of $907s$ and max $|u - u_{exact}|$ is 8.480×10^{-3}.

In this case the fastest execution time for the inexact solver is when the number MS is 100 with $270.3s$, while the exact solver takes $686.9s$ to execute. Notice that the domain is large enough to see the effect of the distributed algorithm (see the execution time for the single domain, that is no workers, $907.0s$).

Table 7. Case 3B: Inexact subdomain solver

MS: # of iter. in worker	# Iterations in Master	Execution Time in seconds	max $|u - u_{exact}|$	Total iterations
3	226	1117.2	1.0211	2712
5	170	835.4	6.782×10^{-1}	3400
10	110	652.8	3.495×10^{-1}	4400
15	84	527.3	2.203×10^{-1}	5040
25	58	395.3	1.270×10^{-1}	5800
50	35	342.7	5.300×10^{-2}	7000
100	21	270.3	2.100×10^{-2}	8400
250	12	376	2.400×10^{-2}	12,000

For both Case 3A and Case 3B, in fact for all of our data, we use the stopping criteria, max $|u^{k-1} - u^k| < \epsilon = 10^{-2}$, to execute the algorithm. Thus the result as it turns out to be much more closer (of order 10^{-3} in Table 8) to the exact solution whereas it is still of order 10^{-2} when it compares with its previous approximation.

Table 8. Case 3B: Exact subdomain solver

# of iter. in Master	# iter. in w1	# iter. in w2	# iter. in w3	# iter. in w4	$\max |u - u_{ex}|$
1	1153	1532	1531	1151	1.370×10
2	1107	1399	1393	1091	4.899
3	944	1243	1240	928	1.7819
4	830	1065	1059	815	6.331×10^{-1}
5	682	903	899	667	2.2237×10^{-1}
6	560	730	725	545	7.460×10^{-2}
7	422	567	563	407	2.130×10^{-2}
8	302	405	401	288	2.400×10^{-3}
9	189	260	256	179	5.900×10^{-3}
Totals:	6189	8104	8067	6071	
Total iter.	23064				
Exec. time	$686.9s$				

4 Conclusions

Our data shows that the size of the linear system (the domain) is the key factor to determine the size of overlap, the number of workers, and the number of iterations, MS, in the inexact solver. In fact, for smaller linear systems, in all three cases relatively small numbers are sufficient to have efficient convergence, whereas for larger systems, relatively large numbers are needed. Our experiments guide how specifically the size of overlap, the number of workers and the number of iterations, MS, in the inexact solver can be chosen for different sizes of linear systems for efficient distributed computing.

References

1. Lucio Andrade, Paramatlab, *http://www.mathworks.com/matlabcentral/ fileexchange/loadFile.do?objectType=file&objectId=217*.
2. P.E. Björstad and O.B. Widlund, To overlap or not to overlap: A note on domain decomposition method for elliptic problems, *SIAM J. Numer. Anal.* 23(6) (1989) 1093-1120.
3. X.-C. Cai, A family of overlapping Schwarz algorithms for nonsymmetric and indefinite elliptic problems. *Domain-based parallelism and problem decomposition methods in computational science and engineering, SIAM*, (1995) 1–19.
4. X.-C. Cai, W.D. Gropp and D.E. Keyes, A comparison of some domain decomposition and ILU preconditioned iterative methods for nonsymmetric elliptic problems, *Lin. Alg. Applics,* (1994).
5. T.F. Chan and D. Goovaerts, On the relationship between overlapping and nonoverlapping domain decomposition methods, *SIAM J. Matrix Anal. Appl.* 13(2)(1992) 663.
6. T.F. Chan and T.P. Mathew, Domain decomposition algorithms, *Acta Numerica*, (1994), 61–143.
7. M. Dryja and O. Widlund, An additive variant of the Schwarz alternating method for the case of many subregions, *Tech. Rep. 339*, Courant Inst., New York Univ., 1987.

8. W. D. GROPP AND D. E. KEYES, *Domain Decomposition on parallel computers*, *Impact of Computing in Science and Engineering*, 1 (1989), pp. 421-439.

9. D. E. KEYES, *Domain Decomposition: a bridge between nature and parallel computers*, *NASA ICASE Technical Report 92-44*, NASA Langley Research Center Hampton, VA 23681-0001, 1992.

10. D. E. KEYES AND W. D. GROPP, *A comparison of domain decomposition techniques for elliptic partial differential equations and their parallel implementation*, *SIAM J. Sci. Statis. Comp.* , 8 (1987), pp. 166-202.

11. P. L. LIONS, *On the Schwarz alternating method II: stochastic interpretation and order properties*, *Domain decomposition methods*, SIAM (1989),47–70

12. PETER RYDESATER, *TCP/IP toolbox, http://petrydpc.itm.mh.se/tools.*

13. B. F. SMITH, P. E. BJORSTAD AND W. D. GROPP, *Domain Decomposition: Parallel Multilevel Methods for Elliptic PDEs*, Cambridge University Press, 1996.

Parallel Image Segmentation in Reconfigurable Chip Multiprocessors

Raphael Fonte Boa, Alexandre Marques Amaral, Dulcinéia Oliveira da Penha,
Carlos Augusto P. da Silva Martins, and Petr Y. Ekel

Pontifical Catholic University of Minas Gerais (Brazil)
Av. Dom José Gaspar, 500 – CEP 30535610 – MG – Brazil
`rfonteboa@ieee.org, alexmarques@ieee.org,`
`dulcineia.penha@ieee.org, capsm@pucminas.br, ekel@pucminas.br`

Abstract. Current image segmentation implementations are not optimized to all kinds of applications. To attend the different application kinds, the solution should allow to be reconfigured to fit their different characteristics and resource needs and to improve performance. Our objective is to present an image segmentation architecture and its implementation that can be reconfigured to execute different application workloads with demanded performance. In order to achieve this objective, our proposal is a parallel image segmentation implementation, which maps a pipelined parallel segmentation software architecture to a reconfigurable pipeline structure composed of reconfigurable chip multiprocessors (RCMPs). In this work, each pipeline stage was composed of a RCMP. Our results and its analysis show that our segmentation implementation provides greater flexibility and scalability and still obtains performance gain when compared to a multiprocessor machine. The main contribution is speedup, scalability and flexibility of the proposed solution.

1   Introduction

Image segmentation operation is applied to several engineering areas, e.g. quality control, computational vision, text fragment recognition [1], robot vision [2], pattern recognition, security systems, Synthetic Aperture Radar [3], etc. These applications can be processed online or offline, and can be static (pictures) or dynamic (video).

Like most of image-processing operations, image segmentation has a high demand of computational resources to store and to process great amounts of data. It requires high performance computers to be applied to four kinds of image applications: static offline, dynamic offline, static online and dynamic online. Among these, static offline applications demand less computational resources while dynamic online applications demand more computational resources. Since these latter are real-time applications, they have a high amount of images to be processed as faster as possible.

Traditional sequential processing architectures usually do not attend image segmentation application requirements considering performance and response times. Hence, the use of parallel processing techniques may reduce the response time of the segmentation operation [4] [5] in the four kinds of image application mentioned. Due to their data independencies, the segmentation processes required for these

G. Min et al. (Eds.): ISPA 2006 Ws, LNCS 4331, pp. 728–737, 2006.

applications can be parallelized. However, a static parallel solution cannot suit all kinds of image segmentation applications since these applications may vary in processing, storage, communication and response time needs. Therefore, the problem considered is that current image segmentation implementations are not optimized to different kinds of segmentation applications. A computational system to attend all these applications should be flexible to support different configurations. These configurations allow the system to improve its performance and to fit different segmentation application features and requirements. Hence, our objective is to present an image segmentation architecture and its implementation (proposed solution) that executes different segmentation application with demanded performance.

Moreover, parallel computer architectures have a significant overhead to perform communication among the processing elements. This overhead is reduced when the parallel architecture is implemented on a single-chip multiprocessor (CMP) [6]. Therefore, the proposed solution is a parallel image segmentation implementation, which maps a pipelined parallel image segmentation software architecture to a pipelined structure composed of reconfigurable single-chip multiprocessors (RCMP).

Our main goals are the design and implementation of the parallel image segmentation filtering phase and the pipelined parallel image segmentation software architecture mapped to a pipeline structure. The speedup, scalability and flexibility is some of the main contributions of the proposed solution, presented in this paper.

2   Image Segmentation

Image segmentation is one of the most important operations within image processing. Currently, several engineering areas demand image analysis in some application that uses alpha-numeric symbols. The image segmentation operation is usually the first one to be executed in the analysis phase. It aims at image division into its parts or objects. Once the image is divided, its parts are able to be separately analyzed.

The image segmentation algorithms can be divided into two classes: discontinuity and threshold detections. The former is based on the borders detection and hard variations of the pixel intensities. A 1D convolution kernel can be used to process the border detections, as represented in (1). After the convolution operation processing, the pixels that compose the borders are detected and a border linkage is processed to separate pixels from different borders. In (1), $B(x,y)$ is the result in each kernel position, N is the kernel size, W is the kernel coefficient and Z is the pixel value.

$$B(x, y) = \sum_{1}^{N} Wi \times Zi \qquad (1)$$

The threshold heuristic is based on the surface texture pattern recognition, targeting to find the object lengths. It can be processed by some tests on the function T, as presented in (2). This function depends on the current position (x,y), the pixel intensity $(f(x,y))$ and some local feature of the current pixel $(p(x,y))$. The tests are also presented in (2). Afterwards, pixels which the function T assumes value '1' could be object pixels, while those which T assumes value '0' could be the background.

$$T = T[x, y, p(x, y), f(x, y)], \quad g(x,y) = \begin{cases} 1 & \text{if } f(x,y) > T, \\ 0 & \text{if } f(x,y) \leq T. \end{cases} \tag{2}$$

There are several methods to perform image segmentation operations. All these methods include two phases: filtering and analysis. Claudino et. al. [1] proposed a method that performs the filtering by convolving the input image and two one-dimensional Gaussian masks (a vertical and a horizontal one). The image convolution operation is characterized by its data independency; hence each convolution operation is possible to be implemented in parallel. In addition, both convolutions can be cascaded, enabling a pipeline structure.

3 Related Works

We did not find any work completely related to the presented solution. We selected some works related either to the research problem or its solution, such as: image segmentation [1], image-filters implemented in FPGA [7] and CMP [6].

Our proposal is based on the implementation of a segmentation method targeting text identification in arbitrary scenes, presented in [1]. This method is separated in two phases: the first one uses some window filters in order to separate the target characteristics, which are vertical details. In the other phase, the regions of interest are segmented and classified whether being or not a text fragment.

There are lots of efforts to improve image preprocessing performances. In [7], the authors presented a parallel image processing architecture and its FPGA-based implementation. It is composed of several layers and each one is responsible for a specific task. The paper concentrates on the image preprocessing layer, which is composed of a parallel array of 16 processing elements and a Direct Memory Access (DMA) channel. The DMA channel addresses the area of interest and the processing elements, which are responsible for data processing. A host processor sends the instructions of control and data manipulation to the processing elements and waits for their output. This architecture, implemented in FPGA, performed a 3x3 convolution in a 256x256 image with a rate of 88.42 frames per second, running at 50 MHz.

Single-Chip Multiprocessors have been currently used since they perform good processing power with high communication speeds. Therefore, its high overall performance makes it possible to decrease the clock frequency enabling low power consumption. This makes these implementations very useful to reach the performance/power consumption required for the most of current applications. In [6], authors made a study around the advantages and disadvantages of these implementations over traditional superscalar and simultaneous multithreading processors. They concluded that even the high evolution of the traditional architectures would not be worthy compared to the novel CMP architectures.

4 Proposed Solution

Traditional sequential solutions, usually do not explore image convolution data independency. In addition, although traditional parallel solutions explore data independency, they usually have flexibility and communication limitations.

Some solutions have integrated multiprocessor elements in a single-chip, developing Chip Multiprocessors (CMPs) [6]. These solutions appeared to enhance the advantages of multiprocessor architectures, allowing higher processing power and communication rates. A CMP integrates several Processing Elements (PEs) and Storage Elements (SEs) connected to each other by high-speed Interconnection Elements (IEs) [6]. Despite their advantages, CMPs have some limitations, such as: low flexibility and low scalability of a static architecture and its implementation, thus not being able to keep high performance for different workloads.

In this paper, a high-performance and high-flexibility image filtering solution is presented, which corresponds to the first phase of the image segmentation method presented in [1]. The proposed solution is an implementation of a reconfigurable architecture organized in two levels: a reconfigurable parallel software architecture mapped to a reconfigurable parallel hardware architecture. The solution has some features to reduce the limitations of the other mentioned architectures. The reconfigurability makes the solution scalable and flexible [8] being able to support different configurations according to the segmentation application requirements. The parallelism improves the performance of the segmentation processing. In order to achieve more performance, flexibility and scalability, the solution was implemented using Reconfigurable Chip Multiprocessors [9].

4.1 Architecture

As mentioned before, the proposed solution architecture is composed of two main levels. The higher level is the reconfigurable parallel software architecture, which is responsible for implementing the convolution operations. This level divides the filtering phase into pipeline stages. Each pipeline stage of the software executes a different filter, required for the correct processing in the second segmentation phase [1]. This enables different stages of the segmentation filtering phase to be executed at the same time. Therefore, this architecture exploits the time parallelism between each filter. Fig. 1 presents in more details the reconfigurable pipelined software architecture composed of n filters, with n being the number of pipeline stages.

The lower level is the reconfigurable parallel hardware architecture organized as a pipeline structure, which stages are composed of Reconfigurable Chip Multiprocessors (RCMPs) [9]. The parallel hardware architecture is responsible for implementing and executing the convolution software. The parallelism and reconfigurability presented in this architecture enables it to achieve a tradeoff between performance and flexibility, supporting a correspondent implementation of the pipelined parallel software. Thus, different numbers of PEs, SEs, IEs and different variations of these elements can be configured.

As presented in fig. 1, the software pipeline organization is flexible, and the number of pipeline stages depends on the application. In this work, the software architecture was divided into three stages, although other applications can divide it into another number of stages. This is possible exploring the reconfigurability of the software architecture, achieving high flexibility and scalability.

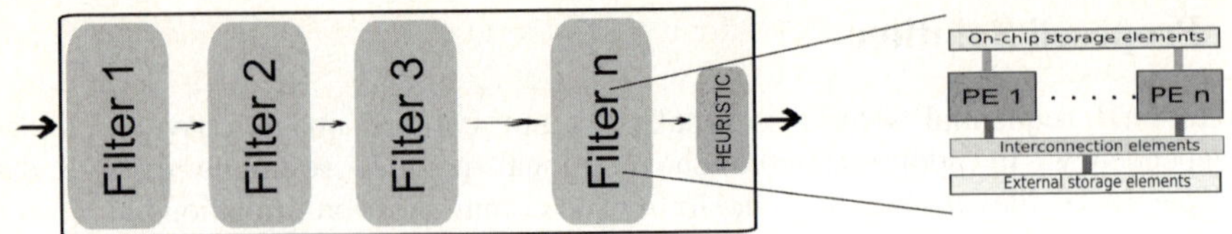

Fig. 1. Reconfigurable text-fragment segmentation architecture   **Fig. 2.** RCMP architecture

The reconfigurable pipelined software architecture can be mapped to the reconfigurable pipelined hardware architecture in different ways. Fig. 1 and fig. 2 illustrate a software mapping to the hardware architecture, which each pipeline stage is composed of a RCMP with a parameterized architecture. However, variations of mapping can be applied. For instance, if the hardware platform does not have enough resources to implement a RCMP in each pipeline stage, each stage can be implemented in a time-multiplexed way. Then, partial results would be buffered to be used by a following filter in a future time slot. Another possibility is to map each software stage to a pipelined hardware platform composed of RCMPs with fewer resources (e.g. number of PEs, storage capacity of SEs and connectivity of IEs). These variations of the architecture and their implementations are due to the reconfigurability feature of the proposed software and hardware architectures, providing flexibility, scalability and high performance for different workloads.

Using pipelined structures and RCMPs, the proposed reconfigurable parallel architecture presents parallel processing in time and space, simultaneously. The pipeline parallelizes the execution in time, while the RCMP architecture parallelizes the application in space. Considering just the time parallelization (pipeline), our architecture obtains a speedup relative to sequential executions showed in (4), where n is the number of images to be processed, T_s is the time relative to the stage execution time and f is the number of filters applied to the images. With the use of RCMPs the filtering process can provide an even greater speedup, as observed during analysis of experimental results.

$$\frac{n \times T_s \times f}{(T_s \times f) + (n-1) \times T_s} \qquad (3)$$

The number of architectural elements may vary in quantity, configuration and type. The proposed solution can have PEs with different architectures and clock frequencies. For instance, to implement the image segmentation operations, the PEs could be vector processors. To suit fine-grained and coarse-grained workloads within the same application, the PEs can have several configurations and the number of PEs can be altered. In this case the pipeline would be heterogeneous. In addition, the topology of the IEs connecting the PEs and SEs can change, providing several forms of communication, thus providing efficient ways to map the filtering phases to the pipelined architecture of RCMPs.

4.2 Implementation

With the software architecture, we were able to efficiently map the filtering phase to the hardware architecture. In order to map the convolution software to the reconfigurable pipelined RCMP structure, we parameterized the software code to use different numbers of PEs in each of the implementations. Each filter was assigned to a RCMP configuration instance. At each hardware stage the software code was divided into n parts, n being the number of PEs, therefore we have temporal and spatial parallelism simultaneously.

Fig. 3 presents an implemented filtering stage using single, dual and quad-cores configurations. This illustrates the flexibility achieved with a reconfigurable architecture and a reconfigurable implementation platform. On all of the software and hardware implementations, the pipeline stages were homogeneous. Heterogeneous pipeline stages, with different RCMPs configurations, could be used if the filters complexity were different. This approach may be explored in further works.

We implemented three configurations of the RCMP architecture (fig. 3) in order to verify the performance gains of the proposed solution. The first configuration has only one PE. This configuration represents the filtering with each pipeline stage running sequentially. The second implementation has two PEs and the third has four PEs, in each pipeline stage. We used Xilinx XC2V1500 FPGA as a reconfigurable platform. All architecture elements are softcores supplied by Xilinx EDK (Embedded Development Kit). We used Xilinx MicroBlaze softprocessor core as the PE.

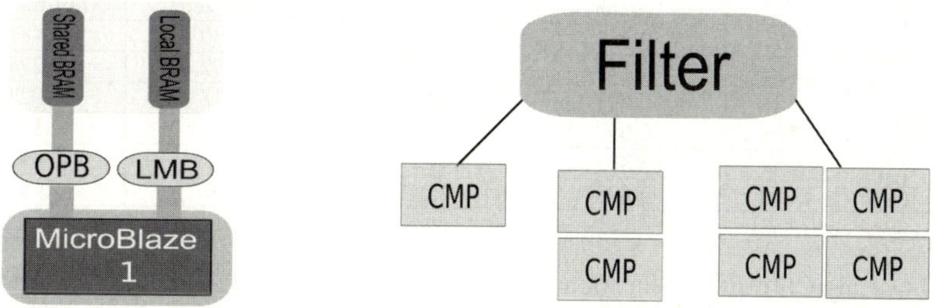

Fig. 3. RCMP MicroBlaze-based configuration with single-processor (left). Filter mapping to single, dual and quad-processor CMPs (right).

All the implemented configurations have each MicroBlaze connected to a 16KB BRAM through LMB (Local Memory Bus) used as program memory. Each processor was also connected to an OPB (On-chip Peripheral Bus) to access peripherals and data outside program address space. We used a 32KB BRAM as an image buffer that feeds Microblaze with data. The 32KB BRAM was a dual port memory with each port connected to an OPB. Depending on the CMP configuration the memory was connected to one or two OPBs.

5   Experimental Results

In this section, we present and analyze the experimental results of the image filters running in our implementation configurations. These filters are essential to the correct processing of the segmentation operation [1]. The implemented configurations are named: single-MicroBlaze, dual-MicroBlaze and quad-MicroBlaze-based CMPs. Besides running at 100 MHz, the chosen processing cores have a 3-stage pipeline and they have neither cache memory nor run operating system. The total memory embedded in the device is 128 KB of BRAMs, and we divide it into 16 KB for each program memories (local) and 32 KB for the image buffer (shared memory).

Targeting compare our implementation results, we also have run the same convolution algorithm in a SMP (Symmetric Multiprocessor) machine, using C programming language and *pthreads* to implement it. The SMP machine is a 1GHz-dual-Pentium III with 10-stage pipeline, 32 KB L1-cache, 256 KB L2-cache and 640 MB main memory. Its operating system is a Linux-based distribution with a SMP kernel. Only the kernel processes were running during tests. Rather than the flexible pipelined structure of our implementation, the dual-Pentium runs the filtering with performance limitation, since its structure is fixed. This gives our version an advantage over the fixed traditional parallel solutions since they cannot always implement a full system spatial pipeline.

Table 1 presents the response times of the convolution filters using either one or two PEs, both in the Pentium-III and in the MicroBlaze-based implementations.

Table 1. Response times (seconds) of Dual-Pentium and the proposed MicroBlaze-based

Image Size	PEs	Pentium-III + cache	Pentium-III - cache	MicroBlaze (non-optimized)	MicroBlaze (optimized)
512 x 512	1PE	0.237	0.267	1.230	0.481
	2PEs	0.159	0.175	0.572	0.224
1024 x 1024	1PE	0.992	1.018	4.918	1.923
	2PEs	0.697	0.681	2.289	0.897
2048 x 2048	1PE	3.871	4.277	19.672	7.692
	2PEs	2.833	2.955	9.155	3.587

We have also run the experiments with the Pentium-III caches, both L1 and L2, disabled. We noticed that without caches, the Pentium SMP was about four times better than our MicroBlaze-based implementation. Thus, our solution had a good performance compared to the Pentium SMP, considering that Pentium architecture has lots of improvements e.g. ten times greater clock frequency, presence of cache memories, superscalar optimizations. These improvements contribute to the Pentium's better performances. However, the MicroBlaze was chosen as a easy implementation of a processor core, since the goal of this paper is to present the advantages of the whole proposed solution.

Furthermore, in the following results, we present the performance gains (speedups) achieved with the proposed solution. Fig. 4-a shows the performance speedups of the dual-processing implementations over single-processor ones, for the Microblaze-based and Dual-Pentium-III solutions. We can observe that the MicroBlaze speedups are better than the Pentium ones since it has less overhead during the application processing. In the MicroBlaze case, this speedup is more than twice since dual-processor configuration takes less clock cycles than the single-processor does. The reasons for this are being investigated in the current solution research phase.

Two configurations of the MicroBlaze-based solution were implemented, differing one from each other in the convolution kernel storage element: main memory (non-optimized) and an internal MicroBlaze register (optimized). Fig. 4-b presents the speedups of the dual and quad MicroBlaze-based implementations over the single PE.

We can notice that, for the non-optimized case, the speedups were better than for the optimized case. This is due to the optimized configuration already has a speedup about 2.56 for single-MicroBlaze, because the kernel is stored in internal registers.

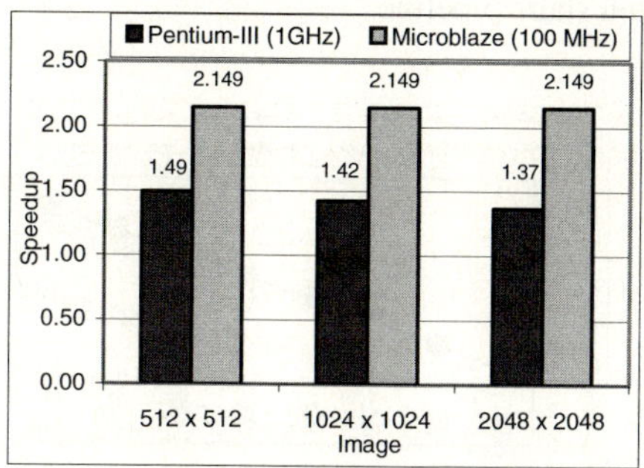

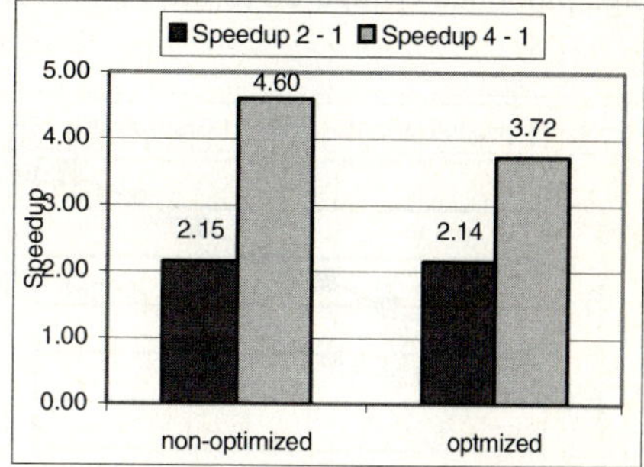

Fig. 4. (a) Speedups of dual-processing versions over the single-processor ones. (b) Speedups of the dual and quad processing MicroBlaze-based configurations over the single one.

Thus, the optimized speedup does not grow as fast as the non-optimized one when the number of PEs varies. Besides, as presented in fig. 4-b, the non-optimized quad-processing has a 15% higher speedup than the number of PEs. This is due to the performance gains when increasing the number of PEs (fig. 4-a). Generally analyzing fig. 4-b we can conclude that the performance gains in the non-optimized cases is greater than in the optimized ones. This occurs since the optimized cases have the kernel accessing time much lower than the non-optimized ones. Therefore the overall accessing times are enhanced with the image size increasing.

Besides the improvements obtained from running the filters in a RCMP architecture, we verified that using a reconfigurable pipeline organization considerably increases the performance. The implemented pipeline organization made our architecture achieve a speedup of almost two (fig. 5-a) related to Pentium's execution time when the number of filters is modified. Such variations are due to the segmentation process and to the application (dynamic or static, online or offline). We segmented 3600 images, which is the number of images in one minute of MPEG-2 video with a display rate of 60 frames-per-second. When varying the number of stages (filters), a 6-stage pipeline was enough to make our implementation achieve the same time Pentium-III took to run a 2048x2048 image with one PE.

Furthermore our implementation took less time than Pentium-III to run the same 2048x2048 image when both of them use dual-PEs. The speedup achieved by our implementation on the pipeline dual-processor implementation was greater than three (fig. 5-a) when compared to the Dual-Pentium-III implementation. That can be explained by the same reasons for which the speedup of our solution compared to itself was greater than two. Since each RCMP runs fewer cycles than the single-processor implementations, the speedup curve, representing the dual-processor implementation, increases faster than the single-PE curve.

The proposed architecture described in this paper, whenever implemented in newer and faster FPGA devices such as Xilinx Virtex-5, could run at higher clock frequencies. Moreover supposing it runs at the above device frequency (1 GHz), and considering the other features unchanged, its performance would be much better than the Pentium-III results, as presented in fig. 5-b. Although we did not considered any Operating System context-switching and pthread creation overheads in our implementation, we have a simpler architecture with no L1 and L2 caches, and a three stage pipelined compared to the Pentim-III ten stage pipeline.

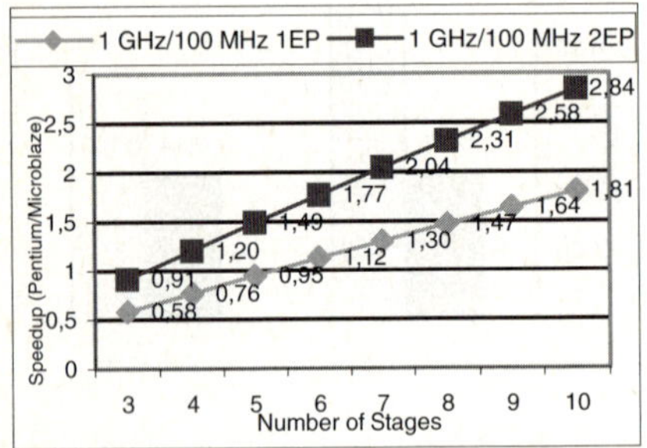
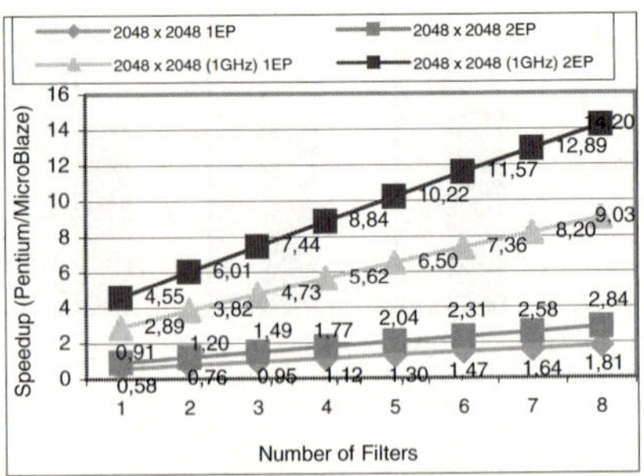

Fig. 5. (a) Speedups of the MicroBlaze-based over Pentium-III, with pipeline stages. (b) Speedups of the MicroBlaze-based over Pentium-III, working at 100MHz and 1GHz.

Analyzing the presented results, we conclude that the proposed image segmentation implementation can have better performance than the Pentium-III SMP. Therefore, although table 1 shows that the Pentium-III results are about five times better than the proposed MicroBlaze-based version, based on the results presented in figs. 4 (a) and (b) and 5 (a) and (b), the proposed solution achieved good speedup results. In addition, we verified that if the numbers of stages and images to process are increased (e.g. frame rate of video), our solution can obtain an equal or better performance compared to Pentium-III, with the same number of PEs. Moreover, if the clock frequency also increases, our solution overcomes Pentium's performances.

Besides performance gains, the proposed solution also has flexibility and scalability to fit different kinds of application requirements. This has been presented in the analysis of the variations of the numbers of PEs, on filter stages and on the number of images. Moreover, performance improvements were presented whenever the number of PEs was increased while keeping fixed the numbers of stages and images. Another result is the increasing of speedups when increasing the stages for static number of PEs and images to be processed. These results confirm the greater flexibility and scalability of the proposed solution.

6   Conclusions and Future Works

In this paper we presented a parallel image segmentation proposal which maps a pipelined parallel image segmentation software architecture to reconfigurable chip multiprocessors. We prototyped three configurations of the RCMP, used as the pipeline structure, and thus we were able to verify our solution's performance.

Even when compared to a solution running at a much higher clock frequency our solution obtained great performance results. Considering our implementation has PEs with simpler architecture, the performance difference was only 5 times worse than Pentium-III with enabled cache and 4 times with disabled cache. Besides, our solution provides greater flexibility and scalability and still presents high performance. Good performance and flexibility, presented by the proposed solution, could be achieved since the whole architecture and its implementation is reconfigurable in its software and hardware levels. Therefore, it is possible to modify the number of PEs in each stage of the hardware pipeline, as shown in presented configurations, targeting suit image segmentation application demands with better performances. This makes our solution flexible while maintaining good performances. In all implementations it obtained a speedup greater than two. This is due to the number of cycles executed by the multiprocessors configurations, in which the multiprocessors executed less than a half of the cycles taken by the single-processor. We are investigating this behavior.

Concerning all the presented results, our main contribution is a parallel image segmentation filtering phase implemented on reconfigurable chip multiprocessors (RCMP) pipeline stages, improving application performance. The further works are: design dynamically RCMPs targeting other applications and an implementation of cache memories targeting performance improvements; perform some tests of the current system in other prototyping platforms, using FPGAs with higher clock frequencies and more resources to implement faster CMPs with more PEs.

References

1. Claudino, L.M.B., Braga, A. de P., Araújo, A. de A. & Oliveira, A.F. Unsupervised segmentation of text fragments in real scenes, Proceedings of the 13th International Conference on Image and Analysis Processing, Cagliari, Italy, LNCS, Springer, vol. 3617, pp 399-406 (2005).
2. DeSouza, G., Kak, A. C.: Vision for Mobile Robot Navigation: A Survey. IEEE Transactions on Pattern Analysis and Machine Intelligence, pp. 237-267 (2002).
3. Strollo, A.G.M., Napoli, E., De Caro, D., Saggese, G.P.: A Reconfigurable 2D Convolver for Real-Time SAR Imaging. Proceedings of the 8th IEEE International Conference on Electronics, Circuits and Systems , pp. 741-744 (2001).
4. Penha, D. O., Corrêa, J. B. T., Góes, L. F. W., Ramos, L. E. S., Pousa, C. V. P., Martins, C. A. P. S.: Comparative analysis of multi-threading on different operating systems applied on digital image processing. In Proceedings of 3rd CSITEA (2003).
5. Hamdi, M., Lee, C.: Efficient Image Processing Applications on a Network of Workstations. In Proceedings of the 4th IEEE Computer Architectures for Machine Perception (1995).
6. Hammond, L., Basem, A. N., Olukotun, K.: A Single-Chip Multiprocessor. In Computer Magazine, IEEE Computer Society, vol. 30, no. 9, pp. 79-85, Sept., 1997.
7. McBader, S., Lee, P.: An FPGA Implementation of a Flexible, Parallel Image Processing Architecture Suitable for Embedded Vision Systems. In Proceedings of the 17th International Parallel and Distributed Processing Symposium - IPDPS, pp. 228.1. 2003.
8. Compton, K., Hauck, S.: Reconfigurable Computing: A Survey of Systems and Software. ACM Computing Survey, Vol. 34, No. 2, pp. 171-210, (2002).
9. Fonte Boa, R., Penha, D. O., Amaral, A. M., Souza, M. O. S., Martins, C. A. P. S., Ekel, P. Y.: RCMP: A Reconfigurable Chip-Multiprocessor Architecture. In Proceedings of the Frontier on High Performance Computing and Networking (ISPA 2006). To appear.

Ensuring Immediate Processing of Real-Time Packets at Kernel Level

Jeong Seob Kim[1], Dae Sung Lee[2], Ki Chang Kim[3], and Jae Hyun Park[3]

[1] Factory Automation Team, Samsung Electronics Co., Ltd., Korea
`jeongseob.kim@samsung.com`
[2] School of Computer Science & Engineering, Inha Univ., Korea
`Xdilemma@naver.com`
[3] School of Information and Communication Engineering, Inha Univ., Korea
`{kchang, jhyun}@inha.ac.kr`

Abstract. Real-Time system is one in which jobs are guaranteed to meet the predefined deadlines. Many researchers have studied real-time systems, and as results, there are numerous commercial real-time systems developed and applied to industry. There are also efforts to transform the Linux system to a real-time system as it becomes very popular and stable. Transforming Linux system into a real-time system, however, is a very difficult and time-consuming task because we have to modify the kernel in many places to ensure its correctness under repeated reentering events. We suggest to limit the effort to a certain specific interrupt, for example network interrupt, instead of trying to provide real-time handling for all interrupts. The scope is limited, and we can control the amount of shared data structures among the reentering kernel threads. We identify a special packet that requires real-time treatment and process it inside the Top Half without delaying. This paper explains the algorithm and shows how it is implemented in Linux.

1 Introduction

Numerous researchers have been working on real-time systems, including real-time operating systems. Linux is one of the popular and widely-used operating systems. However, it was not designed as a real-time operating system, and is not adequate to use as such.

We observe that many real-time systems provide only a few functionalities. Converting a full Linux into a real-time system is an over-kill for such a system. We suggest to tune the Linux code to meet the real-time requirement for the specific function only. In our case, the function is packet processing. Instead of providing real-time capability for all interrupts, we concentrate on the network interrupt, and provide an efficient and painless way tailored to this specific interrupt to handle real-time packets, those that need immediate treatment.

Network interrupt service in Linux is divided into Top Half and Bottom Half as in other interrupt services. Top Half consists of two steps: copying packets from network device to DMA and analyzing their frame types. Bottom Half transfers packets to the TCP layer. The Bottom Half is where most of the packet handling is processed. Since

G. Min et al. (Eds.): ISPA 2006 Ws, LNCS 4331, pp. 738–747, 2006.

Bottom Half is not guaranteed to be executed immediately, Linux is not real-time system. The Bottom Halves are serialized in the order they are activated regardless of their relative importance or timing requirements. Our strategy is to identify real-time packets, those that need real-time treatments, and to ensure their handling is done within Top Half. Identifying real-time packets can be done by marking special field in the packet and modify the kernel to recognize such mark. Handling real-time packet inside the Top Half is done by copying and moving kernel code related with this real-time process from Bottom Half to Top Half. We show how they can be done and what effect they have on the remaining code in following sections.

Section 2 introduces previous researches on real-time processing. Section 3 explains network interrupt processing in Linux systems. Section 4 shows the proposed algorithm for real-time network interrupt processing. Section 5 displays some experimental results, and finally Section 6 gives a conclusion.

2   Related Researches

Existing TCP/IP is a best-effort service and, thus, cannot guarantee differentiated or real-time service. ARP timer, delay due to caching policy, packet collision caused by sliding windows, the problem of TIME_WAIT, etc., all contribute to the unpredictability of TCP/IP. Many researches seek to reduce the degree of unpredictability by changing the behavior of certain layer in TCP/IP. It could be MAC, network, or transport layer. MAC layer modification focuses on removing the unpredictable delay during packet transmission due to packet collision. BRAM (Broadcast Recognizing Access Method)[1], MBRAM (Modified BRAM)[2] are such modifications. They completely remove packet collisions to insure no unpredictable delay. However, they require all network nodes to participate in this new algorithm.

ST-II[3] and RSVP[4] cope with the unpredictable delay at network layer. ST-II is developed for multimedia communication in which data transmission rate and delay should be controlled. It provides a useful mechanism for real-time communication but has compatibility problem with the existing protocols. RSVP controls delay by allocating bandwidth at each network node via reservation. It also requires all participating nodes to follow RSVP algorithm which is in most cases impractical. Transport layer can be also modified to cope with the unpredictability problem. RTP (Real-time Transport Protocol)[5] is one of the well known algorithms. It works on top of UDP which is non-connection-oriented algorithm. It provides a mechanism to control the delay time but is not suitable for industrial network where partial data loss is not tolerable.

Another branch on real-time research is real-time operating system. Processing designated jobs within predictable dead-line is not easy, especially in multi-process systems. Operating systems handle multiple jobs in parallel through time-sharing scheduling. A real-time operating system should be able to stop non-real-time jobs in favor of time-critical jobs. Linux does not have that capability and, thus, is not a real-time operating system. RT-linux [6,7] has been suggested as a way of converting Linux to real-time system. RT-linux inserts RT-kernel between the hardware and the original Linux kernel and treat the Linux kernel as a simple RT-task. RT-linux minimizes code modification and is simple in its concept. However, still the involved code is massive, and requires a full redesign of device drivers if it needs real-time functionality.

3 Network Interrupt Handling in Linux

3.1 Background[1]

An interrupt can occur while another was being served. Linux handles this problem by dividing the interrupt process into Top Half and Bottom Half. The kernel has a data structure connecting device interrupts to the corresponding driver service routines. do_IRQ looks at this data structure and calls the correct device service routine. For the network interrupt, it also performs the copying process of packets from DMA area to system buffer.

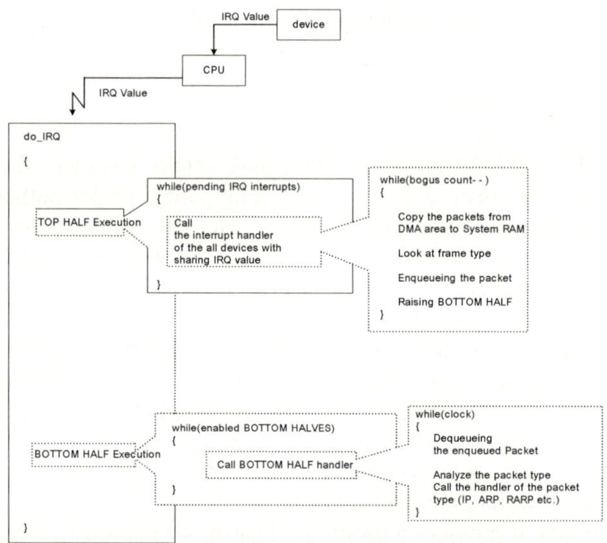

Fig. 1. The inner-working of do_IRQ

Figure 1 shows the inner-works of do_IRQ. The Bottom Half starts some time after the Top Half is done. When the system is returned from Top Half, there could be a multiple of Bottom Halves waiting. This is because the Bottom Half is supposed to be less important than the Top Half and thus can be interrupted anytime, and each Top Half will leave its Bottom Half in the queue during its process.

Top Half consists of code provided by the corresponding device driver. The driver already has registered its handler location in the system data structure which is interpreted as the Top Half location by the kernel for this device.

3.2 Problems and Suggested Solution

Figure 2(a) shows the delay in interrupt processing time. With this delay, it is very hard to provide a fast response to a time-critical packet. Figure 2(b) shows the delay

---

[1] To give a concrete explanation, we use Intel x86 processors as the example system.

time in our real-time scheme. We restrict the real-time packet to be a packet containing a simple command. We modify the kernel slightly to process these packets in real-time. Figure 2(b) removes queue operations, Bottom Half scheduling, and the execution of Bottom Half from Figure 2(a) to achieve real-time performance. For this scheme to work, the Top Half now includes code to analyze the ethernet frame to check if the incoming packet is a real-time one. If it is, the packet is not queued for further processing in Bottom Half; instead, its command is pulled out and processed immediately.

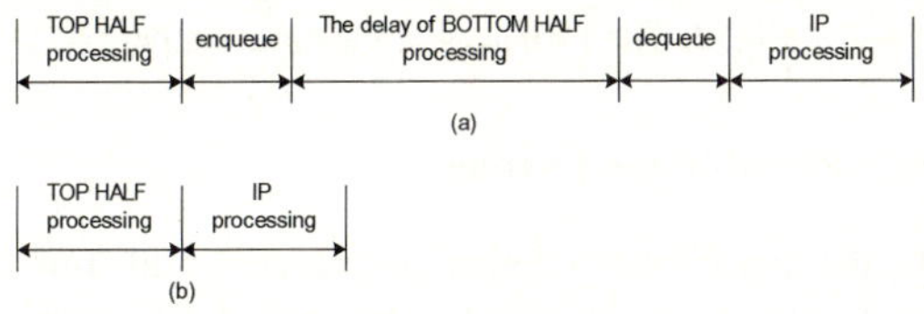

Fig. 2. The delay in interrupt processing time and our scheme

4   Real-Time Network Interrupt Processing

4.1   Real-Time Frame

When a frame is received, the kernel examines the "type" field to determine its frame type. A general ethernet frame has 0x0800 in it. If the type field has a value greater than or equal to 0x0800, it is RFC894; otherwise it is 802.3 [8, 9]. We propose to use this type field to designate a real-time frame. We put some special value in there to identify it as a real-time frame. The actual message for the real-time packet is transferred in IP header. Again, to preserve the original format of the IP header, we re-use some of the rarely used fields in the header: identification and flag field. These two fields are originally for packet fragmentation. When a packet is larger than MTU(Maximum Transmission Unit), it is fragmented before the transmission. The fragmented small packets are numbered using the identification field and reassembled in the order of this number at the final destination. IP_DF(Don't Fragment) flag in the flag field is set to prevent this fragmentation. When IP_DF is set, the identification has no meaning. Our technique uses these two fields to transmit a real-time packet. It sets the IP_DF flag and re-use the identification field as a short real-time message. A shortfall of this method is that the 16 bit size of the identification limits the number of different messages we can send. However by the nature of the real-time packets, it has to be handled at the fastest speed, and thus should be handled in the Top Half of the network interrupt processing. Messages long enough not to be contained within the IP header are already hard to process in the time-critical Top Half anyway. Figure 3 shows the proposed real-time frame. For our purpose, we used 0xff00 for the type field of real-time frames.

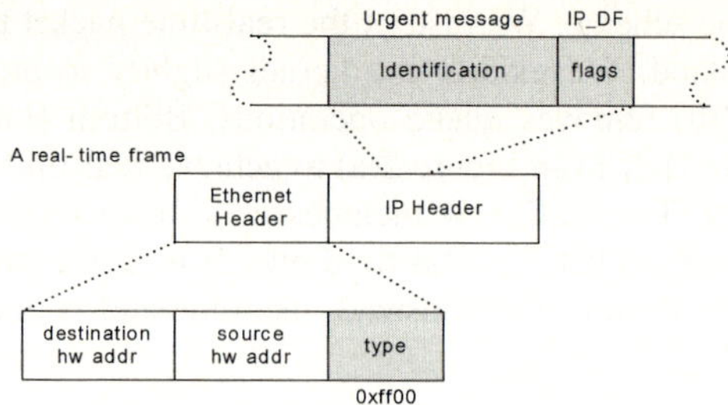

Fig. 3. The format of a real-time frame

4.2   The Processing of Real-Time Frames

In the receiving part, the algorithm to detect and process real-time packets is shown in Code 1. Basically we analyze the frame header and if the packet type is real-time, extract the message and process it immediately. This part was previously done in the Bottom Half. Now we hoisted it to the Top Half, and if the packet needs immediate attention it will be processed here; otherwise it is enqueued to the system buffer and stays there until the network Bottom Half is handled.

Code 1. The pseudo algorithm to detect and process real-time packets

```
while(received frames){
        The allocation of a sk_buff structure
        Copy frame from DMA area to sk_buff structure
        Analyze the ethernet frame header
        if ( frame type == real-time frame ){
            Extract an urgent message from an IP header
            Process the urgent message
        }
        else {
            Enqueue the frame in system buffer
            BOTTOM HALF scheduling
        }
    }
```

For the sending part, general socket libraries won't work because we need to modify ethernet header frame to insert 0xff00 at the type field so that our real-time frame can be differentiated with general ethernet frames at the destination. We need to know how to form our packet frame. We also need to know how to send out packets without the help of TCP/IP stack. Packet frame generation involves two steps: allocating a frame buffer and writing our header onto the frame. Linux manages frame buffers using sk_buff structure. The actual frame buffers are allocated using alloc_skb(). Figure 4 shows the allocated frame buffer attached to sk_buff. The filling of the frame buffer can be done using skb_reserve() and skb_push(). skb_reserve() is used to move the "data" pointer to the IP header and fill it as seen in Figure 5. The ethernet header is also filled in with the skb_push() function. This time the "data" pointer reduced by 14 to point to the ethernet header. figure 6 shows the process.

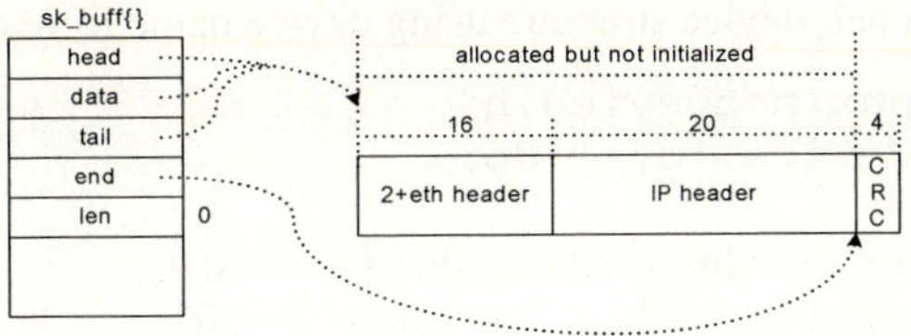

Fig. 4. The allocated frame buffer attached to sk_buff

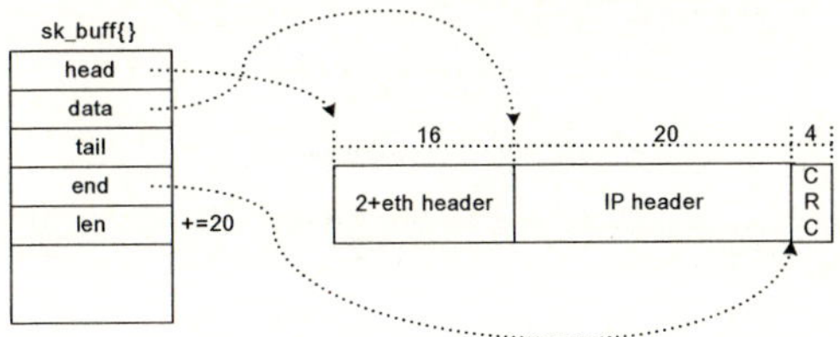

Fig. 5. skb_reserve() : Moving the "data" pointer to the IP header and fill it

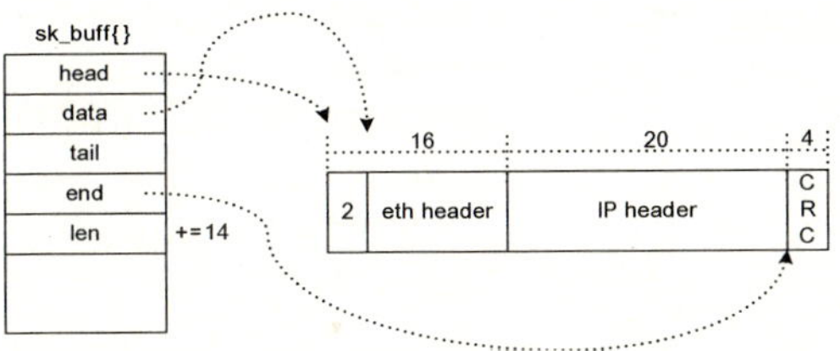

Fig. 6. skb_push() : Moving the "data" pointer to the ethernet header and fill it

To perform a direct I/O for a network device, we need a logical device interface. A global variable "dev_base" is a list of net_device structures allocated for all registered logical network devices. Code 2 shows how we can access to a net_device structure using device name from dev_base. From net_device structure, we can get the target network device's hardware address, which we set into our ethernet header. All this should be coded in a kernel module to access the internal functions and data structures. Figure 7 shows how our kernel module works. The name of our module is "rtx_thread.o" as shown in the figure. Once attached to the kernel, it accesses kernel functions such as skb_push(), skb_reserve(), alloc_skb(), and kernel data structure such as dev_base. Using the kernel functions our module can build a real-time frame, and this frame is transmitted through "eth0" interface using "speedo_start_xmit" function pointed to by the "net_device" structure for "eth0" that we extracted from "dev_base".

Code 2. Access to a net_device structure using device name from dev_base

```
"include/linux/netdevice.h"
struct net_device *d, **dp;

for (dp=&dev_base; (d=*dp) != NULL; dp=&d->next){
    if (strcmp(d->name, "eth0") == 0)
        break;
/* d is a net_device pointer for ethernet device. */
}
```

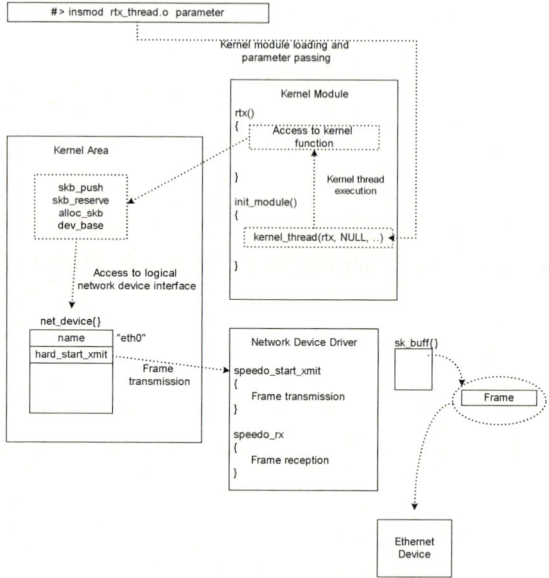

Fig. 7. Overview of the kernel module

5   Experiments

We have implemented the above mentioned kernel modules both for transmission and reception of real-time packets. The transmission module forms a real-time frame according to the given parameters. The parameters are the sender IP, receiver IP, receiver ethernet address, total number of frames to be transmitted, and the rate between real-time frame and regular frame. Only two types of real-time messages are defined: VAR_UP for increasing some kernel variable and VAR_DOWN for decreasing it. The generated real-time frame is inserted into a DMA area via a handler pre-registered by the network device driver. This frame will be transmitted when OUT command is put into the command register of the device. Figure 8 explains this relationship. The receiver side issues an interrupt when the packet arrives. The corresponding Top Half will copy the frame from the DMA area into the system buffer. The frame header is examined. For real-time frame with type being 0xff00, the message is pulled out and processed. Other regular frames are queued into a system queue until Bottom Half handles them as usual.

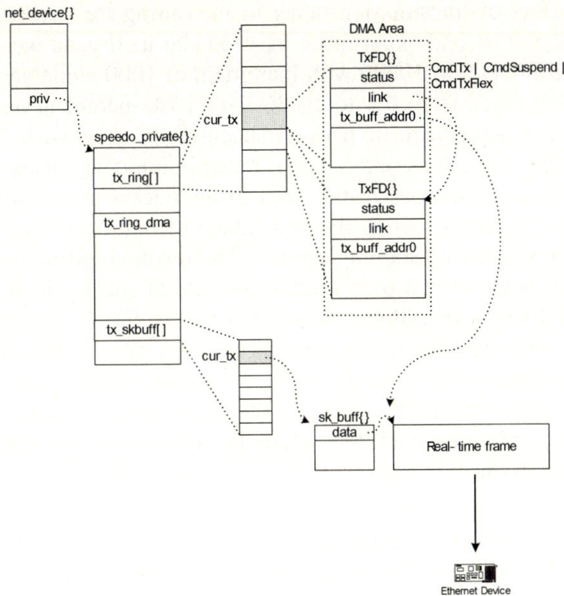

Fig. 8. The data structures for real-time frame transmission

We have measured the packet processing time and successful processing rate with various percentage of real-time frames in the total frames. For the packet processing time, the total number of packets is 1000. These packets are sent every 37 micro seconds. The sender generates random numbers to mark some percentage of the packets to be real-time frames. The percentage varies from 0% to 100% increasing by 10%. Obviously the more real-time frames we have, the faster should the processing time be because real-time frames will be processed without delay. Table 1 shows the results. As expected the processing time decreases as the percentage of real-time frames goes up. But after 40%, the time stays the same. It is because the interrupt handler used in the experiment is very simple such that even with 40% real-time frames, the 37 micro seconds delay at each transmission is long enough to handle every packets sent. With more complex interrupt handler, we expect that the improvement in processing time will continue after 40%.

Table 1. Times in jiffies to process 1000 frames with various percentage of real-time frames

The rate of real-time frames(%) / The number of experiments	0%	10%	20%	30%	40%	50%	60%	70%	80%	90%	100%
1	47	44	41	39	37	37	37	37	37	37	37
2	49	45	42	39	37	37	37	37	37	37	37
3	47	44	41	38	37	37	37	37	37	37	37
4	48	45	41	39	37	37	37	37	37	37	37
5	46	43	40	38	37	37	37	37	37	37	37
6	47	44	41	39	37	37	37	37	37	37	37
7	47	44	41	39	37	37	37	37	37	37	37
8	47	45	42	38	37	37	37	37	37	37	37
9	46	43	40	38	37	37	37	37	37	37	37
10	47	44	41	38	37	37	37	37	37	37	37
average	47.1	44.1	41	38.5	37	37	37	37	37	37	37

To remove the effect of transmission delay in measuring the performance of our real-time scheme, in the second experiment we removed it. Instead we increased the number of frames from 1000 to 10000 with increment of 1000 while varying the percentage of real-time frames from 0% to 100% with 10% increment as before. This time we measured the percentage of packets successfully processed. Since we are sending a large number of packets without any transmission delay, many of them will be dropped at the receiver side due to the limit in the packet processing capacity in given time. Our expectation is that as the percentage of real-time packets increases, the rate of successful processing should improve. The result confirms our expectation as shown in Table 2. With no real-time frames, the rate of success is as low as 3.1% with 10000 packets. Even with 1000 packets, it is only 32.1%. Our technique greatly improves this. For 1000 packets, the processing success rate already reaches 100% with 70% real-time frames. The success rate goes down as the packet number increases. However, even with 10000 packets, the success rate reaches around 90% when real-time frames comprise over 90% while the success rate was only 3.1% when there was no real-time frame.

Table 2. The percentage of successfully processed frames for various combinations of the number of transmitted frames and the percentage of real-time frames among them

The number of transmission frames / The rate of real-time frames	1000	2000	3000	4000	5000	7000	10000
0%	32.1%	15.6%	10.4%	7.8%	6.2%	4.4%	3.1%
10%	42.9%	26.5%	25.5%	18.2%	16.9%	14.9%	13.6%
20%	53.2%	37.0%	31.4%	28.8%	27.7%	25.5%	23.9%
30%	63.9%	46.8%	41.0%	38.3%	36.8%	34.7%	32.5%
40%	72.8%	56.7%	50.9%	48.0%	46.2%	44.2%	43.0%
50%	82.2%	66.1%	62.8%	58.4%	56.9%	54.7%	52.2%
60%	91.0%	75.6%	71.7%	69.2%	66.4%	64.3%	64.3%
70%	100%	87.0%	81.3%	78.1%	76.7%	74.7%	73.8%
80%	100%	100%	92.9%	89.7%	87.9%	85.5%	83.9%
90%	100%	100%	100%	100%	99.0%	96.3%	94.7%
100%	88.0%	88.9%	88.8%	91.0%	87.7%	87.9%	87.9%

One peculiar thing is that the performance with 100% real-time frames is not as good as the one with 90% real-time frames. What happens is with real-time frame we actually spend more time in Top Half where the interrupt is disabled. For non-real-time frame, we put off major job until the Bottom Half and quickly leaves the Top Half resulting shorter period of disabled interrupt. With 90% real-time frames, the 10% non-real-time frames are not instantly handled and pushed over to the Bottom Half, but at least these frames do not block more important real-time frames of entering the system because they have a shorter interrupt-disable period. With 100% real-time frames, all frames spend some time in Top Half once they got into the system, and during this they block other frames entering the system via interrupt disabling.

6 Conclusion

Linux is not well suited for real-time environment. Redesigning it for real-time systems, however, is a very complex and challenging task. In this paper, we suggest an approach to convert a large system like Linux into a real-time system with minimal changes. We observe that most of real-time systems demand real-time performance only for a couple of devices they are targeting for. Our approach focuses on this target device and modifies the original system only where this device is involved. This approach is more practical in that it does not unnecessarily change the whole system and in that it still satisfies the demands of most real-time systems. We picked network device as an example. We assumed the device sometimes got a real-time packet which should be processed immediately. We proposed a technique to ensure this real-time response with a small change in the kernel. The technique is implemented and experimented. The result shows that with 10000 packets poured in, our technique could process 90% of the packets successfully while without real-time handling capacity the inundated system would process successfully only 3.1% of them.

References

1. I. Chlamtac, W. R. Franta, and K. D. Levin: "BRAM: The Broadcasting Recognizing Access Method", IEEE Transactions on Communication vol.27, pp.1183-1189, 1979.
2. R. P. Signorile: "MBRAM – A priority protocol for PC based local area networks", IEEE network vol.2, pp.55-59, 1988.
3. C. W. Group: "Experimental internet stream protocol, version 2 (ST-II)", RFC1190, 1990.
4. R. Braden, Ed., L. Zhang, S. Berson, S. Herzog, and S. Jamin: "Resource reservation protocol(RSVP)", RFC2205, 1997.
5. A.V.T.W. Group: "RTP: A transport protocol for real-time applications", RFC1889, 1996.
6. Victor Yodaiken: "New frontiers for embedded computing", 17th International Conference on VLSI Design, Jan. 5th, 2004, India.
7. http://www.linuxdevices.com/links/LK8662675028.html.
8. J. Postel: "A Standard for the Transmission of IP Datagrams over IEEE 802 Networks", RFC 1042, 1988.
9. W. Richard Stevens: "TCP/IP Illustrated, Volume1 The Protocols", Addison-Wesley, pp.21-37, 1994.

A Parallel Implementation of the Finite Volume Method for the Simulation of the Natural Convection in a Closed Cavity

Elton F.D. Nogueira[1], Luiz J.C. Rocha[2], Alexei Machado[3], Carlos A. Pietrobon[4], Carlos A.P.S. Martins[5], Rose M.S. Batalha[6], and Petr Y. Ekel[7]

Pontifical Catholic University of Minas Gerais (Brazil)
Av. Dom José Gaspar, 500 – CEP 30535610 - BH– MG – BR
DECAT – School of Mines - Federal University of Ouro Preto[2]
Campus Universitário – Morro do Cruzeiro, s/n – CEP 35400000 – OP – MG - BR
`elton@pucminas.br`[1], `ljoaquim@em.ufop.br`[2], `alexei@pucminas.br`[3],
`capietro@pucminas.br`[4], `capsm@puminas.br`[5], `batalha@pucminas.br`[6],
`ekel@pucminas.br`[7]

Abstract. In this work, we present a parallel implementation of an algorithm that simulates the natural convection of fluids in a closed cavity. The method is based on the Boussinesq approximation; and it is numerically solved using the finite volume method, based on the Power-Law interpolating scheme. The pressure-velocity coupling is solved using SIMPLEC algorithm. The software was implemented in Fortran with message passing on a Pentium III processors Linux cluster. The solution is validated upon comparison with experimental results available in the literature. It is shown that the use of parallelism provides a significant speedup and efficiency, without degradation of the quality of the results.

1 Introduction

The study of the natural convection in closed cavities is due in part to the recognition of the importance of this process in some industrial engineering applications, such as collecting solar plates, design of nuclear plants, purification of metals, crystal growth, metal solidification and fusing, among others. Extensive reviews on natural convection in enclosures are available in the literature [1], as well as experiments using liquid metals [2-4] and other numerical results [5]. Many published works deal with natural convection in closed cavities, however the majority of them present relatively coarse computational meshes.

The refinement of those meshes requires the use of high performance computing in order to avoid increased response time. In that sense, there are three basic types of high performance computer architectures that can be applied [6]: vector architecture computers, symmetrical parallel processing computers, and multicomputers.

In view of the growing need for high performance computing, the clusters, a class of multicomputers, constitute a low cost and high performance alternative to solve complex computational problems. There are many different ways to create parallel

G. Min et al. (Eds.): ISPA 2006 Ws, LNCS 4331, pp. 748–757, 2006.

programs, starting from sequential ones, for instance parallel compilers, parallel languages, etc. However, one of the most used programming models is message passing. This model is usually implemented in libraries developed for standard languages, like C, Java and Fortran, each of them widely known. In addition, some of the libraries were created specifically for the development of parallel programs, like Message Passing Interface (MPI) [7], and Parallel Virtual Machine PVM [8].

The main goal of this work is to develop a parallel implementation of the finite volume method using PVM to improve response time. The developed application is used to solve natural convection problems in a square closed cavity.

2 Mathematical Model

The flow of a Newtonian fluid in a closed two-dimensional cavity under the effect of the natural convection is considered. The flow is steady state and laminar. The vertical walls of the cavity are kept under uniform and constant temperatures, but each one with different magnitude. The horizontal walls are perfectly insulated. The cavity model is represented in figure 1.

The physical properties are considered constant with the exception of the specific mass. According to the Boussinesq approximation the specific mass is constant, except in the body force term where it is defined as a linear function of the temperature, as shown in (1), where ρ is the specific mass, β is the coefficient of volumetric expansion and T is the temperature. The subscript C refers to the temperature of the cold wall, T_{cold}.

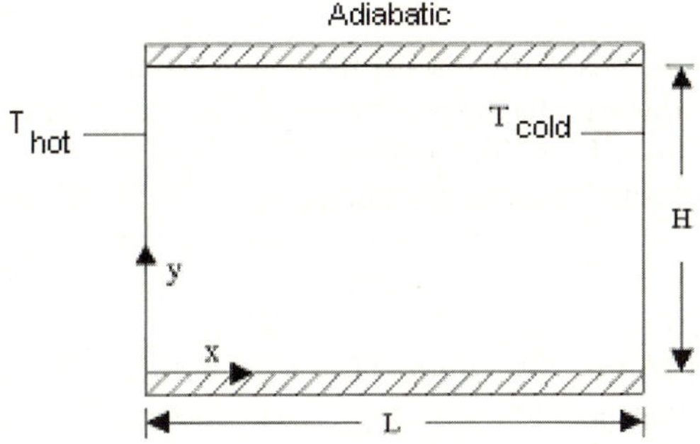

Fig. 1. Cavity model, with geometry and boundary conditions

$$\rho(T) = \rho_c[1 - \beta(T - T_c)] \tag{1}$$

The velocity and temperature fields are governed by (2) to (5), subject to the boundary conditions presented in (6) to (9). The set of equations (2) to (5) need to be solved simultaneously, and they represent the mass conservation, the linear momentum in x direction, the linear momentum in y direction, and the energy conservation, respectively.

$$\frac{\partial u}{\partial x} + \frac{\partial v}{\partial y} = 0 \tag{2}$$

$$\frac{\partial(\rho u u)}{\partial x} + \frac{\partial(\rho v u)}{\partial y} = -\frac{\partial p}{\partial x} + \frac{\partial}{\partial x}\left(\mu \frac{\partial u}{\partial x}\right) + \frac{\partial}{\partial y}\left(\mu \frac{\partial u}{\partial y}\right) \tag{3}$$

$$\frac{\partial(\rho u v)}{\partial x} + \frac{\partial(\rho v v)}{\partial y} = -\frac{\partial p}{\partial y} + \frac{\partial}{\partial x}\left(\mu \frac{\partial v}{\partial x}\right) + \frac{\partial}{\partial y}\left(\mu \frac{\partial v}{\partial y}\right) + \rho_c\, g[1 - \beta(T - T_c)] \tag{4}$$

$$\frac{\partial(\rho u T)}{\partial x} + \frac{\partial(\rho v T)}{\partial y} = \frac{\partial}{\partial x}\left(\frac{k}{c_p}\frac{\partial T}{\partial x}\right) + \frac{\partial}{\partial y}\left(\frac{k}{c_p}\frac{\partial T}{\partial y}\right) \tag{5}$$

$$u = v = 0; \quad T = T_H; \qquad x = 0; \qquad 0 \leq y \leq H \tag{6}$$

$$u = v = 0; \quad T = T_C; \qquad x = L; \qquad 0 \leq y \leq H \tag{7}$$

$$u = v = 0; \quad \partial T/\partial y = 0; \quad y = 0; \qquad 0 \leq x \leq L \tag{8}$$

$$u = v = 0; \quad \partial T/\partial y = 0; \quad y = H; \qquad 0 \leq x \leq L \tag{9}$$

There are also some dimensionless parameters appearing in the problem, they are the aspect ratio, $(AR = H/L)$, the Rayleigh number $(Ra = g\beta\Delta T H^3/\alpha v)$, and the Prandtl number $(Pr = v/\alpha)$.

3 Numerical Method and Sequential Implementation

The numerical method chosen for solving the conservation equations is the method of finite differences with formularization for volumes of control [9], the interpolation method used is the Power-Law [9], and the mesh is uniform.

The coupling pressure-velocity is solved by SIMPLEC algorithm [10]. The dependent variable in the momentum equation is the contra-variant velocity component [11], which is stored staggered of the others variables to prevent the solution from oscillating.

The Tri-Diagonal Matrix Algorithm (TDMA) is used to solve the resultant system of equations. All conservation equations are considered converged when the normalized residue is lesser or equal to 1×10^{-6}.

Following is a FORTRAN 77 fragment code showing the phases of the sequential implementation.

```
 5  CALL INPUT              CALL COEFIC
    CALL GRID               CALL NEWTON-RAPHSON
    CALL GEOMETRY           CALL RESIDUO
    CALL START              IF (REST < delta) GOTO 20
10  CONTINUE                GOTO 10
    CALL BOUND              CONTINUE
    CALL DENSE        20
```

The computation starts with the data input at the INPUT procedure, identified by label 5. The GRID and GEOMETRY procedures compute the mesh and the geometric parameters, respectively. The START procedure starts the computation.

The procedures BOUND, DENSE and COEFIC updates the contour conditions, the density and the coefficients of the equations. TDMA algorithm solves the equation. The residual value is calculated and compared with 10^{-6}. The computation stops or continues depending on the value obtained.

4   Parallel Implementation

The parallel implementation is based on the distribution of the discretized mesh among the processors of the parallel computer. The complete mesh is divided by the number of available processors. The Master process execute this task.

In figure 2-A, we can find a generic mesh distributed among N processors and the communication process among them.

After the data has been distributed for each processor, the computation continues following the same steps of the sequential implementation mentioned above. However, there are some differences due to the fact that the data are distributed among N processors of the parallel computer.

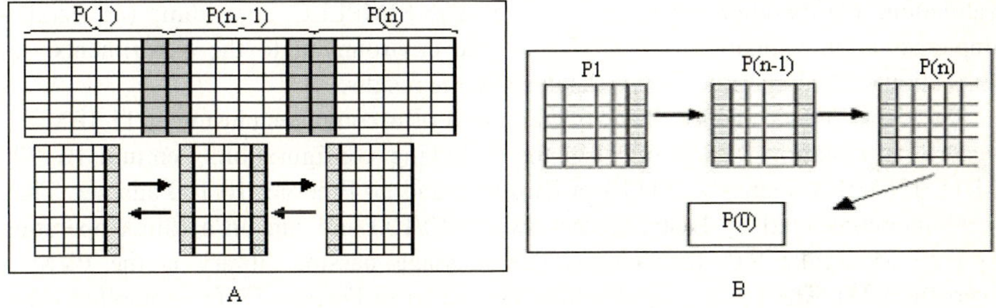

Fig. 2. Discretized Mesh – interprocess communications (A); parallel residue calculation (B)

There are two fundamental differences related to the sequential version:

1) In the parallel implementation, the values are propagated through the computational mesh. Therefore, in the parallel version, communications among the processes are necessary to allow for updating the mesh in each processor.

2) Figure 2-B shows how the residue is computed. The residue is calculated in each processor and the resultant value of each processor must be integrated to get a unique global value. This global value is used to decide whether to stop or not the computation process. The computation of the global residue is executed in the local processor and the resultant parcel is used as an input for the next processor. When the last processor finishes its activities the value of the residue is complete and then it is sent back to the Master process.

This method was adopted to optimize the bandwidth use in the communication channel. If each processor would send the residue directly to the Master process, it could occur a simultaneous transmission of partial residues from several processors, at the same time. Due to the use of our sequential solution, the communication was optimized. We don't overload the communication channel and avoid that the Master process treats a great volume of messages coming from the several processors.

When the application finishes, the outcomes will be distributed among the processors that compose the parallel computer. The results can be reached by Shell Script tools. Another way to collect the data is to insert in the slave code instructions to send outcomes back to the Master Process. The first option described above has the advantage to decrease the size of the Master program. The time spent to collect the outcomes from each processor is insignificant compared with the response time. In this work we use the Shell Script Unix to collect the outcomes from each node.

5   Results

Our experimental method was divided into seven phases: (1) Sequential implementation of the SIMPLEC algorithm; (2) Sequential implementation validation; (3) Parallel implementation of the SIMPLEC algorithm; (4) Parallel implementation validation; (5) Choice of the environment to the experiments; (6) Execution of the experiments; (7) Analysis of the results.

The experimental environment is composed of a computer cluster of 11 IBM-PC generic workstations. Each one has the following configuration: Pentium III 900 MHz, 128MB of memory, 20 GB of hard disk and an Ethernet 10/100 adapter. They were interconnected by Fast Ethernet switch 10/100 and run on a Linux operating system, Mandrake 9.0 distribution. The message passing library is the PVM 3 (version 3.43). The parallel application was coded in Fortran 77 and compiled using GNU Fortran77 (0.5.2.6).

Cluster management uses RSH (Remote Shell) and Shell Script tools. These operating system tools are used to initialize the cluster and to catch the data when the operation ends. A new tool were designed and implemented specially to measure the response time of the sequential and parallel implementations. It made automatic the execution and the computation of the mean time and standard deviation of the response time. After that has been calculated, these values are recorded in a text file.

The tests were designed to show the behavior and performance of the application with different sizes of meshes and nodes. All tests were executed 5 times to avoid external interferences. These interferences can be originated from operating system internal calls and network delays, for example. The final value is the geometric mean of those five values.

The results are organized in two parts: the validation of the parallel implementation and the performance results.

5.1 Validation of the Parallel Implementation

The validation of the parallel implementation is achieved by comparing the results obtained by using the parallel implementation with the results of another simulation program, and also by comparing the simulation results with the data obtained experimentally. Both comparisons are detailed along this section. In order to validate the parallel algorithm, the problem is solved and a test of meshes is initially performed. Figure 3 shows a plot of the variation of the global Nusselt number, defined based on (10), as a function of the mesh size.

$$\overline{Nu} = \int_0^1 -\frac{\partial \theta}{\partial X}\bigg|_{X=0} dY \tag{10}$$

The results show that the solution to the problem stays basically unaltered for meshes of 82x81 or more nodal points, with a maximum deviation of 0.6 % in the global Nusselt number.

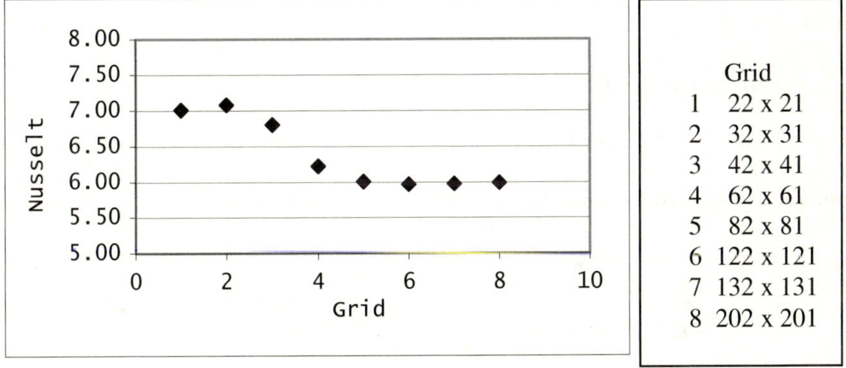

Fig. 3. Nusselt number x Mesh size

The solution is compared to the numerical results of [12] based on the global Nusselt number. In this comparison, the current work uses an uniform mesh with 42x41 nodal points, with a global Nusselt number equals to $\overline{Nu} = 6,804$. Viskanta [12] uses a mesh with 41x41 nodal points, with the global Nusselt number equals to $\overline{Nu} = 6,701$. The results present a deviation of 1.54 %.

The numerical results were additionally compared to the experimental data of [4]. Figure 4 shows the temperature distribution along the horizontal axis in three different positions. It can be seen that the results are consistent and the largest deviations occur in the center and near the superior wall. Notwithstanding, in these regions, the numerical results are qualitatively sound.

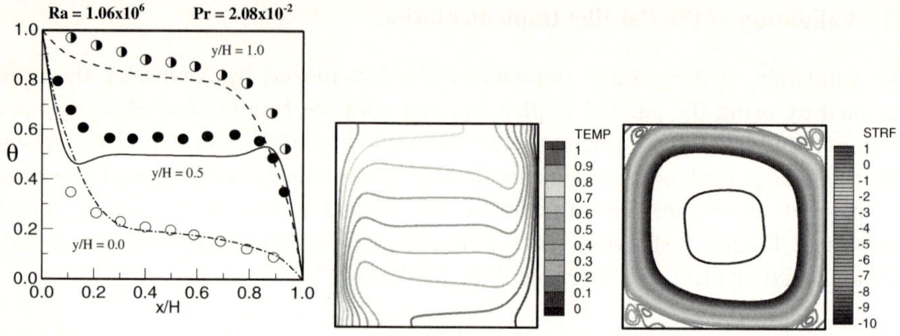

Fig. 4. a- Comparison between the numerical results of the current study and the experimental data obtained by [4]; **b** - Isotherms and current lines

Figure 4.b shows the distribution of isotherms and current lines. These isotherms show places in the cavity with same temperatures. It can be seen that both the increase of temperature at the inferior left corner of the cavity and the decrease of temperature at the superior right corner are caused by subtle re-circulations at those regions. This plot is important since it allows the comparison of visual results with physical photographs of the experiments.

5.2 Performance Results

Figure 5 shows the performance results of this problem. In this plot, the sequential implementation was applied to meshes of different sizes. The mesh sizes are numbered. The response time for each mesh is plotted as a point.

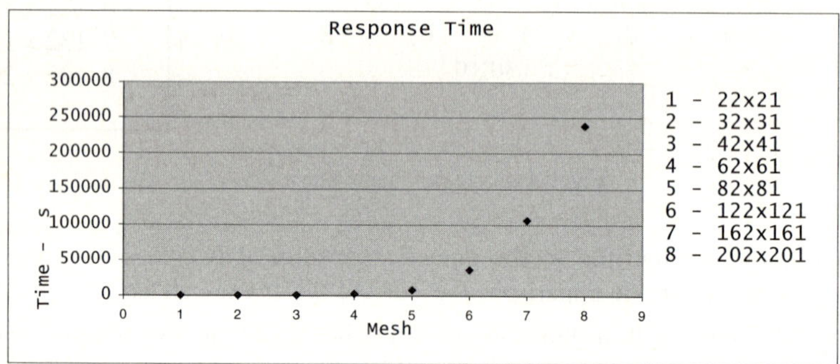

Fig. 5. Response time of the sequential implementation as a function of mesh size

The response time grows with the mesh refining. The plot in Figure 5 also shows that using meshes of size 122x121 or more yields response time in the order of 10 hours or more. This high response time justifies the use of parallel solutions for this problem.

Table 1. Response time in seconds

Mesh/Proc.	1	2	4	5	8	10
22x21	123	263	400	418		
32x31	340	470		642		
42x41	681	760	883	918		
62x61	2396	2052	1925	1887		1910
82x81	7837	4753	3732	3568	3408	3414
122x121	36040	22235	12823	11619	9646	9446
162x161	106124	64949	40039	34210	26451	24389
202x201	238523	141697	90439	79836	61323	55198

Table 1 shows the response time of each configuration of parallel computer and mesh sizes. The bold cells are the number of processors and mesh size, respectively. Empty cell means that tests were not executed. The contents of the table are expressed in seconds.

The speedup of the first three meshes is smaller than one. In this situation the small mesh size causes overhead influenced by operational system, as well as network communication system. The speedup is greater than one for the others mesh sizes. The speedup grows with the mesh size applied. These results are presented in Figure 6. The speedup is plotted for different sizes of the computational meshes.

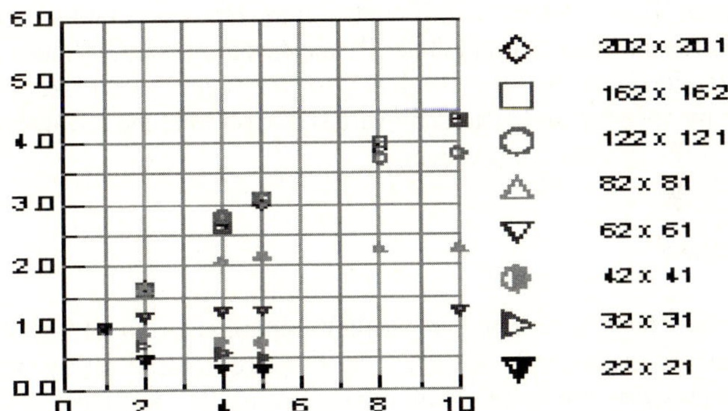

Fig. 6. Speedup x Mesh size

For the 62x61 mesh, the speedup was greater than 1, but still smaller than 1.5. The 82x81 mesh presented a speedup around 2.2. Larger mesh sizes, e.g. 122x121, 162x161 and 202x201 presented more significant speedup.

The best speedup is obtained when the mesh size is 202x201. At this mesh size the response time is 55,198s in parallel implementation and 238,523s for serial implementation. The speedup obtained is 4.32.

The efficiency is calculated and presented in table 2. The first line is the node number in the parallel computer. The first column shows the mesh size applied in the execution test. The value in each cell is the efficiency of parallel computer running with n processor at 'YxZ' mesh size.

Table 2. Efficiency

Mesh/CPUs	1	2	4	5	8	10
22x21	100%	24%	8%	6%		
32x31	100%	36%		11%		
42x41	100%	45%	19%	15%		
62x61	100%	59%	31%	25%		13%
82x81	100%	83%	53%	44%	29%	23%
122x121	100%	81%	70%	62%	47%	38%
162x161	100%	82%	66%	62%	50%	44%
202x201	100%	84%	66%	60%	49%	43%

The efficiency in the small meshes is poor due to the speedup smaller than one. Intermediate mesh values 62x61 and 82x81 present small speedup. The best results are confirmed for bigger mesh sizes. In these tests the processing is enough to overcome operating system and network overhead. Better results of efficiency occur when speedup grows. From the results shown in Figure 6, it can be seen that the speedup between 4 and 5 is not significantly high. However, table 1 shows that the response times for the 162x161 and 202x201 meshes are about 30 hours and 67 hours, respectively. Besides this fact, the efficiency for the bigger mesh size is around 43%. These significant speedup and efficiency values corroborate the advantages of parallel implementation for this kind of problem.

6 Conclusions

In this work, we have developed a parallel implementation of the finite volume method to simulate the natural convection in a squared closed cavity. Validation was achieved by comparing the results with experimental data available in the literature. The parallel implementation performance was verified based on speedup and efficiency analysis.

We show that the use of parallelism reduces significantly the response time without degradation in the results precision, when applied in a classical transport phenomena problem.

The results show that using a cluster and a programming model of message passing successfully solves the problem of the closed cavity. The numerical results were consistent with the ones obtained from a real experiment. The difference between both methods was estimated in 3%. This error can be considered sufficiently small to justify the application of the computational method in real problems of engineering.

The results showed that the use of parallelism did not degrade the precision of the solution and additionally reduced the response time.

The parallel implementation enabled a computational solution to the problem since the time required to achieve a solution without parallelism was 67 hours. The use of parallelism reduced the response time to 13 hours. The speedup of 4.32 is significant in this case, as it represents a time reduction of approximately 55 hours. The performance results with parallelism were not linear; in some cases, using twice as many processors resulted in a small speedup. Thus, it was necessary to make an initial evaluation in order to determine the best configuration for the parallel computer and the size of the problem (size of the simulated mesh).

The solutions obtained with parallel processing were validated and proved to be robust. In all cases of meshes, no significant deviations could be observed. This was evaluated by computing the Nusselt number and the results proved to be trustworthy. All the computational tools used in this work are freely available and can be downloaded from Internet.

Among future works we can highlight: coding the parallel implementation using instruction level parallelism, as MMX, SSE, 3Dnow, for example. These instructions set are available in many modern processors; The Master – Slave model is used in this work. Other kind of parallel model can be experimented.

References

1. S. Ostrach, "Natural Convection in Enclosures", Adv. Heat Transfer, vol. 8, 1972, pp. 161-227.
2. R. Viskanta. A.A. Mohammad, "Transient Natural Convection of Low-Prandtl-Number Fluids in a Differentially Heated Cavity", Int. J. Numerical Methods in Fluids, vol. 13, 1991, pp. 61-81.
3. Y. Wang, K. Amiri, K. Vafai, "An Experimental Investigation of the Melting Process in a Rectangular Enclosure", Int. J. Heat Mass Transfer, Vol. 42, 1999, pp. 3659-3672.
4. F. Wolff, C. Beckermann, R. Viskanta, "Natural Convection of liquid metals in vertical cavities", Exp Thermal Fluid Sci, Vol.1, 1988, pp.83-91.
5. S. Arcidiacono, I. Di Piazza, M. Ciofalo, "Low- Prandtl Number Natural Convection in Volumetrically heated Rectangular Enclosures II. Square Cavity, AR=1", Int. J. Heat Mass Transfer, vol. 44, 2001, pp. 537-550.
6. Hwang, K., Xu, Z., Scalable Parallel Computing: Technology, Architecture, Programming, McGraw-Hill, 1998.
7. MPI Forum, "The MPI message passing interface standard", Technical report, University of Tennessee, Knoxville, 1994.
8. A. Geist et al., "PVM: Parallel Virtual Machine". MIT Press, Cambridge, 1994.
9. S.V. Patankar, "Numerical Heat Transfer and Fluid Flow", Hemisphere, New York, 1980.
10. J.P van Doormaan, G.D. Raithby, "Enhancements of the Simple Method for Predicting Incompressible Fluid Flow", Numerical Heat Transfer, vol.7, 1984, pp.147-163.
11. L. F. G. Pires, A.O. Nieckele, "Numerical Method For The Solution Of Flows Using Contravariant Components In Non-Orthogonal Coordinates", Proc. V Brazilian Meeting on Thermal Sciences, Sao Paulo, 1994, pp. 343-346.
12. R. Viskanta, D.M. Kim, C. Gau, "Three-Dimensional Natural Convection Heat Transfer of a Liquid metal in a Cavity", Int. J. Heat Mass Transfer, vol. 29(3), 1986, pp. 475-485.

A Real-Time and Parametric Parallel Video Compression Architecture Using FPGA

Cássio A. Carneiro[1], Francisco M.P. Garcia[1], Flávia M. Freitas[1],
Zélia M.A. Peixoto[1], Amanda R.M. Diniz[1], and Abraham Alcaim[2]

[1] Pontifical Catholic University of Minas Gerais, Av. Dom José Gaspar 500,
30535-610, Belo Horizonte, MG, Brazil
`cassiomolina@yahoo.com.br`, {`fgarcia, flaviamagfreitas,
assiszmp`}`@pucminas.br`, `dinizamanda@gmail.com`
[2] Pontifical Catholic University of Rio de Janeiro, Rua Marquês de São Vicente 225,
22453-900, Rio de Janeiro, RJ, Brazil
`alcaim@cetuc.puc-rio.br`

Abstract. This paper presents a novel parallel architecture which performs a streamed-based processing of the two-dimensional Discrete Cosine Transform (2D-DCT) for real time video compression applications. This proposal consists in using a programmable device, such as FPGA, to implement kernels of one-dimensional DCT (1D-DCT), referred to as DCT-kernels, which can be instantiated, so many as necessary, to attend the required pixel rate for a specific purpose. The implementation of the architecture proposed for the DCT-kernel also presents some interesting features that represent an advantage over the classical architectures for 1D-DCT available in the literature, mainly when a parallel architecture is supposed to use some of them. Two different applications, standard definition television (SDTV) and high definition television (HDTV), have employed the proposed parallel architecture using different number of DCT-kernels in order to show the potential of its use and real possibilities of enlarging the set of candidate applications.

1   Introduction

Image and video compression has been an area of fast scientific and technological development because of its large employment in many fields of Engineering. Compression techniques offer the possibility to store or to transmit the vast amount of data necessary to represent still image and video in an efficient and robust way. Some of the most important applications are Standard Television (SDTV) [1,2], High Definition Television (HDTV) [3], Interactive Television and 3D-TV [4] and High Definition Digital Video Disc (HD-DVD), among others.

Unfortunately, encoding algorithms with higher performance have come at the price of extraordinarily huge computational complexity and memory access requirement. This makes it difficult to design hardwired encoders for real-time applications. In some cases, the amount of data to be processed may also be too high and so, the bandwidth requirement increases. A typical example is the highly interactive and recreation multimedia (HDTV and HD-DVD), which

G. Min et al. (Eds.): ISPA 2006 Ws, LNCS 4331, pp. 758–768, 2006.

demands much higher compression ratio and quality for video content. In order to achieve the necessary throughput, pipelining and parallel processing techniques have then been employed whenever the required processing is neither sequential nor data-dependent [3,6].

One of the basic strategies for coding still images and video is the Transform Domain Coding, which has become a very popular method for lossy still image and video coding [7]. It consists in quantizing and encoding decorrelated transform coefficients rather than the original pixels of the images. The most popular and well-established transform technique is the Discrete Cosine Transform (DCT) used in the lossy JPEG, MPEG family and H.264 coder standards [8]. The DCT is applied strictly as a block-based approach on blocks of size $N \times N$ pixels (usually, $N = 8$) and it is employed to reduce spatial redundancy at either intraframe or interframe encoding [7]. In this latter case, it is accomplished by motion estimation and compensation techniques to reduce temporal redundancy [7]. Recently, hardwired solutions to implement the DCT have been the focus of research effort. Several evolutions of the original algorithm [8] and implementations have been developed for real-time applications, aiming at reducing costs, improving performance and increasing the throughput [3].

The main motivation of this paper is to present a parametric parallel architecture to compute a block-based DCT scheme for real-time applications. The proposed architecture uses a kernel cell to process the 1D-DCT over a vector of N components. Depending on the application, the required throughput may vary and a different number of these kernel structures may be used (the number of kernels to be used is a parameter of the proposed architecture). The reduction of the hardware resources needed to implement this kernel cell, if compared to recently published works [9,10,6], enables lower circuit area. It is important to note that in block-based DCT scheme there are no data dependencies between neighboring blocks, pointing to the possibility of using parallel processing.

2   The Discrete Cosine Transform

For the block-based DCT approach, the input image are split into disjoint blocks U of $N \times N$ pixels. In general, a linear, separable and unitary 2D-transform can be represented as a matricial operation on each block U in the form $C = AUA^T$, in which C is the $N \times N$ transformed coefficients block, A is a $N \times N$ transform matrix and A^T denotes the transpose of A.

A unitary transform is reversible, since the original block U can be reconstructed using a linear and separable inverse transform, doing $U = A^T C A$. However, in a practical coding scheme, the coefficients will be quantized and the original image block will be only approximated, resulting a lossy compression.

Today, block-based DCT schemes are widely used in most image and video coding due to their high decorrelation performance [7] and the availability of fast DCT algorithms suitable for hardware implementations in real-time applications. These algorithms use the separability property of the 2D-transform that allows its implementation by two 1D-transform operations. This reduces the computational effort and the necessary area for the hardware implementation. In this sense, the block of coefficients may be computed doing:

$$C^T = A(AU)^T = AU^T A^T = (AU^T)A^T = GA^T = (AG^T)^T \qquad (1)$$

That is, first the rows of U are processed to produce the 1D-transformed matrix $G = AU^T$. In the following, the rows of the matrix G are processed to obtain the 2D-transformed matrix $C^T = (AG^T)^T$. Finally, C^T must be transposed in order to produce the final transformed image block C.

Using the separability principle described by Equation 1 in the computation of the 2D-DCT, the 1D-DCT processing over the xth row of $U(U_x), x = [0, \cdots, N-1]$ will produce the xth transformed row of $G(G_x)$, whose components are given by [7],

$$G_{xy} = k_y \sum_{j=0}^{N-1} U_{xj} \cos \frac{(2j+1)y\pi}{2N}, y = [0, \cdots, N-1] \qquad (2)$$

with $k_y = \frac{1}{2\sqrt{2}}$ if $y = 0$ and $k_y = \frac{1}{2}$ if $y \neq 0$. The expression given by Equation 2 is the basis of the fast algorithms proposed in the recent literature to implement the 1D-DCT.

3 Related Works Concerning the 1D-DCT

Several fast algorithms concerning the implementation of the 1D-DCT have been proposed in the literature [11,12,2,6]. The work presented by [5] compares the required number of additions and multiplications in a few of them. In order to reduce the number of multiplications, which is the most expensive operation, all of them use the separability property, while some of them also apply the scaling principle. It consists in excluding the multiplications by constant factors from the DCT algorithm and embedding them in the quantization step.

Table 1 compares the number of multiplications and additions used by some fast 1D-DCT algorithms. It can be observed that the use of the principles of separability and scaling enables the reduction of the required multiplications and, in this sense, the one introduced in [2] was the most efficient.

The algorithm proposed by [2] has been later improved by [9], which reduced from 16 to 12 the number of required two's complement operations, while keeping

Table 1. Fast 1D-DCT algorithms and the required number of operations [5]

Algorithm	Multiplication	Addition
Chen [11] *	16	26
Lee [12] *	12	29
Lee [12] **	11	28
Chen [11] **	8	26
Arai [2] **	5	29

* use separability
** use separability and scaling

the same number of additions and multiplications. The algorithm proposed in [9] has six completely independent stages, which enables the use of parallelism. However, preliminary simulations of the algorithm [9], performed by [10], have pointed to a sintax error in one of the variables. The algorithm introduced in [10] corrected this initial problem and has also proposed simple modifications in the previous architecture, in order to have its latency reduced. The final six stages are showed in the following and the diagram of the proposed architecture [10] is presented in Fig. 1.

Stage A	Stage B	Stage C	Stage D	Stage E	Stage F
$b0 = a0 + a7$	$c0 = b0 + b5$	$d0 = c0 + c3$	$e0 = d0$	$f0 = e0$	$S0 = f0$
$b1 = a1 + a6$	$c1 = b1 - b4$	$d1 = c0 - c3$	$e1 = d1$	$f1 = e1$	$S1 = f4 + f7$
$b2 = a3 - a4$	$c2 = b2 + b6$	$d2 = c2$	$e2 = m3 * d2$	$f2 = e5 + e6$	$S2 = f2$
$b3 = a1 - a6$	$c3 = b1 + b4$	$d3 = c1 + c4$	$e3 = m1 * d7$	$f3 = e5 - e6$	$S3 = f5 - f6$
$b4 = a2 + a5$	$c4 = b0 - b5$	$d4 = c2 - c5$	$e4 = m4 * d6$	$f4 = e3 + e8$	$S4 = f1$
$b5 = a3 + a4$	$c5 = b3 + b7$	$d5 = c4$	$e5 = d5$	$f5 = e8 - e3$	$S5 = f5 + f6$
$b6 = a2 - a5$	$c6 = b3 + b6$	$d6 = c5$	$e6 = m1 * d3$	$f6 = e2 + e7$	$S6 = f3$
$b7 = a0 - a7$	$c7 = b7$	$d7 = c6$	$e7 = m2 * d4$	$f7 = e4 + e7$	$S7 = f4 - f7$
		$d8 = c7$	$e8 = d8$		

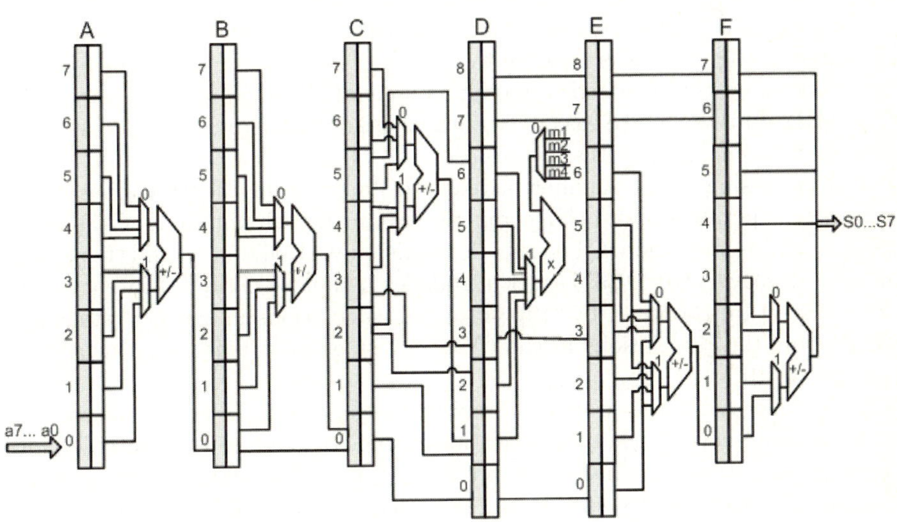

Fig. 1. Diagram of the architecture proposed in [10]

The proposed architecture [10] is basically composed of ping pong buffers and arithmetic operators. The ping pong buffer holds the data so that the operations can be performed. It has two columns of registers: the first one accepts serial data input (ping) and the second one provides parallel data output (pong). In this way, a new pixel is filled in the first buffer (ping) in each clock cycle. After a set of eight pixels has been stored, this set is transferred to the second buffer (pong). In the stages "C" and "D", nine positions are necessary in the respective buffers. Additions and subtractions as previously described for each stage are simultaneously performed in one clock cycle. The five multiplications required to calculate the 1D-DCT over a segment of N elements are computed during six clock cycles.

The algorithm proposed by [10] has been chosen as the basis for the implementation of the 1D-DCT in this paper. It will be modified in order to design a kernel structure for the parametric parallel architecture to be proposed. This modified 1D-DCT kernel structure is going to be introduced in the next section and it will be referred to as DCT-kernel.

4   The DCT-Kernel Architecture

The proposed DCT-kernel aims at using a lower number of flip-flops if compared to [10]. To achieve this, the ping-pong buffers are replaced by simple ping buffers. Due to the elimination of the pong buffers, the data in each stage are not placed in a fixed position, but they move dynamically while the ping buffer is being filled in. To perform the arithmetic operations, it is necessary to properly modify the addresses of the multiplexes. Some stages also had the number of buffers reduced due to the elimination of the unnecessary data storage (i.e. $d0 = e0 = f0$).

The proposed DCT-kernel also offers a speedup in relation to the architecture presented in [10]. This was possible by including a pipelining stage in the arithmetic operators that enabled a maximum simulated operation frequency equal to 80 MHz. This will make easier the parallel use of this kernel structure at video compression schemes for HDTV purposes.

The increasing of the number of required flip-flops for the pipelining in the arithmetic operators has been compensated by the elimination of the pong buffers. In this way, the DCT-kernel demands only 41.66% of the flip-flops used in [10]. Moreover, the DCT-kernel introduces a shorter period of latency than the architecture proposed by [10], since the calculations in the Nth stage can start before the calculations in the $(N-1)^{th}$ stage have finished (which is not possible in [10]).

Figure 2 presents the proposed architecture for the DCT-kernel, where it is possible to observe the reduction of the number of buffers. For example, considering pixels represented with 8 bits, stage "D" in the implementation of [10] requires 198 flip-flops (18 buffers of 11 bits) and, in the DCT-kernel, only 26 flip-flops are necessary (1 buffer of 12 bits plus 14 bits of adder-subtracter pipelining).

Table 2 compares the quantities of flip-flops used by the architecture proposed in [10] and by the DCT-kernel, in which the reduction of 41.66% can be observed. The DCT-kernel has also reduced a single multiplex circuit in stage "E", as showed by Table 3.

The proposed DCT-kernel consists in a state machine composed of sixteen different sub-states. In each of them, some shift registers are enabled and the related operations of the algorithm are performed. It uses a clock with twice the frequency of the input data in order to multiplex the required addition and subtraction operations (each of them occurs during one clock cycle).

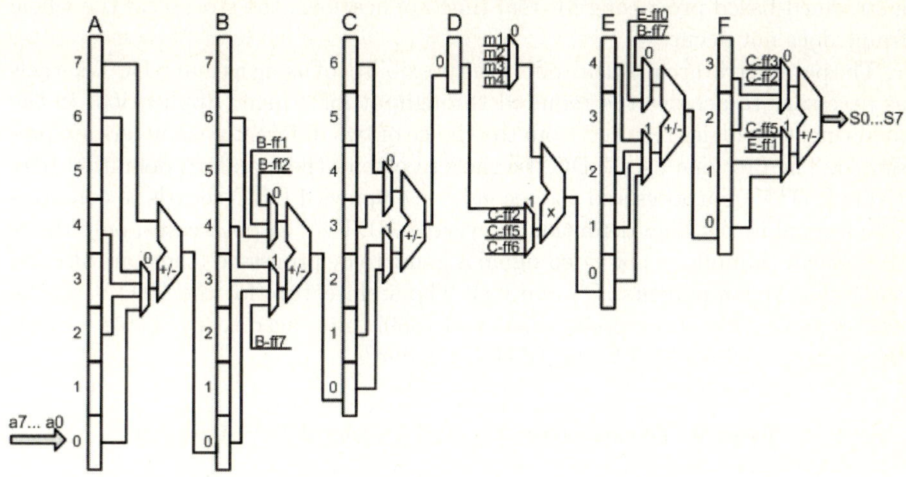

Fig. 2. Diagram of the proposed DCT-kernel

Table 2. Number of required flip-flops

Stage	Arch. [10]	DCT-kernel
A	128	73
B	144	90
C	160	88
D	198	26
E	198	78
F	192	70
Total	1020	425

Table 3. Number of required multiplexes

Multiplex	Arch. [10]	DCT-kernel
Mux0-A	4x1	4x1
Mux1-A	4x1	2x1
Mux0-B	4x1	4x1
Mux1-B	4x1	4x1
Mux0-C	3x1	2x1
Mux1-C	3x1	2x1
Mux0-D	4x1	4x1
Mux1-D	5x1	4x1
Mux0-E	5x1	4x1
Mux1-E	4x1	-
Mux0-F	2x1	4x1
Mux1-F	2x1	4x1

5   The Parametric 2D-DCT Architecture

To implement the 2D-DCT using 1D-DCT kernels, one or more DCT-kernels are
reserved to process the rows, while another set with the same number of kernels
is dedicated to process the columns. The first ones operate with 8 bits input
data and the second one, with 12 bits. The amount of bits is a programable
parameter in the kernel structure. A memory is necessary to save the result of
the 1D processing along 8 consecutive rows of pixels in a frame. These data
constitutes the input for the second 1D processing (along the columns). This
memory is commonly referred to as transposing buffer. In many applications, in
which the whole frame to be coded is previously stored, this transposing buffer
can be just sufficient to store the block of 8×8 pixels that is being coded in
that moment. However, as the goal of the presented architecture is performing

a streamed-based processing for real time applications, the storage of the whole frame does not occur.

The parametric architecture offers the possibility of using as many DCT-kernels as necessary to achieve the required throughput for a given application. In the following, topologies resulted from the choice of two different parameters are presented. The first one uses 2 DCT-kernels to attend the standard definition television (SDTV) purposes and the second one employs 4 DCT-kernels to compress video signal in the high definition television (HDTV). In both cases, only the Y component (luminance) of video signal is going to be processed (there are also the chrominance components, Cb and Cr). The architecture for the HDTV can be used in both 720p (progressive scan) and 1080i (interlaced scan). Table 4 shows the main features of SDTV and HDTV standards.

Table 4. The mains features of SDTV and HDTV standards

Standards	frames/ second	sampling	samples of Y/ second	samples of Cb Cr/ second
SD 720x480i	30/1.001	4:2:2	13,500,000	6,750,000
HD 1920x1080i	30	4:2:2	74,250,000	37,125,000
HD 1280x720p	60	4:2:2	74,250,000	37,125,000

5.1   An Architecture That Attends SDTV Purposes

The first 8 rows of the frame are consecutively processed (in sets of 8 pixels) by just one DCT-kernel. Only when this first step had finished, two 1D processing are simultaneously done, each of them executed by a different DCT-kernel. The first kernel performs the horizontal processing over the following set of 8 rows and the second kernel performs the processing over the columns resultant of the latter horizontal processing. Then, two buffers of size equivalent to 8 complete rows are necessary. These buffers are internal to the FPGA, which means that no external memory is used.

The first buffer is needed for the storage of the horizontal coefficients resultant of the 1D processing of the first set of 8 rows. This buffer will save the horizontal coefficients that will be read during the second step (when they will be processed in the vertical direction). The second buffer, by its time, will be filled in (from this second step on) with the coefficients resulted from the horizontal processing of the second set of 8 rows. In this manner, the simultaneous use of the 2 buffers is such that when one of them is being read, the other one is being written. In each set of 8 incoming rows of pixels, these buffers have their functions inverted. Figure 3 shows the main parts of this proposal for implementing the 2D-DCT for SDTV.

The maximum clock frequency achieved by each DCT-kernel has been 80MHz (12.5ns), as described in Section 4. This limitation is mainly due to the propagation delays of the multiplexes, adders and subtractors. Since both DCT-kernels operate in parallel (there is only a difference of 8 rows to start the processing by the second one), the frequency limit for the parallel architecture using the both kernels keeps the same as that of a particular kernel. As soon as the incoming

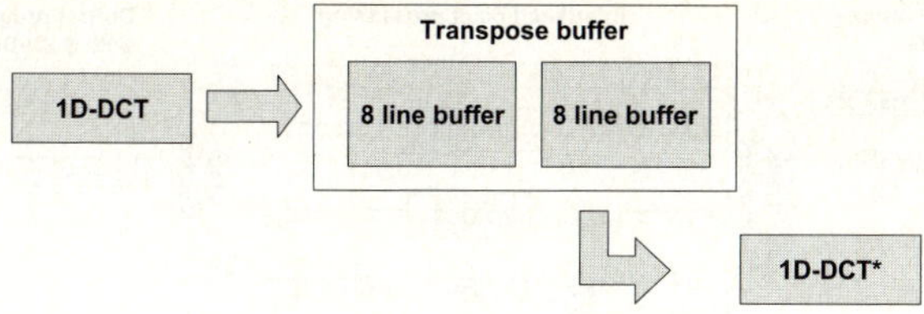

Fig. 3. Parallel 2D-DCT block diagram for SDTV

pixel rate is half this value (as mentioned in the presentation of the DCT-kernel in Section 4), the limit of operation is 40 megapixels/s. This is more than the necessary to attend standard definition video signals (SDTV), for which the pixel rate is 13,5 megapixels/s.

5.2   An Architecture That Attends HDTV Purposes

The rate of 40 megapixels/s is not enough to process high definition video signal, neither in the 720p nor in the 1080i standard. In this case, the required rate is 74,5 megapixels/s. In order to attend HDTV purposes, the present architecture may explore its parametric characteristic, that is, 4 DCT-kernels (instead of 2) may be used in a parallel way. Figure 4 shows the block diagram for HDTV.

Two DCT-kernels are utilized to process, each of them, half the pixels in a particular row. They operate alternatively in sets of 8 consecutive pixels, as shown in Fig. 5. In the same manner, the other two DCT-kernels conjunctly perform the vertical processing in the 8 rows of pixels that have been processed in the horizontal direction in the previous step. In this case, the transpose buffer used by each DCT-kernel has been resized to support only half the pixels of 8 consecutive rows (or columns). For this reason, regardless of the use of 4 DCT-kernels (which is twice the quantity used in the previous architecture), the total memory need for the architecture has been kept unchanged.

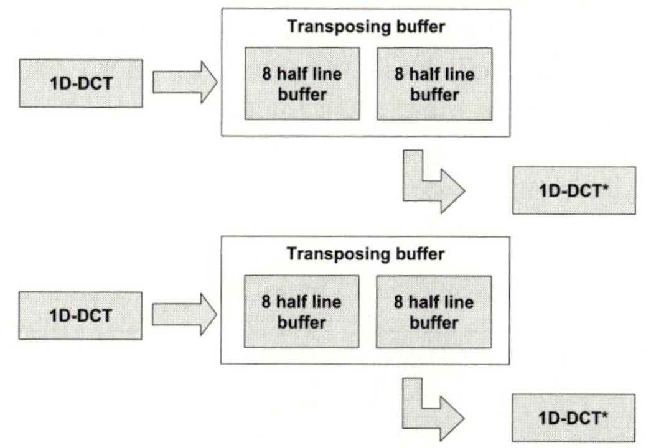

Fig. 4. Parallel 2D-DCT block diagram for HDTV

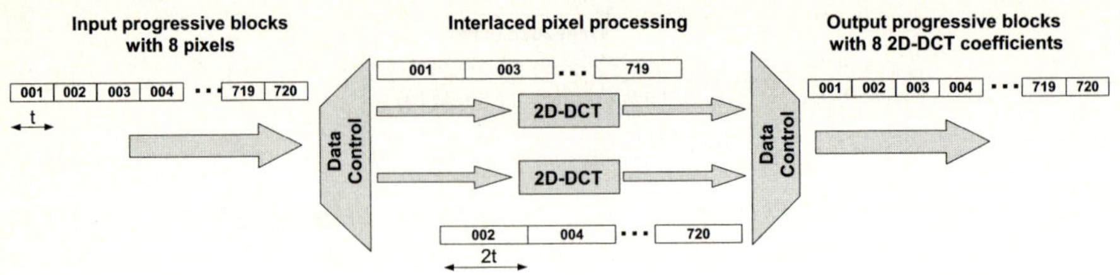

Fig. 5. 2D-DCT parallel processing data stream for HDTV

6   Verification Results

To verify the proposed architecture, the language VHDL (VHSIC - Hardware Description Language) has been employed in the design and the software Altera Quartus II has been used for simulation and synthesis. The target device was the CYCLONE II of Altera. It has been observed a significative reduction in the number of logic elements in the proposed architecture, if it is compared to other schemes reported in the literature.

Figure 6 shows the simulation results of the first unity of DCT-kernel used in the 2D-DCT for the SDTV. The state machine referred to as 'smp_cnt' changes in the rising edge of the 80 MHz clock signal 'clk'. However, a new pixel '$input$' arrives at each two periods of clock and the first coefficient '$output$' is only available after the thirty-second clock cycle. In this figure, the set of 8 pixels [0, 3, 6, 9, 12, 15, 18, 21] has generated the set of 8 1D-DCT coefficients [84, 0 , 0, 0, -77, 1, -6, -2].

For HDTV purpose, a control system has been created to synchronize the job division between the 2 DCT-kernels that alternatively process the same set of 8 rows (or columns). Figure 7 shows the control signals 'in_ena_1' and 'in_ena_2' that enable the data input for the first set of two DCT-kernels. The set of 8 pixels [0, 3, 6, 9, 12, 15, 18, 21] is processed by one of the DCT-kernels and generates the set of 8 1D-DCT coefficients [84, 0 , 0, 0, -77, 1, -6, -2], as shown in the signal '$output\_1$'. The subsequent set of 8 pixels [24, 27, 30, 33, 36, 39, 42, 45] is processed by another DCT-kernel and generates the coefficients [276, 0 , 0, 0,...] (only the first set of four coefficients are shown in Figure 7). The signals '$output\_1$' and '$output\_2$' are the input data for the two transposing buffers shown in Figure 4. The access to the data to be processed by each of them must also be controlled. This task is done by a demultiplex that distributes sets of 8

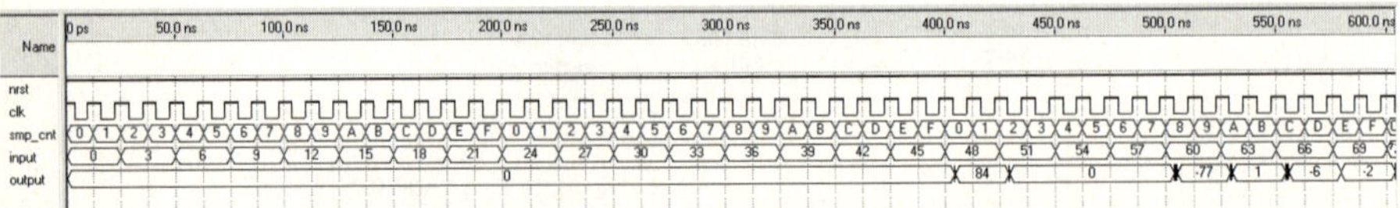

Fig. 6. Simulation results for SDTV

consecutive pixels between the 2 DCT-kernels. Since each DCT-kernel processes a set of 8 pixels in the same row, there is no additional delay (latency) due to the parallel architecture. A speedup of 2 has been obtained.

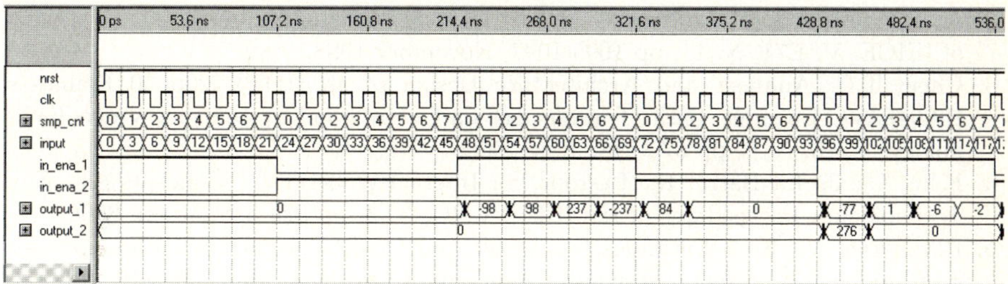

Fig. 7. Simulation results for HDTV

7   Conclusion

The parametric architecture proposed in this paper is expected to be an efficient alternative to provide the pixel rate required by the most of video compression applications. To achieve this goal, it uses as many DCT-kernels as necessary, in a parallel way.

The proposed DCT-kernel is a hardware implementation of the 1D-DCT that presents some advantages over classical implementations in the literature, which are a significative reduction of the number of required flip-flops and the use of a smaller transposing buffer.

The need for a buffer with lower size in the DCT-kernel avoids the use of extended memory while enables the use of a buffer internal to the FPGA. This reduces the circuit area and also prevents from some hardware faults. When two or more DCT-kernels are used to increase the pixel rate, the capacity required for each individual buffer decreases and the total memory keeps unchanged. It is an important to consider that the internal memory available in the FPGAs is restricted and relatively low if compared to the number of equivalent gates provided by them.

This paper has presented two different uses of the proposed parallel architecture. They attend for standard definition television (SDTV) and high definition television (HDTV) purposes, using two and four DCT-kernels, respectively. However, due to its parametric characteristic, this architecture can also provide solutions for other applications that demand higher pixel rates, without changing the hardware device. The number of kernels to operate in parallel is limited to the number of logic elements provided by the device. Then, this architecture promises to be especially useful to the transform approach for video compression in HDTV applications, which are, nowadays, one of the fields with the most expressive appeal for research and development.

References

1. Recommendation ITU-R BT.656-3: Interfaces For Digital Component Video Signals in 525-line and 625-line Television Systems Operating at the 4:2:2 Level of Recommendation ITU-R BT.601 (Part A). (1995).
2. Arai, Y.; Agui, T.; Nakajima, M.: A Fast DCT-SQ Scheme for Images. Transactions of IEICE. V. E71, N. 11, pp 1095-1097, November 1988.
3. Chen, T.C: Analysis and Architecture Design of an HDTV720p 30 Frames/s H.264/AVC Encoder. IEEE Transactions on Circuits and Systems for Video Technology. V. 16, N. 6, pp 673-688, June 2006.
4. Fehn, C.; de La Barré, R.; Pastoor, S.: Interactive 3-DTV - Concepts and Key Technologies. Proceedings of the IEEE. V. 94, N. 3, pp 524-538, March 2006.
5. Bhaskaran, V.; Konstantinides, K.: Image and Video Compression Standards Algorithms and Architectures. Kluwer Academic Publishers. Massachusetts, 1999.
6. Porto, R.; Agostini, L.: Project Space Exploration on the 2D-DCT Architecture of a JPEG Compressor Directed to FPGA Implementation. Design, Automation and Test in Europe Conference and Exhibition, pp 224-229, February 2004.
7. Jain, A.: Fundamentals of Digital Image Processing. Prentice Hall. USA, 1989.
8. Ahmed, N.; Natrajan, T.; Rao, K.R.: Discrete Cosine Transform. IEEE Trans. Comput. V. C-23, N. 1, pp 90-93, December 1984.
9. Kovac, M.; Ranganathan, N.: JAGUAR: A Fully Pipelined VLSI Architecture for JPEG Image Compression Standard. Proceedings of the IEEE. V. 32, N. 6, pp 247-258, February 1995.
10. Agostini, L.: Information Technology Digital Compression and Coding of Continuous-tone still Images Requirements and Guidelines. M. Sc. Dissertation. Computer Science Graduate Program - Federal University of Rio Grande do Sul, 2002.
11. Chen, W.; Smith, C.; Fralick, S.: A Fast Computational Algorithm for the Discrete Cosine Transform. IEEE Transactions on Communications. V. 25, N. 9, pp 1004-1009, September 1977.
12. Lee, B.: A New Algorithm to Compute the Discrete Cossine Transform. IEEE Transactions on ASSP. V. 32, N. 6, pp 1243-1245, December 1984.

A Resource Selection Method for Cycle Stealing in the GPU Grid*

Yuki Kotani, Fumihiko Ino, and Kenichi Hagihara

Graduate School of Information Science and Technology, Osaka University
1-3 Machikaneyama, Toyonaka, Osaka 560-8531, Japan
{y-kotani, ino, hagihara}@ist.osaka-u.ac.jp

Abstract. Modern programmable graphics processing units (GPUs) provide increasingly higher performance, motivating us to perform general-purpose computation on the GPU (GPGPU) beyond graphics applications. In this paper, we address the problem of resource selection in the GPU grid. The GPU grid here consists of desktop computers at home and the office, utilizing idle GPUs and CPUs as computational engines for compute-intensive applications. Our method tackles this challenging problem (1) by defining idle resources and (2) by developing a resource selection method based on a screensaver approach with low-overhead sensors. The sensors detect idle GPUs by checking video random access memory (VRAM) usage and CPU usage on each computer. Detected resources are then selected according to a matchmaking framework and benchmark results obtained when the screensaver is installed on the machines. The experimental results show that our method achieves a low overhead of at most 262 ms, minimizing interference to resource owners with at most 10% performance drop.

1 Introduction

Grid technology [1] has emerged as a new paradigm in computational science. It allows us to share hardware and software resources across multiple organizations, providing us a virtual supercomputer through the Internet. There are many types of grids such as server grids, desktop grids, and data grids [2]. In this paper, we use the term grid to refer to a desktop grid, namely a cycle stealing system that utilizes idle computers at home and the office.

Another emerging paradigm is GPGPU [3], which stands for general-purpose computation on the graphics processing unit (GPU) [4,5]. The GPU is a single chip processor designed for acceleration of compute-intensive graphics tasks, such as three-dimensional (3-D) rendering applications. Modern GPUs are increasing in computational performance at greater than Moore's law [6]. For example, an nVIDIA GeForce 6800 card achieves a peak performance of 120 GFLOPS for single precision data [7]. In addition to their attractive performance, GPUs are becoming more flexible in programmability with supporting branching. Consequently, many researchers are trying to apply the GPU to non-graphics problems [8] as well as typical graphics problems.

---

* This work was partly supported by JSPS Grant-in-Aid for Scientific Research for Scientific Research (B)(2)(18300009) and on Priority Areas (17032007).

G. Min et al. (Eds.): ISPA 2006 Ws, LNCS 4331, pp. 769–780, 2006.

In this paper, we focus on enabling GPGPU applications to execute on desktop grids. This type of grids, named GPU grids, aims at exploiting idle GPUs as well as idle CPUs at home and the office. Thus, we think that desktop grids will become a more attractive computing platform if GPUs are explicitly managed and used as general-purpose resources as well as graphics accelerators.

Since GPUs have been used as dedicated display cards, many technical problems arise if these cards are shared between resource owners and grid users. A resource owner here is the person who contributes resources to the grid while a grid user means the person who desires to run grid applications on donated resources. One typical problem is resource conflicts between owners and users. In particular, the following critical problems must be resolved to achieve our goal of building GPU grids.

P1. The lack of definition of idle resources. GPUs are originally designed to serve their owners who directly see the display output. Therefore, the definition of idle resources has not been considered from the grid users point of view. We must define this to select appropriate resources for grid users. The definition here should be considered from both the owner side and the user side in order to (1) minimize interference to owners and (2) maximize application performance provided to users.

P2. The lack of external monitors for the GPU. Most operating systems are capable of providing CPU performance information such as load average and memory usage. However, current operating systems do not have information on GPU performance. Although modern GPUs have performance counters inside their chips, these internal counters are accessible only from instrumented programs running with an instrumented device driver [9]. Therefore, we need external monitors to minimize modifications to resource configurations and application code.

P3. The lack of efficient multitasking on the GPU. Current GPUs do not support context switching in hardware, so that preemptive multitasking of GPU applications is not available even in Windows XP, namely the most popular system [10]. Instead, multitasking is cooperatively done by software, which results in lower performance. Thus, GPUs are still not virtualized enough to allow multiple applications to be run effectively.

Although problem P3 is critical, it is not easy for non-vendors to give a direct solution to this problem. Therefore, assuming that the GPU grid consists of cooperative multitasking systems, we tackle the remaining problems P1 and P2 to select idle GPUs appropriately from grid resources.

To address problem P1, we experimentally define the idle state of the GPU. For problem P2, on the other hand, we develop a resource selection method based on a screensaver approach with low-overhead sensors. The sensors detect idle GPUs according to video random access memory (VRAM) usage and CPU usage on each computer. Once idle GPUs are detected, they are selected according to a matchmaking framework [11] and benchmark results. The benchmark results here are obtained when the screensaver is installed on each of the resources. Our method is currently implemented on Windows systems, which support the latest GPUs for entertainment use.

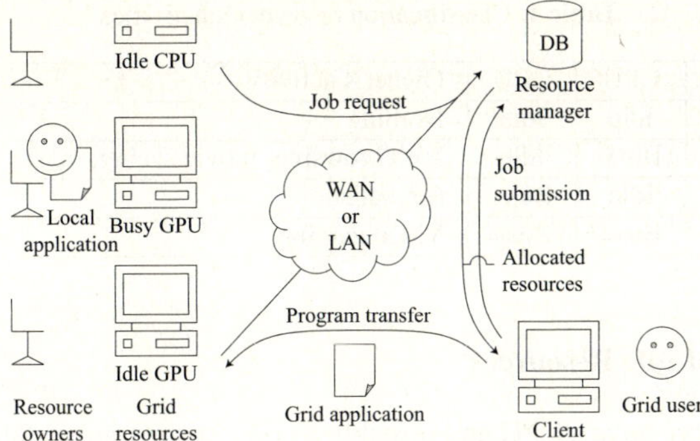

Fig. 1. Overview of the GPU Grid

2   GPU Grid

The GPU grid has almost the same structure as existing desktop grids. The only difference is that the GPU grid explicitly manages the GPU as general-purpose resources. We think that this little difference allows us to easily integrate our resource selection method into existing desktop grid systems.

2.1   System Overview

Figure 1 shows an overview of the GPU grid, which consists of three main components as follows.

- Grid resources. Grid resources are desktop computers at home and the office connecting to the Internet. Ordinarily, these resources are used by resource owners. However, they are donated for job execution if they are in the idle state. Arbitrary computers are considered as grid resources regardless of having the programmable GPU or not.
- The resource manager. The resource manager takes the responsibility for monitoring and selection of registered resources. It also acts as a job manager, which receives jobs from grid users. For each job, the manager returns a list of available resources. This list contains idle resources waiting for job allocation, and thus matchmaking [11] is done using this list (see Section 3.2). We accept arbitrary jobs consisting of GPGPU, GPU, and CPU applications.
- Clients. Clients are front-end computers for grid users, who want to submit jobs to the grid. Clients can also be grid resources. Once the list of available resources is sent from the resource manager, the user program is sent to the resources for job execution.

Thus, the GPU grid is a wider concept of the desktop grid. Therefore, a desktop grid without GPU-equipped computers also can be regarded as the GPU grid.

In the following discussion, we use the term grid application to denote a program submitted by grid users. We also use the term local application to denote a program executed by resource owners using their resources.

Table 1. Classification of owner's activities

Situation	CPU	GPU	Owner's activity
S1	Idle	Idle	Nothing
S2	Busy	Idle	Web browsing, movie seeing, music listening
S3	Idle	Busy	(unrealistic)
S4	Busy	Busy	Video gaming

2.2   Definition of Idle Resources

Since a grid resource have a CPU and possibly a GPU, the resource state can be roughly classified into four groups depending on the state of each unit. Table 1 presents this classification with owner's typical activities. In the following we show the definition of idle resources using this classification.

As we mentioned before, the definition must satisfy the following requirements.

R1. It minimizes interference to resource owners.
R2. It maximizes application performance provided to grid users.

To satisfy the above requirements, we define an idle resource such that it satisfies all of the following three conditions.

$D1.$ The resource owner does not interactively operate the resource.
$D2.$ The GPU does not execute any local application.
$D3.$ The CPU is idle enough to provide the full performance of the GPU to grid users.

Firstly, condition $D2$ is essential to satisfy requirement R1, because the GPU does not support preemptive multitasking. Otherwise, some uncooperative applications will significantly drop the frame rate of the display, making resource owners nervous. Consequently, resource owners are interfered by grid applications if condition $D2$ is not satisfied. Thus, R1 excludes situations S3 and S4 from the idle state (See Table 1).

Secondly, due to the same reason, R1 also excludes situation S2 if the resource owner interactively operates their computer through the display output. We also have experimentally confirmed that the grid application suffers from lower performance if the resource owner gives a window focus to the operating window (see Section 4.1). Therefore, situation S2 does not satisfy requirement R2. Thus, condition $D1$ is needed.

Finally, condition $D3$ is essential to satisfy requirement R2. We have experimentally confirmed this (see Section 4.1). GPU applications generally make the CPU usage go to 100%, because they usually require CPU intervention during GPU execution. Note here that this condition might be eliminated in the future, because Windows Graphics Foundation (WGF) 2.0 will enable GPU processing without CPU intervention [12].

3   Resource Selection Method

In this section, we describe how idle resources are detected and how resources are selected from detected resources.

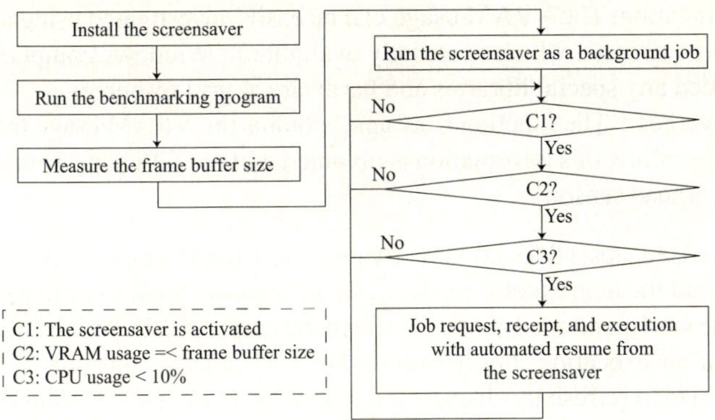

Fig. 2. Resource detection procedure. Steps in the left-hand side are processed only once when the screensaver is installed on the resource.

3.1   Detection of Idle Resources

Figure 2 shows the procedure of resource detection. To detect an idle resource that satisfies conditions $D1$–$D3$, our method checks the resource in the following steps.

C1. The screensaver is activated.
C2. VRAM usage $\leq$ frame buffer size.
C3. CPU usage $< 10\%$.

Steps C1, C2, and C3 here aim at checking conditions $D1$, $D2$, and $D3$, respectively.

The first condition $D1$ is checked by a screensaver approach. The screensaver is currently activated after five minutes of owner's inactivity. This screensaver approach allows us to detect inactivity at a lower overhead. It also allows owners to rapidly resume their activity, as compared with polling-based methods [13].

Due to the lack of preemptive multitasking supports, our screensaver avoids updating the display output. Instead, the display is drawn only when the screensaver is turned on. This intends to avoid increasing the workload of the CPU and the GPU during the screensaver mode, delivering full GPU performance to grid users. The screensaver is implemented using a library scrnsave.lib, which is distributed as a part of Microsoft Visual Studio.

The remaining conditions $D2$ and $D3$ are checked by a sensor program. This program is implemented as a screensaver function ScreenSaverProc(), which is called when the screensaver is activated. Thus, we minimize the monitoring overhead by minimizing the invocation of the sensor program.

The key idea to evaluate condition $D2$ is the VRAM usage check. This idea assumes that the GPU always consumes VRAM for the frame buffer and further VRAM if it executes any GPU programs. Under this assumption, we can evaluate condition $D2$ by comparing the current usage and the default usage, namely the frame buffer size. The default usage here is measured only once when installing the screensaver on the resource. Our VRAM-based monitoring method has two advantages as follows.

- No modification. The VRAM usage can be easily investigated using a Direct Draw function GetCaps(), which is initially available in Windows computers. Thus, we do not need any special libraries and hardware at grid resources.
- Lower overhead. The function GetCaps() obtains the VRAM usage from the device driver. Therefore, this information is obtained without GPU intervention, leading to a low-overhead sensor.

Note here that GetCaps() does not directly give the VRAM usage. This function returns the capacity and the amount of free space, so we subtract them to estimate the usage.

The assumption mentioned above is valid in the current GPU, which allocates VRAM in advance of an execution. Furthermore, the GPU always consumes VRAM for the frame buffer size to refresh the display. Although the amount of this consumption might be computed according to the screen resolution and its color depth, we have found that it varies depending on hardware and software environments, such as the device driver version. Therefore, we directly measure the default usage at screensaver installation.

Finally, condition $D3$ can be evaluated by accessing performance information provided by operating systems. According to preliminary experiments (see Section 4.1), we currently use the CPU usage with a threshold of 10%. As well as the VRAM usage, this information does not require GPU intervention. Our implementation calls PdhCollectQueryData() to access a performance counter in the Windows operating system.

3.2   Selection of Idle Resources

Once idle resources are detected by the screensaver approach, the next issue is the resource selection problem. We resolve this issue by combining two different approaches: a benchmarking approach [14] and a matchmaking approach [11].

The benchmarking approach [14] takes the responsibility for measuring the actual performance for GPGPU applications. The reason why we perform benchmarking is due to the fact that the specification of the GPU does not always represent the actual performance for GPGPU applications. Actually, we have found that a high-end card is outperformed by a commodity card and that the device driver version significantly affects the performance. Therefore, we run a benchmark program at screensaver installation to obtain the actual performance under the idle state. These benchmark results are then collected at the resource manager to give priorities to detected resources.

On the other hand, the matchmaking approach [11] is responsible for providing a flexible and general framework of resource selection. For example, this framework allows grid users to select only nVIDIA GeForce 7800 cards or select only GPUs with having a fill rate of at least 3 Gpixels/s, according to the benchmark results. We think that this flexible framework is essential to run GPGPU applications in grid environments, because the GPU is still not a matured computing environment. We have experienced that some applications running on a GPU do not successfully run on different GPUs, due to architectural differences and driver version differences. Therefore, we think that the framework should allow users to select appropriate resources.

Table 2. Specification of experimental machines

	PC1	PC2	PC3
CPU	Pentium 4 3.4 GHz	Pentium 4 3.0 GHz	Pentium 4 2.8 GHz
GPU	nVIDIA GeForce 7800 GTX	nVIDIA GeForce 6800 GTO	nVIDIA Quadro FX 3400
Core speed (MHz)	430	350	350
Memory speed (MHz)	1200	900	900
Memory bandwidth (GB/s)	38.4	28.8	28.8
Fill rate (Gpixels/s)	6.88	4.2	5.6
Pipeline engines	24	12	16
Graphics bus	PCI Express		
Driver version	79.70	78.01	66.93

4   Experimental Results

Table 2 shows the specification of experimental machines. We use three machines PC1, PC2, and PC3, each with different CPUs and GPUs. PC1 and PC3 provide the highest and the lowest performance, respectively.

For experiments, we use three GPGPU applications: LU decomposition [15], conjugate gradients (CG) [16], and 2-D/3-D rigid registration (RR) [17]. Due to the space limitation, we briefly summarize each characteristic.

- LU decomposition of a 2048×2048 matrix. In this implementation [15], the matrix data is stored as textures in the VRAM. Textures are then repeatedly rendered by the hardware components in the GPU, such as SIMD and vector processing units. The CPU takes the responsibility for computing the working area in textures where the GPU operates.
- CG for solving linear systems with a coefficient matrix of size 64×64. Similar to LU decomposition, this implementation also repeats rendering against textures. From the viewpoint of the workload characteristic, it has less CPU workload than LU decomposition because the GPU is responsible for computing the working area.
- RR for alignment between 2-D images and a 3-D volume. This implementation [17] has the lowest workload of the CPU among the three applications. In contrast, computation at the GPU side is the heaviest because it operates a volume data in addition to 2-D images.

4.1   Evaluating Definition of Idle Resources

To verify the definition of idle resources, we compare the performance of local and grid applications between idle resources and busy resources. The performance is presented by application throughput given by the number of executions per second.

According to the definition presented in Section 2.2, we measure the throughput on busy resources. Busy states here are given by negations of each of conditions $D1$, $D2$, and $D3$ as follows.

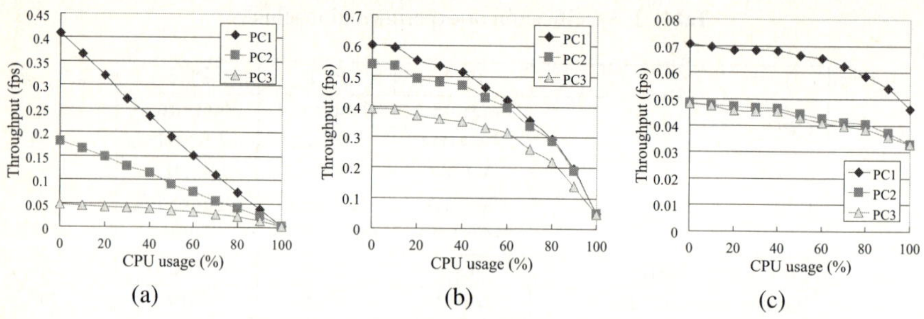

Fig. 3. Measured throughput with different CPU usages for three different GPGPU applications: (a) LU decomposition, (b) conjugate gradients (CG), and (c) rigid registration (RR). These applications are executed as grid applications. Throughput is presented in frames per second (fps).

$\overline{D1}$: The resource owner interactively operates the resource. We measure the throughput of local and grid applications while executing the PCMark05 benchmark [18]. PCMark05 here renders various web pages, and thus this experiment measures interference to owners assuming that they are browsing web pages during grid job execution.

$\overline{D2}$: The GPU executes local applications. We measure the throughput of local applications while executing a grid application. We use LU, CG, or RR application for each side. This experiment also intends to measure the interference to GPU applications instead of CPU applications (web browsing as mentioned above).

$\overline{D3}$: The CPU is not idle enough to provide the full performance of the GPU to grid users. We measure the throughput of grid applications with different CPU usages, ranging from 0% to 100%.

To obtain accurate throughputs, both local and grid applications are executed in an infinite loop during measurement.

Figure 3 gives the results for condition $\overline{D3}$. It shows the throughput of grid applications with different CPU usages. For all applications, we can see that the throughput decreases as the CPU usage increases. One remarkable point here is that LU linearly drops the performance while RR slowly decreases the performance. This is due to the difference of workload characteristics inherent in applications. As compared with CG and RR, LU frequently switches textures, and thus requires more CPU interventions during execution. It also requires more data transfer between the CPU and the GPU. Therefore, LU sharply drops the performance as compared with CG and RR. According to these results, we have determined that idle resources must have a CPU usage of at most 10%.

Figure 4 shows the results for conditions $\overline{D1}$ and $\overline{D2}$. It shows the throughput of grid applications with different activities: web browsing (PCMark05), LU, CG, and RR execution. LU and CG in Figs 4(a) and 4(b) indicate that grid applications significantly drop their performance if owners are seeing web pages. In contrast, the performance drop in RR is not so serious. We think that this is due to CPU interventions required during GPU execution. As we mentioned earlier, LU and CG require more interventions than RR. We also think that the window focus is critical in these cases. Since the focus is

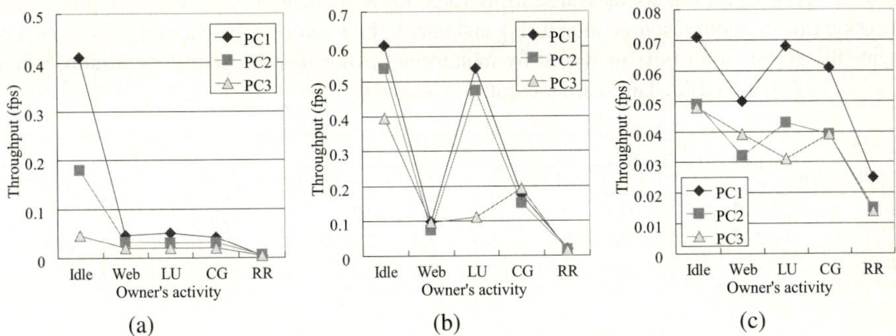

Fig. 4. Measured throughput with different owner's activities for three GPGPU applications: (a) LU decomposition, (b) conjugate gradients (CG), and (c) rigid registration (RR). Applications in the horizontal axis are local applications.

given to owner's operating window, PCMark05 in this case, the operating system gives a lower priority to the background job, namely the grid application. This increases the overhead of CPU interventions, making the GPU in the idle state. Thus, resources in condition $\overline{D1}$ should not be used for job execution. We also confirmed this from the owner side. The rendering performance of web pages is decreased from approximately 2 to 0.5 pages/s.

Finally, we investigate condition $\overline{D2}$. In Fig. 4, we can see that the throughput of grid applications also significantly decreases if the owner executes a GPU application. In particular, RR seems to be an uncooperative application, because it significantly decreases the performance of LU and CG, as shown in Figs 4(a) and (b), respectively. Furthermore, if RR is executed as a grid application, it provides almost the same performance, whether it is executed on an idle resource or a busy resource. Thus, since both the grid users and resource owners can execute uncooperative applications on resources, we think that condition $D2$ is needed to define idle resources.

In summary, we think that the definition is reasonable with minimizing interference to resource owners while maximizing application performance provided to grid users.

4.2   Evaluating Overhead of Resource Selection

We now evaluate our resource selection method in terms of the monitoring overhead. We also investigate how local applications are interfered by the method. In experiments, we use LU, CG, and RR as local applications.

Table 3 shows the execution time of local applications, explaining how local applications are perturbated by the resource monitoring overhead. We first measured the original time T_1 with disabling resource monitoring, and then time T_2 with enabling monitoring. Therefore, the perturbation time $T_2 - T_1$ explains how applications are perturbated by monitoring.

We observe the highest perturbation time $T_2 - T_1$ of 300 ms when executing RR on computer PC1. The perturbation ratio σ also indicates that this time is short enough as compared with the original execution time T_1. Furthermore, our monitoring program is implemented as a CPU program, and thus it avoids making GPU programs slow down.

Table 3. Perturbation effects measured using three local applications. T_1 and T_2 represent the execution time without resource monitoring and that with monitoring, respectively. $T_2 - T_1$ represents the perturbation time increased by monitoring. σ denotes the perturbation ratio, where $\sigma = (T_2 - T_1)/T_1 * 100$. Times are presented in seconds.

| Local | PC1 (s) | | | PC2 (s) | | | PC3 (s) | | |
application	T_1	T_2	$T_2 - T_1\ (\sigma)$	T_1	T_2	$T_2 - T_1\ (\sigma)$	T_1	T_2	$T_2 - T_1\ (\sigma)$
LU	2.4	2.5	0.1 (4%)	5.6	5.7	0.1 (2%)	21.1	21.2	0.1 (1%)
CG	1.7	1.8	0.1 (6%)	1.9	2.1	0.2 (10%)	2.5	2.6	0.1 (4%)
RR	14.2	14.5	0.3 (2%)	18.6	18.8	0.2 (1%)	20.7	21.0	0.3 (1%)

The perturbation time $T_2 - T_1$ of 300 ms is due to the monitoring overhead of 262 ms: 190 ms for activating the screensaver; 2 ms for checking the VRAM usage; and 70 ms for the CPU usage. Although the screensaver activation takes 190 ms at the GPU side, it does not cause critical interference to the resource owner, because the activation guarantee the owner's inactivity. One concern is the interference to GPGPU applications that do not require interaction between owners. However, this is not so critical because our screensaver avoids refreshing the display. The remaining time for checking the VRAM and CPU usages is also a low overhead, because it requires only references to performance information, which is processed at the CPU side. Thus, we think that our method achieves a low overhead monitoring with minimum interference.

5   Related Work

To the best of our knowledge, there is no work on utilizing the GPU as a general-purpose resource in the grid. However, some grid projects use the GPU as a graphics accelerator to achieve large-scale visualization in server grid environments [19,20], in which resources are dedicated to grid users. Due to this dedication, server grids do not have resource conflicts between resource owners and grid users. Therefore, resources can be easily managed by a job management server that receives jobs from grid users. A similar work is presented by Fan et al. [21] who build a cluster of GPUs for fluid simulation and visualization.

There are many projects related to desktop grids. Condor [13] is an earlier system that explores using idle time in networked workstations. This system has a central server that polls every two minutes for available CPUs and jobs waiting. Each workstation has a local scheduler that checks every 30 seconds to see if the running job should be pre-empted because the owner has resumed using the workstation. Thus, owners are interfered for 30 seconds at the worst case. This interfering time is too long for cooperative multitasking systems, which can significantly drop the frame rate of the display.

BOINC [22] is a middleware system of the SETI@home project [23], which demonstrates the practical use of desktop grids. This system has a screensaver mode that shows the graphics of running applications. Although this mode is useful to know that resource owners currently do not operate their computers, it is not sufficient to decide if the GPU is not being used. Thus, some additional monitors are needed for the GPU.

NVPerfKit [9] is a monitoring tool that allows us to probe performance counters in the GPU. This tool gives us important performance information such as the ratio of the idle time to the total measured time. However, it requires modern nVIDIA GPUs with an instrumented version of the device driver to probe the counters. Therefore, this vendor-specific tool is not a realistic solution to our problem, where various GPUs should be monitored without system or code modifications.

Benchmarking tools provide us effective performance information based on direct execution of some small code. For example, 3DMark06 [18] measures GPU performance using a set of 3-D graphics applications. On the other hand, gpubench [14] aims at capturing GPU performance for GPGPU applications. Thus, benchmarking tools might be useful to detect idle GPUs. However, they require a couple of time to finish benchmarking. This high overhead is critical if they are executed every time the resource is checked for availability.

With respect to multitasking of GPU applications, Windows Vista will support pre-emptive multitasking [10]. As compared with cooperative multitasking, preemptive multitasking provides more stable, reliable performance when multiple applications are executed simultaneously. Therefore, our assumption of cooperative multitasking might lead to a strict definition of the idle GPU in the future. However, we think that this assumption is compatible with future systems, because we only have to relax the definition to gather more resources for such preemptive multitasking systems.

6   Conclusion

We have presented a resource selection method for the GPU grid, which aims at executing GPGPU applications on a desktop grid. We also have shown a definition of idle resources in the GPU grid. Both the method and definition works on cooperative (non-preemptive) multitasking systems. The method employs a screensaver-based approach with low-overhead monitors. The monitors are designed to detect idle GPUs with minimum program invocations.

The experimental results show that the definition is reasonable with minimizing interference to resource owners while maximizing application performance provided to grid users. We also find that the method achieves a low overhead of at most 262 ms, which is short enough as compared to the execution time of local applications.

References

1. Foster, I., Kesselman, C., eds.: The Grid: Blueprint of a New Computing Infrastructure. Morgan Kaufmann, San Mateo, CA (1998)
2. Chien, A., Calder, B., Elbert, S., Bhatia, K.: Entropia: architecture and performance of an enterprise desktop grid system. J. Parallel and Distributed Computing **63**(5) (2003) 597–610
3. GPGPU: General-Purpose Computation Using Graphics Hardware (2005)
   http://www.gpgpu.org/.
4. Fernando, R., ed.: GPU Gems: Programming Techniques, Tips and Tricks for Real-Time Graphics. Addison-Wesley, Reading, MA (2004)
5. Pharr, M., Fernando, R., eds.: GPU Gems 2: Programming Techniques for High-Performance Graphics and General-Purpose Computation. Addison-Wesley, Reading, MA (2005)

6. Moore, G.E.: Cramming more components onto integrated circuits. Electronics **38**(8) (1965) 114–117

7. Montrym, J., Moreton, H.: The GeForce 6800. IEEE Micro **25**(2) (2005) 41–51

8. Owens, J.D., Luebke, D., Govindaraju, N., Harris, M., Krüger, J., Lefohn, A.E., Purcell, T.J.: A survey of general-purpose computation on graphics hardware. In: EUROGRAPHICS 2005, State of the Art Report. (2005) 21–51

9. nVIDIA Corporation: NVPerfKit 2 User Guide (2006) `http://developer.nvidia.com/NVPerfKit/`.

10. Pronovost, S., Moreton, H., Kelley, T.: Windows display driver model (WDDM) v2 and beyond. In: Windows Hardware Engineering Conf. (WinHEC'06). (2006) `http://www.microsoft.com/whdc/winhec/trackdetail06.mspx?track=11`.

11. Raman, R., Livny, M., Solomon, M.: Resource management through multilateral matchmaking. In: Proc. 9th IEEE Int'l Symp. High Performance Distributed Computing (HPDC'00). (2000) 290–291

12. Blythe, D.: Windows graphics overview. In: Windows Hardware Engineering Conf. (WinHEC'05). (2005) `http://www.microsoft.com/whdc/winhec/Pres05.mspx`.

13. Litzkow, M.J., Livny, M., Mutka, M.W.: Condor - a hunter of idle workstations. In: Proc. 8th Int'l Conf. Distributed Computing Systems (ICDCS'88). (1988) 104–111

14. Buck, I., Fatahalian, K., Hanrahan, P.: GPUBench: Evaluating GPU performance for numerical and scientific application. In: Proc. 1st ACM Workshop General-Purpose Computing on Graphics Processors (GP^2'04). (2004) C-20

15. Ino, F., Matsui, M., Hagihara, K.: Performance study of LU decomposition on the programmable GPU. In: Proc. 12th IEEE Int'l Conf. High Performance Computing (HiPC'05). (2005) 83–94

16. Corrigan, A.: Implementation of conjugate gradients (CG) on programmable graphics hardware (GPU) (2005) `http://www.cs.stevens.edu/~quynh/student-work/acorrigan_gpu.htm`.

17. Ino, F., Gomita, J., Kawasaki, Y., Hagihara, K.: A GPGPU approach for accelerating 2-D/3-D rigid registration of medical images. (In: Proc. 4th Int'l Symp. Parallel and Distributed Processing and Applications (ISPA'06). (2006)

18. Futuremark Corporation: Products (2006) `http://www.futuremark.com/products/3dmark06/`.

19. Jankun-Kelly, T., Kreylos, O., Ma, K.L., Hamann, B., Joy, K.I., Shalf, J., Bethel, E.W.: Deploying web-based visual exploration tools on the grid. IEEE Computer Graphics and Applications **23**(2) (2003) 40–50

20. Grimstead, I.J., Avis, N.J., Walker, D.W.: Automatic distribution of rendering workloads in a grid enabled collaborative visualization environment. In: Proc. SC'04. (2004) 10 pages (CD-ROM).

21. Fan, Z., Qiu, F., Kaufman, A., Yoakum-Stover, S.: GPU cluster for high performance computing. In: Proc. SC'04. (2004) 12 pages (CD-ROM).

22. Anderson, D.P.: BOINC: A system for public-resource computing and storage. In: Proc. 5th IEEE/ACM Int'l Conf. Grid Computing (GRID'04). (2004) 4–10

23. Sullivan, W.T., Werthimer, D., Bowyer, S., Cobb, J., Gedye, D., Anderson, D.: A new major SETI project based on project serendip data and 100,000 personal computers. In: Proc. 5th Int'l Conf. Bioastronomy. (1997) 729

Parallel High-Dimensional Index Structure Using Cell-Based Filtering for Multimedia Data*

Jae-Woo Chang, Yong-Ki Kim, and Young-Jin Kim

Dept. of Computer Eng., Chonbuk National Univ., Chonju, Chonbuk 561-756, South Korea
jwchang@chonbuk.ac.kr, {ykkim, yjkim}@dblab.chonbuk.ac.kr

Abstract. A large number of high-dimensional index structures suffer from the so called 'dimensional curse' problem, i.e., the retrieval performance becomes increasingly degraded as the dimensionality is increased. To solve this problem, the cell-based filtering scheme has been proposed, but it shows a linear decrease in performance as the dimensionality is increased. In this paper, we propose a parallel high-dimensional index structure using the cell-based filtering for multimedia data so as to cope with the linear decrease in retrieval performance. In addition, we devise data insertion, range query and k-NN query processing algorithms which are suitable for the cluster-based parallel architecture. Finally, we show that our parallel index structure achieves good retrieval performance in proportion to the number of servers in the cluster-based architecture and it outperforms a parallel version of the VA-File when the dimensionality is over 10.

1   Introduction

For the content-based retrieval of a large amount of multimedia data, an object in a multimedia database can be defined as an n-dimensional feature vector. Therefore, it is necessary to research on high-dimensional index structures for efficiently retrieving high-dimensional data in multimedia database applications. Thus, high-dimensional index structures such as K-D-B-tree [1], VAMSplit k-d-tree [2] and TV-tree[3], have been proposed. However, most of them were found to cause the so called 'dimensional curse' problem, i.e., the retrieval performance becomes increasingly degraded as the dimensionality is increased [5][6]. To solve this problem, the cell-based filtering (CBF) scheme and the VA-file scheme were proposed. The VA-file performs filtering by using vector approximation information [7]. The CBF scheme performs filtering by using signatures, and shows good performance by redefining the maximum and minimum distances for good filtering [8]. However, both of these schemes show a linear decrease in performance as the dimensionality increases. In order to alleviate this linear decrease in retrieval performance, it is necessary to make use of a parallel processing technique. In this paper, we propose a parallel high-dimensional index structure using the cell-based filtering for multimedia data so as to cope with the

---

* This work is financially supported by the Ministry of Education and Human Resources Development(MOE), the Ministry of Commerce, Industry and Energy(MOCIE) and the Ministry of Labor(MOLAB) though the fostering project of the Lab of Excellency.

G. Min et al. (Eds.): ISPA 2006 Ws, LNCS 4331, pp. 781–790, 2006.

linear decrease in retrieval performance. For our parallel index structure, we also devise data insertion, range query and k-NN query processing algorithms which are suitable for the shared-nothing cluster-based architecture.

2   Cell-Based Filtering (CBF) Scheme

The existing high-dimensional index structures cause the 'dimensional curse' problem, in that the retrieval performance becomes even worse than that of a sequential scan when the dimensionality is high. To solve this problem, the VA-file scheme [7] and CBF scheme [8] were proposed. The VA-file minimizes the 'dimensional curse' problem by scanning a sequential file in which an approximation of each cell is stored. However, since the distance between the user's query and the cells is not the real distance between the query and the object, the VA-file scheme is affected by the error distance caused by the data distribution within a cell and the size of the cell. Meanwhile, because the CBF scheme minimizes the error distance, it can improve the retrieval performance by filtering out cells effectively using the signature of a feature vector, as well as the distance between the feature vector and the center of the cell containing it. Figure 1 shows the overall architecture of the existing CBF scheme.

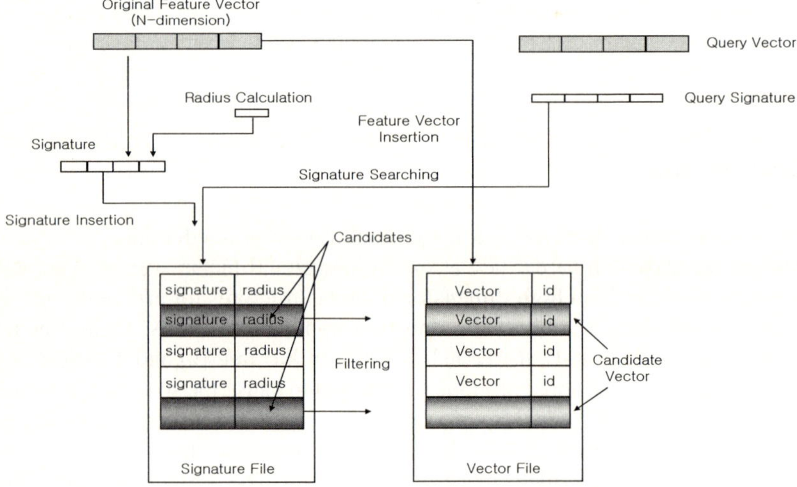

Fig. 1. Overall architecture CBF Scheme

3   Parallel High-Dimensional Index Structure

Though the CBF scheme alleviates the 'dimensional curse' problem, it still exhibits a linear decrease in retrieval performance as the dimensionality increases. To respond to a user query, the CBF scheme sequentially scans signatures and feature vectors, which are stored in a physical disk. However, our parallel high-dimensional index structure distributes signatures and feature vectors over multiple processors by means of a de-clustering technique, and stores them on separate physical disks. In the existing de-clustering techniques, either horizontal or vertical partitioning is employed. In order to design an efficient declustering algorithm for our parallel high-dimensional index structure, it is necessary to consider the two properties of the CBF scheme.

Property 1. All signatures of the CBF scheme should be scanned sequentially in order to respond to a given query. When a query is processed, a parallel CBF scheme scans all of the signatures contained in the signature file. Thus, if the signatures are distributed evenly over multiple servers by a horizontal partitioning technique, the number of page accesses required is approximately equal to B/S, where S is the number of servers and B is the total number of blocks containing all of the signatures. If they are distributed into multiple servers by a vertical partitioning technique, however, we need approximately B/S page accesses and an additional time needed for merging partitioned signatures.

Property 2. The feature vectors corresponding to the candidate signatures in the CBF scheme should be partially searched in order to respond to a given query. When a query is processed, a parallel CBF scheme scans only those feature vectors corresponding to the candidate signatures contained in the data file. Thus, if the feature vectors are distributed evenly by a horizontal partitioning technique, the number of page accesses required is approximately equal to N/S, where S is the number of servers and N is the number of feature vectors corresponding to the candidate signatures. If the feature vectors are distributed by a vertical partitioning technique, however, we need approximately N/S page accesses and an additional time for merging the partitioned feature vectors.

Based on the above two properties, we propose a high-dimensional index structure, i.e., parallel CBF scheme, which distributes both signatures and feature vectors over multiple servers by means of a horizontal partitioning technique. Figure 2 shows the overall architecture of the parallel CBF scheme under the SN cluster-based architecture with four processors, i.e., servers. A special server serves as the master. The mas-ter distributes the inserted data over the multiple servers using a horizontal partition-ing technique, and allows the servers to store the data on their own local disks.

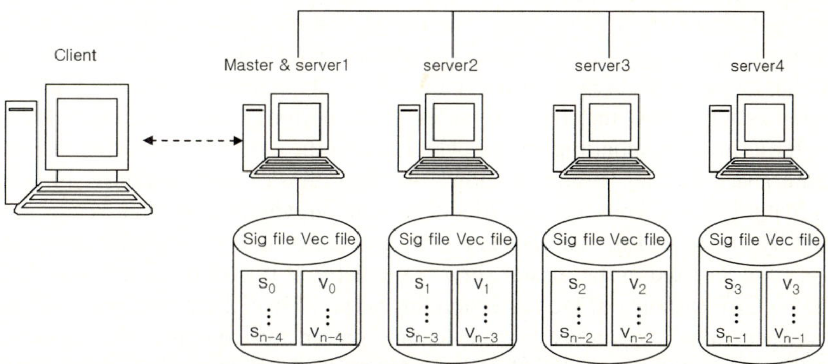

Fig. 2. Overall architecture of our parallel CBF

Mean-while, the master also performs the parallel processing of a query received from a client, by first sending the query to multiple servers and allowing them to process it simultaneously. Then, the master computes the final answer based on the results ob-tained from the servers and transmits the final answer to the client.

3.1 Data Insertion

There are two files in our parallel CBF scheme, i.e. the signature file and the data file. To create the signature file, we first generate a signature from a given feature vector by using a signature generation algorithm. Then, the signature generated is merged with the distance between the feature vector and the center of the cell containing it. Finally, the signature, which has been merged with the distance, is stored in the signature file. To store both the signature and data files in our parallel CBF scheme, it is necessary to distribute them over multiple servers under a SN cluster-based parallel architecture. In order to accomplish the uniform distribution of data over multiple servers, we devise an equation to assign an original n-dimensional vector (Vector$_i$) and its signature (Signature$_i$) into a specific processor by using a horizontal partitioning technique as follows. Here, Pi means a processor to be assigned, Np means the number of processors used for parallelism, and Max_SR means the maximum number of shifting and rotating a signature. The rand-num() function generates a random num-ber ranging from 0 to 1 and makes use of the radius of an n-dimensional vector as its seed. In addition, '>>' means a bit operator to shift and rotate a binary code, and (int)[] means an automatic type conversion from a binary code to an integer.

$$Pi = (int)[Signature_i >> (rand\_num(the\ radius\ of\ Vector_i) * Max\_SR)]\ \%\ Np \qquad (1)$$

Eq.(1) allows for the nearly uniform distribution of a set of vectors in the data file and their signatures over multiple processors (servers) because even some n-dimensional vectors residing on the same cell can be distributed into different processors using the equation. In Figure 2, the master uniformly distributes the inserted data over multiple servers using Eq.(1) and makes the servers to store the data on their own local disks. The master lets the servers operate in parallel, based on both a thread technique and a socket network communication. While a process requires a large amount of data to be stored during context switching, i.e. heavy weighting, a thread requires only light weighting during context switching. The use of multiple threads allows for performing multiple operations in a program simultaneously. When a feature vector is inserted, the master node creates as many threads as the number of servers. Each thread stores the assigned data into its own buffer. If the buffer is full, each thread transmits the buffer to its corresponding server, which stores the associated information into its signature and data files. Figure 3 shows the algorithm of data insertion. Firstly, we read a feature vector from the data file, determine on which server this vector is to be inserted by means of Eq. (1), and then store the vector into the buffer corresponding to this server situated in the master server. Secondly, if the buffer is full, the buffer is sent to the CBF instance of the corresponding server. Finally, the generate_signature() function generates a signature for the feature vector and computes the distance between the vector and the center of cell containing it. Each write_data() function store the signature and the distance in the signature file, and stores the feature vector and its identifier(ID) in the data file.

```
Insertion_MasterNode (Vector data){
  Class server[MAXSERVER];
  Calculate server number Pi to store vector using Eq(1)
  Pi = select_server(MAXSERVER);
  server[Pi].Insertion_ServerNode( data );
}
Insertion_ServerNode (Vector data) {
  signature = generate_signatre( data );
  write_data( signatureFile, signature );
  write_data( vectorFile, data );
}
```

Fig. 3. Data insertion algorithm

3.2 Range Query Search

A range query is expressed as a boundary which has an arbitrary distance from a
given query point and it is processed as a way of searching for all of the objects that
exist within the boundary. For a range query, a user inputs both a query vector and a
dis-tance value. The range query searches for all of the objects included within a circle which is centered on the query vector and whose diameter is equal to the distance
value. We first transform the query vector into a query signature, and then search the
cells within the boundary given by the query signature. To respond to a range query, it
is necessary to access multiple servers simultaneously, since both the signature and
data files are distributed over multiple servers under a SN cluster-based parallel architecture. When a user query is processed, the master node creates as many threads as
there are servers. Each thread sends the query to its own server. Each server searches
its own signature and data files in parallel, thus retrieving the feature vectors that
match the query. By simultaneously searching multiple sets of signature and data
files, our parallel CBF scheme improves the overall retrieval performance. Figure 4
shows the algorithm of range query processing. First, we send the range query to the

```
Range_MasterNode (query) {
  transfer_query_to_server( query );
  list = Range_ServerNode( MAXSERVER );
  return integrate_result( list ); }
Range_ServerNode (qeury) {
  signaturelist = Generate_siglist( signatureFile );
  qsig = generate_signature( query );
  candidatelist = find_sig ( signatureFile, qsig );
  for(;candidatelist!=NULL;) {
    getdata( vectorFile, candidatelist.data );
    if(compute_range( candidatelist.data, query )
     <= query.range ) add_list( resultlist );
    candidatelist = candidatelist->next; }
  transfer_to_master ( resultlist ); }
```

Fig. 4. Range query processing algorithm

CBF instance of each server. Secondly, each CBF instance creates a signature list from its own signature file. Thirdly, we generate a query signature from the query vector and find candidate signatures by searching the signature list. Fourthly, we obtain a result set by retrieving candidate vectors from the data file which corresponds to the candi-date signatures. We also send the result set to the master node. As the last step, we obtain the final result by merging the result sets transmitted from the servers.

3.3 k-Nearest Neighbor (k-NN) Search

The purpose of the k-NN search query is to find the nearest k objects to a query point in data space. The k-NN algorithm of our parallel CBF consists of three filtering phases and an additional phase for integrating the result lists obtained by the three filtering phases. Figure 5 shows the algorithm of k-NN query processing. In the first phase, we first create a thread for each server and send the k-NN query to each thread. Secondly, the CBF instance of each server generates a signature list (sig-buf_list) by searching all of the signatures in its own signature file. Thirdly, we generate the first candidate signature list by inserting signatures sequentially into the candidate list, until the number of signatures to be inserted is k. Once the number of signatures in the candidate list is k, each thread compares the next signature with the k-th candidate signature in the candidate list. If the next signature has a shorter distance from the given query point than the k-th candidate signature, then the k-th candidate signature is deleted from the candidate list and the next signature is inserted into it. Otherwise, we continue to compare the next signature with the k-th

```
KNN_MasterNode (query) {
    transfer_query_to_server( query );   KNN_ServerNode( MAXSERVER );
    list = integrate_result();   return sortlist(list); }
KNN_ServerNode ( query ) {
    sigbuf_list = find_sig ( signatureFile );
    for( i=0; i<query.k ; i++) { // First Phase
        cndlist = add ( sigbuf_list );   cndlist = cndlist->next;
        sigbuf_list = sigbuf_list->next; }
    for(;sigbuf_list!=null;) {
        if(compare_dist(cndlist, sigbuf_list)>0) {
          delete(cndlist);   cndlist = add ( sigbuf_list ); }
        sigbuf_list=sigbuf_list->next; }
    for(;cndlist!=NULL;) { // Second Phase
        if(compare_dist(cndlist.mindist, k_maxdist)>0)   delete(cndlist);
        cndlist=cndlist->next; }
    for(;cndlist!=NULL;) { // Third Phase
        if(compare_dist(cndlist.mindist, k_dist)>0)   delete(cndlist); continue;
        getdata( vectorFile, cndlist.data );
        if(compare_dist( cndlist.data, query ) <= k_dist ) {resultlist = add( cndlist.data );
          delete(cndlist); } }
    transfer_to_master ( resultlist ); }
```

Fig. 5. k-NN query processing algorithm

candidate signature until there are no more signatures to be compared. In the second phase, we reduce unnecessary page accesses by deleting cells whose lower bound is greater than the k-th upper bound (k_maxdist) in the candidate signature list. In the third phase, we obtain a result list by retrieving those real vectors which correspond to the candidate signatures of the candidate list. To accomplish this, we first compare the lower bound of the last candi-date cell with the k-th object distance (k_dist). If k_dist is less than the lower bound of the last candidate cell, the last candidate cell is deleted from the candidate list. Other-wise, we calculate the distances between the query point and the real objects and gen-erate a result list by obtaining the nearest k objects. Next, we transmit the result list to the master node. In the case where the number of servers is N, the number of nearest neighbors obtained from the multiple servers is k*N. Finally, we integrate the result lists obtained from the multiple servers and find the final k nearest objects in the master node.

4 Performance Analysis

For the performance analysis of our parallel CBF scheme, table 1 describes our experimental environment. Here, we make use of 10, 20, 50, and 80-dimensional synthetic data sets, each being obtained by randomly generating 2 million points in data space. At first, we compare our parallel CBF scheme with the conventional CBF scheme in terms of the data insertion time and the search times for both range and k-NN queries. Secondly, we compare our parallel CBF scheme with a parallel version of the VA-File. For this purpose, we implement our parallel CBF scheme under a SN cluster-based architecture with four servers.

Table 1. Experimental environment

System Environment	4 servers (each 450 MHz CPU,HDD 30GB,128 MB Memory) Redhat Linux 7.0 (Kernel 2.4.5), gcc 2.96 (g++)	
Data Set	Synthetic data	2 million data (10,20,40,50,60,80,100-dimensional data)
	Real data	2 million data (10,20,50,80-dimensional data)
Retrieval time	Range query	Retrieval time for searching 0.1% of data
	k-NN query	Retrieval time for searching 100 nearest objects

4.1 Experimental Performance Analysis

To estimate the insertion time, we measure the time needed to insert two millions pieces of synthetic data. Table 2 shows the insertion time for both the existing CBF scheme and our parallel CBF scheme. In the CBF scheme, it takes about 240, 480 and 1860 seconds to insert 10-, 20- and 100-dimensional data, respectively. In our parallel CBF scheme, the same operations take about 250, 450 and 1930 seconds, respectively. It can be seen that our parallel CBF scheme is nearly the same as the existing CBF scheme. This is because our parallel CBF can reduce the time required to insert data by using multiple servers, but it requires additional time due to the communication overhead.

Table 2. Insertion time (unit:sec)

Scheme \ Dimension	10	20	40	50	60	80	100
Existing CBF	236.50	478.89	828.49	992.78	1170.40	1505.90	1862.16
Our parallel CBF	256.12	445.42	824.02	1001.93	1188.42	1543.62	1930.10

As a range query, we use a radius value designed to retrieve 0.1% of the data from the two million synthetic data. Table 3 shows the retrieval time for the range query. The performance improvement metric of our parallel CBF scheme against the existing CBF scheme can be calculated by 1/(PT/CT)*100, where PT and CT refer to their performance measurements (retrieval times) of our parallel CBF scheme and that of the existing CBF scheme, respectively. In the existing CBF scheme, it takes about 13, 16, 38 and 60 seconds to respond to a range query in the case of 10-, 20-, 50- and 80-dimensional data, respectively. In our parallel CBF scheme, it takes about 1.6, 2.2, 7.3 and 11.6 seconds for the same operations, respectively. When the number of dimensions is 80, the performance improvement metric of our parallel CBF scheme is about 520%, being greater than the ideal performance improvement metric, i.e. 400%. This is because our parallel CBF scheme utilizes a large buffer under the SN cluster-based architecture with four servers.

Table 3. Retrieval time for range query

Scheme \ Dimension	10	20	40	50	60	80	100
Existing CBF	13.20	16.42	31.91	37.93	44.96	59.50	74.27
Our parallel CBF	1.59	2.24	5.92	7.27	7.87	11.60	14.04
Improvement	830	733	539	522	571	513	529

For the k-nearest neighbors (k-NN) query, we measure the time needed to respond to a k-NN query for which k is 100. Table 4 describes the retrieval time for the k-NN query using two million synthetic data. In the case of 10-dimensional data, it takes about 3.6 seconds to retrieve the data for the CBF scheme and 1.4 seconds for our parallel CBF scheme. This is because in our parallel CBF scheme, we retrieve objects simultaneously from four servers under the SN cluster-based parallel architecture. In the case of 100-dimensional data, the CBF scheme requires about 76.4 seconds to respond to a k-NN query, while our parallel CBF scheme requires about 25.6 seconds. Thus, it is shown that the performance improvement metric of our parallel CBF scheme is about 300-400%, depending on the dimension of the data. The performance improvement for a k-NN query is relatively low, compared with that for a range query. This is because the overall retrieval performance for a k-NN query is very sensitive to the distribution of the data. That is, it entirely depends on the lowest re-trieval per-formance among the four servers.

Table 4. Retrieval time for k-NN query

Scheme \ Dimension	10	20	40	50	60	80	100
Existing CBF	3.59	17.80	31.92	39.28	46.72	61.60	76.39
Our parallel CBF	1.44	2.62	8.28	10.78	11.02	18.97	25.62
Improvement	249	679	386	364	424	325	298

4.2 Comparison with Parallel VA-File

To verify the usefulness of our parallel CBF scheme as a high dimensional indexing
scheme, we compare our parallel CBF with the parallel version of VA-file. Table 5
describes the retrieval time for a range query using two million pieces of real data. In
the case of the parallel VA-file, it takes about 2.3 seconds to respond to a range query
containing 20-dimensional data and about 13 seconds for 80-dimensional data. In the
case of our parallel CBF scheme, it takes about 1.8 seconds for 20-dimensional data
and 10 seconds for 80-dimensional data. As dimensionality is higher, our parallel
CBF scheme achieves better retrieval performance than the parallel VA-file. This is
be-cause our parallel CBF scheme performs good filtering by redefining the maximum and minimum distances as the dimensionality is increased.

Table 5. Retrieval time for range query using real data

Scheme \ Dimension	10	20	50	80
Parallel VA-File	1.71	2.27	4.37	12.96
Our parallel CBF	1.49	1.82	2.75	10.08

Table 6 shows the retrieval time for a k-NN query. In the case of the parallel VA-
file, it takes about 1.8 seconds to respond to a range query containing 20-dimensional
data and about 11 seconds for 80-dimensional data. In the case of our parallel CBF
scheme, it takes about 1.8 seconds for 20-dimensional data and 10.5 seconds for 80-
dimensional data. Thus, the performance of our parallel CBF scheme is slightly better
than that of the parallel VA-file in case dimensionality is high.

Table 6. Retrieval time for k-NN query using real data

Scheme \ Dimension	10	20	50	80
Parallel VA-File	1.51	1.82	7.17	11.32
Our parallel CBF	1.60	1.77	6.06	10.44

5 Conclusions and Future Work

Most of the conventional indexing schemes work well at low dimensionality, but perform poorly as the dimensionality of feature vectors increases. The CBF scheme was

proposed to overcome the inefficiency of the conventional indexing schemes at high dimensionality. As the dimensionality is increased, the retrieval performance of the CBF scheme decreases linearly. To cope with this problem, we proposed our parallel CBF scheme for multimedia data, which could uniformly distribute both signatures and feature vectors over multiple servers using a horizontal partitioning method under the SN cluster-based parallel architecture. We showed from the performance analysis that our parallel CBF scheme provided a near linear improvement in proportion to the number of servers, for both the range and k-NN queries. We also showed that our parallel CBF scheme outperformed the parallel VA-file when the number of dimensions is greater than 10. In the future work, our parallel CBF scheme is needed to be used as a high dimensional indexing scheme in real multimedia databases.

References

1. Robinson, J.T.: The K-D-B-tree : A Search Structure for Large Multidimensional Dynamic Indexes, Proc. of Int. Conf. on Management of Data (1981) 10-18
2. White, D.A. and Jain, R.: Similarity Indexing : Algorithms and Performance, Proc. of the SPIE : Storage and Retrieval for Image and Video Databases IV, Vol. 2670 (1996) 62-75
3. Lin, H.I., Jagadish, H. and Faloutsos, C.: The TV-tree : An Index Structure for High Di-men-sional Data, VLDB Journal, Vol. 3 (1995) 517-542
4. Berchtold, S. , Keim, D. A. and Kriegel, H-P.: The X-tree : An Index Structure for High-Dimensional Data, Proceedings of the 22nd VLDB Conference (1996) 28-39
5. Arya, S., Mount, D.M. and Narayan, O.: Accounting for Boundary Effects in Nearest Neighbor Searching, Proc. of 11th Annaual Symp. on Computational Geometry, Vancouver, Canada (1995) 336-344
6. Berchtold S., Bohm C., Keim D. and Kriegel H. -P: A Cost Model for Nearest Neighbor Search in High-Dimensional Data Space, ACM PODS Symposium on Principles of Data-bases Systems, Tucson, Arizona (1997)
7. Roger Weber, Hans-Jorg Schek and Stephen Blott: A Quantitative Analysis and Perform-ance Study for Similarity-Search Methods in High-Dimensional Spaces, Proc. of 24rd International Conference on Very Large Data Bases (1998) 24-27
8. Han, S.-G. and Chang, J.-W.: A New High-Dimensional Index Structure Using a Cell-based Filtering Technique, In Lecture Notes in Computer Science 1884(Current Issues in Data-bases and Information Systems), Springer (2000) 79-92
9. Faloutsos, C.: Design of a Signature File Method that Accounts for Non-Uniform Occurrence and Query Frequencies, ACM SIGMOD (1985) 165-170
10. Kim, J.-K. and Chang, J.-W.: Horizontally-divided Signature File on a Parallel Machine Architecture, Journal of Systems Architecture, Vol. 44, No. 9-10 (1998) 723-735
11. Kim, J.-K. and Chang, J.-W.: Vertically-partitioned Parallel Signature File Method, Journal of Systems Architecture, Vol. 46, No. 8 (2000) 655-673
12. Roussopoulos, N., Kelley, S. and F. Vincent: Nearest Neighbor Queries, Proc. of ACM Int. Conf. on Management of Data(SIGMOD) (1995) 71-79

Throughput Aware Mapping for Network on Chip Design of H.264 Decoder

Vu-Duc Ngo, Huy-Nam Nguyen[1], Younghwan Bae[2],
Hanjin Cho[2], and Hae-Wook Choi[1]

[1] System VLSI Lab, SITI Research Center, School of Engineering
Information and Communications University (ICU)
Yusong P.O. Box 77, Taejon 305-714, Korea
[2] Basic Research Laboratory, ETRI, Daejeon, Korea
{duc75, huynam, hwchoi}@icu.ac.kr, {yhbae, hjcho}@etri.re.kr

Abstract. Network-on-Chip (NoC) has been proposed as a new methodology for addressing the design challenges of future massly integrated system in nanoscale. In this paper, we present the queuing theory based model for router to evaluate the performance of NoC in terms of drop probability, throughput and energy consumption. Then we apply the linear programming to optimize the allocation of the heterogeneously functional blocks (IPs) onto the given heterogeneous NoC architecture so as to obtain the maximum throughput as well as to optimize the energy dissipation of whole system. Finally, the three differently heterogenous Tree-based network topologies are proposed as the NoC architectures for the study case of H.264 Decoder. This paper also evaluates the proposed topologies by comparing them to other conventional topologies such as 2-D Mesh and Fat-Tree with respects to throughput, power consumption and size. We use the power modelling tool, known as Orion model to calculate the static powers, areas, and dynamic powers of three topologies. The experiment results show that our Tree-based topologies offer similar throughputs as Fat-Tree does and much higher throughputs compared to 2-D Mesh while use less chip areas and energy consumptions.

1 Introduction

According to [1], the Ultra Large Scale Integration (ULSI) will be the future of chip design. The idea of using NoC as the new design methodology to massly integrate the IPs such as processors, DSPs, as well as memory array was proposed in [2,3]. The packet switching core and the communication protocols are used to replace the complex system of wires or the main factors that lead to the propagation delay exceeding the system's clock period and non-scalable global wire. However, the NoC design methodology poses complex design challenges to meet the requirement of throughput, area, reliability, and power consumption.

The tile-based NoC with various applications and regular topologies such as 2D Mesh, Fat-Tree, and Torus were proposed in [4, 5, 14]. The authors in [6, 7, 8] had different approaches for the NoC design. They proposed the algorithms

G. Min et al. (Eds.): ISPA 2006 Ws, LNCS 4331, pp. 791–802, 2006.

to automatically map IPs onto the target NoC architecture so as to optimize the power consumption. To do that, the authors used the same homogeneous bit energy model for their calculation of power consumption of whole network. The first thing should be mentioned here is that the authors assumed the bit energy consumptions are same for all the routers inside the network. According to our knowledge, the NoC architectures are heterogeneous in terms of router's structure and mounted IPs. Hence, the bit energy consumptions on different routers are obviously different. The second thing is that the accumulated energy on a certain route was calculated without the consideration of actual drop rate of the transactional flits. The drop flits which pass through a lot of intermediate router especially induce a significant amount of energy consumption. This leads to the optimization results might not be precise.

To estimate the power and side of interconnection network, Wang et al. [9] proposed a power-model simulator called Orion. This simulator can be used to estimate the dynamic power of one information bit due to the switched capacitances. It also can be used to estimate the router area and static power with different CMOS technologies.

Recently, the H.264 decoder was designed and evaluated based on 2-D Mesh and Fat-Tree topologies [10]. Authors reported the system-level performance evaluations of two architectures. The optimal mappings that maximize the system throughput were presented as well. According to the authors, with different routing and queuing protocols, the Fat-Tree topologies offers better performance. In fact, because of its irregularity and intensive interconnection wires, the Fat-Tree topology becomes impractical to be implemented on a chip. Moreover, design of NoC for particular application copes with several challenges [11], one of the critical issues is to choose the best suited architecture.

In this paper, we introduce the queuing based calculation for the network throughput of NoC architecture. We also solve the optimization problem of mapping IPs onto the NoC architecture so as to minimize the drop flits at the intermediate router. This minimization of drop flits can not only save the significant energy consumption of unreachable flits but also reduce the energy that needed if we implement the fault recovery mechanism which was strongly suggested by Nurmi [15] for future NoC design. Based on this optimization technique, we propose three heterogeneously optimal Tree-based architectures for the H.264 decoder design and then compare them to 2-D Mesh and Fat-Tree architecture. In Fig. 1 the H.264 decoder's IPs with their pair-to-pair data transactions are presented in Kbps. We simulate the system throughputs of five architectures. Then by using these simulated throughputs and Orion model of differently utilized routers, the system dynamic energy consumptions of five architectures can be exactly calculated. The designs of three architectures also are evaluated and compared with each others and the two mentioned conventional architectures in terms of area and dissipated energy. Our results indicate that the proposed topologies are superior in terms of hardware consumption and energy consumption while offer similar system performance. The rest of this article is organized as follows: Throughput optimization and Power estimation are discussed in

From/To	DB	MC	FR_MEM	ITIQ	LENT	VOM	Proc.	REC	MVMVD	IPRED	IS	DMA
DB	0.0	0.0	0	0.0	0.0	0.0	0.0	0.0	0.0	0.0	0.0	7,098.7
MC	4,465.1	0.0	0	0.0	0.0	0.0	0.0	0.0	0.0	0.0	0.0	344.5
FR_MEM	0	0	0.0	0.0	62.7	4,791.9	0.0	0	0.0	0.0	0.0	13,197.0
ITIQ	0.0	5,936.1	0.0	0.0	0.0	0.0	0.0	641.0	0.0	0.0	0.0	0.0
LENT	0.0	0.0	0.0	6,577.1	0.0	0.0	406.6	0.0	494.7	0.0	0.0	0.0
Proc.	324.9	321.4	0.0	186.0	232.0	11.6	0.0	6.9	990.2	59.2	11.6	0.0
REC	320.5	13.5	0	0.0	0.0	0.0	0.0	0.0	0.0	145.0	0.0	26.7
MVMVD	0.0	0.0	0.0	0.0	0.0	0.0	826.3	0.0	0.0	0.0	0.0	0.0
IPRED	0.0	0.0	0.0	0.0	0.0	0.0	0.0	320.5	0.0	0.0	0.0	0.0
IS	0.0	0.0	62.7	0.0	0.0	0.0	0.0	0.0	0.0	0.0	0.0	0.0
DMA	2,644.3	10,628.0	7470.4	0	0	0	0	39.6	0	0	0	0.0
VOM	0.0	0.0	0.0	0.0	0.0	0.0	0.0	0.0	0.0	0.0	0.0	0.0

Fig. 1. Data transaction between modules of H.264 decoder

Section 2. Proposed topologies construction is presented in Section 3. Simulation model and analysis are introduced in Section 4. Finally, we conclude our contribution and mention about our future work in Section 5.

2 Throughput Optimization and Power Estimation

This section, we firstly introduce the queuing based model of wormhole router then derive the network throughput with respect to the drop rate of data flit. Secondly, we maximize the network throughput by searching the optimal mapping of IPs onto the given architecture. Finally, the Orion power models of router are applied to calculate the network energy consumption and areas of the optimal topology.

2.1 Throughput Optimization

The wormhole router includes p input ports and p output ports. One or some of them can be used for the interconnections with the neighboring routers, the remaining ports are used for the interconnection with the IPs. The wormhole handles the dataflow on a flit level where flit is the smallest flow controlled data unit. The average processing time of the jth router is defined by $x_j = \frac{1}{\mu_j}$. We define the the arrival rates of the independent data flows that enter the ith input port of the jth router as $\lambda_{i1}^j, \lambda_{i2}^j, ..., \lambda_{i\varsigma_i}^j$, where ς_i denotes the number of data flows. The data flows can be generated from the certain IPs or the neighbor routers. To simplify the problem, we assume that all the buffers of the routers have the equal size of k flits. Then if we only consider this input port and the crossbar switch, the probability that m flits exist in the system is

$$p_m = p_0 \prod_{n=0}^{m-1} \frac{\sum_{l=1}^{\varsigma_i} \lambda_{il}^j}{\mu_j} = p_0 \left(\frac{\sum_{l=1}^{\varsigma_i} \lambda_{il}^j}{\mu_j} \right)^m , p_0 = 1 - \frac{\sum_{l=1}^{\varsigma_i} \lambda_{il}^j}{\mu_j}. \tag{1}$$

Since the jth router has p_j inout ports and size of buffers are k, the blocking probability is calculated as follows.

$$P_{block}^j = \left(\frac{\sum_{l=1}^{\varsigma_i} \lambda_{il}^j}{\mu_j} \right)^{(k+1)} \frac{1}{p_j{}^2}. \tag{2}$$

Therefore, the throughput contributed by the ith input port is presented by

$$\tau_i = \left(1 - \left(\frac{\sum_{l=1}^{\varsigma_i} \lambda_{il}^j}{\mu_j}\right)^{(k+1)} \frac{1}{p_j{}^2}\right) \sum_{l=1}^{\varsigma_i} \lambda_{il}^j. \tag{3}$$

Finally, the throughput contributed by all p_j ports or the throughput that outcomes the jth router is

$$\mathcal{T}^j = \sum_{i=1}^{p_j} \tau_i = \sum_{i=1}^{p_j} \left[\left(1 - \left(\frac{\sum_{l=1}^{\varsigma_i} \lambda_{il}^j}{\mu_j}\right)^{(k+1)} \frac{1}{p_j{}^2}\right) \sum_{l=1}^{\varsigma_i} \lambda_{il}^j\right]. \tag{4}$$

Assume that the number of routers in the architecture is N, then the network throughput consequently calculated as

$$\mathcal{T}_\mathcal{N} = \sum_{j=1}^{N} \mathcal{T}^j = \sum_{j=1}^{N} \left(\sum_{i=1}^{p_j} \left[(1 - \rho_i^{(k+1)} \frac{1}{p_j{}^2}) \sum_{l=1}^{\varsigma_i} \lambda_{il}^j\right]\right), \rho_i = \left(\frac{\sum_{l=1}^{\varsigma_i} \lambda_{il}^j}{\mu_j}\right) \tag{5}$$

We can realize that the throughput of network is the function of mapping scheme of IPs onto a given architecture. With the given architecture we have fixed routers or have the values of μ_j unchanged despite of the change of allocation scheme of the IPs onto the routers. Therefore, the value of network throughput depends very much on the applied mapping scheme of the IPs onto the architecture. This leads to the optimization problem of maximizing the network throughput with given set of IPs and fixed routers. We can solve this problem by a welknown linear programming algorithm so called Branch and Bound [12]. Simply described, for certain application, we identify that onto which switch should an IP be mapped so that the of network throughput is maximized under the assumption of the shortest routing algorithm is applied. To do so, we have some definitions as follows:

Definition 1. An IPs Implementation Graph (IIG) $\mathcal{G} = G(V, \lambda)$ is a directed graph where

- Each vertex v_i represents a certain IP.
- Each directed arc λ_{ij} represents the arrival rate of the data packets generated from the ith IP toward j^{th} IP.

Definition 2. An Switching Architecture Graph (SAG) $\mathcal{G}' = G(U, R)$ is a directed graph where

- Each vertex u_i presents a certain switch core, the corresponding $1/\mu_j$ denotes its switch's mean value of processing time.
- Each directed arc r_{ij} represents the route from u_i to u_j in the routing table.

Now we can state our mapping problem as follows:

Given an IIG and a SAG graphs that satisfy $Size(IIG) \leq Size(SAG)$ and after mapping, the arc $\mathcal{T}^j$ denotes the throughput outcoming from j^{th} router calculated in (4). The $Size()$ function presents the number of vertexes on the graph.The shortest path routing is applied in this context and the cost function of found path is the accumulated throughput after every hop.

Find a mapping scheme $map()$ from IIG onto SAG which:

$$\mathcal{T_N}^{Opt} = max\left(\sum_{j=1}^{N} \mathcal{T}^j\right) = max\left(\sum_{j=1}^{N}\left(\sum_{i=1}^{p_j}[(1-\rho_i^{(k+1)}\frac{1}{p_j{}^2})\sum_{l=1}^{\varsigma_i}\lambda_{il}^j]\right)\right) \quad (6)$$

such that:

$$map(v_i) = u_j; \forall v_i \in V, \exists u_j \in U, \forall v_i \neq v_j; map(v_i) \neq map(v_j). \quad (7)$$

Without loosing generality, we assume that $Size(IIG) = p \leq Size(SAG) = q$. Since the number of ways of choosing p switches among q switches of the target NoC architecture for p IPs is C_q^p, and also we can have $p!$ permutational cases of p given IPs. It follows that if we apply the simple Min-Max algorithm to find out the minimum network latency accordingly with the optimum mapping scheme, the complexity can be measured by $Complexity = O(p! \times C_q^p)$ This order of complexity returns the NP-hard search. Therefore, as mentioned above, we apply Branch and Bound technique not only to obtain the optimal mapping but also reduce significantly the complexity of the searching issue.

2.2   Power Estimation

The data packet is divided to a number of flits where the head flit carrying the destination address and the tail flit are important for traversing whole packet through the router. For instant, when the source injects the head flit into input port i and this flit contains the destination address of output port j, firstly the buffer i writes the flit into the tail of it. Secondly, after the request of destination port is read and granted by the arbiter, the arbiter sends the signal to the crossbar switch to emit the data to the output port j by reading flits out of the buffer i. Hence, the energy dissipation of the flit on this router is given by

$$E_{flit} = E_{arb} + E_{xbar} + E_{bufrd} + E_{bufwrt}, \quad (8)$$

where E_{arb} is the arbitration energy, E_{xbar} is the crossbar switch energy, E_{bufrd} and E_{bufwrt} are the read and write to/from buffer energies, respectively. Since the dynamic power of CMOS circuit is calculated as

$$P = E \times f_{clk}, \quad (9)$$

where f_{clk} is the operational frequency of a given router. To calculate this power dissipation we apply Orion model presented in [9]. In this paper, as we mentioned above, the considered topologies are heterogenous in terms of configuration and operational frequency. The operational frequency of each router is decided by the highest data transaction IPs mounted onto it. Without loosing generality, the power dissipation of a particular flit is given by

$$P_{flit}^i = \sum_{R_i} f_{clk}^j \left(E_{arb}^j + E_{xbar}^j + E_{bufrd}^j + E_{bufwrt}^j \right) \times \delta_{ij} \qquad (10)$$

where R_i is the known route that the ith flit goes through, and

$$\delta_{ij} = \begin{cases} 1, & if j^{th} router \in R_i, \\ 0, & otherwise. \end{cases} \qquad (11)$$

Finally, based on the simulated network throughput and the routing table, the power dissipation of the network with respect to routers is presented as

$$P_{Net} = \sum_{\forall i} P_{flit}^i. \qquad (12)$$

In this paper, the wire energy dissipation, $E_{wire} = \frac{\alpha}{2} C_{wire} V_{dd}^2$, is calculated by using the wire model worked out [13]. The C_{wire} denotes the wire capacitance of the interconnection.

3   Proposed Topologies

At first, we briefly discuss about two conventional architectures known as Fat-Tree and 2D Mesh.

The **SPIN** architecture has been proposed by Guerrier and Greiner [4]. It uses Fat-Tree architecture to interconnect IP blocks. In this Fat-Tree, every node has four nodes as its children nodes and this rule is replicated four times at every level of the tree. Let assume N is the number of IPs in the architecture, the size of the network grows as $(N log N)/8$ and the number of switches is $3N/4$. The switches, except for the root switches, are modelled by 4×4 wormhole router. The number of routers depends on the depth of the tree.

The **CLICHE** architecture was proposed by Kumar et al. [5]. This architecture consists of an $m \times n$ 2-D mesh of switches that interconnects $m \times n$ IPs allocated along with the switches. Each switch connects with its for neighboring switches and one IP. Hence, a switch can be modelled by 5×5 wormhole router. The number of routers is also $m \times n$.

In [10], the authors pointed out that even with the optimal design the 2-D Mesh still offers lower performance in comparison with the Fat-Tree architecture. In that paper, the H.264 decoder was designed with the 4×4 Mesh and the Fat-Tree of 16 IPs size. As shown in Fig.1, the number of IPs of H.264 decoder is 12. Hence, there are several unused switches for both architectures. In other words, if we design this particular application on the generic architectures such as 2-D Mesh and Fat-Tree, we have to pay a big penalty on unused hardware. Due to the redundancy of unused switches in designing the H.264 decoder of two mentioned architectures, in this paper, we propose three Tree-based architectures for each application in which the optimal allocation schemes of IPs are implemented. These topologies probably are the best suited architectures for the H.264 decoder.

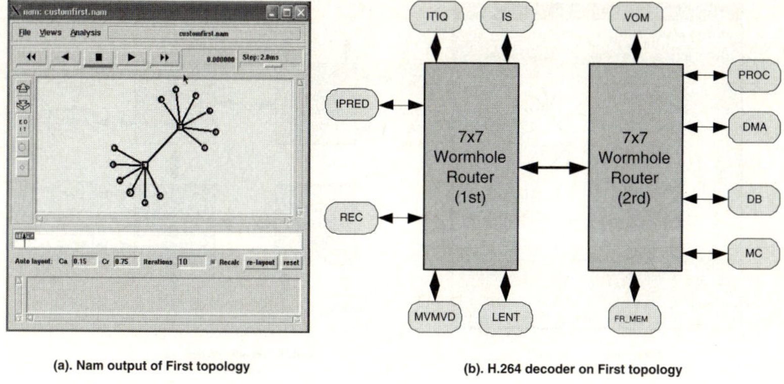

(a). Nam output of First topology   (b). H.264 decoder on First topology

Fig. 2. H.264 decoder on the first topology

3.1   Tree-Based Topologies for H.264 Decoder

In this subsection, we propose 3 tree-based topologies then apply the optimization technique to finally obtain the optimal designs of the H.264 decoder on each topology.

First topology: As shown in Fig. 2, the 12 functional blocks (IPs) of the decoder are mounted on two 7×7 wormhole routers. Each router is used to interconnect six IPs. For this architecture as well as the remaining two architectures, we use optimized technique presented in section 2 to achieve the optimal mapping. This work is done by knowing the required data transactions between IPs, the routing table and the calculation of number of drop flits at all routers. In this article, we also apply the shortest path routing algorithm for the simplicity and practice. This optimal mapping makes the network satisfy the condition of obtaining the highest network throughput. As the optimal mapping shown in Fig. 2, the MC, DMA, ITIQ, DB and FR_MEM are interconnected with the same router. These IPs, as depicted in Fig. 1, are the functional blocks that have the highest data transactions from one to the others.

Second topology: Fig. 3 shows that 12 IPs of the H.264 decoder are optimally mounted on three 5×5 and one 3×3 wormhole routers. The highest data transaction IPs such as MC, DMA, FR_MEM, DB and ITIQ are mounted on two neighboring routers to obtain highest network throughput as well as smallest power dissipation.

Third topology: This topology looks most likely Tree topology. As shown in Fig. 4, there are totally six routers including four 4×4 and two 3×3 wormhole routers. In this topology, the similar technique as applied in above two topologies is used. Hence, the optimal mapping of IPs onto NoC topology can be seen as Fig. 5b. We can easily realize that the IPs such as MC, DMA, FR_MEM, DB and ITIQ are mounted on three neighboring routers so as to obtain highest network

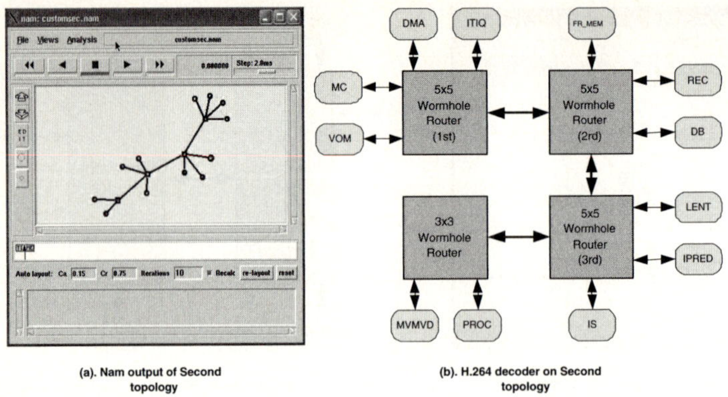

(a). Nam output of Second topology

(b). H.264 decoder on Second topology

Fig. 3. H.264 decoder on the second topology

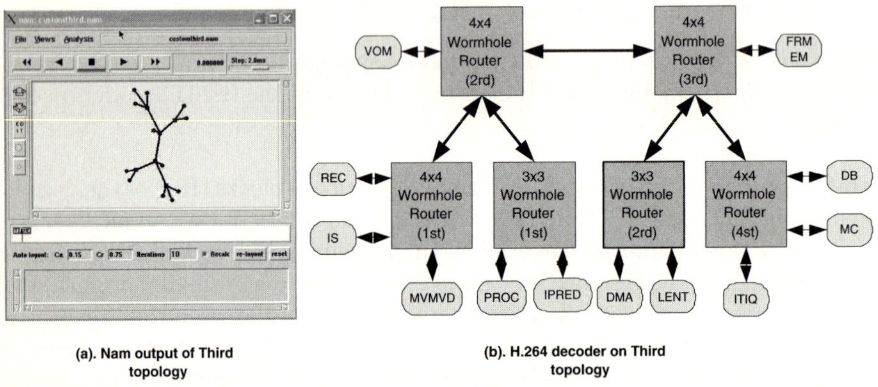

(a). Nam output of Third topology

(b). H.264 decoder on Third topology

Fig. 4. H.264 decoder on the third topology

throughput as well as smallest power dissipation.Now we apply the Orion model for the above three topologies. More particular, we use $0.1\mu m$ technology and supplied voltage of $1.2V$ for the repeated wire model. To calculate the powers for our architectures, we use Orion power model for each individual router in each architecture. We apply $0.1\mu m$ technology, supply voltage of $1.2V$ and flit size of 128 bits for all routers. The operational frequency of each router depends on the IP which has the highest data transaction. Additionally, after calculate the power consumption we can also obtain the router's area of each architecture. Table. 1 presents the power consumption, dynamic bit energy and corresponding used area of two 7×7 wormhole routers of the **first topology**. Table. 2 presents the power consumption, dynamic bit energy and corresponding used area of four wormhole routers of the **second topology**. The power consumption, dynamic bit energy and corresponding used area of six wormhole routers of the **third topology** are presented in Table. 3.

Table 1. H.264: Power, bit energy and area of Routers in First Topology

	First 7×7 Router	Second 7×7 Router
Area (μm^2)	1.19e6	1.19e6
Flit power (W)	0.108289	0.113341
Bit energy (J)	1.76e-10	4.2e-11

Table 2. H.264: Power, bit energy and area of Routers in Second Topology

	1st 5×5 Router	2rd 5×5 Router	3rd 5×5 Router	3×3 Router
Area (μm^2)	993280	993280	993280	374784
Flit power (W)	0.073398	0.0706848	0.070132	0.038102
Bit energy (J)	2.7e-11	1.15e-10	3.65e-10	1.46e-9

Table 3. H.264: Power, bit energy and area of Routers in Third Topology

	1st 4×4 Router	2rd 4×4 Router	3rd 4×4 Router	4th 4×4 Router
Area (μm^2)	647168	647168	647168	647168
Flit power (W)	0.053456	0.053882	0.0542187	0.0556976
Bit energy (J)	2.78e-10	8.775e-11	5.4e-11	2.06e-11

	1st 3×3 Router	2rd 3×3 Router
Area (μm^2)	374784	374784
Flit power (W)	0.0385485	0.0381902
Bit energy (J)	4.43e-11	2.0e-10

4   Simulation and Analysis

In this article, we simulate the designs of H.264 decoder on five architectures including three proposed Tree-based topologies, 2-D Mesh and Fat-Tree. The simulations are done based on the data transaction between IPs depicted in Fig. 1. The transmission protocol is defined as UDP. The exponential traffic generator model is applied. The routing strategy is shortest path. To tolerate with the Orion model, we set the packet size of 64 bytes or four flits of 128 bits. The buffer scheme of DropTail is utilized. As the simulation shows in Fig. 5, our three newly Tree-based architectures offer similar system throughputs in comparison with Fat-Tree and 10Mbps higher than 4×4 Mesh. Among three new architecture, the **first topology** is the best one in terms of system throughput.

Based on the area calculation in previous section, the total router sizes of five architectures are sketched in Fig. 6a. As shown in Fig. 6a, the Fat-Tree topology utilizes biggest chip area, size of $19.8mm^2$ with the $0.10\mu m$ CMOS technology. The second biggest one is 4×4 Mesh, size of $15.9mm^2$. While the biggest one

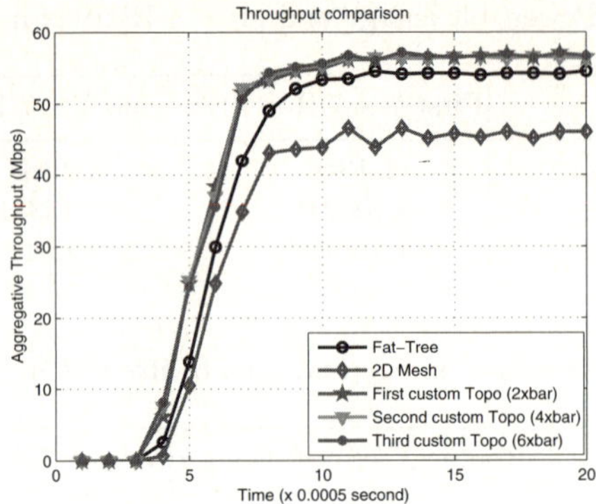

Fig. 5. Throughput comparison of 5 topologies

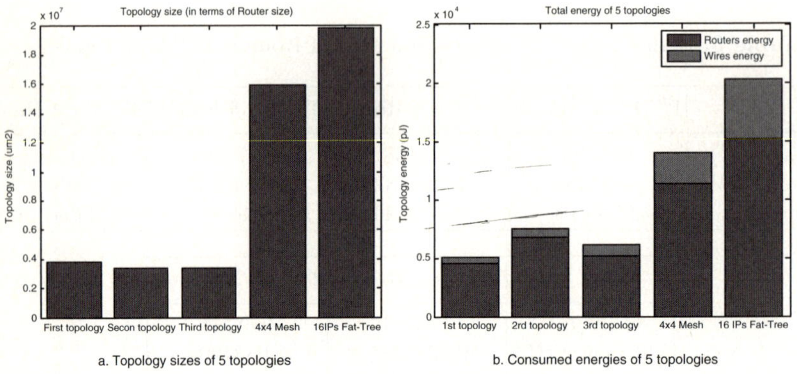

a. Topology sizes of 5 topologies

b. Consumed energies of 5 topologies

Fig. 6. Sizes and Energies of five Topologies

among our three proposed topologies is the **first topology**, size of $3.81mm^2$. This figure also depicts that the router area of three proposed architectures are almost similar. Hence, the **first topology** probably has the smallest chip size due to it's most simplicity in wire interconnection. From Fig. 5 and Fig. 6a, we can conclude that our three proposed topologies offer similar even higher system throughput than Fat-Tree and 2-D mesh but have significantly smaller sizes.

The simulated energy consumptions of five topologies are obtained basically on equations (10, 11, 12). Since we have the system throughput simulation results of five topologies. We also know the in detail about the route of every individual flit. This means that we can point out which routers and wires the given flit goes through. Using the bit energy calculated in Table. 1, Table. 2 and Table. 3, finally we can have the simulated energy consumptions of our proposed topologies as depicted in Fig. 6b. As shown in Fig. 6b, it is interesting that the **first topology** consumes smallest energy compared to two other proposed ones. Due to the complicated flows of flits and big number of switches of Fat-Tree and 2-D Mesh, it is obvious that if we use similar parameters for

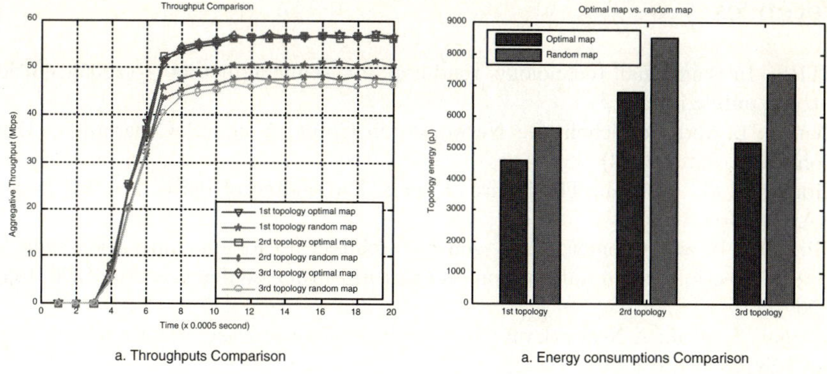

Fig. 7. Throughputs and Energy comparison

simulation, the energy dissipations on these two architectures are much bigger than our three proposed architectures. Finally, we can indicate that the **first topology** consumes less power while offers higher system throughput compared to the remaining two proposed topologies. To show the overperformance of the optimal mappings of our proposed topologies, we also carry out the experiments of three cases of random mappings. The random mappings of our 3 topologies are set up by randomly interchanging IPs in different routers. The throughputs of these three cases are depicted and compared with three cases of optimal mappings in Fig. 7a. The corresponding consumed energies of random and optimal mappings of three architectures are shown in Fig. 7b. It is interesting that the random mappings not only offer less throughputs but consume more power. The main reason for this contradiction is that the random mapping cases create more complicated routes and dropped flits. The more complicated route is, the more energy is consumed. Moreover, the total energy dissipation is calculated by accumulating the flit energy until it reaches the destination or drops out of the network.

5   Conclusion

In this paper, we designed the H.264 decoder with three differently Tree-based architectures. These architectures were designed to not only obtain the highest system-level performance but also reduce the hardware consumption and the intensive interconnections. We also evaluated these architectures in terms of throughput, dynamic and static power consumptions. Then, we compared our proposed architectures to 2-D Mesh and Fat-Tree architectures. The results showed that the newly proposed architectures used less hardware and consumed less power while offered similar throughputs as the Fat-Tree did. The results also showed that our architectures overperformed the 2-D Mesh in three aspects of hardware complexity, power consumption and system performance.

References

1. ITRS. International technology roadmap for semiconductors - (2005) edition, http://public.itrs.net/
2. Benini, L. and DeMicheli, G.: Networks On Chips: A new SoC paradigm. IEEE computer, Jan, (2002)
3. Horowitz, M. A. et al.: The future of wires. Proceeding of IEEE, Vol. 89, Issue. 4 , Apr (2001) 490-504
4. Guerrier, P. and Grenier, A.: A generic architecture for on-chip packet-switched interconnectio. Design automation and test in Europe conference, Aug (2000) 250-256
5. Kumar, S. et al.: A Network on Chip Architecture and Design Methodology. Proc. Int'l Symp. VLSI (2002) 117-124
6. Hu, J. et al.: Exploiting the Routing Flexibility for Energy Performance Aware Mapping of Regular NoC Architectures. in Proc. Design, Automation and Test in Europe Conf, March (2003)
7. Hu, J. et al.: Energy-Aware Communication and Task Scheduling for Network-on-Chip Architectures under Real-Time Constraints. in Proc. Design Automation and Test in Europe Conf, Feb. (2004)
8. Murali, S. et al.: Bandwidth-Constrained Mapping of Cores onto NoC Architectures. DATE, International Conference on Design and Test Europe, (2004) 896-901
9. Hwang, H. S. et al.: Orion: A Power Performance Simulator for Interconnection Networks. IEEE Micro, Nov (2002)
10. Vu-Duc Ngo et al.: Analyzing the Performance of Mesh and Fat-Tree Topologies for Network on Chip Design. In EUC 2005, Lecture Notes in Computer Science Vol. 3824. Springer-Verlag (2005) 300310
11. Dally, W. J. and Towles, B.: Route Packets, Not Wires: On Chip Interconnection Networks. DAC. (2001) 684-689
12. Cormen, T. H. et al.: Introduction to algorithms. Second Edition, The MIT press, (2001)
13. Ho, R. et al.: The future of wires. Proceedings of the IEEE Vol. 89, Issue 4, April (2001) 490 - 504
14. Dally, W. J. and Towles, B.: Route Packets, Not Wires: On-Chip Interconnection Networks. In Proceedings of the 38th DAC, June (2001)
15. Nurmi, J.: Network-on-Chip: A New Paradigm for System-on-Chip Design. Proceedings of International Symposium on System-on-Chip, Nov. (2005)

A Delivery Method for Compound Video Playback in Wireless Network

Kazuya Uyama[1], Morihiko Tamai[1], Yoshihiro Murata[1], Naoki Shibata[2], Keiichi Yasumoto[1], and Minoru Ito[1]

[1] Graduate School of Information Science, Nara Institute of Science and Technology
8916-5, Takayama, Ikoma, Nara 630-0192, Japan
{kazuya-u, morihi-t, yosihi-m, yasumoto, ito}@is.naist.jp
[2] Department of Information Processing and Management, Shiga University
Hikone, Shiga 522-8522, Japan
shibata@biwako.shiga-u.ac.jp

Abstract. In this paper, we propose a method to realize compound video (multiple videos on a layout)delivery service for mobile terminals. In the proposed method, we introduce proxies which receive multiple videos from corresponding servers and produce a composite video from the received videos in real-time according to the layouts which users specify. However, if users require sets of videos with slightly different layouts, multiple similar composite videos will be generated and the wireless bandwidth will be suppressed to transfer them. So, the proposed method identifies the common part in layouts of user requirements, and transmits to each user a composite video corresponding to the common part and remaining videos. We have developed a greedy algorithm which calculates the set of videos to be transmitted within the available bandwidth, so that the sum of satisfaction degrees of all users is maximized. Through experiments, we confirmed that our method can achieve much higher user satisfaction degrees compared to the case that each user terminal receives multiple videos separately and plays them back in parallel.

1 Introduction

In recent years, digital terrestrial broadcasting services have started in many countries. In Japan, digital video broadcasting service for mobile terminals called *1 segment broadcasting* based on ISDB-T [1] has already started since April, 2006. In Europe, US and Korea, similar services based on DVB-H [2], ATSC [3] and T-DMB [4] are going to be available. At the same time, mobile users are awaiting more advanced video services which allow them to watch multiple contents with the specified layout through the same screen like HDTV (we call a set of videos displayed on a screen a *compound video*).

For this purpose, several studies have been conducted so far. [5] describes a method to locate proxies between content server and user terminal so that the resources required for video delivery meet limitation of network resources and user terminal resources by reducing video quality at the proxies. [6] is a method which uses proxies to produce a composite video from multiple video contents

G. Min et al. (Eds.): ISPA 2006 Ws, LNCS 4331, pp. 803–812, 2006.

and forward it to each user terminal. In [7], layout-based video delivery method is proposed, where user can specify any layout of multiple videos.

These existing methods target wired environment where the purpose is to minimize computation resources at proxies and/or network resources of overlay network. Here, minimization of resources of wireless network and/or computation resources of mobile terminals are not considered.

In this paper, we propose a new video delivery method which allows mobile users to watch multiple videos with a specified layout in a typical mobile/wireless environment consisting of a large number of mobile terminals, multiple wireless access points (APs) which cover service area, multiple proxies and a wired network which connects APs and proxies.

The simplest method to realize the target multiple video delivery service is to have each mobile terminal receive multiple video streams from their servers and play back those videos simultaneously after reducing the size, and so on if necessary. This method, however, requires extra processing power at mobile terminal, which may cause so-called *drop frame*. To cope with the problem, many of the existing methods utilize proxies to resize or transcode videos before transmitting to mobile terminals. Although this method mitigates the computation power of mobile terminal to some extent, each mobile terminal still suffers from playing back multiple videos at the same time. This will introduce non-negligible processing overhead such as buffering and synchronization of multiple videos. A more advanced method which is adopted in [7] is to have proxies produce a composite video from multiple videos based on the requested layout and transmits the composite video to each mobile terminal. It minimizes the computation power and/or quality degradation degree at each mobile terminal, whereas the number of composite videos to be transmitted through the same wireless network channel is limited (i.e., when many users request videos with different layouts, most of them cannot receive videos as they want).

For the above problems, our proposed method identifies common part among layouts requested by multiple users, produces a composite video for the part, and transmits it through AP. The remaining videos in each layout are resized and/or transcoded at a proxy and transmitted to the user terminal. Each user terminal receives a composite video and a few small videos, and play them back according to the layout. In general smaller number of videos each user terminal receives, lower computation power is consumed at the mobile terminal. However, the problem to find the best set of transmitted videos which maximize the sum of the user satisfaction degree under limitation of network resources and mobile terminal resource is the combinatory optimization problem. So, we propose a heuristic algorithm to calculate semi-optimal set of videos by introducing a mechanism to predict user satisfaction degrees before transmitting a set of videos. Through some experimnts, we have confirmed that our proposed delivery method outperforms other simple methods in terms of the sum of the user satisfaction degrees.

In the following Sect. 2, we define the problem of multiple video delivery for mobile users. Sect. 3 describes our method. In Sect. 4, our heuristic algorithm to derive a semi-optimal set of videos for broadcasting is given. Sect. 5 and Sect. 6 describe performance evaluation and conclusion, respectively.

2   Problem Definition

In this section, we first describe the assumptions and the target environment, and then we give the formal definition of the problem.

Assumptions. In this paper, we assume that the proposed system is used in conjunction with PDA or mobile phone as user terminal, and IEEE 802.16 WiMAX or cellular phone infrastructure as a means of wireless communication. Each access point (AP) communicates with multiple user terminals, and each user terminal requests a set of videos with a layout (explained later), where the set is different from each other. Each user terminal is assumed to communicate with AP at a time, and the sum of bandwidths between an AP and corresponding user terminals is limited. In this paper, we do not handle handover between APs in consequence of user terminal movement.

We assume that each user terminal accesses a video server or a proxy via an AP. Each video is transmitted from one server. Each proxy has the following three basic services: (1) Transcoding received video stream to stream with the specified picture size, framerate, and bitrate in real time; (2) Composing multiple videos into a video with specified layout; and (3) Transmitting processed video stream towards user terminal. We call the processed video *composite video*, and the raw non-processed video *atomic video*. Each user terminal is capable of changing size of received videos and display them simultaneously at any position on the screen, within the limits of its processing power. Thus, user terminals can receive multiple videos and play them back with any layout within available bandwidth and processing power. If it does not have sufficient processing power, framerate will decrease (which we call *drop frame*). Video stream is sent from AP to user terminals using broadcast, thus even if there are many terminals which receive a same stream, bandwidth usage is equal to the case when there is one receiver. For the sake of simplicity, we assume that bandwidths between video servers and proxies are unlimited, and proxies have unlimited computational power to process video streams.

A layout includes the positions, picture sizes and framerates for displaying multiple atomic videos simultaneously. Fig. 1 is an example of layout. Each user sends a request including a layout to video servers via a proxy. Video servers send the corresponding atomic video to proxies without any processing. Proxies receive videos from servers, process and compose these videos so that the processed videos meet users' requests, and send them to user terminals. Since each AP has bandwidth limitation, all users' requests cannot be always satisfied. If there is bandwidth shortage, the proposed method determines the set of delivered videos to maximize users' satisfaction.

Definition. The set of all available atomic videos is denoted as $C = \{c_1, ..., c_M\}$. A layout includes multiple rectangles to display videos as shown in Fig. 1. We call each rectangle *window*. To each window, picture size and position in the layout are specified. A layout is an ordered set of windows. A composite video generated by using atomic videos $e_1, ..., e_n \in C$ and layout lay_i is denoted as $lay_i(e_1, ..., e_n)$. For example, a composite video generated by specifying atomic videos c_1 and c_2 to windows A and B of layout lay_2 in Fig. 1 is denoted as $lay_2(c_1, c_2)$.

The set of all users connecting to an AP is denoted as $U = \{u_1, ..., u_N\}$. User request from u_i is denoted as r_i. We can assume that the number of APs is one, without loss of generality. The available bandwidth for the AP is A_{bw}. Bandwidth required to deliver video g is denoted as $bw(g)$. The compound video displayed at user terminal u_i is called *user view* and denoted by v_i. Satisfaction degree s_i for user u_i who has requested r_i and is viewing v_i is given by a function $s_i(r_i, v_i)$. The range of the function is between 0 and 1, and larger value means higher satisfaction of the corresponding user. There may be various definition of the function s_i, and we will give a definition based on drop frame rate in Sect. 4.

The definition of problem is as follows. Given a set of user requests $\{r_1, ..., r_L\}$, determine a set D of videos delivered to the users which maximize the sum of user satisfactions $\sum_{i=1}^{N} s_i$ within the limitation of bandwidth $\sum_{d \in D} bw(d) \leq A_{bw}$.

3   Delivery Methods

In order to realize compound video delivery to user terminals, the optimal set of both composite and atomic videos must be determined to satisfy user requests. As we already addressed in Sect. 1, the following three methods are considered as delivery mechanisms: (1) *Method1*: each user terminal receives atomic videos directly from content servers without using proxies; (2) *Method2*: each user terminal can receive atomic videos with reduced quality through proxies after resizing or transcoding the videos according to the user's request; (3) *Method3* and the improved version (proposed method): each user terminal can receive composite videos and/or atomic videos with reduced quality according to the user's request by asking proxies to compose multiple videos to one composite video or to resize/transcode atomic videos. Although Method1 is the simplest approach, many picture frames of a received video can be dropped when a user terminal plays the video back due to increased load for receiving multiple atomic contents, resizing some of them and drawing picture frames on the specified layout. In Method2, in order to overcome the problem of Method1, picture size and/or framerate are reduced at a proxy server and forwarded to user terminal so that the terminal does not consume power for receiving surplus packets and resizing the picture frames and so on. Method3 further reduces computation power required at user terminals by allowing proxies to compose composite videos and forward them to user terminals. With this method, overhead caused by parallel playback of videos could be reduced to a great extent. However, since Method3 may produce many composite videos which cannot be transmitted within the available bandwidth when users request videos with different layouts. So, we propose the improved version of Method3.

Method1: Delivering Videos Without Proxies

Method1 is the simplest delivery method where each user terminal receives atomic videos specified in the user's request from content servers, changes size of received videos, and displays them on windows of the specified layout (Fig. 2). For example, in Fig. 2, we suppose there are three user terminals u_1, u_2 and u_3 which sent the following requests r_1, r_2 and r_3, respectively: $r_1 = lay_2(c_2, c_3)$, $r_2 = lay_2(c_3, c_1)$ and $r_3 = lay_3(c_3, c_1, c_2)$. Here, we suppose to use layouts lay_2 and lay_3 in Fig. 1. With Method1, u_1 will receive atomic videos c_2 and c_3 from the corresponding content servers directly, and reduce the picture size of c_3, and displays c_2 and c_3 on windows A and B of layout lay_2.

Method2: Delivering Videos with Reduced Quality Using Proxies

In Method2, as shown in Fig. 3, proxies which are capable of reducing picture size and/or framerate, are available. Each proxy receives atomic videos from content servers, reduces picture size/framerate of received videos in real time, and forwards them to user terminals. Then, each user terminal displays the received videos on windows of the specified layout. For example, in Fig. 3, user terminal u_1 receives atomic video c_2 from its content server and video c_3 with reduced picture size via the proxy server, and displays those videos on windows A and B of layout lay_2. In Method2, processing overhead on user terminal will be lighter than Method1 since the terminal needs to neither resize the picture size nor process surplus packets of original atomic video. However, similarly to Method1, user terminal still needs to receive all of atomic videos in the request separately and play them back in parallel according to the specified layout.

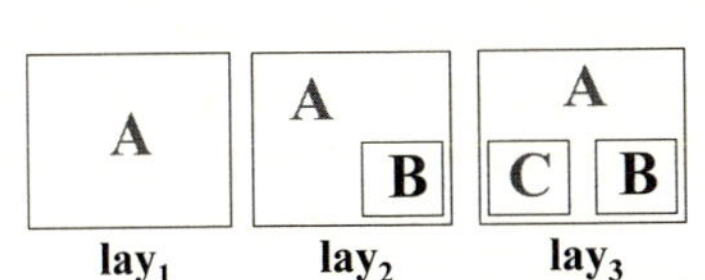

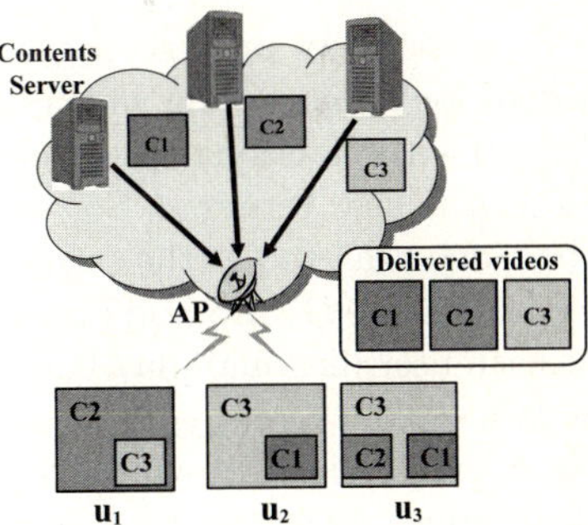

Fig. 1. An example of layout   **Fig. 2.** Video delivery with Method1

Proposed Method: Delivering Composite Videos and Videos with Reduced Quality Using Proxies

In our proposed method, as shown in Fig. 4, each user terminal sends its request to a proxy. Smilarly to Method3, in our proposed method, the proxy produces composite videos which meet user requests as much as possible within the bandwidth limitation, and transmits them to user terminals. The proposed method is different from Method3 in its flexibility that it allows each user terminal to receive and display one composite content, or to receive and display a set of composite and atomic videos on specified layout. For example, in Fig. 4, user terminal u_1 receives a composite video which the proxy server produced from atomic videos c_2 and c_3 using layout lay_2. Similarly, u_2 receives a composite video composed of c_3 and c_1. On the other hand, user terminal u_3 receives an atomic video c_2 with reduced quality and a composite video of c_3 and c_1, and plays the two videos back in parallel, to satisfy u_3's request.

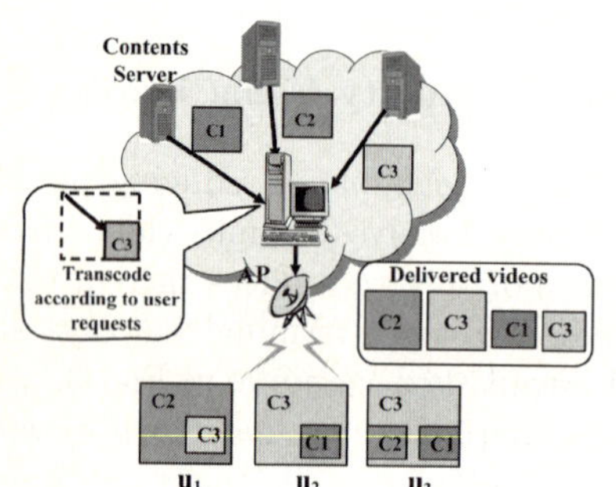

Fig. 3. Video delivery with Method2

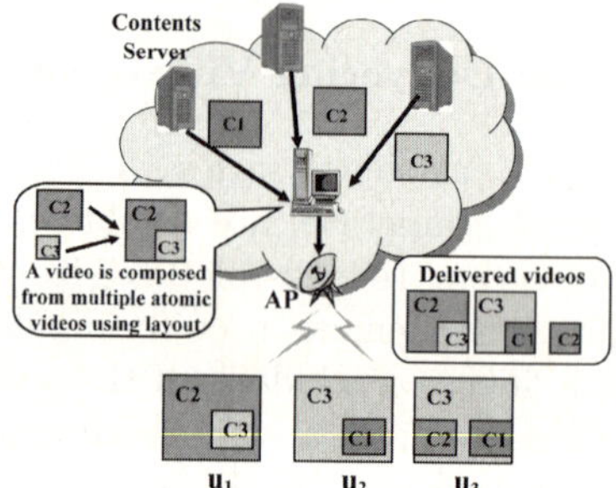

Fig. 4. Video delivery with our method

4   Algorithm to Derive Optimal Set of Videos for Broadcasting

In this section, we propose a greedy algorithm to calculate a semi-optimal set of videos for broadcasting which maximizes the sum of user satisfaction degrees. Each user's satisfaction degree depends on the quality of the displayed compound video at the user terminal. So, we also propose a method to predict the quality of the video achieved at the terminal for the given set of videos for broadcasting.

Either Method1, Method2 or our proposed method described in Sect. 3 may have each user terminal play back multiple videos in parallel. To play back multiple videos concurrently, each user terminal must receive and decode multiple video streams before drawing video frames. In general, as larger number of videos each terminal plays back, more computation power is required. As a result, if the computation power of user terminal is limited, the rate of drop frames called *drop frame rate* will increase as the number of videos increases.

In Method1, user terminals receiving videos with larger picture size (and/or framerates) than in their requests, have to decrease their sizes (and/or framerates) before drawing. In this case, drop frame rate will become larger than Method2. Dropped frames cause quality degradation in user view. In the proposed method, to prevent drop frames at user terminal, we take drop frame rate into consideration to define user satisfaction degree (details are given in

Sect. 4.1). As explained in Sect. 2, the objective function of our target problem is defined as the sum of user satisfaction degrees. So, we need a technique to predict drop frame rates at all user terminals without playing back videos.

In the following subsections, we present a method for predicting drop frame rate and a greedy algorithm to solve the target problem defined in Sect. 2.

4.1 Prediction of Drop Frame Rate

Let p denote the number of pixels processed per unit of time while each terminal decodes videos. We assume that drop framerate denoted by $z(p)$ can be approximated by the equation $z(p) = \alpha p + \beta$[1], where α and β are terminal specific constants. We can obtain these terminal values by measuring drop framerates for different values of p with the Least Square Method. For a compound video q_i, let q_{ij} denote the video assigned in j-th window of layout used for generating q_i. For video q_{ij}, let $w_1(q_{ij})$ denote the product of picture size and framerate of the video received by u_i[2]. If video q_{ij} is not received, $w_1(q_{ij}) is 0$. Let $w_2(q_{ij})$ denotes the product of the picture size and the framerate specified for the window corresponding to q_{ij} in the request. We define the user satisfaction degree as follows. Here, n_i denotes the number of videos which user u_i requests.

$$s_i = z_i\left(\sum_{j=1}^{n_i} w_1(q_{ij})\right) \times \sum_{j=1}^{n_i} \frac{Min(w_1(q_{ij}), w_2(q_{ij}))}{w_2(q_{ij})} / n_i \tag{1}$$

4.2 Greedy Algorithm

The problem to find the optimal set of videos for broadcasting is a combinatory optimization problem, thereby it can be proved to be a NP-hard problem (due to page limitation, we omit the proof).

As a heuristic to solve this problem, we use a greedy algorithm since it is easy to implement and likely to run fast. We show pseudo code of our greedy algorithm to obtain an optimal set of videos for broadcasting in Fig. 5. This algorithm can be used for each of Method1, Method2 and our method. In the algorithm, D denotes the set of videos for broadcasting and $s_i(D - \{d\})$ denotes the satisfaction degree of user u_i when the set of videos for broadcasting is $D - \{d\}$. Here, $d \in D$. As the first step of the algorithm, the initial set of videos D_0 is generated according to user requests. Elements of D_0 differ among Method1, Method2 and our method.

---

[1] In general, several factors such as receiving packets, resizing picture frames, drawing pictures and so on must be considered as a load at terminal. However, these factors can be treated in a similar way to decoding.

[2] In Method1, each user terminal may receive videos with larger picture size (and/or framerate) than in the request, since content servers may retain only a file for each video content. In Method2, each user terminal may receive videos with smaller or larger picture size/framerate than the request due to bandwidth limitation. In our proposed method, q_{ij} may be part of a composite video. In this case, we use the window size in the layout and framerate of the composite video for q_{ij}.

In Method1, D_0 is the set of atomic videos included in user requests. For example, in Fig. 2, $D_0 = \{c_1, c_2, c_3\}$ where c_1, c_2 and c_3 are atomic videos. In Method2, atomic videos with reduced quality are added to D_0 generated by Method1 if some of the users request videos with reduced quality in their layouts. For example, in Fig. 3, $D_0 = \{c_1, c_2, c_3, c_1^s, c_2^s, c_3^s\}$ where c_j^s denotes the video c_j with reduced quality. Our proposed method adds, to D_0 generated by Method2, all composite videos which can be composed by assigning some of atomic contents to windows of all possible layouts. For example, if we assume that there are three possible layouts lay_1, lay_2 and lay_3 in Fig. 1, when user requests are as shown in Fig. 4, $D_0 = \{c_1, c_2, c_3, c_1^s, c_2^s, c_3^s, lay_2(c_1, c_2), ..., lay_2(c_3, c_2), lay_3(c_1, c_2, c_3), ..., lay_3(c_3, c_2, c_1)\}$ where $lay_2(c_2, c_3)$ denotes a composite video generated by assigning atomic videos c_2 and c_3 to 1st and 2nd windows in the layout lay_2. The set D_0 calculated above is assigned to D.

```
Algorithm  GetOptimalSet(D_0, A_bw)
1 D := D_0
2 while D ≠ ∅ and ∑_{d∈D} bw(d) > A_bw do
3       // Find d ∈ D which maximizes ∑_i s_i(D − {d})
4       max := −1
5       foreach d ∈ D do
6           sat := ∑_i s_i(D − {d})
7           if max < sat then
8               d̂ := d
9               max := sat
10          endif
11      next
12
13      D := D − {d̂}
14 next
15 return D
16 end
```

Fig. 5. Algorithm to derive optimal set of videos

As the second step, the algorithm checks if the current set D satisfies the bandwidth limitation or not. If not, it tries to remove every element $d \in D$ from D. It calculates the sum of user satisfaction degrees (denoted by sat) of the set $D - \{d\}$, and finds the element $\hat{d}$ which has the least impact on sat. Then $\hat{d}$ is removed from D and the second step is repeated until the bandwidth limitation is satisfied.

5   Evaluation

In order to evaluate effectiveness of our method, we compared the sum of user satisfaction degrees among Method1, Method2 and our proposed method, varying distribution of user requests.

Table 1. Distributions of user requests

Distribution patterns	A	$AB(AC)$	ABC
Distribution $Dist_1$	5	19	6
Distribution $Dist_2$	5	11	5
Distribution $Dist_3$	5	5	2

Prediction accuracy of drop frame rate. First, we obtained typical values of parameters α and β in function for drop frame rate $z(p) = \alpha p + \beta$, and then we measured drop frame rates using 9 videos with the different picture sizes and framerates. As a result of calculation, the value of α was 5.1 and the value of β was -77.9. We obtained the drop frame rates using the Least Square Method. We used a PDA (SHARP Zaurus SL-C700, CPU: XScale 400MHz, Memory: 32MB, OS: Linux 2.4.28) in the measurement. Fig. 6 shows actual values of drop frame rates and the regression line from the measured values.

From Fig. 6, we can see that the average error between the predicted values from the regression line and the actual measurement values is about 12 %. There is still a room for improvement, but we believe it is enough for practical use.

Result on User Satisfaction Degree. In the experiment, we used configuration of 20 user terminals and 5 atomic videos. Each user selects one of the three layouts in Fig. 1 where the larger window's video quality is 320×240 pixels, 24 fps and 500 kbps, and that of the smaller window is 160×128 pixels, 24 fps and 350kbps. The available bandwidth for wireless network is set to 3000kbps.

The distributions of user requests are shown in Table 1. Labels $A(AB)$ and ABC in the table represent the windows of layouts in Fig. 1, respectively. The numbers in the table show how many different patterns exist in all user requests when we see only the specified window(s) in user requests. The number of each label is counted independently of the other labels. So, the total sum may exceed the number of users (i.e., 20). For example, in distribution $Dist_1$, numbers of different user requests in terms of video(s) to be displayed at the window(s) A, $AB(AC)$ and ABC are 5, 19 and 6, respectively. The total number of different user requests on the same layout depends on which video is displayed on each window of the layout. For example, the total number of user requests using layout lay_2 (which contains two windows A and B) is ${}_5C_2 \times 2! = 20$, and 19 patterns of them are involved in the distribution $Dist_1$. We intentionally set that the total number of different patterns decreases in the order of $Dist_1$, $Dist_2$ and $Dist_3$. Therefore, the number of users who require the same videos is smaller in the distribution $Dist_1$, while the number is larger in the distribution $Dist_3$.

Fig. 7 depicts the user satisfaction degrees achieved by Method1, Method2 and our method under the distributions $Dist_1, Dist_2$ and $Dist_3$.

From Table 1 and Fig. 7, we can see that our method achieves highest user satisfaction degrees in all distributions of user requests. In Method2, user satisfaction degrees are almost constant for all distributions of user requests. This is because sets of videos for broadcasting become almost similar due to the bandwidth constraint. This trend can also be seen in Method1. In our method, we

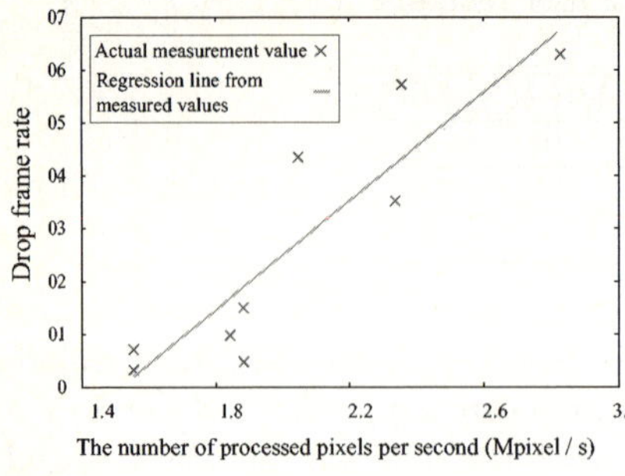

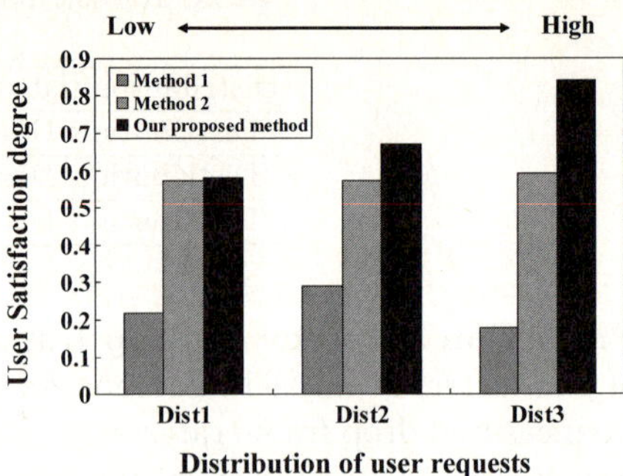

Fig. 6. Actual values of drop frame rate and the regression line from the measured values

Fig. 7. Comparison of user satisfaction degrees

can see that the user satisfaction degree is high, in the order of $Dist_3$, $Dist_2$ and $Dist_1$. This is because the number of users who require similar layouts is large, in the order of $Dist_3$, $Dist_2$ and $Dist_1$. From this result, our method is especially effective when the number of users who require similar layouts is large.

6   Conclusion

In this paper, we proposed a method to realize compound video delivery service for mobile terminals on a wireless network. The proposed method maximizes the sum of user satisfaction degrees, considering both network bandwidth limitation and mobile terminal's computation power limitation. Through experiments, we showed that when a certain proportion of users require similar compound videos, our method which generates a composite video for common part of user requirements increases the sum of user satisfaction degree to a great extent.

References

1. ISDB-T(Integrated Services Digital Broadcasting-Terrestrial).
   http://www.dibeg.org/techp/isdb/isdbt.htm
2. DVB-H Global Mobile TV. http://www.dvb-h.org/
3. ATSC Home Page. http://www.atsc.org/
4. T-DMB Home Page. http://eng.t-dmb.org/
5. J, Jin., K, Nahrstedt.: Source-based qos service routing in distributed service networks. IEEE International Conference on Communications. (2004)
6. J, Liang., K, Nahrstedt.: Service Composition for Advanced Multimedia Applications. Multimedia Computing and Networking (MMCN'05). (2005)
7. K, Nahrstedt., B, Yu., J, Liang. and Y, Cui.: Hourglass Multimedia Content and Service Composition Framework for Smart Room Environments. Elsevier Journal on Pervasive and Mobile Computing. (2005)

A Dynamic Hierarchical Map Partitioning for MMOG

Beob Kyun Kim[1] and Kang Soo You[2]

[1] Dept. of Computer Engineering, Chonbuk National University, South Korea
bkyun.kim@gmail.com
[2] School of Liberal Arts, Jeonju University, South Korea
you.kangsoo@gmail.com

Abstract. Massively Multiplayer Online Games (MMOGs) are characterized by the interaction between a virtual world and an ever-changing worldwide stream of players. Most of them require virtual worlds, significant hardware requirements (e.g., servers and bandwidth), and dedicated support staff. Despite the efforts of developers, users often suffer from overpopulation, lag, and poor support as problems of games. In this paper, a new dynamic hierarchical map partition method for MMORPG based on Virtual Map Information is proposed. This method tries to divide map based on Virtual Map Layer (VML). In order to adapt to dynamic change of population, managers divide or merge fields with the hierarchy of VML. By the simple modification to VML, we can easily manage problems that come from changes of map data (e.g., addition, deletion, and modification of zone), changes of resources, or changes of users' behavior pattern.

1 Introduction

A Massively Multiplayer Online Game (MMOG) is an online game in which a large number of players can interact with each other in the same world at the same time [1]. Usually, MMOGs follow a client-server model. An avatar, a graphically representation of the character that users play, is representing gamers in the game world. The persistent virtual worlds where these gamers reside are hosted by service providers. This interaction between a virtual world and an ever-changing worldwide stream of players characterizes the MMOG genre.

MMOGs are immensely popular with several commercial games reporting millions of subscribers. Most of them require huge virtual worlds, significant hardware requirements (e.g., servers and bandwidth), and dedicated support staffs. So, designers must consider the performance, stability, and scalability of the game while preserving short development cycle and the maintaining convenience. Despite the efforts of developers, users often suffer from overpopulation, lag, and poor support as problems of games. Usually, the virtual world of the game is divided into regions, each of which is assigned to its own respective host. Multiple regions can be contained in a single host but a single region cannot span multiple hosts. As soon as an avatar moves from one region to another region

G. Min et al. (Eds.): ISPA 2006 Ws, LNCS 4331, pp. 813–822, 2006.

which is maintained by another host, its data are automatically transferred to the host responsible for the region which it entered and are deleted from the previous one [2]. While game servers are running, regions which each host maintains are not changed. They can do nothing to manage the situation a single host is over-burdened with too many users.

Designing an efficient distributed virtual environment system is a complex task, since these system show an inherent heterogeneousness. Such heterogeneousness appears in several elements: hardware, connection, communication rate of avatars, data model, communication model, view consistency, and message traffic reduction [3]. Most of those issues are related to the distribution of the workload (avatars) among different servers in the system [4].

In this paper, a new dynamic hierarchical map partitioning method for MMORPG system based on virtual map information is proposed. It tries to divide map based on virtual sub-area hierarchy information, contained in Virtual Map Layer (VML). In order to adapt to dynamic change of population, managers divide or merge fields based on the surveyed load of each sub-area. The divide and merge direction follows the hierarchy of VML. By the simple modification of VML, we can easily manage problems that come from changes of map data (e.g., addition, deletion, and modification of zone), changes of resources' status, and changes of users' behavior pattern.

2   Related Works

Several approaches have been developed for simulating a large set of avatars sharing the same virtual world. Architectures based on networked servers are becoming a de facto standard for large scale MMORPG [4]. In these architectures, the control of the simulation relies on several interconnected servers. When a client orders an action to his avatar, an updating message is sent to its server, that in turn this message must be propagated to other servers and clients. Each field servers must render different 3D models, perform positional updates of avatars and transfer control information among different clients. Thus, each new avatar represents an increasing in both the computational requirements of the application and also in the amount of network traffic. When the number of connected clients increases, the number of updating messages must be limited in order to avoid a message outburst. In this sense, concepts like areas of influence (AOI) [5], locales [6] or auras [7] have been proposed for limiting the number of neighboring avatars that a given avatar must communicate with. All these concepts define a neighborhood area for avatars, in such a way that a given avatar must notify his movements (by sending an updating message) only to those avatars located in that neighborhood. Depending on their origin and destination avatars, messages in a distributed virtual environment (DVE) system can be intra-server or inter-server messages.

OptimalGrid [8] represents a style of middleware for computing large connected problems in a distributed computing environment. When the Optimal-Grid system initializes itself to solve a problem, it automatically retrieves from the grid a list of available computer nodes. It also obtains the grid's performance characteristics. At run-time, OptimalGrid measures ongoing performance, including communication time, computation time, and the complexity of the problem pieces. OptimalGrid uses this information to configure the grid by calculating the optimal number of computer nodes, partitioning the problem, and distributing its pieces in a way that obtains the best possible performance on whatever grid is used.

Lui and Chan suggest an efficient partitioning algorithm for multi-server DVE systems [4]. They exploit a graph partitioning algorithm to answer how to optimally assign users to servers. Their scheme would produce well-balanced partitioning results at a large cost. As the size of the number of servers increase, the overhead of the graph partitioning algorithm exponentially increases. So, it cannot be survive from dynamic change of population. It is not applicable for real-time interactive applications.

3 Design of MMOG System for Dynamic Hierarchical Map Partition

3.1 VML-Based MMOG System

As shown in Fig. 1, the proposed system follows traditional architectures based on networked server. VML Management server is the only new component. It surveys loads of each field servers, checks if the surveyed load is affordable, and tries to divide or merge fields.

A big virtual world has several sub-areas which has different properties. Each sub-area of a big virtual world has different properties to attract gamers. Some of them have popular properties which will lead to over population and some of them have unpopular properties which will be lead to under population. For example, if a sub-area has events or monsters which make gamers easy to get experience points or game money, gamers will like to play in that area. These properties will be considered into the design of VML. A sub-area of the virtual world will be divided or be merged according to the guideline of VML. By the simple modification of VML, we can easily manage problems that come from changes of map data (e.g., addition, deletion, and modification of zone), changes of resources' status, and changes of users' behavior pattern.

3.2 VML

VML is an overlaid version of map which has information about hierarchy of sub-areas. VML consists of Fields, Sector Groups, Sectors, and Cells. Field is an area which is controlled by one game server. And a field consists of sectors or sector groups. VML Management Server tries to divide or merge fields based on the surveyed load of its sectors or sector groups. A sector, which is the smallest unit for partition and incorporation, is similar to OPC(Original Problem Cell) of Optimal Grid [8]. A cell, which is the smallest unit of VML hierarchy, is used

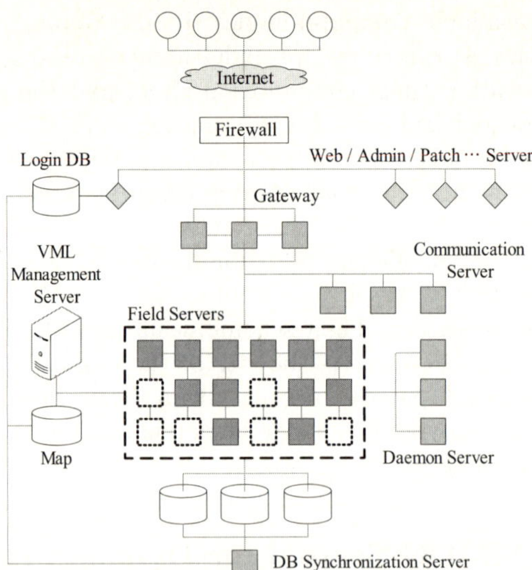

Fig. 1. VML-based MMOG system for dynamic hierarchical map partition

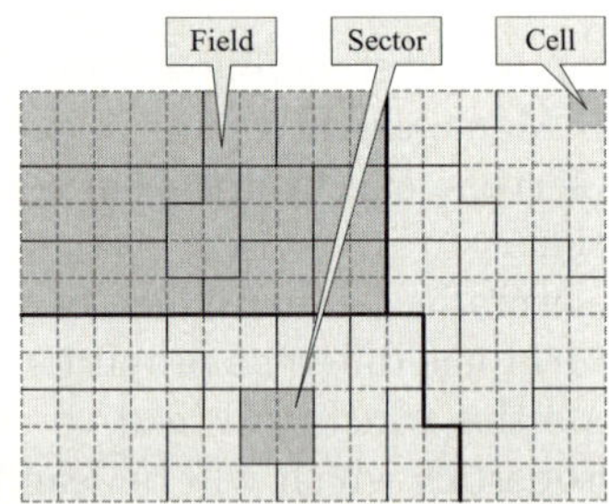

Fig. 2. The hierarchical structure of VML

to define sector and is used to survey load of sector. Sector is defined as a set of related neighbor cells. So, each sector can have different number of cells.

For partitioning and merging fields, $MaxLoF_f$ and $MinLoF_f$ are used as a threshold. VML management server tries to check the load of each field. If the condition where the load of a field exceeds $MaxLoF_f$ is continued above T_{term}, VML management server chooses dividing method by surveying loads of sectors which consist this field. On the contrary, if the condition where the load of a field is not reached $MinLoF_f$ is continued above T_{term}, VML management server tries to merge adjacent fields using dividing history.

Mathematical methods [4] for solving this kind of partitioning problem are possible. But, they cannot provide solution for restoration of partitioned fields and they produce too much traffic overhead between field servers during mergence and partitioning. And also, they don't consider the special relationships between neighbored fields.

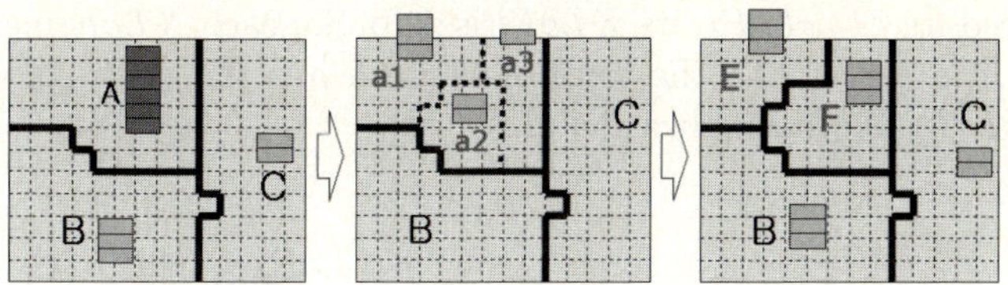

Fig. 3. Map partitioning based on surveyed loads

Fig. 3 shows the map partitioning process based on surveyed loads. Partition and mergence process follows the hierarchy of VML. If a field A is to be divided, the subset of sub-areas and the rest will be new fields. Each sub-area of a big virtual world has different properties to decoy gamers. In VML, this kind of sub-area can be a sector. And their group will be a sector group to compose a field and themselves can compose a field. Usually, geographically neighbored sub-areas have not only geographical relationships, but also other relationships about game philosophy and scenario. VML is designed based on this kind of information and has a hierarchical structure. If a field is needed to be partition, this field will be divided with hierarchical information contained in VML and the partitioning history will be kept to be used in restoration process.

VML has tree-like hierarchical structure. The coverage of a parent node is same to that of union of its children $\{a_1, a_2, a_3, \ldots, a_n\}$. After partition of a field, new fields are subsets of this field.

$$A = \{a_1, a_2, a_3, \ldots, a_n\}$$

$$A \supset E$$

$$F = A - E \tag{1}$$

There are several elements which are included in the load of a field server: the activity of player character (PC), events which tries to access database, weights of each field, computing power of each field server, etc [9]. The load of a field is weighted sum of that of its sub-areas. The weight of each sector is assigned by designer. The bigger value means that this field is important and need high performance. Computation of the load of each sector needs the activity of PC (A_i), the number of events (E_j) which tries to access database, the access time ratio of database to main memory, and other information.

$$LoF_f = \sum_{s}^{n} LoS_s \times W_s \tag{2}$$

$$LoS_s = \sum_{i=0}^{l} A_i + W_{event} \times \sum_{j=0}^{m} E_j \tag{3}$$

Partition process is begun if the load of a field exceeds maximum load ($MaxLoF_f$) of this field. $XLoF_f$ is an excess load of a field. If a field's load doesn't exceed its $MaxLoF_f$, its $XLoF_f$ is zero. So, each $XLoF_f$ means the status of each field server and the total of them means the status of entire game system. $RXLoF_f$ is a normalization of $XLoF_f$.

$$XLoF_f = \begin{cases} LoF_f - MaxLoF_f \\ 0 \end{cases}, \quad \text{if} \quad LoF_f \leq MaxLoF_f \tag{4}$$

$$RXLoF_f = \frac{XLoF_f}{MaxLoF_f} \tag{5}$$

Fig. 4 shows the expected effect of the proposed approach. After partition process (T_{p1} and T_{p2}), the load of the field will not exceed . After mergence process (T_{m1} and T_{m2}), the load of the field will not be smaller than .

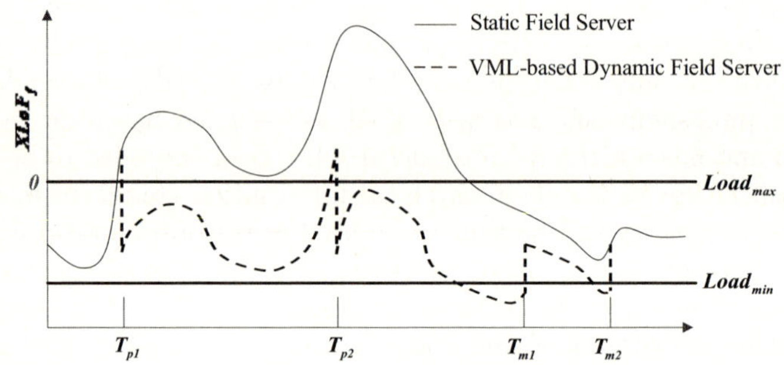

Fig. 4. The expected effect of dynamic hierarchical map partition

4   Implementation and Comparison

We define two variables to control the activity of PC (PA) and the grouping degree of PC (PG).

PCA_i is the activity of i'th PC. So, PA is the average activity of PC and is a factor that affects message traffic. If PA is very high, the system will have very high message traffic. And also, if PCA_i is very high, that PC moves very quickly and frequently. n is the number of PC in the virtual world.

PGG_j is the number of PC which are included into group j. And g is the number of big groups. If g is 30, only the first 30 big groups will be considered for the calculation of group. If these groups have bigger number of PC, the value of PG will be smaller. And also, if the value of PG is smaller, very big number of PCs will show same action pattern and congested region will occur frequently.

Fig. 5 shows a geographic distribution of PC when PA is fixed at 0.3 and PG is variable from 0.3 to 0.7. If PG is set to smaller value, the more congestion and the bigger mean $XLoF_f$ is expected.

Fig. 6 shows the comparison of $RXLoF_f$ between the static management and the dynamic hierarchical map partitioning when PA is fixed at 0.3 and PG is variable from 0.3 to 0.7. The larger number of PC gets more improvements

Table 1. Measures to control the activity and the grouping degree of PC. If PA has values near 1.0, this PC moves very quickly. If PG has values near 0, very large number of PC are acting like just one group.

	PA	PG
Description	The activity of PC	The grouping degree of PC
Min	Usually, don't move	Very large number of PC show same action
Max	Moves very quickly	Each PC show different action
Definition	$\frac{1}{n}\sum_{i=1}^{n} PCA_i$	$1 - \frac{1}{n}\sum_{j=1}^{g} PGG_j$

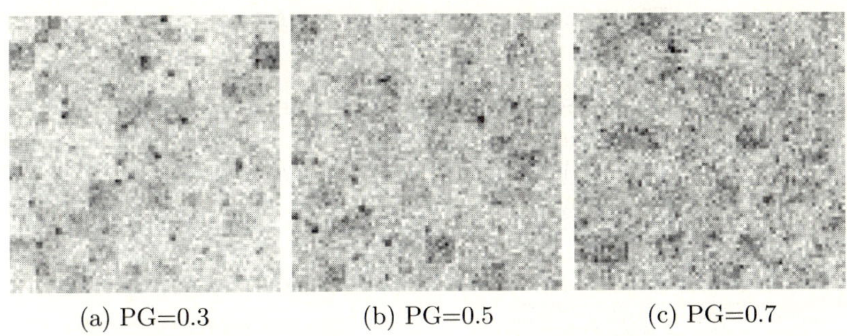

Fig. 5. Geographic distribution of PC $(PA=0.3)$

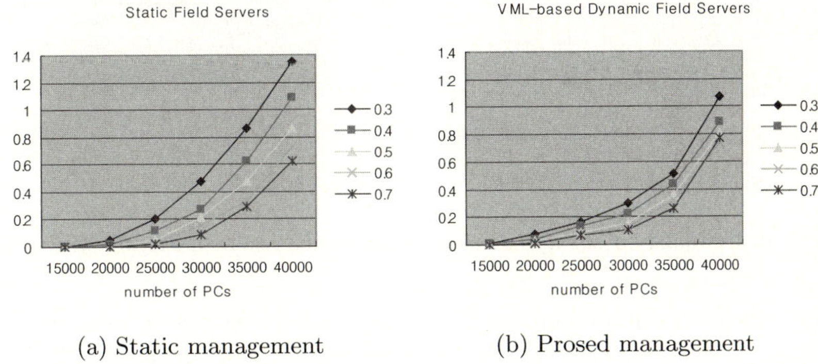

Fig. 6. Comparison of $RXLoF_f$ $(PA=0.3)$

against the static management which don't perform dynamic map partition. If the smaller PG was used, the bigger mean of $RXLoF_f$ was appeared. So, the more congestion leads to bigger mean of excess loads. When PG is 0.3, the dynamic hierarchical map partitioning allow for 23-67% improved performance compared to the static management.

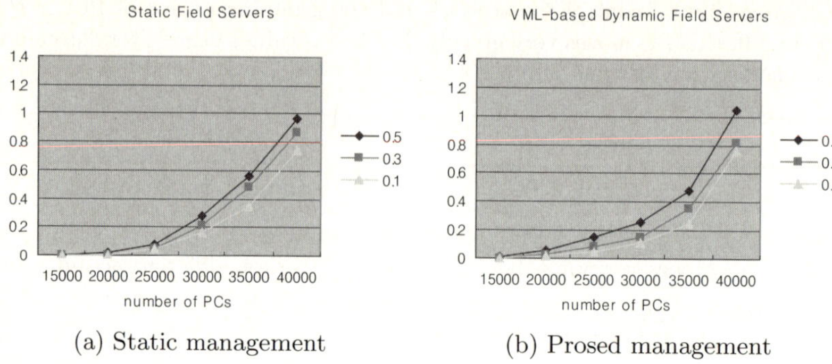

(a) Static management   (b) Prosed management

Fig. 7. Comparison of $RXLoF_f$ (PA=0.5)

Fig. 7 shows the comparison of $RXLoF_f$ between the static management and the dynamic hierarchical map partitioning when PA is variable from 0.1 to 0.5 and PG is fixed at 0.5. If the bigger PA which means the activity of PC was used, the more excess load was appeared.

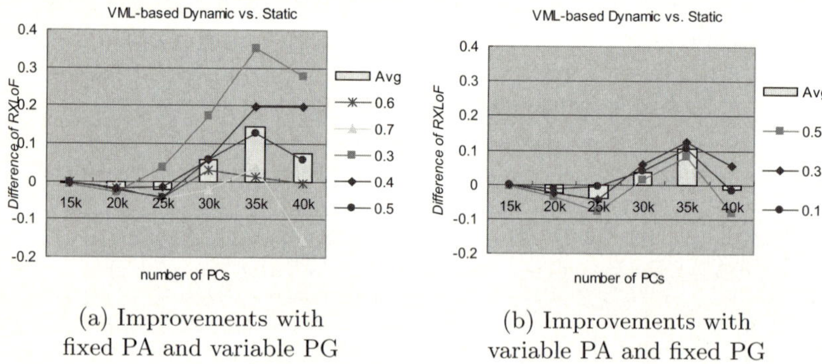

(a) Improvements with
fixed PA and variable PG

(b) Improvements with
variable PA and fixed PG

Fig. 8. Comparison of improvements between the result in Fig. 6 and Fig. 7

Fig. 8 shows the improvement difference between the result shown in Fig. 6 and Fig. 7. We can see that the improvement difference by change of PG is more variable than that by change of PA. But rather, we can see that the improvement at extremely large number of PCs is reduced. It comes from the experimental limit and the special situation where an overpopulated field is just a single sector, and thus cannot be further divided.

The proposed approach may lead to overheads which did not appear in the static management. They may be produced by the monitoring process and the partitioning process. The concept that each field is controlled by the stand-alone field server is same with that of the other MMOGs. Usually in MMOGs, the load of each field server is monitored in realtime and the monitored information is used in other analysis process. The only difference in the proposed system is VML management server which intervenes between monitoring process and recording process. So, the overhead produced by the monitoring process is trivial.

The overhead produced by the partitioning process may include the synchronization of PC information, map data loading for newly divided or merged field, and rerouting of client and daemon server to new field. Considering the synchronization of PC information, it is basic in MMOGs and the only one more pass is added in the proposed system. And because the map data is a kind of static information, each field server can have the entire map data and must have different active area. So, the overhead from map data loading is trivial. Usually, the rerouting of client and daemon server to new field is the same process as the rerouting by PC's migration to neighbor field. So, the complexity of this process is that of the migration process. The only difference from the migration process, the number of PC, can be improved by the improvement of the server architecture or the migration algorithm.

5   Conclusion and Future Works

In this paper, a new VML-based MMOG system for dynamic hierarchical map partition is proposed. It tries to divide map based on virtual sub-area information, contained in VML. VML has a hierarchy which consists of Fields, Sector Groups, Sectors, and Cells. In order to adapt to dynamic change of population, managers divide or merge fields based on the surveyed load of each sub-area. The smallest units of layer are Cells and the largest units of layer are Fields.

For the simulation, we define new measures to model PC's activity. In the experiment result, the proposed approach shows improvement. And it shows more improved performance at highly congested situation. Overheads produced by the monitoring process and the partitioning process arc trivial or can be improved by the improvement of the server architecture or the migration algorithm. The proposed approach has advantages in the game management. By the simple modification of VML, we can easily manage problems that come from changes of map data (e.g., addition, deletion, and modification of zone), changes of resources' status, and changes of users' behavior pattern.

References

1. MMOG, http://en.wikipedia.org/wiki/MMOG
2. N.J.Lee and H.S.Kwak.: The Distributed Server Model for the Evolutionary Online RPG. J. Korea Game Society, Vol. 2. No. 1 (2002) 36-41
3. P.Morillo, J.Orduna, M.Fernandez.: A comparison study of evolutive algorithms for solving partitioning problem in distributed virtual environment systems. Parallel Computing, Vol. 30, No. 5-6. (2004) 585-610
4. J.C.S. Lui, M.F. Chan.: An efficient partitioning algorithm for distributed virtual environment systems. IEEE Transactions on Parallel and Distributed Systems, Vol. 13, No. 3. (2002) 193-211
5. S. Singhal, M. Zyda.: Networked Virtual Environments, ACM Press, New York, (1999)

6. D.B.Anderson, J.W.Barrus, J.H.Howard.: Building multiuser interactive multimedia environments at MERL. Multimedia, Vol. 2, No. 2. IEEE. (1995) 77-82
7. C. Greenhalgh.: Awareness-based communication management in the MASSIVE systems. Distrib. Syst. Engng
8. T. Lehman, J. Kaufman.: Optimal-Grid: middleware for automatic deployment of distributed FEM problems on an Internet-based computing grid. 2003 IEEE Int. Conf. on Cluster Com-puting. (2003) 164-171
9. J. Nam.: IT EXPERT, Online Game Server Programming. Hanbit Book, Korea. (2004)

Generic Framework for Parallel and Distributed Processing of Video-Data

Dirk Farin[1] and Peter H.N. de With[1,2]

[1] University Eindhoven, Signal Processing Systems, LG 0.10,
5600 MB Eindhoven, Netherlands
`d.s.farin@tue.nl`
`http://vca.ele.tue.nl`
[2] LogicaCMG, PO Box 7089, 5605 JB Eindhoven, Netherlands

Abstract. This paper presents a software framework providing a platform for parallel and distributed processing of video data on a cluster of SMP computers. Existing video-processing algorithms can be easily integrated into the framework by considering them as atomic processing tiles (PTs). PTs can be connected to form processing graphs that model the data flow. Parallelization of the tasks in this graph is carried out automatically using a pool-of-tasks scheme. The data format that can be processed by the framework is not restricted to image data, such that also intermediate data, like detected feature points, can be transferred between PTs. Furthermore, the processing can be carried out efficiently on special-purpose processors with separate memory, since the framework minimizes the transfer of data. We also describe an example application for a multi-camera view-interpolation system that we successfully implemented on the proposed framework.

1   Introduction

Video processing and analysis systems pose high demands on the computation platform in terms of processing speed, memory bandwidth, and storage capacity. Requirements grow even further if real-time processing speed is needed for analysis and visualization applications. On current commodity hardware, this processing power is not available. For example, simultaneous capturing of two 640×480@25fps videos from IEEE-1394 cameras already fills the full bus bandwidth. The straightforward solution for this problem is to use computation clusters instead of expensive specialized hardware. However, the design of distributed systems is a troublesome task, prone to design flaws.

Most previous approaches to parallel computation have concentrated on fine-granular data-parallelism. In this approach, the algorithms themselves are parallelized, which requires a reimplementation of the algorithms. This is difficult, especially because computer-vision engineers are rarely experts in distributed processing [6]. Since complex systems are composed of many processing steps, parallelization can also be carried out by keeping the (sequential) algorithms as atomic processing steps. This has two advantages: algorithms are easier to

G. Min et al. (Eds.): ISPA 2006 Ws, LNCS 4331, pp. 823–832, 2006.

implement and algorithm development stays independent of the parallelization. Note that it is still possible to use the distributed-processing framework to also parallelize the algorithms itself by splitting the task into smaller sub-tasks that can be computed independently.

In this paper, we propose a generic framework for distributed real-time processing, into which existing software components (algorithms) can be integrated effortlessly. Algorithm parallelization is achieved by splitting the processing into a set of processing tiles (PT). Each processing tile performs a specific operation on a set of inputs and generates one or several outputs. The inputs and outputs of the PTs can be connected to build arbitrary processing graphs, describing the order and dependencies of processing. The framework software takes care about the appropriate distribution of the algorithms over the processing resources and the control of execution.

The proposed framework provides the following features.

1. **The processing graph is not limited to a certain topology.** (like processing pipelines). In particular, PT outputs can be efficiently connected to the inputs of several PTs.
2. **Automatic parallelization.** While the processing within one PT is considered an atomic operation, parallelism is obtained by running PTs in parallel. The framework also allows to process data from different time instances in parallel, such that not only horizontal parallelism (concurrency of independent tasks), but also vertical parallelism (pipelining) is exploited.
3. **The framework is network transparent.** The processing graph can be distributed over a cluster of computers and still be accessed in a uniform way. If data has to be sent across the network, this is done transparently by the framework.
4. **The framework supports operations on arbitrary data-types.** Hence, not only image data can be processed, but also structured data-types like mesh-based geometry. An important alternative view onto this is that data can be processed in different representations. For example, low-level processing tasks (lens-distortion correction, image-rectification, depth estimation) can be implemented more efficiently on the graphics processor (GPU). In this case, the image data is loaded into the texture memory of the graphics card. Since the overhead of transferring the image data between main memory and the graphics card would annihilate the performance gain of processing on the GPU, it should be avoided whenever possible. This is achieved by passing only handles to the texture data between PTs and doing the conversion to image data in main memory only when necessary.

In this paper, we will first describe the main considerations taken into account when designing the framework software (see Section 2), and we give an overview of the framework architecture. In Section 3, we describe the implementation in more detail. An example application and its implementation using the proposed framework is presented in Section 4.

2   Design of the Distributed Processing Framework

2.1   Design Considerations

The design of our *Distributed Processing Framework* (DPF) was driven by the following requirements.

Fine-Grained Vs. Coarse-Grained Parallelization. Previous work on parallel algorithms has mostly considered parallelization using a fine-granular data-parallelism within a single algorithm. The difficulty with this approach is that it complicates the implementation of the algorithm, because it requires knowledge of the image-processing algorithms as well as knowledge about parallel and distributed programming. On the other hand, large applications consist of a multitude of processing steps. This allows to apply parallel processing on a coarser level, at which every algorithm is (conceptually) implemented in a sequential program (in practice, this does not have to be followed strictly, as we will describe in Section 4). Since we are targeting complex video-processing systems comprising several algorithms, we have chosen the coarse-grained parallelization because it simplifies the implementation of each algorithm. Furthermore, the coarse-grained parallelization has a lower communication overhead, which is usually one of the most restricting bottlenecks.

SMP and Cluster Parallelization. Currently, multi-core processors begin to replace single-core processors because they allow to increase the computation speed more economically than by increasing the processor frequency. While current processors have two or four cores, the number of cores is expected to increase further in the future. But even with multi-core processors, the processing speed is limited because of the limited memory-bandwidth, limited I/O bandwidth, or simply because the computation speed of these processors is still not sufficient for the application. To overcome these limitations, processing in a cluster of computers is a viable approach [1].

For these reasons, the DPF should enable parallel processing in both ways, by exploiting multiple processing cores within one shared-memory system (SMP), and by distributing the work over a cluster of computers.

Automatic Parallelization Vs. Manual Splitting of Tasks. In designing a system using our DPF, it must be decided which processing tiles should be processed on which computer. The optimal design of the processing network can be determined automatically, but we still prefer to specify the assignment of the processing tiles to the computers by hand for the following reasons. First, the number of processing tiles is rather limited for most systems, and the placement of some of these tiles is dictated by the hardware (the camera capturing must take place at the computer to which the cameras are connected). Second, for an automatic optimal distribution of the tasks, exact knowledge about the processing times, the required bandwidths, or the available computation resources is required. These are often difficult to specify formally, particularly in a heterogeneous architecture with special-purpose processors.

Flexibility. Our intention in designing the DPF was to provide a general framework for a wide area of applications. Hence, the design should not impose a specific processing architecture, like a fixed processing pipeline, which might be unsuitable for many applications. Furthermore, the framework should strengthen the reuse of processing tiles for different applications. This is supported by allowing processing tiles to have a flexible number of inputs and outputs, which do not have to be connected all. Unconnected outputs can indicate to the processing tile to disable part of its processing, and optional inputs can be used for optional hints that may help the algorithm.

Special-Purpose Processor Utilization. Many low-level image-processing tasks are well suited for parallel processing, but this parallelism cannot be achieved with standard general-purpose processors. Even though these processors nowadays have support for SIMD instructions, especially designed for multimedia applications, (like MMX on x86, or Altivec on PowerPC architectures), the degree of parallelism is limited and restricted to simple processing.

Additional to the CPU, specific media-processors do exist which offer higher parallelization factors than regular CPUs. When utilizing special-purpose processors with independent memory (like the GPU on graphics cards), it should be considered that the image data to be processed has to be stored in its local memory. The time to transfer the image between different memories is not negligible, and can even exceed the actual computation time. For this reason, it is important to avoid unnecessary memory transfers wherever possible. This has to be considered in the design of the DPF by providing several options how the image data is transferred between successive processing tiles.

2.2   Overview of the Distributed Processing Framework

The core of our distributed processing framework (DPF) is a set of user-definable processing tiles (PT). A processing tile conducts an operation on its input data and generates new output. The number of inputs and outputs is flexible. In order to define the data-flow through the PTs, they can be connected to form a processing graph of an arbitrary topology (without cycles).

A *Processing Graph Control* (PGC) distributes the tasks to carry out in the graph of PTs over a set of worker threads, hereby exploiting multi-processor parallelism in an SMP system. The scheduling is determined by splitting the processing into a set of "(PT, sequence-number)" pairs. Each of these pairs represents a processing task that can be issued to a thread. The scheduler maintains the set of tasks in three queues: the tasks that are currently processed, tasks that are ready to run (all input dependencies are met), and tasks that cannot be started yet because of unmet dependencies. These queues are updated whenever a PT has finished its computation.

For specifying processing graphs that are distributed over several computers in a cluster, the PGC can be wrapped into a *Distributed Processing Graph* (DPG). The DPG provides a uniform access to all PTs even though they might be distributed over different computers. Whenever data is to be transferred between computers, a network connection is established transparently to the user. From a user point-of-view, a DPG looks like a local processing graph, because most of the network distribution is hidden from the user.

It should be emphasized here that the DPF is organized in three separate layers that represent subsets of the features made available by the DPF. The idea is to provide simpler APIs to the programmer when the full-featured framework is not required. The typical usage of these three layers is briefly explained below.

- A system building upon the first layer includes only the PT objects, which are connected to a graph. There is no central scheduler organizing the data processing. Data can be processed directly by pushing new data into some PT input. This will trigger the processing of this tile and also the successive tiles, where additional input is requested as required. On the other hand, the graph of PTs can also be used in a pull mode, where new output data is requested at some PT, which again triggers the processing of the tile. If there is missing input, the PT first acquires the required inputs from the preceding tiles.
- The second layer adds a scheduler (PGC) to the graph of connected tiles. This scheduler manages multiple worker threads to carry out the computations in parallel.
- The third layer adds a network-transparent distribution of the processing graph (DPG) over a cluster of computers. To this end, a server application is run on every computer in the network, and the servers are registered at a central control computer. PTs can be instantiated at any arbitrary computer through a uniform API at the control computer. Connecting two PTs across the network is possible and handled transparently to the user.

3   Implementation Details

3.1   Processing Tiles

All algorithms are wrapped into *Processing Tile* (PT) objects. Each PT can accept a number of inputs and can also create several outputs. For the DPF, a PT appears like an atomic operation (however, the algorithm in the PT may itself be implemented as a parallel algorithm, independent to the parallelization performed in the DPF). Each PT provides the memory for storing the computed results, but it does not include buffers for holding its own input data. The input data is accessed directly from the output buffers of the connected tiles. This prevents that data is unnecessarily copied between PTs, which could constitute a considerable part of the computation time. On the other hand, this blocks the PT that provides the input from already starting the work on the next Data-Unit. If this is a problem, an additional buffering PT can be inserted in-between the two PTs to decouple the data-dependency between these two PTs.

Every output can be connected to several inputs, without any extra cost. Moreover, inputs and outputs can also be left unconnected. While the algorithm within the PT might simply proceed as usual even when there are unconnected outputs, it can be more efficient by disabling generating the data for this output. This feature can be used, for example, to create outputs that provide a visualization of the algorithm. When the visualization is not required, the output can be left unconnected. Connecting only some of the inputs can be used, for example, for operations that work with a varying number of inputs (like composition of images, depth estimation from multiple cameras), or to support additional *hints* for the algorithm (segmentation masks that can help to increase the quality of the result, but which are not required).

Each PT also saves a *sequence-number*, indicating which frame was processed in the last step, now being available at the outputs. Using this sequence-number, a PT can check if all its inputs are available such that it can start processing.

3.2   Data-Units

Data that should be passed between PTs is encapsulated in *Data-Unit* objects. Each Data-Unit provides a uniform interface for communicating with the DPF, but it can nevertheless hold arbitrary types of data. The Data-Unit must provide a function to serialize the data and to reconstruct the Data-Unit again from the serialized data. This is used by the DPF in order to send data across the network, transparently for the user.

3.3   Using a Graph of PTs Without Processing Graph Control

As noted above, it is possible to use a graph of connected PTs without any further central control. For simple pipelined processing, this comes close to the *Decorator* design-pattern [3] used in software engineering. However, processing in our graph of PTs is more flexible than a straight processing pipeline. We do not only allow arbitrary (acyclic) graphs of PTs, but also allow a push-data semantic as well as a pull-data semantic. Using a graph of PTs without a central Processing Graph Control (see next section) is simple to use, but note that parallel processing is not available.

Processing of a new unit of data is triggered at an arbitrary PT in the graph. If new input is fed into the graph, then triggering happens at the moment when the new data is passed into one PT. Whenever a PT is triggered, it checks if the data at its inputs are already available. This is visible from the sequence-numbers in the predecessor PTs. If some input is missing, this predecessor PT is triggered. When all input is available, the tile performs its operation and triggers all output PTs if they are not yet at the same sequence-number (this can happen if triggering one output PT has propagated to another output).

3.4   Processing Graph Control

The *Processing Graph Contol* (PGC) comprises a scheduler that distributes the processing tasks in a graph of PTs over several processors running in parallel. To this end, a *pool-of-tasks* scheme is applied. The PGC maintains a set of PTs that are ready to process the next Data-Unit. A PT is ready if all the input data is available at the connected inputs, if the PT is not internally blocked, and if the outputs of the PT are not required by any other PT anymore. The PGC maintains three sets of "(PT, sequence-number)" pairs to schedule the tasks to the threads. The **to-be-processed** set is initially filled with all tasks for the first sequence-number. Whenever the first task with the latest sequence-number has started, all tasks for the next sequence-number are added to this set. After a PT has finished its processing, the successor and predecessor PTs are examined if they are now ready to be processed. If they are, the corresponding task is moved from the to-be-processed set into the **ready-to-run** set. Whenever a working thread has finished a task, it gets a new task from the ready-to-run set, moves this task into the **in-progress** set and starts processing.

In order to efficiently test if a task can be processed, an **active-edges** set is maintained. An active edge is an edge in the PT graph, connecting an already-processed output of a tile PT_o with a not-yet processed tile PT_i. This active edge represents a data-dependency which prevents that PT_o can process another unit before PT_i has finished using this output data.

An example of this scheduling algorithm is presented in Fig. 1. In this figure, PTs that are *ready-to-run* are indicated with a black bar at the left (input) side. PTs that are currently being processed are depicted in grey color. When they have their output data available, this is indicated with a black bar at the right (output) side. Active edges between PTs are shown with bold lines. The number in the PT denotes the current sequence-number of the outputs. In this example, we have assumed that processing takes equal time-periods for every tile. Note that this is not required by the scheduling algorithm, in which the processing time is not defined. Also note that the shown schedule is not the only possible one. In Fig. 1(b), instead of processing the two top tiles in the second column, any two tiles from the second column would be a valid next step. The step in Fig. 1(f) is similar to (b), just with the sequence-numbers increased to the next frame.

3.5   Network Transfer

In order to connect two processing graphs on two different computers, the data processed on one computer must be sent to the input at the second computer. This is realized with a network-sender PT and a network-receiver PT. The network-sender PT uses the `Serialize` method of the Data-Unit interface to generate a bit-stream representation of the data. This bit-stream is then stored in a FIFO buffer from which it is sent over the network. The sending is carried out in a separate thread which is managed by the PT itself instead of a global scheduler. This has the twofold advantages that (1) streaming can run with maximum throughput because the thread is always active, and (2) the network-connection PTs can also be used without any PGC. Since the sending thread is almost always blocked in the system-function for network transmission, its computation time is negligible.

The network-receiver PT at the other side works similarly to the network-sender. A separate thread is responsible for receiving new data bit-streams from

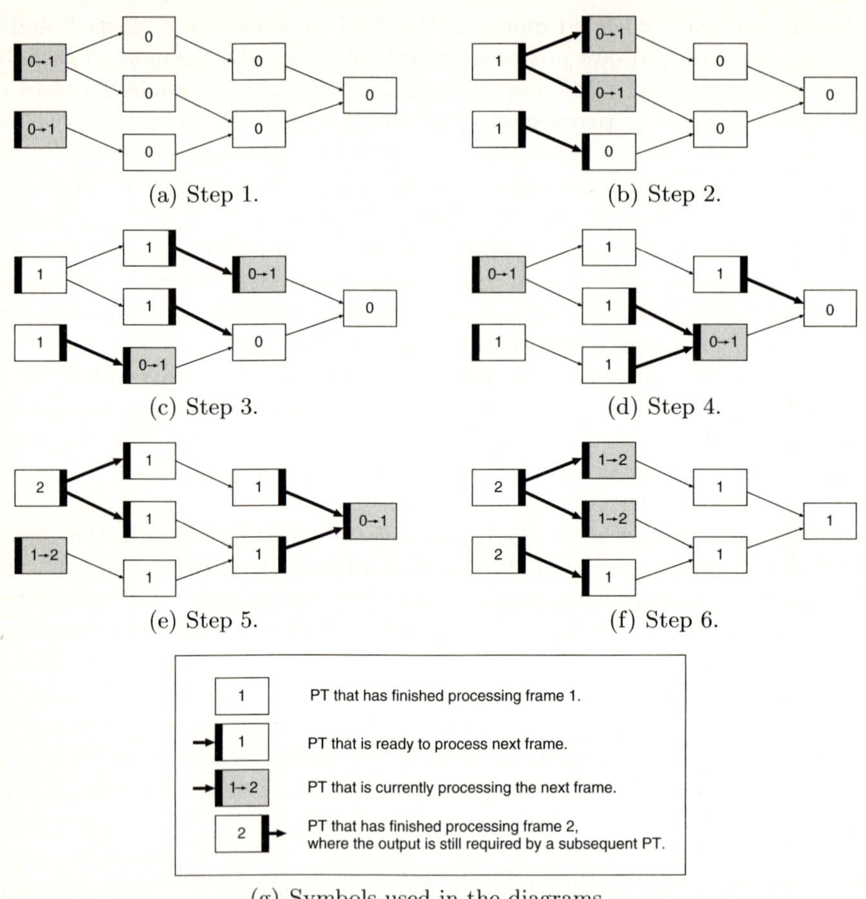

(a) Step 1.

(b) Step 2.

(c) Step 3.

(d) Step 4.

(e) Step 5.

(f) Step 6.

(g) Symbols used in the diagrams.

Fig. 1. Example processing graph running on two CPUs. It is assumed here that processing of each tile takes the same time.

the network. Whenever the PT is triggered, one data packet is removed from the FIFO and used to reconstruct a Data-Unit.

3.6   Distributed Processing Graph

A *Distributed Processing Graph* (DPG) wraps a PGC into a network interface. When DPGs are created on different computers, they can be joined together with a control connection. From that moment onwards, both graphs in the DPGs appear as a joint graph and can also be controlled in a unified way, even though the PTs might be on different computers. New tiles can be created on any computer via the DPG interface by specifying the name of the PT and the system on which it should be instantiated. *Universally Unique Identifiers* (UUIDs) are used to access the PTs in the network.

In the general case, many computers with DPG daemons running on them can be connected into a control tree. Each DPG stores which PTs can be reached via each of its neighboring computers. Control commands for a non-local PT are forwarded to the closest neighbor DPG, which then further handles the request.

The DPG interface can also be used to connect pairs of PTs. If both PTs are on the same computer, a simple direct connection is established like before. If the PTs are on different computers, special PTs are added that serialize the data into a network stream on one computer, and then reconstruct the Data-Unit on the receiving computer (like described in Section 3.5). These network-transmission PTs are connected to the pair of PTs that originally should be connected. This process is transparent to the user of the DPF. Note that the data-transfer connections are independent from the control connections between DPGs. Hence, while the control connections always have a tree topology, data is transferred directly between the involved pair of computers.

In order to run our distributed processing framework on a cluster of computers, a DPG is started as a daemon process on each computer. One computer acts as the control computer, running the actual application program. Note that the DPG daemons are independent of the application program as long as all PTs required by the application are compiled in the DPG daemons. Future work will provide a method to also transmit the PT code over the network and link it dynamically to the DPG.

4   Example Application

As an example application, we implemented a multi-camera view-interpolation system which allows to synthesize images along a set of cameras [2]. For the view-interpolation system, the following tasks have to be carried out.

- Capturing the video streams from the digital cameras.
- Correction for the radial lens distortion.
- Stereo image rectification.
- Depth estimation.
- View interpolation.

These sub-tasks can be implemented in separate PTs. Note that some of the tasks (lens undistortion, rectification, and part of the view interpolation) are implemented on the GPU, while the depth estimation is implemented on the CPU. At the connection between GPU processing and CPU processing, there are conversion PTs to transfer the data between graphics-card memory and main memory.

Because the depth-estimation process is computationally expensive, it is attractive to parallelize this algorithm itself. Even though parallelization *within* one PT is not supported directly by our framework, it can be easily achieved by splitting the PT into separate PTs which compute a partial solution each. The results are then combined into a final solution in a multiplexer PT.

5   Conclusions

This paper has presented a software framework to provide an easy-to-use platform for parallel and distributed processing of video data on a cluster of SMP computers. Existing algorithms can be easily integrated into the framework without reimplementation of the algorithms. The framework organizes the processing order of the algorithms in a graph of atomic processing tiles with unrestricted topology. Parallelization is carried out automatically using a pool-of-tasks scheme.

A specific feature of our framework is that it can be used at three different levels, each comprising comprise a subset of the framework. During the development, PTs can be directly connected without parallelization, to simplify development and debugging. At a second level, a scheduler is added which automatically parallelizes the execution on SMP machines. Finally, in a third level, the processing graph can be distributed over a cluster of computers. As such, the framework provides a scalable approach for distributed processing, without introducing much burden on the programmer.

The framework has been successfully applied on a cluster of multi-processor computers to implement various video-processing tasks, including the described view-interpolation system for multiple input cameras. Because of its flexibility, the framework can be applied to a wide range of applications, probably even in fields other than video processing.

References

1. D. J. Becker, T. Sterling, D. Savarese, J. E. Dorband, U. A. Ranawak, and C. V. Packer. Beowulf: A parallel workstation for scientific computation. In *Proceedings of the International Conference on Parallel Processing*, 1995.
2. D. Farin, Y. Morvan, and P. H. N. de With. View interpolation along a chain of weakly calibrated cameras. In *IEEE Workshop on Content Generation and Coding for 3D-Television*, June 2006.
3. E. Gamma, R. Helm, R. Johnson, and J. Vlissides. *Design Patterns: Elements of Reusable Object-Oriented Software*. Professional Computing Series. Addison-Wesley, 1995.
4. J. Hippold and G. Runger. Task pool teams for implementing irregular algorithms on clusters of smps. In *International Parallel and Distributed Processing Symposium (IPDPS'03)*, pages 54–61, 2003.
5. M. Korch and T. Rauber. Evaluation of task pools for the implementation of parallel irregular algorithms. In *International Conference on Parallel Processing Workshops (ICPPW'02)*, pages 597–604, 2002.
6. F. Seinstra, D. Koelma, and A. Bagdanov. Towards user transparent data and task parallel image and video processing: An overview of the parallel-horus project. In *Proceedings of the 10th International Euro-Par Conference (Euro-Par 2004)*, volume 3149 of *Lecture Notes in Computer Science*, pages 752–759, Aug. 2004.

PSO vs. ACO, Data Grid Replication Services Performance Evaluation

Víctor Méndez[1] and Felix García Carballeira[2]

[1] Universidad de Zaragoza, CPS, Edificio Ada Byron,
Universidad de Zaragoza, CPS, Edificio Ada Byron,
C. María de Luna, 1. 50018 Zaragoza, Spain
`vmendez@unizar.es, eureka@nodo50.org`
[2] Universidad Carlos III de Madrid, EPS, Edificio Sabatini,
Av. de la Universidad, 30, 28911 Leganés. Madrid. Spain
`fgcarbal@inf.uc3m.es`

Abstract. Data Grid replication is critical for improving data intensive applications performance, providing fault tolerance and load balancing. Most of the techniques for data replication use Giggle as a framework for Replica Location Services (RLS), combined with other services for replica selection and optimization. Our previous work have proposed an enhanced Giggle framework, that simplify the location service using a flat catalogue structure, that combined with appropriate heuristic, obtain much better performances than traditional approaches. With this aim, we propose the use of Emergent Artificial Intelligence (EAI) techniques on data replication: Particle Swarm Optimisation(PSO) and Ant Colony Optimisation(ACO). This paper contribution is an experiment comparison between PSO, ACO, a canonical replication algorithm and other state of the art economic model replication algorithm. The experiments are design on two different network topologies. The simulation results confirm that PSO and ACO using the enhanced Giggle, improve performance over traditional solutions.

1 Introduction

Many Grid research groups are focusing on scheduling issue, while data Grid replication systems are still the critical part in final makespan. The assumed framework for data replication, based on OGSA[1] and Giggle[2] *de facto* standards, are giving directions for greedy algorithms with complicated scaling features. Next years Grids are expected to grow in complexity and data size in orders of magnitude, so it is urgent to take up data replication as the critical Grid issue. Our previous work[3] propose an enhanced Giggle framework, that simplified the location service in a flat catalog structure, that combined with suitable heuristic, realize much better performances than traditional approaches. The resulting flat location service is shown on figure 1 and based on Globus middleware[4].

The Giggle location service join with a replica optimisation and catalog services for real Globus infrastructures, like for example EGEE middleware using

G. Min et al. (Eds.): ISPA 2006 Ws, LNCS 4331, pp. 833–843, 2006.

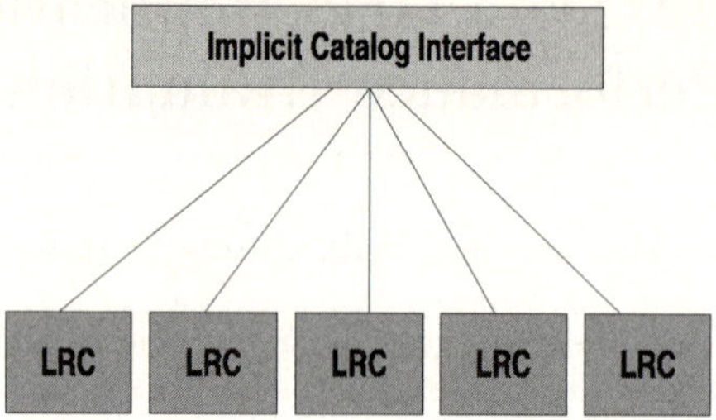

Fig. 1. Flat RLS architecture

ROS and RMC. Our flat Giggle works with simplified versions of those services, supporting optimisation service with Emergent Artificial Intelligent(EAI) algorithms. Given a logical identifier of a file(LFN), the RLS must to provide the physical locations of the replicas for the file(PFN). The traditional RLS consists of two components: Local Replica Catalogs (LRCs) manages consistent information about logical to physical mappings on each site or node, and Replica Location Index(RLIs) provides non-consistent information about the asociated LRCs or others RLIs file entries. With our scheme is possible avoid RLI entities. Figure 1 show a generic example where there is no RLI, but an Implicit Catalog Interface, realice location services based on an emergent algorithm, and without explicit file entries information.

Next section of this paper briefly describes the economic algorithm[5]. We also summarise the PSO[3] and ACO[6] Grid algorithms presented on our previous works.

After background section we show the evaluation methodology, and on fourth we present experimental results on two network topologies. Finally we summarise some conclusions and future work.

2   Grid Replication Background

One of the most famous Grid replication approach is the the economic algorithm proposed by OptorSim group[5], that understand the Grid as a market where data files represent the goods. They are purchased by Computing Elements for jobs and by Storage Elements in order to make an investment that will improve their revenues in the future. The files are sold by Storage Elements to Compute Elements and to other Storage Elements. Compute Elements try to minimise the file purchase cost and the Storage Elements have the goal of maximising profits.

When a replication decision is taken, the file transfer cost is the price for the good. The Replica Optimiser may replicate or not, based on whether the replication(with associated file transfer and file deletion) will result in to reduce the expected future access cost for the local Computing Elements. Replica Optimiser keeps track of the file requests it receives and uses an evaluation function: $E(f, n, r)$, defined in [7] that returns the predicted number of times a file f, will be request in the next n, based on the past r request history base line. The prediction function E is calculated for a new file request received on Replica Optimiser for file f. E is also calculated for every file in the node storage. If there is no file with less value than E for new file request f, then no replication occurs. Otherwise least value file is selected for deletion an new replica is created for f.

EAI is an Artificial Intelligence branch that inspired in the natural social behaviour is used for optimisation. Bees swarm, birds flocks searching food[8], or ant colony[9] are examples of such social beings.

Traditional PSO algorithm was created by Dr. Eberhart. The PSO-Grid algorithm was proposed on our previous work[3]. On Grid environments we introduce some tactic modifications, based on the strategy "follow the closer bird from the food chunk" as social PSO flavour. A bird flock is in a random search for food in an area. For each bird there is only one valid kind of food. The bird does not known where is the food chunk, but its known how long is from the different areas, and it know how many birds are finding they food chunk on this areas, it is called food chirp. This is the social component of our approach, thus the distance to the food chunk is calculated for each bird flock, not for individual birds. The strategy is to follow the closer bird flock with best success food search.

The PSO-Grid uses a performance metric for a file replication between two nodes i, j, defined in equation 1.

$$p_{i,j} = (e_j * c_{i,j}) + ((1 - e_b) * c_{i,b})$$ (1)

The external hit ration, e, is calculated based on N lasts external success request ratio on node j. We use b as the identifier of the node with the best performance metric associated to i, from the evaluated j nodes. Initially b is the producer node of the replica, and in the pseudo-code below is the get producer function.

Considering network access cost, c, we propose the following equation 2:

$$c(i,j) = lt_{i,j} * c1 + (MAX_{BW} - bw_{i,j}) * c2$$ (2)

For our case $c1 = 1$ and $c2 = 0.2$. On the equation 2 $c1$ and $c2$ are coefficients that balance the relative relevance between latency and bandwidth, they also should fit with the bandwidth and latency values of the specific Grid infrastructure, and also fit with their measure relationship (ms. and MB/s.). At the end of the day latency is more important than bandwidth, because latency is always constant, and bandwidth has a variable behaviour depending on sockets allocations and number of network request in a specific moment. MAX_{BW} is the highest bandwidth of all the Grid infrastructure.

The performance function is balancing the probability of find a replica in a node j with the probability of not finding on j, where we may have to reply from the node with best metric, b, initially the producer site.

On the PSO-Grid algorithm the file request is a particle, and the particles in a Site are a swarm. When the file object is found the particle died and the file reply is done with traditional routing methods. The basic algroithm is exposed on the next pseudo-code.

```
Loop
    For each particle not finding file on node i
        Initialize best node as requested file producer site,
            and best metric as performance from i to producer.
        For each node j, not i, from the Grid
            If actual performance(i,j) is less than best one.
                Get new performance(i,j) as best metric,
                    and j as best node.
            End if
        End for each j.
        Launch replica request to best node.
    End for each particle.
Until End Condition.
```

The ACO-Grid algorithm was proposed on our previous work[6]. It is based on ant social behaviour, and for computational purposes is relevant the way of finding paths between food sources and anthill. While walking, ants places on the ground some amount of pheromone. Ants smell pheromone and when choosing their way, they tend in probability to the paths marked with stronger pheromone concentrations. When the time pass the pheromone concentration decrease. Repeating same behaviour they compose optimised trails that are dynamically defining, and they use to find food sources and nests.

The historic algorithm was enunciate by Dr.Dorigo for salesman traveller[10]. This environment is very similar to the Grid, and can be used in a very direct way modifying for Grid dynamic and discrete features. Every Grid request is an ant, when it find its file object, the ant died, and the Grid replies routing is done with traditional methods.

```
Loop
    For each ant not finding file object on actual Grid site.
        Select a neighbour node with state transition rule.
        Change the state to neighbour node placing pheromone on
            the selected conection for path to new node.
        Apply a local updating rule to all conections on
            same original node.
    End for each ant.
Until End Condition.
```

Each edge between node (r, s) has a distance or cost associate $\delta(r, s)$ and a pheromone concentration $\tau(r, s)$. The equation 3 is the state transition rule, that is a probabilistic function for each node u, that has not been visited by each ant on node r.

$$P_k(r, s) = \frac{[\tau(r, s)][\eta(r, s)]^{\beta}}{\Sigma[\tau(r, u)][\eta(r, u)]^{\beta}} \tag{3}$$

The parameter β determine the relevance of the pheromone concentration compared with the distance. The ACO heuristic function $\eta(r, s)$, for our ACO-Grid algorithm is the reverse of τ. The pheromone concentration on equation 4 is the local updating rule.

$$\tau(r, s) = (1 - \alpha)\tau(r, s) + \Sigma \Delta\tau_k(r, s) \qquad (4)$$

Where α is the pheromone evaporation factor between 0 and 1. And $\Delta\tau_k(r, s)$ is the reverse of the distance or cost, if (r,s) is its path and is 0 if it is not in the path.

ACO-Grid does not use global updating rule. Every time a request is processed on a Grid site, tau is update for all the site connections. The Grid distance or cost is defined on equation 5 as a function of network latency lt and bandwidth bw.

$$\delta(r, s) = lt_{r,s} * c1 + (MAX_{BW} - bw_{r,s}) * c2 \qquad (5)$$

On the equation 5 is calculated the same as 2, explained on PSO above.

3   Evaluation Methodology

We have implemented a full simulation toolkit, SiCoGrid, a completed Grid simulation environment as we describe on previous work[3]. SiCoGrid is developed in Parsec[11] that is a combination of C and a simulator parser for creating event driven simulators, and also use DiskSim[12] for the storage disks simulation subsystem.

This paper is a performance evaluation of economic model, ACO-Grid, and PSO-Grid algorithms for two different stages. The replica policy is pure data Grid with computing on the client, thus all the active and passive time is consumed on the Grid client, as show figure 2

(a): The *client* read the request from the log file. (b): The *client* launch a request on the site or node, through the *Local Network* to the *Resource Broker*, that will manage the request in order to return to the client the appropriate data and/or computing results. (c): If the requested file is not on the site, then the RB pass the request to the *node* that depending on the replication and scheduling algorithms, it route to the appropriate *Remote Network* instantiation. (d): Asynchronous data replies from remote sites are received on the *node*, that send it to the corresponding SE. (b)ACK: Requested block file is send from SE to Client data Grid.

This is the case the client has to know the results of the execution with a block requested, to obtain the next block file object to be requested. The process is the same for N request of a job, and after the last job request, the Grid client user will spend a *Passive Time*.

When the Grid Client receives a block file, from local or remote sites, then calculate results for this block along *Active Time*, and after client submit a new request, if the request was the last one of the job, the Grid Client holds a *Passive Time* before a new job starts.

The sites are grouped on three main class as tiers of the grid. Tier of first class has more storage features an also higher bandwidth connection. This split in site classes is the typical EGEE requirements for diferent levels of sites participations.

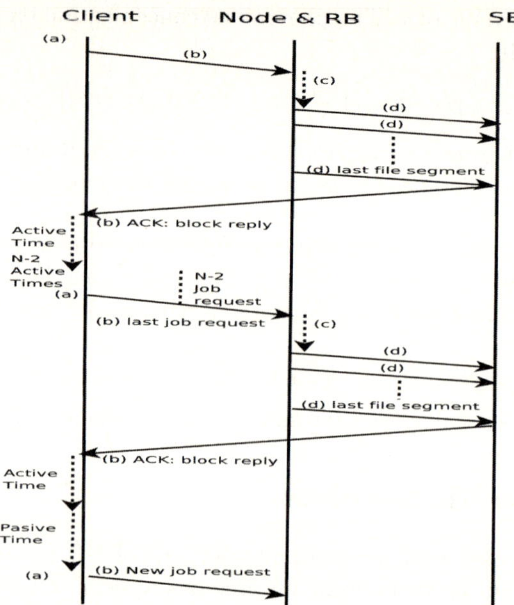

Fig. 2. Pure Data Grid Protocol

The experiment workload are log files created with specific application of the SiCoGrid toolkit, and depends on the following. The number of Grid clients N on each site (traffic density). The number of jobs M that a client do in a simulation (experiment length). Every job has many block file request. We use Gaussian random walk file access pattern, that is the best performance for the state of the art economic OptorSim approach[13].

3.1   Uncyclical Graph Stage

We have configured our SiCoGrid for network topology shown on the Figure 3. The graph disposes a nomenclature where the nodes have a first number that is the tier class, and after the point another identification number. Below there is the storage size of the node in GB. The networks have assigned two numbers, the first one is the latency in ms and the other is the bandwidth in MB/s. The storage capacity, file size, and network bandwidth is scaled in the magnitude of twenty, for time simulation reasons. Therefore the obtained time results will be on the same magnitude.

We have design an experiment with four levels on N and M factors: 4x4, 4x5, 4x6, 4x7, 5x4, 5x5, ... 7x6, 7x7. We repeat for unconditional, market model, PSO-Grid and ACO-Grid algorithms. We perform three statistical occurrences for each experiment instantiation.

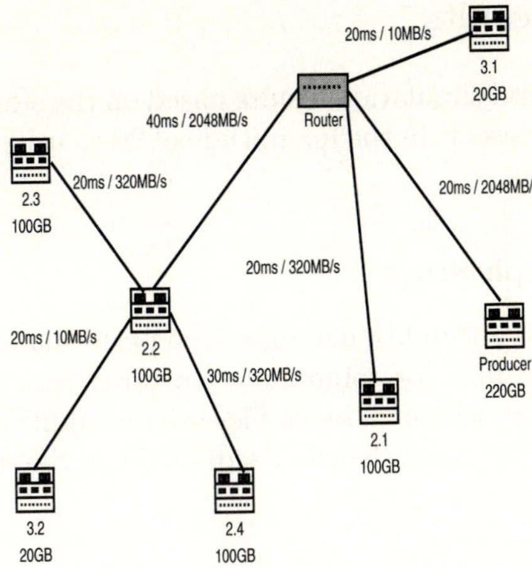

Fig. 3. Simulated Grid Uncyclical Graph Stage

3.2   Cyclical Graph Stage

On the Figure 4 we can see the network topology used on the second experiment. The graph disposes same nomenclature as before.

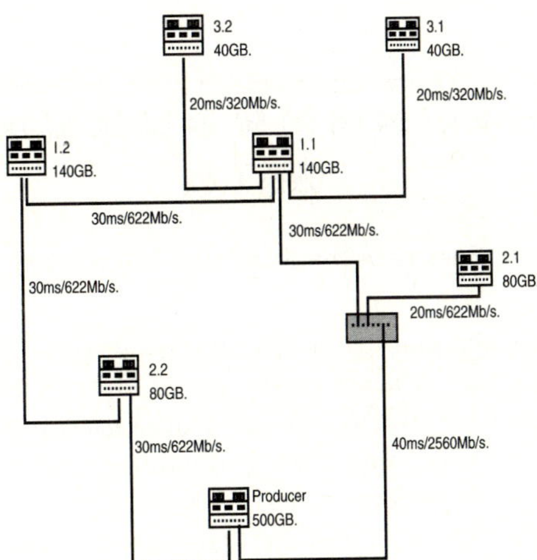

Fig. 4. Simulated Grid Cyclical Graph Stage

We have design an experiment with three levels on N and M factors: 4x4, 4x5, 4x6, 5x4, 5x5, 5x6, 6x4, 6x5, 6x6. We repeat for unconditional, market model, PSO and ACO algorithms. We also do three statistical occurrences for each experiment instantiation.

4 Simulation Results

We following present Grid simulation results based on the stages described above. The job response time is scale in the magnitude of 20 to usual jobs duration from hours to some days.

4.1 Uncyclical Graph Stage

The Figure 5 shows the unconditional algorithm performances on the top of the chart, with black colour line, for comparison purposes as a canonical algorithm for location and selection, where all block files are unconditional requested to the original file producer, with Last Recent Used(LRU) as the deletion algorithm.

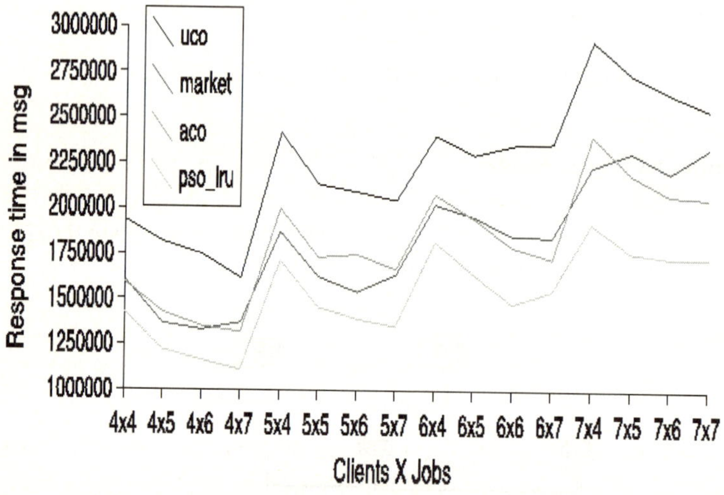

Fig. 5. Experiments Results in the Simulated Uncycled Graph Grid Stage

The bottom lines are the market model on dark gray, ACO on light gray, and PSO on very light gray line. Market model is the OptorSim group optimisation and deletion algorithm. Our ACO-Grid and PSO-Grid approaches use LRU for deletion. The results are very similar for economic model and ACO-Grid algorithms. ACO-Grid improve performances on the half of the simulation series, for 4x4, 4x7, 6x5, 6x6, 6x7, 7x5, 7x6, and 7x7, that are the heavy workloads. Thus ACO-Grid is intuitively expected to performs better on bigger Grid infrastructures. PSO-Grid is the best performances for all simulation series. PSO-Grid response rate performances is around 30% faster than canonical and around 15% faster than economic model and ACO-Grid.

Furthermore we compare canonical line with the others, and we can see that ACO follow the unconditional pattern on lower response time results. Market model start following this pattern, but with heavy workload experiments, on the right part of the chart, market model loses the pattern and it is quickly prone to join with unconditional algorithm line. PSO-Grid is the algorithms that best fits with canonical line, on much less response rate results.

4.2   Cyclical Graph Stage

The Figure 6 show results of clients by site and jobs by client for 4x4, 4x5, 4x6, 5x4, 5x5, 5x6, 6x4, 6x5, and 6x6 simulation series.

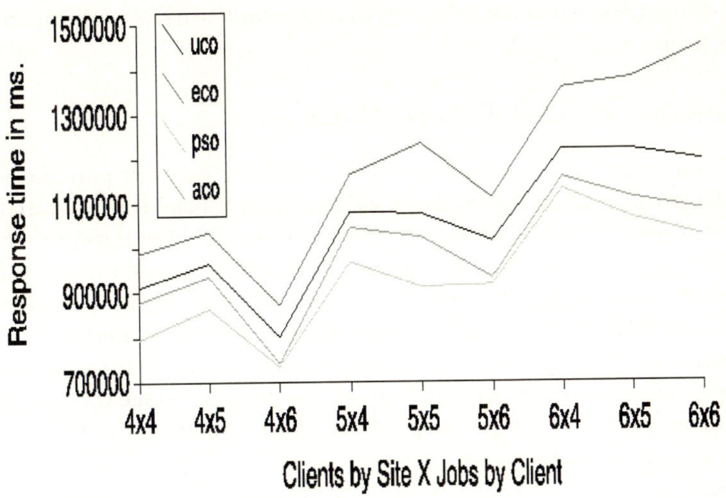

Fig. 6. Experiments Results in the Simulated Cycled Graph Grid Stage

On the top of the chart worst results are for econmic model on dark gray. The canonical algorithm, unconditional replication from producer, is draw on black, the second line from the top. ACO-Grid show better results than unconditional, on the light gray line, and PSO-Grid has the best performances for all simulation series, on very light gray line. PSO-Grid performaces are the best results also in all the repetitions of the experiment. The PSO-Grid improve job response time over canonical around 11%, 21% over economic and 6% over ACO-Grid.

On economic model is relevant the increasing response time on right part of the chart, corresponding to the bigger simulation series. This chart show much better scalability for EAI algorithms, even the unconditional, than the economic market model.

Both experiments, cycled and uncycled, does not consider fault tolerance issues. On a real infrastructures, Grid failures are important for final job response time. Considering fault events, ACO-Grid may even show much better results compared with market model, and other approaches that exploit functionalities dependencies between Grid sites. The reason for expected better ACO-Grid behaviour on fault tolerance, is that our approach does not need any restore time. After a resource failure, the hold system is still working the same as before the failure. On ACO-Grid the control services are flat distributed on the Grid, and all the sites are functionality independent with each others. PSO-Grid needs some control information when a sites fails, so performances considering Grid failures will be between economic model algorithm and the best fault tolerance ACO-Grid algorithm.

EAI Grid algorithms realize this performances due to its features: no control traffic(ACO-Grid) or very little control traffic(PSO-Grid); distributed optimisation, localisation and selection services; autonomous management of each node that will fit best on user and geographical affinities; collaborative strategic against competitive strategic of the economic, that usually performs better on the long term.

5   Conclusions and Future Work

We have presented the first performance evaluation between popular economic model algorithm, and two aproaches based on EAI. It has been evaluated using a full network and disk simulation, SiCoGrid, on two different network topologies, the first an uncycled one, and the second on a cycled graph topology. EAI has been proved as the best performance on this two basic stages. PSO-Grid is the best one over ACO-Grid, for all the experiments and repetitions.

We have seen different behaviours on economic model. Cycled stage results are worst than the canonical algorithm, but on the uncycled stage econmic performs better. Thus we can enunciate that data Grid performances are very dependent from the specific Grid topology.

Nowaday parsecc is crashing with high disk swaping rate, wich is usual on bigger simulations than the presented on this paper. This parsecc bug can not be fixed because the application sources are privative. Future work will focus on a real Grid topology simulation. For this aim we need a SiCoGrid develop with an opensource parsec technology, that give us the posibility of manage the memory allocation on a single machine, or on a parallelized environment, and what it is more important, avoiding the actual parsec memory bugs.

We will present gparsec, a GNU-GPL version of the parsec, that will achieve our goal of a production release for SiCoGrid, that will be published for the research community as the best guarantee for collective contribution scheme. We also plan to introduce parallelisation features to the gparser in order to run real scale simulations, using a cluster or Grid environment with some of the more used techniques like OpenMP or MPI. We like to validate our simulation results on real Grids of big size, such as EGEE.

Another interesting aspect is to introduce real state of the art scheduling policies, and Emergent Artificial Intelligent algorithms following our Data Grid studies.

We also have research targets on fault tolerance issues and depth variable correlations studies.

Acknowledgements

This work has been supported by the Spanish Ministry of Education and Science under the TIN2004-02156 contract.

References

1. Foster, I., Kesselman, C., M.Nick, J., Tuecke, S.: The physiology of the grid an open grid services architecture for distributed system integration. Technical report, Globus Proyect Draft Overwiev Paper (2002)
2. Chervenak, A.L., Deelman, E., Foster, I., Iamnitchi, A., Kesselman, C., Hoschek, W., Kunszt, P., Ripeanu, M., Schwartzkopf, B., Stockinger, H., Stockinger, K., Tierney, B.: Giggle: A framework for constructing scalable replica location services. In: Proc. of the IEEE Supercomputing Conference (SC 2002), IEEE Computer Society Press (November 2002)
3. Méndez, V., García, F.: Pso-lru algorithm for datagrid replication service. In: Proceedings of 2006 International Workshop on High-Performance Data Management in Grid Environments, Springer-Verlag (2006)
4. Foster, I., Kesselman, C.: Globus: A metacomputing infrastructure toolkit. IJSA **11** (1997) 115–128
5. Cameron, D.G., Carvajal-Schiaffino, R., Millar, A.P., Nicholson, C., Stockinger, K., Zini, F.: Analysis of scheduling and replica optimisation strategies for data grids using optorsim. International Journal of Grid Computing **2** (2004) 57–69
6. Méndez, V., García, F.: Ant colony optimization for datagrid replication services. Technical report, RR-06-08. Computer Science Departament, Universidad de Zaragoza. (2006)
7. Capozza, L., Stockinger, K., , Zini., F.: Preliminary evaluation of revenue prediction functions for economically-effective file replication. Technical report, DataGrid-02-TED-020724, Geneva, Switzerland, July 2002 (July 2002)
8. Shi, Y. ;Eberhart, R.: A modified particle swarm optimizer. In: Proceedings of the IEEE International Conference on Evolutionary Computation, IEEE Press. Piscataway, NY (1998) 69–73
9. M., D., Maniezzo, V., Colorni, A.: The ant system: An autocatalytic optimizing process. technical report no. 91-016 revised. Technical report, Politecnico di Milano (1991)
10. Dorigo, M.: Optimization, learning and natural algorithms. PhD thesis, Politecnico di Milano, Italy. (1992)
11. Leijen, D.: Parsec, a fast combinator parser. Technical report, Computer Science Department, University of Utrecht (2002)
12. R.Granger, G., L.Worthington, B., N.Patt, Y., eds.: The DiskSim Simulation Environment. Version 2.0 Reference Manual. University of Michigan (1999)
13. Bell, W.H., Cameron, D.G., Capozza, L., Millar, A.P., Stockinger, K., Zini, F.: Optorsim - a grid simulator for studying dynamic data replication strategies. International Journal of High Performance Computing Applications **17** (2003)

A Markovian Performance Model for Resource Allocation Scheduling on GNU/Linux

Regiane Y. Kawasaki[1], Luiz Affonso Guedes[2], Diego L. Cardoso[1],
Carlos R.L. Francês[1], Glaucio H.S. Carvalho[1], João C.W.A. Costa[1],
and Nandamundi L. Vijaykumar[3]

[1] Department of Electrical and Computing Engineering, Federal University of Pará
(UFPA), 66.075-900,
Belém, PA, Brazil
`{kawasaki, diego, rfrances, ghsc}@ufpa.br`
[2] Department of Computing Engineering and Automation, Federal University of Rio
Grande do Norte (UFRN), 59072-970,
Natal, RN, Brazil
`affonso@dca.ufrn.br`
[3] National Institute for Space Research (INPE), Computing and Applied
Mathematics Laboratory (LAC), P.O. Box 515, 12245-970,
São José dos Campos, SP, Brazil
`vijay@lac.inpe.br`

Abstract. The current paper addresses the problem of quality of service (QoS) provisioning in a general purpose operating system (GPOS), in this case GNU/Linux. Particularly, we propose to change the CPU allocation in that OS by reserving a percentage of a CPU capacity in order to ensure the QoS provisioning according to the QoS demand of each process. In order to investigate the effectiveness of that approach, Markovian models are proposed to represent the dynamics of the systems. Results show that the OS with reservation outperforms the system without it, but also that there is a performance tradeoff in the OS with reservation in such a way that an improvement in the QoS perceived by processes using the reserved capacity is done at a cost of a degradation in the QoS perceived by the other processes.

1 Introduction

As mentioned in the related literature ([1], [2], [3], [4] and [5]) several studies were made on the applicability of Markov models to investigate network technologies and their associated traffic. However, very few discuss the behavior of the front-end computers when the traffic turns into processes in a given operation system. For example, [6] presents a generic model for an Operating System (OS) scheduler for Non-Uniform Memory Access (NUMA) machines using the Stochastic Automata Networks (SAN) formalism. SAN is used to describe processes and processors in the OS and their behavior when processes have to be migrated.

G. Min et al. (Eds.): ISPA 2006 Ws, LNCS 4331, pp. 844–853, 2006.

Due to the necessity of investigating the feasibility of providing QoS to guarantee a minimum of resources to processes that need a differentiated treatment in a general purpose operating system, in case GNU/Linux, a performance model has been developed for the traditional GNU/Linux scheduler. It is important to point out that this model had to be developed as there are no such models available that deal with this issue. This proposal models the host's OS, that allows to verify the direct impact in the performance of distributed applications.

Besides the traditional GNU/Linux model, a different model that reserves a percentage of the processor time for providing attention to priority tasks has also been developed. By solving these models, their performance evaluation was compared to identify the changes in the system behavior due to reserving the resource. The contributions of this paper are: Markov model for Linux scheduler; model to reserve a resource (CPU) in this environment; and the analysis of the performance of these two strategies.

This paper is organized as follows. In Section 2 it describes the current process scheduler used in the GNU/Linux operating system. In Section 3 it shows the analytical model of Linux scheduler architecture and another model with CPU allocation. The performance analysis is based on a detailed mathematical model followed by numerical results that are presented in Section 4, admitted with or without resource reservation models. Finally, Section 5 shows the final remarks of this work.

2   Linux Scheduler

Since version 2.5, the Linux scheduler has been called O(1) scheduler because all of its routines execute in constant time, no matter how many processors there are [7]. The current version of the Linux scheduler (kernel version 2.6.11) brought many advances. Amongst them, the possibility of allowing scheduling processes in multitasking systems such as Symmetric Multiprocessor (SMP) or NUMA [8].

The basic structure of the Linux scheduler is the process queue (*struct runqueue*). This *struct* is defined inside the archive *kernel/sched.c*. The current O(1) scheduler keeps a *runqueue* per processor, which is responsible for containing all the executable processes of a given processor. Thus, if a process is inserted in a *runqueue* of a specific processor, it will only run on that processor [6]. Each *runqueue* contains two priority arrays [7]: active and expired. Priority arrays are data structures composed of a priority bitmap and an array that contains one process queue for each priority.

The search for the higher priority is restricted to this bitmap, which uses a simple and fast algorithm called *sched_find_first_bit()*, that is, to look for the first element one ("1") within the map. When the first bit one is found ("1"), it is verified that in this row, at least one or more processes are ready for execution with that priority; then, the first one of this queue is removed and it will gain access to the processor for a given timeslice. After the execution is finished or by finalizing the task or finishing its execution time, timeslice and priority are recalculated, and it reschedules the current processes to a queue (based on the new priority) in the expired array. Each *runqueue* has two pointers to the priority arrays. When the active array is empty, the pointers are switched: the active array passes to the expired array and vice-versa. The main advantages of this operation are: the avoidance of moving all processes to the active priority array; the execution in constant time; and keeping the scheduling algorithm with $O(1)$ complexity.

3   Analytical Model

Linux scheduler and admission control is depicted in Fig. 1. Higher and lower priority jobs arrive at the system according to two mutually independent Poisson processes with parameters λ_1 and λ_2, respectively. For the sake of simplicity, it is assumed that both services require a negative exponential service time with rate μ.

A job is removed from the active array if: (a) its processing is finished, with rate $qs_1\mu$ (for high priority jobs) and $qs_2\mu$ (for the other processes); or (b) it needs to be rescheduled to the high priority queue or low priority queue in the expired array, with rates $pr_1\mu$ or $pr_3\mu$, respectively. The scheduling of a job in the low priority queue in the active array is tied to the occupancy of the high priority queue in the active array in the sense that it will only be scheduled if the high priority queue in the active array is empty. When the processing queues are empty in an active array and there is a job to be processed in the expired array, these arrays are switched. This switching (via pointer) has an associated time of the $10^{-6}s$ [7].

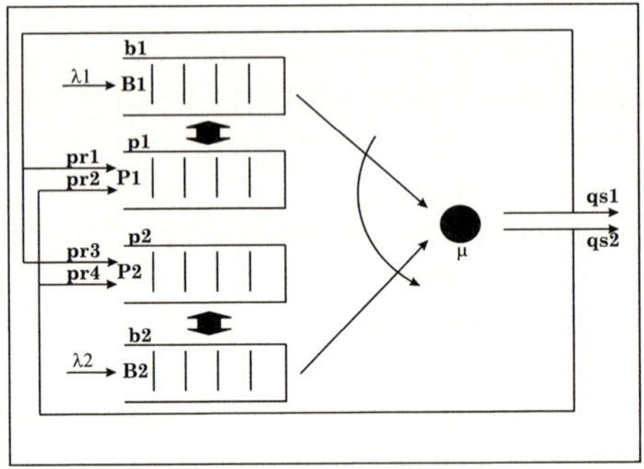

Fig. 1. System model

Given the assumptions presented above, it a Continuous-Time Markov Chain (CTMC) [9] model of the system, whose state is defined as:

$$s = (b_1, b_2, p_1, p_2, ac | 0 \le b_1 \le B_1; 0 \le b_2 \le B_2; 0 \le p_1 \le P_1; 0 \le p_2 \le P_2; ac = 0 \ or \ 1)$$

Where b_1 and p_1 are the number of processes in the high priority queues; and b_2 and p_2 are the number of processes in the low priority queues; and B_i

is the buffer size of the queue i. At time, there is only one high priority queue in the active array and only one low priority queue in the active array, and the remainders are on the expired array. In order to indicate which queues are in these arrays it is used the variable ac, in such a way that if $ac = 0$, then the queues b_1 and b_2 will be in the active array and p_1 and p_2 in the expired array, and when $ac = 1$, vice-versa.

In order to evaluate the performance of the Linux scheduler, some performance measurements may be derived from the steady state probability of that CTMC. Because of the symmetry of the system only the performance measurements associated with the condition $ac = 0$ will be described, i.e., when b_1 and b_2 are in the active array, and p_1 and p_2 are in the expired array. Thus, let $p(b_1, b_2, p_1, p_2, ac)$ be the steady state probability of that Markov model, then the job blocking probability (Pbi) of a job in the queue i, it is given by the probability of its priority queue is full. Eq. (1) shows, for instance, that probability for the high priority queue in the active array. The job blocking probability for other arrays may be computed at the same way.

$$Pb_1 = \sum_{b2=0}^{B_2} \sum_{p1=0}^{P_1} \sum_{p2=0}^{P_2} \pi(B_1, b_2, p_1, p_2, 0) \tag{1}$$

The mean delay of the high priority queue and the low priority queue in the active array may be computed as

$$Wb_1 = \frac{\sum_{b1=1}^{B_1} \sum_{b2=0}^{B_2} \sum_{p1=0}^{P_1} \sum_{p2=0}^{P_2} b_1 \pi(b_1, b_2, p_1, p_2, 0)}{\lambda_1(1 - Pb_1)} \tag{2}$$

$$Wb_2 = \frac{\sum_{b1=0}^{B_1} \sum_{b2=1}^{B_2} \sum_{p1=0}^{P_1} \sum_{p2=0}^{P_2} b_2 \pi(b_1, b_2, p_1, p_2, 0)}{\lambda_2(1 - Pb_2)} \tag{3}$$

where, Pb_2 is the job blocking probability on the low priority queue. Likewise, since, at time, only p_1 and p_2 are in the expire array, the mean delay of the high priority queue and the low priority queue may be, respectively, computed as

$$Wp_1 = \frac{\sum_{b1=0}^{B_1} \sum_{b2=0}^{B_2} \sum_{p1=1}^{P_1} \sum_{p2=0}^{P_2} p_1 \pi(b_1, b_2, p_1, p_2, 0)}{\mu(pr_1 + pr_2)(1 - Pp_1)} \tag{4}$$

$$Wp_2 = \frac{\sum_{b1=0}^{B_1} \sum_{b2=0}^{B_2} \sum_{p1=0}^{P_1} \sum_{p2=1}^{P_2} p_2 \pi(b_1, b_2, p_1, p_2, 0)}{\mu(pr_3 + pr_4)(1 - Pp_2)} \tag{5}$$

Where, Pp_1 and Pp_2 are the job blocking probability on the high sand low priority queue in the expired array. The throughput of the jobs of the high priority queue and low priority queue in the active array are, respectively, given by:

$$X_1 = qs_1\mu \sum_{b1>0}^{B_1} \sum_{b2=0}^{B_2} \sum_{p1=0}^{P_1} \sum_{p2=0}^{P_2} \pi(b_1, b_2, p_1, p_2, 0) \tag{6}$$

$$X_2 = qs_2\mu \sum_{b_2>0}^{B_2} \sum_{p_1=0}^{P_1} \sum_{p_2=0}^{P_2} \pi(0, b_2, p_1, p_2, 0) \tag{7}$$

Here it is considered only jobs that finish their processing and leaving the system.

3.1 Reservation Model

In this section, it is extended the model depicted previously by changing CPU allocation by means of splitting the CPU capacity into two parts: a percentage R is allocated for applications with high priority that demands QoS guarantees; and the remainder capacity $(1 - R)$ is assigned for other process. Fig. 2 shows that scheme.

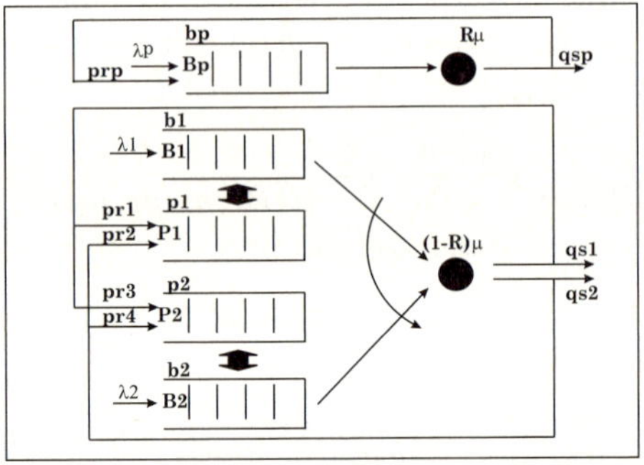

Fig. 2. Resource allocation

The state of the CTMC of that system is defined as: $s = (b_1, b_2, p_1, p_2, bp, ac|0 \leq b_1 \leq B_1; 0 \leq b_2 \leq B_2; 0 \leq p_1 \leq P_1; 0 \leq p_2 \leq P_2; 0 \leq b_p \leq B_p; ac = 0 or 1)$.

Where the main difference between that model and previous one consists in the random variable bp that represents the high priority processes, which demand QoS guarantees. Besides, the rates of the remainder processes have to be multiplied by the factor $(1 - R)$. Table 1 shows that CTMC.

Transitions from state s to all possible successor states are reported in Table 1 along with their rates and conditions under which the transitions exist; the last column indicates the type of event to which a transition refers. When $ac = 0$, if a job is generated in the high priority queue in the active array, the occupancy of that queue, b_1, will increase by one unit. A rescheduled job from that queue will go to the high priority queue in the expired array with rate $pr_1(1 - R)$ or to the low priority queue in the expired array with rate $pr_3(1 - R)$. In the first case the job keeps the same priority and, in the latter, the priority is decreased. A job can leave the high priority queue in the active array, after finishing its processing with rate $qs_1(1 - R)$. An arrival in the low priority queue in the active array takes place with rate and increases b_2 by one unit.

Since the system under analysis is finite, when a buffer (active or expired arrays) is full an incoming or rescheduled job is blocked. After switching, the

Table 1. Transitions from state $s = (b_1, b_2, p_1, p_2, bp)$ to successor state t for jobs in priority policy

Successor State	Condition	Rate	Event
$(b_1 + 1, b_2, p_1, p_2, bp, ac)$	$(b_1 < B_1) \wedge (ac = 0)$	λ_1	A job arrives in high priority class
$(b_1, b_2 + 1, p_1, p_2, bp, ac)$	$(b_2 < B_2) \wedge (ac = 0)$	λ_2	A job arrives in low priority class
$(b_1 - 1, b_2, p_1, p_2, bp, ac)$	$(b_1 > 0) \wedge (ac = 0)$	$qs_1(1 - R)\mu$	A job from high class terminates
$(b_1 - 1, b_2, \theta, p_2, bp, ac)$	$(b_1 > 0) \wedge (ac = 0)$ $\begin{cases} \theta = p_1 + 1, \text{ if } p_1 < P_1 \\ \theta = P_1, \quad \text{ if } p_1 = P_1 \end{cases}$	$pr_1(1 - R)\mu$	A job is rescheduled to high priority class
$(b_1 - 1, b_2, p_1, \theta, bp, ac)$	$(b_1 > 0) \wedge (ac = 0)$ $\begin{cases} \theta = p_2 + 1, \text{ if } p_2 < P_2 \\ \theta = P_2, \quad \text{ if } p_2 = P_2 \end{cases}$	$pr_3(1 - R)\mu$	A job is rescheduled to low priority class
$(b_1, b_2 - 1, p_1, p_2, bp, ac)$	$(b_1 = 0) \wedge (b_2 > 0) \wedge (ac = 0)$	$qs_2(1 - R)\mu$	A job from low class terminates
$(b_1, b_2 - 1, \theta, p_2, bp, ac)$	$(b_1 = 0) \wedge (b_2 > 0) \wedge (ac = 0)$ $\begin{cases} \theta = p_1 + 1, \text{ if } p_1 < P_1 \\ \theta = P_1, \quad \text{ if } p_1 = P_1 \end{cases}$	$pr_2(1 - R)\mu$	A job is rescheduled to high priority class
$(b_1, b_2 - 1, p_1, \theta, bp, ac)$	$(b_1 = 0) \wedge (b_2 > 0) \wedge (ac = 0)$ $\begin{cases} \theta = p_2 + 1, \text{ if } p_2 < P_2 \\ \theta = P_2, \quad \text{ if } p_2 = P_2 \end{cases}$	$pr_4(1 - R)\mu$	A job is rescheduled to low priority class
$(b_1, b_2, p_1, p_2, bp + 1, ac)$	$b_p < B_p$	λ_p	A job arrives in QoS priority class
$(b_1, b_2, p_1, p_2, bp - 1, ac)$	$b_p > 0$	$qspR\mu$	A job from QoS class terminates
$(b_1, b_2, p_1, p_2, bp - 1, ac)$	$b_p > 0$	$prpR\mu$	A job is rescheduled, but before it is decremented
$(b_1, b_2, p_1, p_2, bp + 1, ac)$	$b_p < B_p$	$prpR\mu$	A job is rescheduled, but after it is incremented
$(b_1, b_2, p_1, p_2, bp, ac + 1)$	$(ac = 0) \wedge ((b_1 = 0) \wedge (b_2 = 0)) \wedge ((p_1 > 0) \vee (p_2 > 0))$	mtv	Change of arrays, b_1 and b_2 become expired
$(b_1, b_2, p_1, p_2, bp, ac - 1)$	$(ac = 1) \wedge ((p_1 = 0) \wedge (p_2 = 0)) \wedge ((b_1 > 0) \vee (b_2 > 0))$	mtv	Change of arrays, b_1 and b_2 become active

Table 2. Input data

High Priority	Measures	Low Priority:	Measures
λ_1	7	λ_2	7,3
pr_1	0,1	pr_2	0
pr_3	0,09	pr_4	0,67
Avarage Buffer	5	Avarage Buffer	5

queues that were in the expired array (p_1 and p_2) become active and vice-versa. The variable bp represents QoS jobs. We assumed that $mtv = 10^{-6}$. The system is symmetric, which makes quite natural the match of the other transitions of the model.

Due to the lack of space and for simplicity only performance measurements of the high priority jobs that demand QoS guarantees are presented.

$$W_{pb} = \frac{\sum_{b_1=0}^{B_1} \sum_{b_2=0}^{B_2} \sum_{p_1=0}^{P_1} \sum_{p_2=0}^{P_2} \sum_{b_p=1}^{B_P} b_p \pi(b_1, b_2, p_1, p_2, b_p, 0)}{(\lambda_p + prpR\mu)(1 - Pb_p)} \tag{8}$$

Where Pb_p is blocking probability of high priority jobs that demand QoS guarantees derived as Eq.(1). The throughput is given by:

$$X_{pb} = qspR\mu \sum_{b_1=0}^{B_1} \sum_{b_2=0}^{B_2} \sum_{p_1=0}^{P_1} \sum_{p_2=0}^{P_2} \sum_{b_p>0}^{B_P} \pi(b_1, b_2, p_1, p_2, b_p, 0) \tag{9}$$

4   Performance Study

In this section some numerical results are presented to evaluate how adequate is the Markov model to scheduling GNU/Linux with and without resource allocation policy. First, we present the performance of the Linux Markovian model. For validation purpose, Linux scheduler was simulated by using an academic version of a powerful tool named ARENA©[10]. Some measures were obtained through system calls which collect data for later analysis, minimizing the overhead in kernel (this can be obtained in www.lprad.ufpa.br/parqos). Table 2 summarizes the parameters used.

To validate the probability distributions adopted, models use input data obtained from the real system. In these data, Kolmogorov-Smirinov (K-S) goodness of fit tests were applied, using the trial version of BestFit©tool [11].

These data were used as parameters of probability distributions in question (Poisson for inter-arrivals times). The simulation results were collated with the performance measures obtained from the real system. As the numerical results of that comparison match (very similar), the values may be considered validated for the analytical model.

To implement CPU allocation policy it is important to study the CPU behavior. Assuming the table above, it represents a situation where scheduler is very

Table 3. Performance measurements

	Queue Waiting Time					
	0%	5%	10%	20%	30%	40%
Active High Priority	0,21246	0,21491	0,21687	0,21943	0,22037	0,21995
Active Low Priority	0,59056	0,60058	0,60970	0,62533	0,63785	0,64774
Expired High Priority	6,05108	6,28370	6,48294	6,79442	7,01313	7,16437
Expired Low Priority	0,85739	0,87383	0,88871	0,91386	0,93334	0,94802
	Blocking Probability					
	0%	5%	10%	20%	30%	40%
Active High Priority	0,09701	0,10763	0,11827	0,13925	0,15940	0,17838
Active Low Priority	0,44159	0,44832	0,45431	0,46434	0,47214	0,47817
Expired High Priority	0,43127	0,44343	0,45346	0,46847	0,47854	0,48530
Expired Low Priority	0,45635	0,46216	0,46734	0,47591	0,48241	0,48723

busy and the inputs are Poisson traffic. A new application is added in λ_1, simulating a situation of great workload. Table 3 ilustrates the Markovian model output. As expected, higher the traffic load, bigger the throughput (Fig. 3.a) and, for that reason, longer the mean waiting time, longer is the blocking probability. In the table, 0% represents the system behavior performance with just λ_1 and λ_2. λ_p is derived from λ_1(5%, 10%, 20%, 30%, 40%) and represents the impact of adding an application to the system.

The main objective of modeling kernel scheduling processes is its evaluation and study for future modifications in order to achieve a better performance for QoS applications. The extended model (resource Allocation) is being studied and tested, but it already presents interesting results like the ones in Figs 3.b and 4. It is the same test situation previously used, but with a different scheduling process. Using CPU reservation of 40% means that 40% of process capacity is allocated for QoS applications and 60% for the rest of the applications.

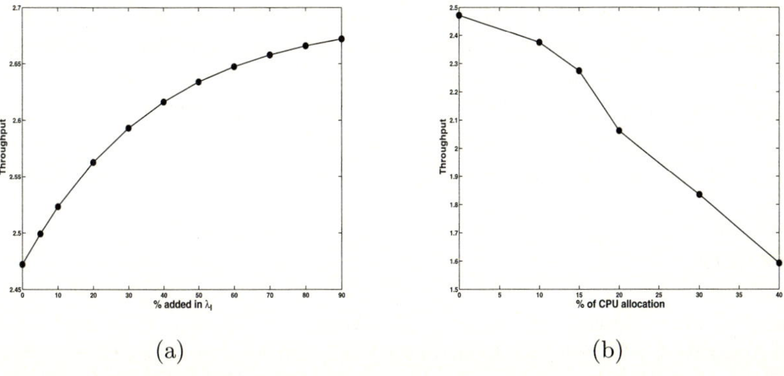

Fig. 3. (a) Throughput behavior (b)Throughput behavior (QoS allocation policy)

Fig. 4 shows the normal system scheduler improvement by limiting the percentage of CPU (100%, 95%, 90%, 80%, 70%, 60%), and it can be observed that, smaller the percentage of CPU used, smaller the system throughput for both priority applications. For QoS application, however, bigger the percentage of CPU used (0%, 5%, 10%, 20%, 30%, 40%), bigger the system throughput.

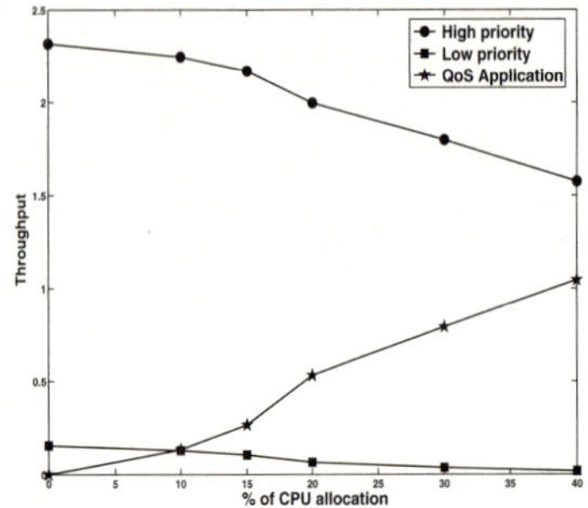

Fig. 4. Throughput behavior per flow

5   Final Remarks

Provision of QoS guarantees in a GPOS scheduler is an open problem. This paper, presented and proposed a Markovian Linux scheduler model for performance study and, in addition, an extended model, which uses static CPU allocation policy. Through the analysis of the results, it has been concluded that the performance of the applications with QoS are greatly improved in its throughput. However, other applications have suffered some limitations. The contributions of this paper are: (1) Proposal of performance models for GPOS (GNU/Linux) scheduler; (2) Proposal of a resource (CPU) allocation scheme in an environment that needs QoS as well as showing through numerical results, obtained from its Markovian model, improvement of performance of QoS applications when compared to other applications.

Currently, we are implementing another extended model which uses dynamic CPU allocation policy. As future work, we performing experiments with Markov decision process to find optimal admission control and scheduling strategies aiming at improving the resource (CPU and memory) allocation.

This work is supported by CNPq and CAPES. Thanks to Dr. Solon Carvalho for giving permission to use the Stochastic Modeling Software (MODESTO) [12].

References

1. Leong, C. W., Zhuang, W., Cheng, Y., Wang, L.: Optimal Resource Allocation and Adaptive Call Admission Control for Voice/Data Integrated Cellular Networks, IEEE Transactions on Vehicular Technology, Vol. **55**, No. 2, March (2006), pp.654-669.

2. Zimmermann, M., Dostert, K.: Analysis and Modeling of Impulsive Noise in Broad-Band Powerline Communications,IEEE Transactions on Electromagnetic Compatibility, Vol. **44**, No. 1, February (2002), pp. 249-258.
3. Yu, J. Y., Chong, P. H. J., So, P. L., Gunawan, E.: Solutions for the Silent Node Problem in Automatic Meter Reading System Using Powerline Communications, in Proc. of the 7th International Power Engineering Conference, IPEC 2005, Nov. (2005).
4. Yuang, M. C., Po-Lung Tien, Shih, J., Chen, A.: QoS Scheduler/Shaper for Optical Coarse Packet Switching IP-Over-WDM Networks, IEEE Journal on Selected Areas in Communications, Vol. **22**, No. 9, Nov. (2004), pp.1766-1780.
5. Levey, D. B., McLaughlin, S.: Calculating Error-Free Seconds in xDSL Systems Corrupted by Impulse Noise, IEEE Communications Letters, Vol. **5**, No. 7, July (2001), pp. 319-321.
6. Chanin, R., Corrêa, M., Fernandes, P., Sales, A., Scheer, R., Zorzo, A.F.: Analytical Modeling for Operating System Schedulers on NUMA Systems, in Proc. of the 2nd International Workshop on Practical Applications of Stochastic Modelling, PASM05, University of Newcastle upon Tyne, UK, July (2005).
7. Love, R.: Linux Kernel Development, SAMS, 1st edn., (2003).
8. Hwang, K., Xu, Z.: Scalable Parallel Computing - Technology, Architecture and Programming, WCB/ McGraw-Hill, (1998).
9. Wei, W., Wang, B., Towsley, D.: Continuous-Time Hidden Markov Models for Network Performance Evaluation, Performance Evaluation, Vol.**49**, (2002), pp. 129-146.
10. Rockwell Automatation - www.arenasimulation.com, accessed in 02/15/2006.
11. Palisade - www.palisade.com/bestfit, accessed in 02/18/2006.
12. Frances, C.R., Oliveira, E., Costa, J., Santana, M., Santana, R., Bruschi, S., Vijaykumar, N., Carvalho, S.: Performance Evaluation Based on System Modelling Using Statecharts Extensions, Simulation Practice and Theory, Vol. **13**, n. 7, (2005), pp. 584-618.

Evaluating Tools for Performance Modeling of Grid Applications

Mariela Curiel*, Gustavo Alvarez, and Leonardo Flores

Universidad Simón Bolívar,
Departamento de Computación y Tecnología de la Información,
Apartado 89000, Caracas 1080-A, Venezuela
`mcuriel@ldc.usb.ve`, {`gjalvarez, floresm.leonardo`}`@gmail.com`

Abstract. A Grid is a collection of heterogeneous distributed computing resources for solving large-scale computational and data intensive
problems. It is a dynamic environment where resources attributes -such
as load- change constantly hindering performance evaluation activities.
Performance models could be a solution to this problem because they
provide a way of performing repeatable and controllable experiments.
Several tools have been developed for modeling scheduling algorithms in
Grids. We believe, however, that if these tools are to be used for modeling application performance they should be improved by adding some
particular features. In this paper, we identify such features and evaluate two modeling tools based on those features. These tools are used to
represent the execution of applications in the Grid SUMA.

1 Introduction

A Grid is a collection of heterogeneous and geographically-dispersed computing
resources connected by a network, possibly at different sites and organizations.
The Grid middleware provides transparent access to resources, and in general it
deals with the physical characteristics of the Grid. Grids have dynamic nature,
i.e., some performance characteristics, such as load, may change over time due
to the fact that resources are shared by other applications. This behavior causes
performance degradation and makes it difficult to evaluate performance. Application performance analysis is crucial to obtain high performance. Although some
factors such as network load or bad scheduling decisions may cause problems,
one of the main source of poor performance comes from wrong design decisions.
One can repair the problems after finishing the application development (tuning) or during the software development process. In the first case, one modifies
algorithms, data structures, compiler options, etc. and then, observe the results.
Additional runs should be done in similar conditions in order to evaluate the
effects of each change. However, it is impossible to get repeatable results in Grid
experiments. Fortunately, modeling allows us to count on a controllable experimentation environment. Additionally, one can use a model to design applications

---

* This work is partially supported by FONACIT, project S1-2002000560.

G. Min et al. (Eds.): ISPA 2006 Ws, LNCS 4331, pp. 854–863, 2006.

whose performance is tailored to the dynamic Grid nature. To construct a representative application model may imply modeling the Grid middleware. Some simulation packages have been developed for modeling Grid scheduling strategies. The objective of this research is to evaluate different tools for modeling Grid applications. The idea is to show drawbacks and strengths that can be useful to improve existing tools or to develop new ones. In this work we start by choosing tools from both Client/Server, distributed applications domain (LQNM analytical [1] and simulation solvers [2]) and Grid domain (GridSim [3]). The tools will be used to model sequential and parallel applications of the Grid SUMA ([4]).

2   Desirable Characteristics in a Modeling Tool

In this Section we present a list of desirable features to support application performance modeling and analysis. This is not an exhaustive list, and it can be enriched along the research. We claim that Grid modeling tools should:

1. Offer capabilities for constructing a representative Grid model: It means to provide facilities for modeling basic Grid elements: (a) Network topology, which includes different graphs, bandwidth and latencies. (b) Compute resources, memories, storage resources and other kind of resources. (c) Aspects related to the dynamic nature of the Grid, i.e. load and unavailability of the resources. (d) Middleware layers. (e) Other particular Grid characteristics such as reservation of resources or location in any time zone.

2. Offer capabilities for easily constructing a representative application model: It includes the possibility of modeling: (a) Simple sequential applications that only need especial resources or services. (b) Different models of distributed and parallel applications. (c) Stochastic behavior. In regards to (b), [5] classifies parallel Grid applications in four groups: loosely coupled (compute intensive with low memory requirements, small amount of data per task and little communication between tasks), pipelined (very memory and data intensive, with coarse-grained inter-task communication), tightly synchronized (frequent inter-task synchronization, significant computation and memory/data usage) and widely distributed (update and/or unify distributed data bases, they have small computational, data and memory requirements)

3. Offer enough metrics for performance analysis: It includes classical metrics such as response times, waiting times, number of I/O operations, number of network communications, bytes transferred in I/O or network communications, residency times, resource utilizations and new Grid metrics. Resultant data should be provided in text format and by means of graphical tools.

4. Be easy to use: Tools should offer wide and clear documentation, user support and user-friendly interfaces. Additionally, it could be interesting to provide high level models closer to the application developers (UML diagrams, MSC, etc.) as well as the algorithms to transform them into performance models.

5. Be efficient: The dynamics of a Grid is complex. It is possible to find NP-complete problems in, for example, routing or scheduling strategies that cannot be treated by analytical techniques. However, diverse kind of programs run on the Grid. Some of them could be very simple, as for example to request a cluster for running a parallel rigid application. In these cases an analytical model could be enough. So, it is recommendable to provide diverse methods to solve a variety of problems. When simulation is the only option, solutions such as parallel simulations should be explored.

3   Selected Tools

Our final goal is to discover the presence or absence of the mentioned characteristics in an important number of modeling tools (mainly oriented to Grid and distributed systems modeling). In order to review each tool exhaustively, it is necessary its installation and use. Due to a lack of time, we start by evaluating a reduced number of tools. BeoSim, Bricks, SimGrid, GridSim, ChicSim and OptorSim are popular simulation tools frequently referenced in Grid related bibliography (see references in [6]). BeoSim, Bricks, ChicSim were discarded because they are not currently available for users. For the time being, we ruled OptorSim out because it is designed for data Grid modeling and we want to model a computational Grid. Although LQNM analytical and simulation solvers are oriented to Client/Server applications they were chose by the possibility of doing analytical models. Between GridSim and SimGrid we first took Gridsim for two main reasons: GridSim is Java based and it apparently has more capacities for Grid modeling. SimGrid, OptorSim and other simulation tools will be subsequently evaluated. The next paragraphs explain in detail characteristics of LQNM solvers and GridSim.

Layered Queuing Network Models are QNM extended to reflect interactions between client and server processes. We choose LQNM (lqns version 3) by the following reasons : 1) The application model can be easily constructed by non experts in performance evaluation: the tools are embedded in a SPE methodology that derives Layered Queuing Network Models (LQNM) from systems scenarios described by means of Use Case Maps (UCM); free software packages are available for process automation under this methodology. 2) Models can be solved by simulation or analytical techniques: The Layered Queuing Network Solver (LQNS) solves the model analytically, whereas the ParaSol Stochastic Rendez-Vous Network Simulator (ParaSRVN) use the simulation technique.

An LQNM can be represented by a graph with nodes for Tasks and Devices, and arrows for service requests. A *Task* (parallelograms in figure 1) is a software object that has its own thread of execution. *Tasks* are divided into three categories: *Client Tasks* (only send requests), *Active Server Tasks* (can receive and send requests) and *Pure Server Tasks* (only receive requests). There are three types of interactions between *Tasks*: asynchronous messages, synchronous interactions and forwarding messages. In a forward call, the sending Client *Task* makes a synchronous call and blocks until it receives a reply. The receiving *Task* partially processes the call and then forwards it to another server, which becomes responsible for sending a reply to the blocked *Client Task*. *Tasks* receive any kind of request message in points called *Entries* (smaller parallelograms in figure 1). A *Task* has a different *Entry* for every kind of service it provides. Internally, an *Entry* could be composed by sequences of smaller computational blocks called *Activities* (rectangles), which are related in sequence, loop, parallel configurations, etc.

GridSim [3] is a toolkit for modeling and simulation of heterogeneous resources, users, applications, brokers and schedulers in a Grid computing environment. GridSim was chosen because of the following reasons: 1) It is one of the most popular simulation tool for Grid research. 2) It is based on Java, which is a popular language. 3) GridSim is an active project. 4) According to the documentation GridSim has interesting features for modeling Grid environments, for example: (a) it allows modeling of heterogeneous types of resources operating under space- or time-shared mode; (b) resources can be located in any time zone and booked for in advance; (c) different parallel application models can be simulated.

GridSim adopts the multi-layered design architecture. The first bottom layer is the Java interface and the JVM. The second layer is SimJava, which provides an event-driven discrete event simulation package on top of JVM to drive the simulation for GridSim. The third layer is the GridSim toolkit that provides the modeling and simulation of Core Grid entities, such as resources and Grid Information Services, using the events of the second layer. The simulation of resource aggregators called Grid brokers or schedulers is provided by the fourth layer. The top layer focuses on application and resource modeling with different scenarios to evaluate scheduling and resource management policies, heuristics and algorithms. Applications in GridSim are modeled as a number of work packets that are called *Gridlets*. A *Gridlet* is a package that contains all the information related to the job and its execution management details, such as job length expressed in MIPS (or SPECs), disk I/O operations, the size of input and output files, and the job originator. Grid resources, users and brokers are modeled as *Entities*, and they communicate via messaging events using the advanced network features. Synchronous and asynchronous messages are allowed.

4   SUMA

SUMA (Scientific Ubiquitous Metacomputing Architecture) [4] is a computational Grid that transparently executes Java bytecode on remote machines, with additional support for scientific computing development. SUMA provides access to both single-process (possibly multi-threaded) and parallel execution agents, according to the JVM and mpiJava execution model. A user invokes the execution of a program in SUMA through the services *suma Execute* (on-line execution mode) or *suma Submit* (off-line execution). We modeled only scenarios associated to *suma execute*. The steps of the *suma execute* services follow: When a Client wants to send an execution request to SUMA, it firstly must find a Proxy, by invoking the *findProxy* method in Scheduler. The Scheduler finds an appropriate Proxy and returns a CORBA reference to the Client. Then the Client invokes the *execute* method in its Proxy, passing the name of the main class as a parameter. This Proxy invokes user authentication methods in User Control and asks for a suitable Execution Agent in Scheduler, getting a CORBA reference for the Execution Agent. Execution Agents run on servers, tipically high performance machines, and execute user applications. Then the Proxy invokes *execute* method in the selected Execution Agent, passing all necessary information for the Execution Agent to start loading applications classes and files; this is done by invoking appropriate methods directly in the Client. As a result of the *execute* method invocation, the Execution Agent starts a Slave (a new Virtual Machine) and obtains its CORBA reference. This reference is sent back to the Proxy and subsequently to the Client. The Client uses this reference to open a connection with the Slave in the Execution Agent. Once the connection is established, the Client orders the execution of the application. When the execution finishes, the Execution Agent sends output files to the Client. Finally, the Execution Agent executes *releaseNode* method in the Scheduler, indicating it is available again. The execution model of parallel applications is similar with an important difference: In the execution of sequential applications, classes and data are loaded/sent directly from/to the Client. In parallel applications, only the Execution Agent loads classes from the Client. Slaves addresses classes requests to the Execution Agent. I/O operations are directly performed between Clients and Slaves.

5   LQNM of SUMA Applications

Figures 1 and 2 show LQN models of the execution of sequential and parallel applications. The sequential model has seven layers. There are *Tasks* in each layer that represent the main SUMA components (Client, SUMA Core and Execution Agent) and the network between each pair of components. *Tasks* contain *Entry* points and *Activities* associated to the main functions of the components. The SUMA Core, for example, finds a suitable Proxy (*findProxy Activity*), verifies User identity (*VerifyUser Activity*), requests an Execution Agent (*RequestEA Activity*) and requests the execution of the application (*RequestExecution Activity*). In the Execution Agent one can observe the *Activities* related to the execution of the application: There is a loop (represented with a circle between *StartExecution Activity* and *EndExecution Activity*), where the JVM executes pieces of computation (*Execution*) followed by a network operation for either loading Classes (*ClassLoading*) or executing I/O operations (*I/O*). The four top layers of the parallel model are similar to the sequential layers. The represented parallel application runs into two nodes: (*Tasks PN1 and PN2*). The Execution Agent creates Slaves in each parallel node (*Activities: a1 and a2*), starts their execution and receives class requests from Slaves (*CV Activity*). The code executed by each parallel Slave is modeled as a loop with the following kind of activities: some instructions (*Execution Activity*) and a network operation for loading classes (*ClassLoading Activity*), communicating with another parallel node (*ComPNi Activity*) or executing I/O operations (*I/O Activity*).

5.1   Model Development, Parameterization and Validation

The main problems during the model development follow. 1) **Too many layers**: Both models have at least seven layers. It was necessary to duplicate the Client in both models because the Client executes a synchronous call (the *execute* command) and it cannot respond requests from the Execution Agent. The Client and its clone run on the same processor. Using asynchronous calls we avoid blocking the Client, but it is impossible to get the application response time (you cannot insert instructions to get starting and ending times). Another possibility is to use forwarding calls. However, these calls are only allowed between *Entries*, making the *Activities* useless. We prefer to use *Activities* because they allow us to clearly represent different functions of SUMA components. There are many copies of the *Network Task* for similar reasons. On the other hand, some single calls were not explicitly represented for avoiding new increments in the number of layers: for example, the callback between the Execution Agent and the SUMA Core to inform the execution end (*released node* method) would require a duplicated of the SUMA Core. 2) **There is not an explicit network model**. 3) **It was difficult to generate the models automatically**: Tools could still have some problems for generating complex systems models. However, the construction of the model was very easy starting from the UCMs and using the method proposed by Petriu in [7]. 4) **LQNM are not suitable for modeling parallel applications**: Because of its complexity, the parallel model cannot be solved by analytical methods. On the other hand, the code of each parallel node must be written explicitly, which can be tedious when there is a large number of nodes.

Model parameters were obtained from Java Grande Forum benchmarks: JGFCryptBench, JGFHeapSortBench, JGFSeriesBench and JGFSparseMatmult (Sizes A and B). We conducted experiments by running SUMA modules in three machines with the following characteristics: Pentium III dual processors, 666 MHz with 504Mb of RAM memory, connected by a LAN (10baseT Ethernet). We ran each benchmark ten times without having interference from other applications. The parameterization process was very easy. Model parameters are expressed in time units, so most of them can be obtained directly from the SUMA monitoring tool. However, we have to have the application for running it and obtaining the parameters. SUMA monitoring tools also offer data about SUMA core components. After parameterizing the model we solved it with the LQNM Solver and with ParaSRVN. Sequential models produced errors below 11.8%. The prediction error in a parallel application was 18 %. Parallel model predictions can be improved by enhancing the input parameters.

6   GridSim Model of SUMA Applications

We use GridSim 4.0 to build the first GridSim models for sequential and parallel applications. In the models, we use elements of the third layer of the GridSim architecture. SUMA components (Client, Scheduler, Proxy, UserControl and Execution Agent) are *Entities* that extend from the *gridsim* class. *Entities* are registered by the *Grid Information Service*. Scheduler, Proxy and UserControl use

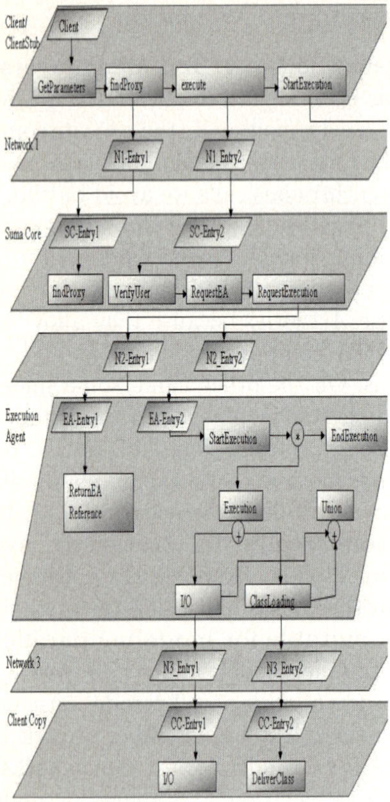

Fig. 1. Sequential LQNM 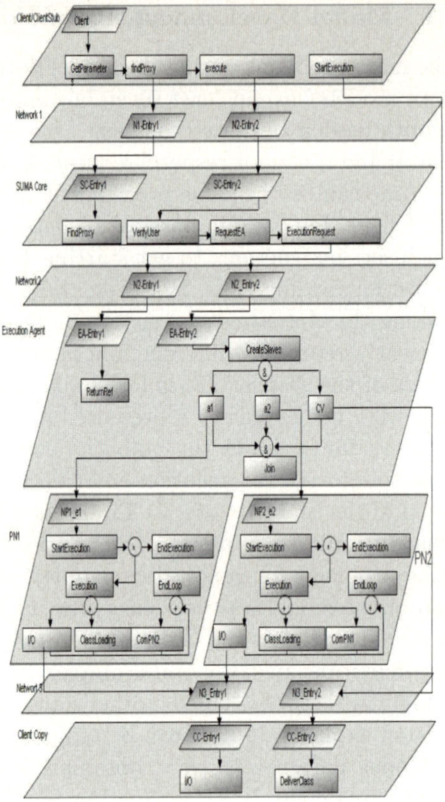   **Fig. 2.** Parallel LQNM

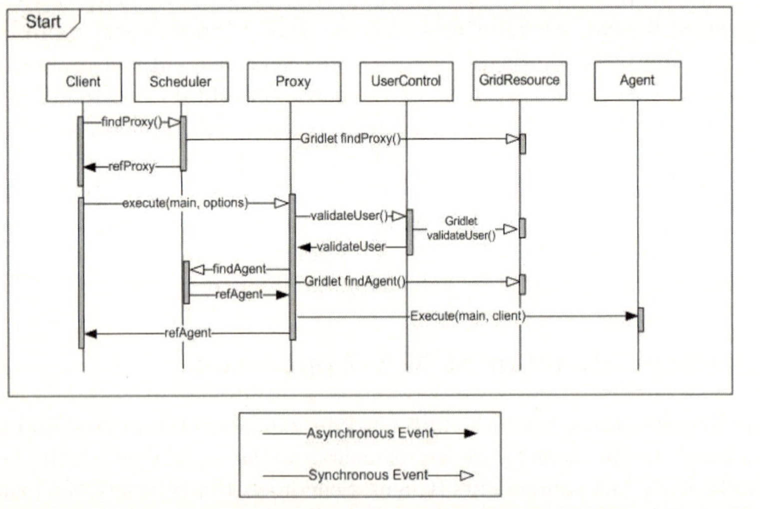

Fig. 3. Preliminary steps of the sequential and parallel execution in GridSim

a *GridResource Entity* to simulate their processing tasks (i.e., to find a Proxy, to validate Users, etc.). The process of creating a *GridResource* is as follows: First, *Processing elements* (PE) objects are created with a suitable MIPS rating. PE are assembled together to create a *Machine*. GridSim *Machine* class represents an uniprocessor or shared memory multiprocessor machine. One or more machines form a *GridResource*. SUMA Core components submit *Gridlets* to the *GridResource SumaCore* (figure 3). In the sequential model, a *GridResource* with a single machine and one or more PEs is bound to the Execution Agent. The execution of one application is modeled by means of a loop where some instructions (simulated by a *Gridlet* submitted to a *GridResource*) are followed by messages to the Client *Entity* to either load classes or execute I/O operations. A network topology was created to allow the *Entities* to communicate. Each *Entity* defines an instance of the *Link* class. An instance of *Router* class is created to forward data from one *Entity* to another. Figure 3 shows the sequence of messages among SUMA Core *Entities* before executing the application. In the parallel model each Slave has associated its own *GridResource*. Each *GridResource* has a *Machine* object and a PE.

6.1   Model Development, Parameterization and Validation

The modeling process was a bit difficult despite the programmers experience in Java. The learning curve of GridSim is slow. Knowledge of object oriented and Java programming is required. On the other hand, once GridSim architecture and philosophy is understood, it was very easy to construct the models because there is a direct correspondence between SUMA components and GridSim *Entities*. The use of asynchronous messages allows us to make calls between *Entities* in both directions: call and callbacks, without copying components. Since the model is a Java program, one can insert special instructions in any place to obtain execution times. Many identical parallel nodes can be added by changing a single parameter.

We execute the benchmarks used to parameterize the LQNM in five machines with the following characteristics: AMD Athlon 64 3800 1GB RAM (runs the Client), Pentium IV 3.4 GHz, 512 RAM (for the Scheduler, the User Control, the Proxy and the Execution Agent); machines are connected by a LAN (10baseT Ethernet). The main *GridResource* static parameters were *architecture, operating system*, MIPS, *number of machines* and *number of PE*. The first two parameters were obtained from OS commands. The SiSoftware Sandra Lite 2007 (http://www.sisoftware.co.uk) was used to compute the MIPS rating per machine. The number of machines and PE depend on the particular Grid architecture. The main parameters of the *Link* class are: delay (*ping* command), MTU (standard Ethernet) and the bandwidth (obtained from router specifications). The main drawback was to obtain the *gridletLength* value for each SUMA component. The *gridletLength* is expressed in MI (Millions Instruction) and it is difficult to know the value of this parameter in a Java Program. The solution was to measure the program, to obtain the execution times and to convert measured times into MI. Prediction errors were below 7.9%.

7   Comparison of Tools

After using the selected tools for developing the SUMA models, it is possible to compare them based on the "desirable characteristics":

1. Capabilities for constructing a representative Grid model: In this aspect **GridSim** is so far one of the most complete tool. Some aspects that could be included are: (a) New classes that allow to model new software components (middleware, operating systems, etc.). (b) Improvements to hardware resources models (more complex network topologies, different network protocols, memory models, etc.) (c) Background load of processors with probabilistic behavior. **LQNM** tools were not designed for modeling Grid systems. They could be useful for modeling small Grids (for example intra-organizational Grids) or other kind of distributed systems, such as clusters with simple application models. Some features could be added to improve distributed systems models, for example: network models.

2. Capabilities for easily constructing a representative model of the application: With respect to this characteristic, **GridSim** also has many advantages: it allow us to model diverse models of parallel and distributed applications. [8] describes GridSim extensions for simulating data Grids. GridSim is based on deterministic simulation where no random events occur. This is a drawback because it limits the type of application to be modeled. However, *GridSimRandom* class and *eduni.simjava.distributions* package can be used for incorporating randomness in data. This randomness would require new outputs processing. **LQNM tools** seem suitable for modeling sequential and some kind of distributed applications. Stochastic behavior can be included in analytical and simulation models by indicating means and variances.

3. Metrics for performance analysis: GridSim provides a small set of metrics. Metrics about *gridlet* processing are: CPU time, wall clock time and waiting time. There are not explicit metrics about throughput or resource utilization. There are, however, a variety of metrics in the new network models. **GridSim** output should be improved by incorporating new metrics. **LQNM** tools offer diverse metrics to evaluate the application performance (response times, waiting times, devices utilizations, etc) and simulation results (confidence intervals).

4. Ease to use: The learning curve of **GridSim** is slow. [9] describes a Java-based Graphical User Interface (GUI) tool for GridSim, which aims to reduce the learning process and enables fast creation of simulation models. Future research projects could be oriented to provide higher level models and methodologies to transform them in GridSim models. Higher level parameters that can be internally transformed should also be included. These features would help application designers and application alvion developers without experience in performance evaluation or Java programming. GridSim documentation is good. **LQNM** could be easily constructed from Use Case Maps, so application developers/designers not need to be queuing network experts.

5. Efficiency: GridSim uses serial simulation. Techniques to reduce simulation times should be incorporated to Grid modeling tools: parallel simulations and to combine analytical and simulation approaches. Analytical **LQNM** meaningfully reduces model execution times. However, approximated analytical techniques only can be used in very simple application models.

8   Conclusions

The aim of our research is to evaluate simulation tools for performance modeling of Grid applications. We have used two set of tools for modeling applications that run in the Java-based computational Grid SUMA. One set of tools solve LQNMs. They were not designed to model Grid environments but offer some advantages for modeling sequential and distributed applications (especially Client/Server applications). These advantages are: 1) Possibility of obtaining analytical and simulation results. 2) LQNM can be derived from Use Case Maps. 3) The tools provide several metrics for evaluating application performance and quality of simulation results. On the other hand, tools like GridSim allow us to model in detail diverse aspects of Grid platforms and a variety of parallel application models. They have many of the "desirable characteristics", but three aspects need to be improved: efficiency, the set of metrics and the ease of use. These features will help designers and application developers construct right models and obtain results in very short times. Future research includes the evaluation of different tools and the modeling of different kinds of Grid applications.

References

1. Franks, G.: Performance Analysis of Distributed Server Systems. PhD thesis, Carleton University (2000)
2. Mascarenhas, E.: A System for Multithreaded Parallel Simulation with Migrant Thread and Objects. PhD thesis, Purdue University (1996)
3. Sulistio, A., Poduval, G., Buyya, R., Tham, C.: Constructing a grid simulation with differentiated network service using gridsim. In: Proc. of the 6th. International Conference on Internet Computing (ICOMP' 05). (2005)
4. Cardinale, Y., Curiel, M., Figueira, C., García, P., Hernández, E.: Implementation of a corba-based metacomputing system. In: Proc. of Workshop on Java for High Performance Computing.LNCS. (2001)
5. Snavely, A., Chun, G., Casanova, H., der Wijngaart, R.V., Frumkin, M.: Benchmarks for grid computing: A review of ongoing efforts and fututre directions. Sigmetrics Perfor. Eval. Rev **30**(4) (2003) 27–32
6. Quétier, B., Capello, F.: A survey of grid research tools: simulators, emulators and real life platforms. In: Proc. of 17th IMACS World Congress (IMAC 2005), France. (2005)
7. Petriu, D.C., Woodside, C.: Software performance models from systems scenarios in use case maps. Proc. of TOOLS, Springer Verlag, LNCS **794** (2002) 159–177
8. A.Sulistio, Cibej, U., Robic, B., Buyya, R.: A Toolkit for Modeling and Simulation of Data Grids with Integration of Data Storage, Replication and Analysis. Technical Report GRIS-TR-2005-13, University of Melbourne (2005)
9. Sulistio, A., Yeo, C.S., Buyya, R.: Visual modeler for grid modeling and simulation (gridsim) toolkit. In: Proc. of the 3rd. International Conference on Computational Science (ICCS 2003), Springer Verlag Publications (LCNS Series) (2003)

A Performance Evaluation of Asynchronous Web Interfaces for Collaborative Web Services

Michele Angelaccio and Berta Buttarazzi

University of Rome Tor Vergata, Rome, Italy
angelaccio@disp.uniroma2.it
http://www.angelaccio.com/

Abstract. AJAX is the latest technology emerged in web development, allowing rich asynchronous dynamic interfaces deployed within a normal web browser. Collaborative web services that aim managing more information throughput among partners, may encapsulate this technology through light Web Interface for sharing data according good service-level. In order to validate the effectiveness of the AJAX technology framework in the design of a Web Interface, we have considered as a case study one of the paradigmatic collaborative applications: a web-chat application. In the paper we have compared the QoS between a traditional client-server web chat model and the asynchronous one implemented using the AJAX-model driven framework chat model.

1   Introduction

Lately there has been a tremendous improvement in the area of web applications and services. One of the main consequence is that simple protocol HTTP (Hypertext Protocol Transfers) with the markup language HTML does not likely satisfy dynamic applications that preview a lot of interaction between client and server ([1], [5]). It is emerging the need of new models for web interface developing ([2]). The aim is that now Web applications are demanding same performances of the programs desktop. Moreover with the always greater spread of the applications distributed on the internet it is emerging the need of previewing application performance for dynamic architectures like P2P systems. For example. the time for the loading of a page or the interaction with the peer becomes an index of the quality of the system (QoS). In this paper we want to demonstrate the performance improvements that can be obtained using technical asynchronous Web Interfaces for P2P-based applications. For this purpose in this paper at first we describe the AJAX technology, subsequently we put the attention on a web Chat case study, relative to putting to comparison an application, that it offers the same service, to forehead of a on one side traditional implementation, from other dynamics, with the attempt to estimate in objective way the entity of the performances. In order to give a level of efficiency we will give some performance measurements . Our analysis, chooses like representative of the new technologies, Ajax, acronym for Asynchronous Javascript And XML, term coined in February 2005 from J.J. Garrett of Adaptive Path [3], to denote not only one new technology, but how much a user uses of the different combination persistent

G. Min et al. (Eds.): ISPA 2006 Ws, LNCS 4331, pp. 864–872, 2006.
© Springer-Verlag Berlin Heidelberg 2006

technologies, each effective in just the field ([4]). The paper is organized in the following way. An outline of Ajax framework and its organization will be given in Section 2. This description will explain the difference between AJAX framework and the traditional one by exploiting the use of interaction diagram. This approach is then used in Section3 for describing our test-case, the web-chat application for which we analyze in section 4 the performance evaluation compared with traditional approach. Section 5 will gives some conclusions and future issues.

2   Overview of AJAX Technology

AJAX is an abbreviation for Asynchronous JavaScript and XML used to describe a framework incorporating several technologies aimed to update web pages without doing a browser refresh. The requests for information update are sent via Javascript background functions and when the results come in.

Ajax Engine includes:

- standards-based presentation using XHTML and CSS;
- dynamic display and interaction using the DOM (Document Object Model);
- data interchange and manipulation using XML and XSLT;
- asynchronous data retrieval using XMLHttpRequest;
- and JavaScript binding everything together.

The architectural organization is described by comparing the traditional Client-Server architecture for a web application interface with the architecture used in the case of one AJAX-based web application interface.

Classical Web-Interface works as shown in Figure 1: a client make an HTTP request to a web server; the server, after some processing action returns an HTML page to the client. While this model is useful for static Web application, it is not

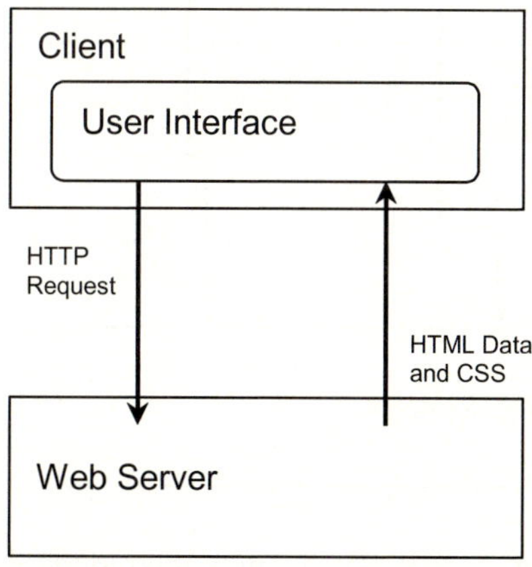

Fig. 1. Traditional web application model

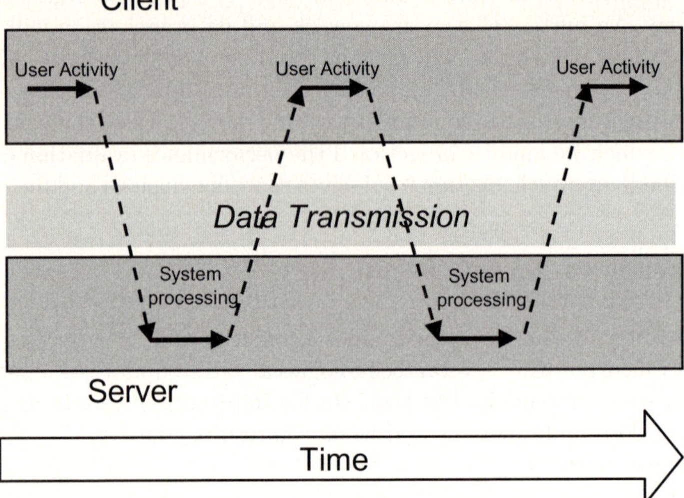

Fig. 2. Interaction Diagram for web application model

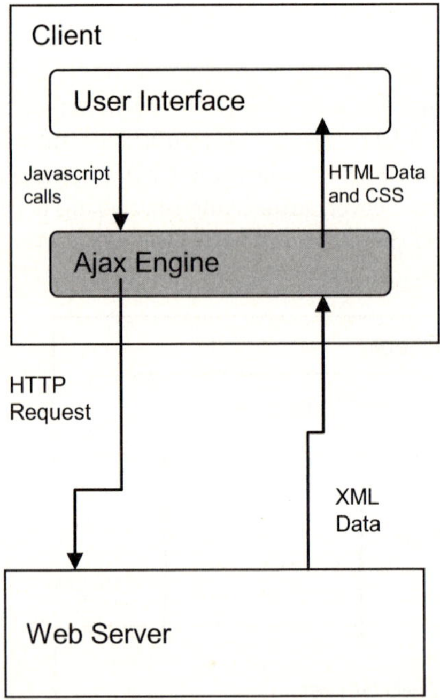

Fig. 3. Ajax-Based Application Model

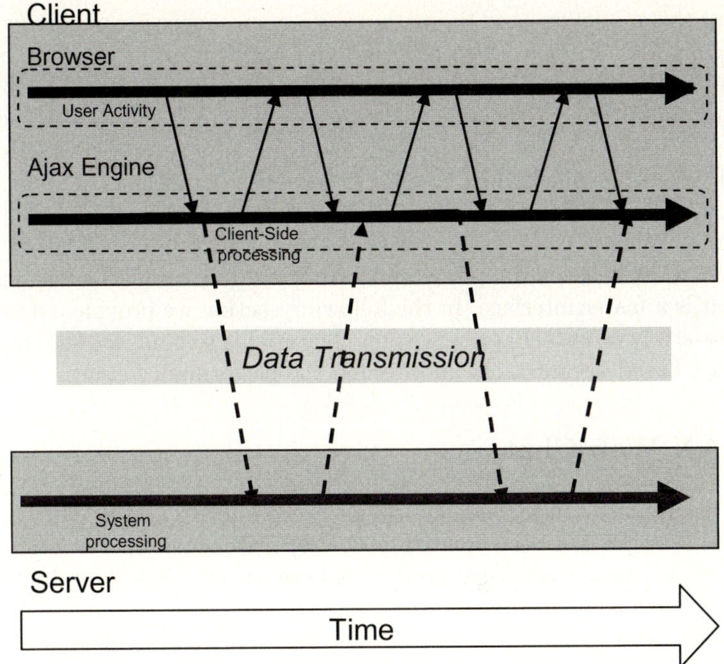

Fig. 4. Ajax-Based Interaction Diagram

suitable for highly dynamic ones. In fact in this case user interaction interrupts the application every time it needs some data from the server (Figure 2).

Asynchronous Web-Interfaces work as shown in Figure 3, where by adding an intermediary software layer - the Ajax engine - between the user and the server, the start-stop nature of interaction on the Web has been modified. In this case instead of loading a webpage, at the start of the session, the browser loads an Ajax engine written in JavaScript. This engine is responsible for displaying data client side and communicating with the server on the user's behalf. The Ajax engine allows the user's interaction with the application to happen asynchronously - independent of communication with the server (Figure 4). So the user is never waiting around for the server to do something. Every user action that normally would generate an HTTP request takes the form of a JavaScript call to the Ajax engine instead. Any response to a user action that doesn't require a trip back to the server - such as simple data validation, editing data in memory, and even some navigation - the engine handles on its own. If the engine needs something from the server in order to respond - if it's submitting data for processing, loading additional interface code, or retrieving new data - the engine makes those requests asynchronously, usually using XML, without stalling a user's interaction with the application. Web application modeling by using AJAX web differs drastically from traditional one. In fact instead of submitting forms to actions and receiving a new page from the server, developers can send small sets of data to the server as soon as the user interacts with the web application. To easy implement this model we used Sajax that is an open source programming toolkit providing an Ajax framework to program web application using PHP as server side scripting language. Thanks to Sajax after the page is loaded as a normal application, a JavaScript function makes a (background) call to PHP script on the server. This JavaScript function sets the name of a second JavaScript function, which will be called when the server response is finished. In short, AJAX builds applications that run inside a Web browser but behave like client-based applications. When a page needs updating, the application uses XML to tell the Web server what it needs to update and JavaScript to process the response. The final result is a faster interface. In the following section we provide a description of our case-study: a web-chat application. The goal is to compare the traditional with AJAX-based organization and discuss the performance issues.

3   AJAX Web Chat

In order to evaluate the technology efficiency we refer to a Web Chat as a case study. The example has been created in two separate versions. The first of these versions, based on a traditional model contains several less-than-desirable usability problems. These problems are tackled in the second example, "Ajax Web Chat " which aims to highlight some of the issues that can be encountered as you move from a page-based application model towards a more dynamic and interactive environment. The two versions of the Web Chat, also having a different implementation (related with the different model of client-server communication), they offer the same services and do the same request to the server. In the development of the chat based on the classic approach, obviously the attention has been focused on refreshing the page only when necessary, to obtain correct performance indices. Clearly not all benefits and advantages related with developing applications using as a template the framework Ajax, are exactly quantifiable. To give a simple interpretation of application performance indices we have considered only the number of byte transferred and the number of request. Figure 5 shows the interaction diagram corresponding to the first version of the Web Chat, based on the classic synchronous approach of Client-Server organization. The diagram shows the activities performed by a user during a chat session composed by a login phase and one message-and-reply phase.

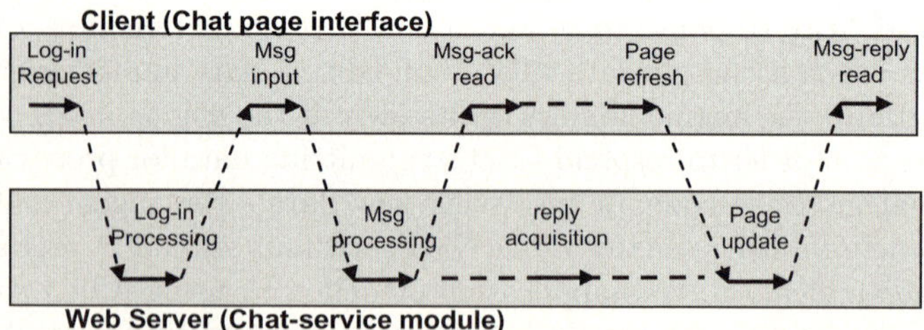

Fig. 5. Traditional Web Chat Interaction Diagram

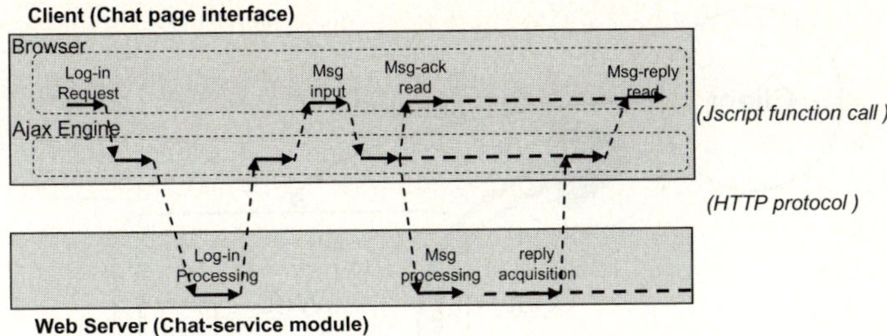

Fig. 6. Ajax-Based Web Chat Interaction Diagram

All communications are performed using HTTP protocol and user is forced to refresh the entire page in order to read information. This is synchronously made in the case of ack-message but must be activated asynchronously in the case of the reply message as shown by dotted lines. In the case of AJAX-based interface as shown in figure 6, the situation is quite different. In this case there are the following advantages:

- (Communication reduction)This is a reduction in the number of HTTP communications thus increasing the efficiency in the use of the HTTP protocol.
- (Message reduction) Some type of message like the one edited from the user are displayed by AJAX engine without sending them to the server. This yields a reduction in the number of bytes transferred from the web server (e.g. ack-msg). These messages could be considered as a local service provide at client in place of web services provided at server side.
- (User activity efficiency) The user avoids refresh operations necessary for reply messages incoming from the server in asynchronous way. Obviously it not always true that a message reduction implies a communication reduction because there are other examples of web application for which could be less expensive to wait for data completion and to update the complete page before to establish a server

Obviously it not always true that a message reduction implies a communication reduction because there are other examples of web application for which could be less expensive to wait for data completion and to update the complete page before to establish a server communication. However under the hypotheses of an high number of user interactions, it is interesting to evaluate the amount of message-size reduction. In the next section we run an experimental chat session by using two different implementation of the same web-chat application. The former (web-chat) is defined in accord to the traditional organization. The latter (ajax-based web chat), instead is implemented by inheriting the traditional template and by rewriting the interface functions using the AJAX toolkit sajax.

4   Web Chat Evaluation

To compare the different performances of two implemented application we have considered the results carried out by analyzing a log file of Apache server

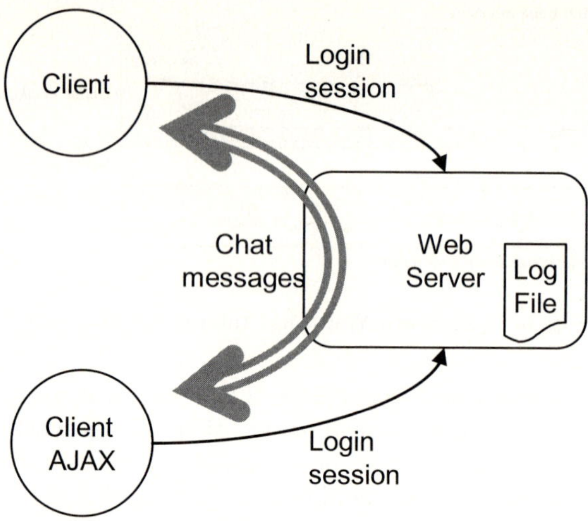

Fig. 7. Experimental scenario

during a chat conversation between two users on two different nodes. We have measured 4 different conversations each one approximately of 400 sec. Figure 7 shows the experimental scenario. The logfile reports for each HTTP connection, a pair (T_i, M_i) that gives the corresponding time instant and transferred message size respectively. Each user talks through a web-chat application but the former makes use of traditional web-chat whereas the latter makes use of Ajax-based web chat. In order to refer a more reliable possible conversation we have been attempted to chat in continuously or without interruptions from users. The average message size is about 80 characters and the frequency is about 0.2 message/sec (or equivalently in terms of speed, 20 sec/chat-message) . The Figure 8 plots the performance measured for each client in terms of transferred bytes as a function of the application time. It must be noted the starting and ending parts of the chart displayed in 8 have a small difference between the two plots. This is due to the fact that the corresponding values are obtained when clients performs login/logout operations. If we restrict instead to the central part of the chart (from about second 30 to about sec 400) it holds that the AJAX client performs better than traditional client. Besides log file data, we have computed also the corresponding percentage of message size reduction obtained by the AJAX client with respect to the traditional client. The resulting values are shown in the chart displayed in Figure 9. Note that under a reasonable assumption of users chatting with an high frequency of message it holds that the performance increase in terms of transmitted bytes obtainable by using AJAX and compared with traditional model tends to the value of 70. We note also that if we stress chat message frequency up to an ideal value of 10 chat-message/sec the the traditional client will soon reach a saturation level in the server communications. This obviously is not relevant for real cases, but may be interesting to evaluate some limit working characteristics. We have compared, in a brief experiment,

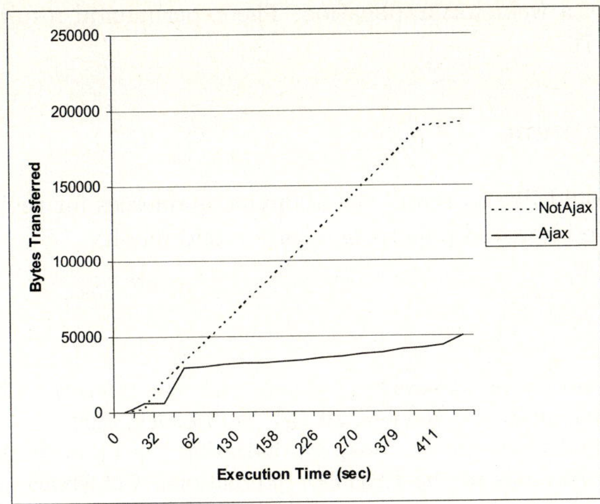

Fig. 8. Web Chat Performance Comparison

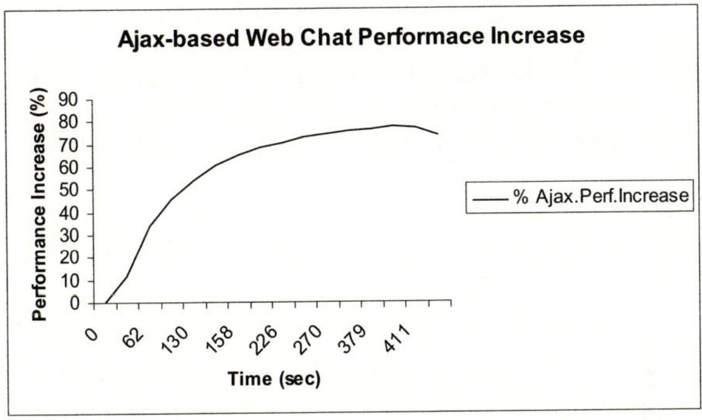

Fig. 9. Performance Increase Evaluation

the AJAX client with the traditional one under a small value of chat message frequency. In particular we have forced values greater than 10 chat-message/sec in the AJAX client by obtaining as saturation level in correspondence of values 18-20 chat-message/sec.

5   Conclusions

The client-level Ajax engine speeds up web server interaction by reducing the latency time caused by unnecessary page reloading. This model gives to web applications a more dynamic behaviour with respect to traditional client-server architecture. In this paper we have evaluated the time-efficiency obtained by introducing Ajax framework in a typical web application with a lot of user interactions, i.e. a web-chat application. The experimental results show a limit value of about 70.

Acknowledgment

The authors would like to thank the anonymous referees for their helpful comments that have improved paper organization and quality.

References

1. J. Wang.: A survey of web caching schemes for the Internet. ACM SIGCOMM Computer Communication Review, **29 (5)** 36–46, Oct. 1999
2. K. Devaram and D. Andresen.: Soap Optimization Via Parameterized Client-Side Caching . Proceedings of the IASTED International Conference on Parallel and Distributed Computing and Systems (PDCS 2003), pp. 785–790, Marina Del Rey, CA, November 3-5, 2003
3. J. J. Garrett: Ajax: A New Approach to Web Applications. http://www.adaptivepath.com/publications/essays/archives/000385.php
4. A. Stamos, Z. Lackey: Attacking AJAX Web Applications. Black Hat security conference 2006
5. W. Li W. Hsiung O. Po K. Hino K. Selc and D. Agrawal: Challenges and Practices in Deploying Web Acceleration Solutions for Distributed Enterprise Systems. WWW2004, May 1722, 2004, New York, New York, USA.ACM

An Adaptive Load Balancing Middleware for Distributed Simulation

Luciano Bononi, Michele Bracuto, Gabriele D'Angelo, and Lorenzo Donatiello

Dipartimento di Scienze dell'Informazione, Università degli Studi di Bologna
Mura Anteo Zamboni 7, 40126, Bologna, Italy
{bononi, bracuto, gdangelo, donat}@cs.unibo.it

Abstract. The simulation is useful to support the design and performance evaluation of complex systems, possibly composed by a massive number of interacting entities. For this reason, the simulation of such systems may need aggregate computation and memory resources obtained by clusters of parallel and distributed execution units. Shared computer clusters composed of available Commercial-Off-the-Shelf hardware are preferable to dedicated systems, mainly for cost reasons. The performance of distributed simulations is influenced by the heterogeneity of execution units and by their respective CPU load in background. Adaptive load balancing mechanisms could improve the resources utilization and the simulation process execution, by dynamically tuning the simulation load with an eye to the synchronization and communication overheads reduction. In this work it will be presented the GAIA+ framework: a new load balancing mechanism for distributed simulation. The framework has been evaluated by performing testbed simulations of a wireless ad hoc network model. Results confirm the effectiveness of the proposed solutions.

1 Introduction

The simulation is useful to support the design and performance evaluation of many complex systems of interest, often composed by a massive number of interacting entities. For a significant performance evaluation, many complex systems would require the implementation of fine-grained models able to include many factors and to capture many causal effects, at many layers of abstraction. Simulation techniques support layered model composition, arbitrarily complex models and fine-grained details [10]. Limitations are mainly given by the long time required to complete the simulation processes, and by the resource constraints of the execution architectures (like computation-power and memory). In the classical approach, computer simulation is monolithic, that is, a single process execution manages one simulation and mimics the evolution of the model state variables. Given the limited amount of memory resources to represent the model data structures, and the limited computation power that can be provided by a single execution unit, the simulation model scalability may be significantly constrained under the monolithic approach. In addition, the time required to complete a simulation analysis over a single Physical Execution Unit (PEU)

G. Min et al. (Eds.): ISPA 2006 Ws, LNCS 4331, pp. 873–883, 2006.

could be long enough to make less practical the analysis. To deal with these limitations, an alternative approach is based on the Parallel and Distributed Simulation (PADS).

In PADS, the model execution is supported by many interacting processes, possibly executed in concurrent way over multiple PEUs, and usually referred to as Logical Processes (LPs) [1]. One or more LPs can be executed over different PEUs. The simulation is obtained as the coordinated, concurrent, distributed execution of LPs. In general, frequent synchronizations are required between computation steps of distributed LPs, to ensure a correct simulation execution. To summarize, with PADS it is possible to use an arbitrary number of PEUs, by aggregating the available memory and the computation power resources of shared clusters. This increases the model scalability supported by the simulation architecture. On the other hand, new bottlenecks are originated under the distributed coordination, synchronization, and communication viewpoints [6]. A typical cluster-based execution architecture for distributed simulation can be a dedicated cluster with homogeneous units, or a cluster of heterogeneous PEUs, connected by a computer network. Heterogeneity is intended here in terms of PEUs' performance characteristics, available resources, and background load. In shared clusters, the effect of load given by unpredictable background-processes may drastically influence the simulation execution performance. This can be avoided in High Performance Computing (HPC) clusters, that can be reserved, resulting more effective than shared clusters in their resource/performance ratio. On the other hand, shared clusters are cost-effective solutions, because they are made by commercial off-the-shelf (COTS) hardware, possibly deployed for students labs, personal workstations and other computing facilities. In this case the execution units can be really heterogeneous, the CPUs can range from entry level up to bleeding edge models, and the communication network can be a high speed LAN up to the Internet. Being shared between a community of users, it is realistic to assume the presence of variable background load, both for the CPUs and for the interconnection networks.

Typically, in PADS each LP manages a subset of the Simulated Model Entities (SME). Intuitively, a SME is a single model component (object) of the simulation model characterized by a state (data structure) and a behavior (methods). The amount of SMEs managed by a LP has some direct relationship with the computation time required between two successive synchronizations involving LPs. To realize load balancing, the number of SMEs allocated over LPs, should depend on the available resources of the PEUs where LPs are executed. A static allocation of the SMEs realized without considering the dynamic SME interactions, and the dynamic background computation and communication loads, could result in dynamic unbalancing of LP executions. The time required to complete the simulation bon runs, usually referred to as the Wall-Clock-Time (WCT), is the metric used for the analysis of the simulation speed. The computation load can be balanced between PEUs, by migrating SMEs from an overloaded PEU to an underloaded PEU. The way to dynamically balance the distribution of computation over the available PEUs, should depend on realtime feedback of current load. This paper proposes and analyzes a distributed mechanism for load balancing based on the realtime adaptive migration of SMEs between LPs in a PADS framework. The preliminary Generic Adaptive Interaction Architecture (GAIA) proposed in [3] has been enhanced in this work, originating the new GAIA+ framework. GAIA+ takes simultaneously into account two main problems of distributed simulation: the computation and communication load balancing issues and the reduction of the communication overheads required to implement the simulation. The two problems are strictly correlated and should not be addressed independently, in order to achieve consistent advantages and results. In addition, GAIA+ introduces heuristics for supporting dynamic load-balancing in simulations over COTS shared cluster systems, characterized by heterogeneous PEUs, and unpredictable background computation and communication loads.

The paper structure is the following: in Section 2 some background concepts and related works about load balancing and the distributed simulation are introduced; in Section 3 we introduce a PADS framework that is adopted as the basis for designing and implementing the GAIA+ load balancing solution; in Section 4 we report some results obtained by the GAIA+ framework adopted for a testbed wireless ad hoc system simulation. Finally Section 5 reports our conclusions and future work.

2   Background and Related Work

The load balancing of parallel and distributed computations has been widely investigated and evaluated. In the simulation field, specific solutions have been proposed to distribute the simulation workload over the processors while reducing the synchronization overhead. In most cases some knowledge is assumed or inferred at compile time about the system and model workload parameters [11]. Some works deal with the opposite assumption: in [6] a process migration mechanism is presented, that reduces the WCT of a parallel simulation. The simulation approach considered is based on an optimized version of the conservative Chandy-Misra synchronization scheme. The proposed mechanism is dynamic and partially distributed. In [7] a stochastic learning automata enables a communication flow control scheme that is used to balance loads in optimistic simulations based on the Time-Warp synchronization algorithm [1]. All these mechanisms are based on the LP migration concept. In other words, LPs are considered the smallest component that can be migrated for simulation load balancing. In general, migrating and re-instantiating LPs between different PEUs may have a significant overhead. Moreover, the adaptation obtained with this approach is coarse grained with respect to the approach obtained by migrating SMEs between LPs. GAIA+ mechanism will adopt the latter approach: we assume the LPs are containers of SMEs, and the load balancing strategy is based on the migration of SMEs between LPs executed over different PEUs.

To the best of our knowledge, our GAIA+ mechanism has the following differences with existing solutions: it improves the computation load balancing and, at the same time, it reduces the communication overheads between LPs by migrating SMEs [3]. In addition, the load balancing mechanism is fully distributed and manages heterogeneous hardware scenarios also in presence of dynamic background load. The latter point represents the main innovation of GAIA+ with respect to preliminary GAIA mechanism introduced in previous works [3,4]. The potential for this innovation is twofold: it enables adoption of COTS architectures by obtaining high performances and by improving the model scalability, and it supports dynamically load balanced simulations without any need for user level configuration.

3   The Adaptive Load Balancing Middleware

The High Level Architecture (HLA) is a general purpose architecture for simulation reuse and interoperability (IEEE Standard 1516) [2]. A HLA-compliant simulation is realized by a set of federates, each federate is a software component that interacts with other federates to form a simulation (federation). Given previous definitions, a federate can be thought of as a LP and viceversa. Many distributed federates can be composed to form simulations, whose interactions are controlled through a distributed middleware called Runtime (RTI). Some implementation criticisms and the lack of basic features as the built-in support for migration-based load-balancing, are the main motivations behind the design and implementation of a new RTI called ARTÌS (Advanced RTI System) [9].

3.1   ARTÌS

The Advanced RTI System (ARTÌS) is a middleware for Parallel and Distributed Simulation (PADS) supporting high degree of model scalability [9]. The design of the middleware is inspired by the IEEE 1516 standard, but new features have been introduced to improve the scalability and the simulation performance. The PADS execution speed is highly influenced by the communication performance: the approach followed by ARTÌS is adaptive and exploits the characteristics of the physical allocation of LPs [5]. ARTÌS supports both the conservative (Chandy-Misra-Briant) and the optimistic (Time Warp) synchronization algorithms. The load balancing mechanism that will be introduced in the following sections is based on a conservative time-stepped synchronization scheme [3]. In [4] it has been shown that the performances of a distributed simulation can be increased by introducing the migration of the simulated entities (SME). A migration based middleware could optimize in adaptive way the simulation execution by reallocating the SME over the LPs. The dynamic reallocation can reduce the communication overhead and moreover can be exploited to improve the computation load balancing. This translates into a reduction of the Wall-Clock Time (WCT) needed to complete the simulation runs. The Generic Adaptive Interaction Architecture (GAIA) is a migration based framework integrated in ARTÌS. The basic task of GAIA is to check the communication pattern of each SME during the simulation execution. A set of heuristics evaluates the communication pattern and triggers the SME reallocation to reduce the communication costs and to improve the load-balancing of the execution architecture. GAIA migrates the highly interacting SMEs within the same LP, by reducing costly inter-LP communication and by increasing the rate of low cost intra-LP communications. The cost of migrating the simulated entities is a key factor to be evaluated in the migration heuristics. An analytic evaluation of this cost is impossible due to the network heterogeneity and the unpredictable behavior of the simulated system.

3.2   GAIA+

The GAIA+ framework is an evolution of the migration mechanism defined in [4]. GAIA+ has been designed and implemented to support the distributed simulation over shared COTS clusters and to enhance the load balancing and communication overheads' reduction in presence of massive models of dynamically interacting SMEs, heterogeneous execution architectures and unpredictable computation and communication (background) loads.

3.3   The Heuristic Migration Policy Definition

The dynamic migration of SME may reduce the message-passing overhead by introducing migration overheads: some analytical or heuristic metrics are required, to be evaluated at runtime, to define "if" and "where" it would be profitable to migrate a SME. The state size of a SME and the amount of "time-locality" of the causal dependencies (LP-local message passing) between correlated SMEs, are the most relevant parameters influencing the migration policy. Specifically, the policy depends on the interaction rate between SMEs, and the overall load balancing policy between the PEUs. By focusing on the network communication-reduction viewpoint, it would be optimal to allocate every SME on a single PEU. Obviously, GAIA+ mechanism has to deal with computation load balancing too, hence the optimal policy would require to dynamically partition in sets the most frequently interacting SMEs, by allocating each set over the available PEUs in load-balanced way. The dynamic load balancing problem is even more complicated by assuming that the CPUs are heterogeneous and subject to unpredictable background load. GAIA+ implements a combination of two low-cost heuristic schemes, that adaptively converge to a balanced solution, under the system assumptions considered in the implementation. The rules for migration heuristic are quite simple and have been improved with respect to the early design of previous work in [3].

3.4   The Heuristic Load-Balancing Policy Definition

The steady state behavior of the migration heuristic in isolation would lead to the asymptotic clustering of all the SMEs over a subset of the available PEUs. This is because the adaptive effect of migrations is focused on the reduction of "external" communication overheads. The migration heuristic must be composed with a computation load balancing heuristic. The load balancing strategy implemented in the previous version of the GAIA framework and defined in [4] was based on some common assumptions: i) each CPU executes one single LP, ii) all the PEUs are homogeneous and every LP manages the same number of SMEs, iii) the execution architecture is dedicated to the simulation and no external background load can interfere with simulation load balancing.

The new version of the framework, GAIA+, has been designed to overcome such limitations. Our previous experience with migration-based distributed simulations shown that a LP overcrowded by many SMEs may be a synchronization bottleneck for the whole simulation. The general load balancing rule that governed the original GAIA migration heuristic allowed only balanced migrations between LPs, in a three-phases migration procedure: in the first phase every LP must claim the number of candidate migrations and their proposed destinations; in the second phase the load balancing condition is evaluated, and in the third phase all the migrations satisfying the load balancing rules are performed. To remove the simplification assumptions described above, it is necessary to introduce some special improvements. Every LP, at each simulation timestep, checks the incoming communication queues to determine which LPs are slow in reaching the synchronization. Some adjacent timesteps are observed to have some confidence on the trends and behaviors of the system, by each LP. The collected data represents a local-LP vision of the foreign-LPs simulation execution. Such information is exchanged by LPs and managed by the distributed GAIA+ middleware components, locally to each LP. GAIA+ middleware infers a global vision and marks the LPs as "slow" or "fast" with respect to the average simulation speed. If the delay between the slow and the fast LPs is significant then the load distribution is not adequate and GAIA+ breaks the adopted general load balancing rule by triggering an *unbalancing exception*, that is, a part of the load has to be migrated from the slow to the fast group of LPs. The *unbalancing exception* allows the LPs marked as slow to migrate a number of SMEs to LPs that are marked as fast, even if this would break the local balancing condition of the involved LPs. However, the implementation of the exception is regulated: the number of SMEs allowed to migrate (referred as *migration set*) is proportional to the difference of speed between slow and fast groups. After defining the size of the migration set, it is necessary to choose the SMEs that will be migrated, and their destinations, in accordance with communication patterns and the migration cost. The implementation of this mechanism has to satisfy a few essential requirements: i) it should quickly adapt to heterogeneous hardware with very different CPUs and network performances, ii) it should quickly adapt to variations of the background load (both computation and communication), iii) it should converge without introducing harmful fluctuations. For the sake of simplicity, in our analysis we assumed that all the SMEs are equivalent in terms of computation-cost per timestep. This assumption is quite common in many simulation models, e.g. in considered wireless ad hoc network models (section 4). If the assumption is not satisfied, the load estimate characterizing each SME has to be taken into account as additional parameter of the heuristic evaluation.

4   Testbed Evaluation

Now we illustrate some key concepts of a testbed model of a wireless system. We assume a high number of Simulated Mobile Hosts (SMHs, that is, the equivalent of general SMEs considered in previous sections), each one following a Random Waypoint (RW) mobility model. This mobility model is far from being real, but this choice was driven by the unpredictable and uncorrelated mobility pattern of SMHs. This is the worst case analysis for the GAIA+ mechanism, because any heuristic definition cannot rely on any assumption about the motion correlation and predictability of SMHs. Space is modeled as a torus-shaped 2-D flat topology, 10.000x10.000 space units, populated by a constant number of SMHs. The torus space topology, indeed unrealistic, is commonly used by modelers to prevent non-uniform SMHs' concentration in any area. The simulated space is without obstacles. The modeled communication between SMHs is a constant flow of ping messages (i.e. constant bit rate), transmitted by every SMH to all neighbors within a wireless communication range of 250 space units.

4.1   Experimental Results

The first set of experiments were executed on a cluster of 3 heterogeneous PEUs: two Dual Xeon Pentium IV 2800 MHz with 3 and 4 GB RAM, respectively, and one Quad Xeon Pentium IV 1500 MHz with 1 GB RAM, connected by a Gigabit Ethernet LAN. We performed multiple runs for each experiment, and the confidence intervals obtained with a 95% confidence level are lower than 5% the average value of the performance index shown. All the performed experiments were initialized with a uniform pseudo-random distribution of 9000 SMHs over a flat topology. The distributed simulation is composed by 3 LPs: each PEU

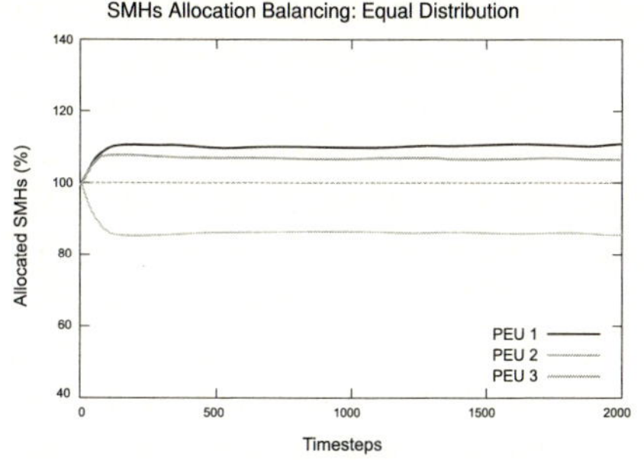

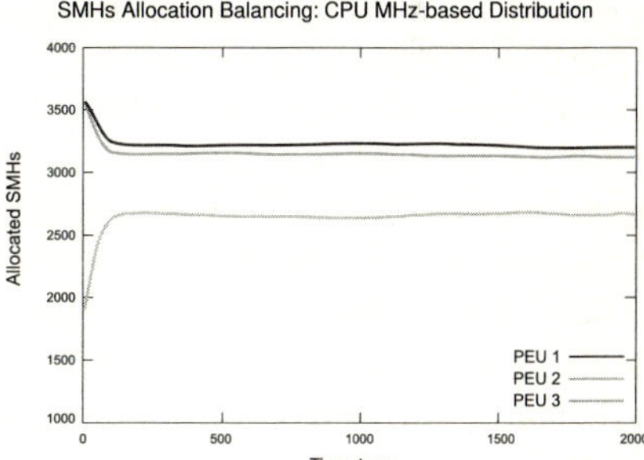

Fig. 1. Initially each PEU simulates the same number of SMHs (3000)

Fig. 2. The initial allocation is based on the CPU MHz of each PEU

manages the execution of one LP. Initially, all the SMHs are randomly and uniformly allocated over the set of PEUs, that is, the model components' allocation is not initialized in a scenario favorable to GAIA+ load-balancing (because PEUs are not homogeneous) and communication-reduction of GAIA+ migration scheme (because modeled wireless hosts with time- and space-correlation are randomly distributed over different PEUs). Testbed evaluation **a**): initially each PEUs allocates the same number of SMHs (3000). All the PEUs are equipped with same generation CPUs (Xeon Pentium IV) but with different clock speed and memory: PEUs 1 and 2 have a 2800 MHz CPU with 3 and 4 GB RAM, respectively, and the PEU 3 has a 1500 MHz CPU with 1 GB RAM. Given the significant difference of speed, we expect that the GAIA+ mechanism will modify the allocation of SMHs for load balancing, reducing the number of SMHs allocated on the slow PEU 3 and increasing the population on the fast PEUs 1 and 2. Figure 1 shows that the expected transient behavior quickly converges to a stable steady state condition, without introducing fluctuations in the number of allocated SMHs. It appears that "fast" PEUs are not homogeneous in performance, as it can be expected due to the difference in the amount of local RAM. The same behavior is confirmed in the results presented in the following.

In the second approach **b**), the initial allocation was based on the nominal performance of the PEUs. In practice, since CPUs are the same generation, it would be possible to roughly allocate the computation load (homogeneous SMEs) proportionally to the clock speed (expressed in MHz). Given this assumption, the 9000 SMEs should be allocated on the fast CPUs (2800 MHz) with 3552 SMHs each, and the slow CPU with 1896 SMHs. In theory, this initial allocation method should be stable under the load balancing viewpoint. Figure 2 demonstrates that this assumption is not confirmed: the GAIA+ framework quickly reacts and reaches a different steady state condition that substantially increases the load on the "slow" PEU. This confirms that load balancing inferred by nominal CPU performance index (like the CPU clock speed) is not adequate.

So far we have considered testbeds with no background load (that is, dedicated cluster). In this case some benchmarks or preliminary simulation tests (like in Figure 1 and 2) could determine a load balanced partition of the SMHs between the execution units involved in the distributed simulation. As discussed in the introduction, this assumption is often unrealistic, as an example with shared clusters with unpredictable background load. In the following we perform some tests of GAIA+ mechanism under the variable background load scenario: the considered system architecture is composed by three Intel Xeon Pentium IV, 2800 MHz, with 2 (PEU1), 4 (PEU2) and 3 (PEU3) GB RAM, respectively. In scenario **c**), we injected a synthetic load over the PEU 1, only. The background load of PEU 1 is shaped as a sinusoidal wave, that is, it is not unpredictable. On the other hand, there is no exploitation of any predictability characteristic in GAIA+: we used this curve because it gradually introduces load variation at different speeds (that is, the derivative of the background load curve shows a variation of slow changes followed by sudden changes). Our analysis goal is to verify the reaction of GAIA+ in presence of slow and fast background load variations. In left-hand figures 3 we show the background load of three PEUs involved in the distributed simulation. The effect on the load balancing mechanism of GAIA+ can be seen on right-hand figures 3: a SMHs re-allocation is realized by GAIA+, by following the shape of the background load in reactive and dynamic way. The right-hand figures report the percentage of allocated SMHs with respect to the initial distribution of 3000 allocated SMH per PEU (100%). SMHs migrated from overloaded PEU1 are fairly re-allocated over PEU2 and PEU3.

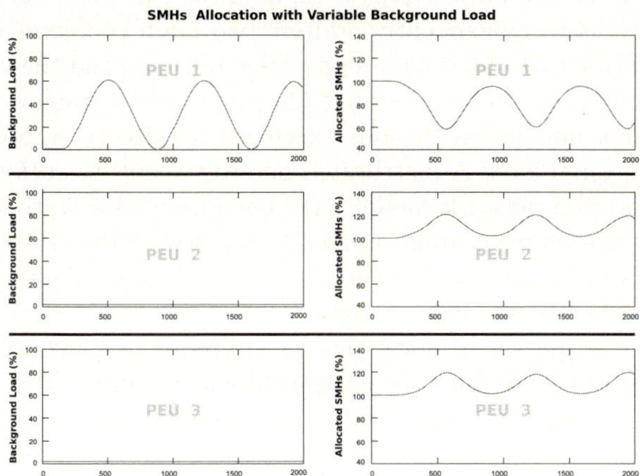

Fig. 3. The effect of the injected background load on the SMHs allocation

These results demonstrate that GAIA+ mechanism can quickly adapt the load partitioning of the SMEs from any initial distributions (e.g. random), and by adaptively reacting to the background load variations. The communication reduction ability obtained by GAIA+ is the same inherited by original GAIA, as shown in [3]. In [3], we also shown that speedup was obtained by the GAIA mechanism with respect to distributed and monolithic simulations. Now we show that GAIA+ mechanism outperforms GAIA under the simulation speedup viewpoint, by reducing the Wall-Clock-Time (WCT) required by simulation runs, under new assumptions that characterize the shared clusters. We analyzed a portion of the execution (1000 steady state timesteps) of the simulation runs of the wireless ad hoc network model, for the three scenarios (a, b and c). Table 1 shows the WCT needed to execute the run portion: we refer to "GAIA+" as a distributed simulation with the new GAIA+ load balancing mechanism enabled and "GAIA" when the old GAIA scheme is used. The results confirm our expectations: the GAIA+ mechanism significantly reduces the WCT in all the analyzed scenarios. The load allocation is quickly balanced over heterogeneous execution scenarios, both in presence of sub-optimal initial allocations (a, b) and in presence of variable background loads (c).

Table 1. WCT (seconds) to complete a simulation run of 1000 timesteps

scenario	GAIA	GAIA+	diff (%)
a	3600	3442	*-4.38%*
b	3983	3568	*-10.41%*
c	5232	4128	*-21.10%*

5 Conclusions and Future Work

In this work we have described GAIA+, a migration-based framework build on top of the ARTÌS middleware. GAIA+ exploits the runtime migration of simulated model entities to concurrently address two main problems of distributed simulation: the reduction of the communication overhead and the load-balancing in the distributed execution architecture. The new GAIA+ framework introduces support for shared and heterogeneous execution architectures possibly characterized by background load. A distributed heterogeneous execution architecture and a wireless ad hoc network model have been used as a testbed for GAIA+ analysis. The performance evaluation has demonstrated that the new heuristics adopted in the GAIA+ middleware can lead to significant reduction in the WCT required to execute the simulation runs.

Future works include new heuristics to address the presence of heterogeneous model entities with different computational requirements, and extended testbed models. Most preliminary Grid-based simulations has revealed poor performances mainly due to the high latency experienced by Internet communications and the lack of control on the nodes. We believe that the ARTÌS and GAIA+ middleware porting on the Grid architecture could possibly contribute to increase the performance of Grid-based simulations.

References

1. Fujimoto, R.M. Parallel and Distributed Simulation Systems. Wiley & Sons, 2000
2. IEEE 1516. Standard for modeling and simulation, High Level Architecture (HLA).
3. Bononi, L., D'Angelo, G., Donatiello, L. HLA-based adaptive distributed simulation of wireless mobile systems. PADS '03: Proceedings of the 17th ACM/IEEE/SCS Workshop on Parallel and Distributed Simulation.
4. Bononi, L., Bracuto, M., D'Angelo, G., Donatiello, L. A New Adaptive Middleware for Parallel and Distributed Simulation of Dynamically Interacting Systems. DS-RT '04: Proceedings of the 8-th IEEE International Symposium on Distributed Simulation and Real Time Applications.
5. Bononi, L., Bracuto, M., D'Angelo, G., Donatiello, L. Analysis of High Performance Communication and Computation Solutions for Parallel and Distributed Simulation. HPCC '05: Springer LNCS Proceedings of the 2005 International Conference on High Performance Computing and Communications.
6. Boukerche, A., Das, S.K. Dynamic Load Balancing Strategies for Conservative Parallel Simulations. PADS '97: Proceedings of the 11th SIGSIM/IEEE/SCS Workshop on Parallel and Distributed Simulation.
7. Choe, M., Tropper, C. On Learning Algorithms and Balancing Loads in Time Warp. PADS '99: Proc. of the 13th Workshop on Parallel and Distributed Simulation.
8. Theodoropoulus, G., Logan, B. An Approach to Interest Management and Dynamic Load Balancing in Distributed Simulation ESIW '01: Proceedings of the 2001 European Simulation Interoperability Workshop.

9. PADS homepage, http://pads.cs.unibo.it
10. Short, J., Bagrodia, R., Kleinrock, L. Mobile wireless network system simulation Wireless Networks 1, 1995
11. Boukerche, A., Tropper, C. A static partitioning and mapping algorithm for conservative parallel simulations. PADS '94: Proc. of the 8th workshop on Parallel and distributed simulation.

Impact of SOAP Implementations in the Performance of a Web Service-Based Application[*]

Elena Gómez-Martínez and José Merseguer

Dpto. de Informática e Ingeniería de Sistemas, Universidad de Zaragoza
C/María de Luna,1 50018 Zaragoza, Spain
{megomez, jmerse}@unizar.es

Abstract. This article recalls, from the literature, a performance study of a web service. That study, based on the layered queuing network (LQN) paradigm, is now addressed following the PUMA approach to obtain a new performance model, in this case in terms of Petri nets, for the target web service. Such Petri net model is used to extend the previous LQN results with respect to some key web service performance aspects: the SOAP toolkit and the XML parsers. Actually, this paper aims to explore through a case study some of the main concerns of web services performance at the middleware layer. The acquired background is meant to start to develop a methodology, based on the SPE principles, useful to analyze web services performance.

1 Introduction

A web service is a collection of protocols and standards used for exchanging of XML messages between applications. Unlike other middleware technologies [2], they allow to communicate heterogeneous environments deployed on the network, offering flexibility and interoperability.

Performance is one of the key aspects and probably the Achilles' heel of web services and in general of services offered over the Internet [28]. However, it has not been adequately addressed from a formal modeling viewpoint in the literature yet. In this work, we try to overcome some aspects of this lack by accomplishing an in-depth study of different key aspects of web services performance at the middleware layer: the SOAP implementations and the XML parsers.

This work is proposed as a first step to develop a methodology to evaluate web service performance, and we start addressing some middleware performance issues. The methodology will use Petri nets (PN) [1] as formal method, and will follow the Software Performance Engineering (SPE) [19] principles and the Performance by Unified Model Analysis (PUMA) approach [30]. PUMA aims translations from different kinds of design models and performance models.

[*] This work was supported by the projects TIC2003-05226 and DPI2006-15390 of the Spanish Ministry of Science and IBE2005-TEC-10 of the University of Zaragoza.

G. Min et al. (Eds.): ISPA 2006 Ws, LNCS 4331, pp. 884–896, 2006.

Our study is based on an interesting performance study of a web service developed, also under the SPE principles, in [3]. We rearchitect this case study following the PUMA approach to get a Generalized Stochastic Petri Net (GSPN) [1]. The GSPN, properly analyzed with the TimeNET tool [23], allows us to offer interesting results about performance middleware key aspects and to contrast them with the results obtained from pragmatic (non-formal) studies.

The rest of the paper is organized as follows. Section 2 revises the state of the art and places our proposal for study performance of web services in the current scene. Section 3 addresses key issues concerning performance of web services at middleware layer. Section 4 recalls the web service under study and we obtain the PN that models the target system. Such net will be useful, in section 5, to accomplish the study proposed in this work. Therefore, the impact of SOAP implementations and XML parsers is studied by means of that formal model. The article ends in section 6 giving the conclusion.

2   Related Work

Performance is an important aspect of web services. Nevertheless, from the best of our knowledge, very few papers focuss on performance evaluation of web service-based applications. And a very few of them follow the techniques proposed by the SPE [19].

Menascé and Almeida [13] developed a methodology from we have learnt the key issues of performance evaluation of web services. While this methodology is focussed on capacity planning using queuing networks (QN), we aim at its performance prediction using PN and the Unified Modeling Language (UML).

Chandrasekaran et al. [4] propose a simulation technique for analyzing performance of composite web services in order to obtain efficient web processes. Menascé in [12] studies QoS issues of composite web services. In [26], Datla and Goševa-Popstojanova present a measurement-based study of performance of e-commerce applications. They study the impact of web services together with other components on integrated applications using benchmark techniques. Ng et al. [14] evaluate diverse SOAP implementations by means of benchmarks of a simple service with three types of message. In contrast to us, they probe that serialization and deserialization are the primary important bottleneck for this application.

Liu et al. [11] propose an approach to predict performance metrics for a middleware-hosted application using QN models. Although, this work is focussed on a J2EE application, their modeling approach is suitable to other middleware technologies, such as CORBA and COM+/.NET.

Verdickt et al. [27] propose a Model Driven Architecture (MDA) model transformation for Platform Specific Models (PSM), including middleware performance details. It is based on SPE and the UML-SPT [15] profile. The transformation process is made by a tool which generates LQN models.

Gilmore et al. [9] propose an UML-based methodology for analyzing security and performance aspects using PEPA models. This method is implemented in the Choreographer design platform.

3   Performance Issues of the Web Services

Web service technology has not been developed with performance as a goal. Performance issues affect several aspects: the XML protocols, such as discovering using UDDI [13], transporting using usually HTTP [7], the latency of SOAP implementations [5] or the use of an XML parser [10]. Furthermore, web services can be provided with dynamic composition of web services, affecting performance in any way [4,12]. The software infrastructure is other significant factor [11].

Although all of these issues are relevant, this paper focusses on those that being closer to the middleware layer can be parameterized in a UML design. Among them, SOAP implementation is one of the key factors that have influence on performance, as previous studies have shown [5,7,10]. Therefore, it is important to determine which particular SOAP toolkit can meet the performance requirements of an application. These studies remark the following topics:

Serialization is the process to convert an in-memory object into an XML stream. This includes to pack the XML message in the SOAP envelope and to build the message which will be sent by the corresponding transport protocol, mainly HTTP [10].

Deserialization converts XML streams in wire-format objects in memory. In this process two phases must be emphasized: (1) unpacking the SOAP envelope and (2) parsing and interpreting the XML document. The most widely models used for parsing are *Document Object Model* (DOM) [6], *Simple API for XML* (SAX) [18] and *XML Pull Parser* (XPP) [8]. DOM parsers are suitable for small documents which must be validated and/or modified. SAX parsers are better for large documents. XPP is optimized when the XML elements are processed in succession and do not need to be visited again. The parser process has a great impact in the performance of SOAP implementation, as previous works have studied [7,10]. Note that XML native parsers and those embedded in SOAP have to be differentiated, since they exhibit different features and performance characteristics [21,8].

However, not only these processes affect the performance of a SOAP toolkit, others such as data structure support, optimizations to handle scientific data or algorithms implementation and protocols have influence too [5,10]. These topics will not be addressed in this work, since they are out of scope of the case study which guides it. Other significant factors that may impact in performance are the service processing time, i.e. the *business logic*, and the XML file size [3].

The goal of this paper is to study the impact of the following aspects in web service performance: (**G1**) XML parsers and (**G2**) SOAP toolkits. Furthermore, other factors that may impact in performance will be studied, such as (**G3**) the sensibility of a web service with respect to the document file size exchanged and (**G4**) the service processing time. The implementations of XML parsers under consideration are: Xerces [24], Xerces2 [25], Crimson [22] and XML Pull Parser (XPP) from [8]. The SOAP toolkits considered are AxisJava and .NET, since they are widely used. We have also included XSUL for its excellent performance for large documents [8].

4   SPE for Web Services

In order to study the impact of the previous goals, we recall a performance case study taken from [3], then section 4.1 summarizes it and its results. In section 4.2 we apply the PUMA approach to obtain a GSPN model from the UML system description.

4.1   Case Study: CDSS Web Service

Catley et al. propose in [3] *"an infrastructure to support artificial intelligence-based clinical decision systems (CDSSs). The system processes multidomain medical data in high-risk medical environments in order to reduce medical errors and alert detection systems"*. It integrates and accesses CDSSs and distributed databases from different medical domains in order to predict medical outcomes. These CDSSs are offered as web-services. The paper models a representative subset of this infrastructure, which invokes a CDSS as a web service and accesses the patient's Electronic Patient Record (EPR). Figure 2(a) depicts the sequence diagram (SD) of such CDSS invocation process, that proposes an *initial system configuration* made of one instance per hardware and software resource.

The system parses XML documents using the Xerces parser through a DOM interface. The *required* response time for 50 users requesting the system should not exceed 8 seconds.

Catley et al. applied the SPE techniques developed in [16] to assess the required metric. Then they modeled the system by means of deployment and sequence diagrams annotated according to the *UML Profile for Schedulability, Performance and Time Specification* (UML-SPT) and translated them into an LQN model [29].

This model was solved with the *initial configuration*, determining that the system can not meet the performance target, see Figure 1(a1) where the response time for 50 users is 39.9 seconds. They identified system bottlenecks and proposed a *new configuration* that replicates processors and threads (10 `WSCoordinator`, 10 `CDSS`, 3 `AppCPU` and a variable number of `EPR`). Figure 1(a2) depicts the results of multithreading the `EPR` task when the system is executed by 50 users. They determined that the target is achieved in this new configuration with 8 threads of `EPR`.

4.2   Applying the PUMA Approach

PUMA [30] was designed as a framework to obtain performance models from design models. Therefore, we use PUMA to obtain a GSPN model from the SD in Figure 2(a), which models the CDSS. The GSPN model aims for validating the CDSS results in [3] and for dealing with the performance goals previously given.

PUMA uses an intermediate model, the *Core Scenario Model* (CSM) [17], which is suited to produce a performance model, such as layered and regular QNs, and stochastic PNs.

The CSM defines a performance *Scenario* as a sequence of *Steps* that are linked by *Connectors*. A Step is a sequential piece of execution. Connectors can include branches, merges, and forks and joins. A scenario has a *Start* point and an *End* point. Start points are associated with *Workload*. There exist two kind of *Resources*: *Active*, which execute steps, and *Passive*, which are acquired and released during scenarios by special *ResAcquire* and *ResRelease* steps. Steps are executed by (software) *Components* which are passive resources.

PUMA gives a translation process to get a CSM model from a UML SD. Figure 3(a) depicts the resulting CSM for our target SD. Observe that this CSM is made of two scenarios, the one corresponding to the CDSS invocation process (left column) and the CDSS processing (right column). The CDSS processing scenario comprises the messages from `processWebService()` to `WebServiceDone()`. The other messages of the SD correspond to the CDSS invocation process.

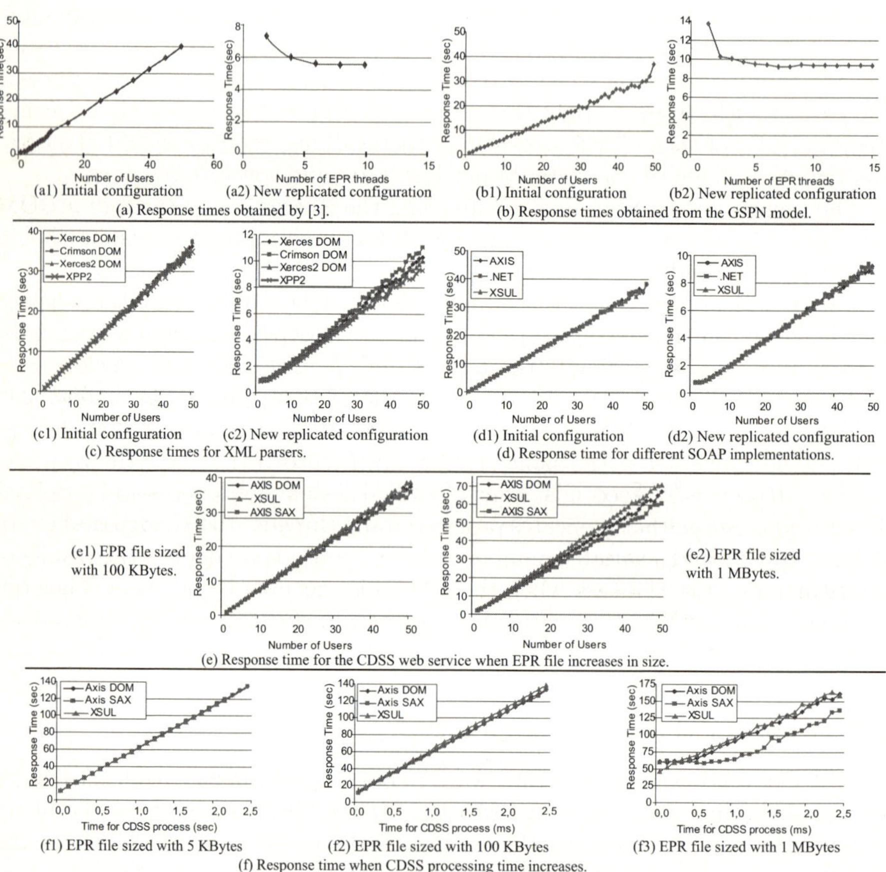

Fig. 1. Results of the experiments

The CSM in Figure 3(a) is translated into a GSPN, see Figure 3(b), by means of a extraction process developed in [30]. So, each class of the CSM corresponds

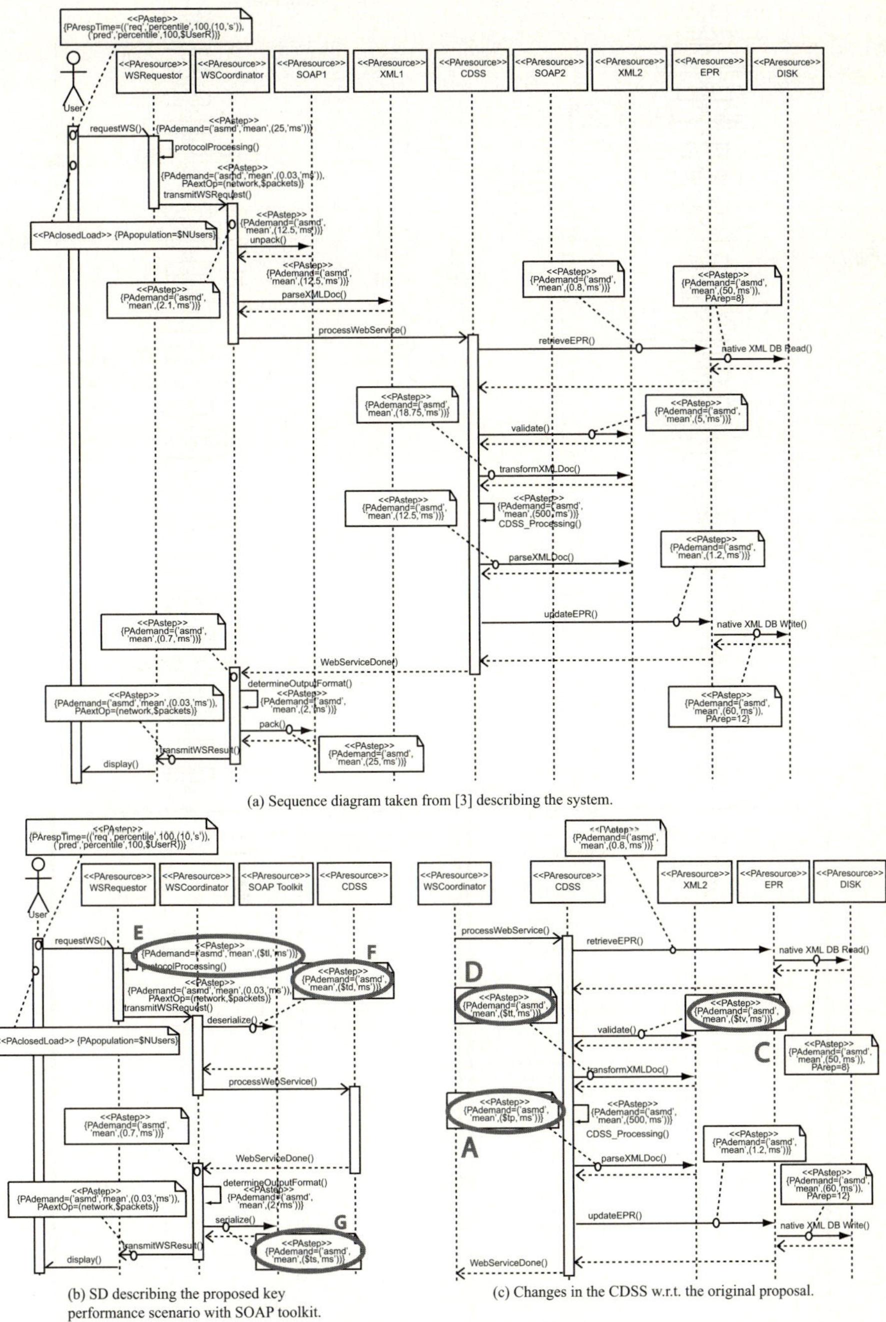

(a) Sequence diagram taken from [3] describing the system.

(b) SD describing the proposed key performance scenario with SOAP toolkit.

(c) Changes in the CDSS w.r.t. the original proposal.

Fig. 2. Sequence diagrams

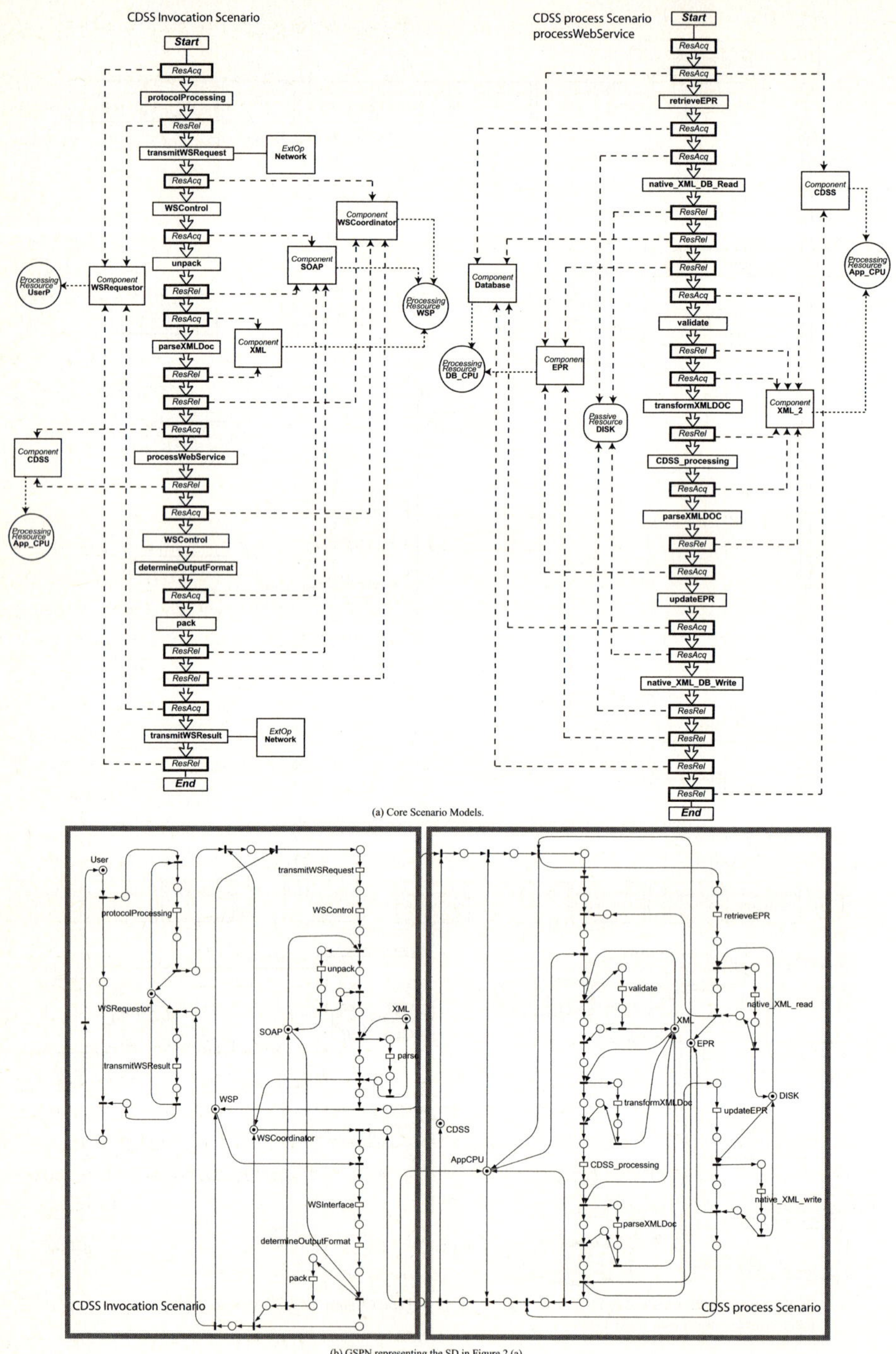

(a) Core Scenario Models.

(b) GSPN representing the SD in Figure 2 (a).

Fig. 3. Core Scenario Model and LGSPN for the SD in Figure 2(a)

with a GSPN pattern. For instance, a step is translated into a timed transition with an input place, where its delay is the demand attribute of the step. All of the GSPN patterns are composed until the GSPN representing the whole scenario is built.

Performance metrics can be obtained using TimeNET [23] to solve this GSPN by means of simulation techniques. Figure 1(b1) and Figure 1(b2) present the same experiments as Figure 1(a1) and Figure 1(a2), respectively, i.e. the response times for the initial and the new replicated configuration. In Figures 1(b2) and 1(a2), the response time for 50 users is stated in 9.23 seconds and 5.4 seconds, respectively. These response times are greater since PNs introduce synchronization in the model. However, both the order of magnitude and the tendency of the results are kept.

Once it has been verified that the results, obtained by the derived GSPN, are similar to those obtained in [3] with LQN, the following step is to study, using this GSPN, the impact of XML parsers and SOAP implementations.

5   Web Services Tunning: CDSS Performance Improvements

In this section we exploit the CDSS case study to deal with the goals **(G1)**, **(G2)**, **(G3)** and **(G4)** proposed in section 3. The final objective is to extract conclusions about those key aspects of web service performance from the case study.

5.1   Impact of XML Parsers

Since XML parsers affect web service performance [7,5,10], we explore different alternatives of them in order to study their impact in the CDSS web service.

We realized that some of the CDSS parameters in [3] should be changed for the following considerations:

A *Document build time* is the time to scan and interpret the XML document [20], but in [3] is assigned to the packing operation. In our experiments, we will assign this value for parsing operations, see Table 1.

B *Document modify time* is the time required to systematically modify the constructed document representation [20], but in [3] is assigned to the parsing operations. We do not assign this value to an operation, since we consider that EPR file is not updated.

C *Document walk time* is the time required to walk the constructed document representation [20]. As [3], we will assign it to validate the XML document, see Table 1.

D *Text generation time* is the time required to output document representations as text XML documents [20]. As [3], we will assign it to transform the XML document, see Table 1.

Table 1. Performance parameters for XML operations from [21]

Operation	parameter in SD	Mean Execution Time (ms)			
		Xerces	Xerces2	Crimson	XPP
(A) `parseXMLDoc()`	$tp	6.957	2.898	9.856	1.159
(C) `validate()`	$tv	$\simeq 0$	$\simeq 0$	$\simeq 0$	$\simeq 0$
(D) `transformXMLDoc()`	$tt	1.055	1.231	1.231	0.703

Table 1 gives the new values taken from an updated benchmark [21]. Figure 2(c) depicts the part of the SD that has been changed to consider the new values in the model.

Figure 1(c1) and Figure 1(c2) depict the response times when the parameters in Table 1 are applied. These results can be compared with those in Figure 1(a1) and Figure 1(a2), as well as with those in Figure 1(b1) and Figure 1(b2), being similar in all cases. Therefore, it does not matter which parser is used.

However, according to [7,21], the response times for Xerces parsers are worse than the obtained ones for Crimson or XPP parsers. Slightly best results are obtained by XPP. The reason for our results is the small size of the EPR file, only 5 KBytes. So, in this case, the XML parser significantly does not affect the performance of the CDSS web service. But in section 5.3 we try to validate the conclusions in [7,21] by varying the EPR file size.

5.2   Impact of SOAP Implementations

Currently, several implementations of SOAP are emerging and their performance differs to a great extent [5,10]. Therefore, it is profitable to determinate what toolkit meets performance objectives in the CDSS invocation web service.

We guess that in [3] the SOAP parameters are taken from [20], but we consider more appropriate to use an specific SOAP benchmark, taken from [10]. Table 2 provides the values of SOAP operations, (F) deserialization and (G) serialization and the overhead that the SOAP toolkit imposes, (E) the latency. Note that they have been calculated assuming that most of the content of the EPR file are strings. Figure 2(b) depicts the part of the SD changed to include in the CDSS these new parameters.

Figure 1(d1) shows that all the SOAP toolkit give similar response time for the CDSS. Only XSUL performs a little better in the replicated configuration, see Figure 1(d2). Comparing these results with those in Figure 1(a1), they are alike. We guess that as the SOAP message, which contains the EPR file, is small, the time taken by processing SOAP is negligible with respect to the CDSS

Table 2. Performance parameters for SOAP toolkits from [10]

Operation	parameter in SD	Mean Execution Time (ms)		
		AxisJava	.NET	XSUL
(E) Latency $\rightarrow$ `protocolProcessing()`	$tl	8.35	3.5	2.435
(F) Deserialization $\rightarrow$ `deserialize()`	$td	10.476	4.797	3.935
(G) Serialization $\rightarrow$ `serialize()`	$ts	16.151	4.481	3.706

processing time. In section 5.4, we try to verify this affirmation by varying this service processing time.

5.3   Impact of the EPR File Size

The previous experiments showed that due to the small size of the EPR file, both the XML parser and the SOAP implementations have no relevant impact for the performance of the CDSS web service.

Table 3. Performance parameters from [21] and [10]

| Parameter in SD | Mean Execution Time (ms) | | | | | |
| | 100 KBytes | | | 1 MBytes | | |
	AxisJava DOM	AxisJava SAX	XSUL	AxisJava DOM	AxisJava SAX	XSUL
(A) $tp	27.68	10.19	40.79	297.8	78.37	501.56
(C) $tv	1.37	$\simeq 0$	0.68	31.34	$\simeq 0$	15.67
(D) $tt	11.36	$\simeq 0$	26.51	282.13	$\simeq 0$	203.76
(E) $tl	8.35	8.35	2.435	8.35	8.35	2.435
(F) $td	44.39	44.39	26.78	917.11	917.11	431.464
(G) $ts	32.00	32.00	35.53	291.82	291.82	265.81

If it would be considered that this file increases in size, the results could be different. Note that the XML-based EPR file is also enveloped in the SOAP message, therefore its size affects both XML and SOAP operations. Table 3 provides the new parameters, considering two sizes for the EPR, they are set in sequence diagrams of Figure 2(b) and Figure 2(c). We have taken into account that XPP is the native parser for XSUL and for Xerces through DOM or SAX interface for AxisJava.

Figures 1(e1) and 1(e2) show the response time with the initial configuration when the EPR file size is 100 KBytes and 1 MBytes, respectively. If we observe the results when EPR file size is 100 KBytes, these are similar to those when it is only 5 KBytes, see Figure 1(d1). However, the response time increases meaningfully with 1 MBytes. As expected [7], comparing the SOAP implementations, AxisJava through SAX interface outperforms AxisJava through DOM. Surprisingly, in spite of the good results of XSUL presented in [10] for large sizes, it performs poorly in this case. It may be due to the time required by XPP to build the document in memory, as suggested in [21].

5.4   Impact of the CDSS Processing Time

Once studied the impact of EPR file size, we come back to section 5.2 to verify if the time required for processing this EPR file (with SOAP and the XML parser) is irrelevant with respect to the time taken by the `CDSS_Processing()` process. In order to validate this supposition, the service processing time will be modified. See the annotation of the `CDSS_Processing()` message self dispatched by the CDSS in the sequence diagram depicted in Figure 2(a).

In section 5.1 and section 5.2, we guess that XML parser and SOAP toolkits have not influence in CDSS web service, since XML-based EPR file size is small.

Therefore, the time required for being processed it by SOAP and XML parser is irrelevant with respect to the time taken by `CDSS_Processing()` process. In order to validate this supposition, the service processing time is modified.

Figure 1(f1) depicts the response times for 50 users with the initial configuration when the `CDSS_Processing()` service time varies from 0.1 to 2.5 seconds and the EPR file is 5 KBytes; in Figure 1(f2) the EPR file is 100 KBytes and in Figure 1(f3), 1 MBytes. The response time of the different SOAP implementations and XML parsers follows the same tendency while sizing EPR file to *"small sizes"*, 5 KBytes or 100 KBytes. However, when EPR file is 1 MBytes, *"big sizes"*, and `CDSS_Processing()` is less than 0.4 seconds, AxisJava through SAX parser performs poorly compared to AxisJava through DOM and XSUL. But, when service time increases, AxisJava through SAX parser outperforms them. We guess that XSUL performs better when the service time is small because it is oriented to slightly processed scientific data. Similarly, we guess that DOM and SAX outperform XSUL when the processing time is greater than 0.4 seconds since they are conceived to process generic information which may be repeatedly accessed.

This experiment shows that the CDSS processing time (`CDSS_Processing()`) and the EPR file size condition the impact of the XML parser and the SOAP implementation.

6   Conclusion

This paper studies some of the main concerns of web services performance through a set of goals established on a CDSS web service. We have focussed on how XML parsers, SOAP implementations, the exchanged file size and the service time influence the web services.

Our experiments indicate that the XML parser choice slightly affects web services performance when the XML-based file size is small, whereas the SOAP implementation influence is even smaller. However, when the EPR file increases in size, the response times obtained are worst and there exist noticeable differences among XML parsers and SOAP implementations. These differences intensify when the service processing time changes.

We can conclude that the impact of the XML parsers and the SOAP implementations is conditioned by both XML-based file size and service time, i.e. the serialization and deserialization processes are not bottlenecks for large data applications and large service times.

Acknowledgments. The authors would like to thank Diego Rodríguez for his help in computing results using the TimeNET tool.

References

1. M. Ajmone Marsan, G. Balbo, G. Conte, S. Donatelli, and G. Franceschinis. *Modelling with Generalized Stochastic Petri Nets*. John Wiley Series in Parallel Computing - Chichester, 1995.

2. G. Alonso, F. Casati, H. Kuno, and V. Machiraju. *Web Services. Concepts, Architectures and Applications.* Springer, 2004.

3. C. Catley, D. Petriu, and M. Frize. Software Performance Engineering of a Web service-based Clinical Decision Support infrastructure. In *ACM WOSP*, pages 130–138, 2004.

4. S. Chandrasekaran, J. Miller, G. Silver, I. Arpinar, and A. Sheth. Performance Analysis and Simulation of Composite Web Services. *Electronic Markets*, 13(2), 2003.

5. D. Davis and M. Parashar. Latency Performance of SOAP Implementations. In *IEEE CCGRID*, pages 407–412, 2002.

6. Document Object Model (DOM). `http://www.w3.org/DOM/`.

7. R. Elfwing, U. Paulsson, and L. Lundberg. Performance of SOAP in Web Service Environment Compared to CORBA. In *IEEE APSEC*, pages 84–96, 2002.

8. Extreme! Computing Lab. Indiana University. `http://www.extreme.indiana.edu/xgws/xsoap/xpp/`.

9. S. Gilmore, V. Haenel, L. Kloul, and M. Maidl. Choreographing Security and Performance Analysis for Web Services. In *EPEW/WS-FM*, pages 200–214, 2005.

10. M. Head, M. Govindaraju, A. Slominski, P. Liu, N. Abu-Ghazaleh, R. van Engelen, K. Chiu, and M. Lewis. A Benchmark Suite for SOAP-based Communication in Grid Web Services. In *IEEE SC*, page 19, 2005.

11. Y. Liu, A. Fekete, and I. Gorton. Predicting the performance of middleware-based applications at the design level. In *ACM WOSP*, pages 166–170, 2004.

12. D. Menascé. Composing Web Services: A QoS View. *IEEE Internet Computing*, 8(6):88–90, 2004.

13. D. Menascé and V. F. Almeida. *Capacity Planning for Web Services: metrics, models, and methods.* Prentice Hall PTR, Upper Saddle River, NJ, USA, 2001.

14. A. Ng, S. Chen, and P. Greenfield. An Evaluation of Contemporary Commercial SOAP Implementations. In *AWSA*, pages 64–71, 2004.

15. Object Management Group, `http://www.uml.org`. *UML Profile for Schedulabibity, Performance and Time Specification.*, 2005.

16. D. Petriu and H. Shen. Applying the UML performance profile: Graph grammar-based derivation of LQN models from UML specifications. In *TOOLS*, volume 2324 of *LNCS*, pages 159–177. Springer, 2002.

17. D. Petriu and C. Woodside. A Metamodel for Generating Performance Models from UML Designs. In *UML*, volume 3273 of *LNCS*, pages 41–53. Springer, 2004.

18. Simple API for XML (SAX). `http://www.saxproject.org/`.

19. C. Smith and L. Williams. *Performance Solutions.* Addison-Wesley, 2001.

20. D. Sosnoski. *XML and JAVA technologies: Document models, Part 1: Performance.* `http://www-128.ibm.com/developerworks/xml/library/x-injava/`.

21. D. Sosnoski. *XMLBench Document Model Benchmark.* `http://www.sosnoski.com/opensrc/xmlbench/`.

22. The Crimson Java Parser. `http://xml.apache.org/crimson/`.

23. The TimeNET tool. `http://pdv.cs.tu-berlin.de/~timenet/`.

24. The Xerces Java Parser. `http://xerces.apache.org/xerces-j/`.

25. The Xerces2 Java Parser. `http://xerces.apache.org/xerces2-j/`.

26. V. Datla and K. Goševa-Popstojanova. Measurement-based Performance Analysis of E-commerce Applications with Web Services Components. In *IEEE ICEBE*, pages 305–314, 2005.

27. T. Verdickt, B. Dhoedt, F. Gielen, and P. Demeester. Automatic Inclusion of Middleware Performance Attributes into Architectural UML Software Models. *IEEE Trans. Softw. Eng.*, 31(8):695–711, 2005.

28. C. Woodside and D. Menascé. Application-Level QoS. *IEEE Internet Computing*, 10(3):13–15, 2006.
29. C. Woodside, J. Neilson, D. Petriu, and S. Majumdar. The Stochastic Rendezvous Network Model for Performance of Synchronous Client-Server-like Distributed Software. *IEEE Trans. Computers*, 44(1):20–34, 1995.
30. C. Woodside, D. Petriu, D. Petriu, H. Shen, T. Israr, and J. Merseguer. Performance by unified model analysis (PUMA). In *ACM WOSP*, pages 1–12, 2005.

Server Allocation in Grid Systems with On/Off Sources

Joris Slegers, Isi Mitrani, and Nigel Thomas

School of Computing Science, Newcastle University, NE1 7RU
{j.a.l.slegers, isi.mitrani, nigel.thomas}@ncl.ac.uk

Abstract. A system consisting of a number of servers, where demands of different types arrive in bursts (modelled by interrupted Poisson processes), is examined in the steady state. The problem is to decide how many servers to allocate to each job type, so as to minimize a cost function expressed in terms of average queue sizes. First, an exact analysis is provided for an isolated $IP/M/n$ queue. The results are used to compute the optimal *static* server allocation policy. The latter is then compared to two heuristic policies which employ *dynamic* switching of servers from one queue to another (such switches take time and hence incur costs).

1   Introduction

Recent developments in distributed and grid computing have facilitated the hosting of service provisioning systems on clusters of computers. Users do not have to specify the server on which their requests (or 'jobs') are going to be executed. Rather, jobs of different types are submitted to a central dispatcher, which sends them for execution to one of the available servers. Typically, the job streams are bursty, i.e. they consist of alternating 'on' and 'off' periods during which demands of the corresponding type do and do not arrive.

In such an environment it is important, both to the users and the service provider, to have an efficient policy for allocating servers to the various job types. One may consider a static policy whereby a fixed number of servers is assigned to each job type, regardless of queue sizes or phases of arrival streams. Alternatively, the policy may be dynamic and allow servers to be reallocated from one type of service to another when the former becomes under-subscribed and the latter over-subscribed. However, each server reconfiguration takes time, and during it the server is not available to run jobs; hence, a dynamic policy must involve a careful calculation of possible gains and losses.

The purpose of this paper is to (i) provide a computational procedure for determining the optimal static allocation policy and (ii) suggest acceptable heuristic policies for dynamic server reconfiguration. In order to achieve (i), an exact solution is obtained for an isolated queue with n parallel servers and an on/off source. The dynamic heuristics are evaluated by simulation.

The problem described here has not, to our knowledge, been addressed before. Much of the server allocation literature deals with polling systems, where a single

G. Min et al. (Eds.): ISPA 2006 Ws, LNCS 4331, pp. 897–906, 2006.
© Springer-Verlag Berlin Heidelberg 2006

server attends to several queues [2,3,4,5,6]. Even in those cases it has been found that the presence of non-zero switching times makes the optimal policy very difficult to characterize and necessitates the consideration of heuristics. The only general result for multiple servers concerns the case of Poisson arrivals and no switching times or costs: then the $c\mu$-rule is optimal, i.e. the best policy is to give absolute preemptive priority to the job type for which the product of holding cost and service rate is largest (Buyukkoc et al [1]).

A model similar to ours was examined by Palmer and Mitrani [10]; however, there all arrival processes were assumed to be Poisson; also, the static allocation was not done in an optimal manner. The novelty of the present study lies in the inclusion of on/off sources, the computation of the optimal static policy and the introduction of new dynamic heuristics.

The assumptions of model are stated in section 2. The analysis of the $IP/M/n$ queue, leading to the optimal static policy, is presented in section 3. Section 4 describes the dynamic heuristics, while section 5 shows the results of experiments comparing the performance of the different policies.

2   The Model

The system contains N servers, each of which may be allocated to the service of any of M job types. There is a separate unbounded queue for each type. Jobs of type i arrive according to an independent interrupted Poisson process with on-periods distributed exponentially with mean $1/\xi_i$, off-periods distributed exponentially with mean $1/\eta_i$ and arrival rate during on-periods λ_i $(i = 1, 2, ..., M)$. The required service times for type i are distributed exponentially with mean $1/\mu_i$.

Any of queue i's servers may at any time be switched to queue j; the reconfiguration period, during which the server cannot serve jobs, is distributed exponentially with mean $1/\zeta_{i,j}$. If a service is preempted by the switch, it is eventually resumed from the point of interruption.

The cost of keeping a type i job in the system is c_i per unit time $(i = 1, 2, ..., M)$. These 'holding' costs reflect the relative importance, or willingness to wait, of the M job types. The system performance is measured by the total average cost, C, incurred per unit time:

$$C = \sum_{i=1}^{N} c_i L_i \,, \tag{1}$$

where L_i is the steady-state average number of type i jobs present. Those quantities depend, of course, on the server allocation policy.

In principle, it is possible to compute the optimal dynamic switching policy by treating the model as a Markov decision process and solving the corresponding dynamic programming equations. However, such a computation is tractable only for very small systems. What makes the problem difficult is the size of the state space one has to deal with. The system state at any point in time is described by a quadruple, $S = (\mathbf{j}, \mathbf{n}, \mathbf{u}, \mathbf{m})$, where $\mathbf{j}$ is a vector whose ith element, j_i, is the number of jobs in queue i (including the jobs in service); $\mathbf{n}$ is a vector whose ith element, n_i, is the number of servers currently assigned to queue i; $\mathbf{u}$ is a vector whose ith element, u_i, is 0 if the ith arrival process is in an off-period, 1 if it is on; $\mathbf{m}$ is a matrix whose element $m_{i,k}$ is the number of servers currently being switched from queue i to queue k. The possible actions that the policy may take in each state are to do nothing or to initiate a switch of a server from queue i to queue k.

A numerical procedure to determine the optimal policy would involve truncating the queue sizes to some reasonable level, discretizing the time parameter through uniformization and then applying either policy improvement or value iterations (e.g., see [11,12]). It is readily appreciated that the computational complexity of that task grows very quickly with the number of queues, M, the number of servers, N, and the truncation level. For that reason, we have concentrated on determining the optimal static allocation policy (which does not involve switching) and comparing its performance with that of some dynamic heuristics.

3   The $IP/M/n$ Queue

If the server allocation is fixed, with n_i servers assigned to queue i ($n_1+n_2+\ldots+n_M = N$), then the M queues are independent of each other. Queue i behaves like an isolated $IP/M/n_i$ queue and may be analyzed as such. To simplify notation, the index i will be omitted in this section.

The state of the queue is described by the pair (j, u), where j is the number of jobs present and u is 0 if the arrival process is in an off-period, 1 if it is on. Let $p_{j,u}$ be the equilibrium probability of state (j, u). Also denote by μ_j the total service completion rate when there are j jobs present: $\mu_j = \min(j, n)\mu$.

The necessary and sufficient condition for stability is that the offered load is less than the number of servers:

$$\frac{\lambda\eta}{\mu(\xi + \eta)} < n \ . \tag{2}$$

When that condition is satisfied, the steady-state probabilities satisfy the following set of balance equations ($j = 0, 1, \ldots$; $u = 0, 1$).

$$[\lambda u + \mu_j + \xi u + \eta(1 - u)]p_{j,u} = \lambda u p_{j-1,u} + \mu_{j+1}p_{j+1,u}$$

$$+ [\xi(1 - u) + \eta u]p_{j,1-u} \ , \tag{3}$$

where $p_{-1,u} = 0$ by definition.

This model can be solved numerically by treating it as a 'Markov-modulated queue'. The Markovian environment that influences the behaviour of the queue is the phase of its arrival process. Then one can compute performance measures by applying either the spectral expansion or the matrix-geometric solution method

900   J. Slegers, I. Mitrani, and N. Thomas

(see [7,9]). However, the present model is sufficiently simple to allow both an explicit exact analysis and an approximate solution in closed-form.

It is convenient to introduce the generating functions of the probabilities corresponding to off and on periods, respectively:

$$g_0(z) = \sum_{j=0}^{\infty} p_{j,0} z^j \;\; ; \;\; g_1(z) = \sum_{j=0}^{\infty} p_{j,1} z^j \;. \tag{4}$$

Then the balance equations (3) can be transformed into a set of two equations for $g_0(z)$ and $g_1(z)$.

$$[\eta z - n\mu(1 - z)]g_0(z) = \xi z g_1(z) - \mu(1 - z)P_0(z) \;, \tag{5}$$

$$[\lambda z(1 - z) - n\mu(1 - z) + \xi z]g_1(z)$$

$$= \eta z g_0(z) - \mu(1 - z)P_1(z) \;, \tag{6}$$

where $P_0(z)$ and $P_1(z)$ are two polynomials involving 'boundary' probabilities (corresponding to states with state-dependent departure rates):

$$P_0(z) = \sum_{j=0}^{n-1}(n - j)p_{j,0} z^j \;\; ; \;\; P_1(z) = \sum_{j=0}^{n-1}(n - j)p_{j,1} z^j \;. \tag{7}$$

From equations (5) and (6), $g_0(z)$ and $g_1(z)$ can be expressed as rational functions whose numerators involve $P_0(z)$ and $P_1(z)$, and a common denominator, $d(z)$. The latter is quadratic and has two real zeros, z_1 and z_2, such that $0 < z_1 < 1$ and $1 < z_2 < \infty$.

The balance equations (3) for $j < n - 1$ supply $2n - 2$ equations for the coefficients of $P_0(z)$ and $P_1(z)$. An additional equation is provided by the normalizing condition $g_0(1) + g_1(1) = 1$. The final equation is obtained by observing that the generating functions are finite in the interior of the unit disc and therefore their numerators must vanish at $z = z_1$.

This determines all unknown probabilities, and hence the full distribution of the queueing process.

The average number of jobs present, L, is given by

$$L = g_0'(1) + g_1'(1) \;. \tag{8}$$

Thus, the procedure for determining the optimal static allocation of servers would use the solution described here to evaluate the cost function (1) for each feasible allocation and then choose the best one. A server allocation $(n_1, n_2, \ldots, n_M)$, with $n_1 + n_2 + \ldots + n_M = N$, is feasible if the stability condition (2) is satisfied for every queue.

It can also be shown that the tail of the queue size distribution is geometric with parameter $1/z_2$ (see [8]). When the queue is heavily loaded, this leads to a very simple approximation for the average queue size:

$$L = \frac{1/z_2}{1 - 1/z_2} = \frac{1}{z_2 - 1} \;. \tag{9}$$

Using that approximation speeds up the search for the optimal static server allocation considerably.

4   Dynamic Heuristics

It is to be expected that a dynamic allocation policy which reacts to changing queue sizes and switches servers when large disparities occur, can achieve lower costs than even the best static policy. However, because of the size of the state space, a computation of the optimal policy is impractical. Hence, our objective is to design heuristic dynamic policies and compare their performance with the optimal static policy.

Two heuristics will be examined. In both cases, switching decisions are made by taking into account the currently observed system state and estimating the costs that would be incurred over some subsequent period of time if (a) no action is taken, and (b) one or more servers are switched from queue j to queue i. The two policies differ by the way they estimate future costs.

The first policy will be referred to as the *Average Flow* heuristic. It ignores the on/off periods and treats queue i as a deterministic fluid which arrives at rate γ_i, given by

$$\gamma_i = \frac{\lambda_i \eta_i}{\xi_i + \eta_i} \, . \tag{10}$$

That fluid is consumed at rate $n_i \mu_i$, where n_i is the number of servers currently allocated to queue i. Suppose that two queues, i and j, have current sizes k_i and k_j, and currently allocated numbers of servers n_i and n_j, respectively. If no further actions are taken, and both queues are stable (i.e., $\gamma_i < n_i \mu_i$ and $\gamma_j < n_j \mu_j$), then those fluid queues would decrement at constant rates and would empty in times $k_i/(n_i \mu_i - \gamma_i)$ and $k_j/(n_j \mu_j - \gamma_j)$, respectively. The total holding costs incurred would be proportional to the areas of the resulting triangles.

Hence, the *Average Flow* heuristic estimates the cost of taking no action with queues i and j as

$$C_0 = \frac{c_i k_i^2}{2(n_i \mu_i - \gamma_i)} + \frac{c_j k_j^2}{2(n_j \mu_j - \gamma_j)} \, . \tag{11}$$

On the other hand, if a decision is made to switch a server from queue j to queue i, and that switch takes time $1/\zeta$ (deterministic), then the service rate at queue j immediately reduces to $(n_j - 1)\mu_j$, while that at queue i remains the same for the duration of the switch and then increases to $(n_i + 1)\mu_i$. Assuming that queue i does not empty during the switch, its size at the point when the switch is completed would be equal to m_i, where

$$m_i = k_i - (n_i \mu_i - \gamma_i)/\zeta \, . \tag{12}$$

The total holding cost incurred in clearing both queues is estimated as

$$C_1 = \frac{c_i(k_i + m_i)}{2\zeta} + \frac{c_i m_i^2}{2((n_i + 1)\mu_i - \gamma_i)} + \frac{c_j k_j^2}{2((n_j - 1)\mu_j - \gamma_j)} \, . \tag{13}$$

At every arrival or departure event, the *Average Flow* heuristic evaluates C_0 and C_1 for every pair of queues i and j, where i is the queue where the arrival occurred, or j is the queue where the departure occurred. If $C_1 < C_0$, a server is switched from queue j to queue i. If that inequality holds for more than one queue i, the switch is made to the queue for which the difference $C_0 - C_1$ is largest. If a contemplated switch would leave queue j potentially unstable (i.e., $(n_j - 1)\mu_j \leq \gamma_j$), then it is not made. If, at a decision instant, a server is in the process of being switched, it is counted as being already available at the destination queue.

The second policy will be referred to as the *On/Off* heuristic. When making allocation decisions, it assumes that that the current phase of each arrival processes, whether it is 'on' or 'off', will last forever. Again queue i is treated as a fluid, but the arrival rate is taken to be $\gamma_i = \lambda_i u_i$, where $u_i = 1$ if the queue i arrival process is in an on-period and $u_i = 0$ if it is in an off-period.

Switching decisions are made not only at arrival and departure instants, but also when an arrival process changes phase from 'on' to 'off' or vice versa. As well as evaluating the estimated costs C_0 and C_1, of doing nothing or switching one server from queue j to queue i, the *On/Off* heuristic evaluates the costs C_s, of switching s servers from queue j to queue i, for $s = 2, 3, \ldots, n_j$. This is necessary because a phase change can make a big difference to the arrival rate at a queue, requiring or releasing more than one server. When calculating C_s for $s > 1$, one could assume that all s servers become available at queue i after a switching interval of length $1/\zeta$. Alternatively, the assumption could be that the s switches complete at different times: the earliest after an interval $1/(s\zeta)$, the next after a subsequent interval $1/((s-1)\zeta)$, etc. The first alternative would be appropriate if the switching times are nearly constant, the second if they are exponentially distributed. In both cases, the costs are evaluated by adding together areas under linear segments.

As before, the switching decision that yields the largest cost reduction is taken. If no reduction is possible, or if all estimated costs are infinite (that can happen, for example, if all arrival processes are in an on-period and the corresponding arrival rates are greater than the available service rates), then no action is taken.

5   Results

To illustrate the behaviour of the dynamic heuristics, and compare their performance with that of the optimal static allocation policy, a cluster of servers was simulated. For completeness, a simpler static policy was also included in some comparisons. The latter is referred to as the ρ-rule: it allocates the servers to job types in proportion to costs, c_i, and offered loads, $\rho_i = \gamma_i/\mu_i$ (γ_i is given by (10)). The ρ-rule is what one would apply without the benefit of the analysis in section 3. Indeed, that was the static allocation used in [10].

The following parameters were kept fixed throughout.

Number of job types: $M = 2$.
Number of servers: $N = 20$.
Average required service times: $1/\mu_1 = 1/\mu_2 = 1$.

In the first experiment, the average 'on' and 'off' periods were equal at the two queues, and so were the average switching times: $1/\xi_i = 1/\eta_i = 100$, $i = 1, 2$; $1/\zeta_{i,j} = 1$, $i, j = 1, 2$. The two arrival rates were also equal, and were increased simultaneously. Some asymmetry was introduced by making type 2 jobs more expensive than type 1: the holding costs were $c_1 = 1$, $c_2 = 1.5$. The simulated time for each run was 10000 time units. Since each arrival process is 'on' for about half of that time, if $\lambda_1 = \lambda_2 = 10$, a total of about about 100000 jobs go through the system. (Note that the simulations were required only for the dynamic policies. The static ones could have been solved numerically, but since the simulation programs could easily be adapted to different policies, they were used in all cases.)

Figure 1 shows the average costs achieved by the two static and two dynamic policies, as the load increases. As expected, at light loads it does not matter very much which policy is adopted. However, differences start appearing at medium loads and become ever larger at heavy loads.

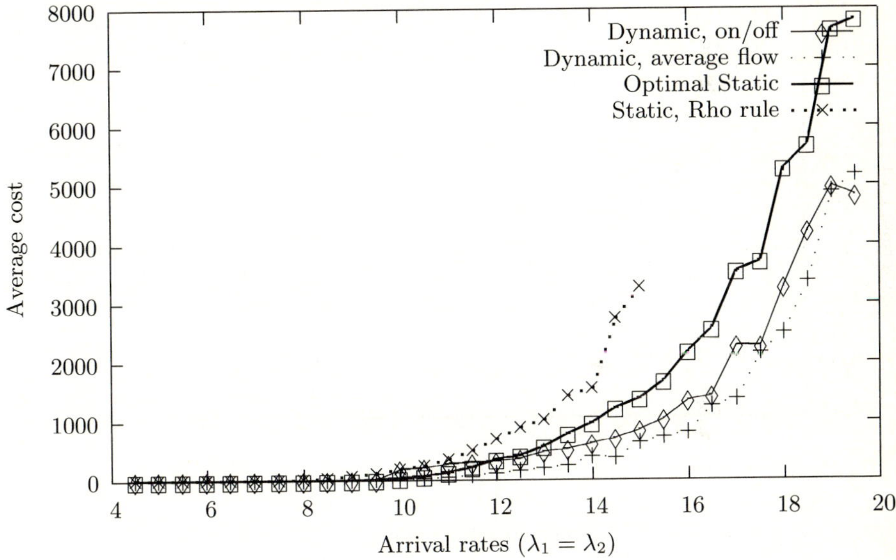

Fig. 1. Policy comparisons: increasing λ_1, λ_2

The ρ-rule has the worst performance. Its application results in 8 servers being allocated to type 1 and 12 servers to type 2 throughout. Hence, when $\lambda_1 \geq 16$, the system becomes unstable and in the long run incurs infinite cost. The optimal static policy allocates 9 servers to type 1 and 11 to type 2 for most of the range, changing to 10 and 10 when the arrival rates become greater than about 17. That policy achieves considerably lower costs than the ρ-rule, and remains stable for $\lambda_i < 20$. The benefits of the dynamic allocation policies become significant for $\lambda_i > 13$. Their performance is similar, although the *Average Flow* policy appears to be consistently slightly better than *On/Off*. We point this out as an observed fact, but cannot explain it. Intuitively, one might have expected that a heuristic which takes into account the current state of the input stream would make better allocation decisions.

Figure 2 shows the effect of increasing the average switching time, in a reasonably lightly loaded system ($\lambda_1 = \lambda_2 = 10$). We observe that the cost of the *Average Flow* heuristic increases initially and then stops changing significantly: it performs slightly better than the optimal static policy (whose allocation does not change) when $1/\zeta < 4$ and then becomes slightly worse. On the other hand, the *On/Off* policy shows an initial steady improvement before its cost also stops changing significantly.

The static allocation policy based on the ρ-rule is not included in these and subsequent comparisons because its performance can only be worse than that of the optimal static policy.

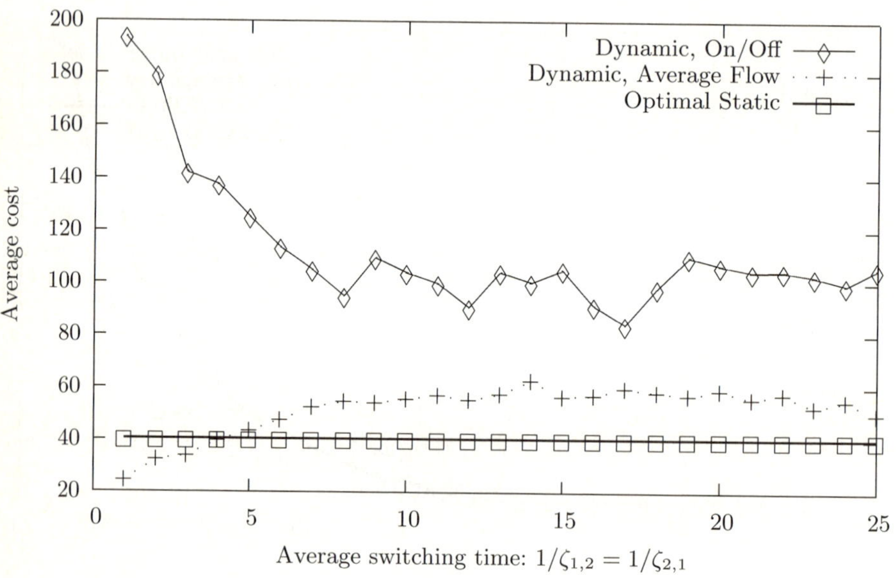

Fig. 2. Performance of different policies for increasing switching times

The last experiment involves a system with asymmetric traffic characteristics. Type 1 jobs arrive in a steam which is 'on' most of the time: $\xi_1 = 1/100000$, $\eta_1 = 1$, $\lambda_1 = 10$. That stream would need at least 10 servers in order to remain stable. Jobs of type 2 arrive in short bursts, with long intervals in between: $\xi_2 = 1/25$, $\eta_2 = 1/500$ (i.e., the arrival stream of type 2 is 'on' for less than 5% of the time). The arrival rate of type 2 during 'on' periods, λ_2, is increased from 20 to 120 in steps of 5. The switching costs are very small.

Figure 3 illustrates very clearly the benefits of using a dynamic allocation policy. Again, there is not much difference between the performance of the *Average*

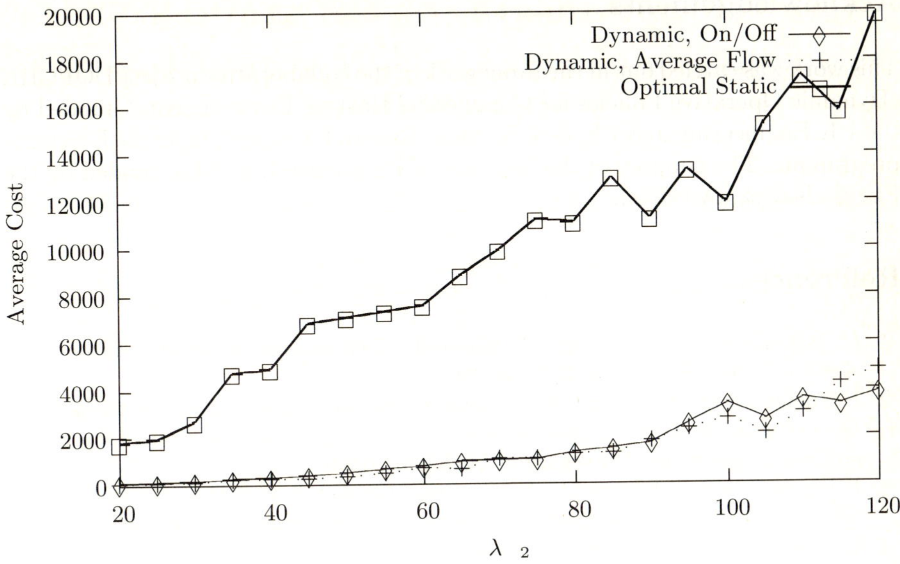

Fig. 3. One steady and one bursty source: increasing λ_2

Flow and the *On/Off* heuristics. However, the average cost achieved by either of them can be an order of magnitude lower that that of the optimal static policy.

6   Conclusions

We have addressed a resource allocation problem that is of considerable importance in the context of distributed computing and grid systems with heterogeneous, bursty demand streams. Under Markovian assumptions, the optimal static allocation policy can be determined quite simply, using the analytic solution provided in section 3. An even simpler approximate solution is also available.

Two dynamic heuristic policies were proposed and evaluated by simulation. When the system is heavily loaded, both achieve large savings in costs, compared to the best static policy.

Further work is required in several directions. First, it is clearly necessary to carry out more extensive evaluations and comparisons for different system configurations (including larger numbers of job types), cost structures and patterns of demand. Next, are there other, better dynamic heuristics that react more promptly and accurately to changes of state? Also, it would be desirable to implement the proposed heuristics in a real grid system and measure their performance. Finally, how would the resource allocation problem change if the servers, too, can be 'on' or 'off' (they may be subject to breakdowns and repairs, or for other reasons become unavailable from time to time)? These and other extensions will be tackled in the future.

RDF is a metadata specification of models providing a structure to organize the web information. OWL is based on RDF, but its contribution is the lexicon to represent semantic information and then to build ontologies. Ontologies manage the knowledge of the semantic web in the upper layer, RDF structures the web documents which are the information on the web [3]. Ontologies are used in semantic systems to interchange knowledge.

An ontology is a specification of a conceptualization [4], i.e. a graph of concepts where nodes are representing concepts and the edges are representing relationships among these concepts. Figure 1 shows the Standard Ontology for Ubiquitous and Pervasive Applications (SOUPA). SOUPA is a set of ontologies for supporting pervasive computing applications. OWL is recommended by the W3C for its use in the conceptual descriptions.

There are different reasons for developing models based on ontologies:

- Knowledge sharing: It permits computational entities, e.g. agents and brokers, using a set of common objects on a specific context whereas they are interacting.
- Knowledge reuse: It builds an ontology integrating in its definitions other well-defined web ontologies from different knowledge bases, e.g. spatial, temporary, etc.
- Logical inference: It uses different reasoning mechanisms to check the consistency of the ontology and its knowledge, e.g. to check for unintended relationships between classes and to automatically classify instances in classes.

On the other hand, a middleware infrastructure for AmI systems must support:

- Extensibility: If new components are detected in the AmI system then they need to communicate each other and offer their services.
- Independency: The new component may be different to the other components belonging to the AmI system.
- Avoidance of central components: In our case, we are developing an AmI system by using a context-broker infrastructure which is simpler but unsafe. In future works we are going to distribute our services among different brokers.

We seize the ontology engineering benefits the support to middleware infrastructures. Thus, it is necessary to include the ontology information in each agent o software element of the AmI system. The extensibility and independency features are obtaining through ontology knowledge sharing, e.g., one ontology may be importing another ontology. Also, the ontology expressiveness permits the interaction and independency among AmI agents. In this way, we are extending the knowledge among system components.

Ambient Intelligent (AmI) systems are based on the ontological description of their contexts [5]. Some implementations of those systems use brokers for managing the distributed information of sensors, monitors and users and transforming this information into knowledge through inference engines (reasoning) [6]. Non-functional information of AmI systems is crucial to their successful operation.

An Agent is the software/hardware that interact in ubiquitous systems and AmIs. The representation language has been a historical problem for the agent

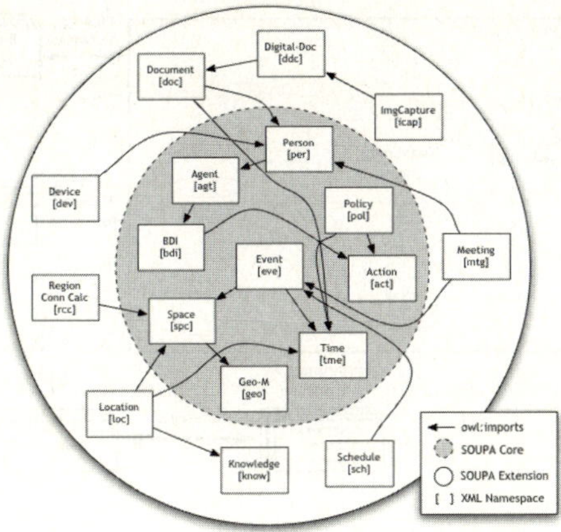

Fig. 1. SOUPA ontology diagram

technology since it is necessary to find out a way to describe common concepts for agents. This representation must be independent of the implementation of the agents, themselves.

In this paper we are going to show how a context-broker architecture may successfully implement an AmI system through mobile agents. Actuality, we are still building the system. This is the prototype. The server of this centralized architecture provides several services for a reduced environment (space) and it is able to communicate with other external agents using ontologies. These ontologies represent AmI knowledge and middleware communication data together. They may help in the task of communicating mobile agents. Our case study is based on the emulation of a Smart Conference Room (SCR) where the external agents are the potential attendants and the speakers (i.e. their portable devices), and the environment (ambient) agents are several sensors and other intermediate agents. The communication among all these actors in the SCR takes advantage of the semantic web knowledge representation by means of the ontological language that agents share.

Therefore, in section 2 we are going to depict the context-broker architecture by means of a layered model. In the next section, some examples of services for the context-broker architecture are shown by means of a Smart Conference Room case study. Finally, we conclude with our present results, open problems and future work.

2   Context-Broker Architecture

Our context-broker architecture is constituted by a central agent (the broker itself), which is in charge of reasoning and communicating with the environment and the external agents. The users will interact with the AmI agents through the central context-broker infrastructure. The ambient and the external agents send

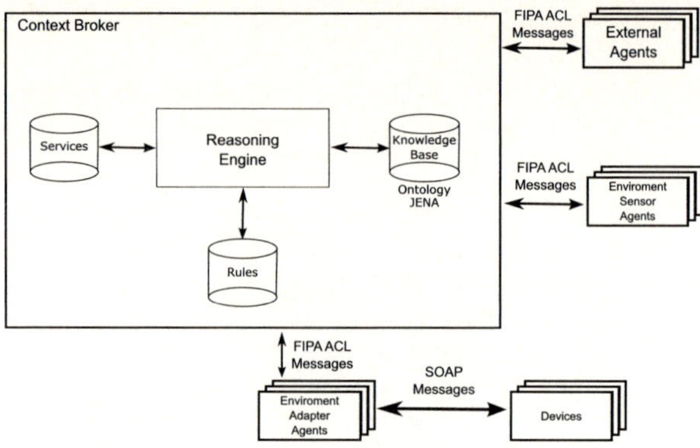

Fig. 2. Context-broker architecture

the necessary information about the environment, e.g. the time, etc. Figure 2 shows the different elements of the context-broker architecture. Our context-broker has three modules, namely: the reasoner, the knowledge base and the services module. The knowledge base stores the information about the ambient through an ontological description. We have used the Jena library to manage the ontology and to create the ontological database. The services define the SCR activity that the context-broker manages. The reasoner infers from the facts based on axioms, laws, rules, etc. and according to the services defined.

The context-broker stores relevant facts about the ambient into the knowledge base by means of concepts which were defined in an ontological way. The reasoner infers new knowledge by reasoning over the knowledge base and the predefined laws [7]. The context-broker communicates with mobile agents by means of ACL messages from the FIPA protocol. As far as we know, mobile devices do not implement an agent architecture. This is the cause why we had to use the SOAP protocol. The SOAP protocol provides an independent layer for the communication among agents.

As we show in figure 2, intermediate agents communicate with the context-broker through ACL messages in SOAP. In fact, the context-broker is another agent but its features are completely different to mobile and ambient agents [8]. Its main difference is the mobility; the context-broker is static whereas the users are potentially mobile. However, the context-broker is managing the ambient and the intelligence of the system. In the SCR case study, the context-broker is part of the conference room and the services it provides are related to the use of this room. The agents are classified in two different groups: those which are sensoring the conference room, and the intermediate agents which are communicating with the context-broker and the devices that are not implementing an agent architecture. As we can see, intermediate agents are only necessary for implementation purposes (unfortunately, most of the devices are not mobile agents).

In order to implement the environment (ambient) agents and the context-broker we use JADE, a middleware for mobile agents (FIPA). Figure 3 shows the different layers of our architecture which is not only suitable for SCR but also for any ambient intelligence system. JADE is between the agents and the devices (in this case the emulation of SCR hardware through a Java virtual machine). In the case of not-JADE agents, intermediate agents are located between JADE and them.

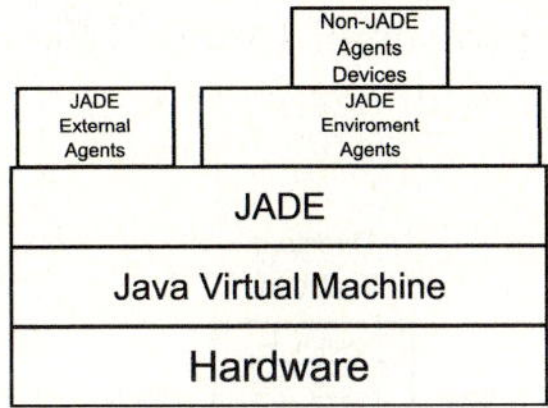

Fig. 3. Layered model

Each ontological concept about the SCR is stored in a database which is only accessed by the context-broker. We have implemented the database and the ontology with Jena, an API written in Java that provides a programmatic environment for RDF, RDFS and OWL. One Jena functionality is to create or load a database from an ontological file, it allows us to have a persistent ontological model. But working directly with Jena can be difficult, this is the reason why we prefer to work also with Jastor on top of the Jena framework. Jastor has the ability to transform any OWL description file into Java Beans enabling convenient, type safe access and eventing of OWL stored in Jena. Jastor generates Java APIs, implementations, factories, and listeners based on the properties and class hierarchies in the ontologies.

There are two ways to access the information stored in the ontological knowledge base: either using Jena or using Jastor. As we mentioned before, Jastor is easy to use but its major drawback is the necessary explicit knowledge of the URIs for conceptualization management.

2.1   Agent Recognition

Another important feature of the AmI systems is agent recognition, especially in the case of external agents. For example, in the SCR case, the agents are running in mobile devices entering and exiting the conference room. The system must provide services only inside the conference room but not outside. JADE provides a structure of *yellow pages* in which the agents are registered when they enter the room and deleted when they leave it. This seems easy, but external agents have to discover the remote platform in which the broker is running. Fortunately each platform has a MTP address named by default *http://[ComputerName]:7778/acc*. If we look around the network we can find the platforms running on it. The *yellow pages* we mentioned before are named in the standard FIPA as *directory facilitators* for agents and services. This directory structure eases the service execution and the recognition of agents by the context-broker. Is possible to contact an agent directly if we know its Agent Identifier (AID), but in intelligent ambients it is difficult to know the AID of all agents. In the SCR case, some ambient agents are intermediate agents due to the absence of agents implemented in mobile devices. The context-broker periodically detects the registered agents in the directory using a special behavior, the `Tickerbehavior`. Thus, the context-broker seeks the directory for the agents and reads the services offered to them. In fig. 4 the context-broker is registering itself in the directory since it is an agent, too.

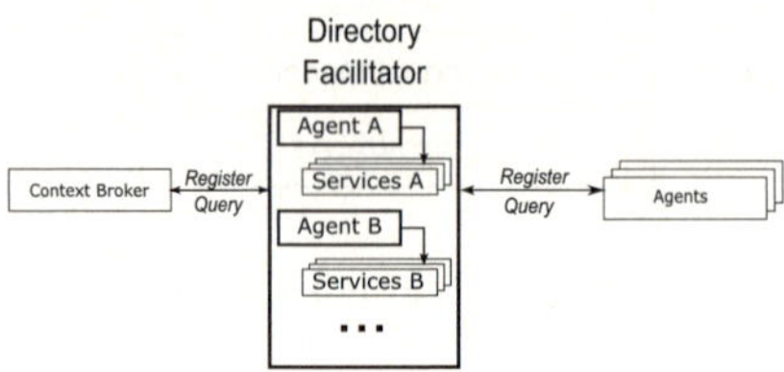

Fig. 4. Directory Facilitator

2.2   Behavior and Performance

While no ACL messages are received, the SCR system is idle in order to reduce CPU consumption. The resources in mobile devices are limited so the less instructions running the more power efficiency of the devices. This is possible thanks to the use of blocking messages. These blocking messages block the behavior thread until a message is received which fits in the template established in the behavior. Another performance improvement is that agents are event-driven: when an event is received the agent performs its tasks and blocks again. This is an advantage of using JADE as a platform to implement agents.

3   Context-Broker Ontology

As we stated before, the context-broker uses an ontology to manage the relevant information to the system. The ontology used for this project is quite simple, but in future works we will increase the ontology domain and complexity. Our ontology consists of three differential concepts: person, appointment and file concepts.

The person concept has three properties, namely: the *name* of the person, their Agent Identifier (*AID*) and the AID of the Directory Facilitator *DFname* in which it is registered. This concept is used to identify the external agents that are presumably managed by a person. All the actions of this person will be registered in the system with this concept.

The appointment concept is shown in fig. 5. Some properties of this concept are used to negotiate an appointment between two or more agents. When the negotiation has finished, these properties are no longer necessary, but we decided

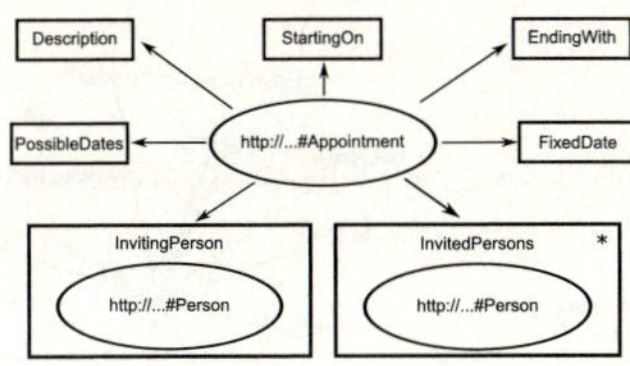

Fig. 5. Appointment ontology

to keep them to have the possibility to renegotiate an appointment in the future. The properties are the *fixedDate* of the appointment, a *description* of the appointment, the *invitingPerson*, the *invitedPerson* that can be more than one. These two last properties are *person* concepts. The negotiation-related properties are *startingOn*, *endingWith* and *possibleDates*.

The file concept has two properties, the *path* where the file can be downloaded and *propertyOf*, the person who owns it.

3.1   Using Performance Ontology

We have incorporated in this project performance information to measure the agents' behavior. This performance information may be used by the agents themselves in order to manage their functional behaviour. Therefore, we have imported a Performance Ontology [9,10,11] in order to use the performance knowledge previously defined by performance engineers in the AmI system. This last feature provides some additional behavioural advantages for AmI agents, for example, the possibility of controlling the waiting service time of agents' requests to the context-broker and, at the same time, the context-broker may balance the agents' workload in order to guarantee a service level agreement. In the fig. 6 we show the measures concept of the performance ontology model. This graph shows the next units: time (intervals, durations, etc.); the abstract concept *number*, this parameter is refers to variable units description, by example the *throughput* concept has not initials units which depends the context ambient; probability and others description units as *typeOfMeasure*.

The services provided by the context-broker together with the behaviour of the functional agents contain performance information related with their execution. This performance information (service time, priority, response time, utilization, etc.) may help to the context-broker to manage the AmI system.

4   Context-Broker Services

In the SCR case, the context-broker provides mainly services for the speakers and the attendants. Of course, other services may be added in the future, at the cost of increased resource consumption in the AmI system. In our present implementation of the SCR, there are three services. In the following sections we will introduce them.

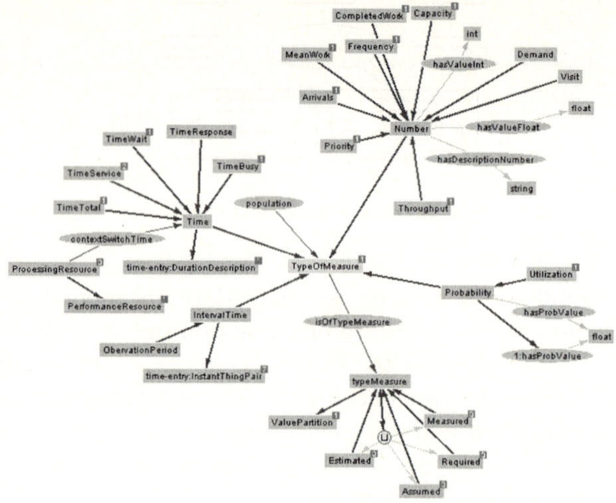

Fig. 6. Measures model in the Performance Ontology

4.1   Intelligent Room Reservation

The context-broker offers a reservation service for external agents. It uses a calendar of the conference room reservations. The external agents ask for the conference room and the context-broker accepts or declines the petitions depending on the room availability. The external agents may offer a flexible petition to allow a better adjustment of the calendar by the context-broker and even negotiate the reservation. This petition may be a set of some possible dates of reservation. We use the appointment class of the ontology to negotiate this reservation. In order for the appointment to be concreted, the agent and the context-broker have to create a temporal appointment concept in their ontological models to make the negotiation possible using semantic information. When the negotiation is finished this temporal must be deleted and a new definitive appointment instance created.

4.2   Upload Presentation

In order to ease the speakers' presentation, it is possible to upload the documentation in the projection service (some PC projector) before the meeting. Once the conference room is reserved, an external agent may send a presentation, ready to be shown, to the context-broker. We use the `file` class to make possible the upload of the file. The *path* property shows the location of the file to upload, when the system has it the projector can get the file. In the example code, the projection service implements the `ProposeResponder` protocol when it receives the presentation document. The storage of the file is controlled by the protocol.

4.3   Download Presentation

The attendants may download the presentation (with the speakers' consent) to their respective mobile devices once the presentation has ended. The presentation can also be broadcasted to all registered attendants. The broadcast uses the `file` class of the ontology, like the above service. Alternatively, this broadcast can be done before the conference.

In the code in fig. 7 we show a part of the context-broker implementation where it looks for receivers which have registered agents in the directory facilitator. These registered agents are users of the service `Appoinment21`. The *File-ConversationBeh* is a behavior that implements the protocol `ProposeResponder` and it sends the documentation file to these registered agents.

```
List receivers=new ArrayList();
myAgent.searchPerson(null,null,
    "Appointment21","personal-agent",
    "cb-ontology",receivers,false);
myAgent.addBehaviour(new FileConversationBeh(
    myAgent,file,receivers));
```

Fig. 7. Searching the agents registered in the service

5   Conclusions and Future Work

Semantic Web can not only be used to implement the next generation of WWW but also to facilitate the creation of new computational environments as AmI systems. In our paper, we have shown that the development of such systems may be delayed in some cases due to the lack of convergence of implementation of several technologies.

An example of that is the SCR case study, where a Smart Conference Room is emulated. This simple case study shows that middleware and mobile agent devices seem to be a step back to ontology development to implement AmI systems. We have provided an architecture circumvallating the problem by using the JADE API and the FIPA standard. Although the project is at an early stage, we can foresee some problems that may arise before the final implementation of SCR. Surely, the main development problems will come from device integration, resource consumption and context-broker performance. However, we are going to build a real SCR, in order to illustrate the power of using ontologies joined to AmI systems and to detect any other potential problems. Another interesting future task will be the research on a complete methodology for the design of AmI architectures. Our immediate future work is to experiment with our SCR implementation in the laboratory in order to measure the different magnitudes of these potential drawbacks and then to simulate the complete network architecture before the final construction of the SCR.

Acknowledgement

The authors acknowledge the partial financial support of this research through the programme *Accions especials del Govern de les Illes Balears* from *Conselleria d'Economia, Hisenda i Innovació*.

References

1. Antoniou, G., van Harmelen, F.: A Semantic Web Primer. The MIT Press (2004)
2. Castells, P.: La web semántica. Sistemas Interactivos y Colaborativos en la Web (2003) 195–212
3. Sanz, I., Pérez, J., Berlanga, R.: Referencia para la integración semántica de información (2002)
4. Gruber, T.R.: A translation approach to portable ontologies. Knowledge Acquisition **5**(2) (1993) 199220
5. Behrendt, W., Goyal, S., Westenthaler, R.: Metokis-towards a seamless content and knowledge exchange infrastructure (2005)
6. Wang, X.: Ontology-based context modeling and reasoning using owl (2004)
7. Lera, I., Juiz, C., Puigjaner, R.: Web operational analysis through performance-related ontologies in owl for intelligent applications. Lecture Notes in Computer Science (2005) 612615
8. Jha, R., Iyer, S.: Performance evaluation of mobile agents for e-commerce applications. In: HiPC. (2001) 331–340
9. Lera, I., Juiz, C., Puigjaner, R., Kurz, C., Haring, G., Zottl, J.: Performance assessment on ambient intelligent applications through ontologies. In: WOSP '05: Proceedings of the 5th international workshop on Software and performance, New York, NY, USA, ACM Press (2005) 205–216
10. Lera, I., Juiz, C., Puigjaner, R.: Performance-related ontologies for on-line performance assessment of intelligent systems. In: Proceedings of the 20th International Conference on Advanced Information, Networking and Applications, Viena, Austria (2006)
11. Lera, I., Sancho, P.P., Juiz, C., Puigjaner, R., Zottl, J., Haring, G.: Performance assessment of intelligent distributed systems through software performance ontology engineering (SPOE). Science of Computer Programming (2006)

Routing Information System and HOIDS for Detection Method of Vicious Attack in Large Networks

Dong Hwi Lee[1], Kyong Ho Choi[1], Kuinam J. Kim[1,*], and Sang Min Park[2]

[1] Dept. of Information Security Kyonggi University,
71 Chungjung-Ro, Sedaemun-Gu Seoul, Korea
dhclub@naver.com, econckh@kyonggi.ac.kr
[2] Dept. of Industrial Engineering Incheon National University,
smpark@incheon.ac.kr

Abstract. The rapid increase of cyber terrorism is threatening the basis of information society; especially, the paralysis of network by malignant traffic could result in national loss in a short period of time which demands a urgent preparatory plans. Related to this, to ensure the urgent preparatory ability against national cyber safety threat, there are many studies being conducted on early alert system for national cyber threat, however, because of the technological problem and limitation of system efficiency, practical research is not on the stage of visibility. The most principal plan in correspondence of new cyber threats is the intensification of awareness of user safety along with establishment of improved detecting system against threat of modification. For this, this study will analyze the problem of existing uniformed detecting method and suggest an upgraded detection method through analysis of correlation of RIS and HOIDS in improved safety system which is the model is currently in operation with development of proto type.

Keywords: Vicious Attack, Early Warining, Intrusion Detection System, Routing Information.

1 Introduction

Although the activation of internet based industry in 21c is creating vast economic values, the rapid increase of cyber terrorism, using the circulation of computer virus as the reverse function of information era, malicious hacking and etc, is threatening the basis of information society and in need of urgent preparatory plans. Especially, as the paralysis of network and interference of electronic transaction, which are now rising as the main issues currently, to ensure an urgent preparation plan for the factors of various cyber threat such as malicious worm, virus and hacking, that could result is enormous national loss, is brought into attention as a very important factor for safety management tasks.

Malicious attack could be named as virus, worm and a comprehensive term that includes hacking techniques applied to social engineering technique which is now

---

* Corresponding author. harap123@daum.net

G. Min et al. (Eds.): ISPA 2006 Ws, LNCS 4331, pp. 917–926, 2006.

getting attention these days and this could result in unintentional information outflow and social/financial damages for users of information communication device and information communication system. Although the existing studies have suggested preparatory plans for these cyber threat factors, this has limitation that each threat factors are separately analyzed. Also, since recent computer virus or worm is mostly manipulated by the creator, the trend of recent cyber threat is resulting in large scale damages in vast areas in short time with automation, dispersion and sophistication. Furthermore, the lack of manpower and technology of safety control institutions and operation of individual information safety system is creating a lot troubles in dealing with safety accidents.

The reality of cyber threat is showing the limitation of existing safety system to new threats or mutation. To overcome this limitation, the need for new detective device is increasing and the study of Honey Net, Honey Pot is not in progress. Honey Systems are decoy servers or systems setup to gather information regarding an attacker or intruder into your system. Therefore, Honey System refers to a system that provides the information that could be helpful for safety intensification only by collecting the information of the attacker which is the system that proves its value by being attacked by the hackers. Honey Pot system as it is shown in its name 'honey pot', is used for tempting someone [1, 2]. The studies related to Honey Net and Honey Pot was used as a method mostly through detecting the action pattern of malicious worm virus. Especially, Honey Net is effective for detecting malicious traffic in large scale network [3].

In this study, to intensify the preparatory ability of cyber threat in mid to large scale network, effective detecting technique is planned and operated with the method of improving the existing detective techniques through analyzing correlation of HOIDS(Honey Net Intrusion Detection System) using RIS(Routing Information System) through routing information. Based on the information extracted from here, the preparatory plan such as blocking of the threat, speculation of packet and network forensics will be executed.

2 Related Work

2.1 Routing Registry System

Routing is providing a route for a packet to reach from the starting point to arrival and it is conducted through the router.

Router always contains routing information and this actually is the network IP address connected to the router or the network IP addresses that is transferred from other routers. The network IP addresses are used as a basic information for the routing at the router and this, generally, is called routing information and the saved routing information and the actual routing information on the Internet is compared as **Fig.1**. and grasp and solve the problem[4].

Since the routing information in this routing registry system is saved to one file, when the routing information is enlarged, it could decrease the performance of this system.

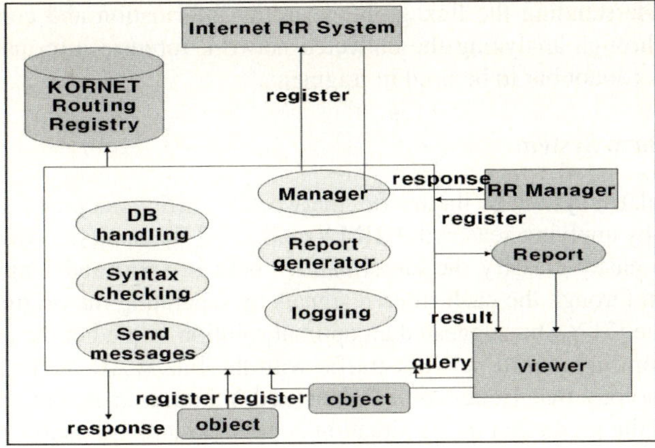

Fig. 1. Routing registry system

2.2   Network Forensics

The existing studies on network forensics were mostly focused on collecting, studying and keeping information of forensic in mid to large scale network. As the area of primary, the collecting of forensic information, analysis and arrangement of linkage of information, and safe keeping of analyzed information. However, until recently, the attention was only on collecting the information safely and rather than the network forensics information, the definition and acquirement of system forensics information that has more detailed information was grabbing the attention.

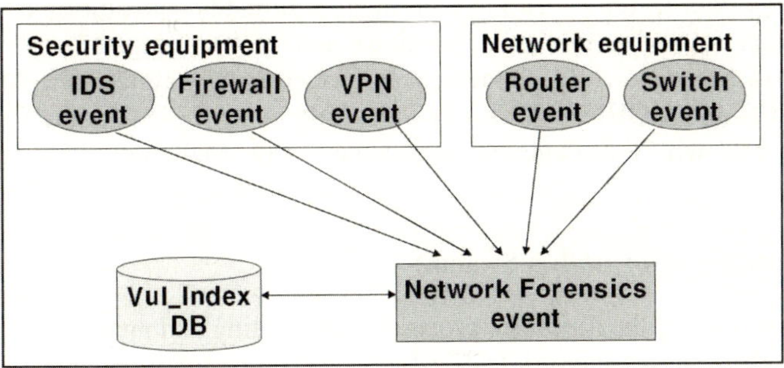

Fig. 2. Network Forensics Information

However, recently, with the need for large scale correspondence system getting enlarged, to judge the current network danger level and rapidly cope with the situation, the studies on the network device is in progress and **Fig. 2** is an important for reproducing the situation when the digital crime has been conducted and includes the status and setup information of the router, the time of accident and version information. The routing protocol and routing table information is the information that could detect the attacker's information safety device circuit possibility. [5].

Without understanding the linkage between the information and consideration of applied plan through analyzing the collected network forensic information, the network forensics cannot but to be used in fragment.

2.3 Early Alarm System

For the early alarm system of the traffic, the weekly traffic amount of wired-network was predicted by applying seasonal ARIMA model. [6] By using the wavelet analysis, the method to easily classify the abnormalities both in short and long term for the traffic situation through the each filtered signals by separating the original traffic into each time frame.[7] Y.Shu suggested an optimal solution to predict the non-linear and non-rectification high speed network traffic with the Fuzzy-AR model.[8] The main common technology that Hellerstein, F.Zang and Y.Shu used is that they suggested the model that the prediction of the situation is possible through analyzing the critical masses for the situation that large scale traffic is congesting and occurrence of abnormality. However, the characteristic of recent traffic congestion occurrence threat is not just a simple port attack or successive attack but evolving into a dispersed attacking method according to artificial intelligence technique and irregular attacking speed [9] which makes hard to predict recent cyber threats with the analysis method reliance to the method that detect the traffic just by measuring. The prediction and alarming of cyber threat through the analysis models in above suggested studies has the limitation considering that it is vulnerable that N-IDS(Network Intrusion Detection System) cannot be detected and approaching method to mutation is the pattern of cyber threat.

3 Proposed Structure

The most important factor in dealing with the new threat is constitution of early detection of attack, following analysis technique and each management technique and mechanism to be organically connected as unified safety system. In this study, by consisting RIS and HOIDS with improved safety system, the optimum system was designed to deal with the technique that detect early malicious virus and mutation virus.

3.1 RIS(Routing Information System)

The study will look at the reporting process of abstracting and analyzing the necessary proofs by collecting the network traffic flows and transmitted contents. The focus of this study is the collection and analysis of real time information for the transmitting data.

Fig. 3. represents the RIS structure. Since the router information is volatile, the router information is saved to the RIS server on the network and each local server. **Fig.4** is consisted of the part that processed the set of procedures saving and canceling the information on routing DB and DB to save the routing information and user interface that enables the users to search the routing information that is saved in routing registry.

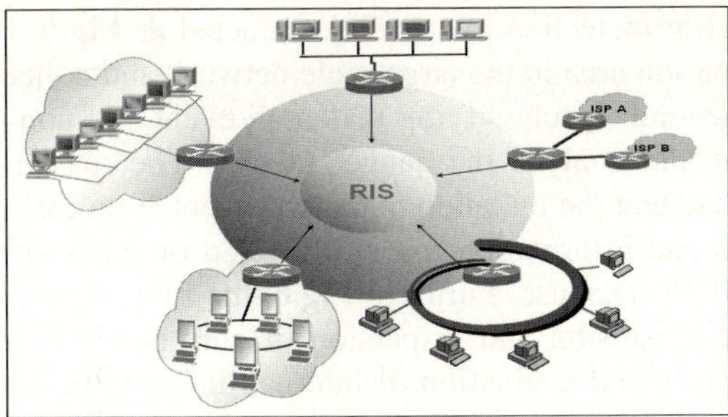

Fig. 3. RIS Structure

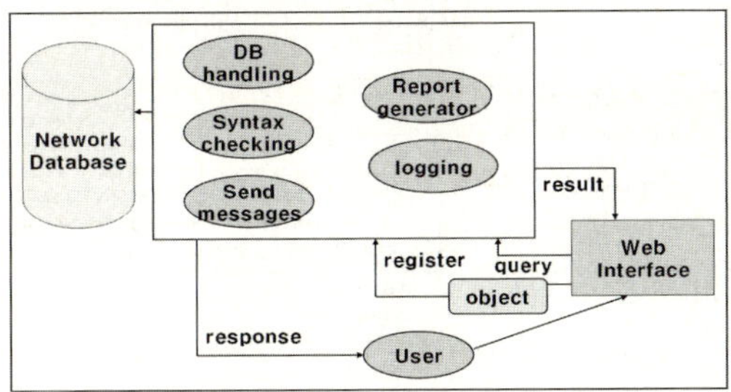

Fig. 4. Routing Information system

To solve the problem of information quantity in large scale network, the 1/16 and 1/32 sampling technique is used. For the sampling technique, the RIS information is periodically received from the local server and automatically produced. The interface part is used for understanding operation situation and performance analysis.

3.2 HOIDS(Honeynet Intrusion Detection System)

The constitution of the HOIDS and operation structure is as **Fig. 5.** The cyber threat factor is analyzed and collected for the event of place of each unusable IP from the place of network. The collected information is compared and analyzed with the event patterns of each safety device and judged of potential weaknesses. The final analysis of expansion of malicious event and multiplication in Honey Pot, the detection method of each safety device would be improved.

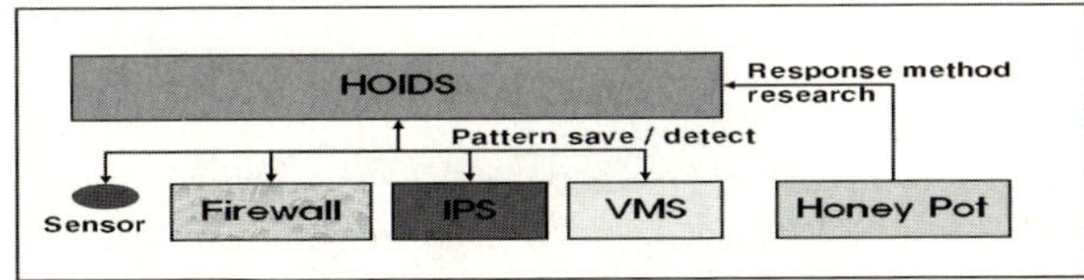

Fig. 5. HOIDS Operating Structure

In HOIDS, the event detection process is conducted as **Fig.6**. First, by classifying the unusable IP detection area in the large scale network and collected by the gateway with each sensor. Second, by classifying matching event and non-matching event for the malicious event and analyze the danger factors. The reason for detecting non-matching event is to detect the mutation malicious event at an early stage.

Third, the events and information that is collected on each safety device and network is sent to HOIDS database. Forth, in **Fig.6**, the rate of fragility of internal network and property, expansion and dispersion of current worm and virus, range of mutation for each virus and evaluation of internal and external threat information is evaluated for total evaluation.

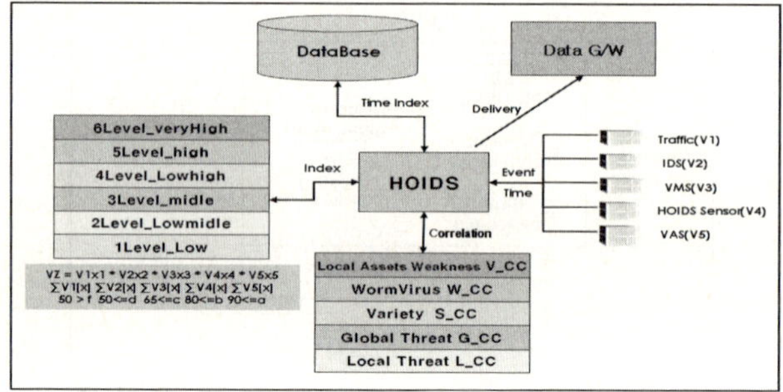

Fig. 6. The Evaluation Method by HOIDS Events

Fifth, by evaluating the rate of threat in each step and classify the level of threat and transfer and block the threatening information to each safety device. Sixth, the evaluated information is sent to the database and indexed by each time frame. The indexed information is accumulated to be defined as the evaluation values in total evaluation to help to make more accurate evaluation.

3.3 The Improved Safety Structure with RIS and HOIDS

The improved safety system structure is consisted as **Fig.7**. First, through early detected information from HOIDS, it is applied to existing safety system to find the information.

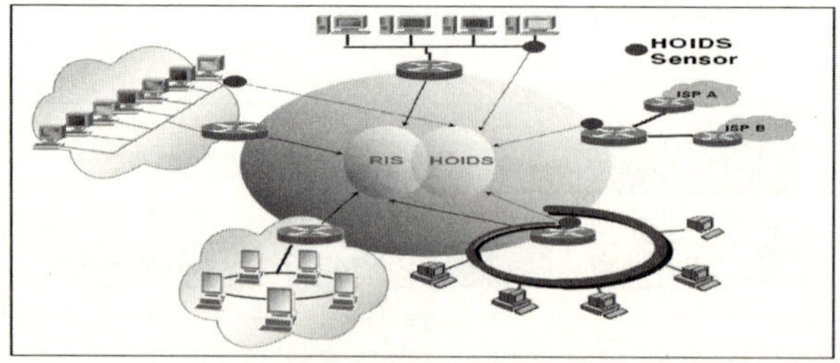

Fig. 7. RIS & HOIDS Structure

Second, as in **Fig.8**, it is detected by finding the applied information and the local IP from RIS or analyzing the expansion pattern of malicious virus event. The early detected information from HOIDS in detail, that is, specific port, pattern of IP expansion, and packet information is compared to existing safety system and detect the non-matching pattern. The detected information is analyzed in RIS about the mutation event through the analysis of correlation and command to block to each safety device.

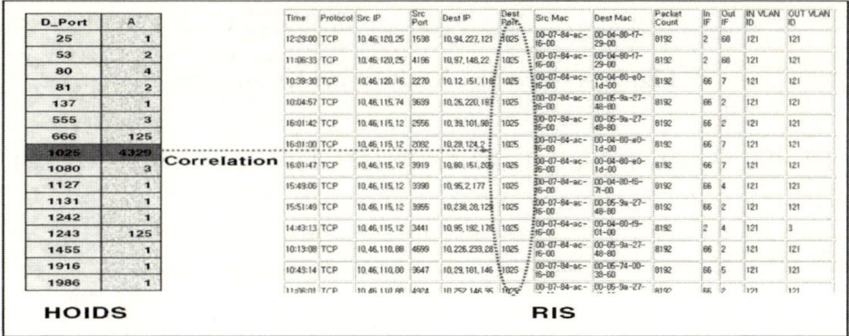

HOIDS

D_Port	A
25	1
53	2
80	4
81	2
137	1
555	3
666	125
1025	4329
1080	3
1127	1
1131	1
1242	1
1243	125
1455	1
1916	1
1986	1

Correlation

RIS

Time	Protocol	Src IP	Src Port	Dest IP	Dest Port	Src Mac	Dest Mac	Packet Count	In IF	Out IF	IN VLAN ID	OUT VLAN ID
12:29:00	TCP	10.46.120.25	1538	10.94.227.121	1025	00-07-84-ac-16-00	00-04-80-47-29-00	8192	2	68	121	121
11:06:33	TCP	10.46.120.25	4196	10.97.148.22	1025	00-07-84-ac-16-00	00-04-80-47-29-00	8192	2	68	121	121
10:39:30	TCP	10.46.120.16	2270	10.12.151.118	1025	00-07-84-ac-16-00	00-04-80-e0-1d-00	8192	66	7	121	121
10:04:57	TCP	10.46.115.74	9699	10.26.220.197	1025	00-07-84-ac-16-00	00-05-9a-27-48-80	8192	66	2	121	121
16:01:42	TCP	10.46.115.12	2556	10.39.101.98	1025	00-07-84-ac-16-00	00-05-9a-27-48-80	8192	66	2	121	121
16:01:00	TCP	10.46.115.12	2092	10.28.124.2	1025	00-07-84-ac-16-00	00-04-80-e0-1d-00	8192	66	7	121	121
16:01:47	TCP	10.46.115.12	3919	10.80.151.20	1025	00-07-84-ac-16-00	00-04-80-e0-1d-00	8192	66	7	121	121
15:49:06	TCP	10.46.115.12	3998	10.95.2.177	1025	00-07-84-ac-16-00	00-04-80-46-7f-00	8192	66	4	121	121
15:51:49	TCP	10.46.115.12	3955	10.238.28.129	1025	00-07-84-ac-16-00	00-05-9a-27-48-80	8192	66	2	121	121
14:43:13	TCP	10.46.115.12	3441	10.95.192.178	1025	00-07-84-ac-16-00	00-04-80-49-01-00	8192	2	4	121	3
10:13:08	TCP	10.46.110.88	4699	10.226.233.28	1025	00-07-84-ac-16-00	00-05-9a-27-48-80	8192	66	2	121	121
10:43:14	TCP	10.46.110.88	9647	10.29.101.146	1025	00-07-84-ac-16-00	00-05-74-00-38-60	8192	66	5	121	121
11:06:01	TCP	10.46.110.88	4924	10.252.146.95	1025	00-07-84-ac-	00-05-9a-27-	8192	66	2	121	121

Fig. 8. Correlation Operating Structure of RIS and HOIDS

4 Performance Analysis

4.1 Analysis Environment

The verification was conducted for real tasks on the K institution network under the condition of common analysis environment in the 2 large scale networks that uses more than 1GB speed. Since it is not equipped with the safety structure design on improved infra structure, it went through the enforcement of measurement objective and environmental preparatory step for the verification. The cited K institute environment is as followings.

The scale of connecting resources into the intra net system is 500 of various kinds of servers, Client: Workstation level PC 10,000, the size of internal users: 20,000, the network structure is connected to intra net and external network and consisted of multiple line network with 500Mbps speed, constructed of attack blocking system at the entrance, for the following sections, the intra net is consisted and in the inner structure of intra net, the server and PC is connected and the separate mail search system is installed in the front of server and the individual virus vaccine is installed for the PC resouces.

As the safety device, 4 of the Giga Bit Firewall (including backup line), 8 units of IDS (Sun V880), 4 units of Giga bit IPS, 2 units of VMS and 1 unit of ESM (Sun ENT3500) is installed.

As in **Fig.9**, in A network, the improved safety structure was established and using the analysis data of VMS and traffic of the 6 months, in January to March it was verified as usual and in April to June the improved safety structure was applied with HOIDS and RIS and posted the cyber threat information through the company network.

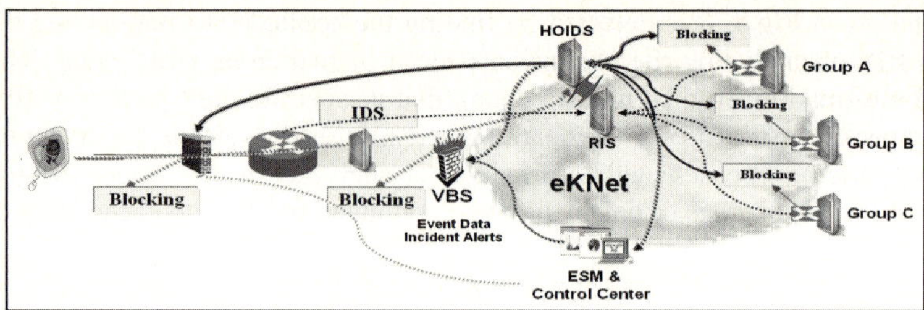

Fig. 9. A Network's analysis model structure

In **Fig.10**, the B network used the existing safety structure to consist identical safety device.

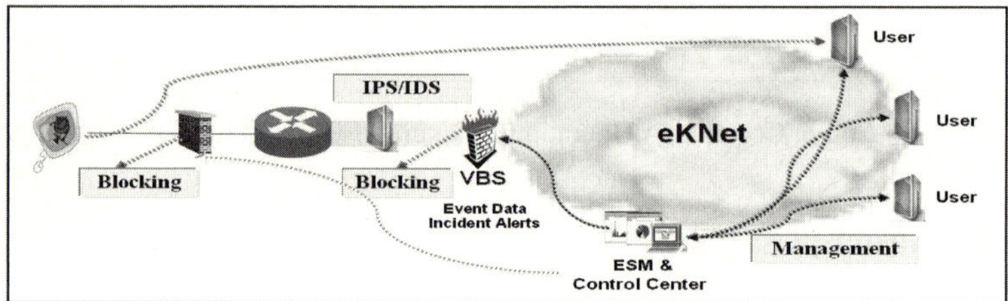

Fig. 10. B Network's analysis model structure

In B network, it was verified with the existing safety structure for 6 months. The following cyber threat information was posted on the company network.

The performance evaluation was done with the verification method through analyzing VMS statistic and traffic. The VMS, F/W, IDS, IPS and etc were constituted identically with the safety device..

4.2 Analysis Result

As the result of **Table 1** and **Table 2**, the average from January to March shows similar characteristics and the A network which used improved safety system in April

Table 1. The number of Virus Infection in the A network

Month	1	2	3	4	5	6
Worm	143,221	112,684	126,892	68,583	52,885	38,187
Trojan	21,682	15,703	18,222	10,393	8,299	5,299
Mail	39,458	38,990	32,222	19,292	20,212	12,391
Total	204,361	167,377	177,336	98,268	81,396	55,877
Vs. pre month	100%	82%	106%	55%	83%	69%

Table 2. The number of Virus Infection in the B network

Month	1	2	3	4	5	6
Worm	138,933	156,129	121,785	100,299	113,329	121,348
Trojan	19,872	12,763	13,165	15,292	13,392	10,392
Mail	51,240	33,150	28,775	31,221	29,942	24,329
Total	210,045	202,042	163,725	146,812	156,663	156,069
Vs. pre month	100%	96%	81%	90%	107%	100%

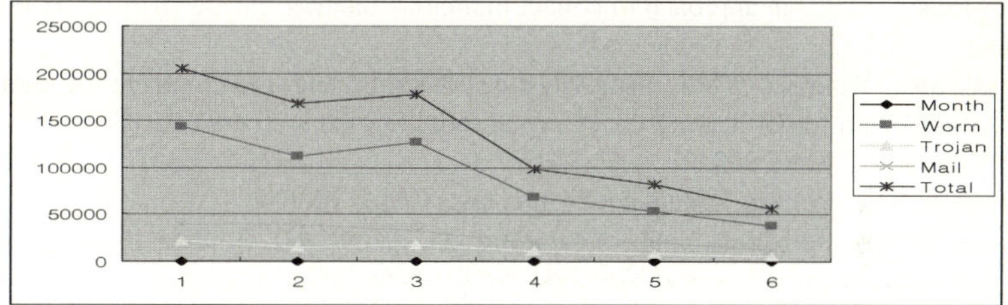

Fig. 11. The graph of Virus in A Network

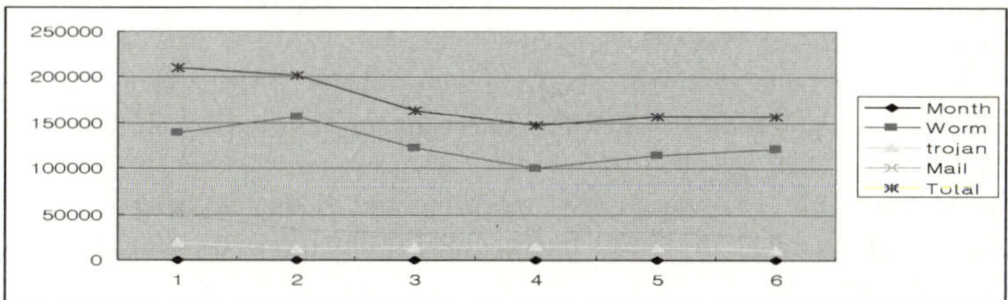

Fig. 12. The graph of Virus in B Network

to June showed the 50% decrease in number of worm virus. In the graphs of **Fig.11** and **Fig.12**, A network was gradually decreased by 50% in April to June compared to January to March. In B network, it was reduced by 20% but had similar characteristics. Therefore, for the worn that induces malicious traffic with specific patterns and malicious events that uses the mail as infecting route, it could be an effective device for blocking.

5 Conclusions and Future Works

In this study, to cope with the cyber mutation attack which the level of threat is increasing, the early detection and detection function was effectively designed by constituting HOIDS and RIS into the existing safety structure. In HOIDS, with this detecting method, the malicious events which were originally impossible to detect could be detected in early stage and through the internal inspection function in RIS, the expansion could have been prevented with rapid blocking. This current trial is to enhance the ability to cope with the situation and gauge the design possibilities of comprehensive early cyber threat system to control the occurrence of large scale damage through intensifying cyber threat preparatory ability and to give the ability to rapidly and actively cope with the occurrence of safety accident with the individual information safety system of safety management facilities.

References

1. Nicolas Vanderavero, Xavier Brouckaert, Olivier Bonaventure, Baudouin Le Charlier. "The HoneyTank : a scalable approach to collect malicious Internet traf-fic".IEEE2004 RTSS04 , Session 1, 2004.12
2. Dong-il Seo, Yang-seo Choi, Sang-Ho Lee. "Design and Development of Real Time Honeypot System for Collecting the Information of Hacker Activity", KIPS 2004, VOL. 10 NO.01 pp.1941~1944, 2003.05
3. http://www.Honeynet.org,"Honeynet Project Overview", 2005.4
4. Hyojung Hwang, Jinhyoun Youn, Youngmin Jin. "KORNET Routing Registry System", Journal of Communications And Networks No.01 pp 665~671, 1997.1
5. JongSeong Park, Jong-sub Moon, UnHo Choi. "A Study on Network Forensics Information in Automated Computer Emergency Response System", Korea Computer Congress 2004(A) pp. 253 ~ 255, 2004. 4
6. J.L Hellerstein, F.Zhang, P. Shahabuddin. "A statistical approach to predictive detection", Computer Networks, vol 35, pp77-95, 2001
7. N.K Groschwitz and G. C. Polyzos. "A Time Series Model of Long-Term NAFNET Backbone Traffic", In proceedings of IEEE International Conference on Communications, 1994. 5
8. Y. Shu, M. Yu, J Liu. "Wireless traffic modeling and prediction using seasonal ARIMA models", In proceedings of IEEE International Conference on Communi-cations,v.3, 2003, 5
9. http://info.ahnlab.com/ahnlab/report_view.jsp?num=416

IPBio: Embedding Biometric Data in IP Header for Per-Packet Authentication

Dae Sung Lee[1], Ki Chang Kim[2], and Year Back Yoo[3]

[1] School of Computer Science & Engineering, Inha Univ., Korea
Xdilemma@naver.com
[2] School of Information and Communication Engineering, Inha Univ., Korea
kchang@inha.ac.kr
[3] Computer Science Department, Montana State University, U.S.A.
yoo@cs.montana.edu

Abstract. Per-packet authentication is a powerful way to authenticate the user. Other authentication mechanisms (e.g. password authentication) verify the user at login time only while per-packet authentication verifies all packets coming from that user. Since every packet is authenticated repeatedly, inserting a fake packet or masquerading as a legitimate user is effectively prevented. Existing techniques for per-packet authentication such as IPSec or PLA, however, is either too expensive or not strong enough. We propose to include biometric data of the user in all packets for per-packet authentication. By collecting the user's biometric data periodically and physically from the user during the session and including it in all packets, we believe that we can provide a cheaper and more secure way of per-packet authentication. A random portion of the biometric data is extracted and used to digest the IP datagram. This technique allows us to control the size of the biometric data and to protect its contents from eavesdropper. This paper explains about the technique and provides experimental results.

1 Introduction

User authentication based on password is vulnerable to MIM(Man-In-the-Middle) attack. For more secure communications, it is recommended to use SSL(Secure Socket Layer) protocol. In SSL, a certificate certified by a trusted third party authenticates the user, and succeeding packets are protected by encryption. However there is no way of telling a stolen certificate. Furthermore, even with a genuine certificate, Burkholder and others [1,2] reports a possible MIM attack in SSL.

Per-packet authentication continuously authenticates all the packets coming from the user. Since it keeps authenticating all packets (not just once at login time), by definition, MIM attack for these packets is impossible. IPSec [3,4] is a one form of per-packet authentication. It stores authentication information in the packet header, and communicating nodes examine this security header to verify each packet. Gennaro and rohatgi [6] suggests a technique in which the sender appends a keyed hash of the next packet in the current one. The receiver verifies each packet by hashing the current packet and comparing the hash value with one sent by the sender last time.

G. Min et al. (Eds.): ISPA 2006 Ws, LNCS 4331, pp. 927–938, 2006.

Kari et al. [5] suggests to include a certificate of the sender in all packets for authentication purpose. The sender also includes a signed digest for the packet contents. The receiver can verify the authenticity of the packet by recovering the digested value with the public key certified in the certificate and compare it with what the receiver gets after digesting the received packet contents.

However, all techniques mentioned above rely on the genuineness of the certificate. If the exchanged certificate is a stolen one, all the processes to check the validity of packets are useless. Even if with a legal certificate, including it on every packet as in Kari et al. [5] is too expensive, and exchanging it only once in the beginning of the communication does not guarantee a complete authentication. The succeeding packets contain a signature that supposedly can be produced only by the legitimate sender, but since we don't have a direct proof of the sender's identity on each packet, it is still not completely reliable.

In this paper, we suggest to use biometric data as a way of authenticating each packet. The sender's biometric data is included in all outgoing packets, and the receiver confirms the validity of each packet by comparing the included biometric data with what it has already. Including the whole biometric data in all packets will cause too much traffic, and sending it in plain text is dangerous. Our technique adopts a challenge-response scheme: the receiver indicates the portion of biometric data to be used, and the sender uses that portion as an encryption key to sign the digested value of the packet contents. Including sender's biometric data in all packets will provide a powerful way of authentication. The live biometric data will ensure that the sender is truly whom he/she claims to be not only in the beginning of the session but throughout all the session.

The organization of the remaining paper is as follows: Section 2 surveys related researches on per-packet authentication; Section 3 explains the details of our technique; Section 4 shows via experimentation that our technique is manageable in cost in terms of packet size and packet processing time. Finally Section 5 gives a conclusion.

2   Related Researches

IPSec [3,4] introduces two new security headers: AH(Authentication Header) and ESP(Encapsulating Security Payload).

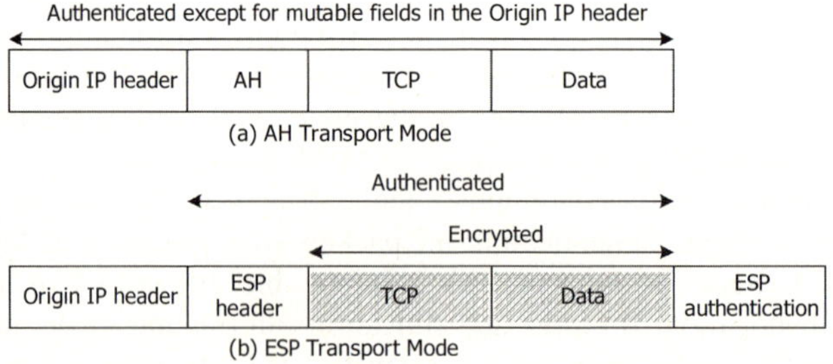

Fig. 1. AH and ESP header in IPSec

Both or one of them can be included in the IP header. AH attaches a digital signature (see Figure 1(a)) for the packet while ESP encrypts the payload (see Figure 1(b)). AH would be more suitable if we care only about the authenticity of the packet. A certificate, however, has to be exchanged to build a session key for the signature. Also, since it depends on the security of the same session key for all the packets during the same session once the initial authentication phase has passed, there is no guarantee that the packet comes from the real user -- an attacker might have cracked the key and tampered the packet.

PLA [5] has been designed for a military ad-hoc network. The purpose of PLA is to authenticate all participating nodes as well as packets. For this purpose, the certificate of the sending node is included for all packets as in Figure 2. It is very secure; however the cost is also very high.

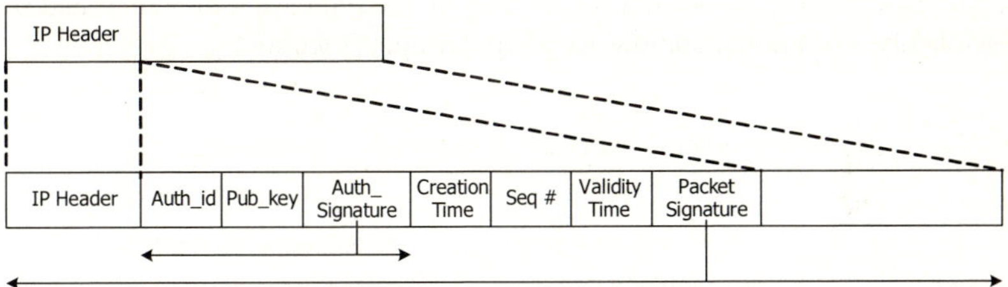

Fig. 2. PLA extension header

The researchers for multicasting techniques also are investigating a suitable method for per-packet authentication. The need for packet level authentication is greater here because the packet is transmitted to multiple receivers and MIM attack is much more easy [7]. Gennaro and Rohatgi [6] proposed an idea that the keyed hash of the second packet is appended to the first packet sent as shown in Figure 3. The receiver can verify the packet by comparing its hash value with the signature included in the previous packet. The danger of this scheme is lost or out-of-order packets which will break the chaining technique [8,9].

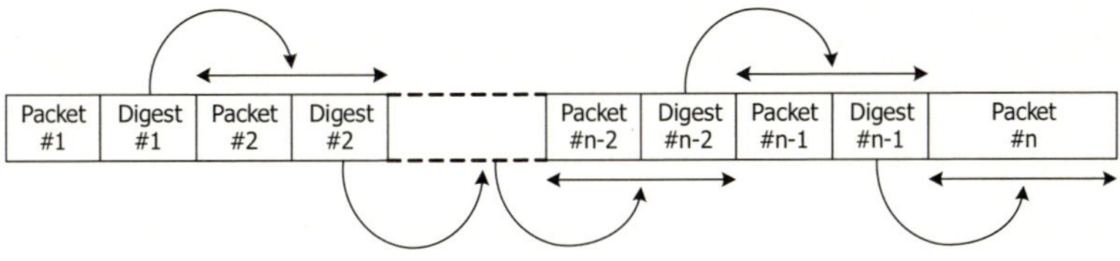

Fig. 3. Source authentication by piggybacking next packets on the current one

3   IPBio

We propose to include biometric data in all packets. Since biometric data is potentially large in size, we split it and send some random portion of it. We propose a protocol that dictates the behaviors of the sender and receiver in choosing the location of partial biometric data. This partial biometric data is used as a key to sign the packet. To verify the existence of the live sender, our scheme forces a periodic extraction of biometric data from the physical sender. This updated biometric data is confirmed by the receiver and used as the original copy for the next time period until the system decides to update it again.

3.1 Exchanging a Session Key

Our scheme requires a session key to encrypt the initial biometric data. Once it is confirmed by the server, this session key is not used; a random portion of the biometric data will be used as a key to encrypt the digested value of the packet payload. The session key is randomly generated by the client. Since the session key is sent to the server for each session, we need a secure way of authenticating the client and sending the session key. For authentication, we adopt Lamport's technique [10,11].

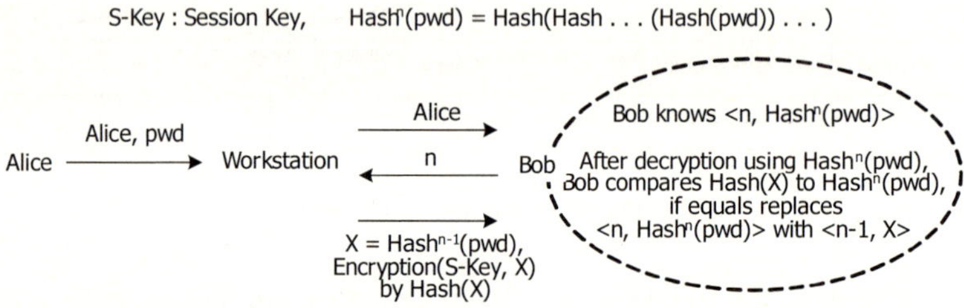

Fig. 4. Generating one-time passwords using Lamport's technique

Lamport [10] describes a technique to generate a sequence of one-time passwords over insecure channel. The client, Alice, pre-generates a sequence of passwords by applying a hash function repeatedly to the initial password as shown in Figure 4. Before the first login, the server, Bob, should already have the last hash value $Hash^n(pwd)$, and n, the number of times the hash function was applied to it. Now for the xth login, Alice sends $Hash^{n-x}(pwd)$, and Bob authenticates her by applying the hash function to it x times and make sure the result matches $Hash^n(pwd)$.

In our case, we require the user to visit and register his or her biometric data[1] at the server site. At this time, the user should provide $Hash^n(pwd)$ and receive his or her user ID. Now for the first login, the user sends <user ID, X($Hash^{n-1}(pwd)$, session key)>, where X is $Hash^n(pwd)$, and X(s) is the encryption of s with key

---

[1] This is the original biometric data. The actual biometric data to be used for authenticating packets will be collected from the user physically during the session. The collected data will be matched against the original one for verification.

X. Note that the client sends a session key and the next encryption key, $Hash^{n-1}(pwd)$, encrypted with $Hash^{n}(pwd)$, the current encryption key. The client has generated n encryption keys by hashing pwd repeatedly and uses them one by one at each session starting from the last generated one, $Hash^{n}(pwd)$, moving backwardly. Each time the client sends a session key, it also sends the next encryption key in this sequence, both encrypted by the current key. The server knows this protocol, and once it decrypts the current session key it discards the current decryption key replacing with one sent by the client -- this new one will be used to decrypt the client's session key in the next session. The server can authenticate the client for the purpose of login process by hashing the next encryption key sent by the client, e.g. $Hash^{n-1}(pwd)$ for the first login, and comparing it with the decryption key it currently has, e.g. $Hash^{n}(pwd)$ for the first login; if they match, the client must be a legitimate user since only the client can know the sequence of hash values. The packet sent by the client is shown in Figure 5. We have defined a new IP protocol, IPPROTO_BIO_KEY for this purpose. The server TCP/IP stack is modified to recognize this protocol: it checks the user_id field, retrieves the decryption key, for this user, and decrypts the session key.

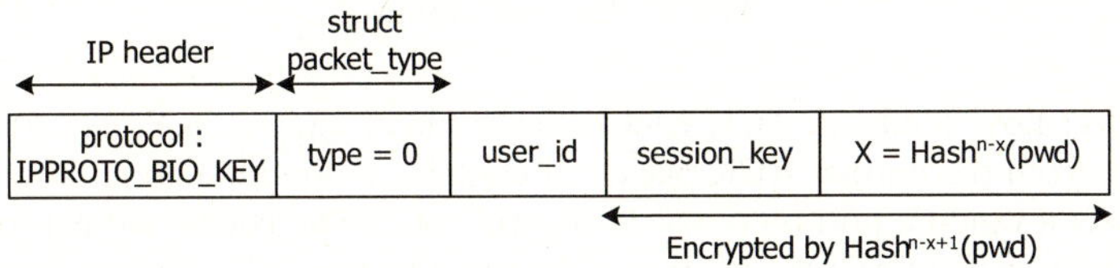

Fig. 5. Login packet format

3.2 Packet Authentication

Once the session key is established by the process in 3.1, the client opens a connection to the server by sending his or her biometric data (collected at run-time) encrypted with the session key. The server verifies the data by comparing it with the pre-registered one for this client and saves it as the current biometric data for this session. If the verification was successful, the server acknowledges the connection request, and the client starts sending packets signed with partial biometric data. The base protocol for this communication is TCP; however to tunnel through the intermediate routers with IPBio header, a new IP header wraps around the packet. The protocol indicated in this new IP header is BIO_CRYPTO.

3.2.1 Basic Design of IPBio
The processing of IPBio packets is shown in Figure 6. The first packet from the client is SYN packet (step 1 in Figure 6). This SYN packet, however, differs from the regular SYN packet in TCP in that it contains the encrypted biometric data of the user at

the client side[2]. The server decrypts it to retrieve and compare the biometric data with what it has (step 2 in Figure 6). If the two match perfectly or differ beyond some threshold, the connection request is refused[3]. If the biometric data is determined to be a legitimate one, the client is listed in the client list at the server side (as client C1 in Figure 6).

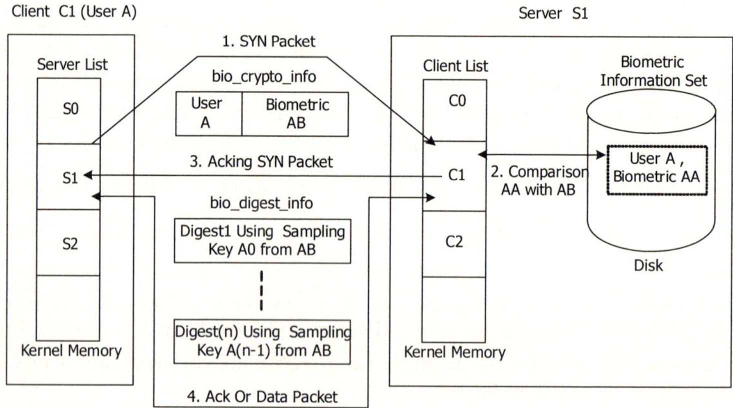

Fig. 6. IPBio packet flow

The server now sends an ACK packet to the client (step 3 in Figure 6). This one also differs from the normal ACK packet: it contains a direction about how the client should select a random portion of the biometric data[4]. The packet format for SYN or ACK is shown in Figure 7: they both use the same format. The client responds with a final ACK, and 3-way handshake is completed. The client generates a random number based on the direction given by the server. 256 bits starting from this random number position is extracted and used as a key to digest the IP datagram (step 4 in Figure 6). The packet format used by the client is shown in Figure 8. The packet contains IPBio header between the new IP header and the original IP header. The IPBio header contains a digested value of the entire IP datagram hashed with the designated portion of the biometric data. Upon receiving this packet, the server knows which portion of the bio-data should be used to decrypt the signature and, therefore, can authenticate the packet's content.

IPBio is implemented in Linux for experimentation using Linux Netfilter. The packets are hooked at IP level, and at the hooking position the sender inserts IPBio header while the receiver removes it. Figure 9 shows the major data structure used for

---

[2] This inclusion of biometric data in SYN packet will effectively block DOS attacks based on SYN flooding. The server can drop the connection request if the bio-data doesn't match with what it has.

[3] The two biometric data should not match perfectly because the one sent from the client must have been taken physically right before the transmission of the SYN packet.

[4] In fact, a structure that contains the direction and other useful information is included, and this whole structure is encrypted with the session key.

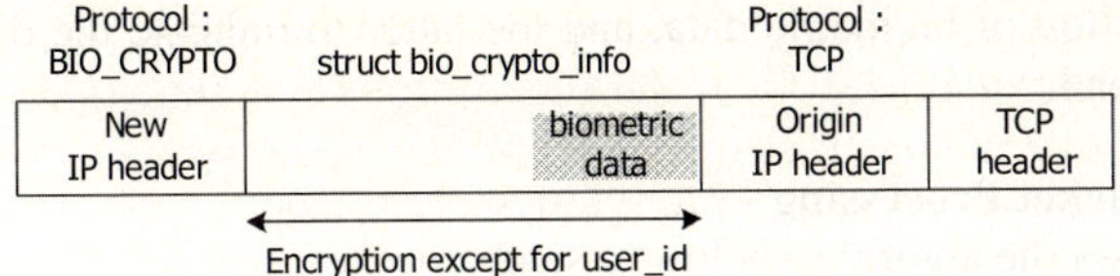

Fig. 7. Packet format for SYN or acknowledging SYN

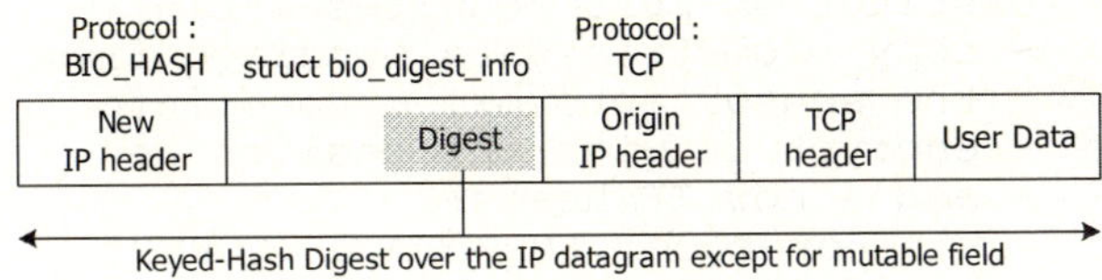

Fig. 8. Packet format for the client side

```
sturct bio_crypto_info {
        char user_id[20];      /*  Not Encrypted. The user  id for searching already exchanged session key  */
        struct bio_crypto_header {                 The Encrypted Area
            unsigned long c_sequence;        //  sequence number for anti-replay attack
            char bio_key_func[64];           //  the starting-bit selecting function from biometrics-data
                                                 for choosing per-packet symmetric-key
        } c_header;
         struct bio_crypto_data {
             unsigned int real_crypto_len;               // the size of biometrics-data
             unsigned char bio_data[BIO_FULL_SIZE];   // total biometrics-data
         } c_data;
};

struct bio_digest_info {
        struct bio_hash_header {
            unsigned long h_sequeunce;        //  sequence number for anti-replay attack
            unsigned int key_startingbitnum;       //  the starting bit number from the biometrics-data used as
                                                         per-packet symmetric-key for message authentication code
        } h_header;
        struct bio_hash_data {
            unsigned int real_hash_len;           // the size of a digested message
            unsigned char HMAC_SHA1_result[SHA1_DIGEST_SIZE];     // the digest over the IP datagram
        } h_data;
};
struct list_head {struct list_head * next; struct list_head * prev; };

struct host_list {
        struct list_head list;              // list chain
        unsigned int isServer : 1;               //  1 : server,  0 : client
        unsigned int list_key[2];        //  the searching key for host_list(source address, port and destination port bitwise-OR)
        unsigned int origin_pmtu;              //  original path MTU(Maximum Transmit Unit)
        unsigned char DES_eKey[16][8];      //  encryption key
        unsigned char DES_dKey[16][8];      //decryption key
        struct bio_crypto_info host_bio;       // the save area for total biometrics-data
} server_list, client_list;
```

Fig. 9. Major data structures for IPBio

IPBio. "bio_crypto_info" contains information for the IPBio header during the 3-way handshake; "bio_digest_info" contains the similar information after the 3-way handshake. The major information in "bio_crypto_info" is "bio_data" and "bio_key_func". "bio_data" contains the biometric data of the client; this field is used when the client sends SYN packet to the server. "bio_key_func" contains a bit-selection function; it is used when the server sends ACK packet to the client, and the client applies it to compute the random position in the user's biometric data. The major information in "bio_digest_info" is "key_startingbitnum" and "HMAC_SHA1_result". They are both used in the packet sent by the client: the former to indicate the starting bit position of the selected portion of biometric data, and the latter to indicate the digested value of the packet payload.

3.2.2 IPBio Packet Processing

The client follows the algorithm below to send a packet.

```
switch (Packet Type){
    case SYN:
        if (destination port requires IPBio){
            - copy biometric data obtained from
              the sensor into bio_crypto_info
            - encrypt it with the session key
            - add a new IP header
              with protocol IPPROTO_BIO_CRYPTO
            - build an IPBio packet and transmit
        }
        else
            - follow normal flow
        break;
    case 3-way Final ACK:
    case normal data:
        if (destination port requires IPBio){
            - select a random portion from
              the biometric data using bio_key_func
            - digest IP diagram using the random portion
              as a key
            - copy the result into HMAC_SHA1_result
            - build an IPBio packet and transmit
        }
        else
            - follow normal flow
        break;
}
```


Fig. 10. Telnet session using IPBio

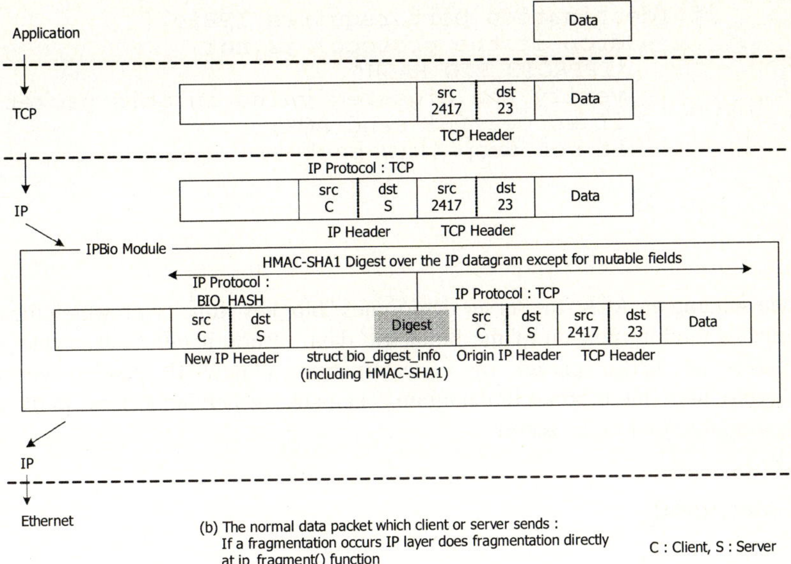

Fig. 10. (*continued*)

As mentioned before, SYN packet includes the whole biometric data; otherwise a portion of it is used to digest the IP datagram. An example telnet session using IPBio is shown in Figure 10. Figure 10(a) shows the packet building process for SYN packet while Figure 10(b) the process for data packets. The dashed line in the figure divides the protocol layers. First at TCP layer, a TCP header is composed: the destination port is 23 because this is a telnet session. This incomplete packet is handed over to IP layer where IP header is added and where, through IPBio module, a new IP header and encrypted biometric data are added. For the data packets, the process is similar except that we have encrypted digest information instead of full biometric data. The packet receiving process in the server is shown below.

```
switch (Packet Type){
   case SYN:
       if (destination port requires IPBio){
           - drop if the protocol is not
             "IPPROTO_BIO_CRYPTO"
           - retrieve user ID from the packet and
             use it to obtain the session key
           - decrypt the biometric data
             using the session key and check its validity
           - if successful send ACK;
             if not drop this packet
       }
       .....
   case 3-way Final ACK:
   case normal data:
```

```
if (destination port requires IPBio){
        - drop if the protocol is not
          "IPPROTO_BIO_HASH"
        - verify the digested value in this packet
        - if successful send ACK;
          if not drop this packet
    }
    .....
}
```

When sending an ACK, the server determines "bio_key_func" with which the client can select a random portion of the biometric data, inserts it into "bio_crypto_info", and builds an IPBio packet by concaternating a new IP header, encrypted "bio_crypto_info, and original IP datagram. The packet receiving process in the client side is similar to that in the server.

4 Experiments

Our scheme increases the packet size by adding IPBio header. Longer packet size will increase the packet processing time. Also the IP layer has to perform additional tasks such as inserting/extracting IPBio header, encrypting/decrypting Biometric data, and digesting IP diagram. We have measured and compared packet transmission time for IPBio packets and non-IPBio packets. The result is in Table 1.

Table 1. Packet transmission time for IPBio packets and non-IPBio packets

bytes transmitted	IPBio		without IPBio	rate of IPBio time over non-IPBio time	
	time for digest	time for enc/dec		enc/dec time included	with digest time only
64Kbytes	0.07Sec	0.13Sec	0.03Sec	6.67	2.33
64Kbytes X 2	0.15Sec	0.12Sec	0.07Sec	3.86	2.14
64Kbytes X 4	0.46Sec	0.12Sec	0.21Sec	2.76	2.19
64Kbytes X 10	1.42Sec	0.11Sec	0.63Sec	2.43	2.25
64Kbytes X 20	4.57Sec	0.12Sec	1.91Sec	2.46	2.39
64Kbytes X 40	11.35Sec	0.13Sec	4.24Sec	2.71	2.68
64Kbytes X 80	23.78Sec	0.12Sec	7.58Sec	3.15	3.14

The size of biometric data in case of fingerprint is between 500 and 4K bytes. In the experimentation, we assumed it is 1K byte. For SYN packet, the whole biometric data is included, but after that each packet contains 20 bytes of digest for the IP datagram. In the table, encryption/decryption time is for the SYN packet: the biometric data is encrypted at the client side and decrypted at the server side. It is one-time cost. After the SYN packet, most of packet transmission time is spent in digestion. The

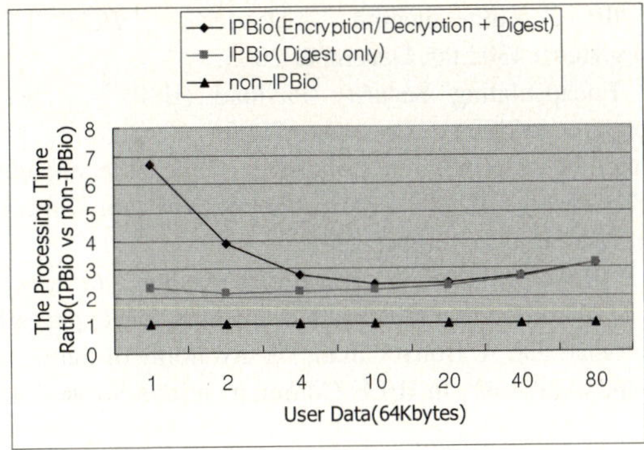

Fig. 11. Comparison between IPBio and non-IPBio

ratio of IPBio packets to non-IPBio ones in terms of transmission time is 2.45 in average.[5]

Figure 11 shows the ratio of IPBio packet transmission times over non-IPBio ones in graph. Two things require explanation. First, the graph shows the encryption/decryption time quickly loses its effect as packet size grows. Second, the ratio is slightly increasing as packet size gets bigger. We suspect the additional 20 bytes is causing another overhead such as more frequent fragmentation other than longer packet size.

5   Conclusion

In this paper, we explained a technique to insert biometric data on every packet starting from the very first one (such as a SYN packet in TCP). A random portion of the biometric data is extracted and used to digest the IP datagram. The receiver can authenticate every packet based on this biometric information. Since every packet is verifiable, attacks based on fake packets such as MIM attack or SYN flooding attack is effectively defeated. The algorithm has been implemented in Linux TCP/IP stack utilizing the hooking mechanism. The additional packet processing time was measured to be about 2.45 times higher than regular packets. We believe this is tolerable in exchange of more secure communication.

References

1. Peter Burkholder: "SSL Man-in-the-Middle Attacks", *SANS institute*, http://www.sans.org/rr/whitepapers/threats/480.php, February 2002.
2. M. Steiner, P. Buhler, T. Eirich and M. Waidner: "Secure Password-Based Cipher Suite for TLS" , *ACM Transactions on Information and System Security (TISSEC)*, v.4 n.2, p.134-157, May 2001

---

[5] It is the figure when we exclude the encryption/decryption time. We believe it is acceptable to exclude it because as the number of packet increases the proportion of encryption/decryption time becomes negligible.

3. S. Kent: "IP Authentication Header", *IETF Working Group*, http://www.ietf.org/rfc/rfc4302.txt, December 2005.
4. S. Kent: "IP Encapsulating Security Payload (ESP)", *IETF Working Group*, http://www.ietf.org/rfc/rfc4303.txt, December 2005
5. Hannu Kari Catharina Candolin, Janne Lundberg: "Packet level authentication in military networks", *In Proceedings of the 6th Australian Information Warfare & IT Security Conference*, Geelong, Australia, November 2005.
6. R. Gennaro and P. Rohatgi: "How to sign digital streams", *In Advances in Cryptology – CRYPTO '97*, vol.1294 of Lecture Notes in Computer Science, pages 180-197, 1997.
7. Y. Challal, H. Bettahar, and A. Bouabdallah: "A taxonomy of multicast data origin authentication : Issues and solutions", In IEEE Communications Surveys and Tutorials, volume 6, October 2004
8. Chung Kei Wong, Simon S. Lam: "Digital signatures for flows and multicasts", *IEEE/ACM Transactions on Networking (TON)*, v.7 n.4, p.502-513, Aug. 1999.
9. A. Perrig, R. Canetti, J. D. Tygar, and D. Song: "Efficient authentication and signature of multicast streams over lossy channels", *In Proceedings of the IEEE Symposium on Research in Security and Privacy*, pages 56 – 73, May 2000.
10. L. Lamport: "Password authentication with insecure communication", *Communications of the ACM*, 24(11):770-772, November. 1981
11. N. Haller: "The S/Key one-time password system" *In Proceedings of the Symposium on Network and Distributed Systems Security*, pages 151-157, February 1994.

Scalable Distributed Scheduling for Quality of Service*

Moohun Lee[1], Sungja Choi[1], Janguk In[2], Changbok Jang[1],
Sunghoon Cho[1], and Euiin Choi[1]

[1] Dept. of Computer Engineering, Hannam University,
133 Ojeong-Dong, Daedeok-Gu, Daejeon, 306-791, Korea
{mhlee, chbjang, shcho, eichoi}@dblab.hannam.ac.kr,
irecomm@dreamwiz.com
[2] Dept. of Computer and Information Science and Engineering,
University of Florida, Gainesville, FL 32611, USA
juin@cise.ufl.edu

Abstract. A grid consists of high-end computational, storage, and network resources that, while known a priori, are dynamic with respect to activity and availability. Efficient scheduling of requests to use grid resources must adapt to this dynamic environment while meeting administrative policies. This paper discusses a framework for distributed resource management. The framework has the following novel features. First, the resource management system is distributed using resource content information that is characterized by system properties. We argue that a distributed system based on resource content is sufficient to satisfy specific scheduling requests for global Quality of Service (QoS) considering workload balance across a grid. Second, the distributed system constructs a hierarchical peer-to-peer network. This peered network provides an efficient message routing mechanism. The simulation results demonstrate that the proposed framework is proficient to satisfy QoS in distributed environment.

Keywords: Scheduling, Grid Computing, Quality of Service, Content-based Resource Clustering, Distributed System.

1   Introduction

The Grid has been a promising way in high performance computing for many data intensive, scientific applications. The challenging computing paradigm allows a large number of competitive and/or collaborative organizations to share mutual resources, including documents, software, computers, data and sensors, to seamlessly process data and computationally intensive applications [1, 2]. The collaboration requires the management of a large number of heterogeneous resources with varying, distinct policies and controlled by multiple organizations. A native approach to distribute scheduling service based on only geographical location cannot properly cover the sophisticated and resource specific scheduling requirement of

---

* This work was supported by a grant from Security Engineering Research Center of Ministry of Commerce, Industry and Energy.

G. Min et al. (Eds.): ISPA 2006 Ws, LNCS 4331, pp. 939–948, 2006.

scientific computing. Many experiments in science projects such as SDSS, LIGO, CMS and ATLAS [3, 4, 5, 6] generate and record data at a rate of the tens of peta-bytes by the near future. We need smart and delicate ways to distribute the resource management systems in order to allow globally dispersed scientists in collaborative teams access and analyze the data rapidly and precisely. A uniform definition of efficient message routing issue is also necessary in a large-scale grid environment. Scalable and effective resource management and request scheduling is a fundamental operation in grid computing.

Even though the issue has been researched comprehensively [7, 8, 9, 10, 11], it is still challenging to fully support the feature in a Peta-scale Virtual Data Grid (PVDG) [1]. A typical grid consists of a fair amount of heterogeneous resources from geographically distanced organizations or individuals. Therefore, it is necessary to distribute the resource management service for the extensibility to the environment. We develop a framework for the distributed service with the following novel features. First, the resource management system is distributed in a hierarchical peer-to-peer network using resource content information that is characterized by system properties. Second, the peered network provides an efficient message routing mechanism to process expressive QoS queries for preventing message flooding and performance bottlenecks.

2 Related Works

2.1 Content Based Network

As a challenging communication framework a content-based network supports the communication mechanisms for large-scale, loosely coupled distributed applications. It complements traditional unicast and multicast addressed-based networks by providing an infrastructure for message flow through the network driven by the content of the messages rather than by explicit addresses which message senders specify. In a content-based network, message receivers declare their interests in message types to the network by means of 'predicates' [12], while senders simply send messages into the network. The network is responsible for delivering messages to receivers declaring the predicate that the messages contain. In traditional address-based networks the delivery function is performed incrementally by passing messages between intermediate nodes in the network. Message routing in a content-based network has been a major issue to prevent message flooding and to provide minimal forward paths for messages [13, 14, 15]. Unlike in an address-based network where messages travels to destinations with explicit addresses, routers in a content based network evaluate the contents of the messages against the predicates in forwarding tables of the routers, and decide neighbor routers to receive the messages.

2.2 Hash Based Peer-to-Peer Network

In a peer-to-peer distributed system [16] autonomous nodes connect to a small set of their neighbors. Queries are recursively propagated to other nodes following the connection over the network to find a corresponding data to the queries. Peer-to-peer systems explicitly or implicitly provide a lookup mechanism that matches a given key to one or more network nodes responsible for the value associated with the key. Simple queries for the lookup by key are assumed in most peer-to-peer systems such as CAN, Chord, Tapestry [17, 18, 19]. These systems guarantee that data can be found with a very small number of message or node hopping. However, these techniques require a specific network structure and total control over the location of the data [20]. Because they are highly centralized content-addressable networks centered on the theme of distributed hash table lookup they cannot support rich and expressive general-purposed queries such as matchmaking [21, 22].

3   A Proposed Framework for Efficient Distributed Scheduling

The proposed framework devises a proficient approach to the demand, which utilizes several distributed computing features. Hierarchically structured computation, storage or network resources contributing to a Virtual Organization (VO) are characterized by system properties such as CPU, memory, storage and bandwidth. A resource is represented with a set of values for the selected properties, and the value set corresponds to a node in a d dimensional property space. The coordinates in the space can be clustered based on their closeness in distance. The clustering procedure implies that resources with similar property values are grouped together. By assigning one or more resource management system to each of the resource clusters, we achieve a fully distributed system based on resource content information. The assigned schedulers autonomously perform the resource allocation to remote or local scheduling requests within the cluster.

The distributed system across the resource clusters constructs a peered network. The network guarantees autonomous resource management within a group and message routing locality with lookup functionality. Especially, the framework provides an efficient routing mechanism to forward a resource property specific request. A scheduling server in the network maintains a request routing table, which contains the information of the service in the other resource clusters.

In order to decide the destination of request forwarding the server performs a logical mapping between the request and the property information representing a cluster in the table. The framework facilitates efficient forwarding of expressive QoS requests on content-based clustering network. Multiple objects of the resource management system can cause resource status and other information such as users' resource usage accounts to be inconsistent among the distributed system. In addition, there may be resource reservation conflicts on a single resource due to the inconsistency. This framework controls the concurrent access to shared resources by using a locking mechanism. A request submission to an intended resource is organized with two steps. First, the request competes for obtaining a lock on the resource. Second, once having the lock, real submission is made to the resource exclusively. The locking supports autonomous scheduling among the multiple servers with keeping information consistency without centralized control.

4 Grid Resource Clustering

The grid resources are organized in a hierarchical infrastructure. A distributed scheduling network is constructed on the base of the resource grouping. In this section we discuss a technique to cluster resources in a VO according to their properties.

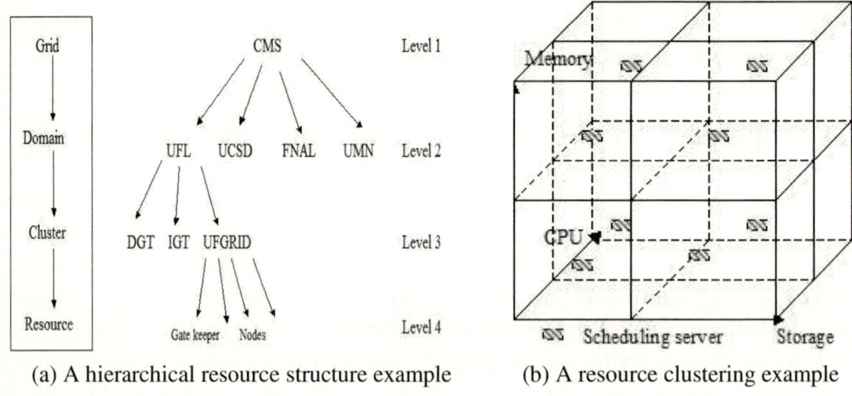

(a) A hierarchical resource structure example   (b) A resource clustering example

Fig. 1. Grid resource hierarchy and resource clustering in property space

4.1 Hierarchical Structure of Grid Resources

Fig. 1-(a) shows an example of the gird resource structure. A grid VO maintains a hierarchical structure of computing, storage and network resources. A resource contributor defines the resource levels that are globally schedulable in the hierarchy tree. For the resources below the levels, a local scheduler of the participant makes scheduling decision. The hierarchy structure may present the globally schedulable resources in the leaf level of the tree. The structure has non-uniform leaf level because globally schedulable resources are indicated in different levels in the tree.

A resource in an intermediate or leaf level of the structure can be characterized with a set of system properties. A group of the properties may include physical information such as CPU, memory and bandwidth, or benchmarking information. A resource identifies itself with its own values to the properties, while an intermediate resource aggregates property information of the resources in lower levels in the hierarchy.

4.2 Clustering of Grid Resource

Heterogeneous resources in a VO are classified in terms of the types or capacities of the properties. The classification is a proficient way to characterize the heterogeneous resources in a dynamically changing grid environment. A set of selected system properties constructs a d-dimensional space in which grid resources can be represented according to their values to the properties. In the resource property space we apply a clustering algorithm to group together the resources with similar properties. Fig. 1-(b) shows an example of the clustering in three-dimensional space, which is constructed with CPU, memory and storage.

5 Peer-to-Peer Scheduling Service Network

In this section we discuss distributed scheduling service in a peer-to-peer network. We talk about scheduling service distribution across a VO, and message routing mechanism among the schedulers.

5.1 Scheduling Service Distribution

Scheduling service modules that are assigned into multiple resource groups construct a distributed scheduling service network. Graph (b) in Fig. 1 shows an example of scheduling service distribution. A set of schedulers for a resource cluster, which is defined with $S_c = \{s_i \mid$ a scheduler, $1 \leq i \leq l\}$, *where l is the number of schedulers,* makes autonomous scheduling decision based on resource status and usage policies within the cluster. The scheduling framework constructs a peered network with the scheduling services that are distributed over all the resource clusters in a VO. Generally, there are $(2^d \times l)$ scheduling service modules in a VO, where d is the number of properties, and l is the number of schedulers within a cluster. It is an overlay network based on the grid that is a network of schedulable resources. Each server has a scheduling service routing table that contains representative resource property information of the clusters and a corresponding scheduling service address within the clusters.

The number of scheduling servers in a resource cluster can be more than one to prevent scheduling failure and congestion caused by a single server. Because the servers within a cluster make scheduling decision to the same set of resources by sharing status and policy information in the region any of the service modules can represent the region for scheduling remote requests. It limits the size of a routing table on each scheduler to 2d, which is equal to the number of clusters. The representative scheduling module is selected randomly among the available servers in a cluster.

5.2 Message Routing

The scheduler performs resource allocation procedure according to its scheduling strategy, when a single user submits request to a scheduler. If the scheduler is able to meet QoS requirement presented by the request then the scheduling work is done, and job submission procedure may start. However, if the QoS cannot be satisfied with the resources in the current region then the scheduler needs to forward the request to schedulers in other resource groups. The framework devises a request routing mechanism in the service peered network. We define three cases where a scheduling server cannot make resource allocation decision to a request.

1. *The scheduler cannot satisfy QoS requirement of the request using the resources within its cluster.*
2. *All the resources in the cluster are overloaded with task execution.*
3. *The schedulers themselves are overloaded with request scheduling work.*

In the cases where resources or schedulers are overloaded the request is simply forwarded to schedulers in a neighbor cluster. However, the forwarding decision might not be easy with the first case where the request requires resource specific QOS. The schedulers should make smart decision to forward the request to the resource group that is able to satisfy the requirement. The decision should prevent request flooding among resource clusters, and shouldn't be a bottleneck in the grid computing performance either.

A user submits her/his scheduling request to the closest server in geographical distance, while a server forwards a request to another server in other resource groups according to the results of a forward function. A scheduling server maintains a request routing table. Each entry in the table represents aggregated property information of resources in a cluster and an address of a scheduler within the cluster. Because resources are clustered according to their property values there is a single value for a discrete property such as OS or architecture, and there is a range value for a continuous property such as memory or CPU speed. When a scheduler needs to find a destination to forward a request with a specific QoS requirement the scheduler performs logical mapping between the QoS and the property information in the table. After finding resource clusters that can satisfy the QoS requirement the request is forwarded to the schedulers specified in the routing table. The scheduling server may interact with the user to negotiate QoS requirement level. [10] discusses the user interaction to the QoS satisfaction.

6 Experiments

We simulate the distributed scheduling discussed in the paper using Java threads and sockets. The simulation shows the performance of request scheduling on the three different network topologies(content-based, geography-based and centralized scheduling networks). We construct the content-based network according to the arguments in the previous sections, while the geography-based is a traditional distributed network based on resources' geographical distance. In the centralized service a single server takes charge of scheduling requests to all the resources in a grid.

6.1 Background

A user submits a task execution request with QoS requirement represented with the properties such as CPU capacity and storage amount. The request contains the property requirement and job completion due time. The experiment assumes a virtual organization in which forty resources are available. Each resource is specified with the property amounts. The experiment uses two properties, CPU and storage for characterizing the resources. We classify the resources into four types according to their values for the properties.

In the experiment we construct the content-based scheduling network according to the resource clustering. A scheduling server is assigned into each of the groups. The server maintains a message routing table that contains IP addresses of the other schedulers and property information of the corresponding clusters. In the geography-based network, a server makes scheduling decision to the resources with various properties in its region. When the server has unsatisfied requests it simply forwards them to a neighbor cluster. In the centralized scheduling service architecture, a single server has property information of all the resources. Users submit requests to the scheduler, which utilizes the resources in the scheduling decision.

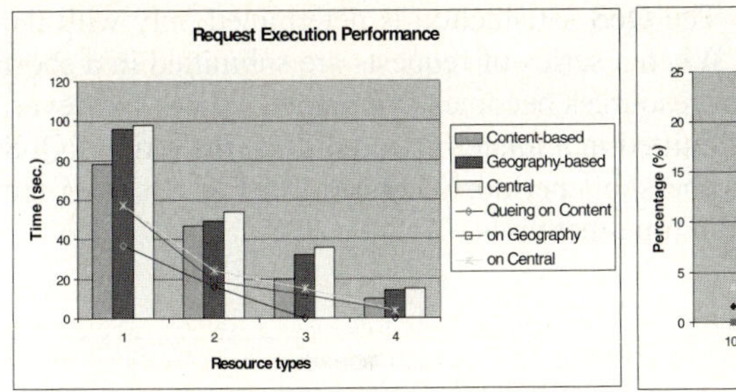

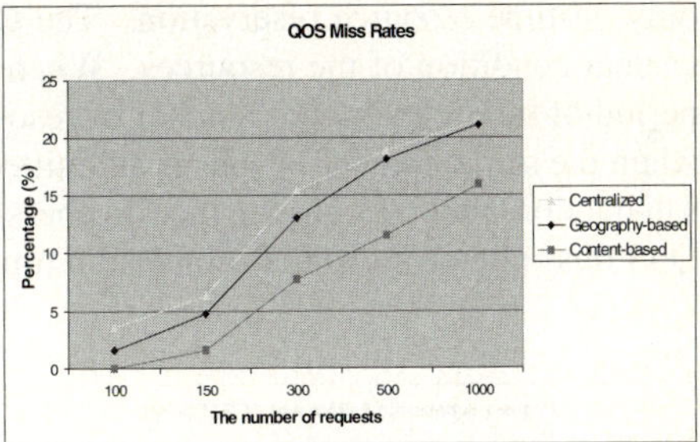

(a) Task execution performance (300 requests)   (b) QoS request missing rates

Fig. 2. Performance comparison among scheduling network topologies

6.2 Scheduling Performance

In this experiment we evaluate scheduling performance on the three network topologies in two aspects. First, we measure job completion time of resources on each of them. Efficient request scheduling reduces workload on a resource, which is represented by queuing time on the resource. Better execution performance increases the possibility to satisfy QoS requirement in on-time reservation. Second, we investigate QoS miss rate with different number of requests on the topologies.

Graph (a) in Fig. 2 shows that completion time of requests is affected by scheduling network topologies. We categorize resource into four different types according to their properties. The graph presents average task completion and queuing or waiting time in each resource category. When we construct the scheduling networks the queuing time makes difference in the performance with the same resources. In graph (a) resources on the content-based has less queuing time than on the others. It indicates that resources on the network are less overloaded than on the others. The content-based scheduling network facilitates QoS satisfaction with the resources over an entire VO, while a scheduler makes the scheduling decision with the resources within its region and the neighbors in the geography-based. The limited utilization makes the resources easily overloaded, resulting in the long completion time.

Graph (b) in Fig. 2 shows that a scheduling service has difficulty to satisfy QoS requirement with a large amount of requests. The graph presents the ratio of failed QoS satisfaction in on-time resource allocation decision for each of the scheduling networks. As the resources are overloaded with the larger number of requests a scheduler can't meet QoS requests with higher possibility. The graph shows that a scheduler in the content-based network has lower miss rate than in the other networks. As shown in graph (a), resources in the network are less overloaded than the others due to the property-based resource clustering that provides a scheduler with all the feasible resources for a QoS request in a VO.

Various request submission patterns can make difference in the resource workload. As we can see in Fig. 2, large percentage of QoS requirements can't be satisfied with congested grid resources in the scheduling networks. In this experiment we perform only on-time resource reservation. The QoS satisfaction is determined only with the current condition of the resources. When a series of requests are submitted in a short period of time, the limited number of resources becomes overloaded easily. However, when the same number of jobs is submitted in a longer period of time the ratio of QoS satisfaction becomes higher than in the short period. Graph (a) in Fig. 3 shows the QoS miss rate drops as the submission time increases.

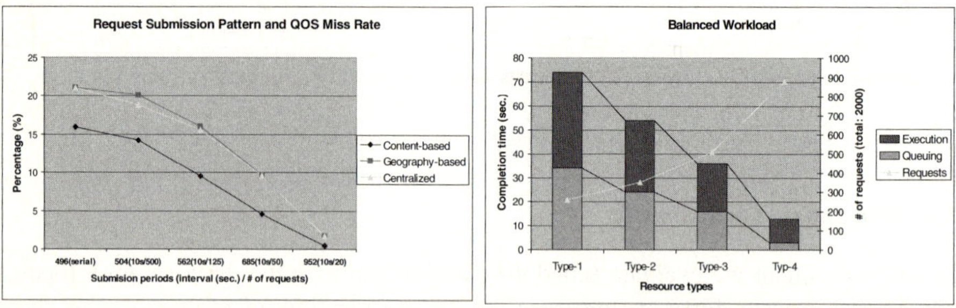

(a)QoS satisfaction rate and request submission   (b)Workload balance and request assignment

Fig. 3. Resource workload and QoS satisfaction

The resource allocation based on on-time scheduling has limitation in overall resource usage and QoS satisfaction. Advanced resource reservation concept facilitates the request scheduling. A scheduler can make the reservation with anticipated resource workload in the near-future time frames.

Graph (b) in Fig. 3 shows an example of balanced workload on different kinds of resources. We submit 2000 requests to four different kinds of resources. We have described the resource types in Section 8.1. Even though average request completion time is different among the resource groups, the ratio of queuing time out of the completion time is similar among the three types, Type-1, Type-2 and Type-3 with the value, 45%. Resources in Type-4 group have lower queuing time than ones in other groups because the number of submitted requests is not large enough to make the resources over all the types busy.

7   Conclusion and Future Works

We present distributed scheduling service framework in this paper. The approach is challenging because network resources are clustered on the base of their characteristics instead of geographical locations, and the services are distributed according to the content-based clustering. The distributed services are connected in a peer-to-peer network. The message forwarding in the peered network is performed using a hash based routing function in order to satisfy QoS requirement of a scheduling request. We are incorporating the distributed scheduling service framework with the proposed policy based scheduling framework and implementing the comprehensive scheduling middleware on a grid testbed. We plan to include several additional core functionalities for grid scheduling. One such important functionality is that of estimating the resources required for task execution. In addition, we plan to investigate scheduling and replication strategies that consider policy constraints and quality of service, and include them in applications to improve scheduling accuracy and performance.

References

1. P. Avery, I. Foster, The GriPhyN Project:Towards Petascale Virtual-Data Grids, GriPhyN Technical Report 2000-1.
2. I. Foster, C. Kesselman, S. Tuecke, The Anatomy of the Grid: Enabling Scalable Virtual Organizations, International Journal of Supercomputer Applications, 2001.
3. Sloan Digital Sky Survey, http://www.sdss.org, 2004
4. Laser Interferometer Gravitational Wave Observatory, http://ligo.caltech.edu, 2004
5. The Compact Muon Solenoid, an experiment for the Large Hadron Collider at CERN, http://cmsinfo.cern.ch/Welcome.html/, 2004
6. The ATLAS Experiment, http://atlasexperiment.org, 2004
7. R. Buyya, Economic-based Distributed Resource Management and Scheduling for Grid Computing, Ph.D Thesis, Monash University, Melbourne, Australia, April, 2002
8. R. Min, M. Maheswaran, Scheduling Co-Reservations with Priorities in Grid Computing Systems, Proceedings of the 2nd IEEE/ACM International Symposium on Cluster Computing and the Grid, 2002
9. D. P. Spooner, J. Cao, J. D. Turner, H. N. Lim Choi Keung, S. A. Jarvis, G. R. Nudd, Localised Workload Management Using Performance Prediction and QoS Contracts, Eighteenth Annual UK Performance Engineering Workshop, 2002
10. J. In, A. Arbree, P. Avery, R. Cavanaugh, S. Katageri, S. Ranka, Sphinx: A Scheduling Middleware for Data Intensive Applications on a Grid, GriphyN Project Technical Report, GriPhyN 2003-17, 2003.
11. J. In, P. Avery, R. Cavanaugh, S. Ranka, Policy Based Scheduling for Simple Quality of Service in Grid Computing, 18th International Parallel & Distributed Processing Symposium, New Mexico, USA, 2004
12. A. Carzaniga, A.L. Wolf, Content-based Networking: A New Communication infrastructure, NSF Workshop on an infrastructure for Mobile and Wireless Systems, Scottsdale, AZ, October, 2001
13. A. Carzaniga, M.J. Rutherford, A.L. Wolf, A Routing Scheme for Content-Based Networking, Proceedings of IEEE INFOCOMM 2004, Hong Kong China, March, 2004.
14. R. Chand, P. Felber, A Scalable Protocol for Content-Based Routing in Overlay Networks, Proceedings of the IEEE International Symposium on Network Computing and Applications, Cambridge, MA, April, 2003.
15. M. Aron, D. Sanders, P. Druschel, W. Zwaenepoel, Scalable Content-aware Request Distribution in Cluster-based Network Servers, Proceedings of the 2000 Annual Usenix Technical Conference, San Diego, CA, June, 2000.
16. D. Doval, D. O'Mahony, Overlay Networks, A Scalable Alternative for P2P, IEEE Internet Computing, August 2003.
17. S. Ratnasamy, P. Francis, M. Handley, R. Karp, S. Shenker, A scalable content-addressable network, ACM SIGCOMM, 2001.
18. I. Stoica, R. Morris, D. Karger, M. F. Kaashoek, H. Balakrishman, Chord: A scalable peer-to-peer loopup service for internet applications, ACM SIGCOMM, 2001.
19. B. Zhao, J. Kubiatowicz, A. Joseph, Tapestry: An infrastructure for fault-tolerant wide-area location and routing, Technical report, U. C. Berkeley, 2001

20. A. Crespo, H. Garcia-Molina, Semantic Overlay Networks for P2P Systems, Technical report, Stanford University, Jan. 2003.
21. W. Hoschek, A Unified Peer-to-Peer Database Framework for Scalable Service and Resource Discovery, Proc. of the International IEEE/ACM Workshop on Grid Computing, Baltimore, USA, Nov. 2002. Springer Verlag.
22. Dan Bradley, Condor-G Matchmaking in USCMS, Condor technical report, University of Wisconsin, Nov. 2003

Analysis of Security Vulnerability Diagnosis in Mobile IP Networks

Dong Chun Lee

Dept. of Computer Science Howon Univ., Korea
ldch@sunny.howon.ac.kr

Abstract. In this paper we design and implement the system that diagnoses security vulnerability in mobile IP networks. The aim of the paper is to interpret the communication network related to security vulnerability reporting process, and focuses on how the information of the vulnerability is received and processed and how the information is managed after the reception in mobile IP networks.

1 Introduction

Mobile IP networks security has become a primary concern in order to provide protected communication between mobile nodes in a hostile environment. Unlike the wire-line networks, the unique characteristics of mobile IP networks pose a number of nontrivial challenges to security design, such as open peer-to-peer network architecture, shared wireless medium, stringent resource constraints, and highly dynamic network topology. These challenges clearly make a case for building multi-fence security solutions that achieve both broad protection and desirable network performance.

The unreliability of wireless links between nodes, constantly changing topology due to the movement of nodes in and out of the networks, and lack of incorporation of security features in statically configured wireless routing protocols not meant for wireless Internet environments all lead to increased vulnerability and exposure to attacks. Security in mobile IP networks is particularly difficult to achieve, notably because of the limited physical protection of each node, the sporadic nature of connectivity, the absence of a certification authority, and the lack of a centralized monitoring or management unit.

The draft for the IEEE 802.11 security architecture recommends that this authentication process be completed using Extensible authentication Protocol-Transparent Layer Security (EAP-TLS), which has been included as the default authentication method in Window XP. Unfortunately, a complete EAP-TLS handshake, including RADIUS messages, requires on the order if 1 s -a number far too large to support ant form of streaming media. To answer this question, the IEEE included "Preauthentication" in the draft, which permits a mobile station to "per-authenticate" itself to the next AP. Unfortunately, pre-authentication has several shortcomings. First, a station can only pre-authenticate to another Access Point (AP) on the same LAN (i.e., the station cannot authenticate beyond the first access router as a single administrative domain might have multiple access routers). Second, a full EAP-TLS authentication

G. Min et al. (Eds.): ISPA 2006 Ws, LNCS 4331, pp. 949–954, 2006.

to all potential next APs is not a scalable solution in terms of the number of stations and the APs as most networks use a centralized authentication server (RADIUS) that can quickly become a bottleneck. This obviously prevents WiFi networks from reaching much of the previously discussed vision.

The above considerations raise the issue of how to better secure mobile IP networks. This will be as critical as securing fixed-line Internet systems in the emerging markets as highlighted above. Each of these security breaches and associate risks can be minimized or negated with the proper use of security policy and practices, network design, system security applications, and the correct configuration of security controls. In this paper we propose system that diagnoses security vulnerability in mobile IP networks.

2   Vulnerabilities in Mobile IP Networks

There are various reasons why wireless Internet networks are at risk, from a security point of view. In traditional wireless networks, mobile devices associate themselves with an access point, which is in turn connected to other wire-line machinery such as a gateway or name server that manages the network management functions. Wireless Internet networks, on the other hand, do not have a centralized piece of machinery such as a name server, which if present as a single node can be a single point of failure. The absence of infrastructure and the subsequent absence of authorization facilities impede the usual practice of establishing a line of defense, distinguishing nodes as trusted and non-trusted. There may be no ground for an a priori classification, since all nodes are required to cooperate in supporting the network operation, while no prior Security Association (SA) can be assumed for all the network nodes. Freely roaming nodes form transient associations with their neighbors, joining and leaving sub-domains independently with and without notice.

An additional problem related to the compromised nodes is the potential Byzantine failures encountered within wireless Internet networks routing protocols where in a set of nodes could be compromised in such a way that incorrect and malicious behavior cannot be directly noted at all. Such malicious nodes can also create new routing messages and advertise nonexistent links, provide incorrect link state information, and flood other nodes with routing traffic, thus inflicting Byzantine failures on the system.

The wireless links between nodes are highly susceptible to link attacks, which include passive eavesdropping, active interfering, leakage of secret information, data tampering, impersonation, message replay, message distortion, and Denial of Service (DoS). Eavesdropping might give an adversary access to secret information, violating confidentiality. Active attacks might allow the adversary to delete messages, inject erroneous messages, modify messages, and impersonate a node, thus violating availability, integrity, authentication, and non-repudiation.

The presence of even a small number of adversarial nodes could result in repeatedly compromised routes; as a result, the network nodes would have to rely on cycles of timeout and new route discoveries to communicate. This would incur arbitrary delays before the establishment of a non-corrupted path, while successive broadcasts of route requests would impose excessive transmission overhead. In particular, intentionally falsified routing messages would result in DoS experienced by the end nodes.

Moreover, the battery-powered operation of mobile IP networks gives attackers ample opportunity to launch a DoS attack by creating additional transmissions or expensive computations to be carried out by a node in an attempt to exhaust its batteries.

Attacks against wireless Internet network's can be divided into two groups: Passive attacks typically involve only eavesdropping of data whereas active attacks involve actions performed by adversaries, for instance the replication, modification and deletion of exchanged data. External attacks are typically active attacks that are targeted to prevent services from working properly or shut them down completely. Intrusion prevention measures like encryption and authentication can only prevent external nodes from disrupting traffic, but can do little when compromised nodes internal to the network begin to disrupt traffic. Internal attacks are typically more severe attacks, since malicious insider nodes already belong to the network as an authorized party and are thus protected with the security mechanisms the network and its services offer. Thus, such compromised nodes, which may even operate in a group, may use the standard security means to actually protect their attacks.

The above discussion makes it clear that mobile IP networks are inherently insecure, more so than their wired counterparts, and need vulnerability diagnosis schemes before it is too late to counter an attack. If there are attacks on a system, one would like to detect them as soon as possible (ideally in real time) and take appropriate action.

3 Design of Vulnerability Diagnosis Systems

Vulnerability diagnosis systems extend to previous vulnerability diagnosis tool so that this system diagnose wireless networks as possible, and to vulnerability between mobile hosts and APs. After diagnosis to vulnerability, mobile host transmit diagnosis results to vulnerability diagnosis manager while connecting on online state. This vulnerability diagnosis follow as: (1) ESSID broadcasting, (2) Open connection authentication, (3)Vulnerability diagnosis of useless WEP, (4) WEP Key generation using RC4 algorithm vulnerability, (5)Vulnerability diagnosis through challenge-response pair collection, and (6)Possibility of attack between wireless clients in Fig. 2.

(1) ESSID broadcasting:

Mobile host must know ESSID of AP for connecting AP. All most AP open to Ap name and ESSID doesn't broadcast. But current security production broadcasts ESSID. AP decides to ESSID broadcasting through the active proving.

(2) Open connection Authentication:

Open connection authentication is method that doesn't use authentication to connect mobile host to AP and obtain mode to use connection authentication through the active proving. This authentication approve of access authority to mobile host, and can do easily packet sniffing.

(3) Vulnerability diagnosis of useless WEP:

If mobile host makes useless of WEP encrypted key, vulnerability diagnosis provides attacker with plain text, user ID, and password through packet collections without hacking in wireless networks. ESSID that obtain from active proving may penetrate to network through opened AP profile, and is be collected to attacker all

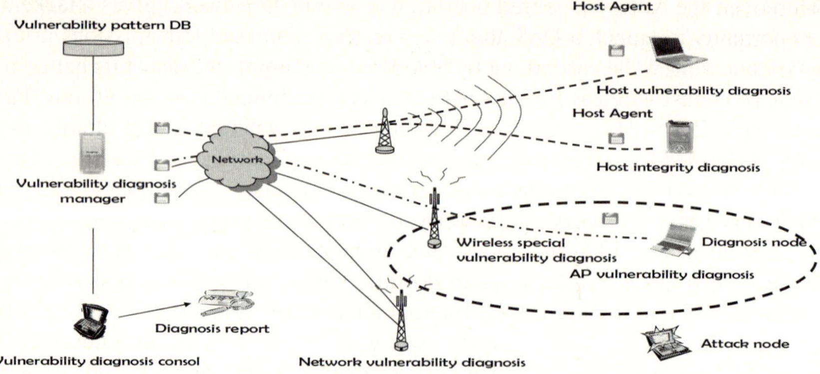

Fig. 1. Vulnerability diagnosis configuration

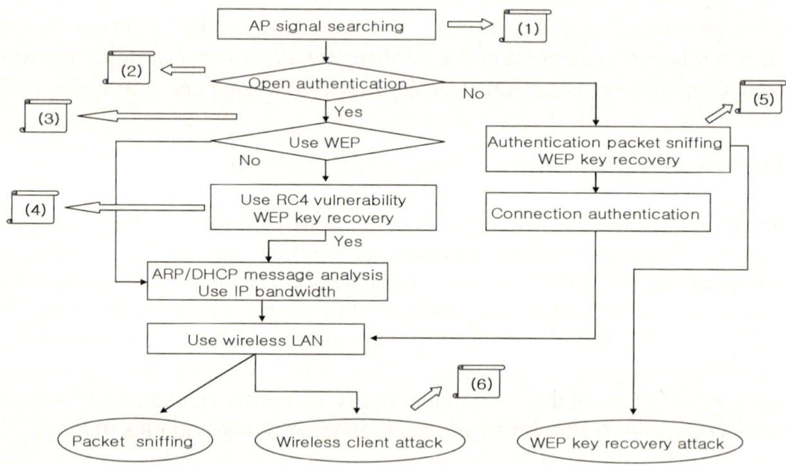

Fig. 2. Procedure of vulnerability diagnosis

messages which transmit on wireless networks. Also, it provides attacker with mobile host's information that has been made use of wireless Internet networks. We will know to use of WEP key considering active proving method to make use of obtaining ESSID broadcasting AP profile and when it approach to AP, it may obtain to WEP key using RC4 algorithm vulnerability through packet collections.

(4) WEP Key generation using RC4 algorithm vulnerability:

WEP key make use of method that seek to analyze through packet collection using powerful PC or Notebook PC. WEP key encryption is based on RC4 stream encrypting algorithm, and test to decryption environment beyond characteristic condition

(5) Vulnerability diagnosis through challenge-response pair collection:

It is security vulnerability to show from authentication method through public key. Vulnerability diagnosis that approaches through challenge-response pair collection collect challenge value that request challenge continuously to AP and response value that encrypted to public key, and when it processes challenge-response using same random numbers, it makes possible response immediately and generation of WEP key using generating packets in initial authentication

In implement environment, proposed system develops vulnerability diagnosis of wireless Internet networks to use easily, and makes use of IPAQ5550 with PDA package including wireless Internet functions which can easily show in popular environment. Also, we use development tool with Microsoft Visual Studio .NET 2003 Professional, Microsoft .NET Compact Framework 1.1 Library, and Microsoft PocketPC 2003 SDK, running HP iPAQ5550 with IEEE 802.11b wireless interface.

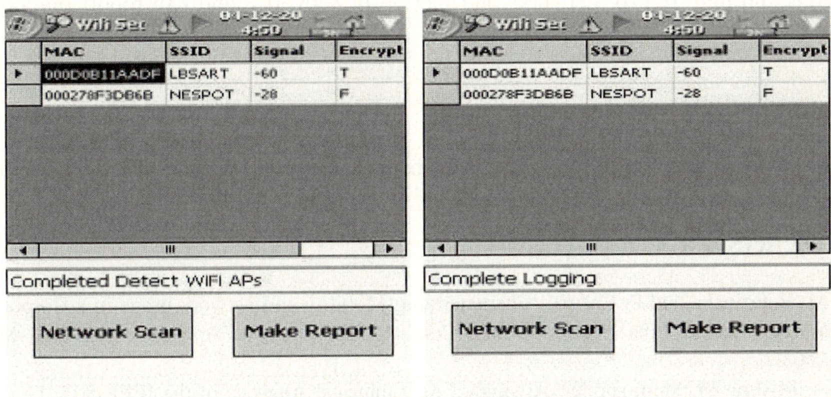

Fig. 3. Screen after scanning network   **Fig. 4.** Screen after making report

In Fig.3, initial execution screen consist of button of making report, upper part of printing data, and button of process scan instruction, and middle text box output to current state. After processing network scan, scan test is discovered two APs, and when it process connection test about each AP, scan test is completed.

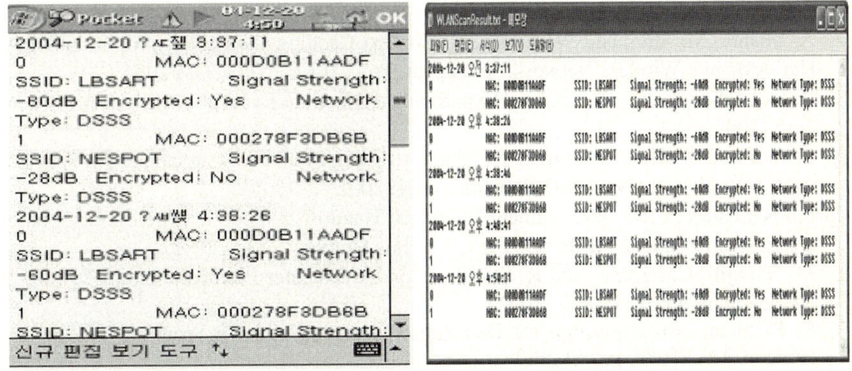

Fig. 5. Screen of report file   **Fig. 6.** Generated report file

Fig. 6 shows report file that processed diagnosis result. In report file, make report instruction process instruction that outputs diagnosis result as report file, and it write down test time and current state situation. In diagnosis result, this shows vulnerability in mobile IP networks.

4 Conclusion

The paper is to interpret the communication network related to security vulnerability reporting process, and focuses on how the information of the vulnerability is received and processed and how the information is managed after the reception in wireless Internet networks. The proposed system can diagnose vulnerability patterns that can generate through TCP/IP networks and mobile IP networks, and can report diagnosis result to network manager rapidly.

Acknowledgement

This work was supported by a fund from Howon University, 2006.

References

1. M. Balazinska and P. Castro, "Characterizing Mobility and network usage in a Corporate Wireless Local Area Network, "Int'l. Conf. Mobile Systems, Apps, and Services, May 2003.
2. A. Mishra, M. Shin, and W. Arbaugh, "An Empirical Analysis of the IEEE 802. 11 Mac Layer Handoff Process, "ACM SIGCOMM Comp. Commun. Rev., vol. 33, Apr. 2003.
3. R. Koodli and C. Perkins, "Fast Handover and context Relocation in Mobile Networks, "ACM SIGCOMM Comp. Commun. Rev., vol. 31, Oct. 2001.
4. IEEE Std. P802. 1X, "Standards for Local and Metropolitan Area Networks: Standard for Port Based Network Access Control," Oct. 2001.
5. J. Edney and W. A. Arbaugh, Real 802.11 Security, Addison Wesley, 2003.
6. IEEE Std. 802.11i, "Draft Amendment to Standard for Telecommunications and Information Exchange between Systems-lan/man Specific Requirements, Part11: Wireless Medium Access Control and Physical Layer(phy) Specifications: MAC Security Enhancements.," May 2003.
7. A. Mishra, M. Shin, and W. Arbaugh, "Context Caching Using Neighbor Graphs for Fast Haridoffs in a Wireless Network," to appear, Proc. IEEE INFOCOM 2004.
8. W. A. Arbaugh and B. Aboba, "Experimental Handoff Extension to RADIUS," Internet draft, 2003.
9. S. Pack and Y. Choi, "Fast Inter-AP Handoff Using Predictive-Authentication Scheme in a Public Wireless LAN," IEEE Networks, Aug. 2002.
10. S. Pack and Y. Choi, "Pre-Authenticated Fast Handoff in a public Wireless LAN based on IEEE 802. 1x Model," IFIP TC6 Pers. Wireless Commun., Oct. 2002.
11. M. Nakhjiri, C. Perkins, and R. Koodli, "Context Transfer Protocol," Internet Draft: draft-ietf-seamoby-ctp01.txt, Mar. 2003.
12. R. Perlman, "An Algorithm for Distributed Computation of a Spanning Tree in an Extended LAN," 1985, pp. 44-53.
13. R. Perlman, Interconnections, 2nd Edition: Bridges, Routers, Switches and Internetworking Protocols, Pearson Education, Sept. 1999.

Virtual Telematics Systems for Distributing Nationwide Real-Time Traffic Information

Bong Gyou Lee

Graduate School of Information, Yonsei University, Seoul, Korea
`bglee@yonsei.ac.kr`

Abstract. This paper is to present why and how to build a virtual Telematics systems. Diverse traffic data are collected, managed and distributed mainly by government agencies. These agencies, however, have their own unique aims, functions, standards and policies with regard to Intelligent Transportation System (ITS) centers for managing and controlling their own transport systems. It becomes obstacles and barriers to overcome for distributing nationwide real-time traffic information. Thanks to the advances of information security and digital convergence technologies, the virtual systems become stable and secure. In this paper we have developed the virtual Telematics systems that can serve as a guideline for other virtual systems.

1 Introduction

The enormous amount of diverse traffic data in Korea is treated and managed mainly by government agencies. Most of these agencies apply their own unique set of standards and policies in collecting, managing and supplying traffic data, to increase the efficiency of the management and control of the transport systems within their ITS centers. Moreover, the various system architectures, including DB, applications, network, hardware and software for each respective ITS center have been partially integrated on an internal level, but a nationwide integration has not yet been achieved. As a result, services for providing real-time traffic information cannot expand across the country, and only a few, limited types of traffic data can be distributed to general users. From a realistic viewpoint, the physical establishment of a fully integrated ITS or Telematics center will require huge amounts of capital and time to develop; there are also other difficulties in building the architecture equipments, such as the hardware, software and network, or employing specialized manpower.

This paper is to present how to build a stable and secure virtual center. The virtual Telemactics center in this study can distribute value-added information including Location-based Services (LBS) and the nationwide real-time traffic information collected from the dispersed ITS centers.

2 Limitations of Existing ITS Centers

Major ITS centers in Korea are operated or supported by government agencies including the Ministry of Construction and Transportation (MOCT), the Korea National Police Agency (KNPA), and the Ministry of Information and Communication (MIC).

G. Min et al. (Eds.): ISPA 2006 Ws, LNCS 4331, pp. 955–963, 2006.

The ITS Center of MOCT collects diverse traffic data including accident information at constant time intervals through associated agencies. These agencies are the Korea Institute of Construction Technology (KICT), the Korea Highway Corporation, Seoul Metropolitan Traffic Broadcasting Service and most local governments. The center also provides specific traffic information via diverse media including the Internet, broadcasting and Variable Message Signs (VMS). However, the center has been built mainly for managing the systems of highway and local expressway by connecting its affiliated agencies. As shown in Fig. 1, most of the collected data are used primarily for management and control purposes, and only a limited portion of traffic data can be provided to private corporations and public users.

The KNPA has managed and controlled nationwide traffic signals and their systems. It also has been in charge of CCTV for monitoring traffic conditions. The KNPA has largely distributed a portion of CCTV traffic information via broadcasting and the Internet.

The Telematics Information Center (TELIC) established by the MIC has been gathering traffic information from other ITS centers. Unlike other ITS centers, the TELIC does not have its own data collection systems including CCTV, roof and infrared detection. It only concentrates on distributing traffic information to Telematics Service Providers (TSP) as well as users of Telmatics services.

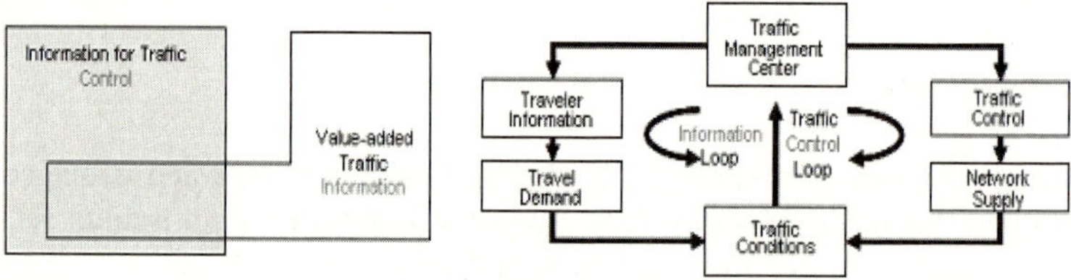

Fig. 1. Usages of traffic data in existing ITS centers

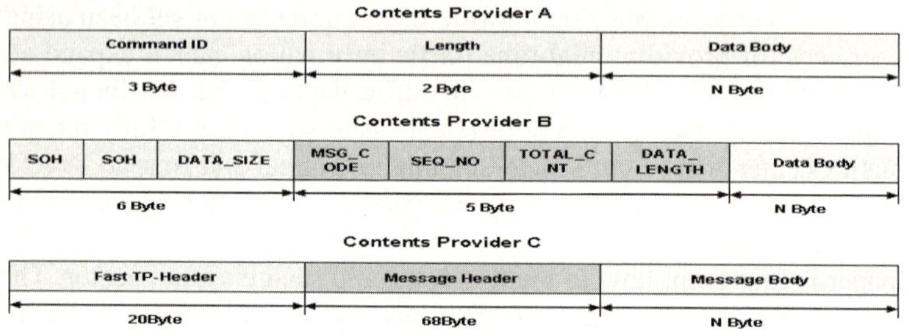

Fig. 2. Examples of receiving message sets in TELIC

Gathering and integrating various traffic data from diverse sources with different standards and formats are extremely complicated and become important issues to distribute real-time traffic information. Most ITS centers have several restrictions for providing real-time traffic information in terms of traffic data formats, data exchange standards and node-link ID structures. That is, like the cases of many other countries, current ITS centers in Korea still have employed different data exchange standards among others, as shown in Fig. 2. Also, in the case of the node-link system, the Center of the MOCT uses the standard of 10-digit node-link ID structure, but other centers employ their own distinctive standards. In other words, taking the number of digits in the current node-link ID format, the MOCT's 10-digit node-link system is used as the standard. Nevertheless, the TELIC uses 8 digits for its node ID and 9 digits for its link ID, while KNPA's Center operates 8 digits for the node ID, and 13 digits for the link.

3   Building the Virtual Telematics Center

3.1   Relationship Between Telematics and ITS

Figure 3 presents the relationship between Telematics and ITS in terms of services, core technologies and international standards. Thanks to the advances of information security and digital convergence technologies, most obstacles and barriers to provide Telematics service can be overcome.

Since the traffic data depended on types of traffic detections include text, audio and video formats, the existing ITS centers have used divergent application software, middleware, DBMS and GIS tools. To share and distribute traffic data efficiently, the Telematics center should have the data standard with regard to data dictionary, data registry, data type, data structure, data element, and so on.

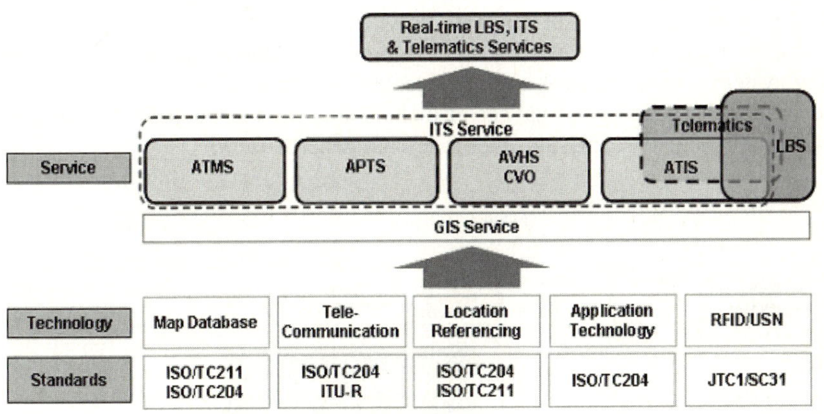

Fig. 3. The relationship between Telematics and ITS

In order to solve the problems of different node-link systems, a matching table must be utilized to initialize the node-link data of other agencies so that it can be compatible with the standard MOCT node-link ID system. An initialized data refers to a matching table that converts link information provided by the KNPA for the Seoul metropolitan area into the standard node format of the MOCT, and the standard link format of the MIC.

958   B.G. Lee

Also, to exchange traffic data effectively, the Telematics center should take the standards for data dictionary, communication protocol, and message sets for semantics and syntax. There are several national and international ITS standards such as "Data Dictionaries for ITS," "Message Set Template for ITS," "On-board Land Vehicle Mayday Reporting Interfaces," "Data Dictionaries for Advanced Traveler Information Systems (ATIS)," and "Message Sets for ATIS."

3.2 Conceptual Framework of the Virtual Center

Establishing another comprehensive ITS or Telematics center to integrate the current ITS centers that are physically apart, obviously incurs huge economic opportunity costs and carries the risk of a redundant investment. Moreover, even if such a comprehensive center is established, expanding the ubiquitous mobile information service nationally cannot be achieved in a short period.

The virtual Telematics center will be operated through linked servers within the system of each of the three agencies, the MOCT, MIC, and KNPA. The purpose of building the virtual center is to make distributed application programs and interoperable ITS/Telematics systems. Using a standardized format, the virtual center integrates traffic and road information collected and possessed separately by public and private sectors. The center manipulates collected traffic data to nationwide real-time traffic information and stores as useful DB. It also distributes the information to government agencies, private Telematics Service Providers (TSP) and general users.

Figure 4 depicts the conceptual framework of the virtual center as a business model. The core-value chain in this framework is the process of integrating and processing the data collected from Contents Providers (CP), then providing the standardized traffic information to TSP. Also, a supportive value chain with regard to the billing system, system control and management is required as a foundation. Participants in the scheme of the virtual center include not only the CP and TSP, but also the relevant public agencies, private enterprises and general users.

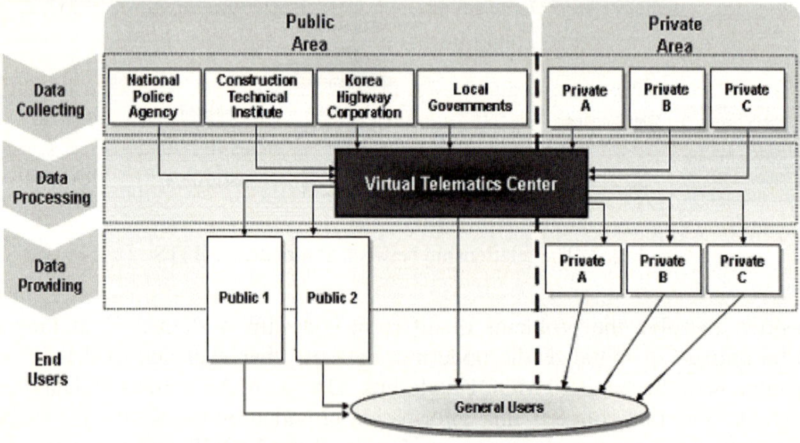

Fig. 4. The conceptual framework of the Virtual Center

3.3 Architecture Flow

The virtual Telematics center does not need a physical alteration of the existing ITS centers' architectures and organizations, and only requires the installation of networks and equipments needed for the integration of traffic information, and the basic operating manpower. It also involves minimal cooperation among the relevant agencies concerning issues of billing, standardization, division of profits, and other business-related issues.

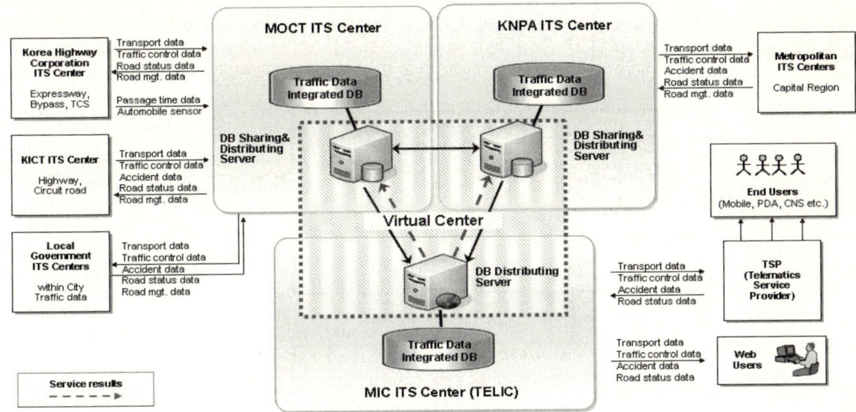

Fig. 5. Architecture flow of the virtual center

Fig. 5 illustrates the architecture flow in the virtual center. The virtual center architecture is essentially a service-oriented, so it enables a step-wise expansion. Thereby the provision of real-time traffic information services, which was previously available to a limited region in the nation, can be extended from the Seoul metropolitan area to the whole nation, and the general user can be expanded in phases.

3.3.1 Data Flow and Data Exchange Standard

Within the three ITS centers of the virtual Telematics center, some traffic data such as accident, vehicle speed, volume and occupancy data can be shared. Each center of the virtual center can make the real-time traffic information using shared data with node-link digital maps and the node-link matching table. Also, each and every agency can provide the information to TSP and general users.

The matching table automatically converts traffic data, from other centers that do not conform to the standard node-link ID system, into the standard node-link traffic information. The information can be searched within the integrated DB server of each agency through various types of EAI adaptors, and will be transferred to, and stored in, other agencies' integrated DB servers. Fig. 6 depicts data flow and the EAI adaptors installed in each agency's systems, the node-link server, the DB server and TCP/IP as a communication protocol.

In order to integrate and exchange traffic data effectively, the virtual center should have the formal standards including data exchange standard, the ASN.1 (Abstract Syntax Notation One) input standard and the standard of node-link ID system.

The virtual Telematics center adopts 'Technology Standard in Basic Traffic Information Exchange' and the ASN.1 input standard. Also, it follows the TELIC node-link ID system that uses 8 digits for its node ID and 9 digits for its link ID. Because the TELIC focus on providing real-time traffic information and has more distributed application programs and interoperable systems compared with other agencies.

The node-link mapping table enables the virtual center to integrate and exchange traffic data based on the node-link ID system. Typical examples of matching schemes are selecting one link that can be considered as the most representative of all, and then matching on a 1:1 basis, or ratio-matching. The latter can be seen as a 1:M matching scheme, as it gives different weights to all targeted links, shown in Fig. 7. Both schemes are based on a readily scalable link distance.

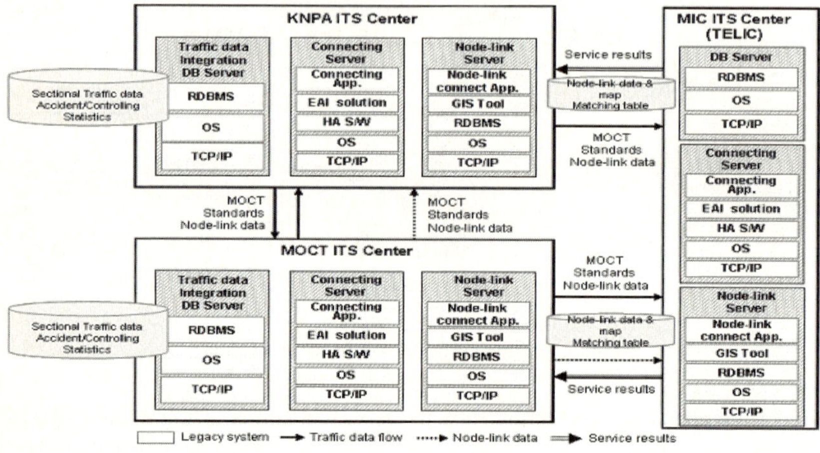

Fig. 6. Data flow and communication protocol in the Virtual Center

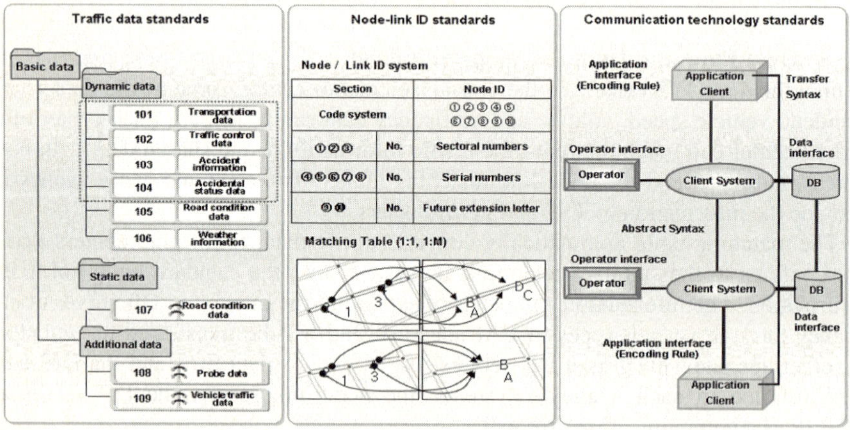

Fig. 7. Standards for the Virtual Telematics Center

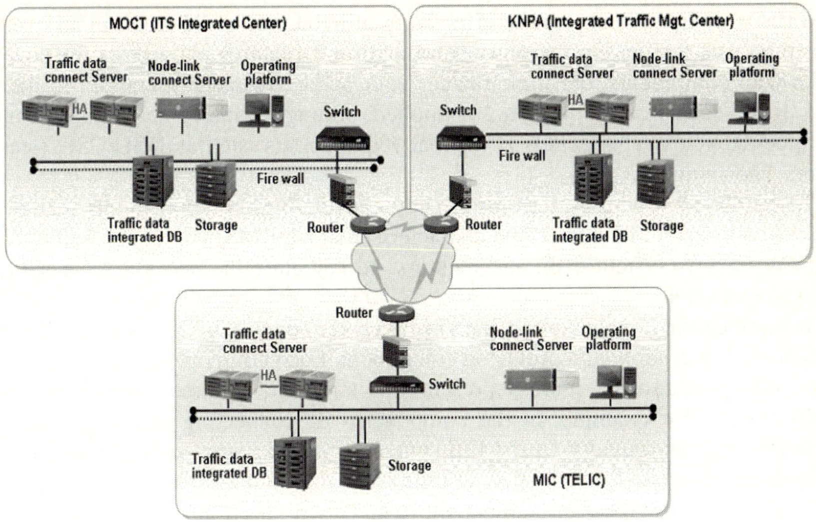

Fig. 8. Hardware and network architecture

3.3.2 Hardware/network/application Architecture

Fig. 8 shows the architecture of hardware and network in the virtual center. The networks of the virtual center can be built either by connecting to a pre-existing network (option 1), or by building a new, exclusive line (option 2). For option 1, existing

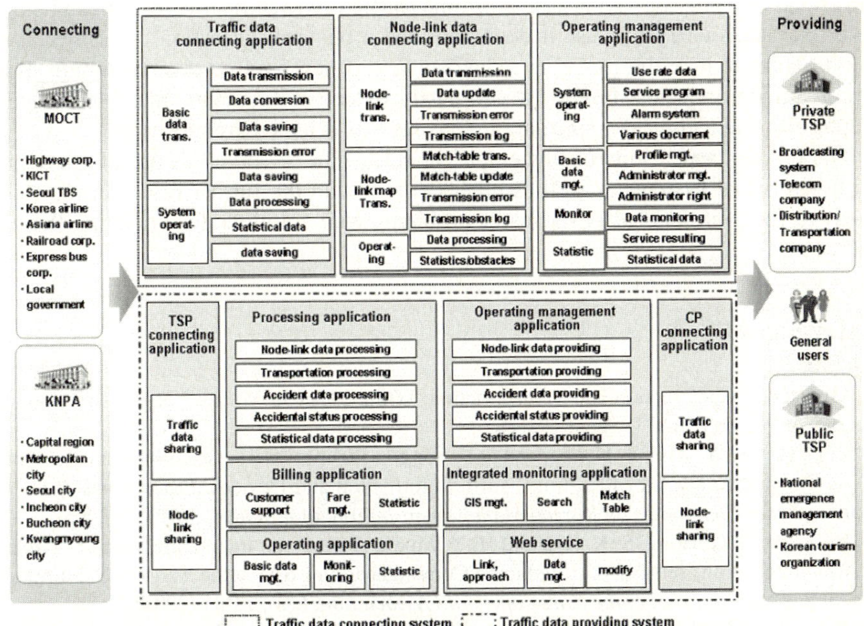

Fig. 9. Application architecture of the Virtual Center

networks with equipments can be effectively utilized, but could result in an overload in security and traffic. On the other hand, option 2 requires extra costs for new networks with equipments, but it guarantees easy and convenient operation. In the first stage of the virtual center, option 2 is applied, adding exclusive networks to connect the three agencies. This entails additional requirements such as DSU/CSU (leased), routers, and switches.

The hardware structures are designed by considering the applications included in the servers of each ITS center, the characteristics of DBMS, and equipments such as CPU, disk array, system disk, and memory, to calculate the necessary capacity and appropriate model.

The application architecture of the virtual center consists of three parts in terms of connecting, integration, and provision component. Each component is composed of its set of sub-applications. Figure 9 presents the structure of three components of the virtual center. For example, in the components of connecting and integration, the traffic information provided by the ITS centers of each agency are integrated into one set, and the integrated information is uniformly distributed to the end users by the applications of the provision component, which is a single information distribution system.

4 Conclusion

This paper addresses the necessity and significant factors of building a virtual Telematics center based on information security systems. Compared to existing ITS centers, the interoperable virtual center has the following several advantages. First, it can effectively provide nationwide real-time traffic information. Second, it can help to save time and money because it does not need a physical alteration or construction. Third, it can reduce the risk of a redundant investment and involve minimum manpower among agencies. Fourth, it can easily extend its contents and services geographically and technically since it employs service-oriented architectures.

The process and results of this empirical study can be served as useful guidelines for other virtual systems as well as other countries. In the further research, the study needs to find out detailed obstacles or problems with solutions for operating the virtual center.

References

1. Ministry of Construction and Transportation, White Paper in Ministry of Construction and Transportation (MOCT, Seoul, 2004).
2. B. G. Lee, K. Y. Kim, T. H. Lee, and J. Y. Song, u-Business Strategies for Telematics based on Demand Analysis of Real-time Traffic Information and Devices, *Proceedings of the International Conference on Korean Management Information System*, 367-370 (2005).
3. B. G. Lee, I. G. Hong, S .K. Ryu and H. Y. Moon, A Study on Integrating Wire & Wireless Communication Networks for Reducing Communication Costs in the National ITS Physical Architecture, *Journal of the Korea open GIS Association*, 6(2), 77-84 (2004).
4. Y. K. Kim, GIS/LBS/Traffic Information Technology, *TTA Journal* 89, 99-104 (2003).

5. Korea Research Institute for Human Settlements, ITS Node-link System, Standardization and Operation Guideline (KRIHS, Seoul, 2005).
6. National Computerization Agency, A Study on Reinforcing ITS Communication Architecture, (NCA, Seoul, 2001).
7. U.S. Department of Transportation, National ITS Architecture: version 5.1 (December 14, 2005); http://www.its.dot.gov/arch.
8. ASN. 1 Information Site (May 3, 2005); http://asn1.elibel.tm.fr.
9. Transport Canada, ITS Architecture for Canada (May 13, 2005); http://www.its-sti.gc.ca.

Scope of Forensics in Grid Computing – Vision and Perspectives*

Syed Naqvi[1], Philippe Massonet[1], and Alvaro Arenas[2]

[1] Centre of Excellence in Information and Communication Technologies (CETIC), Belgium
`{syed.naqvi, philippe.massonet}@cetic.be`
[2] CCLRC Rutherford Appleton Laboratory, United Kingdom
`a.e.arenas@rl.ac.uk`

Abstract. Along with the evolution of Grid technology, the need to protect its resources from malicious activities is becoming more and more important. While robust security architecture provides deterrence, there never be a perfect security mechanism. The Grid security teams must be able to tackle the postattack situation and should be able to read the black-box of the events that led to the failure of the security architecture. Moreover, they should be able to collect the fingerprints of the culprits behind the attack so that necessary legal and judicial actions could be taken. It is only possible when the specific nature of the Grid is kept in mind while developing its forensics techniques. Grid is anewer paradigm and still lacks a number of security features. There is no other work in our knowledge that addresses forensics issues of the grid. This vacuum has overwhelmingly motivated us to take some initiative to fill this gap.

Indexterms: Grid security, forensics techniques, return of security investment.

1 Introduction

The term Forensics is defined in the American Heritage Dictionary as the use of science and technology to investigate and establish facts in criminal or civil courts of law. In the computer world forensics implies using evidence remaining after an attack on a computer to determine how the attack was carried out and what the attacker did [1]. The vast majority of these threats are possible because of the internet. This connection of computers all over the world has brought with it many remotely exploitable threats (e.g. denial of service attacks) [2]. In a networked system, once an attack has succeeded, the attacker generally has complete access to the attacked system. A wily hacker can then remove evidence of the attack making it very difficult to determine what has happened.

The complexity of forensics in the networked systems is further exacerbated by its ever increasing scale with computing resources spread over the diverse administrative and geopolitical domains. The emerging field of Grid computing [3], which intends to

---

* His research work is supported by the European Network of Excellence CoreGRID (project reference number 004265). The network aims at strengthening and advancing scientific and technological excellence in the area of Grid and Peer-to-Peer technologies. The CoreGRID webpage is located at www.coregrid.net.

aggregate all kinds of heterogeneous resources that are geographically distributed, not only requires in-depth security services to protect its resources and data but also entails suitable forensics techniques that can be employed to assess the responsibility of the wrongdoers. Security teams still lack the experience of Grid forensics as being a comparatively newer technology; it has not yet faced any crucial security breach. This is all about to change. The number of people who know about the grid is growing fast as are the worthwhile targets for the potential attackers. This situation makes it imperative that efforts be exerted to explore the scope of forensics in advancing the state of Grid security. This article presents the vision of authors about the Grid forensics and its perspectives.

This article is organized in the following manner: an overview of some forensics techniques in the networked systems is presented in section 2. A forensics lifecycle model is described in section 3. Section 4 briefs the role of honeypots in Grid forensics. Grid forensics is explored in the section 5. A discussion of forensics versus return of security investment is made in section 6. Finally some conclusions are drawn along with our future directions in the section 7.

2   Related Work

2.1   Routing Registry System

There is no existing work that applies forensics in the Grid environments. However, a recent work on distributed forensics [4] describes the two related issues: one is about the attack attribution techniques; the other is about different types of Intruder Detection Systems.

One important type of attribution techniques has been studied is stepping stone correlation based on timing information. In [5-6] several stepping stone correlation methods are discussed. [5] presents the correlation of ON/OFF periods of interactive packets. It is robust to retransmission but not effective to non-interactive traffic and packets with random delay, reorder and chaff. [6] gives active watermark tracing method by actively add watermark into the flows by manipulating inter-packet delays. It can deal with the packets random delay problem. But when the delay is too large and causes packets reorder, or when chaff added, it becomes ineffective.

Another studied attack attribution techniques are IP trace-back and packet marking.

In [7], a Source Path Isolation Engine (SPIE) was developed to do IP trace-back and the Bloom Filter was used as the data storage mechanism. In [8], based on the topology of Internet, a new deterministic packet marking technique was provided and only total 52 bits would be used for marking the whole path.

At the same time, Intrusion Detection Systems (IDS) have been studied extensively over the past few years and the mainstream of work can be categorized into two groups [9], misuse detection and anomaly detection systems. Misuse detection is signature-based methods relying on a specific signature of an intrusion, which triggers an alarm after being found. Such systems cannot detect novel attacks because only known attacks have signature available. On the other hand, anomaly detection systems [10] rely on characterizing normal operations of a network or a host, and attempt to detect significant deviations from the norm to trigger an alarm. Although anomaly detection systems can detect novel attacks to a certain extent, they are difficult to be practical due to the so high false alarms. One solution [11] is to combine signature based systems and anomaly detection systems that can decrease false alarm rates. In this system, currently we use a lightweight IDS, called snort [12] as part of our integrated system as the data filter to find out the attack related data in the network traffic. Snort is a versatile, lightweight and very useful intrusion detection system. It can be used as a straight packet sniffer, a packet logger and a full-blown network intrusion detection system. The drawback here is that snort is still a misuse detection system and it cannot find novel attacks. We need enhance this function in the future.

3   Forensics Lifecycle Model

The first step towards the efficient forensics practice is the recognition of a forensics lifecycle [13]. Digital forensics not only has technical issues but is also a managerial problem. We follow the generic seven stages forensic lifecycle model presented in [14]. This model is shown in Figure 1.

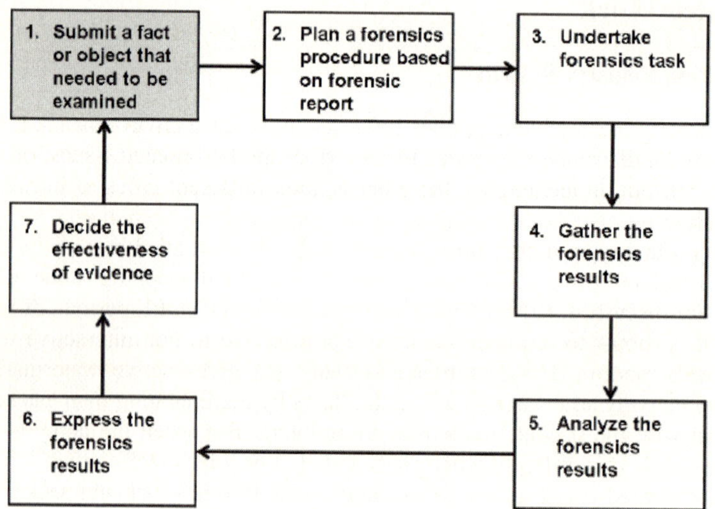

Fig. 1. Generic Forensics Lifecycle Model

The first block of this model is the initialization of the forensics process as well as the re-examination of the previous evidence due to the discovery of new evidences.

This step follows planning of a forensics procedure for producing a legally admissible report. Based on this plan, forensics process in carried out. A general forensics case can be divided into five stages: evidence identification, analysis, verification, individualization, and crime scene reconstruction. Then individual facts or objects are gathered and categorized as one entity where possible. This step eases the analysis of these facts or objects. The analysis is carried out according to the evidence. The result of this analysis constitutes forensics results which are compiled as a forensics report.

This compilation should follow a legally defined procedure and format that is regulated by a court of law. Give an authoritative evaluation of the evidence. The seven stage lifecycle model helps not only to arrange forensics processes but to determine the facilities of a forensics unit of the security team.

The application of this generic model in the Grid environments requires exact determination of the security metrics. Security metrics of the BUGYO project [15] identified in [16] can be employed in the Grid environments.

4   Role of Honeypots in Grid Forensics

Honeypots are computer systems, setup as a trap, which are used to collect data on intruders [17]. The concept of a Honeypot is to learn from the intruder's actions. This knowledge can now be used to prevent attacks on the real, or production systems, as well as diverting the resources of the attacker to a the trap system. If the Honey Pot works as intended, how the intruder probes and exploits the system can now be assessed without detection. This trap appears to contain operating system vulnerabilities that make it an attractive target for hackers. A Honeypot, loaded with fake information, appears to the hacker to be a legitimate machine. While it appears vulnerable to attack, it actually prevents access to valuable data, administrative controls and other computers. Deception defenses can add an unrecognizable layer of protection. There exists a distributed honeypot model for grid computing system security [18]; however, this model is implemented as an intrusion detection system rather than a tool for carryout forensics. Once catched in a honeypot, a considerable amount of malicious entity's information maybe obtained. It includes network information, system activity information, etc. The role of honeypot in forensics is to identify these fingerprints as part of the evidence gathering process.

5   Grid Forensics

Grid specific security requirements [19] should be considered while developing its forensics techniques. Major factors to be considered in the Grid environments are scalability and diverse administrative domains. Besides, there are some other peculiar security requirements of the Grid-based systems which are generally overlooked by the designers. An ideal Grid forensics technique should be able to trace the breach of these Grid-specific security requirements. Their brief description is given in this section.

5.1   Resilience

Resilience is an important requirement as the grid links and nodes are very dynamic in nature and may change over the time. The GDMS security architecture should remain intact and should deliver the promised level of security assurances even if its composition changes over the time. The resilience provides an abstraction layer to hide the architectural changes from the overall security architecture.

5.2 Data Lifecycle Management (DLM)

DLM is the process of managing data throughout its lifecycle from conception until disposal across different storage media, within the constraints of the entire process. The lifecycle is the time from the moment data is created until it is deleted or stored indefinitely. Security assurances require spanning the entire lifecycle of data. GDMS should ensure that the data contents will be protected from the malevolent entities throughout its lifecycle.

5.3 Fault Tolerance

Fault tolerance is a desirable feature especially when transfers of large data files occur. Protocols such as GridFTP [20] allow for resuming transfers from the last byte acknowledged. Overlay networks provide caching of transfers via store-and-forward protocols. However, caching reduces performance of the overall data transfer and the amount of data that can be cached is dependent on the storage policies at the intermediate network points.

5.4 Service Level Agreement (SLA)

SLA is any type of management vehicle between a service provider and a customer that specifies performance requirements, measures, reporting, cost, and recourse. In the context of GDMS security, SLA defines how data is protected while in transit over the service.

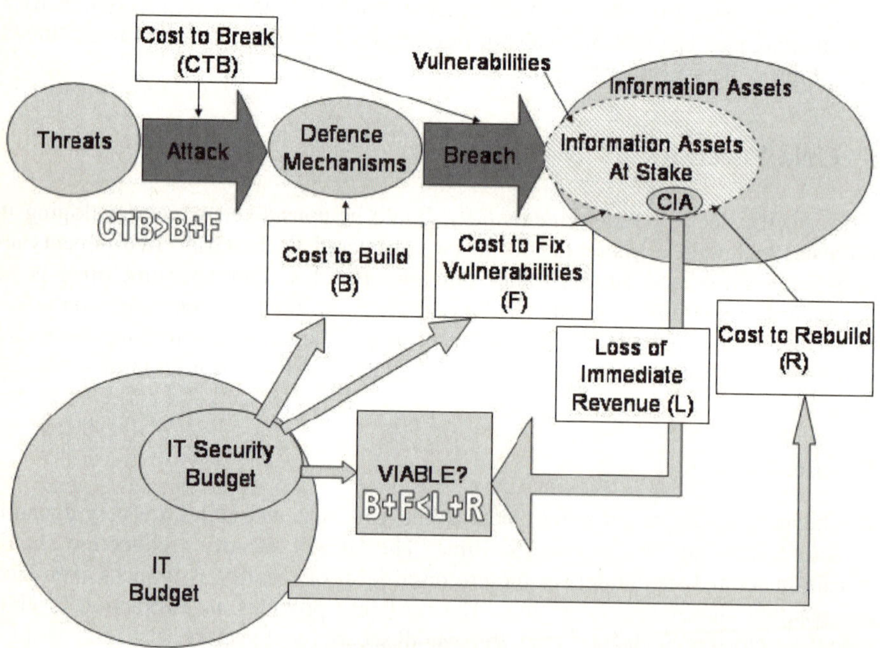

Fig. 2. Viability of an Information Security Investment

5.5 Security Negotiations

Security negotiations are used to establish secure session between the endpoints. A security infrastructure featuring support for negotiations and establishment of end-toend and/or hop-to-hop security associations has broader applicability to general networked environments like grids. Security negotiations require some brokering agent to mediate between the endpoints.

6 Forensics and Return on Security Investment (ROSI)

OSI is an important factor for the companies and other stakeholders. An organization should spend substantially less than the expected loss, no more than one third [21]. Figure 2 depicts the model of to find the viability of an information security program. The methodology strikes a balance between under-spending and overspending [22].

Likewise, the Grid forensics tool should be economically viable yet powerful enough to handle the Grid-specific security monitoring requirements.

7 Conclusions and Future Directions

The term Forensics is not a new collection in the technical dictionaries; however, its application in the Grid computing has no precedence. In this paper, we have explored the utility of forensics in the Grid environments especially to detect the breach of Grid specific security requirements. Evolution of best practices and tools for the Grid Forensics is certainly a nontrivial task. Grid's peculiar nature, such as high scale and distribution of resources across various domains, makes it difficult to determine the precise metrics for the security measurements and for the monitoring of security breaches.

We plan to further investigate the scope of forensics in the Grid based systems and based on the findings, we shall work on the development of Grid forensics best practices and their corresponding tools.

References

1. Laurie B., Digital A., Network Forensics, ACM Queue Vol. 2, No. 4 - June 2004
2. Dixon P., An Overview of Computer Forensics, IEEE Potentials Magazine, Volume 24, Issue 5, Dec. 2005 pp 7-10
3. Foster I., Kesselman C., The Grid: Blueprint for a New Computing Infrastructure, Morgan Kaufmann, 1999. ISBN 1558604758
4. Tang Y., Daniels T., A Simple Framework for Distributed Forensics, IEEE International Conference on Distributed Computing Systems 2005, 6-10 June 2005 pp 163-169
5. Zhang Y., Paxson V., Detecting Stepping Stones, USENIX Security Symposium 2000, 14-17 August 2000, Denver, Colorado, USA
6. Wang X. and Reeves D., Robust correlation of encrypted attack traffic through stepping stones by manipulation of interpacket delays, In Proceedings of the 10th ACM Conference on Computer and Communications Security (CCS 2003), Washington DC, USA, Oct. 2003

7. Snoeren A., Single-Packet IP Traceback, In IEEE/ACM Transactions on Networking (ToN), 2 Volume 10, Number 6, December 2002. Pages 721-734

8. Al-Duwairi B., Daniels T., Topology based packet marking, International Conference on Computer Communications and Networks (ICCCN 2004), 11-13 Oct. 2004, pp 146- 151

9. Carter E., Intrusion Detection Systems, Cisco Press, 15 February 2002

10. González F., Gómez J., Kaniganti M., Dasgupta D., An Evolutionary Approach to Generate Fuzzy Anomaly Signatures, IEEE Systems, Man and Cybernetics Society Information Assurance Workshop, June 18-20, 2003, West Point, New York, USA pp 251-259

11. Kaleton I., Combination of Misuse and Anomaly Network Intrusion Detection Systems, March 2002

12. The SNORT Project - http://www.snort.org

13. Naughton T., Advancing the Science of Forensic Data Management, Proceedings of SPIE -

14. Investigative Image Processing II, vol 4709, July 2002, pp. 60-67

15. Chen P., Tsai L., Ying-Chieh C., Yee G., Standardizing the Construction of a Digital Forensics Laboratory, International Workshop on Systematic Approaches to Digital Forensic Engineering 2005, 7-9 Nov. 2005, pp 40-47

16. The Eureka-Celtic Project BUGYO (Building Security Assurance in Open Infrastructures) http://projects.celtic-initiative.org/bugyo

17. Naqvi S., Riguidel M., Quantifiable Security Metrics for Large Scale Heterogeneous Systems, International Carnahan Conference on Security Technology, Lexington, Kentucky, USA, October 16-19, 2006

18. Martin W., Honey Pots and Honey Nets - Security through Deception. SANS Institute Paper, May 25, 2001

19. Yang G., Rong C., Dai Y., A Distributed Honeypot System for Grid Security, Proceeding of the Grid and Cooperative Computing 2003 (GCC2003), Shanghai, China, 2003, pp 1083-1086

20. Naqvi S., Massonet P., Arenas A., Security Requirements Model for Grid Data Management Systems, International Workshop on Critical Information Infrastructures Security 2006 (CRITIS'06), Samos Island, Greece, August 30 - September 2, 2006

21. W. Allcock et al., GridFTP: Protocol extensions to FTP for the Grid, GGF Document Series GFD.20, April 2003

22. Gordon L., Economic Aspects of Information Security in a Netcentric World, SecurE-Biz CxO Security Summit, Washington D.C. USA, 2004

23. Mizzi A., Return on Information Security Investment, January 2005

Modeling Active Cyber Attack for Network Vulnerability Assessment*

Jung-Ho Eom, Young-Ju Han, and Tai-Myoung Chung

Internet Management Technology Laboratory,
Scool of Information and Communication Engineering,
SungKyunKwan University,
300 Cheoncheon-dong, Jangan-gu,
Suwon-si, Gyeonggi-do, 440-746, Republic of Korea
{jheom, yjhan}@imtl.skku.ac.kr, tmchung@ece.skku.ac.kr

Abstract. In this paper, we considered active cyber attack model to assess vulnerability in network system. As we simulate cyber attack model in the network system, we can identify vulnerabilities, and provide appropriate countermeasures against them. Our model consists of two agents, two modules, and action controller on on-line system, and attack damage assessment analyzer on off-line system. We can minimize a detection probability from target system because we applied 'Sensor to Shooter' concept to our model, and separated information collection agent and attack agent for reduce attack action time. One module analyzes target system's information. Another module develops target system and main point of impact, and builds attack scenario consisted of attack tree and attack pattern. Attack action agents execute the set of attack sequence which consists of attack pattern in attack tree's each node. Action controller controls all execution process of our model's elements.

1 Introduction

A cyber attack is an attack on a computer network system. It consists of computer actions such as remote or local connection, computer database access, or program execution with the intent to compromise the secure operation of the network system by logical or technical means. A cyber attack has become a significant threat to organizations with severe consequences. Because we rely increasingly on network system infrastructures to support critical operations in defense, banking, telecommunication and many other systems [1,2].

Traditionally, cyber attack used only the single vulnerability exploited in the attack. In these days, cyber attacks are complex multi-stage attacks that coordinate the effects of various single-point attacks to achieve their goals. And, as cyber attacks has been various and sophisticated, the level of defense required by security experts has raised [3].

---

* This study was supported by a grant of the Korea Health 21 R&D Project, Ministry of Health & Welfare, Republic of Korea(02-PJ3-PG6-EV08-0001).

G. Min et al. (Eds.): ISPA 2006 Ws, LNCS 4331, pp. 971–980, 2006.

We periodically need to check our network system for defense cyber attacks. The best method to check our network system is actually to simulate attack on them. It is to generate the real synthetic network attack events from cyber attack model. As simulating cyber attack model, it is to identify vulnerabilities, and develop defense mechanism. Our research's goal is to develop cyber attack model for check network system effectively, as simulating real attack method by cyber attacker [9,10].

In this paper, we will describe background and related works in section 2 and cyber attack architecture using 'Sensor to Shooter' concept in section 3. We present a modeling cyber attack in section 4, and conclude in the last section.

2   Backgrounds and Related Works

A government, the military and commercial organizations have widely used network and telecommunication, etc for several decades because of their convenience, ease of use, and the high speed of business processing. With this increasing reliance on internet, network systems comes an increasing vulnerability to cyber attacks. Although attacks can range from cyber attack to physical attacks, the most aspect of cyber attack is to disrupt or disable system's functions and resources that support an organization's operations [2,4,6,7].

Traditionally, network system's defense focuses primarily on prevention; putting controls and mechanisms in place that protect confidentiality, integrity, and availability by stopping users from anomaly behaviors. But, as attack techniques have been diverse and sophisticated, prevention is not enough to protect them. So, defense mechanism has been developing to assure defense goals by such mechanism as detection, isolation, reaction, monitoring, and vulnerability analysis.

Defenses are static in the cyber warfare. That is, after the user has configured their defensive plan, the defense mechanisms will not change. But, as the cyber attacker's behavior is dynamic based on the specific strategy, we have to implement active defense mechanisms [7,10].

Most of the research in the cyber attack modeling has focused on classifying and categorizing exploits and vulnerabilities, and proposed a comprehensive taxonomy of cyber attacks based on effect and intent [10].

We propose active cyber attack model applying 'Sensor to Shooter' and 'OODA Loop' concepts for improve cyber attack model's function.

3   Cyber Attack Architecture

3.1   Cyber Attack Strategy Process

The proposed cyber attack strategy process was designed with systematic framework, as adapting 21st new conventional warfare concepts 'Effects-Based Operation(EBO)' and 'Sensor to Shooter process'. The 'EBO' concept is to identify the center of gravity in enemy's combat organization, and attack it to make massive combat power to unessential factors, and increases the number of enemy's combat factors under control as focusing attack power on effect. The center of gravity is one of the weakest parts of enemy, and it means the part that most definite effect is happened when inflicted attack. 'Sensor to Shooter' concept is a process from target identification to precise strike in real time, which consists of target acquisition, mission tasking, strike planning, mission planning, weapon preparation, and fly-out. Namely, it is to attack on target as soon as target is acquired for reduce total attack time before enemy detects attack. Its process is as Fig. 1 [12,13]. Cyber attack's success is depended on the correct identification of target and the efficient attack strategy development in network system. If attacker identified a center of gravity, he set up attack strategy process to attack it. So, we will apply Sensor to Shooter process to set up our attack strategy process. The Figure 2 is cyber attack strategy process.

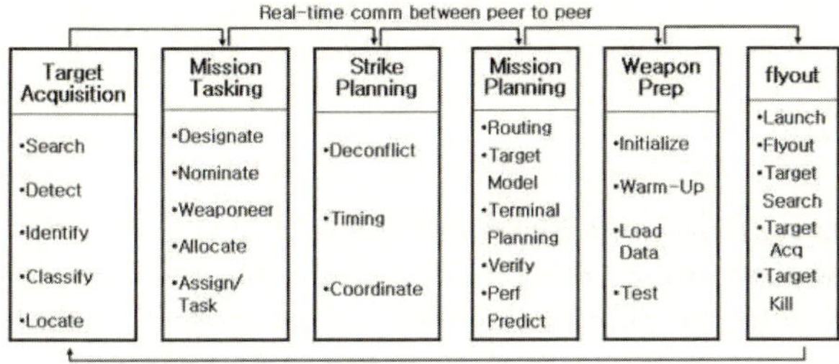

Fig. 1. Sensor to Shooter Process

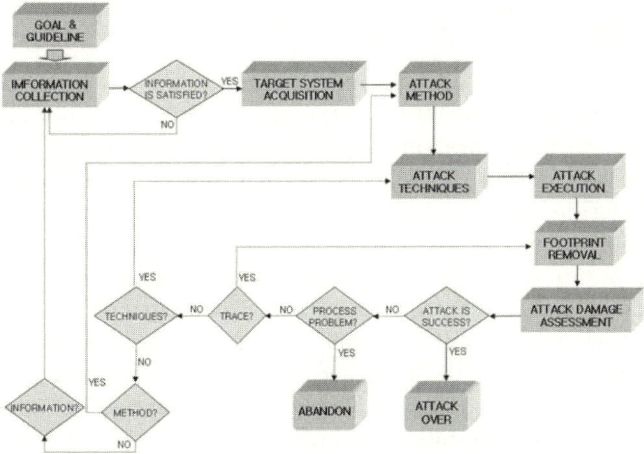

Fig. 2. Cyber Attack Strategy Process

3.2   The Mechanism of Cyber Attack Model

Our cyber-attack model is consisted of 2 agents, 2 modules and action controller in on-line(real-time), and an attack damage assessment analyzer in off-line. This model is adapted by cyber attack strategy process.

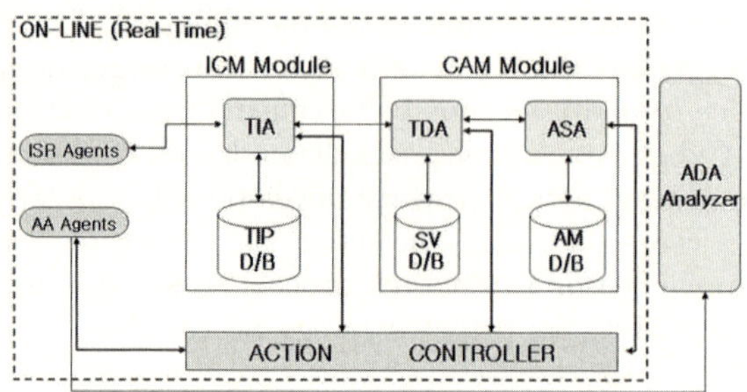

Fig. 3. The Architecture of Cyber Attack Model

Agents

Intelligence, Surveillance and Reconnaissance(ISR) Agents. ISR agents collect information raw data about the target system. They search network environment or configuration properties including target system specifications such as network equipment, security equipment, software and application, IP addresses, etc. They use automatic tools such as network, system and vulnerability scanner, etc. Our model supports the interactions between ISR agents, which connect communication channels between them to exchange knowledge, collected information for collaborate to achieve their goal. They send data to Target system Information Analyzer(TIA).

Attack Action(AA) Agents. AA Agents conduct attack on the weakest vulnerability –main point of impact(MPI)– in target system in real time. The AA agents receive the current target system's information, attack scenario and the attack's ultimate goal from action controller. Once AA agents execute attack scenario, action controller don't concern about AA agent's activities because AA agents are autonomous agents that are able to take decision without action controller's intervention. Action controller only operates when AA agents request. Attack is the actual action which executes attack scenario consisted of attack tree and pattern. After attack finish, they must remove their activities traces, using backdoor or root kits that delete log file or replace commonly used system commands. AA agents send action result to Attack Damage Assessment(ADA) analyzer. When we build attack agents, we must take into account the following challenges [5].

1. Non-traceability: the ability to dissimulate the origin of the attack. To achieve non-traceability, many attack agents will insert intermediate agents between the originating agent and the agents executing the goal or partial goal.

2. Noise acceptance: the level of noise that we allow our agents to make. It can hide main attack agent by other attack agents.
3. Expected attack success: determines the priority which will be given to successfully execute the actions over the other characteristics.
4. Attack execution time: each agent will be given a limit of execution per each action. This is necessary to plan the attack, as it usually consists of a series of dependent steps.
5. Zero-dayness: allowed to use zero-day attack on critical resource that should be used only for main missions.

Information Collection Management(ICM) Module. ICM module consists of 2 components; Target Information Analyzer(TIA), Target Information Profile(TIP) D/B. This module's main function is to analyze data collected by ISR agents, and provide information to Target Development Analyzer (TDA) for exploit vulnerabilities and attack points. TIA compares raw data to profile in D/B. If it is matched up profile in TIP D/B, it sends all information of target system to TDA, if not, it requests further data to ISR agents until TDA satisfy. If ISR agents send data of new network system to TIA, TIA requests to collect information about new network system to other ISR agents. ISR agents will collect all data related to new network system in the other network system infrastructures as well as target system. TIA sends new data to TIP D/B. It updates and stores the data related to all types of information system.

Cyber-Attack Management(CAM) Module. CAM Module consists of 4 components; TDA, ASA, SV D/B and AM D/B. The main function is to develop attack points such as the center of gravity and MPI, and build attack scenario.

Target Development Analyzer(TDA) and System Vulnerability(SV) D/B. TDA acquires a MPI with information from TIA. The MPI is the weakest point that damages the serious impact to target system. A MPI is a point of final action accorded with attacker's goal in a specific attack scenario. Once TDA receives information about target system from TIA, it exploits vulnerabilities of target system and finds MPI. It recommends a MPI priority to attack scenario analyzer. SV D/B stores all network system's vulnerabilities. Whenever new vulnerability is identified, it updates vulnerability list.

Attack Scenario Analyzer(ASA) and Attack Method(AM). D/B It is to analyze the most efficient attack method and technique on MPI. Once it receives MPI from TDA, it builds new attack scenario based on attack tree and pattern in AM D/B, or modifies existent attack scenario. And then, it sends MPI and attack scenario to action controller. AM D/B stores attack scenario with attack trees and patterns. It updates attack scenario for next attack whenever attack agent's action is succeeded or failed.

Action Controller and Attack Damage Assessment(ADA) Analyzer

Action Controller. It controls AA agents and 2 modules. It receives all information related to attack action from 2 modules, and sends them to AA agents.

It doesn't interfere AA agent activities once it sends all attack information to them. If AA agents report problem or malfunction to action controller, it will control them. Action controller follows OODA (Observe, Orient, Decide, Act) Loop to offer promptly necessary information to AA agents for achieve their goal. This Loop's concept is to make a decision promptly and accurately in a cycle of observe-orient-decide-act. Action control observes the condition of all elements, orients AA agent's problem and the state of all elements, decides whether it changes MPI or attack scenario and whether re-attack starts or not, and acts to order decision to AA agents. As using OODA Loop, we can solve problem and malfunction without time-delay, and can reduce re-attack time and action control tasking loads [13].

Attack Damage Assessment(ADA) analyzer. It is to assess attack impact on target system in off-line. Namely, ADA analyzer assesses whether AA agents exactly execute attack scenario on MPI, how deep MPI is damaged, and whether AA agents achieve ultimate goal or not. We excluded ADA in on-line system because our model's performance will be depreciated, and attack time will be extended.

4   Modeling Active Cyber Attack

4.1   Information Analysis and Target Decision

ISR agents collect all information about target system to achieve goal. For example, if ultimate goal is denial of service, ISR agents concentrate on collect network and server equipment such as router, switch, hub, and web server, etc. The example information is as following Table 1.

Table 1. The example of target system information

Equip Type/Name : Router/Cisco 12416	Equip Type: Server
CPU: 665MHz	Equip name: adam.skku.edu
Memory: 2Gb	IP address: 240.1.1.1
OS: Cisco 12000 Manager	OS: SUN Solaris 10
Protocol: ICMP,SSH,RIPv2,IPv4,IPv6,etc.	Service: Sendmail,NTP,BIND 9
Vulnerabilities: TCP Vulnerabilities in Multiple IOS-Based Cisco Products which contain a TCP stack Telnet Denial of Service Vulnerability	Vulnerabilities: Printed arbitrary file deletion Printd demon Transmition control protocol

Once information collection was finished, TDA develops MPI that allows ASA to successfully build a particular attack scenario. If attack goal is a denial of service against target system, TDA recommends server as the center of gravity and TCP vulnerability as MPI to ASA.

4.2   Attack Scenario Analysis

Attack scenario consists of 2 parts; attack tree and attack pattern. Attack tree provides a methodical way based on the types of attack. Figure 4 shows an example attack tree. The root represents an ultimate attack goal. Each node represents a set of sub-goals that must be achieved for top-level goal. It consists of an AND decomposition, an OR decomposition and CON decomposition. AND decomposition means that all the sub-goals of each node must be succeeded. OR decomposition means that one of all, where at least one of the sub-goals must be achieved for upper-level's goal. CON decomposition means that it could be used or not for upper-level's goal according to attack condition or target system's environment [6,7,8,9,11].

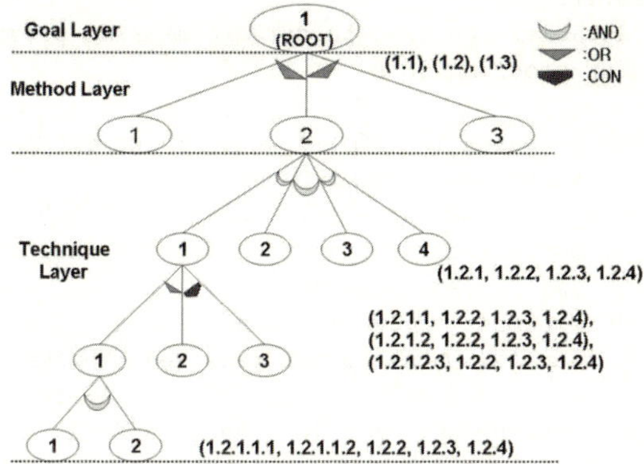

Fig. 4. The relationship between DoS attack tree and pattern

Attack pattern is a generic representation of a deliberate attack that commonly occurs in specific contexts as showing Table 2. Attack pattern includes the attack goal, MPI, pre-conditions, attack execution step, and post-conditions. The goal is the overall goal of the attack specified by the attack pattern. The pre-conditions are assumptions that attacker or the state of target system is necessary for an attack to achieve goal. They include the skills, resources, access, or knowledge that the attacker must know about target system environment and configuration, etc. The attack is the process for carrying out the action on target system. The post-condition is the changes to the target system that result from the successful execution of action. Attack pattern could be listed to illustrate the referential transparency node of attack tree. We can connect action process from root to bottom node because attack tree has hierarchy structure. We use the sequence number $(1, 2, 3, \ldots)$ to represent the attack scenario; attack goal 1, followed by step 2, followed by step 3, ... [6].

We can represent "DoS" attack pattern as following sequence number using each leaf label.

(1.1), (1.2), (1.3)

(1.2.1, 1.2.2, 1.2.3, 1.2.4)

(1.2.1.1, 1.2.2, 1.2.3, 1.2.4), (1.2.1.2, 1.2.2, 1.2.3, 1.2.4), ...

Table 2. The example of attack pattern

```
------------------------------------------------------------------
1. Denial of Service Attack
*Goal: Take TS(Target Server) out of action for a few hours and disrupt
        the services of intermediate routers
*MPI: Server
*Pre-condition: the weak security countermeasures and spoofing TS's IP
*Attack
 OR-Comp. 1. SYN Flooding, 2. UDP Flooding, 3. ICMP Flooding
 Post-condition: the service of TS is interrupted for few hours
 1.2 SYN Flooding attack
*Goal: Exploit TCP Three-way handshaking vulnerability to perform
        overflow Backlog queue
*MPI: TCP vulnerability
*Pre-condition: Attacker can execute certain hacking program on TS
                 for spoofing TS's
*Attack
 AND-Comp.1.Identify source IP address which is unreachable
        OR-Comp. 1. Automated hacking program
                AND-Comp. 1. Use "Ping", 2. Use "Port Scan"
                    2. Social engineering method using insider
        CON-Comp.3. Use "trusted insider"
        2.Send SYN packet to TS for connection
        3.Don't send ACK packet after received SYN/ACK packet from TS
        4.Continue to send a fake connection to TS in the "Half
            Open" state until backlog queue is full
 * Post-condition: Denial of all connection request in this port
------------------------------------------------------------------
```

Figure 4 describes the sequence of attack pattern in the attack tree. So, when AA agents execute attack scenario, they just execute the set of sequence in attack tree. This can reduce a memory load of AA agents. The same attack scenario always has not the same result because target system's structure and security policies are different.

4.3   Attack Action

The attack action is executed by the set of sequence which refers attack tree and pattern. Like Fig. 4, attack action follows direction from left to right and from bottom to top. This allows the action controller to specify ordering of actions that must be performed in sequence. Action controller set up the specific time-stamp between sub-tree and upper sub-tree. This allows AA agents to use attack minimum time to succeed sub-goal without detecting from target system. Let's suppose that attack action's sequence is thick line in the Fig. 5. If attack conditions are not met pre-condition to succeed sub-goal when sub-tree is executed for SYN flooding attack, action controller has to order attack agents to return to former step like (a), and requests TIA to collect needed information about target

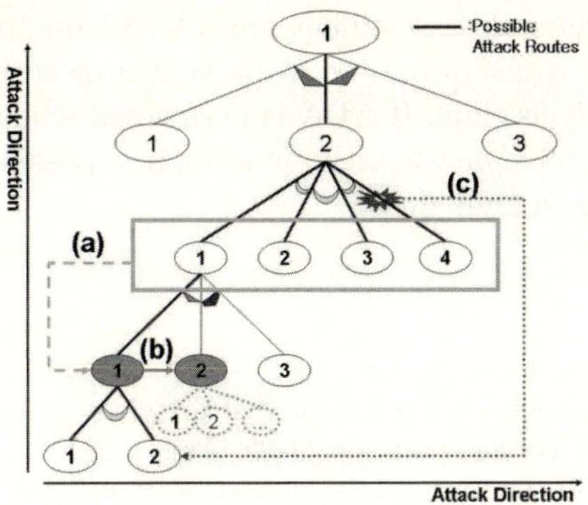

Fig. 5. The example of attack action

system to satisfy pre-condition. If AA agents execute attack scenario without regard for pre-condition, target system is occurred malfunction and may alarm to system administrator. If TIA can not offer enough information or pre-condition, action controller has to abandon the sub-tree's attack action and turn over another sub-tree like (b). When attack is detected like (c), action controller order AA agent to stop attack and return to specific state before starting attack, and AA agent has to delete their activities trace if they have enough time.

4.4 Attack Damage Assessment

In case of DoS attack, ultimate goal is to interrupt system's operation. ADA is to assess how long target system is interrupted by DoS attack. We add our model to assess sub-goals such as '*TCP Three-way handshaking vulnerability to perform overflow backlog queue*' and '*Identify source IP address which is unreachable*'.

In our model, ADA is performed in only off-line system after attack was finished.

5   Conclusions

This paper proposed an active cyber attack model to assess vulnerability in our network system. Our model presents integrated framework for active cyber attack adapting 'EBO', 'Sensor to Shooter' and 'OODA Loop' concepts. As using their concepts, we can structure systematic cyber attack process and mechanism. Also, as using autonomous agents, ISR and AA agents can solve a problem by themselves whenever target system environment and attack process are changed. Action controller is possible to control modules and agents effectively without time delay and performance depreciation as adapting OODA Loop.

When ASA build attack scenario, it uses attack tree and pattern. ASA can substitute sub-tree and pattern actively when action controller requests, because AM D/B has many attack patterns by attack tree.

We added attack damage assessment analyzer to our model. But it doesn't operate with other modules in on-line to prevent unnecessary system resources consumption and analysis time. If ADA is performed when AA agents stand-by on target system to receive new attack scenario, it is possible to detect by target system because of attack time delay.

References

1. Nong ye, et. al: 'A process control approach to cyber attack detection', communications of the ACM Vol.44, No.8, pp.77-82, Aug., 2001.
2. Sushil Jajodia, et. al: 'Surviving Information Warfare Attacks', Computer, Vol.32, Issue 4, pp.57-63, Apr., 1999.
3. Richard E. Overill: 'Information warfare: battles in cyberspace', Computing & Control Engineering Journal Vol.12, Issue 3, pp.125-128, Jun., 2001.
4. Gregg Schudel, et. al: 'modeling behavior of the cyber-terrorist', RAND National Security Research Division, proceeding of workshop, pp.49-59, Aug., 2000.
5. Ariel Futoransky et. al: 'Building Computer Network Attacks', http://www.coresecurity.com/attack/.../planning/Futoransky_Notarfrancesco_Richarte_Sarraute_NetworkAttacks_2003.pdf.
6. Andrew P. Moore, et. al: 'Attack Modeling for Information Security and Survivability', CMU/SEI-2001-TN-001, Mar., 2001
7. Scott D. Lathrop, et. al: 'Modeling Network Attacks', BRIMS 2003, May, 2003.
8. Igor Kotenko: 'Agent-based modelingand simulation of cyber-warfare between malefactors and security agents in internet', ECMS2005, 2005.
9. Kristopher Daley, et. al: 'A Structural Framework for Modeling Multi-stage Network Attacks',ICPPW2002, pp.5-10, Aug., 2002.
10. John R. Surdu, et. al: 'Military Academy Attack/Defense Network Simulation', ASTC:SMGAS, Apr., 2003.
11. Steven J. Templeton, et. al: 'A Requires/Provides Model for Computer Attacks', Proceedings of the New Security Paradigms Workshop, Sept, 2000.
12. ROKAF Combat Development Group: 'Iraq war-Analysis based on Air Operation', Jun., 2003.
13. Tim Grant, et. al: 'Comparing OODA & other models as Operational View C2 Architecture Topic: C4ISR/C2 Architecture', ICCRTS2005, Jun., 2005.

Toward Lightweight Intrusion Detection System Through Simultaneous Intrinsic Model Identification

Dong Seong Kim, Sang Min Lee, and Jong Sou Park

Network Security Lab., Hankuk Aviation University, Seoul Korea
{dskim, minuri33, jspark}@hau.ac.kr

Abstract. Intrusion Detection System (IDS) should guarantee high detection rates with minimum overheads to figure out intrusion detection model and process audit data. The previous approaches have mainly focused on feature selection of audit data and parameters optimization of intrusion detection models. However, feature selection and parameters optimization have been performed in separate way. Several hybrid approaches based on soft computing techniques are able to perform both of them together but they have more computational overheads. In this paper, we propose a new approach named Simultaneous Intrinsic Model Identification (SIMI), which enable one to perform both feature selection and parameters optimization together without any additional computational overheads. SIMI adopts Random Forest (RF) which is a promising machine learning algorithm and has been shown similar or better classification rates compared to Support Vector Machines (SVM). SIMI is able to model lightweight intrinsic intrusion detection model with optimized parameters and features. After determination of the intrinsic intrusion detection model, we visualize normal and attack patterns in 2 dimensional space using Multidimensional Scaling (MDS). We carry out several experiments on KDD 1999 intrusion detection dataset and validate the feasibility of our approach.

Keywords: Intrusion Detection System, Data mining, Random Forest.

1 Introduction

As the amount of information which is interconnecting within networks has been increased tremendously, network security is getting more essential. Among many security methods for protecting network systems such as firewalls and access control, an Intrusion Detection System (IDS) plays a vital role in network security field. The main purpose of the IDS is to inspect all inbound and outbound network activity and identify suspicious patterns that may indicate a network or system attack from someone attempting to compromise a system [4]. IDS should guarantee high detection rates with minimum overheads to figure out intrusion detection model and process audit data. The previous approaches have mainly focused on twofold; parameters optimization of intrusion detection model and feature selection of audit data. The purpose of parameters optimization of detection model is to adjust the value of several parameters and figure out optimal value of them. A lot of researches on parameters optimization have been studied based on data-mining algorithms and machine

G. Min et al. (Eds.): ISPA 2006 Ws, LNCS 4331, pp. 981–989, 2006.

learning algorithms such as Artificial Neural Networks, Support Vector Machines (SVM), and so on. The objective of feature selection of audit data is to remove irrelevant features and find out intrinsic features of audit data. Several wrapper [9, 13] and filter methods [2, 3] have been proposed. However, the feature selection and parameters optimization have been performed in separate way. Several hybrid approaches [8, 14] based on soft computing techniques are able to perform both of them together but they have more computational overheads.

Therefore, in this paper, we propose a new approach named Simultaneous Intrinsic Model Identification (SIMI), which enable one to perform both parameter optimization and feature selection without any additional overheads. SIMI adopts Random Forest (RF) which is a promising machine learning algorithm and have been shown similar or better classification rates compared to SVM. We perform feature selection and parameters optimization together through SIMI. Then, we are able to get intrinsic intrusion detection model with only selected important features. We visualize normal and attacks patterns into 2 dimensional spaces using Multi-dimensional Scaling (MDS). We carry out several experiments on KDD 1999 intrusion detection dataset and validate the feasibility of our approach.

The rest of this paper is organized as follows. The related works are introduced in section 2. Our proposed approach and flow of it is described in section 3. The experiments and their analysis are presented in section 4. Some concluding remarks are given in section 5.

2   Related Works

In this section, we introduce several related works to our approach. As mentioned in section 1, the previous approaches to design and model intrusion detection systems have mainly been studied in twofold: parameters optimization of intrusion detection models and feature selection of audit data. In former case, a lot of studies proposed intrusion detection models using Naïve machine learning algorithms such as Artificial Neural Networks (ANN), Support Vector Machines (SVM). Their main concern is to maximize intrusion detection rates while minimizing false positive rates. They regulated value of parameters of machine learning algorithms, for example, the weight values and number of hidden layers on neural networks, value of parameters of kernel function of support vector machines, and so on. This is can be considered as parameter optimization problems. Moradi *et al.* [11] adjusted Multi-Layer Perceptron neural network (MLP). Mukkamala *et al.* [12] optimized value of parameters of kernel function in SVM. Kim *et al.* [7] also regulated kernel function in using empirical method. In later case, the objective of feature selection is to find out intrinsic important features. All features are not essential to classify network audit data because irrelevant features not only increase computational cost, such as time and overheads, but also decrease the classification rates. Exhaustive analysis requires 2^N experiments if total number of feature is N so that this is effective in terms of computational overheads. There are two representative methods in machine learning: wrapper [9] and filter method [2, 3]. Wrapper method adopts classification algorithms and performs cross-validation to identify important features. Otherwise, filter method utilizes correlation based approaches independent to classification algorithms. Filter method is more lightweight than wrapper methods in terms of computation time and overheads but has lower classification rates than wrapper method since it is performed independent of classification algorithms. In IDS, Sung *et al.* used an empirical method named performance based feature ranking [17]. But the variance of feature importance between each feature is very small and it's infeasible to modeling IDS. Middlemiss *et al.* [10] proposed feature selection using Genetic Algorithm (GA).

In above approaches, both parameters optimization and feature selection were performed in separated way. Several hybrid approaches [9, 15] based on soft computing techniques are able to perform both of them together. Kim *et al.* [8] proposed fusion of GA and SVM for anomaly detection. Park *et al.* [14] proposed which combine filter method with wrapper method based on GA. However, these hybrid approaches sometimes show a little degradation on detection rates with more computations rather than the naïve filter methods, do not provide the variable importance of features and are complicated to implement.

In this paper, we proposed a new approach named Simultaneous Intrinsic Model Identification (SIMI) which performs feature selection and parameter optimization simultaneously without any additional overheads. We adopt Random Forest (RF) which is a stage-of-the-art data mining algorithm comparable to SVM [1]. Zhang *et al.* also [20] proposed a network intrusion detection using RF. But their approach only cut off 3 features after identifying important features and optimized only *mtry* value of RF. We perform feature selection and parameter optimizations based on RF and then only select top *m* numbers of important features and optimize both of *mtry* and *ntree*. Our approach enables one to identify intrinsic model through this procedure. Furthermore, we use Multidimensional Scaling (MDS) to visualize attack and normal patterns with only selected important feature. The next section presents our proposed approach.

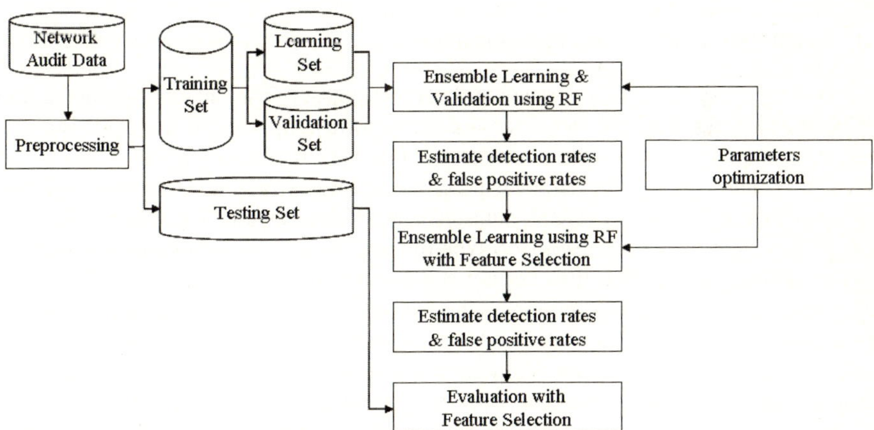

Fig. 1. Overall flow of proposed approach

3 Proposed Approach

The overall flow of our approach is depicted in Figure 1. The preprocessed network audit data is divided into two datasets; training and testing set. The training set is further separated into learning set and validation set. Although we do not need to perform cross-validation to get a balanced estimate of generalization error since RF is robust against over-fitting [1], we adopt n-fold cross validation to minimize that. The learning set is used to generate classifiers and aggregate their results based on RF and find out variable importance of each feature of network audit data and optimal parameters for RF simultaneously. These classifiers can be considered as detection models in IDS. The validation set is used to compute detection rates according to estimating error rates which is Out-Of-Bag (OOB) errors in RF. Feature selection is performed by eliminating the irrelevant features which are low ranked in the ranking of variable importance. In next steps, therefore, only important features that have more effect on classification and optimal parameters are used to build detection models and evaluate by testing set with respect to detection rates. This demonstrates our approach named SIMI. If the detection rates fulfill our design requirement, the overall procedure is finished. To evaluate the feasibility of our approach, we perform several experiments on KDD 1999 intrusion detection dataset. The following section presents the results of experiments and their analysis.

4 Evaluation

In this section, we carry out several experiments on KDD 1999 intrusion detection dataset [5] to verify the feasibility of our approach. We first present the experiments on parameters optimization for RF. Then, we describe the experiments of using random forest to eliminate irrelevant features. Finally, we evaluate our approach. Next section describes experimental dataset and environments and experimental results.

4.1 Evaluation Dataset and Environments

We have used the KDD 1999 intrusion detection dataset. The dataset contains a total of 24 attack types that fall into four main categories [6]: DoS (Denial of Service), R2L (unauthorized access from a remote machine), U2R (unauthorized access to root privileges) and probing. The data was preprocessed by extracting 41 features from the tcpdump data in the 1998 DARPA datasets and we have labeled them as f1, f2, f3, f4 and so forth. We have only used DoS type of attacks since the others have very small number of instances so that they are not suitable for our experiments [16]. According to overall flow presented in section 2, the dataset is divided into 3 datasets; learning set, validation set and testing set. The learning set is used to build the initial detection models based on RF. Then, the Validation set is used to estimate the generalization errors of detection models. The generalization errors are represented as OOB errors in RF. In order to minimize the OOB errors, in other words, maximize detection rates, we have used 10-fold cross validation with 2000 samples. Finally, we have used the testing set to evaluate the detection models that are built by training set.

All Experiments were performed in a Windows environment having configurations Intel® Pentium® 4, 1.70GHz (over 1.72GHz), 512 MB RAM. RF version (R 2.2.0) and MDS algorithm in open source R-project [18] is used to perform several experiments.

4.2 Evaluation Results and Analysis

There are only two parameters in RF to be optimized; the number of variables in the random subset at each node (*mtry*) and the number of trees in the forest (*ntree*). To get the best classification rates, that is, the best detection rates, it is essential to optimize both two parameters. This is considered as parameters optimization. Fortunately, we could get the optimal value of *mtry* using tuneRF() function provided in randomForest package of R-project [18] and it turned out *mtry* = 6. In case of *ntree*, there is no specific function that figures out the optimal value of it. Thus, we got the optimal value of *ntree* by choosing the *ntree* value that has high and stable detection rates. We assume that 350 trees are enough to be the maximum value to evaluate our approach and detection rates are determined by equation "1 – OOB errors". The experimental results for determination of the optimal value of *ntree* are described in Figure 2.

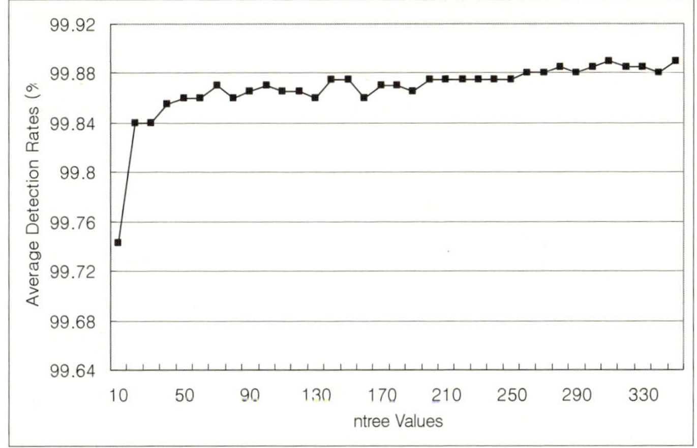

Fig. 2. Average detection rates vs. *ntree* values

According to Figure 2, average detection rates of RF turned out the highest value when *ntree* = 310. As the result of experiments, we set two optimized parameter values; *mtry* = 6, *ntree* = 310. After optimizing two parameters, feature selection of network audit data was carried out employing the feature selection algorithm supported by RF. We ranked features thorough the average variable importance of each feature as the results of 10-fold with 2000 samples. As the results, feature important of each individual feature were decided. The importance value of each feature varies and we rank features with respect to their average importance values of cross validation experiments. We partially show the top 5 important features and their properties in Table 1. Our approach showed reasonable context information for each important feature. f23 represents "number of connections to the same host as the current connection in the past two seconds" property and f6 represents "number of data bytes from destination to source" and so on.

Table. 1. Top 5 important features and their properties

Features	Properties	Average variable importance
f23	number of connections to the same host as the current connection in the past two seconds	0.4023
f6	number of data bytes from destination to source	0.3318
f24	number of connections to the same service as the current connection in the past two seconds	0.3172
f3	network service on the destination, e.g., http, telnet, etc.	0.3163
f5	number of data bytes from source to destination	0.2973

Then, we carried out several times of experiments with elimination of irrelevant features and measure detection rates. The experimental results are depicted in Figure 3.

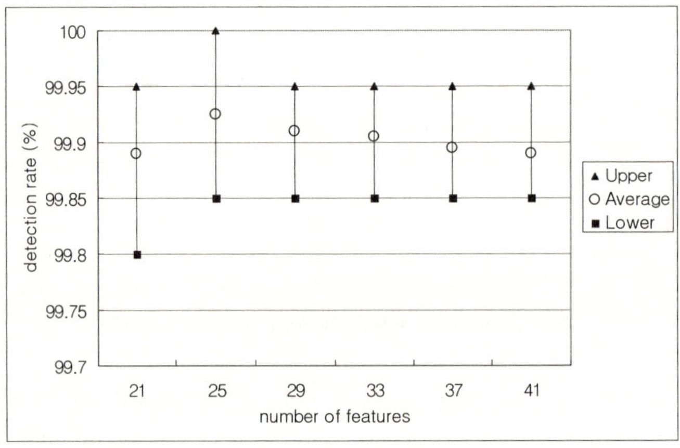

Fig. 3. Detection Rates vs. number of Features

In Table 2, we present comparison results between our approach and other approaches. Our approach showed higher detection rates than others. Even though the detection rates is slightly high than others, our approach only use selected important features and training and testing time is faster than others. We need to calculate computational complexity and compare it to other approaches. But this is out of scope of this paper because both Kim *et al.* and Park et al.'s approach utilized Genetic Algorithm [15]. Although Both Kim *et al.* and Park *et al.*'s approaches have showed "optimal feature set", they didn't show the numeric value as the variable importance

Table 2. The comparison results with other approaches

Approaches	Detection rates	Feature selection		Parameters optimization	
		method	result	method	result
Kim *et al.* [8]	99.85%	GA	Optimal feature set	GA	Optimal parameters value of Kernel function in SVM
Park *et al.* [14]	98.4%	Filter method with GA	Optimal feature set	N/A	Default value of SVM
Zhang *et al.* [20]	99.4%	RF	Individual feature importance /38 features remain	*mtry* only	Partially regulated RF
Our approach	99.87 %	RF	Individual feature importance /*m* features remain	*mtry* and *ntree*	Optimal RF

of each feature. Our approach is able to get individual feature importance so that only important individual features can be used. Zhang et al. also used RF as classification algorithm but they only eliminate 3 features and optimized only *mtry* of RF. We remove irrelevant features and only used *m* number of features to detect DoS type of attacks (see Figure 3). We also optimized *ntree* value of RF to figure out intrinsic model (see Figure 2). In summary, these results proved that our approach is superior to Kim *et al.* [8], Park *et al.*'s approaches [14], and Zhang *et al.*'s approach.

Furthermore, we visualized normal and DoS attacks patterns based on MDS [19] plots in figure 4. These figure 4 plots can easily make one understand about intrusion context information.

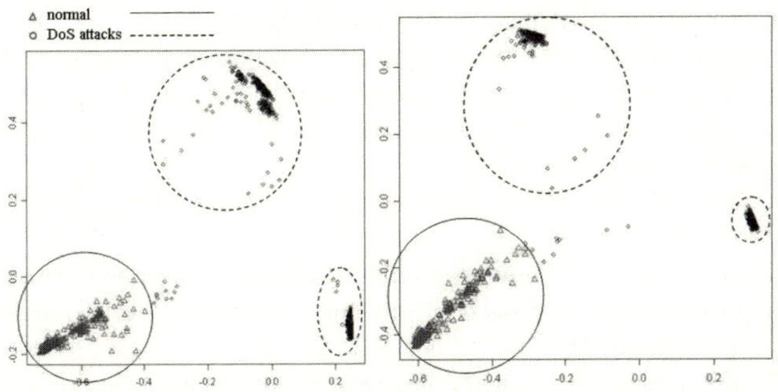

Fig. 4. Visualization of normal and DoS attacks patterns using MDS

5 Conclusions

In this paper, we have presented a new approach named Simultaneous Intrinsic Model Identification (SIMI) for modeling lightweight intrusion detection model. We utilized Random Forest (RF) to perform both feature selection of audit data and parameters optimization of intrusion detection model together without additional overheads. We have evaluated our approach by carrying out several experiments on KDD 1999 intrusion detection dataset and the results have showed that our approach is able to guarantee higher detection rates while figuring out optimal features and intrusion detection model together.

Acknowledgement

This research was supported by the MIC (Ministry of Information and Communication), Korea, under the ITRC (Information Technology Research Center) sup-port program supervised by the IITA (Institute of Information Technology Assessment).

References

1. Breiman, L.: Random forest. Machine Learning 45(1) (2001) 5–32
2. Dash, M.: Feature Selection for Clustering – A Filter Solution. In Proc. of IEEE Int. Conf. on Data Mining (ICDM) (2002) 115–122
3. Hall, M.A. and Smith, L. A.: Feature subset selection: a correlation based filter approach. In Proc. of Fourth Int. Conf. on Neural Information Processing and Intelligent Information Systems (1997) 855–858
4. Intrusion Detection System.:
    http://www.webopedia.com/TERM/I/intrusion_detection_system.html
5. KDD Cup 1999 Data.: http://kdd.ics.uci.edu/databases/kddcup99/kddcup99.html
6. KDD-Cup-99 Task Description.: http://kdd.ics.uci.edu/databases/kddcup99/task.html
7. Kim, D., Park, J.: Network-Based Intrusion Detection with Support Vector Machines. In.: Kang, H. (eds.): Information Networking. Lecture Notes in Computer Science, Vol. 2662. Springer-Verlag, Berlin Heidelberg New York (2003) 747–756
8. Kim, D., Nguyen, H.-N., Ohn, S.-Y., Park, J.: Fusions of GA and SVM for Anomaly Detection in Intrusion Detection System. In.: Wang J., Liao, X., Yi, Z. (eds.): Advances in Neural Networks. Lecture Notes in Computer Science, Vol. 3498. Springer-Verlag, Berlin Heidelberg New York (2005) 415–420
9. Kohavi, R., John, G. H.: Wrappers for feature subset selection, Artificial Intelligence, 97(1–2). (1997) 273-324
10. Middlemiss, M., Dick, G.: Feature Selection of Intrusion Detection Data using a Hybrid Genetic Algorithm/KNN Approach. Third Int. Conf. on Hybrid Intelligent Systems, Melbourne, Australia (2003)
11. Moradi, M., Zulkernine, M.: A Neural Network Based System for Intrusion Detection and Classification of Attacks, In Proc. of IEEE Int. Conf. on Advances in Intelligent Systems-Theory and Applications, Luxembourg (2004)

12. Mukkamala, S., Sung, A. H., Ribeiro, B. M.: Model Selection for Kernel Based Intrusion Detection Systems, In Proc. of Int. Conf. on Adaptive and Natural Computing Algorithms, Springer-Verlag (2005) 458–461
13. Noelia S-M. : A New Wrapper Method for Feature Subset Selection
14. Park, J., Shazzad, Sazzad, K. M., Kim, D.: Toward Modeling Lightweight Intrusion Detection System through Correlation-Based Hybrid Feature Selection. In.: Feng, D., Lin, D., Yung, M. (eds.): Information Security and Cryptology. Lecture Notes in Computer Science, Vol. 3822. Springer-Verlag, Berlin Heidelberg New York (2005) 279–289
15. Rylander, B.: Computational Complexity and the Genetic Algorithm. Thesis for Ph.D., University of Idaho (2001)
16. Sabhnani, M., Serpen, G.: On Failure of Machine Learning Algorithms for Detecting Misuse in KDD Intrusion Detection Data Set. Intelligent Analysis (2004)
17. Sung, A. H., Mukkamala, S.: Identifying Important Features for Intrusion Detection Using Support Vector Machines and Neural Networks. In Proc. of the 2003 Int. Symposium on Applications and the Internet Technology, IEEE Computer Society Press (2003) 209–216
18. The R Project for Statistical Computing, http://www.r-project.org/
19. Young, F. W., Hamer, R. M.: Theory and Applications of Multidimensional Scaling. Eribaum Associates, Hillsdale, NJ (1994)
20. Zhang, J., Zulkernine, M.: Network Intrusion Detection using Random Forests. In Proc. of 3rd Annual Conf. on Privacy, Security and Trust (2005)

The Design of Random Number Generator in an Embedded Crypto Module

Jinkeun Hong[1], Kihong Kim[2], and Dongcheul Son[1]

[1] Division of Information and Communication, Baekseok University,
115 Anse-dong, Cheonan-si, Chungnam, 330-740, South Korea
{jkhong, dcson}@cheonan.ac.kr
[2] Graduate School of Information Security, Korea University,
1, 5-ka, Anam-dong, Sungbuk-ku, Seoul, 136-701, South Korea
hong0612@hanmir.com

Abstract. When using a real random number generator (RNG) with only a hardware component, as required for statistical randomness, it is difficult to create an unbiased and stable random bit stream. Although the hardware generating processor generates an output bit stream quickly, if the software filter algorithm is not efficient, the RNG consumes a relatively large amount of time. This factor becomes the limiting condition when the RNG is applied. Accordingly, this paper proposes a model approach to ensure the model of software filtering in the RNG processor and the chaos function model in the crypto module. Therefore, in the embedded crypto processor, the mixed model guarantees randomness of the output stream, is generated from the combined chaos function with a tent map transformation and a hardware random number generation component in sensor crypto communication.

1 Introduction

At present, ubiquitous computing is advocating the construction of massively distributed computing environments that sensors, global positioning system receives [1] [2]. As such, this case is significantly different from those contemplated by the canonical doctrine of security in distributed computing environments. There are many security issues in the ubiquitous environment, including authentication, authorization, accessibility, confidentiality, integrity, and non-repudiation. Other issues include convenience and speed.

A H/W random number generator (RNG) uses a non-deterministic source to produce randomness. More demanding random number applications such as cryptography, crypto module engines, and statistical simulation also benefit from sequences produced by a RNG, i.e., a cryptographic system based on a hardware component [1]. As such, a number generator is a source of unpredictable, irreproducible, and statistically random stream sequences. A popular method for generating random numbers using a natural phenomenon is the electronic amplification and sampling of a thermal or Gaussian noise signal. However, since all electronic systems are influenced by finite bandwidth, $1/f$ noise, and other

G. Min et al. (Eds.): ISPA 2006 Ws, LNCS 4331, pp. 990–999, 2006.

non-random influences, perfect randomness cannot be preserved by any practical system. Thus, when generating random numbers using an electronic circuit, a low-power white noise signal is amplified and then sampled at a constant sampling frequency. However, when using a RNG with only a hardware component, as required for statistical randomness, it is difficult to create an unbiased and stable random bit stream.

Previous studies [3] [4] [5] have shown that the randomness of a random stream can be enhanced when combining a real RNG, a LFSR number generator, and a hash function. In earlier studies on RNG schemes in the field of security, Fabrizio Cortigiani, et al. (2000) examined a very high speed true random noise generator and S. Rocchi and V. Vignoli (1999) proposed a high speed chaotic CMOS true random analog/digital white noise generator. Adel et al. (2001) conducted a design and performance analysis of a high speed AWGN communication channel emulator. A noise based random bit generator IC for applications in cryptography was also studied (Craig S, et al. 1998[4]).

Our previous paper proposes a random number generator that combines chaos random number and real random number that is not dependent on the security level of the period. Therefore, in particular, it is important in terms of hardware that RNG offers an output bit stream that is always unbiased. In this paper, a combined method of a hardware component and a software chaos function algorithm is designed. However, although the hardware generating processor generates the output bit stream rapidly, if the software filter algorithm is not efficient, the RNG consumes relatively much time and this factor becomes the limiting condition when the RNG is applied. Accordingly, this paper proposes an effective approach to ensuring the method of software filtering in the RNG processor of a crypto module. Thus, to consistently guarantee the randomness of an output sequence from the RNG, the origin must be stabilized, regardless of any change of circumstance elements. Therefore, a RNG that integrates a chaos function and hardware is proposed, and thereby the security characteristics of randomness are guaranteed. Hereinafter, section 2 reviews the framework of the RNG in the embedded crypto module. Section 3 examines the random number generation model and the combined model, that is, the integrated chaos function and hardware component. Experimental results and conclusions are presented in sections 4 and 5, respectively.

2 Framework of the RNG in the Embedded Crypto System

A H/W random number generator includes common components for producing random bit-streams, classified as follows: characteristics of the noise source, amplification of the noise source, and sampling for gathering the comparator [4] [6]. The applied noise source uses Gaussian noise, which typically results from the flow of electrons through a highly charged field, such as a semiconductor junction [7] [8] [9] [10]. Ultimately, the electron flow is the movement of discrete charges, and the mean flow rate is surrounded by a distribution related to the launch time and momentum of the individual charge carriers entering the charged field. An embedded Linux on chip system using a dragonball CPU, MC68328, which is an integrated controller for handheld products based on a MC68EC000 microprocessor core, is used to generate the hardware random bit stream.

The Gaussian noise generated in a PN junction has the same mathematical form as that of a temperature limited vacuum diode. The noise appears to be generated by the noise current generator in parallel with the dynamic resistance of the diode. The probability density of the Gaussian noise voltage distribution function is defined by Eq. (1):

$$f(x) = \frac{1}{\sqrt{2\pi\sigma^2}} e^{(-\frac{x^2}{2\sigma^2})} \tag{1}$$

where σ is the root mean square value of the Gaussian noise voltage. However, for the designed Gaussian noise random number generator, the noise diode is a diode with a white Gaussian distribution. The power density for noise is constant with frequency from 0.1Hz to 10MHz and the amplitude has a Gaussian distribution. Noise originates from agitation of electrons within a resistance, and a lower limit on the noise present in a circuit is set. When the frequency range is given, the voltage of the noise is decided by the factor of frequency. The crest factor of a waveform is defined as the ratio of the peak to the rms value. A crest value of approximately 4 is used for noise. However, for the proposed real random number generator, the noise diode has a white Gaussian distribution. The noise must be amplified to a level where it can be accurately thresholded with no bias using a clocked comparator. Although the rms value for noise is well defined, the instantaneous amplitude of noise has a Gaussian, normal distribution.

$$V_n(rms) = \sqrt{4kTRB} \tag{2}$$

where k is Boltzmann constant $(1.38 \times 10E - 23J/deg.K)$, T is absolute temperature (deg. Kelvin), B is noise bandwidth (Hz), R is resistor (Ohms). If $4kT$ is $1.66 \times 10E - 20$ and R is $1K$, B is $1Hz$, then $V_n(rms) = \sqrt{4kTB} = 4nV/\sqrt{Hz}$. Noise comes from agitation of electrons within a resistance, and it sets a lower limit on the noise present in a circuit. When the frequency range is given, the voltage of noise is decided by a factor of frequency. The crest factor of a waveform is defined as the ratio of the peak to the rms value. A crest value of approximately 4 is used for noise. Hence, when the frequency value is 10MHz, the crest value of a rms value of 0.2mV occasionally occurs.

3   The Random Number Generation Component and the Proposed Combined Model

3.1   The Filter Algorithm in Random Number Generation Component

The filter algorithm in the random number generation component is applied in the next process of the output stream of the sampler so as to reduce the biased statistical randomness [10] [11] [12]. Establishing the optimum buffer size [32bits] and threshold level [γ] are support unbiased and stable randomness. In the conventional filter model, a static buffer memory of 32bits is used to buffer the "pass data" in the decision boundary, and the threshold level for the P value is between 0.9995 and 1.0005.

$$P = \frac{\tau}{T} \tag{3}$$

where the Total_Sum τ is the sum of the number of "1" bit patterns and the Total_Length T is the half value of the Buffer_Length, which is variable from the bits size of 32bits. When the static buffer (S) is fixed at 32bits, the half-value of the static length is 16bits. If the value of (Σ (the number of a pattern 1bit) / the half-value of the static length within the total length) is included in the threshold level, the decision will be the state of "pass". In step 1, if the condition of "pass" is decided, this is added as pass data to the buffer memory. In steps 3-4, if "fail" is decided through the process of conventional filtering, this is decided into the decision process. The process is then completed when the size of the desired bit stream is gathered. The failed bits (32bits) are reduced by a conventional filter (for example, the duty distribution of the bit stream "0" and "1" is normalized). In a conventional model, the output bit stream is expanded by steps of 32bits, evaluated threshold level simultaneously. If the value of the duty cycle of the collected output bit stream, P, satisfies the condition of the threshold level, it is added to the 32bits[S] stream.

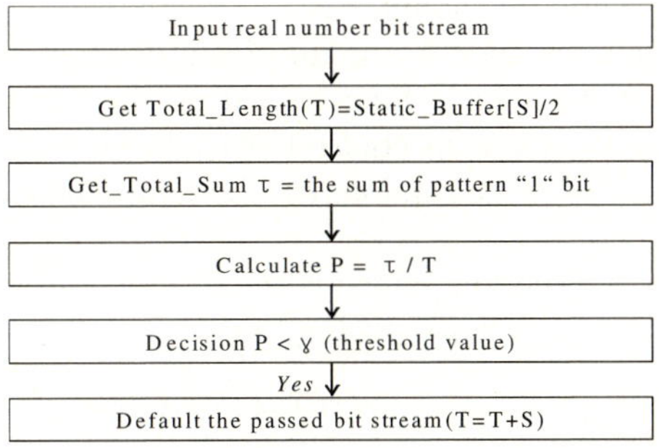

Fig. 1. Process of Filter Algorithm in Random Number Generation Component

If P does not satisfy the condition of the threshold level, it is discarded 32bits stream. Through this filter process, unbiased characteristics of the output bit stream are guaranteed.

3.2   Combined Model of Random Number Generation Component and Chaos Function

The hybrid model combines the output bit stream of the chaos function and the output bit stream of the random number generation component in the next process of the output stream of the sampler so as to reduce characteristics of a biased bit stream. This is typically an efficient method to maintain randomness. In step 1, the real random number is generated from the random number generation component. In step 2 and step 3, the chaos function and tent transformation are applied, and in step 4, the output of the random number generation component and the output of the tent transformed chaos function are mixed at the combined random number generator. In step 5, the randomness of the output stream is evaluated; if the obtained value is distributed within the threshold level of the test item, it is designated a passed stream and saved.

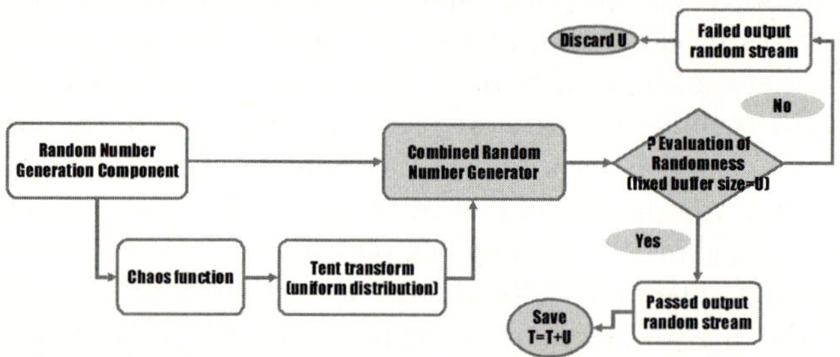

Fig. 2. Process of Combined Random Number Generator

In Fig. 2, the fixed buffer size (U) is fixed 200,000bits. When deciding the size of the fixed buffer, it is used by the measure through the evaluation of passed probability during the setup time interval.

The proposed combined model applies the output of the random number generation component and chaos function, after the process of the hardware random number component is done continuously. The input of the chaos function is driven from the output of the random number generation component through software filtering.

In step 2, the logistic function, which is the discrete chaos map, is applied for the randomized process, as follows (in Fig. 3):

$$X_{n+1} = -\alpha X_n(1 - X_n) \tag{4}$$

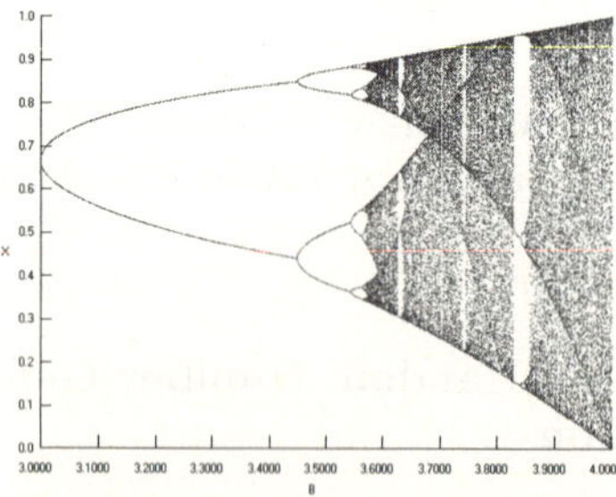

Fig. 3. Logistic Map Equation

where the range of α is $0 \le \alpha \le 4$, and the range of the initial value X_0 is $0 \le X_0 \le 1$. The value of X_{n+1} is derived from the previous state value X_n. Inversely, given X_{n+1}, X_0 has resolved the two values of the solution in an equation of the second degree. The logistic map has the characteristic of irreversibility, and α is the sensitivity parameter that determines the dependence of the next value derived from the initial value. If the value of α is increased, the resulting value varies greatly from the result with slight variation of the initial value after the recursive calculation. For the condition $\alpha < 1$, when the process of X_n is performed recursively, the value of X_n converges to 0. For the convergence to the direction of the chaos domain, which continues to infinity, the value of α must be $\alpha > 3.56$.

In step 3, however, the distribution of the output bit stream of the chaos function has an independent and uniform distribution, and is an integral number between $[0, d-1]$. To apply the random number generator, the integral number between $[0, 1]$ is distributed uniformly by the tent transformation function. By the tent function $x' = h(x)$, the non-linear value of the discrete chaos function becomes a linear value.

$$x' \;=\; h(x) \;=\; \sin^2(\pi x/2) \tag{5}$$

In the tent transformation process, if the initial value is x_0, the transformed value is $x'(0) = h(x_0)$.

$$x(1) = T(x_0), \;\; x(2) = T^2(x_0), \;\; ..., \;\; x(k) = T^k(x_0) \tag{6}$$

Let y_0 be x'_0, it is driven the equation $y_1 = f(y_0)$, $y_2 = f^2(y_0)$, ..., $y_k = f^k(y_0)$. From the f function and T function, it can be driven as follows:

$$f^k(h(x)) \;=\; h(T^k(x)) \tag{7}$$

where k is $0, 1, 2, ...,$. The non-linear value of the x' axis by the tent function is transformed to a linear value of the x axis, which has a uniform distribution. Therefore, the output of the chaos function is uniformly generated by the tent map transportation function on a duty cycle.

In the evaluation of randomness (step5), the bit steam during one period (U) is set at 200,000 bits. When the unit of the output bit stream is 200,000 bits, in the case of the frequency test, the number of "1" pattern bits is t bits. If the value of the duty information within one period is included within the significance level (p), the decision will be considered as a state of "pass".

If the condition of "pass" is determined, this is added as pass data to the buffer memory. If "fail" is determined through the evaluation process, this is not included in the decision process. When the size of the desired bit stream is gathered, the process is then completed. If the value of the duty cycle of the collected output bit stream in the case of frequency test P does not satisfy the condition of the significance level, then the conversion of the bit pattern is started, equivalent to the number of bits, which is included in the significance level.

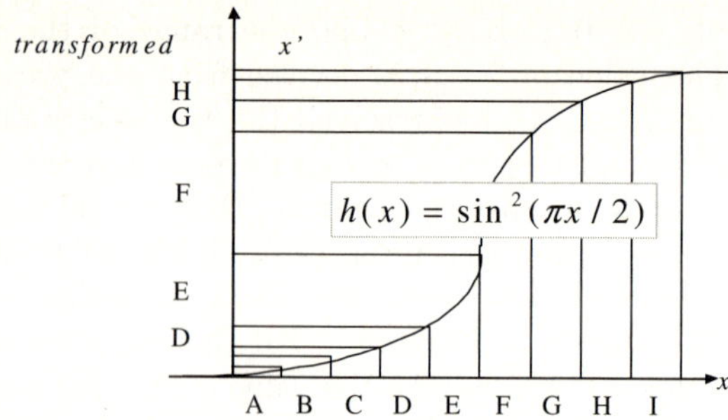

Fig. 4. Tent Transformation Function

4   Experimental results

To generate the output random stream of the chaos function, the chaos function is used through the utilization of a logistic map.

A logistic map when the initial value of X_0 is 0.315001 and the initial value of another X_0 is 0.315002 after 100 iterations. In the initial state, the logistic map according to the initial value is slightly varied; however, with additional iteration rounds, any deviation is magnified by the factor in each iteration. Given an initial deviation, it will eventually become as large as the actual signal itself. After a number of itera-tions, the error will be of the same order of magnitude as the correct values. This section presents the results obtained from the proposed system. First, the effect of the randomness of the output random bit stream was investigated. More quantitative tests for randomness can be found in the literature [9-10]. To guarantee the randomness of the output stream of the chaos function by a necessary condition, a value of α of more than 4.0 must be utilized. If the value of α is less than 4.0, then randomness of the output stream will be beyond the threshold level.

To diagnosis the output bit stream of the hybrid random number generator, randomness test items [10-13] such as a frequency test for verification of the frequency, a permutation test for verification of permutations, a gap test for verification of intervals, and a run test for verification of monotonousness are assessed. The frequency test, this distribution of random numbers should be uniform, is evaluated for successive 200,000 bits out of the random bit stream. If the tested bit stream is included within the threshold level [42.557], the bit stream is evaluated as a non-biased stream. The permutation test, occurrences of permutations of groups of 3 consecutive integers (triplets) and groups of 4 consecutive integers (quadruplets) should be random, is included within the threshold level [35.172]. From Table 1, the stream of the output random number is evaluated as a non-biased stream.

The gap test, are strings of numbers greater than the median, which separate strings of numbers smaller than the median, is included within the threshold level [19.675], and its stream is evaluated as a non-biased stream. For the run test, occurrences of runs up should be random with probabilities based on Knuth,

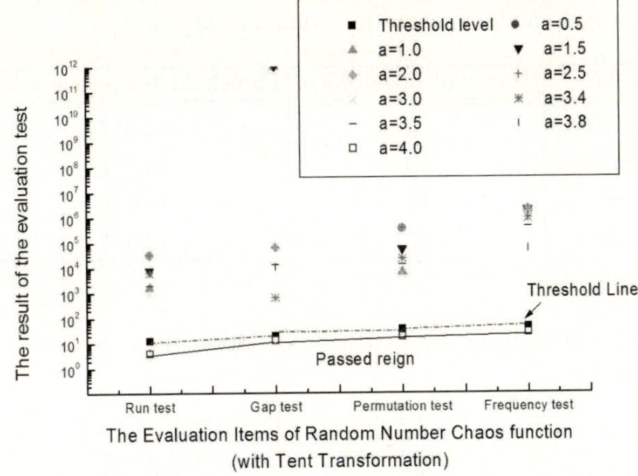

Fig. 5. The Randomness Result According to the Logistic Initial Value of α

is included within the threshold level [12.592], and its stream is evaluated as a non-biased stream. In experiments concerning the randomness evaluation for the combined random number generator, 10 test samples consisting of severely biased and moderately biased streams were statistically evaluated. Therefore, in the ran-domness evaluation, the combined hardware generator, which integrates the chaos function with tent transformation and the random number generation component, always satisfies the randomness test conditions in comparison with the chaos function with tent transformation only. For the output stream of the chaos function, which is not applied to the tent transformation, the probability of the random bit stream being generated successively in a specific pattern is high, and the condition of the threshold level to the frequency test, permutation test, and run test is not satisfied.

Table 1. Results of security randomness evaluation (in condition of chaos function)

Test Item	Degree of Freedom(ν)	Threshold Value($\alpha < 0.05$)	Results
Frequency Test	29	42.557	31929.709
Permutation Test	23	35.172	25418.946
Gap Test	11	19.675	13.701
Run Test	6	12.591	15593.663

In the run test, for the severely biased bit stream, the length of the run is dependent on a specific length, and the tested data from the experiments can be evaluated readily in Table 1 and Table 3. In Table 1, most tests are not satisfied in terms of the randomness of the output random stream of the chaos function only; only the run test is satisfied.

Table 2. Results of security randomness evaluation (in condition of chaos function without transform + random generation component)

Test Item	Degree of Freedom(ν)	Threshold Value($\alpha < 0.05$)	Results
Frequency Test	29	42.557	31929.709
Permutation Test	23	35.172	17.981
Gap Test	11	19.675	12.961
Run Test	6	12.591	3.953

Table 3. Results of security randomness evaluation (in condition of chaos function with transformation)

Test Item	Degree of Freedom(ν)	Threshold Value($\alpha < 0.05$)	Results
Frequency Test	29	42.557	25.623
Permutation Test	23	35.172	25418.946
Gap Test	11	19.675	13.701
Run Test	6	12.591	15593.663

Table 4. Results of security randomness evaluation (in condition of chaos function with transform + random generation component)

Test Item	Degree of Freedom(ν)	Threshold Value($\alpha < 0.05$)	Results
Frequency Test	29	42.557	25.623
Permutation Test	23	35.172	17.981
Gap Test	11	19.675	12.961
Run Test	6	12.591	3.953

Table 2 presents the evaluation results of randomness tests in condition of the chaos function without tent transform or a random number generation component. The test results indicate that the chaos function should be used with a tent transformation: i.e. if the chaos function is not used with tent transformation, a biased bit stream is produced and the randomness of the output stream of chaos function will not be guaranteed. Further, in most cases, the proposed system will not pass all trial tests.

For the condition of the chaos function with tent transformation, the results of most test items, such as frequency test, permutation test, and run test, do not satisfy the threshold level. It is also difficult to satisfy the requirement of randomness, although one part of randomness is included within the thresh-old level. In order to meet the threshold level of randomness, the random number generation component and the chaos function, to which the tent transformation is applied, must be employed, as shown in Table 4.

5   Conclusions

The present work proposes a hardware RNG that combines an RNG and filtering technique that is not dependent on the security level of the period. Therefore, it is important that the RNG hardware offers an output bit stream that is always unbiased. Even though the hardware generating processor generates the output bit stream quickly, if the software filter algorithm is inefficient, the RNG consumes much time, thereby restricting the conditions when the RNG can be applied. Accordingly, this paper proposes a combined model, wherein the random number generation component and the chaos function for an RNG processor are integrated in a crypto module. The combined RNG is not depended on the random number generation component only, and also, the chaos encryption function always guarantees randomness due to the use of a mixed method.

References

1. Alireza h. and Ingrid V. High-Throughput Programmable Crypto-coprocessor. *IEEE Computer Society*, 2004.
2. Jalal A. M, Anand R., Roy C., M. D. M. Cerberus: A Context-Aware Security Scheme for Smart Spaces. *IEEE PerCom'03*, 2003.
3. Robert Davies. True random number. http://webnz.com/robert/true_rng.html.
4. C. S. Petrie and J. A. Connelly. A Noise-Based Random Bit Generator IC for Applications in Cryptography. *ISCAS'98*, 1998.
5. M. Delgado-Restituto, F. Medeiro, and A. Rodriguez-Vasquez. Nonlinear switched-current CMOS IC for random signal generation. *IEE electronic letters*, 1993.
6. http://www.io.com/ritter/RES/NOISE.HTM.
7. http://www.clark.net/pub/cme/P1363/ranno.html.
8. http://webnz.com/robert/true_rng.html.
9. Boris Ya, Ryabko and Elena Matchikina. Fast and Efficient Construction of an Unbiased Random Sequence. *IEEE Trans. on information theory*, 2000.
10. Diehard. http://stat.fsu.edu/geo/diehard.html.
11. Noble, C. and Sugden, S. J. Statistical Tests on Random Numbers I(1 through 80). *A consulting report for Jupiters Network Gaming*, 1997.
12. Noble, C. and Sugden, S. J. Statistical Tests on Random Numbers II(0 through 127). *A consulting report for Jupiters Network Gaming*, 1997.
13. Noble, C. and Sugden, S. J. Stochastic Recurrences of Jackpot KENO. *Computational Statistics and Data Analysis*, 2002.

A Design of Network Traffic Analysis and Monitoring System for Early Warning System

Geuk Lee, Inkyu Han, and Youngsup Kim

Department of Computer Engineering, Hannam University
133 Ojung-Dong, Daeduk-Gu, Daejeon 306-791, Korea
leegeuk@hannam.ac.kr, haik80@nate.com, youksj@paran.com

Abstract. In this paper, we develop network traffic monitoring tool in order to analyze and monitor a network environment effectively. The network traffic analysis and monitoring system is designed based on attack knowledge for EWS(Early Warning System). It consists of an agent for host, a database server and administrator's tool. Each host agent captures and collects network traffic information using WinPcap library, and send those information to the database server. The database server classifies and keeps necessary information from all the information sent, and provides those information when the administrator requests the information. The administrator's tool combines the information from the server, applies the analysis of correlation, and confirms the network attack situation. This system can monitor the network traffics and analyze global traffic stream effectively, and aware various internet attack situations. The system was designed using C++ and ODBC (Open Database Connectivity).

1 Introduction

As internet users and networks are broadly expanded, technologies of cyber attacks have rapidly been changed. Those attacks are more organized and extensive, for example, Win32/Nimda Worm represented a new form of a network attack and SQL-Overflow Worm caused the internet disaster at January 2003, and Blaster Worm showed typical cases which were the most recent internet attack. But capabilities of network administrators are limited to deal with these situations. [1]

Most systems have tools can detect virus or hacking, but these tools can not protect the network itself. Therefore, a technique to analyze and monitor a set of network streams is needed because there is no system to perfectly protect the network itself from whole kinds of cyber attacks. [2]

In this paper, we developed a system which can analyze and monitor a network traffic using the knowledge of previous attack situation. This system is also using Batch and Distributed Correlation technique to reduce overhead.

The outline of this paper is as follows. Section 2, as related works, briefly summarizes analysis technique of network attacks and introduced the analysis of correlation. Section 3 explains a structure of traffic analysis and monitoring system. Section 4

G. Min et al. (Eds.): ISPA 2006 Ws, LNCS 4331, pp. 1000–1005, 2006.

provides simulation results. Finally, Section 5 presents conclusions and a brief summary of the study.

2   Related Works

In this section, we describe the analysis of Network attack situation, and explain the analysis of correlation. The analysis of correlation classifies the characteristics of security warnings of special situations. Using the classified information, flooding state can be prevented and global security analysis for networks is possible.

2.1   Analysis of Network Attack Situation

Analysis of network attack situation is to distinguish special characteristics from network attacks based on the analysis of correlation. This analysis makes it possible to obtain valuable attack information from the flooding stream of security warning, which is can not detected in single host.

Two types of network attack situations are shown in Fig.1 and Fig.2. Fig.1 shows one specific host attacks one target host, and Fig.2 shows more than one host attack the one target host. In the case of Fig.1, warning signal which has the specific source host IP address to the specific destination host IP address may be happened repeatedly. In the case of Fig.2, several warning signals which have same destination host IP address and different source address will be found. In both cases, the purpose and intention of attacks can be clearly detected although real intention is still ambiguous with single host analysis.

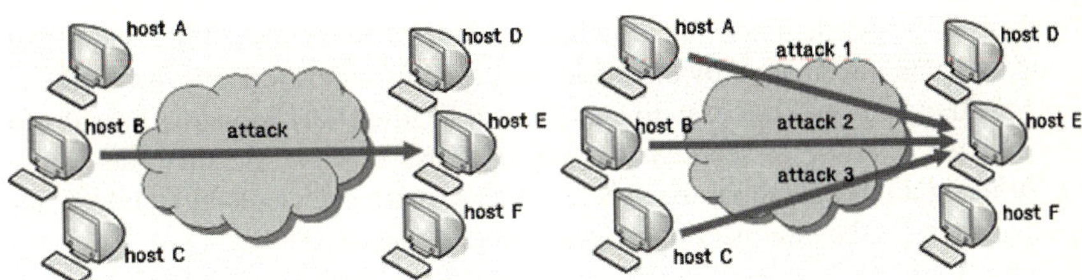

Fig. 1. one-to-one attack   **Fig. 2.** many-to-one attack

2.2   Analysis of Correlation

Debar and Wespi used three factors (source IP address, destination IP address, attack name) for the analysis of correlation. [3] They defined attack pattern into seven special classes using those three factors (Table. 1). When all of three factors are matched, it is the Situation Class 1. If two of three factors are matched, it can be defined as Situation class 2-1, 2-2, and 2-3. Finally, only one of three factors is matched, it is defined as Situation class 3-1, 3-2, 3-3. Applying this to Fig. 1, since both of the

Table 1. Classification of attack pattern

Situation Class	Source IP	Dest. IP	Attack Name	Explanation
1	Match	Match	Match	The situation of a specific attack progressed to a specific host from an attacker. ex) TCP ACK flooding
2-1	Match	Match		The situation of an attacks progressed to a specific host from an attacker. ex) Smurf, Fraggle
2-2		Match	Match	The situation of a specific attack progressed to a specific host. ex) most of the DoS attacks
2-3	Match		Match	The situation of a specific attack progressed from an attacker ex) most of the Scanning attacks
3-1	Match			The situation of a attack progressed from an attacker ex) Kamikaze attack
3-2		Match		The situation of a attack progressed to a specific host ex) DRDoS attack
3-3			Match	The situation of a specific attack progressed to many hosts from many attackers ex) most of the Internet Worm attacks

source IP address and the destination IP address are same, it can be classified into Situation 1 and 2-1. For the Fig 2, it can be classified into Situation 2-2 and 3-2 because only one factor of the destination IP address is same.

Two methods are available to implement Analysis of Network attack situation. The one is to visualize the attack situation using graphics and the other one is to group security warning signals to distinguish a specific pattern from the collection. In the visualization method, same patterns of security warnings can be marked as a same color or symbol such as dot, line, and square. In the grouping method, same patterns are collected into the related group and counted whenever occurred. If a number of the pattern collected within a given time duration exceeds threshold number, it can be considered as the attack situation.

Analysis of Network attack situation has a couple of advantages. First one is that it can find valuable information by distinguishing specific characteristics from stream of security warnings. It was not easy to analyze and handle attack situation in real world because of the flooding of security warning by False Positive. Second one is that it has high recognition rate about the special attack pattern such as DoS attack or Scanning attack against the judgment of attacks is not easy in single host. [4]

3   Traffic Analysis and Monitoring System

3.1   Overall Structure of Traffic Analysis and Monitoring System

Fig. 3 shows the structure of Network Attack Situation Analyzer suggested in this paper. The system consists of agent for Hosts, an Administrator's tool, and a Database server. Each host agent collects network traffic information using WinPcap Library, analyzes the attack propensity, and then sends those collected information to the database server. The database server receives information from hosts, keeps them, and sends them to the administrator's host. The administrator uses the information kept in the database server to analyze network attack situation. In this system, the hosts send

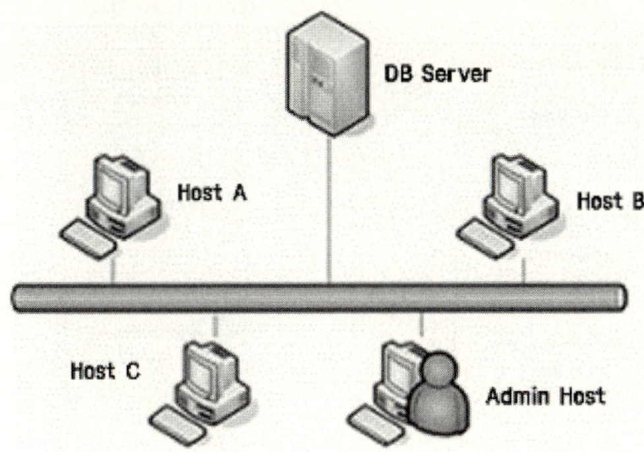

Fig. 3. Overall structure of Traffic analysis and monitoring system

the only information, which is necessary for network attack situation analysis, to the database server. Also hosts will send information when information buffer is full to reduce an overhead of real-time data transmission.

3.2 Host Program Configuration

A agent program for host is organized with three modules. The first module is a traffic capture module which captures all the traffics passing by the hosts. The second module is a traffic analysis module which analyzes the traffics captured to get the attack propensity. The last module is a save and transmission module. This module saves the information obtained by first and second modules, and transfers it to the database server using information buffer. [5],[6]

3.3 Database Server Configuration

A database server merges the information transferred from each hosts and transfers this information to the administrator host. Since the database server has to handle so much information, the database keeps necessary information needed to Network Attacks Situation Analysis (e.g. host-number, time-slot, attack-name, service-pattern) instead of handling all the information.

3.4 Administrator Program Configuration

The administrator's tool analyzes the network attack situation using the information transferred from the database server. It merges both of the information transferred right now and the information used before. But the administrator's tool sets Time-period for information, and discards information timed out because too old information is hard to correctly analyze current attack situation. Communications between the administrator host and the database server are also done in batch mode. Fig. 4 shows a flowchart of Traffic analysis and monitoring system. [7]

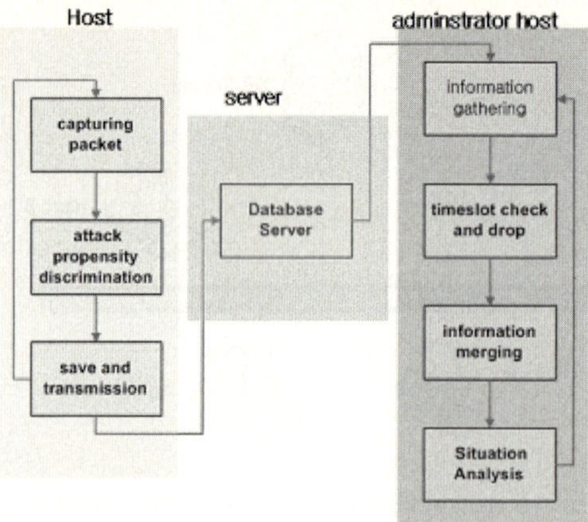

Fig. 4. Flowchart of traffic analysis and monitoring system

4 Simulation Results

4.1 Simulation Conditions

The Simulation was carried out in order to compare performance changes depending on execution of Traffic preprocessing and existence of database server. The traffic preprocessing is that each host keeps some information in advance, such as the attack propensity, required for the network attack situation analysis to reduce host overheads. The database server saves the information from each host, and sends those to an administrator's tool at once. In this simulation, we compared effects of existence of the traffic preprocessing and database server to the overall system performance.

The Simulation was executed with a database server, three host computers, and an administrator's host as in Fig. 3. The result value of the simulation is calculated as an average for consecutive 10 minutes time period.

4.2 Simulation Results

Fig. 5 represents the simulation result. The situation 1 was the simulation with the traffic preprocessing and the database server, the situation 2 was the simulation with only the database server, and the situation 3 was the simulation with no traffic preprocessing and direct communication between hosts and the administrator host without database server.

Fig 5 shows that the CPU time use was reduced when the system executed the traffic preprocessing and included the database server

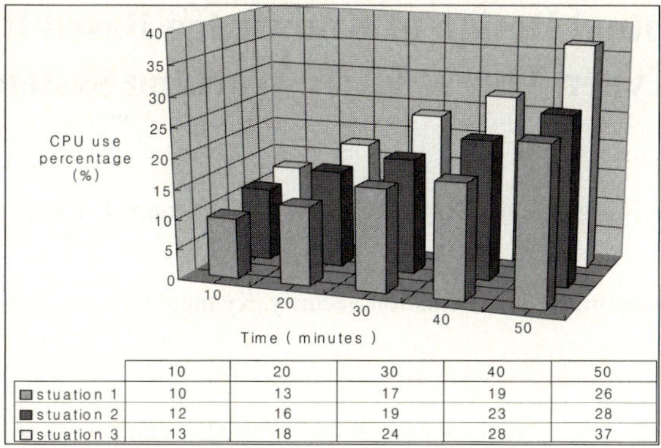

	10	20	30	40	50
stuation 1	10	13	17	19	26
stuation 2	12	16	19	23	28
stuation 3	13	18	24	28	37

Fig. 5. Simulation results

5   Conclusions

In this paper, Traffic analysis and monitoring system using attack knowledge were designed to use in EWS. This system can protect the networks from local or global internet attacks using efficient analyzing and monitoring network traffics captured by host programs. Also the analysis of correlation can improve the accuracy of Network Attacks Situation Analysis. And the use of the decentralization of traffic analysis and the database server improve the system performance.

References

1. Kim, H.A. and Karp, B., *"Autograph: Toward Automated, Distributed Worm Signature Detection"*, 13th Usenix Security Symposium (Security 2004), August, 2004
2. Gatner, *"IDS a failure. firewalls recommanded"*, Web Host Industry Review. June 11.
3. H. Debar and A. Wespi, *"Aggregation and Correlation of Intrusion-Detection Alerts"*, LNCS 2212, pp. 85-103, 2001.
4. D. Schnackenberg. K. Djahandari, and D. Dterene, *"Infrastructure for Intrusion Detection and Response"*, Proceedings of DISCEX, Jan. 2000
5. Matthew V. Mahoney and Philip K. Chan. Phad, *"Packet header anomaly detection for indentifying hostile network traffic"*, Florida Tech, CS-2001-4, 2001
6. Thomas Toth Christopher Krugel and Engin Kirda, *"Service specific anomaly detection for network intrusion detection"*, In Proceeding of Symposium on Applied Computing, March 2002.
7. P. A. Porras and P. G. Newmann, *"EMERALD: Event Monitoring Enabling Responses to Anomalous Live Disturbances"*, Proceedings of the 20th NIS Security Conference, October 1997.

A Conceptual Design of Knowledge-Based Real-Time Cyber-Threat Early Warning System

Sangho Lee, Dong Hwi Lee, and Kuinam J. Kim[*]

Department of Information Security, Kyunggi University, Korea

Abstract. The exponential increase of malicious and criminal activities in cyber space is posing serious threat which could destabilize the foundation of modern information society. In particular, unexpected network paralysis or break-down created by the spread of malicious traffic could cause confusion in a nationwide scale, and unless effective countermeasures against such attacks are formulated in time, this could develop into a catastrophic condition. As a result, there has been vigorous search to develop a functional state-level cyber-threat early-warning system: however, the efforts have not yielded satisfying results or created plausible alternatives to date due to the insufficiency of the existing system and technical difficulties. The existing cyber-threat forecasting depends on the individual experience and ability of security manager whose decision is based on the limited data collected from ESM and TMS. Consequently, this could result in a disastrous warning failure against a variety of unknown and unpredictable attacks. It is the aim of this paper to offer a conceptual design for "Knowledge-based Real-Time Cyber-Threat Early-Warning System, and promote further researches into the subject.

Keywords: Early-Warning, Cyber-threat, TMS, ESM.

1 Introduction

While the birth of information society and burgeoning information business in the 21st century have produced numerous opportunities for accumulation of wealth and national economic growth, such changes also promoted equal growth of criminal and terrorist activities, such as distribution of virus, malicious hacking and cyber terror. In particular, the spread of malicious worm, virus and hacking not only threatens the foundation of modern information society by causing paralysis to the national-wide network and obstruction to electronic-commerce/trade, which many of us come to dependent upon, but could also causes catastrophic failure of national information infrastructure, which most developed nations rely upon in governing and running of a country. Therefore, it is of the highest priority for the network security management to counter against such attacks in timely and pre-emptive manner, and in order to support such activities, it is necessary to adopt and operate credible early-warning

---

[*] Corresponding author. harap123@daum.net

G. Min et al. (Eds.): ISPA 2006 Ws, LNCS 4331, pp. 1006 – 1017, 2006.

system (EWS), which will be a major instrument in insuring daily functions of modern information society.

However, the effort to develop plausible EWS has not yielded significant result yet, because most of the research could not offer alternatives to replacing human experience while only able to issue warnings against a particular or small set of known cyber-attacks. For example, the common feature of the existing EWS depends on the application of traffic-based analysis techniques. In the case of Hellerstein's(2001) study, he attempted the prediction of a weekly traffic volume in baseline-network utilizing "Seasonal ARIMA Model"[1]. Meanwhile, Zang(2000) attempted to predict the traffic volume of wireless network using the same model[2]. Alternatively, Groschwitz suggested a classification method for anomaly detection based on "Wavaelet Analysis." This approach is possible by the application of filtered signals to detect abnormality on both long and short-term network traffic, which were collected by the analysis of original traffic volume using time-cycle division method[3]. Shu proposed an approach to predict the volume of non-linear, irregular high-speed network traffic based on the "Fuzzy-AR Model."[4] The common features of above approaches are utilization of critical-value based analysis technique in EW framework, detecting massive overflowing network traffic and emergence of abnormality. However, the early-detection method based on numeric and quantitative analysis on traffic has limited value for the current technical trends for traffic overflow attack exploits artificial intelligence-based variable tempo approaches, rather than relying on traditional sequential attacks on ports and exploitation of weaknesses[5].

Meanwhile, Zou researched a possibility of adopting an early-warning and surveillance technique on internet worm virus using "Kalman Filter Forecasting Model", which was based on the monitoring of similar activities of pre-collected observation data on the samples of epidemic worm model[6]. However, this approach has limited application since the technique primarily relies on the extraction of sample data that, if an attack exploits multiple vulnerabilities, or utilizes artificial intelligence-based variably distributed worm, the approach won't be able to identify such threats.

Similar limitations have prevented from other researches into a development of EWS yielding plausible results. There were indeed many studies, such as Cabrera's (2003) investigation on the early detection technique of DDoS attack based on the application of "MIB-variation of SNMP-based traffic"[7], Zhai's (2003) study on method of EWS against network disturbance based on "Dempster-Shafer Theory"[8], and Li's (2003) research on the DoS early detection system based on a statistical analysis of a single MIB variation[9]. Nonetheless, while these techniques were offered as alternatives to guard against DoS based threats, they had limited potential.

Moon (2005), in his research on the correlation of network risk and defect through an analysis on cyber threat and vulnerability,[10] suggested an option for EWS based on a correlational analysis of N-IDS and VAS. However, there is a limit in his approach since the suggested system is not able to detect unknown and/or different types of malware, which is common pattern/feature of the recent cyber-threats.

2 Knowledge-Based Real-Time Cyber-Threat Early Warning System

2.1 An Overview

The major weapon against increasing cyber-threat is the capacity to detect and counter attacks before they develop into an epidemic, or better yet, formulates and distribute countermeasures, such as patches and vaccines, before or soon after the related-news or new exploits are introduced. Therefore, it is necessary to develop an effective and comprehensive EWS which is capable of early-detection and warning of attack; analyses of threats and formulation of countermeasures; distribution of necessary vaccines, patches and countermeasures; and sustained capability to analyze and investigate against future variations and threats. As an effort, this research will explore a possibility of developing a new system, tentatively titled as the "EWTMS (Early-Warning and Threat Management System)" to meet above mentioned requirements.

[Picture 2-1] displays the full structure of EWTMS. As shown, this system is comprised of four individual modules. First of all, the events-data collection and processing is carried out by NFIG (News Find Input Gateway), RCEG (Real Critical Event Gateway) and FITM (First Input Threat Module) simultaneously. The NFIG and RCEG modules and FITM are newly developed concept for the designing of EWTMS. The NFIG module collects cyber-threat related information and news from various online sources in real-time, and then formats and standardizes the information into machine recognizable event-data, while RCEG gathers threat events from available security equipment. FITM collects information and variation of vulnerabilities which have not been detected by security equipments. Each data gathering module collects different data and feed them to MN (Data Mining) Database. Then, the collected data from three modules which have been loaded in MN Database is analyzed by KMIM (Knowledge Management Integration Module), and the analyzed data is fed into EWVIM (Early Warning Visual Information Module) for

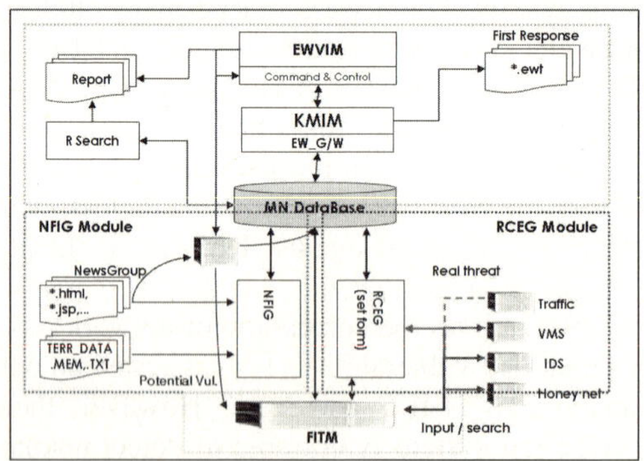

[Picture 2-1]. The Structure of EWTMS

a final review, and results are displayed on easily recognizable graphics and visual displays to provide situational awareness, comprehensive monitoring of threats and quick EW decision making capability by the security specialists. More detailed structure and functions of each module is as follows.

2.2 Structure and Functions

2.2.1 FITM (First Input Threat Module)

[Picture 2-2] describes the structure and functions of FITM. The module collects vulnerability data from NFIG while gathering cyber-threat elements from Honeynet which have not been detected by other security equipment. Finally, comparing the patterns collected from NFIG and Honeynet, and available security equipment, the module evaluates potential weakness and threats.

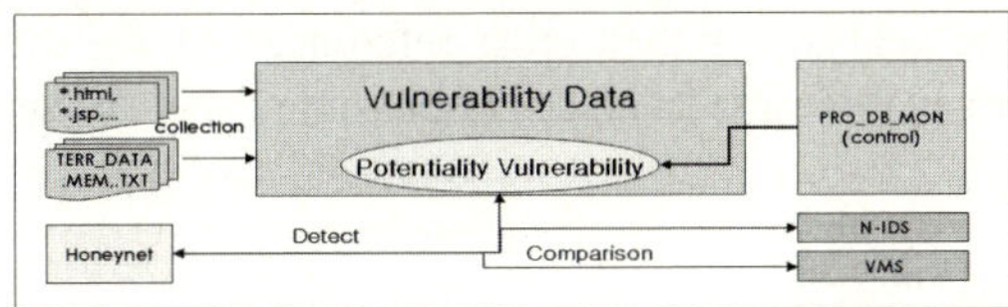

[Picture 2-2]. The Structure and Functions of FITM

[Picture 2-3] displays associated equipment and individual functions of each sub-system in FITM. In short, the module collects the threat and vulnerability data from NFIG and detects threat patterns from Honeynet and various security equipments by pattern matching. In addition, FITM analyses the pattern of the proliferation of cyber-threat elements and then feed the result to the MN Database.

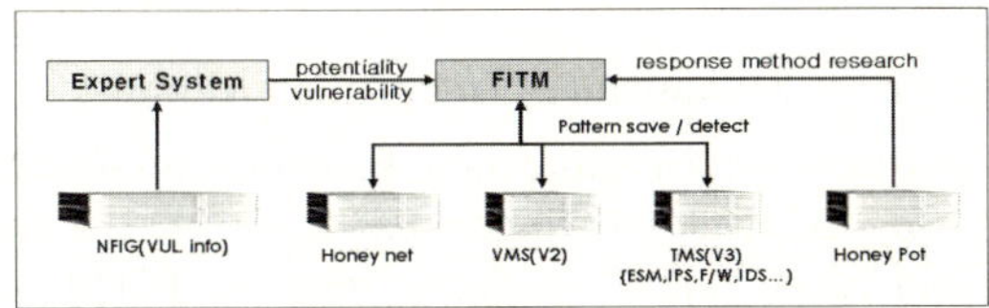

[Picture 2-3]. Associated Equipment and Individual Functions

2.2.2 RCEG (Real Critical Event Gateway)

[Picture 2-4] displays the structure and functions of RCEG. In order to evaluate the levels of threat on the internal network, the module collects security event-feed from four major security equipment in real-time. The data-feed from individual equipment is then given critical-value for determining the level of threat, and are formatted for further analyses before sent to KMIM.

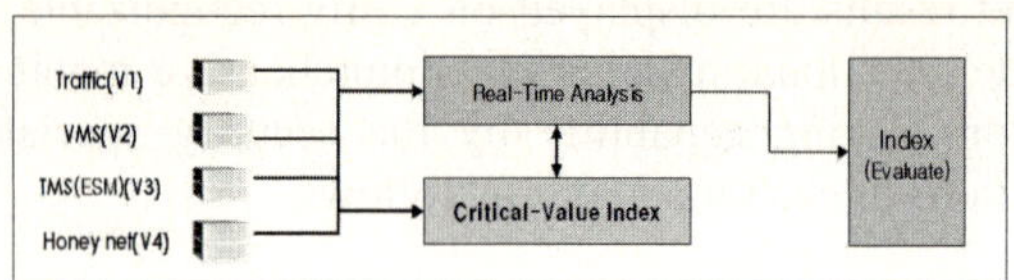

[Picture 2-4]. The Structure and Functions of RCEG

2.2.3   NFIG (News Find Input Gateway)

[Picture 2-5] displays the structure and functions of NFIG. The module's main function is an automatic collection of cyber-threat/vulnerability intelligence and information in real-time. The collected information is fed to a cyber-threat information database, and such values as the nature, characteristics and potential of new cyber-threat elements are analyzed and their potential level of threat is assessed. The result from these analyses is then cross-referenced by the information provided via RCEG in order to enable early analyses of possible cyber-threats.

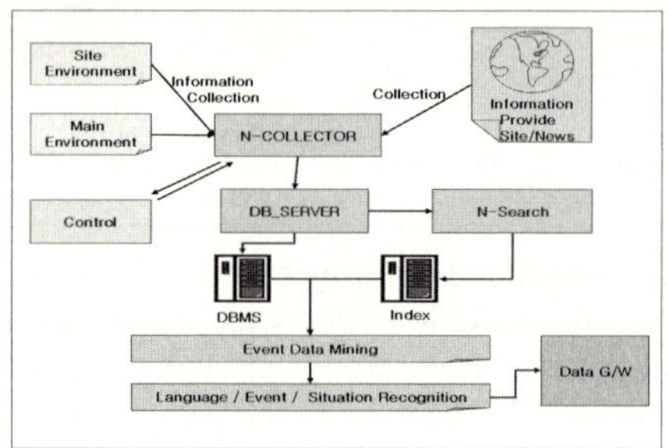

[Picture 2-5]. The Structure and Functions of NFIG

2.2.4   KMIM (Knowledge Management Integration Module)

[Picture 2-6] demonstrates the structure and functions of KMIM. This module's primary function is to calculate EW index based on all the formatted data and information fed from three other modules. Firstly, FITM analyzes potential vulnerability factors based on collected information and data from the internal network. Secondly, the extracted factor is then matched to NFIG's vulnerability data in order to calculate accumulated correlational data in KMIM. Finally, formatted event-data values from NFIG, and RCEG's threat data from security equipment, are standardized to calculated values. The processed information and calculated values from all three modules are then classified in groups using, first, statistical and event-data based knowledge-management analysis methods, and then classification technique by grouping in order to calculate EW index. The fundamental aim of classification technique is to establish a working model for making a similar logical conclusion by a human analyst in making EW decisions.

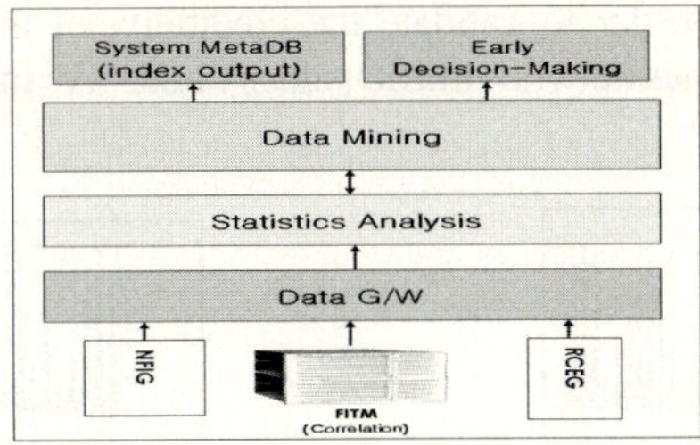

[Picture 2-6]. The Structure and Functions of KMIM

2.2.5   EWVIM (Early-Warning Visual Information Module)

[Picture 2-7] shows the structure and functions of EWVIM. As a main display system for EWTMS, EWVIM provides various graphs and index values for EW decision making.

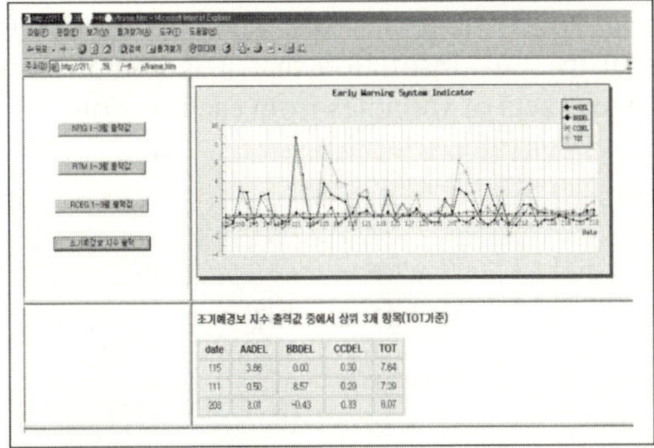

[Picture 2-7]. Display Options of EWVIM

3   The Validity of Suggested System

3.1   Formatted Event-Data Analysis Flow

3.1.1   Traffic Level Analysis on Data Volume

[Chart 3-1] displays a daily traffic graph while [Chart 3-2] does weekly packet volume of the "A" institution, which employs a giga-bit level network. And [Chart 3-3] represents

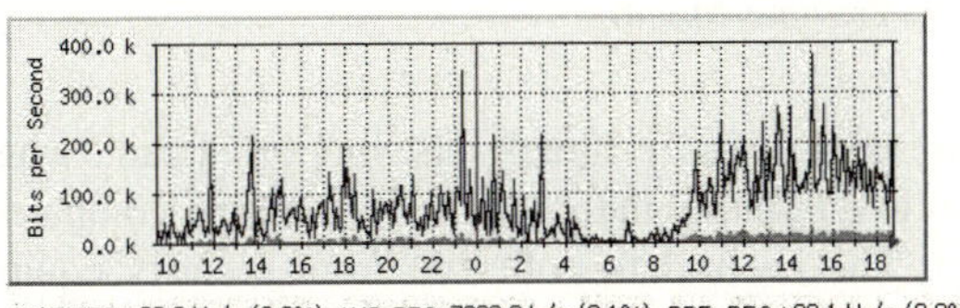

[Chart 3-1]. Daily Traffic Graph

weekly data volume. In order to validate the credibility of the suggested system, this research has utilized various network traffic values of the "A" institution in EWTMS.

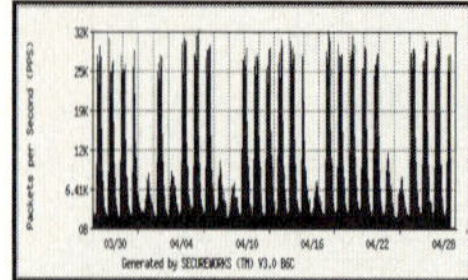 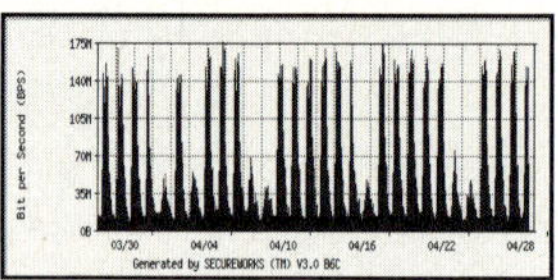

[Chart 3-2]. Weekly Packet Volume Graph   **[Chart 3-3].** Weekly Data Volume Graph

** The values in the graphs are based on the average value of the unit of five-minute traffic in a backbone network*

3.1.2   Information on Other Analysis Tools: VMS, IDS and Honeynet

[Chart 3-4] displays an hourly data of VMS. The data applied to experiment is the actual VMS data from the "A" institution that it is comprised of the correlational weight-added attribute extracts of variables from each section.

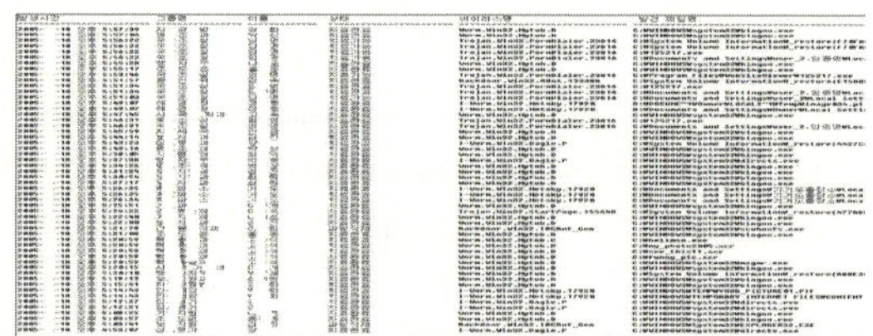

[Chart 3-4]. VMS Data on Hourly

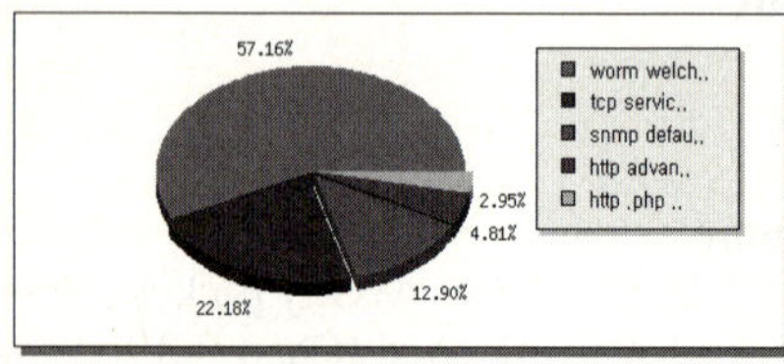 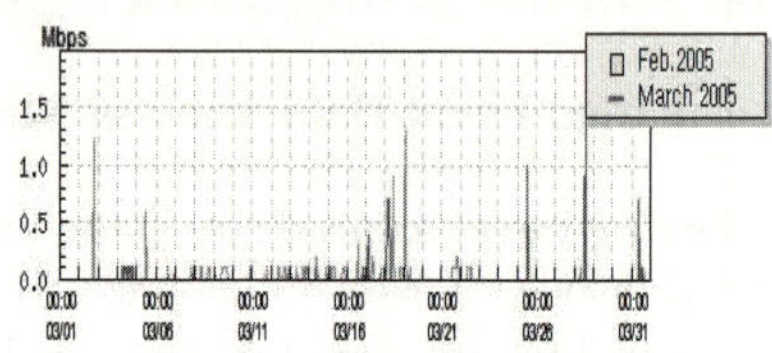

[Chart 3-5 and 6]. The Daily Attack Distribution Chart and Changes in Volumes of Malicious Traffic Compared to the Previous Month

[Chart 3-5] represents a daily attack distribution detail, whereas [Chart 3-6] displays the changes in a monthly malicious traffic volume compared to the data from the previous month. The event-data collected from security equipments events are classified by hourly, daily and monthly bases. Each data is used as a "Data-Set" for statistical analysis of critical-value of model, and it also acts as "Test Data-Set" for the test of critical-value model, while real-time data is used as "Evaluation Data-Set" to evaluate the validity of applied analysis model.

3.1.3 News Data Input

[Chart 3-7] displays a process through which cyber-threat/vulnerability intelligence and information from NFIG is automatically loaded to a Database. The primary data sources of the NFIG module are trusted sites, which provide credible intelligence and information on various cyber-threat/vulnerability, and these collected data is transferred and formatted to text-data which could be loaded to NFIG. Then the converted data is given numerical value through frequency, time-series, and regression analyses, after which data is reprocessed and sent to KMIM after proper weight is added.

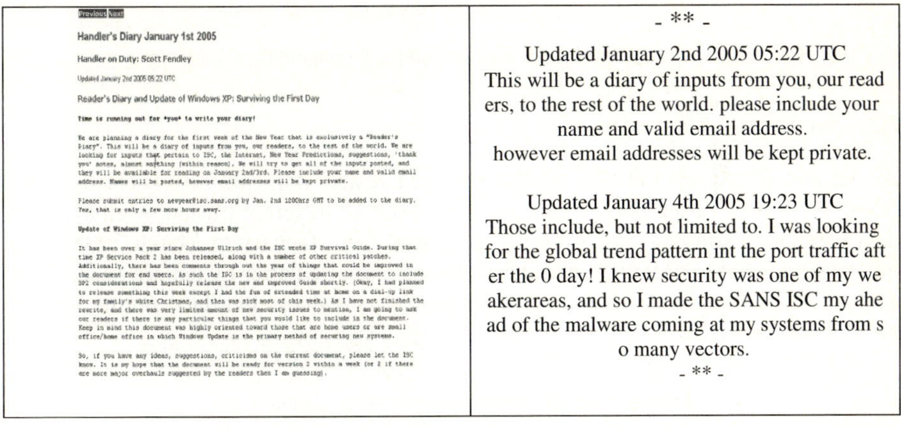

[Chart 3-7]. An Example of News Data Input on Database

3.2 Validation of the Efficiency

3.2.1 Conditions of Experiment

The experiment for the validation of the design was conducted over three month period on a large-scale network with the following conditions: 1) minimum speed is one giga-bit; 2) separate internal and external network; and 3) internal network using virtual IP. The security equipment shown on [Chart 3-8] are applied for the experiment.

Firstly, IPS and TMS are set on the backbone route; and then Honeynet is located on the backbone area to measure information on both internal and external network. VMS is installed on each end-user PC as a client within the main system. The system of "A" network is reconfigured to the EWTMS-based system, and critical-value of each equipment was set based on the last 90 days of data for the test. The same condition was applied to other security equipment, such as VMS, F/W, IDS, IPS and TMS.

3.2.2 Application of Event-Data

In order to verify the credibility of a proposed cyber-threat early-warning system, the existing data from January 2005 to March 2005 was applied to EWTMS and attempted to produce results during the same period. The condition for issuing cyber-threat early-warning is set at momentary traffic (or firewall) volume of 70% of internal or external network sustained over one minute period. This tentative numerical value for EW decision is calculated from the critical-value on which the "A" network is no longer capable of normal functioning.

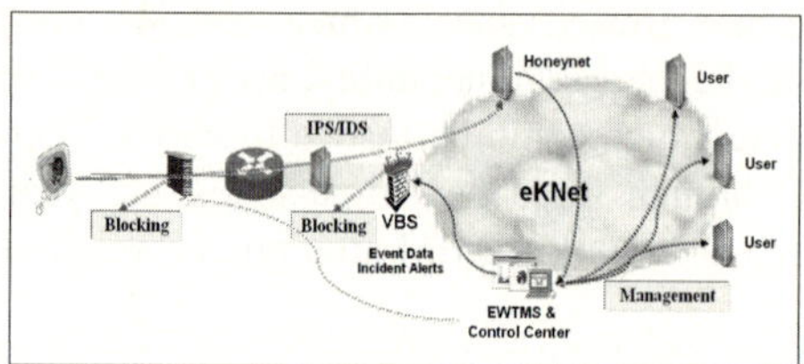

[Chart 3-8]. The Design for Experiment

3.3 The Result of Experiment

At the end of experiment, the NFIG produced results depicted on [Table 3-1] and [Chart 3-9]. NFIG used data values provided from 12 different trusted original event-data generating sources (sites) during the period from January to March 2005. Then the data is loaded to MN D/B, and threat data is classified after by pattern-recognition analysis. This result is again given a set of numerical values after data-mining is taken on MN Database.

[Table 3-1]. The Distribution of NFIG Threat Data

| | 분포 | | | | | |
	1	2	3	4	5	6
표준화(A1)	.9162	.05	1.91998	-.65107	1.06297	1.91998
표준화(A2)	.0000	.36	.83666	-1.67332	3.34664	.00000
표준화(A3)	.6106	-.2700	1.13733	-.80335	1.13733	2.68988
표준화(A4)	3.1449	-.5990	-.08677	-.45990	.65948	-.45990
표준화(A5)	-1.1606	.1828	1.78262	-.30317	3.34696	-.30317
표준화(A6)	-.1129	-.1495	3.99067	-.11129	.57237	-.11129
표준화(A7)	.3596	-1.5066	-.43735	-.43735	.28596	.28596
표준화(A8)	-.5515	-2.7921	-1.39650	1.56891	.08620	.08620
표준화(A9)	-1.3453	-2.5197	-1.03709	.63522	.63522	.63522
표준화(A10)	4.1057	-.0526	2.16798	-1.26656	.69604	-.28526
표준화(A11)	3.1907	-.5661	1.56623	-.46232	.34910	-.46232
표준화(A12)	1.436	-.2703	2.56092	-.92703	-.42875	.56781
표준화(Total)	2.599	-.0258	2.35140	-.92078	1.86057	1.04253
표준화(Avl)	2.0689	-.0224	2.35209	-.92377	1.86169	1.03782
표준화(Avl.old)	.6627	.7724	-.86783	-.10549	.96179	-.86783
표준화(1)	.9162	.0595	1.91998	-.65107	1.06297	1.91998
표준화(2)	.00000	.3666	.83666	-1.67332	3.34664	.00000
표준화(3)	.36106	.2708	1.13733	-.80335	1.13733	2.68988
표준화(4)	.4449	.5990	-.08677	-.45990	.65948	-.45990
표준화(5)	-1.4606	.1828	1.78262	-.30317	3.34696	-.30317
표준화(6)	-.129	-.9495	3.99067	-.11129	.57237	-.11129
표준화(7)	.596	-1.6066	-.43735	-.43735	.28596	.28596
표준화(8)	-.515	-2.7921	-1.39650	1.56891	.08620	.08620
표준화(9)	-1.453	-2.5197	-1.03709	.63522	.63522	.63522
표준화(10)	4.3057	.8526	2.16798	-1.26656	.69604	-.28526
표준화(11)	.8907	.5661	1.56623	-.46232	.34910	-.46232
표준화(12)	.6436	.2703	2.56092	-.92703	-.42875	.56781
표준화(Total)	.0599	-.00258	2.35140	-.92078	1.86057	1.04253
표준화( )	.0689	-.00224	2.35209	-.92377	1.86169	1.03782
표준화(Avl)	.6627	.7724	-.86783	-.10549	.96179	-.86783

상관계수		표준화(A1)	표준화(A2)	표준화(A3)	표준화(A4)	표준화(A5)	표준화(A6)	표준화(A7)	표준화(A8)	표준화(A9)	표준화(A10)
	표준화(A1)	1.000	.20	.270	.082	-.053	.228	-.016	-.124	.097	.140
	표준화(A2)	.20	1.00	.425	.230	.509	.368	-.029	-.192	.011	.274
	표준화(A3)	.270	.25	1.000	.367	.213	.439	.162	-.114	-.008	.441
	표준화(A4)	.082	.30	.367	1.000	-.036	.361	.045	-.144	.032	.781
	표준화(A5)	-.053	.09	.213	-.036	1.000	.415	.017	.054	-.059	.039
	표준화(A6)	.228	.38	.439	.361	.415	1.000	.056	-.135	.000	.535
	표준화(A7)	-.016	-.29	.162	.045	.017	.056	1.000	.166	.016	.041
	표준화(A8)	-.124	-.32	-.114	-.144	.054	-.135	.166	1.000	.278	-.148
	표준화(A9)	.097	.11	-.008	.032	-.059	.000	.016	.278	1.000	-.166
	표준화(A10)	.140	.44	.441	.781	.039	.535	.041	-.148	-.166	1.000
	표준화(A11)	.09	.08	.438	.723	-.078	.344	-.011	-.016	.053	.789
	표준화(A12)	.24	.08	.237	.289	.127	.389	-.123	-.085	-.138	.492
	표준화(Total)	.36	.2	.697	.897	.299	.671	.164	.011	.165	.772
	표준화(Avl)	.36	.12	.697	.698	.289	.672	.164	.010	.164	.772
	표준화(Avl.old)	-.52	.40	.054	.004	.039	-.117	.107	-.037	-.090	-.043
	표준화( )	1.30	.20	.270	.082	-.053	.228	-.016	-.124	.097	.140
	표준화( )	.20	1.00	.425	.230	.509	.368	-.029	-.192	.011	.274
	표준화( )	.70	.25	1.000	.367	.213	.439	.162	-.114	-.008	.441
	표준화( )	.82	.30	.367	1.000	-.036	.361	.045	-.144	.032	.781
	표준화( )	-.53	.09	.213	-.036	1.000	.415	.017	.054	-.059	.039
	표준화( )	.28	.38	.439	.361	.415	1.000	.056	-.135	.000	.535
	표준화( )	-.16	.29	.162	.045	.017	.056	1.000	.166	.016	.041
	표준화( )	-.34	-.32	-.114	-.144	.054	-.135	.166	1.000	.278	-.148
	표준화( )	.7	.11	-.008	.032	-.059	.000	.016	.278	1.000	-.166
	표준화( )	.0	.74	.441	.781	.039	.535	.041	-.148	-.166	1.000
	표준화( )	.8	.18	.438	.723	-.078	.344	-.011	-.016	.053	.789
	표준화( )	.24	.08	.237	.289	.127	.389	-.123	-.085	-.138	.492
	표준화( )	.36	.12	.697	.697	.289	.671	.164	.011	.165	.772
	표준화( )	.36	.12	.697	.698	.289	.672	.164	.010	.164	.772
	표준화( )	-.2	.30	.054	.004	.039	-.117	.107	-.037	-.090	-.043

a. 행렬식 = .000
b. 이 행렬은 양의 유한값이 아닙니다.

[Chart 3-9] displays higher numerical values in the X-coordinate 115-119 and 202-206 compared to the pink line which indicate the level of critical-value. It is clear that when vulnerability data extracted from NFIG is applied, the numerical values of the X-coordinate 111-114, 121-202 and 208 are higher. In particular, the vulnerability on 111 of [Chart 3-10] is a data, the exploit of which was already announced, and is classified as potential vulnerability by FITM.[11] Consequently, it could be assumed that the value on the X-coordinate 115 was influenced by the event as represented on [Chart 3-9].

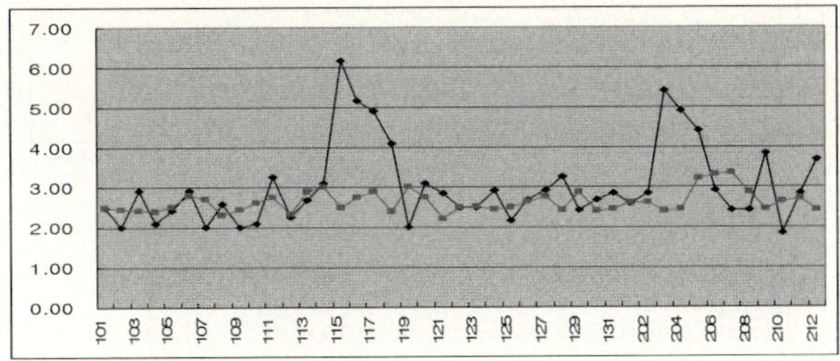

[Chart 3-9]. The Output Value of NFIG (January – March)

[Chart 3-12] is the final test result displayed. According to this, it would have been possible to issue EW against possible threat on three different occasions, the 11th and 15th January, and 3rd February. The credibility of result is based on the fact that NFIG had identified MS05-001, MS05-002 and MS05-003 vulnerabilities, while the attack ratio against FITM identified potential vulnerability was high. According to [Chart 3-11], the increase in potential threat can be identified since the 15th January, and this fact was cross-referenced by a threat assessment report produced by a security manager of the "A" network in that he identified an abnormality of internal network traffic on the 15th January due to the attack by a bot-variation[12]. Consequently, the attacks created potential critical numerical culminating points on the traffic about four times. All in all, it is plausible to assume that, if a proposed cyber-threat early-warning system was in operation, it may had been possible to avoid traffic overflow and prevent threat-factors in the internal network at least four day in advance with EW.

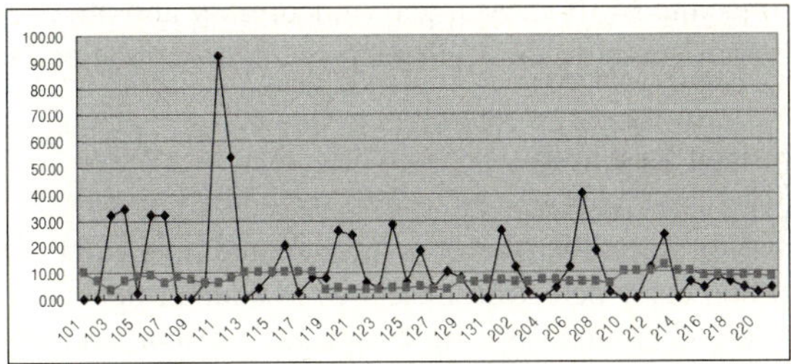

[Chart 3-10]. The Output Value of FITM (January – March)

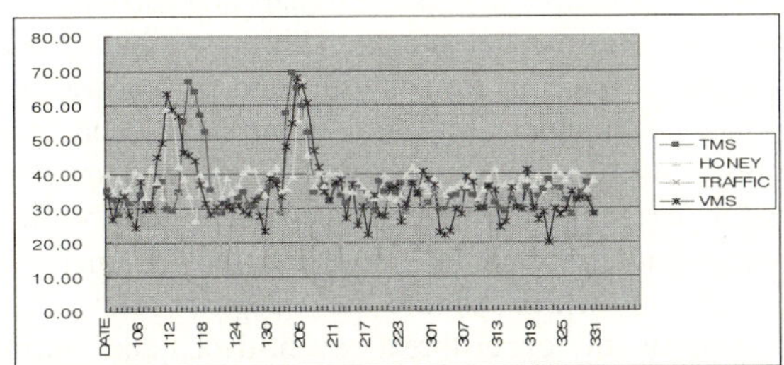

[Chart 3-11]. The Output Value of RCEG (January – March)

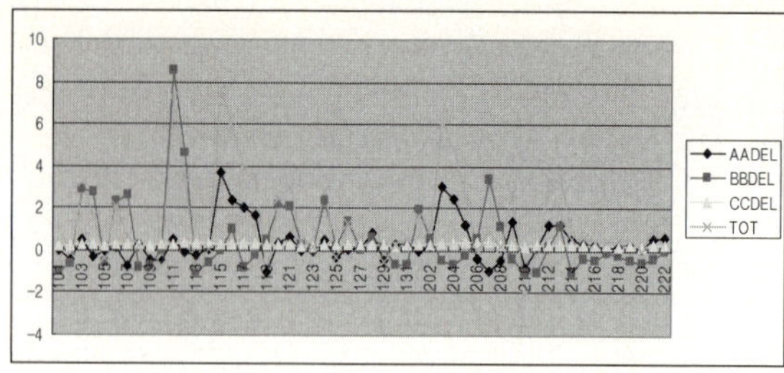

[**Chart 3-12**]. The Output of index of Early Warning and Forecasting

4   Conclusion

4.1   Limits of Experiment

The following limitations were identified during the course of experiment. First of all, despite the fact that the EW indicator appeared on high status on the 15th January, the AA, BB and CC index shown on [Chart 3-12] were low. As a result, it appears that the system reacted to an abnormal traffic of the day rather than acted as the indication of issuing EW. Secondly, although there was a large-scale attack on the MSN messenger platform on the 15th February, such event was only detected by the FITM resulting is a low-level EW indicator posted for the day. It was a result from the fact that the FITM was insufficiently modified to counter the MSN Messenger vulnerabilities since its primary focus was on the diction of web-based abnormal traffic. However, once the MSN messenger vulnerability and attack route are factored in, the system will perform more than sufficiently under such attack scenario.

4.2   Further Required Research

Many nations including Republic of Korea have spared no efforts in search of various crisis management and early detection measures to counter against increasing risks of cyber-attacks. As an alternative to fight against present and clear threats from unknown cyber-criminals and terrorists, this research has proposed a conceptual design of knowledge-based real-time cyber-threat early-warning system. The core of this system is the power to fight against multi-faceted, yet illusive cyber-attacks by early identification and detection of possible threats and early/pre-emptive response to the imminent and/or long-term cyber attacks. This is possible by real-time analyses of a variety of event-data, which in turn is validated by knowledge-based intelligent analytical techniques. Although a few limitations have been identified during the experiment, the result itself is noteworthy as the system demonstrated the potential conceptual basis for designing a working cyber-threat early-warning system. If this system is developed and operated in parallel to the national cyber-security data-warehouse, the asset of which should be adopted solely for the purpose of accumulating a variety of cyber-threat event-data, and sufficient amount of operational experience is accumulated, the proposed system could evolve into a reliable national-level cyber-threat early-warning system.

References

[1] J.L. Hellerstein, F. Zhang, P. Shahabuddin, "A Statistical Approach to Predictive Detection", Computer Networks, vol. 35, pp.77-95, 2001.

[2] F. Zang, J.L. Hellerstein, "An Approach to On-line Predictive Detection", In Proceedings of 8th International Symposium on Modeling, ASCTS, 2000.8.

[3] N.K. Groschwitz and G. C. Polyzos, "A Time Series Model of Long-Term NAFNET Backbone Traffic", In Proceedings of IEEE International Conference on Communications, 1994. 5.

[4] Y. Shu, M. Yu, J. Liu, "Wireless Traffic Modeling and Prediction using Seasonal ARIMA Models", In Proceedings of IEEE International Conference on Communications, Vol.3, 2003, 5.

[5] See http://info.ahnlab.com/ahnlab/report_view.jsp?num=416 for related news.

[6] C. Zou, L. Gao, W. Gong, D. Towsley, "Monitoring and Early Warning for Internet Worms", In Proceedings of the 10th ACM Conference on Computer and Communication Security, p.10, 2003,10.

[7] J.B.D. Cabrera, L. Lewis, X. Qin, C.Gutierrez, W. Lee, R.K. Mehra. "Proactive Intrusion Detection and SNMP based Security Management", In proceedings of IFIP/IEEE Eighth International Symposium on Integrated Network Management, pp.225-254, 2003, 5.

[8] J. Zhai, J. Tian, R. Du, J. Huang, "Network Intrusion Early Warning Model Based on D-S Evidence Theory", In Proceedings of 2003 International Conference on Machine Learning and Cybernetics, Vol. 4, pp.1972-1977, 2003, 11.

[9] J. Li, C. Manikopoulos, "Early Statistical Anomaly Intrusion Detection of DOS Attacks using MIB Traffic Parameters", Information Assurance Workshop, 2003. IEEE Systems, Man and Cybernetics Society, pp.53-59, 2003,6.

[10] Ho Kun Moon, Jin Gi Choe, Yu Kang, Myung Soo Rhee , "Correlation of Network Risk and Defect through an Analysis on Cyber Threat and Vulnerability", KIISC 2005-1, 2005.2.

[11] See http://isc.sans.org/alldiaries.php?month=3&year=2005 for related topic.

[12] The "A" Government Agency's Internal Report, " February 2005 Security Response Report", 2005, 3.

Learning-Based Algorithm for Detecting Abnormal Traffic*

Changwoo Nam[1], Seongjin Ahn[2],**, and Jinwook Chung[1]

[1] Dept. of Electrical and Computer Engineering, Sungkyunkwan Univ., Suwon,
Kyeonggi-do, Korea
{cwnam, jwchung}@songgang.skku.ac.kr
[2] Department of Computer Education, Sungkyunkwan Univ., Seoul, Korea
sjahn@songgnag.skku.ac.kr

Abstract. Modern worm viruses not only tend to promote host attacks, but generate high volumes of traffic and frequently result in network failure. This paper proposes a learning-based algorithm for detecting abnormal traffic, ensuring efficient protection against worm viruses, and promoting network level security. The algorithm identifies abnormal traffic, and learns network level characteristics of this traffic, to prevent in advance factors that may result in network failure. The algorithm presented in this paper was applied to the network system, and simulation results showed that unlike previous network systems, the proposed algorithm more efficiency detects worm viruses, and overall, results in improved network security.

1   Introduction

Network failure rate, due to worm attacks exploiting vulnerability in TCP/IP protocols or operating systems, is increasing. In particular, worm viruses, which spread rapidly and broadly, are an important consideration in network security [7][8].

Technology detecting worm viruses using scanning strategy, common in all worm viruses, is actively being researched, with the goal of preventing damage from worm viruses in a network. Major characteristics in scanning strategy used by worm, include the following. In order to find a target to attack, addresses are randomly generated over a short time period and many connection attempts are made. In attempts to connect to the many generated addresses, it tries to connect to addresses that are not in actual use, increasing the connection failure rate. Due to these two processes, the worm generates considerable network traffic [1][3].

Worm attacks are becoming more sophisticated and intelligent and tend to attack an entire network, rather than attacking and destroying a single host

---

* This work was supported by grant No. R01-2004-000-10618-0 from the Basic Research Program of the Korea Science and Engineering Foundation.
** Corresponding author.

[12]. As host-level security measures are sufficiently strong to prepare for such attacks, host level security management is recommended [2][3].

This paper presents a learning-based method for examining network connections for each host, analyzing worm viruses and unknown traffic attack patterns for efficiently preventing worm attacks and securing the network at a network level. This method uses IP and MAC addresses to examine the connected IP address at each time period. If it exceeds the critical connection value, it is judged as a worm virus. In addition, an increased critical value to promote the efficiency of the algorithm may be applied so that the algorithm can "learn" the normal traffic of the specific network and detect worm viruses during a sudden increase in the number of connections.

2   Worm Virus Detection Algorithm

This paper proposes an algorithm that uses the characteristics of the scanning strategy common in worm viruses, to detect various worms [1][9]. This scanning strategy was chosen because the attack methods of worm viruses may vary widely, and most of the features of the scanning strategy are similar. In order to find an IP address to attack, IP addresses are generated randomly in the scanning strategy, and this causes frequent attempts to connect to IP addresses that are not in actual use[3][9]. Another characteristic is that a large number of IP addresses are searched in a very short time, enabling the worm to quickly spread [1][9]. Using these two characteristics, worm viruses can be detected based on the number of IP addresses that a host communicates to within a time unit.

A network traffic learning method to be utilized during normal times was considered in this paper for more accurate detection of worm viruses. This method periodically analyzes normal network traffic patterns, creates a database of the patterns, and continues to analyze and learn normal traffic patterns. Such a feature makes it possible for the learning-based abnormal traffic detection algorithm to learn flexibly in different network environments. Based on the database records, if the host attempting connection to the network exceeds a certain critical value or if the number of hosts trying to connect increases suddenly, it can be assumed that a worm virus has infected the network.

The selection of items to be analyzed is important in efficiently detecting worm viruses, as the number of items is inversely proportional to system performance, and proportional to detection success rate. To promote the efficiency of the algorithm, this paper uses the worm's characteristic of attempting to connect with many hosts in a short time, and sets packet analysis items as destination port number and IP address of the source and destination [5].

2.1   Packet Capture and Count

The destination port of the packet and IP addresses of the source and destination are used to efficiently detect worm viruses. Well-known port numbers for worm attacks such as port 80, 135 and 445 are defined in advance, to enhance the performance of the algorithm[5][6].

The following Figure.1 shows the procedure for packet capture and count.

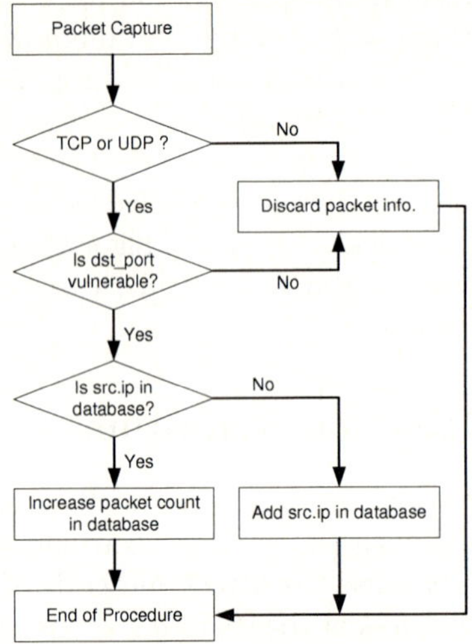

Fig. 1. Packet Capture and Count Procedure

```
        V ← Vulnerable Port List
        D ← Connection Count Database

    Packet-Count-Procedure

1.      Packet ← New Captured Packet
2.      IF ((packet.protocol != TCP) and
                        (packet.protocol != UDP))
3.          THEN Discard packet.
4.      ELSE IF (packet.dst_port ∈ V)
5.          THEN Discard packet.
6.      ELSE IF (packet.src_ip ∈ D[packet.src_ip])
7.          THEN add packet.src_ip in D[packet.src_ip]
8.      ELSE increase ip_count in D[packet.src_ip]
9.      END OF IF

    End of Procedure
```

Fig. 2. Packet Capture and Count Algorithm

The algorithm repeats the above process whenever a new packet is captured. In the packet capture process, only TCP and UDP packets are captured, and those otherwise are discarded. Then, the destination port of the captured packet is analyzed to see if it matches the predefined vulnerable port, and if it does not match, the packet is discarded. The information of the captured packet is compared with the database. If there is no IP address information of the source, IP information is added to the database. Otherwise, the packet count value in the database is increased. Figure.2 shows the packet capture algorithm based on Figure.1.

2.2   Worm Virus Detection

Worm virus detection is performed by the worm virus detection algorithm based on the database set up by the packet capture and count algorithm in Figure.2. This is done by comparison with the database and counting the number of network connections of the same address as the source IP address, to detect abnormal traffic such as worm viruses.

The worm virus detection algorithm is performed periodically. It analyzes all IP information stored in the database and takes account of the same source IP address. If the number of attempted connections by the source IP address for a certain period of time exceeds the connection critical value α, the algorithm detects that the specific host of the source IP address is infected by a worm virus. The following formula (1) can be made for the connection critical value α, by defining each packet from the source IP address as C_i and count value as I_c.

$$\sum_{i=0}^{\infty} C_i = I_c$$
$$I_c > \alpha \rightarrow WormVirus - Detection(1)$$

To increase the efficiency of the algorithm, the increased critical value β is applied so that if attempts to connect to the network increase suddenly, it can be detected that the host of the source IP address is infected by a worm virus. This detection is based on the count value of the specific source IP in the database. Even if the number of attempted connections does not exceed the connection critical value α, if the number is detected to have increased by the increased critical value β times, it is detected as a worm virus. When defining the last count value of the source IP address as j, and the current count value divided by the increased critical value β as d, then the following formula (2) applies.

$$\frac{I_c}{\beta} = d$$
$$d > j \rightarrow WormVirus - Detection(2)$$

As shown in Formula (2), d is derived by dividing the current count value I_c by the increased critical value β, and if d is larger than j, a worm virus is detected. Figure.3 shows the worm virus detection procedure with applied formulas.

The worm virus detection algorithm operates periodically in the above sequence. As shown, the connection critical value α and increased critical value β are criteria for detecting worm viruses in the algorithm, and are required to set appropriate critical values for each network environment.

The following Figure.4 shows the algorithm based on the worm virus detection procedure in Figure.3.

3   Algorithm Test

3.1   Operation of Host Infected by Worm Virus

In order to detect abnormal operation of a worm-infected host, packets of an infected host attempting connection, and the number of attempts, were

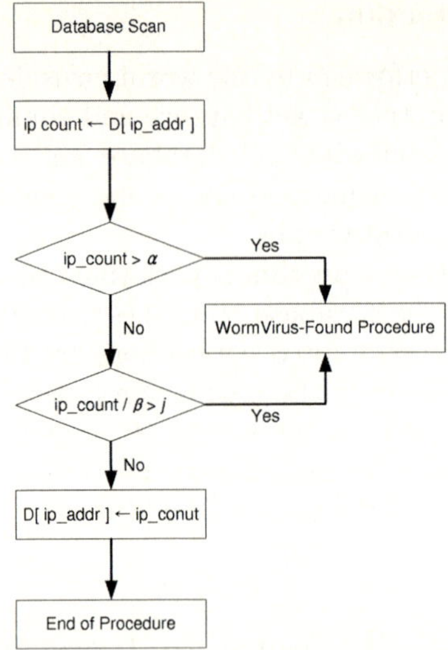

Fig. 3. Worm Virus Detection Procedure

analyzed. A host infected by a type of Sasser virus [4] was chosen as the host to be examined.

Only packets attempting to connect to port 445 were tested. An independent Linux system connected to a dummy hub captured packets using the pcap library. The packet connection was examined each second; the results are shown in Figure.5. In a normally operating network, approximately 2,700 ARP request packets were counted per minute, but were different for randomly generated

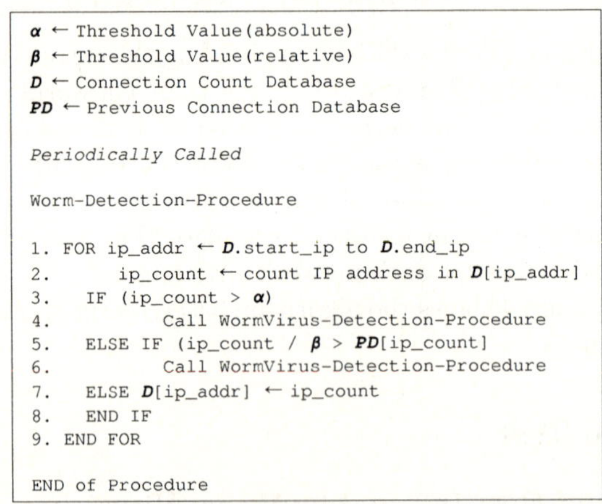

```
α ← Threshold Value(absolute)
β ← Threshold Value(relative)
D ← Connection Count Database
PD ← Previous Connection Database


Periodically Called

Worm-Detection-Procedure

1. FOR ip_addr ← D.start_ip to D.end_ip
2.      ip_count ← count IP address in D[ip_addr]
3.    IF (ip_count > α)
4.          Call WormVirus-Detection-Procedure
5.    ELSE IF (ip_count / β > PD[ip_count])
6.          Call WormVirus-Detection-Procedure
7.    ELSE D[ip_addr] ← ip_count
8.    END IF
9. END FOR

END of Procedure
```

Fig. 4. Worm Virus Detection Algorithm

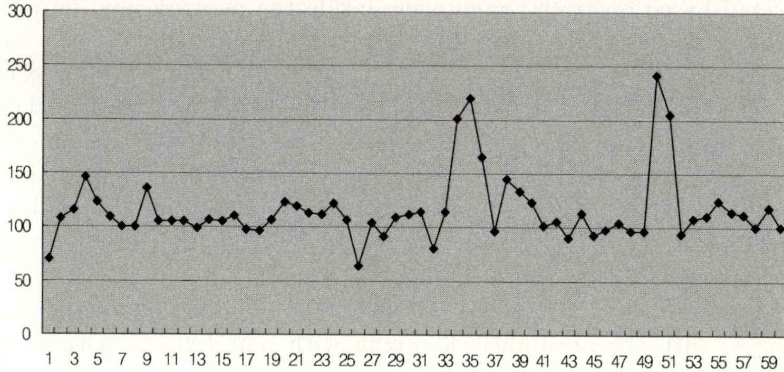

Fig. 5. Number of IP Addresses Attempted for Connection by Worm-Infected Host

addresses, and a host infected by the worm virus attempted connection to over 6,000 hosts per minute[10][11]. Based on these analysis results, it can be seen that an infected host attempts many more connections than a normal host.

3.2   Worm Virus Detection Test

In this paper, critical values were set by the values shown in Table.1 and ARP packets were generated to test the detection of worm viruses[10][11]. The test was repeated five consecutive times, and was performed by attempting connection over the connection critical value and significantly increasing the number of connections from the previous connection in a certain time period.

The connection critical value α in Test 1 was set at 40, but the actual number of host connections was 50, and the connection was judged as a worm virus. Connections in Test 2 to Test 4 did not exceed the critical value, but in Test 5, connections increased by more than 8 times. The increased critical value β, from that of Test 4, was judged as a worm virus even though it did not exceed the connection critical value α.

Table 1. Worm Virus Detection Test

Number	Connection Critical Value (α)	Increased Critical Value (β)	Connected Hosts	Detection Results
1	40	8	50	Detected
2	40	8	5	No Change
3	40	8	20	No Change
4	40	8	4	No Change
5	40	8	35	Detected

4   Conclusion

This paper presented a learning-based algorithm for detecting abnormal traffic, which can protect networks from worm viruses and various attacks. Worm viruses are detected based on traffic monitoring inside the network, and only packets attempting connection to vulnerable ports were examined, to easily increase analysis accuracy at the minimum cost. The number of connections at each host was examined periodically, to detect abnormal operation, and previous data were utilized for accurate measurement, this made it possible to include a method for learning normal usage patterns. However, more test and research are required for setting critical values, and the number of packets to capture and analyze data increased as the size of the network increased, this may have caused problems in the performance of the algorithm-applied system.

The algorithm in this paper is based on the common characteristics of a worm virus, with the advantage of coping with mutated and viruses created in the future. By adding a network traffic analysis factor, a traffic analyzing program based on this algorithm can be created. In addition, this algorithm can develop into a more efficient and secure network management system, through integration with network management systems. In order to enhance this research, traffic sampling methods should be applied and a flexible approach to analysis items is required. Last, establishing an integrated security system using network devices applied to the proposed algorithm should be considered.

References

1. Guofei Gu, Monirul Sharif, Xinzhou Qin, David Dagon, Wenke Lee and George Riley, Worm Detection Early Warning and Response Based on Local Victim Information, Computer Security Applications Conference, 2004. 20th Annual
2. Jason C. Hung, Kuan-Cheng Lin,Anthony Y. Chang, Nigel H. Lin and Louis H. Lin, A Behavior-based Anti-Worm System, Preceeding on AINA'03, China, 2003.
3. Vincent Berk, George Bakos and Robert Morris, Designing a Framework for Active Worm Detection on Global Networks, Preceeding on IWIA'03, 2003.
4. Sumeet Singh, Cristian Estan, George Varghese, and Stefan Savage. Automated worm fingerprinting. In Proceedings of the 6th ACM/USENIX Symposium on Operating System Design and Implementation (OSDI), December 2004.
5. Behrouz A.Forouzan, TCP/IP Protocol Suite 3rd Edition, McGrawHill 2006.
6. W.Richard Steavens, TCP/IP Illustrated, Volume 1 The Protocol, Addision-Wesley, 1999.
7. N. Weaver, V. Paxson, S. Dataniford, and R. Cunningham. A taxonomy of computer worms. In proceedings of ACM CCS Workshop on Rapid Malcode (WORM'03), Octobrt 2003.
8. C. C. Zou, D. Towsley, and Gong, On the performance of Internet worm scanning strategies, J. Performance Evaluation, 2005.
9. Sumeet Singh, Cristian Estan, George Varghese, Stefan Savage. Automated worm fingerprinting. 6th ACM/USENIX symposium on Operating System Design and Implementation (OSDI), December 2004.
10. D.C. Plummer, RFC 0826: Ethernet Address Resolution Protocol, 1982.
11. K. Kwon, s. Ahn, and J. Chung, Network Security Management Using ARP Spoofing, Proc. ICCSA 2004, 2004.
12. X. Qin, D. Dagon, G. Gu, W. Lee, M. Qarfield, and P. Allor. Worm detection using local networks. The recent Advances of Intrusion Detection TAID'04, September 2004.

Energy-Efficient Routing Protocol Depending on Dynamic Message Communication over Wireless Sensor Network

KwangKyum Lee[1], Yongtae Shin[2], and Ara Khil[2]

[1] Dept. of Computing, Graduate School, Soongsil University, Sangdo5-Dong,
Dongjak-Gu, Seoul, Republic of Korea
Goodwin77@cherry.ssu.ac.kr
[2] Dept. of Computing, Graduate School, Soongsil University, Sangdo5-Dong,
Dongjak-Gu, Seoul, Republic of Korea
{shin, ara}@cherry.ssu.ac.kr

Abstract. We propose an energy-efficient routing mechanism for maintaining uniform distribution of each sensor's energy through shorter paths. We define two metrics – energy level and vector information. The energy level describes how much the energy of the sensor remains and the vector information explains whether the direction towards the sink. Using the two factors, we choose leaders with higher energy level and the vector information when any sensor node tries to send the sink some messages. Whenever the sensor node delivers each one message to the sink, the selected leader node may be different dynamically through our defined two metrics. So we expect that the energy level of every sensor node can be maintained uniformly over the entire sensor network. Therefore, sudden sensor failure caused by battery exhaust and network partition caused by some sensor's sudden deaths can be prevented. We analyze our DyMC through evaluating and comparing with existing research such as directed diffusion.

1 Introduction

Wireless Sensor Network (WSN) is composed of many sensors and sinks which collect sensing data. Sensor network is similar to ad-hoc network. However the sensor network is more important for energy consumption than one over the ad-hoc network. Energy efficiency should consider less energy consumption as well as uniform consumption of the energy and both of them are considered at the same time to set a path because much energy consumption threats network survivability and energy consumption of specific nodes incurs network partition. Recently, routing mechanism has studied for energy efficiency over WSN because data delivery is main job. However, most of researches [1, 2, 3] have been considered less energy consumption or uniform consumption, not both.

G. Min et al. (Eds.): ISPA 2006 Ws, LNCS 4331, pp. 1025 – 1033, 2006.

We proposed an energy-efficient routing algorithm for uniformly reducing energy consumption of each node through finding shorter path from the sink and rotating nodes as routers. Chapter 2 introduces some energy efficient routing algorithm [1, 2, 3] and chapter 3 describes our energy efficient routing algorithm. Conclusion and future work is described in chapter 4.

2   Related Works

[1] is efficiently disseminates information among sensors in an energy-constrained wireless sensor network. Nodes running a SPIN communication protocol name their data using high-level data descriptor, called meta-data. Each node use meta-data negotiations to eliminate the transmission of redundant data throughout the network. In addition, nodes can base their communication decisions both upon application-specific knowledge of the data and upon knowledge of the resources that are available to them. This allows the sensors to efficiently distribute data given a limited energy supply.

[2] is data-centric in that all communication is for named data. All nodes in a directed diffusion based network are application-aware. This enables diffusion to achieve energy savings by selecting empirically good paths and by caching and processing data in-network. And data generated by sensor nodes is named by attribute-value pairs. A node requests data by sending *interests* for named data. Data matching the interest is then 'drawn' down towards that node. Intermediate nodes can cache, or transform data, and may direct interests based on previously cached data.

[3] performs restricted flooding. A sensor node sends data to a flooding set in range of two hops. It floods data not to all neighbor nodes but to some nodes which have ability to forward data in flooding area. This mechanism reduces a number of forwarding messages.

3   Energy-Efficient Routing Protocol Depending on Dynamic Message Communication (DyMC)

In this paper, we propose distributed routing mechanism to communicate dynamic message for efficient energy consumption of a sensor node over WSN. Our DyMC can be applied to any topology of WSN and increase energy efficiency of whole sensor network. To increase energy efficiency of sensor network, DyMC controls energy consumption to keep remained energy of sensor nodes to uniform status and avoids traffic concentration. Therefore we propose a mechanism that priority paths are set up based on energy status of neighbor nodes. And when setting up the paths up to the sink, we establish directive paths towards the sink using vector information together with the energy status of them. In case of some node failure, using multi direction vector information up to sink, another path is reset up through comparison of energy status of them. Fig.1 displays proposed network model.

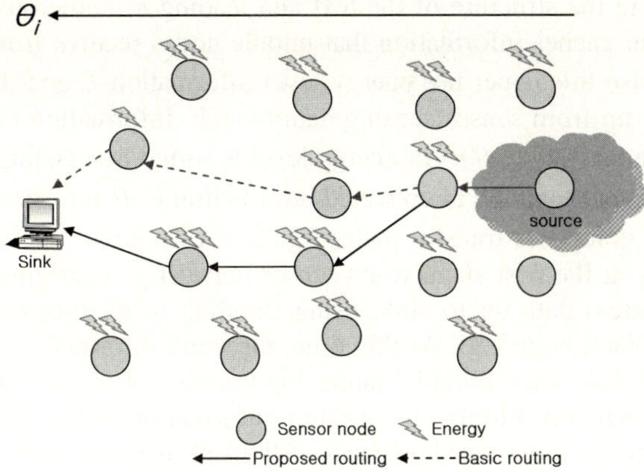

Fig. 1. Proposed Network Model

3.1 Comparison to Energy Level of Sensor Node

We define 3 energy levels depending on remaining energy amount of sensor nodes. Whenever the energy level is changed, the nodes announce their energy level to their neighbors. Depth of the energy levels can be dynamically determined by requests of an application. Suppose that based energy level is N which is total energy value divided by N. and then the energy level is N+D when application request collection of robust and precise time-sensitive information about emergency conditions or battle situations. On the other hands, the energy level is N-D when application request collection of information which regards of less sensitive-time than pre-defined level for a long time about ecology environment investigation such as resource of deep-sea, and changes of the earth's surface. Therefore additional level D is dynamically changed by various application requirement.

For establishing routing paths, sensor nodes advertise their energy levels to their neighbors and determine directions of the neighbors for a sink. So the nodes maintain an energy table containing the energy level and vector information. DyMC selects sink-directive nodes with higher energy level. When the energy levels of nodes are changed, the nodes advertise their energy level. If energy level of the node is lower than one of neighbors, a role of router is changed to a node with higher energy. So as a result of the procedure, the path is reset with nodes of higher energy to maintain shorter path. As each sensor node does not transfer the information periodically but transfers their state information only when there are changes in an energy level, whole energy consumption efficiency increases than flooding their own information periodically. At this time, each sensor node selects a period to maximize efficiency of energy consumption based on a kind of applications.

3.2 Setting Up Path to Make Good Use of Energy Level and Direction Information

Please always cancel any superfluous definitions that are not actually used in your text. If you do not, these may conflict with the definitions of the macro package, causing changes in the structure of the text and leading to numerous mistakes in the proofs. This paper caches information that middle nodes receive from neighbor node to set up path. Also this paper use energy level information $\mathcal{E}_i$ and direction vector θ up to sink, to set up from sensor sensing data to sink. Information of stored nodes at cache is formed a pair of ($\mathcal{E}_i$, θ_i). An energy level is sorted descending series period of ten days from the highest node of collected information $\mathcal{E}_i$. θ_i information mapped into $\mathcal{E}_i$ and is used to composes transfer path of gathered resource. Each sensor node has maximum energy at the first stage when sensor network is configured. At this stage, each sensor transfers data up to sink, using flooding to all direction of directional information that each node had. At this time, direction information is set up to consider direction of sink when initially happening transaction to sink. It is assumed that each node know that sink and its own location information apply GPS coordinateness system. We define location coordinateness of the sink is (0, 0) and coordinateness of source node is (x_i, y_i), then distance is from source node to sink. If vector distance of any sensor node from self-node to neighbor-node is shorter than distance, then the sensor node θ_i information sets 1 that regards of vector direction of sensor towards sink. On the other hands, vector distance is larger than distance   then the sensor node θ_i information sets 0 that regard of the vector direction of sensor is not towards sink.

If path is set up and data transfer is accomplished, process to calculate node's energy amount is stared. In case of energy change, each sensor node advertises their energy information and location information to neighbor node and update cache information of neighbor nodes. At this time, information of direction vector θ_i that node

---

input : *Adv* from neighbors
output : *opt path* that collected data

Procedure *Data delive (i)*
c := 0
If receive *Adv* ($\mathcal{E}_i$, θ_i) from direct neighbors **then**
Begin
Direction:= **Compare location** *(θ_i)*
    If *Direction = 1* **then**
    Begin
        c := c+1
        cache (c) := **cache init** *($\mathcal{E}_i$, θ_i)*
        sort *cache*
        opt path:= **max** *(cache)*
        Deliver packet data through *opt path*
        *recent-energy-level:=***calculate** current-energy-level
        If *pre-energy-level > recent-energy-level* **then**
        Begin
        Advertise *Adv* ($\mathcal{E}_i$, θ_i) to its neighbors
        End
        pre-energy-level := **calculate** *recent-energy-level*
    End
End
Else
  Listen *Adv* ($\mathcal{E}_i$, θ_i)

{opt path is the path that towards the next neighbor node}

Fig. 2. Setting path algorithm

has consists main-direction vector and sub-direction vector that transfer up to sink through node that energy level is high among cache information that node has. Then, sub-direction vectors stores in cache for making a detour against urgent change of node. Fig.2 is algorithm to set up path by using remainder energy amount and direction vector. And table 1 is specification of a variable and a function to be used by algorithm.

Table 1. Function description

Definition	Description
C	Count value of cache information
receive	Received messages form neighbor nodes
cache init(*x, y*)	Cache initialization
Direct	Stored value of location information
Adv(*x, y*)	Advertising message of energy and location information values
Compare-location(*x*)	Comparison Function for location values
sort	Sorting cache information
opt path	Optimized path
max(*x*)	Maximum cache information
Cache	Cache information
Deliver	Transfer data
Recent-energy-level	Value of recent energy
pre-energy-level	Value of past energy
calculate	Calculate energy changes
Advertise	Advertise neighbor nodes
Listen	Stand by received information form neighbor nodes

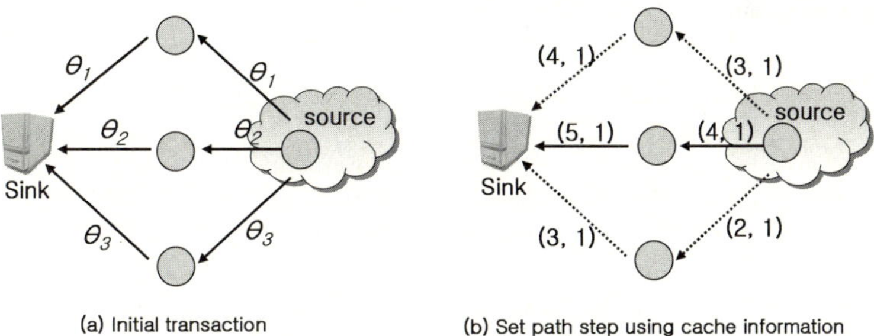

(a) Initial transaction   (b) Set path step using cache information

Fig. 3. Setting path scheme by steps

Fig.3 describes a procedure to create a route hop-by-hop. Each node's energy is full in childhood that compose sensor network at Fig.3-(a). Fig.3-(a) shows a case of not using path establishment. Source node that is passed transaction signal passes collected data to sink through direction vector θ_i's all paths. For example, each nodes transfer data through θ_1, θ_2, θ_3 which are direction vector information from source node that collects sensed information to neighbor nodes. And then nodes that received data from neighbor nodes retransmit data through θ_1, θ_2, θ_3 which are having self information until it reach sink.

Fig.3–(b) shows when energy level of each node is differentiated because consumption of energy is fitful at communication process.

Each sensor transmits sensed data along path that only energy level is high and vector information set by 1, among the pair of energy level information and direction vector. When energy level changed, each node transfer sensed information searching energy and direction vector information from node to sink. And that time each node route energy level is 4 and direction vector information is 1. Grade of own energy of information of node that is passed data which level is 5 and direction vector information transmits data to sink for 1 direction.

3.3 Refresh of Path

Each of nodes broadcasts energy and direction vector information of neighbor node whenever own energy level is changed. This time, each node transmit data using vector information that have high energy level first of organized energy and direction information by descending series period of ten days and remainder of information do cash. If changes occurs and is not used in case schedule node does not operate on network. When transmit data by secondary route using information that have the energy of first highest level of remainder cache information. It updates path without deteriorating efficiency of whole network by data transmission through second path as ambivalent.

4 Performance Analysis

We used NS-2 simulator for performance analysis of DyMC in chapter 3. And then we compare performance of our proposed Energy Distribution Routing scheme with Directed Diffusion.

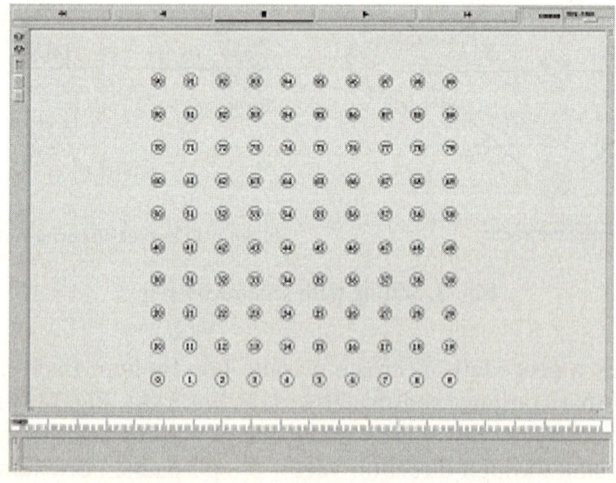

Fig. 4. Network simulation model

Our simulation environment is that 100 node are arranged for grid structure and transmit data to 10^{-6} seconds from number-27 node to number-90 node. Initial energy was established by 26kJ[5], each bits transmission energy when send and received of message calculated 0.021mJ/0.014mJ[5], and transmission data 128 byte 100 times.

Fig. 4 is graph that express mean value of a 10 times simulation for 20 seconds. This simulation result shows that DyMC is better than Directed Diffusion for maximum 4% energy efficient.

And we know that averagely energy decrement of DyMC about 0.4% and Directed Diffusion is about 2%. Therefore our DyMC is better than Directed Diffusion averagely about 1.6% energy efficient.

We know that DyMC is decreasing gently remained energy amount average than Directed Diffusion after 6 seconds in Fig.5. Therefore DyMC is superior to Directed Diffusion in side of whole energy consumption. Table 2 is simulation result that compares with DyMC and Directed Diffusion.

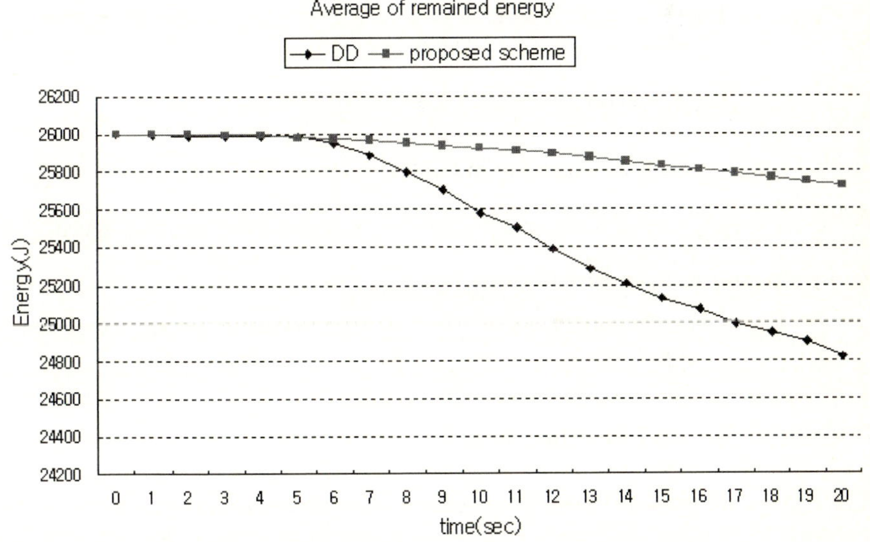

Fig. 5. Average of remained energy through time sequence

Fig. 6 shows that number of exhausted nodes changes by time sequences. Directed diffusion is rapidly changed number of nodes after 12secs. But our DyMC is changed number of nodes after 21secs. So a numerical difference directed diffusion and DyMC are 9secs. This simulation results are show that our DyMC is more robust energy consumption than directed diffusion. But, on the other hands a number of exhausted nodes are similar both of them after 21 sec.

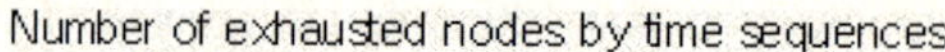

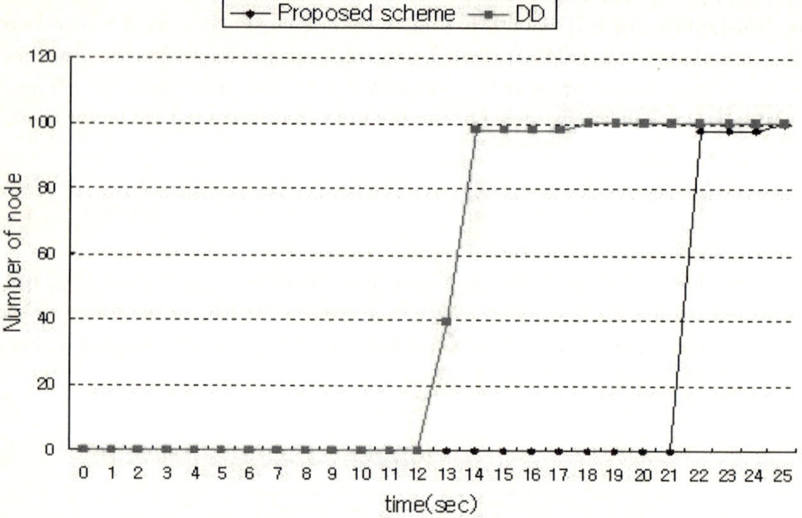

Fig. 6. Number of exhausted nodes according to time sequence

Table 2. Comparison of DyMC and Directed Diffusion

Energy consumption ratio	energy comsumption speed
DyMC<DD	DyMC<DD
Simulation results	
Energy consumption average	Start time when energy exhausted
DyMC<DD	DyMC>DD

5   Conclusion and Further Works

In this paper, we proposed that Energy efficient Distribution Routing scheme considered energy levels and directions. And we do not perform periodic flooding technique which exchange of control messages acquired to distribution effect of energy consumption. Each node floods self-data that is information about direction and energy level when energy level changing.

We used information that set all directions toward sink when data transmitted for initial data collected. Each node sets routing path that energy utilize is maximum using energy level and direction information when energy level changed. Also, in case that some nodes are failed, efficiency of network topology is not affected by nodes failure because of using multi-paths.

At last, we prove that our DyMC is energy efficient for whole network topology by simulations. Furthermore we need to analyze energy consumption of each nodes may have to be achieved subdividing proposal.

If you have supplementary material, e.g., executable files, video clips, or audio recordings, on your server, simply send the volume editors a short description of the supplementary material and inform them of the URL at which it can be found. We will add the description of the supplementary material to the online version of LNCS and create a link to your server. Alternatively, if this supplementary material is not to be updated at any stage, then it can be sent directly to the volume editors, together with all the other files.

References

1. W. R. Heinzelman, J. Kulik, H. Balakrishnan, "Adaptive Protocols for Information Dissemination in Wireless Sensor Networks," Proc. Mobicom '99, pp 174-185.
2. Chalermek Intanagonwiwat, Ramesh Govindan and Deborah Estrin, "Directed Diffusion: A Scalable and Robust Communication Paradigm for Sensor Networks," Proceedings of the Sixth Annual International Conference on Mobile Computing and Networks, August 2000.
3. Taek Jin Kwon; Gerla, M.; Varma, V.K.; Barton, M.; Hsing, T.R., "Efficient flooding with passive clustering-an overhead-free selective forward mechanism for ad hoc/sensor networks," Proceedings of the IEEE , Vol. 91 Issue 8 pp. 1210 - 1220, Aug. 2003.
4. UCB/LBLN/VINT, NS(Network Simulator) Version 2, Online:
   http://www.mach.cs.berkeley.edu/ns/
5. David W. Carman, P. Kruus and B. Matt, "Constraints and Approches for Distributed Sensor Network Security," Technical Report, NAI LABS, 2000.

Design of Authentication Mechanism Using PANA CTP in FMIPv6 Environment*

Insu Kim and Keecheon Kim[**]

Department of Computer Science & Engineering, Konkuk University
Seoul, Korea
{darkguy, kckim}@konkuk.ac.kr

Abstract. MIPv6 working Group in IETF suggests Mobile IPv6 to support host mobility. In order to make MIPv6 to be more practical, FMIPv6 which is a fast handover scheme to optimize the packet delivery route is considered. FMIPv6 protocol assumes layer 2 triggers from the link layer. Through the movement detection and a new CoA configuration using the information in advance, MN can perform a binding update and receive data destined to the MN as soon as a new link to a new access router is established. The routing failure until BU is completed is also addressed by using bi-directional tunnel between the access routers. CTP is used in a bi-directional tunnel between pAR and nAR. nAR must authenticate the MN by using PANA architecture. The authentication process for MN is an associated process of PANA at the wireless link and AAA in the network. Both processes carry messages for authentication. The attendant can be an AR providing the Mobile IP service, and also acts as a PAA to communicate PANA messages with the MN. AAH or HA in a home network can authenticate the mobile node and pAR has authentication information for MN. However, nAR has no authentication information. Therefore, existing authentication mechanism is not acceptable in FMIPv6. For secure FMIPv6, new authentication mechanism should be considered. Our research propose an authentication mechanism using PANA-CTP in FMIPv6 environment.

1   Introduction

In order to support IPv6 mobility in the carrier's network, end-to-end IPv6 mobility needs to be provided. A mobile host is supposed to move with a permanent IPv6 address. Normal IPv6 routing structure based on the longest prefix match algorithm cannot support the host mobility. In order to solve this problem, MIPv6 (Mobile IPv6)[1] working Group in IETF (Internet Engineering Task Force) suggests a Mobile IPv6 for host mobility. Mobile IPv6 structure of IETF is made for IPv6 network mobility, not necessarily for a cellular network. So, MIPv6 WG updates the mobile IPv6 structure to be suitable for a wireless cellular network.

For MIPv6 to be more practical, FMIPv6 scheme, which is for fast handover to optimize the packet delivery route has been introduced.

---

[*] This research was supported by the Brain Korea 21 project.
[**] Corresponding author.

G. Min et al. (Eds.): ISPA 2006 Ws, LNCS 4331, pp. 1034–1043, 2006.

FMIPv6 (Fast Handover support in Mobile IPv6)[2] was proposed to address the problem of handover latency during the host movement. Original mobile IPv6 procedure could not be initiated before layer 2 handover is completed and it may induce unacceptable latency for real-time services. The handover procedure of Mobile IPv6 consists of movement detection, new CoA(Care of Address) configuration, and binding update. If the information for link layer handover could be provided in advance, layer 3 handover, that is, Mobile IP procedure, could be started earlier to reduce the latency related to the handover. FMIPv6 protocol assumes layer 2 triggers from the link layer. Doing movement detection and new CoA configuration using the information in advance, MN can perform a binding update and receive data destined to the MN as soon as a new link to a new access router (AR) is established. Also, the routing failure until the binding update is completed can be secured by using bi-directional tunnel between access routers. CTP(context Transfer Protocol)[3] is used in the bi-directional tunnel between pAR (previous Access Router) and nAR (new access Router). nAR must authenticate MN by using PANA (Protocol for carrying Authentication for Network Access)[4] architecture.

The authentication process for MN is an associated process between PANA at the wireless link and AAA[5] in the network. Both processes carry messages for authentication.

When MN attaches to a network, it discovers AAA attendant by sending PANA discovery message. The detailed messages depend on the selected authentication method decided by the network. Messages are exchanged in the wireless link using PANA, and in the network behind access router using the AAA infrastructure. The attendant can be an AR (Access Router) providing Mobile IP[6] service, and AR also acts as a PaC (PANA Client) to exchange PANA messages with the MN, meanwhile, AR functions as an AAA attendant to communicate with the AAAL(local AAA server) as well. AAAH(Home AAA server) or HA in a home network can authenticate the mobile node and pAR has authentication information for MN. However, nAR has no authentication information. Without knowing the proper information about MN, we can not guarantee secure seamless handover for nomadic users. Therefore, existing authentication mechanism is not acceptable in FMIPv6. In order to achieve a secure FMIPv6, a new authentication mechanism is required. In this paper, we propose a new authentication method using PANA CTP in FMIPv6 environment.

2   Related Works

2.1 FMIPv6 (Fast Mobile IPv6)

FMIPv6 is a package with three components: a support protocol for finding a feasible new access router, a support protocol for IP-address configuration, and a support protocol for an efficient data forwarding during handover. With FMIPv6, a mobile node can determine its next access router without having to connect to it. Instead, FMIPv6 lets the mobile node solicit the relevant information from its current access router.

FMIPv6 defines a signaling protocol between the current and the new access router for an IP address configuration. This signaling protocol allows the mobile node to be configured with a new IP address before it moves to a sub-network where the new IP address will be used. Moreover, FMIPv6 installs a tunnel between the old and the new access router so that the packets that are destined to the mobile node's old access router can be forwarded to the mobile node's new point of network attachment.

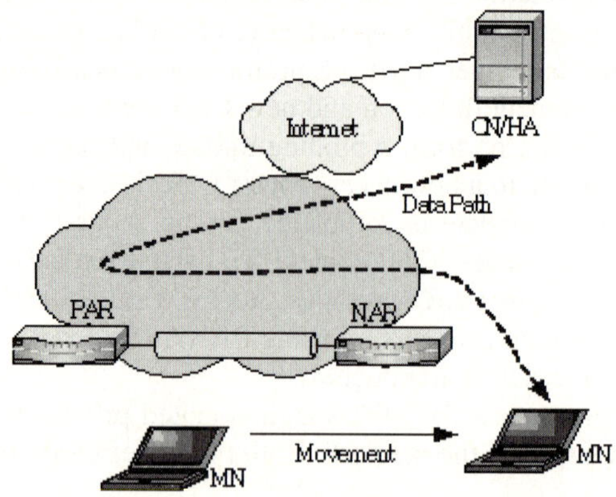

Fig. 1. FMIPv6 data flow

2.2 PANA CTP

PANA is a protocol that carries EAP over IP/UDP to authenticate the users. The PANA Authentication Agent (PAA) is the endpoint of the PANA protocol in the access network. The PAA itself may not be able to authenticate the user by terminating the EAP protocol. Instead the PAA might forward the EAP payloads to the backend AAA infrastructure.

The Enforcement Point (EP) is an entity, which enforces the result of the PANA protocol exchange. The EP can be co-located with the PAA or it can be separated as a stand-alone device. In the latter case, the SNMPv3 protocol is used to communicate between PAA and EP.

A successful EAP authentication exchange results in a PANA security association (PANA SA) if the EAP method was able to derive session keys. In this case, all further PANA messages between PaC(PANA Client) and PAA will be authenticated, replayed, and the integrity is protected due to the AUTH AVP.

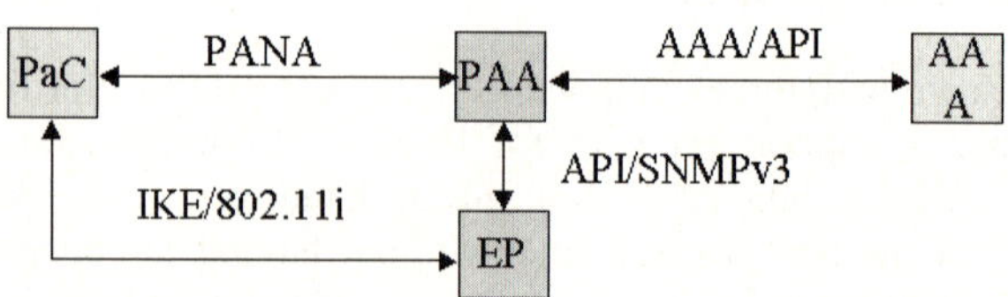

Fig. 2. PANA architecture

After a PaC's IP handover, the PaC changes IP subnet and PAA accordingly. The new PAA (nPAA) does not share any context with the PaC.

For this reason, we use the Context Transfer Protocol (CTP) to transfer the PANA context established between the PaC and pPAA to nPAA.

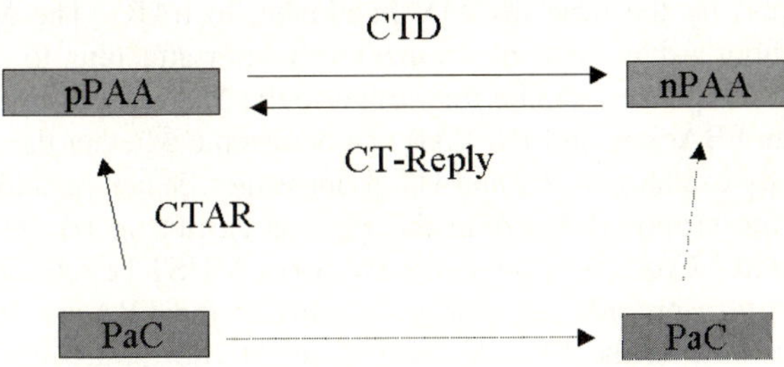

Fig. 3. Handover scheme using PANA-CTP

3   Authentication Mechanism Using PANA CTP

In this paper, we propose a more efficient mobility management mechanism for MN in a visited network of FMIPv6 environment. The movement of MN, which requires mobile IP services, is mostly local within the visited domain.

Binding update is one of the most important function of mobile IP. Binding update enables a mobile node to receive it's data that was transmitted to MN's home address, It requires that binding update needs authentication of mobile node to protect mobile node's data. AAAH or HA in a home network can authenticate the mobile node. However, nAR in FMIPv6 scheme cannot authenticate the MN. Therefore, the existing authentication mechanism is not acceptable in FMIPv6 environment. For secure FMIPv6, new authentication mechanism is required.

3.1   A Handover Scheme in FMIPv6

The protocol begins when a MN sends an RtSolPr (Router Solicitation for Proxy Advertisement) to its access router to resolve one or more Access Point Identifiers to subnet-specific information. In response, the access router   sends a PrRtAdv (Proxy Router Advertisement) message containing one or more fields. The MN may send a RtSolPr at any convenient time, for instance, as a response to some link-specific events or simply after performing router discovery. However, we expect that the MN will discover the available ARs by link-specific methods prior to sending RtSolPr. The RtSolPr and PrRtAdv messages do not establish any state at the access router.

With the information provided in the PrRtAdv message, the MN formulates a prospective nCoA and sends an FBU (Fast Binding Update) message when a link-specific handover event occurs. The purpose of the FBU is to authorize pAR to bind pCoA with nCoA, so that the arriving packets can be tunneled to the new location of the MN. Whenever possible, the FBU should be sent from pAR's link. For instance, an internal link-specific trigger could enable FBU transmission from the previous link. When it is not possible, FBU is sent from the new link. We should be careful to ensure that the nCoA used in FBU does not conflict with an address already in use by some other nodes on the link. For this, FBU encapsulation within FNA (Fast Neighbor Advertisement) must be implemented and should be used when the FBU is sent from nAR's link.

MN receives an FBAck on the previous link. This means that packet tunneling is already in progress by the time the MN handovers to nAR. The MN should send FNA (Fast Neighbor Advertisement) immediately after attaching to nAR, so that the arriving and buffered packets can be forwarded to the MN right away.

Before sending an FBAck to an MN, PAR can determine whether the nCoA is acceptable to the nAR by exchanging HI and HAck messages. When an address assignment by AR is used, the proposed nCoA in the FBU is carried in HI, and the nAR may assign the proposed NCoA. Such an assigned nCoA MUST be returned in HAck, and the pAR must in turn provide the assigned nCoA in the FBAck. If there is an assigned nCoA returned in the FBAck, the MN must use the assigned address upon attaching to nAR.

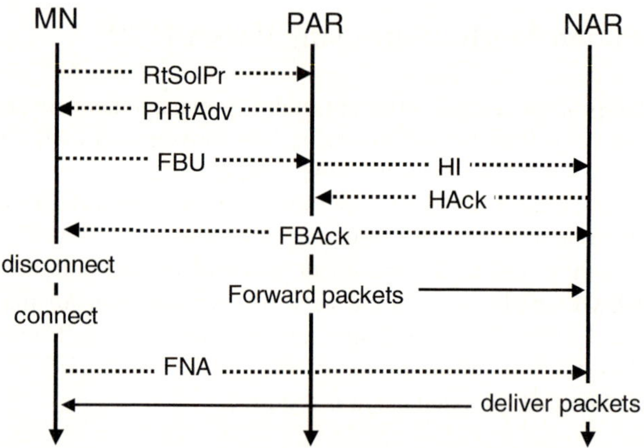

Fig. 4. FMIPv6 handover

3.2 Local Authentication with PANA-CTP

CTP enables context transfers between access routers. The context transfer can be either initiated by a request from the mobile node or by the new or the previous access router. Furthermore it can be performed prior to handover or after the handover.

In a reactive mode, MN sends a CTAR (CT Activate Request) to the nAR. In this message MN includes an   authorization token: this token is calculated based on a secret   shared between the MN and the previous AR (pAR) and it is used in order to authorize the transfer. This means that the MN and the pAR must share a secret.

As soon as the nAR receives a CTAR message, it generates a CT-Request message, which includes the authorization token, and the context to be transferred. This message is received by the pAR that verifies the authorization token and sends a CTD (Context Transfer Data) message including the requested context.

The transfer is triggered using the PANA signalling and CTD message is used to carry the PANA context. In the solution proposed by PANA, the PaC does not use CTAR message to request and to activate the context. Instead, it replies to PSR message with a PSA message containing the   unexpired previous PANA session identifier and an AUTH AVP. This AVP is computed using the PANA_AUTH_KEY shared between the PaC and its pPAA.

For local handover, binding update and authentication must be executed in a local foreign network. Authentication of mobile nodes is based on MN-AAAH security association. A new authenticator is required in local handover. In this paper, we propose a new local authenticator which can be obtained shown below..

Local authenticator:

$$H(sskMA\text{-}AAAH, HC)$$

H( ) : hashing function
sskMN-AAAH : shared secret parameter between a mobile node and home AAA server
HC : home challenge

Mobile node can detect local movement using link-specific event. Mobile node must send FBU message to nAR to update its binding. Then FBU message can include the local authenticator. Local AAA server (AAAL) authenticates the mobile node with a local authenticator that contains a BU message.

3.3 Local Authentication

nAR that receives mobile node's FBU message relays the message to a local AAA server to authenticate the mobile node. Local AAA server decrypts the local authenticator that is included in FBU message and executes the authentication with it's authenticator that is received from the home AAA server. If the authentication is successful, local AAA server sends a FBU message to HA to update the mobile node's binding. pAR delivers PANA session identifier and a AUTH AVP to nAR using CTP.

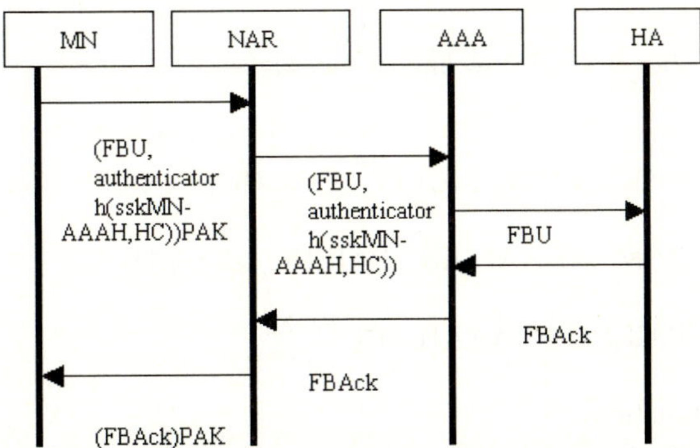

Fig. 5. FBU flow with Local Authentication

The following shows the call flow and its message contents for the local authentication.

1) MN->nAR
        E(FBU, H(sskMN-AAAH,HC)),PAK
2) AR->AAAL
        FBU, H(sskMN-AAAH,HC)
3) AAAL->nAR
        FBAck

E( ) : encryption function
H( ) : hashing function
sskMN-AAAH : shared secret parameter between the mobile node and the home AAA server
HC : home challenge
PAK : PANA_AUTH_KEY

3.4 Distribute Security Parameters

In order to execute the local authentication, each node is required to have some security parameters. The following shows that we need security parameters for AAAL and MN.

AAAL : H(sskMN_AAAH, HC)
MN : HC, PAK

E( ) : encryption function
H( ) : hashing function
sskMN-AAAH : shared secret parameter between the mobile node and the home AAA server
HC : home challenge
PAK : PANA_AUTH_KEY
Home AAA server generates these security parameters, where these parameters are distributed to each node. Each security parameter is encrypted. Home AAA server supports secure delivery mechanism to mobile nodes and local AAA server.

The following shows a call flow and its messages.

1) AAAH->AAAL
        FBAck, (PAK)sskAAAH-AAAL, (PAK,HC)sskAAAH-MN
2) AAAL->nAR
        FBAck, (PAK)sskAAAL-AR, (PAK,HC)sskAAAH-MN
3) nAR->MN
        FBAck, (PAK,HC)sskAAAH-MN

E( ) : encryption function
H( ) : hashing function

sskMN-AAAH : shared secret parameter between the mobile node and the home AAA server
HC : home challenge
PAK : PANA_AUTH_KEY

4 Modeling the Average Delivery Delay

In order to do an accurate performance evaluation for our proposed scheme, when MN is ready to get service after the successful registration on AR1, I started our evaluation. We assume that MN moves to AR2 after AR1 registration is completed. Our simulation ends when the MN finishes its registration to the new location AR2.

It is denoted that the packet delivery delay between HA and MAP, between MAP and AR, and between ARs are T_{HM}, T_{MA}, T_{AA} respectively.

Layer 2 handover happens before BU for the new location is completed. Accordingly, we can compare the effect by analyzing the average packet delay between HA and AR immediately after handover.

Before the completion of the binding update, the packet destined to MN are sent to the previous access router and then forwarded to a new access router. After binding update, the packet data path is now changed to the normal data delivery path. The average delivery delay can be represented as follows.

If $0 < t < T_{BU}$,
Delivery delay $= T_{MA} + T_{AA}$

Therefore, the delivery delay is $3T_{HA}$.

Delivery delay $= T_{HA}$

Accordingly, the average delay is given as follows.

$$Averadge\_delivery\_delay = \frac{T_{BU} + 3T_{MA}}{T_{MT}} + \frac{(T_{MT} - T_{BU})T_{MA}}{T_{MT}}$$

$$= T_{MA} + \frac{T_{BU}}{T_{MT}} 2T_{MA}$$

If we consider that $T_{BU} = 4(T_{HM} + T_{MA})$ in FMIPv6, then

$$Averadg\_delivery\_delay = T_{MA} + \frac{8T_{MA}}{T_{MT}}(T_{HM} + T_{MA})$$

The average delivery delay could be represented following form which is similar to FMIPv6. That is,

$$Averadge\_delivery\_delay = T_{MA} + \frac{T_{LBU}}{T_{MT}} 2T_{MA}$$

5 Performance Evaluation

In this section we analyze the performance of our proposal. We started our performance evaluation of the proposed method, when MN is ready to get service after the
successful registration on pAR. We assume that MN moves to nAR after pAR registration is complete. Our simulation ends when MN finishes its registration to the new
location nAR. We assume that the probability for pAR and nAR to be in a same domain is 50 percent. We randomly select the values for the parameters T, and each test
is run ten times to properly evaluate the new scheme.

Since our authentication scheme with PANA CTP doesn't necessarily send packets
to HA, the more network delays, the better the performance is.

Testing the average registration delay time relies on distance between MAP and
CN shown in figure .6. Where, TCM means the measuring time for an average delivery delay between CN and MAP.

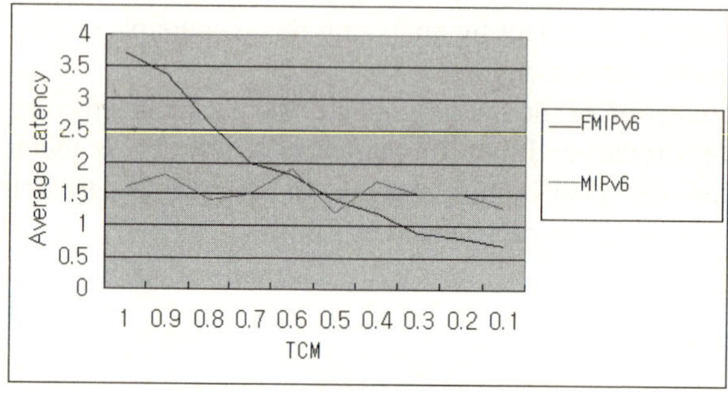

Fig. 6. Comparison of handover latency

6 Conclusion

In this paper, we propose a authentication mechanism using PANA CTP for mobile
hosts in FMIPv6 environment. By using FMIPv6 handover mechanism, we showed
that the handover performance has been greatly improved. Authentication problem of
mobile node in the registration phase is processed in an access router with a local
authenticator and PANA_AUTH_KEY given by the home AAA server. So, the message round trip delay and latency are decreased during the registration process. Local
handoff mechanism based on FMIPv6 can decrease the delay of mobility management
and the load on HA's. Context transfer with CTP requires minimum message exchange. The proposed mechanism is very useful, when the local handoff occurs frequently and inter-domain handoff is needed when a mobile node tries to connect to
the internet in a mobile internet environment.

Acknowledgement

This research was supported by the MIC(Ministry of Information and Communication), Korea, under the ITRC(Information Technology Research Center) support program supervised by the IITA(Institute of Information Technology Assessment).

References

1. D. Johnson, "Mobility Support in IPv6", RFC 3775, IETF, June 2004
2. R. Koodli, "Fast Handovers for Mobile IPv6", RFC 4068, IETF, July 2005
3. J. Bournelle, "Use of Context Transfer Protocol (CXTP) for PANA", draft-ietf-pana-cxtp-01, Internet Draft, IETF, March 6, 2006
4. D. Forsberg, "Protocol for Carrying Authentication for Network Access (PANA)", draft-ietf-pana-pana-11, Internet Draft, IETF, March 3, 2006
5. F. Dupont, J. Bournelle " AAA for Mobile IPv6", draft-dupont-mipv6-aaa-01, Internet Draft, IETF, Nov, 2001.
6. Charles E. Perkins, "Mobile IP", Addison Wesley, 1998.

Bounding Performance of LDPC Codes and Turbo-Like Codes for IEEE 802.16 Broadband Wireless Internet

Kyuhyuk Chung[1] and Jun Heo[2]

[1] Division of Information and Computer Science,
School of Natural Sciences,
Dankook University,
San 147 Hannam-dong Youngsan-gu,
140-714 Seoul, Korea
khchung@dku.edu
[2] College of Information and Telecommunications,
Dept. of Electronics Engineering,
Konkuk University,
143-701 Seoul, Korea
junheo@konkuk.ac.kr

Abstract. We present upper bounds for the maximum-likelihood decoding performance of particular LDPC codes and turbo-like codes with particular interleavers in the application of IEEE 802.16 broadband wireless internet. Previous research developed upper bounds for LDPC codes and turbo-like codes using ensemble codes or the uniformly interleaved assumption, which bound the performance averaged over all ensemble codes or all interleavers. Proposed upper bounds are based on the simple bound and estimated weight distributions including the exact several smallest distance terms because if either estimated weight distributions on their own or the exact several smallest distance terms only are used, an accurate bound can not be obtained.[1]

1   Introduction

Currently the cellular wireless market of circuit-based networks copes with the wireless Internet market of packet-based networks using IP (Internet Protocol) power. One of the most prevailing standards for the broadband wireless Internet market is IEEE 802.16. For the broadband wireless internet standard, the LDPC codes and turbo codes are core technologies.

---

[1] This research was supported by the MIC(Ministry of Information and Communication), Korea, under the ITRC(Information Technology Research Center) support program supervised by the IITA(Institute of Information Technology Assessment) (IITA-2005-C1090-0501-0018).

G. Min et al. (Eds.): ISPA 2006 Ws, LNCS 4331, pp. 1044–1052, 2006.

Iterative detection [1,2] for LDPC codes and concatenated codes with interleavers represents a great advancement in communications theory because of their excellent performance. Parallel Concatenated Convolutional Codes (PCCs, or turbo codes) or Serial Concatenated Convolutional Codes (SCCCs) with interleavers, introduced in [2,3], consist of simple binary convolutional codes connected in parallel or in serial through an interleaver. On the other hand, Low Density Parity Check (LDPC) codes [1] became very popular because of excellent performance and efficient parallel hardware implementation. Numerous simulations and bounds have demonstrated their remarkable performance.

In [4], transfer function bounding techniques were applied to obtain upper bounds on the bit-error rate and the word-error rate for maximum-likelihood decoding of turbo codes constructed with pseudo-random interleavers. Since union bounds are intractable for any particular pseudo-random interleaver, the transfer function bound is developed as a random coding bound based on the uniformly interleaved assumption, i.e., performance averaged over all possible interleaver permutations. Therefore, the transfer function bound can not be used to bound the performance of the turbo code with a particular interleaver.

Since the union bound cannot predict the performance above the cutoff rate, there is a great demand to have bounds on performance that are useful for rates above the cutoff rate. One of those bounds is the simple bound [5]. In [5], the simple bound is used with the uniformly interleaved assumption for LDPC codes and turbo codes. Therefore, bounds on the maximum-likelihood decoding performance of particular LDPC codes and turbo-like codes with a particular interleaver are still unavailable. Note also that simulation performance of LDPC codes and turbo-like codes using iterative detection is suboptimal because iterative detection is approximate to the optimal detection, while all the bounding techniques are for the optimal detection.

In this paper we solve intractability of upper bounds for particular LDPC codes and turbo codes with particular interleavers by using approximate input-output weight distributions. The performance of turbo-like codes at high SNR is well approximated by the expression of the union bound, truncated to the contribution of the several smallest non-zero distance terms [6]. In [6] branch and bound algorithms were developed for finding the several smallest distances and their multiplicities of turbo codes and SCCCs. We include these exact distance spectrum results for the several smallest non-zero distances into the approximate weight distributions, because if either estimated weight distributions on their own or the smallest distance terms only are used, an accurate bound can not be obtained. A particular LDPC code and a particular interleaver of a turbo code are taken into account for both the codewords with small distances and approximate weight distributions.

The paper is organized as follows. Section 2 describes previous bounding techniques and compares transfer function bounds, simple bounds, and simulation results. In Section 3 upper bounds for particular LDPC codes and turbo codes with particular interleavers are presented. Section 4 concludes the paper.

2   A Review of Previous Bounds and Comparison

2.1   Transfer Function Bounds

For maximum-likelihood decoder a union bound on the probability of word error and bit error over an additive white Gaussian noise channel requires the input-output weight distribution. For the overall (N, K) code C with code rate $r = K/N$, $A_{w,d}$ denote the number of codewords for input sequence weight w and output codeword weight d. Then the conditional probability of producing a codeword of weight d given an input sequence of weight w is

$$p(d|w) = \frac{A_{w,d}}{\sum_{d'} A_{w,d'}} = \frac{A_{w,d}}{\binom{K}{w}}. \tag{1}$$

The conditional probability distribution $p(d|w)$ for turbo codes is obtained by using the uniformly interleaved assumption [4]. The divergence properties of the transfer function bounds for turbo codes is observed above the cutoff rate [4].

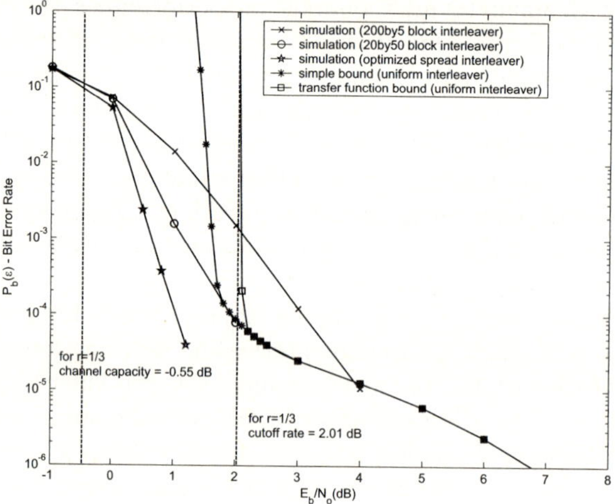

Fig. 1. Upper bounds with uniform interleavers and simulations with various interleavers for turbo codes (r=1/3, K=1000)

2.2   A Simple Tight Bound

The performance of turbo-like codes is close to Shannon's channel capacity limit for moderate to large block sizes, so there is a need for bounds on performance that are useful for rates above the cutoff rate. In [5] such a simple bound on the probability of decoding error for block codes is derived in closed form. This bound is simple because it does not require any integration or optimization in its final version. Consider a linear binary (N, K) block code C with code rate $r = K/N$. For a given code d is the Hamming weight of a codeword. The

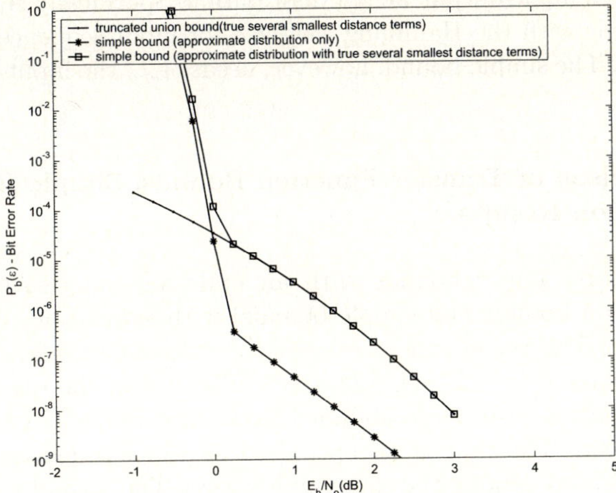

Fig. 2. Comparison of upper bounds of the true several smallest distance terms, the approximate distribution only, and the approximate distribution with the true several smallest distance terms (turbo code with optimized spread interleaver, r=1/3, K=1000)

upper bound on the error rate with maximum likelihood codeword decoding is given by

$$P \leq \sum_{d=d_{min}}^{N-K+1} \min\left\{ e^{-nE(c,d)}, e^{ng(\delta)} Q\left(\sqrt{2ch}\right) \right\} \tag{2}$$

where

$$\text{if} \quad c_0(\delta) < c < \frac{e^{2g(\delta)}-1}{2\delta(2-\delta)}, \tag{3}$$

$$E(c,d) = \frac{1}{2}\ln[1 - 2c_0(\delta)f(c,\delta)] + \frac{c\,f(c,\delta)}{1+f(c,\delta)}, \tag{4}$$

$$\text{otherwise} \quad E(c,d) = -g(\delta) + \delta c \tag{5}$$

$\delta = d/N, \quad c = R_c(E_b/N_0)$, and

$$f(c,\delta) = \sqrt{\frac{c}{c_0} + 2c + c^2} - c - 1 \tag{6}$$

and for the bit-error rate

$$g(\delta) = \frac{1}{N}\ln\left\{ \sum_w \frac{w}{K} A_{w,d} \right\} \tag{7}$$

where $A_{w,d}$ is the input-output weight distribution. Specifically $A_{w,d}$ is the number of codewords with the Hamming weight d for input sequences of the Hamming weight w. The simple bound, however, needs $A_{w,d}$ the input-output weight distribution.

2.3   Comparison of Transfer Function Bounds, Simple Bounds, and Simulation Results

Figure 1 compares upper bounds with an uniformly interleaved assumption (transfer function bounds and simple bounds) with simulation results for various interleavers. The turbo code uses constituent convolutional codes with the generator polynomial $(1 + D)/(1 + D + D^2)$. The rate of the turbo code is 1/3. The three simulation results are obtained from three different interleavers with length $K = 1000$. The first is an optimized spread interleaver, which shows the best performance among the three interleavers. The second is a block interleaver, which reads bits in 20 by 50 rectangular array row-wise and reads out column-wise. The third is an block interleaver with 200 by 5 rectangular array. The transfer function bound and the simple bound use the uniform interleaver assumption, with which only a single bound is obtained. However, simulation results show that performance depends on the particular interleaver. Note that the performance of the iterative decoder can be worse than the upper bound on the maximum-likelihood decoding performance because iterative detection is suboptimal.

Figure 1 also compares the simple bound with the transfer function bound. We observe that the simple bound is tighter than the transfer function bound at the low range of SNR. At a BER of 10^{-1} the simple bound is about 0.7 dB tighter than the transfer function bound. It is well known that the transfer function bound diverges above the cutoff rate. The cutoff rate corresponds to $E_b/N_0 = 2.01$ dB for rate 1/3 codes.

2.4   Truncated Union Bounds

For a linear binary code $C(N, K)$ (N is the codeword length and K the information frame length) with free distance d_{free}, we will denote by N_{free} its multiplicity (the number of codewords with weight d_{free}), and by w_{free} its information bit multiplicity (defined as the sum of the Hamming weights of the N_{free} information frames generating the codewords with weight d_{free}). For very high values of E_b/N_0, where E_b is the energy per information bit and N_0 the one-sided noise spectral density, we can write

$$\text{BER} \simeq \frac{w_{free}}{K} Q\left(\sqrt{\frac{2E_b}{N_0} \cdot \frac{K}{N} \cdot d_{free}}\right). \tag{8}$$

For turbo-like codes, a better approximation can be obtained by including other terms of the distance spectrum [6].

By the symbol UB(j) we will denote the union bound expression, truncated to the contribute of the j-th nonzero distance,

$$\text{UB}(j) = \sum_{i=1}^{j} \frac{w(i)}{K} Q\left(\sqrt{\frac{2E_b}{N_0} \cdot \frac{K}{N} \cdot d(i)}\right) \tag{9}$$

where $d(i)$ is the i-th nonzero distance and $N(i)$ and $w(i)$ are its multiplicities. In [6], branch and bound algorithms for finding the several smallest distances and their multiplicities were developed allowing performance of turbo codes and SCCCs to be approximated by truncated union bounds at the high SNRs. But since these algorithms are based on branch-and-bound method, complexity for finding the whole weight distribution is intractable.

3   Upper Bounds for Particular LDPC Codes and Turbo Codes with Particular Interleavers

The simple bound is the tightest closed-form upper bound on decoding error rate [5]. We use the simple bound for particular LDPC codes and turbo-like codes with particular interleavers. To use the simple bound we need the conditional probability $p(d|w)$ that is defined in Equation (1). But it is intractable to obtain $p(d|w)$ because of complexity. So we want to obtain the maximum-likelihood estimator $\widehat{p}_{\text{MLE}}$ of $p(d|w)$. This problem is the same as estimating the probability of white balls when a ball is drawn with replacement from an urn that contains $A_{w,d}$ white balls and $[\binom{K}{w} - A_{w,d}]$ black balls. The indicator function $I(c)$ is defined by

$$I(c) = \begin{cases} 1 \text{ if } c \text{ is a codeword with } w \text{ and } d \\ 0 \text{ otherwise.} \end{cases} \tag{10}$$

Then $I(c)$ is the Bernoulli random variable with $p = p(d|w)$. If we let k be the number of codewords with the Hamming weight d for input sequences of the Hamming weight w among N_s generated sample codewords, k is the sum of the Bernoulli random variables associated with each of the N_s independent trial. Then k is the binomial random variable with the following probability mass function

$$P(k|p) = \binom{N_s}{k} p^k (1-p)^{N_s - k} \tag{11}$$

for $k = 0, 1, \cdots, N_s$. In order to obtain the maximum-likelihood estimator $\widehat{p}_{\text{MLE}}$, we maximize the likelihood function $P(k|p)$,

$$\widehat{p}_{\text{MLE}} = \max_{p} \ P(k|p) \tag{12}$$

$$= \max_{p} \ \binom{N_s}{k} p^k (1-p)^{N_s - k}. \tag{13}$$

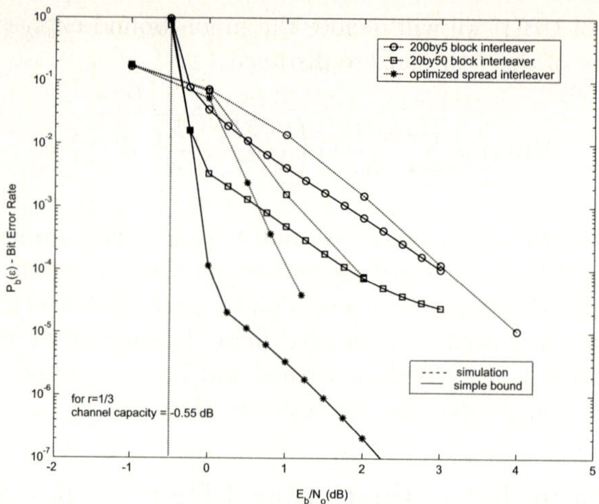

Fig. 3. Simple bounds using approximate distributions with the true several smallest distance terms and iterative decoding simulation results for turbo codes with various interleavers (r=1/3, K=1000)

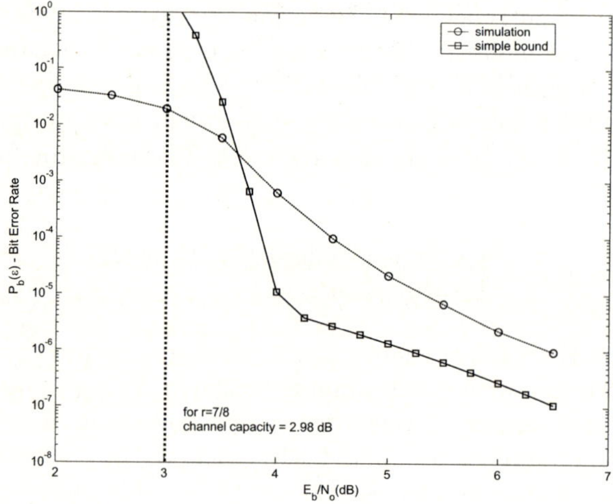

Fig. 4. Simple bound using an approximate distribution with the true smallest distance term and iterative decoding simulation result for LDPC code with $(r = 7/8, (N, K) = (800, 700))$

Differentiating the argument and setting the result equal to 0 give the solution,

$$\widehat{p}_{\mathrm{MLE}} = \frac{k}{N_s}. \tag{14}$$

It is also straightforward to verify that this solution is the global maximum. We approximate $p(d|w)$ by $\widehat{p}_{\mathrm{MLE}}$. Then

$$p(d|w) \simeq \widehat{p}_{\mathrm{MLE}} \tag{15}$$

$$\frac{A_{w,d}}{\binom{K}{w}} \simeq \frac{k}{N_s} \tag{16}$$

$$\frac{\widehat{A}_{w,d}}{\binom{K}{w}} = \frac{k}{N_s} \tag{17}$$

$$\widehat{A}_{w,d} = \binom{K}{w} \frac{k}{N_s}. \tag{18}$$

where $\widehat{A}_{w,d}$ is the estimated weight distribution.

We choose $N_s = 10000$ because the thresholds of simple bounds for $N_s = 1000, 10000$, and 100000 were found to be similar. In order to obtain $\widehat{A}_{w,d}$ we generate $N_s = 10000$ codewords randomly for each input weight w, calculate k from the generated codewords, and obtain $\widehat{A}_{w,d}$ using (18) . The true distribution of several smallest distances $\{A_{w,d}\}_{d=d_{min}}^{d=d_{min}+10}$ is included in $A_{w,d}$ using the algorithm in [6] because for very high values of E_b/N_0 these several smallest distance terms are dominant. Note that a particular interleaver of a turbo code is taken into account for not only the codewords with small distances but also approximate weight distributions. In Figure 2 we compare three cases, i.e.,

- the true several smallest distance terms only,
- the approximate distributions on their own,
- the approximate distributions with the true several smallest distance terms.

By including the true several smallest distance terms $\{A_{w,d}\}_{d=d_{min}}^{d=d_{min}+10}$, we approximate better error floor region at medium to high SNR.

In Fig. 3 simple bounds using approximate distributions with the true several smallest distance terms are compared with iterative decoding simulation results for turbo codes with three interleavers. We obtain three different accurate upper bounds for each interleaver.We also observe that at the low range of SNR the thresholds of the simple bound are approximately the channel capacity of rate $r = 1/3$, i.e., -0.55 dB.

As another application, we consider $(N, K) = (800, 700)$ regular LDPC codes. The rate for this LDPC code is $7/8$. In Fig. 4, the simple bound with both the exact minimum distance term of $d_{min} = 2$ and an approximate weight distribution is compared with iterative decoding simulation performance at fixed iterations 50 for rates $r = 7/8$. Note that a particular LDPC code is taken into account for both the codewords with the minimum distance and approximate weight distributions. At the low range of SNR the threshold of the simple bound is approximately the channel capacity of rate $r = 7/8$, i.e., 2.98 dB.

4   Conclusion

In this paper, we studied and presented upper bounds for the maximum-likelihood decoding performance of particular LDPC codes and turbo-like codes with a particular interleaver for IEEE 802.16 Broadband Wireless Internet. Proposed upper bounds are based on the simple bound and estimated weight distributions including the exact several smallest distance terms because if either estimated weight distributions on their own or the exact several smallest distance terms only are used, an accurate bound can not be obtained. These bounds make it possible to estimate the performance of optimal detection for particular LDPC codes and turbo-like codes with a particular interleaver, which is better than that of suboptimal iterative detection.

References

1. Gallager, R.: Low Density Parity Check Codes. MIT press. (1963)
2. Berrou, C., Glavieux, A.: Near Optimum Error Correcting Coding and Decoding: Turbo-Codes, IEEE Trans. Commun., Vol. 44. No. 10. (1996) 1261–1271
3. Benedetto, S., Divsalar, D., Montorsi, G. Pollara, F.: Serial Concatenation of Interleaved Codes: Performance Analysis, Design, and Iterative Decoding, IEEE Trans. Inform. Theory, Vol. 44. No. 3. (1998) 909–926
4. Divsalar, D., Dolinar, S., Pollara, F.: Transfer Function Bounds on the Performance of Turbo Codes, TDA Progress Reports 42-122., Jet Propulsion Lab, (1995)
5. Divsalar, D.: A Simple Tight Bound on Error Probability of Block Codes with Application to Turbo Codes, TMO Progress Reports 42-139., Jet Propulsion Lab, (1999)
6. Garello, R., Pierleoni, P., Benedetto, S.: Computing the Free Distance of Turbo Codes and Serially Concatenated Codes with Interleavers: Algorithms and Applications, IEEE J. Select. Areas Commun., Vol. 19. No. 5. (2001) 909–926

Design and Performance Analysis of an Enhanced MAC Algorithm for the IEEE 802.11 DCF

Whoi Jin Jung, An Kyu Hwang, Byung Chul Kim, and Jae Yong Lee

Department of Information Communications Engineering, Chungnam National University
220, Gung Dong, Yusung Gu, Daejeon 305-764, Korea
`wjjung@ngn.cnu.ac.kr`, `{akhwang, byckim, jyl}@cnu.ac.kr`

Abstract. In this paper, a performance improving MAC algorithm for the IEEE 802.11 DCF is proposed. The DCF controls the transmission based on carrier sense multiple access with collision avoidance (CSMA/CA), which decides a random backoff time with the range of contention window (CW) for each station. Normally, each station doubles the CW after collision, and reduces the CW to the minimum after successful transmission. This paper proposes an enhanced DCF algorithm that decreases the CW smoothly after successful transmission in order to reduce the collision probability by utilizing the current contention status information of WLAN. In addition, the throughput and delay performance for the unsaturated case is analyzed mathematically. Simulation results show that the suggested algorithm enhances the saturation throughput of WLAN. They also coincide well with the analytical results.

1 Introduction

Lots of efforts have been done to provide high-speed wireless Internet service using Wireless LAN (WLAN) in hot spots with notebook, PDA, and so on. As the standardization of WLAN protocol, IEEE 802.11 was emerged in 1999, and after that, various IEEE 802.11 standards in the 2.4 GHz and 5 GHz frequency bands have been proposed.

The medium access control (MAC) of the IEEE 802.11 WLAN defines two access methods: the Distributed Coordination Function (DCF) and the Point Coordinated Function (PCF). The default access method, DCF, is based on the Carrier Sense Multiple Access/Collision Avoidance (CSMA/CA) principle in which a host wishing to transmit seizes the channel by contention with the same access probability. On the contrary, the PCF allows the station to use the channel based on polling method with the coordination of a Point Coordinator, which resides in the Access Point (AP).

The CSMA/CA uses random backoff time to reduce collisions between stations [2][3][4]. To determine the random backoff time, each station has minimum contention window (CW), CW_{min}, and maximum CW, CW_{max}, respectively. Initially, each station chooses a random CW value between 0 and CW_{min} before accessing the channel, and calculates the random backoff time as a product of the chosen CW value and one slot time. The station counts down its backoff timer while the channel is idle, and it uses the channel for transmission when its reaches 0 first. At that time, other stations stop counting down until the transmission is over. If two or more stations

G. Min et al. (Eds.): ISPA 2006 Ws, LNCS 4331, pp. 1053–1062, 2006.

decrement CWs to zero at the same time, a collision will occur. Then, each station does not receive the ACK frame, and has to select a new backoff time between (0, 2*CW). Each time a station happens to collide, it doubles CW up to CW_{max}. If the transmission fails even after the maximum retry count, that frame is discarded. But, if the transmission is successful, the CW is reset to CW_{min}.

In this paper, an enhanced IEEE 802.11 DCF algorithm is proposed to increase the network efficiency by reducing contention window to half, not reducing it to CW_{min} after successful transmission. The performance is evaluated by analysis and simulation in case that traffic load is saturated and unsaturated, respectively. According to the analysis results, the saturation throughput of the suggested scheme does not decrease after reaching a maximum value, but is maintained to its maximum value because collision probabilities are reduced. In addition, the throughput in unsaturated case is very similar to the original DCF algorithm.

This paper is organized as follows. In Section 2, an 802.11 DCF algorithm is briefly explained. In Section 3, the throughput and delay performance of an enhanced DCF algorithm is analyzed in the saturation condition. Also, throughput is analyzed in the unsaturation condition. The analysis results are verified by simulation in Section 4. A conclusion is given in Section 5.

2   IEEE 802.11 DCF Channel Access Method

The DCF is the basic medium access method of IEEE 802.11 MAC, which follows the CSMA/CA method. If a station with a frame to transmit initially senses the channel to be busy, the station waits until the channel becomes idle for a DIFS period, and then computes a random backoff time. The station decrements its random backoff time until the medium becomes busy again or the timer reaches zero. If the timer finally reaches to zero, the station transmits its frame. But, if the timer has not reached zero and the medium becomes busy, the station freezes its timer. After the medium becomes idle after a DIFS period, the station continues to decrement the frozen timer again. In this case, the frozen random backoff time is likely to be small compared to the newly generated random backoff time, and thus the station has large probability to access the channel. Upon receipt of a correct frame, the receiving station transmits a positive acknowledgement frame (ACK) back to the sending station after a SIFS interval. Upon successful transmission, the CW is reset to the CW_{min} value. Each time a station happens to collide, it doubles CW up to CW_{max}.

Virtual carrier sensing is used to reserve the wireless medium in advance before transmitting DATA frame by exchanging the Request to Send (RTS) and Clear to Send (CTS) frame. A station which generates the shortest random backoff time can access the medium, and send a RTS frame. RTS frames have the duration field. All stations in the Basic Service Set (BSS), hearing the RTS frame, read the duration field and set their Network Allocation Vectors (NAVs) accordingly, while the destination station responds to the RTS frame with a CTS frame. After exchanging RTS/CTS frames, a source station sends a DATA frame and destination station responds with an ACK frame.

3 Design and Performance Analysis of an Enhanced MAC Algorithm

The saturation throughput and access delay of IEEE 802.11 DCF have been mathematically analyzed when transmission queue of each station is assumed to be always nonempty [6][7][8][9]. In this Section, an enhanced DCF algorithm is suggested, and its throughput and access delay are analyzed in both the saturation and unsaturation conditions.

3.1 DCF+ Algorithm

In the original DCF, a station which sends a DATA frame successfully reduces its CW to CW_{min}. But, if we reduce the CW directly to CW_{min} after successful transmission, collision probability won't be reduced in case that the BSS is in a congested state. In addition, if the arrival rate λ increases from unsaturation condition to saturation one, throughput is gradually reduced after achieving a maximum value. This result comes from the high collision probability.

In this paper, a new enhanced DCF algorithm is proposed by modifying CW control algorithm. In the new scheme, the CW will be reduced to half after the successful transmission. The suggested algorithm is called 802.11 DCF+ from now on. The 802.11 DCF+ reduces collision probability by reducing the CW slowly after the successful transmission since the current traffic load cannot be reduced abruptly.

3.2 Frame Transmission Probability of DCF+

The notations for mathematical analysis are shown in Table 1. The $b(t)$ denotes the stochastic process representing the backoff time counter for a given station. $CW_{max} = CW_{min}*2^m$, and $W_i = 2^i*W$, where $i \in (0, m)$ is called "backoff stage" and m is the "maximum backoff stage". The $s(t)$ denotes the stochastic process representing the backoff stage $(0, , , , m)$ of the station at time t. The p means the collision probability seen by a frame transmitted on the channel. It is assumed that each frame collides with constant and independent probability p.

Table 1. Notations used for the mathematical analysis

Notation	Meaning
n	Total number of stations
σ	Slot time size
τ	Probability that the station transmits a frame in a slot time
m	Maximum backoff stage

The contention process can be represented as a two-dimensional discrete-time Markov chain $\{s(t), b(t)\}$ as shown in Fig. 1.

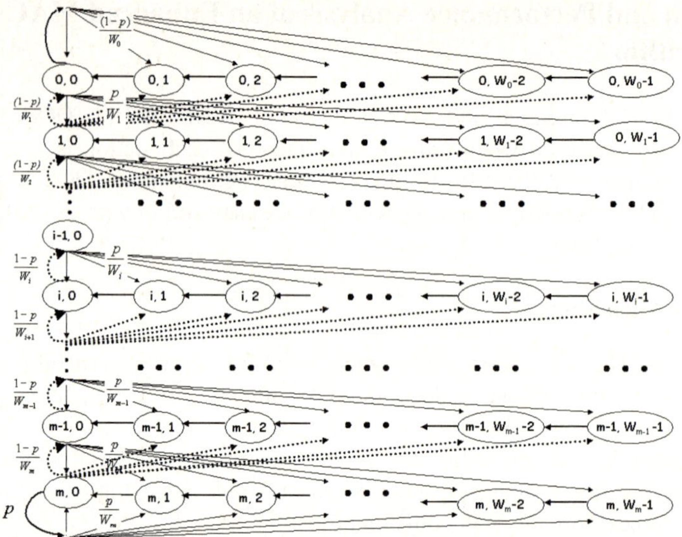

Fig. 1. Markov chain model for the backoff window size

The first frame starts with a backoff stage 0, and the initial backoff is uniformly chosen in the range $(0, W_0-1)$. If a backoff counter is greater than 0, it is always decremented at the beginning of each slot time. If the backoff counter reaches zero, a frame is transmitted and new backoff stage is chosen depending upon whether a collision occurs or not. If a frame is successfully transmitted when the backoff stage is equal to i, a backoff window of next frame is chosen randomly between $(0, W_{i-1}-1)$. When an unsuccessful transmission occurs at backoff state i, the backoff stage increases, and the new backoff window is randomly chosen in the range $(0, W_{i+1}-1)$. However, if the backoff stage reaches the value m, it is not increased any more.

The limiting probabilities of the Markov Chain, $b_{i,k}$, is defined as Eq. (1) where $i \in (0, m)$ and $k \in (0, W_i-1)$. The limiting probability, $b_{i,k}$, when the backoff stage is i and $k \in (1, W_i-1)$, can be obtained by solving usual Markov chain balance equations.

$$b_{i,k} = \lim_{t \to \infty} P\{s[t] = i, b(t) = k\} \tag{1}$$

$$b_{i,k} = \frac{W_i - k}{W_i} \cdot \begin{cases} b_{1,0} \dfrac{1-p}{p} & i = 0 \\[3mm] b_{0,0} \left(\dfrac{p}{1-p}\right)^i & 0 < i \le m \end{cases} \tag{2}$$

$$b_{i,k} = \frac{W_i - k}{W_i} b_{i,0} \qquad i \in (0, m), \qquad k \in (0, W_i - 1) \tag{3}$$

Then, the probability, τ, that a station transmits a frame in a slot time is equal to the sum of the probabilities that the backoff counter is zero. Thus, it can be represented as follows.

$$\tau = \sum_{i=0}^{m} b_{i,0} = \left(\frac{(1-p)\left(1-\left(\dfrac{p}{1-p}\right)^{m+1}\right)}{1-2p} \right. \tag{4}$$

$$\left. \times 2 / \left(\frac{(1-p)\left(1-\left(\dfrac{2p}{1-p}\right)^{m+1}\right)}{1-3p} \cdot W + \frac{(1-p)\left(1-\left(\dfrac{p}{1-p}\right)^{m+1}\right)}{1-2p} \right) \right)$$

We can see that τ depends on the probability p, but p also can be represented as $p = 1-(1-\tau)^{n-1}$ because it is assumed that each station transmits the frame with probability τ. By numerical analysis, p and τ can be obtained from $\tau^{*}(p) = 1-(1-p)^{1/(n-1)}$ and Eq. (4).

3.3 Throughput Analysis Under the Saturation Condition

To compute the normalized throughput, S, P_{tr} is assumed to be the probability that there is at least one transmission in a slot time and P_{s} is defined as the probability that the transmission is successful under the condition that at least one station transmits. The P_{tr} and P_{s} can be obtained as a function of τ and n.

$$P_{tr} = 1-(1-\tau)^{n} \tag{5}$$

$$P_{s} = \frac{n\tau(1-\tau)^{n-1}}{P_{tr}} = \frac{n\tau(1-\tau)^{n-1}}{1-(1-\tau)^{n}} \tag{6}$$

If $E[P]$ denotes the average payload size, the average amount of payload information successfully transmitted in a slot time can be represented as $P_{tr} * P_{s} * E[P]$. Let the T_{s} denotes the average amount of time for transmitting a frame successfully, and the T_{c} denotes the average wasting time due to a collision. Then, the normalized throughput can be obtained from Eq. (7).

$$S = \frac{P_{s}P_{tr}E[P]}{(1-P_{tr})\sigma + P_{s}P_{tr}T_{s} + P_{tr}(1-P_{s})T_{c}} \tag{7}$$

If the frame header size, H, is represented as $H = PHY_{hdr} + MAC_{hdr}$, then T_{s} and T_{c} for basic access and RTS/CTS access methods can be represented as Eq. (8) and (9).

$$T_s^{bas} = H + E[P] + SIFS + \delta + ACK + DIFS + \delta \tag{8}$$

$$T_c^{bas} = H + E[P^*] + DIFS + \delta$$

$$T_s^{rts} = RTS + SIFS + \delta + CTS + SIFS + \delta + H \tag{9}$$

$$+ E[P] + SIFS + \delta + ACK + DIFS + \delta$$

$$T_c^{rts} = RTS + DIFS + \delta$$

3.4 Access Delay Under the Saturation Condition

Let E[D] be the average access delay of successfully transmitted frame under the saturation condition. The access delay means the time interval from the time at which the frame enters into the head-of-line of the queue to the time at which the frame is successfully transmitted. If E[X] is defined as the average number of slots until a frame is successfully transmitted, then E[D] = E[X] * E[Slot]. E[X] can be given by

$$E[X] = \frac{(1-2p)\cdot(W+1) + pW\cdot(1-(2p)^m)}{2\cdot(1-2p)\cdot(1-p)} \tag{10}$$

3.5 Throughput Analysis Under the Unsaturation Condition

To analyze the throughput under the unsaturation condition, we assume that the total input traffic to stations arrives according to Poisson distribution with mean λ. For the saturation condition, throughput, S, can be obtained as the proportion of time interval used to transmit a payload successfully. However, under the unsaturation condition, if p_0 is defined as the probability that a station has no frame to transmit, then S can be modeled as the throughput when there are $n*(1- p_0)$ stations in the saturation condition as shown in Fig. 2.

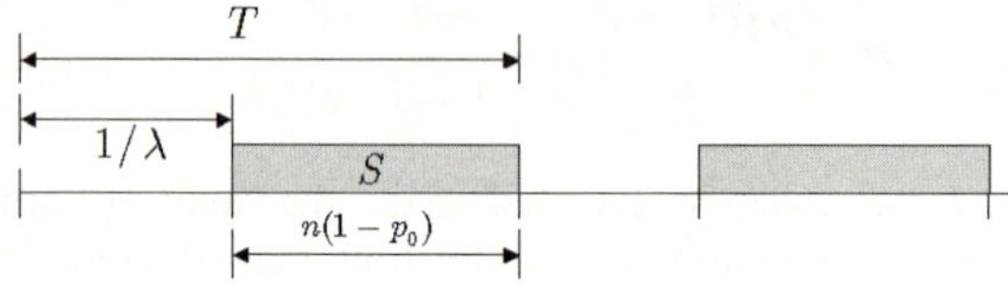

Fig. 2. Throughput analysis under the unsaturation condition

If the arrival rate is λ, the mean idle period becomes $1/\lambda$. Let T be the sum of one busy period and one idle period $1/\lambda$, then the throughput S' under the unsaturation condition is the the proportion of time interval used for successful transmission during T. Thus, the unsaturated throughput S' is given by

$$S' = \frac{S(T - 1/\lambda)}{T} = S(1 - p_0) \tag{11}$$

Fig. 3 shows that S' decreases as p_0 increases. If p_0 is given, the unsaturation throughput at arrival rate λ can be obtained from the saturation throughput $n*(1-p_0)$ stations.

3.6 Access Delay and Waiting Time Under the Unsaturation Condition

We can obtain the mean access delay $E[D]$ by using the same method with one exception that the effective number of stations becomes $n*(1-p_0)$. In addition, if it is assumed that each station queue is independent, we can also calculate the mean waiting time of each frame easily by modeling the input buffer of the station as M/M/1/K queue [10], where K denotes the finite buffer size and the service time is assumed to be exponentially distributed with rate $1/E[D]$

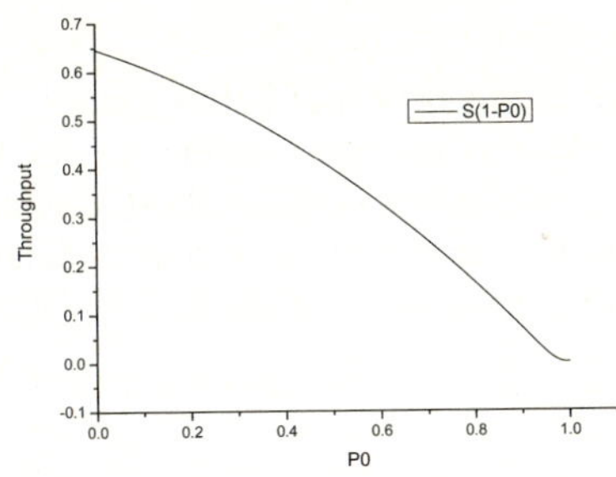

Fig. 3. Throughput with the varying p_0

4 Simulation Results and Performance Evaluation

In this section, throughput and access delay for the 802.11 DCF and 802.11 DCF+ are evaluated and compared by numerical analysis and simulation. A simulator is implemented by using a discrete-event simulator sim++[11]. The channel capacity is assumed to be 1 Mbits/s, and both ACK_Timeout and CTS_Timeout are defined as 300μsec. A MAC Header size is assumed to be 272 bits, and PHY Header is 128 bits long. ACK and RTS size is assumed as 112 bit + PHY Header. A payload size is fixed to be 8,184bits, and Poisson traffic arrival is assumed. Also, it is assumed that all stations can hear other station's transmission and there's no hidden terminal and no transmission error on the channel.

Fig. 4 (a) shows the saturation throughput of the both schemes for varying number of stations. The 802.11 DCF+ shows higher throughput for all the values of CW_{min} and m. In addition, the throughput of the 802.11 DCF is decreased drastically as n increases, but that of the 802.11 DCF+ shows a gradual decrease. Fig. 4 (b) shows the same results for the RTS/CTS access methods. But, in this case, the difference between the two saturation throughputs is not large for varying CW_{min} and m. In case of RTS/CTS access scheme, waste times due to collisions are not large.

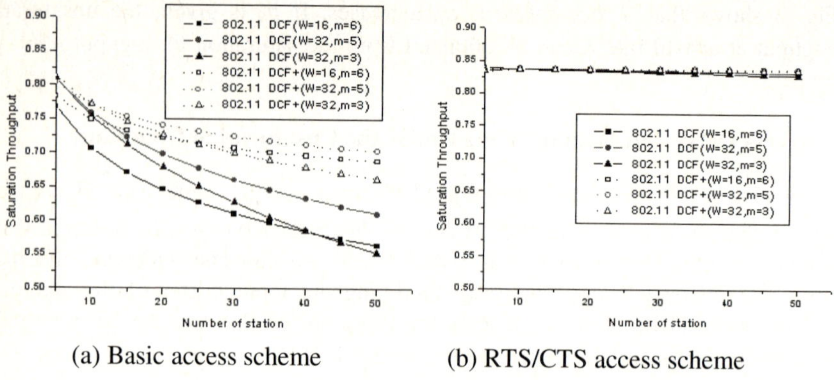

(a) Basic access scheme   (b) RTS/CTS access scheme

Fig. 4. Saturation throughputs of the DCF and the DCF+

Fig. 5 shows the average access delays of both methods. The frame delay increases rapidly as the number of stations increases in the 802.11 DCF. But, in the 802.11 DCF+, since the delay due to collisions is rather short, channel efficiency is high even if the CW is slowly reduced. There is a large access delay gap between the basic access scheme and the RTS/CTS scheme of the 802.11 DCF, but the gap is small in case of the 802.11 DCF+.

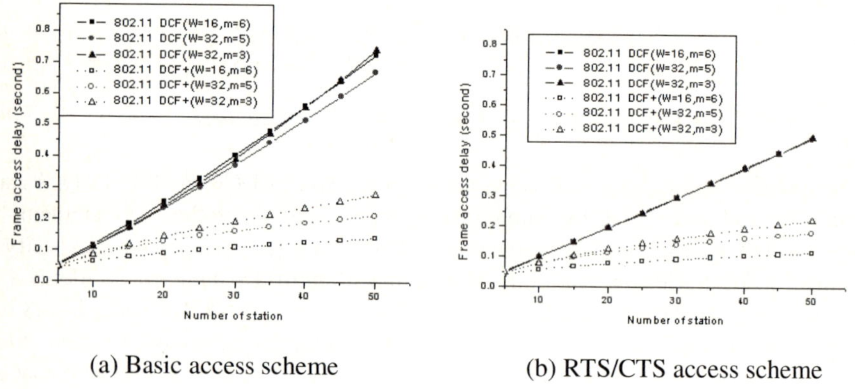

(a) Basic access scheme   (b) RTS/CTS access scheme

Fig. 5. Frame access delays of of the DCF and the DCF+

Fig. 6 (a) shows the throughputs for varying number of stations when $CW_{min} = 31$ and $m = 5$ by simulation. According to the Fig. 6 (a), the throughput is saturated at small λ when n is 50, while it is saturated at large λ when n is 5. The 802.11 DCF+ has an extended unsaturation region compared to the 802.11 DCF under the same number of stations by reducing the collision probability. The throughput is saturated at $\lambda = 0.65$ when n is 50 in the 802.11 DCF, but it is saturated at $\lambda = 0.7$ in the 802.11 DCF+. The 802.11 DCF+ shows even higher throughput for large λ and n value.

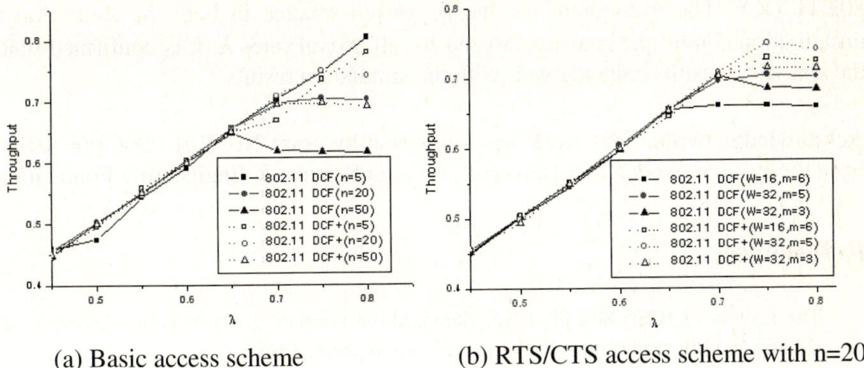

(a) Basic access scheme   (b) RTS/CTS access scheme with n=20

Fig. 6. Throughput of the basic access scheme in the unsaturation condition

Fig. 6 (b) shows the throughput for the RTS/CTS scheme. In the saturation region, the maximum throughput is enhanced by 0.03, 0.045 and 0.07 when m is 3, 5, and 6, respectively.

Finally, the simulation results are compared to the analytical results for the 802.11 DCF+ access. It is assumed that $CW_{min} = 16$, $m = 5$ and payload size = 8,184 bits. Fig. 7 shows the throughput for varying λ when $n = 20$, and $n = 50$, respectively. These two graphs show that analytical results coincide well with the simulation results.

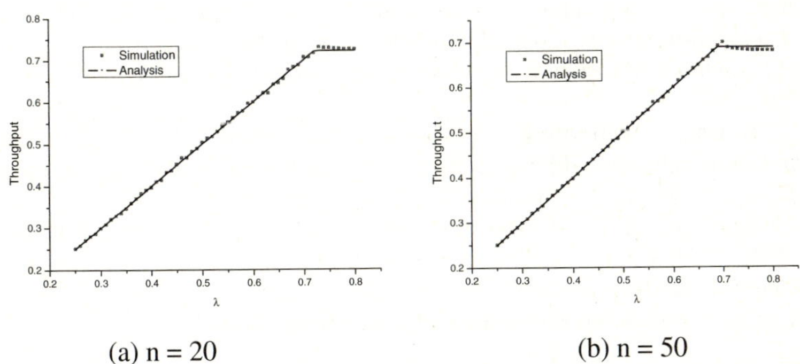

(a) n = 20   (b) n = 50

Fig. 7. Throughput comparison of simulation and analysis results

5   Conclusion

In this paper, an enhanced DCF algorithm, DCF+, is proposed, that reduces the CW gradually after the successful frame transmission instead of reducing it to the minimum value. The 802.11 DCF+ can enhance the channel throughput by reducing the collision probabilities when the number of stations or maximum backoff stage is large, because the current contention stage reflects the contemporary congestion level of the system. The proposed scheme not only enhances the saturation throughput, but also keeps the similar throughput in the unsaturation condition compared to the

802.11 DCF. The throughput for the suggested scheme in both the saturation and unsaturation conditions is also analyzed for all arrival rates λ. It is confirmed that all the analytical results coincide well with the simulation results.

Acknowledgements. This work was supported by grant No. R01-2006-000-10154-0 from the Basic Research Program of the Korean Science & Engineering Foundation.

References

1. The Editors of IEEE 802.11, IEEE Standard for Wireless LAN Medium Access Control (MAC) and Physical Layer (PHY) specifications, Nov. 1997.
2. H. S. Chhaya and S. Gupta, "Performance modeling of asynchronous data transfer methods of IEEE 802.11 MAC protocol", Wireless Networks, vol. 3 (1997), pp. 217-234, 1997.
3. T. S. Ho and K. C. Chen, "Performance evaluation and enhancement of the CSMA/CA MAC protocol for 802.11 wireless LAN's," in Proc. IEEE PIMRC, Taipei, Taiwan, pp. 392-296, Oct. 1996.
4. F. Cali, M. Conti, and E. Gregori, "IEEE 802.11 wireless LAN: Capacity analysis and protocol enhancement", presented at the INFOCOM'98, San Francisco , CA, Mar. 1998.
5. L. Kleinrock and F. Tobagi, "Packet switching in radio channels, Part-II The Hidden Terminal Problem in Carrier Sense Multiple Access Models and the Busy Tone Solution", IEEE Trans. Comm, vol. 23, no. 12, pp. 1417-1433, Dec. 1975.
6. G. Bianchi, L. Fratta, and M. Oliveri, "Performance analysis of IEEE 802.11 CSMA/CA medium access control protocol", IEEE PIMRC, Taipei, Taiwan, pp. 407-411, Oct. 1996.
7. H. Wu, Y. Peng and K. Long, "Performance of reliable transport protocol over IEEE 802.11 wireless LAN: analysis and enhancement", in Proc. INFOCOM 2002, pp. 599-607, Jun 2002.
8. G. Bianchi, "Performance Analysis of the IEEE 802.11 Distributed Coordination Function", IEEE J. Selected Areas in Comm., vol. 18, no. 3, pp. 535-547, 2000.
9. P. Chatzimisios, A. C. Boucouvalas and V. Vitsas, "Packet Delay Analysis of the IEEE 802.11 MAC Protocol", IEE Electronics Letters, vol. 39, pp. 1358-1359, Sep. 2003.
10. L. Kleinrock, 'Queueing systems, volume 1: theory', John Wiely & Sons, 1974
11. URL: http://www.cise.ufl.edu/~fishwick/simpack/simpack.html

Design of an Adaptive DCF Algorithm for TCP Performance Enhancement in IEEE 802.11–Based Mobile Ad Hoc Networks

Gira Lee, Han Jib Kim, Jae Yong Lee, and Byung Chul Kim

Department of Information Communications Engineering, Chungnam National University
220, Gung Dong, Yusung Gu, Daejeon 305-764, Korea
`{gil223, jibi97, jyl, byckim}@cnu.ac.kr`

Abstract. The TCP, which guarantees reliable data transfer, is the most widely used transport protocol for Internet applications. However, because the TCP was designed for wired networks, it degrades the transmission performance in wireless networks. In particular, the difference between the transmission range and the interference range in mobile ad hoc networks produces a hidden terminal problem that seriously deteriorates the TCP performance by constraining the simultaneous transmissions of several stations at a time. We therefore propose a new MAC algorithm for mobile ad hoc networks that can mitigate the effect of the hidden terminal problem by adaptively adjusting the contention window process. While a node in the IEEE 802.11 DCF increases its contention window exponentially whenever the node fails to transmit, the proposed algorithm changes the contention window adaptively according to the probable cause of failure. This change enhances the TCP performance by roughly discriminating hidden terminals and real collisions. The simulation results show that the proposed algorithm enhances the TCP performance by evenly distributing the transmission opportunity to every node in mobile ad hoc networks.

1   Introduction

The Transmission Control Protocol (TCP), which guarantees reliable data transfer, is the most widely used transport protocol for Internet applications. However, because the TCP was designed for wired networks, its transmission performance is degraded in wireless networks and is particularly poor in mobile ad hoc networks. There are several reasons for the performance degradation: the contention for a wireless medium, hidden terminal problems, exposed terminal problems, packet losses at the link layer, unfair transmission opportunity, link disconnection, a waste of bandwidth due to the exponential backoff of a transmission timer, and so on.

In wireless ad hoc networks, the hidden terminal problem severely constrains the number of nodes that can simultaneously transmit data. This constraint arises because the difference between the transmission range and the interference range causes frame collisions. Thus, sufficient distance is necessary between two nodes to transmit their frames safely without mutual interference, which is called *'spatial reuse property'*.

G. Min et al. (Eds.): ISPA 2006 Ws, LNCS 4331, pp. 1063 – 1072, 2006.

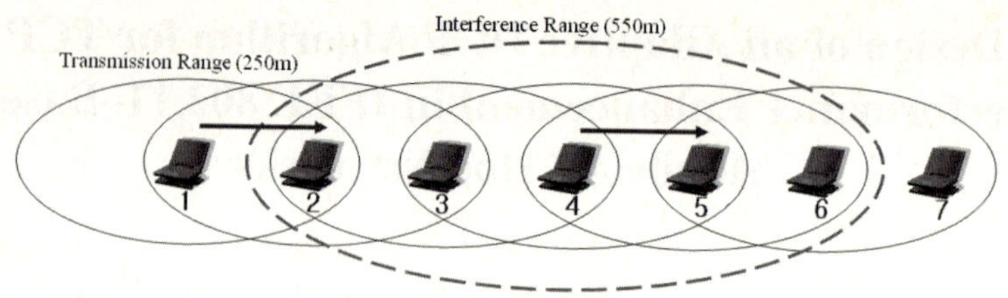

Fig. 1. Hidden terminal problem in mobile ad hoc networks

Figure 1 shows a hidden terminal problem caused by the discrepancy between the transmission range (250 m) and the interference range (550 m); this discrepancy is one of the primary reasons for the degradation of the TCP performance.

All nodes in IEEE 802.11–based mobile ad hoc networks use a Distributed Coordination Function (DCF) to utilize a channel for transmission through a medium contention that is only nominally fair [4]. Although all nodes in mobile ad hoc networks use an RTS/CTS mechanism in a DCF algorithm, the hidden terminal problem cannot be solved. For example, let's assume that node 4 sends an RTS frame to node 5 and receives a CTS frame from node 5, as shown in Fig. 1, and node 4 obtains a transmission opportunity. Because node 1 is located outside the interference range of node 4, node 1 can send an RTS to node 2 in order to get a transmission right. However, node 2 cannot respond with a CTS frame because node 2 is located within the interference range of node 4. Thus, node 1 gets a timeout for an RTS/CTS exchange. This event is regarded as a collision by node 1 and it increases the contention window (CW) according to the exponential backoff process. If node 1 does not receive a CTS frame after it retransmits an RTS frame a maximum number of times, it regards these consecutive failures as a path disconnection and performs a path reestablishment. Originally, the reason a node increases the contention window after transmission failures in the DCF is to avoid the possibility of later collisions with the RTS sender. If the node regards a failure due to a hidden terminal as a collision and subsequently increases its CW, the transmission bandwidth may be wasted due to the long useless waiting time before transmission for a low traffic load. In addition, the next transmission attempt may fail again as a result of the same hidden terminal problem, and this failure may severely degrade performance. The hidden terminal problem becomes more serious when a node moves around as in mobile ad hoc networks [1][2][3]. These problems degrade the TCP performance in ad hoc networks. We therefore propose an adaptive DCF (A-DCF) algorithm, which adaptively evolves the CW in relation to the probable cause of transmission failures in mobile ad hoc networks with hidden terminals.

Our paper is organized as follows: In Section 2, we explain the inherent problems of the IEEE 802.11 DCF protocol. In Section 3, we propose the A-DCF algorithm, which appropriately improves the legacy DCF for mobile ad hoc network environments. In Section 4, we present a simulated evaluation of performance. Finally, in Section 5, we summarize our conclusions.

2   Problems of the IEEE 802.11 DCF in Ad Hoc Networks

The DCF, which is a basic MAC protocol for IEEE 802.11, uses the Carrier Sense Multiple Access with Collision Avoidance (CSMA/CA) algorithm [4]. This algorithm uses a random backoff time mechanism to reduce the link level collision probability between nodes [5][6]. Figure 2 shows the basic access method in the DCF. When the medium becomes idle longer than the Distributed Inter Frame Space (DIFS) after a busy medium state, a node selects a random backoff time and counts it down. If the medium remains idle until the backoff time of a node becomes zero, that node accesses the medium and transmits its frame. If the medium becomes busy before the backoff time reaches zero, the node stops counting down the backoff time until the next idle time. When the backoff time becomes zero, the node sends its frame and waits for an ACK frame to determine the success or failure of the transmission. When the frame is transmitted successfully, it reduces the upper value of the CW selection range to CW_{min}. If the transmission is unsuccessful, it doubles the CW selection range up to CW_{max}.

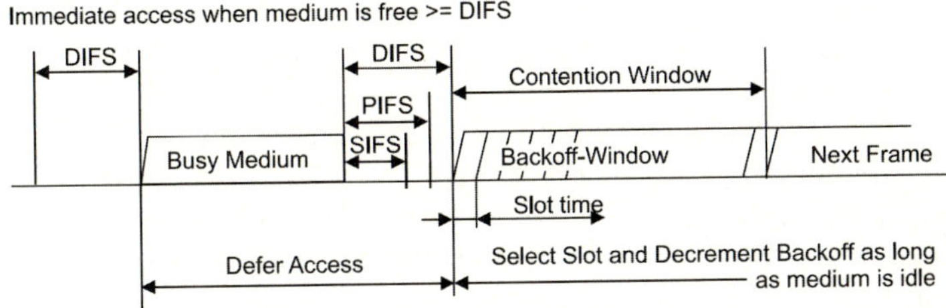

Fig. 2. The basic access method in a DCF

Figure 3 shows the RTS/CTS access method in the DCF. After the random backoff time expires, the node sends an RTS frame ahead of a DATA frame. The RTS frame includes the source address and the duration field used for the setup of a network allocation vector (NAV). The destination node among recipients of the RTS frame replies with a CTS frame, and the other nodes set their NAV values according to the duration field in the RTS frame. The other nodes delay their medium access until the expiration of their NAVs. After the successful RTS/CTS exchange, the sender transmits a DATA frame and the receiver replies with an ACK frame. Every frame has a duration field, and all the nodes that receive a larger duration field than their NAV values update their NAV accordingly. When the NAV becomes zero, the nodes regard the medium as idle and they try to access the medium after their CWs become zero.

Because it can rapidly recognize a link collision, the RTS/CTS access method is more efficient when the packet length is long or the collision probability is high due to a large number of nodes. However, even the RTS/CTS method cannot solve the hidden terminal problem that occurs when the interference range is larger than the transmission range. As explained above, a hidden terminal may prevent nodes from exchanging the RTS/CTS frame, thereby the nodes increase their contention windows exponentially up to the maximum, CW_{max}. In contrast, a successful node selects its contention window randomly between 0 and CW_{min}. Therefore, if a successful node and a node that fails due to a hidden terminal keep contending the medium for their packet transmission in a mobile ad hoc network, the successful node has a higher probability of success due to its smaller contention window. Thus, a successful node is likely to elicit a burst transmission whereas a failed node keeps on failing. In an ad hoc network, when a node fails in its transmission for the maximum number of retransmission times, it regards the failures as a path disconnection and causes the routing process to reestablish another route. If the repeated failure is not due to a path disconnection but a hidden terminal, the routing process need not be used to find another route. If a hidden terminal problem elicits a path reestablishment, the network becomes congested by unnecessary routing packets and the resulting waste in bandwidth causes further deterioration.

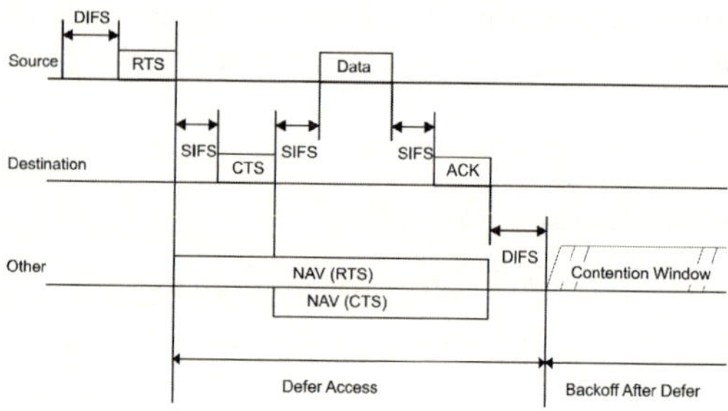

Fig. 3. The RTS/CTS access method in a DCF

3   Design of the A-DCF Algorithm

When a node in a DCF counts down its backoff timer for a frame transmission, the node can sense other frame transmissions or a busy medium. If the traffic load of the entire network is heavy, a node is more likely to sense a number of other frame transmissions while counting down its CW, and the transmission failure may come from a collision rather than a hidden terminal. On the other hand, if the traffic load is low, a node is less likely to experience the frame transmissions of other nodes during the CW countdown, and the transmission failure may come from a hidden terminal. The A-DCF algorithm adaptively changes the CW of a node in relation to the number of frame transmissions (N_{tr}) of other nodes during the CW countdown period of that particular node. The failed transmission most likely comes from a hidden terminal if the node does not experience other frame transmissions during its CW countdown; and this phenomenon occurs because the traffic load is rather low. In the A-DCF, if a transmission failure is due to a hidden terminal rather than a frame collision, the node maintains or even decreases its CW rather than increasing it. The purpose of this action is to ensure that the node catches an early transmission chance because the simple CW doubling after a failure may cause bandwidth waste in a low traffic load condition. This can also improve the transmission fairness among nodes and restrict the burst transmission by one specific node. The A-DCF tries to prevent degradation of the TCP performance by adaptively changing the CW in relation to the cause of failure as determined by N_{tr} during the CW countdown. The simulation results of the next section show that the A-DCF can mitigate the effect of the hidden terminal problem.

In the A-DCF, we selected an initial CW value, CW_{normal}, which was less than the CW value of a DCF. The smaller CW value enabled the A-DCF to be used appropriately in highly mobile ad hoc networks that have severe topology changes. When a node tries to send a new DATA frame or succeeds a frame transmission, the node selects its contention window in a range from 0 to the initial CW value, CW_{normal}. While waiting for a transmission, the node accumulates a number of other frame transmission attempts to N_{tr}. When a transmission fails, the A-DCF guesses the cause of the failure in terms of the following values of N_{tr}:

> For the case of $N_{tr} = 0$

  In this case, since the node does not sense other node transmissions, the transmission failure is attributed to a hidden terminal. Hence, the CW value is reduced to half its current value, until it becomes CW_{min}.

> For the case of $1 \leq N_{tr} \leq 2$

  In this case, the cause of failure is ambiguous. The node keeps the CW unchanged.

> For the case of $2 < N_{tr}$

  In this case, the traffic load is estimated to be heavy and the failure is assumed to be caused by a collision. Hence, the node doubles the CW as in the DCF, until it becomes CW_{max}.

The performance of the A-DCF algorithm depends on the configuration of the three parameters CW_{normal}, CW_{min}, and CW_{max}. In a legacy DCF, CW_{min} is set to 32 and CW_{max} is set to 1024. However, these values are rather large and inappropriate for highly mobile ad hoc networks. Accordingly, on the basis of the simulation results, we propose some suitable values for the three parameters. One thing to be careful about is that the time taken for the maximum retransmission trials when a failure occurs should be longer than the hidden terminal's transmission time for the largest frame. Otherwise, the node keeps trying to send its frame the maximum number of retransmission times, though the attempts fail and the node tries to reestablish the path because the hidden terminal's frame transmission may be still in progress during the retransmission attempts. For example, when node 4 is transmitting a frame to node 5 and node 1 starts trying to send its frame to node 2, the period for the maximum number of trials of node 1 should be longer than the transmission time of node 4. If the total time for seven retrials of an RTS/CTS exchange is shorter than the frame transmission time, the node is likely to fail its transmission attempt and the performance degradation by a hidden terminal would occur in an ad hoc network. In this case, even the A-DCF cannot enhance the performance. In order to mitigate the hidden node problem, we take in this paper the minimum value of CW_{min} in the A-DCF algorithm to be 32, and an appropriate for CW_{normal} to be 64.

4 Simulation Results and Performance Evaluation

To evaluate the performance of the proposed A-DCF algorithm, we performed various simulations by using ns-2 [8] under the chain topology shown in Fig. 1. In the first simulation, the nodes were assumed to be static and the chain length was set to 8 hops. Under this topology, the hidden terminal problem was not serious because the nodes didn't move and the number of neighboring nodes was small.

Figure 4 compares the performance of the proposed scheme with a basic DCF, under varying parameters of the A-DCF algorithm. The DSR [7] was assumed to be an ad hoc routing protocol, and the simulation ran for 500 sec. The bandwidth was fixed at 2 Mbps. In Fig. 4, the parameter M means CW_{max} and S means CW_{normal}. The throughput is enhanced as the number of retries increases because no route reestablishment is required when transmissions fail due to temporary congestion or hidden terminal problems. However, the performance difference between the two schemes is not large with respect to chain topology because the path from the source to the destination does not change dynamically; in the grid topology, on the other hand, the effects of route reestablishment are large.

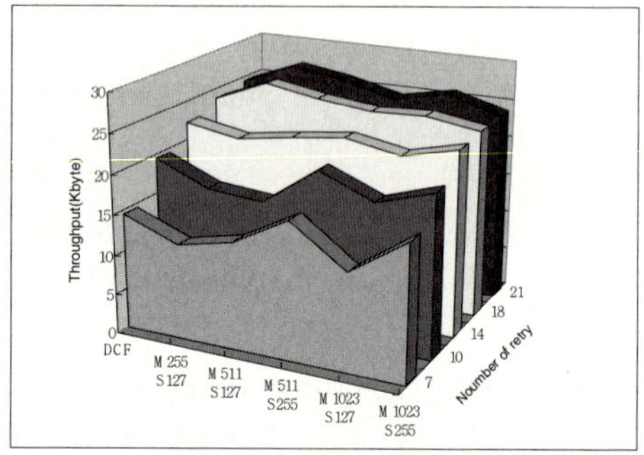

Fig. 4. Throughput of the A-DCF in chain topology

The next simulation was done in a 7 x 7 grid topology. The nodes were initially distributed every 200 m and assumed to move at a predefined speed. We also assumed that the nodes moved at a speed of 5 m/sec or 10 m/sec for each 5 sec interval in an arbitrary direction. To prevent packet transmission failures resulting from path disconnection, we limited the node's movement to a confined area; that is, to within 50 m to 200 m from the initial position. We also fixed the bandwidth to 2 Mbps and ran the simulation for 500 sec.

Figure 5 compares the throughput of the basic DCF and the A-DCF for the grid topology. The throughput of the A-DCF scheme is superior to that of the basic DCF in terms of node mobility. This result is based on the frequent route changes and hidden terminal problems due to node mobility. Because the basic DCF tries to reestablish a new route after attempting retransmissions in relation to the exponential backoff, it does not adapt to the route change quickly. In contrast, if the CW value of the A-DCF is fixed as a small value, then the node can prevent the backoff delay from increasing caused by a hidden terminal problem by quickly adapting the node mobility and, thereby improving the throughput. If there is no mobility, the throughput values of the two schemes are similar because the performance degradation due to route changes, collisions and hidden terminal problems is rather small.

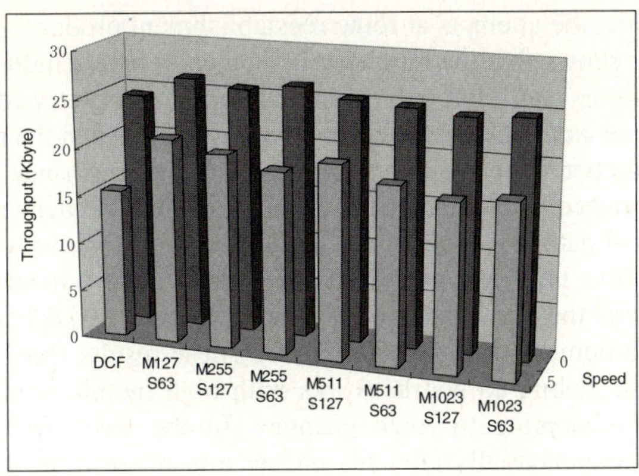

Fig. 5. Comparison of throughput for the basic DCF and the A-DCF

Figure 6 compares the performance of a basic DCF, a constant DCF and the A-DCF for varying node speeds. In the constant DCF and the A-DCF, we selected the optimal parameters for this simulation based on previous simulation results. When the node mobility is not considered, the performance enhancement is only 8% better in the constant DCF and the A-DCF than in the basic DCF. However, if the node mobility becomes high, the performance is enhanced more. That is, the enhancement is 35% greater for the A-DCF than for the basic DCF at a speed of 5m/s speed, and 100% greater at a speed of 10 m/s. The A-DCF also performs better than the constant DCF because the A-DCF has a small and dynamically chosen CW value; thus, the A-DCF has a greater capability of reducing the performance degradation that results from hidden terminals. Moreover, the performance enhancement of the A-DCF is 17% greater than that of the constant DCF at a speed of 5 m/s and 24% greater at a speed of 10 m/s.

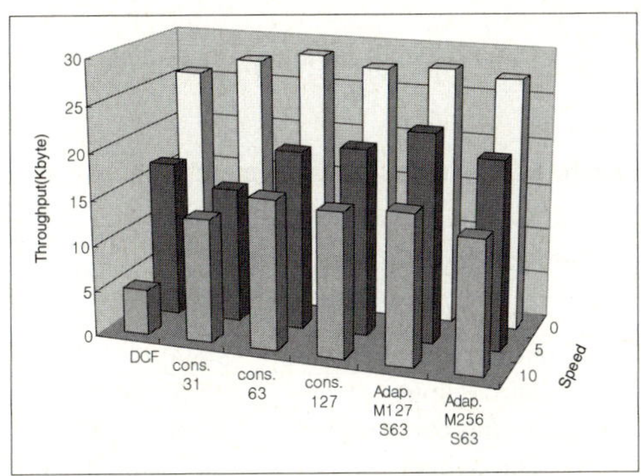

Fig. 6. Comparison of throughput for various node speeds with a retry count of 7

Figure 7 shows changes to the path length for a varying number of retry counts when CW_{max} is 127 and CW_{normal} is 63 in the grid topology. If a packet transmission fails due to temporary interference not by network congestion when all the nodes are assumed to be static, the attempts at route reestablishment produce an overhead in the network. Figure 7 shows that the number of changes in path length was 20 when the number of retry counts was 7 but only 2 when the number of retry counts was 14. The total amount of time using the optimal 8-hop path is small when the number of retry is 7. Thus, if the number of retry counts increases, the performance can be enhanced because of the reduced number of tries at route reestablishment due to temporary problems other than path disconnection. This phenomenon shows how the number of retry counts at the link layer affects the performance of multi-hop ad hoc networks.

Table 1 compares the performance improvement of the A-DCF with that of other schemes when the number of retry counts is 7. These results show that the use of a small CW value in mobile ad hoc networks with high mobility enables a quick and efficient means of adapting to route changes. In the basic DCF, the contention window increases exponentially after the packet transmission fails because it means network congestion. However, if the transmission fails due to a hidden terminal, a reduction in the CW is better than an exponential increase.

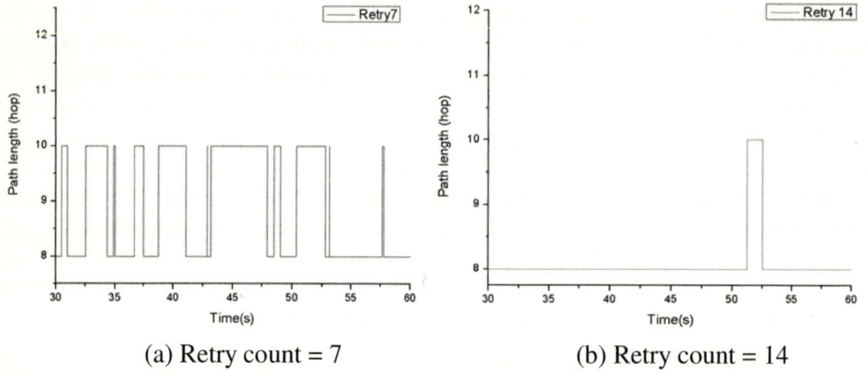

(a) Retry count = 7   (b) Retry count = 14

Fig. 7. Changes in path length for a varying number of retry counts

Table 1. Throughput improvement of the A-DCF

Throughput		Basic DCF	Constant DCF	Adaptive DCF
0 m/s	Throughput	24.6	26.1	26.4
	Throughput improvement ratio	8.6%	1.1%	N/A
5 m/s	Throughput	15.5	18.05	21.25
	Throughput improvement ratio	37%	17.7%	N/A
10 m/s	Throughput	5.2	8.21	10.46
	Throughput improvement ratio	101.1%	24.4%	N/A

[Unit: Kbyte]

Figures 8 and 9 show the fairness of transmission opportunity by each node in the chain topology. We assumed a bandwidth of 2 Mbps, a packet size of 1 Kbyte, and a packet transmission interval of 30 ms. To simulate fairness, we sent UDP traffic from node 0 to node 8. We then set the CW_{max} of the A-DCF to 128 and the CW_{normal} to 63. Figure 8 shows the packet transmission instants in time of each node by successfully accessing the wireless link. In the basic DCF, the hidden terminal problem creates a bursty transmission pattern. In Fig. 8(a), for example, node 0 cannot transmit for a while (for example, from 53 sec to 54 sec) when node 3 transmits because node 3 is a hidden terminal of node 0. In contrast, as shown in Fig. 8(b), the A-DCF halves its CW value when the packet transmission fails due to a hidden terminal; thus, the fairness with respect to transmission opportunity of each node is guaranteed, and utilization of the network becomes highly efficient.

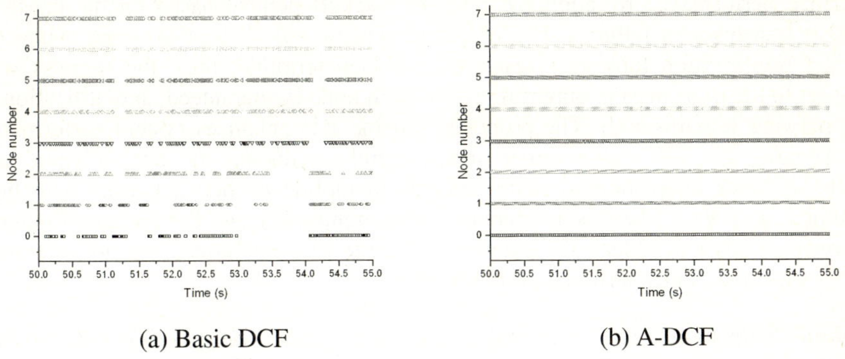

(a) Basic DCF   (b) A-DCF

Fig. 8. Fairness of transmission opportunities between nodes

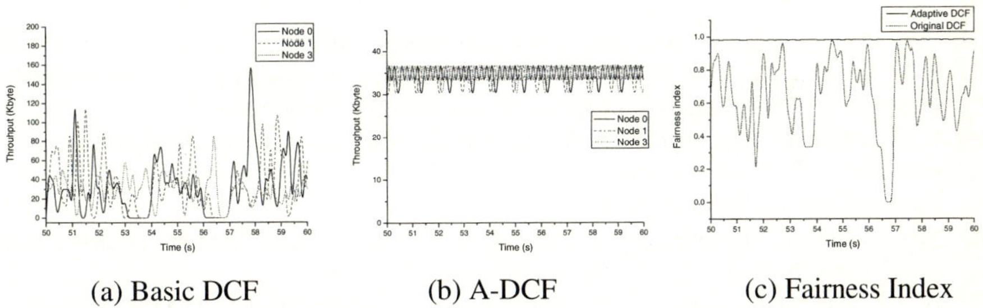

(a) Basic DCF   (b) A-DCF   (c) Fairness Index

Fig. 9. Comparison of fairness between the original DCF and the A-DCF

Figure 9 compares the throughput of each node for a period of one hour. In the basic DCF, the throughput difference of each node is very high, as shown in Fig. 9(a), because of the occurrence of a burst transmission. However, in the A-DCF, as shown in Fig. 9(b), the throughput values of each node are very similar at every moment because of the fair distribution of transmission chances. Figure 9(c) shows the fairness between node 0 and node 3 as measured by Jain's fairness index, which is expressed as follows [9]:   Fairness index $= \left(\sum x_i\right)^2 \Big/ n \times \sum (x_i)^2$.

5 Conclusions

We conducted a detailed investigation of how a hidden terminal problem can hinder TCP performance in mobile ad hoc networks, and we propose a new backoff scheme that reduces the extent to which a hidden terminal can degrade performance. The RTS/CTS access scheme in the 802.11 DCF MAC cannot solve the hidden terminal problem. Furthermore, the method of increasing the backoff time exponentially when a transmission fails as a result of a hidden terminal is inefficient in mobile ad hoc networks and particular nodes may produce a bursty transmission. Our proposed A-DCF, which is based on a modified backoff control algorithm of the basic DCF, can enhance performance by applying a proper backoff control based on the cause of packet transmission failures. The proposed scheme halves its CW value when the packet transmission fails as a result of a hidden terminal; thus, the fairness with respect to the transmission opportunities of each node is guaranteed, and utilization of the network remains high. The proposed scheme also enhances system performance by keeping the CW value rather small, thereby reducing the backoff time and enabling quick adaptation to route changes in mobile ad hoc networks with high mobility. Moreover, there is an increase in throughput because the increased number of retry counts can reduce the overhead of route reestablishment due to temporary congestion and hidden terminal problems.

Acknowledgements. This work was supported by grant No. R01-2006-000-10154-0 from the Basic Research Program of the Korean Science & Engineering Foundation.

References

[1] C. E. Perkins, "Ad hoc networking", Addison Wesley, 2001.
[2] E. M. Royer and C. Toh, "A review of current routing protocols for ad-hoc mobile wireless networks", IEEE Personal Communication, pp. 207-218, April. 1999.
[3] K. Chandran, S. Raghunathan, S. Venkatesan, P. Prakash, "A feedback-based scheme for improving TCP performance in ad hoc wireless networks," IEEE Personal Communications, February 2001.
[4] The Editors of IEEE 802.11. IEEE Standard for Wireless LAN Medium Access Control (MAC) and Physical Layer (PHY) specifications, Nov. 1997.
[5] H. S. Chhaya and S. Gupta, "Performance modeling of asynchronous data transfer methods of IEEE 802.11 MAC protocol", Wireless Networks, vol. 3 (1997), pp. 217-234, 1997.
[6] T. S. Ho and K. C. Chen, "Performance evaluation and enhancement of the CSMA/CA MAC protocol for 802.11 wireless LAN's," in Proc. IEEE PIMRC, Taipei, Taiwan, pp. 392-296, Oct. 1996.
[7] D. B. Johnson, D. A. Maltz, Y. Hu, "Dynamic Source Routing Protocol for Mobile Ad Hoc Networks (DSR)", Internet Draft < draft-ietf-manet-dsr-10.txt >, July 2004.
[8] Network Simulator, ns version 2-29, http://www.isi.edu/nsnam/ns/
[9] R. Jain, D. Chiu, and W. Hawe, "A quantitative measure of fairness and discrimination for resource allocation in shared computer system," Digital Equipment Corporation, Technical Report, DEC-TR-301, Sep. 1984.

Icon-URI Structure with ENUM System for Mobile Device*

Jiwon Choi and Keecheon Kim[**]

Department of Computer Science & Engineering, Konkuk University,
1 Hwayang-dong, Kwangjin-gu, Seoul, 143-701, Korea
`{jackeroo, kckim}@konkuk.ac.kr`
`http://mbc.konkuk.ac.kr`

Abstract. URI has been used for the contents by recognizing them as a page of text, sound, video clip, picture, and animation. However, we need a new URI system and service environment for mobile devices because of the difficulty of inputting information using the mobile devices. Inconvenient interface using a keyboard for the mobile device is one of the major obstacles to the wireless Internet. We can utilize an icon such as bar code or specification image as an alternative plan for the new URI system. We need to work to systemize the Icon-URI. In this paper, we propose a code for Icon-URI system that can be used with ENUM service.

1 Introduction

Wireless communication becomes a vital part of our life by providing various convenient functions such as mobility, high-speed, customized service, and intelligence. According to a recent survey by Korea Investment & Securities, the number of mobile phone subscribers in the beginning of 2006 surpassed thirty seven millions in Korea.

However, there are various restrictions in using internet in mobile environment although the transmission speed has been increased with many different kinds of mobile devices. [9]

The high cost of using mobile internet is an obstacle. However, inconvenience caused by the input function is more serious. It brings about new technologies when we use the internet in mobile environment. URI has been used for the contents by recognizing them as a page of text, sound, video clip, picture, and animation. URL has been used to access and search the information through the character strings that locate the physical position of information resource. However, using URL with hand held devices such as cellular phone or PDA, there are restriction generated by mobile devices. It is not easy to input the characters because of the input capability. In order to access the information resource much easier, Iconic URI can be a solution to this problem. [1][2]

This paper proposes an Icon-URI code that can be used with ENUM service when ENUM service becomes a reality.

---

[*] This research was supported by the Brain Korea 21 project.
[**] Corresponding author.

G. Min et al. (Eds.): ISPA 2006 Ws, LNCS 4331, pp. 1073 – 1079, 2006.

2 Related Works

2.1 DOI (Digital Object Identifier)

DOI is a system to identify content objects in the digital environment. DOIs are names assigned to entities for use in the digital networks. They are used to provide current information, including where they (or information about them) can be found on the Internet. Information about digital objects may change over time, including where to find it, however its DOI will not change.

DOI system provides a framework for persistent identification, managing the intellectual content, and managing the metadata, linking the customers with content suppliers, facilitating electronic commerce, and enabling the automated media management. DOIs can be used for any form of management for any data, whether they are commercial or not.

The system is managed by the International DOI Foundation, an open membership consortium including both commercial and non-commercial partners, and has recently been accepted as a standardization within ISO. Several million DOIs have been assigned by DOI Registration Agencies in the US, Australasia, and Europe.

Using DOIs as identifiers makes managing intellectual property in a networked environment much easier and more convenient, and allows the construction of automated services and transactions. [3]

2.2 QRcode

QRcode is a 2D matrix symbol which consists of square cells arranged in a square pattern. It allows three models - Model 1, Model 2, and MicroQR. Model 1 and Model 2 each have a position detection pattern in three corners while the MicroQR has it in only one corner. The position detection pattern allows code readers to quickly obtain the symbol size, position and tilt. Model 2 is developed for enhanced specification with improved position correction and for the large volume of data capacity. MicroQR model is suitable for small amount of data. A QRcode symbol can encode up to 7,089 characters (numeric data), 4,296 alphanumeric characters, and 2,953 8-bit bytes. [12], [13]

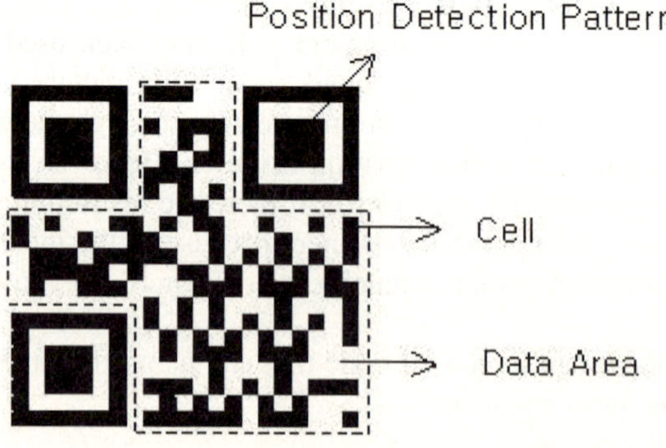

Fig. 1. QRcode structure

2.3 ENUM

ENUM is the abbreviation of Telephone Number Mapping or E.164 Number Mapping, and is a protocol that maps the phone numbers to Internet addresses.

The basis for ENUM is the unification of the existing PSTN (Public Switched Telephone Network) and the IP (Internet Protocol) Network. The phone number and the Internet address operate on a single system. As a result, when a phone number is entered into the computer the number is linked to various communication services such as the Internet homepage, e-mail, fax, cellular phone, instant message etc.

ENUM is only applicable for E.164 numbers. ENUM compliant applications must only query DNS for what it believes to be an E.164 number.

Since there are numerous dialing plans which can be changed over time, it is probably impossible for a client application to have perfect knowledge about all the valid and dialable E.164 number.

Therefore a client application, doing everything within its power, can end up with what it thinks is a syntactically correct E.164 number, even though, in reality it is not actually valid or dialable.

This implies that applications may send DNS queries when, for example, a user mistypes a number in a user interface. Because of this, there is the risk that collisions between E.164 numbers and non-E.164 numbers can occur.

To mitigate this risk, the E2U portion of the service field must not be used for non-E.164 numbers. [8]

KRNIC (Korea Network Information Center) had executed an ENUM test service, which showed that we can connect to E-mail, homepage and internet telephone using one existing telephone number.

3 Icon-URI System Compatible with the ENUM for Mobile Device

3.1 Requirement for Wireless Internet

Present network environment contains various forms of network which includes the latest Internet, traditional PSTN, satellite network, cable network and wireless/wire communication network. This phenomenon has been propelled by the recent internet development and fast deployment of the radio communication technology. The use of the existent network technology is not limited in the area communication. It has been used to connect computers, and now we connect many other electronic devices using network technology. Information-Communication of 21st century may affect all the business activities of our daily lives. At first, circuit switching technology and packet switching technology are integrated, and the existing PSTN and Cellular radio communication network are integrated, and we need to focus on balancing the image and video traffic. Since the number of subscribers for the wireless communication technology using mobile devices has been increased dramatically, wireless communication technology was appeared to be a very important element. Because the current internet only proved a best-effort service, it is not suitable for new Information-Communication business. Since the current internet is designed for data traffic, we need to reinforce other functions to support voice, image, and broadcasting service. It is also very important to use the network resources effectively when heterogeneous network coexist within the environment. Even if the next generation network infrastructure is constructed well, it is very important to test the compatibility and service quality when it coexists with the legacy networks. We must offer different input functions for various kinds of terminals because we must consider various networks. [3], [4], [5], [6]

Two-dimensional codes provide much higher information density than the conventional bar codes. Due to the low information density, conventional bar codes usually function as the keys to databases. However, because of the increased information density of 2D bar code, we can encode the explicit information rather than a database key. A 2D bar code symbol can hold up to about 4,300 alphanumeric characters or 3,000 bytes of binary data in a small area. [12] But 2D bar code is not useful as an input code for ENUM system even if it can hold lots information.

3.2 Icon-URI Structure Based on ENUM System

Because ENUM utilize the existing system as much as possible, it does not require major technical changes. ENUM does not apply the telephone number directly to request a service, it converts the telephone number to a different form such as a domain name database described in RFC 2916.

We do the following conversion to search URL that corresponds to a free E.164 number.

Erase all the characters that is not number except "+" in the telephone number (example: + 82 - 2 - 450 - 3518) including country code.

```
"+" means the number is using E.164 numbering system.

Ex)  +  8224503518

Remove all characters that are not number.

Ex)  8224503518

Dot between numbers

Ex)  8.2.2.4.5.0.3.5.1.8

Overturn the string.

Ex)  8.1.5.3.0.5.4.2.2.8

Add e164.arpa domain in end of string.

Ex)  8.1.5.3.0.5.4.2.2.8.e164.arpa
```

Changed ENUM number can be processed in domain name server which supports the ENUM question. [10], [11]

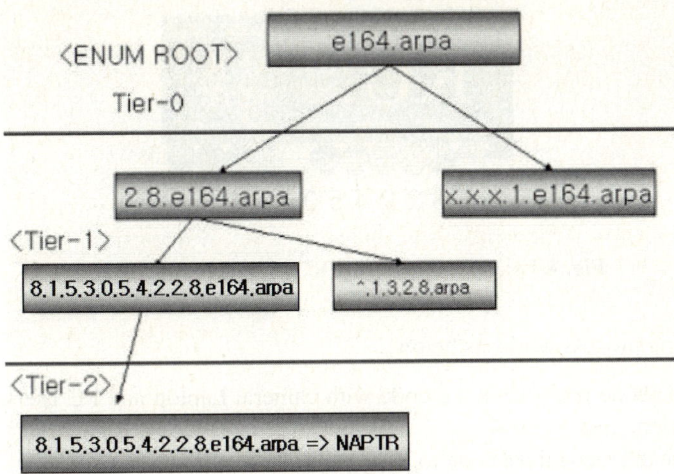

Fig. 2. ENUM layered structure

"arpa" is a root domain that ITU recommends. And in the above example, "2.8.e164.arpa" is an ENUM domain that corresponds to the country code of South Korea (country code 82 that is used in telephone) and other numbers form a layered structure.

If we use the special characteristics of ENUM, we have produced a simpler code form with numbers.

Using this binary code that uses RGB+None, 16 characters can be marked by a code character of 2 ($4^2=16$).

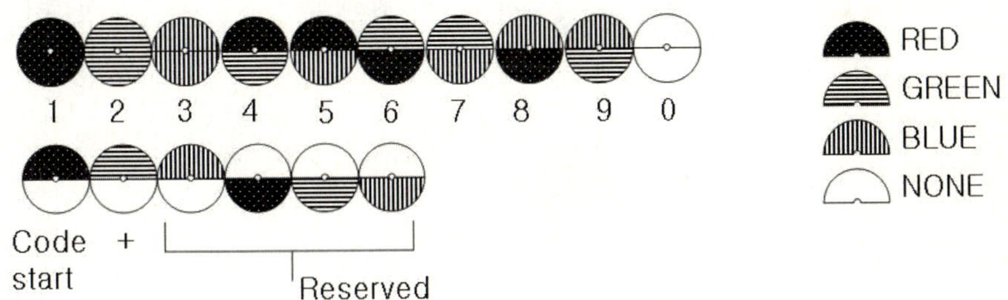

Fig. 3. The structure of Icon-URI

Icon-URI is available for the images like logo. Figure 4 shows an example of an Icon-URI system.

Fig. 4. Example of an Icon-URI compatible with ENUM

The decoding process works as below.

① Cellular phone recognizes the code with camera. Laptop and PC use webcam for recognition.
② Translate the recognized code to ENUM number.
③ Query the number to ENUM DNS.
④ ENUM DNS requests service using URL.
⑤ SP (Service Provider) start service to each terminal.

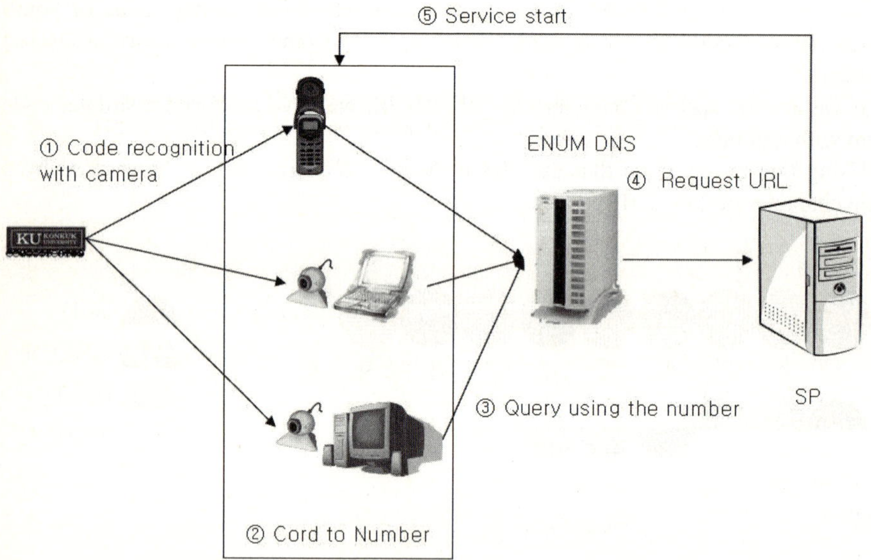

Fig. 5. Icon-URI scheme using the ENUM system

4 Conclusion

Since the information of URN keeps changing from time to time, it is very hard to keep up with the current changes in resolving the URL. Using the bar code as a URL is limited since it requires a private server that needs private management. Since the bar code is allocated locally in the country, it looks hard for a company to handle the general information that must be enforced as a standard.

In order to use Icon-URI, we must establish URI system for Icon-URI that follow the international standard and then design its environment for service.

IETF states that we can register URN without special restriction if some URN fit in IETF URN standard to register URN system, we can make our proposal of using an image through Icon as one of the URI for wireless device.

Through this research, it is expected to propel the use of mobile internet using small devices with limited input capability.

Acknowledgement

This research was supported by the MIC(Ministry of Information and Communication),

Korea, under the ITRC(Information Technology Research Center) support program supervised by the IITA(Institute of Information Technology Assessment).

References

1. T. Berners-Lee.: Uniform Resource Identifier (URI) Generic Syntax draft-fielding-uri-rfc2396 bis-03. Internet Draft IETF (2003)
2. Changyul Lee.: URI structure and conversion technology. URI IT weekly (2003)
3. Norman Paskin.: The DOI Handbook. IDF (International DOI Foundation) (2003)
4. M. Mealling.: The Network Solutions Personal Internet Name (PIN) A URN Namespace for People and Organizations. RFC 3043 (2001)
5. M. Mealling.: A URN Namespace of Object Identifiers. RFC 3061 (2001)
6. M. Walsh.: A URN Namespace for Public Identifiers. RFC 3151 (2001)
7. M. Mealling.: An IETF URN Sub-namespace for Registered Protocol Parameters. RFC 3553 (2003)
8. P. Faltstrom.: E.164 number and DNS. IETF Draft (2000)
9. Korea Investment & Securities.: Sector Analysis, Wireless Telecom Service (2006)
10. P. Faltstrom.: The E.164 to URI DDDS Application (ENUM). IETF work in progress (2003)
11. Richard Shockey.: Privacy and Security Considerations in ENUM, IETF work in progress (2003)
12. Aichi.: QRmaker User's Manual, Denso Corporation, Japan (1998)
13. Kariya.: A Business Case Study QRcode, Denso Wave Inc., Japan (2001)

Efficient Attribute Authentication in Wireless Mobile Networks

Jaeil Lee, Inkyoung Jeun, and Seoklae lee

Korea Information Security Agency,
78, Garak-Dong Songpa-Gu, Seoul, 138-803 Korea
{jilee, ikjeun, sllee}@kisa.or.kr

Abstract. Recent e-commerce requires an attribute authentication that provides users with distinctive and unique internet service, as well as user identification. Despite widespread awareness of the importance of attribute authentication, the attribute authentication service is not yet used widely due to it's inconvenience and inefficiency. These defects especially has a bad effect to mobile users in wireless networks. This paper described the weakness of current attribute authentication mechanisms and proposed a Public Key Certificate(PKC)-based attribute authentication model considering an efficiency and convenience. The user who has a PKC in a mobile device can use the efficient attribute authentication without additional procedure.

1   Introduction

As the information technology is developed so rapidly, e-commerce(EC) like as internet banking, online stock, etc., has been growing quite quickly every year. It is very important to ensure the reliability and security of EC through information networks[1]. Identification of users is the most important technology for EC security. But, some EC requires to combine personal identification technology with attribute authentication. The attribute refers to the qualifications and authority of an individual involved in a business transaction or the like. Based on the generation of attribute information, which represents user's vocations, positions, qualifications, etc., a distinctive and unique access to the internet applications or to individualized services can be provided.

As the methods of providing such attribute information, there are a method for adding attribute information into the public key certificate(PKC) and a method for issuing an attribute certificate (AC). The PKC has been used in EC that require integrity of user information and user identification[2]. The method of using the PKC needs to be reissued the PKC if the user's attribute value changes. If a user uses a mobile phone in wireless network, this is very inconvenient factor. Also, it is necessary to achieve standardization of attributes and attribute values and their corresponding object ID(OID). Attribute Certificate(AC)[3] have been developed and standardized by ANSI X9 committee as an alternative and better approach, to X.509 public key certificates, for carrying authorization information. AC can be used for controlling access to system resources and employing

G. Min et al. (Eds.): ISPA 2006 Ws, LNCS 4331, pp. 1080–1089, 2006.

role-based authorization and access controls policies accordingly[4][5]. But it is necessary to have both PKC verification and AC verification in the method using the AC. Accordingly, it takes a relatively long period of time to verify attributes. On these reasons, despite widespread awareness of the importance of attribute authentication, the attribute authentication service is not yet used widely in the world, especially in wireless networks.

Based on the understanding that it is hard to widespread the attribute authentication service, this paper suggests an efficient attribute authentication mechanism using PKC which is most widely used for user identification in EC. We shall describe the preliminaries for the attribute authentication in Section 2. And we shall assess the current status and problems of attribute authentication mechanisms in Section 3. In Section 4, we shall describe the model of attribute authentication using PKC and compare our proposed model and the current method. And this paper will make a conclusion in section 5.

2   Preliminaries

Before presenting the details about the mechanism, it is also useful for us to define terminologies used in this paper as follows.

Certificate Authority(CA): The party that holds the registration information of the user on its system, and issues certificates to the user.

Registration Authority(RA): The party that applies for certificate issuance. This party is in charge of confirming the identity of the user and delivering the registration information to CA.

Certificates: In general, standard certificates bind a public key and identity. Certificates are issued by a trusted party, the so-called certificate authority(CA). Standard certificates consist of a data part and a signature part. The former contains an identifying string for the entity along with the corresponding public key. The signature part of the certificate contains a digital signature by the CA. Before issuing a certificate for a particular party, it is therefore crucial that the CA ensures proper identification of the requesting party.

Attribute: An attribute represents the position, eligibility, status, etc. of the subject with regards to commercial transactions, regardless of whether they are online or offline. In general, the main purpose of using attribute information in EC or application procedures is to distinguish the services or functions that can be used by the subject, from those of others, through its attributes.

identification: An identification refers to a clear distinguishing of one individual from others in a certain population.

authentication: An authentication means associating the individual with the attribute data of that individual. In an EC, attribute information has been defined as confirmation by others that an identified and authenticated individual has certain attributes.

3   Current Attribute Authentication Mechanisms

For the generating attribute information and providing it, the following methods
have been reviewed and embodied in the application services. One is a method
for adding attribute information into the public key certificate and the other is
a method for issuing an attribute certificate.

3.1   Public Key Certificate(PKC)

This is a method using a public key certificate(PKC) for the system to obtain
the information necessary to make the attributes of a system user certified. The
format of the PKC is defined as ITU-T Recommendation X. 509[2,6]. The application service has two methods of obtaining attributes using the PKC as follows.

Limitation on those who issue the PKC:
   This method considers a PKC as an attribute. The organizations that guarantee attributes issue a PKC only for individuals who have these attributes.
   If a person is verified as a user using the PKC, it is used to certify that the
   user has the attributes and the attribute values.
Method for specifying a attribute value in the PKC:
   This method issues a PKC by writing a users attributes and attribute values
   within the PKC. There are some examples of using a subject or extensions
   as a field of the PKC, in which attributes and attribute values are written.
   That the user has attributes and attribute values is able to be verified by
   checking the attributes and attribute values of the PKC. It is necessary to
   confirm attribute information when issuing the PKC.

As for the method for specifying a user's attribute and attribute value in the
PKC, the extension field inside the certificate, referred to as the *Subject Alternative Name* or *Subject Directory Attributes* extension, can be used to indicate
the attribute.

The hcRole attribute, designated as ISO/TS 17090-2[9], represents the role
of medical staff, and it should be used as *Subject Directory Attributes* extension
when established as a PKC. When we use *Subject Alternative Name* field of the
certificate owner instead of using a separate extension field, the attribute value
is entered into value of Other Name field as below.

```
SubjectAltName ::= GeneralNames,
GeneralNames    ::= SEQUENCE SIZE(1..MAX) OF GeneralName
GeneralName     ::= CHOICE{
    otherName   [0]      OtherName,  ...
}
OtherName       ::= SEQUENCE{
    type-id    OBJECT IDENTIFIER,
    value      [0] EXPLICIT ANY DEFINED BY type-id}
```

This method is difficult to deal with a temporary attribute due to reissuing
of PKC is needed if the attribute is changed. And the method for suggesting

the attributes and attribute values of a user to the PKC is considered by having them simply verify the PKC. Accordingly, it is highly likely that the PKI-related software that is currently utilized is able to be used, making the system relatively easy to establish. Also, It is not easy to prepare in advance the general-purpose certification software that verifies the attributes of the PKC. Even where a person uses the certification software currently used, it will be necessary to customize it for use in the corresponding application.

If it is intended to establish a system with high degrees of interoperability or a globalized system in the method specifying the attributes and attribute values of a user in the PKC, it is necessary to achieve standardization in the industry, and international standardization of attributes and attribute values, and their corresponding OID. However, this is currently insufficient. And The PKC needs to be reissued in case the attributes change. In terms of speed performance, the method of using the PKC is faster than that using the attribute certificate(AC), because the former needs to verify only the PKC.

3.2   Attribute Certificate(AC)

There are a method used for obtaining information for certifying the attributes of system users using an attribute certificate(AC)[6]. The form of the attribute certificate(AC) was defined as ITU-T Recommendation X.509. AC may be user in a wide range of applications and environments covering a broad spectrum of interoperability golds[3].

For the system using the AC, the system issues an AC specified with the attributes and attribute values granted in accordance with a user to those users possessing the PKC. In this case, the trusted party, which we will call the attribute authority, would create AC[10]. These certificates are very like those created by certificate authorities, but instead of relating to the identity of the users in question, they would relate to their behavior[8]. The AC is able to handle multiple attributes and attribute values. In this regard, the system can specify them on an attribute certificate where necessary, or specify them on the multiple attribute certificates separately. The user is certified by the PKC, and the attributes and attribute values are verified using the AC on which the attributes to be verified are specified.

This method has the following characteristics. It is able to explicitly establish and manage the terms of validity of an attribute. And the function of encoding the attribute requiring encryption is provided by the standard. Also, the existence of PKC is a prerequisite to that of AC, because the latter refers to the former. Multiple attributes, as well as unique attributes, are included in the AC. However, it is not easy to prepare in advance general-purpose verification software able to certify AC attributes. Even when using general verification software, it is necessary to customize the software in compliance with its proposed application. And, if one intends to establish a system with high interoperability or a globalized system, it is necessary to achieve the standardization in the industry, and international standardization of attributes and attribute values, and their corresponding OID like PKC method for attribute authentication. However, current systems are insufficient in this regard.

The AC requires reissue in case that attributes changes like PKC method mentions in Section 3.1. In terms of speed performance, it is necessary to have both PKC verification and AC verification in the method using the AC. Accordingly, it takes a relatively long period of time to operate.

4   PKC-Based Attribute Authentication

In this paper, we propose the PKC-Based attribute authentication method. For revitalization of the attribute authentication service, user convenient and efficiency of implementation are most important elements. The user dose not need any more process to use the attribute authentication service.

We consider X.509 v3 PKC for attribute authentication since it is widely used in EC for identification. User has only PKC which is used in EC and the it is used in attribute authentication service for user identity. The attribute information of users are collected and managed by trusted authority, the so-called attribute verification authority(AVA). This is a centralized attribute management scheme and the attribute authentication is executed by an attribute authentication server utilizing an attribute database of trusted authority. The attribute authentication server identifies and authenticates the user by PKC.

4.1   Assumptions and Requirements

The attribute authentication is important for a discriminative internet service in these days. But as we investigated in Section 3, the current attribute authentication mechanisms are not satisfied with user requirements. In this paper, we propose an efficient attribute authentication using PKC. To achieve this, we must consider the next requirements.

- *Convenience:* One of the most important factors when providing an attribute authentication service is easy to use. User hope to use the internet service without regard to change of his attribute information. Also, user should use different certificate by service type, making it difficult for user to use internet service.
- *Security:* There is an exposure risk of attribute information expressed in PKC or AC. If private information like as a position, right, occupation, etc, are disclosed to public, it can be a big harm to user. Therefore, the attribute information should be deal with carefully.
- *Interoperability:* Attribute authentication service should not be limited to specific company or user. Also, the attribute information should be understandable in every service provider.

The main parties of PKC-Based attribute authentication service are;

Attribute Information Provider(AIP): An attribute information provider is a company that provides the necessary attribute information for users when they use EC. It provides users a method for registering attribute information. Also, it manages user's attribute information in a safe manner.

Privilege Verifier(PV): An entity verifying user's attribute to provide an internet services. It can be an internet content providers who offer digital content or services to users.

Attribute Verification Authority(AVA): An authority that collect the attribute information from AIP and manage it. It returns the verification result of attribute to PV. AVA should be operated by trusted authority for the safety of user's attribute information. For this, CA that manages user's database can operate AVA.

User: A subject who uses applications of PV. He already has a PKC and it is used in EC for identify and attribute authentication.

Also, we assume some facts for our propose. First assumption is that the attribute information which is managed by AVA are has a validity period like PKC or AC. AVA should manage the attribute information periodically by asking to PV and update its database before the validity period is expired. Second assumption is a change control of user's attribute. If user's attribute is changed by retirement, promotion, etc., the database of AVA must be updated. To do this, PV sends the information to AVA at proper time if changes of user's attribute information occur.

4.2   Service Model

PKC-based attribute authentication service is constructed 2 steps, one is the registration process of user's attribute information, and second one is the attribute verification process using PKC. The user who register his attribute information to AVA database can use attribute authentication service using PKC at anytime.

For ease of explanation, we use the notations as follows.

A	Alice, the user who use the mobile internet service provided by PV
$sign_{sk}(Doc)$	signature value of Doc signed by sk
sk_A	private key of A
pk_A	public key of A
$Cert_A$	a certificate corresponding pk_A and sk_A
$attribute_A$	attribute information of A
$Att\_Request$	attribute request message for internet service made by PV
$Att\_Response$	attribute verification result made by AVA

The procedure of PKC-based attribute authentication is shown in Fig.1 and the detailed steps for attribute authentication are as follows.

Phase 1: Registration of an attribute information

1. A generates private and public key pair(sk_A,pk_A) and requests the certificate issuing through CA or RA. CA or RA establishes the identify of A to accept

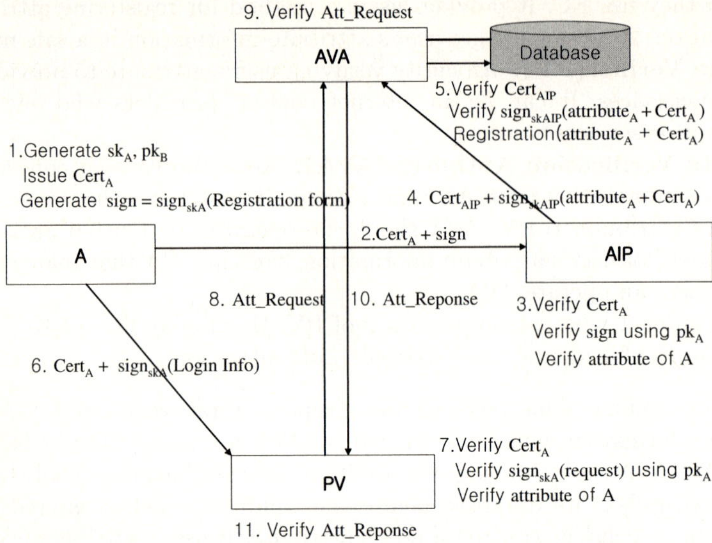

Fig. 1. Attribute Authentication procedure using PKC

the application for the certificate and then issues the certificate. A makes out the registration form which is for registration of attribute information and generates *sign*.

$$sign = sign_{skA}(RegistrationForm)$$

2. A sends *sign* and $Cert_A$ to AIP.
3. AIP verifies *sign* and $Cert_A$. For this, AIP can use OCSP service of CA as well as CRL[7] . In case *sign* and $Cert_A$ are verified, AIP confirms A's attribute.
4. AIP makes signature of $attribute_A$ and $Cert_A$ using its private key sk_{AIP}, and then sends it with $Cert_{AIP}$ to AVA.
5. AVA verifies $Cert_{AIP}$ and $sign_{sk_{AIP}}(attribute_A + Cert_A)$. In case it is verified, AVA registers $attribute_A$ and $Cert_A$ in its database. $Cert_A$ is then used for user identification, $attribute_A$ is used for the verification of access rights for A.

Phase 2: Attribute verification by AVA

6. A presents $Cert_A$ and *sign* to PV for using PV's internet service. *sign* is the signature value of login information.

$$sign = sign_{skA}(LoginInformation)$$

7. PV verifies *sign* by $Cert_A$ using OCSP service or CRL. In case *sign* and $Cert_A$ are verified, PV makes *Att_Request*. *Att_Request* includes a PV's identity information and A's information as below.

```
Att_Request  ::= SEQUENCE {
    tbsRequest                TBSRequest,
    optionalSignature         Signature       OPTIONAL }
TBSRequest   ::= SEQUENCE {
    requestorName             GeneralName     OPTIONAL,
    requestList               SEQUENCE OF UserInfo }
UserInfo        ::= CHOICE {
    userName                  GeneralName     OPTIONAL,
    CertInfo                  Certificiate    OPTIONAL }
```

requestorName can be a PV's ID or subject name. PV can add signature in *Att_Request* for message integrity optionally. *UserInfo* is the user's information for user identity. PV can send the user's ID or certificate using *UserInfo*. User's ID must be registered also like as user's certificate.

8. PV sends *Att_Request* to AVA.
9. AVA received *Att_Request* can distinguish which PV has sent it. After verifying the signature of meesage, AVA extracts *requestList* to know the user's ID or certificate for attribute verification. It examines the necessary attributes on the attribute database and makes *Att_Response* to PV.
   Att_Response structure is :

```
Att_Response  ::= SEQUENCE {
    tbsReqponse               TBSResponse,
    optionalSignature         Signature       OPTIONAL }
TBSResponse   ::= SEQUENCE of Response
Response      ::= SEQUENCE {
    userId      UserInfo,
    result      Attribute }
Attribute     ::= SEQUENCE {
    type             AttributeType,
    values  SET OF AttributeValue }
        --at least one value is  required
AttributeType ::= OBJECT IDENTIFIER
AttributeValue::= ANY DEFINED BY AttributeType
```

10. AVA sends *Att_Response* to PV.
11. After PV received *Att_Response*, it can verify signature value for integrity if *Signature* is included and extract *Att_Response* from the message which is contained the user's attribute. If the attribute is suitable for access right, A is permitted to access the PV's service.

By using this approach, the user who has a PKC does not need to issue an AC additionally. Also, the PKC does not need to include any attribute information and reissue the PKC in case change of attribute value. This model is easy to intensively manage the addition of multiple attributes or changes of attribute values.So it is very efficient in wireless networks. However, there are some defects. Unless the method used for exchanging and managing attribute or attribute value is standardize, interoperability will be excluded. Also, AVA should be trusted authority due to concentration of attribute information.

4.3   Analysis of the Proposed Model

This chapter will analyze and compare the features and security elements of the existing attribute authentication with the one suggested here.

Attribute authentication mechanisms are summarized in Table 1.

Table 1. Comparison of Attribute Authentication Mechanisms

Issue	PKC Method	AC Method	Proposed Method
Change of Attribute	PKC Reissue	AC Reissue	Database Update
Infrastructure	PKI	PKI + PMI	PKI
Verification of Attribute	PKC verification	AC verification	AVA Operation
Number of User Certificate	1	2	1
User Convenience	Middle	Low	High
Exposure of Attribute	Possible	Possible	Impossible
Management	Difficult	Difficult	Easy

PKC method and AC method need to be reissue of certificate in case the attribute values change, but our proposed method dose not need it. It only need to update of attribute database. The infrastructure of PKC and proposed method is PKI. But AC method should build a Privilege Management Infrastructure(PMI) as well as PKI. Our proposed method needs CA and AVA which are operated by trusted authority. Also, verification of attribute information is performed by AVA, not PV or user side, so the management of attribute information is easy than other methods.

In section 4, we mentioned our requirement for efficient attribute authentication. Our first requirement was a convenience. Our proposed method requires only user's PKC which is not included any attribute information. So user can use his PKC in the attribute authentication as well as in the area of e-commerce. These factors will increase a convenience and efficiency, especially in wireless networks. The seconde requirement was security. The certificate is a public information. So, anyone who acquire the user certificate can read the information included in certificate. As a result, the attribute information included in certificate is not any more private information. But proposed model does not include any attribute information in certificate. The attribute information of user are only managed by AVA not user or PV. So there is no risk to exposure of attribute information. The last requirement was interoperability. We presented the detailed process of attribute authentication service and the message format in each process. Our proposed model can be used in almost EC which has ability of verifying a certificate and connects to AVA. Of course, it is necessary an international standardization of attribute type and value like as PKC method and AC method to achieve interoperability.

5   Conclusion

The various e-business by internet revolution now requires users to attribute authentication that provides them with distinctive services as well as their identity certification. This paper analyzed the weakness and problems that current attribute authentication services and proposed the use of an attribute authentication service based on public key certificate for wireless networks.

For attribute authentication services, we can use PKC which is include the attribute information or issued to limited individual and AC which is issued by attribute authorities. But these mechanism require an reissuing of certificate of the attribute value is changes. Also, the AC user also should be issued the PKC and if the attribute information is changed, he should reissue the AC as well as PKC. This can be a restrictions to mobile user in wireless networks. To solve these drawbacks, we propose PKC-based attribute authentication service using AVA. AVA can manage and update of user's attribute information, so user has not something to do with management of attribute information.

We sincerely hope that this paper herald further efforts adopting attribute authentication service and lead to promoting the PKC in attribute authentication services in wireless mobile networks.

References

1. ECOM(Next Generation Electronic Commerce Promotion Council of Japan), *Attribute Authentication Handbook*, http://www. ecom.jp, 2005
2. R.Housley et al., *Internet X.509 Public Key Infrastructure Certificate and Certificate Revocation List (CRL) Profile*, RFC3280, IETF, April, 2002
3. S.Farrel et al., *An Internet Attribute Certificate Profile for Authorization*, RFC3281, IETF, April, 2002
4. R.Oppliger et al., *Using Attribute Certificates to Implement Role Based Authorization and Access Control Models*, SIS2000, Oct. 2000
5. Georgios Kambourakis et.al, *Introducing Attribute Certificates to Secure Distributed E-learning or M-learning Serivces*, WEB2004, Feb.2004
6. ITU-T Recommendation X.509 (1997) | ISO/IEC 9594-8:1998, *Information technology - Open Systems Interconnection - The Directory : Authentication Framework*, 1998
7. M.Myers el al., *Internet X.509 Public Key Infrastructure Online Certificate Status Protocol-OCSP*, RFC2560, IETF, June, 1999
8. Markus Jakobsson, *Efficient Attribute Authentication with Applications to AdHoc Networks.*, ACM, 2004
9. ISO/TS, *Health Informatics-Public Key Infrastructure - Part2 : Certificate Profile*, ISO/TS 17090-2, 2002
10. ECOM(Next Generation Electronic Commerce Promotion Council of Japan), *Handbook of Attribute*, http://www. ecom.jp, 2005

Group Key Agreement Protocol Among Mobile Devices in Different Cells

Jeeyeon Kim[1], Seungjoo Kim[2], Kilsoo Chun[1], Jaeil Lee[1], and Dongho Won[2,*]

[1] Korea Information Security Agency,
78, Garak-Dong, Songpa-Gu, Seoul, 138-803, Korea
`jykim@kisa.or.kr`
[2] Information Security Group, Sungkyunkwan University,
300 Cheoncheon-dong, Jangan-gu, Suwon-si, Gyeonggi-do, 440-746, Korea
`www.security.re.kr`, `dhwon@security.re.kr`

Abstract. Mobile communication has become more pervasive and it is considered as one of main concerns of IP telephony, video conferencing, multi-user games and etc. in mobile environments. These applications require secure group communication between a multitude of mobile devices owned by group members. Most of the published group key agreement protocols are based on a model which consists of a stationary base station and a cluster of mobile devices. In this paper, we assume a more realistic scenario in which secret group key is established between several base stations and mobile devices in different cells. We present new group key protocol among mobile devices in different cells and analyze its security.

Keywords: Group communication, Mobile device.

1   Introduction

Mobile communication has become more pervasive and it is considered as one of main concerns of IP telephony, video conferencing, multi-user games and etc. in mobile environments. Many of these application needs group-oriented security mechanisms. These security mechanisms are achieved through some form of group key management. Group key agrement protocols are favorable to efficiently implement secure multicast channels for a group of parties communicating over a public network by providing them with a shared secret key called a *session key*.

There are two methods to share a session key according to key generation party. : key transport and key agreement. While one party determines the resulting shared key in the key transport, communicating parties contributed to the resulting shared key in the key agreement. Since the key transport is unilateral to the party who received the key, key agreement is generally likely to be preferred.

Over the years, several group key agreement protocols have been offered [2], [4], [7], [8], [9], [10]. Most published protocols are based on 2-party Diffie-Hellman(DH) key exchange protocol.

---

* Corresponding author.

G. Min et al. (Eds.): ISPA 2006 Ws, LNCS 4331, pp. 1090–1097, 2006.

Recently mobile communication has become more pervasive and group key agreement protocols in a mobile environment have been studied [2], [8], [9]. Borisov *et al.* pointed out that IEEE 802.11 standard does not specify how distribution of keys is to be accomplished in Wired Equivalent Privacy(WEP) protocol [5]. In 2003, Bresson *et al.* presented an efficient authenticated group key agreement scheme that can complement the WEP protocol and showed that their protocol has been proved secure in the random oracle model under the computational DH assumption [2]. However Nam *et al.* showed that Bresson-Chevassut-Essiari-Pointcheval's group key agreement protocol does not have the main security properties such as implicit key authentication, forward secrecy, and known key security. Then they proposed an improved version [8]. In 2005, Nam *et al.* proposed an efficient, asymmetric group key agreement protocol. Then they showed that their protocol achieved perfect forward secrecy and had been proven secure against an active adversary in the random oracle model under the Decisional DH assumption [9]. Until now, their protocols are based on a model which consists of a stationary base station and a cluster of mobile devices.

In a wireless environment, due to the mobility, the communicating mobile devices are placed in different cells. Therefore the group key agreement protocol across the boundaries of base stations is required.

In this paper, we have focused on the extended model of which participants are several base stations and mobile devices in different cells. We present a new group key protocol among mobile devices in different cells and analyze its security.

The paper is organized as follows. In Section 2 we begin with a description of the requirements for group key agreement protocols among mobile devices in different cells. In Section 3 we present a new group key agreement protocol among mobile devices in different cells and analyze its security.

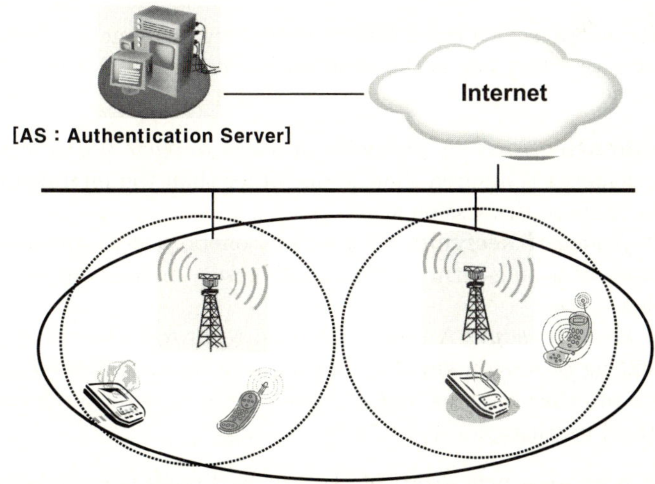

Fig. 1. A comparison between previous model and proposed model

2   Requirements for Group Key Agreement Among Mobile Devices in Different Cells

Our proposed group key agreement protocols consist of several base stations and a cluster of mobile devices connected to different base stations. The followings are the requirements for the protocol.

- ***Communication via the base station***: Mobile devices are connected with the base station of the cell to which they belong. The mobile devices cannot establish a direct connection between them, they communicate via the base station.
- ***Asymmetry of computational power***: The mobile computing architecture we visualize is asymmetric in the sense of computational capabilities of hosts. That is, the base stations has sufficient computational power and mobile hosts has limited computational resources.
- ***Contributory key agreement***: Providing a truly (physical) random source in a slow-computing mobile device may not always be possible or cost effective. In particular, it may be the case that a cryptographically weak (physical) random number generation is provided, or that some "random" seed is pre-loaded in the phone at manufacturing time [6]. Thus we have focused on contributory key agreement protocols in which the session key is derived as a function of contributions provided by all parties. In contributory key agreement protocols, a correctly behaving parties is assured that as long as his contribution is chosen at random, even a coalition of all other parties will not be able to have any means of controlling the final value of the session key.

3   Group Key Agreement Protocol Among Mobile Devices in Different Cells

In this section we present a contributory group key agreement which meets the main security properties: key authentication, perfect forward secrecy and known key secrecy.

- ***Key authentication***: A protocols provides *implicit key authentication* if each participants is assured that no one other than the intended parties can learn the value of the session key.
- ***Perfect forward secrecy***: A protocol offers *perfect forward secrecy* if compromise of a long-term key(s) cannot result in the compromise of past session keys.
- ***Known key secrecy***: A protocol is said to provide *known key secrecy* if compromising of session key does not allow a passive adversary to compromise keys of other sessions, nor an active adversary to impersonate one of the protocol parties.

Before we propose a new protocol, we briefly discuss two trivial approaches using a previous group key agreement in a cell to design a group key agreement among mobile devices in different cells.

Approach 1: A base station B_j $(1 \leq j \leq n)$ generates a group key K_j with its mobile devices by a group key agreement protocol. Then B_j encrypts K_j with the public key of B_k $(1 \leq j \neq k \leq n)$ and sends the ciphertext to all the base station B_k's. Upon receiving the ciphertext, the base station B_k decrypts the ciphertext to get the key K_j and then computes a final group key $K = H(K_1, \cdots, K_n)$, where H is a secure hash function. The base station B_k sends $E_{K_k}(K)$ to its mobile devices, where E is a secure symmetric encryption algorithm. Finally, all mobile devices obtain K by decrypting the receiving ciphertext.

Approach 1 doesn't provide perfect forward secrecy and key authentication. If the public key of the base station is compromised, the attacker can compute all previous group keys. In case that malicious base station can send $E_{K_k}(R)$ instead of $E_{K_k}(K)$, the mobile devices have no method to verifying a valid group key K, where R is a random number.

Approach 2: A base station B_j $(1 \leq j \leq n)$ generates a group key K_j with its mobile devices by a group key agreement protocol. Then B_j shares a group key BG with B_k $(1 \leq j \neq k \leq n)$ by using a group key agreement protocol. The base station B_j sends $E_{BG}(K_j)$ to all the base station B_k's. Upon receiving the ciphertext, the base station B_k decrypts the ciphertext to get the key K_j and then computes a final group key $K = H(K_1, \cdots, K_n)$. The base station B_k sends $E_{K_k}(K)$ to its mobile devices. Finally, all mobile devices obtain K by decrypting the receiving ciphertext.

Unlike Approach 1, Approach 2 provides perfect forward secrecy. But like Approach 1, it doesn't provide key authentication. Furthermore, Approach 2 is inefficient since it requires the group key agreement between base stations per session.

Now, we present a contributory group key agreement protocol among mobile devices in different cells.

3.1   Computational Assumption

- Mobile devices $U_i^{(j)}$ $(1 \leq i \leq m)$ are connected with the base station B_j $(1 \leq j \leq n)$ of the cell to which they belong. The mobile devices can also communicate with the authentication server(AS) via the base station.
- Mobile devices, AS and base stations have a pair of public key and private key for digital signature.
- All arithmetic is performed in the cyclic group G of prime order q and generator g which is subgroup of $\mathbb{Z}_p^*$ for a prime p such that $p = 2q + 1$. Note that p, q and g are public and common to all participants.
- Mobile devices and base stations use secure hash function H, secure symmetric encryption algorithm E and signature algorithm secure adaptive chosen ciphertext.

3.2   Protocol Description

1. (a) Each client (mobile device) $U_i^{(j)}$ $(1 \leq i \leq m)$ chooses a random number $r_{U_i(j)} \in \mathbb{Z}_q$, computes $z_{U_i(j)}$ and sends $m_{U_i(j)}$ with the signature $\sigma_{U_i(j)}$ of $m_{U_i(j)}$ to the base station B_j.

$$z_{Ui(j)} = g^{r_{Ui(j)}}, \; m_{Ui(j)} = (U_i^{(j)}, z_{Ui(j)})$$

   (b) Other base stations $B_k (\neq B_j)$ $(1 \leq k \leq n)$ also choose a random number $r_{Bk(j)} \in \mathbb{Z}_q$ and send $m_{Bk(j)} = (B_k, z_{Bk(j)} = g^{r_{Bk(j)}})$ with $\sigma_{Bk(j)}$ to the base station B_j. $\sigma_{Bk(j)}$ is the signature on $m_{Bk(j)}$.

2. Upon receiving the messages and the signatures, the base station B_j verifies the signatures, chooses random $r_j, r_{Bj(j)} \in \mathbb{Z}_q$, and computes

$$z_j = g^{r_j}, \; K_j = (\textstyle\prod_{i=1}^m z_{Ui(j)} \times \prod_{k=1}^n z_{Bk(j)})^{r_j} = g^{r_j(\sum_{i=1}^m r_{Ui(j)} + \sum_{k=1}^n r_{Bk(j)})}.$$

Then B_j computes $X^{(j)} = \{x_l^{(j)} | 1 \leq l \leq m\}$ and $Y^{(j)} = \{y_l^{(j)} | 1 \leq l \leq n\}$ where

$$x_l^{(j)} = \left(\frac{\prod_{i=1}^m g^{r_{Ui(j)}} \times \prod_{k=1}^n g^{r_{Bk(j)}}}{g^{r_{Ul(j)}}} \right)^{r_j}, \; y_l^{(j)} = \left(\frac{\prod_{i=1}^m g^{r_{Ui(j)}} \times \prod_{k=1}^n g^{r_{Bk(j)}}}{g^{r_{Bl(j)}}} \right)^{r_j}.$$

B_j broadcasts $m_{Bj} = (B_j, z_j, X^{(j)}, Y^{(j)})$ and σ_{Bj} to its connected clients and the other base stations. σ_{Bj} is the signature on (B_j, K_j).

3. (a) Upon receiving the broadcast, each client $U_i^{(j)}$ $(1 \leq i \leq m)$ computes $K_j = x_i^{(j)} \times z_j^{r_{Ui(j)}}$ and verifies the signature σ_{Bj}.

   (b) Base stations $B_k (\neq B_j)$ $(1 \leq k \leq n)$ also computes $K_j = y_k^{(j)} \times z_j^{r_{Bk(j)}}$ and verifies the signature σ_{Bj}. Then B_k broadcasts

$$E_{K_k}(\{K_j | 1 \leq j \neq k \leq n\})$$

and σ_{Bj} to its connected clients $U_i^{(k)}$ $(1 \leq i \leq m')$.

4. The mobile device decrypts the receiving ciphertext to obtain K_j and verifies the signature σ_{Bj}. Finally all of the participants compute their session key as $K = H(K_1, K_2, \cdots, K_n)$.

3.3 Security Analysis

In this section, we show that our proposed protocol provides desired properties for a practical key agreement protocol. The security of our protocol is based on the security of the underlying signature algorithm and symmetric encryption algorithm and on intractability of the CDH(Computational Diffie-Hellman) problem. Computing g^{ab} (mod p) given g^a and g^b is called CDH problem.

– *The proposed protocol is a contributory authenticated key agreement protocol.*

From the construction of the resultant group key K and K_j, each K_j is derived as a function of the ephemeral random values $r_{Ui(j)}$, $r_{Bk(j)}$ and r_j contributed by the base stations and the mobile devices.

$$K = H(K_1, K_2, \cdots, K_n), \; K_j = g^{(\sum_{i=1}^m r_{Ui(j)} + \sum_{k=1}^n r_{Bk(j)})r_j}$$

Therefore we can see that the proposed protocol is contributory group key agreement protocol.

Let *Eve* be an adversary who can modify, delay, or inject messages. *Eve*'s goal is to share a key with group members, mobile devices or base stations, by masquerading as some group members.

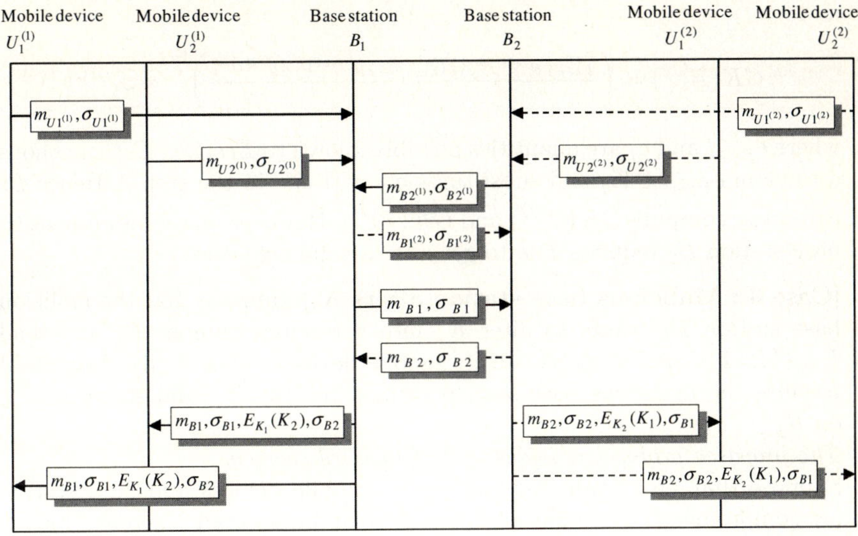

Fig. 2. An execution of the proposed protocol between two different cells

[**Case 1: *Eve* masquerades as $U_i^{(j)}$ or $B_k^{(j)}$**] Assume that *Eve* wants to send message purporting to come from the valid $U_i^{(j)}$ or $B_k^{(j)}$. Let $GK(B_j)$ be the partial group key computed by the base station B_j. It can be expressed as:

$$GK(B_j) = \left(\prod_{i=1}^{m} g^{e_{Ui(j)}} \times \prod_{k=1, k \neq j}^{n} g^{e_{Bk(j)}} \times g^{r_{Bj(j)}} \right)^{r_j}$$

where $e_{Ui(j)}$ and $e_{Bk(j)}$ are values possibly known to *Eve*, i.e., *Eve* can substitute any $g^{r_{Ui(j)}}$ and $g^{r_{Bk(j)}}$ with $g^{e_{Ui(j)}}$ and $g^{e_{Bk(j)}}$ respectively in the step 1. Since *Eve* knows all $e_{Ui(j)}$ and $e_{Bk(j)}$, *Eve* can easily compute $GK(B_j)$:

$$GK(B_j) = \left(\frac{\prod_{i=1}^{m} g^{e_{Ui(j)}} \times \prod_{k=1, k \neq j}^{n} g^{e_{Bk(j)}} \times g^{r_{Bj(j)}}}{g^{e_{Ui(j)}}} \right)^{r_j} \times z_j^{e_{Ui(j)}}$$

or

$$GK(B_j) = \left(\frac{\prod_{i=1}^{m} g^{e_{Ui(j)}} \times \prod_{k=1, k \neq j}^{n} g^{e_{Bk(j)}} \times g^{r_{Bj(j)}}}{g^{e_{Bk(j)}}} \right)^{r_j} \times z_j^{e_{Bk(j)}}$$

However, Eve masquerading as group members can be reduced to the attempt to breaking the signature algorithm secure against adaptive chosen ciphertext attack.

[**Case 2 : *Eve* masquerades as B_j**] Let $GK(U_i^{(j)})$ and $GK(B_k^{(j)})$ be the partial group keys computed by $U_i^{(j)}$ and $B_k^{(j)}$. They can be expressed as :

$$GK(U_i^{(j)}) = \left(\frac{\prod_{i=1}^{m} g^{r_{Ui(j)}} \times \prod_{k=1, k \neq j}^{n} g^{r_{Bk(j)}} \times g^{e_{Bj(j)}}}{g^{r_{Ui(j)}}} \right)^{e_j} \times z_j^{r_{Ui(j)}}$$

and

$$GK(B_k^{(j)}) = \left(\frac{\prod_{i=1}^{m} g^{r_{Ui(j)}} \times \prod_{k=1,k\neq j}^{n} g^{r_{Bk(j)}} \times g^{e_{Bj(j)}}}{g^{r_{Bk(j)}}} \right)^{e_j} \times z_j^{r_{Bk(j)}}$$

where $e_{Bj(j)}$ and e_j are quantities possibly known to Eve, i.e., Eve can choose a random $e_{Bj(j)} \in \mathbb{Z}_q$ and substitutes g^{r_j} with g^{e_j} in the step 2. Hence Eve can easily compute $GK(U_i^{(j)})$ and $GK(B_k^{(j)})$. However, masquerading as the base station B_j requires Eve to generate a valid signature.

[Case 3 : Malicious base station alters K_j] Suppose that the malicious base station B_k wants to alter K_j into a random number R_j and sends $E_{K_k}(\{R_j | 1 \leq j \neq k \leq n\})$ to its mobile devices. That is also intractable because the malicious base station cannot generate a valid signature σ_{Bj} on R_j.

- *The proposed protocol provides perfect forward secrecy.*
  Suppose that all private signing keys of mobile devices and base stations are compromised. Then our attacker, Eve can masquerade the base stations or mobile devices to compute a new group key. However, it is intractable to compute earlier group key because compromise signing keys are used for implicit authentication only and not for hiding the group key. In other words, Eve with private signing keys knows $(\prod_{i=1}^{m} z_{Ui(j)} \times \prod_{k=1}^{n} z_{Bk(j)})$, g^{r_j} and $E_{K_k}(\{K_j | 1 \leq j \neq k \leq n\})$. If the CDH problem in prime-order subgroup is hard, computing K_j from g^{r_j} and $g^{(\sum_{i=1}^{m} r_{Ui(j)} + \sum_{k=1}^{n} r_{Bk(j)})}$ is intractable. And decrypting $E_{K_k}(\{K_j | 1 \leq j \neq k \leq n\})$ can be reduced to the attempt to breaking the underlying symmetric encryption algorithm.
- *The proposed protocol provides known key secrecy.*
  Each group key is derived as a function of the ephemeral random values $r_{Ui(j)}$, $r_{Bk(j)}$ and r_j contributed by mobile devices and base stations respectively. Thus, each run of the proposed protocol computes a unique group key K. Therefore a compromised group key does not help adversary Eve to compute another group key.
  Moreover the group keys do not contain any information for authentication. So it is intractable for Eve to masquerade as group member.

3.4   Efficiency

While $m + 2(n + 1)$ exponentiations, 1 signature generation and $m + 2(n - 1)$ verifications per base station are needed by the proposed protocol, 2 exponentiations, 1 signature generation and n verifications per client are needed. That is, it is designed the protocol so that base stations have more computational load than mobile devices.

Bresson *et al*'s protocol[2] and Nam *et al*'s protocol[9] are well suited for a wireless network environment. As pointed out before, Bresson *et al*'s protocol has critical security flaws.

Both our protocol and a three-round group key agreement protocol by Nam *et al* require 2 exponentiations per client. Furthermore, if base station $B_k(\neq B_j)$

of our protocol is honest in sending K_j, only 1 verification is needed per client. Therefore our protocol is efficient since computation costs per client are the same as that of Nam *et al*'s protocol.

4   Conclusion and Future Work

In this paper, we presented new group key agreement protocol which allows a set of heterogenous mobile devices in different cells to form a secure group. Then we show that our protocol offers the desired properties including key authentication, perfect forward secrecy and known key secrecy for a practical key agreement protocol. An open question is whether our protocol is provably secure in the standard definition even in the random oracle model.

References

1. N. Asokan, and P. Ginzboorg, *"Key Agreement in Ad-hoc Networks"*, Expanded version of a talk given at the Nordsec'99 workshop, Februry 2000.
2. E.Bresson, O. Chevassut, A. Essiari, and D. Pointcheval, *"Mutual Authentication and Group Key Agreement for Low-Power Mobile Devices"*, International Conference on Mobile and Wireless Communications Networks, Springer-Verlag, LNCS 1514, pp.59-62, 2003.
3. E.Bresson, O. Chevassut, and D. Pointcheval, *"Group Diffie-Hellman Key Exchange Secure Against Dictionary Attacks"*, Advances in Cryptology Asiacrypt'02, Springer-Verlag, LNCS 2501, pp.497-514, 2002.
4. M. Burmester, and Y. Desmedt, *"A secure and efficient conference key distribution system"*, Advances in Cryptology - Eurocrypt'94, Springer-Verlag, pp.275-286, 1995.
5. N. Borisov, I. Goldberg, and D. Wagner, *"Intercepting Mobile Communications: The Insecurity of 802.11"*, ACM MobiCom 2001, 2001.
6. C.Carroll, Y.Frankel, and Y.Tsiounis, *"Efficient key distribution for slow computing devices: Achieving fast over-the-air activation for wireless systems"*, IEEE Symposium on Security and Privacy (S&P '98), May 3-6 1998, Oakland, CA.
7. I. Ingemarsson, D. T. Tang, and C.K. Wong, *"A conference key distribution system"*, IEEE Transactions on Information Theory, IT-28(5), pp.714-720, September 1982.
8. J. Nam, S. Kim, and D. Won, *"A Weakness in the Bresson-Chevassut-Essiari-Pointcheval's Group Key Agreement Scheme for Low-Power Mobile Devices""*, IEEE Communications Letters, Vol.9, No.5, May, 2005, pp.429-431.
9. J. Nam, J. Lee, S. Kim, and D. Won, *"DDH-based Group Key Agreement in a Mobile Environment"*, Journal of Systems and Software, Volume 78, Issue 1, Elsevier Science Inc, October, 2005, pp.73-83.
10. M. Steiner, G. Tsudik, and M. Waidner, *"Diffie-Hellman Key Distribution Extended to Group Communication"*, Proc. of the 3rd ACM Conference on Computer and Communication Security(CCS'96), pp.31-37, March 1996.

A Novel Approach to Link Utilization Measurement*

Cui Yidong[1], Zhang Bin[2], and Ma Yan[2]

[1] P.O. Box 95, Telecommunication Engineering School, Beijing University of Posts and Telecommunications, 100876, Beijing, P.R. China
nathan@x263.net
[2] Information Network Center, Beijing University of Posts and Telecommunications, 100876, Beijing, P.R. China
{zhangbin, mayan}@bupt.edu.cn

Abstract. In this paper a novel approach to link utilization measurement is proposed. In the network, the source workstation sends IP packets (namely, probes) that have the time stamp options being set to an arbitrary ICMP-enabled destination. Each router that the probes traverse across will record a timestamp in the packets. The timestamps are collected and further processed to gain the link utilization. By analyzing the model of the single hop delay, it is observed that the packet processing delay, propagation delay, the clock skew greatly affect the timestamps. So, the LUS (Link Utilization Statistic) algorithm is proposed to remove the disturbance. The LUS algorithm computes the queuing delay of each probe by processing multiple timestamps jointly. Then being quantized and smoothed with slide window, the queuing delay is transformed into link utilization. This approach is verified through simulation.

1 Introduction

Network measurement provides powerful tools to monitor the internet for NPs (Network Provider). This field has attracted more and more attentions. According to the way of obtaining measurement data, network measurement can be classified into two categories: active and passive measurement. According to the locations of the measurement point, it can be classified into three categories: end-to-end measurement (E2EM), router-based measurement (RBM) and router-cooperated measurement (RCM). The NPs usually adopt the RBM scheme. However, the network information obtained with RBM can not be shared due to the incooperativity among the NPs. Moreover, the measurement data consume much bandwidth while they are transferred from the routers to the network management center.

Recent years, many active measurement techniques are developed: 1) end-to-end delay measurement [1], [2], mainly focusing on the clock skew and and clock reset; 2) available bandwidth measurement and bottleneck locating [3], [4], [5]; 3) packet loss rate measurement [6]; 4) network performance and topology inference [7].

---

* This work is partially supported by the research fund of CNGI-04-8-1D, NSFC(NO. 90604019 and NO. 90204003).

G. Min et al. (Eds.): ISPA 2006 Ws, LNCS 4331, pp. 1098–1106, 2006.

The general way used by the above techniques is to design a sequence of packets, which is called a packet train. When the packet train traverses the network, the intervals among the packets are changed. By studying the characteristics of the intervals, the network status is obtained. We also follow the above way to develop our new method. The main idea is, 1) the packet (namely, a probe) records the router's clock hop by hop; 2) by collecting and processing the records, the queuing delay of each hop can be obtained; (3) quantizing the queuing delay and processing with slide window, the link utilization are finally obtained.

Our method avoids the security issue that brought by SNMP (Simple Network Management Protocol) in direct access to the devices. Moreover, it takes very low cost (the bandwidth consumption over a 2Mbps-link is less than 2.7%). This technique can be used to cooperate with several end-to-end measurement techniques to evaluate the quality of the network, including the end-to-end measurement of the bottleneck bandwidth, the delay and jitter measurement, packet loss rate measurement and the topology measurement.

However, the problem is, how to acquire the time during which the probe traverses across two routers? Fortunately, RFC 781 defines the time stamp option in the IP header which is helpful in solving this problem. When a probe traverse the network along a certain path, the routers that belong to this path will check the time stamp option in the packet header and record current clock value into the options. The clock value is the cumulative milliseconds starting from the midnight. Each clock value occupies 4 bytes. The time stamp options may hold maximum 9 items. Most of the routers and operating systems have implemented this RFC. Windows XP, Linux 2.4 and the later versions provide "ping" command which supports time stamp options (FreeBSD 4.7 is an exception). Usually, the time stamp options work together with ICMP. An ICMP packet of "echo request" with the time stamp options set is sent from the source to the destination. After receiving the ICMP packet, the destination generates an ICMP packet of "echo" and sends it back to the source. Then the source can collect the clock values. The destination must support ICMP protocol which is easily fulfilled.

Before we discuss the measurement algorithm, the method of link utilization calculation should be first given. The router computes the link utilization as follows. During the period of W, the link status (busy or idle) is sampled at frequency f. Thus the number of samples is $n = Wf$. We define the sample result as X_i, $i = 1 \ldots n$. If the link is busy, $X_i = 1$. Otherwise, $X_i = 0$. Hence, the link utilization is:

$$u = n^{-1} \sum_{i=1}^{n} X_i \qquad (1)$$

where W is named as "sample window".

In this paper, a new approach to the link utilization based on time stamp is proposed. It is router-cooperated active measurement. The probes are sent from the source workstation and the per-hop delay is recorded. By analyzing the delay data, the sequence, $\{X_i\}$, can be obtained. With further processing using "slide window", we finally get the link utilization. This approach requires no special functionality for the destination, and up to 9 links can be monitored with one group of probes. The rest of this paper is organized as follows. In section 2, the model for IP packets in a single hop is analyzed. In section 3, based on the analysis in section 2, the link utilization statistic algorithm is detailed. In section 4, the simulation and the corresponding analysis are presented. In the last section, section 5, we summarize.

2 Single Hop Delay Model

As detailed in Fig. 1, the delay budget of the IP packet "Probe" that traverses across Router1 and Router2 is: 1) T_{prcs} , the time during which the router processes the packet. The router should read the packet header, search the routing table, process the IP options and put the packet into proper output queue; 2) T_{queue} , the queuing delay that the packet suffers in the output queue; 3) T_{tran} , the transmission delay, which is the ratio of packet length to link rate; 4) T_{prop} , the propagation delay, which is the ratio of link length to the velocity of light. Hence, we can get:

$$T = T_{prcs} + T_{queue} + T_{tran} + T_{prop} \tag{2}$$

By inspecting the packet marked as "Probe" in Fig. 1, we may infer intuitively that, the busy-idle status of the router is able to be obtained if the queuing delay $T_{queue}^{(i)}$ at t_i can be probed. Apparently:

$$X_i = \begin{cases} 1, & T_{queue} > 0 \\ 0, & T_{queue} = 0 \end{cases} \tag{3}$$

where X_i denotes the busy-idle status of the link (i.e. if the queuing delay of Probe is zero, the link is idle when the probe arrives the output queue. Otherwise, the link is busy).

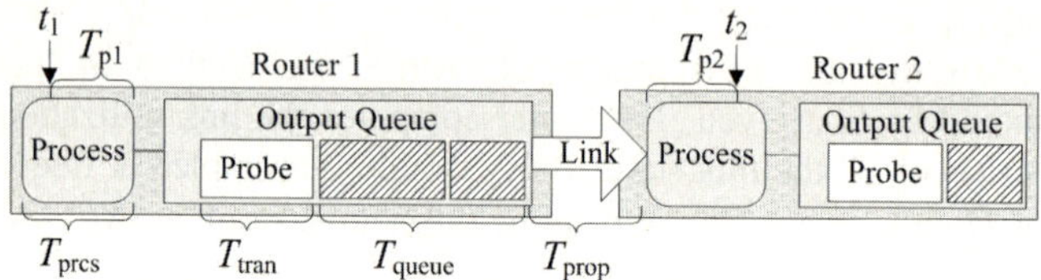

Fig. 1. Single hop delay model

Now, we'll analyze the delay budget of the single hop more completely. The previous sections have mentioned that according to RFC 781, the i-th probe records two time stamps $t_1^{(i)}$ and $t_2^{(i)}$ when it traverses Router1 and Router2. Let

$$T^{(i)} = t_2^{(i)} - t_1^{(i)} \tag{4}$$

Then we will question, is $T^{(i)}$ equal to T in Equation (2)? Obviously, the answer is no. The reason is: a) due to the drifting of the router clock, the time stamp $t_1^{(i)}$ and $t_2^{(i)}$ may be far from the real time. For example, if the clock of Router1 is 2 seconds faster than that of Router2, then $T^{(i)} < 0$ is not impossible. Even when the routers are synchronized with NTP (Network Time Protocol), there's still relatively big error due to the poor precision (about millisecond-level) of NTP over the wide area network. To achieve the microsecond-level precision, only GPS synchronization technique can be adopted which adds great cost to the implementation [2][3]. We will discuss the impact of the clock precision upon the measurement results later in Section 3. b) Router1 and Router2 may be of different types, even manufactured by different vendors. What's more, Ref. [8] has pointed out the packets with the IP options being set may cost more processing time than other packets in high speed routers. Thus, when the router processes the time stamp options will greatly affect $T^{(i)}$. Considering a), we get the relationship between the time stamps and the real time:

$$\begin{cases} \tau_1^{(i)} = t_1^{(i)} - \xi_1^{(i)} \\ \tau_2^{(i)} = t_2^{(i)} - \xi_2^{(i)} \end{cases} \tag{5}$$

where $\tau_k^{(i)}$ represents the real time when the k-th router records the time stamp $t_k^{(i)}$ into the i-th probe, and, $\xi_k^{(i)}$ represents the clock offset of the k-th router at the moment of $\tau_k^{(i)}$. $\xi_k^{(i)}$ will be positive if the clock of the k-th router is ahead of the real time. Otherwise, it will be negative. Considering b), as well as detailed in Fig. 1, we can get:

$$\tau_2^{(i)} - \tau_2^{(i)} = T_{p1}^{(i)} + T_{queue}^{(i)} + T_{tran}^{(i)} + T_{prop}^{(i)} + T_{p2}^{(i)} \tag{6}$$

where $T_{p1}^{(i)}$ (or $T_{p2}^{(i)}$) represents the processing delay which the i-th probe must suffer after (or before) its time stamp option is set by Router1 (or Router2).

By Equation (4), (5) and (6) we can get the single hop delay:

$$T^{(i)} = t_2^{(i)} - t_1^{(i)} = T_{p1}^{(i)} + T_{queue}^{(i)} + T_{tran}^{(i)} + T_{prop}^{(i)} + T_{p2}^{(i)} - \xi_1^{(i)} + \xi_2^{(i)} \tag{7}$$

3 Link Utilization Statistic Algorithm

In Equation (7), only $T^{(i)}$ is measurable while $T_{queue}^{(i)}$ can not be obtained directly. So, we develop LUS (Link Utilization Statistic) algorithm to get $T_{queue}^{(i)}$.

To have a convenient depiction, let $\delta^{(i)} = T_{p1}^{(i)} + T_{p2}^{(i)} + T_{tran}^{(i)} + T_{prop}^{(i)}$ and $\xi^{(i)} = \xi_2^{(i)} - \xi_1^{(i)}$. Equation (7) is transformed into:

$$T^{(i)} = t_2^{(i)} - t_1^{(i)} = T_{queue}^{(i)} + \delta^{(i)} + \xi^{(i)} \tag{8}$$

Let

$$T^{(ik)} = T^{(i)} - T^{(k)} = T^{(i)}_{queue} - T^{(k)}_{queue} + \delta^{(i)} - \delta^{(k)} + \xi^{(i)} - \xi^{(k)} \qquad (9)$$

Considering two probes P_i and P_k, where $i, k \in [1, N]$, if the packet length satisfies $len(P_i) = len(P_k)$, then $\delta^{(i)} = \delta^{(k)}$. Next, we define $\psi = \xi^{(i)} - \xi^{(k)} = (\xi_2^i - \xi_2^k) - (\xi_1^i - \xi_1^k) = \xi_2^{ik} - \xi_1^{ik}$ as the clock variance resulted from the router clock skew. If the interval between the sending time of P_i and P_k is short enough (i.e. $\left| \tau_0^{(i)} - \tau_0^{(k)} \right| < D$), ψ is smaller than the resolution of the time stamp (1 ms) and can be neglected. In the above equation, D is defined as AEW (Allowable Error Window) for clock skew. Then we get:

$$T^{(ik)} = T^{(i)}_{queue} - T^{(k)}_{queue} \qquad (10)$$

If the packet P_k satisfies $T^{(k)} = \min(T^{(1)}, ..., T^{(N)})$, then $T^{(k)}_{queue} = \min(T^{(1)}_{queue}, ..., T^{(N)}_{queue})$. According to Equation (10) we can conclude that $T^{(i)}_{queue}$ can be calculated if $T^{(k)}_{queue} = 0$ because $T^{(ik)}$ has already been known.

Since the final result depends on $T^{(k)}_{queue}$, we inspect the condition of $T^{(k)}_{queue} = 0$ next. Suppose a link that has the average utilization u during the period of D. We get $P(X_t = 1) = u$, where t is an arbitrary time within D and X_t is the link status. Then, the probability of such a case, in N samples there are at least one sample satisfies $X_k = 0$, is:

$$P_{idle} = 1 - u^N \qquad (11)$$

By (3), we can infer that (11) just gives the probability of the case, that at least one probe out of the N probes does not need to wait in the output queue. In Fig. 2, the relationship between the sample number N and the average link utilization u is shown. We can see clearly that when N reaches 100, P_{idle} is not less than 99.9% provided that the average link utilization is not greater than 90%.

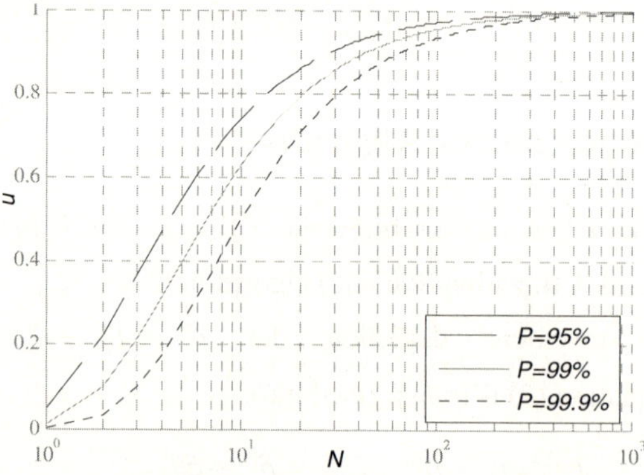

Fig. 2. Sample number and average link utilization

The LUS algorithm is depicted as follows:

1. Split the timestamp data into M segments by the allowable error window D. Process the j-th segment.

2. Calculate the delay sequence of the m-th hop $\{T^{(i)} = t^{(i)}_{m+1} - t^{(i)}_{m}\}$, $i \in [1, n]$

3. Find the minimum delay of the m-th hop $\ \ T^{(k)} = \min\{T^{(i)}\}$

4. Calculate the queuing delay sequence of the m-th hop $\{T^{(i)}_{queue} = T^{(i)} - T^{(k)}\}$

5. Transform the queuing delay sequence into link status sequence $\{X_i\}$ according to Equation (3)

6. Use the slide window method (the window is W) to calculate the link utilization of the m-hop according to Equation (1).

7. Repeat 2 to 6, until all segments are processed.

4   Simulation and Analysis

Since the queuing delay of the probes varies inversely as the link rate, multiple link rates are designed in the simulation environment. The loss of the probes due to the congestion of the link will not make the LUS algorithm ineffective, so the loss of the packet is not considered.

Simulation Model

The simulation model is shown in Fig. 3. There are three subnets in the first level topology and the connections are TJ_Net ↔ BJ_CLOUD ↔ GZ_Net. The rates of the links that connect devices include 2M/10M/55M/100M/155M. Five types of applications run over the network including WWW, FTP, E-Mail, Telnet and custom application. The source workstation is the node named Ping_Src located in TJ_Net

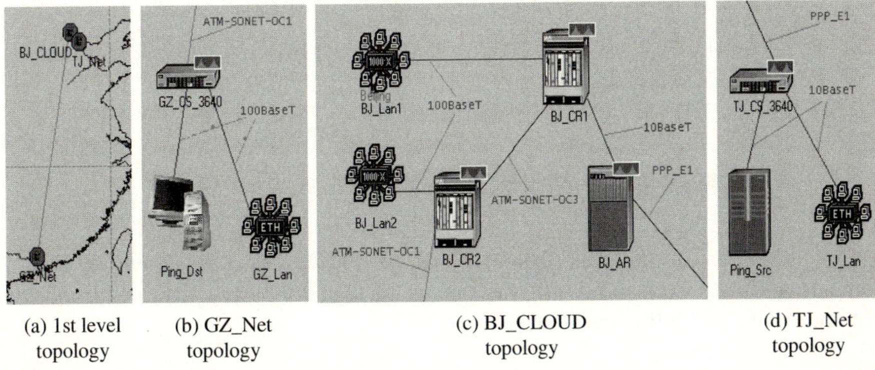

(a) 1st level topology   (b) GZ_Net topology   (c) BJ_CLOUD topology   (d) TJ_Net topology

Fig. 3. Network topology

and the destination is the node named Ping_Dst located in GZ_Net. The probes traverse the path: Ping_Src $\rightarrow$ TJ_CS_3640 $\rightarrow$ BJ_AR $\rightarrow$ BJ_CR1 $\rightarrow$ BJ_CR2 $\rightarrow$ GZ_CS_3640 $\rightarrow$ Ping_Dst. The packet length of the probe is 56 bytes and the frequency is $f = 100$.

4.1 Analysis of the Simulation Result

The link utilization from TJ_CS_3640 to BJ_AR is shown in Fig. 4. The curve in Chart 4-(a) shows the data collected from the router. The ordinate of the hemline is 2.69, which is generated by the probes. The curve in Chart 4-(b) shows the result of the active measurement in which the size of the slide window is 30 ms. Comparing 4-(a) and 4-(b) we notice that: 1) low link utilization (<20%) is not easy to be probed because the queuing delay of the probe is smaller than the resolution of the time stamp (1 ms); 2) the utilization burst at Time=106.116 sec is not probed. The reason may be it occurs in the interspaces between two adjacent probes. 3) The sub-charts in 4-(a) and 4-(b) zoom in the data between 100.35 sec and 100.81 sec. Comparing the two sub-charts, we can conclude that the result reflects the trends of the link utilization variation. However, since the size of the slide window (30 ms) is only three times of the interval between two probes, the curve is of a three-step form.

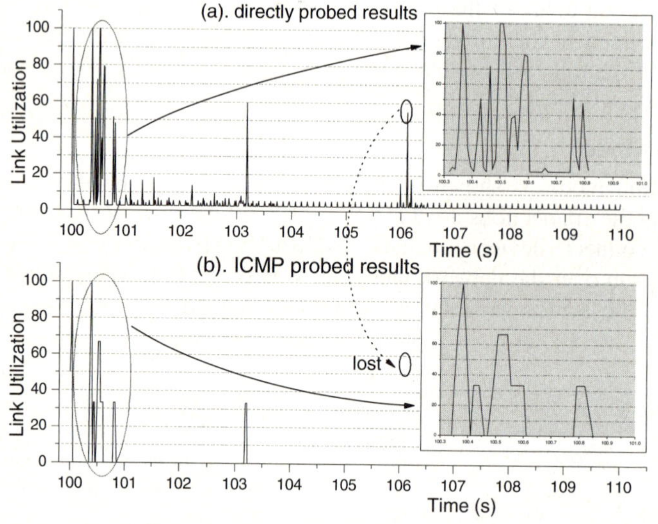

Fig. 4. Utilization of the link from TJ_CS_3640 to BJ_AR

The utilization of the link from BJ_AR to TJ_CS_3640 is shown in Fig. 5. Comparing Chart 5-(a) and 5-(b), we can see that under heavy load condition, the probing results match the real state well.

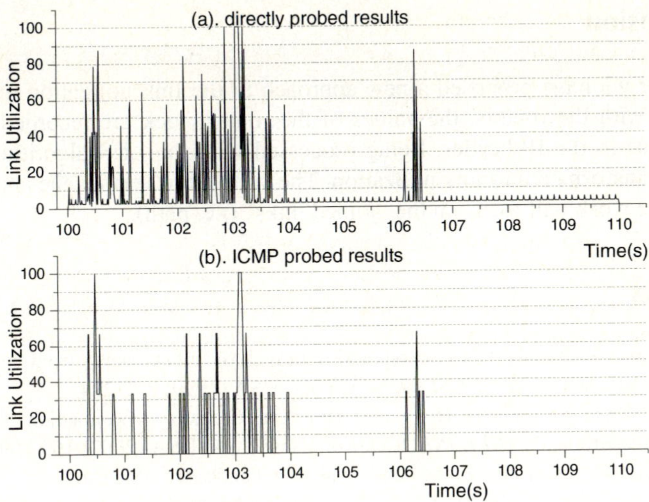

Fig. 5. Utilization of the link from BJ_AR to TJ_CS_3640

In Fig. 6 the utilization of the link from BJ_CR1 to BJ_AR is shown. The curves in Chart 6-(b) and 6-(c) are calculated with slide window W=30 ms and W=50 ms respectively. By observing the charts we can conclude if the utilization is low over a high speed link, our method may only show the peak of the utilization roughly. Due to the sparseness of the probing data, larger sliding windows size may only smooth the peak-value of the sampling result curve, but can hardly reflect the data variation within a short period of time ($10/f$).

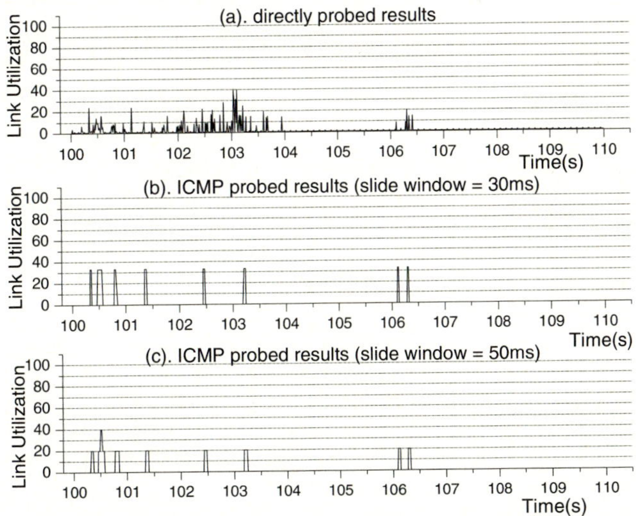

Fig. 6. Utilization of the link from BJ_CR1 to BJ_AR

5 Conclusion

In this paper we have proposed a new approach to the link utilization measurement. Cooperated with the routers, the values of the router clock are recorded in the time stamp options in the IP header. Being processed with the LUS algorithm, the clock values are transformed into link utilization. The simulation verifies the approach.

Our future work will focus on the "joined links" (i.e. path).

References

1. S. B. Moon, P. Skelly: Estimation and removal of clock skew from network delay measurements. *IEEE INFOCOM'99*, New York, USA (1999) 227-234
2. Li Zhang, Zhen Liu, Cathy Hong and Hui Xia: Clock synchronization algorithms for network measurements. *IEEE INFOCOM'02*, New York, USA (2002) 160-169
3. M. Jain and C. Dovrolis: End-to-end available bandwidth: Measurement methodology, dynamics, and relation with TCP throughput. *ACM SIGCOMM'02*, USA (2002) 295-308.
4. N. Hu and P. Steenkiste: Evaluation and characterization of available bandwidth probing techniques. IEEE JSAC Special Issue in Internet and WWW Measurement, Mapping, and Modeling, Vol. 21(6), USA (2003) 879-894
5. N. Hu, L. Li and Z. M. Mao: Locating Internet Bottlenecks: Algorithms, Measurements, and Implications. *ACM SIGCOMM'04*, USA (2004) 41-54
6. N. G. Duffield and F. L. Presti: Inferring link loss using stripped unicast probes. *IEEE INFOCOM'01*, Alaska, USA (2001) 22-26
7. Bestavros, J. Byers and K. Harfoush: Inference and labeling of metric-induced network topologies. *IEEE INFOCOM'02*. New York, USA (2002) 628-637
8. Konstantina Papagiannaki, Sue Moon, Chuck Fraleigh, Patrick Thiran and Christophe Diot: Measurement and Analysis of Single-Hop Delay on an IP Backbone Network. IEEE JSAC Special Issue in Internet and WWW Measurement, Mapping, and Modeling, USA (2003) 908-921

A Joint MAC Discovery-Routing Protocol for Self-Organizing Hierarchical Ad Hoc Networks*

Hyukjoon Lee, Yong-Hoon Choi, Young-uk Chung, and Seomin Yang**

Kwangwoon University, Seoul, Korea
{hlee, yhchoi, yuchung}@kw.ac.kr
** Samsung Electronics Co., Ltd., Korea
Seomin.yang@samsung.com

Abstract. Self-organizing hierarchical ad hoc network (SOHAN) is a new ad-hoc network architecture designed to improve the scalability properties of conventional "flat" ad hoc networks. This network architecture consists of three tiers of ad-hoc nodes, i.e., access points, forwarding nodes and mobile nodes. This paper presents a joint topology discovery and routing protocol for the self-organization of SOHAN. We propose a cross-layer path metric based on link quality and MAC delay which plays a key role in producing an optimal cluster-based hierarchical topology with high throughput capacity. The topology discovery protocol provides the basis for routing which takes place in layer 2.5 using MAC addresses. The routing protocol is based on AODV with appropriate modifications to take advantage of the hierarchical topology and interact with the discovery protocol. Simulation results are presented which show the improved performance as well as scalability properties of SOHAN in terms of throughput capacity, end-to-end delay, packet delivery ratio and control overhead.

1 Introduction

There has been a tremendous influx of research interest in wireless multi-hop networks (mobile ad hoc networks) during the past several years. Many routing protocols have been proposed for ad hoc networks. These protocols are designed to operate in traditional flat ad hoc networks and optimized in terms of end-user performance measures such as delay and packet delivery ratio. More recently, research issues related to the system capacity of wireless multi-hop networks, such as power consumption and throughput capacity, are drawing much attention. One of the fundamental problems of the flat ad hoc networks is that they do not scale well. Gupta and Kumar described that the throughput of an ad hoc network is bounded above and decreases as $O\!\left(1/\sqrt{n}\right)$ as n becomes large [1]. This motivates the investigation of a new ad hoc network architecture based on hierarchical structure.

In [2], Ganu *et al.* propose a novel hierarchical ad hoc network architecture called SOHAN (Self-Organizing Hierarchical Ad-Hoc Wireless Network) of three tiers, i.e., *access points* (APs), *forwarding nodes* (FNs) and *mobile nodes* (MNs). In this architecture, the APs are connected together by high-speed wired links and FNs and

---

* This work was supported by Research Grant of Kwangwoon University in 2006.

G. Min et al. (Eds.): ISPA 2006 Ws, LNCS 4331, pp. 1107–1116, 2006.

MNs self-organize themselves to form a hybrid wired-wireless multi-hop network. This architecture is designed to increase the system capacity, while retaining the robustness, coverage and power advantages of ad hoc networks.

It is desired that a topology discovery protocol taking into account the cost in routing produce a network topology that provides high throughput capacity. The authors of [2] propose a MAC-layer topology discovery protocol in which they simply use the received signal strength as a discovery metric to determine the network topology. They also present a distance vector-based routing protocol which periodically exchanges the neighbor tables constructed by the topology discovery protocol. However, this routing protocol has a limited capability in that it only supports outbound traffic from the MNs to the APs.

In [3], Zhao *et al.* evaluate the applicability of two popular ad hoc routing protocols, DSR [4] and AODV [5], to this architecture with some modifications and present some simulation results that show about four-fold improvement in throughput capacity compared to the conventional flat architecture. However, they do not specify a routing protocol that takes into account the efficient use of the hierarchical architecture.

In this paper, we present a joint topology discovery and routing protocol for SOHAN which produces an optimal cluster-based hierarchical topology with high throughput capacity and increased scalability. This paper is organized as follows. In section 2, we present the architecture of self-organizing hierarchical ad-hoc network. In section 3 and 4, we describe the joint topology discovery and routing protocols. In section 5, we give some simulation results that demonstrate the improved scaling properties of SOHAN. Section 6 summarizes this paper.

2 Hierarchical Ad Hoc Network Architecture

SOHAN is a novel self-organizing hierarchical ad hoc network architecture designed to improve the scaling properties of conventional flat ad-hoc networks [2]. This network architecture consists of three-tiers of wireless nodes: low-power end-user mobile nodes (MNs) at the lowest tier, high-power forwarding nodes (FNs) at the mid-tier, and wired access points (APs) at the highest tier (Fig. 1(a)). The MN operates on a single radio such as 802.11 and can attach to a FN and/or AP. As a user device, it does not forward packets for other nodes. Instead of directly connecting to each other, the MN connects to an AP or FN of the best link quality. The main function of the FN is to forward packets for other nodes using multi-hop routing. The FN can have a direct radio connection with all three types of nodes. It can be equipped with a single 802.11 interface or two radio interfaces, one for FN-MN traffic and the other for inter-FN and FN-AP traffic. The FN can be either fixed or mobile. The AP has both a radio interface and wired interface to the Internet. The AP can be configured as an *access router* (AR). Therefore, it is responsible for routing packets between the wired Internet and SOHAN. Multiple FNs and MNs can be directly connected to the AP in ad hoc mode. The APs are connected to each other by wired links, and hence, it provides the transmission speed of orders of magnitude faster than that of wireless links as well as more natural integration with the Internet.

3 Topology Discovery Protocol

3.1 Discovery Protocol

Topology discovery is a distributed process through which a node associates with its neighbor nodes to form a logical network topology in a self-organizing manner. Our discovery protocol organizes the FNs and MNs to form a logical cluster around an AP in such way that the multi-hop communication cost between each node within a cluster and the AP is minimized.

The topology discovery protocol is based on beacons. These beacons can be made as an extension to existing beacons (e.g. 802.11) or as an application layer beacons. The APs and FNs use these beacons to identify their one-hop neighbors. The beacons also carry various kinds of information that can be used in determining the network topology. Upon bootstrapping, the APs and FNs enter a self-organizing phase by transmitting the beacons on their predetermined channels and repeat this phase periodically (e.g., 200 ms in our simulation). Based on the beacons received, the FNs and MNs update their *neighbor table* and transmit the *association messages* to the best one-hop parents. In this way, a tree structure is formed from top to bottom with the AP at the root and the MNs at the leaf level.

The message format of the beacons is given in Fig. 1(b). *Msg Type* field is used to specify the message types used in the topology discovery phase. There are four types, i.e., *beacons, association requests, association acknowledgement and disassociation requests*. *Node Type* contains the information about the type of node that transmits the message. *Node ID* uniquely identifies a node which can have multiple *interface IDs*. *Channel* specifies the radio channel used for transmitting the beacon. *Cost to AP* represents the expected routing cost metric to the AP. This value is used in selecting the best parent node in terms of routing cost to an AP. *Beacon No.* is a sequence number for the beacons and is used to detect the duplicate association messages. *BSSID* and *AP IPv6 Addr* are the BSSID and IPv6 Address of the AP to be used in IPv6 address autoconfiguation [6] of the FNs and MNs.

A neighbor table is constructed for each node based on the information gathered from the beacons and association request messages. It contains the information about the parent and child nodes in the tree structure. Thus, the neighbor table can provide the routing protocol with a basis for building a local routing table. It provides each node with the minimal next hop routing information for outbound traffic towards the AP. The routing table entries for the other nodes of the same cluster are built up on-demand by the modified AODV routing protocol.

The neighbor table is updated when a new neighbor node is found or an association request is received. The cost to an AP can be calculated by adding the communication cost to the neighbor node and the neighbor node's communication cost to an AP carried in the beacon. The neighbor table is updated also when a node moves out of the radio range, i.e., the corresponding entry is purged if a beacon is not received in three successive scans. Periodically, each node selects one of its neighbors as its candidate parent node. That is, a neighbor node that has the lowest communication cost to an AP is selected.

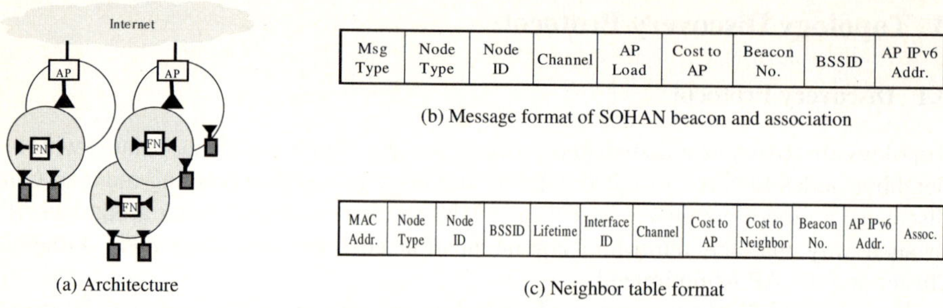

(a) Architecture

Msg Type	Node Type	Node ID	Channel	AP Load	Cost to AP	Beacon No.	BSSID	AP IPv6 Addr.

(b) Message format of SOHAN beacon and association

MAC Addr.	Node Type	Node ID	BSSID	Lifetime	Interface ID	Channel	Cost to AP	Cost to Neighbor	Beacon No.	AP IPv6 Addr.	Assoc.

(c) Neighbor table format

Fig. 1. SOHAN architecture and message format

After determining its candidate parent node, the node transmits an *association request message* to it. Upon receiving the association request message, the candidate parent node creates an entry for a child node in its neighbor table and stores the information received in the association request message. It also sets the *lifetime* and transmits an *association acknowledgement message*. If the child node receives the association acknowledgement message, it makes the candidate parent node its parent node. Otherwise, the child node repeatedly transmits the association request message up to three times. If the child node fails to receive an acknowledgement, it purges the neighbor table entry for the candidate node, selects the next candidate node and repeats the association steps. Association steps are also taken when a child node fails to receive three successive beacons from its parent node in order to prevent the node from being disconnected from the rest of the network.

Each entry of the neighbor table includes some information received from a neighbor node in the beacon message, i.e., *Node Type, Node ID, Channel, Cost to AP, Beacon No., BSSID* and *AP IPv6 Addr* (Fig. 1(c)). *MAC addr* is the 48-bit MAC address of a neighbor node. *Interface ID* is used to distinguish among multiple radio interfaces attached to the node through which a neighbor node can be communicated. *Cost to Neighbor* represents the cost associated with the radio link to a neighbor node. *Assoc.* represents the three kinds of association the node has with a neighbor node, i.e., *parent, child* and *no association*.

Discovery Metric

One of the main goals of the topology discovery protocol is to produce a logical topology that is efficient for inter-cluster communication via APs in order to make the best use of the high throughput capacity of wired backbone links. Therefore, we use the communication cost between an AP and a node as the discovery metric. In other words, a path metric to an AP is used by each node in determining its parent node via which it can communicate with an AP which would then forward inbound/outbound data for that node. Based on the assumption that physical link quality between a pair of nodes is symmetric, the same paths are used for both inbound/outbound traffic.

It has been widely discussed in the literature that the minimum hop-count does not guarantee to give a route with high throughput, although it has been used mostly by traditional routing protocols for flat ad-hoc networks such as DSR and AODV [7-9]. Hence, rather than using minimum hop-count as our path metric, we define a new path metric based on the traffic load and link quality, i.e., expected delivery delay (EDD). The EDD of a path, EDD_{path}, is the sum of EDD of a link, EDD_{link}, between a pair of nodes, which is defined as:

$$EDD_{link} = c_1 D_q + c_2 \frac{D_c}{r},$$

where c_1 and c_2 are scaling coefficients, D_q is the average queuing delay of packets within the radio interface of a sender, D_c is the average MAC contention delay experience by the sender, and r is the delivery ratio of beacons. Since D_q is associated with each node, its value can be computed locally in each node. On the other hand, D_c and r are associated with a link between two nodes. The value of D_c depends on the characteristics of packets generated by an application at either end of the link, and hence is likely to be asymmetric in practice. However, if the applications at both ends of the link generate a fairly large number of packets over a certain period of time, the value of D_c would become symmetric. In addition, based on the assumption that the underlying physical link has a symmetrical channel quality, we have the same value of r in both directions. Thus, they can be also measured locally at either end of the link. The values of D_q and D_c can be computed directly in the interface driver, while the value of r is computed by dividing the number of beacons received by the number of beacons expected to be received over a period of time. EDD_{link} represents the MAC delay and directly affects throughput. Transmission and propagation delays are not included since the amount of variation in their relative values would be small enough to be ignored. The reciprocal of a beacon delivery ratio implies the expected number of transmissions required to send a packet over a link. The EDD of a path is the sum of EDD_{link} over all links in a path, i.e.,

$$EDD_{path} = \sum_{all\ links\ in\ a\ path} EDD_{link}.$$

Conceptually, the summation can be obtained by accumulating EDD_{link} values as links are added to the tree structure. The EDD of a path represents the predicted end-to-end delay experienced in sending a packet from a node to an AP or vice versa, which directly affects throughput.

4 Routing Protocol

As discussed in the previous section, the topology discovery protocol of SOHAN performs self-organization which produces an optimal topology in terms of throughput capacity. The routing protocol operates based on the topology found by the topology discovery protocol. We make the routing protocol operate in the same layer as the topology discovery protocol, i..e., layer 2.5. There are several advantages with this approach:

- The topology information can be shared by routing protocol easily.
- The routing can be performed transparently to the IP routing protocols, hence, make the ad-hoc network be integrated with IP-based network seamlessly.
- The ad-hoc network can appear as a single LAN segment which makes plug-in-play type of deployment possible.

Our routing protocol is based on AODV with appropriate modifications such as addressing scheme and routing table management. It sets up the initial routing table based on the neighbor table and adds an entry as a new route is found on-demand. A neighbor table generated by the topology discovery protocol contains information about the next hop node (i.e., parent node) for each node to reach an AP. This information is used to initialize and periodically update the routing tables where it is specified as the default routes. Entries for the other nodes are created on-demand according to AODV route discovery. The MNs do not participate in routing, i.e., they do not forward packets for other nodes. They can only be a source or destination of packets. Therefore, they have only one entry in their routing table, i.e., the default route entry with their parent node (a FN or AP) as the next hop.

The FNs and MNs use MAC addresses as their identifier for routing, while they can use IP addresses at the network layer which are locally acquired through an address allocation mechanism such as IPv6 address autoconfiguration. The IP-to-MAC address resolution operation requires broadcast on a single-link, which can be mapped to flooding over the ad-hoc network. The loss of radio resource due to flooding can be substantial. Therefore, the flooding is confined within the subset of nodes that are associated with the same AP. This operation is called *limited-scope broadcast* (*LSBC*). The node can determine whether it is associated with the same AP as the source of flooding by checking the Basic Service Set ID (BSSID).

Provided that each AP is configured as an AR, each tree rooted at an AP can be mapped to an IP subnet. In this approach, each node in the tree is configured with an IP address with the same prefix. Packets are routed to an AP if the destination is out of the subnet of the source. The normal IP delivers the packet to the destination network. Hence, a packet sent across the boundaries of two subtrees would be routed via wired links. This approach is based on the suggestions given in [1].

1) Inbound routes: An IP packet originated from outside a subnet and destined to a FN/MN is received by the AP (i.e., AR) by normal IP routing. As all nodes appear as they were a single hop away from the AP, the IP layer of the AP hands the packet over to the MAC routing layer for ad hoc routing. Before the MAC route table is searched, the destination IP address must be translated into a MAC address, i.e., address resolution must be performed by looking up the ARP table, in case of IPv4, or the neighbor cache, in case of IPv6. If an entry is not found, an address resolution message is flooded using LSBC. If the destination node exists within the subnet, the MAC address is returned within address resolution reply message by unicast. Using this MAC address, the AP searches the route table for the entry of the destination node. It should be noted that it is guaranteed to find a route table entry if the address resolution succeeds. This is because a new entry can be added to the MAC routing table for a destination node by reverse path set up when an address resolution reply message arrives from the node. A new route table entry is added when an outbound data packet is received by the AP. If IPv6 is used, a new route entry is also created when a router solicitation message arrives at the AP. Hence, the AP never floods RREQ messages for destination nodes within its subnet. Based on the route table entry found, the AP forwards the packet to the next hop node for further delivery towards the destination node. If an entry is a stale one, the AP would receive a RRER message. In this case, the AP should flood a RREQ message to find an alternate path.

2) Outbound routes: Outbound packets are sent to the AP along the path determined by the topology discovery protocol. A source node uses the default route to send the packet to its parent node which further will deliver the packet towards the AP. The first step the source node must take is to determine whether the destination is within the same subnet. If the source node determines the destination is located outside the subnet by examining the destination prefix, it uses the default route to send the packet to the AP and hand it over to the MAC layer ad-hoc routing.

3) Internal routes: A packet originated from a MN and destined to another within the same subnet of SOHAN is forwarded purely by ad-hoc routing. The network layer performs normal AODV route discovery operations with the same path metric used in topology discovery for normal packet delivery between two hosts in the same subnet. The address resolution and route discovery are performed using LSBC.

5 Simulation Results

5.1 Simulation Model

We used the Monarch extension of ns-2 simulator to evaluate the performance of the joint topology discovery and routing protocol for SOHAN. Following the result presented in [10], we maintain the number of APs above the square root of the number of FNs and MNs combined. In all scenarios, there are twice as many MNs as FNs. The APs are placed in the center of rectangular sub-areas of the equal size that covers the entire simulation area. The FNs and MNs are randomly placed within the sub-areas. The APs are fixed whereas the FNs and SNs are mobile in random way point model, the max. speed of 20 m/s, the pause time of 30 sec. The MNs are the source and destination of all traffic flows. The traffic flow from/to an Internet host is not considered in this simulation. The MNs generate CBR traffic with varying packet generation rates. The key simulation parameters are summarized in Table 1.

Performance Evaluation

Several scenarios were set up with the different number of APs, FNs and MNs and packet generation rates. For each scenario, simulations were repeated 10 times with different node placements and move patterns. In order to assess the simulation results, we use system throughput, average end-to-end delay, packet delivery ratio and normalized control overhead. For each scenario, we set up a flat AODV ad-hoc network which had the same number of nodes and node locations as SOHAN in order to compare the performance of the two networks with respect to system load and scalability.

Table 1. Simulation parameters

Simulation area	1500*m* × 1500*m*				
Number of APs	4	6	8	10	12
Number of FNs	6	12	22	34	48
Number of MNs	10	24	42	66	96
Number of nodes	20	42	72	110	156
Number of pkts/sec generated	5, 10, 20, 30, 40, 50, 60, 70, 80 pkts/sec				
Packet size	512 bytes				
Number of communication pairs	20				
Simulation time	1000 sec				

1) System load: In order to evaluate the performance of SOHAN at varying the system load, we fixed the number of total nodes to 110. In case of SOHAN, the number of APs, FNs and MNs are 10, 34 and 66, respectively. All of 110 nodes are ad-hoc nodes in case of the flat network. As illustrated in Fig. 2, the control overhead of SOHAN is decreased by 69.1%. The improvement is mainly due to the reduced amount of routing packets flooded in the network. That is, instead of flooding route discovery packets to find a new route, SOHAN mainly uses topology information discovered based on beacons and association messages. Furthermore, even in case the SOHAN floods control packet, the scope of flooding is limited within a cluster. As will be seen below, the improved control overhead of SOHAN has positive impact on the other performance metrics.

Fig. 3 shows how throughput changes as the system load increases. In the static scenario, flat network saturates at about 40 pkts/sec while SOHAN saturates at about 60 pkts/sec, to reach the peak throughput of 150 Kbps and 250 Kbps, respectively. The average number of hops is 3.50 and 4.12 for flat network and SOHAN, respectively, which implies SOHAN selects routes with high throughput capacity instead of one with less number of hops. In Fig. 4 one can observe the packet delivery ratio of SOHAN is higher than that of the flat network.

2) Scalability: In order to study the scalability properties of SOHAN, we measure the same performance metrics while increasing then number of nodes with 20 CBR traffic flows of 30 packets per second. In Fig. 5, one can see the amount of control overhead of SOHAN increases more slowly than the flat network although they both increase linearly.

Fig. 6 and Fig. 7 show the behavior of throughput and packet delivery ratio. The curves in the two graphs clearly indicate that SOHAN has better scalability properties than the flat network. Notice that both the throughput and packet delivery ratio of SOHAN is lower than those of flat network when the number of nodes is 20.

In this case, SOHAN has only 10 nodes that are capable of packet forwarding, and some MNs lose connection with these nodes when they happen to be out of a coverage area. Since all nodes are capable of forwarding in flat networks, the loss of connection is less likely to happen. This observation motivates further research in the minimum number of APs and FNs required to maintain a certain level of throughput capacity in a given service area.

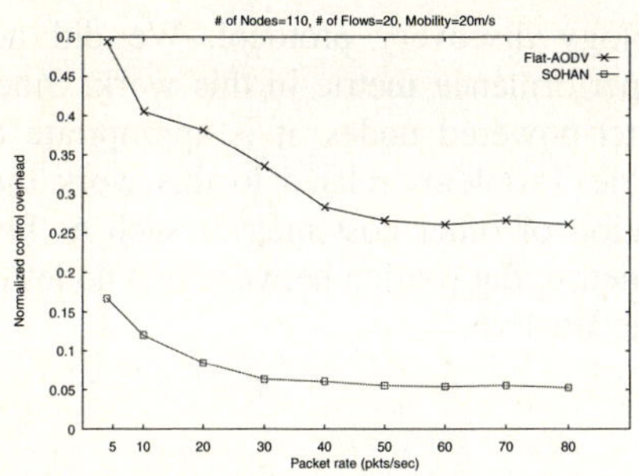

Fig. 2. Routing overhead vs. System load

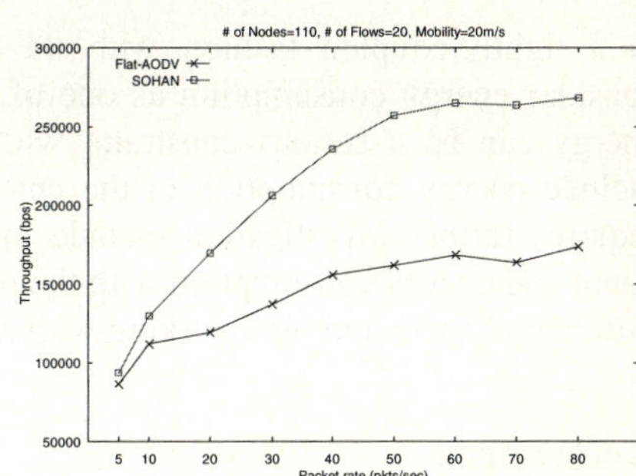

Fig. 3. Throughput vs. System load

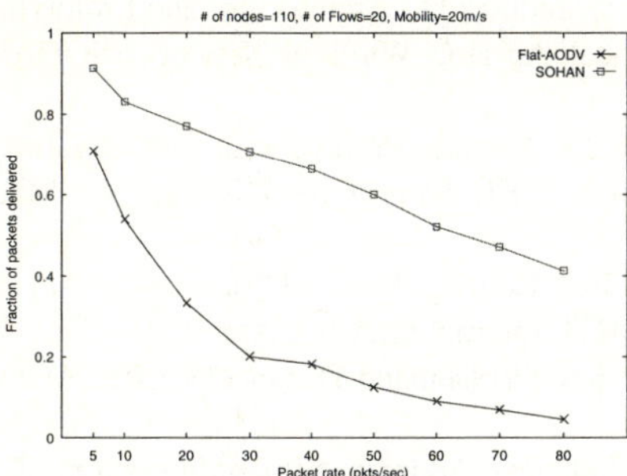

Fig. 4. Delivery ratio vs. System load

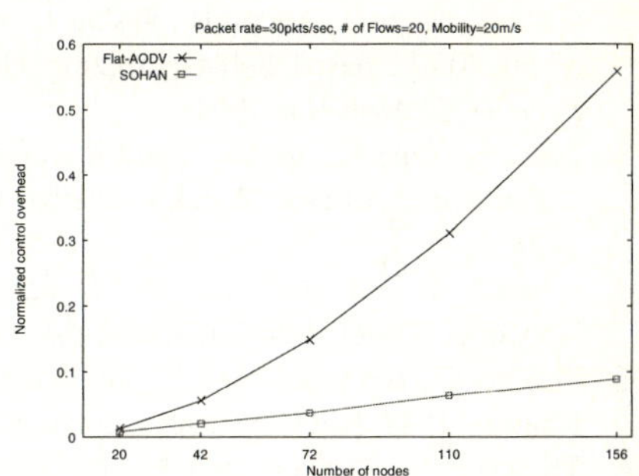

Fig. 5. Routing overhead vs. No. of nodes

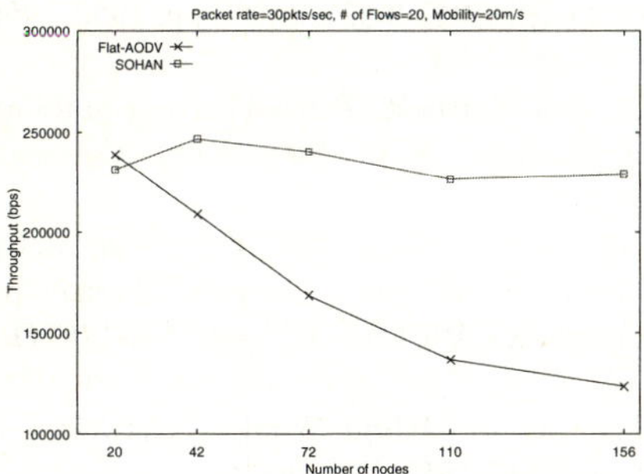

Fig. 6. Throughput vs. No. of nodes

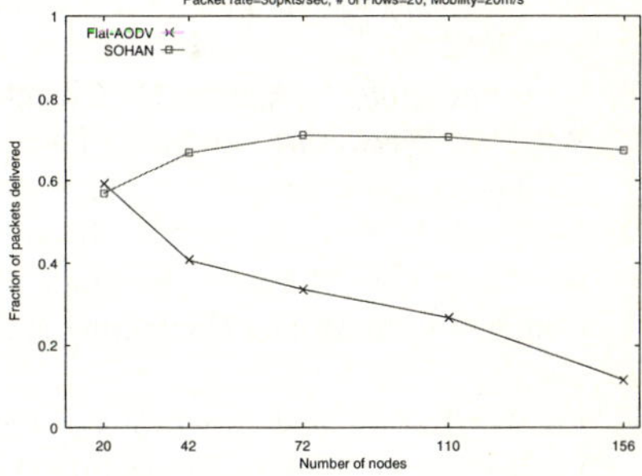

Fig. 7. Delivery ratio vs. No. of nodes

6   Conclusion

We presented a joint MAC topology discovery and routing protocol for self-organizing ad-hoc networks. We also proposed a cross-layer path metric based on link quality and MAC delay which plays a key role in producing an optimal cluster-based hierarchical topology with high throughput capacity. We also showed that significant improvement in performance can be achieved by having the routing protocol operate in a tightly-coupled fashion with the topology discovery protocol. We did not consider energy consumption as one of the performance metric in this work. Since energy can be a serious constraint with batter-powered nodes, it is appropriate to include energy consumption in the cost metric. Problems related to this work that requires further investigation include integration of other cost metrics such as hop count and energy consumption with the path metric, flat routing between two nodes of different clusters and interworking with Mobile IPv4/v6.

References

1. Gupta P. and Kumar P. R.: The Capacity of Wireless Networks, IEEE Transactions on Information Theory, vol. IT-46, no. 2, pp. 388-404, March 2000.
2. Ganu S., Raju L., Anepu B., Seskar I. and Raychaudhuri D.: Architecture and Prototyping of an 802.11-based Self-Organizing Hierarhical Ad-Hoc Wireless Network (SOHAN), *Proc. IEEE MobiHoc* 2004.
3. Zhao S., Tepe K., Seskar I. and Raychaudhuri D.: Routing Protocols for Self-Organizing Hierarchical Ad-Hoc Wireless Networks, Proc. IEEE Sarnoff Symposium, NJ, March 2003.
4. Johnson D. and Maltz D.: The Dynamic Source Routing Protocol for Mobile Ad Hoc Networks (DSR), draft-ietf-manet-dsr-09.txt, IETF Internet draft, 15, Apr. 2003.
5. Perkins C., Belding-Royer E. and Das S.: Ad hoc On-Demand Distance Vector (AODV) Routing, IETF RFC 3561, July, 2003.
6. Thomson S., Bellcore and Narten T.: IPv6 Stateless Address Autoconfiguration, IETF RFC 2462, Dec. 1998.
7. Yuen W. H., Lee H. N. and Anderson T. D.: A Simple and Effective Cross Layer Networking System for Mobile Ad Hoc Networks, In 13th IEEE int. symposium on personal indoor and mobile radio communications (PIMRC 2002), vol. 4, pp. 1952-1956, Sep. 2002.
8. De Couto D. S. J., Aguayo D., Chambers B. A. and Morris R.: Performance of Multihop Wireless Networks: Shortest Path is Not Enough, ACM SIGCOMM Computer Communication Review, vol. 43, pp.43-48, Jan. 2003.
9. De Couto D. S. J., Aguayo D., Bicket J. and Morris R.: A High-Throughput Path Metric for Multi-hop Wireless Routing, Proceedings of the Ninth Annual International Conference on Mobile Computing and Networking, MOBICOM 2003, pp. 134-146, Oct. 2003.
10. Liu B., Liu Z. and Towsley D.: On the Capacity of Hybrid Wireless Networks, in Proceedings of the IEEE Infocom 2003, vol. 2, pp. 1543-1552, Mar. 2003.

An Effective Path Recovery Mechanism for AODV Using Candidate Node*

Sang-min Lee and Keecheon Kim[**]

Dept, of Computer Science & engineering, Konkuk University,
Gwang-jin Gu, Seoul, Korea
{leesm, kckim}@konkuk.ac.kr

Abstract. We propose an effective path recovery scheme for AODV in mobile ad-hoc network environment. Even though the existing path recovery scheme for AODV routing protocol can recover the disconnected path in some ways, however, they can not utilize the pre-connected routing nodes when we handle the nodes in Ad-hoc environment. In order to utilize the pre-connected routing nodes in recovering the path more effectively, we use a designated candidate nodes. The candidate nodes are used to recover the disconnected path using the pre-connected routing information. This scheme produces better results with less control packets with faster path recovery time.

1   Introduction

The Mobile Ad-hoc Network is a mobile network composed of more than two mobile terminals without fixed infrastructure. Legacy table driven routing protocol such as OSPF and RIP can not be applied to MANET because of its lack of mobility supporting capability. Therefore, several reactive routing approaches have been studied.[3][4]

AODV Routing algorithm is a reactive routing algorithm in Ad-hoc network. AODV provide a high performance for Ad-hoc network. But, AODV has a problem of local repair. So, we propose a new local repair algorithm in AODV[1]. The algorithm provides an effective local repair using candidate nodes.

2   AODV (Ad Hoc On-demand Distance Vector) Routing Protocol

The AODV algorithm enables dynamic, self-starting, and multi-hop routing among the participating mobile nodes wishing to establish and maintain an ad-hoc network. AODV allows mobile nodes to obtain routes quickly for new destinations, and does not require nodes to maintain routes to destinations that are not in active communication. AODV using RREQ, RREP, RERR massages to establish and maintain an ad-hoc network. AODV uses a local repair to maintain the established link[1].

---

[*] This research was supported by the Brain Korea 21 project.
[**] Corresponding author.

G. Min et al. (Eds.): ISPA 2006 Ws, LNCS 4331, pp. 1117 – 1125, 2006.

3 Path Recovery Problem of AODV

AODV provide the path-recovery algorithms. Local repair is a main idea in AODV path recovery algorithms. But the local repair shows low performance in large networks. Local repair can not utilize pre-connected routing nodes, and increase the number of control packets as networks grows.

3.1 Destination Sequence Number[1]

Every route table entry at every node must include the latest information available about the sequence number for the IP address of the destination node. This sequence number is called the "destination sequence number (DSN)". DSN is updated whenever a node receives new information from RREQ, RREP, or RERR messages that are related to that destination. The AODV depends on each node in the network to own and maintain its destination sequence number to guarantee the loop-free routes towards that node.

The AODV Using the DSN ensures loop free routes. However, DSN causes the problem. The local repair using DSN can not utilize pre-connected routing nodes.

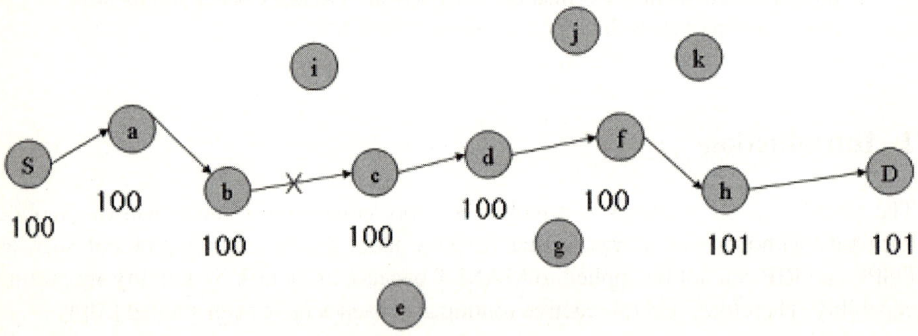

Fig. 1. The problem of the Destination Sequence Number

In Fig 1, AODV shows the problem with DSN. The exiting algorithm can not utilize the pre-connected routing nodes (c, d, f).

4 An Effective Path Recovery in AODV

We propose more effective path recovery scheme that uses the Candidate Node. This scheme provides the solution that utilizes the pre-connected routing nodes.The proposed scheme needs to change the routing table and change the massage formats.

4.1 Routing Table Format

The existing Routing table can not support the candidate node. Therefore, we need to change the routing table. The candidate node address is added in the routing table to

Table 1. Routing Table[1]

Table Name
Destination IP Address
Destination Sequence Number
Valid Destination Sequence Number flag
Other state and routing flags(ex., valid, invalid, repairable, being repaired)
Network Interface
Hop Count (Number of hops needed to reach destination)
Next Hop
List of Precursors
Lifetime (expiration of deletion time of the route)

support the candidate node. And the massage format needs to be changed to be used as candidate node.

4.2   Changed Massage Formats

The RREQ (Route Request) Massage format is changed. We added The Origin-destination IP address and flag C. The Origin-destination IP address is the destination IP address before being disconnected.

Type	J	R	G	U	D	C	Reserved	Hop count
RREQ ID								
Destination IP address								
Destination Sequence Number								
Originator IP address								
Originator Sequence Number								
Origin-Destination IP address								

Fig. 2. New RREQ Massage Format

Type	R	A	C	Reserved	prefix sz	Hop count
Destination IP address						
Destination Sequence Number						
Originator IP address						
Lifetime						
Candidate Node IP address						
Origin-Destination IP address						
Origin-Hopcount						

Fig. 3. New RREP Massage Format

The RREP (Route Reply) Massage format is changed. We added a candidate node IP address, Origin-destination IP address, Origin-hop-count and flag C. The Origin-destination IP address is the destination IP address before being disconnected. Origin-hop-count is number of hops before the disconnected link.

5   The Scenario for Local Repair Using Candidate Node

In figure 4, it explains the link repair scenario when it detects a broken link for the next hop of an active route in its routing table.

1. Node d detects a broken link to Node f.
2. Node d chooses to execute the Local repair or reconfiguring the Link by Source Node.
3. If it selects to do a Local repair, Node d broadcasts RREQ Massage to Node h to repair the link
4. If Node h receives a RREQ massage, Node h creates RREP massage and sends the message to Node d.
5. If Node d receives RREP massage, Node d reconfigures the link.

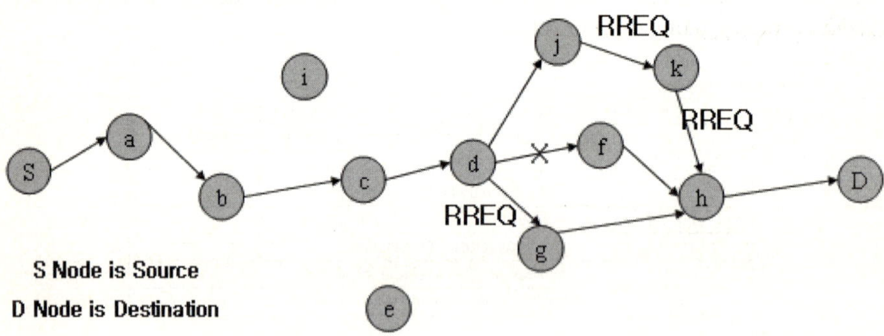

Fig. 4. The RREQ massages broadcast for local repair

6   Performance Evaluation

We compare the existing algorithm with proposed algorithm using the mathematical expression. We compare the recovery time, the number of packets (RREQ massages) and the overhead in the routing table.

6.1 Parameters Defined in RFC

The RFC3561 defines the parameters[1]. This paper uses these parameters.

Table 2. Parameters in RFC[1]

Parameter Name	Value
ACTIVE_ROUTE_TIMEOUT	3,000 Milliseconds
ALLOWED_HELLO_LOSS	2
BLACKLIST_TIMEOUT	RREQ_RETRIES * NET_TRAVERSAL_TIME
HELLO_INTERVAL	1,000 Milliseconds
LOCAL_ADD_TTL	2
MAX_REPAIR_TTL	0.3 * NET_DIAMETER
MIN_REPAIR_TTL	See note below
MY_ROUTE_TIMEOUT	2 * ACTIVE_ROUTE_TIMEOUT
NET_DIAMETER	35
NET_TRAVERSAL_TIME	2 * NODE_TRAVERSAL_TIME * NET_DIAMETER
NEXT_HOP_WAIT	NODE_TRAVERSAL_TIME + 10
NODE_TRAVERSAL_TIME	40 milliseconds
PATH_DISCOVERY_TIME	2 * NET_TRAVERSAL_TIME
RERR_RATELIMIT	10
RING_TRAVERSAL_TIME	2 * NODE_TRAVERSAL_TIME * (TTL_VALUE + TIMEOUT_BUFFER)
RREQ_RETRIES	2
RREQ_RATELIMIT	10
TTL_START	1
TTL_INCREMENT	2
TTL_THRESHOLD	7

*The MIN_REPAIR_TTL should be the last known hop count to the destination.

6.2 Delay Time

Delay time of the exiting local repair can be calculated as below. LR-PATH-DISCOVERY-TIME means the time required to finish the local repair.

LR_PATH_DISCOVERY_TIME =
2 * NODE_TRAVERSAL_TIME * 2 * LR_RREQ_TTL

LR_RREQ_TTL =
MAX (MIN_REPAIR_TTL, 0.5 * #hop) + LOCAL_ADD_TTL

Since the minimum LR_RREQ_TTL is bigger then 4, the maximum LR_RREQ_TTL is 0.3 * NET_DIAMETER + 2.

Delay time of propose scheme is calculated as below, in which NEW_PATH_DISCOVERY-TIME is the time required to finish the repair with our scheme.

NEW_PATH_DISCOVERY_TIME =
2 * NODE_TRAVERSAL_TIME * 2 * 4

New scheme fixes the broadcasting range for RREQ massage by 4 hops. Therefore we know that the new discovery scheme needs less time than local repair scheme.

NEW_PATH_DISCOVERY_TIME =< LR_PATH_DISCOVERY_TIME

The path discovery time influences the range of a broadcast massage. However, the proposed scheme doesn't influence the range of a broadcast massage since the proposed scheme fixes the range of the broadcast massage.

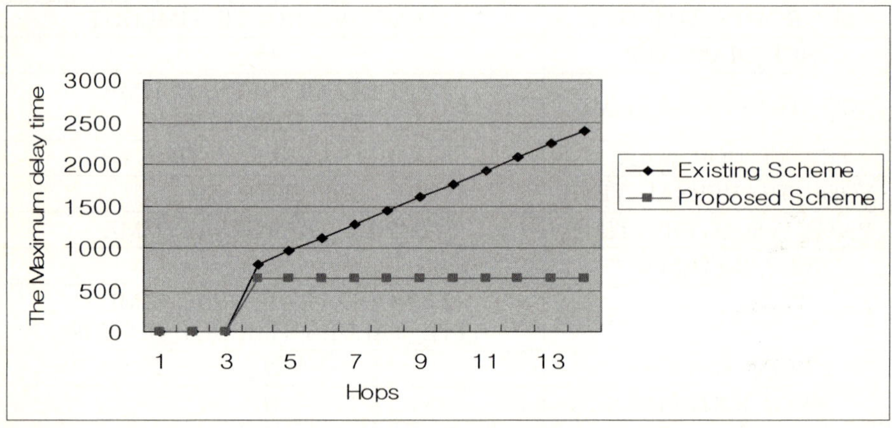

Fig. 5. The Maximum delay Time comparison for local repair

We check the maximum delay time of ad-hoc network. We use the network of size 12-45 hops. As the size of the network increased, maximum delay time increases in the existing scheme. But, the proposed algorithm never changes the maximum delay time, because, the scheme fixed the range of the broadcast massage.

The delay time in the Existing scheme = OPDT (Old_Path_Discovery_Time)
The delay time in the Proposed scheme = NPDT (New_Path_Discovery_Time)

OPDT (Old_Path_Discovery_Time) = 2 * NODE_TRAVERSAL_TIME * 2 * h

$$\sum_{h=4}^{h \to 16} = OPDT = 20160$$

Average recovery time = 1680

NPDT (New_Path_Discovery_Time) = 2 * NODE_TRAVERSAL_TIME * 2 * 4

$$\sum_{k=4}^{k \to 16} = NPDT = 7680$$

Average recovery time = 640
As we have proved, the proposed algorithm is more effective than the existing algorithm. The maximum delay time is smaller than the existing algorithm.

6.3   The Number of Flooded RREQ Massages

We evaluate our new scheme using the candidate node in terms of the number of Flooding RREQ message.

For the existing Scheme,
SCOPE_DELIVERY_LR_RREQ=∏ * (LR_RREQ_TTL)2

For the propose Scheme,
NEW_SCOPE_DELIVERY_LR_RREQ =∏ * (4 hop)2

LR_RREQ_TTL >= 4 hops

So, NEW_SCOPE_DELIVERY_LR_RREQ=<SCOPE_DELIVERY_LR_RREQ

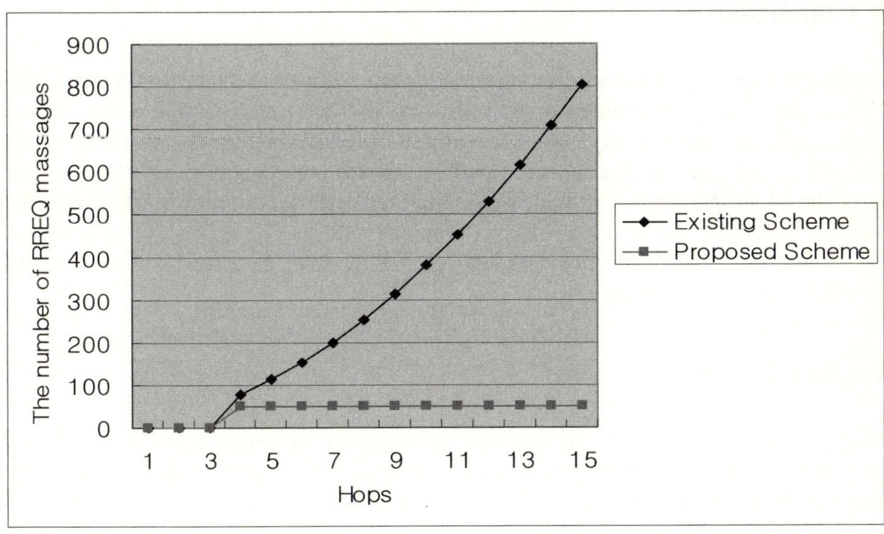

Fig. 6. The Number of flooded RREQ massages

As the size of the network increases, the number of flooded RREQ massages in the existing algorithm. But, the proposed algorithm never change the number of flooded RREQ massages, because the algorithm fixes the range of the broadcast massage

The number of flooded RREQ massages in the Existing Scheme =
OSD (OLD_SCOPE_DELIVERY)
The number of flooded RREQ massages in the Existing Scheme =
NSD (NEW_SCOPE_DELIVERY)
OSD = $\prod$ * (h)2

$$\sum_{h=4}^{h \to 16} = OSD = 4603$$

The average = 383.

NSD = $\prod$ * (4)2

$$\sum_{h=4}^{h \to 16} = NSD = 603$$

The average= 50.24

Even the proposed scheme causes the routing table overhead using the candidate node. But the overhead is very small since it is only a couple of bytes, which is a lot smaller than the normal packet size. By reducing the number of packets, our scheme shows the better performance.

7 Conclusion

In this paper, we propose an effective local path recovery scheme for AODV. The existing path recovery scheme can not utilize the pre-connected routing nodes. But we propose scheme improves performance using the candidate node. The candidate nodes are used to recover the disconnected path using the pre-connected routing information. The proposed scheme provides a good result with less control packets and fast path recovery time. Ad Hoc Network is organized with mobile nodes. Ad hoc network needs more effective Algorithm. Our next goal is to make an effective routing protocol for ad-hoc sensor network.

Acknowledgement

This research was supported by the MIC(Ministry of Information and Communication), Korea, under the ITRC(Information Technology Research Center) support program supervised by the IITA(Institute of Information Technology Assessment).

References

[1] RFC3561, Ad hoc On-Demand Distance Vector (AODV) Routing. C. Perkins, E. Belding-Royer, S. Das. July 2003.
[2] RFC 3626, Optimized Link State Routing Protocol (OLSR). T. Clausen, Ed., P. Jacquet, Ed.. October 2003.

[3] RFC 2501, Mobile Ad hoc Networking (MANET): Routing Protocol Performance   Issues and Evaluation Considerations. S. Corson, J. Macker. January 1999.

[4] D. B. johnson, D. A. Maltz, Yih-chun Hu and J. G. Jetcheva. "The Dynamic Source Routing Protocol for Mobile Ad Hoc Networks(DSR)", Internet Draft, IETF MANET Working Group, draft-ietf-manet-dsr-07.txt. February 2002.

[5] Z. J. Haas and M. R. Perlman, "The Zone Routing Protocol(ZRP) for Ad Hoc Networks", Internet Draft, IETF MANET Working Group, draft-ietf-manet-zone-3.txt. March 2000.

[6] http://www.netmeister.org/misc/zrp/zrp.html

[7] Young-Bae Ko and Nitin H. Vaidya, "Location-Aided Routing(LAR) in mobile Ad-hoc network", Wireless Networks, Vol.6, No.4, July 2000, pp.307-321.

[8] S. Basagni, I. Chlamtac, V.R. Syrotiuk and B.A. Woodward, "A distance routing affect algorithm for mobility(DREAM)," Proc. of the ACM/IEEE International Conf. on Mobile computing and Networking, 1998, pp.76-84.

[9] B. Karp and H. T. Kung, "GPSR: greedy perimeter stateless routing for wireless networks," Proc. of the international conf. on Mobile computing and networking, Aug., 2000, pp.243-254.

[10] W. Liao and J. Sheu and Y. Tseng, "GRID: A Fully Location-Aware Routing Protocol for Mobile Ad Hoc Networks," Telecom. Systems, Vol.18, 2001, pp.37-60.

Analyzing Correlation Between Flow Data and AS Paths in BGP Routing

Yoshiaki Harada[1], Koji Okamura[1], Takashi Chiyonobu[1], and Youngseok Lee[2]

[1] Kyushu University, Kyushu, Japan
`harada@ale.csce.kyushu-u.ac.jp`,
`oka@ec.kyushu-u.ac.jp`,
`chiyonobu@ale.csce.kyushu-u.ac.jp`
[2] Chungnam National University, Daejon, Korea
`lee@cnu.ac.kr`

Abstract. The big picture of Internet could be depicted with the AS map made from BGP routing tables. The traffc distribution statistics on this AS map will be usefule for understanding of Internet dynamics. Particularly, it is interesting to find which AS path are used for Internet traffic exchange between two ASes. The correlation between Internet traffic and AS path will be also important for future Internet design. Therefore, in this paper, we aim at analyzing the correlation between the AS path length and flow data. For the analysis, the BGP routing tables and flow data collected at QGPOP for more than 1 year have been used. As a analysis result, there is the relationship between the AS path length and the traffic usage. In addition, we can find the traffic distribution monitored at Kyushu Univerisity.

Keywords: BGP, AS, Flow Data.

1   Introduction

Due to the explosive growth of Internet usage and 'always on' wireless connectivity to Internet, a huge amount of computers and equipments are being connected to the Internet. Typically, the global picture of Internet could be depicted with the AS map where each AS node will be connected with other ASes with BGP peering links. On this AS map, the correlation between traffic and AS path will be interesting. For example, the traffic density will not be uniformly distributed over ASes, which implies the heavy tail distribution or self similar charactersitics. Thus, in this paper, we aim at finding traffic distribution over reachable ASes which is observed at a BGP router of a specific AS.

Though IP prefixes could be a more useful metric for representation of global Internet, the number of IP prefixes is so large that AS-level analysis has been employed in this paper. An AS is a collection of IP network systems and routers under the control of one entity (or sometime more) that runs a common routing policy. The current total number of unique ASes is estimated to be more than 20,000, and it is continuously increasing. Usually, an AS has a BGP peering with a neighboring AS through which reachability information will be exchanged. If

G. Min et al. (Eds.): ISPA 2006 Ws, LNCS 4331, pp. 1126–1135, 2006.

an AS is to communicate with a non-neighboring AS, ASes along the AS path will provide the transit service that traffic will be forwarded to the appropriate destination.

One of our objectives concerning BGP routing policies is how to decide the AS path toward the destination AS. In BGP routing, traffic will be delivered to the destination AS through the minimum AS hop path. Thus, if an AS path has a large amount of traffic volume, routing optimization could reduce the AS path hop for improving Internet performance. The BGP routing protocol will select a long AS path if the destination AS could not be connected with short AS paths. However, it will be an inefficient routing choice from the view point of traffic engineering.

In our work, we assume that the average AS path length will decrease while the Internet connectivity spans globally. if a new BGP peering is established between ASes, this BGP peering link will reduce the existing AS path length, because a new link added to a graph will minimize the average hop per path. Thus, it will be important for designing future Internet to analyze the trend of AS-level reachability on the AS map with the BGP routing table for a long term. Furthermore, the correlation between traffic usage and the AS path will be investigated. As an example of the result, we found that Kyushu University has a lot of traffic usage with other Universities in Japan and related institutes and that traffic usage between Kyushu University and organizations which do not have close relationships with our university is not much reported.

This paper verifies the relationship between the AS path length and the traffic usage through analyzing the BGP routing table and NetFlow data collected for the long observation period. In addition, this paper shows the traffic distribution monitored at our organization.

The remaining of this paper is organized as follows. The backgrounds on Internet routing and AS path are explained in Section 2. Next, in Section 3, we present how to analyze the BGP routing table and flow data. We show the results of analysis in Section 4. Finally we conclude the paper in Section 5.

2   Backgrounds

2.1   BGP Routing

An Autonomous System (AS) [1] is a collection of IP network systems and routers under the control of an administration entity that shares a common routing policy. A unique AS number is assigned to each AS. Since the AS number an 16 bit integer, 65536 ASes could exist in maximum. Information on the AS number and its IP prefixes could be known by using the WHOIS protocol. The WHOIS is a TCP-based query/response protocol which is widely used for querying a database in order to determine the owner of domain names, IP addresses, or AS numbers.

Routing protocols used within an AS are called Interior Gateway Protocol (IGP), whereas routing protocols used between ASes are known as Exterior

Gateway Protocol (EGP). The most commonly used IGPs are RIP, OSPF, and IS-IS, and BGP4 for EGP.

BGP [3][4][5] is used to exchange routing information between ASes. A BGP routing table contains information on how to reach all the advertised prefixes throughput the Internet. A prefix is a part of a 32-bit IP address that is a block of IP addresses with the masking prefix length. Each routing information in the routing table contains a prefix and AS path attributes, which is the actual list of ASes along the path to the destination. BGP prefers the shortest AS path. And BGP table have associated properties that are used to determine the best route to a destination when multiple paths exist toward a particular destination. The length of an AS path is the number of ASes to the destination. Therefore, we regard the AS path length as a network distance between ASes.

2.2   AS Path

The length of an AS path is one of the important points to the Internet architecture. Generally, it is believed that the shorter the distance between communicating parties is, the less it will take to transmit data. Therefore, there have been many studies on the AS-path length [6][7][8]. We analyze the correlation between AS path length and flow data to get information which is useful for designing Internet topology.

The number of packets is considered as traffic volume, and the number of flows as the frequency or density of communication. We analyze the relationship between flow data and AS path length. In this analysis, we calculated the average AS length and deviation per packet, flow.

Regarding the communication pattern of an organization, we analyze the total number of ASes that our university has sent/received data to/from. By analyzing the communication pattern, we could improve the performance of the network by optimizing the AS map or topology. For our analysis, we used the HTTP flow data as well as all the flow data.

3   Analysis Method of Flow Data

3.1   BGP Table and Flow Data

In this paper, we analyzed the flow data and BGP table data that have been collected for a long term. We describe the method of collecting flow data and BGP table.

Our analysis method uses the BGP table exported from a router in AS 2523 (QGPOP), and the flow data exported from routers in AS 2523 and AS 2508 (Kyushu University). QGPOP [9] is a transit AS between KOREN (Korea advanced Research Network) and SINET (Science Information Network). QGPOP communicates IIJ (Internet Initiative Japan) and KOREN. We use the collected flow data exported from QGPOP and Kyushu University. These flow data are sampled at the rate of 1/10. Flow Data is used to analyze the Internet traffic. Therefore, There have been many studies on analysis of Flow Data [10][11][12].

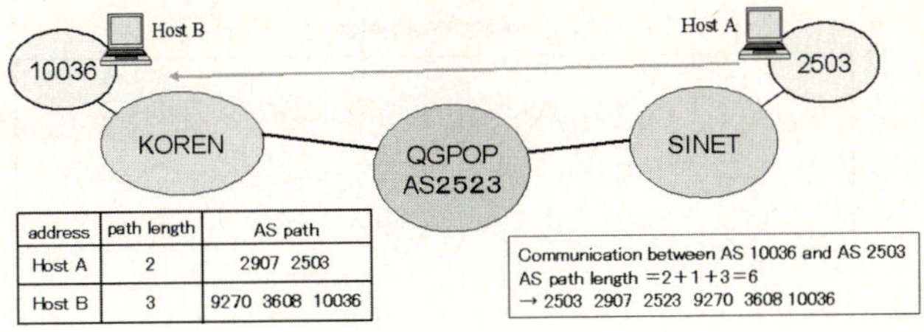

Fig. 1. How to calculate the AS path length

A flow is a stream of unidirectional packets that shares the same 5-tuples of (src IP, dst IP, src port, dst port, proto). A network port is a special number, ranging from 0 - 65535, recognized by the TCP and UDP protocols. These protocols use the ports to demultiplext incoming packets to a particular process running on a host. In this paper, port numbers are used in order to classify application traffic.

Next, we explain BGP routing table data. A BGP routing table includes prefixes and AS paths of reachable ASes. An AS path is a list of ASes. In the AS path, sometimes, the same AS number might be included such as "300 100 100 200". It is called a 'prepended AS path', and it is often used for manipulating the AS path according to BGP routing policy of preferring the shorter path.

3.2   How to Analyze Flow Data

Relationship between Flow Data and AS Path Length. This paper analyze the relationship between the change of AS path length and flow data. If ASes which have long AS path communicated frequently, it means that wasting packets flows between the two ASes. In this case, we can reduce the traffic by shorten AS path between these ASes. Analyzing Flow Data with AS path lead to reducing data traffic. In this section, we explain how to analyze the relationship between Flow Data and AS path length. We analyze the flow data observed at QGPOP on Wednesday in every fourth week from 2004/10/13 to 2006/01/04. Flow data for a day is collected at 0-5 minutes in every hour.

We explain the method of calculating AS path length. A BGP table has AS path for destination ASes. Therefore, we should calculate the full AS path by using the AS path for source AS. An AS path is directional, because a route might be changed according to the routing policy at each AS. However, most of routes will be selected as the shortest one. Therefore, we add a source AS to the outbound AS path, and calculate the full AS path length. Figure 1 shows an example of calculating the full AS path length. It is assumed that the source AS path equals to backward AS path. For example, communication from AS 2503 to AS 10036 could be possible as seen at at Fig. 1. We add the contrary source AS path "2907 2503" and AS 2523 (QGPOP) to the destination AS path "9270 3608 10036". In this case, the AS path length is 6.

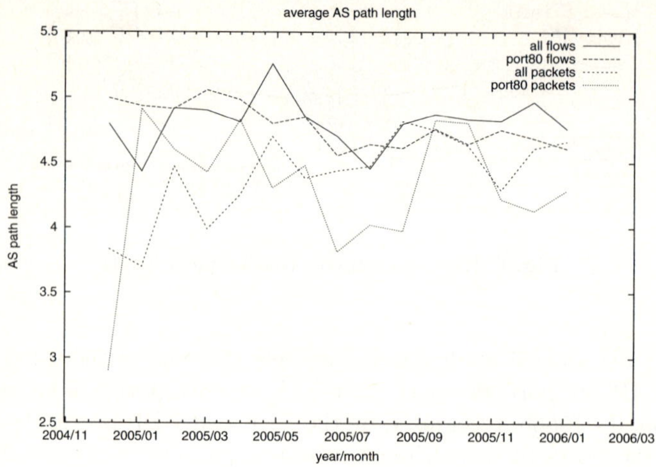

Fig. 2. Temporal changes of AS path lengths per flow, packet, and AS pair

We calculate the average AS path length per one packet, per flow, and per AS pair to find the correlation. When we examine AS path length, we use the flow data with the reduced prepend path of AS 2497 (IIJ). IIJ is an AS neighboring to QGPOP, and IIJ appends a prepended AS path to its own AS path in 2005/08. IIJ communicate with QGPOP frequently so that the AS path dynamics of IIJ affects the BGP table of QGPOP. we analyze the flow data with the reduced IIJ prepended path in this paper.

Flow data might include illegal access such as Internet worm or viruses. If anomaly traffic is included for analysis, the correlation of actual communication data could not be correctly found. Therefore, we consider port 80 traffic in flow data.

Distribution of Destination ASes. We use the collected flow data in Kyushu University and BGP table in QGPOP. While analyzing the distribution of communication targets, we use the flow data on Wednesday in every week from 2004/10/13 to 2006/02/01. Since we could not collect BGP tables in Kyushu University, we used BGP tables in QGPOP to find AS numbers of communication targets.

4   Analysis Results

4.1   Relationship Between Flow Data and AS Path Length

We analyzed the average AS-path length per packet, flow, and AS pair to find correlation between flow data and AS path length. Figure 2 shows the temporal changes of the average AS path length on all traffic and port 80 traffic. Port 80 is the typical port for HTTP. The AS path length per packet was shorter than

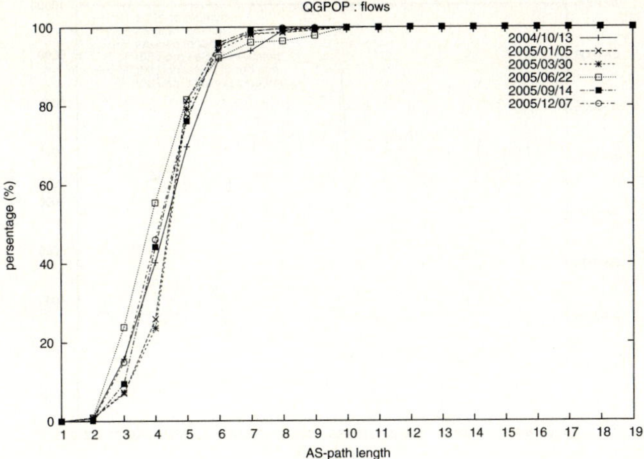

Fig. 3. CDF of port 80 flows per AS path length

the other data through a year. It represents that network routing is effective from the view point of traffic volume, because routing is to reduce the total number of packets in Internet. On the other hand, the average AS path length has increased for a year. Next, we explain the time change of AS path length on port 80 traffic. On 2005/12, the average AS path length per flow has been changed when compared with others on port 80 traffic. However, the average AS path length of packets is extremely short. It is estimated to be the influence of the communication between AS 2523 (QGPOP) and AS 2970 (SINET) with AS path length of 2. Since this communication data includes a large amount of packets per one flow, it affected the average AS path length per packet. The average AS path length has increased for a year in all flows. Yet, it has decreased in port 80 flows as shown in Fig2. It is considered that the number of flows represents the frequency of communication. Therefore, communication with shorter AS path length has increased in port 80 flows. However, we could not find relationship between AS path length and packets on port 80 traffic, because dynamics of packet volume changes significantly day to day.

Figure 3 shows the relation between the percentage of flows in port 80 traffic and AS path length. The graphs are shifted to left in Fig. 3. It shows that the communication with the short AS path length has increased. The AS path length of port 80 flows was not short. Yet, overall, the average AS path length was shorter than that of all flows. Recently in port 80 flows, the AS path length of 3 accounts for about 20% of traffic volume. The AS path length of 4 explains about 40% of flows. However, there are low percentages about AS path lengths of 4 and 5. It shows that flows are transmitted evenly between AS path 2 and 6.

As shown at port 80 flows, the average AS path length has decreased, and flows with the short AS path length has increased through one year. Therefore, we investigate the ASes with a large number of flows through the year in order to figure out what are reasons of decreasing the average AS path length. One

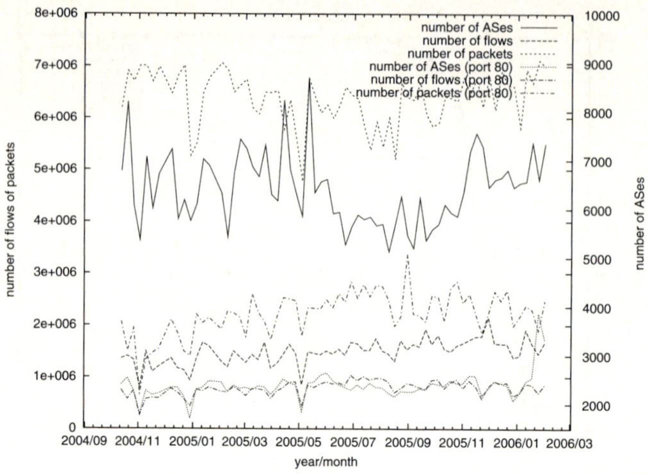

Fig. 4. Temporal changes of flows, packets, and communication target

of reasons is the AS related with Microsoft. Microsoft has ASes from 8068 to 8075, and integrate AS 8072 in AS 8075. Traffic for AS 8072 was transmitted through AS 8072. Therefore, the AS path of traffic for AS 8072 was shortened. Microsoft communicated with AS 2508 (Kyushu University) frequently, and AS 2508 connected to AS 2523 (QGPOP) directly. The AS path between AS 6075 and AS 2508 is 4, which is shorter than the average AS path length. Thus, the average AS path length has decreased. On the other hand, traffic of AS 18088 has been observed. This AS was included in BGP table in 2004/10, and there are a few incidents of communication at that time. However, the communication with this AS has increased gradually, and it became one of the most communicating ASes since 2005/05. Most of communication traffic of AS 18088 are to AS 2508, whose AS path length is 3. This AS path length is shorter than the average AS path length. Hence, the average AS path length of flows has decreased.

4.2   CDF of Destinations

Figure 4 shows the temporal changes for the number of flows, packets, and target ASes that communicate with Kyushu University on all traffic and port 80 traffic. As shown in Fig. 4, when the number of target ASes was small, both the number of flows and packets tends to be small. The dates of 2004/11/03, 2005/05/04 and 2005/11/23 were holiday. On these days, the number of target ASes was specifically small, and both of the number of flows and packets are small. Similarly, 2004/12/29, 2005/12/28 and 2006/01/04 shows small traffic volumes. From July to September, the number of target ASes are small. It is estimated that there are more than 20,000 ASes in Internet. It is seen that Kyushu University communicated with about a half of whole ASes in the global Internet. Next, we explain port 80 traffic. On 2006/01/25, the number of target

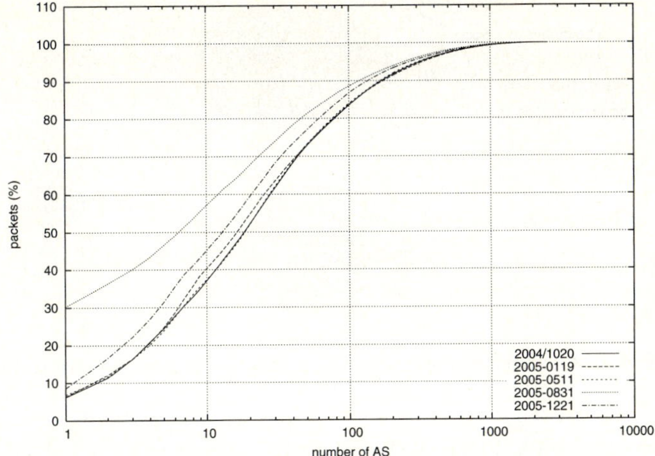

Fig. 5. CDF of communication (log scale)

ASes was especially large, 3,871 ASes. Assuming that the average number of target ASes was about 2,400, the number of ASes on these days was about 1,400 larger than the average number of ASes. However, the number of flows and the number of packets are not so much different from the others. We considered that the data with small packets or flows transmitted from (to) Kyushu University. Port 80 is generally used as web with a moderate volume of flows or packets. Thus, it is inferred that anomalay traffic has occurred such as scanning a lot of ASes with the small traffic. On 2006/02/01, the number of the target ASes is significantly large, 3,325 ASes because of same reason. In web traffic, Kyushu University communicated with 2,200 to 2,500 AS on average. There is a bias of anomaly traffic toward ASes.

As shown in Fig. 4, the number of flows and packets has increased throughout a year. The HTTP traffic has increased, too.

Figure 5 shows the CDF of packets, and the vertical axis is the percentage of packets. On 2005/08/31, only one AS accounts for 30% of packets. This AS is Kyoto University AS, which AS number is 2504. The top 20 ASes communicated with Kyushu University explain 50% of packets, and the top 80 ASes accounts for almost 80% packets. 80 ASes is 0.4% of total ASes in Internet. It shows that communication targets of Kyushu University are strongly biased to a few ASes.

We found a tendency that Kyushu University communicates with 2,200 to 2,500 AS on average in port 80 traffic. Thus, we examine ASes communicated with Kyushu university through a year. We analyzed the details of ASes by comparing traffic patterns between 2004/11/10 and 2005/11/09. Figure 6 shows which ASes have been communicated with our university throughout a year.

Table 1 shows the details of ASes communicated with Kyushu University. The number of ASes which have communicated with Kyushu University on both 2004/11 and 2005/11 are 1,365. The number of ASes communicated on only

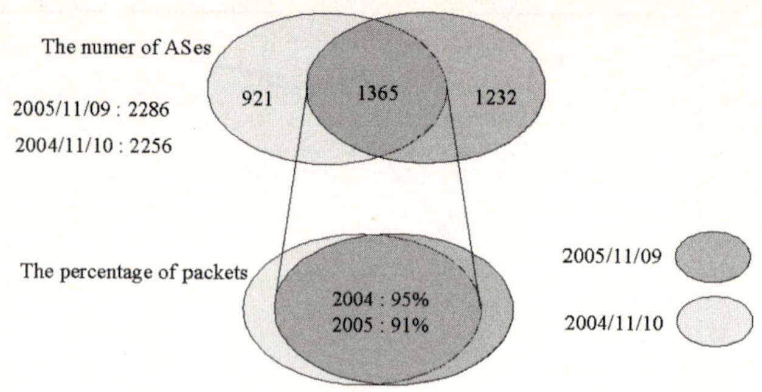

Fig. 6. Changes of communication targets in port 80 flow data

2004/11 and only 2005/11 are 921 and 1232, respectively. A half of ASes have been changed for a year.

Table 1. Details of communication AS targets compared between 2004/10 and 2005/10

	2004		2005	
	only	duplication	only	duplication
flow (num)	23,519	548,140	58,776	875,022
flow (%)	4.1	95.9	6.3	93.7
packet (num)	61,509	1,276,678	226,662	2,377,060
packet (%)	4.6	95.4	8.7	91.3

As shown Table 1 and Fig. 6, ASes communicated with our University for a year have a lot of traffic. In 2005 and 2004, the ASes communicated with us account for more than 90% of packets. ASes in 2004 explains only 4.6% of packets. Yet, new ASes which have been contacted to in 2005 take 8.7% of packets. As a result, ASes communicated with us for a year have a large volume of traffic, and new ASes and disappeared ASes have a small volume of traffic.

5   Conclusion

In this paper, we investigated the correlation between the traffic patterns and AS path. Specifically, it is observed that the average AS path length per packet, flow has been increased during one year from the date of QGPOP in the opposite our assumption. The average AS-path length per flow for HTTP has not been decreased, because the number of flows with shorte AS paths have increased, and AS-path length between ASes that communicates frequently has been reduced. It is seen that Kyushu University has communicated with about a half of ASes on the Internet for one year. However, when we consider HTTP flow data, 80% of flows belong to 0.7% of total ASes. A half of ASes communicated with Kyushu

University were changed for one year. However, ASes that have a large amount of communication traffic with Kyushu university did not changed throughout one year. That is, 50% of packets is transmitted by the most frequently accessed 20 ASes. We have found that Kyushu University frequently communicated with Kyoto University and some particular commercial ISPs.

We could find the relationship between AS path length and flows, but we could not find the relationship between AS path length and packets in port 80 traffic. We think that we should decrease data collecting interval to analyze more in detail. Generrally, finding relationship between traffic pattern on the AS map in the global Internet is versy difficult. However, this will be important for designing future Internet.

References

1. RFC 1772 - BGP-4 Application, http://www.ietf.org/.
2. IANA (Internet Assigned Numbers Authority), http://www.iana.org/.
3. RFC 1771 - A Border Gateway Protocol 4, http://www.ietf.org/.
4. Stephen A.Thomas, "IP Switching and Routing Essentials", WILEY, p181-219, 2001.
5. Sam Halabi, Danny McPherson, "Internet Routing Architectures, Second Edition", Cisco Press, 2000.
6. Huffaker Bradley, Marina Fomenkov, Daniel J.Plummer, David Moore and K claffy, "Distance Metric in the Internet", IEEE International Telecommunications Symposium (ITS), 2002.
7. L.Amini and H.Schulzrinne, "Observations from router-level internet trace", in DIMACS Workshop on Internet and WWW Measurement, mapping and Modeling, 2002.
8. Toshiyuki Kawasaki, Koji Okamura, "Evaluation on Scalability of Conference System using Request-Routing", 18th International Conference on Advanced Information Networking And Applications, p533-534, 2004.
9. QGPOP (Kyushu GigaPOP Project), http://www.qgpop.net/.
10. C.Estan and G.Varghese, "New Directions in traffic measurement and accounting", ACM SIGCOMM '02, 2002.
11. Y.Zhang et al, "On the characteristics and origins of Internet flow rates", ACM SIGCOMM '02, 2002.
12. Connie Logg, Les Cottrell, "Passive Performance Monitoring and Traffic Characteristics on the SLAC Internet Border", PAM2001 A workshop on Passive and Active Measurements, 2001.

Printing: Mercedes-Druck, Berlin
Binding: Stein+Lehmann, Berlin

Lecture Notes in Computer Science

For information about Vols. 1–4230

please contact your bookseller or Springer

Vol. 4331: G. Min, B. Di Martino, L.T. Yang, M. Guo, G. Ruenger (Eds.), Frontiers of High Performance Computing and Networking – ISPA 2006 Workshops. XXXVII, 1141 pages. 2006.

Vol. 4329: R. Barua, T. Lange (Eds.), Progress in Cryptology - INDOCRYPT 2006. XXXXX, 454000 pages. 2006.

Vol. 4318: H. Lipmaa, M. Yung, D. Lin (Eds.), Information Security and Cryptology. XI, 305 pages. 2006.

Vol. 4313: T. Margaria, B. Steffen (Eds.), Leveraging Applications of Formal Methods. IX, 197 pages. 2006.

Vol. 4312: S. Sugimoto, J. Hunter, A. Rauber, A. Morishima (Eds.), Digital Libraries: Achievements, Challenges and Opportunities. XVIII, 571 pages. 2006.

Vol. 4311: K. Cho, P. Jacquet (Eds.), Technologies for Advanced Heterogeneous Networks II. XI, 253 pages. 2006.

Vol. 4307: P. Ning, S. Qing, N. Li (Eds.), Information and Communications Security. XIV, 558 pages. 2006.

Vol. 4306: Y. Avrithis, Y. Kompatsiaris, S. Staab, N.E. O'Connor (Eds.), Semantic Multimedia. XII, 241 pages. 2006.

Vol. 4304: A. Sattar, B.-H. Kang (Eds.), AI 2006: Advances in Artificial Intelligence. XXVII, 1303 pages. 2006. (Sublibrary LNAI).

Vol. 4302: J. Domingo-Ferrer, L. Franconi (Eds.), Privacy in Statistical Databases. XI, 383 pages. 2006.

Vol. 4300: Y.Q. Shi (Ed.), Transactions on Data Hiding and Multimedia Security I. IX, 139 pages. 2006.

Vol. 4296: M.S. Rhee, B. Lee (Eds.), Information Security and Cryptology – ICISC. XIII, 358 pages. 2006.

Vol. 4295: J.D. Carswell, T. Tezuka (Eds.), Web and Wireless Geographical Information Systems. XI, 269 pages. 2006.

Vol. 4293: A. Gelbukh, C.A. Reyes-Garcia (Eds.), MICAI 2006: Advances in Artificial Intelligence. XXVIII, 1232 pages. 2006. (Sublibrary LNAI).

Vol. 4292: G. Bebis, R. Boyle, B. Parvin, D. Koracin, P. Remagnino, A. Nefian, G. Meenakshisundaram, V. Pascucci, J. Zara, J. Molineros, H. Theisel, T. Malzbender (Eds.), Advances in Visual Computing, Part II. XXXII, 906 pages. 2006.

Vol. 4291: G. Bebis, R. Boyle, B. Parvin, D. Koracin, P. Remagnino, A. Nefian, G. Meenakshisundaram, V. Pascucci, J. Zara, J. Molineros, H. Theisel, T. Malzbender (Eds.), Advances in Visual Computing, Part I. XXXI, 916 pages. 2006.

Vol. 4290: M. van Steen, M. Henning (Eds.), Middleware 2006. XIII, 425 pages. 2006.

Vol. 4289: M. Ackermann, B. Berendt, M. Grobelnik, A. Hotho, D. Mladenič, G. Semeraro, M. Spiliopoulou, G. Stumme, V. Svatek, M. van Someren (Eds.), Semantics, Web and Mining. X, 197 pages. 2006. (Sublibrary LNAI).

Vol. 4288: T. Asano (Ed.), Algorithms and Computation. XXXX, 753333 pages. 2006.

Vol. 4285: Y. Matsumoto, R. Sproat, K.-F. Wong, M. Zhang (Eds.), Computer Processing of Oriental Languages. XXXX, 55000 pages. 2006. (Sublibrary LNAI).

Vol. 4284: X. Lai, K. Chen (Eds.), Advances in Cryptology – ASIACRYPT 2006. XIV, 468 pages. 2006.

Vol. 4283: Y.Q. Shi, B. Jeon (Eds.), Digital Watermarking. XII, 474 pages. 2006.

Vol. 4282: Z. Pan, A. Cheok, M. Haller, R.W.H. Lau, H. Saito, R. Liang (Eds.), Advances in Artificial Reality and Tele-Existence. XXIII, 1347 pages. 2006.

Vol. 4281: K. Barkaoui, A. Cavalcanti, A. Cerone (Eds.), Theoretical Aspects of Computing - ICTAC 2006. XV, 371 pages. 2006.

Vol. 4280: A.K. Datta, M. Gradinariu (Eds.), Stabilization, Safety, and Security of Distributed Systems. XVII, 590 pages. 2006.

Vol. 4279: N. Kobayashi (Ed.), Programming Languages and Systems. XI, 423 pages. 2006.

Vol. 4278: R. Meersman, Z. Tari, P. Herrero (Eds.), On the Move to Meaningful Internet Systems 2006: OTM 2006 Workshops, Part II. XLV, 1004 pages. 2006.

Vol. 4277: R. Meersman, Z. Tari, P. Herrero (Eds.), On the Move to Meaningful Internet Systems 2006: OTM 2006 Workshops, Part I. XLV, 1009 pages. 2006.

Vol. 4276: R. Meersman, Z. Tari (Eds.), On the Move to Meaningful Internet Systems 2006: CoopIS, DOA, GADA, and ODBASE, Part II. XXXII, 752 pages. 2006.

Vol. 4275: R. Meersman, Z. Tari (Eds.), On the Move to Meaningful Internet Systems 2006: CoopIS, DOA, GADA, and ODBASE, Part I. XXXI, 1115 pages. 2006.

Vol. 4274: Q. Huo, B. Ma, E.-S. Chng, H. Li (Eds.), Chinese Spoken Language Processing. XXXX, 8000 pages. 2006. (Sublibrary LNAI).

Vol. 4273: I. Cruz, S. Decker, D. Allemang, C. Preist, D. Schwabe, P. Mika, M. Uschold, L. Aroyo (Eds.), The Semantic Web - ISWC 2006. XXIV, 1001 pages. 2006.

Vol. 4272: P. Havinga, M. Lijding, N. Meratnia, M. Wegdam (Eds.), Smart Sensing and Context. XI, 267 pages. 2006.

Vol. 4271: F.V. Fomin (Ed.), Graph-Theoretic Concepts in Computer Science. XIII, 358 pages. 2006.

Vol. 4270: H. Zha, Z. Pan, H. Thwaites, A.C. Addison, M. Forte (Eds.), Interactive Technologies and Sociotechnical Systems. XVI, 547 pages. 2006.

Vol. 4269: R. State, S. van der Meer, D. O'Sullivan, T. Pfeifer (Eds.), Large Scale Management of Distributed Systems. XIII, 282 pages. 2006.

Vol. 4268: G. Parr, D. Malone, M. Ó Foghlú (Eds.), Autonomic Principles of IP Operations and Management. XIII, 237 pages. 2006.

Vol. 4267: A. Helmy, B. Jennings, L. Murphy, T. Pfeifer (Eds.), Autonomic Management of Mobile Multimedia Services. XIII, 257 pages. 2006.

Vol. 4266: H. Yoshiura, K. Sakurai, K. Rannenberg, Y. Murayama, S. Kawamura (Eds.), Advances in Information and Computer Security. XIII, 438 pages. 2006.

Vol. 4265: L. Todorovski, N. Lavrač, K.P. Jantke (Eds.), Discovery Science. XIV, 384 pages. 2006. (Sublibrary LNAI).

Vol. 4264: J.L. Balcázar, P.M. Long, F. Stephan (Eds.), Algorithmic Learning Theory. XIII, 393 pages. 2006. (Sublibrary LNAI).

Vol. 4263: A. Levi, E. Savas, H. Yenigün, S. Balcisoy, Y. Saygin (Eds.), Computer and Information Sciences – ISCIS 2006. XXIII, 1084 pages. 2006.

Vol. 4262: K. Havelund, M. N\'u\~nez, G. Ro\csu, B. Wolff (Eds.), Formal Approaches to Software Testing and Runtime Verification. XXXXXX, 24555555 pages. 2006.

Vol. 4261: Y. Zhuang, S. Yang, Y. Rui, Q. He (Eds.), Advances in Multimedia Information Processing - PCM 2006. XXII, 1040 pages. 2006.

Vol. 4260: Z. Liu, J. He (Eds.), Formal Methods and Software Engineering. XII, 778 pages. 2006.

Vol. 4259: S. Greco, Y. Hata, S. Hirano, M. Inuiguchi, S. Miyamoto, H.S. Nguyen, R. Słowiński (Eds.), Rough Sets and Current Trends in Computing. XXII, 951 pages. 2006. (Sublibrary LNAI).

Vol. 4257: I. Richardson, P. Runeson, R. Messnarz (Eds.), Software Process Improvement. XI, 219 pages. 2006.

Vol. 4256: L. Feng, G. Wang, C. Zeng, R. Huang (Eds.), Web Information Systems – WISE 2006 Workshops. XIV, 320 pages. 2006.

Vol. 4255: K. Aberer, Z. Peng, E.A. Rundensteiner, Y. Zhang, X. Li (Eds.), Web Information Systems – WISE 2006. XIV, 563 pages. 2006.

Vol. 4254: T. Grust, H. Höpfner, A. Illarramendi, S. Jablonski, M. Mesiti, S. Müller, P.-L. Patranjan, K.-U. Sattler, M. Spiliopoulou, J. Wijsen (Eds.), Current Trends in Database Technology – EDBT 2006. XXXI, 932 pages. 2006.

Vol. 4253: B. Gabrys, R.J. Howlett, L.C. Jain (Eds.), Knowledge-Based Intelligent Information and Engineering Systems, Part III. XXXII, 1301 pages. 2006. (Sublibrary LNAI).

Vol. 4252: B. Gabrys, R.J. Howlett, L.C. Jain (Eds.), Knowledge-Based Intelligent Information and Engineering Systems, Part II. XXXIII, 1335 pages. 2006. (Sublibrary LNAI).

Vol. 4251: B. Gabrys, R.J. Howlett, L.C. Jain (Eds.), Knowledge-Based Intelligent Information and Engineering Systems, Part I. LXVI, 1297 pages. 2006. (Sublibrary LNAI).

Vol. 4250: H.J. van den Herik, S.-C. Hsu, T.-s. Hsu, H.H.L.M. Donkers (Eds.), Advances in Computer Games. XIV, 273 pages. 2006.

Vol. 4249: L. Goubin, M. Matsui (Eds.), Cryptographic Hardware and Embedded Systems - CHES 2006. XII, 462 pages. 2006.

Vol. 4248: S. Staab, V. Svátek (Eds.), Managing Knowledge in a World of Networks. XIV, 400 pages. 2006. (Sublibrary LNAI).

Vol. 4247: T.-D. Wang, X. Li, S.-H. Chen, X. Wang, H. Abbass, H. Iba, G. Chen, X. Yao (Eds.), Simulated Evolution and Learning. XXI, 940 pages. 2006.

Vol. 4246: M. Hermann, A. Voronkov (Eds.), Logic for Programming, Artificial Intelligence, and Reasoning. XIII, 588 pages. 2006. (Sublibrary LNAI).

Vol. 4245: A. Kuba, L.G. Nyúl, K. Palágyi (Eds.), Discrete Geometry for Computer Imagery. XIII, 688 pages. 2006.

Vol. 4244: S. Spaccapietra (Ed.), Journal on Data Semantics VII. XI, 267 pages. 2006.

Vol. 4243: T. Yakhno, E.J. Neuhold (Eds.), Advances in Information Systems. XIII, 420 pages. 2006.

Vol. 4242: A. Rashid, M. Aksit (Eds.), Transactions on Aspect-Oriented Software Development II. IX, 289 pages. 2006.

Vol. 4241: R.R. Beichel, M. Sonka (Eds.), Computer Vision Approaches to Medical Image Analysis. XI, 262 pages. 2006.

Vol. 4239: H.Y. Youn, M. Kim, H. Morikawa (Eds.), Ubiquitous Computing Systems. XVI, 548 pages. 2006.

Vol. 4238: Y.-T. Kim, M. Takano (Eds.), Management of Convergence Networks and Services. XVIII, 605 pages. 2006.

Vol. 4237: H. Leitold, E. Markatos (Eds.), Communications and Multimedia Security. XII, 253 pages. 2006.

Vol. 4236: L. Breveglieri, I. Koren, D. Naccache, J.-P. Seifert (Eds.), Fault Diagnosis and Tolerance in Cryptography. XIII, 253 pages. 2006.

Vol. 4234: I. King, J. Wang, L. Chan, D. Wang (Eds.), Neural Information Processing, Part III. XXII, 1227 pages. 2006.

Vol. 4233: I. King, J. Wang, L. Chan, D. Wang (Eds.), Neural Information Processing, Part II. XXII, 1203 pages. 2006.

Vol. 4232: I. King, J. Wang, L. Chan, D. Wang (Eds.), Neural Information Processing, Part I. XLVI, 1153 pages. 2006.

Vol. 4231: J. F. Roddick, R. Benjamins, S. Si-Saïd Cherfi, R. Chiang, C. Claramunt, R. Elmasri, F. Grandi, H. Han, M. Hepp, M. Hepp, M. Lytras, V.B. Mišić, G. Poels, I.-Y. Song, J.D. Trujillo, C. Vangenot (Eds.), Advances in Conceptual Modeling - Theory and Practice. XXII, 456 pages. 2006.